Myra Clark Gaines, Versus Richard Relf, Beverly Chew, and Others

P.C. Wright

Myra Clark Gaines, Versus Richard Relf, Beverly Chew, and Others

U.S. Circuit court, in Chancery - Myra Clark Gaines versus Richard Relf, Beverley Chew and Others - Record - 1819
P.C. Wright, Jno. R. Grymes, J.A. Campbell, Greer B. Duncan, Isaac T. Preston
HAR04811
122
Court Record
Harvard Law School Library
New-Orleans: Printed by Hinton & Co., 107 Poydras Street 1849

The Making of Modern Law collection of legal archives constitutes a genuine revolution in historical legal research because it opens up a wealth of rare and previously inaccessible sources in legal, constitutional, administrative, political, cultural, intellectual, and social history. This unique collection consists of three extensive archives that provide insight into more than 300 years of American and British history. These collections include:

Legal Treatises, 1800-1926: over 20,000 legal treatises provide a comprehensive collection in legal history, business and economics, politics and government.

Trials, 1600-1926: nearly 10,000 titles reveal the drama of famous, infamous, and obscure courtroom cases in America and the British Empire across three centuries.

Primary Sources, 1620-1926: includes reports, statutes and regulations in American history, including early state codes, municipal ordinances, constitutional conventions and compilations, and law dictionaries.

These archives provide a unique research tool for tracking the development of our modern legal system and how it has affected our culture, government, business – nearly every aspect of our everyday life. For the first time, these high-quality digital scans of original works are available via print-on-demand, making them readily accessible to libraries, students, independent scholars, and readers of all ages.

The BiblioLife Network

This project was made possible in part by the BiblioLife Network (BLN), a project aimed at addressing some of the huge challenges facing book preservationists around the world. The BLN includes libraries, library networks, archives, subject matter experts, online communities and library service providers. We believe every book ever published should be available as a high-quality print reproduction; printed on-demand anywhere in the world. This insures the ongoing accessibility of the content and helps generate sustainable revenue for the libraries and organizations that work to preserve these important materials.

The following book is in the "public domain" and represents an authentic reproduction of the text as printed by the original publisher. While we have attempted to accurately maintain the integrity of the original work, there are sometimes problems with the original work or the micro-film from which the books were digitized. This can result in minor errors in reproduction. Possible imperfections include missing and blurred pages, poor pictures, markings and other reproduction issues beyond our control. Because this work is culturally important, we have made it available as part of our commitment to protecting, preserving, and promoting the world's literature.

GUIDE TO FOLD-OUTS MAPS and OVERSIZED IMAGES

The book you are reading was digitized from microfilm captured over the past thirty to forty years. Years after the creation of the original microfilm, the book was converted to digital files and made available in an online database.

In an online database, page images do not need to conform to the size restrictions found in a printed book. When converting these images back into a printed bound book, the page sizes are standardized in ways that maintain the detail of the original. For large images, such as fold-out maps, the original page image is split into two or more pages

Guidelines used to determine how to split the page image follows:

• Some images are split vertically; large images require vertical and horizontal splits.
• For horizontal splits, the content is split left to right.
• For vertical splits, the content is split from top to bottom.
• For both vertical and horizontal splits, the image is processed from top left to bottom right.

U. S. CIRCUIT COURT,
FIFTH CIRCUIT DISTRICT OF LOUISIANA

IN CHANCERY.

NO. 122.

MYRA CLARK GAINES
versus
RICHARD RELF, BEVERLY CHEW, AND OTHERS

RECORD.

P C WRIGHT, *Solicitor for Complainant*
JNO R GRYMES, J A CAMPBELL, *and*
GREER B. DUNCAN ISAAC T. PRESTON, *& OTHERS*
Solicitors for Defendant

NEW-ORLEANS
PRINTED BY BAYTON & CO. COMMERCIAL

1 3

INDEX TO RECORD

TESTIMONY.

UNITED STATES OF AMERICA, } ss.
EASTERN DISTRICT OF LOUISIANA, CITY OF NEW ORLEANS,

Be it remembered, that on the several days hereinafter set forth in the year of our Lord one thousand eight hundred and forty-nine, before me, William H Hunt, a commissioner, duly appointed by the Circuit Court of the United States, in and for the Eastern district of Louisiana, under and by virtue of the acts of Congress, entitled, "an Act for the more convenient taking of affidavits and bail in civil causes depending in the courts of the United States," passed February 20th, 1812, and the act of Congress, entitled, "an act in addition to an act entitled 'an act for the more convenient taking of affidavits and bail, in civil causes depending in the courts of the United States," passed March 1st, 1817, and the act entitled "an act to establish the Judicial Courts of the United States," passed September 24th, 1789, personally appeared Ph Baron Boisfontaine, T D Harper, James Gardette, Gallien Preval, and Peter K Wagner, all persons of sound mind and lawful age, and witness for the complainants in civil suit now depending in the Circuit Court of the United States, in and for the Eastern district of Louisiana, wherein Edmund P. Gaines and wife are complainants, and Richard Relf, B Chew, and als, are defendants, and the said witnesses being severally and apart by me first carefully examined and cautioned, and sworn to testify the whole truth and nothing but the truth, did depose and say, as follows in the schedules annexed.

UNITED STATES CIRCUIT COURT, FOR THE 5TH CIRCUIT, WITHIN AND FOR THE EASTERN DISTRICT OF LOUISIANA.

In Chancery

Depositions of witnesses produced, sworn and examined on the 3d day of May, in the year of our Lord one thousand eight hundred and forty-nine, and at divers days and times hereinafter named, at the Court room of the United States Circuit Court, in the city of New Orleans and State of Louisiana, by virtue of an order of said Court in chancery sitting, to me the undersigned, a commissioner of said Court, directed, for the examination of witnesses in a certain cause there depending and at issue, wherein Edmund P Gaines and Myra Clark, his wife, are complainants, and Richard Relf, Beverly Chew, and others, are defendants, designated on the docket of said Court as No 122, I, the said commissioner, having first taken the oath prescribed by law

Philippe B Boisfontaine, aged twenty-eight years, a clerk by occupation, produced, sworn and examined, on the part and behalf of said complainants, deposeth and saith as follows

I am the son of the late Baron Boisfontaine my father died on the seventh of January, 1836

PH BARON BOISFONTAINE.

Examination taken, reduced to writing, and by the witness subscribed and sworn to this, 3d day of May, 1849, before me,

WILLIAM H. HUNT, U. S Comm'r.

Thomas D. Harper, by occupation a merchant, twenty-six years of age, produced, sworn and examined on the part of said complainants, as follows

I am twenty-six years of age, by occupation a merchant, and a resident of New Orleans   I am the son of the late Mrs Harriet Smyth, formerly Mrs Harper I know her handwriting, (a document is shewn to the witness, being testimony taken in the case of Wm W Whitney and Myra C Whitney vs. Relf Chew and others, being the same suit in which this testimony is now taken and marked No. 1), the signature to this document I know to be that of Mrs Smyth.   Mrs Smyth died in the early part of last January   T D HARPER.

Cross examined on behalf of Messrs. Chew & Relf.

It was in 1834 I think, that Mrs Smyth was married I think my father, Mr Harper, died in 1829   I know. from family information, that my mother was in New Orleans in 1801, and that at that time she had one or two children I make these statements from what my mother has told me. My mother had eight children, all by Mr. Harper none by Dr Smyth. I could not tell from reputation in the family, when these children were born I was born in 1822   My brother, Henry Sidney Harper, is now in this city, and was born in the year 1806. I do not recollect having heard in what part of the year. I am slightly acquainted with Mrs Gardette, the mother of the complainant, Mrs Gaines I have heard Mrs. Gaines spoken of as the daughter of Mrs Gardette   I know her very well, and I know Dr. Gardette, also, very well, a son of Mrs. Gardette I should take Dr Gardette to be a man of 35 years, the Dr Gardette I refer to, is James Gardette, I think I have heard him spoken of as the legitimate child of Mrs Gardette My mother's maiden ties complainant, and the defendants Relf and Chew, I have resided 39 years in New Orleans, I knew the late Daniel Clark, he died in 1813, as near as my memory serves me, he resided at his death at his house on the Bayou Road, I was, at his death, justice of the peace for the city of New Orleans. I was called upon to affix the seals to the effects of Mr Clark on the day of his death

Question—State what you did, and what transpired at the time of the affixing of the seals to the effects of Daniel Clark? (Defendants' counsel object to this question, on the ground that the proces verbal of the affixing the seals is the best evidence, complainants' counsel insisting, the witness saith)

Answer—I went to the house of Daniel Clark, situated as above stated, I then proceeded to affix the seals upon his property, in presence of witnesses who were present, but whose names I do not now recall in affixing these seals I looked particularly for the last will of Daniel Clark, and I looked more particularly in a certain trunk which he had in his bed room, because I had been informed that his last will was to be found in that trunk, but I did not find any I made the proces verbal after having affixed the seals upon the effects on which I thought proper to affix them, and then I caused the said proces verbal to be signed by the witnesses, and signed it myself, and appointed a person to keep the seals, as the law directs After that was done, as I was about to retire, Mr Richard Relf came to me and handed to me a package, sealed, telling me that he thought it was the last will of Daniel Clark, and telling me to take charge of it and deliver it to the Court of Probates I then made a little memorandum at the bottom of the proces verbal, of what had passed, stating in the memorandum that I had taken charge of the sealed package to be by me delivered to the Court of Probates; and, as well as my memory serves me, I requested the witnesses to sign the memorandum and I then carried the said package to the Court of Probates, where it is to be found

I was acquainted with Mr D Clark, but not intimately I frequently attended his parties, and visited his house, this was the extent of my intimacy Judge Pitot was very intimate with Daniel Clark, I got this information by conversation with Judge Pitot, I also know it by personal knowledge I had no knowledge of Mr Clark's intimacy with Col Bellechasse, although I knew Col Bellechasse himself I often heard Mr Clark speak of Mr Baron Boisfontaine I knew Mr De la Croix

Question—What have you heard pass in conversation between Judge Pitot and Mr De la Croix in regard to the last will of Daniel Clark? (Defendants' solicitors object to this question on grounds to be stated before the Court complainant' counsel insisting, the witness saith) 12

Answer —I have heard no such conversation

Question —What has Judge Pitot said to you in respect to the last will and testament of Daniel Clark? (Defendants solicitor objects to this question on the grounds 1st, That the will of Daniel Clark is not in controversy in these actions, complainants having themselves abandoned all claim under any pretended will whatever, made by the late Daniel Clark 2d, That it is hearsay testimony, which is inadmissible 3d, That the party referred to was not under oath at the time of the statements And *lastly*, that the statements, if any, were made, if at all, out of the presence and hearing of the parties to these actions. Complainants solicitor insisting, witness saith),

Answer —Judge Pitot very often spoke to me about the last will of Daniel Clark On that matter, he told me that Clark had informed him, Pitot, that in case of his death, his last will would be found in a trunk which he had in his bed room. He told me, also, that Clark had informed him, Pitot, that a certain negro, by the name of Lubin the confidential servant of Mr Clark, had been instructed by him, Clark to carry, in case of his death, that trunk to the house of De la Croix, if De la Croix should be in town, or to Pitot's residence if De la Croix should be absent He further told me, that Clark had informed him, that in the said last will, he had appointed as his executors, Mr Bellechasse. Mr De la Croix, and himself. Pitot. These conversations of myself with Mr Pitot, took place at different times , sometimes at my house, sometimes at his house, perhaps within three or four months before Clark's death Judge Pitot is dead, and has been so for many years I was very intimate with Judge Pitot; perhaps more intimate than any one else I have had no other conversation, to the best of my recollection, with any other person on this subject I knew Lubin the servant of Mr Clark, spoken above , I think he is dead, the general report is that he is dead ave not seen him for many years, he was Mr. Clark's confidential servant

GALLIEN PREVAL

Cross examined

Question —Have you, or not, a very indistinct recollection of anything that occurred at the time of the affixing of the seals, as stated in your chief examination, further than that which appears in the proces verbal? (Here complainants' solicitor showed the witness the proces verbal in question, and to this defendants' solicitor objected, and requested that of the objection note might be made, on the ground that the witness had not asked for the same, and that it was an interference with the cross examination, which complainants solicitor had no right to make.)

name was Harriet Dover She was married twice, to Mr. Harper and Dr. Smyth My mother had three sisters I think; only one is now living, she is a Mrs Thomas, residing in Philadelphia the wife of Moses Thomas T D HARPER

Examination taken, reduced to writing, and by the witness, subscribed and sworn to this 3d day of May before me, at New Orleans WILLIAM H HUNT, U S Comm r

The defendants, by their counsel, except to the filing of the deposition of Mrs Smyth, as an exhibit in the cause against them, on the ground that it was taken *en parte* as to them and before issue joined, and the publication thereof was made, without notice to the defendants

WILLIAM H HUNT U S Comm r

After the examination of John H Holland a witness in behalf of defendants the examination here closed before the undersigned, and was adjourned until Monday the 7th day of May, 1849 at 5 o clock. P M

WILLIAM H HUNT, U S Comm r

And on Monday, the 7th May, 1849 appeared before me the undersigned Commissioner, P C Wright, Esq Solicitor for Complainants, and G B Duncan, Esq, Solicitor for Relf, Chew and Devereux, defendants, and Jules Lavergne Esq, Solicitor for James Hopkins, defendant, and Martin Blache Solicitor for Norbert Louque, defendant, at which time Complainants produced James Gardette as a witness in their behalf

James Gardette, Doctor of Medicine, residence in New Orleans, and aged thirty-nine years, a witness produced and sworn, and examined on the part and behalf of said complainants, deposeth and saith, as follows '

My name is James Gardette I am a Doctor of Medicine aged thirty-nine years, and a resident of New Orleans, I know the parties complainant to this suit, and the defendant Mr R Relf I knew Madame Louisa Binguerel formerly residing in Louisiana perfectly well and have known her since 1831 She resided in Opelousas and died there about five months ago I know of my own personal knowledge that Madame Binguerel testified in this cause a few years ago She told me so, since she gave her testimony JAMES GARDETTE

Cross Examined

I was born in Philadelphia, in 1809 I am the eldest child of my father and mother My father and mother were married in 1807 or 1808 as I understand About a year after the marriage I was born, as I learn I understand they were married in Philadelphia My father was a widower before he married He died in Bordeaux From this marriage there were three children My father died, I think, in 1831 My mother was with him at the time of his death My mother always continued to reside with him from the marriage to the time of his death My father lost everything in the Revolution in France, in 1831, and left no estate at his death My mother continued to reside in Bordeaux until 1835 My father and mother went to Bordeaux in 1829 They resided in Philadelphia until they removed to Bordeaux in about 1829 For a long time previous to their removal to Bordeaux they resided in Philadelphia, at the corner of Ninth and Chesnut Sts My mother was the mother of Mrs Gaines, one of the complainants in this case   JAMES GARDETTE

Examination taken, reduced to writing, and by the witness subscribed and sworn to, at New Orleans, this 7th day of May, 1849, before me   WILLIAM H HUNT, U S Comm'r.

After the examination of the above named witnesses the examination here closed before the undersigned, and was adjourned until Wednesday, 9th May, 1849, at 5 o'clock, P M.

        WILLIAM H HUNT,   U S Commissioner

And on Wednesday, the 9th of May, appeared before me, the undersigned commissioner, P C wright, Esq, solicitor for complainants, and G B Duncan, Esq, solicitor for Relf, Chew, and in behalf of C Roselius, Esq, solicitor for M Devereux, defendants, at which time, no witnesses being produced, either on behalf of complainants or defendants, the examination was adjourned until Thursday, the 10th of May A. D 1849, at 5 o'clock, P M

        WILLIAM H HUNT, U S Commissioner

And on Monday, the 14th of May, 1849, appeared before me, the undersigned commissioner, P C. Wright, Esq., solicitor for complainants, and Martin Blache, Esq, solicitor for Norbert Louque, Esq, defendant, and M Taylor, Esq, and M Labarre, Esq, solicitors for several defendants

At which time, complainants produced Gallien Preval as a witness in their behalf

Gallien Preval, gentleman, residence New Orleans, aged —— years, a witness, produced, sworn, and examined on the part and behalf of said complainants, deposeth and saith as follows My name is Gallien Preval, my residence New Orleans my occupation gentleman my age sixty-eight years, I know the par-

I saw Mr Clark, sometimes his servants, sometimes his friends I often went to inquire after his health

Question —Upon the occasion of one of your visits to Mr Clark at his house, some short time prior to his death were the defendants Relf and Chew, or either of them a subject of conversation by Mr Clark? If yea what did Mr Clark say respecting them, or either of them?

Answer —It was in the spring of 1813 I think I cannot exactly say what month, I called on Mr Clark I had an account against him Clark was an off-hand kind of a man, and told me 'Wagner I have no change' We, here in the city of New Orleans had here, then, a plenty of paper money, but little gold and silver He had been in the habit of giving me a draft on Chew and Relf in paying my accounts, whose counting room was in St Louis street, at that time, as I believe I told Mr Clark it was all the same thing, 'Give me a draft on Chew and Relf' He told me, as nearly as I recollect, "That fellow Chew is such a damned rascal, I dont speak to him' I am certain he used these words, damned rascal and said he did not speak to him, and that in consequence, he could not give me a draft on that house I knew the account was good, and went away after that I saw Mr Clark several times after that, but never mentioned the subject of Mr Chew or Mr Relf to him, that I recollect

PETER K WAGNER

Cross examined

I think either Chew or Relf lived on the Bayou Road which one I do not recollect but I think Mr Chew, at the time of my arrival in this city

Question —Do you know whether or not at any time after your arrival in this city Mr Clark resided during a portion of his time in the family of Mr Chew?

Answer —I do not Whenever I saw him at home, he was at his own house

Question —Do you know whether or not, at any time after your arrival in this city, Mr Relf resided any portion of his time with Mr Clark, at Clark's house, on the Bayou Road?

Answer —Not to my knowledge I never saw him at Mr Clark's house I visited Mr Clark frequently

Question —You have stated, in your chief examination, that you had an account against Mr Clark for collection please to state what that account was for

Answer —It was for business done in my printing office

Question —Do you know whether or not Mr Chew was in New Orleans during any time of the spring of 1813?

Answer—I cannot say—it is so long ago. I think he was, but I am by no means sure.

Question—Do you know if he was here at the battle of New Orleans, in 1815?

Answer—I know he was. I saw him in the lines.

PETER K WAGNER

And it is here admitted on the part of the counsel for the respective parties to this suit, that Mrs Mary R Davis wife of Colonel Samuel B Davis formerly of the city of New Orleans, and now residing in the city of Wilmington State of Delaware departed this life some years since and that she is the same lady whose testimony was taken heretofore in the suit of Whitney and Wife vs Eleanor O'Beirn and others in which the said Relf and Chew were parties lately pending in the Probate Court of the city of New Orleans and this stipulation is made by Greer B Duncan Esq, solicitor for Relf and Chew and De la Croix, and on behalf of C Roselius Esq solicitor for M Devereux and it is made also by Julian Seghers, Esq solicitor for J J Jeandeau

Examination taken reduced to writing and by the witness subscribed and sworn to this 1st day of June, A D 1849 at New Orleans before me

WILLIAM H HUNT, U S Commissioner

After the examination of the above named witness the examination before the undersigned commissioner closed and was adjourned sine die

WILLIAM H HUNT, U S Commissioner

———

No 1   Offered and filed by complainant, 23d June 49

J W GURLEY Com

COURT OF THE UNITED STATES FOR THE EASTERN DISTRICT OF LOUISIANA

To any Judge or Justice of the Peace in the Parish of St Landry

Know ye, that reposing special trust and confidence in your integrity and ability we hereby authorize and require you that you call and cause to come before you certain witnesses, and them duly examine on oath touching and concerning certain matters and things in a cause now depending in the said court, wherein W W Whitney and wife are plaintiffs and Richard Relf and others are defendants and the same examinations so taken and reduced to writing, you certify under your hand and seal and send enclosed to this court without delay to be read in evidence on the trial of said cause and send also this writ

Answer —I have a very distinct recollection of everything relative to the affixing the seals, but not of any facts which might have occurred at the same time, which had nothing to do with the affixing of the said seals

Question —Have you not heretofore stated that your recollection was very indefinite, or words to that effect, of anything which occurred at the time of the affixing of the seals except by referring to the proces verbal itself?

Answer —If I said so, at that time I have said just what I say now

Question —Was not Judge Pitot spoken of in the chief examination, Judge and ex-officio Judge of the Court of Probates, and the same Judge who ordered the probate of the will of Daniel Clark?

Answer —I think that he was   I was at the funeral of Daniel Clark   I was at the funeral of Daniel Clark   The funeral started from Conti street, if my memory is correct   This is my impression   I may be mistaken   I cannot recollect on what day of the month this was, but I think it must have been on the 14th of August, 1813   I was not present at the time he died

Question —You have stated, in your chief examination, that you made particular search in a specified place for the will of Daniel Clark, and assigned as a reason that you had been previously informed that the will would probably be there   Now please state who it was that gave you this information

Answer —I received the information from Judge Pitot

I did not see Mr Relf or if I did I do not recollect it, after the death of Clark and previous to my meeting him at Clark's house when I went to affix the seals   I did not see Mr Chew there   I do not recollect the superscription of the package handed me by Mr Relf   I was not at that time acquainted with the handwriting of Mr Clark

Question —When did you first become acquainted with Mr Daniel Clark?

Answer —It must have been in the year 1811 or 1812   The first time I saw him was at Mr Pitot's house   I dined once or twice as well as I recollect, at Daniel Clark's house. I used to attend his soirees   I never on any of these occasions, met with a lady recognized as Mrs Clark

Question —Was not Mr Clark's standing reputation in New Orleans, from the time you knew him until his death, that of a high minded and honorable man?

Answer —Yes

Question —Did Daniel Clark ever state to you or in your presence and hearing, that he had a wife?

Answer —No never

Question —Did you see any lady presenting herself as his widow at his death or funeral?

Answer —No

Question —Did you know or ever hear of any lady presenting herself as the widow of Daniel Clark, and claiming any rights in the court in which his succession was opened?

Answer —No

Question —Did not Daniel Clark, from the time you knew him, at these parties and dinners and elsewhere, act and hold himself out to his friends as a bachelor? (Complainants counsel objects to this interrogatory on the ground that it has no reference to the matter of the direct examination, and therefore is a direct question objected to as being leading, and thereupon defendants solicitor modified their question, and before the answer was given, so as to read as follows)

Question —Did or did not Daniel Clark, from the time you knew him at these parties and dinners and elsewhere, act and hold himself out to his friends as a bachelor? (And complainants' counsel objected to this interrogatory, as thus amended on the same ground that had been urged against the original question. Defendants counsel insisting the witness saith)

Answer —In going to Mr Clark's soirees and to dine with him, it never crossed my mind to ascertain if Mr Clark was a married man or not.

GALLIEN PREVAL.

Examination taken, reduced to writing, and by the witness subscribed and sworn to, before me, this 14th May, 1849, at New Orleans.

WILLIAM H HUNT, U S Commissioner

And on Friday, the 1st day of June, 1849, appeared before me the undersigned commissioner, P C Wright, Esq solicitor for complainants, and Greer B. Duncan, Esq, solicitor for Relf and Chew and in behalf of C Roselins and Theodore Seghers, Esq, solicitor for defendants, at which time, complainants produced as a witness in their behalf Peter K Wagner, Esq, gentleman, aged   years, sworn and examined on the part and behalf of said complainants, who saith and deposeth as follows:

Peter K. Wagner is my name, my age 63 years, my residence New Orleans, my residence has been in New Orleans since March or April, 1812 I know the complainants, and the defendants Relf and Chew I knew the late Daniel Clark I was on very friendly and familiar terms with him I was at his house several times during his last illness I am not sure that I saw him every time I went there Sometimes

Witness the Honorable Sam'l H Harper, Judge of said court, at the city of New Orleans this 18th day of March Anno Domini 1837, and the sixty-first year of the Independence of the United States of America

T W COLLINS, Dy. Clerk

WILLIAM W WHITNEY AND MYRA C WHITNEY, COMPLAINANTS, *against* RICHARD RELF BEVERLY CHEW, AND OTHERS, DEFENDANTS	IN CHANCERY IN THE DISTRICT COURT OF THE UNITED STATES, FOR THE EASTERN DISTRICT OF THE STATE OF LOUISIANA

Interrogatories to be propounded on behalf of the complainants to Joseph Deville Degoutin Bellechasse, Mrs Harriet Smith, Samuel B Davis, Mrs Eliza Clark, and Chevalier Delacroix

1st, Were you, or not, acquainted with the late Daniel Clark of New Orleans?

2d Were you, or not, at any time, upon terms of intimacy with him? and did you, or not, enjoy his confidence?

3d Do you know, or not, whether the said Clark at the time of his death, left any child living? If so, state who that child is how you derived your information or knowledge upon the subject, and particularly all that you may have heard the said Clark relate touching that matter, and his conduct towards and treatment of said child

4th Do you know whether the said Clark, at any time during his life, made any provision for said child? If so, state particularly all you may know upon that subject

5th If you have any information or knowledge touching a will of said Clark, made about May, 1811, relate all you may know of the said will and the circumstances under which it was made and whether, or not, the said Clark did not thereafter express his determination to make another will State all you may have heard him say upon that subject

6th Did, or not, the said Clark make a last will and testament about the year 1813? State all you may know touching that matter, or what you may have heard from him relative thereto, and the contents of the will, as far as you can recollect

7th If you know any thing further material to the controversy herein, of interest to the complainants or defendants, relate it

(Signed) GRYMES CHINN &c., for Complainants

Filed 6th February, 1837

(Signed) T W COLLINS Dy Clerk

Clerk's Office, United States Court,)
New Orleans, March 17th, 1837)

I do hereby certify the foregoing to be a true and correct copy of the original, on file in this office

T W COLLINS, Dy Clerk

No 1   Offered and filed by complainant, 23d June, 1849

J. W. GURLEY, Con

WILLIAM W WHITNEY, AND
MYRA C WHITNEY
against
RICHARD RELF, BEVERLY CHEW,
AND OTHERS

IN EQUITY

No 3823, IN THE DISTRICT COURT OF THE UNITED STATES, IN AND FOR THE EASTERN DISTRICT OF LOUISIANA

Cross interrogatories to the interrogatories filed by the complainants on the sixth of February, 1837, and by them propounded, in their behalf, to Joseph Deville Degoutin Bellechasse, Mrs Harriet Smith, Samuel B Davis, Mrs Eliza Clark, and Chevalier de la Croix

The commissioner who may receive the answers to the interrogatories of the complainants, and to the cross interrogatories, is notified that it will be required of him to certify that the said several interrogatories, and cross interrogatories, were answered by the deponents separately and apart from each other, and from other person, and that neither the chief or cross questions were shown to or read by the deponent, or by either of them, and that *each question* under each separate chief and cross interrogatory, was answered in the order in which the several questions are propounded, and that he did not permit any deponent to see or read any succeeding interrogatory, until his answer to the preceding had been fully taken down, and especially, that no communications or suggestions were made in the presence of the commissioner, or to his knowledge or belief, by any attorney or agent of either of the parties to either of the defendants. and also to certify that he carefully cautioned each witness to distinguish accurately in each answer, what he or she stated, from his or her personal knowledge, and what from hearsay and let it so be written down in the answers—what is of personal knowledge and what of hearsay

The *complainants are notified* that all legal exceptions are reserved to each one of their interrogatories, and especially do the respondents, in propounding these cross-interrogatories, reserve to themselves the right to demur, plead or answer, hereafter, as they shall be advised, and at all times to declare and show, that this honorable court hath not, either in equity or at law, any jurisdiction of the matter of the present bill of complaint, the same being only cognizable by the Probate Court of the Parish of Orleans in the State of Louisiana, which Court is already seized of the succession of Daniel Clark, the pretended ancestor of the complainant Myra the same being a Court, where a plain adequate and complete remedy may be had at law, by the complainants for any and all their supposed claims against the succession of the said Daniel Clark, and full redress for their many grievances, set forth in their said bill of complaint, protesting therefore against this proceeding, and not intending to waive any right or to admit any claim of the complainants in the premises, but merely desiring and intending to provide against the effect of error, accident, surprise, or fraud and wishing to advertise the complainants of the purposes of such of the respondents only as sign these cross interrogatories, said respondent here acting in his, her, and their own behalf only, and each one acting for him or herself separately, propound the following cross interrogatories

1st Will you and each one of you, answering any interrogatory of the complainants state your name, age and present residence and where you resided during each year, from 1800 to 1814 and state your employment and mention your means of acquaintance with Mr Daniel Clark, formerly of New Orleans, and who is said to have died in that city in the summer of the year 1813? Mrs Harriet Smith and Mrs Eliza Clarke two of the witnesses proposed to be examined by the complainants, are particularly requested to state what were their names before marriage and if they were married more than once, to state the names of their several husbands

2d If you say you were upon terms of intimacy with Mr Clark, state, if you please how you came to be thus intimate with him when that intimacy commenced under what circumstances, and in what place it commenced and how long it continued, when it ended, and whether it was ever interrupted and if it was, for what cause?

3d If you answer the third interrogatory in chief, affirmatively, state the name, sex and age of the child, and *where* and *when* the child was born Be very particular, if you please, in stating these matters with great accuracy and mention in detail, what circumstances enable you to recollect, with accuracy, the matters about which you are interrogated

4th Was Mr Daniel Clark, about whom complainants interrogate you, ever married? If you answer affirmatively, state *when*, *where*, and to *whom*, by what priest, clergyman, or magistrate, and who were the witnesses present ? were you among the witnesses, and if so who was present with you ? Answer with great particularity

5th Did Mr Clark (if you say he was married) introduce his wife to his friends and acquaintances, and was she received and recognized in New Orleans as his lawful wife? If you answer that she was not so received, state why she was not, and mention the reasons which did, in your opinion, induce Mr Clark not to introduce her in society Or was his marriage private? If so why was it private, or what circumstances could or did induce him to keep that marriage secret from his friends and the public ?

6th If in answering the sixth interrogatory of the complainants, you say that Mr Clark made any provisions for the child whom you are to state he left, at his death, state what the provision was, and in what did it consist—lands houses lots, slaves, stocks, bonds, mortgages, or what ? State particularly, and mention the amount, and state how you happened to know all these matters

7th Will you state whether you have ever had any correspondence or conversations with the complainants or with either of them, on the subject of the pretensions of the complainant, Myra C Whitney to be the daughter and heiress of the estate of Mr Daniel Clark? and if you have had any such correspondence annex it to your answer or any such conversation, state the nature of it—what was desired and what it was intimated to you it was important you should prove ? Mention when you last saw the complainants or either of them, and which of them, and whether you were not then or at some other time, informed that your testimony would be wanted and required touching the matters about which you have now been interrogated ?

8th Did you or not ever hear Mr Clark acknowledge that he had any natural children in New Orleans, and, particularly, did you or not ever hear him acknowledge two female children, the one named Caroline and the other named Myra and is or not that Myra one of the complainants in this case ? Did you ever hear him say that he intended to leave, by will, money or property enough to Myra to take the stain of her birth ? If you heard him use such expressions, or those of a similar character, state what you suppose he meant by taking off the stain from the birth of his own legitimate daughter ?

9th. Will you state who was the mother of the complainant, **Myra**, and did the mother nurse Myra ? if not why not, who did nurse her did her mother die and leave her an infant, or was she too sick and too feeble to nurse that child ? did the mother of Myra, the complainant nurse and raise her or not ?

if not, who did? Mention particularly and all the circumstances

10th If you know when the complainant, Myra, was born, state the precise date and place, and state if you know, by whom and where she was raised and whose name she bore and why she bore that name?

11th Was not the last will of Mr Clark admitted to probate in the proper tribunal at New Orleans? If you undertake to say anything about a will which it is supposed Mr Clark made either in 1811 or 1813 or any other time state nothing but what is of your own personal knowledge and be careful to avoid stating anything which is in the way

12th If you state anything about any supposed will of Mr Clark or any of its provisions state whether you are sufficiently with the ordinances and law of the Territory of Orleans, and State of Louisiana to form a correct opinion as to the legality of the will in form and in its different provisions Have you ever studied the laws of Louisiana? if so how long if not how can you express any opinion about them? Have you not frequently conversed with the complainants respecting the supposed provisions of a will supposed to have been made by Mr Clark in 1813, and if you have in your conversation you have expressed in your answer to these interrogatories of the complainant, be somewhat attached to such conversation and state what are your feelings and affections towards the complainants whether you are attached to or connected with either of them and if you are how and in what manner connected and whether you have any interest in the result of this suit

13th Will you, Col Bellechasse and Mr Passion Drian, for yourselves, personally in addition to the foregoing interrogatories, be pleased to state whether or not from your during the year 1810, or thereabout, or some time before to the year 1806 and the period of his death at New Orleans, Mr Daniel Clark the gentleman about whom you have now been interrogated, did or not, convey to you certain lots of land in what is called the Bayou Road in the rear of the city of New Orleans, and if so state as nearly as you can collect the numbers of these lots, and for what purpose Mr Clark conveyed them and whether you have accomplished that purpose, and if so, where Were not said lots in fact and in truth conveyed to you in trust for the complainant Myra, and if they were, will you be pleased to state what motive induced Mr Clark to convey property in trust for his supposed legitimate daughter, the sole heiress of his estate?

14th Will you, Col *Bellechasse* and Mr *Delacroix*, state further in addition whether or not said trusts were not confided to you for the purpose, in part, of being conveyed to another supposed natural child of Mr Clark, named Caroline and if so, state whether or not the sum has been so conveyed to the said Myra and Caroline?

15th Will you, Col *Belleehasse*, particularly, and in addition, for yourself, individually, state whether or not, some time during the year 1822 and at other times you corresponded on most friendly terms with Mr Richard Relf, one of the respondents in this case, and whether you ever alluded to two female children named Myra and Caroline of whom Mr Daniel Clark supposed himself the father and state particularly, if you recollect having used in one of these letters to Mr Relf such expressions as the following "Neanmoins et relativement a M lle Caroline, je puis dire et meme jurer que Clark avait une trop belle ame et le cœur trop bien placé pour avoir été capable, ayant deux enfans qu'il adorait, d'en avoir voulu favoriser une, en laissant l'autre exposée à mendier son pain, et livrée aux vicissitudes qu'entraine la misere' Will you now, sir, be pleased to state if you could say, and were, indeed, ready to swear, in 1822, and at other times, that Mr Clark had two children whom he adored, one of them being named Caroline, how you can declare that the complainant, Myra, is the legitimate daughter and only daughter of Mr Daniel Clark If you had occasion to change your opinions on these points, state when you so changed your mind and what reasons induced such change, mention the names of the persons who induced such change, and when you first knew or believed Mr Clark was a married man

16th To Mrs Harriet Smith particularly, and in addition to the first twelve interrogatories, will you, Madame be pleased to state, whether you knew the mother of Myra, the complainant intimately and if so, how long, and whether you associated familiarly with her? pray mention whether you were present at the birth of Myra, and whether you saw the child frequently after her birth and how soon thereafter State, also, whether Myra was nursed by her mother, if not, why not, and by whom nursed, and why, and whether, also, Myra's mother was known and received publicly in New Orleans as the lawful wife of Mr Daniel Clark, and whether you knew or believed then that Mr Clark was married to Myra's mother? If you did know of any such supposed marriage, did other persons know the facts as well as yourself? if so, who? Mention the names of all persons whom you may recollect who knew these matters as well as yourself, state all circumstances with great particularity

17th To all the witnesses Will each one of you, answering any of these direct or cross interrogatories, state whether you have seen, examined, read, or heard read any one of them, or copies of them, at any time or place before you were called upon by the commissioner to answer them? if aye, state where, when, and by whom they were thus so shown or read to or by you, and for what purpose? State, also, each one of you, whether you have had any conversation or correspondence within the last three or four years with the complainants, or with either of them, respecting their supposed claims, against the estate of the late Daniel Clark, and, if you answer affirmatively, state why, when, and where such conversations or correspondence occurred, and the nature and amount of them, as far as your memory will serve you, and who was present at such conversations, if you have any letters from the complainants, or from either of them, on the matters referred to in these direct and cross interrogatories, annex them to your answers, if possible, and if not possible, state why? and then, if you have preserved and cannot annex them, give true extracts from them, and if that is not possible, state your recollections

18th. What is your own maternal language? If not English, do you understand that language perfectly, and if you do not understand English, how have you contrived to answer these chief and cross interrogatories? Who has translated them to you?

[Signed]	L. C. DUNCAN, for R. Relf and B. Chew,
	J. J. MERCIER, for the Mayor and Aldermen of New Orleans, Soniat Dufossat and Louis Desdunes
[Signed]	R. M. SHEPARD, for P. A. Sorbe and Rene Lemonier
"	P. A. ROST, for Maria Holliday and Dussuau Delacroix
"	H. LOCKETT, for James Field
"	JOHN SLIDELL, for John Minturn, George Kenner, and Duncan Kenner
"	JULIEN SEGHERS, for for F. H. Petitpain, Claude René Samory, and Louis Lalande Ferrier
[Signed]	ISAAC T. PRESTON, for Widow Jaubert, Luke Vigneau, Charles Patterson, Mr. Callaway, Charles Fonde, Belfine Berdule, Antoine Piernas, and John Matthews, Ramon Mansana, Manuel Marquez

Clerk's office, United States Court, New Orleans, 17th March, 1839

I hereby certify the foregoing to be a true copy of the original, on file in this office

T. W. COLLINS, Deputy Clerk.

WILLIAM W WHITNLY AND MYRA C WHITNEY, COMPLAINANTS, *against* RICHARD RELF, BEVERLY CHEW AND OTHERS, DEFENDANTS	IN CHANCERY In the District Court of the United States for the Eastern District of the State of Louisiana

STATE OF LOUISIANA, PARISH OF ST LANDRY

Pursuant to a commission from the District Court of the United States for the Eastern District of the State of Louisiana, dated the 18th day of March, Anno Domini, 1837,—

I, George King, parish judge in and for the aforesaid parish of St Landry have this day the twelfth of April, in the year one thousand eight hundred and thirty eight, caused to come before me Mrs Harriet Smyth, a witness in the above entitled suit, who being first sworn on the Holy Evangelists of Almighty God, to make true answers to the interrogatories and cross-interrogatories propounded to her and annexed to the said comission, to the best of her knowledge, she made the following answers, to wit —

Answer to the first interrogatory

Yes, I became acquainted with the late Mr. Daniel Clark shortly after my arrival in New Orleans in eighteen hundred and four, which acquaintance continued to the period of his decease, in August, eighteen hundred and thirteen

Answer to the second interrogatory

I was on terms of intimacy with Mr Clark, as the particular friend of my late husband, Wm Harper, and have every reason to believe I enjoyed his confidence. Mr. Clark and my late husband were intimate friends. In eighteen hundred and five the firm of Davis & Harper was formed, and except the sum of money advanced to my late husband by my father, I understood that Mr Clark's credit was the basis of the firm. I suckled in her infancy, Mr Clark's daughter Myra. I did it voluntarily in consequence of her having suffered from the hired nurses. Mr Clark considered that this constituted a powerful claim on his gratitude and friendship and he afterwards gave me his confidence respecting her

Answer to the third interrogatory

Yes, Mr Clark left, to my knowledge, but one child only, a daughter, named Myra Clark, whom I suckled in her infancy, and who is now Myra Clark Whitney. I was residing with my late husband in the family of his uncle, Col S B Davis, when the infant Myra was brought into the family by Col and Madame Davis. I had at that time an infant of my own. I was solicited by them to suckle the infant they had brought, which I refused to do, unless they first disclosed to me the name of her parents both Col and Madame Davis then told me, she was the child of Daniel Clark, and that he, Mr Clark, was particularly anxious that his child should be under the care of Madame Davis Mr Clark afterwards assured me that she was his child, and always told me she was his only child She was always called Myra Clark by the whole family I never knew her by any other name, till her marriage Mr Clark, during his continual attentions to, and while caressing her ever called her his dear little daughter Myra his affection and attentions to her seemed to increase with her age, in fact, he showed and seemed to feel all the paternal regard for her, that the most affectionate father could show to an only child Her clothing and playthings, which were of the most extravagant and costly description, were provided for her by Mr Clark, he also purchased for her a valuable servant Mr Clark invariably spoke of her to me, as his only child, and as destined to inherit his splendid fortune I witnessed the continued and increasing paternal solicitude of Mr Clark for his daughter Myra, from her early infancy, till her departure for Philadelphia, with the family of Col Davis, in 1812 Mr Clark continued his frequent visits to my husband and self, till his last and fatal sickness, his last visit was on the day that fatal sickness commenced he then complained of being very unwell, and requested the favor of a bowl of tea, which was provided for him Up to that period he always spoke of his daughter Myra with the most enthusiastic affection

Answer to the fourth interrogatory

I always understood from Mr Daniel Clark himself, that he destined his daughter Myra to be the sole heiress of his large fortune, and on the occasion of his duel with Gov Claibourne, in I think 1807, he told me after that affair, that he had previously, by way of precaution, secured to his daughter Myra the amplest provision, in case he should have fallen, and that he had also left documents so arranged, as to manifest every thing of interest to her Afterwards in 1811, when he was about to visit Philadelphia, in order, as he said, to settle some commercial affairs with D. W Coxe of that place, of whose conduct he complained, he told me he had made arrangements by means of confidential transfers of property to secure the interests of his said child Myra, which consisted of a very large amount of notes, and titles to real estate Mr. Clark told me his reasons for going to Philadelphia, were, that he heard that D W. Coxe was about to fail, and that although his partnership with him had been dissolved a considerable time, yet as the dissolution had not been made legally public, he feared he would be made liable

Answer to the fifth interrogatory

When Mr Clark was on the point of departure from New

44

Orleans, for Philadelphia, in May, 1811, in consequence, as he told me, of the pecuniary embarassment of D W Coxe, he said to me that he had well protected his daughter Myra by confidential trusts, and had also left with Chew and Relf a will, in favor of his mother; that this will **was** the result of his situation at the time.

After his return he told me the report was not true to the extent that he had feared.

He complained very much of the conduct of Coxe. He referred to the will he had made previous to his departure in May, 1811, as being made to meet the circumstances, in which he had been placed by Coxe, but that now he had finally closed all transactions with said Coxe, and had made great pecuniary sacrifices in order to secure himself against all possible future claims.

Answer to the sixth interrogatory

In eighteen hundred and thirteen, some few months before Mr. Clark's death, he told me, he felt he ought no longer to defer securing his estate to his daughter Myra by a last will.

Near this period he stopped one day at my house, and said to me he was on his way to the plantation of Chevalier De la Croix, for the purpose of requesting him to be named in his will one of his executors, and tutor to his daughter Myra On his return, he told me, with much apparent gratification, that De la Croix had consented to serve, and that Judge Pitot and Col. Bellechasse, had consented to be the other executors. About this time, he told me he had commenced making his last will Between this period and the time he brought his last will to my house, Mr Clark spoke very often of being engaged in making his last will, he always spoke of it in connection with his only and beloved daughter Myra, said he was making it for her sake, to make her his sole heiress, and to insure her being educated according to his wishes At the times Mr Clark spoke of being engaged in making his last will, he told me over and over again, what would constitute its contents that he should in it acknowledge the said Myra as his legitimate daughter, and bequeath all his estate to her, but direct that an annuity of 2000 dollars a year, should be paid his mother during her life; and an annuity of 500 dollars a year to a young female, at the north of the United States, named Caroline De Grange, till her majority; then it was to cease, and 5000 dollars were to be paid her as a legacy; and that he would direct that one year after the settlement of his estate, 5000 dollars should be paid to a son of Judge Pitot, of New Orleans, as a legacy; at the same period 5000 dollars as a legacy to a son of Mr. Du Buys, of New Orleans; that his slave, Lubin, was to be freed, and a maintenance provided for him.

In his conversations respecting his being engaged in making his last will, he talked a good deal about the plan of education to be laid down, in his will, for his daughter Myra, he expressed, frequently, his satisfaction that the Chevalier Delacroix would be her tutor in his will, he often spoke with earnestness of the moral benefit to his daughter Myra from being acknowledged by him in his last will as his legitimate daughter, and he often spoke of the happiness it would give his mother He expressed the most extravagant pride and ambition for her, he would frequently use the emphatic language, that he was making her a bill of rights he mentioned, at these times, that this will would contain a complete inventory of all his estates, and explanations of all his business, so as both to render the administration on his estate plain and easy to his friends, Chevalier Delacroix, Judge Pitot and Col Bellechasse, and as a safeguard to his estate in case he should not live long enough to dissolve and adjust all his pecuniary relations with others About four weeks before his death, Mr Clark brought this will to my house, as he came in, he said, ' Now my will is finished my estate is secured to Myra, beyond human contingency, now if I die to-morrow, she will go forth to society, to my relations, to my mother acknowledged by me, in my last will as my legitimate daughter, and will be educated according to my minutest wishes under the superintendence of the Chevalier Delacroix, and her interest will be under the care of Chevalier Delacroix, Judge Pitot, and Col Bellechasse, here is the charter of her rights it is now completely finished, and I have brought it to you to read " He left it in my possession until the next day I read it, deliberately, from beginning to end In this will, Mr Clark acknowledged Myra Clark as his legitimate daughter, and only heir, designating her as then living in the family of S B Davis · Mr Clark, in this will, bequeathed all his estate to the said Myra, but directed that an annuity of 2000 dollars should be paid to his mother during her (his mother's) life, and an annuity of 500 dollars should be paid to Caroline Degrange till she arrived at majority, when the annuity was to cease and 5000 were to be paid her as a legacy He directed that, one year after his estate was settled, 5000 dollars should be paid, as a legacy, to a son of Judge Pitot, of New Orleans, and that one year after his estate was settled, 5000 dollars should be paid, as a legacy, to a son of Mr Dubuys, of New Orleans He provided for the freedom and maintenance of his slave Lubin he appointed Mr Dusuau Delacroix tutor to his daughter Myra he gave very extensive instructions in regard to her education This will contained an inventory of his estate, and explanations of his business relations, he appointed Mr Dusuau Delacroix, James Pitot, and J.'D D Bellechasse, executors the whole of this will was in Mr

Clark's handwriting it was dated in July, 1813, and was signed by him, it was an olographic will it was dated in July, 1813, and was signed by him I was well acquainted with said Clark's handwriting The last time Mr Clark spoke to me about his daughter and his last will was on the day he came out for the last time (as far as I know) from his house, which was the last time I saw him He came to my house about noon, complained of feeling unwell, asked leave to have prepared for him a bowl of tea he made his visit of about two hours duration talking the whole time of his daughter Myra and his last will he said a burthen of solicitude was removed from his mind, from the time he had secured to her his estate beyond accident, by finishing his last will he dwelt upon the moral benefit to her, in society, from being acknowledged by him, in his last will as his legitimate daughter he talked about her education said it would be the greatest boon from his God, to live to bring her up, but what was next to that were his comprehensive instructions, in his will, in regard to her education, and her being committed to the care of the Chevalier Delacroix, who would be a parent to her After Mr Clark's death, Col Bellechasse stopped at my house and told me Mr Clark's last will was suppressed, and that the old provisional will of 1811 was brought forward he repeated what Mr Baron and Lubin said (as he said) about the matter Knowing well the unbounded confidence reposed in Lubin by Mr Clark, I sent for him, he came and related to me what he said occurred Soon after said Clark's death I understood that the notaries of New Orleans were summoned in court on the petition of Mr Dusuau Delacroix, to swear whether they had a duplicate of Mr Clark's last will The late John Poultney, of New Orleans deceased, who, at the time of Mr Clark's death was transacting my late husband's business under a general power of attorney, (he, the said Mr Harper, having gone to the north about two months or a little more previously) came with several friends to examine an iron chest of Mr Clarks, that stood in my house, in the faint hope, as they said, of finding a duplicate of Mr Clark's last will, that is, the will of 1813 this was immediately subsequently to Mr Clark's death

To the seventh interrogatory she answers Mr Clark was a man of powerful and acknowledged talents, towering ambition, great pride and dignity of character, strong feelings and affections, the spectacle of such a man, absorbed in one object that seemed to engage all his faculties, was of itself highly impressive To the excessive love for his child, all who were intimate with him could bear witness, but when he came to frame his last will, arrange his plans for her future aggrandisement, for her education, and embody principles and advice for her government through life, his wish and effort, by means of his last will, to carry himself beyond the grave in all the relations of parent to his sole and orphan child, these scenes are as vivid to my mind as if they had lately occurred   Mr Clark, having for several months been dwelling on his being employed in making his last will, had prepared my mind to see it finished and when he brought it to me he exclaimed, "Now my will is finished," and when, next day, after having read it carefully, I returned it to Mr Clark, I, playfully, said to him, since the charter of Myra's rights, as you call your last will, is dated in July, what a pity you did not finish it soon enough to bear the date of the Fourth of July, the anniversary of the day the Americans promulgated their charter   Mr Clark told me that he wished the existence of this will to be known only to a few friends, for the present he mentioned that he had given it to Col Bellechasse, Governor Derbernais, Judge Pitot, Chevalier Delacroix, and Mr J Lynd, to examine   The mysterious disappearance of Mr Clark's last will produced great excitement among Mr Clark's friends   A short time after the death of Mr Clark, I heard with surprise that the Chevalier Delacroix, the tutor of Myra, in the last will, in whom Mr Clark had so confidently trusted, became very friendly with Mr Relf, and received from him a large number of Mr Clark's negroes, and other favors   Thus were the fond hopes of Mr Clark ended

To the first cross interrogatory she answers, my name is Harriet Smyth, my age is fifty years, my present residence is Opelousas   In 1804, I removed to Louisiana prior to this I resided in and near Philadelphia   From 1804, till some time in 1814, I resided in New Orleans, with the exception of an occasional visit, which I made to Philadelphia   Prior to removing to New Orleans, I married William Harper, of Philadelphia, who died in 1828   In 1834, I married George Morris Smyth, M D   My name before marriage, was Harriet Dover   I have been married twice   My present husband is a cotton planter, and exercises his profession

To the second cross interrogatory   This has been already answered

To the 3d cross interrogatory   The name of the said child was Myra Clark, she is a female   I understood from her father that she was born in New Orleans, she was born in 1806

To the 4th cross interrogatory.   I do not know whether Mr Daniel Clark was ever married or not

To the 5th cross interrogatory.   I have answered that I do not know whether Mr. Clark was married or not, that is to say, I was not present at his marriage, and, therefore, do not know whether he was married, it was asserted that he was married to the mother of Myra, whether the unblemished character which she had borne, forbid the idea that she could form any connection, except under the sanction of marriage, contributed to form this opinion, I cannot say   I am acquainted with the circumstances that produced the separation between Mr Clark and the mother of his child, namely when Mr Clark departed for Washington, as a delegate in Congress, he left with her Lubin's wife   While Mr Clark was absent, individuals had or supposed they had, a great interest in dissolving his connection with the mother of his child, commenced a plan of breaking it up by writing to Mr. Clark imputations against her, and by filling her mind with unfavorable impressions against him, till at length his mind was so poisoned, that when he arrived at New Orleans, he and she had a severe quarrel and separated she, immediately after this, left New Orleans   If Mr Clark was married and had not promulgated it, there were strong interests opposed to the promulgation.   If he was not married, strong interests were opposed to his marrying the mother of his child

To the 6th cross interrogatory.   This has already been answered.

To the 7th cross interrogatory   I have at different times conversed with Myra Clark Whitney, and her husband, about Daniel Clark, and his testamentary dispositions in her favor   I considered it my duty to make her acquainted with all that I knew about her father, that could be interesting to her, her history was communicated to her a very short time before her marriage, she believing herself to be the daughter of Colonel and Mrs. Davis.   As to epistolary communication with her on that subject, as well as I recollect there has been little or nothing I last saw them in 1837   They never made any suggestions to me incompatible with delicacy and propriety

To the 8th cross interrogatory   I never heard Daniel Clark acknowledge any other child than the said Myra, whom he called his legitimate daughter, he told me she was his only child ; that the mother of Myra had another daughter, named Caroline, six or seven years older than Myra, who was the child of Mr Degrange   I never heard Mr. Clark say, that he had any natural children.   I never heard him say there was any stain upon the birth of his daughter Myra.

To the 9th cross interrogatory   I have already before mentioned that I always understood that a Miss Carriere was the mother of Myra Clark, but whether she was married or not to Daniel Clark, I cannot say, but I did hear that at the time of Mr Clark's marrying the mother of Myra, the bigamy of Degrange in marrying her had not been judicially established, and that, therefore, the marriage was private   I understood that subsequently Degrange was condemned criminally for bigamy in marrying Miss Carriere, while he had a living wife. this was previous to my arrival in New Orleans. After my arrival, I understood, that the same fact was established in a civil action Mr. Clark had papers to prove this fact which I do not doubt would have been found with his last will, if that will had not been fraudulently suppressed after his death I never saw Degrange, he had fled from Louisiana, as I understood, several years previous to my arrival in New Orleans Myra was not nursed by her mother Mrs Davis, the wife of Col. Davis, as I have before mentioned, had charge of Myra Clark from her extreme infancy, until her father's death, and, indeed, I have sufficient reason to know that Myra continued with Mrs Davis, until her marriage with Mr Whitney, the plan of her education, traced out and provided for by her father in his last will of 1813, having been frustrated by the suppressing or purloining of that will Mr Clark never specified to me his reasons for placing his daughter Myra under the care of Mr. Davis, this lady possessed distinguished merit, and in every way fully justified Mr Clark's unbounded confidence

To the 10th cross interrogatory I have already spoken of the time, as well as I recollect, of Myra's birth, she was born in New Orleans, and bore the name of Myra Clark, when I lived in that city

To the 11th cross interrogatory. Mr Clark's last will (which was dated in July, 1813,) was not admitted to probate, but instead of that last will, the former provisional will of 1811, of which I have already before spoken was admitted to probate

To the 12th cross interrogatory I never studied law, but always understood that a father could leave property to his children consistently with law. Myra Clark Whitney and her husband might very naturally have taken up ideas about her father's testamentary dispositions from me, for the reasons already stated, but I certainly never took up any ideas from them, about those dispositions, my feelings towards Daniel Clark's daughter, are those of disinterested friendship, I am not connected with her by ties either of affinity or consanguinity, and have nothing to gain or lose by the result of this suit.

To the 16th interrogatory I have already said that I knew Myra Clark within a few days after her birth, and that I suckled her · as to her mother, I knew her only from report, and judged her to be a lady of respectable standing from her intimacy with Mrs Relf, the first wife of Richard Relf, now cashier of the Louisiana State Bank. I was not present at the birth of Myra. I know not, as I have already said, if Mr. Clark was married with her; there were rumors of a private marriage between them.

To the 17th cross interrogatory. I have neither seen, or heard read the interrogatories or cross interrogatories referred to, before called upon to answer the same. I have already before stated my conversations with Mr and Mrs Whitney about Mr. Clark's testamentary dispositions, and recollect nothing to add upon that subject.

To the 18th cross interrogatory   The English language is my mother tongue

                                                 HARRIET SMYTH

Sworn and subscribed to, at Opelousas,) Before me,
in the aforesaid parish of St Landry, this } GEORGE KING,
12th day of April, 1838, as aforesaid.   )   P Judge

Referred to in the depositions of T D Harper, at page No 3 of the depositions taken before me.

           WILLIAM H HUNT, U S Commissioner

          STATE OF LOUISIANA, PARISH OF ST LANDRY

Pursuant to the aforesaid commission, appeared before me, George King, parish judge in and for the aforesaid parish of St Landry, Mrs Harriet Smyth, wife of Doctor George M Smyth, of said parish, who, being first sworn as the law directs, gave the preceding answers to the interrogatories in chief, numbered 1 to 7, and to the cross interrogatories, numbered 1 to 18, annexed to said commission, which answers, reduced to writing, and signed by the said Harriet Smyth, are contained in the foregoing thirteen pages, and annexed to said commission, and therewith returned

Given under my hand and private seal, at Opelousas, this 12th day of April, 1838

           GEORGE KING, Parish Judge [Seal]

——————

          CONSULATE OF THE UNITED STATES OF AMERICA,
                                                 Matanzas.

I, C. P. Traub, Vice Consul of the United States of America, at this port, and residing within the same, do certify, that in pursuance of the annexed commission and interrogatories to me directed by the Circuit Court of the United States for the eastern district of the State of Louisiana, in a suit in chancery therein pending, wherein Wm. W Whitney and wife are complainants and Richard Relf, and others are defendants, I proceeded on the twenty-first day of August last, to the sugar estate of Colonel Joseph Deville Degoutin Bellechasse, to take his deposition to be read in evidence in said case, and the foregoing deposition

was then and there taken subscribed and sworn to before me.
All which is hereby certified to said court

[L. s.] Witness my hand and seal of office, this 6th day of
September, 2827.

[Signed] CHARLES P. TRAUB, Vice Consul

WILLIAM W. WHITNEY AND MARY C. WHITNEY COMPLAINANTS, *against* RICHARD RELF, BEVERLY CHEW AND OTHERS, DEFENDANTS	IN CHANCERY In the District Court of the United States for the Eastern District of the State of Louisiana

Interrogatories to be propounded in behalf of the complainants, to Joseph Deville Degoutin Bellechasse, Mrs. Harriet Smith, Samuel B. Davis Mrs. Eliza Clark and Chevalier Delacroix

1st. Were you or not acquainted with the late Daniel Clark, of New Orleans?

2d. Were you or not at any terms of intimacy with him and did you or not enjoy his confidence?

3d. Do you know or not whether the said Clark, at the time of his death left any child living? if so, state who that child is, how you derived your information or knowledge upon the subject, and particularly all that you may have heard the said Clark touching that matter and his conduct towards and treatment of said child.

4th. Do you know whether the said Clark, at any time during his life made any provision for said child? if so, state particularly all you may know upon that subject.

5th. If you have any information or knowledge touching a will of said Clark made about May, 1811, relate all you may know of the said will and the circumstances under which it was made and whether or not the said Clark did not thereafter express his determination to make another will. State all you may have heard him say upon this subject.

6th. Did or not the said Clark make a last will and testament about the year 1813? State all you may know touching that matter, or what you have heard from any relative thereto, and the contents of it as you can recollect.

7th. If you know ... herein and of intere ... late it ... ... nal to the controversy ... ndants re-

Signed, ...

Filed 6th February
Signed,

WILLIAM W. WHITNEY AND MYRA } IN EQUITY
C. WHITNEY, } No. 3823, IN THE DISTRICT
against } COURT OF THE U. STATES
RICHARD RELF, BEVERLY CHEW } IN AND FOR THE EASTERN
AND OTHERS, } DISTRICT OF LOUISIANA

Cross-interrogatories to the interrogatories filed by the complainants on the 6th February 1837, and by them propounded in their behalf to Joseph Deville Degoutin Bellechasse, Mrs. Harriet Smith, Samuel B. Davis, Mrs. Eliza Clark and Chevalier Delacroix.

1st. The commissioner who may receive the answers to the interrogatories of the complainants and to the following cross-interrogatories is notified that it will be required of him to certify that the said several interrogatories and cross-interrogatories were answered by the deponents separately, and apart from each other and from other persons, and that neither the chief or cross questions were shown to or read by the deponents or to or by either of them and that *each question*, under each separate chief or cross interrogatory was answered in the order in which the several questions are propounded and that he did not permit any deponent to see or read any succeeding interrogatory until his answer to the preceding had been fully taken down, and especially that no communications or suggestions were made in the presence of the commissioner or to his knowledge or belief, by any attorney or agent of either of the parties touching the deponents, and also to certify that he carefully cautioned each witness to distinguish accurately in each answer what he or she stated from his or her personal knowledge, and what from hearsay, and keep in the written down in the answers what is personal knowledge and what of hearsay.

2nd. The complainants insist, *at the outset*, that all legal exceptions are reserved to each one of them interrogatories, and especially do the respondents in propounding these cross-interrogatories, reserve to themselves the right to demur thereto and whenever after taken, shall be filed and it shall appear or be argued and shown that this honorable court hath not either in equity or at law, any jurisdiction of the matter in the present bill of complaint, the same being only cognizable in the probate court of the parish of Orleans in the State of Louisiana, which court is already seized of the succession of Daniel Clark, the pretended ancestor of the complainant Myra, the same being a court where a plain, adequate and complete remedy may be had at law by the complainant Myra, and all their supposed claims against the succession of the said Daniel Clark, and full redress for their many grievances set forth in their said bill of complaint, protesting, therefore against this proceeding, and not intending to waive any right or to admit any claim of the complainant in the premises but merely desiring and intending to provide against the effect of error, accident surprise or fraud and wishing to advertise the complainants of the purposes of several the respondents only as to these cross interrogatories. Said respondent here acting in his, her and then own behalf only and each one acting for him or herself separately proposed the following.

Cross Interrogatories

1st Will you in each one of you answering any interrogatory of the complainants state your name age and present residence and whether you resided from each year from 1800 to 1813 your age and profession and occupation your places of residence and if Mr Daniel Clark, briefly in New Orleans, and whether or not he married privately in the summer of the year 1801?

Mr Harrison and Mr Chas Clark were of the witnesses proposed to be examined by the complainants are particularly requested to state what were their residences before marriage and children were married how long ago, state the names of their children?

2d If you say you were upon terms of intimacy with Mr Clark at that period how you came to be thus intimate with him and at what time you comment it and under what circumstances and in what place of circumstances and how long it continued and whether it was ever interrupted and if it was for what cause.

3d If you answer the third interrogatory in chief affirmatively, state the sex, name and age of the child and whether and when the child was born. Be very particular, if you please in stating these matters with great accuracy and mention in detail what circumstances enable you to recollect with accuracy the matters about which you are interrogated.

4th Was Mr Daniel Clark at the time when complainants interrogate you, ever married? If you answer affirmatively, state when where and to whom, by what priest, clergymen, or magistrate, and who were the witnesses present? Were you among the witnesses and if so, who were present with you? Answer with great particularity.

5th Did Mr Clark (if you say he was married,) introduce his wife to his friends and acquaintances and was she received and recognized in New Orleans as his lawful wife? If you answer that she was not so received state why she was not, and mention the reasons which had in your opinion induce Mr Clark to introduce her into society or was his marriage private? If so why was it private?   And what circumstances could or did induce him to keep that marriage secret from his friends and the public?

6th If in answering the sixth interrogatory of the complainants, you say, that Mr Clark made any provisions for the child, whom you are asked to state he left at his death, state what that provision was, and in what did it consist? lands, houses, lots, slaves, stocks, bonds, mortgages, or what?   State particularly, and mention the amount, and state how you happen to know all these matters

7th. Will you state whether you have ever had any correspondence or conversations with the complainants, or with either of them on the subject of the pretensions of the complainant, Myra C Whitney, to be the daughter, and heiress of the estate of Mr Daniel Clark, and if you have had any such correspondence, annex it to your answer, or any such conversation, state the nature of it, what was desired, and what it was intimated to you it was important you should prove mention when you last saw the complainants, or either of them, and which of them, and whether you were not then, or at some other time, informed that your testimony would be wanted and required touching the matters about which you have now been interrogated

8th. Did you or not ever hear Mr. Clark acknowledge that he had any natural children in New Orleans? and particularly, did you or not ever hear him acknowledge two female children, the one named Caroline, and the other named Myra, and is or not, that Myra one of the complainants in this case? Did you ever hear him say that he intended to leave by will money or property enough to Myra to take the stain off her birth? If you heard him use such expressions, or those of a similar character, state what you suppose he meant by taking off the stain from the birth of his own legitimate daughter?

9th. Will you state who was the mother of the complainant, Myra, and did the mother nurse Myra, if not, why not? Who did nurse her? Did her mother die and leave her an infant, or was she too sick and too feeble to nurse this child? Did the mother of Myra, the complainant, nurse and raise her, or not? If not, who did? Mention particularly, and all the circumstances

10th. If you know when the complainant Myra was born, state the precise date, and place, and state, if you know, by whom and where she was raised, and whose name she bore, and why she bore that name

11th. Was not the last will of Mr. Clark admitted to probate in the proper tribunal at New Orleans? If you undertake to say anything about a will which it is supposed Mr Clark made either in 1811, in 1813, or at any other time, state nothing but what is of your own personal knowledge, and be careful to avoid stating anything which is of hearsay

12th It you state anything about any supposed will of Mr Clark or of any of its provisions, state whether you are sufficiently acquainted with the ordinances and laws of the territory of Orleans, and state of Louisiana, to form a correct opinion as to the legality of the will in form, and in its different provisions

Have you ever studied the laws of Louisiana? if aye how long? If not, how can you express any opinion about them? Have you not frequently conversed with the complainants respecting the supposed provisions of a will supposed to have been made by Mr Clark in 1813, and if you have, may not the opinions you have expressed in your answers to the sixth interrogatory of the complainants, be somewhat influenced by such conversations? And state what are your feelings and affections towards the complainants, whether you are related to or connected with either of them; and if you are, how, and in what degree or way, and whether you have any interest in the event of this suit

13th Will you, Col *Bellechasse*, and M *Dussuau Delacroix* for yourselves, personally, in addition to the foregoing interrogatories, be pleased to state whether or not, sometime during the year 1810, or there about, or some other time between the year 1806 and the period of his death, at New Orleans, Mr Daniel Clark, the gentleman about whom you have been interrogated, did or not convey to you certain lots of land, situated on what is called the Bayou Road, in the rear of the city of New Orleans and if so, state as nearly as you can recollect the number of these lots, and for what purpose Mr Clark conveyed them and whether you have accomplished that purpose, and if so, when? Were not said lots in fact and in truth conveyed to you in trust for the complainant, Myra? and if they were, will you be pleased to state what motive induced Mr Clark to convey property in trust for his supposed legitimate daughter, the sole heiress of his estate?

14th Will you, Col *Bellechasse* and Mr Delacroix, state further, in addition, whether or not said trusts were not confided to you for the purpose in part of being conveyed to another supposed natural child of Mr Clark, named Caroline, and if so, state whether or not the same has been so conveyed to said Myra and Caroline.

15th. Will you, Col *Bellechasse*, particularly, and in addition for yourself, individually, state whether or not, sometime during the year 1822, and at other times, you corresponded on most friendly terms with Mr Richard Rell, one of the respondents in this case, and whether you ever alluded to two female children named Myra and Caroline, of whom Mr Daniel Clark supposed himself the father and state particularly if you recollect having used in one of these letters to Mr Relf such expressions as the following "Neanmoins et relativement à M'll Caroline, je puis dire et même jurer que Clark avait une trop belle âme, et le cœur trop bien placé, pour avoir été capable, ayant deux enfans qu'il adorait, d'en avoir voulu favoriser une en laissant l'autre exposée à mendier son pain et livrée aux vicissitudes qu'entraine la misère"? Will you now, sir, be pleased to state if you could say, and were indeed, ready to swear in 1822, and at other times, that Mr. Clark had two children whom he adored one of them named Caroline how you can declare that the complainant Myra, is the legitimate daughter and only daughter of Mr. Daniel Clark? If you had occasion to change your opinions on these points, state when you so changed your mind, and what reasons induced such change Mention the names of the persons who induced such change, and when you first knew or believed Mr Clark was a married man

16th To Mrs Harriet Smyth particularly, and in addition to the first twelve interrogatories Will you Madame, be pleased to state whether you knew the mother of Myra, the complainant, intimately and if so, how long? and whether you associated familiarly with her, pray mention whether you were present at the birth of Myra, and whether you saw the child frequently after her birth, and how soon thereafter. State, also, whether Myra was nursed by her mother, if not, why not, and by whom nursed, and why, and whether, also, Myra's mother was known and received publicly in New Orleans as the lawful wife of Mr Daniel Clark, and whether you knew or believed then that Mr. Clark was married to Myra's mother If you did know of any such supposed marriage, did other persons know the facts as well as yourself? if so, who? Mention the names of all persons whom you may recollect who knew these matters as well as yourself State all circumstances, with great particularity

17th To all the witnesses Will each one of you, in answering any of these direct or cross interrogatories state whether you have seen, examined, read or heard read any one of them or copies of them, at any time or place before you were called upon by the Commissioner to answer them, if aye, state where, when and by whom they were thus so shown or read to, or by you, and for what purpose? State also, each one of you whether you have had any conversation or correspondence, within the last three or four years, with the complainants or with either of them, respecting their supposed claims against the estate of the late

Daniel Clark, and if you answer affirmatively, state why, when and where such conversation or correspondence occurred, and the nature and amount of them, so far as your memory will serve you, and who was present at such conversations? If you have any letters from the complainants or from either of them on the matters referred to, in these direct and cross interrogatories, annex them to your answers if possible, and if not possible, state why? And then if you have preserved and cannot annex them, give true extracts of them, and if that be not possible state your recollections

18th What is your own maternal language, if not English, do you understand that language perfectly? And if you do not understand English, how have you contrived to answer these chief and cross interrogatories? Who has translated them to you?

(Signed)   L DUNCAN, for Richard Relf and Beverly Chew

"   J. J. MERCIER, for the Mayor and Aldermen of New Orleans, Soniat Dufossat and Louis Desdunes

R M SHEPHARD, for P O Soibé and Réné Lemonier.

P A ROST, for Maria Holiday and Dussuau Delacroix

H LOCKETT, for James Field

ISAAC PRESTON, for widow Lambert and Luke Vigneau, Charles Patterson, Mr Callaway, Charles Fonde Belfaie Berdule, Antoine Prinas, John Matthew, Ramon Mansana and Manuel Marquez

JOHN SLIDELL, for John Minturn, George Kenner and Duncan Kenner.

JULIEN SEGHERS, for F O Petitpain, Claude Reme Samory and Louis Lallande Ferrier

Endorsed Filed 9th March, 1837

(Signed)   T W COLLINS, Deputy Clerk

CLERK'S OFFICE, UNITED STATES COURT

I do hereby certify the foregoing to be a true and correct copy of the originals on file in this office.

T W COLLINS, Deputy Clerk

New Orleans this 5th August 1837.

To the first interrogatory

1st I knew the late Daniel Clark, of New Orleans

To the second interrogatory

2d I enjoyed his friendship and confidence many years

To the third interrogatory

3d I knew, from what Clark told me in repeated conversations, that he had a daughter named Myra, now the wife of W W Whitney, and that he treated her with the utmost paternal affection Clark carried me with him on divers occasions to see Myra, and in my presence he manifested for her the most ardent love Said Daniel Clark always gave me to understand, as well by reason of his extraordinary affection for said Myra, as by his positive declaration to that effect, that she would be the heiress of his fortune

To the fourth interrogatory

4th In 1811, when said Clark was about to make a visit to the north, in a formal act or deed of sale before a notary public, he conveyed to me some lots, perhaps fifty, as if I had paid the due price for them, when in truth nothing had been paid, for the sale was made with or under the confidential understanding that I should hold them for the sole use and benefit of said Myra, in the event of the death of said Clark before his return

To the fifth interrogatory

5th That in the same epoch, in 1811, said Clark made known to me that on account of a special emergency that called him to the north, he had made a will, (to the best of my recollection, in the month of May, in that year,) which he merely designed as a provisional will, in which Richard Relf and Beverly Chew were named as executors, and that although he did not mention his said daughter Myra in that will, yet by confidential modes he had amply provided for her, and that will, said Clark told me he had deposited in the hands of said Relf On the return of said Clark, I wished to reconvey to him the said lots, but Clark would not allow me to do so, wishing, as I suppose, to give another proof of his confidence in my honor and rectitude; particularly as he, Clark, never wished to receive any written acknowledgment of the confidential nature of said sale

To the sixth interrogatory

6th. That in the year 1813, said Clark told me he was thinking of reducing to order his affairs, that were various and complicated, and of making his last will, so as not to leave any longer exposed to risk the standing and fortune of his child, and that he wished me to consent to become one of his executors I did so consent Said Clark spoke of Judge Pitot and Chevalier Delacroix, as persons whom he contemplated to have associated with him, with much reflection and deliberation said Clark spoke of his being occupied in preparing his last will. On these occasions, in the most impressive and emphatic manner, he spoke of the said Myra as the object of his last will, and that he should in it declare her to be his legitimate child and heiress of all his estate, and he accordingly so made his last will. A very short time before the sickness that ended in his death he, Clark, conversed with us about his said daughter Myra, in the paternal and affectionate terms as theretofore; he told us that he had completed and finished his last will. He, Clark, therefore, took from a small black case his said last will, and gave it open to me and Judge Pitot to look at and examine. It was wholly written in the handwriting of said Daniel Clark, and it was dated and signed by the said Clark in his own handwriting. Pitot, De la Croix and myself were the executors named in it, and in it the said Myra was declared to be his legitimate daughter, and the heiress of all his estate. Some short time afterwards, I called to see him, Clark, and learned from said Relf that the said Clark was sick in bed too sick to be seen by me; however, I, indignant at an attempt to prevent me from seeing my friend, pressed forward into his room. He, said Clark took me by the hand and with affectionate reprehension, said, "How is it, Bellechasse, that you have not come to see me before, since my sickness? I told Relf to send for you." My answer was, that I had received no message on account whatever of his sickness from Relf. I said further, My friend, you know that on various occasions I have been your physician, and on this occasion I wish to be so again. He looked at me and squeezed my hand. Fearful of oppressing him, I retired, and told Relf that I would remain to attend occasionally to Clark; Relf said there was no occasion for it, that the doctor or doctors had ordered that he, Clark, should be kept as quiet as possible, and not be allowed to talk. I expressed apprehension for the situation of Clark, but Relf expressed a different opinion; and on his, Relf, promising to send for me if there should appear to be any danger, I departed. On the next day, without receiving any message from Relf, I went and found Clark dead. I continued my way till I reached Pitot's, whom I found much afflicted by the death of Clark, and very indignant at the conduct of Relf, as well for having always prevented the assistance of Clark's other friends, as for not having notified them, (particularly him, Pitot, who lived near Clark), of his approaching dissolution; that by their presence the fraudulent suppression of the last will of Clark might have been prevented. What! I said, has Clark's last will disappeared? Yes, my friend, it was not in the case in which he had placed it, and the succint and *provisional* will, of a dozen lines, which he pre-

46

viously made when about sailing for the north, and which he
delivered to Relf, has been brought forward by Relf.   Pitot, as
well as othres, always spoke with the utmost indignation of the
fraudulent suppression or destruction of the said last will of
1813, and the fraudulent substitution in its place of the provisional will of 1811, all of which we attributed to interested villany
    7th To the seventh interrogatory.

In the autumn of 1831, I saw in a newspaper a letter
of said Relf, being an answer to some remarks on the verdict
that had been awarded against him in a suit with R. R. Keene
for libel, in accusing him, Relf, with the suppression of said
Daniel Clark's last will, and embezzlement of his estate   In
that letter, said Relf declares that said Myra, if she be the child
of said Clark, is the offspring of an adulterous bed   Knowing
that this was a calumny, and a most shocking one, on the name
and memory of my deceased friend, and a most cruel and
wicked one on the birth and name of his child, I, the contem-
porary of Clark, and acquainted with the facts, wrote to Mr
Whitney that this statement of said Relf was untrue, and that
before the birth of said Myra, De Grange had been condemned
for bigamy in marrying Miss Carriere, and requested that my
letter be published   Mr Whitney did not think proper to publish this letter, which I regret, as I feel that justice had not been
rendered the grave of my departed friend, against whom, if
living, no one would have uttered such a calumny   Dead, Mr
Relf is the last person who should asperse his ashes for though
he had withdrawn his confidence from him, still Mr Relf had
received from him, not only the greatest pecuniary favors, but
taking him out of obscurity and indigence, Clark, with the
nobleness of soul which distinguished his character, extended
to him his kindness.   I was the more shocked with this statement of Relf, because Relf knew to the contrary   I think it
my duty now to declare, what I know to be a fact, that said De
Grange was condemned for bigamy in marrying Miss Carriere,
(subsequently the mother of Myra), several years prior to the
birth of said Myra   The prosecution and condemnation of
said De Grange for said crime of bigamy, took place at New
Orleans towards the close of the Spanish domination in Louisiana, his first and lawful wife, whom he had married previous
to his coming to Louisiana, (as it was proved), coming
to New Orleans in pursuit of him   When said De Grange
practised the infamous deception of marrying Miss Carriree, it
was the current opinion in New Orleans, that he was a bachelor
or single man
    To the cross interrogatories he answers
    1st To the first cross interrogatory
My name is Joseph Deville Degoutin Bellechasse   I was

born in Louisiana, in 1760, and followed the profession of arms there, until it was transferred to the United States: after the transfer to the United States I held various important civil and military offices under the American Government, and managed my own affairs, which were extensive and related principally to real estate I continued to live in Louisiana until 1814, and then established myself in this Island, where I reside, on my sugar estate, and enjoy the rank of lieutenant colonel, in the service of her Majesty the Queen of Spain My means of acquaintance with said Clark were various friendly intercourse, business connexion, and political connexion

2d To the second cross interrogatory

My friendship and intimacy with said Clark began towards the end of the last century, and lasted with uninterrupted harmony and confidence till his death which happened in August, 1813 I was intimate and intimately connected with him under a variety of circumstances For several, years previous to the transfer of Louisiana to the United States, I had been in habits of the greatest intimacy with said Clark, this was commenced, I suppose, by our liking each other, and was cemented and made permanent by proving ourselves worthy of confidence and friendship Our business and political connexion only drew closer the cords of friendship Such was my respect for him said Clark that when, in November 1803 I was solicited by *the French Colonial Prefect*, Mons Laussat to accept the command of the militia of the Province of Louisiana, then about to be delivered to him by Spain, and not knowing with what view the Prefect was actuated resisted his offer and communicated the same to the said Daniel Clark, then United States Consul at New Orleans who disapproved of my refusal, and earnestly recommended that, if it was not too late, I should accept the proffered command giving as a reason that he believed the tranquillity of the country would be insured by so important a trust being confided, at such a juncture to a man attached to good order, and who possessed the confidence of his fellow citizens, and that he was persuaded such conduct would be agreeable to the Government of the United States in consequence of which, I informed the Prefect that I would take the command of the militia, which was given me as soon as Spain surrendered the country So, also, when the American commissioners arrived in New Orleans, and possession of that city was given to them, I yielded to the wishes of said Clark in accepting the command of the militia then again offered me I was one of those intimate friends whom, in 1806, said Clark assembled at his house, and, after informing them of the imputed intentions of Colonel Burr, advised to exert their influence with the inhabitants of the country to support the United States Government, and notwithstanding the incapacity of the Governor, to rally around him and afford him every aid, and to prevent, if possible, a meeting of the Legislature, in case Colonel Burr should gain possession of the city, and such meeting should be called, and attempt to assemble—regretting that he must leave for Washington   I was a member of the legislative council of Louisiana, and I was a member of the convention that assembled in 1812, and framed the constitution of that State.   Said Daniel Clark was the head of that political party of which I belonged. I have explained at least some of the causes and circumstances of my intimacy with said Clark

3d   To the third cross interrogatory

The said Myra, the daughter of the said Daniel Clark, was born in New Orleans, as well as I recollect, in 1806

4th   To the fourth cross interrogatory

I cannot swear that Clark was married to Miss Carrière, the mother of his child, although many persons affirmed that such was the fact . but I am well assured that, if he was not married to her, he was never married to any other woman

5th. To the fifth cross interrogatory

If Clark had been married to Miss Carrière, the cause for concealing his marriage might have been found, perhaps in the suggestion of his pride, alarmed on account of her misfortune, resulting from the deception practised upon her by said De Grange, when, according to his coat of arms (which he did not fail to lay considerable stress upon, though he was a republican citizen), he carried his pedigree up to the ancient kings of Ireland

6th   To the sixth cross interrogatory

From said Daniel Clark himself, in repeated conversations, and from his last will of eighteen hundred and thirteen I know that he said Clark, left to his daughter Myra all his estate, which consisted of plantations, of lands of immense value, of numerous slaves of many debts that were due to him, and other various classes of property, which altogether made him a man of great wealth

7th To the seventh interrogatory

To fulfil my sacred duty towards said Clark and his daughter, said Myra, I wrote and sent her, many years before I saw her, in Matansas, in 1833 two letters by a safe conveyance to Philadelphia one of which went to the care of Colonel Davis, with whose wife said Myra was then living, and the other was directed to the care of Mrs Hulings, of same city   In these letters, I informed her of the confidential trust held by me for her from her father and of the fraudulent suppression of her father's last will, made in her favor   But neither of these letters, although sent by a safe conveyance, got into her hands, as she assured me afterwards, in Matansas   In that place, I spoke at length with her and her husband of her rights, and of the cruel suppression of those rights   Since that time, I have never seen them, but I often afterwards wrote to them both, particularly to console them for the cruel imprisonment which Mr Whitney had suffered, in New Orleans for taking some preliminary steps for the investigation of his wife's rights   On some occasions, I wrote to them again, always assuring them of my friendly and almost paternal feelings towards the child of my old friend. With great pleasure, I would see all my letters published, but as I am ignorant of any right on the part of Mr Relf, and those who are associated with him in this cause, to wrest from me private letters, written in the way of mere friendship (now that there is no inquisition in the Spanish dominions, and if there should be a holy office in Louisiana, I am not subject to its jurisdiction), I am not disposed to acquiesce in so unreasonable a pretension, even if I retained copies of my own letters, and the letters themselves that have been written to me, neither of which I am not quite certain is the case   But I give full permission to Myra and her husband to publish or carry into court for judicial inspection, any letters which I may have written to them or either of them

8th   To the eighth cross interrogatory

I never heard said Daniel Clark speak of having any other child besides the said Myra   I never heard him say that she was a natural child   I never heard him speak of any stain upon her, or her birth, but on the contrary, he styled her, in his will of 1813, his legitimate daughter   He told me that she was his only child

9th   To the ninth cross interrogatory

The answer to the cross interrogatory No 9 in reference to the mother of Myra, is anticipated in the answer to the interrogatory in chief, No 7   I saw said Myra in her childhood in the house of Mrs Davis, a respectable lady the wife of Col Davis, to whom Clark had rendered many favors   Said Clark never made known to me his motive for placing said Myra under the care of Mrs. Davis.

10th   To the tenth cross interrogatory

Said Myra Clark was born in New Orleans, according to the best of my recollection, in 1806 and lived with Mrs Davis as just mentioned   I always thought and believed, that in the lifetime of her father, said Daniel Clark she bore his name.

11th   To the eleventh cross interrogatory

The last will of said Daniel Clark, made in 1813, was never admitted to Probate in New Orleans, or in any other place, but that will was fraudulently suppressed, and Clark's old *provision-*

al will of a dozen lines of 1811, that was deposited in the hands of said Relf, was the one which he, Relf, delivered up for Probate, instead of the last will of Clark of 1813

12th To the twelfth cross interrogatory

My profession was that of a military man and not of a lawyer, yet from my extensive business transactions in Louisiana from the civil offices which I held under that government, from my duties as a member of the legislative council of Louisiana, from my associations, and &c., I became acquainted with many of the laws of that country and on so plain a subject as an olographic will I consider myself competent of judging of the legality of such will The last will of Clark, viz his will of 1813, was legal in form, because it was written wholly in his (Clark's) handwriting, and was dated and signed by him It was legal in its provisions because Clark had the power, even supposing his child not born in marriage of giving her all the rights of a child born in marriage by declaring her in his last will his legitimate daughter for she had the capacity of acquiring those rights, as the bigamy of De Grange in marrying Miss Carriére, left her in a free condition, and Myra was born several years after the detection and establishment of De Grange's bigamy in marrying Miss Carriére, the mother of Myra This was the plain and positive law of Louisiana, and known to be so by every intelligent person The subject of one's last will, is a subject which he soon makes himself acquainted with when there is a sufficient motive Few men were equal to Clark in talents and intelligence he was well instructed in the principal matters that appertain to a gentleman and the proprietor of vast possessions; and the future happiness, fortune, and standing of his child, were the objects dearest to his heart, and he satisfied himself that there was no obstacle to his bestowing his fortune upon her Pitot, the Judge of the Court of Probate at New Orleans was one of the Executors in Clark's last will, viz that of 1813 Pitot examined the said will after it was finished and he should have known whether the said last will of Clark's was legal in form, and in its provisions Few lawyers in Louisiana were better acquainted with the laws than Clark, and had he not been, he numbered among his intimate friends some of the ablest lawyers of that State, and he was the last man to neglect any means necessary to accomplish an object which he was so intent upon I consider myself capable of relating facts with which he is acquainted, with as much clearness, (though less ornament) as any jurisconsult I am not related to or connected with the complainants or with either of them. I have no interest in the event of this suit It would be impossible for me to receive impressions about a subject with which I am familiar, and so peculiar a kind as this, from other persons, much less from those who would have to come to me for information My only desire is that the issue be conformable with justice

13th To the thirteenth cross interrogatory

In 1811, by a formal act of sale before a Notary Public, Clark transferred to me some fifty lots of ground within the limits of New Orleans, near the bayou road of St John, and acknowledged the receipt of a due legal consideration for the same.— But it was confidentialy understood that the lots so sold and conveyed to him, were for Myra, and her alone , and that to her he would convey them, in the event of his Clark's death, before his return from the North, for he was then about to make a visit there After his return, I wished, and offered to reconvey to him the aforesaid lots, but Clark would not allow me to do so thus evincing his delicacy, and the full confidence he had in my honor and integrity I understood that about the same time in 1811, Clark made trusts for his child with other friends, that he made a deposit with Mr Delacroix and that with, or under a receipt, he deposited in the hands of Col Davis, title papers for real or immovable estate, or property and claims due to him, of great value, for Myra Respecting the motive of Clark in acting thus, I am of opinion that Clark, overtaken by a sudden emergency, and with or without cause, doubted of the integrity of Relf and Chew, and of their good faith towards him in the management of his affairs, and being aware of the uncertainty of life, placed out of the reach of those persons, Relf and Chew the interests of his daughter by means of said confidential trusts and deposit of titles, when he made his summary will, viz of 1811, of some dozen of lines, and put it into Relf's hands, calling them, in it, his executors And this summary was true will, as he feels assured, because the emergency that called Clark to the North was so sudden, as not to allow him to make a detailed will, like that of 1813

14th To the fourteenth interrogatory

That Mr Clark never entrusted any to me, but for his daughter Myra, whom he acknowledged to be his daughter

15th To the fifteenth interrogatory It will be necessary to enter into many details in answering this interrogatory Mr Clark had always been a patriot, and an enthusiastic lover of liberty, and under the influence of these feelings always refused to become a Spanish subject, and when the United States acquired Natchez, he became a citizen of that country, although he continued to reside in Louisiana On various occasions he exerted his influence in favor of that country, at the hazard of his life and fortune. With that sagacity and foresight for which he was so distinguished, said Clark appreciated the physical advantages of

Louisiana, and pressed upon the attention of the U. S. government the importance of purchasing that territory. At great expense and labor, he procured information concerning the interior, forwarded to that government the results. For their benefit he translated from Spanish and French into English original documents. He pointed out the future value and greatness of that region and at length the American government was stimulated to obtain it. The United States owe the acquisition of Louisiana to Daniel Clark. Previous to the purchase of Louisiana by the United States, he possessed an ascendancy over the people of Louisiana, and they, deriving their opinions principally from him, passed under the American government with the strongest impressions of its wisdom and justice. But unhappily, the Governor appointed the province at this important period, was very weak minded, and the policy adopted was neither wise nor conciliatory. Jealousies and almost civil strife were the immediate consequences, and bloodshed was often prevented solely by the personal interposition of said Clark. Such was the weight of his character, such the purity and greatness of his mind. The final effect of this was to produce hostility between said Clark and Governor Clayborne, and two political parties arose, one sustained by all the influence of a Governor invested with the almost absolute powers of a Spanish Governor, and by the aid of the general government, and after said Clark, in obedience to a call on him in Congress, exposed General Wilkinson's corrupt practices by all the influence he could add, the other party rallied under Mr. Clark, whose power consisted in his great talents, great name, and the unlimited confidence reposed in his opinions and integrity. Such characters as Edward Livingston moved subject to Mr. Clark's orbit. I was a native of Louisiana, and it so happened that I had, or was considered to have, extensive influence, and I was the intimate friend of Clark, politically as well as personally, consequently, I shared in the political warfare, and I experienced a large share of the hostility and hatred that were felt for him, and after his death was transferred to me. After said Clark's death I left New Orleans on business, and while absent, said Relf made known to me that my enemies had now devised, what they would have been far from daring if I had been present, a wicked scheme by which they hoped and expected to destroy my fame and fortune, and, perhaps, my life that I was charged with no less a crime than I had gone to lead the British to New Orleans; that I was denounced to be taken dead or alive, that such tyranny then ruled in New Orleans, that my life would be the certain forfeit of returning at that time, and that he, Relf, risked his own safety in making the communication. The charge was absurd and ridiculous enough, when I had left my family and fortune behind me in Louisiana, but after the bitter warfare and hatred to which I had been so many years exposed, I readily believed my enemies capable of any injury or injustice to me, however base and black and I did believe that Relf had written the truth, and could not help entertaining grateful feelings towards him. Thus kept away from New Orleans I was ruined in the mean time by the fraudulent conduct of my agent there. At a subsequent period I wrote to said Relf, to Colonel Davis, to Mr Dubourg, Mr Edward Livingston, that I might have said Myra put into possession of the aforesaid lots. Thinking that said Relf would feel remorse for the great injury and injustice he had committed against the said Myra in suppressing her father's last will, I expected that he would cheerfully invest her with the same, but I was deceived. In a letter written by said Relf to me in 1822, he professed to give the news (as indeed it was altogether new information) of another daughter, called Caroline, of Clark's, which daughter, he, Clark, (as Relf affirmed,) had placed in a boarding school, at the North, under the care of Mr Hulings, and represented it as his opinion that she was entitled to the half of the aforesaid lots of Myra, and said Relf in said letter, requested me to annul the act made by said Clark, and put him, Relf, into possession of the same. In answer to that letter, he having before him this new advice of the extension of Clark's paternity to Caroline, and speaking in a conditional or hypothetical sense, said that Clark had a soul too good and a heart too well placed having (according to Relf) two daughters to be loved and adored by him as a father that upon this supposition his affectionate heart and generous soul would not abandon the other. In my said letters previously written, I had positively declared that said Clark had only designated said Myra, but as Mr Relf holds my letter, why does he not present it to judicial view? I not only give permission to publish that letter, but any other that he can hold of mine, including that which I wrote to his brother-in-law, Mr Zacharie, in 1835, respecting a judicial declaration made by me in the libel suit of Relf against R R keene

16th To the sixteenth. That Mrs Smith's answer is only required for the cross interrogatory, No 16

17th To the seventeenth. Before I became notified of the aforegoing interrogatories and cross interrogatories by the commissioner, I never saw them nor heard them read, consequently, could not have examined them. Respecting my correspondence and conversations, I refer to my answer given to the cross interrogatory, No 7

18th To the eighteenth. I was educated in Louisiana; both

the Spanish and French languages were current there, so that I can say that both are my maternal tongues. My knowledge of the English language is limited, but, as I have three daughters, one son and two sons-in-law who understand it, and some of them perfectly well, when I require an English translation, I avail myself of the services of some one or more of my own family.

JOSEF DEVILLE DEGOUTIN BELLECHASSE

Interrogatories and answers of Pierre Baron Boisfontaine, 28th May, 1835.
Filed April 25, 40

D. N. HENNEN, Clerk
By F. A. Foygnet, Dy. Clerk

Offered by complainants, and filed 23d June, 1849.
J. W. GURLEY, Commissioner

COURT OF PROBATES

WILLIAM WALLACE WHITNEY,
AND MYRA, HIS WIFE,
vs
E. O'BEARNE AND OTHERS

Interrogatories to be propounded to witnesses, on behalf of the complainants in this cause.

1st. Where you acquainted with the late Daniel Clark, deceased, of New Orleans? If so, were you at any time on terms of intimacy with him?

2d. Did the said Daniel Clark leave, at his death, any child acknowledged by him as his own? If so, state the name of such child, whether said child is still living, and if living, what name it now bears, as also state when and where and at what times said acknowledgment of said child was made.

3d. Have you any knowledge of a will said to have been executed by said Clark shortly before his decease? Did you ever read or see the said will, or did Daniel Clark ever tell you that he was making said will, or had made said will? If so, at what time and place, and if more than once, state how often, and when and where.

4th. If you answer the last question affirmatively, state whether the said Daniel Clark ever declared to you, or to any one in your presence, the contents of said will, and if so, state the whole of said declarations and the time, place, and manner in which they were made, before whom, and all the circumstances which occurred when such declaration was made

5th State how long before his death you saw the said Daniel Clark for the last time, how long before his death he spoke of his last will and what he said in relation to his aforesaid child

6th State whether you ever heard any one say he had read the said will, if so state whom, what was said, and whether the said person is now living or not

[Signed] WM W WORTHINGTON,
For Plaintiff.

Cross examined

1st Each witness examined and answering any one of the foregoing interrogatories, is desired to state his name, age, residence, and employment, and whether he is in any manner connected with or related to any of the parties to the suit, or has any interest in the event of the same

2d How long did you know Daniel Clark and under what circumstances? And if you presume to state that Daniel Clark left any child at his decease, state who was the mother of said child, and who was the husband of that mother State all the circumstances fully, and in detail, and whether said Clark was ever married, and if so, to whom, when, and where

3d If said Clark ever acknowledged to you that he supposed himself to be father of a child, state when and where he made such an acknowledgment and all the circumstances of the recognition of such a child or children and whether the act was public or private

4th Did said Clark consider you as an intimate friend, to whom he might confide communications so confidential as those relating to his will? If aye, state what you know of your own personal knowledge of the contents of said will, and be careful to distinguish between what you state of your own knowledge, and what from hearsay

The defendants propound the foregoing interrogatories with a full reservation of all legal exceptions to the interrogatories in chief the same not being pertinent to the issue, and the last of said interrogatories being calculated merely to draw from the witnesses hearsay declarations.

[Signed] L C DUNCAN, for defendants

In pursuance of the annexed commission, directed to me, the

undersigned, justice of the peace, personally appeared Pierre Baron Boisfontaine, who, being duly sworn to declare the truth on the questions put to him in this cause in answer to the foregoing interrogatories says

1st In reply to the first interrogatory he answers

I was acquainted with the late Daniel Clark of New Orleans, and was many years intimate with him

2d In reply to the second interrogatory, he answers

Mr Clark left at his death, a daughter named Myra whom he acknowledged as his own, before and after her birth, and as long as he lived In my presence he spoke of the necessary preparation for her birth, in my presence asked my brother's wife to be present at her birth, and in my presence proposed to my sister and brother in law Mr S B Davis, that they should take the care of her after her birth After her birth he acknowledged her to me as his own constantly and at various places He was very fond of her, and seemed to take pleasure in talking to me about her When he communicated to me he was making his last will, he told me he should acknowledge her in it as his legitimate daughter The day before he died, he spoke to me about her with great affection and as being left his estate in his last will The day he died he spoke of her with the interest of a dying parent, as heir of his estate in his last will She is still living and is now the wife of William Wallace Whitney

3d In reply to the third interrogatory he answers

About fifteen days before Mr Clark's death I was present at his house, when he handed to Chevalier Delacroix a sealed packet, and told him that his last will was finished, and was in that sealed packet About ten days before this he had told me that it was done Previous to this commencing about four months before his death, he had often told me he was making his last will He said this in conversations to me on the plantation, and at his house and I heard him mention this subject at Judge Pitot's I frequently dined at Judge Pitot's with Mr Clark on Sundays The day before he died he told me that his last will was below in his office room, in his little black case The day he died he mentioned his last will to me

4th In reply to the fourth interrogatory he answers

I was present at Mr Clark's house, about fifteen days before his death, when he took from a small black case a sealed packet, handed it to Chevalier Delacroix, and said, my last will is finished it is in this sealed packet with valuable papers as you consented, I have made you in it tutor to my daughter If any misfortune happens to me, will you do for her all you promised me, will you take her at once from Mr Davis? I have given her all my estate in my will an annuity to my mother, and some

legacies to friends—you, Pitot and Bellechasse, are the executors.
About ten days before this, Mr Clark, talking of Myra said that
his will was done. Previous to this he often told me, commencing about four months before his death, that he was making his
last will. In these conversations he told me that in his will he
should acknowledge his daughter Myra as his legitimate daughter, and give her all his property. He told me that Chevalier
Delacroix had consented to be her tutor in his will, and had
promised, if he died before doing it, to go at once to the North,
and take her from Mr Davis that she was to be educated in
Europe. He told me that Chevalier Delacroix, Judge Pitot and
Col Bellechasse, were to be executors in his will. Two or
three days before his death, I came to see Mr Clark on plantation business he told me he felt quite ill. I asked him if I should
remain with him, he answered that he wished me to. I went to
the plantation to set things in order, that I might stay with Mr
Clark, and returned the same day to Mr Clark, and stayed with
him constantly till he died. The day before he died, Mr Clark,
speaking of his daughter Myra told me that his last will was in
his office-room below in the little black case that he could die
contented, as he had assured his estate to her in the will. He
mentioned his pleasure that he had made his mother comfortable
by an annuity in it, and remembered some friends by legacies.
He told me how well satisfied he was that Chevalier Delacroix,
Judge Pitot and Bellechasse were executors in it, and Chevalier
Delacroix Myra's tutor. About two hours before his death, Mr
Clark showed strong feelings for said Myra and told me that he
wished his will to be taken to Chevalier Delacroix as he was
her tutor as well as one of the executors in it. and just afterwards, Mr Clark told Lubin, his confidential servant, to be sure,
as soon as he died, to carry his little black case to Chevalier
Delacroix. After this and a very short time before Mr Clark
died, I saw Mr Relf take a bundle of keys from Mr Clark's armoire, one of which, I believe, opened the little black case. I had
seen Mr Clark open it very often. After taking these keys from
the armoire, Mr Relf went below. When I went below I did
not see Mr Relf, and the office room door was shut. Lubin
told me that when Mr Relf went down with the keys from the
armoire, he followed, saw him then, on getting down, go into
the office room, and that Mr Relf, on going into the office room,
locked the office room door. Almost Mr Clark's last words
were that his last will must be taken care of on said Myra's account.

5th. In reply to the fifth interrogatory, he answers

I was with Mr Clark, when he died, I was by him constantly for the last two days of his life. About two hours before he

died, he spoke of his last will and his daughter Myra in connection, and almost his last words were about her, and that this will must be taken care of on her account

6th In reply to the sixth interrogatory, he answers

When, after Mr Clark's death, the disappearance of his last will was the subject of conversation, I related what Mr Clark told me about his last will in his last sickness Judge Pitot and John Lynd told me that they read it not many days before Mr Clark's last sickness, that its contents corresponded with what Mr Clark had told me about it, that when they read, it was finished, was dated and signed by Mr Clark, was an olographic will, was in Mr Clark's handwriting that in it he acknowledged the said Myra as his legitimate daughter, and bequeathed all his estate to her, gave an annuity to his mother and legacies to some friends the Chevalier Delacroix was tutor of said Myra, his daughter, Chevalier Delacroix Colonel Bellechasse, Judge Pitot, were executors Judge Pitot and John Lynd are dead The wife of William Harper told me she read it Col Bellechasse told me that Mr Clark showed it to him not many days before his last sickness that it was then finished Colonel Bellechasse and the lady, who was Madame Harper, are living

In reply to the first cross interrogatory, he answers

My name is Pierre Baron Boisfontaine, my age about fifty eight, I have been some time in Madisonville, the place of my family abode is near New Orleans, opposite side of the river, I was eight years in the British army, I was several years agent for Mr Clark's plantation since his death I have been engaged in various objects I now possess a house and lots, and derive my revenue from my slaves, cows, &c I am in no manner connected with, or related to any of the parties of this suit, I have no interest in this suit

In reply to the second cross interrogatory he answers

I knew Daniel Clark between nine and ten years, I knew him as the father of Myra Clark she was born in my house, and was put by Mr Clark when a few days old, with my sister and brother-in-law, Samuel B Davis I was Mr Clark's agent for his various plantations—first the Sligo and the Desert, then the Houmas the Havana Point, and when he died, of the one he purchased of Stephen Henderson He respected our misfortunes, knowing that our family was rich and of the highest standing in St Domingo before the revolution The mother of Myra Clark was a lady of the Carriere family Not being present at any marriage, I can only declare it as my belief, Mr Clark was her husband To answer this question in detail as is **demanded,** it is necessary that I state what was communicated to me It was represented to me that this lady married **Mr. De Grange** in good faith but it was found out some time afterwards that he already had a living wife, when the lady, nee Carrierre, separated from him Mr Clark, some time after this, married her at the north When the time arrived for it to be made public, interested persons had produced a false state of things between them, and this lady being in Philadelphia, and Mr Clark not there, was persuaded by a lawyer employed, that her marriage with Mr Clark was invalid which believing, she married Monsieur Gardette Some time afterwards, Mr Clark lamented to me that this barrier to making his marriage public, had been created He spoke to me of his daughter, Myra Clark, from the first, as legitimate and when he made known to me that he was making his last will he said to me that he should declare her in it as his legitimate daughter From the above, I believe there was a marriage

In reply to the third cross interrogatory, he answers

Mr Clark made no question on this subject before and after her birth, and as long as he lived, he exercised the authority of a parent over her destiny He was a very fond parent he sustained the house of Mr Davis and Mr Harper, because my sister had her in care, and Mrs Haraper suckled her He sustained Harper as long as he lived and conferred great benefits on my brother-in-law He spoke of her mother with great respect, and frequently told me after her marriage with Mr Gardette, that he would have made his marriage with her public, if that barrier had not been made, and frequently lamented to me that this barrier had been made, but that she was blameless He said he never would give Myra a step-mother When in 1813, he communicated to me that he was making his last will for her, he showed great sensibility as to her being declared legitimate in it While I was with him at his death sickness, and even at the moment he expired he was in perfect possession of his senses, and no parent could have manifested greater affection than he did for her in that period Nearly his last words were about her, and that his will must be taken care of on her account She, the said Myra, is the only child Mr Clark ever acknowledged to me to be his She was born in July, 1805

In reply to the fourth cross interrogatory he answers

I was a friend of that confidential character from the time of said Myra's birth Mr Clark treated me as a confidential friend in matters relating to her and to his affairs generally

In reply to the fourth interrogatory

I have stated what I knew concerning Mr. Clark's last will My recollection of these facts is distinct The circumstances connected with them were of such a character that my recollection of them could not easily be impaired

(Signed)   P BARON BOISFONTAINE

Which answers being reduced to writing, were sworn to and signed by the said witness in my presence, in testimony whereof, I have hereunto affixed my hand and private seal at the parish of St Tammany, in the state of Louisiana, this twenty seventh day of May, eighteen hundred and thirty-five

(Signed)   DAVID B MORGAN,
                        Justice of the Peace   (L S)

A true copy of commission for interrogatories, (and answers thereto,) propounded to Pierre Baron Boisfontaine, on file in Court of Probates, in and for the parish and city of New Orleans

          W F C DUPLESSIS, Register of Wills

New Orleans, 20th April 1840

———

Copy of the Testimony of Mrs Col Davis, in the case of William W Whitney and Myra C Whitney vs Eleanor O'Beain Filed April 25 1840

          D N HENNEN, Clerk,
          F A Foignet Dy Clerk

Offered by Complainant, and filed 23d June 1849
          J W GURLEY Commissioner

WM W WHITNEY AND WIFE ⎞
                        vs   ⎬
ELLANOR O BEARN AND OTHERS ⎠

Interrogatories propounded on the part of the Plaintiffs

1st Were you acquainted with the late Daniel Clark, of New Orleans?

2d Were you, at any times, upon terms of intimacy with the said Daniel Clark? If yea, were you so intimate with the said Daniel Clark as to enjoy his private confidence?

3d Do you know whether the said Daniel Clark, at his decease, left any child?

4th Have you heard the said Daniel Clark claim and acknowledge any child as his own?

5th If the last question is answered in the affirmative, please state when and where you have heard the said Daniel Clark claim and acknowledge the said child as his own

6th Please state where the said child then was, whether it was protected by the said Daniel Clark what became of it, and where it is at present

7th By what name was the said child called?

8th Do you know Myra Clark Whitney? If yea say whether she was the said child whom the said Daniel Clark claimed and acknowledged as his own

9th Are you acquainted with the circumstances of the said Daniel Clark, during his life, and at the time of his death?

10th Do you know whether the said Daniel Clark, at any time during his life made any provision for the said child in the event of his death? If yea state particularly under what circumstances

11th Did the said Daniel Clark, at any time, place property in your hands, for the use and benefit of the said child? If aye, state under what circumstances and how that property was disposed of

12th Did not the said Daniel Clark always manifest the fondest affection for the said child, and did he not express the intention to make her his heir?

13th Have you not often heard the said Daniel Clark say that he intended to leave to the said child his estate?

14th What intentions of pecuniary advancement have you heard the said Daniel Clark express in regard to the said child?

15th Are you acquainted with the circumstances under which the said Daniel Clark made a will in the month of May, in the year eighteen hundred and eleven? If yea, state the particulars of this subject, and whether, at that time, he had not otherwise provided for the said child

16th Was the said will of May, 1811 made by the said Daniel Clark, a short time before his departure for the north? If yea, did the said Daniel Clark, after his return from the north, express to you his intention to make another will, and did the said Daniel Clark, after his return from the north, refer to the circumstances of the will of 1811?

17th Have you heard the said Daniel Clark subsequent to the date of the said will of May, 1811 claim and acknowledge the said child as his daughter? If yea at what times?

18th Have you heard the said Daniel Clark subsequent to the month of May, 1811, say that the said child was his heir, or that he would leave his estate to the said child? If yea, state particularly when and the terms in which the said Daniel Clark spoke in regard to the said child

19th Had you subsequent to the month of May, 1811, much intercourse with the said Daniel Clark?

20th Have you often heard the said Daniel Clark speak o

the said child, subsequent to the month of May, 1811? If yea, state the particulars of his language, in regard to the said child

21st   How long before the decease of the said Daniel Clark, did you see him for the last time and in your last interview with the said Daniel Clark, did he speak of the said child? If yea state the particulars of his conversation in relation to the said child

22d. How long before his decease, did the said Daniel Clark, for the last time, speak to you, in regard to the said child, and what did he say at this time, in regard to the said child?

23d   Have you heard the said Daniel Clark, subsequent to the month of May, 1811, say that he was about to make, or that he was engaged in making, or that he was about to make, or that he was engaged in making, or that he had made his last will? If yea state the particulars of any conversations on this subject

24th   Do you recollect at what time or times the said Daniel Clark spoke of being engaged in making his last will, or at what time he spoke of having made his last will?

25th   Did you ever see the said will, or any writing said, by the said Daniel Clark, to be his last will? If yea, when, and where?

26th   Was the will in the handwriting of the said Daniel Clark, and was it signed by him? or was his name written in any part of it, and was it dated?

27th   Did you hear the said Daniel Clark say that, in his said last will, he had left his estate to his daughter Myra? Recollect, as well as you can his precise expressions

28th. When and where, for the last time, did you see the said will?

29th   When and where, for the last time have you heard the said Daniel Clark speak of the said will and what did he say?

30th   Did you hear the said Daniel Clark say who were named executors in said will? If yea, state who

31st   Did you hear the said Daniel Clark say who was named, in said will tutor to his said daughter Myra? If yea, state all you know on this head

32d   Did you or not ever read the said will? If so, state the contents as particularly as you recollect them and whether the said will was not in the handwriting of the said Daniel Clark and dated and signed by him

(Signed)   WM M WORTHINGTON,

For Plaintiffs

Cross interrogatories

1   Will you be pleased to state your name, age, residence, and employment

2   Will you state whether you have any interest in the event of this suit the object of which to annul the will of the late

Daniel Clark, that is, a will made by him, in the month of May, 1811, and which, at the point of his death in August, 1813, was duly admitted to Probate, in the Courts of Louisiana?

3. Will you state whether or not you are related to, or connected with the plaintiffs or with either of them? If aye, state in what degree

4. Will you state where you were in the spring and summer of the year 1813 and where Mr Daniel Clark was at the same time?

5. If you state that you were intimate with the said Clark, mention the circumstances which led to that intimacy how the same was formed, what was its particular character and how long the same continued

6th. Was the said Daniel Clark in the habit of consulting you about his affairs, whether personal mercantile, or political? State fully and particularly

7th. If you answer any of the interrogatories in chief, affirmatively as to your knowledge of the will of Mr Clark, state all the circumstances—the time when and the place where, and what was the occasion of his mentioning the subject to you

8. If you say that you saw the will of Mr Clark state where and when you saw it and state who was present and why he exhibited the same to you? Did you ask him whether he had made a will, and request him to show it to you? If not, state particularly, and in detail, the reasons why the same was shown to you

9. If you answer that you saw the will about which plaintiffs interrogate you, will you state how you can at this distant day, relate with precision the date of that instrument so as to enable you to speak with confidence of the year the month, and the day? Did you take a copy of the will or any memorandum, to enable you to speak positively of the date? If you did annex that copy or memorandum to answer and when and why you made such copy or memorandum?

11. Was Mr Daniel Clark ever married, to your knowledge? If aye when where and to whom?

12. If Mr Clark was not married, state if you please, all the circumstances attending the birth, the maintenance and education of the child Myra, whom you are asked whether he did not acknowledge State when and where she was born, whether, to your knowledge she was ever christened. If so, by whom, and where, and who were the sponsers?

13th. Will you state how or why it was, that Mr Clark came to acknowledge as his own the child called Myra? Was she born in his house, or where if not under his roof? Who was her mother, and where did she reside?

14. Did you or not ever hear said Clark acknowledge as his own, any other child than this Myra? If aye, state the name of that child, and whether or not he did not appear to have as much affection for the one as for the other? If not, what was the occasion for the one, as for the other? If not, what was the occasion of this difference of feeling towards his own reputed offspring? And why did he acknowledge the one to the exclusion of the other, as the heir of his estate?

☞ These cross interrogatories are propounded by the defendants with the full reservation to them of all legal exceptions to each and any of the interrogatories in chief, and any other legal exception thereto

LUCIUS C DUNCAN, Attorney of Chew & Relf, and *Curator at hoc* to the other defendants

WILLIAM WALLACE WHITNEY, }
AND MYRA C WHITNEY, } COURT OF PROBATES AND STATE
vs } OF LOUISIANA
ELEANOR O'BLARNE }

Marian Rose Davis, a witness for the plaintiffs, being sworn, answers:

To the first interrogatory, on the part of the plaintiffs, she answers as follows

1st I was several years acquainted with Mr Clark

To the second

2d. I was upon terms of intimacy with Mr Clark only so far as he was in the habit of coming very often to my house to caress his daughter Myra, who was placed by him in the charge of my husband and myself

To the third interrogatory on the part of the plaintiffs, she answers as follows

3d. When Mr Clark died, his daughter Myra was living in my family.

To the fourth interrogatory on the part of the plaintiffs, she answers as follows

4th I have heard Mr Clark often claim and acknowledge, as his own child, the said Myra He placed her in our family as his own child He uniformly acknowledged her, with pride and uncommon affection, as his own child.

To the fifth interrogatory, on the part of the plaintiffs, she answers as follows

5th Mr. Clark himself placed his daughter Myra in charge of my husband and myself, when she was about six or eight days old; and from that till our departure from Louisiana in 1812, he was accustomed to spend much of his time with his daughter Myra He always claimed and acknowledged her as his own child

To the sixth interrogatory, on the part of the plaintiffs, she answers as follows

6th. This child was placed in my family by Mr Clark when she was six or eight days old, and she remained with us till her marriage with Wm Wallace Whitney she is now, with her husband, on a visit in our family, she was protected by Mr Clark.

To the seventh

7th She was named Myra

To the eighth

8th I know Myra Clark Whitney, she is the very same person whom Mr Clark placed in care of our family as his own child, and whom he always claimed and acknowleged to us as his own child

To the ninth

9th I am not

To the tenth

10th In May, 1811, at the time he heard that D W Coxe of Philadelphia had become very much embarrased, and went to that city on that account, Mr Clark placed with my husband a large amount of property, to be appropriated for the benefit of his daughter Myra, if misfortune befel him, if not, they were to be returned to Mr Clark Also, after his arrival in Philadelphia, as he was about to sail for New Orleans, Mr Clark wrote a letter to my husband, dated July 28th, enclosing, we supposed written authority to invest his daughter with more property in case of his death before his arrival in New Orleans

To the eleventh

11th Mr Clark never placed any property in my hands for his daughter

To the twelfth

12th Mr Clark showed wonderful affection for his daughter Myra, and often spoke of her as the heir of his estate

To the thirteenth

13th. I have often heard him say that he would leave his estate to her

To the fourteenth

14th I have heard him speak of her as the heir of his estate

To the fifteenth

15th I have no knowledge of any will of Mr Clark

To the sixteenth

16th I have no knowledge of any will of Mr. Clark

To the seventeenth

17th After Mr Clark's return from Philadelphia, in 1811, and until our departure from Louisiana, in 1812, he came to our house very often to see his daughter Myra, and he always claimed and acknowledged her as his daughter

To the eighteenth

18th When we were about to depart from Louisiaua, in 1812, Mr Clark said that she would be his heir; that he intended to leave his estate to her, he spoke in terms of great affection and pecuniary ambition about her.

To the nineteenth

19th After Mr Clark's return to New Orleans from Philadelphia, in 1811, until our departure from New Orleans, in 1812, he was in the habit of coming to our house very often to see his daughter Myra

To the twentieth

20th After Mr Clark's return to New Orleans, in 1811 as long as we remained in New Orleans, he came very often to see his daughter Myra, he spoke of her with great affection, said that he should leave her all his estate his ambition was stimulated to make her very rich

To the twenty-first

21st It was when we left New Orleans, in or near March, 1812, that I saw Mr Clark for the last time I, with his daughter Myra, sailed about two months before my husband On this occasion Mr Clark said, that as she was of an age to receive instruction, he wished that on our arrival at the north, teachers should be provided for her He spoke of her as his heir, and, in speaking of her education, said that he wished her educated in a manner suitably to take in society the standing of the heir of his estate

To the twenty-second

22d I never saw Mr Clark after I left Louisiana in the spring of 1812 On this occasion, he spoke of his daughter Myra as the heir of his estate manifested the intensest affection and solicitude for her, and pride and ambition for her

To the twenty-third

23d I never heard Mr Clark speak of any will.

To the twenty-fourth

24th I never heard Mr. Clark speak of any will

To the twenty-fifth

25th I never saw any will of Mr Clark, or any writing called by him his will

To the twenty-sixth ·

26th. I have no knowledge on this head

To the twenty-seventh

27th I never heard Mr Clark speak of any will of his own

To the twenth-eighth.

28th. I never saw any will of Mr Clark's

To the twenty-ninth

29th I never heard Mr Clark speak of any will

To the thirtieth

30th I never heard him speak of any will

To the thirty-first

31st I never heard him speak of any will

To the thirty-second

32d I never saw any will of Mr Clark's

To the first cross interrogatory on the part of the defendants, she answers as follows

1st My name is Mary Ann Rose Davis, wife of Samuel B. Davis I reside in Philadelphia I have no employment

To the second cross interrogatory

2d I have no interest in the event of this suit

To the third cross interrogatory

3d I am in no degree connected with either of the plaintifs

To the fourth cross interrogatory

4th I was at Lewistown in the spring and summer of 1813 I do not know where Mr Clark was

To the fifth cross interrogatory

5th My intimacy with Mr Clark was only so far as was produced by having in my family his daughter Myra, this continued till my departure from New Orleans, in 1812

To the sixth cross interrogatory

6th. He was not

To the seventh cross interrogatory

7th I have no knowledge of any will of Mr Clark's

To the eighth cross interrogatory

8th I never saw any will of Mr Clark's

To the ninth cross interrogatory

9th I know nothing of any will of Mr Clark's

To the tenth cross interrogatory

10th I know nothing of any will of Mr Clark's

To the eleventh cross interrogatory

11th I do not know whether Mr Clark was married or not

To the twelfth cross interrogatory

12th Before the birth of this child, Mr Clark came to my husband, and requested him to have a house prepared for the reception of the child's mother She was born in New Orleans This child lived in our family till her marriage Before we left New Orleans she had never had teachers, nor till Mr Clark's death it was then alone at my husband's expense I do not know that she was ever christened Mr Clark purchased a servant for her gave her costly dresses and playthings

To the thirteenth cross interrogatory

13th I can only suppose it was from natural affection I believe that she was born in a house which my brother then held, which was not the house of Mr Clark's residence. Her mother's family's name was Carriere, I do not know where she then resided, the child was born in New Orleans

To the fourteenth cross interrogatory

14th His daughter Myra is the only child Mr Clark ever acknowledged to me as his own.

her

(Signed)   MARIAN ROSE ⋉ DAVIS

mark

Indisposition prevents Mrs Davis from signing her name
(Signed)   M SWEFT

A true copy of the answers of Madame Marian Rose Davis to interrogatories propounded to her, filed in my office
New Orleans, 21st April, 1840

W F C DUPLESSIS,
Register of Wills

WILLIAM W WHITNEY, AND
MYRA C WHITNEY,
vs   COURT OF PROBATES
                                          AND
ELEANOR O'BEARN, *et al*   STATE OF LOUISIANA
A B C

Samuel B Davis, a witness for the plaintiff, being sworn, answers.

To the first interrogatory on the part of the plaintiff he answers, as follows

1 I was

To the second interrogatory, on the part of the plaintiffs, he answers, as follows

2 I was

To the third interrogatory on the part of the plaintiffs, he answers as follows

3 At the time of Mr Clark's death, he left a daughter named Myra, who was then living in my family

To the fourth interrogatory on the part of the plaintiff he answers, as follows

4 I have often heard Mr Clark acknowledge the said Myra as his child

To the fifth interrogatory on the part of the plaintiffs, he answers as follows

5 Before her birth Mr Clark acknowledged her to me as his own child Before her birth, Mr Clark came to me, requesting me to make preparations for her birth. After her birth, he

placed her in charge of my family He always claimed and acknowledged her to me as his own child He not only claimed and acknowledged her to be his child, but manifested the fondest paternal affection for her

To the sixth interrogatory on the part of the plaintiff, he answers as follows

6 This child, a few days after her birth was placed in my care, and has been brought up in my family, where she remained till her marriage with Mr William Wallace Whitney She and her husband are now on a visit in my family

To the seventh interrogatory on the part of the plaintiffs, he answers, as follows

She was named Myra In Mr Clark's papers respecting her, he called her Myra Clark

To the eighth interrogatory on the part of the plaintiffs, he answers as follows

8 I know Myra Clark Whitney wife of William Wallace Whitney She is the identical child whom Mr Clark claimed and acknowledged as his own

To the ninth interrogatory on the part of the plaintiff, he answers as follows

9 In the month of May 1811, Mr Clark requested me to go with him to his house He appeared to be much agitated, and I thought, in trouble He informed me that he was apprehensive, or that he had heard that Danl W Coxe of the city of Philadelphia with whom he had been a partner in business had become embarrassed by some bad speculations to the north of Europe, and that he (Mr Clark) was fearful of suffering severely, if it were so for though he was not really a partner at that time, yet the dissolution of the partnership had not been done in legal form He showed me at the same time a schedule of the property possessed by him, and the debts for which he was liable in Louisiana by which, it appeared there was a balance in his favor of about five hundred thousand dollars, to the best of my recollection after all his debts were paid The impression is the stronger on my mind, as a coolness had subsisted between us for some time, and this was the first mark he gave me of his renewed confidence

To the tenth interrogatory on the part of the plaintiffs, he answers as follows

10 In one instance, Mr Clark being about to leave Louisiana, placed to my order in the bank property to the amount of about twenty eight thousand dollars, which he said was contained in a trunk, for which I gave him receipts and received instructions from him, that in case of accident to him, (the said Daniel Clark) to have the said property above mentioned, secured for

49

his daughter's benefit He returned in safety, and gave me up my receipts Some short time before I left New Orleans, Mr Clark induced me to retain in my hands, twelve thousand three hundred and sixty dollars, the interest of which was to go towards the education of his daughter Myra, for which I gave him my note This note was sued for, shortly after Mr Clark's death, by Chew and Relf, and recovered with interest, while I was at the North with the army, and the child lost the use of it. On the twenty-seventh of May 1811 Mr Clark wrote me from the Balize the following letter

Dear Sir—We are preparing to put to sea, and I hope I shall have a pleasant passage My stay will be but short in Philadelphia, unless a forced one In case of any misfortune to me, be pleased to deliver the enclosed to Gen Hampton I count on him as a man of honor, to pay the amount of notes mentioned in my letter to him which in that case you will dispose of as I have directed It will naturally strike you that the letter to the General is to be delivered only in case of misfortune to me Remember me kindly to Mr Davis and all your family Yours

(Signed,) DANIEL CLARK

P S—Of the enclosed letter you will say nothing unless in case of accident when you may communicate it to Chew and Relf.

S B Davis

His instructions to me were, to place the money to the best advantage for his daughter Myra's interest Mr Clark proceeded to Philadelphia, and when he was about to sail for New Orleans, wrote to me the following letter respecting his daughter Myra

Philadelphia, 12th July, 1811

My dear Sir,

In case of any accident or misfortune to me, be pleased to open the letter addressed to me, which accompanies this, and act with respect to the enclosures as I directed you with respect to the other affairs committed to your charge, before leaving New Orleans To account in a satisfactory manner to the person committed to your honor, will, I flatter myself, be done by you, when she is able to manage her own affairs, until when, I commit her under God to your protection I expect to sail to-morrow for New Orleans in the ship Ohio, and do not wish to risk these papers at sea

(Signed) Yours, DANIEL CLARK.

S. B Davis, Esq

In this letter was the packet referred to by Mr Clark, in this letter, which on his safe arrival in New Orleans, I gave to him unopened, as also the letter addressed to General Hampton, in Mr Clark's letter from the Balize

11th The tenth and eleventh interrogatories are intended to be answered by this

To the twelfth interrogatory on the part of the plaintiffs, he answers as follows

12th Mr Clark did always manifest the warmest affection and deepest interest towards his daughter Myra He has repeatedly told me that he intended to leave her his property, and never doubted that he was entirely sincere

To the thirteenth interrogatory on the part of the plaintiff, he answers as follows·

13th I have heard Mr Clark repeatedly say that she was his heir

To the fourteenth interrogatory on the part of the plaintiff, he answers as follows

14th In answer to this, I can only repeat, what I have already said in the preceeding interrogatories, that he intended to leave her his property

To the fifteenth interrogatory 🖤 the part of the plaintiffs, he answers as follows

15th I have no knowledge of any written will At the time of Mr Clark's death I was absent in the army at the North, and had been absent from Louisiana more than a year I have perfect knowledge that the property owned by him, commonly known as the Bayou property, had been secured to her by a sale to Mr Delacroix and D D Bellechasse, in separate portions, wherein he confided in blind confidence to their honor This same property he had previously transferred to me in a bona fide sale in the same blind confidence, but in consequence of a coldness before mentioned in my reply to a former interrogatory, I gave it up

To the sixteenth interrogatory on the part of the plaintiffs, he answers as follows

16th I never heard of any will until after his death

To the seventeenth interrogatory on the part of the plaintiffs, he answers as follows

17th I have always before and after her birth, up to the last hour I parted with him, heard him acknowledge her as his daughter, and received instructions from him relative to her education in the minute particulars, about which he manifested the greatest anxiety

To the eighteen interrogatory on the part of the plaintiffs, he answers as follows

18th I have heard him on all occasions express himself in favor of her as his daughter and heir It was an every day conversation when we met

To the nineteenth interrogatory on the part of the plaintiffs he answers as follows

19th Mr Clark came, as he always had to my house, to see his child Our intercourse was as usual I cannot pretend to say whether I possessed his confidence, in the same degree that I thought I did, before our estrangement

To the twentieth interrogatory on the part of the plaintiffs, he answers as follows

20th I have very often heard him speak of her She was always the subject of his conversation when he visited my house, and he manifested, if possible, more interest in his child in proportion as she grew older His language was always the same, but expressed with more enthusiasm as she became more interesting

To the twenty-first interrogatory, on the part of the plaintiffs he answers as follows

21 I had not seen Mr Clark for upwards of a year before his death, being absent in the army as already related At his last interview with his child, it was impossible for any father to have manifested more solicitude and affection than he did In my last interview with Mr Clark, his conversation turned almost exclusively on the subject of his child It was then I received instructions relative to her education about which he seemed very solicitous, and alluded to the place that he wished her to take in society when arrived at the age of maturity

To the twenty-second interrogatory, on the part of the plaintiffs, he answers as follows

22d As I have already related, I did not see Mr Clark for more than a year before his death The conversations were always the same, when on her subject as I have so repeatedly said

To the twenty-third interrogatory on the part of the plaintiffs he answers as follows

23d I have no knowledge on the subject of any written will

To the twenty-fourth interrogatory on the part of the plaintiffs he answers as follows

24th I have no knowledge on this subject

To the twenty-fifth interrogatory on the part of the plaintiffs, he answers as follows

25th I have no knowledge on this subject

To the twenty-sixth interrogatory, on the part of the plaintiffs he answers as follows

26th I have no knowledge on this subject

To the twenty-seventh interrogatory, on the part of the plaintiffs, he answers as follows

27th I have no knowledge on this subject

To the twenty-eighth interrogatory, on the part of the plaintiffs, he answers as follows.

28th I have no knowledge on this subject

To the twenty-ninth interrogatory, on the part of the plaintiffs, he answers as follows

29th. I have no knowledge on this subject

To the thirtieth interrogatory, on the part of the plaintiffs, he answers as follows·

30th I have no knowledge on this subject

To the thirty-first interrogatory, on the part of the plaintiffs, he answers as follows·

31st I have no knowledge on this subject

To the thirty-second interrogatory, on the part of the plaintiffs, he answers as follows

32d I have no knowledge on this subject

To the first cross interrogatory, on the part of the defendants he answers as follows

1st My name is Samuel B Davis, gentleman, residence Philadelphia, age sixty-eight

To the second cross interrogatory, on the part of the defendants, he answers as follows:

2d I have no interest whatever in the event of this suit; that is, in a pecuniary point of view

To the third cross interrogatory, on the part of the defendants, he answers as follows.

3d. I am in no degree whatever related to or connected with either of the plaintiffs

To the fourth cross interrogatory on the part of the defendants, he answers as follows

4th I was, in the spring and summer of 1813, commanding officer at Lewistown, State of Delaware. first aid-de-camp to the Commander-in-Chief of the State of Delaware I believe Mr. Clark was at that time, in Louisiana

To the fifth cross interrogatory, on the part of the defendants, he answers as follows

5th I was very intimate with the said Daniel Clark The circumstances that led to it were these I commanded the ship General Washington, of sixteen guns, and came to New Orleans, consigned to Mr Clark, in the year 1799 At this time, our commerce had been much interrupted. and we were then in a state of open warfare with France, in the service of which nation I had been several years, where I had acquired some reputation as an officer I had resigned my commission in the service as lieutenant de vaisseau and had lately returned to my country, very poor and this was my first command Louisiana was then under the Spanish Government The standing of Mr Clark in society, at that time inspired every stranger that came to the country with the highest respect for his character and acquirements, the kind reception which I met with from him naturally gained my confidence, and my confidence was confirmed by the delicate attention which he showed me on all occasions and the interest which he took in every thing that related to me My intimacy continued with Mr Clark, uninterrupted, till 1809 or 1810 when from some cause, of which I have been ignorant our mutual confidence was suspended

To the sixth cross interrogatory on the part of the defendants, he answers as follows

6th I was in partnership with Mr Clark for several years in the Rope Walk establishment Mr Clark naturally conversed with me on the subject of our establishment

To the seventh cross interrogatory on the part of the defendants, he answers as follows

7th. I know nothing on this subject

To the eighth cross interrogatory on the part of the defendants, he answers as follows

8th. I never saw any will of Mr Clark's

To the ninth cross interrogatory on the part of the defendants, he answers as follows

9th I have no knowledge on this subject

To the tenth cross interrogatory on the part of the defendants, he answers as follows

10th. Answered in the preceding interrogatory

To the eleventh cross interrogatory on the part of the defendants, he answers as follows

11th I do not know whether he was or not

To the twelfth cross interrogatory on the part of the defendants, he answers as follows

12th I was not present at the birth of the child, Myra, but at Mr Clark's request I had the necessary arrangements made for her birth I have maintained and educated the child, Myra, at my expense She was born in New Orleans in June, 1804 or 1805. I did not see her mother before her birth, nor had she any communication with me The terms on which Mr Clark and myself were at that time precluded the possibility of his speaking to me of his child, in respect to the expense of her maintenance, I had been under so many obligations to him, and I believe he knew my character too well to suppose that I would have tolerated such an allusion Time rolled on and the child grew, and as she grew, she gained on our affections, and no con-

versations ever passed between me and Mr Clark, relative to
the expense of her maintenance, until we were about leaving
that country for the North in 1812, when her education became
an object of deep interest to him, then he insisted on my retaining in my hands the two thousand three hundred and sixty dollars, which I have already mentioned the interest of which
was to go towards her education the requisite balance for her
education was to have been remitted to me yearly I never
wrote to Mr Clark on the subject of her expenses, nor ever
should His death put an end to our correspondence, had he lived,
I am sure he would have attended to it I cannot say whether
the child was ever christened or not she was not christened at
my house

To the thirteenth cross interrogatory on the part of the defendants, he answers as follows

13th It is impossible for me to answer this question in any
other way than that he, believing her to be his child felt as a
father towards her She was not born at his residence This
question has been answered in my reply to a former interrogatory. Her mother's family name was Carriere I do not know
where her place of residence then was but the child was born
in New Orleans

To the fourteenth cross interrogatory on the part of the defendants, he answers as follows

13th On one occasion Mr Clark spoke to me of a child called
Caroline, then living in New Jersey, but we had no conversations on her subject, if I remember rightly, but on one occasion,
it was not for me to enquire what could produce a difference of
feeling or attribute to him any cause of this difference of feeling

SAML B DAVIS

A true copy of interrogatories propounded to Samuel B Davis
and to Madame Marian Rose Davis, and the answers of Samuel
B Davis thereto on file in the Court of Probates in and for the
parish and city of New Orleans

New Orleans, 21st April, 1840

W F C DUPLESSIS,
Register of Wills

Deposition of Madame Louisa Benguerel, 27th May, 1836

Offered by complainant, filed 23d June, '49,

J W GURLEY, Commissioner

DISTRICT COURT OF THE UNITED STATES FOR THE EASTERN
DISTRICT OF LOUISIANA

RICHARD RELF,	INTERROGATORIES TO BE PRO-
vs	POUNDED TO MADAME LOUISA
WILLIAM WALLACE WHITNEY	BENGUEREI

Mr. Louis Louailher, and Madame vve Despau, Madame vve Carriére, vve. Gradenigo, and others

FIRST —Will you please to state your name, age, occupation, and place of residence ?

SECOND—Are you acquainted with, or have you known or heard of, Myra C Whitney, wife of the above named William Wallace Whitney, and the daughter of the late Daniel Clark, of New Orleans ?

THIRD—Are you, or have you been acquainted with Zulime née Carriere, the mother of the said Myra ? If yea, please to state when and where you were acquainted with her, and whether the said Zulime was or was not married to the said Daniel Clark, and all that you know on that subject, the time and place where such marriage took place, if at all

FOURTH.—Did or did not, one Jerome DeGrange, representing himself to be an unmarried man, impose himself as such, in marriage, upon the said Zulime née Carrière, at a time when in fact he had a lawful wife, to whom he was previously married still living ? If aye, please to state, whether, after the said DeGrange had so imposed himself upon the said Zulime, as above enquired of, his said lawful wife did or did not come to New Orleans and detect and expose the bigamy of which he had been guilty in marrying the said Zulime, as has been enquired of in the first part of this interrogatory?

FIFTH—If you answer affirmatively in reply to the last preceding interrogatory, please to state the time at which the said bigamy of the said DeGrange was detected and exposed, and was it not many years before the birth of the said Myra?

SIXTH—Was it not proved and believed at that time and afterwards, amongst the friends and acquaintances of Madam the said Zulime and the said DeGrange, that he had a lawful wife living at and before the time of his marriage with the said Zulime?

SEVENTH—If you have answered affirmatively in reply to the fourth of these interrogatories, please to state whether, when the said lawful wife of the said DeGrange came to New Orleans as enquired of above, he, the said DeGrange, did or did not confess or acknowledge that she was his lawful wife, and that he had been guilty of bigamy in marrying the said Zulime?

EIGHTH—If you have answered affirmatively the fourth of the above interrogatories, please to state whether the said De Grange did or did not escape or flee from Louisiana when his said bigamy was detected and exposed, and many years before the birth of said Myra? If aye, please to state whether the said DeGrange did or did not return again to Louisiana. Describe the person of the said DeGrange

NINTH—Do you know of any other matter or thing of benefit or importance to the said William Wallace Whitney, the defendant in this suit, which is instituted for an alleged libel said to have been uttered by him when asserting or claiming for his wife the said Myra Whitney, a right to inherit and to interfere with the settlement and administration of the succession of the said Daniel Clark? If aye, please to set forth the same fully and particularly

    (Signed)   JAMES W WHITE, Attorney for def't

WILLIAM W WHITNEY AND MYRA C WHITNEY, COMPLAINANTS *vs* RICHARD RELF, BEVERLY CHEW AND OTHERS, DEFENDANTS.	IN THE NINTH CIRCUIT COURT OF THE UNITED STATES, IN AND FOR THE EASTERN DISTRICT OF LOUISIANA

Cross interrogatories to the interrogatories filed by the complainants, on the 25th July, 1837, and by them propounded in their behalf to Madame Beaugeron and Mr Cowper

In propounding these cross-interrogatories, the respondents, who now appear to cross the same, especially reserve to themselves the right to demur or plead, or answer hereafter, as they shall be advised, and at all times to declare and show, that this honorable Court hath not, at law, or in equity, any jurisdiction of the matter of the present bill of complaint, the same being only cognizable by the Probate Court of the parish of Orleans, in the State of Louisiana, which court is already seized of the succession of Daniel Clark, the pretended ancestor of the complainant Myra, the same being a court where a plain, adequate, and complete remedy may be had, at law, by the complainats, for any and all their supposed claims against succession of said Daniel Clark, and full redress for their many grievances set forth in their said bill of complaint. Protesting, therefore, against this proceeding, and not intending to waive any right, or to admit any claim of the complainants, in the premises, but merely intending and desiring to provide against the effect of error, accident or surprise, and especially of fraud on the part of the complainants, and wishing to advertize the said complainants of the purposes of all of the respondents as sign these cross interrogatories, said respondents, here, acting in their own behalf separately

☞ The commissioner who may receive the answers to the interrogatories of the complainants, and the following cross interrogatories, is notified that it will be required of him to certify that the said several interrogatories and cross interrogatories were answered by the deponents separately, and apart from each other, and from other persons, and especially, that no communications or suggestions were made, to the knowledge or belief of the commissioner, by the attorney or agent of either of the parties, to either of the deponents

1 Will you be pleased to state your name, age and residence, your occupation and employment, and whether you are related to, or connected with the complainants? if aye, how?

2 Did you ever reside in New Orleans? if aye, when? in what year? in what street? and what was your business? and whether Mr Daniel Clark, about whom the complainants ask you, frequented your house, and what was the *particular motive* for his visits to your house? were his visits frequent? and made generally by day, or by *night*?

3 Did you know the said Daniel Clark intimately? if aye, how long did you know, and what was the occasion of your intimacy?

4 Was Mr Clark a married man? if aye, to whom was he married, and when and where? were you present at the marriage? if not, how do you know he was married?

5. It has been some times represented and pretended that Mr Clark was married to one Madame DesGranges, whose maiden name was Carriere, and who was married, several years before Mr. Clark's death, to one Dr Gardette, of Philadelphia. Will you state whether you know anything about that Madame DesGranges? if aye, state everything you know about her, from the time you first knew her, up to the present period If you say, or think, that Mr Clark was ever married to Madame DesGranges, mention when, where, by what priest or magistrate, and who was present at the marriage Did Mr Clark introduce Mrs. Clark to the community in New Orleans as his wife, and was she so received by society? if not, why not? Was the marriage clandestine? if so, why so? What motive, suppose you, would have induced Mr Clarke to contract a private marriage?

6. The complainants ask you about one Jerome DesGranges,

what do you know about that man ? and how do you know he was ever married to any other person than Zulime Carrière ? You will be pleased to be very careful to state nothing of hearsay, but let everything you do state, be of your own personal knowledge, and mention if you please, have you distinguished between hearsay, and your personal knowledge ? Has not this subject often been introduced to your notice, within the last two or three years ? if aye, by whom, and for what purpose ? Mention particularly, and state whether the complainants, or one of them has not visited you, or corresponded with you, on this very subject ? If they have written to you any letters, annex them, if possible and if not possible, state why, and then give copies, and if that be not possible, then state the substance of their communications

7 Have not the complainants stated to you frequently, or by correspondence that you were expected to prove DeGrange's bigamy, and the subsequent marriage of his wife with Mr Daniel Clark ? State fully

The respondents reserve all legal exceptions

L C DUNCAN, for R. Relf and Bev Chew

I, Michael Perrault, Justice of the Peace in and for the parish of St Landry, county of Opelousas, and State of Louisiana, and one of the commissioners named in the annexed commission, issued from the district Court of the United States for the Eastern district of Louisiana in the cause of Richard Relf vs William Wallace Whitney have caused to appear before me Louisa vve Benguerel who, being duly sworn to declare the truth on the questions put to her in this cause, answers

To the *first* interrogatory My name is Louisa vve Benguerel, age about fifty-seven years, gentlewoman, place of residence, Opelousas.

To the *second* interrogatory I have heard of both

To the *third* interrogatory I am acquainted with Zulime nee Carriere, the mother of the said Myra I knew her in New Orleans a long time ago I have no personal knowledge of such marriage.

To the *fourth* interrogatory Mr Jerome DeGrange married the said Zulime which proved on his part bigamy, for, after his marriage with the said Zulime the lawful wife of said DeGrange, whom he had married previous to his marrying the said Zulime, came to New Orleans, and he was thrown into prison, from which he escaped and fled from Louisiana this was in the year 1802 or 1803, since that period I have never seen the said DeGrange, and do not believe that he ever returned to Louisiana

To the *fifth* interrogatory This interrogatory is answered under the preceding one

To the *sixth* interrogatory   It was the said lawful wife of the said DeGrange brought with her to New Orleans proofs of her marriage with the said DeGrange.   The exposure at that time of the said DeGrange's bigamy in marrying the said Zulime was notoriously known in New Orleans

To the *seventh* interrogatory   My husband and myself were very intimate with said DeGrange, and when we reproached him for his baseness in imposing upon the said Zulime, he endeavored to excuse himself by saying, that at the time of his marrying the said Zulime, he had abandoned his said lawful wife, and never intended to see her again

To the *eighth* interrogatory   I have answered all this interrogatory in my answer to the fourth interrogatory, except as to DeGrange's personal appearance   he was about six feet English, stout built, light complexion, blue eyes

To the *ninth* interrogatory   As well as I can judge, I do not know.

To the general cross interrogatory   I am not related to, nor connected with defendant, nor with either of them, nor with the mother of the said Myra, nor am I interested at all in this suit   I was in New Orleans, where I obtained my information

It will be seen by my answers how I know the facts   I was well acquainted with the said DeGrange and the said Zulime, and I knew the lawful wife of the said DeGrange, whom he had married previous to his imposing himself in marriage upon the said Zulime

(Signed)　　　　　　　Vᵥᶠ BENGUEREL

Sworn to and subscribed before me this, 27th day of May, 1836, at Opelousas, parish of St Landry   In testimony whereof I have hereunto set my hand and private seal, the day and year above written   I am not related to nor connected with any of the parties to this suit, nor with their relatives nor with the witnesses   I am not interested in this suit, nor of counsel

(Signed)　　　　　　　M PERRAULT,
[L S]　　　*Justice of the Peace of the parish of St Landry*

Deposition of C W Drechsler, New Orleans, April 24, 1840
Filed April 25, '40

D. N HENNEN, Clerk,
By F A. FOYGNET, Dy. Clerk

Offered by complainants, and filed 23d June 1849
J. W GURLEY, Commissioner

I heereby certify, that, at the request of General Edmund P

Gaines, I have been engaged for several days, assisted by a gentleman who understands the Spanish and French languages well in making very extensive and most diligent search at all others, &c, in the different parts of this city, where records are kept and could be looked for for the purpose of obtaining a copy of prosecution against one Jerome DeGrange, convicted for the crime of Bigamy, in the year 1802 or 1803, when Louisiana was under the Spanish government, and Cassacalvo, the governor, by whose order the said DeGrange was arrested, imprisoned &c, in this city but that I have not been able to find the Spanish records of the aforesaid criminal proceedings because most all the Spanish documents, up to the 20th December, 1803, when Governor Claibourne issued his first proclamation, were taken away by the Spanish authorities, sent to Spain, and to the Island of Cuba and the few papers left in this city are in a loose or bad condition, as also, because, many books and papers having been destroyed by fire, and lost by removing them on account of fire, during two occurrences of that kind.

I am informed that Governor Claibourne made several ineffectual applications to the Spanish government to return the papers taken away, to New Orleans that persons have had to go to Havana for documents titles to land, &c

In the Archives of the old corporation I looked for the files of the "Moniteurs de la Louisiane," the onlynewspaper published up to 1804, in New Orleans, and found the files up to 1802, vol 1 and 2, and vol 4, of 1804 but the files of 1803, vol 3, was missing

I have in my possession a piece cut out of a printed publication, which reads as follows

'Zulime Carriere, at the early age of sixteen, married in New Orleans, in the year 1796, one Jerome DeGrange, a younger member of a noble French family About the year 1800, Zulime was informed that Mr DeGrange had a former wife then living DeGrange was charged by Zulime's family with his baseness in thus marrying her while his first wife was living, and, although he at first denied the charge, he subsequently admitted it Zulime left him on the instant, and he fled the country

' About 1803 DeGrange's first wife came to New Orleans, from France, and her husband happening to come to New Orleans at the same time, she prosecuted him for the offence of bigamy, and had him arrested by the order of the governor, and thrown into prison DeGrange affected his escape, and never afterwards returned"

I herewith annex three papers which were handed to me by

the persons who signed them, viz Certificate A, from Wm C
C. Claibourne, Esq: Certificate B, from the Spanish Consul
Certificate C, from the Keeper of the Archives of the old cor-
poration

New Orleans, April 25th, 1840.

Sworn to before me, this 25th April, 1840,

C W DREBHSLER.

HENNEN, Clerk.

———

Filed April 25th, 1840.

D N HENNEN, Clerk.

By F A Foignet Dy Clerk

Offered by Complainants, and filed 23d June 1849

J W GURLEY, Commissioner

(B)

I, Don Antonio Argote Villalobos, her Catholic Majesty's
Consul at New Orleans, do hereby certify that no part of the
records of this city and province of Louisiana, at the time it
was a Spanish colony, was ever brought into this office of consulate nor do I know in what manner those records were
disposed of, when the Spanish authorities delivered up the
country

In testimony whereof. I have, at the request of Mr Charles
W Drechsler set hereunto my hand and seal of office, at New
Orleans this 25th day of April, in the year one thousand eight
hundred and forty

[L S]   ANTONIO ARGOTE VILLALOBOS.

———

Filed April 29th, 1840

D N HENNEN, Clerk,

By F. A. FOYGNET, Dy Clerk

Offered by complainants, and filed 23d June, 1849

(A)   J W GURLEY, Commissioner

At the request of Gen Gaines, I hereby certify, that I have
no public documents of the Spanish Colonial Government of Louisiana in my possession, and that I have understood that they had
been taken away by the last Spanish Governor, my father, after
the cession of the country by the French, having made ineffectual attempts to obtain them from the Spanish authorities

W C C CLAIBOURNE

New Orleans, 25th April, 1840

Filed April 25, '40

D N HENNEN, Clerk.
By F. A FOYGNET, Dy Clerk

Offered by complainants, and filed 23d June, 1849
J W GURLEY, Commissioner

I, Eugene Lasere, Keeper of the Archives of the General Council of the city of New Orleans, and of the old corporation, do hereby certify, that the files of the newspaper called the *Moniteur de la Louisiane*, said paper being the official Gazette of the corporation of New Orleans, in the year one thousand eight hundred and three, vol No 3, when Casacalvo was then Governor, during the Spanish government, are missing, the previous files, No 1 and 2, up to 1802, and the subsequent files, No 4, &c, are now among the archives of said corporation And I further believe, that said file of papers was lost, with others, during confusion of fire

EUGENE LASERE,
Keeper of the Archives of the Old Corporation

Two words interlined and approved

EUGENE LASERE.

———

Offered by complainants, and filed 23d June, 1849
J W GURLEY, Commissioner

To the Honorable the Judge of the Court of Probates of the Parish of New Orleans

The petition of Francis Dussuau Delacroix, of this parish, planter, respectfully showeth

That your petitioner has strong reasons to believe, and does verily believe, that the late Daniel Clark has made a testament or codicil posterior to that which has been opened before your honorable Court, and in the dispositions whereof, he thinks to be interested

And whereas, it is to be presumed, that the double of this last will, whose existence was known by several persons, might have been deposited with any notary public of this city

Your petitioner, therefore prays, that it may please your honor to order, as it is the usual practice in such cases, that every notary public of this city shall appear before your honorable Court within the delay of twenty-four hours, in order to certify, on oath, if there does or does not exist, in his office, any testament or codicil, or any sealed packet, deposited by the said late Daniel Clark

And your petitioner, as in duty bound, will ever pray

[Signed]   SEGHERS, of counsel for petitioner

Francis Dussuan Delacroix, the above petitioner, maketh oath, that the material facts in the above petition set forth, are true, to the best of his knowledge and belief

(Signed)   DUSSUAU DELACROIX

Sworn to before me, August 18th, 1813
(Signed)   THOS. BEALE, Register of Wills

ORDER

It is ordered, That the several notaries of this city do appear before this Court, at the office of the Register of Wills, to-morrow, the 19th instant, at 9 o'clock A M precisely, in order to comply with the prayer of this petition

(Signed)   J PITOT, Judge
New Orleans, August 18th, 1813

I certify the foregoing to be a true copy from the original, on file in the Court of Probates in and for the parish and city of New Orleans

Clerk's office in New Orleans, 22d of April, 1848

And D DORICOURT,

Filed and opened by written consent, filed this day, 23d June, 1849   J. W GURLEY, Dy Clerk

EDMUND P GAINES AND MYRA ⎞   IN CHANCERY.
  CLARK GAINES, HIS WIFE,   ⎟   IN THE CIRCUIT COURT OF THE
         vs   ⎬ UNITED STATES, IN AND FOR THE
RICHARD RELF, BEVERLY CHEW, ⎟   DISTRICT OF LOUISIANA
FRANCOIS DUSSUAU DELACROIX   ⎠

Interrogatories to be propounded to Madame Sophie Despau, and Madame Rose Caillavet, witnesses to be produced, sworn, and examined, on the part of the complainants.

1st interrogatory. What is your age, and where is your residence?

2d interrogatory Do you know the complainant, in the above entitled suit, Myra Clark Gaines? If yea, how long have you known her?

3d interrogatory Did you reside in the city of New Orleans, about the year 1800? If yea, state how long your residence continued in that city

4th interrogatory. Did you know Daniel Clark, late of the city of New Orleans, deceased? If yea, when did you first know him?

5th interrogatory. Do you know if the said Daniel Clark was married? If yea, when, where, to whom was he married? and was there any issue of that marriage? If there was any, who is such issue? State fully and particularly all you know, or may have heard from said Clark, upon the subject of said marriage

6th interrogatory Did you know a man, in the city of New Orleans by name of Jerome DeGrange? If yea, when and where did you first know him? When and where did you last know or hear of him? State particularly what came to your knowledge respecting said DeGrange having been married before he came to New Orleans and also all you may have heard touching said marriage

7th interrogatory Do you know, or can you set forth any other matter or thing which may be a benefit or advantage to the parties at issue in this cause or either of them, or that may be material to the subject of this your examination, or the matters in question in this cause? If yea, set forth the same, fully and at large in your answer

P C WRIGHT,
Complainants' Solicitor

Cross Interrogatories

With reservation of all legal exception, other than those I may hereafter expressly and in writing waive, I propound the following cross interrogatories

1st If you state, in answer to the complainants' fifth interrogatory that Daniel Clark was married, then answer the following questions, under this first interrogatory How do you know that fact? Were you present at his marriage? Where did his marriage take place? If you state that it took place in Philadelphia then answer Did said marriage take place in a church? What was the name of the church? In what street did said church stand? According to the forms of what church was he married? By whom was the marriage service performed? name the person Was said person magistrate, judge, priest, or minister, or what office did he hold? If he was a minister, or priest, then state the name of the church at which he preached, or otherwise officiated

2d If you state that you were present at the marriage of Daniel Clark, then answer the following In what year did his marriage take place? In what month did it take place, and what was the day of the month? If you cannot state the month, and the day of the month, then state why you cannot What season of the year was it, winter, spring summer, or fall? If you state that it was in the winter, then state whether or not it was in the early part of the winter, about mid-winter, or the latter part of winter If you state that it was in the spring, then, was it early, middle, or the latter part of the spring? If you state that it was in the summer, then was it in the early middle, or latter part of summer? If you state that it was in the fall, then, was it in the first part, the middle, or latter part? State particularly

3d If you state that Daniel Clark was not married in a church, then state whether the house was a public or private house If the former what was it called? If the latter whose house was it? And what family resided in the house, of whom the bride and bridegroom were guests?

4th If you state that Daniel Clark was married in Philadelphia then answer—how long he had been in that city immediately preceding said marriage? Did he reside in a private family, at that time, during his sojourn in Philadelphia? If so, with whom did he reside? Did he put up at a hotel? If aye, what hotel was it? If at a private boarding house, whose boarding house was it?

5th If you state in answer to the complainants' interrogatories, that Daniel Clark was married to Zulime nee Carriere, then answer How old was this woman at that time? How many children had she previously had? Who was the father of those children? Was the father of her child or children living at the time she was married to Clark? Where did Daniel Clark reside, when at home, at the time you say he was married in Philadelphia? Where did the woman reside to whom you say he was married? How many days, weeks, or months, had she been in Philadelphia preceding this alledged marriage with Daniel Clark? What was her business in Philadelphia? What did she go to Philadelphia for? Did she stop at a hotel, boarding house, or private house in Philadelphia, previous to the marriage of which you speak? If at a hotel, or boarding house, then what was it named or called? and by whom was it kept? If she stayed at a private house, whose house was it? and what family resided in it?

6th Did you accompany the lady of whom you speak as having been married to Daniel Clark, from New Orleans to Philadelphia, previous to the said supposed marriage? If aye, by what conveyance did you leave New Orleans, for the North? Did you go by sea, or land? If by sea, what was the name of the vessel, and for what port did she sail? Did Daniel Clark accompany the lady to the North? If not, which of the two reached Philadelphia first? How long had the lady been in Philadelphia, previous to the marriage?

7th Have you not, heretofore, stated or sworn that Daniel Clark and the lady of whom you speak met, in New York, and there became satisfied that there was no legal obstruction to their marriage? Why, therefore, were they not married in New York? What was their motive for going to Philadelphia, to consummate their purposes?

8th If you state that Daniel Clark was married in Philadelphia, state—how long did he remain in Philadelphia, after said marriage? Did he introduce that woman, in Philadelphia, as his wife? To whom did he introduce her as his wife? Was not the mother of Daniel Clark residing, at that time, in or near Philadelphia? Was Mr Clark's mother present at the wedding? Do you know or believe that Daniel Clark ever introduced the woman in question, to his mother, as his wife? If aye, when and where was that done? Who was present at Daniel Clark's marriage besides yourself? State the names and residences of all such as were present

9th. If you state that Daniel Clark was married in Philadelphia, answer What sort of a wedding party was there on the occasion? Was his wedding conducted in a style equal or becoming his rank and circumstances? Was it announced in the public newspapers of the day? How long did the parties remain in Philadelphia after the marriage? At whose house did they remain after said marriage? Are you aware, and are you to be understood as swearing, of your own knowledge, that Daniel Clark ever remained one night with the lady in question, while in Philadelphia? Please state explicitly, so that there may be no misunderstanding your answer How many days did Mr. Clark remain in Philadelphia after the marriage? Did he take his wife with him when he left? Did you accompany them or either of them when they, he, or she left Philadelphia? Did they travel together as man and wife? To what place did you accompany them, him, or her after the marriage? How long was it after you left New Orleans before the marriage took place in Philadelphia? How long after the marriage before the parties reached New Orleans? Were you present when they, or either of them, reached New Orleans? Did they come together? If not, which reached home first, and who travelled with Madame Clark? under whose protection was she?

10th After Daniel Clark reached New Orleans did he keep house? Did he and his wife occupy the same house? Did they live together, at any time, in New Orleans as man and wife? Where did they live? In what street was Clark's house in which he kept his wife, and between what streets? state explicitly. How many weeks, months or years, as near as you can remember, did Daniel Clark live with the lady, to whom you say he was married, in New Orleans? Did Daniel Clark ever introduce that woman into society in New Orleans as his wife? If aye, state how and where? Was it generally known among Daniel Clark's friends in New Orleans that he had been married?

11th Did Daniel Clark ever keep house in New Orleans with the lady to whom you say he was married, as his wife?

12th When did Daniel Clark die? Was his wife living with him at the time of his death?

13th How long did the lady to whom you say Daniel Clark was married live in New Orleans, after said marriage, and previous to the death of Clark?

14th How many children had the mother of the complainant, Myra, after you say that she was married to Daniel Clark, and previous to the death of said Clark? Name each one of them who was their father, respectively?

15th Was the mother of the complainant Myra ever divorced from Daniel Clark? If so, when? Did she ever marry previous to the death of Daniel Clark? Was she ever married subsequent to the time you say she was married to Clark and previous to the death of Clark? If aye, state to whom she was married? By whom was she married? At what place was she married? and the month and year of her said marriage? How often has the mother of the complainant, Myra, been married, according to the best of your knowledge, information and belief? State the names of each of her husbands If she was married to Clark, had she not three living husbands at the same time, and without being divorced from either?

16th. With whom was the mother of the complainant, Myra, living, at the time of the death of Daniel Clark, in the character of wife? How long previous to the death of Daniel Clark had the mother of said complainant, Myra, been living with another man as *his* lawful and wedded wife?

17th. Did the mother of the complainant, Myra, go into mourning for the loss, at the time, of the death of Daniel Clark? If not why did she not? Did she ever present herself and claim any rights as the widow of Daniel Clark? and if not, why did she not?

18th How many children had the mother of Myra by Mr Gardette? Did she not live with Mr Gardette, as his wife, for many years previous to the death of Clark? Did she not go into mourning for Mr Gardette at *his* death? Did she not act as the widow of Mr Gardette? Did she not both claim and receive rights as the widow of Mr Gardette? Where and when did Mr Gardette die?

19th Was Daniel Clark considered an honorable man? Was he such a man as to submit to the indignity of having another man take his wife off and marry her? Would he have allowed Mr. Gardette to be imposed upon by marrying a woman under bonds of matrimony to himself?

20th Were you in New Orleans at the time of the birth of the complainant, Myra? If aye, state *why* it was that the child was so soon removed away from her mother? *Why* was the mother not allowed to take care of the child? Why was she not subsequently allowed intercourse with her said child?

21st State why it was that the mother of Myra allowed her to remain in ignorance of her present imputed parentage ? Why was it that she allowed her child to remain in ignorance of the rights which she now claims and pretends to have as the legitimate child of Daniel Clark ?

22d Why was it that the mother of Myra never claimed *her* rights as the widow of Daniel Clark ? State fully

23d What relation are you to the mother of the complainant Myra ? Where is she now ? Where has she resided, and with whom, since 1806 ? Who now supports her?

24th In what year were you born ? What time in the year ?

25th Did Daniel Clark ever furnish apartments for your sister, the mother of the complainant Myra ? If aye, state where those apartments were situated the name of the street, and between what streets the house was situated ? Did he make his *home* with her or only visit her there ? State particularly

G B DUNCAN,
Att'y for Chew, Relf and Delacroix

I join in the foregoing cross interrogatories on behalf of the defendants whom I represent

New Orleans, February 20th, 1846

ISAAC T PRESTON Solicitor for them

GAINES & WIFE,
   vs.
A & Z CAVALIER *et al*

I join in the above cross interrogatories on behalf of the defendants, Antoine and Zenon Cavalier

THOMAS GIBBES MORGAN,
Solicitor for A & Z. Cavalier

I join in the above and foregoing interrogatories on behalf of Gerasime Richard, Maddison Lyons Abraham Harman, Sr, Abraham Harman, Jr and Adolphe Richard

THOS H LEWIS Solicitor for them

New Orleans, March 16th, 1849

UNITED STATES CIRCUIT COURT,
FIFTH CIRCUIT AND DISTRICT OF LOUISIANA,
14th *day of March,* 1849

The Court met pursuant to adjournment
   Present—the Honorable Theo H McCaleb
   The Honorable J McKinley, absent

GAINES & WIFE,
   vs.   No 1731
RELF, CHEW, & DELACROIX

In consideration of stipulations between the parties hereto re presented by the solicitors, P C Wright and G B Duncan, on file in this cause it is ordered that William H Cleaveland, Esq, of Biloxi, in the State of Mississippi Attorney and Counsellor at Law, be appointed a commissioner to take the testimony of Madam Rose Caillavet née Carriere and Madam Sophie Despau née Carriere, two witnesses to be produced and examined on behalf of the complainants. And that said Cleaveland shall return the commission directed to him, with the testimony taken by virtue thereof, under his seal to the Clerk of the United States Circuit Court for the District of Louisiana

CLERK'S OFFICE, }
Circuit Court of the United States, District of Louisiana }

I hereby certify the foregoing to be a true Copy from the Original of Record in this Office

Witness, my hand and seal of said Court, at the City of New Orleans, this 14th day of March, 1849

ED RANDOLPH, Clerk

CIRCUIT COURT OF THE UNITED STATES
For the Fifth Judicial Circuit }

Holding Sessions in and for the District of Louisiana

To William H Cleaveland, residing at Biloxi, State of Mississippi ·

Know ye, That reposing special trust and confidence in your integrity and ability, we hereby authorize and require you, that you call and cause to come before you, Madam Sophie Despau, and Madam Rose Caillavet, and them duly examine on oath touching and concerning certain matters and things in a case now depending in the said Court wherein Edmund P Gaines and wife are plaintiffs, and Richd Relf Bev Chew, F Dussuau Delacroix, *et als.*, are defendants and the same examinations, so taken and reduced to writing, you certify under your hand and seal, and send enclosed to this Court, without delay, to be read in evidence on the trial of said cause, and send also this writ.

{ L.S }

Witness, the Honorable Roger B Taney, Chief Justice of the Supreme Court of the United States at the City of New Orleans, this thirteenth day of March Anno Domini, 1849, and the seventy-third year of the Independence of the United States of America

ED RANDOLPH Clerk

By WM ANDRY Dy Clerk

Edmund P. Gaines and Myra Clark Gaines, his Wife,
vs
Rich'd King, Beverly Chew, Francois Dussuau Delacroix

IN CHANCERY
In the Circuit Court of the United States, in and for the District of Louisiana

In pursuance of the annexed commission to me directed, issued from the Circuit Court of the United States, for the Fifth Judicial Circuit, holding sessions in and for the District of Louisiana, I, William H Cleaveland, residing at Biloxi, in the State of Mississippi, have caused to come before me Madame Sophie Despau, who, being duly sworn to dec'are the truth in answer to the interrogatories and cross interrogatories accompanying said commission, says.

Answer to the first interrogatory

I am seventy-one years of age. My present place of residence is Biloxi, Harrison county, Mississippi

Answer to the second interrogatory

I am acquainted with the complainant in this suit, Myra Clark Gaines I was present at her birth, and, with some intervals, I have been well acquainted with her up to the present time.

Answer to the third interrogatory

I was residing in the city of New Orleans in the year eighteen hundred My residence continued there, up to the year eighteen hundred and seven

Answer to the fourth interrogatory

I was well acquainted with Daniel Clark, late of the city of New Orleans, deceased. My acquaintance with him commenced about, or not long after, the year seventeen hundred and ninety-seven My acquaintance and intimacy with him continued until the interruption of friendly relations between him and my sister Zulime, about the year eighteen   and seven

Answer to the fifth interrogatory

I do know that the said Daniel Clark was married. He was married in the city of Philadelphia, by a Catholic priest, to my sister Zulime, née de Carrière I was present at this marriage This to the best of my recollection, was in the year eighteen hundred and three, although there are some associations in my memory, which make me think it not improbable that the marriage may have taken place in the year eighteen hundred and two. My impression, however, is that the marriage took place in eighteen hundred and three It was, I remember, a short while previous to Mr Clark's going to Europe. There was one child, and to the best of my knowledge and belief, only one child born of this marriage, to wit, Myra Clark, who married William Wallace Whitney, now deceased, and

who is now the wife of Gen Edmund P Gaines   The circumstances attending the marriage of the said Daniel Clark with
Zulime de Carriere, were these —She had previously been married to a man named Jerome DeGrange, with whom she lived
several years, until she heard that he had another living wife at
the time of his marriage with her   This information, confirmed
by the subsequent admissions of DeGrange himself, led to a
separation, when Zulime returned to her family   These circumstances were known to the public   While thus residing with her
family, Mr Clark made proposals of marriage with her   These
proposals were made with the full knowledge of all the family
But it was considered essential, before any marriage could take
place, that record proof of the invalidity of her marriage with
DeGrange should be first obtained   To obtain this proof from the
records of the Catholic church in New York, where De-
Grange's prior marriage was celebrated, my sister and myself
embarked for that city   It was agreed and understood, that
Mr Clark should follow after us   On our arrival in New York,
we learned that the registry of marriages of which we were in
search had, in some way, been destroyed   Mr Clark arrived
after us   We were told that a Mr Gardette, then living in
Philadelphia, was one of the witnesses to DeGrange's prior
marriage   We proceeded to Philadelphia, and found Mr Gardette, who told us that he was present at said prior marriage of
DeGrange   that he afterwards knew DeGrange and his wife by
this marriage, and that this wife had gone to France   Mr
Clark then said to my sister, you have no longer any reason to
refuse being married to me   It will, however, be necessary to
keep our marriage secret until I have obtained judicial proof of
the nullity of your marriage with DeGrange   They, the said
Zulime, and the said Clark, were then married   Soon afterwards,
our sister, Madame Caillavet, wrote to us from New Orleans,
that DeGrange's former wife, (the one he had at the time of marrying Zulime,) had arrived at New Orleans   We hastened our
return to New Orleans, where DeGrange was prosecuted for
bigamy   Father Antoine, of the Catholic church in New Orleans, took part in the proceedings against him   Mr DeGrange
was condemned for bigamy in marrying the said Zulime, and
was cast into prison, from whence he secretly escaped by connivance of the Governor, as it was understood, and was taken
down the Mississippi river by Mr LeBreton D Orgenois, where
he got to a vessel, and escaped from the country   This happened not a great while before the cessation of the Spanish government in Louisiana   Mr Clark told us that before he could
promulgate his marriage with my sister, it would be necessary
that there should be brought by her an action against the name
of DeGrange   The change of government, which took place

about that time, created delay, but at length, in eighteen hundred and six, Messrs, James Brown and Elijah Fromentin, as the counsel of my sister, brought suit against the name Jerome De-Grange, in, I think, the City Court of New Orleans The grounds of said suit were, that DeGrange had imposed himself upon her in marriage at a time when he had a lawful living wife Judgment in said suit was rendered against DeGrange But Mr Clark still continued to defer promulgating his marriage with my sister, which very much fretted and irritated her feelings Mr Clark became a member of the United States Congress in eighteen hundred and six While he was in Congress, my sister heard that he was courting a Miss Caton, of Baltimore She was distressed, though she could not believe the report, knowing herself to be his wife Still, his strange conduct in deferring to promulgate his marriage with her, had alarmed her, and she and I sailed to Philadelphia to get the proof of his marriage with my sister We could find no record of the marriage and were told that the priest who married her and Mr Clark was gone to Ireland My sister then sent for Mr Daniel W Coxe and mentioned to him the rumor above stated He answered that he knew it to be true that Mr Clark was engaged to the lady in question My sister replied that it could not be so He then told her that she would not be able to establish her marriage with Mr Clark, if he were disposed to contest it He advised her to take the advice of legal counsel, and said he would send one A Mr Smith came, and, after telling my sister that she could not legally establish her marriage with Mr Clark, pretended to read to her a letter in English, (a language then unknown to my sister,) from Mr Clark to Mr Coxe, stating that he was about to marry Miss Caton The marriage between Mr Clark and my sister was a private one Besides myself, there was present at the marriage a Mr Dorsier, of New Orleans, an Irish gentleman, a friend of Mr Clark's, from New York. whose name I do not recollect Mr Clark told me in his lifetime that he had informed Col Samuel B Davis, Mr Daniel W Coxe, and Mr Richard Relf of this marriage It was known only to a few friends

Answer to the sixth interrogatory

I became acquainted with Jerome DeGrange in seventeen hundred and ninety-three, when, as I understood, he first came to New Orleans He then passed for a single or unmarried man, and, as I have already stated, in answer to the preceding interrogatory, imposed himself in marriage upon my sister Zulime. I have already stated the fact of his prosecution and conviction for bigamy, and of his escape, before the sentence was executed, from the country To the best of my knowlegde and belief, he never afterwards returned to Louisiana

Answer to the seventh interrogatory·

I am not aware of any thing further that would be material to the parties in this suit, unless it be to state that by the marriage of my sister with Mr DeGrange there was born two children, a boy and a girl The boy died The girl lived, and was named Caroline. She afterwards married a phisician named Barnes She was born in the year eighteen hundred and one. I have understood that she is dead within the last three years I was present at her birth, as well as that of her brother It may, also, be proper to state that my sister afterwards, in the year eighteen hundred and eight, married, in Philadelphia, Dr James Gardette, of that city

Answer to the first cross interrogatory

I was present at Mr Clark's marriage with my sister Zulime The marriage was privately celebrated at a house in Philadelphia, rented by Mr Clark for my sister, but I am unable to remember the name of the street on which it was situated, or of the priest who officiated

Answer to the second cross interrogatory·

The great lapse of time which has taken place since these events, renders it impossible for me to answer with the precision the question demands As well as I can remember, it was in one of the early months of spring in 1802 or 1803.

Answer to the third cross interrogatory

This has been already answered

Answer to the fourth cross interrogatory

Mr Clark was several weeks in Philadelphia before the marriage I did not know, or cannot now remember where he lived during that time

Answer to the fifth cross interrogatory

I have already stated that my sister has had two children by Jerome DeGrange, and the object of her going to Philadelphia.

On our arrival there we stopped first at a boarding house kept by an American lady, I think a widow, whose name I cannot remember We were in Philadelphia but a short time previous to the marriage. My sister was about nineteen or twenty years old at the time of her marriage with Mr Clark After the marriage we resided together in the house provided for my sister, as I have already stated.

Answer to the sixth cross interrogatory

I have already answered this interrogatory, except as to the name of the vessel, which I do not remember

Answer to seventh cross interrogatory

I have already given the reason in answer to the fifth direct interrogatory

Answer to the eighth cross interrogatory

I was not acquainted with the mother of Daniel Clark I do not know of Daniel Clark's introducing my sister to any one in

Philadelphia as his wife I have already stated that the marriage was a private one, and have stated that only myself, Mr Dorsier of New Orleans, and a friend of Mr. Clark's, whose name I do not remember, was present at it

Answer to the ninth cross interrogatory

I have already stated fully my recollection of all that concerns the marriage Not a great while after the marriage Mr. Clark set out for Europe Soon after his departure, in consequence of information received from our sister, Madame Caillavet, at New Orleans, in regard to the arrival there of the first wife of DeGrange, we set out for that city We arrived there, I think, in the summer I do not remember the precise time of Mr. Clark's arrival there, but it was afterwards It is impossible for me to recollect with certainty the precise time occupied by each one of so many events that happened so many years ago.

Answer to the tenth cross interrogatory

Mr Clark did not give publicity to his marriage with my sister He furnished her with a handsome house in New Orleans, in which she and I resided together and where he frequently visited my sister, taking his tea with us almost every evening This house was situated on a corner, and, I think, near what was then called the Bayou Road but I cannot recall the name of the street, or fix, with certainty, the precise locality. I do not know whether the marriage was generally known among Mr Clark's friends at New Orleans, or not I always supposed it was known to but a few persons Mr Clark told us that he had informed Daniel W Coxe, Samuel B Davis, and Richard Relf of it My sister and myself resided, as above stated, in the house provided by Mr Clark, until the rupture between her and him, a period, as well as I can remember, of between three and four years.

Answer to the eleventh cross interrogatory:

This is already answered.

Answer to the twelfth cross interrogatory

I was not living in New Orleans at the time of Mr Clark's death, which took place in eighteen hundred and thirteen, as I have understood Previous to this time, a rupture and separation had taken place between him and my sister, growing out of his delay in promulgating their marriage

Answer to the thirteenth cross interrogatory

The information called for by this interrogatory has been already given

Answer to the fourteenth cross interrogatory

The information called for by this interrogatory has been already given

Answer to the fifteenth cross interrogatory,

The mother of Myra was never divorced from Daniel Clark within my knowledge As her marriage with him was never made public, I never heard the necessity of her being divorced made a question She married Mr Gardette before Mr Clark's death, as I have already stated, under the impression that she could not establish her marriage with him, Clark She was married to Mr Gardette in Philadelphia, according to my information, but, as I was not present, I do not know by whom, or in what month I have already sufficiently answered the rest of this interrogatory

Answer to the sixteenth cross interrogatory

The information called for by this interrogatory, has been already given

Answer to the seventeenth cross interrogatory

I have no knowledge on this subject

Answer to the eighteenth cross interrogatory

My sister had two children by Mr Gardette, with whom she lived as his wife from the period of their marriage at Philadelphia, in 1808, to the time of his death, which took place, as I have been informed by my family, in France, in the year eighteen hundred and thirty-two or thirty three

Answer to the nineteenth cross interrogatory

Mr. Clark enjoyed throughout Louisiana, as far as my knowledge extended, the character of a highly honorable man He had great pride of character, and was as quick to resent and punish any personal indignity as any man I have known I have always believed that his feelings and purposes towards my sister were sincere and honorable, and that he would have proven this by giving her her true position before the world as his lawful wife, if it had not been for the unfortunate state of feeling that was produced between them I do not believe he was a man to impose designedly upon any one, or to suffer it to be done where he was concerned. What would have been his course in the matter if he had been apprised of the contemplated marriage between her and Gardette, it is impossible for me to say My sister has told me that in an interview, had with him in Philadelphia, after the marriage with Mr. Gardette, he expressed the deepest regret that that barrier had been placed between them ; stating that he had become thoroughly satisfied that things he had heard in regard to her, and which had influenced him to postpone the promulgation of his marriage with her, were calumnies ; that he acquitted her of all blame ; and that but for the marriage with Gardette, he would then have claimed and recognized her before the world as his wife

Answer to the twentieth cross interrogatory

The marriage being a secret one, and not as yet promulgated, the child was put in the family of Col. Samuel B. Davis, with whom arrangements to that effect had been previously made It was visited frequently and constantly by the mother, at the house of Col Davis

Answer to the twenty-first cross interrogatory

I cannot undertake to give all the reasons or motives which may have actuated my sister under these painful circumstances I have always supposed, and now suppose that it was because the child being under the charge of its father, Mr Clark, who alone possessed the power of establishing her legitimacy, she left it to him to judge of the propriety of telling her the history of her birth   Previous to her (the child's) removal to Philadelphia in the family of Col Davis, she was of so tender an age that her mother may have well thought it premature to talk with her on such a subject   I am not prepared to state, of my own personal knowledge, what considerations may have governed my sister subsequently to her marriage with Mr. Gardette, as I was separated from her many years, and the subject being a painful one, has not often been the subject of conversation between us.   I remember, however, having heard, either from her or from some one of the family to whom she had stated the facts, that she had solicited from Col Davis the privilege of taking her daughter home to live with her—her then husband, Dr Gardette, having given his free consent for her to do so.   Col Davis represented to her that Myra was happily ignorant of her parentage, that she believed herself to be his and Mrs. Davis' daughter, that they both loved her as if she were their own child, and that he intended to leave her his fortune, that she was then happy in her ignorance of the painful circumstances connected with her history, and that she would be as well provided for as it was possible she could be by giving her up to her real mother She yielded to these considerations, for the benefit of her child

Answer to the twenty-second cross interrogatory ·

I have no further information on this subject.

Answer to the twenty-third cross interrogatory

I have already stated that the mother of Myra is my sister She now resides in New Orleans, and is supported by her son, Dr. James Gardette.   She has resided since 1806 in New Orleans, Philadelphia and France

Answer to the twenty-fourth cross interrogatory:

I was born in the year 1778.

Answer to the twenty-fifth cross interrogatory

This has been answered

CARRIERE Vᶠᵘᵛᵉ DESPAU

Which answers having been reduced to writing under my direction, and by me read to said witness, Madame Sophie Despau, and approved by her, have been signed and sworn to by her in my presence this 19th day of March, A D., 1849   In testimony whereof, I hereto set my hand and seal, this, the day and year last above written

WH H. CLEVELAND Com   [Seal]

EDMUND P. GAINES AND MYRA } IN CHANCERY
CLARK GAINES, HIS WIFE, }   IN THE CIRCUIT COURT OF THE
vs } UNITED STATES, IN AND FOR THE
RICHARD RELF, BEVERLY CHEW, } DISTRICT OF LOUISIANA
FRANCOIS DUSSUAU DELACROIX }

In pursuance of the annexed commission, to me directed, issued from the Circuit Court of the United States, for the Fifth Judicial Circuit, holding sessions in and for the District of Louisiana, I, William H. Cleaveland, residing at Biloxi, in the State of Mississippi, have caused to come before me, Madame Rose Caillavet, who, being duly sworn to declare the truth in answer to the interrogatories and cross interrogatories accompanying said commission, says.

Answer to the first interrogatory

I am in my eighty-third year of age, my residence is Biloxi, Mississippi.

Answer to the second interrogatory

I am well acquainted with the complainant in the above entitled suit, Myra Clark Gaines. My personal acquaintance with her is of about fourteen years duration. My knowledge of her may be said to date from the period of her birth.

Answer to the third interrogatory

I did reside in the city of New Orleans, about the year eighteen hundred, and for many years previous. My residence continued there until I went to France, about the year eighteen hundred and seven.

Answer to the fourth interrogatory.

I was well acquainted with Daniel Clark, late of the city of New Orleans, deceased. My acquaintance with him commenced about the year seventeen hundred and ninety-seven. My intimacy with him, growing out of his marriage with my sister, continued during my residence in New Orleans.

Answer to the fifth interrogatory

I was not present at the marriage of Zulime de Carrière (who is my sister) with Mr. Clark, but it is within my knowledge, both from information derived from my sisters at the time, and from the statements of Mr. Clark, made to me during his lifetime, that a marriage was solemnized between them. It is to my personal knowledge, that Mr Clark about the year eighteen hundred and two, or three, made proposals of marriage with my sister Zulime, with the knowledge of all our family. These proposals were discussed, and the preliminaries of the marriage arranged by my husband, at his house, in my presence. But my sister, having been previously married to one Jerome De-Grange, who was found to have had a lawful wife living at the time of his (DeGrange's) marriage with her, the marriage with

Mr Clark could not take place until proofs of the invalidity of her marriage with DeGrange were obtained. To procure these proofs from public records, my sisters Zulime and Madame Despau went to the north of the United States, where De-Grange's prior marriage was said to have taken place. While there my sister Zulime wrote to me that she and Mr. Clark were married. There was born of this marriage one, and only one child, a female, named Myra who was put by Mr Clark, while an infant, under the charge of Mrs Sam'l B Davis, in whose family she was brought up and educated. Having suffered from the hired nurses, she was nursed, through kindness, for some time after her birth by Mrs Harriet Harper, wife of William Harper, the nephew of Col Sam'l B Davis. Mr Clark stated to me, frequently, that Myra was his lawful and only child. This child is the same person who was married to William Wallace Whitney, son of Gen Whitney, of New York, and who is now the wife of Gen Edmund P Gaines, of the United States Army. I have always understood that the marriage between my sister and Mr Clarke was a private one, and that it was not promulgated by Mr Clark, in his lifetime, unless he did so in a last will made a short time previous to his death. I have heard that such a last will was made, but it was believed to have been suppressed or destroyed, after his death.

Answer to the sixth interrogatory.

I was acquainted with Mr Jerome DeGrange, for the first time, in New Orleans, about the year seventeen hundred and ninety-five. He passed for an unmarried man, and as such imposed himself on my sister Zulime. Some years after this marriage, it became known, in New Orleans, that he had a prior lawful wife living. My sister immediately separated from him and came to reside with her family. At a later period, Mr DeGrange was prosecuted found guilty of bigamy in having married my sister Zulime, and cast into prison. He escaped from prison, as it was reported at the time by the Spanish Governor's connivance. I understood that Mr Le Breton D Orgenois aided him to escape from the country. This happened some time before the transfer of the government of Louisiana to the Americans. The flight of DeGrange from New Orleans is the last I know of him. I did not myself know the first wife of DeGrange but it is within my knowledge that she came to New Orleans, and while there, fully established her pretensions as his lawful wife.

Answer to the seventh interrogatory.

I am not aware of having omitted anything material to the parties in this suit, in the foregoing answers. It may, however, be an advantage to the complainants for me to state, as I do under the solemnities of my oath, that my deposition taken in the year eighteen hundred and thirty-five, by virtue of a commission from the Probate Court of New Orleans before Galien Preval, in the presence of L C Duncan, and C Roschus is as it has been translated to me from the English copy filed in the court, in very material parts a garbled and mistranslated statement of what I then and there stated—particularly in answer to the cross examination Witness never did state, as it is there put down, that '*there has been no children of that marriage,* meaning the marriage between Zulime De Carriere and Jerome DeGrange Nor did she then testify as it is there set forth that her sister had written to her about the marriage with Daniel Clark, *since* witness return from France (in 1835 fifteen days before the taking of said deposition) or that her sister had ' afterwards,' to wit after witness return from France at the period above mentioned. "informed witness that she (witness' sister) ' had a child by that marriage' &c It is impossible that witness could have deposed to any such statements for the birth of two children by the marriage with DeGrange was well known to witness, of her own personal knowledge Further witness and her sister had resided together in France, and were passengers on the same ship returning therefrom, to this country thereby leaving no occasion for written communication between them, especially on that subject And further the information of witness, so far as derived from her sister, in regard to said marriage with Daniel Clark was derived at the time the event took place, as I have already stated and not after the return of witness to this country in eighteen hundred and thirty-five I further declare that said deposition was not read nor translated to me after being reduced to writing, neither by the commissioner, the counsel of the opposite party, nor by the counsel of the party in whose behalf I was called—which last mentioned counsel, as I was told and have reason to believe, very soon after the taking of my deposition abandoned his then clients and took a fee from the opposite side I make these declarations and desire they may go on record as a correction of the mistranslations and misstatements of my deposition I am unwilling that my integrity should be called in question in my old , when I am conscious of having given no ground for it

Answer to the first, second, third, and fourth cross interrogatories

I answer that I have already stated all I know on this subject
Answer to the fifth cross interrogatory

She had had two children by the marriage with Jerome DeGrange a boy and a girl The first, a boy, died very young My sister was, as well as I recollect, about nineteen or twenty years of age, when she married Mr Clark Mr Clark, as well as my sister, then resided in New Orleans Upon the other branches of this interrogatory, I have no knowledge further than I have already given

Answer to the sixth, seventh, eighth, and ninth cross interrogatories

I answer that not having been present at the marriage, nor at Philadelphia, at the time, I have no knowledge on the subject.

Answer to the tenth cross interrogatory

On the return of my sister Zulime to New Orleans, after her marriage with Mr Clark, at Philadelphia, she kept house with her and my sister, Madame Despau The house was provided by Mr Clark, who visited my sister frequently He did not keep house with her Their marriage being secret, was a sufficient reason to the family for his not doing so and for his not introducing her into society as his wife. I *think* this house was on Dauphine street but I cannot state positively that in this particular my memory is correct

Answer to the eleventh cross interrogatory

This is already answered

Answer to the twelfth and thirteenth cross interrogatories

I answer, that, as I left New Orleans in 1807, I had no personal knowledge

Answer to the fourteenth cross interrogatory

I have already answered *one* who is now Mrs Gaines

Answer to the fifteenth, sixteenth, and seventeenth cross interrogatories

I answer that being in France, I had no personal information, further than I have already given, except it is to add that my sister, having married Dr Gardette of Philadelphia, lived with him for a number of years in France as his wife—until the period of his death which took place in the year 1831 or 32

Answer to the eighteenth cross interrogatory

She had two children, by Mr Gardette. She went into mourning, and acted as his widow, after his death, and claimed and received rights as such

Answer to the nineteenth cross interrogatory

Daniel Clark was considered an honorable man I so esteemed him, and believe that the wrongs which my sister suffered at his hands had their source in the evil designs and misrepresentations of others, and not from any want of attachment to her or from any dishonorable purpose I do not think he was a man to submit to any kind of indemnity but he was of a confiding as well as a proud and sensitive nature and his mind was poisoned by those in whom he placed confidence

Answer to the twentieth cross interrogatory

I was in New Orleans at the time of Myra's birth I know of no other reason than that the marriage was a secret one not then made public She was not denied intercourse with her child, but visited it frequently

Answer to the twenty-first and twenty-second cross interrogatories.

I answer, that I can give no information, on this point, further than may be found in the facts and circumstances I have already narrated

Answer to the twenty-third cross interrogatory

She is my sister She has resided, since 1806, in New Orleans, Philadelphia, and France—while in France, with Dr Gardette, until his death She now resides in New Orleans, with her son, Dr. James Gardette

Answer to the twenty-fourth cross interrogatory

I was born in Opelousas, Louisiana, on the 2d of April, 1766.

Answer to the twenty-fifth cross interrogatory .

I have already answered this, as far as my memory serves me.

R CAILLAVET née CARRIERE

Which answers having been reduced to writing, under my direction, and by me read to said witness, Madame Rose Caillavet, and approved by her, have been signed and sworn to by her, in my presence, this 19th day of March, A D 1849. In testimony whereof, I have hereunto set my hand and seal, this the day and year last above mentioned

WM H CLEVELAND, Com

UNITED STATES OF AMERICA, } ss
SOUTHERN DISTRICT OF NEW YORK.

I, Alexander Gardiner, Clerk of the Circuit Court of the United States of America, for the Southern District of New York, Second Circuit, do hereby certify, that I am well acquainted with the handwriting of Alexander Gardiner, whose name is subscribed to the annexed depositions, and that the signature to the same is in his proper handwriting And I do further certify, that he was, at the time of signing the same, a United States Commissioner, duly appointed under, and by virtue of the acts of Congress in that behalf, by the Circuit Court of the United States of America, for the Southern District of New York

In testimony whereof, I have hereunto subscribed my name, and affixed the seal of the said Circuit Court, this

{ Seal. } ninth day of May, in the year of our Lord one thousand eight hundred and forty six, and of the Independence of these United States, the seventieth

ALEX'R GARDINER, Clerk

In the Circuit Court of the United States for the Eastern
District of Louisiana

Edmund Pendleton Gaines and Myra
Clark Gaines, his Wife, Complainants,
against   IN EQUITY
Beverly Chew, Richard Relf, and
others, Defendants

UNITED STATES OF AMERICA, } ss
Southern District of New York

James W. White, of the City of New York, Counsellor at
Law being sworn, deposes and says that he is of counsel,
and also attorney in fact for the complainants in the above entitled cause, that as deponent is informed and believes to be
true, said cause is depending in the Circuit Court of the United
States, for the Eastern District of Louisiana, and that the
place of trial of said cause is at New Orleans, in the State of
Louisiana, and that Ellen Guinan, John Power, and Charles
E Benson, are, and each of them is, a material and necessary
witness and then, and each of their testimony, is material and
necessary for said complainants in said cause, in the prosecution thereof, and that all the said witnesses reside and live in
the city of New York except said Benson, who lives in Brooklyn; and they all live more than one hundred miles from the
said place of trial, and that the defendants in the said cause
all reside more than one hundred miles from the city of New
York, and reside, as deponent is informed and believes, in New
Orleans, in the State of Louisiana, aforesaid, and have not, as
deponent verily believes, any attorney, solicitor, or counsel within one hundred miles of the said city of New York, and deponent further says that he is informed and believes the said complainants are at present at and residing in the said city of New
Orleans   JAMES W WHITE.
Sworn, this 8th day of May, 1846, before me,
ALEX R GARDINER, U. S. Com'r.

In the Circuit Court of the United States for the Eastern
District of Louisiana

Edmund Pendleton Gaines and Myra
Clark Gaines, his Wife, Complainants,
vs.   IN EQUITY
Beverly Chew Richard Relf, and
others, Defendants.

Let Elen Guinan, one of the witnesses named in the within
affidavit, be examined *de bene esse*, before me, accordingly, at

my office, at the new City Hall of the city of New York, on Friday, the 8th day of May, 1846

ALEX'R GARDINER, U S. Commissioner

May 8, 1846

Let John Power, one of the witnesses named in the within affidavit, be examined *de bene esse*, before me, accordingly at his residence, No 15 Barclay street, in the City of New York on Saturday, the ninth day of May, 1846

ALEX R GARDINER, U S Commissioner

May 8, 1846

Let the within named Charles L Benson be examined de bene esse before me, at No 15 Barclay street, in the city of New York, on Saturday, the 9th day of May, 1846,

ALEX GARDINER, U S Commissioner

May 9, 1846

UNITED STATES OF AMERICA

SOUTHERN DISTRICT OF NEW YORK,
CITY, COUNTY, AND STATE OF NEW YORK } SS

Be it remembered, that on this eighth day of May, in the year of our Lord one thousand eight hundred and forty-six, I, Alexander Gardiner, a commissioner, duly appointed by the Circuit Court of the United States, for the Southern district of New York, in the second circuit, under and by virtue of the acts of Congress entitled "an act for the more convenient taking of affidavits and bail in civil causes, depending in the courts of the United States," passed February 20, 1812, and the act of Congress entitled "an act, in addition to an act, entitled 'an act for the more convenient taking of affidavits and bail in civil causes, depending in the Courts of the United States,' " passed March 1, 1817, and the act entitled "an act to establish the judicial Courts of the United States," passed September 24, 1789, did call and cause to be and personally appear before me, at my office, at the United States Courts in the city of New York, in the said Southern District of New York, in the State aforesaid, Ellen Guinan, to testify, and the truth to say, on the part and behalf of the Complainants in a certain suit or matter of controversy, now depending and undetermined in the Circuit Court of the United States for the Eastern District of Louisiana, wherein Pendleton Gaines, and Myra Clark Gaines, his wife, are complainants, and Beverly Chew, Richard Relf, and others, defendants

And the said Ellen Guinan, being about the age of fifty-two years, and having been by me first cautioned and sworn to testify the truth, the whole truth, and nothing but the truth, in the matter of controversy aforesaid, I did carefully examine the said

Ellen Guinan, and she did thereupon depose, testify and say, as follows, viz

1 Question   What is your present place of residence?

Answer   No 57 Warren street, in the city of New York

2 Question   Do you know any of the parties, complainants or defendants, in this suit?

Answer   I do not

3 Question   How long have you resided in the city of New York?

Answer   Since I was nine years old

4 Question   Do you know who was the pastor of the Catholic Church of St Peter, in the city of New York, when you first came to that city?

Answer   I do   My uncle, William Vincent O'Brien

5 Question   How long was he pastor of that church?

Answer   For thirty years he preached there

6 Question   Is he now living?

Answer   No, sir

7 Question   About what time did he die?

Answer   On the fourteenth of May, about the year eighteen hundred and fourteen or fifteen, I should think.

8 Question   Have you ever seen him write?

Answer   During my residence with him, I was accustomed to see him write several times a day

9 Question   How long did you reside with him?

Answer   I resided with him from the time I was nine years old until he died

10 Question   Please to look at the paper now shown to you, marked Exhibit A, and state whether the signature to it, Gulielmus V o Brien is in the handwriting of the said William Vincent O Brien, pastor of St Peter's Church, and your uncle?

Answer   It is his hand writing

11. Question   Is the whole of the document preceding the signature in his hand writing?

Answer   It is   the whole of it is his hand writing

12 Question   How was he accustomed to sign his name to such documents?

Answer   In the manner in which it is there signed, viz "Gulielmus V. o Brien, pastor Ecclesia S. Petri, ut supra"

(The exhibit referred to by the witness and marked exhibit A is annexed to this deposition)

13 Question   Do you know the persons named in the body of this exhibit, Joannes O'Connell, Carolus Bernardi and Victoria Bernardi?

Answer.   I have heard of them and think they are dead, but never knew or saw them that I know of

14 Question   Did you know Jacobum Degrange and Barbara M Orci, named in the body of said exhibit?

Answer   I did not—never have known them

15 Question   Do you know whether the books or records of St. Peter's Church were at any time destroyed?

Answer   I heard they were

16 Question.   When did you hear they were, and on what occasion?

Answer   A gentleman from Ireland, Mr Cruse, who married the sister of Sir John Johnston, of Johnstown and Warrenstown in Ireland, came to inquire about the marriage of one of his family whom he had understood was married by my uncle   I told him to go to the church as we had given up uncle's books after his death to Bishop Connelly, Catholic bishop of this city   He came back and told us that he had found that the books had been destroyed by fire

17 Question   About how long ago was it that you thus heard that the books were destroyed?

Answer   To the best of my recollection, about thirteen or fourteen years ago

18. Question.   What did you hear of Joannes O'Connell, Carolus Bernardi and Victoria Barnardi, named in the exhibit shewn you, and mentioned in a previous question?

Answer.   I heard from my aunt Louisa Jane O'Brien, that they were all attached to the Spanish ambassador's suit   I think O'Connell was his chaplain

19. Question.   Was Louisa Jane O'Brien, of whom you have spoken, related to your uncle William V. o'Brien?

Answer   She was his brother's daughter

20. Question   Where did she reside?

Answer.   She resided with my uncle, William V O'Brien, from her infancy till his death

21 Question   Did she live with him before you went to live with him?

Answer   She did many years before

22 Question.   Is she now living? and if she is not, when and where did she die?

Answer.   She is not she died at No 57 Warren street, in this city, last Easter Monday, I think the 13th of April

23. Question   How are you related to the said William V o'Brien?

Answer   I am his grand niece   I am the daughter of the sister of Louisa Jane O'Brien, above spoken of

24. Question.   What was the profession of the said William V O'Brien?

Answer.   He was a Catholic priest.

25. Question   Where did he die?

Answer   He died at No 57 Warren street, in this city.

26 Question.   Are you acquainted with or do you know any person now living who was acquainted in 1790 with the pastor of St Peter's church?

Answer   I do not all that I know that were acquainted with him at that time are dead or gone away

27 Question   Had or had not the said pastor, William V o'Brien, full and legal power to solemnize and perform the ceremonies of marriage, during all the time that he was pastor of St Peter's Church, aforesaid?

Answer   He had

28 Question   In what manner did he usually write his marriage certificates and sign his name to them, in English, in the usual way, or in Latin?

Answer   Mostly in Latin it was his favorite language, and the language of the church

29 Question   How did he usually form the letter *O* prefixed to the word Brien, in writing his name?

Answer   He wrote a small O with a comma or mark over it, just as it is in the Exhibit marked A, excepting that the letter is a little blotted there

30 Question   Do you know, and are you well acquainted with the handwriting of the said William V o Brien?

Answer   I do   I am well acquainted with it.

31 Question   Does the marriage of DeGrange, which is certified in said Exhibit A, appear by said exhibit, to have been performed according to the usages and formalities of the said Church, at that time?

Answer   It does the certificate appears to be in the usual form.

32 Question   Have you or not seen such certificates given by your said uncle?

Answer   I have frequently

33 Question Do you know, or can you set forth any other matter or thing, which may be of benefit or advantage to the parties a issue in this cause, or either of them.—or that be material to the subject of your examination or the matters in question in this cause, if yea, set forth the same fully and at large in your answer?

Answer.   I don t think I know anything more except that I think I have heard my aunt, Louisa Jane O Brien, mention such a person as DeGrange, as having been married by my said uncle Upon consideration I know I did, for my aunt mentioned to me something about the dress of Mrs Bernardi at the wedding, as being so remarkable.

ELEN GUINAN

UNITED STATES OF AMERICA, } ss
SOUTHERN DISTRICT OF NEW YORK }

I, Alexander Gardiner, a commissioner, duly appointed by the Circuit Court of the United States, for the Southern District of New York, in the Second Circuit, under and by virtue of the Acts of Congress, entitled "An act for the more convenient taking of affidavits and bail in civil causes, depending in the Courts of the United States" passed February 20th., 1812, and the Act of Congress entitled "An act, in addition to an act, entitled ' An Act for the more convenient taking of affidavits and bail in civil causes, depending in the Courts of the United States,' " passed March 1st, 1817 and the Act, entitled " An Act to establish the Judicial Courts of the United States," passed September 24th, 1789, DO HEREBY CERTIFY, that the reason for taking the foregoing *deposition* is, and the fact is that the *witness* Elen Guinan, lives at a greater distance than one hundred miles from the place of trial of the cause depending.

I further certify, that no notification of the time and place of taking the said deposition signed by me, was made out and served on the opposite parties, nor their attorney or attorneys, to be present at the taking of the deposition and to put interrogatories, if he or they might think fit, neither the adverse parties, nor their attorney or attorneys, being within one hundred miles of the place of such caption, as appears by the affidavit of James W White, hereunto annexed

I further certify that on the eighth day of May, A D, 1846, I was attended by James W White, solicitor for complainants, and by the witness, who was of sound mind and lawful age, and witness was by me carefully examined and cautioned, and sworn to testify the whole truth, and the deposition was by me reduced to writing, in the presence of the witness, and after carefully reading the same to the *witness*, she subscribed the same in my presence I have retained the said deposition in my possession for the purpose of sealing up the same, and directing the same with my own hand to the Court, for which the same was taken

I further certify, that I am not of counsel or attorney for either of the parties in said deposition and caption named, or in any way interested in the event of the said cause named in the caption

In testimony whereof, I have hereunto set my hand and seal this eighth day of May, in the year of our Lord one thousand eight hundred and forty six and of the independence of the U States the seventieth

ALEX R GARDINER, [L.S]
U S commissioner, Circuit Court of the
U S, for the Southern district of N York

UNITED STATES OF AMERICA,)
SOUTHERN DISTRICT OF NEW YORK, CITY, } SS.
COUNTY AND STATE OF NEW YORK)

Be it remembered, that on this ninth day of May, in the year of our Lord one thousand eight hundred and forty-six, I, Alexander Gardiner, a commissioner, duly appointed by the Circuit Court of the United States, for the Southern district of N. York, in the second circuit under and by virtue of the acts of Congress, entitled, 'an act for the more convenient taking of affidavits and bail in civil causes depending in the courts of the United States," passed February 20th, 1812, and the act of Congress, entitled, "an act in addition to an act entitled 'an act for the more convenient taking of affidavits and bail in civil causes, depending in the courts of the United States'' passed March 1st, 1817, and the act entitled, "an act to establish the judicial courts of the United States, passed September 24th, 1789, did call and cause to be and personally appear before me at his house, No 15 Barclay street, in the city of New York, in the said southern district of New York in the State aforesaid, John Power, to testify and the truth to say, on the part and behalf of the complainants in a certain suit or matter of controversy now depending and undetermined, in the circuit court of the United States for the Eastern district of Louisiana, wherein Edmund Pendleton Gaines and Myra Clark Gaines, his wife are complainants, and Beverly Chew, Richard Relf, and others are defendants

And the said John Power being about the age of fifty-five years, and having been by me first cautioned and sworn to testify the truth, the whole truth and nothing but the truth, in the matter of controversy aforesaid, I did carefully examine the said John Power, and he did thereupon depose, testify and say as follows, viz

1 Question Please to state your residence, and your profession or occupation

Answer I reside at No 15 Barclay street, in the city of New York and am by profession a clergyman of the Catholic church I am vicar general of the diocese of New York, and pastor of St Peter's church in the city of New York

2 Question How long have you been pastor of St Peter's church?

Answer I have been officiating as clergyman in that church twenty-six years, and pastor of it about twenty years

3 Question Have records been kept in said St. Peter's church of the marriages solemnized by the clergymen officiating there?

Answer There have been with more or less regularity there have been frequent omissions arising either from neglect or accident
51

4 Question   Is there any written record now existing of the marriages solemnized by the clergymen of the said church previous to the year 1800?

Answer   I don't know that such a record exists   I have heard that it was missing, but have made no particular personal search for it   I don't know that I ever saw it

5 Question   Have you known, personally or by reputation, William V o'Brien now deceased?

Answer   I have no personal knowledge of him   He was dead when I came to this country, but his memory was then fresh in the minds of people, and he was held in high repute

6 Question   What was his profession, and what place or office did he hold here?

Answer   He was pastor of St Peter's church

7 Question   How long had he been pastor of St Peter's church?

Answer   Many years   I cannot say the precise time.

8 Question   Do there appear to be any records in said church kept by him of the baptisms which he solemnized while pastor of said church?

Answer   There do

9. Question   Have they been universally and at all times received as genuine and authentic?

Answer   They have been always received as genuine and authentic, and I have no doubt that they are so

10 Question   Have you any knowledge of the hand-writing of said William V o Brien, and if so, whence have you derived it?

Answer   I have a knowledge of his hand writing, which I have derived from the register of baptisms in St Peter's church, which have always been received as —— hand writing

11 Question   From the knowledge which you have thus derived of his hand-writing do you believe the signature Gulielmus V o Brien, in the Exhibit marked A, now shown you, to be in the hand-writing of said William V O Brien

Answer   I believe it to be his hand-writing   It is identically the same hand-writing with that of the records now in the church of which I have spoken

12 Question   In whose hand-writing do you believe the writing in said exhibit preceding said signature, that is, the body of the marriage certificate, to which said signature is affixed, to be?

Answer. In the hand-writing of said Rev William V. o'Brien

13 Question   In what language did said Rev Mr O'Brien keep his records before spoken of?

Answer   In the Latin language.

14 Question   How did he sign his name when writing in the Latin language?

Answer. In the same manner as it is signed in the Exhibit marked A, which you have shown me, Gulielmus V o'Brien.

15 Question Had said Rev Mr O'Brien full and legal power to solemnize and perform the ceremonies of marriage while he was pastor of St Peters church?

Answer He had.

16 Question Have you a knowledge of and are you versed in the Latin language?

Answer I am versed in the Latin language

17 Question Please to read said certificate of marriage marked exhibit A, now shown you, and state whether the marriage of DeGrange therein certified to, was performed according to the usages and formalities of the said church at the time of the date of the said certificate, so far as the same appears in and by virtue of the said certificate

Answer The certificate is absolutely in due form, and it is to be presumed that the marriage was solemnized according to the rites and ceremonies of the Catholic church Previous to giving this, my answer, I have, as requested, read the said certificate, and understand its contents

18 Question Do you know anything of the witnesses to the marriage, mentioned in said certificate, or any of them?

Answer I do not

19 Question Do you know, or can you set forth any other matter or thing which may be of benefit or advantage to the parties at issue in this cause, or either of them, or that may be material to the subject of your examination, or the matters in question in this cause, if yea, set forth the same fully and at large in your answer?

Answer No sir, I do not

JOHN POWER,
V G of New York

UNITED STATES OF AMERICA,
SOUTHERN DISTRICT OF NEW YORK } SS

I Alexander Gardiner, a commissioner, duly appointed by the Circuit Court of the United States for the Southern District of New York, in the Second Circuit, under and by virtue of the acts of Congress entitled "an act for the more convenient taking of affidavits and bail in civil causes, depending in the courts of the United States," passed February 20th, 1812, and the act of Congress entitled 'an act in addition to an act entitled 'an act for the more convenient taking of of affidavits and bail in civil causes, depending in the courts of the United States,'" passed March 1st, 1817, and' the act entitled "an act to establish the Judicial Court of the United States," passed September 25, 1789, DO HEREBY CERTIFY, that the reason for taking the foregoing dep-

osition is, and the fact is, that the witness, John Power, lives
at a greater distance than one hundred miles from the place of
trial of the cause depending

I further certify, that no notification of the time and place of
taking the said deposition, signed by me, was made out and
served on the opposite parties, nor on their attorney or attorneys, to be present at the taking of the deposition, and to put
interrogatories, if he or they might think fit, neither the adverse
parties, nor their attorney or attorneys being within one hundred miles of the place of such caption, as appears by the affidavit of James W White, hereunto annexed

I further certify, that on the ninth day of May, A. D 1846, I
was attended by James W White, solicitor for complainants,
and by the witness, who was of sound mind and lawful age,
and the witness was by me carefully examined, and cautioned, and
sworn to testify the whole truth, and the deposition was by me
reduced to writing, in the presence of the witness, and after
carefully reading the same to the witness, he subscribed the same
in my presence   I have retained the said deposition in my possession for the purpose of sealing it up, and directing the same
with my own hand to the Court for which the same was taken

I further certify, that I am not of counsel or attorney for either of the parties in said deposition and caption named, or in any
way interested in the event of the said cause named in the
caption

In testimony whereof, I have hereunto set my hand and seal,
this ninth day of May, in the year of our Lord one thousand
eight hundred and forty-six, and of the independence of the
United States the ——

                    ALEX GARDINER,   [Seal]
    U S Commissioner, Circuit Court of the U S for the
Southern District of New York

The certificate marked Exhibit A, referred to in the above
deposition of John Power, is the same with that referred to in
the deposition of Elen Guinan, and hereunto annexed.
                    ALEX'R GARDINER, U S Com'r

———

UNITED STATES OF AMERICA.   ⎰
    Southern District of New York,   ⎱ SS
City, County and State of New York ⎰

Be it remembered, that on this ninth day of May, in the year
of our Lord one thousand eight hundred and forty-six, I, Alexander Gardiner, a Commissioner, duly appointed by the Circuit
Court of the United States, for the Southern District of New
York, in the Second Circuit, under and by virtue of the acts of

Congress, entitled "An act for the more convenient taking of affidavits and bail, in civil causes, depending in the Courts of the United States," passed February 20th, 1812, and the act of Congress, entitled, "An act in addition to an act, entitled 'An act for the more convenient taking of affidavits and bail in civil causes, depending in the Courts of the United States,'" passed March 1st, 1817 and the act entitled "An act to establish the Judicial Courts of the United States," passed September 24, 1789, Did call and cause to be, and personally appear before me at my office at the United States Courts in the City of New York, in the said Southern District of New York, in the State aforesaid, Charles E. Benson, to testify and the truth to say, on the part and behalf of the complainants in a certain suit or matter of controversy now depending and undetermined, in the *Circuit* Court of the United States, for the Eastern District of Louisiana, wherein Edmund Pendleton Gaines and Myra Clark Gaines, his wife, are complainants, and Beverly Chew, Richard Relf and others are defendants

And the said Charles E. Benson, being about the age of thirty-two years, and having been, by me, first cautioned and sworn to testify the truth, the whole truth, and nothing but the truth, in the matter of controversy aforesaid, I did carefully examine the said Charles E. Benson, and he did thereupon depose, testify, and say as follows, viz

1 Question What is your present business or occupation, and where do you reside?

Answer I am Clerk of St Peter's (Roman Catholic) Church, in the city of New York, and my residence is at No 219 Jay street, in the city of Brooklyn

2 Question Have you the custody of the records of marriages and baptisms solemnized by the pastors and clergymen of said St Peter's Church?

Answer I have

3. Is there existing now, among those records, any record or written memorandums of marriages solemnized by the pastors and clergymen of the said Church, previous to the year 1800?

Answer There is now none existing of any date previous to the year 1802

4 Question Have you any knowledge of the handwriting of William V O'Brien, Catholic Priest, formerly Pastor of said St Peter's Church?

Answer No other knowledge than such as I derive from the records of the church, which were kept by him Those records have been always received as authentic and genuine, and as being in his handwriting

5 Question From the knowledge which you have thus derived of his handwriting, do you believe the certificate of mar-

riage, marked *Exhibit A*, now shown you, to be in his hand-writing, including the signature, Gulielmus V. O'Brien?

Answer I do. I have not the slightest doubt about it

6 Question. Are there any records of baptisms solemnized by the Pastors of St. Peters Church?

Answer There are.

7 Question Are there any such records of baptisms belonging to said Church, kept by said William V O'Brien?

Answer There are. from the year 1787 to the year 1808 in one register, and from 1808 to 1816, in another There are, in each of these registers, other entries by other clergymen attached to the church

8. Question In whose handwriting are the first entries in the oldest register spoken of by you?

Answer In the handwriting of said Mr O'Brien

9. Question. Are these entries in that register of baptisms in the handwriting of said William V O'Brien in each of the years, 1787, 1788, 1789 and 1790 and in each year subsequently down to 1808?

Answer In some of those years there are not There are entries in his handwriting in 1787, 1788, and most of the subsequent years

10. Question Have you made diligent search for the register of marriages solemnized by the clergymen of said St Peters church previous to the year 1802?

Answer I have

11. Question When and where did you make that search?

Answer. I have made several searches for it for different purposes, during the last two years, in all the places in the church, where records would proabably be

12. Question. Did you search elsewhere than in St Peters church for it, and if so where and why did you search elsewhere?

Answer. I did I searched in the house of a Mr Flanden, an old French gentleman, whom I was told had a register of the church. I searched there in the month of March last, for the purposes of this cause

13. Question What was the result of that search?

Answer I did not find the register I discovered on going to Mr. Flandens, that the register which he had had was an old register of baptisms, which I found upon the information which I received from him

14 Question How long have you been clerk of said St Peters church?

Answer. Nearly two years

15. Question Had said Rev. William V. O'Brien, full and legal power to solemnize and perform the ceremonies of marriage during the time he was pastor of said St Peter's church?

Answer. So far as I can know from the general practice of the church, he had

16 Question   Was the marriage of DeGrange mentioned in the said certificate, marked exhibit A performed according to the usages and formalities of the said church at that time as the same appears in and by virtue of the said certificate?

Answer   It was. the said certificate is in the form usual to this day

17 Question   Do you know anything of any of the witnesses to the marriage mentioned in the said certificate?

Answer   I do not

18 Question   In what language did said Rev Mr O'Brien usually keep his records and make out his marriage certificates?

Answer   He kept the records and made out his marriage certificates in the Latin language

19 Question   How long was the said Rev William V O'Brien pastor of St Peter's church?

Answer   It appears from the records of the church that he was pastor of the church from the year 1787 to the year 1816, the time of his death, such also is the tradition of the church and the general reputation

20 Question   Do you know of any other matter or thing which may be of benefit or advantage to the parties at issue in this cause or either of them or that may be material to the subject of your examination or the matters in question in this cause if yea set forth the same fully in your answer

Answer   I don't know anything that I am aware of excepting that I have heard from different persons connected with the church, that the marriage register referred to, for which I made search was lost many years ago, and I do not believe it can be found

CHARLES E BENSON,
Clerk of St Peter's Church, New York.

UNITED STATES OF AMERICA,
SOUTHERN DISTRICT OF NEW YORK } ss

I Silvanus Rapalje, a commissioner, duly appointed by the Circuit Court of the United States for the Southern District of New York, in the Second Circuit, under and by virtue of the Acts of Congress, entitled " An Act for the more convenient taking of affidavits and bail in civil causes depending in the Courts of the United States,' passed February 20th, 1812, and the Act of Congress, entitled ' An act in addition to an act entitled ' An act for the more convenient taking of affidavits and bail in civil causes, depending in the Courts of the United States,' passed March 1st, 1817, and the act, entitled " An act to establish the Judicial Courts of the United States,' passed

September 24th, 1789, Do HEREBY CERTIFY, that the reason for taking the foregoing *deposition* is, and the fact is, that the *witness*, Charles E Benson, lives at a greater distance than one hundred miles from the place of trial of the cause depending

I further certify, that no notification of the time and place of taking the said *deposition*, signed by me, was made out and served on the adverse parties, nor on their attorney or attornys, to be present at the taking of the *deposition*, and to put interrogatories, if he or they might think fit, neither the adverse parties, nor their attorney or attornies, being within one hundred miles of the place of such caption, as appears by the affidavit of James W White, hereunto annexed

I further certify, that on the ninth day of May, A D., 1846, I was attended by James W. White, solicitor for complainants, and by the *witness*, who was of sound mind and lawful age, and the *witness* was by me carefully examined and cautioned, and sworn to testify the whole truth, and the *deposition* was by me reduced to writing, in the presence of the *witness* and after carefully reading the same to the *witness* he subscribed the same in my presence   I have retained the said *d'position* in my possession for the purpose of sealing it up and directing the same with my own hand to the Court for which the same was taken

I further certify, that I am not of counsel or attorney for either of the parties in said deposition and caption named, or in any way interested in the event of the said cause named in the caption

In testimony whereof I have hereunto set my hand and seal, this ninth day of May, in the year of our Lord, one thousand eight hundred and forty-six, and of the Independence of the United States, the seventieth.

ALEX GARDINER,   (L S)

U S Commissioner, Circuit Court of the U S
for the Southern District of New York

The certificate, marked Exhibit A, referred to in the preceding deposition of Charles E Benson, is the same with that referred to in the deposition of Elen Guinan, and hereunto annexed

ALEX. GARDINER, U. S Commissioner

†

OMNIBUS HAS LITERAS, INSPECTURIS SALUTEM IN DOMINO. Ego infrascriptus sacerdos Catholicus et Apostolicus, pastor Ecclesiæ S. Petri Apostoli, hinc Præsentibus, notum facio et attestor omnibus, et singulis quorum interest, quod die sexta mensis julij, A D 1790, in matrimonium conjunxerum Jacobum Degiange et Barbaram Orci, Testes præsentes fuerunt, Joannes o'Connell, Carolus Bernardi, et Victoria Bernardi.   In quorum fidem, has manu propria scripsi, et subscripsi, vigilloq muniri   Datum Neo Eboraci, vulgo New York hac die 11d mensis Septembris, A D. 1806.

GULIELMUS V o' BRIEN,

Reg pag , '45.   Pastor Ecclesiæ S. Petri ut supra.

Nous, Gabriel Rey, Général Divisionnaire, Commissaire des Relationes Commercia e France, à New York, certifione que Monsieur Guillaume O'Brien dont la signature est apposé a l'extrait de Mariage en l autre part, est Prétre et Curé de l'Eglise Catholique de Ste Pierre in cetté ville de New York, et qu en cette qualité foi doit être ajouter à sa dite signature tant en jugement que hors,

En témoin de quoi nous avons signé le présente et scelle **fait** apposer le timbre du Commissariat.

[SLAL]   à New York, le 13 Septembre, 1806
                                                         REY.

On motion of Wright, Esq , Solicitor for Plaintiffs, agreeably to stipulation, opened and filed 20th July, 1849.

                    J W GURLEY, D. C.

CIRCUIT COURT OF THE UNITED STATES,

For the Fifth Judicial Circuit, holding Sessions in and for the Eastern District of Louisiana.

To William H Rawle, of the city of Philadelphia, Commissioner of the State of Louisiana know ye, that reposing special trust and confidence in your integrity and ability, we hereby authorize and require you that you call and cause to come before you Samuel B Davis, and him duly examine on oath, touching and concerning certain matters and things in a case now depending in the said court, wherein Edmund P Gaines and Myra Clark, his wife, are plaintiffs, and Richard Relf and Beverly Chew et al. are defendants , and the same examinations, so taken and reduced to writing, you certify under your hand and seal, and send enclosed to this court without delay, to be read in evidence on the trial of said cause, and send also this writ Witness the Honorable Roger B Taney, Chief Justice of the

{ L. S. }   Supreme Court of the United States, at the city of New Orleans, this twenty-sixth day of May, Anno Domini 1849, and the sixty-third year of the Independence of the United States of America

                    ED RANDOLPH, Clerk.
                    Per J W GURLEY, Dy Clerk

The execution of this commission appears in a certain schedule hereunto annexed. I certify that the examination was conducted as appears therein, all the interrogatories and cross interrogatories having been severally put to the witness, and severally answered under oath as therein set forth

Witness my hand and seal of office, this eleventh day of July, Anno Domini one thousand eight hundred and forty-nine.

WILLIAM HENRY RAWLE, Commissioner   (Seal.)

The expense of executing this commission is seventy-five dollars. [$75.00]

EDMUND P. GAINES AND MYRA CLARK, HIS WIFE, *vs.* RICH'D RELF, BEVERLY CHEW, AND OTHERS.	IN CHANCERY. U S CIRCUIT COURT, FIFTH CIRCUIT, EASTERN DISTRICT OF LOUISIANA No 122.

Interrogatories to be propounded to Samuel B. Davis, residing at Wilmington, in the State of Delaware, a witness to be produced on the part of complainants, and sworn and examined in the above entitled suit

Interrogatory 1st. Do you know the complainants in the above entitled suit, and the defendants Relf and Chew?

Interrogatory 2d. What is your age? occupation? and where do you reside?

Interrogatory 3d. Did you, at any time, reside in the city of New Orleans, and State of Louisiana? If yea, at what period did you go there to reside? When did you cease to reside there? and where did you reside, after leaving New Orleans?

Interrogatory 4th Did you know Daniel Clark, late of the city of New Orleans, now deceased? If yea, did you know him intimately? Did you enjoy his confidence and friendship? When and where did you last see him? State what you know respecting his business and pecuniary affairs at that period

Interrogatory 5th. Do you know whether the said Daniel Clark left a child living, at the time of his death, which he acknowledged as his own? If yea, state who is that child; who is the mother; when and where it was born, by whom reared and educated, and under what circumstances; state fully and particularly.

Interrogatory 6th Did the said Daniel Clark ever make any declaration or acknowledgment to you respecting said child? If yea, when, and what was such declaration or acknowledgment? Did he make any provision for the education of said child? If yea, what? how? Did he express any intention of disposing of his fortune or any portion thereof in favor of said child? If yea, what intention was so expressed? Did he do any act in the performance of such intention so expressed?

If yea, what act? when and where done and performed? State particularly

Interrogatory 7th. Do you know if the said Daniel Clark, sometime in or about the year 1811, made a voyage from New Orleans to Philadelphia by sea? If yea, state what was the occasion of said voyage, the date of his departure, and the date of his return to New Orleans. Did you receive any letter or letters from the said Clark, about the time of his departure, or any paper, writing, memorandum, or document? If yea, annex such letter or letters to your answer to this interrogatory; and state what was or were such memorandum, paper, writing, or document. Did you receive from said Clark any letter or letters with any paper or papers or memorandum enclosed, addressed to you from Philadelphia, prior to Mr. Clark leaving there to return to New Orleans? If yea, annex it or them to your answer to this interrogatory, and state particularly what was or were enclosed in such letter or letters.

Interrogatory, 8th Do you know or can you set forth any other matter or thing, which may be a benefit or advantage to the parties at issue in this cause, or either of them, or that may be material to the subject of this, your examination, or the matter in question in this cause? if yea, set forth the same fully and at large in your answer

P. C. WRIGHT, Sol for Complainants

Cross interrogatories in behalf of Messrs. Richard Relf, Beverly Chew and Dussuau Delacroix

The defendants, aforenamed, reserving to themselves all manner of objection to the foregoing interrogatories and all exception in the premises, now propound the following cross interrogatories:

1st. When did you first become acquainted with Daniel Clark, and where?

2d. Were you in New Orleans in the years 1802 and 1803? If aye, was Daniel Clark absent from that city any part of either of those years? If aye, state how long he was absent where did he go? at what precise time did he return at New Orleans?

3d. Do you know whether or not Daniel Clark was in Europe any part of 1802? if aye, state what part.

4th Were you present when Laussat, the French colonial prefect, arrived in Louisiana? When did he arrive? Was Daniel Clark present in Louisiana at that time? If aye, how long had he been then back from Europe? Do you know whether Daniel Clark sailed from Liverpool, or elsewhere in Europe, directly for New Orleans? Did he not come in the Thomas Wilson, a ship belonging to Daniel W. Coxe, of Philadelphia?

Do you know Mrs. Zulime Gardette, widow of the late Dr

James Gardette, whose maiden name was Carrière? Who was she *first* married to? Was it not to Jerome DeGrange? When was she married to James Gardette? Where did this latter marriage take place? Where did Mr James Gardette and his said wife reside, after their marriage? Did they not continue to reside in Chesnut-street, at or near 9th street, Philadelphia, from the time of their marriage in 1807 or 1808 until 1829?

5th. Did not Dr. James Gardette, and his said wife, Zulime, née Carrière, live together in Philadelphia, as aforesaid, openly and notoriously as husband and wife, from 1808 to 1829, or from the time of your return to Philadelphia, in 1812, when you can speak personally? Was she not introduced into the society in which Dr Gardette moved, as his wife? Did he not, by every act by which a man can manifest a woman to the world as his wife, thus, and in that capacity proclaim her as such? Did she not also, in the same manner, own, acknowledge, and proclaim the said Gardette as her husband?

6th. Did not the said Dr. James Gardette and his said wife, Zulime, nee Carrière, raise a family of children by him, of her begotten, and did they not both manifest to the world by their conduct and declarations that their said children were honorably and legally born in lawful wedlock?

7th Did not the said Gardette and his said family remove from Philadelphia in 1829, or thereabouts, to Bordeaux, in the then kingdom of France?

8th. Did you have any intercourse with Mrs. Gardette, née Carrière, after you removed to Philadelphia? If aye, was she not called, known, and generally received as the lawful wife of Dr. Gardette? Did she not herself so represent and hold herself out to the community?

9th. Were you or were you not acquainted with Mrs De-Grange, to wit, Zulime, nee Carrière, while you resided in New Orleans? Was that acquaintance personal or by reputation in the community? How long had you thus known her?

10th. Did you, or did you not ever hear Daniel Clark speak of Zulime, née Carrière, subsequently Madame DeGrange, as being his wife? Have you not, on the contrary, heard him speak of that woman as holding a very different relationship to him, than that of his accepted and lawful wife? If aye, state distinctly and fully what that relationship was? What was Clark's position or connection with her, if any,—as you understood it, either from Clark or public repute in New Orleans? State fully.

11th. Did you ever know of Daniel Clark presenting the said Zulime to the community of New Orleans, or any other community, as his wife? State fully. Did Daniel Clark keep house in New Orleans before you departed from said city? If aye state how long he had kept house, and in what part of the city? If you answer that he kept house, then answer these questions .—Were you in the habit of visiting Mr Clark at his house? Did you ever see at Mr Clark's house any woman, especially the said Mrs DeGrange, acting, and being presented by Mr. Clark in the relation of his wife, as Mrs. Clark?

12th. Was the father of Mrs. DeGrange living at the time you knew her? Did she live with her father? With whom did she live? Who was she kept or supported by? Who maintained her? State fully Was it her father or brother, or other members of her own family? State fully.

13th Where was the house situated in which the complainant Myra was born? whose house was it? who owned it? who lived in it at the time of the birth of the complainant Myra?

14th. Some short time after the marriage of the complainant Myra with the late Mr. Whitney, and shortly after his arrival in Louisiana with the complainant Myra, in a judicial proceeding, he, the said Whitney, caused it to be stated on the records, that about the period of his marriage with the complainant Myra, he was informed that Mr Daniel Clark had expressed his intention of *adopting* Myra as his child ;—assuming this statement to be true, be pleased to state whether or not it was you who gave the said information, or words to that effect. If aye, be pleased to state whether or not such was the full extent of any and all information, which you ever gave to said Whitney or to Myra? Was or was not the information which you gave said Myra and her husband, to the effect that Daniel Clark had informed you, that believing that he was the father of the complainant Myra, by an illegitimate connection with her mother, that, therefore, he had or intended to make proper provision for her under such circumstances, or words to this effect? Please state fully

15th Did or did not Daniel Clark ever inform you that the complainant Myra was an illegitimate child by him, the said Clark, begotten, or words to that effect?

16th Do you or not believe that it would be a matter of self abasement and degradation in a man, lawfully to marry a woman, and after a child should be born unto him of said marriage, to take the child away from the mother,—to abandon the mother,—to allow the mother to intermarry with another man during his own lifetime, under her maiden name, without protest and resistance on his own part? From your knowledge of Daniel Clark, do you believe he was a man to have acted in the manner herein spoken of, or to have allowed of such indignities? Speak fully, if you please.

17th Will you be pleased to state whether or not Mr. Bellechasse ever wrote to you a letter previous to 1830, respecting property which Clark had put into his name for the use and benefit of Myra? And particularly, did he write to you one previous to the 23d of September, 1822, on this subject? If aye, please annex hereto the original of said letter or letters, if in your power, and if not in your power, state why it is not, and state the substance or contents of said letters as fully as you can? Did not one of those letters speak of the said property as intended by Clark for " little Myra, one of the fruits of our poor friend's indiscretions?" or words precisely to that effect? Did he, the said Bellechasse, in the same letter, refer you to Mr. Richard Relf, as one who knew all about the circumstances, and to whom he, the said Bellechasse, had offered to transfer the property in question? State fully.

18th. In the year 1817 a suit was instituted in the then first judicial district Court of the State of Louisiana, before the Honorable Joshua Lewis, Judge of said Court, against Beverly Chew and Richard Relf, as executors of Daniel Clark, by you, for, in the name of, and for the use of the present complainant, Myra, in which suit you presented a petition as " her curator *adlitem*, specially appointed," in which petition it is averred that the petitioner (Myra) " is the natural daughter of Daniel Clark, late of the city of New Orleans, deceased, acknowledged by him as such," and praying among other things, " that an adequate allowance for her education and support be paid out of the estate of her said father " Will you be now pleased to state whether or not, according to the information which you had previously from Daniel Clark, the averment in said petition that the present complainant, Myra, was the natural daughter of Daniel Clark, is, or is not true? The petition referred to in this interrogatory, was signed by " Davis & Pierce, attorneys for petitioner." State whether or not said gentleman, the partner of Mr. Pierce, was your son. It is also stated in the said petition, which was filed on the 24th day of June, 1817, that the said Myra was then thirteen years (13) of age. Is *that* statement true? When was she in fact born? What *was* the year? what the month? and what the day of the month? Was there ever any entry in your family Bible respecting her birth? If aye, state what the entry was. Was there entries in said Bible as to the births of your own children?

G. B. DUNCAN,
Att'y for Chew & Relf and Dussuau Delacroix.

MARTIN BLACHE,
Solicitor for N. Louque.

ROBERT PREAUX,
Att'y Municipality No. 1.

Cross interrogatories:

1. If you say that Madame Gardette is Myra's mother, where did she live immediately prior to the birth of Myra? Describe the street and house, if you can, and state who resided in the same house with her, and for what purpose, and at whose instance was a different house procured for her accouchement?

2. How many days after Myra's birth elapsed before she was removed from her mother and taken out to nurse? who was that nurse? where did she then reside? Why was Myra removed from her mother in that infant state, and put to nurse? at whose instance was it done? How many days had Myra been out to nurse before Mrs. Davis and yourself had her removed to your house to be better taken care of? Was Mrs. Harriet Harper then living in your family? Did she suckle Myra? If yea, for what length of time? Which of Mrs Harper's children was then at the breast? or had she then recently lost a child? If yea, state the name

3. Did Madame DeGrange visit Myra, while she was out to nurse? or did she ever visit her at your house from the time you received her up to the time of your leaving Louisiana, (the spring of 1812.) If yea, how often? If you say no, why did she not visit her? Did you forbid her your house? If yea, why? Did she never demand to see the child? was she never taken to see her? If yea, how often? Is it within your knowledge that Madame DeGrange ever saw or expressed a desire to see Myra, from the time she was taken from her up to the time of your leaving Louisiana in 1812?

4th At what time, particularly, did you remove with your family from Louisiana to Philadelphia? Did you take Myra with you? For what length of time did you reside in Philadelphia? Had not Mrs DeGrange, before you reached there, been married to Mr. Gardette, of that city, and was she not then living there? How long a time was your family and Mr. Gardette and wife living there in the same city? Did Madame Gardette ever visit Myra at your house while you lived in Philadelphia? If yea, how often? If nay, why not? Did you forbid her your house? and if yea, why? Did she visit her elsewhere in Philadelphia? Has not Mrs Gardette denied to you that Myra was her daughter? and has she not also denied that Myra was Mr. Clark's daughter?

5th. Have you not strong and cogent reasons to believe that Myra is not *in fact* the daughter of Daniel Clark? If yea, state them. Had you any other reason to believe that she was, except that Mr. Clark so believed? Was there the slightest resemblance between Mr. Clark and Myra, during her minority and his life?

6. During the time that you lived at New Orleans, did or did not Mr. Clark visit your family often ?   By what title did Myra designate him ?   Was it " Mr. Clark" or otherwise ?   Did she or not designate at all times Mrs Davis and yourself by parental titles ?   What occurred between yourself and Mr Clark in relation to Myra, about the period of your removal from Louisiana ?   Did he assent or dissent to your taking Myra with you ?   Did he or not refuse to acknowledge her as his daughter ?   Did he ever see her from the time you took her away, up to the period of his death ?   Did he make any inquiries of Mrs. Davis or yourself after your removal, in relation to Myra, her health, her education, accomplishments, disposition, talents, &c. &c., if by letters, please annex them, and state, if you please, whether the whole of Myra's expenses, apparel, education and all have not been defrayed out of your own pocket and without any reimbursement whatever, before or since Mr. Clark's death.

7th. How long after Mr. Clark's death was it before you returned to New Orleans, and how much of your time between the years of 1815 and 1820, were spent there ?   Was your family and Myra with you ?   Did you, as the guardian of Myra, attempt, in 1817, to procure alimony for her of Mr. Clark's executors, by virtue of her being his *natural* child ?

8th. Did you or did Madame Gardette or her sisters, Madames Despau or Caillavet, or any one else, to your knowledge, attempt to obtain anything for her from Mr. Clark's estate, by virtue of her being Mr Clark's *legitimate* daughter ?   Did Madame Gardette or either of her sisters inform you, that Mr Clark had been married to Mrs. Gardette, at any time, and that Myra was his *legitimate* child ?   And did they urge you on that ground to claim the estate for her ?   And had you known from any source, or even believed that Myra was his *legitimate* daughter, would you not on that ground have asserted and prosecuted her claims to her full share of Mr. Clark's estate.

9th Have you any knowledge of Mr. Clark's ever having been married ?   Did he ever tell you so ?   If yea, when and to whom was he married, and at what time ?   Did you not know from him or from current report, that early in 1808 he paid his addresses, with a view to marriage, and was actually engaged to Miss Louisa Caton, of Baltimore, the grand daughter of Charles Carroll, of Carrollton, and the present marchioness of Carmarthen, and state, from your knowledge of Mr Clark's honorable principles, his high standing and character, if you think it credible, that he would have made such proposals to that young lady, if he was at that time a married man ?

10th. Did not Mr Clark, in the spring or summer of 1811, and shortly prior to his going to Philadelphia convey to you in trust and confidence a certain portion of Bayou property and various other effects for Myra, in the event of his death, and which Bayou property you afterwards reconveyed, at his request, to Dussuau Delacroix for a like purpose? If yea, be pleased to state, whether or not Mr Clark did not tell you at the time that he had consulted Mr Etienne Mazureau and other eminent counsel, and that they had advised him that under the circumstances of Myra's birth, (being his child by a woman then married to another person,) he could not provide for her by will, or gift, or any mode, but by a secret confidential and simulated trust under the laws of Louisiana, and did you not learn from the same source that this had occasioned his confidential conveyance to Col Bellechasse? And if you knew at the time, the motive and the necessity of those confidential conveyances, could or did Mr. Clark or yourself deem Myra at that time a legitimate child of Mr. Clark?

11th. Be pleased to state as near as you can the age of Myra, (Mrs. Gaines) Was she or was she not born about the 21st of June, 1803 not far from the time when New Orleans was surrendered to the United States? Did not your son, Col Horatio Davis, of this city, leave your house for college in August 1805, and was not Myra at that time smartly grown, and running about with activity? And state whether Mr Clark was not during the greater part of the year 1802, and part of the year 1803, absent in Europe

12th. Please to state any thing else within your knowledge or memory to show that Mrs Gaines was not the legitimate daughter of the late Daniel Clark, as fully as if thereto specially interrogated

ISAAC T PRESTON,
Solicitor for defendants.

No cross interrogatories   All exceptions to admissibility of testimony reserved.

JANIN & TAYLOR,
Solicitors for Carrollton R R Co, and others.

Deposition of Samuel B Davis, a witness produced, sworn, and examined by virtue of the annexed commission, on the tenth day of July, in the year of our Lord one thousand eight hundred and forty-nine, at the residence of the said S B Davis near the City of Wilmington, and State of Delaware, before me, the said William Henry Rawle, the Commissioner named in the annexed commission, and also the commissioner for the State of Louisiana, to take testimony in the State of Pennsylvania, in a certain cause now depending in the Circuit Court of the United States for the fifth judicial circuit, holding sessions in and for the

Eastern District of Louisiana, wherein Edmund P. Gaines and Myra Clark, his wife, are plaintiffs, and Richard Relf and Beverly Chew, et al, are defendants

Samuel B Davis, of New Castle county, in the State of Delaware, gentleman, aged eighty-one years and upwards, being duly sworn, answers as follows to the interrogatories propounded to him in this cause.

1 To the first interrogatory he answers :

I am well acquainted with both the complainants and defendants in the above entitled suit

2 To the second interrogatory he answers

My age is eighty-one years and upwards I have been both a soldier and sailor, but have now no occupation, and I reside in New Castle county, in the State of Delaware.

3 To the third interrogatory he answers·

I began to remain permanently in New Orleans in the year 1803 I first went there (in a ship) in 1799. I sold my estates in Louisiana in the year 1822, or thereabouts, and after that time came to reside in Philadelphia.

To the fourth interrogatory he answers :

I did well know and enjoy the confidence and friendship of Daniel Clark, late of the city of New Orleans, now deceased. I knew him intimately. I last saw Mr. Clark in New Orleans in the year 1812. He was almost the last person I saw there before leaving there at that time. About a year before my leaving New Orleans he showed me a schedule of his property, in which it appeared that after the payment of all his debts, there remained to him a balance of ($500,000) five hundred thousand dollars I had no other means than this of knowing his business and pecuniary affairs, except the general reputation that he was a very rich man.

5 To the fifth interrogatory he answers

I know that Mr. Clark left a child living at the time of his death, which he acknowledged as his own That child is Mrs Edmund P Gaines Her mother was Mrs DeGrange It was born in New Orleans, on the last day of June, (to the best of my knowledge,) in the year 1804, about the time of taking possession of Louisiana She was raised and educated by myself Until she grew up, she never knew any other mother or father than Mrs Davis and myself The reason was that inasmuch as no provision had, to my knowledge, been made for her, we thought it an act of cruelty to treat her in all respects otherwise than as our child Before her birth, I had provided, at Mr Clark's request, a proper place for the accouchement of her mother, Mrs DeGrange It was the house of my brother-in-law, Baron Boisfontaine After her birth there, on going to see her, with Mrs Davis, when she was but a few weeks old we found the child not properly provided for, and as Mr Clark was then absent from New Orleans, (I think in Mexico,) we had the child taken to my own house. She (the child) afterwards remained with my family, with the concurrence of Mr Clark up to the time of her marriage with Mr Whitney, and afterwards

6. To the sixth interrogatory he answers,

Mr Clark always, at all times, spoke of said child, which was called Myra, as his daughter. He was very fond of her, as much so as a father could be. He has often conversed with me to the effect that all his property was to be for her, at least, such was my understanding. I cannot distinctly say that he ever said that he intended to leave her all his property, but the impression always left on my mind was, that she was to inherit his property. I never heard him speak of any one else than Myra being the recipient of his property, and I have constantly heard him so speak of her, in words that could leave no other impression. When I was about to leave New Orleans, in 1812, Mr Clark placed in my hands two thousand three hundred and sixty dollars, ($2360,) or thereabouts. He drew up an agreement whereby it was provided that the interest of that money was to be by me applied to her education and support, and the balance that might be required was to be remitted by him to me every year. He died in August of the next year, and, consequently, I never received anything. Before that time I had never received one cent towards Myra's education and support. That agreement was left with him, and I took no copy of it. After Mr. Clark's death, I was sued for the money so received by me by Messrs Chew and Relt, and I paid over three thousand dollars for satisfaction of the judgment obtained against me by them

7. To the seventh interrogatory he answers;

I recollect that Mr Clark made a voyage by sea from New Orleans to Philadelphia, about the year 1811: the occasion of said voyage was to see after the affairs of his partnership with Mr Daniel W Coxe, of Philadelphia. I think his departure was in the summer. He was not long away. I do not remember when he returned. I received a letter from him written by him on board ship at the mouth of the river, when about leaving, and I received a letter from him before he left Philadelphia. In these letters he mentioned that there was to my order, in the Bank, a trunk, containing notes of Mr Wade Hampton, and other property, to a large amount, which he requested me to take care of, (in case of any accident happening to him,) and manage for the benefit of his daughter Myra, till she was old enough to take care of herself. Upon search, I have been able to find copies of these letters

The originals of these letters have been given by me, some years ago, to Mr Whitney, or to a person named White, who came from New York, at the instance of Mr Whitney, to get from me all the letters written to me by Mr. Clark   I do not recollect, particularly, any thing further respecting this matter. The copy of the letter from Mr Clark to me, written from the Balize, I hereunto annex (marked "A," verified by my signature), and the copy of that addressed to me from Philadelphia I also annex (marked "B," and verified by my signature)   I do recollect that before Mr Clark left New Orleans, he gave me instructions respecting a large amount of his property in my hands   A large amount of real estate stood absolutely in my name as owner—that is to say, between two or three hundred lots—I can't recollect the exact quantity, it was the Bayou property The amount of his instructions to me was, that I was to use and place this property to the best advantage for his daughter Myra's interest.

The trunk I have spoken of I now recollect was placed to my order in the bank, before he left New Orleans, and at my request, I gave him a receipt for it, which on his return was given up to me again   The instructions respecting this trunk were the same as those respecting the real estate I have referred to.   I am unable to answer the interrogatory more fully or particularly.

8   To the eighth interrogatory he answers

I know of no other matter or thing material to the subject of this my examination

To the cross interrogatories he answers as follows

1   To the first cross interrogatory he answers.

I first became acquainted with Daniel Clark in the summer of 1799, at New Orleans

2   To the second cross interrogatory he answers.

In the years 1802 and 1803, I was in command of a ship in the Liverpool trade, and was in New Orleans at different times. In the year 1802, I was there for some time.   Mr Clark may have been absent during those years, but I always found him at New Orleans on my return there.

3   To the third cross interrogatory he answers.

I have a faint recollection of Mr Clark being in Europe at some time, but I could not say what time   I now recollect that the ship I commanded was sold in New Orleans, in 1802, and I think Mr Clark was absent then, but I will not be positive.   I do not think it was long after the ship was sold before I went into partnership with Mr Clark, which was on his return

4   To the fourth cross interrogatory he answers

I was present when Laussat, the French colonial prefect, arrived in Louisiana   Mr Clark was then in New Orleans. This was, I think, in the beginning of 1804   Having nothing to refer to, I cannot say how long Mr. Clark then had been in New

Orleans   I cannot answer this interrogatory more particularly as to Mr Clark s absence or return

I did know Mrs Zulime Gardette   that is to say, I have seen and spoken to her.   I know no more of her marriage with De-Grange or with Dr Gardette than by hearsay—by reputation I have understood she was married to Jerome DeGrange, but do not know when.   I have understood she was married to Dr Gardette, but do not know when   I presume that Gardette and his wife resided in Philadelphia   I know they lived in Philadelphia for some time   I cannot tell how many years   I think it was in Walnut street that they lived at one time   I think they did, for some time, live at the corner of 9th and Chestnut streets, but cannot say how long, not being in the habit of visiting them.

5 To the fifth cross interrogatory he answers:

Never being on terms of visiting acquaintance with Dr James Gardette and the said Zulime, I am entirely unable to answer this interrogatory particularly   I know nothing of the terms on which they lived, or the society in which they moved

6 To the sixth cross interrogatory he answers

I have no knowledge whatever of the matters inquired of in this interrogatory.

7. To the seventh cross interrogatory he answers ·

I have no knowledge whatever of the matters inquired of in this interrogatory

8. To the eighth cross interrogatory he answers .

I have no knowledge of the matters herein inquired of

9 To the ninth cross interrogatory he answers

I knew the said Mrs. DeGrange, very well by sight, but not personally, for a long time   I cannot tell how long   I never knew her to speak to until after the birth of Myra—that is, to the best of my knowledge.   The fact is, I never was acquainted with her till after the birth of Myra.

10 To the tenth cross interrogatory he answers ·

I never did hear Mr. Clark speak of said Zulime as his wife. It was never a subject of conversation between us   I never did hear Mr Clark at any time, speak of her as holding a very different relationship to him than that of his accepted and lawful wife.   I never conversed with Mr. Clark on this subject, and no one ever spoke to me of his position or connection with her. I was too intimate with him   I do not know what was the public repute, if any, at New Orleans, as to this matter.

11 To the eleventh cross interrogatory he answers

I know nothing of Mr Clark presenting the said Zulime to the community in New Orleans or elsewhere as his wife   Mr Clark always kept house in New Orleans from the time I knew him.   At one time he lived in Church street, but when I first went there he lived in the street that runs up from the Old Exchange to the rue Royale   I was at his house every day   I never saw any woman in his house, except the wife of his body servant—a black woman

12 To the twelfth cross interrogatory he answers·

I have no knowledge whatever of any of the matters inquired of in this interrogatory

13 To the thirteenth cross interrogatory he answers

The house in which Myra was born was near the Esplanade It was my brother-in-law's, as I have stated. I do not know who owned it. My brother-in-law then lived in it.

14. To the 14th cross interrogatory he answers

I could not have made the statement set forth in this interrogatory, inasmuch as Mr Clark never spoke to me of *adopting* her; he never used any such term He always spoke of her as his own child, and treated her as such on all occasions, showing the most devoted affection to her Mr Clark never made use of any expression to me which would convey the idea that she was an illegitimate child The information which I gave Mr Whitney and his wife was what I have stated in my previous answers I told them that "She was Daniel Clark's daughter, and he had always, and a thousand times, spoken of her as such" The information given by me to them was not to the effect set forth in this interrogatory.

15. To the fifteenth cross interrogatory he answers.

Mr Clark never did make any expression to lead to any belief that said Myra was an illegitimate child of his, or ever make use of any words to that effect.

16. To the sixteenth cross interrogatory he answers:

The first question embraced in this interrogatory being a question of abstract morality, I am unable to give a definite answer respecting it. Before I could form an opinion, I would take care to make myself master of all the facts. On the statement of facts here presented, I should think it would all depend on the character, conduct, &c., of the mother. From my knowledge of Mr. Clark's character, I am entirely at a loss to know how to answer the second question embraced in this interrogatory.

17 To the seventeenth cross interrogatory, he answers·

Mr Bellechasse wrote me two letters on the subject of Myra's property. I do not remember the dates. I have not these letters They have been given by me to Mr Whitney and Myra — The substance of these letters was, that he had been asked to divide the property in his hands, between Myra and some other person, but that he had refused to do so ; that his friend Clark had left the property to him in blind confidence for Myra, and that he would let it go to no one else I do not not know that he made use of the expression set forth in the interrogatory I have no knowledge whatever of it Had such been used, I should have remembered it The substance of the letters I cannot now remember more particularly I do not remember anything of the reference to Mr Richard Relf

18 To the eighteenth cross interrogatory, he answers:

If the petition referred to in this interrogatory contained such words as herein made use of to-wit that said petitioner (Myra) was "the natural daughter of Daniel Clark, late of the city of New Orleans, deceased, acknowledged by him as such," said words or word to that effect were never made use of with or by my knowledge or consent According to the information which I had previously from Mr Clark, such an averment would not be true The Mr Davis referred to as one of the firm of Davis and Pierce, was my son I first spoke to Davis and Pierce on this subject, by the advice of Mr Edward Livingston, and within a day or two after, the petition was withdrawn, in consequence of an assurance from either Mr Chew or Mr Relf, that they would do all that was right if they could have a little time ; that it was not worth while to have a suit about it I never knew or heard, before, that there had been any question or mention made of legitimacy or illegitimacy I have stated in a former answer, the age of Myra, her birth, &c.

I had no family bible, and never entered the birth of any of my own children. I will not be positive as to whether Myra was born in 1804 or 1805. It was on the last day of June, in one of these two years.

To the additional cross interrogatories, he answers as follows :

1. To the first cross interrogatory, he answers·

I do not know where Myra's mother lived immediately prior to Myra's birth. All I know is, that Mr Clark desired me to procure for her a house for her accouchement, which I did, as before stated.

2. To the second cross interrogatory, he answers

I do not know how many days elapsed before Myra was taken out to nurse It might have been two or three weeks — The nurse was the wife of a coachmaker named Gordon — Myra did not stay with her more than ten or twelve days She (Mrs Gordon) had a child, also, of her own, and Myra was neglected I then had her taken to my house. Mrs Harriet Harper was then living in my family, and she suckled Myra — She (Myra) was suckled by her (Mrs Harper) until such time as we could get another nurse I do not remember which of Mrs Harper's children was then at the breast It was the first child after she came to New Orleans She had not recently lost a child.

3. To the third cross interrogatory, he answers:

I do not know whether Mrs. DeGrange went to see Myra

while she was out to nurse, but she often came to see her at my house I cannot say how often, it was frequently I never forbid my house to Mrs DeGrange She often expressed a desire to see Myra, and often did come to see her while she (Mrs De-Grange) was in New Orleans

4 To the fourth cross interrogatory he answers

I have before stated the time of my removal to Philadelphia It was in 1812 My family went on before I did, and Myra went with them My family resided there for many years until I came down here where I now am. I cannot say how long I think we moved here somewhere about 1822 We have moved backwards and forwards several times

I think Mrs. DeGrange was living with Dr Gardette, in Philadelphia, when we reached there I do not know when they (the Gardettes) left Philadelphia Mrs Gardette was at my house once, while we were living in Philadelphia I never forbid my house to Mrs Gardette Mrs Gardette did not visit Myra elsewhere, to my knowledge Mrs Gardette once met me in the street with Myra, and she stopped to speak to me — She did not speak to Myra, or take any such notice of her, that the latter might remark, but she looked very hard at her Mrs Gardette never denied to me that Myra was her daughter, or that she was Mr. Clark's daughter On the contrary, she has always acknowledged her to be her own child, and to be Mr. Clark's child. I have seen her, when Myra was a little creature, manifest every feeling which a mother could do towards a child.

5 To the fifth cross interrogatory, he answers .

I have no reason to believe that Myra is not in fact the daughter of Mr Clark I have no other reason to believe that she is the daughter of Mr Clark, further than that Mr Clark has over and over told me so, and that her mother, Mrs DeGrange, has told me so I thought there was a very strong resemblance to Mr Clark Myra resembled Mr Clark more in figure than in face, and more in character than in figure. In figure and character, she strongly resembled him

6 To the sixth cross interrogatory he answers

Mr Clark visited my family nearly every day Myra never knew that Mr Clark was her father at that time, and she always called him "Mr Clark ' She, at all times, designated Mrs. Davis and myself by paternal titles. Nothing but what has been already stated occurred between Mr. Clark and myself, at the period of my removal from Louisiana He assented to my taking Myra with me and my family He requested me not to put her to a public boarding-school. He desired that she should remain under Mrs. Davis' eye. He never did refuse to acknowledge her as his daughter. He was always proud of her. Mr Clark never saw her from the time she went from New Orleans, up to the time of his death, as he died shortly after. After our removal from New Orleans, I never got a letter from Mr Clark, in relation to any subject. He may have written, but I was then in the army, and not stationary in any one place for any length of time. All the expenses of Myra's apparel, education and all, have been defrayed out of my own pocket, just as if she had been my own child. I never doubted but that some arrangement had been made by Mr Clark in relation to her and I never made any difference as to the manner in which she was educated.

7. To the seventh cross interrogatory he answers

I returned to New Orleans alone, just towards the close of the war. My family came out to me in 1816, I think shortly after the war—that is, Mrs Davis, Myra remained at Philadelphia at that time. I spent a considerable time on my estate then, from the time my family (except Myra) came on till the time I sold my estates,—or rather before that time, I remained there. I have already answered the remaining part of this interrogatory, respecting the suit against Mr Clark's executor

8. To the eighth cross interrogatory he answers

Further than what has been stated, I never made any attempt to obtain for Myra any part of Mr Clark's estate. I have no knowledge of any efforts made by Mrs Gardette or her sisters, Mesdames Despau or Caillavet, to obtain anything from Mr Clark's estate, by any means whatever. I never had any conversation with any of these three ladies in connection with Myra's legitimacy. They never urged me to claim the estate for her. Could I have had the satisfactory means of proving that Myra was Mr Clark's legitimate child, and could I have had reason to believe, that anything would have been gained from out of the estate, I certainly should have taken legal advice, and should have followed it. It was reported that Mr Clark's estate was insolvent, and before I had any means of ascertaining the precise situation of the estate, Myra was married

9. To the ninth cross interrogatory he answers

I have no particular knowledge of Mr Clark's ever having been married. He never told me so. It was never a subject of conversation between us. I have heard from public report, (and from that only) that Mr Clark was paying attention to Miss Caton, of Baltimore. I never heard that he was engaged to be married to her. I am entirely unable to answer the latter part of this interrogatory. I have no means of answering it. I do not think Mr Clark would have been likely to marry two wives

10 To the tenth cross interrogatory he answers.

I have already mentioned the circumstances connected with the transfer of the Bayou property and the other property to me, in trust for Myra. This property I afterwards conveyed to Dussuau Delacroix, for a like purpose. Mr Clark never did tell me that he had consulted Mr Mazureau or any other, and never told me of any advice that had been given him on this subject. The conveyance so made by me to Mr Delacroix was during a period of some coolness between Mr Clark and myself. The property stood in my name in fee simple. I was about also leaving the country. I never knew the reasons of his conveyance to Col Bellechasse. He never consulted me about it, and I never knew. I cannot answer this interrogatory more particularly

11 To the eleventh cross interrogatory, he answers

I have already stated the time of Mrs Gaines' birth. It was not, I know, before 1804, because Mrs Harper was not in New Orleans before that time, and could not, therefore, have suckled her. I do not remember when my son Col. Horatio Davis, left my home for college. It was the first year that Mr Clark went to Congress, as a representative of the territory, he took my son on with him. I think it was in 1805. It was the first year in which a representation was sent. At that time Myra was about a year old,—in the nurse's arms,—not able to sit alone,—a very sickly child. I have already stated all I know about Mr Clark's absence in Europe, in the years 1802 and 1803

12 To the twelfth cross interrogatory he answers

I know nothing further on the subject matter of this interrogatory. I have already stated all I know on this subject fully and particularly. The length of time which has occurred, must account for any inaccuracies, in any part of this, my testimony, of which, however, I am not aware, and I have had no notes wherewith to refresh my memory

                              SAM B DAVIS

Sworn and subscribed before me, on the day and year aforesaid

              WILLIAM HENRY RAWLE, Commissioner

                              A

Dear Sir—We are preparing to put to sea, and I hope I shall have a pleasant passage. My stay will be but short in Philadelphia, unless a forced one. In case of any misfortune be pleased to deliver the enclosed to Gen. Hampton. I count on him as a man of honor to pay the amount of notes mentioned in my letter to him, which in that case you will dispose of as I have directed. It will naturally strike you that the letter to the General is to be delivered only in case of misfortune to me. Remember me kindly to Mrs Davis and all your family

Yours,

(Signed) DANIEL CLARK.

P S Of the enclosed letter you will say   unless in case of accident, when you may communicate it to Chew and Relf

S. B. Davis

This is the paper marked 'A,' referred to in the deposition of the witness.   SAM B DAVIS

WILLIAM HENRY RAWLE, Commissioner.

B

PHILADELPHIA, 12th July, 1811

MY DEAR SIR—In case of any accident or misfortune to me, be pleased to open the letter addressed to me which accompanies this, and act with respect to the enclosures as I directed you with respect to the other affairs committed to your charge before leaving New Orleans. To account in a satisfactory manner to the person committed to your honor, will I flatter myself be done by you, when she is able to manage her own affairs, until when, I commit her under God to your protection. I expect to sail to-morrow for New Orleans, in the ship Ohio and do not wish to risk these papers at sea

Yours,

(Signed) DANIEL CLARK

S. B. Davis, Esq

This is the paper marked B," referred to in the deposition of the witness   SAM B DAVIS

WILLIAM HENRY RAWLE, Commissioner

I, William Henry Rawle, the commissioner named in the annexed commission, and also the commissioner for the State of Louisiana, do hereby certify that the deponent Samuel B Davis, was, by me, duly sworn to declare the truth on the questions put to him in this cause that the interrogatories and cross interrogatories were produced to him and his answers thereto taken in writing by me and subscribed by him in my presence on the day and at the place in that behalf first aforesaid

In testimony whereof, I have hereunto set my hand and affixed my seal of office, this eleventh day of July, Anno Domini one thousand eight hundred and forty-nine

[L S]   WILLIAM HENRY RAWLE.

Commissioner.

Filed 20th June, 1847, and opened according to stipulation and order thereon   J W GURLEY, D'y Cl'k

UNITED STATES CIRCUIT COURT)
FIFTH CIRCUIT AND DISTRICT OF LOUISIANA }
          Tenth day of April, 1849   )

The Court met pursuant to adjournment
Present the Honorable Theo H McCaleb, district Judge
Absent the Honorable John McKinley, presiding Judge
Ed P Gaines and wife vs. Relf, Chew et als   No 122
Ed P Gaines and wife vs Ant J Cavelier et al. " 1728
'   '   "   '   "   vs Delacroix et als   " 1731
"   "   "   "   '   vs Norbert Louque et al " 1785
"   "   "   "   "   vs John S Minor et als " 1729
"   "   "   "   "   vs Rob't R Barrow et als ' 1784
"   "   "   "   "   vs Madison Lyons et als. " 1408

Interrogatories and cross interrogatories having been filed in the above entitled causes, to be administered to Philander Chase, of Peoria county, of the State of Illinois, a witness to be sworn and examined on the part of the complainants It is ordered, on motion of P. C Wright, solicitor for complainants, that a commission be issued to Onslow Peters, Esq, att'y and counsellor at law of Peoria, Peoria county, in said State of Illinois, to take the testimony of said witness, according to the rules and practice of this Court to be used on the hearing of the said causes.

CLERK'S OFFICE NEW ORLEANS, LA   )
CIRCUIT COURT OF THE UNITED STATES, DISTRICT OF LOUISIANA }

I hereby certify the foregoing to be a true copy from the original of record in this office

Witness, my hand and seal of said Court at the city of New Orleans, this eleventh day of April, 1849

          [LS]   ED RANDOLPH, Clerk
                    By WM ANDRY, D'y Clerk

CIRCUIT COURT OF THE UNITED STATES,)
FOR THE 5TH JUDICIAL CIRCUIT, HOLDING SESSIONS IN }
    AND FOR THE EASTERN DISTRICT OF LOUISIANA   )

To Onslow Peters, attorney and counsellor at law at Peoria, Peoria county, State of Illinois

Know ye that reposing special trust and confidence in your integrity and ability, we hereby authorize and require you, that you call and cause to come before you Philander Chase, and him duly examine on oath, touching and concerning certain matters and things in a case now depending in the said Court, wherein Ed P Gaines and wife are plaintiffs and R Relf, B Chew et als are defendants, and the same examinations, so taken and reduced to writing, you certify under your hand and seal, and send enclosed to this Court without delay, to be read in evidence on the trial of said cause, and send also this writ

Witness the Honorable Roger B. Taney, Chief Justice of the Supreme Court of the United States, at the city of New Orleans, this thirty-first day of March, Anno Domini, 1849, and the 73d year of the Independence of the United States of America

[L S] ED. RANDOLPH, Clerk

By Wm Andrs, Dy Clerk

U. S. CIRCUIT COURT, 5th CIRCUIT,
Within and for the District of Louisiana

IN CHANCERY,

Edmund P. Gaines and Myra Clark his Wife
vs
Richard Pitt Beverly Chew, James Hopkins and others
} No 122

Same Complainants,
vs
Antoine J. Cavelier and others
} No 1728

Same Complainants
vs.
Francois Dusuau Delacroix and others
} No 1731

Same Complainants vs Norbert Louqul and others.

Same Complainants vs Charles Matthews and others.

Same Complainants vs John S. Minor and others

Same Complainants vs Robert R. Barrow and others

Same Complainants vs Madison Lyons and others

Interrogatories to be propounded to Right Reverend Philander Chase, Presiding Bishop of the Protestant Episcopal Church in the United States, residing in the County of Peoria, in the State of Illinois, a witness to be produced, sworn, and examined on the part of the complainants in the above entitled suits

Interrogatory 1st. Where do you reside, and what is your age and occupation?

Interrogatory 2d. Do you know the parties complainants in the foregoing entitled suits, and either and which of the defendants? if yea, how long have you known them?

Interrogatory 3d. If you say that you know the complainant, Myra Clark Gaines, state when you first knew her? Where? What was her age? With whom did she reside, and under whose care and protection was she at that time? and where did you reside at that time?

Interrogatory 4th Were you acquainted with Daniel Clark, Esquire, late of the city of New Orleans now deceased? If yea, at what period did you become acquainted with him, and was your intercourse with him intimate and friendly, or otherwise? How long did it continue? What was his position and character in the community where he resided?

Interrogatory 5th Who was the reputed father of the complainant Myra? If you know state what you saw of the conduct of such reputed father towards the said Myra? Did you, at the time to which the foregoing interrogatories refer, ever hear the paternity or the legitimacy of the said Myra called in question, or doubted by any one? State particularly, what you heard at the time referred to, respecting the said Myra and her father, and what you saw of the intercourse between the said Myra and her said father and his friends

Interrogatory 6th Were you acquainted with a Mr Samuel B Davis at the period above referred to? If yea, where did he reside? Who were the members of his family? Were you on intimate and friendly terms with them? State what you saw and may have known respecting the relations and intercourse of the said Daniel Clark with the said Samuel B Davis and his family

Interrogatory 7th Do you know, or can you set forth any other matter or thing, which may be a benefit or advantage to the parties at issue in the foregoing causes, or either of them, or that may be material to the subject of this your examination, or the matters in question in these causes? if yea, set forth the same fully and at large in your answer

P C WRIGHT
Complainants' solicitor.

The defendants, Beverly Chew, Richard Relf, and Francois Dusnau Delacroix, each reserving all legal objection in the premises, and to the foregoing interrogatories, by protestation, &c, propound the following cross interrogatories, to be answered by the said witness

1st If you answer the third interrogatory propounded by complainants in the affirmative, then please answer the following questions Do you know any of the facts so stated by you from your personal knowledge, or have you stated them from hearsay, information or belief? If you have stated any fact from your own personal knowledge, please now state which fact you have so stated How, and under what circumstances did you first become acquainted with the complainant, Myra? In whose family was said Myra then residing? By what name was she then called in addition to Myra?

2d If you answer the fourth interrogatory of complainants in the affirmative then answer the following Did you ever know from general reputation in the city of New Orleans, that Daniel Clark was a married man? Was the general reputation which said Daniel Clark had in New Orleans, at any time previous to his death, that he was a married man? Did Daniel Clark keep house in the city of New Orleans during the time of your acquaintance with him? If aye, where was his house situated, and had he a wife living with him? Do you believe, from the knowledge which you had of Daniel Clark, and from the position and character which he had in the community, where he resided, that he was an imposter? Do you believe, from such knowledge as you had of Daniel Clark, his character and standing in the community, that he would have imposed a woman on society as his lawful wife who was not in truth so, or refuse to own, acknowledge and present to society a lady living in the same place with himself who was in truth and fact his lawful? Do you believe that if Daniel Clark had had a wife, that he would have failed to give her all of the protection, position, and comfort due to that holy relationship, which it might be in his power to give? From your knowledge of the character and standing of Daniel Clark during his lifetime, do you believe that if he had been a married man, he would have silently allowed another man to marry her, while she was his wife?

3d. If you answer the fifth interrogatory of complainants affirmatively, then answer the following Who was the reputed mother of the complainant, Myra? Where did she live at the time you were acquainted with Myra, in the days of said Myra's childhood? Had the mother ever the charge of Myra? If aye, for how long a time, when, and where? When was Myra removed from New Orleans? By whom and to what place was she so removed? How old was Myra when she was removed from New Orleans? Do you know anything of Daniel Clark's family? Were they, his mother and sisters, abundantly able to take charge of the education and sustenance of Daniel Clark's child, if he had any, without imposing her upon a family with whom he had no family ties? Were you intimate in the family of Col. Samuel B. Davis, who resided in New Orleans at the time spoken of? Have you not often heard the paternity of the complainant, Myra, attributed to another gentleman than Clark? If aye, name him What was the character and standing of the mother of the complainant, Myra, at the time of which you have spoken of Daniel Clark's character and standing? Was she the open and well known wife of Daniel Clark? Did he ever receive her into his own house and home as his wife?

4th. Have you ever received any letters or communications from either of the complainants in reference to this suit? If aye, annex them to this interrogatory?

5th. As you have been asked about the character and stand-ing of Daniel Clark in the community of New Orleans, so the said respondents will be pleased to have you state, fully and par-ticularly every thing you know of their standing in the commu-nity at that and at any other time. Please state

Was not one or more of them a member of your vestry, in the church over which you presided in New Orleans, as early as the year 1805, and did he not so continue during the entire period of your residence in New Orleans? Do you not know that the same gentleman has been a member of said vestry, by annual election, made by the pew-holders, from that period to the present day, a term of upwards of forty years? Was not another a member of the convention that formed the first State constitution of Louisiana? Did you ever hear a word of re-proach to his character except by the complainants? Has not the third held various public offices of confidence and trust in the city of New Orleans, both under the federal and State govern-ments? And have you ever heard his character for integrity and honor called in question except by the complainants, or by per-sons deriving their impressions from statements and publications made by complainants, or with them connected

6th Do you know where Daniel Clark was during the latter part of the year 1802, and commencement of 1803? Can you remember these dates particularly and is there any circum-stance by which you can fix the date? State particularly

G B DUNCAN, for Richard Relf, Beverly Chew, and Fran-cois Dusuau Delacroix

ISAAC T PRESTON, for John S. Minor and others, defend-ants represented by him

THOMAS GIBBES MORGAN, for Cavelier

THO H. LEWIS, for Eugene Richard, and other represen-ted by him,

J. H HOLLAND, for Relleaux, Dusnan Picou, Drisuard & Eller

ROBERT PREAUX, for P Soule, Att'y Municipality No .1

T. LAVERGNE, for James Hopkins

W A LABABRE, for the Minors Dauphin

MARTIN BLANC, for Norbert Louque

JANIN & TAYLOR, for Carrollton Railroad Company, and for the defendants represented by him in No 1728.

UNITED STATES OF AMERICA, }
  DISTRICT OF ILLINOIS, } SS

I do hereby certify, that in pursuance of the authority and requirements of the annexed commission, I did on the third day of May, in the year of our Lord eighteen hundred and forty-nine, call and cause to come before me, at my office in the city of Peoria, State of Illinois, the Right Reverend Philander Chase, to be examined, and give evidence touching and concerning the matters and things in the suits entitled in the annexed commission and interrogatories, and the said witness being unable to continue his examination on that day, the further examination of said witness was adjourned to Jubilee College, in said county of Peoria, at which place, on the ninth day of June, A D 1849, the examination of said witness was completed, as follows, to wit.

Interrogatory 1st Where do you reside, and what is your age and occupation?

Answer I reside at Jubilee College, Peoria county, State of Illinois, my age is seventy-three on December 14th, 1848 I am *Præcess in officio* of the said (incorporated) institution, and presiding Bishop of the Protestant Episcopal Church in the United States of America

Interrogatory 2d Do you know the parties complainants in the foregoing entitled suits and either and which of the defendants? If yea, how long have you known them?

Answer I am unacquainted with all of the persons named, except Messrs Relf and Chew and Myra Clark, now, as I hear, the wife of General Edmund P Gaines, her I knew when a child, as the following narrative in answer to the next interrogatory will show

Interrogatory 3d If you say that you know the complainant Myra Clark Gaines, state when you first knew her; where? what was her age? with whom did she reside? and under whose care and protection was she at that time? and where did you reside at that time?

Answer In the autumn of the year eighteen hundred and five, I went, unaccompanied by my family, from New York to New Orleans, and obtained, from the Legislature of Louisiana, the charter of Christ Church, in that city In the summer of eighteen hundred and six, I returned to New York, and in the fall of that year, my wife accompanied me to Louisiana we sailed in one vessel, and our household furniture, etc, was left in New York to come by another The latter vessel was shipwrecked on Cuba This made it necessary that we should accept the kind invitation of my friend, Andrew Burl, in New

58

Orleans, and we remained for some time in his house, on the levee, in the faubourg St Mary.

While here, the project of moving into the country was agreed on . and accordingly, I hired of Mr. Joseph McNeil, one of the two houses which he had lately built "down the coast," about three miles from the city, on a small piece of land which he had divided into two equal parts, and on which he had erected two small dwelling houses, one on each part or lot, both set back from the levee road about two hundred feet. There was an entrance gate to each, and a fence between The house I lived in was built on pillars, raising the same and its gallery about eight feet above the ground; there was a garden between me and the levee road

Nearly opposite me, and on the other side of the dividing fence, about thirty or forty feet off. was the other house spoken of above, and in this house lived Myra Clark, under the nursing care of *Mrs* Samuel B Davis *Mr* Samuel B Davis, her husband, and his family were not then, apparently, in affluent circumstances, being, as was generally believed, dependent on Daniel Clark for favors and friends, into their care the said Daniel Clark committed his daughter, Myra Clark, then, as I should judge, (from her being brought out almost every day to meet her father's caresses, as he approached the house,) to be a year and a half or two years old, at that time This I saw during the period of six months or more

Interrogatory 4th. Were you acquainted with Daniel Clark, Esquire, late of the city of New Orleans, now deceased? If yea, at what period did you become acquainted with him ? and was your acquaintance with him intimate and friendly, or otherwise? how long did it continue ? what was his position and character in the community where he resided?

Answer I was acquainted with Daniel Clark. Esquire, but not intimately He spoke to me. and I to him, as two gentlemen would address each other, having no particular acquaintance. His character was good, so far as I ever knew One failing, however, was admitted on all hands, viz . that a weakness (amiable it was termed by some) in confiding too much in those who would flatter him, but who, as it was thought, served him with sinister views

His position was that of a wealthy man, as much so as any man in Louisiana This acquaintance with him was during the period of my residence in Louisiana, which was, the last time, from 1806 to 1811

Interrogatory 5th Who was the reputed father of the complainant Myra ? If you know, state what you saw of the conduct of such reputed father towards the said Myra ? Did you, at the time to which the foregoing interrogatories refer. ever hear the paternity or the legitimacy of the said Myra called in question, or doubted by any one? State particularly what you heard, at the time referred to, respecting the said Myra and her father, and what you saw of the intercourse between the said Myra and her said father and his friends

Answer—Daniel Clark was the reputed father of his child, Myra Clark her, he openly cherished as such he embraced her in the presence of his friends as his child in my sight Other paternity, to my knowledge or belief, was never spoken of or thought of in New Orleans She was spoken of as his heiress

Interrogatory 6th. Were you acquainted with a Mr Samuel B Davis at the period above referred to? If yea, where did he reside? who were the members of his family? were you on intimate and friendly terms with them? State what you saw or may have known respecting the relations and intercourse of the said Daniel Clark with the said Samuel B Davis and his family

Answer—I was *somewhat*, but not *intimately* acquainted with Mr Samuel B. Davis His attempts at familiarity with me were unpleasant, by reason of his bad character Andrew Burk, my senior warden, had told me while I lived in his family, that Mr Samuel B Davis, having been a privateer under French colors, had taken his (Mr Burk's) vessel at sea · and that he was sorry to see him made harbor master of the port of New Orleans After Mr Samuel B. Davis had moved into the other house of Mr Joseph McNeil, I found his servant cutting up, on the opposite side of the levee, and disposing of, a Kentucky flat boat, belonging to me, which I had bought a few days before, for ten dollars, in New Orleans, and caused to be floated down the river for domestic purposes I asked the servant by whose orders he was doing so. He answered, "by my master's orders," and added such language, as to give me to understand that a quarrel was the object aimed at In this I was determined to disappoint him, and suffering the pecuniary loss, gave up the matter.—Remembering what good Mr. Burk had told me, I shrunk from the thought of contending with Mr Samuel B Davis · especially as he had gained the patronage of the rich Daniel Clark

While said Davis resided in the house of Mr McNeil, as before stated, Daniel Clark was intimate there, as I very frequently saw Mr and Mrs Davis had two nieces; one was Mrs Harper, but the name of the other I do not recollect, the latter lived with her aunt in the McNeil house From neither of these, nor from any one else, did I ever hear a word contradicting the general opinion that Myra was the daughter of said Daniel Clark, and his intended heiress.

Interrogatory 7th Do you know, or can you set forth any other matter or thing which may be a benefit or advantage to the parties at issue in the foregoing causes, or either of them, or that may be material to the subject of this your examination, or the matters in question in these causes? if yea, set forth the same fully and at large in your answer

Answer.—Mr Samuel B Davis was reputed in New Orleans a poor man before the death of Daniel Clark   Since that event, he has been reputed to be a rich man   as the following narrative will show   In the summer, I think of 1809 I moved up into the city of New Orleans   In the year 1811, myself and family left New Orleans for the northern States —As Rector of Christ Church Hartford in the State of Connecticut, I resided there (at Hartford) about six years   In the year 1817 I went to Ohio and organized a diocese, to which I was duly appointed Bishop; and in Philadelphia, on the 11th of February 1819, was consecrated by the venerable Bishop White and his assistants

Pending the examination of testimonials for this office, I was told that a Col Samuel B Davis, a rich man in Philadelphia, had made oath, as evidence against me, to the fact that I had written him a letter, threatening his life   He was called on to produce the said letter   this he did not do, and in my presence, said he could not do   I had never, to my remembrance, written him a note or letter of any sort   I thought proper to ask legal advice, and for that purpose went to the city of New York, and laid the matter before the Hon Cadwallader D Colden, Mayor of that city   This learned gentleman wrote an opinion concerning the premises, and sent the same to Bishop White and his counsel, the standing committee of the diocese   The said opinion stated that he knew of no judge, either in England or America, who had admitted such evidence without producing the letter itself; the only exception was, the infamous Jeffries. This settled the matter

Some time after, enquiring of my brother, Dudley Chase, who had been senator in Congress of the U. States, in the (then) late war with England, how it came to pass that he voted for the appointment of Mr Samuel B Davis, as Colonel of the Regiment raised, or to be raised for the defence of the Chesapeake Bay, he answered, that the parties at that period ran high, and he went with his friends, though he remembered that there was a hard struggle , Mr. Fromantine, the senator from Louisiana, voting against him, as a man of bad character

I learned while in Philadelphia, that said Davis (now Col Davis) had a daughter living with him by the name of Myra Davis   This deception of the public being consistent with his character, created no surprise in my mind, should she prove, at last, to be the real Myra Clark, whom I had seen her father own and caress in the year of our Lord 1807-8, when receiving her from the arms of Mrs Davis, her nurse, as related above

This opinion of said Davis having deceived the public, was confirmed some time after in my mind, by calling on Rev Dr Edmund Barry, in New Jersey city He told me that a Mr Whitney had just left his dwelling, and had gone, or was going to New Orleans, to claim the fortune of his wife Myra, left her by her father, the late Daniel Clark that when he married her he thought her, as then reputed, the daughter of Col Samuel B Davis but now having been repudiated as such, and proved to be the daughter of Daniel Clark he was going to seek her inheritance According to what I had already seen and known, I gave full credence to the statement, and told Dr Barry so

The cross interrogatories annexed to said commission on behalf of Beverly Chew, Richard Relf and Francois Dussuau Delacroix, were then severally propounded to said witness, who thereto answered as follows, to wit

Cross interrogatories

1st If you answer the third interrogatory propounded by complainant in the affirmative, then please answer the following questions Do you know any of the facts so stated by you from your personal knowledge, or have you stated them from hearsay, information or belief ? If you have stated any fact from your own personal knowledge, please now state which fact you have so stated How and under what circumstances did you first become acquainted with the complainant, Myra ? In whose family was said Myra then residing ? By what name was she then called in addition to Myra ?

Answer What I have stated in answer to such of the direct interrogatories as within my own knowledge or observation, I have, to the best of my recollection, correctly stated; what purports to be from information or belief, I apprehend, sufficiently appears from the answers above given

My personal knowledge of Myra Clark was when she was from one to two years old, as I should judge, she was then frequently brought out of the house of Mr and Mrs Samuel B Davis, to enjoy the caresses of her father, Daniel Clark, then (in 1807 or 8) a constant visitor there She was an inmate of the house, and under Mrs Davis' care, and the same house being so near that in which I resided, I would see and hear what I supposed was never intended to be private, viz . the evidences of a father's affections for a loved child. This little girl had no other name, to my knowledge, **but that of Myra Clark**

Cross interrogatory

2. If you answer the fourth interrogatory of complainant's in the affirmative, then answer the **following** Did you ever know,

from general reputation in the city of New Orleans, that Daniel Clark was a married man? Was the general reputation which said Daniel Clark had in New Orleans, at any time previous to his death, that he was a married man? Did Daniel Clark keep house in the city of New Orleans, during the time of your acquaintance with him? If aye, where was his house situated, and had he a wife living with him? Do you believe, from the knowledge which you had of Daniel Clark, and from the position and character which he had in the community where he resided, that he was an impostor? Do believe from such knowledge as you had of Daniel Clark, his character and standing in the community, that he would have imposed a woman on society as his lawful wife, who was not in truth so, or refuse to own, acknowledge and present to society a lady, living in the same place with himself who was in truth and fact his lawful   Do you believe, that if Daniel Clark had had a wife, that he would have failed to give her all the protection, position and comfort due to that holy relationship which it might be in his power to give? From your knowledge of the character and standing of Daniel Clark, during his lifetime, do you believe that if he had been a married man, he would have silently allowed another man to marry her, while she was his wife?

Answer. I never knew, nor do I now recollect of ever having enquired, whether Daniel Clark was married or not, nor do I know of any general reputation on that subject I never was at his house, nor do I recollect any thing of his residence. I knew nothing of his wife, whether he had one or not, or whether she was living or not. what Daniel Clark would have done in certain cases I know not—his character was good so far as I knew, except in the case of weakness in yielding to the influence of flatterers, &c., as before stated in one of my former answers. I never thought that Daniel Clark was an impostor, nor do I believe he deserved that appellation. All parts of this interrogatory, referring to fictitious cases, and a supposititious state of facts, are beyond my power to answer. And I can only say, that from my knowledge of Daniel Clark, I had no reason to suppose or believe he would be guilty of any grossly improper conduct

Cross interrogatory

3d. If you answer the fifth of complainant's interrogatories affirmatively, then answer the following Who was the reputed mother of the complainant, Myra? Where did she live at the time you were acquainted with Myra, in the days of said Myra's childhood? Had the mother ever the charge of Myra? If aye, for how long a time, when and where' When was Myra removed from New Orleans? by whom and to what place was she so removed? How old was Myra when she was removed from New Orleans? Do you know anything of Daniel Clark's family? Were they, his mother and sisters, abundantly able to take charge of the education and sustenance of Daniel Clark's child, if he had any, without imposing her upon a family with whom he had no friendly tie? Were you intimate in the family of Col Samuel B Davis, who resided in New Orleans at the time spoken of? Have you not often heard the paternity of the complainant, Myra, attributed another gentleman than Clark? If aye, name him What was the character and standing of the mother of the complainant, Myra, at the time of which you have spoken of Daniel Clark's character and standing? Was she the open and well known wife of Daniel Clark? Did he ever receive her into his own house and home as his wife?

Answer I know nothing of the mother of Myra Clark. If she were alive, I knew nothing of her, or her residence, or whether she had any charge of her daughter, Myra Clark. I knew not when she was removed from New Orleans; I knew not by whom removed, nor to what place, except as herein before already stated, nor how old she was when removed. I knew nothing of Daniel Clark's family, except Myra, as herein before, in this deposition, fully stated. I was not intimate with the family of Samuel B. Davis, as I have already fully stated. I had never heard the paternity of Myra Clark attributed to any other person than Daniel Clark, until it was insinuated by this interrogatory, except so far as that may have been implied by the reports of said Davis, as before herein stated by me.

4th Interrogatory by said respondents

Have you ever received any letters or communications from either of the complainants in reference to this suit? if aye, annex them to this interrogatory

Answer. I never received any letter from either of the complainants, but I did receive a letter from one, whom I supposed to be the counsel for the complainants, a copy of which, with a copy of my answer thereto, is hereto annexed, marked A & B, and made part of this, my deposition; these copies are in my own handwriting, and I believe them to be true copies; and this letter is the only letter ever received by me, from any person, relative to the subject of these suits, or the parties thereto.

5th Cross interrogatory.

As you have been asked about the character and standing of Daniel Clark in the community of New Orleans, so said respondents will be pleased to have you state fully and particularly everything you know of their standing in the community at that, and any other time? Please state, was not one or more of them a member of your vestry, in the church 'over which you presided in New Orleans, as early as the year 1805; and did he not so continue during the entire period of your residence in New Orleans? Do you not know that the same gentleman has been a member of said vestry, by annual election made by the pewholders, from that period to the present day, a term of upwards of forty years? Was not another a member of the convention that formed the first constitution of Louisiana? Did you ever hear a word of reproach to his character, except by the complainants? Has not the third held various public offices of confidence and trust in the city of New Orleans, both under the Federal and State Governments? and have you ever heard his character for integrity and honor called in question except by the complainants, or by persons deriving their impressions from statements and publications made by complainants, or with them connected?

Answer Messrs. Chew and Relf were gentlemen of good *reputation and standing* when I lived in *New Orleans*, and during the whole time either one or both of them were members of Christ Church, of which I was rector I never heard a word of reproach against either of them whilst I was in New Orleans. Of all the other defendants in said suits, I have no knowledge or recollection, nor have I, hence, any personal knowledge of the residue of the subjects embraced in the remainder of said fifth interrogatory

6th. Cross interrogatory

Do you know where Daniel Clark was during the latter part of the year 1802 and commencement of 1803? Can you remember these dates particularly, and is there any circumstance by which you can fix the date? State particularly.

Answer I have already as fully answered this interrogatory as I am able, having had no knowledge of said Daniel Clark, till after the years 1802 and 1803

PHIL'R CHASE.

And I do further certify, that before proceeding to the examination of said witness, he was by me duly sworn upon the Holy Evangelists, the truth, the whole truth, and nothing but the truth to speak touching and concerning the matters and things in said entitled suits, that I then propounded to said witness each of the said direct interrogatories of the complainants in the order they above appear, and accurately wrote down his answers to each, that I then propounded to him, in the order they appear in the foregoing deposition, the interrogatories of the respondents, and in like manner I wrote down the answer to each question, as given by the witness; that the said witness thereupon in my presence subscribed his name thereto. In witness whereof, I have hereunto set my hand and seal, at said Peoria, on this ninth day of June, in the year of our   one thousand eight hundred and forty-nine.

ONSLOW PETERS, Commissioner.

Fees of commissioner, for taking foregoing deposition
Two journeys to Jubilee, 60 miles, expense $10,00
Three days,   . 3 ',00
                                          ——————
                                             $40,00

O PETERS, Commissioner

Copy (A)

NEW ORLEANS, 27th Jan , 1849.

RT REV. BISHOP CHASE

DEAR SIR—Mrs Gaines, daughter of the late Daniel Clark of this city, received a few days since a letter from Mr Baker, a member of Congress from your State, from which I make the following extract .

" I have heard, upon authority in which I confide, that Bishop Chase (Jubilee College, Peoria, Illinois,) possesses information which he thinks very important in your case '

The Gen and Mrs Gaines have been unwell since their arrival, and cannot, therefore, address you in person   I suppose it propable, that Mr Baker alludes to conversations you may have had with Mr. Clark, when residing in this city   The U. S Court have decided in one case, there being several defendants in one bill, that Mrs. Gaines was the legitimate child and forced heir of Mr. Clark, which decision is by some lawyers thought final, but doubted by others   At all events, the other bills must all go thro' the forms of a trial, and hence, any facts you may possess may become important

I suppose that your conversations with Mr Clark embrace the subject of his marriage and the child, with his intentions in regard to that child, &c , which conversations or written evidence, if you have them I would thank you to communicate, that they may be submitted to the counsel for his judgment as to their importance at this juncture. I would suggest that dates given by Mr Clark as to the marriage or birth be given ; as, also, when the conversations occurred, be stated   As I may be absent from the city when your reply is received, please address it to Major Gen E P Gaines, New Orleans

An early reply is most respectfully solicited

I am, with high consideration and respect,
Your obedient servant,
VIRGIL WHITNEY

Copy of the answer, (B)

JUBILEE COLLEGE. Feb 15th, 1849

To VIRGIL WHITNEY, ESQ

MY DEAR SIR,—I received by last mail your favor of the 27th
of January, dated in New Orleans In answer to your inquiries, I reply . that I knew Daniel Clark, of New Orleans, but
not intimately We spoke together but seldom, when we did
so, always as friends

I lived, in the year 1808 or 1809, down the River Mississippi,
about three miles from the city A Mr Samuel B Davis the
harbor-master of the port of New Orleans, appointed by Gov.
Claibourne, was my next door neighbor Our respective dwel-
lings being built on one lot, divided in twain by Joseph
McNeil, the owner, to rent, were very near each other, so that
the visitors to the inmates of the one were perceived by those
of the other There was a wide space between the houses and
the road, which was the only one leading down the coast on the
levee.   Each half lot had its separate gate near this road.
Through that which led to Mr Davis' dwelling, I often saw
Daniel Clark ride to visit his daughter *Myra*, then a little girl apparently about two years old I saw them meet and caress as
father and daughter repeatedly Mrs Davis was then in charge
of this interesting babe, and cherishing her for Daniel Clark,
her father Mrs. Harper, the niece or wife of the nephew of
Mr. S. B. Davis, was a frequent visitor, and Mrs. H Lister was
an inmate of the family, and neither from them, nor any other,
friends or foes, did I ever hear of Myra's being an illegitimate
child. All whom I did hear speak, reported her as the acknowledged daughter and heiress of the wealthy Daniel Clark I
never doubted of this fact, nor do I doubt it at the present moment.

Some years passed away, and when Daniel Clark was reported to be no more, I heard that Myra Clark was domiciliated
in the house of a Col. S B Davis, in the city of Philadelphia, and that she was known as Myra Davis, and he reported
to be a rich man The same, when I knew him in New
Orleans, was apparently far from being wealthy.

Be pleased, sir, to present my most respectful regards to Gen.
Gaines and his lady, once Myra Clark, and believe me
            Your faithful friend and ob't serv't
                              PHILAN'R CHASE

Deposition filed 10th September, 1849, and opened 25th September, 1849, at request of Mr Wright, in accordance with stipulation on file

J W GURLEY, D C

CIRCUIT COURT OF THE UNITED STATES,

FOR THE FIFTH JUDICIAL CIRCUIT, HOLDING SESSIONS IN AND FOR THE EASTERN DISTRICT OF LOUISIANA.

To William H Cleveland Know ye, that reposing special trust and confidence in your integrity and ability we hereby authorize and require you that you call and cause to come before you Mrs Nixon, Madame Leoni Blondeau, Doctor Beyrenheidt, Mr Renoir Madame Rainoi nee Hugon, and Monsieur le Cure Guinand, and them duly examine on oath, touching and concerning certain matters and things in a case now depending in the said court, wherein Myra Clark Gaines is plaintiff, and Relf, Chew, et al are defendants and the same examinations, so taken and reduced to writing, you certify under your hand and seal and send enclosed to this court without delay, to be read in evidence on the trial of said cause, and send also this writ.

Witness the Honorable Roger B Taney, Chief Justice of the Supreme Court of the United States, at the city of New Orleans, this twentieth day of July, Anno Domini 1849, and the sixty-third year of the Independence of the United States of America

{ L.S }

ED RANDOLPH, Clerk
Per J W GURLEY, D y Clerk

MYRA CLARK GAINES, *vs* RICH D RELF, BEVERLY CHEW AND OTHERS	IN CHANCERY U S CIRCUIT COURT, FIFTH CIRCUIT, LOUISIANA No 122.

Interrogatories to be propounded to Mrs Nixon, Madame Leoni Blondeau, Mr Beyrenheidt Madame Rainoir née Hugon, and Monsieur le Caré Guinand, all of whom reside at Biloxi in Hancock county, State of Mississippi respectively, witnesses to be called and sworn, and examined on the part of the complainant in the above entitled suit, before William H Cleaveland, Esq, a commissioner appointed for that purpose

Interrogatory 1st What is your name in full? The females will state also their maiden names What is your age, residence, and occupation?

Interrogatory 2d Do you know the complainant in this suit, and either of the defendants and which of them?

Interrogatory 3d Do you know Madame Sophie veuve Despau née de Carrière? If yea, how long have you known her? and where did you first become acquainted with her?

Interrogatory 4th Do you know what is and what has been the standing and estimation of Madame Despau in the place or community or communities where you have known her, for truth and veracity, chastity and virtue? State fully and particularly

Interrogatory 5th and last Do you know or can you set forth any other matter or thing which may be a benefit or advantage to the parties at issue in this cause, or either of them, or that may be material to the subject of this your examination, or the matter in question in this cause? If yea, set forth the same fully and at large, in your answer

P C WRIGHT, Solicitor for Comp'ts

Cross interrogatories

1st How long have you known Madame Sophie Despau? Where has she resided during that time? Has she constantly resided   ? and if not, where and how long?

2d Is she not entirely without means of support within herself? And is she not entirely dependent upon her family connexions for her support? If not, state what means of support, to your knowledge, she has

3d State when, where, and under what circumstances, you became acquainted with Mrs Sophie Despau and mention the nature of your acquaintance, whether intimate or otherwise State also, if you know, what is   present age, or her probable age

4th Do you know whether or not Mrs Despau ever resided in New Orleans? If aye, at what period? and whether her husband was then living Do you know any thing of her character, conduct, and social position in New Orleans, at the time of her residence in that city?

5th Have you in answering any one of these interrogatories, either those in chief and cross, or in answer to any part or parts of them, stated any thing that is not of your own personal knowledge? If you say you have, distinguish, if you please, in all your statements what is of hearsay, or rumor, from is of your direct knowledge

6th Have you conversed with any person or persons touching the subject matter of your answers to these interrogatories? If aye with whom and for what purposes did you hold such conversation or conference?

7th You have been asked by the complainant, what has been the standing and estimation of Madame Despau, in the place or community or communities where you have known her, for truth and veracity, chastity and virtue? Will you now be pleased to state, what would be your opinion, and the opinion of the community or communities, about which you have been asked concerning the truth and veracity chastity and virtue of a woman, accused and charged in a court of justice by her own husband, in the following words "with scandalously and clandestinely leaving the territory, (her residence,) leaving her children to the care of nobody, leading a wandering, rambling life. without regard to the principles of honor or decency,—living in open adultery." Upon which accusation and charge the court rendered judgment, declaring "that the wife had forfeited her rights to the property acquired, and that the same vested in, and belonged to the husband."

How, it is again asked would a person thus described, in a Judicial Record be considered by you or by any community you ever knew, or ever resided in? How, say you, this being the character given by Mr Despau of his wife, Mrs Sophie Despau? L C DUNCAN, of counsel for the Defendants

MYRA CLARK GAINES	IN CHANCERY.
vs	
RICHARD RELF, BEVERLY CHEW, AND OTHERS	U. S CIRCUIT COURT FIFTH CIRCUIT LA. No 122.

The testimony and depositions of Madame Leonide Blondeau, Doctor Byrenheidt, Mrs Nixon, Mr. Reynoir, Madame Reynoir nee Hugon, and Monsieur le Cure Guinand, witnesses for the complainant, called, sworn, and examined before me, William H Cleveland, the commissioner in the annexed commission named, at Biloxi, in the county of Harrison, and State of Mississippi.

Mrs. Leonide Blondeau, being first duly sworn, says, in answer to—

Interrogatory 1st My name is Leonide Blondeau nee Jourdain, my maiden name was Leonide Jourdain; my age is thirty-one years, I reside, at present, at Biloxi, with my husband

Interrogatory 2d I have known the complainant for a short time only, I do not know the defendants

Interrogatory 3d I know Madame Sophie veuve Despau née de Carière I have known her about three or four years. I think I first became acquainted with her at Biloxi.

Interrogatory 4th I have never heard anything bad of her. I have never heard anything against her truth, veracity, chastity, and virtue

Interrogatory 5th I know nothing about the suit

Cross interrogatory 1st I have said about three or four years. she has resided at Biloxi the most of that time

Cross interrogatory 2d I am not acquainted with her means

of existence. 1 have always known her to reside at her nephew's I do not know that she is dependent upon her family
connexions for support I have already said I do not know

Cross interrogatory 3d. I think I became acquainted with
her here at her nephew's My acquaintance with her is not
very intimate I have seen her repeatedly at Mr Caillavet's
house. I do not know her parentage. I do not know exactly,
she is aged.

Cross interrogatory 4th I have heard that she resided at New
Orleans. I do not know when, or whether her husband was alive.
I do not know.

Cross interrogatory 5th. I have just said that I heard she
resided in New Orleans. As to the rest of my answers, they
are of my knowledge.

Cross interrogatory 6th No, I never have had any such
conversation.

Cross interrogatory 7th. If such were the truth I could not
form a good opinion of her. I do not know whether it is true
or not, I have never heard of it before.

LEONIDE BLONDEAU.

Sworn to and subscribed this 21st day of August, A D. 1849.
before me,

WM. H. CLEVELAND, Commissioner   [Seal]

Doctor Byrenheidt, being first duly sworn, says, in answer to

Interrogatory 1st. Alexander Byrenheidt I am sixty-four
years of age, my residence is Biloxi, at present, occupation,
physician.

Interrogatory 2d. I know the complainant I do not know
Mr. Chew; I only know Mr Relf as cashier of the Louisiana
State Bank, in which Bank I had my deposits

Interrogatory 3d I know Madame Sophie Veuve Despau,
née de Carrière I have known her, I think, since about 1833
I first became acquainted with her at Judge Caillavet's, in Biloxi I was an inmate of his family a short time in 1833 There
were some old ladies there, I think Mrs. Despau was one of
them, but I can't say positively

Interrogatory 4th I always heard her spoken of with respect
I never heard any body say anything against her truth, veracity,
chastity, and virtue—to the best of my knowledge, never

Interrogatory 5th I know nothing further

Cross interrogatory 1st I have already answered I think
since 1833. I think that she has resided most of the time at Biloxi.
I can't say whether she constantly resided there or not

Cross interrogatory 2d I know nothing about her circumstances I do not know that she is dependent upon her family

connexions for support   I know nothing of her means of support, except from hearsay.

Cross interrogatory 3d   I became acquainted with Madame Despau first, I believe, while I was staying at Judge Caillavet's, and afterwards, since 1844, as an attending physician in cases of disease in his family   My acquaintance is not intimate, not more than that of an attending physician in a family where she resided   I do not   She appears to be very aged

Cross interrogatory 4th   I do not know.

Cross interrogatory 5th   This will appear from my answers

Cross interrogatory 6th   No, I have not; I was surprised that the interrogatories were proposed to me

Cross interrogatory 7th   I think the answer to this question ought to be left to a judge or jury, and not to a witness   As a witness, I will state facts within my knowledge, but cannot give opinions   •

A BYRENHEIDT

Subscribed and sworn to this 21st day of August, A D 1849, before me,

WM H CLEVELAND, Commissioner.   ]Seal]

Mrs. Adeline C Nixon, being first duly sworn, says, in answer to

Interrogatory 1st.   My name in full is Adeline Cecelia Nixon my maiden name was Copp ; my age is fifty, my residence Biloxi , I have no occupation at present but my domestic concerns.

Interrogatory 2d.   I do not know the complainant. I only know Mr Chew by sight, I was formerly well acquainted with Mr Relf

Interrogatory 3d   I am acquainted with Madame Sophie Veuve Despau nee de Carriere   I have known her for the last seven or eight years, about eight years, probably.   I first became acquainted with her in Biloxi.

Interrogatory 4th   I have never heard anything that would be exceptionablae gainst her , her standing and estimation is that of a respectable lady, and good as to those points, as far as I know. I have never heard anything against her truth, veracity, chastity, and virtue.

Interrogatory 5th.   I know nothing of my own knowledge

Cross interrogatory 1st   I have known her about eight years; during that time she has resided in Biloxi   I do not recollect of her being absent but about a month, a year or two ago, and this spring about two months, on a visit in New Orleans   I now am not certain as to the first visit I speak of, whether she was absent, or her sister, Mrs Caillavet

Cross interrogatory 2d. That I do not know I am not reacquainted with her circumstances. I do not know of her having any resources whatever, but always understood she was dependent upon her friends

Cross interrogatory 3d In the latter part of 1841, or the beginning of 1842, I became acquainted with her on a transient visit at Mrs Reynoir's house The acquaintance is not very intimate, but sociable; such as passes between neighbors in the common intercourse of social life. I should suppose her probable age to be between sixty and sixty-five years

Cross interrogatory 4th No, I do not; I have heard her speak of residing at New Orleans, I was not acquainted with her then. I do not.

Cross interrogatory 5th All that I have stated on hearsay is in regard to Mrs. Despau's circumstances, that I have understood that she was dependant upon her friends The rest of my answers are from my own observation and personal knowledge

Cross interrogatory 6th. No

Cross interrogatory 7th If her husband represents the truth, I should say she forfeits all claims as a wife or mother, she would be so considered in any moral community.

                                    A. C NIXON

Sworn to and subscribed, this 22d day of August, A. D 1849, before me,

WM. H CLEVELAND, Commissioner   [Seal]

Mrs. Louise Reynoir being first duly sworn, says, in answer to interrogatory 1st My name is Louisa Reynoir, my maiden name was Louise Hugon, my age is about forty-five years, residence Biloxi; my occupation is attending to my domestic concerns.

Interrogatory 2d. I know the complainant but slightly: I do not know the defendants

Interrogatory 3d. I have known Madame Sophie Despau née de Carriere ever since I have resided at Biloxi I first became acquainted with her about seven years ago.

Interrogatory 4th. I have always known Madame Despau to be a person of good conduct She is well esteemed, her standing and estimation for truth, veracity, chastity and virtue is and has been good in the community where I have known her

Interrogatory 5th I know nothing more.

Cross interrogatory 1st I have known her about seven years

She has resided at Biloxi She has, I believe, constantly resided at Biloxi during that time, except a short time she was absent last winter I am not sure that she may not have been absent before.

Cross interrogatory 2d. I think she is entirely without means of support within herself I think she is entirely dependent upon her family for her support.

Cross interrogatory 3d. I first became acquainted with Mrs Despau in going to Mr. Caillavet s, where she resided My acquaintance with her is intimate I do not know her age, her probable age is about seventy years

Cross interrogatory 4th I do not know whether Mrs Despau ever resided in New Orleans I did not know her before I came here I do not know

Cross interrogatory 5th What I have stated is of my own knowledge

Cross interrogatory 6th. I have not. I did not know the commissioner was coming to take my testimony

Cross interrogatory 7th I ought to first know whether these statements were true, before I can give my opinion.

LOUISE REYNOIR.

Sworn to and subscribed, this 22d day of August, A D, 1849, before me,

WM H CLEVELAND, Commissioner. [Seal.]

Mr. Reynoir being duly sworn, says, in answer to interrogatory 1st. My name in full is Frederick Reynoir, age 47; residence Biloxi, and live upon my income

Interrogatory 2d I know the complainant slightly. I know the defendants, Chew and Relf, slightly

Interrogatory 3d I know Madame Sophie Despau née de Carrière I have known her about seven years. I first became acquainted with her at Mr Caillavet's, in Biloxi

Interrogatory 4th. Her standing and estimation in the community, where I have known her. for truth, veracity, chastity and virtue, is and has been very good

Interrogatory 5th. I know nothing

Cross interrogatory 1st. About seven years She lived in Biloxi at Mr Caillavet s, constantly, with the exception of short absences of a few months

Cross interrogatory 2d She is, in my opinion I believe she is entirely dependent upon her family connections for support

Cross interrogatory 3d I became acquainted with Mrs Sophie Despau, by visiting Mr Caillavet. My acquaintance is quite intimate. I believe her to be about seventy years of age

4th cross interrogatory I do not know

60

5th cross interrogatory. I have not stated anything that is not of my personal knowledge

6th cross interrogatory. No, not at all

7th cross interrogatory I can give no opinion upon this subject, without being acquainted with the nature of the case

F REYNOIR.

Sworn to and subscribed, this 22d day of August, A D 1849, before me.

WM. H CLEVELAND, Commissioner [Seal]

Monsieur le Cure Guinand being first duly sworn, says, in answer to

Interrogatory 1st Synphorien Guinand is my name in full my age, 49 years, residence, at Biloxi, generally occupation, Catholic priest.

Interrogatory 2d I am personally, only slightly acquainted with the complainant I do not know the two defendants, at all

Interrogatory 3d I have known Madam Sophia Veuve Despau about five years. I first became acquainted with her at Biloxi

Interrogatory 4th Since I have had the advantage of knowing Madam Despau, I have never remarked anything in her that did not deserve the esteem of honest and well-thinking persons From what I know of her, this is the general opinion of her here. Her standing and estimation in this community, where I have known her, for truth, veracity, chastity, and virtue, is excellent

Interrogatory 5th. I know nothing asked for in this interrogatory

Cross Interrogatory 1st I have known her about five years She generally remained at Biloxi, during that time and last winter spent a few months in New Orleans

Cross Interrogatory 2d I have no knowledge whether she has property or not I do not know whether she is entirely dependant upon her family connexions for support or not, I have heard that she was, I have no knowledge of her means of support I have heard several persons say that she was supported by her family

Cross interrogatory 3d Having been a priest here five or six years I in this capacity became acquainted with her shortly after coming here I think I should be well acquainted with her during the time I have been here, for I have visited her quite frequently In my opinion, her present age is 66 or 67 years, or 68.

Cross Interrogatory 4th I do not know whether she formerly resided in New Orleans or not

Cross interrogatory 5th   All I have stated, is of my own knowledge

Cross interrogatory 6th   I have never spoken with any person touching my answers to these interrogatories   My answers are dictated from my own knowledge

Cross interrogatory 7th   From the acquaintance I have had with Madam Despau during the last five years, and from what I have heard respecting her, I think that others would have formed the same opinion of her as I did   Not knowing anything about her life or conduct before that time, I am incapable of giving an opinion concerning it   Before that time I resided in Florida, and had no knowledge of her nor her family.

SY GUINAND, Prêtre Catholique

Sworn to and subscribed, this 23d day of August, A D. 1849, before me,

WM H CLEVELAND, Commissioner

[Seal]

THE STATE OF MISSISSIPPI, } SS
HARRISON COUNTY

I, William H Cleveland, Commissioner in the herein above entitled case, acting under and by virtue of the annexed commission to me directed, do hereby certify, that I caused to come before me, at Biloxi, in said county, Madam Leonide Blondeae and Dr Brunheidt, on the 21st of August, instant, Mrs Nixon Mr Reynon and Madame Reynoir née Hugon, on the 22d day of August, instant, and Monsieur le Cure Guinand, on the 23d of August, instant   all witnesses in said commission named, and did then and there severally examine on oath, by propounding to them the interrogatories and cross interrogatories herewith annexed, and their answers thereto, did reduce to writing in their presence, and after having carefully read to them their respective answers, did cause the same to be signed by them, which answers are the foregoing

Given under my hand and seal, this 23d day of August A. D. 1849   WM H CLEVELAND, Commissioner

[Seal]

Returned, filed, and opened under stipulation, at request of P C. Wright, this 18th October 1849.

J W GURLEY, D C

CIRCUIT COURT OF THE UNITED STATES, }
FOR THE 5TH JUDICIAL CIRCUIT, HOLDING SESSIONS IN AND FOR THE EASTERN DISTRICT OF LOUISIANA

To any Judge or Justice of the Peace in the Parish of St James, Louisiana

Know ye, that reposing special trust and confidence in your

integrity and ability, we hereby authorize and require you, that you call and cause to come before you Madame Silvère Cantrelle, and her duly examine on oath, touching and concerning certain matters and things in a case now depending in the said Court, wherein Myra Clark Gaines is plaintiff, and Relf, Chew, et al are defendants, and the same examinations, so taken and reduced to writing, you certify under your hand and seal, and send enclosed to this Court without delay, to be read in evidence on the trial of said cause, and send also this writ

Witness the Honorable Roger B Taney, Chief Justice of the Supreme Court of the United States, at the city
[L S] of New Orleans, this twentieth day of July, Anno Domini 1849, and the 74th year of the Independence of the United States of America.

ED RANDOLPH, Clerk.
Per J. W 'GURLEY, D'y Clerk.

U. S. CIRCUIT COURT, 5TH CIRCUIT,)
DISTRICT OF LOUISIANA. }

IN CHANCERY,
MYRA CLARK GAINES
vs.
RICHARD RELF, BEVERLY CHEW, AND OTHERS. }
No 122

Interrogatories to be propounded to Madame Sylvère Cantrelle, a witness to be produced on the part of the complainant in the above suit, sworn and examined before

which witness resides in the parish of St. James

Interrogatory 1st. What is your age and occupation, and where do you reside?

Interrogatory 2d. Do you know Madame Sophie vve. Despau née Carrière, who now resides at Biloxi, State of Mississippi? If yea, when did you first become acquainted with her, and where? and how long did your acquaintance with her continue?

Interrogatory 3d. What was the standing of the said Madame Sophie in society? and what was her reputation for chastity, truth and veracity in the community, while you were acquainted with her? State fully and particularly.

Interrogatory 4th. Were you or not accustomed to meet Madame Despau and associate with her in the first society where you or she resided? If yea, how was she esteemed in such society?

Interrogatory 5th and last. Do you know, or can you set forth any other matter or thing, which may be a benefit or advantage to the parties at issue in this cause, or either of them, or that may be material to the subject of this your examination, or the matters in question in this cause? if yea, set forth the same fully and at large in your answer

P C WRIGHT, Complainants solicitor

Cross interrogatories under reservation of all legal exceptions:

1st If you state that you ever met Madame Sophie Despau née Carrière in society, mention the year, or years; the place, or places and the names of the families where you thus met her Be as particular in your answer, if you please, as your memory will permit. Stating, also whether or not she resided any length, and what length, of time in the place where you say you met her

2d Whether there were or not, at the period, and in the place of which you speak, distinct circles or classes of society, with which persons of both sexes, of unquestionable individual respectability, associate, but which are not, what the complainant in her fourth interrogatory, calls "the first society?"

3d Was Mrs Despau a maiden or married lady, or a widow, at the time you knew her? Mention particularly the *time* and place of your acquaintance with her, and whether or not you are in any, and if any, in what way, connected with or related to the said Madame Despau, or to the complainant in this cause?

4th You have been asked what was the standing of the said Madame Sophie in society, and what was her reputation for chastity, truth and veracity, in the community while you were acquainted with her? Will you now be pleased to state what would be your opinion, and the opinion of the first society, where you or she resided concerning the chastity, truth and veracity of a woman accused and charged by her own husband, in a Court of Justice, in the following words. "with scandalously and clandestinely leaving the territory, ' (her residence);' leaving her children to the care of nobody; leading a wandering, rambling life, without regard to the principles of honor or decency. living in open adultery,' Upon which accusation and charge, the Court rendered judgment, declaring "that the wife had forfeited her rights to the property acquired, and that the same vested in and belonged to the husband" How, it is again asked, would a person thus described in a judicial record, be considered by you and by *the best* society of any community you ever knew, or ever resided in? How say you, this being the character given by Mr. Despau of his wife, Mrs. Sophie Despau'

L C. DUNCAN,
Of counsel for def'ts

MYRA CLARK GAINES }
vs } STATE OF LOUISIANA, PARISH OF SAINT
RELF, CHEW, ET AL } JAMES

By virtue and in pursuance of the hereto annexed commission, issued from "the Circuit Court of the United States, for the 5th Judicial Circuit, holding sessions in and for the Eastern District of Louisiana and addressed to any judge or justice of the peace in the parish of Saint James, directing and empowering any such magistrate to reduce to writing the answers of certain witnesses to the interrogatories and cross interrogatories annexed to said commission, and whose depositions are to be taken and used as evidence in the case in which Myra Clark Gaines is plaintiff, and Relf, Chew, and others are defendants, pending before the aforesaid Court

I, Benjamin Severin Webre, duly elected, sworn, and qualified *Justice of the Peace in and for the 6th ward of the parish of* Saint James, did, accordingly, cause to come before me Madame Sylveré Cantrelle, witness, residing in aforesaid parish, and, in the aforesaid entitled suit, and after swearing her to declare the truth on the questions put to her in said cause, did reduce to writing her depositions, as follows, to wit

To the first, witness answers   That she is fifty-one years of age, that she is a planter, and resides in the parish of Saint James on her own plantation

To the second, witness answers   That she knows Madame Sophie Veuve Despau née Carriere, who now resides at Biloxi, State of Mississippi, as she is informed   Witness knew her for the first time at Opelousas, since about thirty-eight years ago Her acquaintance with her lasted about seven or eight years, whilst they were in Opelousas.

To the third, witness answers   That Madame Sophie Despau used, while she was in Opelousas, to come to the house of witness ; she used, also, to visit some other families, and to attend the balls, in which were to be found the most respectable ladies of Opelousas. She cannot say anything against the chastity truth, and veracity of Madame Sophie Despau, nor does she recollect to have then heard any body speak badly of her at that time

To the fourth, witness answers   That she refers herself to the answer in the third interrogatory

To the fifth, witness answers not

S'RE CANTRELLE

Sworn to and subscribed, at the parish of Saint James, this 11th day of October, 1849, before me,

B S WEBRE, Justice of the Peace

Cross interrogatories

To the first, witness answers   That she refers herself to her *examination in chief* she, however, must say, that she does not now recollect the names of the diverse families where she used to meet Madame Sophie Despau

To the second, witness answers   That she cannot say anything about that, she does not recollect

To the third, witness answers   That at the time she knew

Madame Sophie Despau, said Sophie Despau was a widow ; she was residing at Opelousas, it was about thirty-eight years ago, witness says she is not in any manner connected or related with said Sophie Despau

To the fourth, witness answers That she does not understand the meaning of this interrogatory, and she cannot give any answer to it

S RE CANTRELLE.

Sworn to and subscribed at the parish of Saint James, this 11th day of October 1849, before me,

B S WEBRE, Justice of Peace

I, the aforenamed and undersigned magistrate, do hereby certify, that the aforenamed witness did appear before me, and was duly sworn by me, did make and sign her foregoing depositions, by her subscribed, after due reading thereof, and by me faithfully taken and reduced to writing, all of which I do now draw, and return my present proces-verbal, by me written, dated, signed, and annexed to the aforesaid commission and interrogatories and cross interrogatories

Witness my hand and signature, set and affixed at the parish of Saint James, this 11th day of October, 1849

B S WEBRE, Justice of Peace.

Eight words erased and null, and six words interlined and approved good

B S WEBRE. Justice of Peace.

Ret'd filed, and opened, under stipulation, at request of P. C. Wright, this 18 Oct, 1849

J W GURLEY, D C.

CIRCUIT COURT OF THE UNITED STATES,

For the Fifth Judicial Circuit, Holding Sessions in and for the Eastern District of Louisiana

To any Judge or Justice of the Peace in or near the Town of Plaquemine, State of Louisiana

Know ye that reposing special trust and confidence in your integrity and ability we hereby authorize and require you, that you call and cause to come before you, Madame Evariste Lauve nee Brunet, and her duly examine on oath touching and concerning certain matters and things in a case now depending in the said Court, wherein Myra Clark Gaines is Plaintiff, and Relf, Chew, et al, are Defendants and the same examinations so taken and reduced to writing you certify under your hand and seal, and send enclosed to this Court without delay, to be read in evidence on the trial of said cause, and send also this writ

Witness, the Honorable Roger B Taney Chief Justice of the
Supreme Court of the United States at the city of
New Orleans, this twentieth day of July, Anno Domini, 1849, and the 74th year of the Independence
of the United States of America

{ Seal }

ED RANDOLPH Clerk
      per J W GURLEY, D y Clerk.

U. S CIRCUIT COURT, 5th CIRT DIST, LA

IN CHANCERY

Myra Clark Gaines,
       vs
Richard Reif, Beverly
Chew, and Others
          No. 122

Interrogatories to be propounded to Madam Evariste Lauve
née Brunet, a witness to be produced on the part of the complainants, in the above suit, sworn and examined before
          , which witness resides upon ' the Coast, near the
town of Plaquemine, State of Louisiana

Interrogatory 1st   What is your age and occupation, and
where do you reside ?

Interrogatory 2d   Do you know Madame Sophie Vve Despau née Carrière, who now resides at Biloxi, State of Mississippi ? if yea, when did you first become acquainted with her,
and where? and how long did your acquaintance with her continue ? Be pleased to answer the same questions in reference to
Madam Zulime Gardette née Carrière, who now resides in New
Orleans

Interrogatory 3d   What was the standing of the said Madam
Sophie Despau in society, and what was her reputation for chastity, truth, and veracity in the community, while you were acquainted with her? State fully and particularly

Interrogatory 4th   What was the standing of the said Madam
Gardette in society, and what was her reputation for chastity
in the community, while you were acquainted with her? State
fully and particularly

Interrogatory 5th   Were you not accustomed to meet these
ladies, or either of them, and associate with them, in the best
society in the community, in which you or they resided? if yea,
how were they, and each of them, esteemed in such society ?

Interrogatory 6th and last   Do you know, or can you set
forth, any other matter or thing which may be a benefit or advantage to the parties at issue in this cause or either of them
or that may be material to the subject of this, your examination, or the matters in question in this cause? if yea, set forth
the same fully and at large in your answer

          P C WRIGHT, Sol r for Complainant.

Cross Interrogatories, under reservation of all legal exceptions.

1st. If you state that you were acquainted with Made Sophie Despau nee Carriere and Zulime Gardette nee Carriere, mention the place or places, the year or years, and whether they lived together or separate, in what particular city and in what street of the city. Whether they were then or either of them was, then, maiden or married or widows, and if widows, with whom they resided and where and how long you knew them, or either of them, in the particular place of which you speak.

2d. You have been asked whether you had been accustomed to meet Mrs. Zulime Gardette in the best society in the community where she resided, and how she was esteemed. If you answer that question affirmatively, will you please state the precise time of your acquaintance with her,—particularly, whether it was between the year 1790 and 1808, and what you understand by the complainant's question "the best society in the community." Mention the names of the families whose society she frequented, and the names of the persons who visited her. Mention the names of as many families and persons as your memory will permit you to recollect and state the name which she bore in society.

3d. You have been asked whether you were not accustomed to meet Mrs. Sophie Despau in the best society in the community where she resided, and how she was esteemed, and what was her reputation for chastity, truth, and veracity in the community. Will you now be pleased to state what would be your opinion and the opinion of the best society of the community concerning the chastity, truth and veracity of a woman accused and charged by her own husband in a Court of Justice, in the following words: 'with scandalously and clandestinely leaving the territory (her residence,) leaving her children to the care of nobody, leading a wandering, rambling life, without regard to the principles of honor or decency, living in open adultery." Upon which accusation and charge, the Court rendered judgment, declaring "that the wife had forfeited her rights to the property acquired, and that the same vested in and belonged to the husband."

How, it is again asked, would a person thus described in a Judicial Record, be considered by you and by the best society of any community you ever knew, or ever resided in? How say you, this being the character given by Mr Despau of his wife Mrs Sophie Despau?

L. C. DUNCAN, of Counsel for Defendants.

MYRA CLARK GAINES
vs
RELF, CHEW, ET AL

Be it remembered that on this day the 11th of October, 1849, by virtue of a commission issued by the Hon Circuit Court of the United States for the Fifth Judicial District, dated the 20th day of July, 1849, authorizing me to take and receive the deposition of Mrs Evareste Lauve nee Brunet, the said Mrs E Lauve, nee Brunet came and appeared before me, and after being duly sworn, has answered as follows, to the first interrogatories propounded to her, and annexed to the said commission

To the first She answers that she is fifty-eight years of age, that she is a planter and resides in the parish of Iberville

To the second She answers that she knows Madame Sophie V Despau, nee Carriere, who resides now at Biloxi, as she is informed That she first knew her about fifty years since, at New Orleans, her acquaintance continued seven or eight years at the city of New Orleans She was acquainted with Madame Gardette, nee Carriere, and then Mrs DeGrange at about the same time as with Mrs Sophie V Despau, and her acquaintance with Mrs Gardette lasted as long as that with Mrs Despau

To the third She answers that she cannot say anything about the standing of Mrs Despau in society, nor what was her reputation for chastity, truth and veracity in the community She, witness, was a young girl while she was acquainted with said Mrs Despau, and had no opportunity to ascertain what was her reputation She can say this much, that Mrs Despau and Mrs Gardette used to visit the house of her parents.

To the fourth. She answers that she cannot say what was the standing of Mrs Gardette in society, nor any thing about her chastity, or her reputation in the community during her acquaintance, but she knows that she was in the habit of visiting many families in New Orleans, among which was that of witness

To the fifth Witness answers that she was not accustomed to meet these ladies, or either of them, and associate with them in the best society in the community She was very young and did not pay any attention to the said facts She knows that Mrs Gardette, then Mrs DeGrange, has some time resided with Madame Reynaud, the mother-in-law of Mr Valery Landry

To the sixth She knows nothing else material, which may be a benefit or advantage to the parties at issue in this cause

Cross interrogatories. To the first.

Witness answers that she was acquainted with both Mrs Sophie Despau and Mrs Gardette, nees Carriere, in the city of New Orleans, about fifty years age, but cannot say where they were living, and in what street; she thinks, however that Mrs Gardette then Mrs DeGrange, was living in Royal-street, Madame Despau was then married, and Madame Gardette was then married with Mr DeGrange; and cannot tell whether Mrs Despau was a widow. Witness says that she knew them about seven or eight years, and always in New Orleans.

To the second. Witness answers that she has already answered that question in her examination in chief. She knew them between the years 1799 and 1808. Her memory does not permit her to recollect the names of the families they used to visit. They were called Mrs Despau and Mrs DeGrange.

To the third. Witness answers that she would entertain the worst opinion of a woman charged as stated in this interrogatory, if the facts charged should prove to be true, and that she could not believe any thing that she might say.

Vve E LAUVE

Sworn to and subscribed before me, in the parish of Iberville, this 11th day of October, 1849.

J H RICHARD, Justice of the Peace

I, the undersigned, J H Richard, Justice of the Peace, in and for the parish of Iberville, do hereby certify, that pursuant to the commission hereto annexed, I have on this day, the 11th October, 1849, taken and received the above deposition and answers of Mrs Evareste Lauve, nee Brunet, on her plantation, situated in the above parish.

J. H RICHARD, Justice of the Peace

―――――――

Filed 16th August, 1849, and opened at request of Dr Gardette, as per stipulation on file.

J W GURLEY, D. C

CIRCUIT COURT OF THE UNITED STATES, }
For the 5th Judicial Circuit, holding Sessions in }
and for the Eastern District of Louisiana }

To any Judge or Justice of the Peace in Mandeville State of Louisiana.

Know ye that reposing special trust and confidence in your integrity and ability, we hereby authorize and require you that you call and cause to come before you Madame Azalie Fauchet and her duly examine on oath, touching and concerning cer am matters and things in a case now depending in the said Court, wherein Myra Clark Gaines is plaintiff, and Relf Chew, et al are defendants, and the same examinations, so taken and reduced to writing, you certify under your hand and seal, and send enclosed to this Court without delay, to be read in evidence on the trial of said cause, and send also this writ

Witness the Honorable Roger B Taney, Chief Justice of the Supreme Court of the United States, at the city [L S] of New Orleans, this twentieth day of July, Anno Domini 1849, and the 74th year of the Independence of the United States of America

ED RANDOLPH, Clerk
Per J W. GURLEY, D'y Clerk

U S CIRCUIT COURT 5th CIRCUIT /
District of Louisiana (

IN CHANCERY
Myra Clark Gaines } No 122
vs
Richard Relf, Beverly Chew and others)

Interrogatories to be propounded to Madame Azelie Du-chel, a witness produced on the part of the complainant in the above suit, sworn and examined before

which witness resides near New Orleans and is now sojourning at Mandeville, in the State of Louisiana

Interrogatory 1st — What is your age and occupation, and where do you reside?

Interrogatory 2d — Do you know Madame Sophie ve Despau nee Carrière, who now resides at Biloxi, State of Mississippi? If yea when did you first become acquainted with her, and where? and how long did your acquaintance with her continue? Be pleased to answer the same questions in reference to Madame Zulime Gardette nee Carrière, who now resides in New Orleans

Interrogatory 3d — What was the standing of the said Madame Sophie Despau in society? and what was her reputation for chastity, truth and veracity in the community, while you were acquainted with her? State fully and particularly

Interrogatory 4th — What was the standing of the said Madame Zulime Gardette in society, and what was her reputation for chastity in the community while you were acquainted with her? State fully and particularly

Interrogatory 5th — Were you or not accustomed to meet the e ladies, or either of them, and associate with them in the best society in the community in which you or they resided? If yea how were they and each of them esteemed in such so-

Interrogatory 6th and last Do you know, or can you set forth any other matter or thing which may be a benefit or advantage to the parties at issue in this cause, or either of them, or that may be material to the subject of this your examination or the matters in question in this cause? if yea, set forth the same fully and at large in your answer

P. C. WRIGHT, Complainants' Solicitor

Cross interrogatories under reservation of all legal exceptions

1st If you state that you were acquainted with Madame Sophie Despau née Carrière and Zulime Gardette née Carrière, mention the place or places, the year or years and whether they lived together or separate, in what particular city, and what street of the city whether they were then, or either of them was, then, maiden or married ladies or widows Distinguish carefully if you please, what you state, as to one and another of these ladies If widows, with whom they resided, and where, and how long you knew them, or either of them, in the particular place of which you speak

2d You have been asked whether you had been accustomed to meet Mrs Zulime Gardette, in the best society in the community where she resided, and how she was esteemed? If you answer that question affirmatively will you please state the precise time of your acquaintance with her, particularly whether it was between the years 1799 and 1808, and what you understand by the complainant's question, the *best society* of the place? Mention the names of the families whose society she frequented, and the names of the persons who visited her mention the names of as many families and persons as your memory will permit you to recollect, and state the name which she then bore in society.

3d You have been asked whether you were not accustomed to meet Mrs Sophie Despau in the best society in the community where she resided, and how she was esteemed and what was her reputation for chastity, truth and veracity Will you now be pleased to state what would be your opinion and the opinion of the best society of the community, concerning the chastity, truth and veracity of a woman accused and charged by her own husband, in a Court of Justice, in the following words 'with scandalously and clandestinely leaving the territory, (her residence), leaving her children to the care of nobody, leading a wandering, rambling life, without regard to the principles of honor or decency; living in open adultery," upon which accusation and charge the Court rendered judgment, declaring ' that the wife had forfeited her rights to the property acquired and that the same vested in and belonged to the husband ' How it is again asked would a person thus described in a judicial record, be considered by you and by the best society of any community

you ever knew, or ever resided in? How say you, this being
the character given by Mr Despau of his wife, Mrs Sophie
Despau?   L C DUNCAN,
                                              Of counsel for def ts

Myra Clark Gaines	Before the Circuit Court of the
vs	United States, for the Fifth Ju-
Relf, Chew, et al	dicial Circuit, holding sessions in
	and for the Eastern district of
	Louisiana

Be it remembered that on this day, the thirteenth day of August, in the year one thousand eight hundred forty-nine, by
virtue of a commission issued by the said Court, dated the
20th of July, 1849, authorizing me to take and receive the deposition of Madame Azelie Foucher, residing temporarily at
this moment at Mandeville, in the above entitled case

Personally came and appeared before me, the undersigned
Justice of the Peace, the said Madame Azelie Foucher, who
being duly sworn, answers as follows to the interrogatories annexed to the said commission:

To the first She answers that she is sixty-five years of age,
that she lives upon her income, and resides in the city of New
Orleans.

To the second · She answers that she is acquainted with Mrs
Sophie, widow Despau, born Carrière, that she has known her
since about five years up to this day, that she saw her for the last
time, about a month since, when she was leaving New Orleans
to go to Biloxi With regard to Mrs Zulime Gardette, born
Carriere, witness states that she has known her since about
forty-eight years She used to see her in the balls, and also in
other places.

To the third She answers that she knew Madame Sophie
Despau more particularly, when she was living at Madame
Verlouin De Gruy, the witness' sister, that she, Madame Sophie
Despau, resided one year at her sister, Mrs Verlouin De
Gruy, and that during that time, she never heard or saw anything which could affect her reputation for chastity, truth, and
veracity, as to her own opinion, witness says that she has
always considered Mrs. Sophie Despau as a good honest, and
chaste woman, and that her sister (of witness) entertained the
same feeling towards the said Mrs Despau

To the fourth She answers that she knows nothing about
the facts set forth in this interrogatory relative to Mrs Zulime
Gardette.

To the fifth She answers that she was not accustomed to
meet Mrs Zulime Gardette in society, but she often saw, as
already stated, Mrs Sophie Despau at her sister's house, and

the said Mrs. Sophie Despau used to come often with Mrs. Ver-loin De Gruy at witness' house.

To the sixth. She answers that she knows nothing else than she has already stated; she may only add that she entertains the best feelings towards Madame Sophie Despau as being an honest and upright lady.

Answers to the cross interrogatories annexed to the commission.

To the first. She answers that she has already answered this interrogatory in her examination in chief; that she cannot say whether Mrs. Zulime Gardette and Mrs. Sophie Despau have ever lived together at any time; that they may have but it is not to witness' knowledge; that when she first knew Mrs. Despau, she was a widow; and that she had known Mrs. Zulime Gardette under that name, and also under the name of Madame DeGrange.

To the second. She answers that she knew Madame Gardette at the time she was Madame DeGrange, and cannot state positively whether it was between the years 1799 and 1808. She, witness, considers unnecessary to say what is meant by the words "best society of the place," having stated that she does not know the families nor the names of the persons she used to frequent, so long time having elapsed since she has lost sight of her.

To the third. She answers that it is impossible for her to answer this interrogatory in the way that it is propounded, for the facts charged by the husband of Mrs. Despau in his petition might not be true, and the decree of the Court expresses no opinion as to the said facts, which can authorize witness to form any opinion herself, relative to the character of a woman, against whom such facts might have been alleged in a petition.

AZE L FOUCHER

Sworn to and subscribed before me,

LS COQUILLON, Justice of the Peace
Mandeville, 13th of August, 1849

I do hereby certify, that pursuant to the commission issued by the Hon. the Circuit Court of the U S for the Fifth Judicial Circuit, holding sessions in and for the Eastern District of Louisiana, dated the 20th July, 1849, I have on this day, the 13th of August, 1849, taken and received the deposition of Mrs. Azelie Foucher in the above entitled case, at Mandeville, on the day, month and year aforesaid

LS COQUILLON, Justice of the Peace

Depositions of Madame Brasier and Latour returned, filed, and opened under stipulation on file, at request of P C Wright Esq, this fifth November, 1849

J W GURLEY, D C

CIRCUIT COURT OF THE UNITED STATES,

For the Fifth Judicial Circuit, holding Sessions in and for the Eastern District of Louisiana

To William H Rawle, commissioner for State of Louisiana at Philadelphia, Pennsylvania

Know ye, that reposing special trust and confidence in your in egrity and ability, we hereby authorize and require you that you call and cause to come before you Madame Brasier and Madame Latour, and them duly examine on oath, touching and concerning certain matters and things in a case now depending in the said Court wherein Myra Clark Gaines is plaintiff, and Relf Chew, et al, are defendants and the same examinations so taken and reduced to writing, you certify under your hand and seal, and send enclosed to this Court without delay to be read in evidence on the trial of said cause, and send also this writ Witness the Honorable Roger B Taney Chief Justice of the Supreme Court of the United States at the city of New Orleans, this twentieth day of July Anno Domini 1849, and the seventy-fourth year of the Independence of the United States of America

[L S]

ED RANDOLPH, Clerk

Per J W. Gurley, D y Clerk

The execution of this commission appears in a certain schedule hereto annexed   WILLIAM HENRY RAWLE,
Commissioner

The expense of executing this commission is five dollars

Myra Clark Gaines,	IN CHANCERY
vs.	U. S. Circuit Court Fifth Cir-
Rich'd Relf Beverly Chew,	cuit, Louisiana
and Others	

Interrogatories to be propounded to Madame   Brasier, and Madame   Latour, witnesses to be produced on the part of the complainant, in the above suit, sworn and examined before William H Rawles, Esq, commissioner for the State of Louisiana, residing in the city of Philadelphia, both of which witnesses reside at or near Philadelphia, in the State of Pennsylvania

Interrogatory 1st What is your age and occupation and where do you reside ?

Interrogatory 2d. Do you know Madame Zulime ve Gardette, née Carriere, who now resides in New Orleans, in the

State of Louisiana? If yea when did you first become acquainted with her, and where? and how long did your acquaintance
with her continue?

Interrogatory 3d What was the standing of the said Madame
Gardette in society, and what was her reputation for chastity in
the community, while you were acquainted with her? State fully
and particularly

Interrogatory 4th Were you or not accustomed to meet
Madame Gardette and associate with her in the first society
of Philadelphia, during her residence there? If yea, how was
she esteemed in such society?

Interrogatory 5th. What was the character and standing of
Madame Gardette, as a step-mother and wife, as far as you had
knowledge, or heard from others?

Interrogatory 6th and last Do you know or can you set forth
any other matter or thing, which may be a benefit or advantage
to the parties at issue in this cause or either of them, or that may
be material to the subject of this, your examination, or the matters
in question in this cause? If yea, set forth the same fully and at
large in your answer   P C WRIGHT,

Sol r for complainant.

Cross interrogatories, under reservation of all legal exceptions

1st State when, where, and under what circumstances your
acquaintance with Madame Gardette commenced. Did you
and she interchange visits familiarly? Was she married to Mr
Gardette, when you first became acquainted with her? and did
you know her before that marriage?

2d If you say that you knew Zulime Carriere before her marriage to Mr Gardette, state whether she was then considered
and received as a maiden lady, or as a widow, and if a widow,
of whom, and if neither maiden nor widow, but a divorced women, from whom divorced, and how did from whom do you derive your knowledge of such divorce. Be very particular if
you please in your answer and state if you know, in this
country and in what tribunal such divorce was obtained. If
you know nothing personally, then is it that you have stated
more hearsay? and then whom, pray, was such hearsay derived?

3d. Do you know when and where Zulime Carrier now
Madame Gardette, was born and in what country town or city
she passed the first thirty or thirty-five years of her life? If you
answer affirmatively state the consideration and standing she
enjoyed during these years. Was she then and there considered a woman of fair reputation, and received in the respectable
circles of the society where she passed her youthful and mature
years?

4th Do you know whether or not this Mrs Zulime Carrier

62

widow Gardette, ever resided in New Orleans? If aye, what was her reputation and particular social position in that city? and was she there received or admitted into society deemed respectable?

5th. You have been asked by the plaintiff, complainant in this case whether Mrs Gardette associated with the first society of Philadelphia, while she resided there. Will you now be pleased to state what was considered the *first* society of that city, at the period of which you speak? Mention, if you please, with as much particularity as possible, the names of the persons and families with whom Mrs Gardette held friendly and familiar intercourse in Philadelphia mention as many names and families as you can now recollect

6th. State, if you know, whether there were or not, at the period of the marriage of Mr and Mrs Gardette and long before and afterwards, and now, distinct circles or classes of society in Philadelphia, with which persons of both sexes, of unquestionable individual respectability, associate but which circles or classes are not what the complainant, in her fourth interrogatory calls "the first society"

L. C. DUNCAN,
Of Counsel for defend'ts.

Deposition of Elizabeth Brasier, a witness produced, sworn, and examined by virtue of the annexed commission on the twenty-sixth day of October, Anno Domini one thousand eight hundred and forty-nine, at the residence of said witness, in the borough of West Philadelphia in the county of Philadelphia, and State of Pennsylvania, before me William Henry Rawle, the commissioner named in the annexed commission, and also commissioner in the State of Pennsylvania for the State of Louisiana, in a certain cause now depending in the Circuit Court of the United States, for the fifth Judicial Circuit, holding sessions in and for the Eastern District of Louisiana, wherein Myra Clark Gaines is plaintiff, and Relf Chew, et al, are defendants

Elizabeth Brasier, aged sixty-eight years, or thereabouts, being produced, sworn, and examined on the part of the plaintiffs, answers as follows to the interrogatories propounded to her in this cause

1 To the first interrogatory, she answers as follows

I am sixty eight years of age; I follow no occupation and I reside in the borough of West Philadelphia, near the city of Philadelphia

2 To the second interrogatory she answers as follows

I know Madame Gardette and first became acquainted with her in Philadelphia about forty years ago, and was acquainted with her until she left Philadelphia, a period of about twenty years

To the third interrogatory she answers as follows

The standing of the said Madame Gardette appeared to me as good as that of any other person, and her reputation for chastity was never canvassed before me

1 To the fourth interrogatory she answers as follows

I answer that I cannot take upon myself to define what is meant by "first society," and I was not in the habit of going to balls and assemblies, but I did understand that Madame Gardette went to the parties of distinguished and fashionable persons

5 To the fifth interrogatory she answers as follows

The character and standing of Madame Gardette as far as I had knowledge, or heard from others was that of a kind and affectionate step-mother, as a wife, I had no occasion to hear or know of anything which could cast a slur upon her character

6 To the sixth interrogatory, she answers as follows

I have nothing to state in my answer to this interrogatory

To the cross interrogatories she answers as follows

1 To the first cross interrogatory she answers as follows

I first became acquainted with Madame Gardette as I have before stated about forty years ago when she was introduced to me by her late husband immediately after her marriage, and we interchanged visits occasionally more frequently on her part as I was not in the habit of going out much I did not know her before her marriage

2 To the second cross interrogatory she answers as follows

I did not know Zénon Carrière before her marriage to Mr Gardette and I know nothing of the other matters and things mentioned in this interrogatory

3 To the third cross interrogatory she answers as follows

I know nothing of the matters mentioned in this interrogatory

4 To the fourth cross interrogatory she answers as follows

I have only heard that Madame Gardette resided in New Orleans before coming to Philadelphia Of the other matters inquired of I know nothing

5. To the fifth cross interrogatory she answers as follows

I have already stated that I could not take upon myself to define what was meant by "first society" and I cannot be expected to recollect, at this remote period matters which were and are of no interest to me

6 To the sixth cross interrogatory, she answers as follows

For the reasons above stated I have no answer to make to this interrogatory

Upon further recollection, I desire to alter my answer to the second cross interrogatory, as I now remember that Mr. Gardette married a widow, but I did not know then whose widow she was.

ELIZABETH BRASIER

Sworn and subscribed before me, on the day and at the place in that behalf first aforesaid,

WILLIAM HENRY RAWLE, Commissioner

I William Henry Rawle, the commissioner named in the annexed commission, and also the commissioner for the State of Louisiana in the State of Pennsylvania, do hereby certify, that the deponent, Elizabeth Brasier, was by me duly sworn to declare the truth on the questions put to her in this cause, that the interrogatories and cross interrogatories were produced to her and her answers thereto taken in writing by me, and subscribed by her, in my presence, on the day and at the place in that behalf first aforesaid. And I do further certify, that I have made constant and frequent attempts to take the testimony of Madame Latour, the other witness named in said commission, but that all such efforts have been ineffectual, it having been represented to me, by members of her family, and others, that said witness was very old and infirm, that she had nearly lost her hearing, and that it was with difficulty that she could bring her memory to bear upon the most ordinary matters; said witness was confined to her room, and I had no opportunity of seeing her. And I further certify that the delay in the execution of this commission was caused partly by the above reasons, and partly because I was unable to find the residence of the other witness named in said commission until within the last few days, she not residing in Philadelphia.

In testimony whereof I have hereunto set my hand, and affixed my seal of office, on the twenty-sixth day of October, Anno Domini one thousand eight hundred and forty nine.

[L. S.]

WILLIAM HENRY RAWLE, Com

Deposition of Rev Sen Vicar Garcia Don Andres de Torres, Don Pepe de Torres, Don Zamore and others

Under cover to the address of Robert Morison, Esq, of Havana, I the undersigned, deposited this packet in the Post Office, at Matanzas, this 18th day of October 1849

NATH L CROSS, Commissioner

Ret'd and filed 29 Oct, 1849, and opened at request of P C Wright, Esqr, under stipulation on file, this 31 Oct 1849

J W GURLEY, D C

Postage, 1,25, paid by P C Wright, Esqr

CIRCUIT COURT OF THE UNITED STATES,

For the Fifth Judicial Circuit, Holding Sessions in and for the Eastern District of Louisiana

To the Consul of the United States at Matanzas, Island of Cuba

Know ye that reposing special trust and confidence in your integrity and ability, we hereby authorize and require you, that you call and cause to come before you, Rev Sen the Vicar Garcia, Don Andres de Torres Don Pepe de Torres, Don —— Zamore Don —— Sarazin, Don Antonio Mendez (now or formerly Notary) Mons —— Ruelle, Madame Ruelle, Madame Clara de Truffin and Doctor Ulmo and them duly examine on oath, touching and concerning certain matters and things in a case now depending in the said Court, wherein Myra Clark Gaines is Plaintiff and Relf Chew et al are Defendants, and the same examination so taken and reduced to writing you certify under hand and seal, and send enclosed to this Court without delay to be read in evidence on the trial of said cause, and send also this writ

Witness, the Honorable Roger B Taney Chief Justice of the Supreme Court of the United States, at the city of [Seal] New Orleans, this twentieth day of July Anno Domini 1849 and the 74th year of the Independence of the United States of America

ED RANDOLPH, Clerk
per J W Gurley, Dy Clerk.

U S CIRCUIT COURT, 5th CIRT DIST, LA

IN CHANCERY	⎫	
MYRA CLARK GAINES,	⎬	
vs	⎬ No. 122	
RICHARD RELF BEVERLY	⎬	
CHEW AND OTHERS	⎭	

Interrogatories to be propounded to the following witnesses, to be produced on the part of the complainant in the above suit, sworn and examined before the Consul of the United States at Matanzas, in the Island of Cuba, all of whom, the said witnesses, reside at or near Matanzas, aforesaid, to-wit Rev Sen the Vicar Garcia, Don Andres de Torres, Don Pedro de Torres, Don —— Zamore, Don —— Sarizan Don Antonio Mendez, (now or formerly Notary,) Mons —— Ruelle, Madame —— Ruelle, Madame Clara de Triffin, and Doctor Ulmo

Interrogatory 1st What is your age and occupation, and where do you reside ?

Interrogatory 2d Do you know Madame Sophie Vve Despau née Carriere, who now resides at Biloxi, State of Mississippi ? if yea, when did you first become acquainted with her and where ? and how long did your acquaintance with her continue ?

Interrogatory 3d What was the standing of the said Madam Sophie Despau in society and what was her reputation for chastity, truth, and veracity in the community, while you were acquainted with her ? State fully and particularly

Interrogatory 4th Were you or not accustomed to meet Madam Despau, and associate with her in the first society of Cuba in and around Matanzas, during her residence there ? if yea, how was she esteemed in such society ?

Interrogatory 5th and last Do you know or can you set forth, any other matter or thing which may be a benefit or advantage to the parties at issue in this cause or either of them or that may be material to the subject of the your examination, or the matters in question in this cause ? if yea set forth the same fully and at large, in your answer

P C WRIGHT, Sol'r for Complainant

Cross Interrogatories, under reservation of all legal exceptions

1. If you state that you ever met Made Sophie Despau née Carriére in society, mention the year or years, the place or places, and the names of the families where you thus met her Be as particular in your answer, if you please as your memory will permit Stating also whether or not she resided any length, and what length, of time, in the place where you say you met her

2d Whether there were or not, at the period and in the place of which you speak distinct circles or classes of society with which persons of both sexes, of unquestionable individual respectability, associated, but which are not what the complainant calls, in her fourth interrogatory, the first society

3d Was Mrs Despau a maiden or married lady, or a widow, at the time you knew her Mention particularly the time and place of your acquaintance with her, and whether or not you are in any, and if any in what way, connected with, or related the said Mad Despau or to the complainant in this cause

4th You have been asked what was the standing of the said Madame Sophie Despau in society, and what was her reputation for chastity truth and veracity in the community, while you were acquainted with her Will you now be pleased to state what would be your opinion and the opinion of the first society where you or she resided, concerning the chastity, truth, and veracity of a woman accused and charged by her own husband in about in the following words " with scandalously and clandestinely leaving the territory, (her residence,) leaving her children to the care of nobody leading a wandering and rambling life without regard to the principles of honor and decency, living in open adultery' upon which accusation and charge, the court rendered its judgment, declaring, that the wife had forfeited her rights to the property acquired, and that the same vested in and belonged to the husband "

How it is, it is asked, would a person thus described in a judicial record be considered by you, and by the best society of any country that you ever knew, or resided in? How, say you, do bring the character given by Mr Despau of his wife, Mrs Sophie Despau?

L C DUNCAN, of Counsel for Defendants.

CONSULATE OF THE U. S OF AMERICA, MATANZAS

1 Nathaniel Cross acting consul of the United States of America, for Matanzas do hereby certify, that under and by virtue of a commission numbered 122, dated 20th July, A. D 1849, and issued out of and under the seal of the Circuit Court of the United States for the 5th judicial circuit, holding sessions in and for the Eastern district of Louisiana, to the consul of the United State, at Matanzas, Cuba, I, the said acting consul, have collected, reduced to writing, and hereunto annexed the answers of Dr Antonio Uhno, Maria Clara Lassabe de Truffin, Antonio C. Mendez, Rev Manuel F Garcia, D D, Andrew or Andres de Torres, Francis Ruelle, Eliza L Ruelle, John B Sarazin, Peter or Pedro de Torres, and Joseph or José G Zamora, to the interrogatories and cross interrogatories appended to the said commission, to be read in evidence on the trial of a certain cause in the said Court, wherein Myra Clark Gaines is plaintiff and Relf, Chew, et al are defendants To the due execution of the said commission, an act of me, the said acting consul, being required by the said Court I hereby grant the same, to serve and avail as occasion may require.

In testimony whereof, I have hereunto set my hand and affixed the seal of the consulate of the United States, at Matanzas, this 15th day of October, in the year of our Lord one thousand eight hundred and forty-nine, and of the Independence of the United States the seventy-fourth year

[L.S]

NATH'L CROSS, Acting Consul

Depositions of witnesses produced, sworn and examined at the office of the United States consul, in the city of Matanzas, in the Island of Cuba, under and by virtue of a commission issued out of the Circuit Court of the United States for the fifth judicial circuit, holding sessions in and for the Eastern district of Louisiana, to the consul of the United States, at Matanzas, Island of Cuba, for the examination of witnesses touching and concerning certain matters and things in a case now depending in the said Court, wherein Myra Clark Gaines is plaintiff, and Relf, Chew, et al. are defendants

Dr Antonio Ulmo being produced, sworn and examined, doth depose and say as follows, viz

First   To the first interrogatory on the part of the complainant, the witness saith that his age is forty-four years, by profession is a physician, residing in Matanzas

Second   To the second interrogatory, witness saith, that he knows Madame Sophie veuve Despau née Carriere, that he first knew her in or about the year 1829, and that his acquaintance with her continued until she left the Island, does not now recollect where he first met her

Third.   To the third interrogatory, witness saith, that the standing of Madame Sophie Despau was highly respectable in society; that her reputation for chastity, truth and veracity was untarnished, and to his knowledge was never called in question during his acquaintance with her

Fourth   To the fourth interrogatory, the witness saith that during Madame Despau's residence in Matanzas and its vicinity, he was accustomed to meet and associate with her in good society, in which she was esteemed and respected, that she was connected and associated with some of the first families in Matanzas; but that he never met her in the first society

Fifth and last   To the fifth and last interrogatory, witness saith, that he can set forth no other matter or thing beneficial to the parties at issue, or either of them, or material to the subject of his examination, or the matters in question in this cause

First   To the first cross interrogatory on the part of the defendant, witness saith, that he first met Madame Sophie Despau née Carriere in or about the year 1829, that he often met her during her residence in Matanzas; but is unable to specify dates, that he met her in the family of Dr Garcia, rector of the parish church of St. Charles in Matanzas, in that of Antonio Mendez, that of Mrs. Campuzano and that of Mr Ruelle, all of them families of the first respectability in Matanzas, and also in the family of Mr Sarazin, a worthy and respectable man who resides in the country near Matanzas, witness cannot state what length of time Madame Despau resided in Matanzas and its vicinity

Second To the second cross interrogatory witness saith, that there are, at this time, in Matanzas, and ever have been, distinct classes or circles of society, as described in this second cross interrogatory, which are not the first society.

Third To the third cross interrogatory the witness saith, that at the time he knew Madame Despau, she was a widow, that he first saw her in or about the year 1829, in the district of Limonar, on a coffee estate belonging to her son-in-law, witness further saith, that by marriage, he is related to Madame Despau and the complainant, the former being a great aunt and the latter a second cousin of his (witness') wife

Fourth. To the fourth cross interrogatory witness saith, that the charges against Madame Despau, as set forth in this interrogatory, are to him entirely new, although he has been connected with the family nearly 19 years, that having justly conceived a good opinion of Madame Despau for chastity, truth and veracity, he is not prepared hastily to alter it; that such was her exemplary conduct during her residence here, such her kindly feelings, and such her devotedness to her children, and knowing, as does, the charitable disposition of this community towards an unfortunate female, he does not believe that Madame Despau will suffer, in the opinion of the best society here, until all the evidence against her is made known

ANT'O ULMO

Sworn to and subscribed, this 18th day of August, 1849, before me,   NATH'L CROSS, Commissioner

Madame Maria Clara Lassabe de Truffin, being produced, sworn and examined, doth depose and say as follows, viz.

First To the first interrogatory, on the part of the complainant, witness saith, that her age is sixty years, has no occupation, is a widow, and usually resides in Matanzas

Second To the second interrogatory witness saith, that she knows Madame Despau née Carrière, but cannot name the year in which she first became acquainted with her, witness first knew her in New Orleans, has known her from her (witness')

youth, and that her acquaintance with her continued until she (Madame Despau) left this Island

Third   To the third interrogatory witness saith, that Madame Despau's character for chastity, truth and veracity was never to her knowledge, aspersed, that she was regarded by all who knew her as a very worthy woman, and as such, she was esteemed and respected in society

Fourth   To the fourth interrogatory witness saith, that she never met Madame Despau in the first society in Cuba, which is composed of the rich and affluent, she being poor, did not, consequently, go into such society, witness often met her in highly respectable families, in which she (Madame Despau) was much esteemed and beloved

Fifth and last   To the fifth and last interrogatory, witness saith that her aunt, Madame Despau, is a virtuous woman, and has ever demeaned herself as such

First.—To the first cross interrogatory on the part of the defendant, the witness saith, that she cannot name the year in which she first saw Madame Despau in society ; that she has known her from her (witness') youth ; remembers first to have seen her in her (witness') mother's house, thinks that Madame Despau left New Orleans in or about the year 1816, and came to Matanzas, that in New Orleans she met Madame Despau in the family of Madame Renau, in that of Madame La Branche ; in that of Madame Tremolie, and in many other respectable families in that city   Witness has met and associated with Madame Despau in Matanzas, in the families of Mons Ruelle Señor de Mendez, and Señora de Campuzano, and in the country, near Matanzas, in the families of Mr. Zamore, Mr Sarazin, Mrs Jimene, and Mr Morejon, all of them families of the first respectability· To the best of witness' recollection, Madame Despau resided in Matanzas, and its vicinity, about twenty years.

Second.—To the second cross interrogatory witness saith!, that there were in Mantanzas, during Madame Despau's residence here, and are at this time, distinct circles or classes of society, such as are described in the second cross interrogatory, which are not the first society ; that the first society being made up of the wealthy, and Madame Despau being poor, she did not visit in such society, but visited and associated with families of the first respectability in Matanzas.

Third.—To the third cross interrogatory witness saith, that when she first knew Madame Despau, she was a married woman ; that when she came to Matanzas, she was a widow ;

witness first saw Madame Despau in New Orleans, in her (witness') mother's house . cannot name the year in which she first saw her, has known her from her (witness') youth; is related to Madame Despau and the complainant, the former being her aunt, and the latter, her second cousin

Fourth.—To the fourth cross interrogatory witness saith, that the husband of Madame Despau, in his lifetime, was an unprincipled man, that if the charges against her in the fourth cross interrogatory are not supported by other and better testimony than his, she gives them no credence whatever; that she fully confirms all that she has said in this deposition, in favor of Madame Despau, allowing others to judge of her (Madame Despau. as they may think proper.

MARIA CLARA LASSABE TRUFFIN.

Sworn to and subscribed, this 15th day of August, 1849, before me, NATH'L. CROSS, Com'r

Hallandose presente Dñ Antonio C Mendez y despues de haber sido juramentado y interrogado dice lo siguiente·

Primero Al primer interrogatorio de parte de la demandante, como testigo dice que su edad es la de 59 años, que es vecino de Matanzas, y que su profesion es la de Escribano de su Majestad Católico Doña Isabel Segunda, Reina de España.

Segundo Al segundo interrogatorio dice· que conoce á la Señora Dña Sofia Carrière, viuda de Despau, y que la conoció por primera vez en Matanzas, en el año 1822, que su amistad con ella continuó hasta que esta salió de la Ysla

Tercero Al tercer interrogatorio dice que la reputacion de la Señora de Despau en la sociedad era respetable, que contra su castidad, verdad y veracidad, nunca oyo una palabra que la perjudicase

Cuarto Al cuarto interrogatorio dice que durante la reisdencia de la Señora de Despeau en Matanzas, el acostumbraba á verla y á asociarse con ella en el circulo de su familia, que tanto él como su familia y todas las personas que la conocian la respetaban y estimabanpero, que nunca la vió en la primera sociedad de Matanzas

Quinto y ultimo Al quinto et ultimo interrogatorio dice que no puede decir mas en la materia que sea favorable á las partes en cuestion, ó á cualquiera de ellas en particular, ó que sea material al particular de su declaracion, o á las matérias que se ventilan en esta causa

Primero Al primer interrogatorio en contra de parte del demandado el testigo dice que por primero vez vió á la Señora de Despau en Matanzas, en el año 1822, pero ne recuerda en qui casa particular, o en qui familia El testigo la veia con frecuen cia—pero no lo es posible designar el tiempo y los lugares La Señora de Despau visitaba á la familia del testigo y esta á la de ella El testigo la ha visto con frecuencia en las familias de sus hijos politicos, Doñ Luis Gayare, antes Commandante del Castillo de San Severino de esta, y de Doñ Francisco U. de Moréjon, como tambien en las familias de Doñ Pedro y de Doñ Andres de Torres, que raras veces la vió fuera del circulo de su familia, y que la Señora de Despau residió aqui como viente años

Segundo. Al segundo interrogatorio en contra dice, que en Matanzas hay y siempre ha habido distintas clases ó circulos de sociedad, tales como se han especificado en este segundo interrogatorio en contra, que no se llama primera sociedad.

Tercero Al tercer interrogatorio en contra dice que cuando él conoció a la Señora de Despau por primera vez, era viuda—que la vió por primera vez en Matanzas en el año 1822, que no puede decir en que familia ó en que casa la vió por primera vez—que no tiene relaciones de ninguna clase, ni parentesco con la Señora de Despau ni con la demandante en esta causa.

Cuarto Al cuarto interrogatorio en contra dice que aunque que oye con sorpresa y sentimiento los cargos contra la Señora de Despau en este cuarto interrogatorio en contra, se vé obligado á manifestar que una mugar de un carácter representado del modo que se ha hecho, no merece la buen opinion del publico

ANTONIO C MENDEZ

Jurado y firmada á 25 de Agosto, de 1849, ante mi,

NATH CROSS, Comisionado

TRANSLATION OF THE FOREGOING DEPOSITION

Antonio C Mendez, being produced, sworn, and examined doth depose and say as follows, viz

First.—To the first interrogatory, on the part of complainant, the witness saith that his age is 59 years, resides in Matanzas, and by profession, is a notary of her Catholic Majesty, Isabella second, Queen of Spain

Second.—To the second interrogatory he saith, that he knows Madame Sophie Veuve Despau nee Carrieré, that he met her for the first time in Matanzas, in the year 1822, that his acquaintance with her continued until she left the island

Third.—To the third interrogatory he saith, that Madame Despau's standing in society was respectable, that against her reputation for chastity, truth, and veracity, he never heard a word to her injury

Fourth.—To the fourth interrogatory he saith, that during Madame Despau's residence in Matanzas, he was accustomed to meet and associate with her in the circle of her family, that by him, and his family, and all who knew her, she was esteemed and respected, but never met her in the first society of Matanzas.

Fifth and Last —To the fifth and last interrogatory he saith, that he can set forth no other matter or thing beneficial to the parties at issue, or either of them, or material to the subject of this examination, or the matters in question in this cause.

First.—To the first cross interrogatory, on the part of the defendant, the witness saith. that he first met Madame Despau in Matanzas, in 1822. in what particular house or family, does not recollect Witness often met her; is unable to designate times and places Madame Despau visited in witness' family, and he in hers; has often seen her in the families of her sons-in-law, Lewis Gayere, formerly Commandant of the Castle of Saint Severino, in Matanzas, and Francis U. Moréjon; also, in the families of Peter and Andrew Torres; seldom met her beyond the circle of her family, that Madame Despau resided here about 20 years.

Second —To the second cross interrogatory he saith, that there are in Matanzas, and ever have been, distinct classes or circles of society, such as are described in this second cross interrogatory, which are not called the first society.

Third —To the third cross interrogatory he saith, that at the time he first knew Madame Despau, she was a widow: saw her for the first time in Matanzas, in 1822, cannot say in what family or house he first saw her. Witness is in no wise connected with or related to Madame Despau, or the complainant in this cause

Fourth —To the fourth cross interrogatory he saith, that although he learns with surprise and regret the charges against Madame Despau in this fourth cross interrogatory, he feels bound to say, that a woman of the character thus portrayed, is not entitled to the good opinion of the public

[Signed]   ANTONIO C. MENDEZ.

Sworn to and subscribed, this 25th day of August, 1849, before me,   [Signed]

NATH'L CROSS, Commissioner.

A faithful translation   Attest:
NATH'L CROSS, Commissioner

Hallandose presente el Reverendo Doctor Don Manuel Francisco Garcia, y despues de haber sido interrogado, dice y declara, verbo sacerdote, lo siguiente

Primero. Al primer interrogatorio de parte de la demandante,

Gaines vs Relf, Chew, and Others

como testigo dice : que su edad es la de 54 años, que es vecino de esta ciudad y cura párroco de la Yglesia Parroquial de San Carlos de Matanzas.

Segundo Al segundo interrogatorio dice que conoce á la Señora Doña Sofia Carrière, viuda de Despau, y que la conoció por primera vez en esta, pero, no recuerda en que año fué, ni puede decir con certeza cuanto tiempo continuó su amistad con ella

Tercero. Al tercer interrogatorio dice : que el lugar en la sociedad que ocupaba la Señora de Despau era respetable—que su reputacion de castidad, verdad y veracidad era sin muncha, y que su conducta durante su residencia en Matanzas era irreprensible.

Cuarto. Al cuarto interrogatorio dice· que los deberes de su ministerio público nunca le han dejado mucho tiempo para visitas sociales—que durante la residencia de la Señora de Despau en Matanzas, el acostumbraba verla y asociarse con ella de cuando en cuando en él circulo de su familia—que tanto él como su familia la respetaban y estimaban pero, que nunca la vió en la primera sociedad de Matanzas.

Quinto y ultimo Al quinto y ultimo interrogatorio dice que no puede decir mas en la matéria que sea favorable á las partes en cuestion, ó á cualquiera de ellas en particular, ó que sea material al particular de su declaracion, ó á las matérias que se ventilan en esta causa

Primero. Al primer interrogatorio en contra de parte del demandado dice: que por primera vez vió á la Señora de Despau en Matanzas, pero, que no le es possible designar el tiempo y los lugares en que se encontró con ella La Señora de Despau visitaba á la familia del testigo y esta á la familia de ella Que la veia de cuando en cuando en el circulo de la familia de dicha Señora, y que no lo es possible designar las familias de que se componia ese circulo, ne sabe cuanto tiempo residió en Matanzas.

Segundo. Al segundo interrogatorio en contra dice que en Matanzas hay y siempre ha habido distintas clases ó circulos de sociedad, tales como se han especificado en este segundo interrogatorio en contra, que no pertenecen á la primera sociedad.

Tercero Al tercer interrogatorio en contra dice que no recuerda si la Señora de Despau era soltera, casada ó viuda cuando él la conoció—que no puede decir en que año fué, ó en que familia ó casa la vió por primera vez—que no tiene relaciones de ninguna clase, ni parentesco con la Señora de Despau, ni con la demandante en esta causa

Cuarto. Al cuarto interrogatorio en contra dice que no sabe nada de los cargos contra la Señora de Despau en este cuarto interrogatorio en contra—que dichos cargos le son enteramente desconocidos—que, en esta declaracion, como es de su deber, ha dado testimonio á su favor—que ha hallado de ella tal como la conoció durante su residencia en Matanzas, y como una Señora que gozaba de una reputacion sin mancilla, y que no tiene otra cosa que decir.

Dor MAN FRAN GARCIA, Cura Párroco

Declarado y firmada á 7 de Setiembre de 1849, ante mi,

NATH. CROSS, Comisionado

TRANSLATION OF THE FORGOING DEPOSITION:

Rev Manuel F. Garcia, D D., being produced and examined, doth declare and say on the word of a minister at the altar, as follows, viz·

First To the first interrogatory on the part of the complainant, the witness saith, that his age is 54 years, resides in Matanzas, and is rector of the Parish Church of St. Charles, in Matanzas aforesaid

Second To the second interrogatory he saith, that he knows Madame Sophie, veuve Despau, née Carrière Saw her, for the first time, in Matanzas,—does not recollect the year,—cannot state, with certainty, the length of time he was acquainted with her.

Third To the third interrogatory he saith, that Madame Despau's standing in society was respectable, that her reputation for chastity, truth and veracity was unblemished, and her conduct, during her residence in Matanzas, irreprehensible.

Fourth To the fourth interrogatory he saith, that the duties of his public ministry have never left him much time for social visiting; that he was accustomed, occasionally, to meet and associate with Madame Despau in the circle of her family; that by him and his family she was respected and esteemed. Witness never saw her in the first society of Matanzas.

Fifth and last To the fifth and last interrogatory he saith, that he can set forth no other matter or thing beneficial to the parties at issue, or either of them, or material to the subject of his examination, or the matters in question in this cause.

First To the first cross interrogatory on the part of the defendant he saith, that he first met Madame Despau in Matanzas—cannot designate the time and place of meeting her. Madame Despau visited in his family and he in hers. Met her occasionally in her family circle—is unable to designate the families composing that circle Does not know what length of time she resided in Matanzas.

Second To the scond cross interrogatory, he saith, that there are, and ever have been, in Matanzas, distinct classes or

circles of society, such are described in this second cross interrogatory, which do not belong to the first society.

Third. To the third cross interrogatory, he saith, that he does
not recollect whether Madame Despau was a maiden, married
lady, or a widow, at the time he knew her;—is unable to state
in what year, family or house, he first saw her —is not conect-
ed with or related to Madame Despau, or the complainant in
this cause.

Fourth. To the fourth cross interrogatory he saith, that he
knows nothing of the charges in this fourth cross interrogatory, against Madame Despau,—that to him they are entirely
unknown;—that in this deposition, as in duty bound, he has
borne witness in her favor;—has spoken of her as he knew her
during her residence in Matanzas—as a lady who enjoyed a
spotless reputation, and further saith not

> Signed, DR MAN'L FRAN'CO GARCIA, Rector
> Declared and subscribed, this 7th day of Sept 1849, before me,
> Signed, NATH'L CROSS, Commissioner.

A faithful translation ·

> Attest,   NATH'L CROSS, Commissioner.

Andrew de Torres, being produced, sworn and examined,
doth depose and say, as follows, viz :

First. To the first interrogatory, on the part of the complainant, he saith, that his age is 36 years, is a capitalist, and resides in Matanzas.

Second. To the second interrogatory, he saith, that he knows
Madame Sophie veuve Despau née Carrière, that he first became acquainted with her in Matanzas, in the year 1832 ; that
his acquaintance with her continued until she left the Island.

Third. To the third interrogatory, he saith, that during his
acquaintance with Madame Despau, her standing in society
was highly respectable, and her reputation for chastity, truth,
and veracity, was without reproach.

Fourth To the fourth interrogatory, he saith, that during
Madame Despau's residence in Matanzas, he was accustomed
to meet and associate with her in good society, in which she
was much esteemed and respected ; but that he never met her in
the first society of Matanzas

Fifth and last To the fifth and last interrogatory, he saith,
that Madame Despau is a lady of great moral worth, and as
such, was deservedly esteemed and respected during her residence in Matanzas.

First To the first cross interrogatory on the part of the defendant, he saith, that he first met Madame Despau in her own house
in Matanzas in 1832, that he visited in her family from that
time until she left the Island, that during the same period, he

met her, occasionally, in Matanzas, in the families of Antonio C Mendez and Francisco Ruelle, also, in the family of Mr Sarazin, who resides in the country, near Matanzas. Witness is unable to state what length of time Madame Despau resided in Matanzas

Second To the second cross interrogatory he saith, that there are in Matanzas, and ever have been distinct classes or circles of society, such as are described in this second cross interrogatory, which are not the first society

Third. To the third cross interrogatory, he saith, that at the time he knew Madame Despau, she was a widow, that he became acquainted with her, at her house, in Matanzas, in 1832, that he is related to her, and to the complainant in this cause, the former being the grandmother, and the latter the second cousin, of his wife

Fourth To the fourth cross interrogatory, he saith, that he does not alter or change the opinion he has expressed of Madame Despau, in this deposition that she will continue to enjoy the good opinion of this community until further proof of the immoral conduct with which she is charged in this fourth cross interrogatory shall be adduced.

ANDRES DE TORRES

Sworn to and subscribed, this 17th day of September, 1849, before me NATH'L CROSS, Commissioner

Francis Ruelle, being produced, sworn and examined, doth depose and say as follows, viz

First To the first interrogatory on the part of the complainant, the witness saith that his age is 60 years, is a planter, and usually resides in Matanzas.

Second To the second interrogatory he saith, that he knows Madame Sophie veuve Despau née Carrière, that he became acquainted with her in Matanzas, in the year 1830, that his acquaintance with her continued until she left the Island

Third To the third interrogatory he saith that, during his acquaintance with Madame Despau, she held a respectable rank in society, that her reputation for chastity, truth and veracity was never, to his knowledge, assailed or called in question.

Fourth. To the fourth interrogatory he saith, that during his acquaintance with Madame Despau, he was accustomed often to meet and associate with her in good society, in which she was respected and esteemed, but never met her in the first society of Matanzas

Fifth and last. To the fifth and last interrogatory he saith, that he ratifies what he has said in this deposition in favor of Madame Despau, who, in his opinion, is an excellent woman.

First To the first cross interrogatory, on the part of the defendant, he saith, that he met Madame Despau, for the first time. in 1830, at her house in Matanzas, that during his acquaintance with her, she visited in his family, and he in hers, and that he often met her at Mrs Truffin's and Dr Ulmo's Witness does not know what length of time Madame Despau resided in Matanzas, cannot speak more definitely

Second To the second cross interrogatory he saith, that there are in Matanzas, and ever have been, distinct classes or circles of society, such as are described in this second cross interrogatory, which are not the first society.

Third. To the third cross interrogatory, he saith, that at the time he knew Madame Despau, she was a widow, that he became acquainted with her in 1830, at her house in Matanzas, is not connected with or related to her, or the complainant in this cause

Fourth. To the fourth cross interrogatory he saith, that he never before heard a word against Madame Despau that, in this deposition, he has spoken of her, as she was when he knew her, as a lady of a good reputation, that the charges against her in this fourth cross interrogatory do not induce him to alter the opinion he has expressed, that he does not believe she will suffer in the opinion of her Matanzas friends, until further evidence against her shall be adduced

FRANCIS RUELLE

Sworn to and subscribed, this 20th day of September, 1849, before me, NATH'L CROSS, Commissioner

Eliza L. Ruelle, being produced, sworn and examined, doth depose and say as follows, viz

First To the first interrogatory, on the part of the complainant, she saith, that her age is 49 years, is the wife of Francis Ruelle, a planter, and usually resides in Matanzas

Second To the second interrogatory, she saith, that she knows Madame Sophie veuve Despau, née Carrière, that she became acquainted with her in Matanzas in the year 183 , that her acquaintance with her continued until Madame Despau left the Island

Third To the third interrogatory she saith, that Madame Despau's standing in society was reputable, that her reputation for chastity, truth and veracity was irreproachable, during witness' acquaintance with her

Fourth To the fourth interrogatory she saith, that during her acquaintance with Madame Despau, she was accustomed to meet and associate with her in good society, in which Madame Despau was esteemed and respected, but never met her in the first society of Matanzas.

Fifth and last. To the fifth and last interrogatory she saith, that Madame Despau is a good woman, and is so regarded by all who know her in Matanzas.

First. To the first cross interrogatory, on the part of the defendant, she saith, that she first met Madame Despau in Matanzas, in 1830, in her (Madame Despau's) house; that during her acquaintance with her, Madame Despau visited in witness' family, and witness in hers, during the same period; witness often met her at Mrs. Truffin's and Doctor Ulmo's; does not know what length of time she resided in Matanzas; cannot be more definite in her answer.

Second. To the second cross interrogatory she saith, that there are and ever have been, in Matanzas, distinct classes or circles of society, such as are described in this second cross interrogatory, which are not the first society.

Third. To the third cross interrogatory she saith, that at the time she knew Madame Despau she was a widow. Met her, for the first time, at her (Madame Despau's) house in 1830, in Matanzas; is not connected with or related to her or the complainant in this cause.

Fourth. To the fourth cross interrogatory she saith, that in this deposition, she has spoken of Madame Despau, as she was when she knew her in Matanzas, as a lady of an unblemished reputation; that she does not change the opinion she has expressed, that such was Madame Despau's deportment during her residence here; she does not believe she will suffer in the opinion of this community, until further evidence against her shall be adduced. ELIZA L. RUELLE

Sworn to and subscribed, this 20th day of September, 1849, before me, NATH L CROSS, Commissioner.

John B Sarazin, being produced, sworn, and examined, doth depose and say as follows, viz:

First. To the first interrogatory, on the part of the complainants, he saith, that his age is 69 years; by occupation is a planter, and resides in Limonar.

Second. To the second interrogatory he saith, that he knows Madame Sophie veuve Despau née Carrière; that he became acquainted with her on her arrival in the Island, and that his acquaintance with her continued during her residence in it; does not now recollect the time and place of his first acquaintance with her—thinks it was about the year 1820.

Third. To the third interrogatory he saith, that during his acquaintance with Madame Despau, her standing in society was respectable, and her reputation for chastity, truth, and veracity was blameless.

Fourth To the fourth interrogatory he saith, that during Madame Despau's residence in Matanzas, he was accustomed to meet and associate with her in the first society in which she was esteemed and respected for her amiable and interesting qualities

Fifth and last To the fifth and last interrogatory he saith, that he can set forth no other matter or thing beneficial or advantageous to the parties at issue, or either of them, or material to the subject of his examination, or the matters in question in this cause

First. To the first cross interrogatory, on the part of the defendant he saith, that he cannot designate the time and place of his first acquaintance with Madame Despau, that during her residence in the Island, he visited in her family, and she in his, that he often met her in the families of her sons-in-law, Lewis Gayaré, formerly commandant of the Castle of San Severino, in Matanzas, and Francis U Morejon, also, in the family of Mis Truffin Witness does not know what length of time Madame Despau resided in the Island cannot be more particular in his answer

Second To the second cross interrogatory he saith, that there are in Matanzas, and ever have been, distinct classes or circles of society, such as are described in this second cross interrogatory, which are not the first society

Third To the third cross interrogatory, he saith, that at the time he knew Madame Despau she was a widow that he cannot designate the time and place of his first acquaintance with her: is not connected with or related to her or the complainant in this cause.

Fourth To the fourth cross interrogatory he saith, that he does not alter the opinion he has expressed of Madame Despau in this deposition, that he has spoken of her as she was when he knew her—a lady enjoying an unblemished reputation, that she will not suffer in the opinion of this community until further evidence against her shall be adduced

J B SARAZIN

Sworn to and subscribed this 24th day of Sept, 1849, before me

NATH'L CROSS, Commissioner

Peter de Torres, being produced, sworn and examined, doth depose and say, as follows, viz :

First To the first interrogatory on the part of the complainant, he saith, that his age is 35 years, by occupation, a storekeeper, in the employ of a Rail Road Company, and resides in Limonar.

Second To the second interrogatory he saith, that he knows Madame Sophie veuve Despau née Carrière, that he first became acquainted with her in Matanzas, between the years 1830 and 1833, that his acquaintance with her continued with her until she left the Island

Third To the third interrogatory he saith, that during his acquaintance with Madame Despau, her standing in society was respectable and her reputation for chastity, truth, and veracity without stain

Fourth To the fourth cross interrogatory he saith, that during Madame Despau's residence in Matanzas he was accustomed to meet and associate with her in the first society, in which she was much and deservedly esteemed and respected

Fifth and last To the fifth and last interrogatory he saith, that he can set forth no other matter or thing, beneficial or advantageous to the parties at issue, or either of them, or material to the subject of his examination, or the matters in question in this cause

First To the first cross interrogatory on the part of the defendant, he saith, that he first met Madame Despau, between 1830 and 1833, in Matanzas, at the house of her son-in-law, Lewis Gayaré, formerly commandant of the Castle of San Severino, in Matanzas, that during his acquaintance with her, he often met her there, and in the families of Antonio Mendez and Francisco Ruelle, does not know how long she resided in Matanzas, cannot be more definite in his answer

Second To the second cross interrogatory he saith, that there are and ever have been, in Matanzas, distinct circles or classes of society, such as are described in this second cross interrogatory, which are not the first society, but that the families in which he met and associated with Madame Despau are, and were, of the first society, in his opinion.

Third To the third cross interrogatory he saith, that at the time he knew Madame Despau, she was a widow, that he first became acquainted with her between the years 1830 and 1833, in Matanzas, at the house of Lewis Gayaré, formerly commandant of the Castle of San Severino, in Matanzas. that he is related to Madame Despau and the complainant in this cause, the former being the grandmother, and the latter the second cousin of his wife

Fourth To the fourth cross interrogatory, he saith, that the charges in this fourth cross interrogatory, against Madam Despau, do not induce him to alter or change the opinion he has expressed in this deposition, that he has spoken of her. as she was when he knew her, a lady of a spotless reputation ;

that she will continue to enjoy the good opinion of this community, until further proof of her guilt shall be adduced

                                        PEDRO DE TORRES

Sworn to and subscribed this 28th day of Sept 1849, before me.   NATH L CROSS, Commissioner

Joseph G Zamora, being produced, sworn, and examined, doth depose and say as follows

First. To the first interrogatory on the part of the complainant, he saith, that his age is 56 years, by occupation is a planter, and resides in Limonar

Second To the second interrogatory he saith that he knows Madame Sophie veuve Despau née Carriere that he first became acquainted with her in New Orleans in what year, cannot determine, that his acquaintance with her continued until she left this Island

Third. To the third interrogatory he saith, that during his acquaintance with Madame Despau, her standing in society was respectable, and her reputation for chastity, truth, and veracity without blemish.

Fourth To the fourth interrogatory he saith, that during Madame Despau's residence in Matansas and its vicinity, he was accustomed to meet and associate with her in the first society, in which she was much esteemed and respected

Fifth and last. To the fifth and last interrogatory he saith, that he can set forth no other matter or thing beneficial or advantageous to the parties at issue, or either of them, or material to the subject of his examination, or the matters in question in this cause.

First. To the first cross interrogatory, on the part of the defendant, he saith, that he first became acquainted with Madame Despau in New Orleans, does not recollect the year nor the family in which he first met her has known her from his childhood; that in New Orleans, he has met her in the families of Madame Caillavet and Madame Saba, in Matanzas, from time to time, at Mr Duet s. in the country, near Matansas, in the families of Francisco V. Morejon, George Bartlett, and Mr Sarazin, that during her residence in the Island, he often met her : can't say how many times he met her in society, does not know how long she resided in New Orleans or Matanzas; regrets that he cannot be more definite in his answer

Second To the second cross interrogatory he saith, that there are in Matanzas, and ever have been, distinct classes or circles of society, such as are described in this second cross interrogatory, which are not the first society.

Third. To the third cross interrogatory he saith, that at the time he knew Madame Despau in New Orleans, she was a married lady that when she come to Matanzas, she was a widow become acquainted with her in New Orleans does not recollect the year nor the family in which he first met her is not connected with or related to her or the complainants in this cause

Fourth To the fourth cross interrogatory he saith that he never before heard a word against the reputation of Madame Despau that the charges against her in this fourth cross interrogatory do not induce him to alter or change the opinion he has ever entertained of her, and which he has expressed in this deposition that the opinion of the community will remain in her favor, until convincing proof of her guilt shall be shown

JOSE G ZAMORA

Sworn to and subscribed this 11th day of October, 1849, before me

NATH L CROSS, Commissioner

To the honorable court I consider it my duty to remark, that the Rev Manuel F Garcia D D, (whose deposition is hereunto annexed) declined giving testimony under a formal oath, remarking that the courts of Spain do not require gentlemen of his profession to swear or affirm—that they require them to ' say and declare, verbo sacerdote,' that in this manner he would give testimony in this cause In this manner, after a little reflection, I took his deposition, it being the prerogative of the court to decide upon its legality as evidence in the courts of the United States NATH L CROSS, Commissioner.

Matanzas, 17th Oct , 1849.

Returned and filed 30th October, 1849, and opened at the request of P C Wright, Esq , under stipulation on file, this 31st October, 1849

J W GURLEY, Deputy Clerk.

CIRCUIT COURT OF THE UNITED STATES,

For the Fifth Judicial Circuit, holding Sessions in and for the Eastern District of Louisiana

To William H Martin, Opelousas, parish of St. Landry, Louisiana.

Know ye, that reposing special trust and confidence in your integrity and ability, we hereby authorize and require you, that you call and cause to come before you Madame Thompson, nee de la Chaise, Madame Dupre nee   , widow of Dupre, Madame Celeise Louailher, Madame Garrigues Flaujac

Mr. Etienne Lamorendier, Mr. Lasty Dupré, Mr. Cyprien Dupre, Madame Clementine Deballlon, née Benguerelle, Madame
de Carrière, and Madamoiselle M Chretien, J J Louaillier.
Madame M ve Lamorendier, and them duly examine on oath
touching and concerning certain matters and things in a case now
de pending in the said Court, wherein Myra Clark Gaines is plaintiff and Relf, Chew, et al, defendants, and the same examinations, so taken and reduced to writing, you certify under
your hand and seal, and send enclosed to this Court without
delay, to be read in evidence on the trial of said cause, and send
also this writ

Witness the Honorable Roger B Taney, Chief Justice of the
    Supreme Court of the United States, at the city of New
    Orleans, this twenty-sixth day of July, Anno Domini
[L S] 1849, and the seventy-third year of the Independenc
    of the United States of America

                    ED RANDOLPH Clerk
                 Per J W Gurley D y Clerk

Myra Clark Gaines, *vs* Rich'd Relf, and Others No. 122.	IN CHANCERY U S Circuit Court, Fifth Cir- cuit, District of Louisiana.

Interrogatories to be propounded to Madame Sydalise
Thompson nee de la Chaise, Mr J J Louaillier, Madame M
Vve. Lamorendier, Madame Garrigues Flaujac, Madame Dupré nee   widow of Dupre, Madame Célise Louaillier,
Mr. Etienne Lamorendier Mr Cyprien Dupre, Mr Lastie Dupré, Madame Clementine Deballlon nee Bengeurelle, Madame
de Carrière, and M'll M Chrétien, all of whom reside at Opelousas, in the State of Louisiana, witnesess to be produced by
complainant, and sworn and examined in the above entitled suit.

1st interrogatory. What is your age? where do you reside?

2d interrogatory Do you know either of the parties to this
suit? if yea, which of them?

3d Interrogatory Are you acquainted with Madame Sophie
Veuve Despau, nee de Carrière? if yea, when did you first become acquainted with her, and where has she, and where have
you resided since that period? State particularly

4th interrogatory. Do you know what has been the character
and reputation of Madame Sophie Despau, née de Carriere in
the community where she has resided since you have known
her, as regards chastity, virtue, truth and veracity? if yea, state
particularly.

5th interrogatory. Do you know, or can you set forth any
other matter or thing which may be a benefit or advantage to
parties at issue in this cause, or either of them, or that may be

material to the subject of this your examination, or the matters in question in this cause? if yea, set forth the same fully and at large in your answer

P C WRIGHT,
Solicitor for complainants.

Cross interrogatories.

First. Have you ever resided in New Orleans? if aye, be pleased to state when, and for how long a time? In what street did you reside? between what streets? With whom did you reside, and for how long?

Second Where were you born? When were you born? Were you ever married? if aye, to whom? Is your husband, (if you ever had any,) yet living, and where does he live? Have you always rasided with him from the period of your marriage until his death or the present time?

Third If you speak of the character of Madame Despau do you speak of your own personal knowledge, or from hearsay?

Fourth If you answer complainants interrogatories by saying that you know anything about the reputation of Madame Despau in the community where she has resided, then answer the following questions What community do you refer to? Do you speak of the character of Madame Despau as known to you among ladies, or gentlemen? What were your means of knowing the reputation which Madame Despau had among gentlemen in the community where she resided?

Fifth Is it not possible for a woman to have an exceedingly bad reputation among men in the community, and ladies of chastity, virtue, truth and veracity, know nothing on the subject?

Sixth Was it not notorious in the community of New Orleans, that Madame Despau, between the years 1800 and 1807, was in the habit of going to balls of an exceedingly doubtful character in New Orleans, and where no ladies, caring for their reputation, would have ventured to go?

Seventh Do you not know, and have you not heard, that Madame Despau has, in her younger days, been in the habit of visiting places to meet gentlemen, where no lady, having a regard to her reputation, would go?

Eighth. Please name one or more respectable families in New Orleans, where any of the members are now living, into which Madame Despau was ever received as an acquaintance and visitor, after the year 1800

Eighth Where was Madame Despau in the year 1802? How do you know that fact? Was she there all of the time? Where was she in the years 1805, 1806, and 1807? State fully and particularly.

65

Ninth Did you associate in the same company with **Madam** Despau after the year 1800 ? State particularly

Tenth How many children has Madame Despau ever had ? Did she raise them, and attend to their support, and why not ? Are any of them living ? Name them ? Where do they reside? Did Madame Despau continue to live with her husband from the time of her marriage until death separated them ? if not, why did she not ?

Eleventh Was not Madame Despau openly and publicly accused of violating the marriage bed ?

Twelfth Do you not perfectly well know that Madame Despau was regarded among gentlemen in New Orleans as a *femme gallante* ?

Thirteenth State all you know about certain matters touching the character of Madame Despau, which were brought before the Vicar General in New Orleans, many years ago ? In the face of such facts, can you say that the community of New Orleans received and regarded Madame Despau in society as chaste, virtuous, truth-telling, and as a person of veracity ? state fully ?

> G B DUNCAN, for his clients of Record.
> ISAAC T PRESTON, Solicitor for defts.
> L JANIN, Solicitor

MYRA CLARK GAINES,	PENDING IN THE CIRCUIT COURT OF THE
vs	UNITED STATES FOR THE FIFTH CIRCUIT IN
RICHARD RELF, ET AL	AND FOR THE EASTERN DISTRICT OF LA

By virtue of a commission addressed to me in the name of William H Martin, in the above entitled cause, dated at the city of New Orleans, the 26th day of June, 184 , and 73d year of the Independence of the United States of America, I, Edmund H Martin, residing in the parish of St Landry, and town of Opelousas, have caused to appear before me the witnesses hereinafter named and examined, on the days and year herein set forth, who being first duly sworn to testify the whole truth touching their knowledge of any thing relating to the matters in controversy between the said parties, have answered the interrogatories and cross interrogatories as hereinafter taken down and written by me.

Appeared this 9th day of August, 1849, Madame Carrière, who answers as follows, to wit

To 1st interrogatory My age is sixty-eight years. I reside in the parish of St Landry

2d I do not know the parties to this suit.

3d I am I knew Madame Despau when I was quite young. My first acquaintance with her was some five or six years after her marriage I formed her acquaintance in the parish of St Landry She has resided since that time in the parish of S. Landry, New Orleans, and Havana With the exception of three years residence or thereabouts in New Orleans, I have always resided in the parish of St Landry

4th I have always esteemed Madame Despau as irreproachable in character, being a good mother and kind relation Her chastity and integrity of character I never doubted or heard doubted

5th and last interrogatory I know nothing

Cross Interrogatories

1st interrogatory I lived in New Orleans three years, opposite Place D Armes street not recollected I lived with and at the residence of my husband

2d I was born in the parish of St Landry about the year 1781 I was married to Louis Carriere now deceased late of said parish I always resided with my husband, from the date of our marriage until his death

3d I lived in the same house with Madame Despau about seven years, and I speak of her reputation from long personal knowledge as well as from general character

4th I allude to the most respectable families of the parish of St Landry Madame Despau was esteemed by both sexes I acquired my knowledge of Madame Despau's standing as stated in answer to third cross interrogatory

5th It is possible but I think it improbable

6th During my residence in New Orleans which was about the time of the death of Governor Gayoso (the only event recollected to fix the date) Madame Despau, to my knowledge, never visited either ball or theatre

7th I never knew or heard it She was a modest woman, and I never knew her to contravene the proprieties of life

8th I do not recollect dates so long passed with accuracy

9th I do not recollect those dates, but I have always lived on the most intimate terms with Madame Despau

10th She had five children, one died young She raised the other four herself Her daughter Sophie alone survives She lives at Biloxi, as I am informed Madame Despau was separated from her husband during marriage I know not the cause, but I do know that he was a bad (mechant) man

11th Never to my knowledge

12h I know no such thing on the contrary, she bore quite a different reputation

13th I know nothing and have heard nothing in relation to the subject of of this interrogatory

Signed, her mark ⋈ LISI CARRIERE

Appeared also, this 9th day of August, 1849, Madame Clementine Debaillon, who answers as follows, to wit

To first interrogatory in chief I shall be forty-six years of age in September next, and reside in Opelousas

2d I do not know any of the parties to the suit

3d I know her more from reputation than personal knowledge I first became acquainted with her in or about the year 1836 She has since resided in New Orleans, I in St Landry.

4th Her reputation in the community in which she has resided, since my first acquaintance with her, has been irreproachable

5th I know nothing more in relation to the matter

Cross interrogatories

First interrogatory I was born in New Orleans, and resided there until the year 1819 I resided in St Louis street between Levee and Chatres streets I resided with my father and mother, and was sixteen years of age when they left New Orleans

2d I was born in New Orleans, in September, 1803 I was married to J M Debaillon, now deceased, late of the parish of St Landry, with whom I resided from my marriage until his death

3d I speak of Madame Despau from general report or hearsay

4th I know nothing from personal knowledge—all derived from the opinions and knowledge of others

5th It is scarcely possible

6th In 1800, I was not born, in 1807, I was too young to know.

7th I have never heard such accusations or (propos).

8th I cannot answer, because I was not acquainted with Madame Despau, in New Orleans

9th I do not recollect

9th. I was then too young

10th I do not know how many children she had, the only one with whom I am acquainted is Madame Sophie Moréjon, who, I believe, resides at Biloxi I did   know Madame Despau's husband, or of their separation

11th. I never knew.

12th No.

13th I know nothing nor have heard anything in regard to this interrogatory

C DEBAILLON

Appeared also, this 17th day of October, 1849, Miss Margaret Chretien, who answers as follows, to wit:

To first interrogatory in chief. **I am seventy-seven years of age. I reside in Opelousas.**

2d I do not know either of the parties to the suit

3d I knew Mr and Madame Despau when they resided in the parish of St Landry, but do not recollect the exact period of their residence in said parish Madame Despau left here for New Orleans, but her residence since I know not. I myself have always resided in Opelousas, parish St Landry

4th Madame Despau was my neighbor I saw her almost every Sunday She bore a good and respectable character.

5th I know nothing

Cross Interrogatories

First cross interrogatory. I was never in the city of New Orleans

2d I was born in the parish of St Landry I do not know in what year I was born tho' I am seventy-seven years of age I was never married

3d I speak of my own knowledge She was my neighbor for several years, and no one could know her character better than I

4th Madame Despau visited and associated with the best families at the post of of Opelousas She associated as other ladies, and was equally respected by both sexes My means were limited as I visited seldom public places, yet I have never heard anything as coming from lady or gentleman reflecting upon Madam Despau's character

5th Of this I cannot say anything

6th I know nothing I never was in New Orleans.

7th Of this I know nothing

8th I cannot—inasmuch as I was never in the city.

9th I know not I do not remember these dates.

9th I do not recollect during what year she resided in the parish of St Landry It is the only place where I knew her

10th I recollect three—Sophie, Meranthe, and a son they were tolerably grown the reason why I recollect them—her children were with her here, they left for New Orleans with her, Meranthe and the son are dead, Sophie, I am informed, survives, and lives at Biloxi. I know not if Mr. and Mrs Despau were ever separated

11th I know not.

12th I do not.

13th. I nothing know, and have never heard anything of the matter   MARGUERITE CHRETIEN

Appeared also, this 22d day of October, 1849, Mr Jean J. Louaillier, who answers as follows, to wit

To first interrogatory in chief I am sixty-nine years of age. **I reside in the parish of St. Landry, near the village of Opelousas.**

2d I am not acquainted with the parties to this suit

3d. I am   I made her acquaintance during her residence in this parish about the year of 1809, to the best of my recollection She left this parish for New Orleans   since then, I know not of my own knowledge where she has resided   I myself have resided at my present abode

4th Her character was always good whilst I knew her.

5th I cannot

Cross Interrogatories

First cross interrogatory Never

2d. At Paris   In July, 1780   I have been married to Marie Celise Carriere

3d. From my own knowledge

4th She associated with the best families in this country — I speak of my own knowledge and observation.   I visited her residence almost every week.

5th It is not probable.

6th I know not

7th I do not

8th. I cannot, never having resided there

8th I know not

9th I knew and associated with her during her residence in this parish only

10th I knew but two daughters. She did   Only one survives   Madam Moréjon   She resides alternately at New Orleans and Biloxi as I am informed.   I know not

11th. Never, to my knowledge

12th. I do not.

13th. Of this I know nothing

J. J LOUAILLIER

Appeared, also, this 23d day of October 1849, Madam Marie C Carrière, wife of Jean J Louaillier, who answers as follows, to wit

To first cross interrogatory: I am fifty-one years of age, and reside near Opelousas.

2d I do not

3d Yes   Whilst she resided with my father at Opelousas, about the year 1808, or thereabouts.   Subsequently she resided both at Philadelphia and Havana.   I was in correspondence with her whilst she was at those places   She now resides at Biloxi   I have always resided near Opelousas.

4th. It was always good

5th Nothing.

Cross interrogatories.

To the 1st cross interrogatory. I was born in Néw Orleans, but left there before I could recollect

2d In New Orleans, in 1798, in the month of July Yes I have been married to J J Louaillier He still lives, and we have always lived together

3d Of my own knowledge

4th The best society I speak from my own knowledge We resided together seven years

5th It is not probable

6th I know not.

7th I do not.

8th I have not resided there since infancy

8th I do not

9th Yes

10th She had four children She raised her children Sophie, her daughter, alone survives She resides at Biloxi Her son went to sea young and has not since been heard from He is supposed to be dead I know not

11th Never to my knowledge

12th I do not

13th I know nothing, nor have heard anything of this matter before   MARIE C LOUAILLIER

The witnesses who have been examined by me as heretofore stated, having signed their names to the testimony, I have closed the process verbal of the taking of such depositions, which are hereunto annexed to the commission, the whole of which are enclosed, sealed and directed to Ed Randolph, Esq, Clerk of the Circuit Court of the United States, for the Judicial Circuit holding sessions in and for the Eastern District of Louisiana In testimony whereof I have hereunto signed my name this 23d day of October, 1849   E. H MARTIN.

Filed Nov 29 1849

By virtue of a commission issued from the Circuit Court of the United States for the Fifth Judicial Circuit, holding sessions in and for the Eastern District of Louisiana, addressed to me in the name of W H Martin, for the purpose of taking the testimony of certain witnesses therein named, which when taken, to be read in evidence in behalf of the plaintiff in the cause where Myra Clark Gaines is plaintiff, and Relf, Chew, et al are defendants, which commission is dated at New Orleans, November 6th 1849 I, E H Martin, of the town of Opelousas, parish St Landry, have caused to appear before me the witnesses hereinafter named at the dates herein specified, who, being first duly sworn, answered to the interrogatories and cross interrogatories accompanying said commission as stated hereafter, appeared Mr Lastie Dupre, this 13th day of November, 1849, who answers as follows, to wit.

To first interrogatory. I am fifty-four years of age, and reside in the parish of St Landry.

2d No

3d I knew her when I was about eleven years of age first—I knew her intimately well for about ten or eleven years thereafter I have always resided in the parish of St Landry Where she resided after she left this parish, I know not, of my own knowledge

4th I have always known her as an honest woman I visited her frequently, and she visited my relations

5th I know nothing further

Cross Interrogatories

1st I resided six months in New Orleans, but Madame Despau resided here at that time

2d I was born as before stated, in St Landry I am a married man

3d I speak of my own knowledge

4th She was received as a lady of character at all public and private places with both sexes

5th It is possible

6th I know not

7th I have not known or heard any such thing

8th I know none

9th I do not recollect dates sufficiently well to state if I ever knew

9th It was since then I knew her in the parish of St Landry

10th I knew but three whilst she resided here Sophie is the only that I know who survives She was my first sweetheart. I know not if Madame Despau separated from her husband

11 Never to my knowledge

12. I do not

13th. Of this I know nothing

LASTIE DUPRE.

Appeared this 16th day of November, 1849, Mr Cyprien Dupré, who answered as follows, to wit

First interrogatory in chief I will be forty-eight years of age the 18th of the present month I reside in the parish of St. Landry

2d I do not

3d I knew her as well as recollected about the years 1810 and 1811. Since Madam Despau left this parish I do not know of my own knowledge where she has resided. With the exception of two or three years which I spent in New Orleans at school, I have always resided in the parish of St. Landry.

4th. I have heard nothing derogatory to her character whilst she resided in the Parish of St Landry, or since she removed from thence

5th I cannot

Cross interrogatories

1st I went to New Orleans in 1817 and returned in 1819 — I resided with Mr Delacourt, at the corner of Burgundy, and, I believe, St Louis Streets. She kept a school

2d I was born in the Parish of St Landry, and am a married man, having always resided happily with my wife, Marcelite Geudy

4th I knew her intimately well. She resided about a mile and a half from my father's house. I speak of my own knowledge, when I say she bore a good character in this Parish

4th She visited the *best* families in the parish of St Landry, and was esteemed equally by both sexes in the best company.

5th It is possible, but not probable

6th I know not

7th. I do not

8th I did not know Madam Despau in New Orleans.

8th I know not

9th I associated in the same society with Madam Despau, when I knew her in the Parish of St. Landry

10th When she resided here, I recollect but two children— Sophie and Madam Poincy, then a widow. I know not if any of her children survive of my own knowledge. I do not know if Madam Despau was separated from her husband.

11th I know not.

12th I do not

13th Of this I know nothing

CYP DUPRE

Appeared, this 18th day of November 1849, Mr Etienne Lamorandier, who answered as follows, to wit

To first interrogatory I am fifty-two years of age, and reside in the Parish of St Landry

2d I do not

3d I knew Madame Despau well when I was about ten years of age. I boarded with her, and went to school to her about three years when she resided in this Parish. After she left here I know not, of my own knowledge, where she has resided. I myself have always resided in the Parish of St Landry

4th I have always known her as a perfectly honest woman. She was well esteemed by all. At all *reunions* amongst the most respectable families, she was the first to be invited

5th. I know nothing further

Cross interrogatories

1st I never resided in New Orleans

2d I was born in the Parish of St Landry. I am a married man I have always resided with my wife, Felicite Robin since my marriage

3d I speak of my own personal knowledge and acquaintance with her

4th She associated with the best families in the Parish, and was respected by both gentlemen and ladies My means of knowing were, as stated before that I resided with her family

5th I think not

6th I know not

7th I have not

8th I know not I never resided in New Orleans

8th I, I knew, I do not recollect I was then quite young

9th I resided with her after that period, as before stated

10th I knew but three She took care of them whilst I was acquainted with her I know but one living Her name is Sophie The last time I saw her she was in New Orleans — I know not where she resides of my own knowledge I do not know Her husband was not with her when I knew her I know not if he was dead or alive

11th Not to my knowledge

12th I do no

13th Of this I know nothing

ETNE LAMORANDIER

Appeared, this 18th day of November 1849 Madam Marguerite Gradrego, widow Etienne Lamorandier

First Interrogatory I am about seventy-two years of age — I reside in the Parish of St Landry

2d I do no

3d I am well acquainted with Madam Despau My first acquaintance with her was in this Parish The date of its commencement I do not recollect I know not, of my own knowledge, where Madam Despau has resided since she left here My residence has always been in this Parish

4th She was considered an estimable woman when she resided here

5th I cannot

Cross Interrogatories

1st I never resided in New Orleans.

2d I was born in Point Coupee I was married to Etienne Lamorandier pere in the Parish of St. Landry He is now dead. We lived together during his lifetime

3d I speak of the character of Madam Despau, from personal knowledge of her character

4th I refer to the best families then living in this Parish — She was well considered and received by both sexes I frequently met with her in society and at public assemblies, such as at balls dinners &c

5th I think not

6th I did not know Madam Despau in New Orleans

7th I do not

8th I cannot

8th Cross interrogatory I do recollect, if I ever knew

9th It was since the year 1800 that Madame Despau resided in this parish where I knew her

10th She had seven or eight She raised them herself as I recollect I knew but Sophie, who now lives I am told she lives at Biloxi They were separated, for what reason I know not

11th Never to my knowledge

12th I do not

13th I know nothing

Her mark ✗ MARGUERITE GRADNEGO,
Veuve Lamorandier

Appeared, Marie Louise Fontenot, widow Garrigues Flaujac the 21st day of November, 1849

1st interrogatory I am sixty two years of age and reside in the parish of St Landry

2d. I do not

3d I knew Madame Despau whilst she resided in this parish, where I formed her acquaintance it was about forty years ago, as well as I can recollect Since she left this parish, I do not know where she has resided I have always resided in the parish of St Landry

4th She bore a good and respectable name whilst I knew her

5th I do not

Cross interrogatories

1st I never resided in New Orleans

2d I was born in the parish of St Landry the year I do not recollect I was married to Garrigues Flaujac, deceased, late of the parish of St Landry We lived happy together during his lifetime

3d I speak of my own knowledge.

4th She was respected and visited by the best families. My means of knowing were, that I met her frequently in society She was esteemed both by gentlemen and ladies

5th I do not know

6th I do not know.

7th I do not know

8th I cannot, as I never resided there.

8th. I do not recollect.

9th I knew her here since that time

10th. I do not but three, two girls and a boy The son was not with her here, although I was informed she had a son elsewhere I do not know if she raised or supported them Madame Moréjon is the only one who survives, as I am informed I do not know where Madame Moréjon resides. *I heard* they were separated, the reason I do not know.

11th Not to my knowledge.

12th I dot not

13th Of this I know nothing.

Her mark ✕ MARIE LOUISE FOUTENOT,
Veuve Garrigues Flaujac.

Appeared, this 24th day of November, 1849, Madam Sydalise Thompson, who answers as follows, to wit

1st interrogatory I am fifty-eight years of age, and reside in the parish of St. Landry.

2d I do not know either of the parties

3d I knew Madame Despau when she resided here, parish St Landry It was here I formed her acquaintance I was about twelve years old at the time Since she left here I do not know where she has resided My residence has always been here

4th Her reputation was good whilst here. She was an intimate friend of my mother and aunt.

5th. I know nothing more

Cross interrogatories

1st I never resided in New Orleans.

2d I was born in the parish of St Landry The year I do not recollect I was married to John Thompson He is now dead We always lived together during his lifetime after our marriage

3d Of my own knowledge

4th She associated with the best families here I speak of her reputation as being known to both ladies and gentlemen. My means of knowing were, that she resided near the plantation of my father, and she having a daughter about the same age as myself, I went frequently to see the family

5th I do not know

6th. I do not know

7th. I do not know, nor have I heard any such report

8th I never resided in New Orleans, as before stated

8th. I cannot recollect these dates, I was quite young at those epochs

9th I knew her after that period in this parish

10th I knew but three, she may have had more children, as well as I can recollect, she gave the same attention to her children as other mothers do　Her daughter Sophie alone survives I do not know where Sophie resides.　I do not know if Madame Despau ever separated from her husband.

11th. Never to my knowledge.

12th I do not

13th Of this I know nothing.

SYDALISE THOMPSON

Appeared, this 24th day of November, 1849, Madam Theotiste Roy, widow Jacques Dupre, who answered as follows, to wit.

1st interrogatory　I am seventy-six years of age, and reside in the parish of St Landry.

2d I do not.

3d I knew her whilst she resided in the Parish of St Landry I formed her acquaintance about the year 1810, in this parish. I do not know where she has resided since　I, myself, have always resided here

4th Her character was good whilst I knew her.

5th I do not

Cross interrogatories.

1st Never

2d In Point Coupee　I came to this parish at the age of seven years　I was born in the　1773, the 22d day of July.　I was married to the late Jacques Dupré　He is now dead　We lived happily together, during our marriage

3d I speak of my own knowledge

4th. I refer to the best society in our neighborhood.　I speak of her as regards both ladies and gentlemen　My means of knowing were, that I met her casually in society, and heard nothing against her character

5th I know not

6th I know not.

7th. I know not, nor have I heard it.

8th I cannot.

8th. I know not

9th I was since then　I knew, as before stated.

10th I knew but two—Madame Poincy and Madame Sophie Moréjon　She acted the part of a good mother, whilst I knew the family　I am told Sophie now lives.　Where she resides I know not, but am told she resides alternately at New Orleans and Biloxi. I know not if Madame Despau was parted from her husband

11th Not to my knowledge.

12th I do not

13th Of this I know nothing

her
THEOTISTE × ROY
mark
VEUVE JACQUES DUPRE

STATE OF LOUISIANA,)
  PARISH OF ST LANDRY   )

I, Edmund H Martin, of the parish of St Landry town of Opelousas, hereby certify, that the answers to the interrogatories and cross interrogatories, herein before contained were reduced to writing by me, as given and detailed by the witnesses who signed the same in my presence, either by writing their names or making their ordinary marks and having closed the process verbal of taking the deposition, have annexed the same to the commission, the whole of which are enclosed sealed and directed to the Clerk of the Court whence said commission was issued In testimony whereof, I have signed my name this 24th day of November, 1849   E H MARTIN

COMPLAINANT

Depositions of —1 Louis Bringier   2 Madame Marie Désirée Vignaud 3d Mrs M. S Outlaw   4 H S Harper 5 Madame Veuve Matias Alpuente 6 E F Brasier 7 James Gardette.

For complainant—Louis Bringier

And afterwards, to wit, on the 28th June, 1849, appeared Louis Bringier, a witness for complainant, who, being duly sworn, did depose and say

I am sixty-six years of age. I am surveyor general of Louisiana I was born in Louisiana, at Carrollton and have resided here ever since I have been a surveyor in this State since 1825 I know Mrs Gaines, the complainant, and Relf and Chew. I knew the late Daniel Clark I knew Mr. Rossignac when he was mayor here. He was a man of best standing, as I understood. I knew the family of Madame Rossignac, the Montiguts; they were one of the best families here at that time I have known Madame Despau for about ten or eleven years I have seen her now and then. She lives in Biloxi I know nothing against her charcter I never heard anything said against her character I always looked upon her as a lady of first respectability

I have known Madame Gardette since 1815 I dined with her in Philadelpia, in company with Louis Labranche and Zenon Roman it was on this occasion that I first made her acquaintance I thought she had a very fine establishment She had company of the first respectability Her husband, Gardette, was then living, and mingled in society of the first respectability in Philadelphia Dr Gardette had two or three daughters there at the time I know nothing of Madame Gardette at all When I hear any one spoken bad of, I never listen I know no one's business in the world Mr Zenon Roman, of whom I have spoken, and Mr Labranche, were of the first French families in the State The ex-Governor Roman, of this State, was in Philadelphia at the time referred to, and would have dined with us, but for business engagements which prevented him These gentlemen were in the habit of visiting the nouse of Madame Gardette when they went to Philadelphia

L BRINGIER

Cross examination

I frequently visited Mr Clark, at his house, on the Bayou Road It was I who brought those presents to him from Mexico gold medals from the Countess Perez Galvez—the Count de Casarol—the Count de Valenciana I went to Clark's one or two times to breakfast I was very intimate with Clark in 1802 and 1803 and 1801, and I visited his house in 1806 and 1807 I never saw a lady at his house as his wife I went there one or two times to breakfast—never took notice I never heard from him that he had a wife. I have been acquainted with Messrs Relf and Chew since 1802 and 1803 I never knew nothing against their reputation myself—as I told you before, I pay no attention to rumors I always found them fair in the dealings I had with them I was a near neighbor and intimate acquaintance of the late Alexander Milne, who died about ten or twelve years ago. It is in my knowledge that Mr Relf was one of his executors—and as such, was in possession of a large sum of money—but I do not know the amount I never heard any complaint against Mr Relf as executor Mr Milne had the greatest confidence in him

L. BRINGIER.

J W Gurley, Commissioner.

Madame Marie Désirée Vignaud—witness for complainant.

And afterwards, to wit, on the 29th June, 1849, came Madame Marie Désirée Vignaud, a person of sound mind and law.

...always appearing modestly... who... Life..., lives with
his sister, Mrs. Cail...... I have ... known M... e Despau,
of her visit to New Orleans, and on the visit I made to B.low...

J. S. OUTLAW

J. W. GURLEY, Com'r.

H. S. Harper——for Complainant

And afterwards, to wit on the 4th day of July, 1849, personally appeared Mr. H. S. Harper a witness on behalf of complainant a person of sound mind and of lawful age who, being duly sworn, did depose and say

I know the complainant in this suit, Mr. Cain. I was born in 1806, and I am now forty-three years of age. I reside in New Orleans. I am one of the inspectors of the Custom House. I know Madam Sophie Despau and Caroline. I became acquainted with her near Matanzas, in Cuba. She was then living with her son-in-law on his estate. I went to Cuba in 1817, and became acquainted with her immediately after my arrival there. She stood as highly in Cuba as any lady could; she mingled in the best society in that section of the country, and some of the most wealthy planters of the country lived there. She was received at parties there, and was reckoned among the elite. I have also known her since her return here. I have known her for several years past. I have always understood her reputation and standing here to be very good, have never heard anything to the contrary

H. S. HARPER

Cross Examination

I am the third child of my mother, Mrs. Harper, the late Mrs. Smith. I had a sister and brother older than myself. I think my sister was born in Philadelphia, and my brother in New Orleans. I do not know whether it was my brother or myself that my mother suckled with Mrs. Gaine. My sister of whom I have spoken my eldest sister is Widow Bartlette and my brother, of whom I have spoken, was Gustavus H. Harper, and is now dead. I lived with my brother-in-law in Cuba who was a coffee planter, and returned to New Orleans in 18... My father and Madame Despau and D. Fechasse, all lived in the neighborhood of Matanzas

H. S. HARPER

J. W. GURLEY, Commissioner

Madame Alpuente—for complainant

And afterwards, to wit on the 5th day of July, 1849, personally appeared Madame Veuve Marie Alpuente, a witness on behalf of complainant a person of sound mind and lawful age

who being sworn, did depose and say (P B Boisfontain.
sworn as interpreter)

My maiden name was Elizabeth Chouriach I am seventy
five years of age I reside in the parish of St Bernard, about
nine miles from the city of New Orleans I was born in the city
of New Orleans, and have always resided there except for the
last fifteen years that I have resided in the parish of St Bernard
I know Madame Despau, Madame DeG__ge, now Madame
Gardette, and Madame Caihavet all née Carriere I have known
them since I was eleven years of age The witness being asked
the standing of the Carriere family in society, when she knew
them, answers they were in a high respectable position Witness being asked the position in society which the ladies, she
has named, have always occupied answers they were highly respectable I have always known them to be highly respectable
and have always heard them so spoken of by all their acquaintances Madame Caihavet occupied a house directly opposite
mine in New Orleans at was here I first became acquainted
Madame DeGrange she was a sister to Madame D Grange
I was about twenty-two years of age at the period last spoken
of At the time I knew Madame Despau she came frequently
to my house I never heard anything said against her She
was visited by the first Creole ladies of that day I never knew
DeGrange I was told that he was very rich and that he kept
a confectionary store I cannot state at what time DeGrange
left New Orleans I was ill at the time Witness being asked
to state what she recollects of the events that transpired at about
the time DeGrange left New Orleans and the occasion of his
leaving says It was said that he left in consequence of the
arrival of the Havre of the woman he had formerly married.
The public generally pitied Mrs DeGrange his wife here and
were much incensed with DeGrange, for imposing upon her

                   VVE ALICENIE

J W Gurley, Com r

E F Brasier—for complainant

And afterwards, to wit on the 6th July, 1849, appeared Emi-
leus F Brasier, a witness on behalf of complainant a person of
sound mind and lawful age who being sworn, did depose and
say

I am just fifty years of age I was born in Philadelphia I
left Philadelphia in 1832, and came south I knew Doctor James
Gardette and his wife Madame Gardette, of Philadelphia Dr.
Gardette was a dentist I think I heard mentioned, that Madame Gardette was née Carriere At the time I knew Dr Gardette and his wife in Philadelphia they were looked upon as

genteel and respectable people, he was a man of eminence in his profession, and was thought to be wealthy. I cannot pretend to classify the kind of society they were in, and I was not sufficiently intimate to state altogether the peculiar nature of their acquaintance, but from all I can recollect, and be aware of, they went into good society, respectable society. I never heard the character of Madame Gardette called in question until I came to New Orleans, and in reference to these suits.

E F BRASIER

Cross Examination

I did not know Dr Gardette and his wife intimately, but I knew them very well. by 'intimately,' I mean, I did not visit there frequently. I cannot call to mind any one that visited there intimately and frequently. I cannot now recall what families respectable or otherwise, they visited. I have known Mr Gardette ever since I was a child. I can recollect Mrs Gardette for about the time of her marriage with Mr Gardette. I think the marriage must have occurred when I was about ten years of age. When I first knew Mr and Mrs Gardette, they lived in Walnut street below Third. They subsequently went to live at the corner of Chestnut and Ninth street.

Q. You have spoken of Mr Gardette's wealth, please state how he was ...

A. ... I believe I expressed he was wealthy because he had ... a respectable profession of dentist. I did not know Mrs Gardette ... but I heard she came from ... I was too young to know how long she had been in Philadelphia before she married Mr ... whether Mr and Mrs Gardette ... absence the year previous ... Virginia, Philadelphia ... having been absent ... recollection not ... as respects ...

... Mrs Garde ... that at ... marriage. He had ... and his ... no intimately ... name of the last Mrs Gardette when she ... a man of that name Mr Gilbert ...

An____ I did not know. But the lady I saw in New Orleans
in 1812, is the same lady I saw in Philadelphia.

                                C. P. BRASIER.

J. W. GURLEY, Commissioner.

No. 2. December term 18__

MANDATE SUPREME COURT UNITED STATES

Patterson vs Gaines.
Ordered by complainants, and filed 25th June, 1849.

                J. W. GURLEY, Commissioner.

Filed 11th April 1848,

                ED. RANDOLPH, Clerk.
        By J. G. A. HOIT, Deputy Clerk.

Decree ordered June 26th, 1848.

                DOWNS, Deputy Clerk.

UNITED STATES OF AMERICA, SS.

The President of the United States of America.

To the honorable the Judge of the Circuit Court of the United
[L. S.] States for the Eastern District of Louisiana greeting.

Whereas lately, in the Circuit Court of the United States for
the Eastern District of Louisiana, before you, or some of
you, in a cause between Edmund P. Gaines and Myra
Clark Gaines his wife, complainants, and Charles Patterson and
others defendant, the decree of the said Circuit Court was in
the following words, viz:

'This cause having come for final hearing, by consent of the
complainants, and the defendant Patterson, upon the bill, answer, replication, exhibits, depositions, and documents on file
herein, and on the admission of the parties that the estate in
controversy in this case exceeds in value the sum of two thousand dollars, and the said complainant, and the defendant, Patterson expressly waiving and dispensing with the necessity of
any other parties to the hearing or decision of this cause than
themselves and agreeing that the cause shall be determined
alone upon its merits, and the Court being now sufficiently advised of and concerning the premises, does finally decree and
order that the defendant, Patterson, do, on or before the first day
of the next term of this Court, convey and surrender possession
to the complainant, Myra Clark Gaines, all those lots or parcels
of land lying and being in the city of New Orleans, and particularly described in this answer and exhibits, and to which he

claims title under the said will of (1811) eighteen hundred and eleven said conveyance shall contain stipulations of warranty against himself only, and those claiming under him. It is further decreed and ordered that the defendant pay the complainants so much of their costs expended herein as has been incurred by reason of his being made a defendant in this cause.

As by the inspection of the transcript of the record of the said Circuit Court which was brought into the Supreme Court of the United States, by virtue of an appeal agreeably to the act of Congress, in such case made and provided fully, and at large appear.

And whereas in the present term of December, in the **year of** our Lord one thousand eight hundred and forty-seven, this appeal having been heard by this Court upon the transcript of the record from the Circuit Court of the United States for the Eastern District of Louisiana, and upon the arguments of Counsel, as well for the appellant as for the appellees this Court, upon consideration of the premises, doth now here adjudge, order, and decree that the decree of the said Circuit Court be and the same is hereby reversed with costs, and that the said Charles Patterson recover against the said complainants three hundred and fifty-nine dollars and nineteen cents, for his costs herein expended, and have execution therefor and that such other decree in the premises be passed as is hereinafter ordered and decreed.

And this Court thereupon proceeding to pass such decree in this cause as the said Circuit Court ought to have passed, doth now here adjudge order, and decree, that it be adjudged and declared and is hereby adjudged and declared upon the evidence in this cause, that a lawful marriage was contracted and solemnized at Philadelphia, in the State of Pennsylvania between the same Daniel Clark in the bill and proceedings mentioned, and the same Zulent or Zuliene Carriere in the bill and proceedings mentioned, and that Myra Clark, now Myra Clark Gaines, and one of the complainants in this cause, is the lawful and only issue of the said marriage and was, at the death of her said father, Daniel Clark, his only legitimate child and heir at law; and, as such, was exclusively invested with the character of his forced heir, and entitled to all the rights of such forced heir.

And this Court doth further adjudge, order, and decree, that all the property described and claimed by the defendant, Patterson, in his answer and supplemental answer, and in the exhibits thereto annexed, is part and parcel of the property composing the succession of said Daniel Clark that the defendants Richard Relf and Beverly Chew, at the time and times when under the pretended authority of the testamentary executors of the said Daniel Clark, and of attorneys in fact of the said Mary Clark, in the bill and pro-

ceedings mentioned, they caused the property so described and
claimed by the defendant Patterson, to be set up and sold at public auction in December, 1820 and when they executed their act
of sale, dated on the 18th February 1821 to Gabriel Correjolles
for the two lots therein described (which two lots constitute the
same property described and claimed by the defendant Patterson,
as aforesaid) had no legal right or authority whatever so to sell
and dispose of the same, or in any manner to alienate the same
that the said sale at auction and the said act of sale to Correjolles, in confirmation of the previous sale at auction were wholly
unauthorized and illegal and are utterly null and void and that
the defendant Patterson at the time and times when he purchased the property so described and claimed by him as aforesaid, (part from the said Correjolles the vendee of the defendants
Relf and Chew and the residue from Etienne Mesnier, the vendee of said Correjolles himself the vendee of the same defendants,) was bound to take notice of the circumstances which rendered the actings and doings of the said defendants in the premises illegal null and void and that he ought to be deemed and
held, and hereby is deemed and held, to have purchased the property in question with full notice that the said sale at auction
under the pretended authority of the said defendants and the
said act of sale to Correjolles, were illegal null and void and
in fraud of the rights of the person or persons entitled to the
succession of the said Daniel Clark.

And the Court doth further adjudge order and decree that
all the property claimed and held by the defendant Patterson as
aforesaid, now remains unaliened and undisposed of as parts
and parcel of the succession of the said Daniel Clark, notwithstanding such sale at auction and act of sale as the added
right or under the pretended authority of the defendants Relf
and Chew.

And the Court doth further adjudge order and decree, that the
complainant Myra Clark Gaines is justly and lawfully entitled
as the only forced heir of said Daniel Clark, to her legitimate
portion of four-fifths of the said succession, and to have four-
fifths of the property so claimed and held by the defendant Patterson, as aforesaid, duly partitioned, assigned and delivered,
or paid over to her together with four-fifths of the yearly rents
and profits accruing from the same, since the same came into the
said defendant's possession, and for which the said defendants is
hereby adjudged, ordered, and decreed to account to the said
complainant.

And the Court doth now here remand this cause to the said
Circuit Court for such further proceeding as may be proper and

necessary to carry into effect the following directions; that is to say

1 To cause the said defendant, Patterson, forthwith to surrender all the property so claimed and held by him, as aforesaid, into the hands of such curator, commissioner, or trustee, as the said Court may appoint for the purpose whose duty it shall be, under the directions of the Court, to manage the said property to the best advantage all the whole matter and apportionment of the said two portions (being the said 4–5 and 1–5) of the said property shall have been completed and finally liquidated as a part of the succession of the said Daniel Clark, and in the meantime to collect and receive all the rents, issues and profits of the same and to account and bring the same into Court, to be there apportioned and paid over, or in part retained for further directions

2 To cause a complete of the property, so claimed and held by the said defendant Patterson as aforesaid, to be duly partitioned, apportioned and delivered or paid over to the said complainant and account and in the same subject to further direction for said property of the same which other party shall be at may move or in case the same be proved and found indivisible that the same cannot be conveniently divided, to cause it to be sold by public auction after the time of notice and advertisement and as near as may be, in the manner prescribed by law of the judicial sale of the property or successions and, in case of such sale by auction, to apportion and pay over four-fifths of the net proceeds of such sale to the said complainant and to retain the residue subject to further directions, as aforesaid

3 To cause an account to be taken by the proper officer of the court, and under the authority and direction of the court, of the yearly rents and profits accrued and accruing from the said property since it came into the possession of the defendant Patterson and four-fifths of the same to be accounted and paid to the said complainant, and the residue to be retained subject to such further directions, as aforesaid

4 To give such directions and make such orders, from time to time, as may be proper and necessary for carrying into effect the foregoing directions, and for enforcing the due observance of the same by the parties and the officers of the court.

You therefore, are hereby commanded that such execution and further proceedings be had in said cause in conformity to the opinion and decree of this court as according to right and justice and the laws of the United States ought to be had, the said appeal notwithstanding Witness the Honorable Roger B Taney, Chief Justice of said Supreme Court, the first Mon-

day of December in the year of our Lord one thousand eight
hundred and forty seven

Cost of Petitioner—Clerk's $9 15 .... Cost.....—$372 77
Paxed by   WM. THOS. CARROLL
Clerk of the Supreme Court of the United States

Statement of property belonging to Daniel Clark, including
sums owing to him for lands sold, &c &c

DEBTS			
		J. Mignon,	1 200
John McDonough,	$110 000	H. Turner & Co	32 000
Henry Hunt,	13 000		
Remy's estate	12 000		$330 873
George Hart,	7 000	Lots sold on the Bayou	
Benjamin Farar	12 500	road	117 640
Patrick Walsh,	1 500		
Charles Mawdesley	4 000	Dollars	448 513
James Wilson	4 000	Lands and slaves Hou-	
Edward Turner	8 000	mas estate and 100	
Pierre Derbigny	3 860	slaves	170 000
Jean Mercier,	1 538	Sugo and 100 slaves	110 000
Robert Semple,	6 000	Half of Clarksville and	
J. Winfrey,	1 200	30 do	2 000
Adon Sides	800	Houmas Point estate,	
Joseph LeBlanc	4 000	advances made on	
Thomas Power	8 000	and payment on	300 000
James Brown,	1 500	12 000 acres of land in	
D C Dier,	1 350	Ouachita,	52 000
C Keyser,	1 600	40 000 Bilhol claim	16 000
Carmie La Tour,	5 000	5 000 in Opelousas	5 000
Seth Lewis and W			
Turner,	18 000	Dollars	863 513
Isaac Guion,	6 000	8 500 acres in the Ba-	
		you Boeuf	8 700
Dollars	268 448	Plantation on the Ger-	
		man coast, 13 1-2	
		acres front	10 000
Brought forward,	$268 448	Do on the Fourche 6	
Robert Munson,	1 000	acres front	3 000
Pierre Biron and C		Do on the Mississippi	
Ment	11 600	1 league above the	
Jacques Bieu,	875	Fourche, 11 acres	
D Boulignv	10 500	front,	1 000
John Morris	1 750	Land at Terre aux	
James Storrell	5 200	Boeuffs	7 500

10,000 acres on waters of Thompson's creek,	20,000	for the present, only estimated at 30,000
180 acres on the canal of Carondelet and extending to the Bayou road, now selling in lots, and		House on the Bayou road, 12,000
		Dollars, 967,013

On the whole of the above landed property and slaves, I owe but $5,500   DANIEL CLARK.

New Orleans, 27th February, 1810.

———

STATE OF LOUISIANA, FIRST DISTRICT

PETITION OF CHEW AND RELF)
AND CLARK'S EXECUTORS, }
vs }
THEIR CREDITORS)

To the honorable the Judge of the said District, the petition of Beverly Chew and Richard Relf, acting for themselves, and as executors of the last will and testament of Daniel Clark Esq., deceased, of the city of New Orleans, respectfully showeth

That owing to the peculiarity of the times, the scarcity of money, and the stagnation of commerce arising from the oppressive political condition in which the United States have for some time been involved, as well as from the peculiar nature of their estate, they find it utterly impossible to produce, either from sales or from collection, a sufficiency of ready money to meet their debts as they become due.

They represent, that although they believe the assets to be very abundant to discharge every debt due and owing to them, and to leave a large surplus to themselves and the heirs of the late Daniel Clark, yet they are apprehensive that if sales are coerced at this time for payments for ready money or even at short credits, the whole landed and mortgaged property would be sacrificed at merely a nominal price by which means speculators might enrich themselves on the ruin of your petitioners and to the great loss of their creditors. Your petitioners further represent to your honor that they deem it their bounden duty, as well to the creditors as to the heirs of the said estate to claim of them a respite from the payment of their debts and from all suits and prosecutions for the same until they can bring into action the vast sums that are in the hands of debtors, residing in various parts of this State and the Mississippi Territory, and until they can call to their aid the proceeds of the large tracts of uncultivated lands which belong to them, on sales to be made on such credit as will insure a fair price

To this end, they pray your honor, the premises considered, to order a meeting of their creditors to take place, after the usual delay and notice, in John Lynd's notary's office in this city to take into their consideration the affairs of the said estates and the objects of this petition, when and where your petitioners will be ready to make a full exposition of the situation in which the affairs of the estate are involved, and inasmuch as your petitioners are threatened with law suits, which would be a useless expenditure of the moneys of the estate, they pray that all such proceedings against them may be stayed, &c., and annex hereto a schedule &c., but as the same is not complete, they reserve the privilege of rendering a supplementary schedule in due time

Signed,   TURNER, P. Qe

PARISH OF ORLEANS

Richard Relf maketh oath that all the material facts and allegations contained and set forth in the foregoing petition are true, to the best of his knowledge and belief

Signed,   RICHARD RELF.

New Orleans, March 2d, 1814.

Sworn to before me,

Signed,   JOHN P SANDERSON,
                                    Justice of the Peace.

STATE OF LOUISIANA,
       First Judicial District Court

I certify the foregoing petition and affidavit to be copies from the originals on file in the office of the clerk of this court, as the matter of Chew and Relf for themselves, and as executors of Daniel Clark *vs.* Their Creditors, No. 412 of the docket of this court

Signed,   P L. BLANC [L S]
                                    Deputy Clerk

Clerk's Office, 22d April, 1840.

———

Deposition of James Gardette, and documents offered by complainant

Be it remembered, that on this 23d June, 1849, the complainant offered in evidence and filed the following documents, to wit

1 Deposition of Joseph D D Bellechasse, taken in the suit of W. W. Whitney and wife vs Relf, Chew, et al, taken in this cause, No 122, in this Court, opened and filed agreeably to rule of Court, 7th December, 1837

2 Testimony of Pierre Baron Boisfontaine, taken in the probate court, parish and city of New Orleans, in the suit of W. W Whitney and Myra his wife vs. Ellena O'Bearne et al, No 843, of the docket of said suit, filed in this cause in this court, April 25th, 1840

3 Testimony of Colonel Samuel B Davis and Mary Ann Rose Davis, his wife, taken in suit of W W Whitney and Myra, his wife, vs Ellena O'Bearne et al in the probate court of parish and city of New Orleans, No 843 of docket of said court, filed in this court, April 25th, 1840

4 Testimony of Madame Louise Benguerel, taken in suit of W W Whitney and wife vs Ellena O'Bearne et al, No 843, of the docket of the court of probates for parish and city of New Orleans, filed in this court 25th April, 1840

5 Testimony of Mrs Harriet Smith, taken in this cause by Charles A. Folsom, justice of the peace of Hancock county, Mississippi, on the 14th day of May, 1846

6 Testimony of Ellen Guman and others, taken in this cause by Alexander Gardiner, U S commissioner for the Southern district of New York, on the 9th May, 1846

7 Deposition of C W Dreschler, taken in this cause on the 25th April, 1840, and filed in this cause same day

8 Certificate of Antonio Argote Villalobos, filed in this cause April 25th, 1840

9 Certificate of W. C C Claiborne, dated New Orleans, 25th April 1840, and filed in this cause the same day

10 Certificate of Eugene Lasere, filed in this cause, 25th April 1840

11. Petition of Francois Dussuau Delacroix, filed in the court of probates for the parish and city of New Orleans, August 18th, 1813

12 Decree and mandate from United States Supreme Court, entitled Patterson vs Gaines and wife, on appeal, rendered December term, 1847, filed in this court 11th April, 1848.

13 Statement made by Daniel Clark, in his own hand writing, of his private affairs, dated New Orleans, 27th February, 1810

Letters offered by Complainant

And on this 23d day of June, 1849, the complainant introduced the following letters, which, under the stipulation on file, are admitted to be genuine

Defendants reserve all legal exceptions

1 Letter from Mrs Ann Relf to Daniel Clark, dated Philadelphia, 20 June, 1795.

2 Letter from Daniel Clark, to Chew and Relf, 11 March, 1802

3 Letter from Daniel W Coxe to Chew and Relf, dated 7th April 1 1802 Also, one other from the same to the same, dated Philadelphia, 22 September 1802 Also, one other from the same to the same, dated Philadelphia, 15 November, 1802.— All referring to the same subject matter.

4 Letter from Daniel W Coxe to Daniel Clark dated Philadelphia, 11 June, 1802

5 Letter from Daniel Clark to Chew and Relf dated Balize, 29 June, 1802

6 Letter Daniel W Coxe to Daniel Clark Philadelphia, 1 July, 1802

7. Letter dated Plaquemine, 7 June, 1803, from Richard Relf to D Clark

8 Letter dated Philada. 5 Jan'y 1805 D W C, to ———

9 Letter dated Philadelphia 6 Jan'y, 1808, from D W. C to Daniel Clark

10. Letter dated Philadelphia, 16 July, 1807, from D W Coxe to Dan. Clark

11 Letter dated New Orleans, 28 Oct, 1809, from Richard Relf to Daniel Clark

12 Letter dated Philadelphia. 9 Feb'y, 1808, from J. H Imlay to Mr Clark

13 Letter dated Philada 12 July 1810 from D W C to —.

14 Letter dated New Orleans, 9 Feb'y, 1810, from Dan Clark to Thomas Wilkins, Esqr

15 Letter dated Philadelphia 20 April, 1810, from W. F Hulings to Dan Clark

16 Letter dated Philadelphia, 20 Sept'r, 1810, from D. W Coxe to D Clark

17 Letter dated Philada 19 May, 1812 from Eliza Clark to Daniel Clark

[No 1]   PHILADELPHIA, June 20th, 1795

Sir—It will not appear improper to you, sir, that a mother, acquainted with your uninterested kindness to a son, should endeavor to express the sincerity of her gratitude for the generous obligation   g, sir, after hearing of the improper situation of Richard and the contracted trade of Mr Hulings, has more tended to ease my anxious apprehensions, than the account of his having entered into your employment

Placed in a foreign country, unknown, unfriended, young and helpless, your timely favors have supported him
midst of his difficulties, and when all his prosperous hopes seemed to vanish, your generous friendship enlivened him   Next to his being in your service, my most fervent wish is, that as he is young and inexperienced   ill condescend to instil into his mind the principles of a man of honor and integrity   But I need not attempt to request of you that which every man of your character will readily perform, as thro' an instinct of duty   Your past favors to Richard convinces me that   hopes for a continuance of his g   conduct will insure a contin
also of your patronage and friendship

   With grateful respect, I am, sir, &c

        ANN RELF

[No 2]   PHILADELHHIA, 11th March, 1802.
 Messrs Chew & Relf—Gentlemen   Mr Pershouse, of the house of Clegg & Pershouse, of Manchester, being desirous of trying your market, has requested an introduction to some respectable house in Orleans, and I have recommended yours as the most likely to give him satisfaction. I request you will attend to any business he may commit to your care, and punctually follow his orders with respect to remittances. I have no doubt of your dispositions to serve your friend, and, confident of every exertion being made use of in their behalf ,and of your integrity, I have offered Mr Pershouse, to guarantee all transactions between you and them, and flatter myself the present will be but the beginning of a more extensive and advantageous intercourse between you   I remain, with esteem, gentlemen,

      Your most obedient servant,

        DANIEL CLARK

[No 3]   PHILADELPHIA, 7th April, 1802
 Gentlemen—Since my last I have received your letter of the 19th February and 2d ult   I regret extremely the measure you have adopted of sending the New York to this port, which will be attended with great delay, and request you will, in future, unless you hear from Messrs Green or Barclay to the contrary, send my ships to Liverpool direct   Cotton is admitted, by order of council, free of duty, but I was doubtful of the measure, and until lately could not with certainty advise you   Whenever a change takes place, you will be informed of it by the Messrs Greens, who will in future give you ample information on every subject that comes within their knowledge   On the subject of frauds committed in packing cotton they will write you, and they advise their intention of forwarding certificates of the old marks

and numbers of the bales, with samples of the quality   I hope you will expose the villains, and if the fraud has been committed in the Natchez, have the gin advertised as an example , if in your own country, apply to the Governor for redress.

The molasses, by the Sophia, was of excellent quality, but by the annexed sale, you will perceive that it is a ruinous business, you must not, on any account, until I advise you to the contrary, give more than 25 cents per gallon on board, including casks With respect to sugar, you must not exceed 5 cents per lb., if purchased for my account, and they must be of the very best quality and no other, as inferior sugars will not sell here   You mention that you had taken molasses in payment for sugar works , was it for any sold since 1st November last, or before By the advices I had previously received, I knew of but one payment to be made in produce, and that was by a Mr Hanchicope   You are certainly under no obligation to receive any more, and you must not do it, unless at such prices as will, at least, leave no loss   The molasses, I perceive, has overrun the measurement, which will pay a part of the charges, but the duty and freight are entirely lost   I believe I before recommended to you to measure molasses by the French velt in preference to our gauge, and you would do well to attend to it   You would also do well, whenever you have molasses filled as the sugar works, to let the casks remain a night in the cool air, and measure them in the morning, as the filling causes it to ferment and increases the measurement

I am glad the charter of the Matilda has not been effected, she would have been loaded at Mobile with casks of peltries of a large size, which she would not stow to advantage, and would consequently have made a very small freight   I effected no insurance on her, and you will, therefore, have nothing to demand on that account of the freighters

April 22d   The schr. Eliza, on board which Mr Clark has taken passage, goes to-morrow morning for your port, and takes an invoice of goods to your address of about $27,000. She will probably reach you before this letter.

Your assured friend,
D W. COXE

Messrs. Chew & Relf

[No 4.]   PHILADELPHIA, June 11, 1802
DEAR CLARK —The brig Harriet, in which your father's family came passengers, arrived 5 days ago, at the Lazaretto, and they are all well, tho', unfortunately, will be obliged to ride out the quarantine of fifteen days from the time of anchoring, notwithstanding all my exertions and interest made with the Board of

Health to permit them to land   I even presented a request to the Board, before they arrived, for leave to land, I was answered, that leave might possibly be granted if the vessel, on her arrival, proved healthy   On her arrival, I repeated my supplications, with every prospect of success, the President of the Board being in my favor; but as the law is pointed against such indulgences, I was frustrated, altho I offered to give bonds under any penalty that they should not come within the city for any length of time that might be prescribed   All the indulgence I could obtain was permission to visit and converse with one of them on shore, for an hour, which I did the day before yesterday, when I saw your mother, who was better able to leave the vessel than your father, owing to his rheumatism   I satisfied your mother fully of the necessity of your returning to New Orleans, and convinced her of the uncertainty we were all in of the family coming to Philadelphia, indeed, both Huling's and Chew's letters to you, received a short time previous to the arrival of the Harriet, were conclusive as to the determination of your family to remain at New Orleans   'Twas not till I received duplicates of the Harriet's letters, per the Br Samuel, (10 days since,) that I knew of their coming

Some previous intimation ought to have been given, and a faster sailing vessel to have been selected, as the Harriet had 3 months passage out to Orleans, and was well known to be a very dull sailer   However, they are now arrived, and in good health, and every care and attention shall be paid them   I have just succeeded in obtaining permission for your aunt to visit them, to-morrow, when she will go down   Our plan is, at present, to take lodgings at Germantown or Frankford for your aunt and them, for the summer, as *we* are *all* of opinion that it will be best not to be precipitate in deciding on a permanent residence, respecting which I consulted your mother, fully. For the present, they are provided with all necessary comforts and fresh provisions, and will be at liberty in 10 days, before which time, your aunt and myself will have prepared lodgings for them and herself

As they are fully satisfied of the necessity of your return to Louisiana, they are likewise aware, from the extent of your concerns, and apprehensions of the French going to New Orleans, that you may not be back for some months, so that on that score you may be perfectly easy

The determination of your aunt to make one of their family will be highly consoling and satisfactory, both to them and me

In regard to business, I refer you to my letter to C and R, of this date, and will add some information for yourself. I got through my heavy payment last month, being altogether about $95,000, by means of shifts, contrivances, and drawing

This month, I have $50,000 to pay, and about $45,000 to $50,000 the next In August, my payments will be very heavy There will be near $30,000 within one week, being Butler's acceptance for $12,700, and sundry other drafts of C and R, and Turner falling due together I imagine the total may be $90,000 for that month Barclay cautions me to draw sparingly on account of the bad cotton and low prices of the good, which was only 16 to 17d, the 1st May The measure of accepting 4 days per bill payable per the Ohio and T Martin, seems best, tho' my own funds are thereby kept back, but it leaves in your power the detection of the frauds that have been practised in the cotton, which I feel convinced the arrival of the A French and Thomas, with the proofs and certificates and sales of the bad marks, will enable you to effect, in which case you will be able to reject the cotton bought high, and yet to be delivered, and to buy afterwards at very reduced prices

I have uniformly opened all letters to you, perused and re-sealed them, to be laid by for you, whereby I have obtained some necessary information I have thought proper to forward Huling's statement of his difficulties with the S Government to the Secretary of State I will take some able medical opinion on Mr Dunbar's case of a strangury, &c, and forward it to him, as he requests you I shall write to Turner not to go higher than 16 cts for cotton, and to be careful in the quality of the cotton on account of the frauds and you doubtless will make public in the most impressive manner the information forwarded you by Green & Son The Definitive Treaty will, I trust, affect the price of goods favorably at Orleans, and I should prefer your obtaining good prices on credit, to sacrificing for cash. If sugars are cheap and good, 'twould answer to send back the Sophie here with a cargo of them, putting cotton on deck The parcel shipped by George, per brig Friendship, brought 10 3-4 dollars the charges you are acquainted with I presume, by the tenor of Barclay's letters, that the Indian goods will go out in the Thomas which Green says is waiting for the goods ordered by him The Gen Washington was spoken well the 16th ult, long. 54, lat 38. The freight per Matilda wont pay her disbursements on the voyage. Chew and R are silent on the subject of the suplus articles of nails, Russia and Raven's duck and R. and F.'s cordage which twas expected the intendant would take.

T Brunet has behaved infamously, as from letter to C. and R

From the enclosed extracts from our newspapers, you will be able to judge as well as myself, of the probable fate of Louisiana

which yet seems wrapt in mystery The French **article looks
very suspicious,** and also Windham's speech of 3d **May.**

The Aurora, however seems to deny it altogether, **God grant**
he may be in the right

I remain your faithful and affectionate friend,

D. W COXE,

[No 5] BALIZE 29 June, 1802

Messrs CHEW & RELF —*Gentlemen* I wrote you from Plaquemines recommending the letter to the care of Mr Duplessis
to forward by first opportunity and inclosed you a note in it
which I now mention, that if the letter does not shortly get to
hand, you may cause enquiry to be made for it I have heard,
since we came here that a person who was passenger on board
a ship bound for New York died at the Balize and just before
his death wrote to me It is said that Gerique, who was the
officer in command here, took charge of the letter and I am
given to understand there was some property left which I wish
you would speak to him about For God's sake get the Creole
off as fast as possible—push those who owe you to pay, and
try to relieve your friend in Philada from all embarrassments.
If on my arrival there, I should not immediately set off for
Europe you may count on my return to Orleans, in the fall,
to assist in disposing of the shipping and this once effected, I
shall feel easy but till then will know no peace That on my
arrival with you I may know what to depend on, I entreat you
will, by every opportunity, write to Madan & Drake on the subject of molasses and freights, and have such other information
as may be necessary to regulate me I shall rely on this being
done, and shall be much disappointed if you neglect it The
Rover sailed on the 24th the sloop Sally with the Polacre, for
Pensacola, are still here a brig from Malaga came in yesterday

July 1st I expect you will receive letters for me from Mr
Coxe and Mr Kings on on private business—those from the
latter, I wish on no account should be opened Should any
from Mr Coxe get to your hands without a private mark on
them and they treat of any private business I know your
delicacy will forbid you reading them and I only mention this
to put you on your guard, that if you open his letters you may
be careful in perusing the contents Now that I am on the
subject of letters I have to mention, with regret, an accident
which happened to two of those you committed to my care I
was desirous of paying particular attention to them, and therefore put them in my pocket book having one day opened it on
deck a sudden puff of wind carried off all the papers I
thought I had got them all again, but this morning discovered

that a letter from each of you had remained under the hen-
coops, and were almost consumed by the wet in washing the
decks I send you back the letters in their present state, that
you may again write to your friends to whom I will apologise
for not hearing from you, and beg you will not impute the accident to neglect, which I am sincerely sorry for

I left last year, in your iron chest some notes of people living
in Natchez, who are indebted to Capt McFaden Please to
take an account of them, and have them forwarded to Turner
for collection

On the arrival of the Fame and Sophia, unless very good
freights can be obtained I think, considering the embarrassments our mutual friend may be in, it would be best you should
send them here loaded with sugar, provided it can be had at
6 dollars and a long credit and that it is of superior quality,
which you must yourselves judge of, and trust to nobody to act
for you it may be necessary to come to an immediate determination on their arrival, as I fear the Port will be shut and
our vessels will not be suffered to load with Spanish produce
This could easily be got over by naturalizing the vessels, if they
were afterwards permitted to clear out for the Ports of the U
S, but this, I fear, will not be the case If obstacles should be
laid in the way endeavor to get permission to load for St
Thomas, or any place from whence it may not be necessary to
bring a Consul's Certificate —you know the consequences, and
I wish you to be on your guard Let what will happen, let me
know that I may be prepared in time

When the Thomas arrives, send her back without delay let
the Creole have as little repairs as possible, and let not Mag-
nen take out a plank, if it can in any way be avoided

We are here, tired of waiting, eat up by mosquitos and con-
suming our provisions we live, however in perfect good humor with each other and old Ronquil or is very civil and polite
constantly dividing his milk and vegetables with us I would
thank you to take notice of it by sending him a small present of
something agreeable, in my name, by return of the bearer, or
first good opportunity All our people are well on board —
Even's sloop has buried one man on the name of Thomas, and
another is I fear, on the point of dying A schooner is now in
sight, coming in another schooner a brig and a ship were said
to have been seen yesterday from the Tower, but are not now
visible

For God's sake write to Mr Coxe by every vessel, particularly, and give him constant advice of the state of the market, regulations, &c, &c

With compliments to Debuys and Hulings, and their families and all friends, I remain yours sincerely,

DANIEL CLARK

Monsr St Venant had not paid for his stores in town, and therefore, as Mr Coxe or myself will have to pay the Cap[tain] for them, I enclose you his ____ on Leathers for the amount, which pay to Mr Coxe cred[it]

[No 6] Philadelphia, July 1st, 1802.

Dear Clark —My last letters to Chew and Relf are of 25th ult, and this day per mail Your family remain well and pleasantly situated at Germantown with your aunt at their leisure, and when better acquainted with the place they will select a house suitable to their tastes and wishes, of which there are several to rent, of convenient sizes, and at reasonable rents They are so fully convinced of the necessity of your returning to New Orleans that they now only feel the desire (which is so natural) of seeing you, and the period of which they know solely depends on your business Your father who is the only invalid among them is no further so than arises from his rheumatic pains, which incommode him, though without depriving him of a very florid appearance for a man of his years, his hearing is not good, which occasions him to converse less than he would otherwise do He seems to have that yearning after his native spot which is natural to a person who has never left it till late in life, and I am rather inclined to believe that the happiness of your family will, ultimately, be best promoted, by indulging a desire which may, probably, increase, of returning to Ireland, though of this, I have not heard your mother and sisters say anything

The most interesting topic to you and myself, next to my pecuniary wants, (which are heavily pressing on me, and becoming more embarrassing,) is the fate of Louisiana, which, though yet a matter not positively ascertained, bears every appearance of a cession to France Our newspapers, from north to south, teem with a spirit of opposition to the event on both sides of the question, with the single exception of the Aurora which, a few days since again asserted that Spain not only held Louisiana in undisturbed sovereignty, but says that by the most recent advices from Europe, matters in regard to that colony, remained in statu quo

If the cession to France does take place one good consequence amidst its disastrous effects will be a union of party in opposing the hostile views of France and keeping a watchful eye over her movements in that quarter Mr Jefferson's election will I think, be very unfavorably affected by such an event His party have deprived the country of the only sure means of defence and protection, in case of a quarrel with France I mean the repeal of the internal taxes which takes place this day The motive for this measure will, in case of war, become apparent and forcibly felt, for these taxes must be resorted to again if our commerce is attached, or diminishes from other causes   My anxiety to hear of your arrival in New Orleans and to learn from yourself the state of our affair there and my prospect of relief, is inexpressible, though easily to be imagined by your knowledge of my situation   Fearful (after b   bills) of drawing, except now and then, a very small bill in a long sight my resources have been chiefly factitious, which undermines my credit and weaken confidence, or in vain to expect that a repetition and increase of these means of raising money will not gradually be discovered   I however bear up against my difficulties, and got tolerably through my last month's payments

This month, (July,) I have $70,000 to pay and the next I suppose at least $70,000

I feel every reliance on your exertions, in some way or other to afford me relief either by the continuance of shipment to Barclay, or by shipment to her   My bills on Barclay, up to this day, together with all his shipments for my account to New Orleans, draw to the departure of the Ohio from Liverpool and inclusive of her cargo will be barely covered or balanced by all the shipments from New Orleans this year, including the Gys' Mars and New York's cargoes, estimated at the rate of cotton by the latest advices and also debiting Barclay with the freight of flour of the Thos Wilson and Ohio and the proceeds of my account per the Providence

The shipments of Barclay by the A Creole and Thomas, on their present voyages, and also by the Matilda, if she returns from London will be all an advance by them, supposing our accounts previously balanced This statement may form the basis of any calculations you wish to make

You shall hear further from me by the brig Spanish Lady to sail in a few days for New Orleans, and in the meanwhile remain your faithful and affectionate friend

                                                            D W C

P. S   The value of shipping has lately revived a little, and there are now but few good ships for sale in this port You may, probably have heard, through the medium of the newspapers, that your acquaintance, Capt Izard, was severely wounded in a duel he fought with a French gentleman, on the Jersey shore, about two weeks since.   The ball passed through the fleshy part of his right arm, and grazing the upper rib, entered his right breast, and passed thence into his back, or dropped into the trunk of his body   His fate was very desperate till the third day, when his wounds began to suppurate, and he is now in a fair way of recovery, sitting up   I saw him yesterday, when he inquired after you   The dispute which produced the duel is of long standing, and of a very delicate nature, relating to the

Frenchman's sister, now in South Carolina, and to whom. Izard is said to have given a promise of marriage, which the Frenchman is said to have thought Izard was either unwilling to comply with, or to have postponed too long. The delicacy of the subject prevents Izard from saying more than that he has promised marriage, and intended fulfilling his engagement when his circumstances should enable him; but the Frenchman, viewing the matter, as he thought improperly, and having come here for the express purpose of forcing a compliance, or fighting, Izard would not be said to be bullied into anything by coertion. They therefore met, both behaved very gallantly, and the second exchange of shot Izard was wounded, as related. The affair, 'tis thought will be renewed on his recovery.

Affectionately yours D. W. C.

[No 7] PLAQUEMINE, 7th June, 1803

Dear Sir—I must apologize for my leaving town without waiting on you. It was my intention, but Capt Black hurried us off at so early an hour, that I thought you would have been still abed. I however requested Mr. Chew to acquaint you of the circumstance and make an excuse, which I hope he has done. I have the letters you sent down by Lubin, and shall take care of them, with the others recommended to my care by you. We arrived here last evening late, and are now preparing to get under way the Balize, where we hope to pass the night met in the river the Carlisle, from Amsterdam in 9 weeks who informed us that the debou was actually blockaded, and all appearances of war in Europe. I have likewise this morning seen Francois Girod who has arrived in a brig from Havre which he left the 5th April. He is firmly of opinion that there will be a war, and was pleased to learn his brother had not despatched the *Bonne Mere*, as every thing is to be apprehended. He knows nothing of the Expedition, more than it was to sail on the 25th March. There is a gentleman with him who comes out, I believe, in some official capacity, but I had not time to make particular inquiry. There are yet several other vessels at the Balize, which I shall endeavor to speak, and if any thing interesting is brought by them, will inform you by this opportunity, which is the *Feluca del Jobierno*, expecting to pass up from the Diligencia, which may probably arrive before any opportunity. The day previous to my leaving town, wishing to adjust my account, I made an entry in your books of what appeared to me reasonable for six and half years salary in the house, and intended to have spoken to you on the subject myself, but did not see you. It has since occurred to me that a few observations on that head would not be improper, which I beg you will permit me to make. The last time I spoke to you on this busi-

ness, if I recollect right, you remarked that I ought to bear in
view, in my calculations, the favorable situation I was left in by
you, which I ought to consider an important circumstance. No
doubt it was so, but was it ever considered by you as a recompense for my services? or did you in the arrangement, suit only
my interest, or even give it a preference? Certainly not. Why
then, should you be desirous of curtailing an emolument justly
due to a long series of services, for what you would at that time
have, with the same advantages, allowed any stranger possessing
equally your confidence? In my opinion, I think my attachment
shewn to you by remaining with you at a salary, altho' not stipulated, whilst I was receiving offers easy and advantageous propositions making to me for establishment, ought to be a sufficient merit to counteract what you hinted to me. With regard
to the sums charged, I cannot think you can find any difficulty.
In allowing the two first years of my services-you are a better judge
of the worth of than myself, and if you find them improper are at
liberty to alter, tho' I think if you consider what was allowed the
other young men, and take into view our services, it is not out of the
way. The remainder I have regulated by what I could have obtained of several, and which was offered to me in 1796. Mr
Coxe, moreover, has himself mentioned to you that my services
ought not to be regulated by those of a common clerk, and
larly recommended an augmentation   salary. I make this
remark, not with a wish that it should be done, but merely to assist me in my charge. You will observe that for the last year
I have charged at   rate of $1000 in consequence of my not
      g in the house, and of course no   pense to i. I beg you
will pardon me if   hese remarks I have not met your ideas, or
should have let escape any opinion in opposition to yours. You
must be sensible of the necessity I am in of knowing what I
have to depend upon, and   any unfortunate accident
happening to me, what I expect for those I leave behind. I
thought it prudent for your and Mr Coxe's interest, before I left
town, to make a will, which is filed in Pedesclaux's office, and
is merely an avowal of the partnership appointing persons in the
case of   accident to me, to arrange the business and   t
any judiciary proceedings. In doing   I have taken the liberty
to mention   jointly with my wife, and hope you   find
it proper. I cannot conclude without recommending to your
care, in case   any misfortune to me, my wife and children,
your attention to whom will be gratefully acknowledged by your
faithful friend,   RICHARD RELF.

[No. 8]   PHILADELPHIA, January 5th, 1807
  MY DEAR FRIEND —You are too much occupied in great
national concerns, to take an interest in the ruinous difficulties

which you have thrown upon my hands. I have in vain endeavored (even by foregoing the perusal of my own papers) to please you in forwarding them, tho' in the most regular manner, put up by myself and that always on the very day on which they were received. Shall I direct these papers in future to be forwarded to you by the Aurora and Relf offices? You have brought the Abolition Society on my back. The wench was yesterday taken, under an alderman's warrant, to be embarked for Charleston for which place, I informed her she could not be legally sent. She collected, by her cries, a mob of 500 persons about her tho it was night; the constable fled, and left Thos. Lewop with her who however persevered, and put her into jail. The Abolition Society has got wind of the business; the wench has refused to bind herself to her mistress, which I recommended to-day and they are both summoned before an alderman to-morrow and I suspect by some mere legal quirk, the woman will be liberated as 'tis now said, a foreigner or stranger, coming here with slaves, and taking a house manumits by that act.

I must sneak out of business in which no person durst show his face here and Madame Carriere must bear the brunt. 'Tis really an unfortunate thing, in every point of view, that this lady should have come here, under a fallacious hope which can no be realized and still more so that she should remain in a land of strangers a tax on yourself and a burden to herself and me. Had she not best return to New Orleans? I submit it to your better judgment.

The John and Concordia have both arrived here, and if the river remains open, the Felicity may be soon looked for. The Mary with 3750 qtls of logwood, arrived at the Balise 2d December, and I have got 8000 dollars insured on it to this port, as Relf proposes sending her on. He writes me, on 2d and 8th December, that he had received your and my letters of 3d and 11th November but was too unwell to reply to yours.

He seems to anticipate nothing but difficulties, and utters great complaints at the delay in shipping the German goods, and thinks they will now command no profit, as nothing will sell other goods having arrived and fears of war with Great Britain changed the complexion of affairs.

Enclosed are $200 for you. I shall after 1st January, cease underwriting on any but my private account and you must allow me a little discretion in what shall not in future affect you you therefore have my promise and may consider that as evidence of my determination not to involve you in any of my underwriting accounts.

I have Parish's sales of mortgaged cotton, which, after paying all charges whatever, excepting only insurance, leaves $17,000. I hope if your orders to Relf are the cause of the embargo

catching and locking up a cargo of cotton, which might have
been ready and got away, that I shall be able to devise some
ways and means of meeting the heavy engagements which that
remittance and shipment was intended to aid me in   I could,
at this moment, sell out to 25 per cent profit, any shipments of
cotton made prior to the embargo   The suspension of purchases
after knowledge of the embargo and until the price fell again
was right, and recommended likewise by myself   but to permit
a cargo to be caught, that might have been away, and given
the chance of an immense profit, I cannot discover the policy
of   I am, yours, affectionately
                                             D W C

I concealed nothing from you when I consulted you about
flour, none is bought.

I hope your fears about others which last year prevented
purchases and a fortune being made may not this year prove
as unfortunate to our interests

[No 9]   PHILADELPHIA, January 6th, 1808
My Dear Sir—I have received your two letters of 3d and 4th
inst.   I hope I have escaped the abolition inquisition, and that
matters will to-morrow be settled, by binding the negress for 5
years to her mistress.   Thos Jew op has actually left town thro'
fear, for a few days   You say nothing about writing Duralde,
and if you mean that he shall not mock my authority you will
immediately enclose me a letter instructing him to return to Orleans   I keep his letters to send his father with proper explanations, as in his last he acknowledges that he has falsified and deceived me by misstatements   I have letters from Hope & Co to
30th October, on which day they sold 15 hhds coffee at 21, and 87
hhds at 21 1-2 stevers, equal to 23 and 23 1-2 in Bags   Jones
will clear $50,000 by his coffee per the Bainbridge   The sales
must then have been nearly closed, and I durst now predict
that 5 to 10 per cent, which gain must be made on sugar per F.
Augustus, as prices by advices from Bremen had risen higher
than in Holland   I conclude the Caroline's sales must have been
closed to advantage

I have insured $8,000 on 160 tons logwood, per Mary, from
the Mississippi or Balise to Philadelphia at 5 per cent and
am trying to get the vessel covered   I fear the air of Washington does not agree with either your spirits or temper, and the
effects appear to fall on me, for your late letters, in addition to
your heavy complaints of me, contain not a syllable of your engagement to Miss C, which two letters from Baltimore, received
in this city, state in positive terms.   On this last subject Mrs.
Cox complains of your breach of promise in not communicating

the event to her Confidence once lost between friends is not
easily regained Yours affectionately. D W C

I rejoice at the investigation of Gen W's conduct, but suspect
that the Court of Enquiry (if under executive influence) may
smother facts, and end in his acquittal

[No 10] PHILADELPHIA, July 16th 1807

My Dear Clark—The fortunate result of your affair with Claiborne, first came to my knowledge thro' a newspaper which fell
into my hands on the road returning from the sea shore a few
days since, and while I feel unfeigned satisfaction at the happy
termination of your long standing differences with the governor,
I am deeply anxious to learn from yourself the particulars which
could have led to it especially after (according to your own letters) attempts were made to effect a compromise. This is the
point which to me is very material. However a letter from you
at Natchez must shortly relieve me as I learn that after the matter
ended you continued your journey to your plantation and did
not return to town as one of the papers states. None of the
public prints have animadverted on the affair, but merely state
the occurrence and issue. While at the shore, one of the Miss
Smith's of Princeton, said before several persons (addressing
herself to Mrs Coxe) that one of her friends had a letter from
New Orleans, mentioning that you and Claiborne were going
up the country in a few days to have a duel and asserted the
matter with so much positiveness, that tho' Mrs C discredited
it altogether, I thought it very probable but would not say so.
Mrs C will therefore, in hearing of it, learn that the issue was
favorable, and you unhurt. Your family are all well, and I shall
to-day go out to see them. Madam Carriere and sister handed
me your letter of introduction which shall be attended to. They
have taken a snug house on little Swansom st which suits them
perfectly, and wait your arrival which they assure me I may expect in 4 or 5 weeks. Your own letters indeed, lead me to
hope it, and your next will I trust, confirm it. I therefore
write this without touching on business, but refer you to mine
to C & R., should you not be away when this arrives. We
shall have no war with Great Britain, unless the principals
bring it on some months hence. In the mean while you will
attend Congress, and we can settle our future operations. Your
two letters of 25th and 29th May were received in my absence,
and T Jessop opened that which contained the paragraphs respecting you, which were previously published by Ren as also
those you sent me before. Your reception, popularity and
standing in Louisiana, appears now as well known here as
there, and the eclat which a brilliant *affaire d honneur* will give
you with the French creoles will be among the good effect

produced by it.   It is far from being a subject of regret with me, and I think you view it in the same light

Turner's clerk is here looking at goods, and I hope to receive your letter before it becomes necessary to purchase   He must be now supplied with an assortment, and his assiduity entitles him to our confidence   The unanimity throughout the country, and among all parties, are a pledge for the zeal with which we shall act against Great Britain, if we become her foes   Preparation is going on as well of a voluntary as governmental nature The fortification of vulnerable points will, I expect be attended to without regard to the limitation of means given by the act of Congress, last session, and the President seeing the general enthusiasm, need not fear to transcend his powers on the occasion   On Friday evening I shall expect letters from you

I remain ever and affectionately yours

D W COXE

[No. 11]   NEW ORLEANS 28 Oct, 1809

DEAR SIR —You will no doubt be surprised that I should have delayed till your departure from town, communicating to you the subject of the present letter   and I beg you will not think it has proceeded from indifference, or a want of desire of obtaining your favorable opinion of it   The fact is, that from the moment I conceived the idea, I have been anxious of acquainting you with it   but an insuperable embarrassment has always prevented me to account for which, and your extreme candor to me I find impossible   And I have resolved to change my situation and again enlist under the banner of matrimony, and have fixed my choice on Miss Ann Zacharie, the worth of whom is only known to them who have cultivated her acquaintance, and little becomes me to speak of   I do not know whether you are sufficiently acquainted with the character of the young lady, to give an opinion, but if you were to form it from the opinion of every one who is intimately acquainted with her, I anticipate a favorable one   Her circumstances in life are certainly not as brilliant as many others to whom probably, I might without arrogance pretend, but she has qualities possessed by few in the circle of my acquaintance.   Her personal deformity is certainly a misfortune, but not an objection In making this choice I have consulted, not principally the happiness of my children, to whom, I feel convinced, she will prove an affectionate mother, and it has afforded me no small satisfaction to find that Mrs Quinones most heartily approves my determination   In fact, none to whom the subject has been communicated, but commend it.   I would, however, wish you to understand that I have as yet only communicated it to Mr. Harper, and of my family, it is true it has generally been supposed that the engagement was made and when I have been spoken to have never contradicted it. It was my wish previous to forming this new engagement to have had an idea of my future prospects which from the complicated nature of our business it is impossible to form Your late communication has however set me at ease on that head and I feel now no desire but to obtain your approbation which if given I shall on your return conclude the business otherwise shall wait a more auspicious moment

   I am, Dear Sir
    most affectionately yours,
     RICHARD RELF.

DANIEL CLARK, Esq.

[No 12]   PHILADELPHIA Feb 9th 1808.

MY DEAR SIR.—Although it may be uncertain whether you will have any recollection of the person who has now the honor of addressing you yet be I willing to hope, from the vivid remembrance he has of yourself that his memory has not wholly escaped your recollection Let however unpleasantly for him this should prove the occasion permit me to refer to the commencement of our acquaintance, which although quite accidental was in no respect the less acceptable This was at New York in the winter of 1791-2 Our acquaintance tho' only of some 12 or 15 days duration was continued, and has been cemented by a present to me of a watch key and seal of value—the which I have ever since (when I was accidentally not deprived of them) was worn as an appendage of my watch And permit me also to observe, that on more occasions than one in consequence of some recent and important occurrence in which yourself have been not an unimportant actor, it has been my pride and pleasure to say "This key and seal were presented to me by the same Mr Clark"

The object of this letter, however is not alone to remind you that you have such a friend as myself in existence. Its object is of greater magnitude I find, and I presume you are not wholly ignorant the of that efforts, tho' feeble and unsuccessful are making by the tools and minions of Wilkinson and another great per——age, to impeach your character and impair the credibility of your testimony in the serious and damning charges exhibited against *the Commander-in-Chief* &c., &c It is indeed a painful, mortifying, and disagreeable truth that a man whose character and ———— ———— late vicious and corrupt, should no h—— should so long have held an appointment so important in the Government of this country But he is now gone——gone beyond recovery—even in the hope of such if such there can be who are yet his friends.

And allow me my dear sir, to assure you, which I do with
with equal pleasure and truth that all the efforts of his aiders
and abettors— and the advocates of even the P————t himself,
will prove unavailing against you—that your conduct through
the whole of this business is approbated by judicious and
....
....the my friend because I
well know when a man is exposed to the storm of malice and
detraction by ....tyrants
....
him...
approbation and thanks of the ....and respectable part of his ....

I...........you this from the place where I have been for some
weeks past. Should your avocation permit you to acknowledge
its receipt, please to direct to me at Allentown, New Jersey
and do me the favor to accept the assurances of my best friendship and good will.   I am &c,

                                        JO. H. IMLAY

The Honorable Mr Clark

[No 13]   BURLINGTON, July 21. 1811

My Dear sir.—I have no letters from you by the ship Or-
lean, and mail of 22d and 29th January though I perceive
by C. and Relf's letters that you intended sending a parcel of
molasses, for the prospect of which I refer you to my letter to
C and R.

Until I get my account and sales from Europe, I can't send
you the statement which is however, all ready to be closed and
forwarded the moment I obtain those papers. The numerous
seizures of our property at   originated, as you will see
by the enclosed paragraph, from the villanous prostitution of our
flag by the British merchants. Of our sugars I have no advices
since the 25th of October, when they were not sold. The Hamburgh houses are so jealous of each other that, in general none
will receive and forward letters except to their own correspondents, hence every body complains of the supposed neglect of
his friend in not writing. I fear much the effect of the stagnation of prices of colonial produce, and on our sugars which,
however having passed the duty and being in Parish's possession, at Frederickstadt run no risk of confiscation in the worst
event. Of the report respecting the exclusion of cotton, I place
no reliance, as it is well known to be a favored article everywhere; therefore, C and R, need not be uneasy if they have
shipped cotton to Fanning, as Parish expressly states that under any circumstances it will always find admission.

Stephen Kingston lately got himself into a serious situation at

London in consequence of having defamed Thomas Wilson's
and Baring houses who both brought actions against him for
damages to an enormous amount but he contrived to procure
bail. I believe Mr G L ley in connection with whom I learn
he purchased the ship Havana Capt Robinson at Cadiz, and is
sending her from thence to New Orleans where I think it likely
from his former acquaintance with you he will endeavor to draw
you into some adventure or responsibility and I therefore caution you against committing yourself or Chew and Pell. Your
friends and Mrs Coxe are all well and I remain

Affectionately yours   D W COXE

You asked me my idea of settling with C and R. If our
bad sales and assets at New Orleans turn out well, I should be
disposed to allow them only in a lump 25 30, or 40 dollars according to our ability presuming they have nothing to do with
the fund. Their losses in the cotton shipments were, together
with our own very severe. I have no idea that any
sum like the above could be coming to them on a fair settlement,
notwithstanding the subsequent profits. We should further establish and leave them in credit each with Bank directorships

Turn over   D. W. C.

Moses Myers & Son of Norfolk, state to me in confidence that
they had so bad an opinion of Jno Dev Delacey, who applies
to them to do his business that they declined it. He was gone
and I shall forward you   letters for him to my friend at
Kingston

[No 14]   New Orleans, 9 Feb y, 1810

My Dear Sir —In conformity to my promise, I made the necessary enquiries here since my arrival, respecting the state of
the business with the assignees of Morgan's creditors, and have
understood that on account of some law quirk, it was not possible to compel Minor to answer any interrogatories, as it could
not be proved that he actually had any property of yours in
his hands. Thus the affair remains in statu quo

I again, my dear Wilkins, take the liberty of recommending to
you either to compromise this business, or bring it to an issue
You must be sensible that while it remains undecided, you are
prevented from leaving the Mississippi Territory, for fear of
being pestered about it, and I think this ought not to be submitted to by a man of your principles or fortune. You ought to
seek not deprive yourself of enjoyment and certainly the sphere
is much limited by your remaining buried at Natchez I have no
interest in advising you to throw money away, nor do I wish to do
it I am on bad terms with those you have to deal with, and hold
no communion with them, but if ever you have to come to a settlement with them, the sooner it is done the better, and you

wou'd do well to consign to me or some other friend, a few bales of cotton, that it may be attached, and the merits of the cause tried. Your lawyer is acquainted with the merits of your case and should the matter, as I hope and expect, be given in your favor, it will free you from a dependence and trust on another, which you never ought to be in or have confided to any one. Those who advise you to a contrary line of conduct have no regard for your honor, but seek merely their own interest, and it is the duty of friendship to advise you on it. When it may please Heaven, at a remote period to call you from the world, leave your fortune to those you like, but remain master of it while you live, and let it never be said that you did anything to keep it from the eve of the public. Were I in the situation of Minor with respect to you I would advise what I now have done although I should lose your friendship by the act, and if he merits any mark of your regard it ought to be by endeavors to dispel every appearance or shadow of imputation which might be injurious to your name or character. I do not wish you to take the trouble of replying to this letter which may probably displease you, because advice that is not asked or should be different to our own opinion is generally displeasing, and ill received. But I should look on as well as a false friend to you, if I did not offer it, and prove that regard of which you have often given me proof. Were you however be inclined to take any steps in the way I wish you will only have to inform me of your intentions to have them executed.

I have, thank God, been more than commonly successful, in my last year's shipments and have now the pleasing perspective, of retiring from business with a handsome competence. I know you will be pleased with the news, and therefore advise you of it. I have resolved on having no more interest in any mercantile transactions and as my debts come in, I shall lay out the money in ornamenting a place for my retreat. Altho' I scarce expect to have the pleasure of seeing you at the Houmas, yet I sincerely wish it, and my happiness would be much augmented by it, for however we may differ on some occasions, yet we generally think alike of men and measures, and I flatter myself, I could succeed in keeping *ennui* far from you, while we were together. If you ever visit me, you will find good books, good cheer, a good horse a good gun, and the most heartfelt welcome from   Your sincere friend,

DANIEL CLARK

P. S.—You have probably heard of a loss I lately experienced by an ill-placed confidence in the Collector. Report has exaggerated it; it will amount to 8000 dollars only, and since my return here, I have cleared more than that sum by the purchase and sale of an estate, without disbursing a cent.

THOMAS WILKINS, ESQ'R

[No. 15]   PHILADELPHIA, 20th April, 1810

DAN'L CLARK Esq—*Dear Sir* I received your favor of the 10th ult, with the bill on our friend, Daniel Coxe, to whom I announced the circumstance He observed to me that, if it was convenient to me he would be glad that I should let it remain under the arrangement I had made with him for the payment of the first bill, which was to be on the 10th of next September and said that I might hold this last one, as it was a matter of convenience, and could not prejudice any of the parties. I cheerfully consented to his request and the business remains in statu quo

Mr Coxe accepted your draft for the periodical payment of the interest, which I receive punctually I am, indeed, much pleased to hear, that you are about to act as I have long wished you to and as a man ought to do who reflects that the life of mortals seldom exceeds the short term of three score and ten years, and that of this poor pittance, the latter part affords little that can be called pleasure

The sources of pleasure vary according to the difference of constitution of men's minds, nor can any one, with propriety, say that *his* idea of happiness ought to be adopted by another Yet there is one point in which most men are agreed; that is that a mind harrassed with unceasing exertions to overcome difficulties, or to accumulate wealth, and a body worn down by mental or muscular action can never be a fit recipient for the *genuine* delights of life These take up their abode in the pure unsullied bosom of the man who, contented with an honest competency, remembers that this earth is not man's abiding place, who, using its good things, abuseth them not and who calls to mind, that if the vigor of life has been spent in obtaining the decline of it has a right to enjoyment

Now, my good friend, I do sincerely believe, that you possess *all* the chief requisites for happiness You are temperate in eating and drinking you have a comprehensive mind, and a social benevolent spirit But this fertile soil that produces so many valuable plants bears one, I fear, that you will not so easily *prune* to a sufficient degree, (for I would not wish you to eradicate it totally) I mean ambition, the desire of being the first, the richest When I see this luxuriant vine restrained within due bounds, I shall have hopes that you will effectually carry your plan of retirement from mercantile affairs into execution, and will reap from your determination all the satisfaction you expect Sally joins me in affectionate friendship, and good wishes for your health and happiness

We heard from Germantown the other day all the family were well but Mary, who was indisposed I am, respectfully, your most obedient &c.,   WM. E HULINGS.

[No 16]　　　　　　　　　Philadelphia, Sept 20th 1810

My Dear Sir—I have no letters from you by last mail Yesterday Relf set off on his return home with his family via Pittsburg and I feel very apprehensive that Mrs R's accouchment will take place before he arrives, and retard his journey I set out to-morrow, after great exertions, to enable me to go and meet Mrs Coxe and the bridal party at New York, on the 22d, on their return from Boston I have sent C & R by this opportunity, all the remaining sales of cotton in which you or they are concerned, and not knowing precisely which are yours, you must select them, if I have made any mistake Your account from April, 1807, is also enclosed together with theirs, for the last 17 months, merely to show the state of them in justification of my request, that neither you or they would draw any more on me, without the most urgent necessity forces you to it, which I can hardly suppose will happen I have lately remitted $1400 cash to Mr Jno Miller, towards paying the expenses of the negroes which, for forms sake, I charge to your account, together with the bonds given, in order that you may know how to settle with him This is independent of the former sum advanced him for expenses, which is also charged I believe I informed you that he had recently made another purchase of six slaves, which makes the whole number he is to take down about 116 I know of nothing that can prevent your coming on here to spend the winter with us, after Relf returns, and therefore trust you will come on, which in the present prospects of a final winding up, will be particularly gratifying to Mr C and myself, and indeed necessary to a more perfect and complete understanding on all points I hope you will find my proposal an acceptable one If not, I must strive to improve my fortune in the best way I can

At the urgent solicitation of Mr Skipwith, I have advanced Mrs S $1000, over and above the balance due them, which you must have refunded in the spring He wanted $3000, but I told him the dissolution of my commercial copartnership with you and C & R, rendered it impossible to go beyond $1000 The affair of the Brothers, which I mentioned to you, has not proved a chimera and I shall positively clear 20, and perhaps between 30 and 40,000 dollars, as Relf will explain to you The 20,000 are certain, and the money received The remainder depends on the underwriters at Loyd's, where I am ensured My subsequent shipments, you will say, may deprive me of my *precious* profits, which is possible

Your aunt hinted to me the other day, that Massey (who is much at your mother's) is fond of your niece Sally Anderson, and as he really appears to be a good creature I should think him a safe match for her The family are all well, and the mor desirous to see you, as I believe the plan of going to Liverpool will not be executed without your approbation and presence

I remain yours affectionately

D W COXE

D CLARK, Esq

[No 17] PHILADELPHIA May 19 h, 1812.

Mr CLARKE—Sir I have received a letter from Davis, dated the 28th March, saying he should leave New Orleans, the first of April, in consequence of which I write you, knowing how much you are interested for Mira she is in good health, and, be assured, very happy she is beginning to read, you will find her much improved when you have the happiness to see her. Davis is also well They often speak of you I have taught them to write your name

May peace, health and happiness be yours, is the prayer of your friend.

ELIZA CLARKE

And afterwards, to wit, on the tenth July, 1849, appeared Dr. James Gardette, a witness, heretofore called and examined on behalf of complainant, and now by them recalled doth depose and say

Witness being shown document No 6, filed with the commissioner by complainant, on 23d June, 1849, being a certificate of marriage of one Jacobum DeGrange and Barbara Orci, he was asked to state when and where the same was found Witness says My mother and myself were looking over the papers of Dr Gardette, my father, several papers fell on the floor, and among them this paper was found This paper was found after the decision of the Patterson case in the Circuit Court of the United States, and before the decision of the same case in the Supreme Court of the United States And it was handed by my mother to General Gaines or his wife immediately after it was found

JAMES GARDETTE

Cross examination waived by Louis Janin, Esq, of counsel for defendants

J W. GURLEY, Commissioner

Letters offered by complainant, 26th June, 1849

A. Letter dated 15th July, 1834, from Madame de Roffignac, to Madame Gardette, at Bordeaux, France

B. Letter from same to the same, dated 15th October, 1834, at
   Angouleme, France

C Letter from same to same, July, same year

D Letter from same to same, dated 14th January, 1835

E. Letter from Madame de la Roche née Boulgny to Madame
   V Gardette née Carrière, dated 1st July, 1833

F Letter from same to same, dated 16th June, 1833

G Letter from same to same, dated 4th August, 1833

H Letter from same to same, dated 3d March, 1833

I. Letter from same to same, dated Bordeaux, 12th September,
   1839, directed to New Orleans

J. Letter from Fanny Duchaufour née Gardette to Madame Gardette née Carrière, dated 28th November, 1833, directed to
   Bordeaux, France.

K Same to same

L Same to same, dated 4th May, 1839.

M Same to same, 26th November, 1838

N Same to same, 22d August, 1838

O Same to same, 23d November, 1839.

P. Same to same, 5th September, ——

Q Same to same, 24th April, ——

R Same to same, 17th August, ——

S Same to same. 24th January, 1839

T. Same to same, 23d January, 1840

U Same to Dr Jas Gardette, N Orleans, May 31st

V. Letter from L'Abbe Moni, dated New Orleans, 27th March,
   1826, to Jacque Gardette, dentist, Philadelphia

W Letter from Emile Gardette, son of late Dr Jas Gardette,
   Philadelphia, to Madame Zulime Gardette nee Carrière,
   dated 1st January, 1822

X. Letter from same to same, Philadelphia, 2d July, 1829

Y. Letter from same to same, dated 30th January, 1835

Z Letter from same to same, dated 4th September, 1832

A. 2 Letter from same to Jos Gardette, dated Philadelphia, 22d
   June, 1822

A

15 JUILLET.

En te recommandant ma jeune cousine et son aimable oncle,
je te dirais qu'ils sont, l'un et l'autre, si parfaits que tu regret-
teras de les perdres-it t, ils car resteront que peu de tems à Bordeaux, où ils vont chercher un jeune petit creole qui viens faire
son education, recommendé à M le Chevalier de Vas-agne, qui
le remettra à . . . . et qui a déja fait élevé trois frères du
jeune qui est à Bordeaux. Si nos voyageurs restent plus de

tems que je le suppose, tu leurs feras faire la connaissance du
G n ral DeClouet et de sa famille, et chez Madame de la Roche,
notre amie Tu lui exprimeras mes regrets de la mort de Madame de Bouligny Reçois pour toi les vœux sincères de mon
tendre attachement Mon mari et mes enfans se portent bien.

SOLIDELLE DE ROFFIGNAC.

B

19 8 BRE, ANGOULEME.

MA BONNE ZULIME—Je suis depuis un mois très souffrante
d'une névralgie à la tete, du moins, on le craint J'ai si longtemps pleuré ma famille et mon mari, que je devrais m'attendre
à faire une maladie.

La bonne Madame Castex te fera le detail du motif de mon
voyage a Paris C'est en route que je tombait malade, pour
avoir pris un bain froid avec un catarrhe a la tete Enfin patience parlons de mon amie Madame Castex, elle te dira le
but de mon voyage a Bordeaux, et j'espere que tu la seconderas
de tout ton pouvoir, que tu la recommenderas à nos bonnes
créoles, à Gittere, qui a des amis,—enfin je suis convaincue
que tu feras tout pour lui etre utile

Mon mal de tete est affieux Je n'ai que le tems de t'embrasser SOLIDELLE DE ROFFIGNAC.

C

20 JUILLET, ANGOULEME.

C'est avec plaisir, ma chere Zulime, que je t'engage à faire la
connaissance de la famille Faild, qui vont se fixer à Bordeaux.
Ils sont tous trois d'une société sure et agréable. Ce sont des
amis rare, et qui laisseront ici d'éternelle regret Je te prie, donc,
de leur faire faire quelques bonnes connaissances Ils sont d jà
bien connus, mais je veux te dire que vous faites une très bonne
acquisition, à nos d pens.

Il est bien vrai, ma bonne amie, que j'attend mes filles. Pour
moi, je ne serai heureuse que lorsque je serai fixée à Paris ou à
Bordeaux, que j'aime tant, et chez qui je trouverai des compatriotes qui me d dom nage de l'absence de la patrie.

Dis moi si tu a vu le Chevalier de Vassagne et sa m're; si tu
as reçu la lettre où je te parle de ma caisse, envoyée par le navire (*La Jeune France*)

Donne moi de tes nouvelles On dit que le choléra avait reparer chez nous, mais que ce n'etait rien Cependant Mlle.
Poultney en a ete victime Les banqueroutes ont été commencees Notre pauvre pays est bien changé à son desavantage.
Ne m oubliez pas, et donne moi souvent de tes nouvelles.

Monsieur Fayd est le médecin des dames Je ne sai pas si
à Bordeaux il continuera son état, ici il le fesait que pour ses
amies, qui le regrette bien

Albin Michel est arrivé à Paris, et beaucoup de créoles.

Embrasse pour moi ta bonne soeur, amitiés a MM les fils pour ton amie

S De ROFFIGNAC.

D

14 Janvier, 1835, Angoulême

Eh bien ma chère Zulime, est tu encore sur cette terre étrangère, où deja bien loin mes vœux t'accompagnes.

Un Monsieur nommé Castex, qui va dans le nouveaux monde, desire partir dans le meme navire que ta famille, nous le connaissons peu, mais il est bien recommendé ici, et c'est beaucoup Ce sera un passager de plus, et que vous ne serez pas faché d'avoir.

Mon mari lui à donné plusieurs lettres Bon voyage chère amie, répond moi de suite, c'est la troisième sans reponse

S De ROFFIGNAC

E

Cauterets, 1er Juillet, 1833

Madame et bonne amie —J'ai reçu votre chère lettre du 24 Juin Je suis bien sensible à tout interet que vous prenez à tout ce qui nous interesse

Je partage, ma chere amie, toutes vos inquiétudes je désire bien sincerement, que vous receviez de l'eveque de Baltimore des nouvelles satisfesantes de votre cher fils Vous avez eu une bonne idée de vous adresser à l'évêque Esperons qu'il vous repondra de suite, et que sa reponse sera des plus heureuse, c'est le vœu que forme votre sincère amie.

J'ai reçu une lettre de mon fils Henry, qui me confirme la mort de mon cher frère, comme vous le disait Madame de Duchaufour, d'une attaque d'apoplexie, il a succombé à sa premiere maladie Henry me fait part de son mariage, vous savez ce que j'en pense, mais la chose est faite, il faut se resigner et prendre son parti, ce ne sont pas toujours les mariage les plus riches qui sont les plus heureux, l'exemple de ma chere Justine en est une preuve

M St Avide, qui est à Paris, a ecrit à M Blanc que M Garnier etait arrivé au Havre avec sa femme et tous ses enfants, et qu'il lui avait ecrit du Havre de lui retenir des appartements à Paris. Je n'ai pas encore reçu de lettre de ma chere fille, j'attends le moment heureux où je pourrai la presser sur mon cœur, ainsi que tous mes chers petits enfants

Si les dames Declouet sont parties quatre jours après votre lettre, elles arriveront aujourd'hui ici, j'attends avec impatience, leur arrivee me fera plaisir

Mon mari continue à bien se trouver des bains qu'il prend et

de l'eau qu'il boit a la Raillere 'e me me trouve aussi beaucoup mieux j'ai pris 9 bains et deux verres d'eaux minerales
tous les jours, dont j'avais un grand besoin pour ma poitrine,
car le rhume que viens d'avoir m'avait fatigué beaucoup.

Je ne puis pas precisement vous dire le temps que nous res-
terons ici, si Mr Laroche continue a bien se trouver des eaux,
je l'engagerai a y passer toute la saison J'ai eu le plaisir de
voir Mr. Cazenave, mon gendre, qui a passé deux jours avec
nous Adele se portait bien, ainsi que le petit Edouard

Mon mari desire que vous veuilliez agreer ses respects, ainsi
que Madame Caillavet Adieu mes cheres et bonnes amies, je
vous embrasse toutes deux d'intention, et pense bien souvent
a vous, ainsi qu'à Edmond, à qui je renouvelle mon amitie

Si j' recois quelqu' nouvelle de Madam Roungaud, je vous
en ferai part

Ma lettre n'ayant pas ete mise a la poste ce matin, je vous
dirai que je viens de recevoir une lettre de Madame Garnier, du
23 uin, ils ont eu un traversee des plus heureuse, ils l'ont faite
dans trente huit jours Ils resteront un mois a Paris pour faire
voir à Othli et Agala tout ce qu'ils y a de beau ils iront
aussi passer quelques jours chez M Pontalba, a Mo t l'Eveque,
une campagne tres agreable, ou ils se delasseront des fatigues
du voyage

Les dames Declouet sont arrivees a 4 heures cet apres midi,
tres fatiguees Je recois votre lettre a l'instant

Mon mari se rappelle à amitie de Mons. Edemont
1er Juillet   L e BOULIGNY
Le courier ne partira que demain a 10 heures

F

CAUTERETS, 16 JUIN. 1833

MADAME ET BONNE AMIE —Vous sommes arrives a Cauterets
le 3, 14 jours qui se sont ecoules sans que j'aie pu vous donner
de mes nouvelles Je n'ai aucun doute de l'interet que vous
prenez a nous, aussi je regrette de n'avoir pas pu vous écrire
plutôt, un mal de gorge suivi d'un rhume occasione par les
fortes chaleurs, que nous avons eprouvees en route, en a été la
cause Je me trouve mieux depuis deux jours, mais n'ai pas
encore pu me baigner, j'attends que mon rhume soit gueri, pour
prendre des bains a la Raillere

Mon mari a mieux soutenu le voyage que je n'aurais cru, il
a eu la fievre en route, mais il avait a Bordeaux sans sortir, il
a deja pris six bains d'ont il se trouve bien, je trouve que ses
forces reviennent, il a bon appetit et dort bien, j'espere qu'il
laissera ici toutes ses douleurs

Et vous mes bonnes amies comment vous portez vous ? donnez moi de vos nouvelles Madame Caillavet était indisposee

quand je partis   J'avais fait le projet d'aller vous voir la veille de mon d part, mais Madame Rival et Madame Latapie, étant venues passer la soirée avec moi, lorsqu'elles se retirent il était trop tard.

Avez-vous eu des nouvelles de Mons votre fils ? faites le moi savoir   Madame Tuchaufour vous a t'elle écrit ? vous m'obligerez infiniment de m'en faire part, ainsi que si vous apprenez arrivée de Mlle., la jeune Gabrielle, à la Nouvelle Orléans

Donnez moi, je vous prie, des douvelles de Madame Bartte et de Mlle. Victorine, comment ne se décide t'elle pas à venir prendre les eaux de Cauterets elle trouverait ici leur guérison. Rappellez moi au souvenir de Madame Déclouet et de sa famille.

Mes amitiés à Edemond   Adieu mes bonnes amies, aimez moi comme je vous aime, et donnez moi de vos nouvelles Mon adresse, Hôtel du Lion d Or, chez le traiteur Cazenave, a Cauterets

Avez-vous su si Madame Roufignac est à Paris ? vous a t'elle écrit ? Si elle est à Paris, vous savez ma bonne amie, que je compte sur vous pour avoir son addresse.

L nee BOULIGNY.

G

BAGNERRES, 4 Aout, 1833

MA CHERE ET BONNE AMIE,—J'ai reçu votre chere lettre dans son temps. Si je n'ai pas répondu de suite, c'est le manque de temps,—ici les matinees passent pour le bain, ou à attendre, l'après d ner il faut faire un peu d'exercice pour faire passer les eaux, ensuite il   recevoir on aller visiter les personnes qui vienent vous voir, j'ai voulu profiter aussi des navires qui vont partir pour la Nouvelle Orléans Si je n'ai pas eu le temps de vous écrire, celui de penser à vous, ma chere amie, et de m'occuper de toutes vos peines, tant physiques que morales, ce temps, dis-je, ne m'a jamais manqué J'ai appris par M Declouet les tristes nouvelles que vous avez reçu de votre famille ; croyez, mes chere amies, que je partage vivement toutes vos peines et inquietudes. Aux décrets du ciel il faut se soumettre et se résigner J'espere que vous êtes en bonne convalescence. Donnez moi de vos nouvelles, ainsi que de votre chere sœur et Edemont, je pense que la gripe n aura pas pu l'atteindre dans ses courses.

J'ai laisse les dames Déclouét bien portantes ; les eaux ont fait beaucoup de bien à Madame Barthe et à Victorine ; Laure a de temps à l'autre la fievre

Nous sommes arrivés ici le 1er Aout Les 15 premiers jours après notre arrivée à Cauterets, les eaux ont paru faire beaucoup de bien à mon mari, ses forces revenaient à vue d'œil ; et en suite les bains et surtout les douches le fatigaient beaucoup, et dernièrement il prit un rhume dont il n'es pas encore gu'ri. Je n'ai point reçu d'autres lettres de Madame Garnier, cela me donne de l'inqui tude, je craint qu'elle soit malade ou ses enfans, car on respire un si mauvais air à Paris

J'ai reçu une lettre de Madame Brueys, qui me prie de la rappeller à votre souvenir.

Je vais vous prier de me rendre le service de faire parvenir cette lettre à mon fils, je ne voudrias pas qu'elle soit mise dans le navire le Bolochant, par raison que j'ai envoy, il y à 8 à 10 jours, à Mons. Cazenave deux lettres pour maman et une autre pour Madame Brueys, en priant Mons Cazenave de les mettres dans le Bolochant, ou de les remettres au capitaine, qu'il connait. Si la Zelia n'était pas encore partie, vous pourriez l'envoyer par ce navire, ou le premier qui partira pour notre pays, vous obligerez ma chere amie, cell qui pense souvent à vous, ainsi que la bonne Madame Caillavet.

Je me propose d'écrire à Madame Garnier, et de lui donner votre adresse, si el va à Bordeaux, je désire qu'elle fasse votre aimable connaissance.

Adieu mes cheres amies, je vous embrasse de tout mon cœur

6 Août   L née DE BOULIGNY.

C'est avec le plus grand plaisir ma chere amie que je viens d'apprendre que votre cher fils est arrivé à Bordeaux, c'est du plus profond de mon cœur que je vous félicite, et partage tout votre contentement, je ne puis vous exprimer combien je partage tout votre bonheur, dite je vous prie à Mons. votre fils, les choses les plus amicalles de notre part.

M La Roche vous présente ses respects

H

BORDEAUX, 3 MARS, 1833.

MADAME ET CHERE AMIE,—Combien il est flatteur pour moi de voir qu'au milieu des tourbillons de plaisir qui vous environnent, vous vous rappellez de votre triste amie, et que vous avez trouve le temps par le moyen d'un stratagème de vous entretenir avec moi ; soyez persuadée que vous etiez payee de retour, il ni a pas de jours que je n'aie dit à mon mari, il me semble qu'il y a un siècle que je n'ai vu Madame Gardette, je voudrais la voir de retour

Je partage tous les plaisirs que vous avez eu en revoyant votre aimable niece, mais je vois par votre lettre que le moment de votre séparation s'approche, moment de peines, mais vous avez l'espoir qu'elle viendra s'etablir à Bordeaux, l'espérance console toujours

Votre chere et bonne sœur ainsi que votre cher fils se portent bien. Madame Gaillavet donne des soirés ; à été au bal, je sai qu'elle s'y est bien amusée : j'ai sai de ses nouvelles tous les jours Nous n'avons pas eu le plaisir de nous visiter depuis plusieurs jours, le temps est affreux, la pluie ne discontinue pas.

Nous sommes toujours ingenieuses, vous et moi, a nous tourmenter pour nos enfants nous avons été convaincues, vous et moi que quand nous ne recevons pas de leurs nouvelles, c'est un peu de paresse de leur part, ainsi pour quoi vous allarmer ni troubler votre tranquillité et alterer votre santé, ne cherchons pas ma bonne amie a prevoir des malheurs qui n'existent pas

Rappellez moi moi, je vous prie, au souvenir de Madame Anita, dite lui les choses les plus amicales, je vous avais priée de la remercier du joli tuelle qu'elle m'envoya, dites lui que j'en ai fait garnir un bonnet qui me coiffe tres bien, cette garniture fait un joli effet.

Adieu ma chere et bonne amie, soyez persuadée de mon sincere attachement, je ne puis rien ajouter aux sentimens que je vous ai voués.   Mon mari désire d'etre rappellé à votre souvenir, ainsi qu'à celui de votre interessante niece

Madame Caillavet m'ayant dit qu'elle pensait que vous deviez être partie de Bruge, c'est ce qui m'a empechée de faire partir celle-ci, pour la mettre dans la sienne, afin qu'elle vous parvienne Je puis vous assurer, que votre cher fils n'a pas perdu l'appétit, je l'ai vu faire son second déjeuner il s'en acquitta bien

LA ROCHE, née Bouligny.

I

BORDEAUX, le 12, 7bre, 1835

MES BONNES ET CHERES AMIES,—Nous avons été dans de grandes inquiétudes sur votre compte, on faisait courier la nouvelle ici pendant quelque temps, que le Bolochant était peu corps et bien, vous jugez, mes cheres amies, de tou les moments douleureux que tous ceux qui vous sont attachés ont éprouvés, jusqu'au moment que nous avons eu la certitude que tous ces bruits étaient faux, et que le Bolochant était arrivé à bon port Je fus a l'église remercier Dieu de l'heureuse nouvelle que e recevais, cela me fit faire une bonne action, je trouvai une malheureuse femme qui me tendit la main, je lui donnai une piece de 2 fr, et lui dis, allez entendre la messe et priez Dieu pour le remercier de ce que le navire est arrivé à la Nouvelle Orleans, elle se mit à courir, en criant oui, Madame, je vais prier pour la Nouvelle Orléans, je ne pouvais pas m'empecher de rire quand je la vis courir ainsi

Peu de jours apres j'ai reçu votre aimable lettre, qui m'a fait le plus grand plaisir, je vois que vous avez passé un temps des plus cru l, nous avions à cette époque, presque tous les jours des tempetes terribles, je pensai que vous deviez vous en ressentir.

Tout ce que vous avez dit a ma chere Justine à produit un

bon effet, elle m'a écrit deux fois depuis votre arrivee ; soyez bien persuades de toute ma reconnaisance   Vous ne me parlez pas de ma chere Josephine, lui avez vous fait parvenir ma lettre ? Je pense qu'elle était à la campagne, et que plus tard vous me parlerez d'elle

Les trois lettres de M. D...., ne seraient elles pas imitées par le serpent, qui tant de fois vous a donné des preuves de sa fourberie ? ah, *méfiez vous de lui*

Vous recevrez celle-ci par le frère de Jeannette, qui sûrement ira à Biloxi pour voir sa sœur, et il me promet de vous la remettre à vous-même.   Vous avez du être etonnés, mes bonnes amies, de n'avoir pas encore reçu de mes lettres, j'ai eu pendant trois mois une douleur à la main, je l'avais enflée, c'était une douleur rheumatismale, lorsque ma main a desenflé, la douleur s'est portée sur les reins, il a fallu me mettre des sangsues, et me purger, j'ai eté encore deux mois tres souffrante, ensuite, mon mari m'occupa beaucoup, il est tout-a-fait devenu infirme ; pour aller de sa chambre au salon, il faut que je lui donne le bras, tout souffrant qu'il est, il vous prie d'agreer ses amitiés, ainsi que la bonne Madame Caillavet.

Je suis bien aise de vous savoir à Biloxi, vous ferez bien d'y rester toute la mauvaise saison ; Edmon passera un temps agréable, il se baignera, montera a cheval, et mangera des huitres, je pense qu'il a toujour bon appétit   Gardette, est-il de retour ? faites leur, je vous prie, mes amities à tous deux

Adieu mes cheres et bonnes amies, croyez que vous n'avez pas une amie plus sincère que moi, je vous embrasse de tout mon cœur.   Madame Declouet m'a fait part de celle du 12 Mai, je ne puis vous exprimer combien votre souvenir me fait plaisir.

Mons. Garnier est a Nantes, il viendra nous voir   Nos affaires avec Rival sont toujour la même choses, comme quand vous avez parti d'ici.   L. née BOULIGNY

J

Nouvelle Orleans, le 28 Novembre, 1833.

Ma chere Zulime,—J'ai reçu, il y a que trois semaines, ta lettre du 26 Août, m'annonçant l'heureux retour de James auprés de toi, soit persuadee que j'ai partagé la joie que tu as dus éprouver.   Je relève d'une maladie très grave, je ne suis pas encore sortie de ma chambre, je suis encore très faible, et m'a vue me fait beaucoup souffrir, tu dois t'en apercevoir à mon écriture ; quoique cela, je ne puis laisser partir la bonne occasion du Belochant, s'en t'écrire un petit mot.   Je ne puis plus rester dans ce pays, chère Zulime, il deviendra mon tombeau, j'y suis constamment malade, aussi, je fais tout mon possible pour décider mon mari à partir pour France, j'espère y réussir, et qu'au printemps je verrai cette France, pour laquelle je sou-

pire depuis si longtemps   Je me flatte de l'idée que tu resteras
aussi à Bordeaux, je t'y verrai surement.   Ne me parle pas de
retourner au Nord, rien ne pourrait m'y decider, j'aime encore
mieux mourir ici, ce qui en arrivera, si j'y reste encore longtemps, je suis encore d'une faiblesse extreme.

Mon Emma se porte bien, ainsi que le gros Alphonse   Emma
se fait une fête d'aller en France, de te revoir, ainsi que son
cher oncle Edmond   je suis sure, me dit telle, que ma tante
Zulime me mordera encore l'oreille mais j'aime cela parce
qu'elle m'aime

Mes enfans t'embrassent tendrement, et mon mari te fait ses
amitiés   nous nous joignons tous en amitiés à James et Ep-
mond   Les enfans de Louisa se portent bien   ils sont toujours
chez Adèle

Rappelle moi, je te prie, aux souvenirs des dames Desclouet,
Martique, &c, et dit leur que j'espere avoir le plaisir de les voir
dans le courant de l'année prochaine

Milles choses aimables de ma part à Mad Caillavet, dit lui
que ses fils se portent bien et l'attendent avec impatience

Je suis, chere Zulime, ton affectionnee amie pour toujours
　　　　　　　　　　　　　　　　　　　FANNY

K

NOUVELLE ORLEANS, LE 22 Oct
CHERE ZULIME.—Quoique je t'ai ecris Samedi, par le Velocipede, j'apprend à l'instant que le *Suiss Boy*, un petit bateau,
part aujourd'hui, et va jusqu'à Nachitoches   je ne puis manquer cette occasion, qui me parait certaine   Nous sommes
très inquiets de Mons Sy   aucune nouvelle de lui depuis ta lettre, et le bruit court en ville qu'il est mort —qu'elle annee cruelle
Je suis aussi inquiete de James, car tu me dis qu'il a rechute,—
quand finira donc nos malheurs

Croirais-tu, chere Zulime, que la mort meme ne peut trouver
grace auprès de J———h, il s'occupe encore de ce malheureux
Valliere et en dit toujours des horreurs.   Tu dois penser si je
suis indignee   Ah ! il y a un Dieu qui est juste, et qui lui rendra
dra tout cela   Il quitte la maison de Madame Avart cette semaine, et en a pris une superbe, rue Royale, à cent piastres par
mois   Sa fille se marie le 7 Decembre   Tout semble leur
sourire, excepte à la pauvre Azélie, qui semble une martyre sur
la terre   Que j'aurais de choses à te dire que je ne puis écrire,
mais j'espere que nous nous verrons cet hiver   Nous sommes
tous en bonne santé, mais comme tu le pense bien triste   Je
t'envoye, ci-inclus, un hécrologe sur notre pauvre ami, tu verras
par cela que quoiqu'il a un ennemi, il avait aussi des amis, qui
le pleuront longtemps

Ecris moi, chere Zulime, et dis moi ce que decide James sur ce que je lui propose dans ma derniere lettre

Emma et Emile te font leurs amities, ainsi qu'a James, Duchautour se joint a eux

Les maladies ont presque totalement disparu Les etrangers arrivent de toute part

Adieu, chere Zulime, toute à toi d'amitie,

FANNY

Ta famille ici se porte bien Emile a mis a bord du Velocipede une lettre pour toi de Madame Caillavet

L

Mai, le 4, 1839

J'ai reçu hier, chere Zulime, ta lettre du 30, par un jeune homme à qui James la remit a bord, il s'est acquitte de sa commission tres ponctuellement et m'a promis de venir prendre ma reponse aujourd'hui s'il repart par le Velocipede, il a fait le voyage avec Jh, et le hazard a voulu qu'ils couche dans la meme cabine, il te dira sans doute toute la conversation qu'ils ont eu concernant James, donc ce monsieur parait l'ami il est tres indigne de la maniere que Jh a parle, et pense comme tout le monde que cela ne peut que lui faire du tort dans l'opinion des gens qui pense bien

J'espere, chere Zulime, que James se decidera a venir ici dans l'automne, d'ici là, il verra si la chantelle des Nachitoches vaut la peine d'y rester D'apres ce que m'a dit le porteur de la lettre, James est beaucoup aime la bas, il exerce la profession de medecin, il fait tres bien avec ses talents je suis sure qu'il reussira, et se fera un nom comme medecin, et pourra plus tard continuer ici que je serai heureuse de vous avoir aupres de moi J'ai toujours l'intention de passer l'ete à la campagne, je mettrai de cote quelque argent pour renouveller quelques meubles à l'automne, et j'espere que nous pourrons bien monter une maison entre nous Je crains de me bercer meme de cette idée qui me parait pourtant bien fondée Chere Zulime que je serai heureuse de pouvoir te donner les soins d'une fille chere a mon coeur Oui j'espere qu'entre James, moi et mon Emma nous te ferons passer encore des jours heureux

Je n'ai pas vu Sophie depais 15 jours j'irai ce soir la voir, et m'acquitter de ta commission qu'elle sera heureuse d'aller aupres de toi

On dit en ville qu'Eugenie se marie le mois prochain, je ne sai si cela est vrai

Mon Emma t'embrasse bien tendrement ainsi que son oncle, et desire autant que moi que nous soyons reunis Duchautour vous fait milles amities Toutes tes amies se rappellent a ton souvenir Aimée Canonge va demenager, elle a pris maison avec sa belle-sœur, Madame Léphine, c'est une bonne personne, et ces dames seront heureuse ensemble

Je devais t'écrire par le même bateau ou est monte Jh , mais Dieu ne l'a voulu, je n'avais pas une feuille de papier à la maison, et il était trop tard pour en faire prendre jusqu'en ville, ainsi, donc je n'ai pas pu écrire.

Le monsieur vient à l'instant prendre ma lettre, je l'achève sans avoir vu Sophie , je t'écrirai encore bientôt

Adieu, chere Zulime, toute à toi d'amitié sincere.

FANNY

M

NOUVELLE ORLEANS, LE 26 NOVEMBRE

Je reçois à l'instant, ma chere Zulime, ta dernière lettre du 28 Octobre, tu vois qu'elle a été assez longtemps en route, ainsi je pense que toutes celles que je t'ai écrites, ont subit le meme sort ; il parait que les postes sont affreusement tenus de ces côtes, car je reçois des lettres du Nord dans moins de temps   Je t'ai dejà marque, chere amie, bien des choses que tu me demande dans ta dernière

Enfin, chere amie, nous serons je crains éternellement les martyres du sort ; patience, chere Zulime, il se lassera de nous persecuter, il faut espérer   Je me voyais à la veille d'embrasser mon fils cheri, mon Emile, éh ' bien, par la méchancéte de ——, tu sais bien qui, il l'a fait envoyer dans le Connecticut, comme un esclave dans une manufacture de cassinet   Ah ! chere amie, je suis révoltée d'une telle barbarie, tu sais bien que ce n'est pas l'intérêt qu'il prend à mon malheureux enfant, mais seulement pour me déchirer l'âme.   Aussi, ma bonne amie je souffre en silence, et mon cœur de mère est un gouffre de douleur , tu peût me comprendre, chere Zulime, et toi seule ; si je pouvais verser mes larmes dans ton sein, je serais soulagée

Quant à nous, nous n'irons pas au bal cet hiver ; Emma ne le desire pas plus que moi, nous pensons trop à notre Emile, qui peut-être souffre

J'embrasse bien mon cher James, je lui ecrirai ces jours-ci

Toujours, chere Zulime, ton aime de cœur.

FANNY.

N

NOUVELLF ORLEANS, IE 22 AOUT

J'ai reçu hier, chere Zulime, ta petite lettre , je suis contente de te savoir heureuse, ayant notre cher James auprès de toi. Je regrette qui le steamboat ait resté si peu de temps, mais j'espère que la prochaine fois tu m'écriras plus longuement

Quand tu écriras à ta sœur Caillavet, chere Zulime, recommende lui mon fils , il a porté un petit paquet pour elle, de la part de Madame Despau   Vaillière a un lettre d'elle pour toi

Embrasse bien de notre part notre cher James ; j'ai toujours espoir qu'au mois de Novembre il viendra ici se fixer, quelque chose me dit cela, quelle bonheur ! nous serons encore réunis, et j'espère pour longtemps

Duchaufour te fait mille amities, ainsi qu'à James. Ne nous oubliez pas auprès de la bonne Jeanny et Gautier

Madame Narcotte se rappelle à ton souvenir

Adieu, chere Zulime, aime moi comme je t'aime, ton amie sincère FANNY.

O

Nouvelle Orleans, le 23 Novembre

Chere Zulime, j'ai reçu hier ta lettre datee le 25 du mois passé, comme tu vois, elle à eté presque un mois en route. Je t'ai ecris par la poste deux fois depuis la mort de notre ami, toutes tes lettres me sont parvenus, j'ai verifié toutes les dates d'après ta derniere, elles sont toutes ici.

Je t'ai marque dans toutes mes dernières lettres, ma chere Zulime, tout le plaisir que tu me ferais en venant ici, pourquoi fais-tu des cérémonies avec moi ? tu sais que je n'aurais qu'un morceau de pain, que je le partagerais avec toi de tout mon cœur Viens, chere Zulime, quand cela te fera plaisir, je te recevrai de tout mon cœur, le plutôt ne sera que le mieux ; ne manque pas la bonne occasion de Madame Robinson. Dis à Jenny qu'elle me fera aussi bien plaisir en venant avec toi, j'ai pour elle un amitié qui ne finira qu'à la mort Pourquoi est-ce que James ne se decide pas de venir ici de suite, ou peut-être vaut-il mieux que tu vienne seule avant, nous verrons a nous deux ce qu'il y aurai á faire plus tard pour lui,—viens donc, j'ai cinquante projets en tête, mais suis decidée a faire quelques choses pour gagner de l'argent, pour te mettre ainsi que moi-même dans l'aisance, et je crois réussir

Duchaufour te fait ses amities ainsi q'á James

Adieu chere Zulime, toute a toi d'amitié sincère

FANNY

P

Jeudi, 5 Sept.

Voilá le Têche de retour ma chere amie, et pas de lettre de toi ; je suis d'une inquiétude très grande, pourquoi ne me pas faire écrire deux mots par Vaillière.

J'ai presque envie de gronder, mais crains quelques malheurs, car je suis un peu comme toi, chere Zulime, j'imagine toujours le mal avant qu'il n'arrive.

Rien de nouveau depuis la dernière, qui était Lundi par le Vélocipéde ; as-tu reçu celle par le Têche ?

Ta sœur, &c, se portent tous bien, je leur fera t'écrire le prochaine voyage du Vélocipéde.

Milles amitiés de notre part á James Dufauchour est perce
de douleur ce matin, d'avoir couché avec la fenetre ouverte, la
nuit passee il a fait très froid, et le jour une chaleur etouffiante,
aussi les maladies augmentent Je te quitte, car le bateau part
dans une heure

Toute a toi, chere Zulime, d'amitie sincere   F D

Q

Le 24 Mai

J'ai reçu chere Zulime ta dernière lettre, du 12 ce mois, c'est
Sophie qui me la apportee, elle me dit que c'est Mons Lemec
qui lui a remise, et qu'il devait partir ces jours-ci, et qu'elle doit
ecrire par lui, comme j'ai la bonne occasion de Mr Robinson,
gendre de Madame Narcot, je la prefere il te portera aussi tes
porte-bouteilles et corbeille Je t'ai écrit par le dernier voyage
du *John Linton*, et t'ai envoye des gazettes

Je savais, chere amie, par Mr Robinson que James avait intention de vendre, je sai bien qu'il en a fini, car je le voyais avec
régret quitter son etat, ou il doit faire fortune avec le talent qu'il a
J'espère d'ici a l'automne il pourra venir ici, et j'en suis sure
J'ai toujours l'intention de passer mon ete a la campagne, et
j'espère arriver jusqu'aupres de toi

Mon Emma est toujours bonne et aimable, elle ne pense et ne
rêve que talent. Nous avons entendu ces jours-ci une forte
pianiste, Madame Yarerand, je ne m'etais pas imaginee qu'on
pouvait jouer comme cela Emma est decidee a ce qu'elle dit
d'arriver jusqu'à ce point A notre retour de la campagne, je
la ferai prendre des lecons avec cette dame J'espere qu'a cette
epoque nous serons reunis Son oncle James lui donnera beaucoup d'emulation parcequ'elle l'aime extremement, et fera tout ce
qu'il voudra Elle fera son entree dans le monde cet hiver, et
elle dit qu'elle espere avoir son oncle pour chevalier

Mon mari te fait milles amities, ainsi qu'a James Emma
vous embrasse tendrement Elle etudie son piano à cote de moi
Mon Alphonse est aussi bien

Sophie est toujours chez Madame Woorster nous avons intention de diner là cette semaine Myra est chez Mons Bringier
avec son mari, mais elle va rester a l'Hotel St Louis, a la fin de
la semaine Je n'ira pas la voir, excepté qu'elle ne vienne me
voir, car elle croirai que je veux lui faire la cour, etant a present dans la grandeur,—elle fait grand etalage Je t'envoye une
gazette ou on annonce son mariage Je pense qu'elle ira aux
Nachitoches bientôt avec le Général

Madame Narcotte te fait ses amities, ainsi que toutes tes amis
elles demandent toujours de tes nouvelles Adieu chere Zulime,
pense à moi, écris moi souvent, j'en ferai de meme, ton amie de
cœur,   FANNY

R

VENDREDI, LE 17 AOUT

Tu as été sans doute surprise, ma chere Zulime, de ne pas recevoir une réponse de moi par le jeune homme qu'a apporta ta lettre, mais n'accuse que lui car il est parti sans nous prévenir Gautier a été chez lui le jour convenu pour porter ma lettre, et les objets que tu lui demandais il était déja parti une autre lettre de moi ci-incluse chere Zulime, te prouvera ce que je te dis est vrai, quoique vieille je te l'envoye pour ne pas récrire plusieurs choses qui y sont

Les amours sont toujours la meme chose on a donné un diner l le 15 fête de la mere et la fille, c'est aussi la tienne, chere Zulime je voudrais pouvoir te la souhaiter de plus près, mais quoique de loin je te la souhaite heureuse, et qu'a l'avenir tes chagrins soient finis, et te donne l'assurance, que si l'amitié et le respect d'une fille et d'un fils, qui te sont sincerement dévoués peuvent te rendre le bonheur tu peut conter sur celle de James et moi Il me tarde de nous voir réunis et nous disputer a qui te prodiguera le plus d'attentions et d'amitiés —ce jour viendra chere amie Et mon Emma cette enfant chérie réclamera aussi sa part te ton amitié.—oui, tu seras heureuse, chere Zulime nous pleurerons avec toi quelquesfois et te consolerons toujours

Comme tu t'interesse à ce qui me fait plaisir, je t'apprendrai que j'ai reçu une longue lettre de mon Emile, il me marque qu'il est d'une santé parfaite, qu'il a 5 pieds 4 pouces, et pese 152 livres Il me demande la permission d'encore aller en mer ; je suis sure que c'est un ordre qu'il a reçu de M E, car surement cet enfant ne peut pas desirer encore courir les mers, après tout ce qu'il a souffert , non cet *etre* veut encore me faire de la peine, en tachant de me séparer pour toujours de mon fils bien aimé Je lui ai écrit de suite, que je ne voulais pas qu'il aille en mer, mais qu'il revienne ici si le plan que j'ai pour son avenir ne lui plait pas, il sera toujours temps de partir d'ici pour se faire marin Mais le plan est qu'il ne revienne pas ici, car il pourra me dire beaucoup de choses que le pauvre enfant ne peut pas m'écrire. J'ai donc le faible espoir, chere Zulime de presser mon fils sur mon cœur dans le mois d'Octobre ou Novembre Je crains d'en mourir de joie

Il y a un mois que je n'ai reçu de nouvelles de mon mari, tu es près de lui, tache donc d'en avoir des nouvelles pour moi, écris lui quelques mots et marque lui mon inquiétude sur sa negligence , je crains qu'il soit malade.

Emma vous embrasse milles fois, ainsi que mon gros Alphonse Fais bien mes amitiés à James. Je pense que tu n'osas écrire par le Teche, parceque tu n'avais pas reçu de lettre de moi. Tu devais bien penser que c'était un malentendu, car tu sais que je ne suis ni paresseuse pour écrire, ni négligente envers ceux que j'aime,—la preuve, ces deux longues lettres

Gautier me charge de te dire qu'il n'a pas pu toucher un sou de son mois d'appointement au corps-de-garde, c'est perdu pour lui, et il a couru au moins trois jours sans pouvoir travailler, pour tâcher d'avoir cet argent.

Maintenant il fait son état, et pense de ramasser de l'argent pour aller te rejoindre, s'il n'a pas la place a l'église

Répond moi par le retour du Têche, soit sure que je négligerai aucune occasion de t'écrire

G. a trouvé ce paquet de gazettes et lettres chez M Jourdain, je pense que tes sœurs les enverront toujours la   Si tu as quelques choses à leur envoyer, met tout sous mon envelope, et j'enverrai aussi chez M Jourdain. Pas de lettres à la poste pour toi; Gautier en demande toujours.

Gautier fait bien ses amitiés à sa sœur, et se rappelle à votre souvenir.

Je suis ton affectionée amie,   FANNY.

S

NOUVELLE ORLEANS, LE 24 JANVIER, 1839

CHERE ZULIME,—Je regrette de ne pouvoir te voir, j'ai tant de choses à te dire, mais j'espère que si James se decide de venir faire un tour ici, tu l'accompagneras, je ne veux pas de refus, et je t'attend avec lui, et cette fois j'espére ce sera moi que tu viendras voir; j'ai été désappointée deux fois, dans l'espoir de t'avoir auprès de moi ; pour la troisième, je mérite, j'espère, par ma patience de t'avoir; ainsi point de refus

J'enverrai celle-ci par le steam boat "Alexandrie," ainsi que quelques gazettes que je t'ai ramassés. Les dames Canonges ont éte bien du tracas et chagrin, Léphine a été à l'article de la mort, il est mieux depuis hier, il a la disantrie : Mr. Albin Mihel père, est mort depuis 15 jours ; le vieil Juge Martin est aussi mort.

Emma t'embrasse mille fois ainsi que son oncle. Duchaufour toi fais aussi ses amitiés. Alphonse est bien et t'embrasse. J'ai reçu une lettre de mon Emile, du 1er Janvier, il se portait bien mais désire beaucoup revenir auprès de moi.

Adieu chère Zulime, Je suis ton affectionée amie, FANNY.

T

JANVIER, 23, 1840.

CHERE ZULIME,—Encore j'ai manqué le Teche sans être de ma faute comme tu le pense bien. J'ai t'écris une longue lettre par le John Linton, que tu recevras mes lettres par tous les bateaux, mais j'espère qu'un mois ne se passera pas sans que je te voye, d'ailleurs bientôt les eaux seront encore trop basse; il faut donc profiter du prochain voyage du Teche.

Depuis la lettre par Madame Buard, je n'ai pas eu de tes nouvelles, j'espère que la cause n'est pas maladie, donne moi des nouvelles de James et s'il est décidé a venir se fixer ici Je n'ai pas vu ta sœur depuis ma dernière lettre, je t'en donnerai des nouvelles dans ma prochaine parceque j'irai la voir.

Emma te fais mille amitiés et t'embrasse ainsi qu'a son oncle, je me joins a elle

Duchaufour se rappelle a votre souvenir les dames Gachet aussi Seline est au lit dans ce moment d'une fausse couche de trais mois, c'est la troisieme qu'elle fait e depuis sa derniére petite, le bras de sa mere est presque gueri, ils ont beaucoup de pensionnaires et font de l'argent et vive bien

Bournos est toujours ici, il a diné avec nous deux fois sans façon, et le petit Eugéne qui est venu nous voir hier (parcequ'il repart pour le college aujourd'hui,) nous dit, que Bournos dine chez eux presque tous les jours—les miracles ne cesserons jamais—qu'il me tarde de te voir tous ce que j'ai a te dire, ne peut pas s'ecrire

On vient me dire qu'un bateau part a quatre heure, je te quitte a la hâte

Adieu chére Zulime, je t'embrasse de cœur, FANNY

U

NEW ORLEANS, May 31st.

I have just learned from Gautier, my dear James, that a steamboat leaves here, this morning, for Nachitoches, I avail myself of the opportunity

You have, no doubt, learnt all the new difficulties I have gone through Poor mamma has I expect, suffered much. Gautier tells me, she has written to you of course has given you a long and correct detail of all When I heard that she had learnt the death of our unfortunate Edmond, I thought it as much my duty as my inclination prompted me to go see her, which I did I spent two afternoons with her The second, I met Joe, as I left the house He addressed me the phrase which follows, and many others, which, of course I did not stop to hear. "You must have the impudence of the devil, Madam, to come here; this is the second time, and, damn, let it be the last time"

What think you, my dear, brother, of this reception? However, it did not astonish me as I partly expected it Knowing the man so well I am persuaded it does not surprise you. Béon has called on me to give me news of mamma, she has more courage than I had dared to hope. her trials are indeed great She has not yet been out of the house, and, Gautier tells me, but seldom goes down stairs Hurry, my dear James, to make money, and come back to her she needs consolation, at this

73

trying moment of her life   I am on the search of a house.   I hope to find one which will suit us both, before you return to town

Write to me   Let me know if you are doing well, and tell me how I am to act with regard to mamma   Shall she remain where she is—lonely, unhappy? or shall I take her with me—and, by my attention try to sooth her sorrows?   Be frank with me, dear James, you know my heart.   I will do as you say; I think it for the best.

Emma embraces you tenderly; she devotes all her time to study   I have a thousand things to tell you, which I cannot write   Believe, however, that, tho' absent, you are not forgotten.

The news are, that Mr Delachaise is dead, and is to be buried to-day   He leaves 12 hundred thousand dollars to his children.

Duchaufour Froe, and Sinson beg to be affectionately remembered to you, they long, as well as myself, to see you return here

I have received several letters from Carrida.   She expects to see you at her dwelling, and seems to regret the city very much.

I expect Gautier, every moment, to come for my letter.   I embrace tenderly.

Your affectionate Sister,
FANNY.

V

New Orleans, 27 Fevrier, 1826

Monsieur —Je n'ai l'honneur de vous connaitre que de reputation, Monsieur, mais j'ai bien l'avantage de connaitre tout bien votre famille, qui est tres respectable, et qui jouit ici de l'estime, de la confiance, et de la consideration des premières familles. Monsieur, votre fils est desolé   que, malgré les demarches de soumission et de respect qu il a fait, et qu'il fait sans cesse, auprès de vous, il n'obtient pas votre pardon.   Monsieur, je me joint a lui, on voyez a vos pieds, pour vous conjurer de lui écrire en marque de votre satisfaction, et d'avoir oublié les torts, qu'il a envers vous; et je puis vous l'assurer que ce n'a éte que l effet de sa vivacité, et nullement de sa volonté, et de son cœur, qui en est tout sincerement repentant, et que lui est necessaire votre attention pour etre heureux. J espére fermement que vous ne rejetterez pas mon priere, et que vous aurez la bonté de faire une reponse favorable a la présente pour consoler Monsieur votre fils, et Madame Avare sa et celui qui a l honneur d'etre avec respect et consideration,

Votre trés dévoué serviteur, L'Abbé MONI.

Le 6 Avril, 1826.

Monsieur,—Je reçus il y a 4 jours la lettre que vous me fites l'honneur de m'écrire le 27 Fevr. dernier, et je m'empresse d'y

repondre, quoique d'après une lettre que j'ai reçus de mon fils
il y a 10 jours en date 22 du même mois, je suppose qu'il ne
sera point à la N Orléans lorsque vous recevrez celle-ci, puis
qu'il me dit qu'il devait partir pour le *Kentucky* le 15 mars
cette lettre et une autre qu'il m'écrivit le 7 Dec 1824 sont les
seules que j'ai reçus de lui depuis qu'il quitta ma maison, *a mon
insu*, le 21 Septembre 1821

Il écrivit a son frere le 21 juillet dernier, et lui annonça son
depart prochain pour Louisville lui donnant son adresse aux
soins d'un negociant de cette ville j'en profitai, et lui écrivis à
cette addresse au mois d'avril il parait d'après sa dernière lettre,
qu'il n'a pas reçu la mienne Je vais lui écrire de nouveau poste,
et s'il n'est pas à la N Orleans lorsque ma lettre arrivera, on
pourra la lui envoyé ou il se trouvera pour lors Je l'ai pardonné trois fois, comme je le fais a present et je n'ai jamais cessé
de lui souhaiter bonheur et prosperité, quoique dans une lettre
qu'il écrivit à son frere quelques jours apres son marriage il dit
*"although, I suppose, I have the malediction of my father yet I am
perfectly happy and very well contented with my lot*

Puis que vous avez la bonté Mr de vous interresser a ce jeune
homme, il a sans doute comme il le doit toute confiance en
vous; Je puis par consequent inclure dans cette lettre une copie
de celle que je lui écrivis au mois d'aout dr a Louisville, ce que
je fais; vous y verrez Mr que je l'ai pardonné plusieurs fois,
comme je le fais a present, mais je ne puis oublier certains torts,
qu'il a eu envers moi et ma femme, desquels je suis bien persua-
dé, il ne vous a point informé il sont bien graves, ces torts!
Mr ils ont cependant tous été pardonnés Si je pouvais avoir
l'avantage de m'entretenir avec vous *ma voce* je pourrais vous
dire bien de choses à son sujet, que je n'ose confier au papier, et
qui vous prouverait que ce n'est pas l'etourderie qu'il a toujours
dirige sa conduite, comme il veut nou le faire croire

S'il est vrai que mon fils jouisse de l'estime, de la confiance,
et de la consideration des premieres familles, (j'entends par la
des gens honnetes de la N O.) il ne peut manquer de faire ses
bonnes affaires, Pourquoi est-il donc toujours a voyager? Il
est desolé dites vous, voyant que malgré les demarches de soumission et de respect qu'il a fait et ne cesse de faire auprès de
vous, il n'obtient pas encore votre pardon Vous savez, sans
doute, M l'Abbe, qu'un pére est toujours enclin a pardonner
les fautes de ses enfans mais il en est qui sont si graves, qu'il
est impossible de les oublier, quoiqu'on les aye pardonnés—ces
demarches de soumission et de respect sont sans doute contenues
dans les deux lettres que j'ai reçues de lui si cela est ainsi, je
puis vous assurer Mr qu'elles sont tres insignifiantes

Je crains beaucoup que les parents de sa femme n'ayent un
grand tort negligent de s'informer, par des voies sures, si ce

jeune homme etait capable, par son industrie, de fournir aux besoins d'une famille, qui augmentent ordinairement beaucoup plus vite que les rentes.¹ J'en sais quelque chose, M. l'Abbe, moi qui ai eleve douze enfans, et qui travaille depuis quarante ans, pour tacher de me procurer une petite independance dans ma viellesse, à quoi je n'ai pu parvenir. Je suis donc toujours obligé de travailler sans l'aide d'aucun de mes enfans. C'etait mon fils Joseph, comme l'ainé de ceux qui me restent sur qui j'avais fixé mes vues pour me remplacer dans une pratique tres lucrative pour un jeune homme, recommandé par moi mais il aurait fallu pour cela, qu'il restat aupres de moi, et qu'il attendit qu'il fut bien etabli pour se marier.

Je vous prie Mr d'etre l'interprete de mes sentiments respectueux etc., auprès de Madame Avart, quoique je n'ai pas l'honneur de la connaitre mais pour qui d'apres ce que j'ai appris de la bonte de son caractere, j'ai la plus grande veneration. Ma fille, Madame Le Roy qui me charge de vous presenter ses respects, m'a dit que Mad Avart avait l'intention de venir passer l'eté prochain à Philadelphia. Si cela ainsi, Madame Gardette serait extrenement flattee que Madame Avart voulut accepter une chambre chez nous, je me joins a ma femme pour prier cette respectable dame d'accepter son offre, comme sa ma femme espere que Madame Avart ne lui refusera pas cette faveur.

Recevez, je vous prie Mr mes remerciments bien sinceres pour l'interet que vous avez la bonte de prendre à mon fils, je desire bien sincerement qu'il le merite, c'eut eté bien heureux pour lui, si a son arrivee a la N. O. il eut eu le bonheur de faire la connaissance d'un homme respectable, de qui, comme vous, la sainte profession conduit toujours à donner des avis salutaires a la jeunesse, lui qui en avait tant besoin.

Soyez bien persuade, je vous prie, Monsieur, de la vive reconnaissance, du respect, de la haute consideration, avec lesquels j'ai l'honneur d'etre Votre tres oblige et devoué Serviteur

Recu le 31 Mars—et repondu le 6 Avril, 1826

W

Ma chere Maman —Je t'aime, te souhaite cinquante années heureuses, et j'espère qu'à la fin de tes jours tu pourra dire que depuis le 1 Jan, 1822, je me suis comporte envers toi de manière à meriter ton amitie et estime. J'espère te prouver que je ne suis pas un ingrat, et que le mauvais example n'aura pas d'effet sur moi, pour te remercier de tes bontes sans nombres, **pour tonjours ton**

fils EMILE

1er Jan 1822

X

Philadelphia, July 2d, 1829

Chere Maman —Tu ne sera point surprise que je t'écrive une

lettre courte, comparree a celle que j'addresse en anglais à pappa ce n'est pas que je manque de sujets ou que je j'eprouve moins de familiaritee envers toi mais simplement parceque je m'exprime avec difficulte, et suis constantinent en crainte, lorsque j'ecrit le français Il est tems que nous recevions des nouvelles de ton arrivee au Havre, si tontefois tu n'a pas oublie ta promese de m'ecrire de suit je ne puis te faire comprendre combien je suis inquiet de l'etat d'incertitude dans la quelle il me faut rester peut etre encore pendant quelques semaines—milles dangers qui peuvent survenir en mers, et autant qui ont leur sources dans l'etat de santé dans la quel mon pere quitta l'amerique me rendent triste, et je me pursuade en vain que ces craintes sont mal fondees

Le 30 Juillet—J'avais commencé cette lettre dans la supposition que Mr Phiquepal devait partie de suit pour France et Agen, il a remis son voyage, et pendant ce delai, j'ai reçu la, lettre tant desiree qui m'annonca votre arrivé au Havre Mais, Maman, elle n'etait point de ta plume Pappa qui n'ecris pas souvent voyant que tout le monde devait recevoir des lettres excepter Emilie, a pris pitie de moi, et me donna les detailes amusantes du voyage Comment vais-je te gronder et te punir? En te faisant lire mon mauvais français—ne t'ecrivant pas, serait une pauvre vengeance, puis que je ne puis produire une lettre en francais, sans causer des sensations pénibles a celui ou celle qui doit me lire J'ai presqu'envie de t'en donner une douzaines de pages Mais non—ce serait une trop grande punision pour une petite offense Je vais être plus généreux— et sans te pardonner tout de suite, je veux t'ecorché les oreilles avec de villains mots mal arranges—et quand tu m'aura envoyé quatre pages dans ton style coulant et agreable, je t'enverrai mon pardon par écrit Consent-tu a ce jugement de la cour supreme, viz *l'offense?*

Si tu veux t'amuser chere Maman étudiéz l'anglais je te recommande a lire ma petite lettre a pappa—tu y trouvera toutes les nouvelles du jour Je veux t'en donner une suite ici Dévine qui marie? non—non—non—non—non—allons, tu ne dévinera pas—Abadie l'aine

Je te prie de dire a James et Edmond de m'ecrire—et si tu veux recevoir de *bonnes* lettres tu sais a qui il faut que tu écrive —je serai toujours exact a répondre, mais si tu na m'ecris point, je t'enverrai quatres longues lettres par chaque paquet Ma femme est un peu mieux qu'elle n'a ete depuis notre délogement —elle te fais bien des amities ainsi qu'a pappa—quand elle sera bien elle écrira a pappa en anglais

J'attends beaucoups, de detailles d'Agen dans tes lettres, et jespère connaitre tout mes parens et me faire connaitre par ton entremise. Je t'embrasse de cœur, ton fils et amie EMILE.

Y

ALEXANDRIA, Jan 30th, 1825.

Je m'empresse de répondre a ton aimable lettre du 23, chère maman, pour t'exprimer combien je suis sensible à la peine que tu t'ai donné, pour me faire connaître mon injustice envers mad G— Si je me suis trompe a son egard, j'en suis vraiment bien aise. j'ai une estime tres sincere pour toute cette famille, et me trouve heureux de recevoir des assurances de leur amities Le faux jugement que j'ai porté provient de pleusieurs circonstances qui m'ont été rapportes par une personne que je crois être mon ami, mais je suis plutot porte a croie le bien que le mal de n'importe qui, et surtout de ceux dont je voudrais posseder l'estime.

Ce que tu nomme ton barbouillage, chère Maman, ne procure d'autant plus de plaisir qu'un joli abandon dans le style èpisto-laire *de ceux qui me sont chère, semble à mon cœur une* embleine de leurs sincerité Les mots jettés sur le papier, sans cette attention particuliere a former les lettres, donne l'assurance que les idees partent directement du cœur C'est meme une satisfaction d'être oblige de retire et chercher avant de pouvoir bien decouvrir le sentiment que l'on aime ; les pières précieuse ne se trouvent, tu sais, qu'a force de piocher Je ne veux plus entendre d'appologies, pour ta mauvais ecriture, et surtout ne pas être prive de ta correspondence parceque je ne suis pas là pour te tailler des plumes

Une lettre de Louisa que me parvint hier m'apporte la nouvelle affligeantes de l'indisposition de mon cher Pere; tu m'avait donner des nouvelles de lui bien plus agreables, en me disant qu'il était aller déjeuner chez le conte Survilliers.

Je n'ai pas vu mon aimable ami Guegan depuis mon départ de Washington, dont il y a huit jours, j'ai reçu une longue lettre de lui hier, par la qu'elle j'apprends que ses affaires en sont la cause. Il me dit qu'il était sur le point de t'écrire, ainsi qu'a pappa.

Je te prie d'être mon intérprete aupres de toutes mes aimables connaissances et amis a Philadelphia Je serais tres peine si je croyez avoir mal agit envers la *petite demoiselle au tourter elles·* ce qui je lui dit chez mad—B—fut simplement avec le but de me justifier dans une demarche que j'avais fait par pure complaisance, et que sa mere semblais avoir mal intèrpreter. J'espère que l'on n'en parlera plus, car cela y domerai trop de conséquence J'en ai fait si peu de cas, que je fut parler à la mère D—quand elle se trouva au bal d'enfant, avec moi, comme si rien n'était

Adieu, ma chère Maman, porte toi bien et crois à l'attachement bien sincère de ton fils et ami.   EMILE.

Mes amitiés a pappa, Louisa, James et Edmond.

Ma plus grande depense pour mes plaisirs, est en tabac—je porte tabatière, et prise comme un grenadier priseur—cela vaut mieux que chiquer, fumer, ou boire et il me faut absolument avoir un habitude quelconque, pour me consoler dans mon exile.

Z

————"parcequ'il est generalement convenu qu'on ne doit pas aimer une belle mere"————je ne crois pas que j'aurai pu ecrire de telles bêtises„ dans n'importe quelles circonstances, et certainment des sentiments semblables n'ont jamais eu place dans mon cœur je ne suis pas dans l'habitude de faire de grandes professions d'affections, mais depuis l'age de raison, je crois avoir rempli mes devoirs envers mes parens.

Elizabeth se rappelle à ton souvenir et nous faisons bien des amitiés à Edmond, nous serons très heureux de te revoir. Dites bien des choses, je te prie à Madame Caillavet de notre part, et à ceux de tes amis à Bordeaux qui me connaissent, Madame et Monsieur Bouchon, et d'autres qui sont souvent nommé par James sont des personnes pour les qu'elles je sens un grand intéret, si jamais quelqu'un deux, ou le Docteur Beulatour, venait dans mon pays, je serai tres heureux de l'occasion qui s'offrirai pour leur faire voir ma sincère reconnaissance pour les attentions et les bontes qu'ils ont eu pour ma famille.

Adieu ma chere mere, n'oublie pas de me laisser savoir l'epoque de ton depart de Bordeaux, et le nom du batiment.

Je ne sais pas si je te dis tout ce que je desire ici, car j'ai la tête boulversee par trop d'occupation, non seulement dans mon état, mais également pour les autres. Tu pardonneras les fautes que tu trouve dans ma lettre, car je ne puis la relire.

Avec affection ton fils et ami,   E B GARDETTE.

A---2

Philadelphia, Juin le 22, 1822.

Monsieur Joseph Gardette, à Agen

Mon cher Oncle.—Mon père m'ayant communiqué votre lettre du 15 Oct 1821, j'ai vu qu'il y était question de moi et de ma jeune sœur et je ne crois pas pouvoir me dispenser de vous écrire quelques mots pour rendre justice a la verité.

Je dois donc vous dire, mon cher oncle, que ce que mon frère peut vous avoir dit relativement à la conduite de Maman envers lui, moi et ma sœur cadète, est sans verité, et qu'au contraire, elle a montré beaucoup d'amitié pour lui particulièrement, et nous à toujours donné de bons conseils à touts.

Comme pappa vous écrit, je suppose qu'il vous donne des détails sur Joseph—qui cependont ne doivent pas vous étonnées d'apres ce que vous savez de sa conduite et la manniere qu'il vous à remercié de toutes les bontées que vous lui avez prodigue

Je vous dirai seulement qu'il a décampe de la maison, et á été
à la N'lle Orléans, où il s est marie, il faut espèrer que quand il
sera père qu'il verra ses torts et fera son possible pour les
reparer

Presentez, je vous prie, mes amitiés respecteuses a ma chere
Tante, ainsi qu à mes aimable cousines et cousins, et croyez
moi avec des sentiments

d'estimes et de considerations, votre

affectionnee et respectueux neveu,

E B GARDETTE, S D

Deposition of Doctor James Gardette, for Complainant.

And afterwards, to wit: on the 27 June, 1849, Doctor James
Gardette, a witness on behalf of complainant, heretofore examined, being recalled, did depose and say

Madame Solidelle de Roffinac's Letters

That he knew the late Madame Solidelle de Roffignac. She
died in France She was from her infancy an intimate friend
of my mother She was a creole of New Orleans. I am the
son of Madame Zulime Gardette I have looked upon the letters
handed me, designated by letters from A to D, inclusivo,
and recognize them to be in the hand writing of Madame Roffignac, and were received by my mother, Madam Gardette.

Madame Louise la Roche's Letters.

I knew Madame Louise de la Roche née Bouligny. She
was an intimate friend of my mother from her infancy I have
often seen her at my mother's house in Bordeaux I know her
husband perfectly well, he was a nobleman, a count if I am not
mistaken. I have looked on the letters designated by the letters from E to I, inclusive, and recognize them to be in the
handwriting of Madame de la Roche

I know Madame Fanny Duchaufour; she is a half-sister of
mine I have seen her write, and know her hand writing perfectly. I have looked on the letters handed to me designated by
the letters from J. to U, inclusive, and recognize them to be in
the hand writing of Madame Duchaufour.

I know Emile Gardette perfectly well; he is a half brother of
mine I have seen him write, and know his handwriting I
have looked upon the letters designated by the letters from **W.**
to A., inclusive, and also A 2, and recognize them to be in the
handwriting of Emile Gardette. these were directed to and
received by my mother.

I have looked on the letter handed to me marked **V**, a letter from Abbe Mori, and recognize on one of the pages the reply thereto, in the handwriting of my father

JAMES GARDETTE

Cross examination waived by defendant's counsel

J. W GURLEY, Commissioner

[Duplicate] PHILADELPHIA NOVEMBER 24, 1819

MONSIEUR,—Mon nom ne manquera pas sans doute de vous rappeler celui de notre ami réciproque le feu Monsieur Daniel Clarke

Lorsque j'étais à la Nouvelle Orleans, l'hiver passé, pour régler quelques affaires avec les sieurs Chew et Relf, les exécuteurs testamentaires de notre dit ami il fut convenu entre eux et moi que Monsieur Richard Relf vous écrivit pour vous prier de passer une acte de vente à Caroline Clark, la fille illegitime de Monsieur D Clark des 51 terrains, dont il vous avait passé la vente il y a plusieurs années au bureau de Monsieur Pedesclaux, à la Nouvelle Orleans

L'objet de cette lettre est de vous repeter cette affaire, en cas que la lettre de Mr Relf ne vous soit pas parvenue, et de vous prier de ne perdre pas de tems en nous l'expediant Vous pouvez la faire dans toutes les formalités legales, ayant toujours rapport dans l'acte que vous devez envoyer aux mème 51 terrains situés sur le bien de notre ami sur le chemin de Bayou St Jean, dont il avait passé la vente chez Monsieur Pedesclaux, à la Nouvelle Orleans Comme la pauvre Caroline n'a aucune autre heritage que ces dits terrains, il est tres urgent à cause de son etat pitoyable, de l'expédier au plutot, et pour mieux assurer qu'elle nous parvienne, je vous prie de la faire par *Duplicata*, dont l'une peut être envoyé à Mons Relf a la Nouvelle Orleans, et l'autre a moi a Philadelphie, ou Caroline se trouve actuellement

Je vous prie, Monsieur, d'agreer les sentiments amicales et respectueux, avec lesquelles, j'ai l'honneur d'etre

Votre tres humble Serviteur,

DANIEL W COXE

Monsr Joseph de Ville Degoutin de Bellechasse, à Matanza l'Ile de Cube

TRANSLATION

[Duplicate] PHILADELPHIA, Nov 24th, 1819

SIR.—My name cannot fail to recall to you that of our mutual friend, the late Mr Daniel Clark

When I was in New Orleans last winter to arrange some affairs with Messrs, Chew & Relf the testamentary executors of our said friend, it was agreed, between them and me that

Mr Richard Relf should write you to ask you to pass an act of sale to Caroline Clark, the illegitimate daughter of Mr D Clark, of 51 lots, of which he (Clark) had passed you the title, several years since, in the office of Mr Pedesclaux, in New Orleans

The object of this letter is to make you acquainted with the affair, in case the letter of Mr Relf should not reach you, and to beg you to lose no time in consummating it You may do it with all the legal formalities specifying in the act you are to send the same 51 lots situated on the property of our friend, on the Bayou Road, the titles which he had passed you before Pedesclaux, in New Orleans As the poor Caroline has no other heritage than these lots, it is extremely desirable, on account of her necessitous, pitoyable condition to attend to it at once and to make sure of the act reaching us, I beg you to make it in *duplicate*—sending one to Mr Relf, at New Orleans, and the other to me, at Philadelphia, where Caroline now is

I pray you, sir, to accept the friendly and respectful sentiments with which I have the honor to be

Your very humble servant,
DANIEL W COXE

Mr Joseph de ville Degoutin Bellechasse
Matanzas, Cuba

NOUVELLE ORLEANS, ce 21 AOUT 182

MON CHER BELLECHASSE,—Il s'est écoulé un lapse très considérable de temps, depuis que j'ai eu le plaisir d'avoir de vos nouvelles directes ; je n'ai pas manque néanmoins de prendre toutes les informations que vos amis ont reçu de vous , et j'appris avec une peine sincère les afflictions domestiques qui vous sont survenues, que j'en partage en vrai ami

J'ai essayé aussi beaucoup de contre-temps, trop nombreux pour vous entretenir dans une lettre, et comme ils sont irréparables, il faut tacher de les oublier

L'objet de la présente, est pour vous entretenir de l'affaire des terrains réclamés par Davis, pour la fille Myra , vous ignorez peut-être que Clark avait deux enfans naturelles, l une qu'il avait confie aux soins de Davis, nommée Myra, et l'autre qu'il plaça lui-même en pension au Nord, sous les soins de notre ami commun Hulings, qui depuis la mort de Clark en a eu tous les égards possibles Ignorant entièrement moi-même les intentions du défunct, à l'égard de ces enfants, peu de temps après sa mort, en réponse à une lettre de Hulings a ce sujet, je lui instruisit de l'affaire des terreins passés à votre nom et celui de La Croix : et ce que vous me dites à ce sujet, me donnent, mon opinion, que les intentions de Clark ne pouvaient êtres autres que de donner la moitié a chaques, je voudrais qu'en réponse vous me disiez positivement, si dans l'entretien que

Clark eut avec vous, il vous a déclaré que les **objets** furent exclusivement p   Mira, et s'il la designee par nom ou autrement, et comme les pieces que vous m'aviez envoyé dans le temps, ne peuvent pas suffire pour passer la vente, je vous prie de m envoyer un pouvoir special, duement authentique et légalise, par l'agent de commerce Américain à Matanzas, s il en existe un   Le pouvoir peut etre pur & simple, m'autorisant a résilier la vente, et declarant que c était une affaire de confiance entre les parties

Je serais charme en recevant votre reponse, d'apprendre votre réussite dans les affaires qui vous occupent, et que votre famille jouit d'une bonne santé, souhaite tres aidemmen votre ami   **RICHARD RELF**

TRANSLATION

New Orleans, 21st August, 1820

My Dear Bellechasse   A very considerable time has elapsed since I had the pleasure of hearing from you direct.   I nave not failed, however, to exact all the information that your friends have received from you   I learn with sincere pain the domestic afflictions that have happened to you, in which I truly sympathize

I, also, have been exposed to many disappointments   They are too numerous to relate to you in a letter, and. as they are irreparable, it is best to try and forget them

The object of this is to speak to you of the affair of the lots claimed by Davis for the girl Myra   You do not know, perhaps, that Clark had two natural children; one that he had confided to the care of Davis, named Myra, and another that he himself placed at boarding in the north under the charge of our common friend, Hulings, who, since the death of Clark, has taken all possible care of her   Entire y ignorant, myself, of the intentions of the deceased in regard to these children, a little while after his death, in reply to a letter from Hulings on this subject, I informed him of the lots passed in your name and that of Delacroix and of what you tell me on that subject, giving him, my opinion that the intentions of Clark could not have been otherwise than to give the half thereof to each   I wish you, in reply, to tell me then, positively if in the talk had with you, Clark declared that they were exclusively for Myra, and if he designated her by name, or otherwise   And as the writing you sent me at time is not sufficient to authorize me to pass the title, I pray you to send me a special power of attorney, duly authenticated by the American Consul at Matanzas, if there is one there   The power might be pure and simple, authorizing me to annul the sale, declaring that it was only an affair of confidential trust between the parties

I shall be delighted, in receiving your response, to learn your success in the business with which you may be occupied, and that your family may be in the enjoyment of good health, is the ardent wish of your friend,

RICHARD RELF

DEFENDANTS

Depositions of—1 Louis Lesassier   2. Henry W Palfrey 3 R D Shepherd   4 Vve Barbin De Bellevue   5 Francois Dussuau Delacroix   6 Louis T Caire.

UNITED STATES OF AMERICA,

EASTERN DISTRICT OF LOUISIANA—CITY OF NEW ORLEANS

Be it remembered, that on this 24th day of May, A. D 1849, before me, John W Gurley, a commissioner, duly appointed on the twenty-fourth day of April, A D 1849, by the Circuit Court of the United States, in and for the Eastern district of Louisiana, under and by virtue of the several acts of Congress, and in pursuance of a written agreement this day entered into by the counsel in the suit of E. P. Gaines and wife *vs*. Relf, Chew et al, No. 122 of the docket of said Court, which said agreement is on file and of record in said suit, I caused to come before me, at the Clerk's office of the said Court, Louis Lesassier, a person of sound mind and lawful age, witness for the defendant in the said civil suit now depending in the said Court, and the said Louis Lesassier, being by me first carefully cautioned, examined and sworn, did depose and say, as follows

That he is fifty three years of age, came to this city in 1805, is acquainted with Relf & Chew, knows the plaintiff's by sight, has no particular acquaintance with them, knew Daniel Clark well, has seen him frequently, had no particular acquaintance with him, means by this that they did not visit each other, knew his general reputation in the community, he stood high as a man of business; he was a gentleman very well known in the community was a leading man as a politician and man of business never heard of Mr Clark's being a married man; witness was a very young man, and Mr Clark much above him in age and standing, never heard of his having any family here, was clerk at that time in the house of Thorn & Co, in St Louis st, between Chartres and Royal   Chew & Relf kept nearly opposite   Saw Mr Clark frequently about the house of Chew & Relf. His standing in the community, as a man of honor and probity, was very high

Question. Judging from the reputation which Daniel Clark

enjoyed in the community in which he lived, for honor and probity, would you or would you not suppose him capable of addressing a lady with a view to marriage, if at the same time he had a living lawful wife?

To the propounding of this interrogatory, on part of the defendants, the complainants objects. The defendants persisting in their interrogatory, the witness answers from what I recollect of the character of Daniel Clark at that time and what I have heard of it since, I should think not. Does not know or recollect of any other fact or circumstance which would be of benefit or advantage to either of the parties to this suit

L. LESASSIER.

Cross Examination

At the period alluded in the principal examination, witness was a clerk in a mercantile   situated in the neighborhood of Chew & Relf.

Question. What was your age at the time you state you were acquainted with Mr Clark, in your principal examination?

Answer. I think I was about thirteen years of age, when I first began to know him, that was about the year 1008 or 1809.

L. LESASSIER.

J W Gurley, Com'r

And on this 25th day of May, 1849, personally came and appeared Henry W Palfrey, a person of lawful age and sound mind, a witness on behalf of defendants, who, being by me first duly sworn, did depose and say as follows, Is fifty-one years of age, having been born on the 8th February, 1798, came to New Orleans in the fall of 1810, is acquainted with the complainants Gen Gaines and lady, and with Messrs Richard Relf Beverly Chew, and Francois Dussuau Delacroix, defendants to this suit, was acquainted with the late Daniel Clark, of New Orleans, was engaged in the house of Chew & Relf, a commercial house at New Orleans, in the capacity of Clerk, went into said house in that capacity, some time in the winter of 1811 1812, was very well acquainted with the hand writing of Richard Relf, Beverly Chew, and Daniel Clark, from having seen them write. The letter now handed to witness, and marked A, he says was written and signed by Daniel Clark. The defendants here present the letter, and to identify it, it is signed by the undersigned commissioner, and by the witness, and the defendants now offer it as part of this deposition.

The defendants here present the letter marked B, which witness says is written and signed by Daniel Clark, and to identify it, it is signed by the witness and by the undersigned commissioner, and the defendants now offer it as part of this deposition.

The letter now handed to witness, and marked (C), witness says is in the hand writing of Daniel Clark, and signed by him The defendants here present the letter and to identify it, it is signed by the witness and by the undersigned commissioner, and the defendants now offer it as part of this deposition

The letter marked (D), witness says, is written and signed by Daniel Clark The defendants here present the letter, and to identify it, it is signed by the witness, and me, commissioner, and the defendants now offer it as part of this deposition

The letter marked (E), witness says, is entirely in the handwriting of Daniel Clark The defendants here present the letter, and to identify it, it is signed by the witness and the undersigned commissioner and the defendants now offer it as part of his deposition

The letter marked (F), witness says, is entirely in the handwriting of Daniel Clark The defendants here produce the letter, and to identify it, it is signed by the witness and by the undersigned commissioner, and the defendants now offer it as part of this deposition

The letter marked (G), witness says, is entirely in the handwriting of Daniel Clark The defendants now produce the letter, and to identify it, it is signed by the witness, and me, commissioner, and the defendants now offer it as part of this deposition

The letter marked (H), witness says, is entirely in the handwriting of Daniel Clark The defendants now produce the letter, and to identify it, it is signed by the witness, and by me, commissioner; and the defendants now offer it as part of this deposition

The letter marked (I), witness says, is entirely in the handwriting of Daniel Clark The defendants now produce the letter, and to identify it, it is signed by the witness, and me, commissioner, and the defendants now offer it as part of this deposition

The letter marked (K), witness says, is in the handwriting of Daniel Clark The defendants now produce the letter, and to identify it, it is signed by the witness, and me, commissioner, and the defendants now offer it as part of this deposition

The letter marked (L), witness says, is in the handwriting of Daniel Clark The defendants now produce the letter, and to identify it it is signed by the witness, and by me, commissioner, and the defennants now offer it as part of this deposition.

The letter in French, marked M witness says, is in the handwriting of Daniel Clark The defendants now produce the letter, and to identify it, it is signed by the witness and by me, commissioner, and the defendants now offer it as part of this deposition

Witness has examined the three copies now produced, with the originals which copies are marked N, O, P, the originals of which were wholly written and signed by Daniel Clark, and are annexed to a commission in the suit of Barnes et al, vs Gaines et al No 19 150, of the late First judicial District Court of the State of Louisiana, and to identify them they are signed by the witness, and me, commissioner, and the defendants now offer them as part of this deposition

Objection The complainants except to the said letters, produced by defendants from A to P inclusive, as irrelevant, and as inadmissible in evidence, on other grounds

Question Will you have the goodness to look upon the document now presented to you, purporting to be a notarial certified copy of articles of agreement and partnership between the late Daniel Clark, Richard Relf, and Beverly Chew and state whether or not you have compared said copy with the original, and if so, where the original is, in whose handwriting is the body thereof, and state also whether or not you are one of the attesting witnesses to said instrument, and whether or not the signatures of Daniel Clark, Richard Relf, and Beverly Chew to the said original, are true and genuine signatures of those persons respectively?

Objection Complainants object to this interrogatory The defendants persisting in the interrogatory, the witness, answering, saith

Answer Having looked upon the said copy witness says he has compared it with the original The original is at Mr' Caire's, the notary office, in Exchange Alley The original is all in the handwriting of witness except three words, the words are "fourteen thousand dollars" These are in the second article of the agreement, and are in Mr Relf's handwriting.

On the original paper, below the signatures of the respective parties, are the following words written "It is further understood, that the plantation lately purchased by D Clark, of S. Henderson, on account, of which nothing has, as yet, been paid is to remain on his private account" and which said words are in the handwriting of Richard Relf, and are not signed

Witness was one of the attesting witnesses to the said instrument, and witness believes the signatures to the said instrument of Daniel Clark, Richard Relf and Beverly Chew, to be the genuine signatures of those persons Witness says that the signatures of those gentlemen could not be easily mistaken Witness has no doubt at all about the genuineness of those signatures (The copy here referred to is here identified, by being signed by the witness, and me commissioner, and marked (Q)

Objection. The complainan's object to the introduction of the instrument here produced, marked Q, as inadmissable under the state of the pleadings, and as to the manner of proving the same.

Mr Clark lived, during the latter day of his life, at his large house, at the forks of the Bayou Road, in fauburg St John Mr Clark died at that house Thinks that was his town residence during all the time witness knew him The store of Chew & Relf was then in St. Louis street, between Royal and Chartres Mr Clark was frequently at their store, thinks he was there every day when he was in the city', came in after breakfast, and went home to dinner Witness thinks Mr Relf lived with Mr Clark during the latter part of his life, that is to say, the last three or four months of it Mr Relf had a room at Mr Chew's house in the winter but is not certain whether it was the winter last preceding Mr Clark's death, or the following one. Mr Relf was at the north in 1811, and on his return, witness thinks he had a room at Mr Chew's house

Question Do you know whether or not Mr Daniel Clark and Mr. Richard Relf were in the habit of riding out from their store in St Louis street, during the last three or four months of Mr Clark's life, every day for dinner, and returning together in the following morning to the store, if so, state fully what you know on the subject.

Answer. They used to get into the gig to go to their dinner every day, or almost every day, during that time At the time witness first became acquainted with Beverly Chew, he, Chew, was a man of family. At the time witness became acquainted with Mr. Relf, sometime in the winter of 1811 and 1812, he, Relf, was a widower At the time witness became acquainted with Daniel Clark, in 1811 or 1812, he was not, to witness' knowledge, a married man

Question Up to the time of Mr. Clark's death, had you ever heard of his being a married man'

Objection. Question objected to by complainants counsel. The defendants insisting on their interrogatory, witness saith Up to the time of Mr Clark's death, he had not heard of his being a married man

Question What was the standing of Mr. Clark in the community up to the time of his death'

Answer I thought that Mr Clark and Mr Relf and Mr Chew were three of the principal men of New Orleans, and I never had heard any body say any thing to the contrary, but being then only 15 years of age, I did not think myself competent to give an opinion on the matter Continued in the employ of the house of Chew & Relf, and kept the books of the house for four years af-er the death of Mr Clark, and also for some months previous to his death

Question   Do you remember whether or not after the agreement marked (Q) there was a new set of books opened by the house of Chew & Relf?

Objection   Question objected to by counsel for complainants, and the defendants insisting upon the interrogatory the witness saith—

Answer   Yes sir there was a new set of books opened a short time afterwards a few days or a few weeks afterwards, the books were in witness' handwriting the precise number of days after the date of the instrument witness does not recollect Knew the servant named Lubin, a negro man belonging to Mr Clark at the time of his death

Question   What was the character of this negro?

Objection   This interrogatory objected to by complainants' counsel, the defendants insisting on it the witness answers

Answer   He was Mr Clark's confidential servant his master and his friends had a high opinion of his character   But in the spring of 1815 that was about two years after Mr Clark's death witness caught him stealing cotton from the cotton bales in the cotton warehouse of Chew & Relf, at the corner of Burgundy and Toulouse streets

Objection   To this statement of the witness the complainants object as improper evidence   Does not know from whom Mr Clark purchased Lubin   H W PALFREY

J W GURLEY, Com r.

And also appeared on this 28th May, 1849, H W Palfrey, a witness on behalf of defendants who heretofore appeared, and whose examination in chief is now resumed

Being shown documents marked R he states it is all in Daniel Clark's handwriting and the signature of Daniel Clark thereto is genuine   Being asked whether he is acquainted with the signature of Daniel W Coxe says, that he has never seen said Coxe sign his name, but that from his acquaintance with the correspondence of said Coxe with the house of Chew & Relf, during the five years he was in the employ of said Chew & Relf he believes the signature of said Coxe to the document marked R, is genuine, which said document, to identify it, is signed by witness and the commissioner, and defendants now offer it as part of this deposition   Being shewn the schedule annexed to said document R, says, he does not know in whose handwriting the body of the said schedule is, but believes the signatures thereto of Daniel Clark and Daniel W Coxe, are genuine

Objection.   To the introduction of this instrument complainants object   H W PALFREY.

J W GURLEY, Com r
76

Cross Examination of H. W Palfrey

Question   In your principal examination on the 25th instant, you were examined in respect to a document, marked (Q), were you present, and did you see Daniel Clark sign that document?

Answer   It is so long since, that I do not remember whether I actually saw him sign it or not; but I am under the impression, that I did see him sign it   I think I did   There is not an instance in my recollection, that I put my name to an instrument, as a witness, without seeing the person sign, or without their acknowledging their signatures in my presence

Question   Did you see Richard Relf and Beverly Chew sign that instrument?

Answer   I make to this the same answer as I made to the last preceding interrogatory

Question   Have you now any distinct recollection of having seen Daniel Clark, Beverly Chew, and Richard Relf sign that document, or their having each and every of them separately acknowledged their signatures to it to you?

Answer   I can't say positively   My impression is that they came to my desk, each of them, and signed the paper on the desk that I was in the habit of using

Question   Was that addenda, or writing underneath the signatures, put to it then?

Answer   I believe not   have no recollection of it   does not remember to have seen the addenda until he saw it three or four days ago at the notary's office

Question.   Did you see Mr Deutillet sign that instrument?

Answer   Does not remember to have seen him sign it

Question   Do you know his handwriting?

Answer   No, sir

Question   You have said that Mr Relf, for the last three or four months of Mr Clark's life, lived with him   Will you be good enough to state whether Mr Relf was a married man at the time of Mr Clark's death?

Answer   He was not a married man at that time

Question   How long after Mr Clark's death was Mr Relf married?

Answer.   Think it was one or two years

Question   At the time of Mr Clark's death, had not Mr. Relf an establishment of his own in the near neighborhood of Mr Clark's house on the Bayou road?

Answer   He had a house, which I believe he owned, in the neighborhood of Mr Clark's house   He owned this house in 1811   does not remember when he sold it; he sold it some years afterwards   I believe he never lived in this house after the death of his wife in 1811

Question You have no certainty upon any of these matters have you? but merely speak as to your belief?

Answer Am certain as to his owning the house in 1811, but am not certain as respects the other matters included in the last question

Question How long was Mr Clark sick and confined to his house before his death

Answer I do not remember exactly it was not very long it was not more than two or three weeks, it was from one to three weeks, at least I believe it was

Question How many clerks were employed in the house of Chew & Relf, in June, 1813

Answer I believe I was the only one then there was one who had been turned off a few months previously

Question Were you at that period the chief book-keeper in in the house of Chew & Relf?

Answer. Yes sir, I was—the only one.

Question Did you keep the books yourself?

Answer I kept them myself, under the instructions of my employers

Question How old were you then?

Answer At the death of Mr Clark, I was fifteen and a half years of age but commenced keeping books previous to that time, how long before does not remember

Commenced in the house of Chew & Relf in April or May, 1812, and as to the time of his going into the house of Relf & Chew, witness is able to correct the statement made in his previous examination, by information he has obtained since his previous examination He obtained this information from examination of the letter book of the house of Relf & Chew When he first went to the house, his occupation was copying letters into the letter book and I find, by referring to the letter book, that I commenced in April or May, 1812

H. W. PALFREY

Examination in chief resumed

Question. Will you be pleased to state whether or not there is the least doubt upon your mind that you wrote the original of the document marked (Q), as stated in your examination in chief, and that the signatures of Daniel Clark Richard Relf and Beverly Chew, as principals and your own as a witness, are genuine and true?

Objection Objected to by complainants as a leading question The defendants persisting, the witness says

Answer There is no doubt in my mind, and I am sure that the document is in my handwriting, and that my name, signature as a witness, is genuine

There is no doubt in my own mind that the signatures of Daniel Clark, Richard Relf, and Beverly Chew are genuine; and as to my own, there can be no doubt; it does not admit of a doubt.

Question   Is the other witness to the document (Q), Mr Dutilhet living or dead?

Answer   He is dead

Question   Has he any surviving children living in this State, known to you? and if so, where?

Answer   I believe he has one, who lives in the parish of Plaquemine, a son

Question   At the time of this transaction, in June 1813 what was the business of Mr Francois Dutillet, the witness to this instrument?

Answer   He was an auctioneer and kept his auction store on the opposite side of the street from Chew & Relf.

Question   State whether or not, very soon after the date of the document marked (Q), a new set of books were opened by the house of Chew & Relf

Answer   Yes, sir, there was

Question   Having stated that you wrote the articles of co-partnership being document (Q) state whether or not you are to be understood as meaning that you composed them of your own volition, or merely that it is in your handwriting as clerk of the house, and in the manner stated in your chief examination

Answer   I copied them from a draft that was furnished by Mr Relf, and in his handwriting

Question   One of the articles of co-partnership providing that one of the members of the house should proceed to the north for the purpose of establishing a branch of the concern, will you state whether or not either Daniel Clark, Richard Relf, or Beverly Chew did proceed to the north shortly after the signing of that instrument and if so, which of them went on?

Objection   Objected to by complainants, and defendants persisting the witness say

Answer   Mr Chew removed with his family from New Orleans to Philadelphia or New York, in the course of a month afterwards

                                        H W PALFREY

J W GURLEY, Commissioner

And afterwards, to wit on this 26th day of May 1849, personally came and appeared before me the undersigned commissioner, at the Clerk's office of the Circuit Court, R D Shepherd, a person of lawful age and sound mind, a witness on behalf of defendants, who being duly sworn did depose and say

Arrived at New Orleans on seventh day of September, 1802. **Was acquainted** with Mr Relf and Chew they were doing business at that time under the firm of Chew & Relf. Was well acquainted with the late Daniel Clark.

Question. Do you know whether or not Daniel Clark was in New Orleans during any part of the autumn of the year 1802, after your arrival?

Answer. He was not, not in the early part of it.

Question. Do you know where he then was? either from your then knowledge or from what you subsequently knew from Clark himself?

Answer. He was in Europe, attending to the sale of cotton and other business of the house of Chew & Relf.

Question. Do you know whether or not Daniel Clark was interested in the shipments of cotton made to Europe by the house of Chew & Relf, referred to in your last answer?

Objection. This question objected by complainants' counsel, and being persisted in by the defendants, the witness saith.

Answer. I have no knowledge of the shipments being made myself, as I was not here, but after Mr. Clark's return, I understood from himself that he had suffered severely from heavy losses on the shipments of cotton made the previous year, principally owing to fraud in packing, of which he complained most bitterly.

Question. Do you know of your own knowledge, or from information derived from Daniel Clark himself how he returned from Europe, and whether or not he came from thence in a vessel directly to this city?

Answer. I know he arrived here in mid winter in the year of 1802-3 in a vessel direct from Europe and he was very much excited in consequence of the fraud which had been practiced on him in the packing of cotton, and of this he spoke to almost every one in the city.

Was well acquainted with Mr Clark subsequently, and up to the time of his death and had a great many business transactions with him. During the latter days of his life, he resided in his house out on the Bayou road. Was frequently there at Mr Clark's house, he visited there. Mr Clark was a man of considerable note here, was of great consequence and influence, and of wealth, and was   the most prominent men here.

Question. Did you ever hear, during the lifetime of Mr Clark, of his being a married man?

Objection. Objected to as irrelevant and incompetent. Defendants insisting upon his interrogatory, the witness saith.

Answer. I never did hear of his being a married man, until since his death.

Question. In any of your visits which you ever made to the house of Mr. Daniel Clark, did you ever see any lady about the house having the appearance of a wife of Mr Clark, in charge of the mansion

Objection   Objected to by complainants, and the defendants persisting, the witness saith.

Answer   I never did

Question   After the death of Mr Clark, did you ever hear of any lady presenting herself as the widow of Mr Clark?

Objection   Objected to by complainants, and the defendants persisting, the witness saith ·

Answer.   No, never.

Question   Do you know whether or not Mr Clark brought back with him from Europe any of the cotton, in bales or otherwise, of which he had complained of having been falsely and fraudulently packed?

Answer.   He told me that he had brought back, I think the stones or bricks, or some parts or some other evidence to prove the fraudulent packing of the cotton, and expressed his determination to prosecute the owners of the gins from whence the cotton came   R D. SHEPHERD

Cross Examination

I am sixty-five years of age, reside in New Orleans in the winter, and on my farm in Virginia in the summer   Have no occupation, farmer, if you choose   Was born in 1784, and arrived here in 1802, consequently, was about eighteen years of age   Never knew Mr Clark before coming to New Orleans   Came to this city at first on a special mission in September, and left in April   Returned again to New Orleans in January, 1804, to establish myself, and did so, and have been here ever since, up to 1817, since which time I have been here at intervals   My principal place of business and property has always been here   I was introduced to Mr Clark immediately on his arrival here, at the time before mentioned, and was in constant social intercourse with him.   Mr. Clark's most prominent and confidential friends were Chew & Relf, Le Croix, Petayvin, John McDonough, Shepherd Brown, Bellechasse, Judge Pitot, the two latter were among his most intimate friends   Witness was not very intimate with Daniel Clark· have dined in his house, and have met him very frequently, at dinners and parties and socially, in other houses   Became acquainted with Mr Relf immediately on my arrival here in 1802   Mr Chew was then absent in Europe, and as soon as he returned, I became acquainted with him

                               R D SHEPHERD

J. W. GURLEY, Com'r

Madame Veuve. Barbin de Bellevue

And afterwards, to wit   on the 28 May, 1849, personally came and appeared Delphine Trepagnier, widow of Barbin de Bellevue, a witness on behalf of the defendants, who being duly sworn, did depose and say

Is fifty-six years of age My husband was in the service of the United States, about eighteen or twenty years since My husband has been dead five years from last November — Witness' family left their residence on Bayou road, in 1813 or 1814 where they had resided for three or four years previously. Knew the late Daniel Clark was acquainted with him Daniel Clark lived three or four squares from the residence of Witness' family that is, from the family of her mother and her sisters and brothers Daniel Clark paid a visit every day, to the house of witness' family this was during the time that witness' family resided near Daniel Clark's, and witness was a member of the family In thus speaking of her family she means to designate her mother's family she being an unmarried lady at the time, and living with her mother

Had two sisters living at home with her mother at the time she speaks of One of these was older, and the other was younger than witness One of them had been married, and had been divorced at the time she speaks of This sister's maiden name was Heloise Tupagnier, and had been married to Mr Francois Lambert, from whom she had been divorced, as above stated The sister here spoken of was the elder sister The name of the younger sister was Hortense Trepagnier

Question Do you know whether or not the late Daniel Clark ever paid his addresses to either of your sisters, with the view to marriage ? And if so, to which one of the two ?

Objection Complainants object to this question

Answer He paid his addresses to the sister which had been divorced, that is to say, to Madame Lambert These addresses were evidently paid with a view to marriage

Question Do you remember in what year Daniel Clark paid his addresses to your sister, Madame Lambert, as stated in your last answer and if so, state the same

Answer He paid his addresses, and was engaged to Madame Lambert, in 1813 and was engaged up to the time of his death.

Question State, if you please, whether or not the late Daniel Clark always represented himself in the family of your mother as a bachelor or whether he ever stated himself to be a widower ?

Objection Complainants object to this question, as a leading question The defendants persisting in their interrogatory, the witness says

Answer He never represented himself as a widower but always as a bachelor

Question Do you know whether or not Daniel Clark spoke

the French language with ease and fluency? and if so, state
Answer   He spoke French as well as English
VE BARBIN DE BELLEVUE

Cross Examination

Question.   State at what period, in the year 1813, Mr Clark commenced to pay his addresses to your sister. ?

Answer   He commenced to pay his addresses to her about one year or eight months previous to his death

Question   At what period of the year did the engagement take place?

Answer   The engagement took place about eight months or one year before his death

Question   When did the courtship begin?

Answer   About one year before his death

Question   How old were you at that the time the engagement took place?

Answer   Was twenty pears of age at that time

Question   Were you present, and did you hear the engagement made by Mr Clark, with your sister

Answer   Was present and recollects the answer of her sister

Question   As this engagement took place a year before the death of Mr Clark, do you know why the celebration of the marriage was delayed until the time of his death?

Answer   It was delayed for causes which she does not particularly understand, from time to time, and was to have been celebrated within about two months, when it was put an end to by the death of Mr Clark

Question   Do you know, or did you ever hear of any cause which prevented the immediate celebration of the marriage

Answer   Does not know, and has never heard any cause assigned, why the marriage was not celebrated immediately after the engagement took place

Question   Do you know at what period your sister was divorced?

Answer.   Does not know

Question   How do know that she was divorced

Answer   Heard so, and it was published in the paper

Question   In what manner was she divorced?   Was it by a decree of court, or how?

Answer   By a judgment of a court

Question   What court?

Answer   Does not know what court

Question   Was your sister afterwards re-married? and if yea, at what time?

Answer   In the year 1815

Question   Whom was she remarried with?   Was it not with

the same François Lambert, from whom she had been divorced?

Objection Defendants object to this question, on the ground 1st Of its irrelevancy to the issue in this case 2d That marriages are to be proven in Louisiana, by documentary evidence

Answer Mr Lambert returned to this city in 1815 There was no marriage—ecclesiastical marriage—or marriage in the church but that they passed a civil contract before a notary, and lived together as man and wife

Question Do you know before wha notary that contract was passed?

Answer Saw the notary arrive and pass the act, but does not recollect who he was

Question At what period was this act passed?

Answer It was in the months of March April, or May, 1815

VI BARBIN DE BELLEVUE

J W Gurley Com

And afterwards to wit, on the 11th June 1848, personally came and appeared François Dussuau Delacroix a person of sound mind, a witness on behalf of the defendants, in all the suits except No 1731, who being duly sworn, did depose and say

Objection Witness objected to on the part of complainants as incompetent on the ground of interest, as being a defendant in the suit of Mrs Gaines for certain slaves in his possession, which belonged to the estate of the late Daniel Clark, which suit is now pending and at issue in this Court, designated as suit No 1731

Mr Louis Felix Maxent sworn as translator

Note —By way of preface to this examination, witness desires to state, that from thirty-six to forty years having elapsed since the period when the facts of which he is about to testify transpired there may be some variation in the mode in which he may now express himself from that he has formerly used, but there can be none in the testimony itself, as the facts are strikingly impressed on my mind

Question When did you arrive in Louisiana

Answer I arrived in New Orleans in 1793

Question What is your age?

Answer A little over seventy-three

Question What is your present occupation?

Answer I am a planter

Question Have you held any office in Louisiana?

Answer In 1806 or 1807, a member of the legislature of the territory of Orleans

Question Did you hold any office in any monetary institution here? and if so, how long?

Answer   I was one of the directors of the Planters Bank in Louisiana, and president of the Louisiana State Bank, president of the State Insurance company

Question   Do you know Richard Relf and Beverly Chew? and if so, how long?

Answer   I do know Richard Relf and Beverly Chew, since all the time I have been residing in New Orleans

Question   What has been their reputation for honesty and integrity.

Objection   Objected to by complainants as irrelevant, and defendants persisting, witness says

Answer   Messrs Relf and Chew I have always considered honest, and, if it had been otherwise Mr Daniel Clark, who knew human nature a a perfect Judge, would not have employed them in his commercial house

Question   Have or not Beverly Chew and Richard Relf held monetary offices in this city? and if so, what offices, and how long?

Objection.   Objected to by complainants as irrelevant

Answer   Mr Relf has been cashier of the State Bank since the foundation of that Bank to the present time   I am not so well informed of Mr. Chew   but I know he was in one of the banks, but I do not know whether he was then as president or director. nor do I recollect which bank it was

Question.   Did you or not ever, provisionally or absolutely, appoint R Relf your attorney in fact during your absence from this country?

Objected to by complainants as irrelevant

Answer   I recollect in one voyage I made in France, perhaps in 1819, I do not recollect positively, I appointed two men here to be my attorneys, and Mr Richard Relf, in case of the death of one of them

Question   Would you have done so in case you had entertained any suspicion of his integrity?

Objected to by complainants as irrelevant

Answer   My answer is already made   certainly no

Question   Did you know the late Daniel Clark? and if so, was your acquaintance with him intimate or general?

Answer   My acquaintance with Daniel Clark was of the greatest intimacy

Question   Was he a man of integrity and honor?

Answer   Mr Clark would never have been my friend had he not been a man of integrity and honor   In my opinion, he was a man of honor and integrity

Question   Was he a married man or a bachelor?

Objected to by complainants

Answer   Mr Daniel Clark, in my opinion, was never married; and I was too much intimate with him not to have been informed of it had he contracted marriage with anybody.

Question. Did Daniel Clark ever tell you that he had a child? and if so did he tell you whether that child was legitimate or illegitimate?

Answer. Mr Clark told me that he had a child with a married woman, an adulterous child.

Question. Who is that child?

Answer. That child was placed by Daniel Clark in the house of Samuel Davis in Terrebonne, and the name of that child was Myra. I suppose that Myra is the same Myra who married with Mr Whitney, and after the death of Mr Whitney married with Mr Gaines.

Question. Did Daniel Clark ever place property in your hands as his confidential friend for that child? and if so, when and what property?

Objected to by complainants.

Answer. I do not recollect, positively, the time, but it was probably one or two years before Daniel Clark's death he placed in my hands two portions of land on the Bayou Road, to be remitted to Myra in case of his death; which portions of land witness remitted to Myra the first time she came here with Captain Davis. I recollect at that time of that first voyage of Captain Davis. I met with him in the Exchange, and I asked him if Myra was here, and he answered yes. Then I told him I would be glad to remit to her the two portions of land which were confided to me by Daniel Clark to be remitted to Myra. The answer of Captain Davis was, "she will not receive that from you, because she is entirely ignorant that she is the natural or bastard child of Daniel Clark." That was the answer of Captain Davis. But, a few days after she accepted, and the business was settled before a notary.

Question. Did you see Daniel Clark shortly before his death? and if so, how long before?

Answer. I saw D. Clark I believe the day before his death, he was laying on a mattrass, on the floor of his parlor. When I entered some persons who were present retired on the gallery. I came close to him. I put my knees on the mattrass where he was laying, he took my hand, kissed my hand one hundred times perhaps, covered my hand with his tears; and in that supreme instance, not one single word escaped from his bosom. In that moment, when the most profound secrets escaped involuntarily, he did not tell me one single word about his pretended marriage.

Question. Did you or not very frequently during his life time visit his house, and especially at dinners, and on evening soirees?

Answer. I visited very frequently Daniel Clark, as I lived in the country, every time I came from the country, frequently I dined with him and breakfasted sometimes with him

Question   Was Madame DeGrange ever in his house at breakfast, at dinner, or at soirees?

Objected to by complainant

Answer   I never saw her

Question   Did you ever hear in society in New Orleans before Clark's death, even a rumor of his marriage?

Objected to by complainant

Answer   Never never

Question   Did or not Daniel Clark, shortly before his death, ever speak to you of Myra? and what did he say of her?

Answer   He spoke to me of Myra, as his illegitimate daughter or bastard, and never spoke otherwise of her to me

Question   What were the pecuniary circumstances of Daniel Clark previous to his death? Was he or not embarrassed in his pecuniary affairs?

Objected to by complainants as irrelevant

Answer   I think that the pecuniary circumstances of D Clark were very much embarrassed before his death, and I recollect myself he sent me a letter to my plantation, I believe in 1810 to pray me to endorse for him a note of six thousand dollars to pay some many small debts, for which he was tormented I endorsed that note for him, and a few months before his death, he told me confidentially, that he was very much embarrassed, and he was very much afraid to be obliged to fail, that as a proof of my intimacy with him, and I kept that secret

Question   Had he or not a great mania to buy real property, either on credit or for cash?

Objected to by complainants

Answer   Yes, Mr Daniel Clark was always tormented by that spirit of speculation, and I recollect myself, a few years before his death, that D Clark proposed to me to buy a sugar plantation that was to be sold at two or three leagues from the city I went myself to the plantation the day of the sale, the plantation was adjudicated to witness and Daniel Clark for seventy-two thousand dollars twenty five thousand cash, when I returned to N Orleans when I told D Clark, he tells me that he had not a cent to pay his part of those twenty-five thousand dollars I was obliged to raise the money myself, and fortunately for me two months after we sold the plantation to Mr Farrar, I believe to Farrar & Williams, who paid us about one hundred and twenty five thousand dollars. But that benefit was nothing for Mr Daniel Clark, who was too much embarrassed

Question   Did or not the war of 1812, 13 and '14 produce **a scarcity** of money in Louisiana?

Answer   I believe it was about that epoch that the scarcity of money was such that the banks were forced to suspend the payment in specie, I do not recollect positively

Question Did property in the city of New Orleans, during the three years of war depreciate in value?

Answer Yes, it very much depreciated during that period

Question Was or not Clark a partner of Chew & Relf?

Objected to by complainant, on ground that if there was a partnership, there is better evidence of its existence

Answer Daniel Clark to my knowledge, was in partnership with Chew & Relf, witness endorsed several notes for the house

Question Were not Chew & Relf obliged to suspend payment shortly after Clark's death?

Answer I do not recollect

Question Do you recognize the letter (marked (M,) referred to by Mr Palfrey in his deposition and) now handed to you?

Answer Yes, perfectly well It was sent by Daniel Clark to me at my plantation, and received by me

Question Did you know Madame DeGrange, by reputation or otherwise?

Answer. I knew Madame DeGrange, to have seen her frequently in the streets, during my residence in New Orleans.

Question What was her reputation for chastity about the time of the change of government?

Objected to as irrelevant by complainants

Answer The reputation of Madame DeGrange was the reputation of "une femme gallant, as we call it in French I do not know how it is expressed in English.

DUSSUAU DELACROIX

Cross Examination

Question Are you interested in the event of this suit?

Answer Certainly, no I am not interested in this suit Mrs Gaines instituted suit against me, but I have nothing to do with this one, that is, the suit against Chew & Relf I do not believe I have anything to do with it.

Question Did not P A Rost, Esq. appear for you in a suit in this court in chancery, in which you were a party defendant, whilst you were absent in France?

Answer At that time I was in France Mr Cavellier was my agent in this country, and I think it would be more proper to put that question to them than to me I know that Mr Rost was employed by Mr Cavellier to defend me I have never read what Mr. Rost has done, it was entirely confided to my agents

Question Are you satisfied that Mr Rost did his duty as your attorney?

Answer. I was very satisfied with the appointment of Mr. Rost, but do not know what he has done in the case

Question Do you approve of act of your agents in employing Mr. Rost?

Answer I was very much satisfied that Mr Rost was employed by my agent

Question Do you or not, intend to repudiate or accept the acts of Mr Rost as your attorney?

Answer I was very satisfied of the appointment of Mr Rost by my agents, in that suit, because I know Mr Rost as a man of talents and integrity, it is all I have to answer

Question In case the present suit should result in establishing the claims of Mrs Gaines the complainant as the heir at law of the late Daniel Clark in what manner would that result affect yourself?

Answer I answer to this question, that I have never reflected on the consequences which might result from the loss of this suit, so monstrous and iniquitous

Question Has a suit been commenced against yourself since you returned from France, by the complainant, and if so, for what property?

Answer I do not know of any other suit instituted against me by Mrs Gaines, but the suit in this Court in which I have filed my answer and the property for which I am sued is fully described in that answer—being slaves

DUSSUAU DELACROIX.

J. W. Gurley Com r

And afterwards to wit, on the 12th day of June, 1849, personally appeared Louis T Caire a witness on part of the defendants, heretofore examined a person of lawful age and sound mind, who being duly sworn did depose and say

'I am fifty-five years of age, and reside in New Orleans I am a Notary Public I have very carefully examined the certified copy of document marked (Q) referred to in Mr Palfrey's testimony, with the original, and it is a literal copy now on file in my current register No 197—date, 12th April, 1841 I was personally acquainted with the late Mr F Dutillet. He appeared personally before me, and made the affidavit, a copy of which forms part of document (Q) I recollect the circumstances very well I showed the original document, purporting to be articles of agreement between Daniel Clark, and Beverly Chew, and Richard Relf, to Mr Francois Dutillet at the time he made his affidavit I know that Mr Francois, the subscribing witness to that instrument is dead I am myself personally acquainted with the signatures of Richard Relf and Beverly Chew, having frequently seen them write The signatures of Richard Relf and Beverly Chew to the original act purporting to be articles of agreement, as above stated, witness believes to be genuine. When I first knew Francois Dutillet he was engaged in business as a commission merchant, and was subsequently an auctioneer. **LEWIS T. CAIRE**

Cross examination waived by Mr. P. C. Wright, solicitor for complainant.

J. W. GURLEY, Commissioner

DEFENDANT'S EVIDENCE.—No. 2

1 Germain Musson   2 Zenon Cavellier   3 Theodore Zacharie   4 Etienne Carraby   5 Louis Bouligny

And afterwards to wit: on the 29th May, 1849, personally came and appeared Germain Musson, a person of sound mind and lawful age, a witness on behalf of defendants, who, being duly sworn, did depose and say:

Came to the city of New Orleans in 1803—previous to the change of government. Was a clerk for several years then became a western country merchant. Knew Daniel Clark, from the time I arrived here, almost, until he died.

Question. Was he, or not, a married man?

Objection. Objected to by complainants and defendants persisting, the witness says:

Answer. Not to my knowledge. means he was not married to his knowledge.

Question. Had you or not, much intercourse with the people of New Orleans during the period of which you speak as being acquainted with Daniel Clark?

Objection. Objected to by complainants, as irrelevant, and defendants persisting, witness says:

Answer. The population of merchants and men of business being small at that time, we knew each other and saw each other very often.

Question. Did you, or not, ever hear, from any one, of Daniel Clark being a married man until after his death?

Objection. Objected to by complainants and defendants persisting, witness says:

Answer. No, sir.

Question. Was or not Daniel Clark represented to be impotent?

Objection. Objected to by complainants as wholly irrelevant, impertinent and scandalous and defendants persisting, witness says:

Answer. I cannot answer this question.

Question. Were you acquainted with Zulime deGrange? and at what period? what was her reputation as to virtue and purity of life?

Objection. Complainants object to this question as imperti

624 Gaines vs Relf, Chew, and Others

nent, irrelevant, and scandalous, and defendants persisting, witness says ·

Answer. Cannot answer this question

G. MUSSON

Cross Examination

Was sixteen years of age when I arrived in this city, will be sixty-three next November, could not be very intimate with Mr. Clark, as there was so great a difference in our ages, but as men of business, we met very often, very seldom visited Mr. Clark at his house. Mr Clark stood high in this community as an honorable man, and a man of fortune In his operations in the canal de Carondelet, I believe he was interested with Dussuau Delacroix, they were very often together—I mean the old Dussuau Delacroix, and not his sons Knew Col. Joseph Bellechasse This gentleman went, after the death of Mr Clark, to the island of Cuba, and established one or two sugar plantations there Bellechasse is dead, but witness does not remember when he died Mr. Bellechasse was considered a high minded and honorable man in this community. I believe he was one of Mr Clark's intimate friends, because at that time all those old men associated much together Knew the late judge Pitot of New Orleans He was considered a high minded, honorable man, in this community Does not know of his being one of the intimate friends of Mr Clark, but suppose he was, from his position and that of Mr. Clark's Knew Edward Livingston very intimately, both here and in France Cannot say that Mr Livingston was one of Mr Clark's intimate friends, but supposes he was. Mr. Clark was associated at that time with all the men of note or distinction in the country, to the best of my knowledge.

G. MUSSON

J. W Gurley, Commissioner

And afterwards, to wit, on this 30th hay of May, 1859 personally came and appeared Zenon Cavellier, a person of lawful age and sound mind, a witness on behalf of the defendants, who, being duly sworn, did depose and say

Question. What is your age?
Answer, I am upwards of seventy years of age
Question. Where were you born?
Answer. In New Orleans.
Question. Have you lived in New Orleans ever since your birth to the present time?
Answer. Yes sir—have been temporarily absent
Question. Were you acquainted with the late Daniel Clark?
Answer Yes sir
Question How long were you acquainted with the late Daniel Clark?

Answer Almost from the time he came to this country

Question. Was your acquaintance with him intimate?

Answer I was intimately acquainted with him There was, for a short time, a coolness existing between him and myself, arising from political matters

Question Did you ever hear from Daniel Clark, or any of his friends or from any other person of the community in which he lived during the lifetime of said Clark, that he the said Clark, was, or ever had been, a married man?

Objection Objected to by complainants as a leading interrogatory and irrelevant, and defendants persisting the witness says

Answer I never knew him as a married man and never heard of his being a married man

Question What was the general reputation which Daniel Clark had in New Orleans, from the time you first knew him until his death, as to the fact of his being a married or unmarried man?

Objection Objected to by complainants as leading and irrelevant and defendants persisting witness says

Answer I always knew him as a bachelor, and a man of good reputation

Question Did you ever hear anything to the contrary of this opinion from any person previous to the appearance of Mrs Gaines in this community claiming to have been the legitimate child of Daniel Clark?

Objection Objected to by complainants as leading and irrelevant and defendants persisting, witness says

Answer Never heard anything to the contrary previously

Question Did you know Jerome DeGrange?

Answer Yes sir I mean the first husband of Madame DeGrange

Question What was the occupation or business of Mr Jerome DeGrange?

Objection Objected to by complainants as irrelevant,, defendants persisting witness says

Answer He was a confectioner

Question In what part of the city did he carry on his business?

Answer In St Ann street, between Royal and Condé, at the time I knew him

Question Were you acquainted with Mrs DeGrange?

Answer Was acquainted as I am with a thousand persons, never went in the house except when I went there to buy something

Question. What was the general reputation of Mrs De-

Grange in this community, as to virtue and chastity ?

Objection. Objected to by complainants as irrelevant. impertinent, and scandalous, and defendants persisting, witness says

Answer I am here under oath and am bound to say the truth, which I regret very much, but I am obliged to say what I said many years ago, when I was before the other courts. I do not wish to hurt the feelings of any one Her reputation was not good, she was a "femme gallante".

Question. What was the relationship or connection which existed between Daniel Clark and Madame DeGrange according to the public understanding or reputation ?

Objection Objected to by complainants as irrelevant, and impertinent, and scandalous, and defendants persisting witness says

Answer He was considered as the lover of Mrs DeGrange

Question Did you ever hear the names of Daniel Clark and Madame DeGrange spoken of in connection with each other as man and wife ?

Objection Objected to by complainants, and defendants persisting, witness says

Answer No sir

Question Did Mrs DeGrange continue to reside in New Orleans up to the period of Mr Clarks death ?

Answer No sir She went to the North before Daniel Clark's death I believe it was to the North

Question. Do you know where she went after she left New Orleans ?

Objection. Objected to by complainants, and defendants persisting, witness says

Answer Cannot say precisely '

Question What was the maiden name of Madame De-Grange ?

Answer Zulime Carriere

Question. Was she a native of this city ?

Answer. I do not know whether she was a native or came here from abroad, but, if she came from abroad, she came here very early Z. CAVELLIER.

Cross examination.

Question Are you or not interested in the event of this suit ?
Answer I believe not sir.
Question What was the name of your father ?
Answer. Antoine Cavellier
Question When did he die
Answer In 1826,
Question Did one of your sisters marry Zenon Maxent
Answer No My sister married Celestine Maxent.

Question   Did your daughter marry a Maxent.

Answer   Yes, she married Zenon Maxent, son of Celestine Maxent

Question,   Did your father have any interest in a certain plantation in East Baton Rouge, once the property of Daniel Clark?

Answer   I was always told that he had an interest with some others   I have never been acquainted with the matter of the plantation   had never any interest

Question   Did your father leave a last will and testament?

Objection   Objected to by defendants on the ground that testaments, being instruments of writing, can only be proved by their production or official   And complainants persisting, witness says

Answer   Yes sir

Question   were you one of the heirs or devisees named in that testament?

Objection   Defendants make the same objection to this interrogatory as is noted in the foregoing, and complainants persisting, witness says

Answer   Being one of his sons, I was named, of course, but never received anything from his succession

Question   Did you ever accept or renounce that succession? and if so, in what manner?

Answer   I have never accepted nor renounced it, have never received anything from it, since long time I have declared that I would not take a cent from the succession

Question.   Have not your children been benefitted by the succession of your father?

Answer.   It is not to my knowledge that they have received anything   No sir, not a cent.

Question   Is it your intention that they shall be benefitted by the succession of your father?

Answer   I have no intention and no opinion, because I have never reflected on the subject

Question   Is Zenon Maxent, and his wife, your daughter, still living?

Answer   They are

Question   Do you know of a suit having been commenced by the heirs of Fletcher against yourself, Antoine Cavellier, and others

Answer   Have never been aware that there was a suit instituted against me by the heirs of Fletcher, but there have been various suits running through the last 25 years against Davenport and against my brother, who had a small part of the ground, but as to myself, never until about a year ago, when I was made a party to a suit in which I have no interest.   This is my belief

Question   Do you know of any part of the estate of Daniel Clark situate in the fauburg St John, in the city of New Orleans, having been sold by virtue of an execution against the heirs of Daniel Clark, at said sale purchased by your son-in-law, Zenon Maxent ?

Answer.   I was told so, that he was in suit about some lots he bought there, from the sheriff, I believe

Question.   Are you not a party to a suit brought by General and Mrs Gaines, involving the same property, in the fauburg St John ?

Answer   No, I am not a party to any suit

Question   Do you now hold, or have you at any time, held any property, real or personal, which belonged to the succession of the late Daniel Clark or which was derived from or through Relf & Chew, representing themselves as his executors, or either of them ?

Answer   No, sir

Question   Are you a member of the house of A & Z Cavellier ?

Answer   Yes, sir

Question   How long has that house existed ?

Answer   I believe since 1822

Z CAVILIER.

And hereupon adjourned, in consequence of the fatigue and indisposition of Mr Cavelier, until to-morrow the 31st of May inst, at 12, M   J W GURLEY, Com'r.

MAY 31, 1849.

Cross examination resumed

Question   You say in your examination in chief, that you were intimately acquainted with Daniel Clark, do you mean to be understood, that this intimacy was a business, or social intimacy ?

Answer   It was not a business intimacy a friendship

Question   Was the late Daniel Clark in the habit of conferring with you confidentially, in regard to his private affairs ?

Answer   No sir, he was not

Question   In your examination in chief, you speak of a coolness having existed between you and the late Daniel Clark, at what period did this coolness take place ?

Answer   It was a very long time ago, it was after the time of the Spanish government, but on the occasion of an event which took place under the Spanish government.

Question   How long did this coolness, of which you speak, continue ?

Answer   A very short time

Question   Was not the late Daniel Clark, reputed to be a

high minded and honorable man, and **was he not considered** among the first men in this country, at the period in which he lived?

Answer   He was considered an honest man, a man of good reputation   it is for that very reason, that I think he was never married to that woman, because he knew well the conduct of that woman, and was himself a man of delicacy of feeling

Question   Were you in the habit of meeting Mr Clark socially at his house during the last years of his life?

Answer   No sir

Question   Were you at any time, during his life, in the habit of visiting him socially at his residence?

Answer   When he lived here in Toulouse street, I was in the habit of taking tea with him very often at night with **Chew & Relf,** and some other gentlemen

Question   Did you know the late Col Joseph D. D. Bellechasse?

Answer   Yes sir

Question   What was his character and standing in this community at the time you knew him?

Answer   An honest man   Under the Spanish government he was Captain in the Louisiana Regiment; he was, after, made or appointed Colonel by Governor Claiborne. Always considered Col Bellechasse as an honest man   does not know whether it is true, that the report that he had given information to the British General, respecting the manner of coming and landing here   Does not know whether this report was true as regards Colonel Bellechasse   This was in December, 1814

Question   At what period did Col Bellechasse leave this country for Cuba?

Answer.   Cannot say

Question   Was Colonel Bellechasse one of Daniel Clark's most intimate and confidential friends?

Answer   I knew that they were well together, but do not know that they were in such intimacy, did not often meet Col Bellechasse at D Clark's house

Question   Were you at all times, during the residence of Col Bellechasse in this country on terms of friendship and intimacy with him?

Answer.   I am sure I knew him, but there was no intimacy between him and myself, he was a great deal older than I was at that time

Question.   Was there, at any time, any coolness or enmity between you and Col Bellechasse, and if so, at what period?

Answer   No sir, there was none.

Question   Did you know the late Pierre Baron Boisfontain?

Answer   Knew him by sight, was not intimate with him

I believe he was an honest man, never heard any thing against him

Question Did you know the late Judge Pitot?

Answer Yes sir, I believe he was an honest man, was so respected in this community, was a merchant here, and my neighbor for a long time

Question What is your maternal language?

Answer French I understand and speak the English language tolerably well

Question Was your intimacy with Daniel Clark such that if he had been privately married, he would have communicated to you the fact?

Answer I was not so intimate with him, that he would communicate to me the fact for that is only communicated to intimate friends such as Pitot and Delacroix were I saw him often at Pitot's house Chew & Relf were his best friends, he had great confidence in them.

Question You speak in your direct examination of having known one Jerome DeGrange, formerly of the city of New Orleans At what period did you first know him, as near as you can remember?

Answer Cannot say positively believe he was here under the Spanish government he was a long time here, but he runaway when it was discovered he had been married in France

Question At what time did he runaway from this country?

Answer Cannot say.

Question. Can you describe his person?

Answer He was a very ugly man I believe he was about five feet six or seven inches, and stout, a very common looking man

Question Do you remember, very nearly the time of the marriage of Jerome DeGrange in this city

Answer Does not

Question Did you know the lady to whom he was married in this city, prior to his marriage?

Answer Yes sir, Zulime Carriere

Question Do you know if Jerome DeGrange was arrested in this city and tried for bigamy in marrying Miss Carriere

Answer Does not know, I heard that he was a bigamist, may have been tried, but I do not know may be I was absent at the time

Question In your direct examination, in answer to an interrogatory by the defendants, concerning the character of Madame DeGrange née Carriere, you use this language—I am oblige to say what I said many years ago in other courts—she was a "**femme** gallante" To what courts do you refer, when you use this or similar language, in respect to the character of said Zulime Carriere?

Answer I believe it was in the case of Kean *vs* Relf, or Relf *vs* Kean I believe it was in Judge Lewis' court, about twelve or thirteen years ago

Question On what other occasions have you used such language respecting that lady?

Answer I have never been called, except this time this is the second time

Question Did you ever hear Daniel Clark speak of Zulime Carriere if so what language did he use?

Answer Never said anything to me on the subject.

Question Did you ever hear any of the persons whom you have before named, as the intimate friends of Daniel Clark, speak of her during Mr Clark's life?

Answer No

Question Who have you heard speak of her during Mr. Clark's life?

Answer. Many persons, it was public If I was forced to it, I can name two individuals, who are now dead, who told me they had slept with her

Question. Do you know the complainants in this suit, General and Mrs Gaines? and if yea, how long have you known them?

Answer I am not acquainted with them, except by sight

Question Do you know Francois Dussuau Delacroix? and how long have you known him?

Answer I know him, and have known him since he arrived in this country Cannot say in what year he arrived here, but it is many many years

Question Have you been for a number of years the agent and attorney in fact of Dussuau Delacroix?

Answer Yes, sir Since, I believe, in 1829 or 1830

Question At what time did Mr. Delacroix leave this country for France?

Answer He left here for France twice The first time in May, 1829, and came back some time afterwards; remained here a very short time and went away again in August, 1833 Have always continued to hold his power of attorney since that time, and still hold it

Question Has there not been for years, and is there not still, a strong intimacy and friendship subsisting between yourself and Mr. Delacroix?

Answer Yes, sir.

Question Is there not a suit pending in which General and Mrs. Gaines are complainants, and Mr. Dussuau Delacroix is defendant, respecting certain property which belonged to the succession of the late Daniel Clark?

Answer. I know there is a suit, but can say nothing more than that.

Question. Did not Mr Delacroix purchase a large number of negroes from Relf & Chew, which belonged to Daniel Clark at the time of his death?

Answer. I have seen that in the suit. Know that he was sued for some negroes which were purchased when the canal was digging there.

Question. Have you not often conversed with Mr Delacroix, respecting this suit?

Answer. Not often—sometimes. Mr Delacroix is always on his plantation, and comes very little in town, and less now, being blind.

Question. Did you know the late Governor Claiborne, formerly Governor of Louisiana? and if so, were you intimate with him, and did you hold any, and what, office under him?

Answer. I knew and was intimate with him. I was a representative at the time there was another party here against him. He offered me several offices, but I refused all but a very trifling one—that was, directory of the State library. I was appointed by him major and colonel.

Question. Did there not a strong enmity exist between Daniel Clark and Governor Claiborne?

Answer. I know that they fought together. They had a duel.   Z. CAVELIER.

Examination in Chief resumed.

Was, or was not, Daniel Clark embarrassed in his pecuniary affairs, shortly before his death, to your knowledge? and, if so, how do you know?

Objection. Objected to, as impertinent and irrelevant.

Answer. Yes, sir. I know it, because there were many of his notes in circulation sold at twelve per cent. per annum interest—a very high discount at that time. but I have seen them in the hands of brokers.

Question. Was, or was not, Daniel Clark a partner of Chew & Relf, before his death?

Objection. Objected to by complainants, as irrelevant and impertinent and proved at all can be proved by better evidence.

Answer. It was reported so—that he had an interest in the house of Chew & Relf—but he was still a partner.

Question. How long have you known Richard Relf and Beverly Chew? and what is the reputation they have enjoyed in this community as to integrity?

Objection. Objected to by complainants.

Answer Always a good reputation I have known them since they arrived in this country and more particularly Relf, since he was a boy, and never knew any thing against them

Z CAVELIER.

J W GURLEY, Commissioner

Examination in chief —Theodore Zacharie

And afterwards to wit, on the first day of June, 1849, personally came and appeared Theodore Zacharie a person of lawful age and sound mind a witness on behalf of defendants, who, being duly sworn, did depose and say

Question. Please look upon the letter now handed to you, marked A A and state whether or not, you ever presented the same to the late Colonel Bellechasse and if so when you presented it where you presented it and whether or not, said Bellechasse acknowledged the same to have been written and signed by him

Objection Objected to by complainants, as irrelevant, and defendants persisting witness says

Answer I presented this, sir at his plantation, about four or five miles from Matanzas, island of Cuba, in February 6th, 1835 He acknowledged his signature to it and that the whole of it was written by him

Question Look upon the letter now handed to you, marked B B, and state whether, or not you ever presented the same to the late Colonel Bellechasse and if so when you presented it, where you presented it and whether or not, said Bellechasse acknowledged the same to have been written and signed by him

Objection Objected to by complainants as irrelevant, and defendants persisting witness says

Answer Yes I presented it to Colonel Bellechasse—presented it on the 6th of February, 1835—presented it at his plantation, four or five miles distant from the town of Matanzas, island of Cuba He acknowledged the same to have been written and signed by him

Question Look upon the letter now handed to you, marked C C, and state whether, or not you ever presented the same to the late Colonel Bellechasse, and if so, when you presented it; where you presented it and whether, or not, said Bellechasse acknowledged the same to have been written and signed by him.

Objection Complainants make the same objection to this as to the foregoing interrogatory, and defendants persisting, witness says

79

Answer I handed this letter to him, presented it on the sixth of February, 1835—presented it to him at his plantation, four or five miles from the town of Matanzas, island of Cuba, and he acknowledged the same to have been written and signed by him

Question Look upon the letter, marked D D, and state whether, or not you ever presented the same to the late Colonel Bellechasse, when you presented it where you presented it, and whether, or not, he stated it had been written under his direction or dictation, and if so, by whom he stated it had been so written, and whether or not he acknowledged the signature thereto to be his own genuine signature

Objection Complainants make the same objection to this as to the foregoing, and defendants persisting, the witness says

Answer I presented this letter to the late Colonel Bellechasse —presented it on the sixth of February, 1835—presented it to him at his plantation four or five miles from Matanzas, in the island of Cuba He stated it had been written under his direction or dictation, by one of his daughters he thought he acknowledged his signature thereto as genuine

Question Please to look at the certificate on each of the foregoing letters to wit those marked A A, B B, C C, and D D, and state whether, or not they were written by you, and if yea, whether they were severally written at the time and place they respectively bear date

Answer Those certificates were written by my own hand They were written by me, at the time and place they respectively bear date

Question Please read the several certificates annexed to said letters, and state whether, or not, you now confirm the statements therein contained under your oath now taken as containing the facts as they then occurred

Answer Having read the certificates, witness says yes, sir, I now confirm under oath the statements as therein contained
THEO ZACHARIE.

Cross Examination

I am forty-one years of age, was born in the city of New Orleans, and have lived here all my life Have no interest whatever in the result of this suit

Question At whose request did you present these letters to Colonel Bellechase?

Answer At Mr Relf's request   THEO ZACHARIE.

Examination in chief of Etienne Carraby

And afterwards, to wit on the fourth day of June, A. D 1849, personally came and appeared, Etienne Carraby, a witness on behalf of the defendants a person of sound mind and lawful age, who being duly sworn doth depose and say

Question. What is your age?

Answer About seventy-four years

Question How long have you lived in New Orleans?

Answer Seventy-four years. I was born in New Orleans.

Question Do you know the complainants in this suit, General Gaines and his wife, and the defendants Beverly Chew and Richard Relf or either of them and which?

Answer Does not know the complainants, but knows the defendants, Beverly Chew and Richard Relf

Question How long have you known Beverly Chew and Richard Relf?

Answer I have known them upwards of fifty years

Question Did you know the late Daniel Clark and if so how long did you know him?

Answer Knew him very well, and my acquaintance with him commenced in the year 1799

Question Did your acquaintance with Mr Clark continue from your first acquaintance with him until his death in 1813?

Answer Yes, it continued until his death

Question What was your own occupation or business at the time you became acquainted with Mr Clark, and always thereafter?

Answer I was a merchant, and continued a merchant until 1806 or 1807

Question Did you ever have any business connection or relationship with the said Daniel Clark?

Answer I had some business with him at different times, and particularly, in 1799, when we had an operation on joint account, from here to Nassau, New Providence I even believe that operation was made by Clark for and on account of the commercial house of Knox, in New Providence

Question What was the business, occupation or employment of the late Daniel Clark

Answer He was a merchant

Question What was the general reputation which Daniel Clark had in the community of New Orleans among his acquaintances and friends and the public generally, from the time you first became acquainted with him until the period of his death, as to his being a married or unmarried man?

Objection Objected to by complainants, and defendants persisting, witness says:

Answer Mr Clark enjoyed a very good reputation, and witness never heard Clark or any one else say that he was a married man

Question Did you ever hear any one previous to the death

of Mr. Clark, intimate or express a contrary opinion to the fact
of Mr Clark being a bachelor or unmarried man?

Objection. Objected to by complainant, as leading and irrel-
event, and defendants persisting, witness says

Answer   Never heard any one express the opinion, before
Clark's death, that he was not a bachelor

Question   Were you acquainted with, or did you know, Jerome DeGrange?

Answer   Yes, I knew him

Question   What was his business or employment in this
city, at the time you knew him?

Answer   He was a manufacturer of syrups and liquors, and
lived in St Ann Street, between Royal and Conde Streets.

Question.   Were you acquainted with Madame DeGrange?

Objection   Objected to by complainants as wholly irrelevant
and impertinent to the issue in this cause   The same objection
is made to the two last preceding interrogatories; and defendants persisting, witness says

Answer.   I was acquainted with Madame DeGrange

Question   What was her general reputation in the community of New Orleans for virtue and chastity?

Objected   Objected to by complainants, as irrelevant, impertinent, scandalous, and as indicating unmitigated malice, and defendants persisting, witness says

Answer   Her reputation was bad.

Question   Was or was not the reputation of Madame De-
Grange, in the community of New Orleans, so well and generally known, that Daniel Clark must have known of this reputation of Madame DeGrange?

Objection   Objected to by compl'ts, on the same ground as
the last preceding interrogatory, and compl't's, counsel takes
this occasion on himself and his clients, to enter his solemn protest against the course of the examination of witnesses, directed
against the character of an individual entirely disconnected with
this suit, and whose character, be it as it may, has nothing to
do with the matters in controversy in this suit   And the counsel
for the defendants, thereupon protest against the assumption of
facts contrary to the record of this cause, as they aver will be
there seen that the complainants claim in this case, not only as
heir at law of the late Daniel Clark, under an alleged marriage
between the said Daniel Clark and the said Madame DeGrange,
but, also, as assignees under a notarial act of the said Madame
DeGrange of the supposed rights of Madame DeGrange as
widow in community of the late Daniel Clark

Complainants hereby declare, in answer to the above, that they
make no claim by virtue of said notarial act, from Madame Gardette, as alluded to above

Answer   It was known enough not to have been misunderstood by Clark

Question   Did Madame DeGrange continue to reside in New Orleans up to the period of Daniel Clark's death ?

Answer   Does not remember

Question   What was the relationship, according to public reputation, which existed between Daniel Clark and Madame DeGrange, if any ?

Objection   Objected to by complainants, in addition to the objections before stated, as leading, and defendants persisting, witness says

Answer   It was generally reported in New Orleans, that Mr. Clark lived with Madame DeGrange

Question   In what capacity or character was it so reported, that Daniel Clark lived with Madame DeGrange ?

Objection   Objected to by complainants, and defendants persisting, witness says

Answer   In an amorous and illicit connection   And witness understands by this, that he lived with her as her lover   This was the general report

Question   What was the maiden or family name of Madame DeGrange ?

Answer   Her family name was Carriere   Witness does not recollect her maiden name.

Question.   Were you acquainted with the general reputation of Madame Despau, a sister of Madame DeGrange ? and if so, state what that public reputation was

Objection   Objected to on the same ground as the preceding interrogatories respecting Madame DeGrange, and defendants persisting, witness says

Answer   Did not know, personally, Madame Despau, but nothing good was said of her

Question.   Was or was not the reputation of Daniel Clark in New Orleans, that of an honorable and high-spirited gentleman ?

Answer   Yes, it was

Question   Judging by the reputation which Daniel Clark enjoyed in New Orleans, as a high spirited, aspiring man, do you, or do you not, believe that he would have connected himself in marriage with any lady who did not enjoy a spotless reputation in the community in which she lived

Objection   Objected to by Complts; and defendants persisting, witness says

Answer   Mr Clark was a too high minded man, to contract marriage with his paramour

E'NE CARRABY

Complainant waives cross examination at present, of this witness, and makes no objection on that account, in case the witness should die before cross examination

P C WRIGHT, Compl'ts' Solicitor.

Examination in Chief of Louis Bouligny

And afterwards to wit, on the 4th day of June, 1849, personally came Louis Bouligny, a person of sound mind, a witness for defendants who being duly sworn doth depose and say —

Question   What is your age ?

Answer   Sixty-eight years.

Question   How long have you resided in New Orleans?

Answer   Since sixty-eight years I have been residing in New Orleans, or the immediate neighborhood

Question   Do you know the complainants General Gaines and his wife, and the defendants, Beverly Chew and Richard Relf, or either of them, and if so, which of them?

Answer   Does not know the complainants, but knows the defendants

Question   How long have you known the said defendants, Richard Relf and Beverly Chew?

Answer.   Has known Relf since 1798 or 1799, and Mr Chew a few years afterwards

Question   Did you know the late Daniel Clark?

Answer   Knew him, and was very intimate with him

Question.   How long did you know the late Daniel Clark, and did your acquaintance with him continue until his death?

Answer   Was acquainted with Daniel Clark in 1791 or 1792   Daniel Clark used to visit witness' brother   In 1803 witness got intimately acquainted with Clark, and had some business transactions with him then, and this intimacy continued up to Daniel Clark's death

Question   State whether or not your acquaintance with Daniel Clark grew into very close terms of intimacy and friendship, and if so, whether you frequently visited his house on terms of intimacy

Answer.   In 1803 witness had a business transaction with Daniel Clark   We went together to Ouachita, where there was a tract of land which witness had sold to Clark.   We laid on the same bear skin during the night, and traveled on horseback during the day   From that moment, my intimacy commenced with Clark, and continued up to his death.   Witness used to take dinner with Clark, and Clark used to reciprocate, but witness was oftener at Clark's, than Clark was at his house   During several years, witness used to go and sleep at Clark's house, who was a bachelor, in order not to wake his, witness' mother late in the night.

Question   What was your occupation or employment from the time you became acquainted with Daniel Clark, up to the time of Clark's death, in 1813?

Answer   I was a military man up to 1803, and from that time a planter

Question   What position or office did you hold in the military service in the year 1803, and under what government?

Answer   I was a cadet, and afterwards an officer under the Spanish government   In 1803 I held the position of second lieutenant

Question   At what place were you stationed in the months of February and March, 1803?

Answer   In February, 1803, I was stationed at the Balize, and on the first days of March, 1803, I started from the city of New Orleans, to go and receive the prefect, Laussat, and General Victor who was expected   but the latter did not arrive

Question   Do you know, whether, or not, Daniel Clark was in the city of New Orleans when you left for the Balize in the early days of March, 1803, as stated in your answer to your last foregoing question?

Answer   I left Mr Clark in the city of New Orleans when I started for the Balize, and had a conversation with Mr Clark at the moment I left

Question   Do you know whether or not Daniel Clark held any office under the American government at the time last above referred to, (1803) in the city of New Orleans, and if so, what office was it?

Objection   Objected to by complainants, on the ground that it is not the best evidence, and the defendants persisting, witness says

Answer   Mr Clark was American Consul, but does not know when he was   In the year 1803 Mr Clark held no office under either the Spanish or American Government

Question   Do you know whether or not Daniel Clark had been absent from New Orleans during the latter part of the year 1802, and if so, whether you knew from him that he had been to Europe during his absence?

Answer   Yes, he was absent about some cotton transactions in Liverpool. This fact he knows from public conversation, and from Mr Clark himself.

Question.   Do you know whether or not Daniel Clark sailed from Europe directly for this port of New Orleans, and did you learn this fact from Mr. Clark himself?

Answer   Mr Clark told me he came from Europe; I do not know whether he had sailed from France or Liverpool, and sailed directly to this port

Question   How long had Daniel Clark been in New Orleans on his return from Europe previous to your departure for the Balize, in the early days of March, 1803, as before stated by you?

Answer   Only a few days

Question   What was the general reputation of Daniel Clark in the community of New Orleans from the time you became acquainted with him up to the period of his death. among his acquaintance and friends, and the public generally, as to his being a married or unmarried man?

Objection.   Objected to by complainants; and defendants persisting, witness says—

Answer   It was, that he was a bachelor

Question   During any of your visits to the house of Mr. Clark, did you ever see any lady to whom you were presented, or who seemed to be conducting herself as the wife of Daniel Clark?

Objected   Objected to by complainants, and defendants persisting, witness says

Answer.   I never met with any such lady Mr Clark always kept bachelor's house, but nothing else   He very often gave soirees, and gentlemen and ladies were invited, and came to his house   Never met any lady on any of those occasions who conducted herself as the wife of Mr Clark.

Question   Did you ever hear it intimated by any one, previous to the death of Mr Clark, that he, Clark, was, or ever had been, a married man?

Objection.   Objected to as impertinent and irrelevant; and defendants persisting, witness says—

Answer.   No, never, and if Clark had been married, he, witness, would have been aware of it   Witness was so very intimate with him, that he is sure Clark would have informed him of the fact

Question.   Were you acquainted with Jerome DeGrange?

Objection.   Objected to on the same grounds as to the interrogatory propounded to the witness Caraby; and defendants persisting, witness says

Answer   By sight only

Question   Were you acquainted with Madame DeGrange?

Objection   Objected to on same grounds as the preceding; defendants persisting, witness says.

Answer   Knew her by sight, and danced with her sometimes, at balls.

Question   What was her general reputation in the community of New Orleans, for virtue and chastity?

Objection   Objected to by complainants, same grounds as above stated; and defendants persisting, witness says.

Answer   It was bad

Question   Did Madame DeGrange continue to reside in New Orleans up to the period of Mr Clark's death?

Answer   Witness does not know.

Question   What was the relationship, according to public reputation, which existed between Daniel Clark and Madame DeGrange, if any?

Objection   Objected to by complainants on grounds already stated to similar questions propounded to witness Caraby, and defendants persisting, witness says

Answer   Public opinion was, that Mr. Clark was the lover of Madame DeGrange, but I must add, that Mr Clark never spoke to me of Mrs DeGrange, as being either his wife or his mistress

Question   What was the maiden or family name of Madame DeGrange?

Answer   Her family name was Carrière. does not recollect her maiden name.

Question   Were you acquainted with the general reputation of Madame Despau, a sister of Madame DeGrange? and if so, state what that public reputation was.

Objection.   Objected to on same grounds as stated to similar interrogatory propounded to Mr Carabuy and defendants persisting, witness says

Answer   Only knew Madame   by sight only, and knew nothing of her reputation

Question   Judging by the reputation which Daniel Clark enjoyed in New Orleans, as a high spirited and aspiring man, do you, or do you not, believe that he would have connected himself in marriage with any lady who did not enjoy a spotless reputation in the community in which she lived?

Objection   Objected to on grounds mentioned in a similar one propounded to Mr Caraby, and defendants persisting, witness says

Answer   Witness says, no, Clark would not have married such a lady   L BOULIGNY.

Examination in chief resumed —Louis Bouligny
June fifth, 1849

Examination in chief resumed, William Andry sworn as interpreter

Question Have you or not any knowledge from Daniel Clark or otherwise, of his addressing any lady in New Orleans with a view to matrimony and if so what lady, and at what time?

Objection Objected to by complainants, as irrelevant and impertinent, and defendants persisting witness says

Answer A young lady of this country a widow by the name of Miss Trepagnier, being divorced from Mr. François Lam

80

bert, was courted by Mr Clark, as Mr. Clark told witness himself, with a view to marriage This was in 1809, 1810, or 1811 ; am not positive as to the date It will be very easy to ascertain the date, by referring to the divorce, as it was subsequent to thh divorce

Question Were you or were you not a creditor of Daniel Clark at the time of his death ; and if so, in what sum ?

Objection Objected to by complainants and defendants persisting, witness says

Answer. Mr Clark owed witness ten thousand dollars at the time of his death Witness was paid this sum by the executors of Daniel Clark Witness gave them time to pay the same, but does not recollect what time he gave them

Question Was or was not Daniel Clark embarassed in his pecuniary affairs, previous to and at the time of his death ?

Objection Objected to by complainants.

Answer Daniel Clark was so much embarassed before his death, that he told witness he had only taken the contract of the canal for fifty thousand dollars, as he was much in need of that sum The canal referred to, is the Canal de Carondelet. Daniel Clark himself told witness he only took the contract on account of the fifty thousand dollars, as he was in great need of the money

Question Was or was not Daniel Clark in partnership with Chew & Relf before his death ?

Objection Objected to by complainants, as impertinent and as not the best evidence that can be adduced of the fact of partnership, if any existed , and defendants persisting, witness says .

Answer There was a house here under the style of Clark and those gentlemen, but witness does not know whether it existed at the time of Clark's death Does not know when it was dissolved All the moneyed transactions between witness and Daniel Clark were disconnected with mercantile business, and was altogether personal between them

Question. How long have you known Richard Relf and Beverly Chew, and what has been their character in this community for honor and probity of character, from the time you first knew them until this time ?

Objection Objected to by complainants

Answer I have known Richard Relf from 1798 or 1799, and became acquainted with Beverly Chew a few years afterwards I have always known them as honorable men and enjoying great confidence in the community

Question What office do you hold yourself, and how long have you held it ?

Answer I am recorder of mortgages of the parish of Jefferson, and have held that office since 840 or 1841

L. BOULIGNY

Cross examination

Question What is your maternal language?
Answer Spanish.

Question Have you fully understood the questions propounded in your examination in chief, as they have been translated to you, and are you satisfied that your answers to those interrogatories have been properly translated to the commissioner?

Answer Yes, and had I not understood them, I would have had them repeated to me

Question Are you interested, directly or indirectly, in the result of this suit?

Answer No, the estate owed me, and has paid me

Question. Who paid the debt the estate owed you, and in what manner was it paid, and when?

Answer The debt was paid to witness by Mr. Zenon Cavellier, who bought property on the Materie Road from Daniel Clark, which said property was mortgaged in favor of witness At the death of Daniel Clark he owed witness ten thousand dollars, eight thousand of this was paid by Zenon Cavellier, and the balance by Richard Relf, of the house of Relf & Chew He was paid in about two years after the death of Clark

Question In your direct examination you speak of having sold land in Ouachitta to Daniel Clark in 1803 what tract of land was this? how was it designated?

Answer I had inherited a tract known under the name of Maison Rouge concession I sold half of it under private signature in 1803 to Mr Clark, and the act of sale was passed in 1804 Mr Pierre Sauvé and Dussuau Delacroix were witnesses to the act under private signature The other half I also sold to Daniel Clark in 1812 It was thus that Daniel Clark became indebted to me in the balance of ten thousand dollars

Question Did you warrant the title of this concession, or any part of it, to Mr Clark in your sale in 1803, or in that of 1812?

Answer It will be necessary for me to have the act of sale to answer all these particulars I think there was warranty.

Question From whom did you inherit this Maison Rouge concession, and in what manner? Was it as heir at law, or by will and testament?

Answer By testamentary donation, from the Marquis de Maison Rouge

Question What age were you when you first sold this land to Daniel Clark in 1803?

Answer I was twenty-two years of age

Question Of what age was Mr. Clark at that time, 1803 ?

Answer Clark was eight or nine years older than witness

Question Have you, at any time since the death of Daniel Clark, held or disposed of, or do you now hold, any property, real or personal, belonging to his succession ?

Answer No, sir

Question Can you name some of the most prominent men who lived in New Orleans during Mr Clark's residence here ?

Answer The family of Cavellier, the two Urquhart, Michel Fortier, Doctor Dow, J B Labatut, Major Nott, Bellechasse, Destrehan, Governor Villere, Governor Derbigny, General Laronde, Dussuau Delacroix

Question In what estimation was Daniel Clark held by these gentlemen, whom you have named ?

Answer They were the friends of Daniel Clark. They all held him in high estimation If they had not had a good opinion of him, they would not have acted as his friends

Question Were you on terms of close intimacy with Colonel Bellechasse ?

Answer Yes, I served as an officer with him, and I was a friend of his until 1818, when I saw him in Matanzas, Cuba This friendship continued up to the death of Colonel Bellechasse I have the highest opinion of the character of Colonel Bellechasse, he was a very honorable man He was commanding the militia of New Orleans, and was president of the Senate under the territorial government. He was one of the most intimate and confidential friends of Daniel Clark

Question. Did you know the late Judge Pitot, of New Orleans ?.

Answer Yes, but not so well as Colonel Bellechasse. He was an honorable man, and a man of very good reputation He was mayor under the territorial government, and afterwards parish judge

Question. Did you know the late Pierre Baron Boisfontaine ?

Answer I knew Pierre Baron Boisfontaine he was an honorable man He managed a plantation of Daniel Clark, and Daniel Clark treated him as a friend He had previously managed a plantation at Natchez, known as the Desert plantation, and he afterwards came with the negroes to establish the Houma planation

Question. In answer to an interrogatory in your examination in chief, you say, respecting Madame DeGrange, that you knew her by sight, and danced with her sometimes at balls At what epoch was this ?

Answer It was between 1798 until 1804 I saw her at every public ball, but not at society balls There was only one public ball room at that period

Question You speak also, in answer to an interrogatory in your direct examination, of an intimacy between Mr Clark and Madame DeGrange At what epoch did this intimacy commence?

Answer The rumors say that the intimacy begun during the presence of her husband here,—it was in 1800, and continued for a long while

L BOULIGNY

Examination in chief resumed

Question Did you ever meet with Madame DeGrange at the soirées given by Daniel Clark, or at any other private parties or soirées given in the circe of society in which Daniel Clark held position or rank

Objection Objected to by complainants.

Answer Never.

Question Do you know whether or not there existed a warm friendly relationship between D Clark and Beverly Chew and Richard Relf, up to the period of said Clark's death.

Objection Objected to by complainants

Answer. Previous to Clark's death, Chew and his family were living with Clark on Bayou road Clark had given Chew the upper part of his house there to live in, and Chew and Relf were always very friendly with Clark until his death

Question What was the character and standing of Beverly Chew and Richard Relf from the time you first became acquainted with them to the present period, for honesty and integrity of character?

Answer I have already stated that they had the reputation of men of honor They were men of honor, enjoying the highest reputation

Question Have they or have they not held offices and places of public trust and confidence at various periods, from the time of your first acquaintance with them to the present time

Answer. Mr. Chew has been Collector of the Customs Mr Relf has been appointed cashier of the Louisiana State Bank from its creation, and still holds the office Mr. Chew was collector for many years—at least four years, but witness cannot state exactly

L BOULIGNY.

J. W. GURLEY, Commissioner

DEFENDANTS.

Depositions of—1 Madame Villerie Ducaunau. 2 Seaman Field 3 P J Tricou 4 Horatio Davis 5 Jacob Hart 6. J. Canon

MYRA CLARK GAINES)
      vs   } No 122
RELF, CHEW ET AL.)

Interrogatories propounded on behalf of defendants to Madame Ducournau, to be by her answered under oath, before J W Gurley, commissioner herein appointed to take testimony in the city of New Orleans

Question 1st Please state your age and residence, and how long you have resided in New Orleans?

Question 2d Were you acquainted with the late Daniel Clark? if yea, when did you become acquainted with him, how long did you continue your acquaintance with said Clark?

Question 3d Do you know whether or not Daniel Clark was ever married? State all you know on this subject, either on the affirmative or negative side of the question, according to your knowledge, as fully and particularly as if you had been thereto specially interrogated.

Question 4th. What was the general reputation of Daniel Clark in the community of New Orleans, from the period of your first acquaintance with him until his death, on the subject of his being a married or unmarried man? State fully

Question 5th Were you acquainted with Madame Zulime DeGrange nee Carriere, either personally or by general reputation? If yea, state what her general reputation was in New Orleans Did you ever hear of said Madame De Grange being married to Daniel Clark?

Question 6th Did you know Madame Sophie Despau, the sister of Madame DeGrange? if yea, what was her reputation in New Orleans?

Question 7th. Do you know, or can you set forth, any other matter or thing which may be a benefit or advantage to the parties at issue in this case, or either of them, or that may be material to the subject of this your examination, or the matters in question in this case? if aye, set forth the same fully and at large in your answer   G B DUNCAN,
                     For Chew, Relf, et al

Cross interrogatories propounded to the aforementioned witness, on the part of Myra Clark Gaines, the complainant in the foregoing entitled suit

Cross question 1st What is your maiden name; where were you born, and what is your maternal language?

Cross question 2d. If you say you knew the late Daniel Clark, at what period did you first know him ? was you on intimate terms with him ? did he ever visit you, or did you ever visit him ? did you enjoy his confidence ?

Cross question 3d. At what period were you first married ; have you been more than once married, and if so, to whom on each occasion ? have you a husband now living ? if yea, where does he live, and what is his age and occupation ?

Cross question 4th. You are inquired of respecting the general occupation of two ladies. If you state any thing unfavorable, state from whom particularly you heard what you state, and whether these persons were or were not on intimate terms with the persons of whose character and reputation you are interrogated, state whether you were on terms of intimacy with any prominent persons residing in Louisiana, during the lifetime of the said Daniel Clark, if yea, what are their names ; who of them are living, and who are dead ?

> P. C. WRIGHT,
> Complainants' solicitor.

New Orleans, 14th June, 1849.

Note.—The solicitor for the defendant will take notice, that since the foregoing interrogatories seek to impeach the character of two persons, the complainant reserves to herself the right to re-examine the said witnesses orally, at any time, upon giving due notice of such examination.

> P. C. WRIGHT, Comp's sol

A true copy J. W. GURLEY, Com'r.

Madame Mary Villerie Ducaunau, in answer to written interrogatories in chief.

And afterwards, 22d June, 1849 appeared Mary Villerie Ducaunau, a person of sound mind and lawful age, a witness for defendants, who being sworn, did depose and say (William Andry, sworn as interpreter.)

In answer to Interrogatory—

1st. I am eighty years and six months of age, my residence is New Orleans, I was born in New Orleans, and never went further from it than to the Lake.

To 2d. I knew the late Daniel Clark very well, I knew Daniel Clark when he was eighteen or twenty years of age, and my acquaintance continued until the time of his death.

To 3d. I never heard that Daniel Clark was married, he was never married positively. I know that he was never married, because I always heard that he was never married, and that he had good reasons not to marry. I always heard that he could not be married, because at about the age of sixteen or seventeen he was afflicted with a disease, the result of which was, to prevent his ever after being married, but, fortunately, he had the money to pay his "*soi-disant maitresses*"

To 4th Daniel Clark was always reputed, in the community of New Orleans, to be an unmarried man, his reputation was that of a man "*comme il faut*" I never heard that Daniel Clark was married, and, as I said before, I always heard that he could not be married

To 5th I knew Madame Zulime DeGrange née Carrière by reputation only, her reputation was very equivocal I never heard that Madame DeGrange was married to Daniel Clark, the reputation of Madame DeGrange was not that of an honest woman, but, perhaps, it was not true

To 6th. I knew Madame Sophie Despau, sister of Madame DeGrange, her reputation was about that of her sister

To 7th. Knows nothing more of these parties The ladies named did not mingle in the same society that witness did; but Clark did.

Witness cannot sign her name, being paralyzed in her right hand　　　　　　　　　　J W GURLEY, Com'r

In answer to cross question—

1st. My maiden name is Mary Roy Villeré, I was born in New Orleans; my maternal language is French

To 2d I knew him when he was about the age of sixteen or eighteen years, cannot recollect the year, I was not on terms of intimacy, but on such terms of intimacy, as are general in society; Daniel Clark used to visit my house, but I never visited him, I was in the habit of visiting his aunt, Mrs Clark, who lived next to him, I never enjoyed his confidence

To 3d I was seventeen years of age when I was married; I have been married but once, my husband's name was Simon Ducaunau, my husband is dead, he was a planter; a justice of the peace, &c &c

To 4th I cannot state from whom I heard, those ladies, already mentioned, were of equivocal reputation, but it was generally said; cannot say whether the persons from whom I heard the reputation of those ladies were on terms of intimacy with them or not, I was acquainted, and on terms of intimacy, with persons of high standing and prominence in Louisiana, during the lifetime of Daniel Clark Among those dead, I was intimate with Edmund Forstall, Edward Forstall, Eran Jones. I knew Relf and Chew, but was not intimate with them, I knew them, by reputation, as honest merchants.

Witness, as before stated, is not able to sign this, her deposition.　　　　　　　　　J. W GURLEY, Com'r.

And afterwards, to wit on the 23d June, 1849, personally appeared Mr. Simon Field, a person of sound mind and lawful age, a witness for defendants, who, being duly sworn, did depose and say

I reside in New Orleans; I am fifty years, and upward, of age, I have resided in New Orleans since 1813; I knew Mrs Gaines, and also Mr Chew and Mr Relf. In the fall of 1813, I met Mr Chew in Philadelphia, and crossed the mountains with him to Pittsburg. Mr Chew was on his way to New Orleans. We separated at Pittsburg. Mr Chew and his party came down in a barge. I came down in a small steamboat that was fitted up for the purpose. I think it was in November that we crossed the mountains. I think that at that time, it took about fifty or or sixty days to come down in a barge from Pittsburg to New Orleans.

S FIELD

Cross examination

My first acquaintance with Mr Chew commenced on our passage from Philadelphia to Pittsburg, in the stage

S. FIELD

And afterwards, to wit, on the 23d day of June, 1849, personally came and appeared Mr P J Tricou, a person of sound mind and lawful age, a witness on behalf of the defendants who, being duly sworn, did depose and say

I was born on the fourth of January, 1788, in the city of New Orleans. I went first to the north, when I was about seven years of age, and remained there 3 or 4 years, and in 1802 I went to France' and returned on the 20th August, 1806, and since that time I have constantly lived in the city of New Orleans. I know Messrs Chew and Relf very well. I have known those gentlemen since the year 1801 or 1802. I do not know the complainant, Mrs Gaines. I knew the late Daniel Clark. I knew him since about the year 1801, 1802, or 1806, cannot recollect precisely. Chew and Relf used to live near my father's counting house, so my father was very intimate with them, and with Clark also. Mr Clark came very often to my father's counting room. My acquaintance with Clark continued up to the time of his death, in 1813

Question. What was the general reputation which Daniel Clark had in the community of New Orleans, among his acquaintances and friends, and the public generally, from the time you first became acquainted with him until the period of his death, as to his being a married or unmarried man?

Objected to by complainant

Answer. I never, for my part understood that he had ever

81

been married I always took him for a single man I never heard any one intimate or express the opinion that he was a married man, on the contrary, I always heard that he was a single man

Question Was or not the late Daniel Clark generally reputed among his friends and acquaintances to be impotent?

Objection. Objected to by complainants as wholly irrelevant and that witness is incompetent to prove such a fact if it existed.

Answer I heard so It was said so by women whom I visited myself at that time, I was then young I was at least twenty years of age at that time

I saw Madame DeGrange several times I saw her in my mother's saloon Knowing that Mrs DeGrange had a bad reputation, I informed my mother of it, and since that time have never seen her except in the streets

Objection Complainant objects to the testimony above, referring to Madame DeGrange's reputation

Question What was the relationship, according to public reputation, which existed between Daniel Clark and Madame DeGrange, if any

Objected to by complainant as irrelevant and as incompetent testimony

Answer She was considered as the mistress (amante) of Daniel Clark

Question Were you acquainted with the general reputation of Madame Despau, the sister of Madame DeGrange and if so state what that public reputation was

Answer Her reputation was on the same footing as that of Madame DeGrange

Objection The above objected to by complainant

Question From the knowledge you had of the late Daniel Clark's reputation, do you believe that he would have connected himself in marriage with any lady who did not enjoy a spotless reputation?

Objected to by complainant

Answer I do not, really, believe that he would have done so

Question What has been, and is, the reputation of Messrs Chew and Richard Relf in the community of New Orleans ever since you knew them to the present time, for integrity and honorable conduct

Answer They have always enjoyed the best character in the community

Question Have they or not, each of them at various times held public offices in the banks of this city?

Answer Mr Relf has been cashier of the State Bank since the establishment of the Bank which, I believe, was in the year 1818. Mr Chew has been collector of customs here in the city, and has also been cashier of the Canal Bank.

Question. Did you ever hear, either from Daniel Clark or from any one else during said Clark's lifetime, that he, the said Clark, was or ever had been a married man?

Answer. No sir. I never heard any such thing. I always heard to the contrary.

Question. Do you know whether or not an intimate friendship existed between Daniel Clark, Beverly Chew and Richard Relf from the time you first knew these gentlemen until the death of Daniel Clark?

Answer. Mr Clark always considered those young men as his children.

One day I heard a conversation between my mother and Daniel Clark (not sooner than 1806 nor later than 1810) in which she was teazing him for not being married and told him he should get married, and he answered that it was *trop tard* — the time was over.

Question. Did Daniel Clark in the conversation which you have just detailed, intimate, in any manner, that he was then a married man or ever had been?

Answer. No sir. Nothing was said about that.

P. J. TRICOU.

J. W. GURLEY, Com'r.

Cross Examination.

I am not interested in the event of this suit.

Question. Were you so intimate with Daniel Clark and on such terms of close intimacy with him, that had he been married secretly he would have confided that secret with you?

Answer. No I believe not. I was too young a man at that time. P. J. TRICOU.

J. W. GURLEY, Com'r.

Examination in chief of Horatio Davis.

And afterwards to wit on the 25th day of June, 1849 personally came and appeared Horatio Davis a person of sound mind and lawful age a witness in behalf of defendants herein, who, being duly sworn, did depose and say as follows to wit.

Question. Look upon the printed remembrancer, with handed to you and state whether or not that publication was made by you if aye when was it made?

Answer. I made the publication. It was made in May 1844.

Question. State whether or not you ever saw the original, of which the letter therein forming part, purporting to be a copy of a letter dated at New Orleans 14th October, 1805 from Daniel Clark to his sister, if yea by whom was it written or signed?

Objected to by complainant.

Answer   The original of the letter was handed to me by Mr. Barton, at present our Charge at Chili or by Dr Barnes, the husband of a lady claiming to be a daughter of Mr Daniel Clark   After having copied the letter, I returned it to those gentlemen, who were both in my office at the time of the letter being given to me   Mr Barton was acting as the counsel of Dr Barnes and wife   I believe the original to have been written and signed by Daniel Clark   I am sufficiently acquainted with Mr Clark's signature to say so

Question   State whether or not this printed copy is an exact copy of the original letter as compared at the time by yourself?

Answer   I collated the copy that I made from the original, but did not compare the printed copy with either the original or the manuscript copy   I, however, carefully read the whole of the printed statement, and noticed the inaccuracies of language in the printed copy of the statement, and if there had been any discrepancy between the printed letter and the original, I would have observed it

Question.   State whether or not you know the character in which Myra, the complainant was introduced into your father's family, when an infant   If aye, state whether it was in the character of a legitimate child of Daniel Clark or otherwise, please state fully

The infant Myra was brought to my father's house some time in the year 1804, I did not, at the time, know whose child she was, I, however, before long, heard her spoken of, by members of the family, as the child of Daniel Clark.   I was too young to have noted whether it was as a natural or legitimate child, or to be able to distinguish between what was a natural or legitimate child   I left New Orleans in the summer of 1806, to go to the North for an education   My mother arrived in Baltimore with Myra, then a little girl, in the year 1812, while I was at college at that place.   From that period up to the present time. I have never had any reason to believe that any member of the family ever looked upon her in any other light than as the natural child of Mr Clark

Myra was always treated by every member of the family as my sister   Neither directly or indirectly was it ever communicated to her, by any member of the family or by any of the servants, in my presence, that she was any other than the daughter of my father and mother   We seldom spoke of her relation to Mr Clark, but when she was so spoken of, it was as his natural daughter

Question   Do you now re-affirm the statement made in the printed publication already referred to

Answer   Ye

I am the son of Samuel Boyer Davis and Mary Ann Rose Baron, his wife, now deceased. I was born on the 23d July, 1795, and am a resident of New Orleans.

Objection. All the foregoing testimony objected to by complainant, as irrelavent and incompetent evidence.

HORATIO DAVIS

Cross examination waived by P C Wright, Solicitor for complainant.

J. W. GURLEY, Commissioner

Referred to by Gen Horatio Davis in his deposition.

J. W. GURLEY, Com

Messrs Editors:—In a statement by Mrs Gaines published in your paper of the 11th inst., I am charged with leaguing with her enemies, in the year 1817. The charge is one affecting honor, and as it appeared in your columns, I pray that you will have the goodness to insert the following defence.

Yours, respectfully, H D.

"Statement written and signed by Myra Clark Gaines, and read by her in the District Court, May 7, 1841.

"Richard Relf and Beverly Chew, in the year 1817, having learned that their victim had found, in the wife of Colonel Samuel B Davis, a benevolent friend and an adopted mother, apprehended that she could not be *safely disposed of*, so as to prevent her future growth and improvement. for they learned that *Myra Clark*, though known to her immediate associates only as *Myra Davis*, was receiving from Mrs. Davis the care and kindness of a devoted mother, and though in the eleventh year of her age, had made such progress in the attainment of knowledge as to fill these lawless executors of my father, Daniel Clark, with serious apprehensions that they might ere long find in his only child a power of mind and moral courage that would drag them out of their *Banks of ill got gold*, in which they were then fortifying themselves. These miserable men, who had often quailed under the evanescent frown of the high-spirited but generous father, naturally feared to meet at mature age the injured daughter, lest she should inherit too much of the *mind and spirit* of her father for their repose or safety. After due deliberation, aided by counsel worthy of such clients, they determined *to get up a case of alimony*, by which they could make it appear that this orphan child of their deceased benefactor had made admissions, in her eleventh year, which would enable them to abuse and calumniate her *when of age!* This extraordinary proceeding, got up in 1817 for after use, was published by Richard Relf, in 1835; and since, anonymously, in the year 1839. This alimony case, which follows, will be seen by every honest mind to contain irrefragible evidence of the weakness of a cause that could require, or even palliate, the enormities of

such a proceeding   In examining this case, it is proper to bear
in mind the fact that at the time this case was got up in New
Orleans Mrs Clark was not only unconscious of her being
any other than Myra Davis the daughter of Colonel S B Davis
and Mrs M A R Davis whom she had considered as her
parents, and by whom she had been treated as their daughter
from the earliest moments of her childhood to which her memory
could revert but she was during the summer of 1817 with her
supposed mother, Mrs Davis, in the City of Philadelphia, in the
enjoyment of every comfort nor did she know anything about
this extraordinary almony, or of it more than twelve years
after its *commencement and discontinuance*'

Myra! Did you write, sign and read this statement before
the District Court—in the presence of a gay—a crowded
audience?

Are you the Myra I have seen in her helplessness resting on
the breast from which you in infancy received the sustenance
that brothers give their children? Are you the Myra I have
seen nestling on the manly bosom of my father? Are you the
Myra that I have so often talked to step with all a brother's
love, and whose infant steps I have supported?

Are you that Myra? And could you *deliberately write with a
view publicly to read* these words After due deliberation, aided
by counsel *worthy of such counsel* they determined to get up a
case of almony by which they could make it appear that this
orphan child of their deceased benefactor had made admissions,
in her eleventh year, which would enable them to *abuse and
calumniate* her when of age!

The two petitions you publish were signed, Davis and Pence
You knew that *I* had written and presented these petitions
claiming almony for you and in support of the baseless charge,
by which you seek to fasten dishonor upon me and upon a name
that had been lent to you, my father's authority is brought to
bear against me—' *Colonel Samuel B Davis has publicly declared
that he never authorized or sanctioned such a suit,* thereby placing
me in the alternative of either submitting in silence to a false
and disgraceful imputation, or of publicly raising a question of
veracity between my father and myself!

Have you a heart, and could you do this? Did not your eye
wander from this disavowal of my father to another part of his
public letter where he says 'Connected with Mr Clark by
great intimacy, I became acquainted with the birth of his
daughter when it occurred He desired that the circumstance
should be kept secret, and so it was by me The child was
placed where it was supposed she would be properly attended
to, and Mr. Clark leaving New Orleans for a short time, very
soon after I consented to see that this was done. *It was soon*

apparent that the infant was neglected, and after some hesitation, I communicate the facts to my wife. She went at once to see the child was touched with compassion at her forlorn and desolate situation and gave orders immediately to take her at once to her own house." Could not these public expressions bring better feelings to your bosom, and a restoration to the avowed purpose of arraying against each other the husband and son of your benefactress. Was there no inward sense of gratitude to restrain you? On, shame! shame! It is true that I made the application in behalf of my father—but I did so by his direction; he furnished me with the grounds for the application.*

After a lapse of twenty years, that he should have forgotten the part that he took in the transaction is not so remarkable as that one who *had made such progress in the attainment of knowledge,* should have been misled by your memory, when you state that at the time of filing the petition you were in Philadelphia with my mother *enjoying every comfort.* In 1817 my mother was on the sugar estate in the parish of St. Bernard, and did not return to Philadelphia till the spring of 1818, after my father had sold the estate. You were going to school in Philadelphia and resided with Mrs. Patterson.

Even your excellent memory sometimes deserts you not only in the way of forgetfulness of benefits but also in the forgetfulness of records. You seem to have forgotten that in answer to a cross interrogatory propounded by Mr. Whitney your late husband to my father in the case of Richard Relf vs W. W. Whitney, and filed on the 19th December 1836, my father said

"I have no recollection of any such suit (the alimony suit) as is enquired of being instituted nor how it came to be brought, though my name may have been used therein as curator *ad litem.* I remember only that Mr. Edward Livingston said to me, that alimony might be obtained for Myra, and I remember that Mr. Chew or Relf, but I believe Relf, spoke to me, and said—'The affairs of the estate were so unsettled, that nothing could be done for her then, but that when settled they might be able to do something for her,' and if the suit was discontinued it was in consequence of this statement. Mr. Clark did frequently express to me, his intention of educating and supporting Myra in his own rank of life and of providing for her, but I never heard him say when he meant to do it.'

The bringing of the suit was the consequence of his conver-

_____

*The two petitions were signed by me, Davis & Pence because we were printer. Mr. Pence, as well as I can now remember was, at the time of filing the petition, ill of the fever.

sation with Mr. Livingston, who was to have given me his assistance in conducting it

After the conversation with Mr. Relf, by direction of my father, I moved for its discontinuance.

You have alleged, and by the testimony of your aunt, Mrs. Despau, now on record, have endeavored to prove, that Daniel Clark was married in Philadelphia in the year 1803, to Mrs. Desgrange, your mother, and you take offence, and accuse me, because you were styled in the petition, a natural daughter of Daniel Clark. Let what follows show. From your infancy I had never heard you designated otherwise. I believed you to be his natural daughter, and so named you, in the petition *to establish your title to alimony.* That I was not singular in this belief, I refer you to the testimony of one of your own witnesses, Mr de la Croix, the *intimate friend of your father*, and who, under the *last* will, *was to have been your tutor.* Page 282. (printed edition,) in the answers to interrogations 4th and 5th, he twice calls you *the natural daughter* of Mr Clark, and in answer to the 6th interrogation, he says—"Mr Clark asked my consent, also, to become the tutor of the said child, Myra, and told me that his intention was, to *leave her a fortune sufficient to efface, if possible, the dishonor of her birth.*'

In the case of Barnes and wife *vs* Gaines and wife, in the First District Court, by the testimony of Mr and Mrs Baron Boisfontaine, (in whose house you were born,) it is proved that you were born in 1804. That such was the fact, I have a personal knowledge. In November 30th, 1805, *seventeen months after your birth*, Mrs. Degrange presented the following petition to the County Court of New Orleans.

To the Hon. James Workman Judge of the County Court of New Orleans.

The petition of Zuhme Carrère Desgrange, an inhabitant of the city of New Orleans, humbly sheweth,—

That whereas it is provided by the first section of an act, entitled, "an act concerning alimony, and for other purposes," that the County Court shall have jurisdiction on applications from wives against their husbands, for alimony, on the husband deserting his wife for one year, successively, and in cases of cruel, inhuman, and barbarous treatment, and whereas your petitioner may adduce proofs before this honorable court that she has been cruelly and barbarously treated by Jerome Desgrange, *her husband*, and likewise that she has been deserted by him for three years past, to wit from the 2d day of September, 1802, even unto this day, although she has been told that the said Jerome Desgrange returned from France to New Orleans, sometime in the course of last month, and is now in the city of New Orleans.

Therefore, these are to pray, that it may please your Honor to order that Jerome Desgrange, *your petitioner's husband*, be condemned to pay to your petitioner a sum of $500 per annum, and that your petitioner be likewise entitled to all the other benefits and advantages belonging to her, in virtue of the law of this Territory, in that case made and provided and your petitioner, as in duty bound will ever pray

(Signed,)   EICHUS FROMENTIN

Attorney for plaintiff

A true copy of the original English part of the petition, filed in the County Court in the case of Zulime C Desgrange vs Jerome Desgrange, on the 30th of November 1805.

Clerk's Office of the Parish Court, }

New Orleans, May 13, 1841 }

[SEAL]   (Signed,)   J OLIF, Deputy Clerk

Now hear Mr Clark's voice. One month before your mother's application for alimony from her husband Desgrange he writes to his sister, Mrs Green of Liverpool as follows

NEW ORLEANS 14th October, 1805

My Dear Sister —I have received your letter of the 3d May and thank you kindly for the pains you took in filling the toilette *I assure you that it would have given me infinite pleasure to have offered it either to Mrs Clark, or any person likely to become Mrs Clark, but this will not be the case for some time to come* for, as long as I have the misfortune to be hampered with business, *so long will I remain single,* for fear of misfortune or accident."

To the public, before whom you have so unnecessarily dragged me I leave to determine whether or not I have repelled your accusation   HORATIO DAVIS

STIPULATION

It is agreed, in the presence of me, commissioner by the respective solicitors of the complainant and defendants, that the copy of the letter from Daniel Clark, dated 14 October, 1805, referred to in the testimony of H Davis, shall be read in evidence on the trial of this case, provided the original cannot be had before the trial, from Mr Barton or Dr Barnes, provided, Dr Barnes and Mr Barton shall swear that they have not the original, and cannot produce it, but that they have seen said original and that commissions shall at once issue to Dr. Barnes and Mr. Barton (Issued 25th June, 1849)

J. W. GURLEY, Commissioner.

NOTE —Be it remembered, that after the testimony of Gen H Davis had been closed, he, the said Davis, made application to the solicitors for complainant and defendants, for permission to file, in this record, a statement, to be prepared by himself, in reference to statements contained in the deposition on file, of Philander Chase, and that thereupon, G B Duncan, solicitor for defendants, gave his consent thereto and P C Wright, Esq, solicitor for complainant, objected, on the ground that it will be an ex parte statement, and wholly irrelevant and impertinent to the issue of this cause

I. W. GURLEY, Commissioner

And afterwards, to wit on the 28th day of June, 1849, personally came and appeared, Jacob Hart, Esq, a person of sound mind and lawful age, a witness on behalf of the defendants, who, being duly sworn, did depose and say

I knew Madame DeGrange in the year 1805 or 1806   I knew her husband, Gerome DeGrange, by sight, was not personally acquainted with him   He was pointed out to me a number of times, as the husband of Madame DeGrange, and was well known as such   As far as my memory serves me, I think he was here in 1806 or 1807   He was publicly in the streets.

Question   What was the the reputation of Madame DeGrange as to her chastity?

Objected to by complainant.

Answer   At that time, Madame DeGrange was in the habit of going into the best society here   I became acquainted with her in a private family

Question   What was her reputation as to chastity, some years subsequent to your first acquaintance with her?

Answer.   It did not stand as fair   she had the reputation of intriguing with gentlemen a great deal,—this is only hearsay

Question   What years do you refer to, that she had this reputation for intriguing

Answer   I think it was about the years 1808 and 1809, because I left here in 1810, and it was before I went away

I do not know Madame Despau, I knew Daniel Clark intimately

Question   Was Clark a married or a single man?

Objected to by Compl't

Answer   I always understood he was a single man, up to the time of his death

Question   Had or not Daniel Clark the reputation of being impotent, both among women and men?

Objected to by compl't.

Answer   It was so reported

Question   Was or not the report general?

Answer   I heard it a number of times. I heard it from females, I will not be particular as to the number of times, I heard it probably a dozen times, I will not be precise as to the number of times, I heard it repeatedly

I arrived in New Orleans, 1804 in October. My occupation has been a merchant and broker.   JACOB HART

Cross Examination

I was sixty-eight years of age on the 30th of last March, 1849

Question. What was the occupation of Jerome DeGrange?

Answer. Of that I cannot inform you

Question. What was his personal appearance?

Answer. He had the appearance of a common man. I suppose his height was about five feet six inches in height. Rather thinly inclined. It appears to me he was pox-marked. I think he had light hair, do not remember the color of his eyes; he had a very common look, he was ugly. I think he wore powder on his hair. I suppose at that time DeGrange was about thirty-six or thirty-eight years of age, according to my judgment

Question. Can you name any individual who pointed out Mr DeGrange to you?

Answer. I cannot

Question. Can you name the place or circumstances in which you first became acquainted with Madame DeGrange?

Answer. I boarded in a family by the name of Gautier, whom Mrs DeGrange was in the habit of visiting, at least three or four times a week

Question. Did you ever meet her in society?

Answer. Repeatedly. This was the first society in the city of N Orleans at that time. I occasionally met Daniel Clark in the same society.

Question. You mention in your direct examination, having seen Mr DeGrange here in 1806 or 1807. Can you name any circumstance which has fixed this fact on your memory?

Answer. No, I cannot

Question. Do you know when Mr DeGrange first left New Orleans?

Answer. I do not

Question. In your direct examination, you state that the reputation of Madame DeGrange, a few years after I first knew her, was not as fair as when you first became acquainted with her. Can you name any person or persons who spoke of her at the period last mentioned? and if so, what did they say?

Answer. I cannot recollect the particular persons

Question. Do you recollect at what time Madame DeGrange first left New Orleans?

Answer. I do not recollect

Question. Name any women or men whom you heard speak of the impotency of Daniel Clark, and what did they say upon that subject?

Answer. I cannot, sir.

Question Were you invited by said Daniel Clark, at his house, at social parties?

Answer Yes, I have been at parties at Mr Clarks', but not often I have dined with him He was not in the habit of giving parties at that time, he lived retired

Question Have you ever heard of Gerome DeGrange since the time you last spoke of seeing him in New Orleans?

Answer No, sir JACOB HART

Examination in chief resumed

Please look at the paper handed to you, marked A A, and state whether you know merchants and business men whose names are thereto signed and state whether or not they were among the most prominent and intelligent business men in New Orleans, at that time

Answer Yes, sir, they were.

Objection Compl't object to the above mentioned document as evidence

I suppose I saw DeGrange about a half dozen times I never saw him anywhere but in N Orleans, and I arrived in New Orleans, for the first time, in 1804 JACOB HART

W Gurley, Com'r.

And afterwards, to wit, on the 28th June, 1849, personally appeared Jean Canon, a person of sound mind and lawful age, a witness for defendants, who, being duly sworn, did depose and say

I am sixty-three years of age, was born in N Orleans; knew Daniel Clark intimately, knew also the complainant, Mrs Gaines, knew her when a child, her mother was Madame widow DeGrange, and Daniel Clark always passed for her father. Daniel Clark frequently spoke to witness of this child, witness bought, by D Clark's order, a choctaw pony for her, he bought the pony from Mr Delery, who is now a planter in the parish of Plaquemine, and had a saddle and bridle made by James Martin, a sadler in New Orleans I took the pony up to Mr Davis' and when I arrived there, the child was asleep, they woke her up, and I took her, and put her on the pony, and held her in the saddle with one hand, and led him around the yard with the other. Previous to this incident, and before the child was placed in charge of Mr. Davis, she was in that of Mrs Harper One day, during this period, D Clark met me in the street and told me to go and send Dr Watkins to Mrs Harper's, to see the child who was sick I did as requested, and went to the house with Dr Watkins, and, after hearing his opinion, went to the Bank, of which Clark was at that time a director, and made my report. Being asked why Mrs DeGrange did not suckle her child, he says that it was said, that she wanted to get away from her husband, DeGrange others say, that she wanted to get out of the way of DeGrange's first wife, who was then in the country

Being asked what Clark said of Madame DeGrange, witness said, that whenever Clark spoke of her, he spoke of her as a beautiful woman, he always admired her as a beautiful woman, and witness adds, very deservedly, for she really was a beautiful woman

Clark sent for me one day about 2 o'clock, P M When I entered the house, I found Clark sitting on a small canopy, and holding in his hand a grape. The servant was arranging his bed on the floor I asked him how he felt, and he replied, ' Badly, I am not well" He then said he had sent for me to take and deliver to Jno McDonough some six or seven old negroes, whom he had sold to him I delivered the negroes to McDonough, overseer on the Gentilly plantation, which afterwards belonged to Judge Martin In returning, I reached Clark's house a little before sundown was surprised to see all the doors and windows opened, and feared something had happened On reaching the house, I saw Mr Relf standing on the gallery, he was weeping, and he said to me, " he is dead ' Baron Boisfontaine was at the house, and also Cadet d Jean The latter said to me, send me your razors and soap box as I wish to shave Mr Clark I went across the street, to my house, and sent the razors over, as requested, otherwise, I should have gone up stairs to see Clark once more, as I was very much attached to him

Being asked, whether Clark was not very fond of pretty women, witness answers, he was

Being asked, whether he kept Mrs DeGrange, or lived with her, answered their connection was kept very secret, Clark kept such things concealed as much as possible, as he had several such connections, and it would have given him trouble, had his particular female friends had known of them

Being asked whether Clark was married, he said, he does not know If Clark was married he was not married here, it must have been at the North, otherwise Chew & Relf would have known it, as they were very intimate with him, and every body else would have known of it Clark never told me that he was married. I always forbore questioning him about Madame DeGrange, as I knew that Clark had an intrigue with her, but frequently in conversation, in speaking of beautiful women, Clark would ask me what I thought of Madame DeGrange. D Clark courted a great many ladies in N Orleans When Clark saw a pretty woman, he fell in love with her.

J. CANNON.

Cross Examination

Jerome DeGrange was a short, thick set man, with a round, red face, his hair was light or auburn. He sold liquors and confectionary, his establishment was at the corner of St Ann and Royal streets; it was here that witness saw him the last time, and, as soon as DeGrange's other wife arrived here, he disappeared. Witness does not recollect in what year he saw him last. Witness knows Madame Caillavet, but does not know Madame Despau.   J CANNON

J W GURLEY, Commissioner

Depositions of Octave De Armas, Louis T Caire, William Christy, Isadore A Quemper, W W Montgomery, Madame Fanny Duchatoui, Madame Adile Tauzia Boumos, Charles Paterson, Henry W Palfrey, Joachim Courcelle

MYRA GAINES   )
        vs   } CIRCUIT COURT OF THE UNITED STATES
CHEW, RELF, AND OTHERS)

Interrogatories to Louis T Caire, William Christy, and Octave De Armas, Esquires, notary publics of New Orleans

1   What notarial offices were kept in New Orleans, previous to the cession of Louisiana from Spain to the United States?

2   Do you keep one of said offices and which one? Are there not deposited with you, as keeper of said office, records of civil and criminal prosecutions before the Spanish tribunals previous to the cession of the country?

3   Is there in your office any record of the prosecution of Jerome DeGrange, for bigamy, from the beginning of the year 1801 until the change of Government?

ISAAC T PRESTON, Solicitor for Defendants.

The complainant, reserving all right of legal exception to the testimony of the above witnesses as evidence in this suit, declines propounding cross interrogatories

P C WRIGHT, Solicitor for Complainant.

Octave de Armas, for Defendants

Octave de Armas answers, to the foregoing interrogatories.

To 1st   The offices now held by him, by Louis T Caire and W Christy   Before the cession, they were held by divers.

To 2d   Yes   This answer and the foregoing, reply to the rest of the interrogatory

To 3d   From a careful examination of the index of the judicial proceedings kept in my office, it does not appear that such prosecution therein exists.

OCTAVE DE ARMAS

Sworn to and subscribed before me, at **New Orleans,** this 24th July 1849

J W GURLEY, U S Com

And afterwards, to wit on the 29th day of June 1849, personally appeared Louis T Caire, Esq, a notary public of New Orleans a witness heretofore examined, on behalf of the defendants, and now recalled by them, who in answer to the written interrogatories propounded to him, did depose and say

To 1st interrogatory At that time, there were in New Orleans, within the knowledge I have obtained since I came to this country, three notaries to wit Carlox Ximenes, Narcissus Brutin, and Pierre Pedesclaux

To 2d interrogatory Yes, I keep one of said offices, to wit the office of Peter Pedesclaux, whose papers are now in my custody, and by the perusal of said papers, and the inspection of the indexes I see that they were then in the habit of lodging in the offices of notaries public, and namely, in the one alluded to of Pedesclaux civil and criminal prosecutions

To interrogatory 3d No After a careful examination of my indexes

LOUIS T CAIRE.

J W. GURLEY, Com.

And afterwards, to wit on the 30th day of June, 1849, personally appeared William Christy, Esq, a notary public of New Orleans a witness on behalf of defendants, a person of sound mind and lawful age, who, being duly sworn, did depose and say, in answer to the written interrogatories propounded to him, as follows

To 1st interrogatory That now occupied by Louis T Caire: his predecessors were Phillipe Pedesclaux, Pierre Pedesclaux, Fernandez Rodriguez, Leonardo Mazony, and J B Garie

That now occupied by Octave de Armas, his predecessors were Christoval de Armas, Stephen de Quinones, Carlos Ximines, Rafael Perdome Andres Almonaster Joseph Fernandez

That now occupied by myself, my predecessors were Hughes Lavergne, Francis Newhall Varcisse Broutin Francisco Broutin These are all the notarial offices which existed in this city, previous to the cession of Louisiana to the United States, of which I have any knowledge

To 2d interrogatory I do keep the office lately occupied by the said Hughes Lavergne, and I am in possession of the records of the said office as far back as the year 1774 And there are in my possession, records of civil and criminal prosecutions before the notaries who preceded me, under the Spanish Government, and previous to the cession of this State to the United States

To 3d interrogatory There is no such record that I have been able to find, after a careful examination of the indices of the said old records.

WM CHRISTY

J W GLELLY, Commissioner

And afterwards, to wit, on the 18th day of June 1849, personally came and appeared Isadore A Quempei a person of sound mind and lawful age, a witness on behalf of defendants, who, being duly sworn, did depose and say

I am about thirty-two years of age, and was born in New Orleans, and have always resided here I am the keeper of the records of the Cathedral St Louis, of this city Witness being shown paper marked A A A, and signed by him and me, commissioner, to identify it with this testimony says, that he has compared it with the original now in his possession as keeper of the records of the church of St Louis, commonly called the Cathedral of New Orleans, and that the said paper is an exact and literal copy of the original

Objection Complainant reserves all legal exceptions to the introduction of these documents as evidence in this cause

Question. Who is the present curate of the Church of St Louis, commonly called the Cathedral of New Orleans?

Objected to by complainant

Answer Constantine Maenhaut

Question Is the signature to the said document, marked A A A, the genuine signature of the said curate? and if yea, state how you know that fact

Answer The signature is genuine I saw him sign it myself

Question Is the impression on said document A A A the genuine seal of the said church?

Answer It is I have the custody of the seal, and put it on this document myself

Question Is it, or not, customary among the French and Creoles, to give children soubriquet, or nicknames? and if so, whether or not, you have found, in the examination of the records of the aforesaid church, great confusion and difficulty in finding the record of baptisms marriages, and deaths, when applied to, and those soubriquets or nicknames given as the names applied for?

Objected to by complainant

Answer It is customary, among the French and Creole population of New Orleans, to give nicknames or soubriquets to their children ; and witness has found great difficulty and confusion in consequence, in examining the records of the church to find

the real name intended because they generally apply for the
soubriquet, or nicknames This state of facts arises in part
from the fact that the Catholic priests will not christen a child,
nor baptize nor marry parties, by family nicknames, or soubriquets

Question Is the name Zulime a Christian name or what is
called a soubriquet, or nickname?

Objected to by complainants

Answer It is a soubriquet or nickname

ISADORE A QUEMPER

Cross Examination

Question How long have you been keeper of the records of
the society of the Church of St Louis?

Answer Since the beginning of 1839

Question How do you know that the name Zulime is a
nickname?

Answer Because I have heard it from the different priests
who were there, and I do not think there is a saint by that
name

Question Are not Catholic children sometimes named otherwise than by the names of saints

Answer I do not think I ever saw any

Question Have you conversed with any of the priests in
regard to any of the names given in the document marked A A A?
and if yea, which one?

Answer I have not conversed with any of the priests I
merely gave it to Mr Maenhaut to be signed that is all

Question In your direct examination you speak of the customs of the church respecting the records of the deaths baptisms,
and marriages only by their real names Are you to be understood as speaking from your own knowledge or from information derived from others?

Answer From my own knowledge

Question Has application been made to you to record a
baptism, marriage, or death, by any other than the real name?

Answer I record no acts The priests who perform the
ceremony draw the acts I have a blank book in which the
priests who perform the ceremony record the acts, whether of
deaths, baptisms, or marriages Some of these records are kept
double I copy from the original of the act made by the priest
into another book Since a few years, this has been discontinued They were kept double to guard against loss from fire

J A QUEMPER

J W GURLEY, Com

And afterwards, to wit on the 18th June 1849, personally
came W W Montgomery, a person of lawful age and sound

83

mind, a witness for defendants, who, being duly sworn, did depose and say

I have been in this city ever since the fall of 1803 I am seventy years of age. I was acquainted with Henry Turner formerly of Natchez He is dead I had business connection and slight correspondence with Mr Turner during his life The correspondence which I had with Mr Turner during his life was recognized by him.

Question Look at the letter marked B B B, and state whether or not you believe, from your knowledge of Mr Turner's handwriting, that it is his?

Answer To the best of my recollection I believe it is his handwriting It is a good many years since.

Objection Complainants object to the introduction of the letter B B B, as wholly irrelevant to the issues in this cause Complainant makes no objection to the proof of the genuineness of the letter.

Question Are you acquainted with the signature of the late Judge Dick

Answer Yes I am acquainted with it Have often seen him write. He was Judge of the Federal Court in this State

Question Look upon the two letters marked C C C and D D D, and state whether you believe them to be in the handwriting of the late Judge Dick?

Answer Witness having looked on the said two papers, says he has no doubt they are in his handwriting Judge Dick is dead

Objection Complainants object to the said two letters C C C and D D D, as irrelevant but does not object to the sufficiency of the proof of genuineness of the said letters

Question Were you acquainted with the late Governor Robertson, of Louisiana, and with his handwriting? and if yes, look at the letter marked E E E and state whether or not you have seen him write and if so, whether you believe said paper to be in his hand-writing?

Answer I was acquainted with him Have seen him write, and believe said letter is in his handwriting Governor Robertson is dead

Question Were you acquainted with James Brown, formerly a lawyer in New Orleans, and subsequently the United States Minister to the Court of France?

Answer Yes, I was

Question Were you acquainted with his writing?

Answer. Yes, I have seen him write frequently.

Question Look on the two letters now shown you, marked F F F and G G G, and state whether or not you recognize them to be in the handwriting of Mr Brown?

Answer I believe they are both in the handwriting of Mr Brown Mr Brown is dead

Question Are you acquainted with the hand-writing of the late Josiah S Johnson, formerly senator of the United States, from the State of Louisiana? if so look upon the letter marked H H H, and state whether or not you believe the same to be in the genuine handwriting of the said Johnson?

Answer I was acquainted with the late J S Johnson, and believe the letter to be in his hand-writing

NOTE.—The defendants here offer in evidence the five commissions emanating from the Presidents of the United States, James Madison, James Munroe, and John Q Adams, appointing Beverly Chew, one of the defendants in this case, Collector of the port of New Orleans, the genuineness of which documents is admitted by the complainant, with reservation made to their admissibility as evidence in this case These commissions are marked J J J, K K K, L L L, M M M, N N N

Question Are you acquainted with the signatures of Thomas Urquhart, William Nott, Stephen Henderson, J H Shepherd, J Linton, L Millaudon?

Answer Yes, I am acquainted with their respective signatures, having seen them frequently write They are all dead, except L Millaudon

Question Look at the letter marked O O O, and state whether the signatures thereto are genuine?

Answer Having looked upon the letter, witness says the signatures are genuine

Question Are you acquainted with the signature of Mr Samuel Jaudon, formerly cashier of the branch of the United States Bank in New Orleans?

Answer I was, having seen him sign almost daily, for two or three years

Question Look on the letter now shown you, marked P P P, and also on the document marked Q Q Q, and state whether or not said letter is wholly written and signed by Mr Jaudon, and whether or not the document is signed by Mr Jaudon?

Answer Having looked on the letter and document, witness says that the said letter is wholly written and signed by Mr Jaudon, and that the said document is signed by Mr Jaudon

Question State, if you please, whether or not Mr Jaudon was cashier of the branch of the United States Bank in New Orleans, at the date of the letter and document last referred to?

Answer He was

Question Are you acquainted with the handwriting of Nicholas Biddle, formerly president of the United States Bank at Philadelphia?

Answer I am

Question Look on the letter marked R R R, and state whether it is wholly written and signed by Mr Biddle ?

Answer It is

Question Were you acquainted with the late Daniel Clark ?

Answer Yes sir

Question Were you or your house of W & J Montgomery, a creditor of Chew & Relf or Daniel Clark, at the time of said Clark's death in August, 1813 ?

Objected to by complainant

Answer Yes, Mr Clark borrowed some money a few days before his death from us which remained unpaid at the time of Mr Clark's death   I think it was about two thousand dollars

Question How long have you been acquainted with Beverly Chew and Richard Relf

Answer Became acquainted with Beverly Chew shortly after I arrived in this city, in 1803   I am not positive, but I think Mr Relf, at that time, was absent, but returned some time afterwards, and I became acquainted with him shortly after his arrival

Question What was the business of those gentlemen at that time ?

Answer They were commission merchants, and I have been acquainted with them up to the present day, I believe I was security for Mr Chew while he was collector of the port of N Orleans, and has been security for Mr Relf since his appointment as cashier of the Louisiana State Bank, to the present time.

Question Did Mr Chew ever hold any office in the Branch Bank of the United States in this city ?

Answer Yes, he was the president of that institution for a number of years, and until he was appointed cashier of the Canal Bank in this city

Question Have you ever known or heard of the integrity or honesty of Mr Chew, in any of these offices of collector of the port of N Orleans president of the Branch Bank of the U States, or cashier of the Canal Bank, impugned or called into question ?

Objected to by complainant

Answer No, I never did.

Question. How long has Mr Relf been cashier of the Louisiana State Bank ?

Objected to by complainant.

Answer. I do not recollect, but for a number of years.

Question Will you please to state, whether or not you have ever heard or known the integrity and honesty of either Richard Relf or Beverly Chew doubted or called in question, from the period of your first acquaintance with them to the present time, except it may have been by parties connected with this suit?

Objected to by complainant

Answer No I have not, except by persons connected with the suit of Mrs Gaines

Question What was the character and standing in the community of N Orleans of the late Daniel Clark?

Answer A high minded honorable man, chivalrous &c

Question State whether or not from your knowledge of the character and standing of Daniel Clark in N Orleans, you believe him capable of addressing a young lady with a view to marriage if, at the same time, he had been, in truth, a married man?

Objected to by complainant

Answer No, I do not believe he would for my part, he had too much honor

Question What was the position or character which Daniel Clark held in the community of N Orleans, with his friends and the public generally, as to his being a married man or a bachelor?

Objected to by complainant

Answer He was always considered a bachelor, by his friends and acquaintance in general I think

Question Did you ever hear Daniel Clark spoken of in this community as a married man?

Objected to by complainant

Answer No I did not during his lifetime

Question Where did Mr Clark live at the time of his death?

Answer On the Bayou road, at the forks of the Bayou road and the Gentilly road, where he had built him a house

Question Do you know whether or not Mr Daniel Clark was on intimate personal terms and business relations with Beverly Chew and Richard Relf up to the period of his death?

Objected to by complainant

Answer Yes, he was also, Mr Delacroix was his personal friend, Samuel B Davis was also one of his proteges

Question Are you acquainted with Mrs Gaines, the complainant in this case, and if so, how long have you known her?

Answer Yes, I have been acquainted with her from childhood, I first saw her in the family of Samuel B Davis, where she was regarded as an adopted orphan child, she was then taken or sent to the North, and witness did not see her until some years after, when she had become Mrs Whitney

Question State whether or not it is to your knowledge, that both Beverly Chew and Richard Relf have, ever since the period of Mr. Clark's death, been supporting themselves and families by means of their own personal exertions?

Objected to by complainant, as wholly irrelevant

Answer   Yes, I believe they have, for my part, it is a general belief

Question   Have Beverly Chew and Richard Relf or either of them, ever been regarded in this community as men of any very considerable means or as persons of wealth'

Objected to by complainant

Answer.   No, neither of them.

Question   Have not both of them raised large families in this city?

Answer   Yes, sir

Witness knows that Mr Chew was at the lines at the time of the invasion, and was in the battle of the 23d December, 1814, as a member of the rifle company, and continued in service until the evacuation of the British   Mr Relf was, at that time, a member of the fire company, and that the firemen had turned out, at that time, to assist the police in the protection of the city, they were the active police

W W MONTGOMERY

Cross Examination of W W Montgomery

Question   Please to name some of the most intimate and confidential friends of the late Daniel Clark'

Answer.   Delacroix, Judge Workman, Judge Pitot Harper, Henry Turner, and a great many others, whom witness cannot remember

Question.   State whether you knew the late Colonel Bellechasse, and if yea, state what was his character and standing here?

Answer   I knew Mr Bellechasse, but did not know much about his character or standing either

Question   What was the character of the late Judge Pitot?

Answer   Very good, he stood nigh, was one of the prominent men

Question.   Do you now hold, or have you any interest in, or have you at any time held or been interested in, any property, real or personal, belonging to or found in the succession of the late Daniel Clark?

Answer   No, sir, none   I have no interest, direct or indirect, in the event of this suit   W. W. MONTGOMERY.

J W Gurley, Com r

And afterwards, to wit on the 19th day of June, 1849, personally came Madame Fanny Duchaufour, a person of sound mind and lawful age, a witness for defendants, who, being sworn, did depose and say .

I reside in New Orleans, and have resided here for the last twenty-eight years   I was born in Philadelphia, I am about fifty-two years of age my maiden name is Fanny Gardette, my father's name was Doctor James Gardette, formerly dentist in Philadelphia my mother is dead, she died in 1807

About eight or nine months after my mother's death, my father married Mrs DeGrange At the time he married her, she went by the name of Carriere He was married to Madame De-Grange in Philadelphia, as witness understood Witness was not there but was away at school My father subsequently presented her to us as our step-mother After this, she always resided with him as his wife They resided in Philadelphia until they went to France, in 1829 My father died in Bordeaux, on the 11th August, 1831 Knows nothing, personally, of Mr DeGrange. Did not know Daniel Clark

Question. State, if you please, whether or not you knew anything of the reputation of Madame DeGrange née Carriere and if so, state what that public reputation was.

Objected to by complainant

Answer I was very young at that time, and did not pay much attention, it is very positive that her reputation was not good

Question Is it not, on the other hand positive that it was very bad?

Answer It is so

Question. Will you state whether or not you are acquainted with the public reputation of Madame Sophie Despau? and yea, state what that public reputation is

Answer Well, sir I never heard anything of her until she came to my father's house. I then heard as much bad of her as I did of her sister, Zulime Carriere

Question Did you ever hear from Madame DeGrange, after she became the wife of your father Doctor Gardette, that she had ever been married to Daniel Clark?

Objected to by complainant

Answer No—most positively.

Question Did you ever hear that Madame DeGrange née carriere had been the mother of a child or children previous to her marriage with Doctor Gardette.

Objected to by complainant

Answer I did hear that she had a child, a girl. I asked her about it, and she most positively denied it, and said that child was Madame Lambert's and Daniel Clark's I think Madame Lambert was Miss Trepagnier She made this denial, (on the subject of the child,) in the presence of my father.

Question Was the name of the child mentioned at the time of the conversation referred to in the preceding interrogatory?

Answer There was no name mentioned at that time, but I afterwards heard it was Myra

Question.   How many children were born of the marriage between Dr. Gardette and Madame DeGrange née Carriere?

Answer.   Three boys   James, Alvarez, and Edmund

Question   Were those children always regarded as the legitimate offspring of the marriage between your father and Madame DeGrange née Carrière? and were they so esteemed and received in the community in which they lived?

Answer   Certainly they were—always

Question   In what year did the marriage take place between your father and Madame DeGrange née Carrière?

Answer   I think in 1808

FANNY DUCHAUFOUR.

Cross examination.

I have been three times married   I was fifteen years of age when I was first married. My first husband's name was Delauny, and lived in Philadelphia   I was married in Philadelphia, at my father's house.   I was married a little more than a year, when my husband died   I then returned to my father's house, and remained there, a widow, about three years, when I was married, a second time, at my father's house, in Philadelphia, to Mr LeRoy   I was married, the third time, in New Orleans, to my late husband Mr Duchaufour

Question   In your direct examination, you speak of a conversation with Madame Gardette respecting a child said to have been born of her prior to her marriage with your father   Was this conversation prior to your marriage with your first husband, or subsequent?

Answer   It was when I was a widow of my first husband

Question   Was not your father in good standing in the society of Philadelphia, recognized and received in that society as a gentleman of good repute for honor and integrity?

Answer   Yes, sir, assuredly he was   and every one was much astonished that he should have married again, as he did

Question   What was the position of your father in society in Philadelphia, after his marriage with Zulime Carriere?

Answer   His position continued the same, that did not alter his position, it did not make him less respected

Question.   Was your father a man of wealth?

Answer   He was always considered a man well off, without being excessively wealthy

Question   In what manner did Madame Gardette née Carrière treat you in the relation of step-mother?

Answer.   She had very little to do with me   I was married very soon after she was; and I was at school until three or six months previous to my marriage.

Question.   Did Madame Gardette nee Carrière go to France

with your father and remain there as his wife until after his death?

Answer. Yes, she did.

FANNY DUCHAUFOUR.

J. W. Geary, Commissioner.

And afterwards to wit on the 19th June, 1849 personally came Madame Adele Panzia Bournos nee Gardette a person of sound mind and lawful age, a witness for defendants, who, being duly sworn, did depose and say:

I reside in New Orleans, have resided here for thirty years. I am fifty years of age. My father was Doctor James Gardette, dentist in Philadelphia. My father was married, I believe, in 1808, to Mrs Zulime Carriere, at least he told me so, and I always lived in his house, and believed her to be his wife. He married her in Philadelphia. I believe that Madame DeGrange nee Carriere lived with my father up to the time of his death. I left them in 1817, and went to Nashville. For two years father and myself corresponded. Since then I have heard nothing from them—not a word. I have received nothing from my father's estate. It was settled in Bordeaux.

Question. Did you know Madame DeGrange nee Carriere, and if so state what her public reputation was?

Objected to by complainant.

Answer. I was very young at the time she was married—When she was married I was 9 years of age. I never heard any good of her. She was always very unkind to me, and unjust. I suffered greatly under her, and the first chance I got, I went away, never to return, never saw my father afterwards.

Question. Will you state whether or not you are acquainted with the public reputation of Madame Sophie Despau, and if so state what that public reputation is?

Answer. She lived two years at my father's house. I always heard that she was no better than her sister.

Question. Did you ever hear from Madame DeGrange nee Carriere, after she became the wife of your father, Doctor Gardette, that she had ever been married to Daniel Clark?

Objected to by complainant.

Answer. No, sir.

Question. Did you ever hear that Madame DeGrange had been the mother of a child previous to her marriage with Doctor Gardette?

Objected to by complainant.

Answer. Yes sir. The child was named Myra.

Question. Do you know who that child is now, and where she is?

Answer. I have been told she is now Mrs. Gaines.

84

Question   Did you ever hear Madame DeGrange née Carrière speak of having had a child previous to her marriage with
your father?

Answer   She always denied having had one

Question   Did you ever hear her speak of Myra; at that time
called Myra Davis?

Answer   Yes sir, but not as her child

Question   Did Madame DeGrange née Carriere ever tell you
who she believed the mother of Myra to be? if yea, name the
person whom she said was the mother

Answer   She did· she said her mother was Madame Lambert.

Question   How many children were born of the marriage of
Madame e Grange nee Carrière and octor Gardette?

Answer   Three boys.

Question   Were those children always regarded as the legitimate offspring of the marriage between your father and Zulime
nee Carrière, and were they so esteemed and received in the
community in which they lived?

Answer   They were always regarded as the legitimate children of that marriage I left them so young that I do not know
what their standing was after I left

Question   In what year did your father die?

Answer.   In the year 1831

Question   In what year was your father married to Zulime
nee Carrière?

Answer As well as I can recollect, it was in the year 1808,
in Philadelphia.

Question   Do you know whether or not, at the death of your
father, Zulime nee Carrière took possession of the effects and
property he left behind, as his widow?

Objected to by complainant

Answer   I have no personal knowledge on the subject.

ADELE TAUZIA BOURNOS.

Cross examination waived by P. C. Wright, Esqr, of Counsel
for complainant   J W GURLEY, Commissioner

, And afterwards, to wit on the 20th June, A. D 1849, personally appeared Henry W Palfrey, a witness heretofore examined, and now again called by defendants, for defendants, a
person of sound mind and lawful age, who, being duly sworn,
did depose and say:

Question.   Do you, or not, on examination, recognize the
signatures purporting to be the signatures of the late Daniel
Clark, in the records of Narcisse Broutin, late Notary Public in
New Orleans, to notarial proceedings executed, and to be found
in the bound volume of notarial acts, for the year 1803 Vol 12

at pages 401 and 405, now in the office of William Christy, Notary in New Orleans, dated 7th June, 1803, at New Orleans,—to be his genuine signatures?

Answer Those signatures are genuine, but whether they were signed, or not, on the day they purport to be signed, I cannot say

Question Is, or not, the signature purporting to be the signature of Daniel Clark, to notarial act in said office, to be found in the volume above mentioned, at page 621, and dated at New Orleans, 3d November, 1803, the genuine signature of Daniel Clark? And also the signature on page 617 dated New Orleans, 17th November 1803, in said volume? And also, the signature purporting to be his on page 632, dated 11th November, 1803 at New Orleans the genuine signatures of the late Daniel Clark?

Answer Yes, they are and the signature purporting to be Daniel Clark's, to a will to be found in said volume, recorded at page 407, and which will is dated 5th February, 1801, is the genuine signature of said Clark

Question Do you or not, recognize the signature purporting to be that of Daniel Clark, to notarial act dated 8th of February 1804 at page 131, of bound volume of notarial acts of the year 1804, of the late Peter Pedesclaux Notary Public of New Orleans, now in the office of L T Caire, Notary in said city, to be the genuine signature of the late Daniel Clark? And also, the signature purporting to be his, to act dated 2d March, 1804, on page 218 of said volume?

Answer They are both the genuine signatures of the late Daniel Clark

H W PALFREY

Cross-examination of Mr Palfrey waived, by P C Wright, Esq, of counsel for complainant

J W GURLEY, Com'r

And afterwards, to wit on the 20th June, 1849, personally came Joachim Courcelle, a witness for defendants, a person of sound mind and lawful age, who, being sworn, did depose and say: (William Andry, Esq., sworn as interpreter)

I am seventy-three years of age, I was born in New Orleans, and have always resided here Does know Chew and Relf, but does not know Gen. Gaines, except by sight. Have known Mr Relf for nearly fifty years, Mr Relf occupied a room in my house in 1801 Has known Chew when he was in partnership with Relf I became acquainted with Daniel Clark about the same time that I became acquainted with Relf. I knew Clark from the time I first became acquainted with him up to the time of his death. I was particularly acquainted with Clark, when

Clark was young, but afterwards not so much. I was never very intimate with Daniel Clark, but I have met Clark in society and at parties. This was about 1801 or 1802.

Question. What was the general reputation which Daniel Clark had in the community of N Orleans among his acquaintances and friends and the public in general, from the time you first became acquainted with him until the period of his death, as to his being a married or unmarried man?

Objected to by complainant

Answer. Daniel Clark was never married as far as I know. I have said that Daniel Clark was never married, because the population was so small that we knew every thing that took place. I speak of the time under the Spanish government

Question. Did you ever hear any one, previous to the death of Mr Clark, intimate or express an opinion to the fact, that he, Mr Clark was a married man?

Objected to by complainant

Answer. No, sir, I never did

Question. Were you acquainted with Jerome DeGrange?

Answer. Yes

Question. What was his business or employment in this city, at the time you knew him?

Objected to by complainants, as wholly irrelevant

Answer. He was a watchmaker

Question. Did he or not keep a confectionary shop in this city?

Objected to as irrelevant by complainant.

Answer. I knew his brother-in-law, who kept a confectionary store, but not Jerome DeGrange, his brother-in-law was named Callavet

Question. Were you acquainted with Madame DeGrange?

Answer. Yes

Question. What was her general reputation in the community of New Orleans for virtue and chastity?

Objected to by complainant

Answer. I have been in certain circles, where her reputation was spoken of very slightly, but I cannot give any positive testimony about it, she was very " coquette et legère "

Question. Was or was not the reputation of Madame De-Grange, in the community of New Orleans, so well and generally known, that Daniel Clark must have known of her reputation?

Objected to by complainants

Answer. I think Daniel Clark must have known it.

Question. What was the relationship, according to public reputation, which existed between Daniel Clark and Madame DeGrange, if any?

Objected to by complainants

Answer   I do not know

Question   Were you acquainted with Madame Despau, sister of Madame DeGrange? and if so, what was her general reputation?

Objected to by complainant.

Answer   I knew her, but cannot answer further than I stated of Madame DeGrange   What they stated of the one, they stated of the other, but witness does not attack their reputation

Question   Was or was not the reputation of Daniel Clark in N Orleans, that of an honorable and high spirited gentleman?

Answer   Daniel Clark was an honorable and estimable man in all his conduct

When I stated that Daniel Clark was not married, I was, perhaps, wrong, because, at the time spoken of, Daniel Clark was visiting a young lady living in one of my houses adjoining my dwelling house, and that it was said, that he, Clark, was going to be married to that young lady   This lady was Miss Trepagnier, who had been married to Francois Lambert and then divorced from him, and was then living with her mother.

Question   Judging from the reputation which Daniel Clark enjoyed in New Orleans, as an honorable and high spirited gentleman, do you believe that he would have connected himself in marriage with any lady, who did not enjoy a spotless reputation in the community in which she lived?

Objected to by complainant, as irrelevant, improper, and is considered, by counsel for complainant, as a direct violation of all the well settled rules of testimony, attempting to introduce the mere opinion of the witness in place of matters of fact within his own knowledge and belief.

Answer   It is a very difficult question to answer, but I think that Daniel Clark was not a man to contract a marriage which would dishonor him, and which might have been a subject of reproach to him in the society in which he moved.

J'IM COURCELLE.

Cross examination

Question. What is your occupation?

Answer   Landlord, living on my income.

Question. What was your occupation previous to 1813, at the time you say you knew Daniel Clark?

Answer   My occupation was the same then as now.   I was then rich

Question   Were you at any time on terms of close friendship and intimacy with Daniel Clark? and if so, at what time?

Answer   I was never intimate with Daniel Clark, but often met Mr Clark, Madame DeGrange and Madame Despau in parties. Then Clark was young, and had not much to do This was under the Spanish Government

Question Were you acquainted with Madame Lambert, nee Trepagnier? and if so, what can you say of her reputation while you knew her?

Answer. I knew her Cannot say any about her reputation

Question Did you see her at the parties of which you have spoken of having seen Mr Clark?

Answer. No When I speak of Madame Lambert, it was 15 or 18 years after those parties I have spoken of, and when Mr Clark had purchased that property on Bayou St. John, which property he afterwards divided into a faubourg.

I knew Colonel Joseph Deville Degoutin Bellechasse He was a brave honorable man,—very respectable. He was first a military man, and afterwards occupied a property on the faubourg St Mary I knew the late Judge Pitot, of New Orleans. He stopped at my father's when he arrived here He was an honorable man. Was afterwards a merchant here.

J'IM COURCELLE

J W. Gurley, Commissioner.

And afterwards to wit on the 19th day of June, 1849, personally came Charles Paterson, a person of sound mind and lawful age, a witness for defendants, who, being sworn, did depose and say

I am about seventy years of age Came to New Orleans in 1805. I have had a suit with Mrs Gaines in this Court It was for a house and lot on which I resided when the suit was brought. I still reside in that house and lot, and have resided on it ever since the suit was brought. Mrs Gaines succeeded in the suit. According to the judgment of the Court, that house and lot belongs to her but they told me that they would not take it from me

Question If the creditors of Mrs. Gaines should attach or seize that property under execution for her debts, would you not take legal steps to prevent them doing so?

Objected to by complainant.

Answer I believe that Mrs Gaines would give me a title to the property If her creditors should attach or seize it, I suppose I should stand a suit.

Question If Mrs Gaines or her creditors should attempt to take the property, would you have any ground on which to resist their claim?

Objected to by complainant.

Answer. General Gaines and his wife gave me in writing, under their hands, that they would not take the property from me, and that they would make my title good. The property has always been assessed as mine, and I have always paid the taxes on it

Question Did Gen or Mrs. Gaines ever ask possession of the property from you after judgment ?

Objected to by complainants

Answer No. The decision of the Court was, that the property should be sold or divided.

Question Did they ever ask you to sell or divide it ?

Answer They talked of having it done The Court must do it I cannot do it .

Question. Who paid the costs of that suit ?

Answer. I paid most of the costs—but they paid me again ; that is, Gen. and Mrs Gaines paid me

Question Was there or not an understanding or agreement between Gen and Mrs Gaines and yourself, that they should pay the costs, even should the suit be decided against you ?

Objected to by complainant

Answer Yes, sir. They made the same offer to Judge Martin.

CHARLES PATERSON

Cross examination

Question. Did you not, in defending the suit brought against you by Mrs Gaines, referred to in your direct examination, make the best effort in your power, with the aid of the most able counsel you could employ, to defeat Mrs. Gaines in her suit.

Answer Yes, sir

CHARLES PATERSON

J W Gurley, Commissioner

And afterwards, to wit. on the 20th June, 1849, came and appeared Charles Paterson, a witness heretofore examined on behalf of defendants, whose cross examination being resumed by complainant, did depose and say.

Question Look upon the document handed to you, marked A, and state whether you know the handwriting of the late Gen. Gaines, and whether or not the signature of said document is in the handwriting of Gen Gaines, and whether you received that, or a communication of which that is a copy, prior to your withdrawing your dilatory pleadings in the case of Gaines and wife against yourself, Relf, Chew, et al., and filing your answer to the merits in that case ?

Objection. Defendants, represented by G. B. Duncan, protest against said paper going upon the record of this case, on the ground that it contains false, malicious and gratuitous imputations against parties in no wise connected with this suit.

Answer I know the handwriting of the late General Gaines,

having received several letters from him, and have seen him write The signature to said document is in the handwriting of the late Gen Gaines. I received two or three communication, of which that is a copy, prior to my withdrawing my dilatory pleadings in that case, and answering to the merits

Question   Look on the letter, now handed to you, marked B and state whether you know the handwriting of the body thereof and the signatures thereto?

Answer   The handwriting of the body thereof, is that of Gen Gaines. I was present when he wrote it, and saw both the General and Mrs Gaines sign it

Question   At the trial of your cause with Gaines and wife, did or did not your counsel make a request of the counsel of Mrs Gaines, to be permitted to introduce the record from the probate court of New Orleans, of all the proceedings of Mrs. Gaines in the prosecution of her rights in that court?

Answer   Yes, sir, her counsel objected to that and I then made application to General and Mrs Gaines to introduce said record They replied to me to get all the evidence possible—the stronger the better General Gaines remarked it would be more glorious to have it as strong as possible. I then caused the proceedings to be introduced

Objection   The defendants object to the foregoing testimony, and especially that part which details the conversations of the complainants with the witness, and that part which details what was done in a judicial proceeding, on the grounds, among others, that it is incompetent for the complainants to make evidence for themselves, and that what has been done in judicials proceedings, must be shown by the record.

CHARLES PATERSON

Note.—The counsel for defendants object to the cross examination of Mr Paterson, by complainant, as a part of the cross examination of the witness introduced by the defendants but insist that it should be considered as his examination in chief by the complainant, to which defendants have the right to cross examination; and the facts now agreed upon by both parties are these, that the defendants called and examined said witness on the 19th instant, and he was, at the same time, cross examined by complainant, and the witness having signed his examination in chief, and cross examination, when the parties both announced that they had concluded the examination of said witness, and on this 20th June, the same witness was brought back for examination by complainant.

Examination by defendants:

Question. Do you remember at what time your suit with General and Mrs. Gaines was tried in this court?

Answer   I think it was nine years ago, last month

Question   Had you, or not, interviews with General and Mrs. Gaines, previous to that trial, and in reference to the same ?

Answer   Yes, sir

Question.   How long before the trial of your case in the Circuit court was it that you employed the attorney, who appeared in your defense on the trial ?

Answer   Well, I do not recollect now long it was   It took some time to get the copy of the record from the Probate court He was employed immediately before the record was obtained from the Probate court

Question   Who was that counsel ?

Answer   Mr John McHenry, now Judge of the First District Court of New Orleans

Question   Did he, the said John McHenry, to your knowledge, hold any consultation with counsel, previously employed by you in the cause ?

Answer   I do not know.   Not to my knowledge

Question   Did either the said counsel, John McHenry or you, consult with Messrs Chew & Relf, or either of them, or their counsel employed in defending the suit, or with any other attorneys engaged in defending the suit, or obtain any testimony or documents from them, or either of them ?

Answer   No I did not apply to any of them, and I do not know whether he did or not

Question   What was the name of the counsel employed by you in that case, previous to Mr. McHenry's being employed ?

Answer   Mr Isaac T Preston

Question   What was the name of the counsel employed by you, to defend your interests in that suit, before the Supreme Court at Washington ?

Answer   Mr Brent, the old gentleman, formerly member of Congress from Louisiana

Question   Has he ever been paid for his professional services in that case ?

Answer   On the first trial he was paid   The son of Mr Brent took charge of the case on the second trial, and he was paid, he and Mr May, by draft on me for a hundred dollars each, through the hands of Mr May's brother, in this city

Question   Has not that amount been reimbursed to you ?

Answer   Yes, sir, by General Gaines

Question.   Who took up the record from the Circuit court to the Supreme court at Washington, in your case ?

Answer   Well, I took it out here, and sent it on, but do not recollect how.

Question   You have stated, in answer to the last foregoing

85

question propounded on behalf of Mrs. Gaines, that on the trial of your cause before the Circuit court of the United States, your counsel applied to the counsel of Mrs Gaines, to be permitted to introduce the record from the Probate court of N Orleans, of all the proceedings of Mrs Gaines in the prosecution of her rights in that court, and that Mrs Gaines' counsel refused said permission, that you then made application to General and Mrs Gaines, to introduce said record   Are you to be understood that you were not, at that time, in possession of the transcript of that record? and in truth, had you it not then in said Circuit court on the trial?

Answer   I explained at first that Mr McHenry could not bring on the case without the copy of the record and he procured it before the trial commenced   I was in possession of the record, at the time of the trial

Question   Do you know whether or not the transcript of the record from the Probate court, referred to had been offered in evidence previous to your application to General and Mrs Gaines, to be permitted to put it in evidence?

Answer   I understood it had been.

Question   Was it or not agreed by Gen Gaines and wife, with you that if you would go to trial on the merits of the case they would indemnify you against all fees and costs, and that your property should not be taken in case they succeeded in their suit?

Answer   Yes, it was

The letters I have spoken of, as having been received by me from General Gaines, were all on the subject of this suit, or on subjects connected with it   I do not recollect whether I received the document marked A, from General Gaines himself, or from Mr. Dolbear, whom, witness thinks, was agent of Gen Gaines The document or letter, marked B, was delivered by Gen Gaines and lady, to witness

Question by counsel for complainant

Question   Were you not particularly requested by the General and Mrs Gaines, to use your best exertions, with the aid of the best counsel you could employ, to make every defense in your power to this suit, and of which it was susceptible?

Answer.   Yes, and I did so

I consider the agreement with General and Mrs Gaines, as an act of liberality on their part, growing out of a desire to come to a speedy trial with some one or more of the defendants, on the merits of the case   CHARLES PATERSON

J. W Gurley, Com'r.

DEFENDANTS

Depositions of—1 Mrs Sarah H Smith   2. Louis Bouligny,
3 Madame Eulalie Watkins   4 Jean B Dejan, sen   5 Hilary J Domingon   6 Charles Harrod

Interrogatories to Mrs Smith

GAINES	IN CHANCERY
vs	Circuit Court of the United States,
CHEW RELF, ET AL,	District of Louisiana
No 122	

Interrogatories propounded to Mrs Sarah H Smith, residing in New Orleans on behalf of defendants

Direct interrogatory 1st Please state your age and residence

Direct interrogatory 2d Are you acquainted with the parties to this suit, or any of them ' and if yea, which parties are you acquainted with?

Direct interrogatory 3d State whether or not you were acquainted with the late Daniel Clark ?

Direct interrogatory 4th Do you know when and where the defendant Beverly Chew was married, and to whom was he married? if yea, be pleased to state the same fully and particularly

Direct interrogatory 5th In whose house was Beverly Chew married ?

Direct interrogatory 6th State whether or not Daniel Clark was present at the marriage of Beverly Chew as his particular friend

Direct interrogatory 7th State whether or not Beverly Chew went to house-keeping immediately or soon after his marriage; if yea, in what street was his house and was it near your own residence ? Had you constant and intimate friendly intercourse, at the house of Mr Chew, with his family ? If yea, state whether or not Daniel Clark was very intimate in the family of Mr Chew, and whether or not Mr Clark had not a room at Mr Chew's house and a seat at his table

Direct interrogatory 8th State whether or not you know of Beverly Chew having left New Orleans for the North any time in the year 1813 If aye state the time he departed, the conveyance he took, at what port he arrived, and state how you know these facts

Direct interrogatory 9th State whether or not you know of Mr Daniel Clark having been on board of the vessel on which Mr Chew sailed from New Orleans, in 1814, at the time of his departure, and having then taken friendly parting with Mr Chew's family

Direct interrogatory 10 When and where did you hear first of the death of Daniel Clark ?

Direct interrogatory 11th Do you know, or can you set forth any other matter or thing which may be a benefit or advantage to the parties at issue in this cause, or either of them, or that may be material to the subject of this your examination, or the matters in question in this cause? if yea, set forth ths same fully and at large in your answer

G B DUNCAN.

Solicitor for Chew, Relf, et al

NOTE.—The complainant, reserving all legal rights of exception, decline propounding cross interrogatories

P. C. WRIGHT,

For Complainant.

New Orleans, 26th June, 1849
J. W. GURLEY Commissioner

And afterwards, to wit. on the 30th day of June, 1849, personally appeared Mrs Sarah M Smith, a person of sound mind and lawful age, a witness on behalf of defendants, who, being duly sworn, did depose and say, in answer to the written interrogatories propounded to her, as follows

To 1 int I am upwards of sixty-two years of age—nearly sixty-three, I reside on Apollo street, in New Orleans, I have resided in New Orleans since 1806

To 2 int I am acquainted with Mr Chew and Relf, Mr. Chew is my brother-in-law I am not personally acquainted with Mrs Gaines.

To 3d int I was very well acquainted with the late Daniel Clark

To 4 int Beverly Chew was married at my house, in St. Louis street, in 1810 I think in June He was married to my sister, Maria Theodora Duer He was married by Philander Chase, who was afterwards Bishop Chase

To 5 int. In my house, near the corner of Royal street and St Louis street.

To 6 int That Daniel was present at the marriage I cannot state on oath, but there is no doubt in my mind that he was present, as he was a particular friend of Mr Chew's

To 7 int Beverly Chew went to house-keeping immediately after his marriage with my sister His house was in St. Louis street, the next house to the one in which I resided. I had constant and friendly intercourse, at the house of Mr. Chew, with his family. Daniel Clark lived in Mr Chew's house, and had a seat at his table always. He was his intimate friend

To 8 int. Beverly Chew left here for the North in 1813, in the brig Astrea, (I believe that was the name of the vessel) I accompanied him in the same vessel, as did also my sister, Mrs. Thomas Callender and Mr and Mrs William Brand were of the party also Mr Brand and Mr Chew had purchased this vessel to take the party on There were a number of passengers They all paid their fare It was during the embargo The vessel was a small one We sailed from here, I think, in the month of June, 1813 I remember we were at sea on the *Fourth of July* We sailed from here for Philadelphia, but were obliged to put in at Havana in Cuba, for provisions, and from there we sailed direct to Philadelphia Our passage was a long one from here to the Havana and an unusually short one from there to Philadelphia

Int 9 I cannot state positively whether Mr Clark was on board the vessel to take leave of Mr Chew and family or not but, from his friendly and intimate relations with Mr Chew and family, I have no doubt he was I had a sick child with me at the time, and my whole attention was engaged with her

Ans to int. I first heard of the death of Daniel Clark in **New York**, I think it was a short time after I arrived there I remained a short time in Philadelphia and then went to **New York** It was shortly after my arrival there that I heard of Mr. Clark's death It was among the first news that we had from New Orleans, after our arrival

To 11 int I only know that Mr Clark was supposed to be a single man , he was always said to be an unmarried man , and I recollect hearing that this child, Myra, lived with a Mr Davis, an Englishman on the other side of the river, as his adopted child I think I saw her when she was quite a child I was then living with a brother-in-law of mine, Judge Prevost, he was the first American Judge on the bench here

SARAH H. SMITH.

J W Gurley, Commissioner

And afterwards to wit on the 3d day of July, 1849, personally appeared Louis Bouligny, a witness heretofore examined on behalf of the defendants, and now by them recalled, who, being duly sworn, did depose and say

Statement That he now exhibits the private contract between himself and Daniel Clark, in relation to the Maison Rouge grant It is in the handwriting of Daniel Clark, and was signed in the city of New Orleans, on the 16th July, 1803 (The contract is, by consent of parties, returned to the witness, the date and place of signature being the only matter to be proved J. W G. Com'r)

Question Is it, or not, within your knowledge, that the late Daniel Clark was impotent?

Objection Objected to by complainant, as irrelevant, impertinent, and incompetent to be proven by the witness

Answer Mr Clark had the reputation of courting a great

many women But it was said by some '*femmes gallantes*,' that Clark was impotent, but whether it was true or not, witness cannot say As a friend, I have often defended Daniel Clark, as to that Clark was strong, of great energy and courage he had that reputation

L BOULIGNY

Cross-examination

Question Had you a sister who married one De la Roche? and if so, is she living, and where does she reside?

Answer I have a sister who married De la Roche, she is living, and now resides at Pau, department at Bearn France Her husband, under the Spanish government, was the second officer in the custom house, he was afterwards a planter He left Louisiana in 1820

L BOULIGNY

J. W GURLEY, Com'r

And afterwards, to wit on the 6th July, 1849, appeared Madame Veuve Eulalie Watkins, a witness on behalf of defendants, of sound mind and lawful age, who, being duly sworn, did depose and say (John Watkins sworn as interpreter.)

I knew the late Daniel Clark I cannot say I knew him intimately, though he often came to the house to see my husband My husband was a physician, and was the physician of Daniel Clark My husband and Daniel Clark were on terms of intimacy

Question Do you know whether or not Daniel Clark was a married man?

Objected to by complainant

Answer I do not know that he was married

Question From the terms of intimacy on which your husband was with Clark, would you not have been likely to know, had he been married?

Objected to by complainant

Answer I knew they were on terms of intimacy, but I do not know whether I should have been likely to have heard it, or not

Clark always enjoyed a reputation for honor and integrity

Question. Judging from the reputation which Clark enjoyed in the community, do you think he would have paid his addresses to a lady, had he at the time been a married man?

Objected to by complainant

Answer I do not think he would

I do not know Madam DeGrange, I only saw her once, I was then a young lady, unmarried, she was pointed out to me at the theatre, she having the reputation of being a handsome woman She was remarkable for her beauty

Question State whether, at that time, or at any other time, Madam DeGrange had the reputation of being the mistress of D Clark or of any one else, and state also whether or not she was received in society in New Orleans

Objected to by complainant

Answer At the time I saw Madame DeGrange I did not hear it but since I have heard it rumored that she was the mistress of D Clark I do not know whether she mingled in society here, or not

Question Do you know, or did you ever hear that she had a child by Mr Clark?

Objected to by complainant

Answer Not by own knowledge but I have heard it spoken of in public as such things are spoken of in the world

Question Did you ever hear from your husband that Mr Clark was impotent?

Answer I never did

Question Do you know whether your husband was called upon by Daniel Clark to attend professionally the accouchment of a lady? If yea state what season of the year it was, and the year and to what part of the city he was called

Objected to by complainant

Answer Yes my husband was once called upon by Daniel Clark to attend professionally a lady who was about being confined I believe this was in the year 1804, but do not recollect in what season of the year, nor in what section of the city It was at night that Mr Clark called on my husband My husband afterwards told me that the lady whom he had been called on to visit was a sister of Madam DeGrange I do not recollect the name, but I believe it was the one called Madame Despau

EULALIE WATKINS

Cross Examination

My maiden name is Eulalie Trudeau I am a native of New Orleans and have always resided in this State I am near sixty-three years of age

EULALIE WATKINS

J W. Gurley, Com'r.

And afterwards, to wit on the 6th July, 1849, appeared Jean B Déjan, Sr, a witness on behalf of the defendants, a person of sound mind and lawful age, who, being duly sworn, did depose and say.

I am near seventy-two years of age I was born in New Orleans I was well acquainted with the late Daniel Clark I knew him from 1797 up to the time of his death, in 1813. He stood high in the opinion of all the respectable families in New Orleans

Question. Was Daniel Clark a married or a single man?

Objection. Objected to by complainant.

Answer. He was a single man.

Question Did you ever hear, from any person, up to the time of his death, that he was a married man?

Answer I did not.

Question In the situation in which the community then was, and the prominent position of Daniel Clark, could he have concealed the circumstance, had he been married?

Objected to by complainant.

Answer No, he could not have concealed the circumstance in this community

Question Was it, or not, understood in this community that Daniel Clark was impotent?

Objected to by complainant

Answer There was such a rumor

Question Judging from your knowledge of Daniel Clark, state whether or not he would have connected himself by marriage with a woman of bad reputation

Objected to by complainant

Answer I do not think he would

Question State whether or not, Daniel Clark was capable of paying his addresses to a young lady, with a view to marriage, had he himself been married at the time?

Objected to by complainant

Answer I believe he was not

I know well the signature of Francisco Caisergues, to the record marked Z. It is his genuine signature He was the Syndic of the Cabildo, under the Spanish Government.

I have known Richard Relf and Beverly Chew, well, ever since they came to this country Their reputation for integrity has been very good, they have been very much esteemed by the population in New Orleans.

                                        DEJAN, aîné.

Cross Examination

I was on terms of close intimacy with Daniel Clark I have dined frequently with him, and he dined frequently at my sister's, Madame Gaspar Dubuys, and took tea there I was then living with my sister I had not Mr Clark's private confidence. I was very young, and he was ten or twelve years older than I was.

                                        DEJAN, aîné

J. W. GURLEY, Com.

And afterwards, to wit: on the sixth day of July, 1849, personally appeared Hilary Julien Domingon, a witness on behalf of defendants, a person of sound mind and lawful age, who, being duly sworn did depose and say

I am sixty years and seven months of age I have lived in New Orleans for sixteen years ten days and nine hours I knew the late Daniel Clark as well as a young man of fifteen years and some years could know a man of about forty years. I first knew Daniel Clark in 1804 I believe he died in 1812 I always thought Daniel Clark was a single man Clark was much before the public, in those days—his character much discussed in the public papers

Question Was it ever rumored or said, in public, that Daniel Clark was a married man?

Objected to by complainant.

Answer No sir

Question Were you about the time spoken of, in the habit of reading the paper called the Louisiana Courier? and if yea, state whether or no, you ever read in that paper certain interrogatories propounded to Daniel Clark, asking him how much money he had offered a certain physician to give him a certificate of his potency

Objection Objected to by complainant as wholly irrelevant.

Answer I cannot recollect

I do not know Madame DeGrange—never knew her I heard her spoken of, in the years 1806, 1807, and 1805 Her reputation, about that time, was that of a *"femme galante*

Objection. Complainant objects to any question respecting the character of Madame DeGrange

Question From your knowledge of the character of Daniel Clark, do you suppose that, had he been married, he would have kept the marriage secret

Objected to by complainant

Answer The population then was so few, that, if he had married, every one in the city would have known it

Question. Was it, or not generally understood, in this community, that Daniel Clark was impotent?

Objected to by complainant

Answer. I know that he always liked the company of ladies —he was always with them and it was said that the reason of his being so much with them was that he was impotent He, however, had the reputation of having several mistresses I do not recollect that at that time Madam DeGrange was reputed t be his mistress

H J DOMINGON

Cross Examination

I never saw Madame DeGrange I knew such a name was in town, but never saw the lady I never saw Mr DeGrange

I cannot mention the names of any persons whom I heard speak of Madame DeGrange. I cannot recollect them

H J DOMINGON

J W. GURLEY, Com.

And afterwards, to wit on the 4th July, 1849, personally appeared Charles Harrod, a person of sound mind and lawful age, a witness on behalf of defendants, who, being duly sworn, did depose and say ·

I have resided in the city of New Orleans, for the last forty years, altogether, have never been absent more than six months at any time I am sixty years of age I knew the late Daniel Clark intimately. His reputation as a man was that of an honorable man, and as a merchant, was respectable and was considered rich

Question Was Daniel Clark a married man ?

Objected to by complainants

Answer Not to my knowledge

Question Can you state the reasons which induce you to believe he was an unmarried man ?

Answer I have always heard him speak of himself as a bachelor And we frequently jocked with him about a lady in Baltimore, whom we supposed he was going to marry Frequently when dining together we conversed on such subjects, and the course of conversation was that of bachelors,—it led me always to believe he was a bachelor I think he was considered a bachelor by the community of New Orleans

Question Did you ever hear any one, during his lifetime, suggest the idea that he was married ?

Objected to by complainants

Answer I think not The lady whom we joked about was Miss Catron, of Baltimore

Question Was he a man capable of addressing a lady, if he had been married at the time ?

Answer I think not He was an honorable man Knew Messrs Chew and Relf from 1809, when I first came to New Orleans

Question What has been the reputation of Richard Relf for integrity, from that period to this ?

Answer. Very respectable, so far as I know of He has stood high among merchants and bankers, as a man of integrity I know nothing to the contrary Mr. Chew enjoys the same reputation

Question. Has it ever been suspected in this community, that they were capable of suppressing a will or plundering an estate ?

Objected to by complainant

Answer I can only answer this by saying, that I should not

suspect them, or either of them, as being capable of acts of that kind

Question Do you know anything of the reputation of Madame DeGrange ?

Answer I do not   I do not know the lady.

CHARLES HARROD

Cross examination

I knew the late Judge Pitot   His standing in the community was very respectable   Did not know late Col Bellechasse, nor Pierre Baron Boisfontaine   At the time of D Clark's death, I was in Massachussets

Question Who were the prominent men of that day, who were the intimate friends of Daniel Clark ?

Answer The gentlemen whom I was accustomed to meet at Daniel Clark are most all dead   Among the living are Mr. Chew and Relf, Colonel Davis, of Philadelphia   I first landed in this city on the 14th day of July, 1809

CHARLES HARROD

J W Gurley Commissioner

Postage $6 60   Filed 15th September, 1849, and opened at request of P C Wright, Esq , under stipulation on file, this 18th September 1849   ED RANDOLPH, Cl'k

Per J W Gurley, D y Cl'k

CIRCUIT COURT OF THE UNITED STATES,

For the 5th Judicial Circuit, holding Sessions in
and for the Eastern District of Louisiana

To William H Rawle, or any other commissioner of Louisiana in Philadelphia

Know ye, that reposing special trust and confidence in your integrity and ability, we hereby authorize and require you, that you call and cause to come before you Daniel W Coxe, and him duly examine on oath, touching and concerning certain matters and things in a case now depending in the said Court, wherein E P Gaines and wife are plaintiffs, and Relf, Chew, et al , are defendants , and the same examinations, so taken and reduced to writing, you certify under your hand and seal, and send enclosed to this Court without delay, to be read in evidence on the trial of said cause, and send also this writ

Witness the honorable Roger B Taney, Chief Justice of the Supreme Court of the United States, at the city of New Orleans this 4th day of June, Anno Domini 1849, and the 73d year of the Independence of the United States of America

[LS]

ED. RANDOLPH, Clerk
Per J W Gurley, D y Clerk

The execution of this commission appears in a certain schedule hereto annexed. I certify that the examinations were conducted as appear therein all the voir dire interrogatories interrogatories in chief and cross interrogatories, having been severally put to the witness, and severally answered under oath as therein set forth.

WILLIAM HENRY RAWLE, Commissioner.

The expense of executing this commission is fifty dollars.

E. P. GAINES AND WIFE vs CHEW, RELF DELACROIX, ET AL	No. 122 IN CHANCERY CIRCUIT COURT OF THE U. S. AND DISTRICT OF LOUISIANA

Interrogatories propounded on behalf of Richard Relf, Beverly Chew and Dussuau Delacroix, to Daniel W Coxe Esq., residing in the city of Philadelphia

1st Are you acquainted with the complainants, E P Gaines and Myra Gaines his wife and with the defendants, Richard Relf, Beverly Chew and Dussuau Delacroix? If aye, state how long you have known them, and each of them.

2d Were you acquainted with the late Daniel Clark, formerly of New Orleans? If aye, be pleased to state how long you had known him previous to his death, which occurred in the month of August, 1813. Were you particularly intimate with the said Clark?

3d Were you ever associated in business with Mr Daniel Clark? If aye state the nature, purposes and objects of your business connections with him. When did you first form a business association with the said Daniel Clark? How long did it continue? Was there ever any final settlement of your business with said Clark, previous to his death? If aye state when that settlement took place. If there never was any such final settlement during the life of Clark, then state whether or not there was an agreement between you and him, fixing the basis of a final settlement? Whether in the one case or the other, will you be pleased to annex to this commission the original writing evidencing the said settlement or agreement between you and said Clark? If you cannot annex the original, then please annex a copy, stating first the reason why you can not annex the original, and then state whether you know the copy, which you annex, is a true and exact copy. Were there any attesting witnesses to said paper writing? If yea state their several names, and whether they are now living or dead, and if living, where they reside.

4th Which of the two was found indebted, one to the other, on your settlement with Daniel Clark, if you had such a settlement, you to Clark or Clark, or Clark to you? In what amount was said indebtedness? If you state that Clark was found indebted to you then be pleased to state whether or not he paid it before his death State whether or not he made repeated statements to you of his utter inability to pay you the debt he owed you, or even any considerable part thereof State whether or not Clark stated his utter insolvency, and whether or not his pecuniary situation was not so gloomy and hopelessly insolvent, that he was induced to write to you as late as the 15th of June, 1812 that if he ' could sacrifice the little I (he) had left, and after paying every thing, only reserve wherewith barely to keep me (Clark) from starving in any other country, I would do it in an instant, to escape from the hell I have lived in for the last 18 months State also whether or not every letter which you received from Mr Clark, after his return to New Orleans from Philadelphia, in 1811 did not contain statements of reasons, excuses, explanations and protestations of deep regret that he did not and could not comply with his pecuniary obligations to you State fully whether this be or be not so, or whether or not, on the other hand, he complied and paid you, as his obligations became due

5th Do you know whether or not Daniel Clark was in Europe any parts of the years 1802 and 1803 ? If aye, please state all you know about it When he left New Orleans, what port he sailed from, in what vessel he was a passenger, to what port he sailed, and any fact connected with this branch of the inquiry which you may remember

6th Did you correspond with Daniel Clark, at the time of his visit in Europe ? Can you state the occasion of his visit to Europe ? If aye please do so as fully and particularly as you can

7th Do you know the period of the departure of Daniel Clark from Europe, on his return to the United States, in 1802 or 1803 ? If yea, be pleased to state the period with all of the exactness in your power, and state the circumstances or facts which enable you so to fix the precise period, if you do fix it.

9th Did or did not the said Daniel Clark sail from Europe at the time inquired about in the last interrogatory, in a vessel belonging to you ? If aye, state the name of the vessel, also the name of the port from which she sailed, and whether or not she sailed at that time directly for the port of New Orleans Can you fix the time of her sailing by any of said ship's papers now in your possession , or, perhaps, by reference to the books of the insurance office, where you effected insurance at that time , if you can, in any manner, to place the matter beyond cavil or question, please do so, and state whether or not the said vessel put into Kingston, in the Island of Jamaica, or elsewhere, on her said return trip to New Orleans If she did then state how long she was delayed there Did you receive letters from Clark, dated at Kingston ? If aye, state the dates

10th What time did the ship in which **Daniel Clark came in** from Europe to New Orleans, reach New Orleans? State the day, month and year, if you can

11th Do you know whether or not Daniel Clark was in Philadelphia, during any part of the year eighteen hundred and three? If he was, then state what part of the year he was there, and how long he remained.

12th Do you know whether Daniel Clark was in Philadelphia in eighteen hundred and two? If aye, state when he arrived, whether he had pressing and important business of great magnitude on hand, occupying his entire time, while he remained in said city With whom did he stay during his sojourn? Did you have occasion to see him every day, and did you see him every day? Was he or not there chiefly at your suggestion and request? Was he or not then on his way to Europe? From what port did he sail for Europe? In whose vessel did he sail?

13th What were your personal relations with Mr Clark in 1802 and 1803? Do you or not believe that it would have been possible, that Daniel Clark standing in the business relations, and in the personal relationship of frank and cordial confidence, which he did towards you, to have been married in Philadelphia, at the time mentioned, without his having informed about it, and invited you to his wedding? If you state that it **was** *possible,* then state whether or not it was probable

14th. Did Daniel Clark ever speak to you, or write to you about his relationship with Madame DeGrange, the reputed mother of the complainant Myra? If aye, state what that conversation was, the circumstances connected with it, and all about it

15th Did Daniel Clark ever consult or speak to you, on the **subject** of his marriage, or his contemplated or projected marriage with any lady? If aye, state who that lady was, when he spoke to you on the subject and all of the circumstances attending the same

16th Did Daniel Clark ever speak or write to you of his purposes or intentions of addressing any lady with a view to marriage? If aye, state all about it, as fully and particularly as if you had been thereunto specially interrogated; especially, state the name of the lady, the time when this took place, and if he addressed you any letters on the subject, please annex the originals hereto, if you can, and if you can not, then please state why you can not, and in that case, please state the substance thereof as fully and particularly as if you had been thereunto specially questioned, and as fully as you can remember

17th Do you know any thing of the mother of the complainant, Myra Gaines? If aye, be pleased to state all you know of her. State whether she ever came consigned to your care If aye, state by whom, the time when, and the circumstances under which this took place. State who consigned her to your care, the purposes, &c., and state whether or not the person who sent her to you addressed you a letter on the subject. If he did, please annex it if you yet have it, and if you have not got it, state what became of it, and then state, as fully as you can remember the contents of said letter.

18th. Did you ever hear Daniel Clark speak of being the father of any child, by the mother of the complainant Myra? If aye, state what was the name of said child, and state all you know about her as fully and particularly as if you had been specially interrogated. State especially, all that you have heard Clark say about his being the father of said child, and what he said about her legitimacy and illegitimacy.

19th. State whether or not you knew the mother and other relations of Daniel Clark? If aye, state how many of them you knew, how long you knew them, where they lived, and if they are dead, state where they died. Was your acquaintance with them personal, frequent and intimate? If aye, be pleased to state whether or not the mother of Daniel Clark, or any of his relations ever spoke of said Daniel as a married man. Did Daniel Clark enjoy the reputation, among his family or friends, of being a married man? Or was the contrary the truth?

20th. What became of Mrs. DeGrange after she came to you in 1802? Do you know of her ever being subsequently married? If aye, to whom was she married, when was she married, where was she married and what evidence have you of the fact? State fully.

21st. Have you ever seen or examined any church records, in Philadelphia in reference to the marriage of Mrs. DeGrange, that is to say, Zulime Née Carrière? If aye, be pleased now to procure a copy of any certificate which may exist on the church records of her marriage in Philadelphia, and state whether or not you have verified the copy with the record, and know it to be correct.

22d. If, in answer to the last interrogatory you state that Zulime née Carrière was married in Philadelphia, state where she and her husband subsequently resided. If they resided in Philadelphia state in what part for how long a time, and where they subsequently went. State also, whether said Zulime née Carrière, alias Madame DeGrange had any children by her said marriage and if so, whether or not they were not regarded in the community as the lawful and legitimate children of their father and mother.

23d. If you state that Zulime née Carrière—Madame DeGrange married, be pleased to state whether or not she did not hold herself out to the world or community in which she lived as the lawful wife of the man she had married, and did not the gentleman, in like manner, hold her out as his lawful wife to the community in which he lived? Do you believe they would have been allowed to live in the society in which they moved, but for this general belief, made manifest by the conduct of both parties, or if it had been believed and known that she was not the wife of the gentleman she was living with, as such? Would the moral tone of Philadelphia society have tolerated such a thing?

24th Do you know of Daniel Clark having been in Philadelphia after the marriage of Zulime nee Carriere—Madame De-Grange—with Dr James Gardette? Did you ever hear him make any objection or protest against her being the wife of said Gardette? Speak fully

25th What was the temper or disposition of Daniel Clark? Judging from that, can you express any decided belief, whether or not he would have quietly submitted to the indignity of allowing any man to take away his lawful wife, if he had had one, and appropriating her to himself? If you can, please do so fully and particularly

26th If, in answer to the last interrogatory, you state that you were acquainted with Daniel Clark's temper and disposition, will you be pleased to state whether you can express any decided opinion, judging from said knowledge, on this point, to wit —Supposing Daniel Clark to have had a lawful wife living, would he, or not, have held himself out to the community, and in the social circles, as an unmarried man? Would he, in the case supposed, or would he not, have approached a young lady with overtures of marriage? Would he have, do you suppose, announced to his friends an intention, on his part, of addressing a young lady with a view to marriage, if he had been, himself, at the time, a married man? State fully

27th Is there any other matter of fact, or circumstance, within your knowledge, not related by you in answer to the foregoing interrogatories, and which you believe would be of any use or advantage to the complainants or defendants in this suit? If yea be pleased to state the same as fully and specially as if you had been thereunto specially interrogated, stating particularly, all you know of the complainant, Myra,—her birth, the name she bore, by whom, and where she was brought up, when and whom she married, under what maiden name she was married, whose daughter she was publicly announced to be, at the time of her marriage, etc.   G B DUNCAN,

Counsellor and Solicitor for Beverly Chew, Richard Relf, and F. Dussuau Delacroix

The complainants, reserving all and all manner of exceptions to the foregoing interrogatories, specially, except to the said witness on the ground of interest, and require the commissioner, before proceeding to propound the interrogatories above, to propound the following interrogatories to said witness, upon his voir dire—that is to say.

Interrogatory 1st   Are you interested, in any degree or manner, in the result of this suit?

Interrogatory 2d   Have you, at any time since the death of the said Daniel Clark, alluded to in the foregoing interrogatories in chief, had any transaction with the defendants in this suit, Richard Relf and Beverly Chew, or either of them, respecting any property real or personal, which was found in the estate or succession of said Daniel Clark, or in which he had any interest at the time of his death?   If yea, state particularly what were such transactions, respecting what particular portion or portions of property, where it is situated when such transactions were made, with whom, and with what motive, purpose, intent or consideration   State fully **and particularly**

Interrogatory 3d   Have you not, and do you not now assert, some claim, or title to, or interest in, some real estate in Louisiana, which was found in the succession of said Daniel Clark?   if yea, was not said property derived through the said defendants, Relf and Chew, or one of them?   Describe said property particularly, who now holds the same, or any part thereof?

Interrogatory 4th   Have you not, within the year past, given out, that you contemplated prosecuting the complainant, Myra Clark Gaines, and others, claiming to be entitled to the estate or succession of said Daniel Clark, for certain indebtedness which you pretend said estate is under to you?

Interrogatory 5th   Did you know the mother of said Daniel Clark?   Where did she reside at the time of her death?   When did she die?   Did she leave a last will and testament?   Who wrote or dictated that will and testament?   Where was it written, and what was its date?   Did you make any suggestions to the testatrix, or any other person, with regard to the contents of said will?   If yea, what were such suggestions, and to whom made?   State fully and particularly

P C WRIGHT,
Solicitor for Complainants

Cross Interrogatories

The complainants, reserving to themselves all and all manner of exceptions to the foregoing interrogatories on the **part of** defendants, as well to the ability and competency of the witness, as to the matter and form of said interrogatories, and especially excepting to interrogatories numbered 3, 4, 13, 25, and 26, as **leading** and wholly irrelevant and impertinent to the issue **in this suit,** propound the following cross-interrogatories

Cross Interrog 1st   Have you in your possession, or under your control, the papers, documents, and letters referred to in the interrogatories in chief propounded to you by defendants?   If yea, annex them and each of them to your answers to said inte -

rogatories, respectively, or state at length why you cannot so annex them, or either of them

Cross Interrog 2d   Do you know what were the pecuniary circumstances of the mother of said Daniel Clark, during the last eight or ten years preceding her death?   If yea, state fully what you know of them, and your means of knowing them

Cross Interrog 3d   If you answer the 15th and 16th direct interrogatories affirmatively, state if you know of any reasons why such marriage was not consummated   What were those reasons, and from   did you derive any knowledge, or any information, respecting them?   State fully and particularly

Cross Interrog 4th   If you state that you know Zulime née Carriere, and that she came to Philadelphia in 1802, or thereabouts, then state how long she remained there at that time, where did she go on leaving there, and when did she again visit Philadelphia, and what part did you perform toward her as a friend of herself or others, interested in her welfare and comfort? State minutely and particularly, all that at that time transpired, the part which you acted, and at whose instance and request you acted, and where the said Daniel Clark was, at this period last mentioned, and whether you advised him of what you had done in the premises; and if you have any letters from him upon the subject of the said visit of said Zulime at Philadelphia, on the occasion enquired of, annex them to this commission, with your depositions   In speaking of the acts or sayings of the said Daniel Clark, in your answer to this cross interrogatory, you will confine yourself to what you know of your own knowledge and observation, and what you heard verbally, or by letter, from Mr Clark himself, and not give expression to your own opinion, or that of others

Cross Interrog 5th   When and where did you first become acquainted with Daniel Clark?   At this time how old was he, and how old were you?   How long after this period did he come to Louisiana?   If he came after that time, in what station or capacity was he then employed, upon coming to Louisiana? At what period did he enter upon mercantile and commercial pursuits, and in connexion with whom if with any one?   How old was he, when he first came to Louisiana?

Cross Interrog 6th   What were the most prominent and striking traits of character which distinguished Daniel Clark, as developed in his eventful life?   State fully, according to the best of your knowledge and belief   Was he not always actuated by the highest sense of honor, integrity, and justice?   At the same time, was he not proud, ambitious, and aspiring, and did he not possess remarkable spirit and energy?   and were not his social feelings cordial, and his natural affections strong and ardent?

Cross Interrog 7th   If you state, in answer to the 5th inter regatory in chief, that Daniel Clark was in Europe, in any portions of the years 1802 and 1803, state what was the purpose and object of said visit to Europe

Cross Interrog 8th What were your pecuniary circumstances in the year 1811, when Mr Clark visited Philadelphia, or about that time?

P C WRIGHT, Complainant's Solicitor

Deposition of Daniel W. Coxe, a witness produced, sworn and examined by virtue of the annexed commission, on the twenty-fifth day of August, in the year of our Lord one thousand eight hundred and forty-nine, at the office of William Henry Rawle, No 93 South Third Street, in the City of Philadelphia, and State of Pennsylvania. before me, the said William Henry Rawle commissioner named in the annexed commission and also commissioner for the State of Louisiana, to take testimony in the State of Pennsylvania in a certain cause now depending in the Circuit Court of the United States for the Fifth Judicial Circuit, holding sessions in and for the Eastern District of Louisiana, wherein E P Gaines and wife are plaintiffs, and Richard Relf, Beverly Chew et al are defendants.

The said Daniel W Coxe being duly sworn, upon his voir dire, answers, as follows, to the voir dire interrogatories proposed to him in this cause

1 To the first of said interrogatories he answers as follows

It is impossible for me to answer this interrogatory categorically by a simple yes, or no, as I am not informed what the issue is in this case but I am perfectly willing to answer fully as to any facts I may be enquired about, and then the Court can best determine whether I have any interest or not I have no interest in the result of this suit, that I am aware of

2 To the second of said interrogatories, he answers as follows

Since the death of Daniel Clark I have had a transaction with the defendants named in the interrogatory, to wit Richard Relf and Beverly Chew, respecting property which was found in the estate or succession of Daniel Clark and in which said Clark had an interest at the time of his death The transaction which I had with them was this in the early part of the year 1819, I went to New Orleans, with a view of arranging with the said Chew and Relf, in their capacity of executors of Daniel Clark, and as agents of Mrs Mary Clark, the mother of the said Daniel Clark, and the said Daniel Clark's only heir and legatee under his will, for the claim which I had against the estate or succession of Daniel Clark under the agreement between the said Clark and myself, dated on the 12th of July, 1811, a copy of which is hereto annexed marked "1" After my arrival in New Orleans, it was agreed that the said Chew and Relf in their capacities aforesaid should sell certain properties belonging to said succession of Daniel Clark, under and by authority of the Court of Probates in New Orleans, and that if, at the public sale made of said property, no other person or persons would run the same up to a certain specified sum, that I should undertake to do so, and that the same should be charged to me in account current at the price at which the said properties might be struck off to me, and that an account should be immediately stated between the estate of Daniel Clark and myself, and my claims adjusted and settled. Accordingly, a public sale of a portion of the real estate of the succession of the said Daniel Clark was made on, as I believe, the 24th of February, 1819, by Mr Mossy, public auctioner, then of the city of New Orleans, which sale took place at Maspero's Coffee-house, which was the usual place of public sales at that time, in said City. At said sale I did purchase a portion of said land, so sold. Subsequently, the said Richard Relf and Beverly Chew, as executors aforesaid, did state an account current between the estate of Daniel Clark and myself, up to the 27th of January, 1819, in which I was charged with the lands which I had purchased at the aforesaid public sale, a copy of which said account current I hereto annex, marked "A.," and for greater certainty and perspicuity, I make the same a part of my answer to this interrogatory. The particular portions of property which I acquired of said estate, are referred to in said account, and more full and particular description of the same must have been given in the act of transfer which those gentlemen made of that property to me, and which I think may be easily found, before a notary in New Orleans at that time, though which one I do not particularly remember at this time.

The said property lies in Louisiana, one item of which was an undivided moiety of the Maison Rouge grant, and is situated in Wachita Country, the other was fifty thousand arpents of what was called Florida lands, and situate in the Florida Parishes. That purchase by me at public auction was made, as before stated, on the 24th of February, 1819, and the account current and final settlement was made, as before stated, on the 27th of February, 1819. My motives, purposes and intentions in said transactions were to effect a settlement with the estate of Daniel Clark, of a very large debt which the said succession owed to me, and which I was unwilling should remain longer unadjusted, my purpose being, in order to accomplish this end to bid upon said real estate, to an amount much greater than its true value, which I in fact did. The considerations of the transaction are fully set forth in the account current before referred to, and a copy of which I have furnished, and hereto annex. The amount is $172,950.

3. To the third of said interrogatories, he answers as follows:

I have, and do now assert, title in some real estate in Louisiana, which was found in the succession of Daniel Clark. The said property was purchased by me at public auction, made of a portion of the estate of Daniel Clark, in the manner I at the time stated in my answer to the last foregoing interrogatory. The said Relf and Chew were at that time acting as the representatives of the succession of Daniel Clark, and as agents of the mother of the said Daniel Clark, and who was his sole legatee I have no memorandum or means at hand, at this time, of giving a more full and particular description of said property, than I have already done I yet own a portion of said property, and I have sold various parts and parcels thereof to divers and sundry people in the Wachita country, and if the complainants in this case wish for a list of said purchasers, and a more particular description of the said property which I yet hold, and of the lots which I have sold, they are respectfully referred to Robert Maguire, of Monroe, and Richard King, of Caldwell Parish, my agents, who both reside in the Wachita country, and who are in possession of all the papers and documents necessary to enable them to give the required testimony on these points

4. To the fourth of said interrogatories, he answers as follows.

I have, within the year past, given out that I contemplated prosecuting the complainant, Myra Gaines, and others, but not for a debt which I claim now to be actually due, but what I have said and claim, is this that I acquired the real estate mentioned in the account current from the succession of Daniel Clark, for a good, just, full and valuable consideration, to wit the extinguishment of a just debt, to the amount of said purchase, which I held against the estate of said Daniel Clark, and that if my said purchase was set aside by the said Mrs. Gaines, for, or on account of any defect in the conveyance made to me, or if my title thereto should be otherwise set aside by the United States, or any other parties, inasmuch as the said Mrs Gaines declared herself to be the heir at law of the said Daniel Clark, I unquestionably would prosecute her for the restoration of the consideration money, with such interest, costs, and damages as I might be entitled to under the laws of Louisiana And I most unquestionably would prosecute her, or any other persons who might legally represent the succession of Daniel Clark, for it is a matter of perfect indifference to me who represents the estate, for it is against the legal heirs of the estate of the said Daniel Clark that my claim would be interposed, and if I had any desire to make the said Mrs. Gaines particularly and personally responsible, I should be then interested in establishing the fact that she is the legal heir of the late Daniel Clark

5. To the fifth of said interrogatories, he answers as follows.

I did know the mother of the late Daniel Clark, she resided at Germantown, near Philadelphia, at the time of her death, she died in the year 1823, she did leave a last will and testament, Mrs Clark dictated her own will, and it was written by Joseph Reed it was written, I think, at the house of Mrs Clark, it was dated on the 22d day of November, 1817, I did make, in conjunction with the late Dr William Hewlings, certain suggestions to Mrs Clark, in relation to the propriety of her making her will, and in it to make suitable provision for Caroline Clark, an illegitimate child of her son, Daniel Clark, inasmuch as she, the said Mrs Clark, had succeeded to the entire estate of her son Daniel Clark, under his will, and we also informed Mrs Clark of a communication which had been made to us by Col Samuel B. Davis, to the effect that a young female then in the family of the said Davis, and who had been raised in the family of the said Davis as his own child, and who was called and known as Myra Davis, was, according to the representations of the said Davis, also an illegitimate child of said Daniel Clark. We, at the time, informed Mrs Clark that we had no evidence of the truth of Myra's being the child of Daniel Clark, than what had been stated to us by the said Col Davis, but, relying on those representations, we persuaded Mrs Clark to mention her in her will These are the only suggestions which I made to Mrs Clark in reference to her will

And thereupon, the said Daniel W Coxe, of the said city of Philadelphia, aged eighty-one years, or thereabouts, being produced, sworn and examined on behalf of the defendants, answers as follows to the interrogatories and cross interrogatories propounded to him

1. To the first interrogatory in chief, he answers as follows

I am acquainted with the parties named in said interrogatory I have known Richard Relf since he was about fourteen years of age, at which time he went from this city to New Orleans in the employ of the late Wm E Hewlings, Esq, who was subsequently Consul of the United States in Louisiana I have known Beverly Chew since the year 1797, I first saw said Myra Gaines in the year 1818, when I met her on board of a vessel commanded by Captain Simon Toby, she and I both being passengers from Philadelphia to New Orleans, she being with and under the charge of Mr. Samuel B Davis, whose name she bore, being named and called Myra Davis. General Gaines I have known by public reputation for many years, but never made his personal acquaintance until after his marriage with the said Myra. I have known the said Delacroix since the year 1797

2. To the second interrogatory in chief he answers as follows:

I was acquainted with the late Daniel Clark, formerly of New Orleans, I was acquainted with him from the year 1791 until the time of his death, in August, 1813 The last time I saw him was in 1811, in the city of Philadelphia. I was particularly and intimately acquainted with the said Clark

3. To the third interrogatory in chief he answers as follows

I was associated in business with the late Daniel Clark the

nature, purposes and objects of our business connection were
general commercial business and speculations in lands This
connexion commenced in 1792, and continued until July, 1811
There was a settlement between Daniel Clark and myself, revious
to his death That settlement took place on the 12th of July, 1811
I am unable to annex the original written evidence of settlement
between said Clark and myself, as the same was left by me several
years since in the hands of Louis Jannin, Esq, New Orleans,
and I understand that the same has been filed in Court, as evidence in this cause.

I annex hereto a copy of said agreement (marked No 1, and
verified by my signature), which I know to be a true and exact
copy There were two attesting witnesses to said agreement,
viz James Morphy, Jr, and Thomas Sparhawk. The said
Sparhawk is dead Whether Mr Morphy is living or dead, I
cannot say When I last knew him, he resided in Custom-house
street, New Orleans, and was then, or had been, acting as Spanish
Vice Consul

4 To the fourth interrogatory in chief he answers as follows

In the settlement which took place between Daniel Clark and
myself, in July, 1811, the said Clark was found largely indebted
to me. The nature and amount of that indebtedness will be
seen by reference to a copy of the agreement or settlement with
the said Clark and myself, hereto annexed, marked "1." Said
Clark did not pay or otherwise discharge his said indebtedness
to me, previous to his death. He did make repeated statements
to me of his utter inability to pay the debt which he owed me,
or any considerable part thereof His letters to me were couched
in terms of deep gloom, owing to his inability to comply with
his engagements to me I cannot say whether, or not, the
said Clark wrote to me a letter dated on the 15th of June, 1812,
in which he made use of the terms indicated in this interrogatory no such letter being now before me, but I can say that I
furnished G B Duncan, Esq, of New Orleans, and my counsel
in certain matters in that country, with a number of letters
written to me by the said Clark, which said letters, I understand,
have been filed, and are on record in this case. They are in the
handwriting of Daniel Clark, and I beg leave to refer to the
same as my answer to this part of said interrogatory. I cannot
say whether, or not, *every* letter which I received from Mr Clark
after his return to New Orleans, in 1811, contained statements
of reasons or excuses for his not complying with his pecuniary
obligations to me, but certainly a larger portion of them were
couched in such terms, and he at all times expressed his deep
regret because of his inability to comply with his engagements

5 To the fifth interrogatory in chief he answers as follows

Daniel Clark was in Europe during a part of the year 1802.

He arrived in this city, in a vessel from New Orleans during the last days of July, 1802 He was at Wilmington, below this city, on the 22d of July, 1802, as will be seen by his letter to me, of that date, (herein annexed, marked "2," verified by my signature,) but owing to quarantine regulations then in force, he was not allowed to come up to Philadelphia for, I believe, some five or six days thereafter. On his arrival in Philadelphia, he commenced making preparations for an immediate departure for Europe, on business of importance, and left this city, in a few days, for New York, from whence he sailed for Europe, in a very short time—on what precise day, I cannot here say, but am quite certain that it was previous to the middle of August 1802, nor can I say in what vessel he sailed Mr. Clark remained in Europe until, I think, the latter days of November, 1802, at which time he sailed directly from Europe to New Orleans, where he arrived in the latter part of the winter, as I understood, the last days of February, 1803, but as to the time of his arrival in New Orleans, I refer to his letter, addressed to me, on the 31st day of January, 1807 (hereto annexed, marked "3," verified by my signature)

6. To the sixth interrogatory in chief he answers as follows

I did correspond with Daniel Clark, at the time of his visit to Europe. The occasion of his visit to Europe was urgent business, connected with our commercial transactions, making it necessary that he should arrange certain business matters with our mercantile friends in that country, our business at that time rendering it necessary for us to know the existing and probable future political state of England, and the continent generally

7. To the seventh interrogatory in chief he answers as follows

I do not know the precise period at which Daniel Clark left Europe, on his return to the United States, but believe that it was in the latter part of November, 1802.

No eighth interrogatory in chief has been annexed to this commission.

WILLIAM HENRY RAWLE, Com.

9. To the ninth interrogatory in chief he answers as follows,

My impression is, that Daniel Clark did sail from Europe, at the time spoken of in answer to the last interrogatory, in a vessel belonging to me It was either ship Thomas or ship Thomas Wilson—I am not certain which. She sailed from Liverpool directly to the port of New Orleans. I am unable to fix the precise time of her sailing by any papers now in my possession, or by reference to the books of any insurance office; the most of my papers and letters were destroyed by fire, in the year 1806 The vessel in which the said Clark sailed from Europe to New Orleans put in at Kingston, Jamaica, from some cause not now remembered by me, and which, of course, caused her to make a longer passage than she otherwise would have done. How long the said ship remained at Kingston, I cannot now state, nor can I now find any letters addressed to me by Mr. Clark from Kingston

10 To the tenth interrogatory in chief he answers as follows

I cannot state the precise time of Daniel Clark's arrival in New Orleans but to the best of my knowledge, information, belief, and recollection, it was in the last days of February, or early in March, 1803

11 To the eleventh interrogatory in chief he answers as follows

Daniel Clark was not in Philadelphia at any time during the year 1803, to my knowledge, and I believe if the said Daniel Clark had been in Philadelphia, I would have known it; it could scarcely have been otherwise

12 To the twelfth interrogatory in chief he answers as follows

Daniel Clark was in Philadelphia in the year 1802, on two several occasions he was in Philadelphia in April, 1802, at which time he left with me a power of attorney, which is annexed to a commission, by virtue of which my testimony was taken in a suit instituted by Dr Barnes and his wife and others against General Gaines and his wife, in the First Judicial District Court, in New Orleans, which testimony was, I think, taken in the year 1841, by William Rawle, Esq. Commissioner, and I now refer to said power of attorney as a part of my answer to this interrogatory Immediately thereafter, Mr Clark left for New Orleans where he remained until June and then sailed from thence to Philadelphia, on his way to Europe and arrived in Philadelphia, as before stated during the last days of July, 1802 I do not recollect with whom he stayed Said Clark had pressing and important business of great magnitude, which occupied his entire time during his stay in Philadelphia My impression is, that I saw him every day during his stay in Philadelphia I do not know whether he came to Philadelphia particularly at my suggestion or request When Mr Clark arrived here, in July, 1802, he was on his way to Europe, he sailed from New York I do not know the vessel in which he sailed

13 To the thirteenth interrogatory in chief he answers as follows

My personal relations with Daniel Clark, in the years 1802 and 1803 were of the most intimate and confidential character I do not believe it possible that Daniel Clark, standing in the business and personal relationship of unlimited and cordial confidence which he did to me, would have been married in the city of Philadelphia or any where else where I was at the time mentioned in the interrogatory, without his informing me of it, and inviting me to the wedding. Such a thing is, of course, possible, but I can imagine few events in life less probable

14 To the fourteenth interrogatory in chief he answers as follows:

Daniel Clark did both write and speak to me about his (the said Clark's) relationship or connexion with Madam DeGrange, the reputed mother of the complainant Myra In the early part of the year 1802, the said Madame DeGrange presented herself to me, with a letter from Daniel Clark, introducing her to me, and informing me in confidence that the bearer of that letter, Madame DeGrange, was pregnant with a child by him, and requesting me, as his friend, to make suitable provision for her, and to place her under the care of a respectable physician, requesting me at the same time to furnish her with whatever money she might want and stand in need of, during her stay in Philadelphia As the friend of Mr Clark I undertook to attend to his request, and did attend to it I employed the late William Shippen, M D, to attend to her during her confinement, and procured for her a nurse Soon after the birth of the child, it was taken to the residence of its nurse That child was called Caroline Clark, and, at the request of Mr Clark, the child was left under my general charge and exclusive care until the year 1811. After that period, she was not so exclusively under my charge but I had a general charge over her, which continued up to the period of her marriage with Dr John Barnes, formerly of this city She is now dead, as is also Dr Shippen, before spoken of Daniel Clark arrived in this city within a very short time after the birth of said Caroline, which was, I believe, in April, 1802, when I received from him the expression of his wishes in reference to this child He left here shortly afterwards, as before stated by me. During Daniel Clark's subsequent visits to Philadelphia, he always visited that child, acknowledged and caressed it as his own, and continued to give me the expression of his wishes in reference to her On the occasion of Mr Clark's visit to Philadelphia, immediately after the birth of Caroline, in conversation with me in reference to Madame DeGrange, he confirmed what he had stated in his letter of introduction, stating to me that he was the father of this illegitimate child, Caroline, and that he wished me to take care of her, and to let the woman have what money she stood in need of, until she returned to New Orleans.

15 To the fifteenth interrogatory in chief he answers as follows:

Daniel Clark did both write and speak to me on the subject of the projected marriage which he desired to bring about between himself and a lady of Maryland That lady's name was Louisa Caton She was the granddaughter of the late Charles Carroll, of Carrollton. Daniel Clark did **address** that lady with the view of marriage, in the year 1807 or 1808, and there was, as I was informed by Mr Clark, a partial **engagement** existing between him and that lady Mr Clark **informed** me that this engagement was subsequently dissolved, in **consequence** of high pecuniary demands made by the friends of **that** lady, to be made in the form of settlement on her behalf, **and** beyond his means to comply with Mr Clark also informed me that there was a subsequent effort made to renew this engagement with Miss Caton, made chiefly through the instrumentality of Robert Goodloe Harper, Esq, who had married an aunt of Miss Caton. The same obstacles interposed, and I may **add that** as Mr Clark consulted me upon this subject, I also **interposed** my objections to his encumbering himself with heavy **pecuniary** stipulations, as it would greatly embarrass him, **and me also**, in our business relations In my testimony before **referred** to, taken in the case of Barnes and others against Gaines and wife, in the First Judicial District Court, at New Orleans, there are several original letters written by Daniel Clark to me upon this subject, and to which I now beg leave to refer, as a part of my answer to this interrogatory

16. To the sixteenth interrogatory in chief he answers as **follows:**

My **answer** to this interrogatory is fully set forth in my answer to the 15th interrogatory in chief, and I refer to it as an answer to this interrogatory

17 To the seventeenth interrogatory in chief he answers as follows

I do **know** the mother, or, at least, the reputed mother of the complainant, **Myra Gaines.** Chiefly what I know of her is already set forth in my answer to the 14th interrogatory, or, at least, the manner in which I became acquainted with her To which answer I now refer She did come consigned to my care by Daniel Clark, in the spring of the year 1802, and the circumstances connected therewith I have already stated in my answer to the 14th interrogatory Mr Clark did write to me a letter on the subject, which was handed to me by the said mother of Mrs Gaines I have not got that letter at this time; owing to the nature of its contents, I think I destroyed it at once, or it may have been destroyed with my other papers at the time my store was burned, in 1806, or, at all events, I cannot now find it. I have already stated its contents, as near as I can remember them, in my answer to the 14th interrogatory

18 To the eighteenth interrogatory in chief he answers as follows

I have heard Daniel Clark speak of being the father of a child by the mother of the complainant, Myra The name of that child was Caroline. I have already stated the leading incidents of what I know respecting her, but, for more full and particular account of what I knew and know respecting her, I again refer to my testimony taken as by me stated in the case of Barnes and others against Gaines and wife I have heard Daniel Clark repeatedly say he was the father of that child, but he never intimated to me that she was a legitimate child but, on the contrary, always spoke of her, the said Caroline, as his illegitimate child Nothing ever occurred, to my mind, either from the letters or conversations of Daniel Clark, than that this child, Caroline, was a bastard child, whereof Madame DeGrange was the mother, and Daniel Clark was the father

19 To the nineteenth interrogatory in chief he answers as follows

I knew the father and mother of Daniel Clark, as also his uncle, Daniel Clark, his aunt, and two of his sisters, and a niece. I think I became acquainted with these parties about the year 1797. My acquaintance with the uncle of Daniel Clark and his wife, was but casual and limited They lived, at the time, in Natchez, Mississippi The other individuals above named I think I first became acquainted with in New Orleans. They subsequently, to wit in 1802, came on to Philadelphia, and settled in Philadelphia The father of said Daniel Clark died a few years before his said son His mother survived him, and died about the year 1823 The date of his sisters' death, I do not particularly remember His niece is still living, in Germantown. The father, mother, and sisters whom I knew, died in Germantown My acquaintance with the family of Daniel Clark, except as above mentioned, was personal, frequent, and intimate. I never heard either the mother, or any other relation of Daniel Clark, speak of him as a married man. His reputation with his family and friends was, that he was an unmarried man, until the day of his death One of the sisters of Daniel Clark married a Mr Anderson The niece spoken of was named Sarah Campbell, she was the daughter of Mrs Anderson

20 To the twentieth interrogatory in chief he answers as follows

Mrs DeGrange left Philadelphia, soon after the birth of Caroline, for New Orleans that is, as soon after her confinement as it was prudent for her to travel, in the spring of 1802. She subsequently returned to Philadelphia, according to the best of my recollection, in the autumn of the year 1807, and did not again leave until after her marriage with James Gardette, surgeon dentist of this city of Philadelphia. She was married in this city, at St Joseph's church, by the Right Reverend Michael Egan, on the second of August, 1808. She was married to the said Gardette by her maiden name, Marie Zulime Carriere   I annex hereto a certificate from the said church, marked No. "4", verified by my signature

21   To the twenty-first interrogatory in chief he answers and says

I have seen and examined the church records of St Joseph's church, in Philadelphia, in reference to the marriage of Madame DeGrange, that is to say, Zulime nee Carriere   I have procured a copy of the marriage record from said church records, and have verified the same, and I know it to be correct. It is hereto annexed, marked "4"   It was certified to by the pastor of the church, in my presence, and his signature thereto is genuine.

22. To the twenty-second interrogatory in chief he answers as follows

The said Zulime ree Carréire, from the time she was married, in 1808, to Dr James Gardette, continued to reside in Philadelphia, with her said husband, Dr Gardette, until the year 1829 or 1830, at which time they removed to France.   I know nothing subsequently of her personally, but have understood that she resides in New Orleans, with one of her sons born of her marriage with Dr Gardette   During her residence in Philadelphia, after her marriage with Dr. Gardette, they resided in Chesnut street, at the corner of Ninth street   The said Zulime nee Carriere alias M de DeGrange, alias Mrs Gardette, had children after her marriage with Dr Gardette   I never heard any suggestion to the contrary of those children being legitimate

23   To the twenty-third interrogatory in chief he answers as follows

Having stated that Zulime n c Carriere did intermarry with Dr Gardette, she did always subsequently thereto hold herself out to the community in which she lived as the lawful wife of the said Gardette, and he, the said Gardette, did in like manner hold her out in the community as his lawful wife   The balance of this interrogatory seems to require but the expression of an opinion   I can, therefore. only say, that I do not believe that any man would be tolerated in the society of Philadelphia who would attempt to palm off on the community a woman as his lawful wife, if it were known that she was not so.

24   To the twenty-fourth interrogatory in chief he answers as follows

I do know that Daniel Clark was in Philadelphia on several occasions after the marriage of Zulime nee Carriere, alias Madame DeGrange, to Dr. James Gardette.   I never heard Daniel Clark make any objection or protest against her being the wife of the said Gardette

25   To the twenty-fifth interrogatory in chief he answers as follows.

Daniel Clark was a high tempered and chivalrous man, and his disposition was quick and impetuous. I have known no man who would have more promptly resented an imputation against his honor or integrity. I can express most decided belief that he would not have submitted to the indignity of allowing a man to take from him his wife, if he had any, and appropriating her to, himself

26 To the twenty-sixth interrogatory in chief he answers as follows.

I can express a decided opinion upon the point enquired of in the interrogatory, and it is this: That I am perfectly sure that if Daniel Clark had been in truth a married man, whether that marriage had been public or private, and that wife still living, he would never have held himself out to the community and the social circles in which he moved, directly or indirectly, as an unmarried man. I am equally sure that in the case supposed, Daniel Clark would never have approached a lady with overtures of marriage, *nor would he have announced to his friend an intention* of addressing a young lady with a view to marriage, if he had been at the time a married man. There ought to have been no doubt upon the mind of any man, who knew anything of Daniel Clark, on this subject, that he would neither have been guilty, or even conceived of acts so atrocious

27. To the twenty-seventh interrogatory in chief he answers. as follows.

It is difficult for me to say whether or not there are any other facts within my knowledge, and not related by me in my answer to the foregoing interrogatories, which would be of any use or advantage to the complainants or defendants in this suit; but there are some things, which I desire to state as illustrative and corroborative of my foregoing answers, and as part of my answers to said interrogatories in general

In the first place, I annex hereto original letters addressed to me and written by Daniel Clark. They are all genuine letters, as well known to me, being intimately acquainted with Daniel Clark's handwriting. The same are numbered from "9" to "80", inclusive. They all refer, in whole or in, part, to the several subject matters stated in my foregoing answers. The one dated on the fourth day of January, 1808, contains a paragraph commencing with the words "I am happy to learn," (the same being in exhibit marked ("39"), which refers to his relationship to Miss Caton. That lady resided at the time at Anapolis, in Maryland. Others of said letters are annexed to show our business relations and connexion, and our personal and confidential position in respect to each other.

In the next place, I wish to state, that some years since, having heard much about a supposed will, alleged by the complainants in this case to have been made by Daniel Clark, subsequent to the one which he had made in 1811, and having understood, also, that the late Stephen Mazureau, then a distinguished lawyer of New Orleans, was cognizant of certain matters connected therewith and having, in the month of February, 1842, conversed with Mr Mazureau on the subject, and being anxious not to rely on my recollection of his conversation, I addressed him a letter, in reply to which he addressed to me a communication, dated at New Orleans, on the first of May, 1842. I now annex the original communication of Mr Mazureau, as a part of my answer to these interrogatories, (the same being numbered "5") It is wholly written and signed by Mr Mazureau, whom, I understand, departed this life during the present year, 1849. The contents of this document I deem important, and it will speak for itself. The annexed letter, marked '6,' is a genuine original letter, addressed to me by Mrs. P Alexander, and the girl Caroline therein referred to, is Caroline Clark, born of Madame De-Grange, at the time spoken of by me. I also think it proper to state, that in the year 1808, after Madame DeGrange had returned to Philadelphia from New Orleans, and when lodging in Walnut street, she sent for me, and during a private interview with her, at Mrs Rowan's, where she lodged, she stated that she had heard Mr Clark was going to be married to Miss Caton, of Baltimore, which, she said, was a violation of his promise to marry her, and added that she now considered herself at liberty to connect herself in marriage with another person, alluding, doubtless, to Dr. Gardette, who, at the moment of this disclosure, entered the room, when, after a few words of general conversation I withdrew, and her marriage to Mr Gardette was announced a few days after

I also have found, and annex hereto, (marked "7," and verified by my signature, a notarial copy of the act of sale of the lands in the Wachita country, before referred to in my deposition. I mean the lands which were a moiety of the Maison Rouge grant

I also now recollect when Mr. Clark visited Philadelphia, in the year 1802, he stayed part of the time at Germantown, part of his time at my house, where he had a room, and occasionally at a hotel. On further recollection, it was on his subsequent visits that he stayed with his family, at Germantown, as, at the time I first referred to, his family had not yet removed to Germantown. On all of Mr Clark's visits to Philadelphia, he had a room at my house

D W COXE.

I also annex hereto an agreement, dated 18th of April, 1807, between said Daniel Clark and myself, the said agreement being in the handwriting of said Clark, the same being numbered "8," verified by my signature

D W. COXE.

To the cross interrogatories propounded to him on the part of the complainants, the witness answers as follows

1 To the first cross interrogatory he answers as follows

I have in my possession a part of the pape s, documents and letters, referred to in the interrogatories in chief, propounded by the defendants, and where I have them, I have annexed them, and where I have not been able to annex them, by reason of my not being in possession of them, I have stated the facts at length, as suggested in this interrogatory

2 To the second cross interrogatory he answers as follows

I have but little personal knowledge of the pecuniary circumstances of the mother of Daniel Clark, for the last eight or ten years of her life, as I was not her agent, but I believe they were limited

3 To the third cross interrogatory he answers as follows

Having answered the 15th and 16th interrogatories, I now state, in reply to this 3d cross interrogatory, as requested, that I do know some of the reasons at least, why the marriage of Daniel Clark was not consummated, those reasons were the unreasonable exactions made on behalf of the lady in the matter of a pecuniary settlement, which they desired should be made and settled upon her by said Daniel Clark, previous to the consummation of said marriage Mr Clark also having consulted me upon the subject, I interposed my decided objections to his cramping himself with such pecuniary obligations while he was connected with me in business Mr Clark informed me that upon reflection he thought the match not an eligible one, under the circumstances My knowledge and information upon the subject of Daniel Clark's engagement were derived exclusively from Daniel Clark himself

4 To the fourth cross interrogatory he answers as follows

Having stated that I knew Zulime, nee Carriere, and that she did come to Philadelphia in the year 1802, I now state, in answer to this cross interrogatory, that I am unable to answer as to the precise time that she remained in Philadelphia I do not think it was long after her arrival that she was confined, and gave birth to the child, Caroline; and she left Philadelphia, I think, as soon thereafter as it was prudent for her to travel. I have no personal knowledge where she then went to, but understood that she returned to New Orleans She returned again to Philadelphia, according to the best of my recollection, in the year 1807 I did not act towards her as *her* friend, but as the friend of Daniel Clark, who appeared interested in her welfare and comfort I have already stated, in answer to the 14th interrogatory in chief, as minutely and particularly all that transpired, connected with this particular matter, as my recollection at this time will enable me to do, and I refer to that answer, as my answer to this branch of the inquiry in this 4th cross interrogatory. The part which I acted in the matter, was that of a friend to Daniel Clark, and I acted at the instance and request of Daniel Clark. Daniel Clark arrived at Philadelphia a short time after the birth of the child Caroline. I did advise Daniel Clark of what I had done in the premises. I had a letter from Daniel Clark, on the subject of the visit of said Zulime to Philadelphia in 1802. but I cannot annex the same, because it has been destroyed; my impression is, that owing to its nature, I destroyed it at the time, or soon after reading it.—if I did not, it is probable that it was destroyed at the time my store was burnt in 1806. In speaking of the acts and sayings of Daniel Clark, I have, as suggested, confined myself to what I know of my own knowledge and observation, and what I have heard verbally and by letter from Daniel Clark himself.

5. To the fifth cross interrogatory he answers as follows:

I first became acquainted with Daniel Clark in the year 1791, in New Orleans. I do not know how old he was at that time but have understood and believe that he was about 22 or 23 years of age. I was about the same age. Daniel Clark was in Louisiana at the time I made his acquaintance. I do not know in what station or capacity he was employed when he went to Louisiana. It was in 1791 that he entered into mercantile and commercial pursuits in connection with me. I do not know how old Daniel Clark was, when he first went to Louisiana, but I have understood, and I believe from himself, that he was 14 years of age.

6. To the sixth cross interrogatory he answers as follows:

It is difficult to say what were the most prominent striking traits of character which distinguished Daniel Clark. He was a high minded, honorable man, quick in his impulses, ardent in his temperament, actuated, as I believe, by the highest sense of honor, integrity and justice; he was a proud, ambitious, and aspiring man; he did possess remarkable spirit and energy; his social feelings were cordial, and his natural affections strong and ardent. As an illustration of this. I refer to his expressions to me, contained in his letters, annexed to my answers to the interrogatories in chief, which were written at a time of great pecuniary distress and in which he shows his natural affections for his mother and family, in very strong terms.

7. To the seventh cross interrogatory he answers as follows:

Having stated that Daniel Clark was in Europe in the year 1802, I now state that the purpose and object of his visit there, was to arrange certain mercantile matters, in which he and I, as well as Chew & Relf, were deeply interested; and also to promote our mercantile interests and those of the house of Chew & Relf, at points of commercial importance both in Eng-

land and on the Continent He was especially concerned to arrange difficulties, arising out of certain cotton transactions,
which cottons had been purchased in Louisiana and shipped to
Europe, it turning out, that immense frauds had been practised
in the packing of said cotton at the gins in Louisiana, by the
planters and others

8 To the eighth cross interrogatory he answers as follows

My pecuniary circumstances in 1811 were very limited and
embarassed, at the time Mr Clark visited Philadelphia

D. W COXE

Sworn and subscribed before me on the day and at the place
first aforesaid

WILLIAM HENRY RAWLE, Commissioner

The exhibits hereunto annexed, numbered ' 9" to ' 80" inclusive, are the letters referred to by me, in my answer to the
twenty-seventh interrogatory in chief, the exhibits numbered " "
is the notarial copy of the act of sale referred to in said answer

D W. COXE

The exhibits above referred to are all identified by the signature of the commissioner   The number of the exhibits and
the age of the witness, rendering the further identification of
the same, by the signature of the witness to each, impracticable

WILLIAM HENRY RAWLE, Commissioner

Exhibits numbered 1, 2, 3, 5, 6 and 8 are identified on the
back thereof

I, William Henry Rawle, the commissioner named in the
annexed commission, and a commissioner for the State of
Louisiana, to take testimony in the State of Pennsylvania, do
hereby certify, that the deponent, Daniel W Coxe, was by me
duly sworn to declare the truth, upon the questions put to him
in this cause   That the voir dire interrogatories were first propounded to him, and then also the interrogatories in chief and
the cross interrogatories, and his several answers thereto taken
in writing by me and subscribed by him in my presence, on
the day and at the place in that behalf first aforesaid.

In witness whereof, I have hereunto set my hand and affixed
my seal of office, on this twenty-fifth day of Augnst, Anno Domini one thousand eight hundred and forty-nine

WILLIAM HENRY RAWLE, Commissioner

Exhibit A, referred to by the witness, in his deposition
WILLIAM HENRY RAWLE, Com'r

D. W. Coxe

Account Current between Daniel W. Coxe, and the Executors
of Daniel Clark dated 27th February, 1819, settled on the
principles of the agreement of July 12th, 1811, by Mr. Coxe
becoming a purchaser, at public auction, of the property debited
in this account

Dan'l Wm. Coxe, in account with the Estate of Dan'l Clark, dec'd

1813   Dr

Nov 9	To B. Chew, for the two payments per contra, to Mrs			
	Alexander,	378	25	
	" W. E. Hulings,	200	"	578 25
1814				
Aug 1	" Daniel Clark, for balance of account, rendered the 19th May, 1813,			15,397 54
	' Interest on do from 1st August, 1813 to this day, 12 month,			923 85
	To balance per contra,			11,083 89
1815				
March 30	" Amount received from J. Ingersoll, for compromised recovery, from J & J Clifford less fees to attorney,			4,400 '
	' Interest on above, balance $11,083 89 from 27th September, 1814 to August 1st, 1815 is three years 10 months	2,549	17	
	' Do on $4,100,	880	'	3,429 17
1819				
Feb'y 24	" An undivided moiety of the Maison Rouge Grant, sold him,			100,000 "
	' 50,000 arpents Florida lands,			50,000 "
	" R. W. Meade, for an assignment of a debt due Chew & Relf			4,036 94
				$172,000 00

1813.   CR

Oct 14.   By the following sums paid to
          Mrs. Alexander, 13th July
          last,   100 "
          23d September,   50 "   150 "
                                                          ──────────

          ' Payment to B Chew, for
          Mrs Alexander,   378 25
          " A do do W E Hulings,   200 "
Dec 6   " Joseph Reed, for drawing
1814   Mrs C s will,   20 "
Jan'y 28 " Cash paid Mrs Clark,   100 "
Feb'y 17. "   do   do   do   200 "
Ap'l 1   "   do   do   do   50 "
May 21   "   do   do   do   100 "
July 7   "   do   do   do   50 "
Aug 1   " One year s annuity, viz
            six months, due Feb'y last, 2250 "
            This day,   2250 "   4500 "
                                                          ──────────

          " Six months interest on first
          half year s interest,   67 50
          " Balance to new account,   11 083 89
                                                          ──────────

          " This sum due him, per con-
   -        tract, dated Philadelphia,
1818   July 12th, 1811,   150,000 "
Aug 1   " Four year's annuity from
            1st August, 1814, to this
            day,   18 000
          " Interest on annuity, $4,500,
1819   for 4, 3, 2, and 1 year,   2,700 "
Feb'y 1. " Six months annuity, due
            this day,
                                                          ──────────
                                                          $172,950 "

New Orleans, 27th February, 1819
       (Signed)   RICHARD RELF, ⎫
                      BEV CHEW,   ⎬ Executors
                                   ⎭

Exhibit 1," referred to by the witness

WILLIAM HENRY RAWLE, Con'r

D W Coxe

Articles of Agreement made and concluded by and between Daniel W Coxe, of the city of Philadelphia, of the one part, and Daniel Clark of the city of New Orleans, of the other part, witness, that whereas a connexion has subsisted between the parties in certain mercantile transactions in New Orleans, and purchases of real property on the river Mississippi, and territories thereto adjacent and it being the wish of both parties, finally, to close all their said concerns, and adjust their accounts, they have agreed, as follows

That all the property, whether real or personal, in lands, slaves, bonds notes book debts, accounts or claims, in which the aforesaid Daniel W Coxe had an interest, and which were under the management of Daniel Clark and Chew & Relf, in New Orleans, and Henry Turner, in Natchez, shall be solely vested in, and from henceforward considered as the sole property of Daniel Clark, the said Daniel W Coxe, hereby forever quitting all claim thereto and resigning it to the aforesaid Daniel Clark, and in like manner the aforesaid Daniel Clark quits claim and renounces all claims to all or any property, whether in debts owing, goods, real estate, or other property, which the said Daniel W Coxe may possess in this country or elsewhere, they mutually binding themselves to discharge their debts respectively, so that neither shall have any claim on the other therefor

2d In order to leave as little room for doubt as possible, respecting what may be considered as the property in which the aforesaid Daniel W Coxe is interested and which he hereby resigns to the said Daniel Clark and forever quits all claim thereto, it is designated in the schedule of this date, signed by both parties, annexed hereto but it is particularly understood, that any other property, held by Daniel Clark, except that enumerated in the schedule, before mentioned, is, and shall remain, his sole and distinct property for which he is in no wise accountable to the said Daniel W Coxe

3d In consideration of the aforesaid cession of Daniel W Coxe to Daniel Clark the latter hereby engages to pay to the former, the sum of one hundred and fifty thousand dollars in three notes, and bonds of General Wade Hampton, secured by mortgage in the territory of Orleans, dated the 25th of February, of this year, and payable in two, three and four years from the date, and further, to pay annually to the said Daniel W Coxe, in half yearly payments of two thousand two hundred and fifty dollars each, the sum of four thousand five hundred dollars, during his natural life, to commence from the first day of August next, and furthermore, to pay to the said Daniel W. Coxe, an additional sum of one hundred and fifty thousand dollars, in Philadelphia, so soon as it can be collected out of the property, specified in the schedule, mentioned in the second article of this agreement, and which is to be paid in the manner and on the conditions stated in the ensuing article

4th. The sum of one hundred and fifty thousand dollars, last mentioned, which Daniel Clark obliges himself to pay to Daniel W. Coxe, being the stipulated value of his half of the lands and debts, mentioned in the annexed schedule, is to be paid only in proportion, as the lands are sold, and their amount, with the debts recovered by Daniel Clark, who obliges himself to pay to Daniel W Coxe, in Philadelphia, on account thereof one half of all the sums he may so receive until they amount to the sum before specified, a correct list of which sales, receipts, and recoveries, he engages to forward to said Coxe annually

5th In case the half of the schedule of property, hereto annexed, should not produce to Daniel Clark the sum of one hundred and fifty thousand dollars, it is well understood by the parties, that in no case is Daniel Clark to pay to Daniel W Coxe, more than one half of the sum he may receive   It is besides understood, that Daniel Clark shall never be compelled to sell or dispose of the whole, or any part of the property, mentioned in the schedule, at rates inferior to the value set thereon, and shall not be called on for payments of any sales he may make, until he shall have received the amount thereof

6th The aforesaid Daniel Clark stipulates and agrees to settle and pay off the balances, which may be respectively due in Philadelphia, to Reed & Forde, on account of former joint transactions, and to the executors of John Craig for the amount of certain Spanish duties, whenever the said Daniel W Coxe, may be called on therefor

7th Daniel W Coxe agrees to allow to Daniel Clark an interest of six per cent on such sums as the latter may pay him on account of the one hundred and fifty thousand dollars, which interest shall be annually deducted from the amount of the annuity granted to said Coxe until the payments amount to the sum of seventy-five thousand dollars, when the interest and annuity shall respectively cease

8th It is understood that the first payments made by Daniel Clark to Daniel W Coxe, independent of the annuity, shall be applied to extinguish the claims of Reed & Ford, and of the executors of John Craig's estate, which sums shall be afterwards reimbursed to said Daniel W Coxe, by Daniel Clark

And for the true and faithful performance of all and each of the foregoing articles, the parties hereto bind themselves their heirs, executors and assigns, each to the other in the penal sum.

of two hundred thousand dollars, and have hereunto set their hands and seals, having first signed duplicates in the presence of the undersigned witnesses in the city of Philadelphia, this twelfth day of July, one thousand eight hundred and eleven

(Signed)   DANIEL CLARK
                   DANIEL W COXE

(Signed) witnesses.
   JAMES MORHIIX Jr
   THOMAS SPA IAWK

Received from Daniel Clark, the three notes and bonds of Wade Hampton, for the sum of fifty thousand dollars each, referred to in the foregoing agreement

(Signed)   DANIEL W COXE.

$150,000.

Chew and Relf's Statement

	C_R		D_R

	Cr		Dr
Bills payable.	$43,700	Bills receivable.	$35,500
Dunbar's estate,	800	Fletcher's Synhes,	2,000
Wm S Stone,	1,900	St Marc,,	1,600
T & W Sperry,	1,800	Lafon,	621
Pratt & Kintsing,	1,000	Steele	650
Jones & Magrath,	300	Wright	350
F L Turner,	1,000	Miller,	2,300
Charles Delacroix,	9,600	Coffee	2,000
Thomas Urquhart,	6,600	Wine	5,000
Balance,	80,040	Villeneuva,	200
		Godberry,	212
		Dewees	1,100
		Francis Word,	209
		Book account,	3,000
		L Bank Stock,	2,800
		Planter do	800
		Navigation do.	4,900
		Insurance do	400
		Pedesclaux do	1,300
		Theatre do	600
		Simple,	5,000
		Michael Jones,	600
		Randolph,	12,000
		Welsh, of Havana,	2,200
		Cowall, of Vera Cruz,	1,100
		B Bosque, est, in N O	6,000
		Sterrett,	6,000
		H Remy,	1,000
		Derbigny,	1,930
		Orso,	1,800
		Balance due in per	
		J Miller,	11,250
		Nine negroes unsold,	2,000
		Clay's estate,	
		Bourgand's,	
		Lands in Ouachita,	20,000
	$146,740		**$146,740**

Property belonging to Daniel Clark in Territory of Orleans

Land sold on ground rent near New Orleans, -	$90,000
Maison Rouge grant, - - - - -	26,000
Lands in Opelousas, eight thousand arpents - -	8,000
Tract of eleven arpents, front on the Mississippi, near the Fourche, - - - - - - -	4,000
Do of six arpents on the Fourche, - - - -	2,000
Lands at the Terre aux Bœufs, - - - -	5000
Do in Florida, one hundred and sixteen thousand five hundred arpents, - - - - - - -	120,000
Metaire, near New Orleans, sixteen arpents front, -	10,000
Two-thirds of the tract, supposed to contain one hundred and eighty arpents, on the Canal of Carondelet, behind New Orleans, - - -	30,000
Lands on Bayou Bœuf, eight thousand six hundred arpents, - - - - - - - -	17,200
	$312,200

Moneys due to Daniel Clark in New Orleans

By Seth Lewis - - - -	$18,000
" Henry Hunt, - - - -	13,500
" Joseph Le Blanc, - - -	3,000
" George Hart, - - - -	6,000
" Manuel Perez, - - - -	10,000
" T Kimball, - - - -	3,200
" E Johnson, - - - -	8,000
" Isaac Guion, - - - -	6,000
" C Maxent - - - -	7,000
" T Skipwith, - - - -	6,600
" C La Tour, - - - -	5,000
" John Watkins, - - - -	5,000
" Thomas Power, - - -	7,500
	$98,800
Balance due on Chew and Relf's statement herewith, - - - - - -	80,040
Private property of Chew and Relf, consisting of cotton estate, house, lot, and negroes at Bayou, - - - - -	40,000
Supposed balance due by H Turner, - -	20,000
Brought down lands and ground rents, -	312,200
	$551,040

This paper, which is annexed to an agreement between

Daniel Clark and Daniel W Coxe, is signed by them for the purpose of identifying the same.

[Signed]   DANIEL CLARK
                             DANIEL W. COXE

[2]   WILMINGTON, 22 July, 1802.

MY DEAR FRIEND —I have rec'd your letter by Earle, and will accompany him as far as the Bell Tavern, in hopes of seeing you   The explanation you require about the statement of affairs in Orleans is easily given—the house there may be looked on to owe nothing, as I deducted from the sum mentioned to be due to D. C, a sum fully equal to all they might owe, so that what appears on the statement forwarded you is all clear   I shall say nothing more, till we meet   My respects to Mrs. Coxe, Mr and Mrs Burd and family.

                             DANIEL CLARK

MR DANIEL W COXE, Philadelphia.

[3]   WASHINGTON, 31 January, 1807

SIR —I shall, in consequence of your advice, see Mr Tilghmar, and implicitly follow his advice.   -

Davis' note, which you mention to be in Jas Yard's possession, I believe to have been given for a plantation he bought on the Mississippi and that it went into the hands of the person who passed it over to James Yard, in consequence of his being the attorney of a creditor of the latter   The note, in my opinion, was given for value received, and Mr Yard will be perfectly safe in advancing money on it, as Davis has amply wherewith to pay any engagement

The person who gave you the clue you mentioned is totally deceived or misinformed on the subject, and you may, if you think proper, communicate to that person the following statement of the only proposition I believe I ever made to Governor Claiborne, which was done in presence of the late Mr Trist and Mr Kean, of New Orleans   When I returned from Europe, in the beginning of the year 1803, found the deposit at New Orleans suspended, and the French making immediate preparations to take possession of Louisiana, which I believed would be attended with ruinous consequences to the United States   I waited on Gen Wilkinson and Governor Claiborne, separately, to propose to them to take possession of New Orleans, if they thought the measure would be approved of by the Executive, and assured them of a certainty of success in consequence of the proffered assistance of the people of the country.   Claiborne was doubtful whether the thing would be approved of, but asked 24 hours to consider of it   I told him that the business would infallibly be disavowed by the Executive, but that it would afford it an opportunity of availing itself of the circumstance, should it afterwards be found expedient. At the end of the 24 hours, I waited again on Claiborne for his answer, when he asked what were the means which could be provided for the support of the people engaged in the expedition. This I pointed out by engaging with my friends to furnish him in provisions and money, a sum of $150,000, to be applied, under the direction of a Council, to the payment of all expenses. Claiborne then said that if the expedition failed, I had a resource in my estate, whereas, he, being an officer dependent on the public, would be ruined. I then asked him whether that was his only objection, and if it were removed, whether he thought he could, without acting against the wishes of the President, enter heartily into the measure. He assured me he would. I then proposed to him to put my whole estate in trust, to be equally divided between him and me, in case the expedition failed. He then retracted— told me he was afraid of consequences, and we parted. This conversation took place, I think, in March of 1803, after which, I never saw Claiborne until the 18th December of the same year, when he arrived to take possession of Orleans. My letters to him, in the intermediate period, were all forwarded to Government, so that no other communication, either verbal or written, was made but what Government was in possession of. It follows, therefore, that I never made Claiborne a proposition for any thing to be done for the benefit of Spain. And if the proposition I did make, and which I know Claiborne communicated immediately to the President, was then disapproved of by the latter, why did he, for 9 months after, place an implicit confidence in me, and all on a sudden, at the end of that period, neglect me? There is, therefore, some other reason, and the true one is, my violent opposition and outcry against Claiborne's imbecile measures. But it suits better to give a reason which is injurious to me, than bring forward the real one. I never spoke to any of Claiborne's relations, nor did I know any one of them at the time you mention. I am glad the Hunter's affair was likely to end so well.

I think it would be prudent to make a conditional insurance on specie, as mentioned by Relf, but as the shipment is doubtful, you might probably annex a condition to return the whole premium, if no shipment is made. It would, however, be better to pay a trifle, than run any risk whatever. I therefore recommend the insurance to be done.

I remain, sir, your very humble servant,
DANIEL CLARK

Daniel W Coxe, Philadelphia.

[4]
Married, by the Right Rev Michael Egan, James Gardette and Mary Zulma Carriere, in the year of our Lord, eighteen

hundred and eight, August 2d   Witnesses. John Monges, John Dubarry, William Martin, Jane Rowan, and Isabel Rowan

The above is a faithful extract, taken from the marriage register, kept in St Joseph's Church, Philadelphia

            J. T BARBELIN, Pastor of said Church

St. Jos, Aug 20, 1849

[5]   NEW ORLEANS May 1st 1812

SIR —In the conversation with you, in February last, I mentioned, in reply to your enquiries, that the late Daniel Clark once consulted me and the late Edward Livingston, Esq, not "to ascertain whether he could make some provision by will for Myra, his supposed illegitimate daughter" but whether a certain will, of which he showed me a rough sketch, would be valid in law in this then territory   The will thus intended to be made, stated Myra to be his *natural child*, and instituted her his universal heir, leaving to his own mother an annual rent of, I believe three thousand dollars   Upon asking Mr Clark what the name of the mother's girl was he answered me   "You know the lady, it is Madame Desgranges"   But that woman was married and Desgranges was alive when the girl was born   I recollect having heard a good deal of talk about it at the time, but never heard your name mentioned as connected with that love affair   Yes, said Clark, she was married, I know, and what matters it ?   The ruffian (who kept a confectionary shop here) had deceived that pretty woman , he was married when he courted her and became her husband, and, as it was reported, he ranaway afterwards from fear of being prosecuted   So, you see this marriage was null   That may be, but, until so declared by a competent tribunal, the marriage exits, and the child is of such a class of bastards* as not to be capable, by our laws, of receiving, by will, from her supposed father, anything beyond what may be necessary for her sustenance and education   Such are the positive provisions of our code   The Spanish laws were somewhat more favorable   They permitted the father to leave to such a child one-fifth of the whole of his estate , but our code has restricted that to mere alimony

I showed Clark both our codes and the Spanish laws, and, though apparently disappointed, he expressed his satisfaction that he could not make the will he intended to make   I went further, and showed him the girl could not be legitimated, or even acknowledged as his child, by subsequent marriage or otherwise   I showed him, also, that, if his mother survived him, she was his forced heir, and that in supposing that he could leave to the *child* anything beyond what is necessary for her sustenance

---

* An adulterous bastard

it could not be of the value of more than one-third of **his** estate, as his mother was entitled to take and receive two-thirds clear of all charges or dispositions

What shall I do, then? asked Mr Clark Sir, if you have friends in whom you can place your confidence, you probably have some, convey them secretly some of your property, or give them money for the use of the child, to be given to her by them when she becomes of age That I'll do, said Mr Clark, and we separated

I heard, afterwards, from him, and from Mr Bellechasse, that he, Clark, that done what he told me he would do

I may add here, that the first husband of Myra wanted to retain me as her counsel to sustain her claim under the pretended will, (which I sincerely think never was executed,) as universal heir of Mr Clark That I declined, from the motives above expressed, and, as he confessed to me that the friends of Clark had conveyed to her the property which he had trusted them with for her use I advised him to be contented with what he had

The present husband of Myra came once to ask me whether I had any knowledge of a will in favor of his lady by the late Clark, and in that case, whether I had any objection to appear as one of her witnesses My answer to him was this I have seen no such will of Mr Clark but he has consulted me upon a will of which he showed me a rough sketch Well, that will will answer our purpose, said the General Very little, I believe for, if I was to give my testimony, I am inclined to think it would demolish all your pretensions. Never mind said the General, I will have you subpœnaed Upon this, I stated to him all that had occurred between Clark and myself on the subject, the opinion I had given him, and the determination which he did say he had taken, &c, &c And he retired, and I never was subpœnaed

Before concluding I must observe, that having once been of counsel, for Mr Relf in the case of libel brought by him against Myra's first husband in the Federal Court, I felt a very natural delicacy, and declined to appear as a witness for him in the suit that has since made so much noise

As this is written in haste, I would not like it to meet the eye of the public, though every particle of it is most substantially true

I remain, with great respect, sir, your most obedient servant,
MAZUREAU

D W Coxe.

[6.]   TRENTON, May 23d, 1814
SIR.—The disappointment in not receiving the money from Mrs. Clark, places me in such a situation that I do not know what I shall do without assistance. I owe some money in the Bank, likewise part of my last quarter's rent, which I must pay

immediately I had placed full reliance on her paying it, and it will be impossible for me to keep house without it I have 5 boarders, beside Caroline, to provide for. and everything so dear, that it takes all I receive from them to furnish the table

I have taken the liberty of making known my situation to you, sir, as a friend of Mr. Clark's, with the hope that you, with your former goodness, will assist me with the money for the last six months that I have had Caroline I beg, sir, you will consider if nothing can be done for me in my truly distressed situation. It i really hard for me to break up house keeping, as I have a prospect now of doing better, if I could get through my present embarrassment. I beg you will favor me with your directions, in case I can not get through it, where it is best for my beloved Caroline to be placed My heart bleeds at the thought of parting with her. She is recovering from the measles, and has had them light, but they have left her with sore eyes

With respect, I remain, sir, your obedient servant,

P. ALEXANDER

Daniel W. Coxe, Esq , Merchantee, Philadelphia.

Exhibit 7.

Be it known, that this day, before me, Carlisle Pollock, in and for this city of New Orleans, came Beverly Chew and Richard Relf, both of this city, acting herein as well for themselves, as in their respective qualities of executors testamentary of the late Daniel Clark, and as attorneys in fact of Mary Clark, sole heiress and devisee of the said late Daniel Clark , and the said appearers declared, that for and in consideration of the sum of one hundred thousand dollars, to them in hand paid, receipt whereof they hereby acknowledge, renouncing the exception non numerata pecunia, they do, by these presents, grant, bargain, and sell, unto Daniel William Coxe, of the city of Philadelphia, here present, and accepting, one undivided half part of a tract of land, situate in the parish of Ouachita, in this State, which was granted by the Spanish government of Louisiana to the Marquis of Maison Rouge, on the twentieth day of June, one thousand seven hundred and ninety-seven, the whole containing two hundred and eight thousand, three hundred and forty four, or thereabouts, and all the right, title, claim and demand of them, the said Beverly Chew and Richard Relf, the succession of the late Daniel Clark, and the said Mary Clark, of, in, and to the same, and every part thereof.

To have and to hold the said undivided half part of said land, to the said to the said Daniel William Coxe, his heirs and assigns, to their proper use and behoof forever And they, said Beverly Chew and Richard Relf, hereby bind themselves, respectively, and their respective heirs, and the succession of the said late Daniel Clark, and their constituent, the said Mary Clark, and her heirs, that they, and each of them, shall and will forever warrant and defend the said land to the said Daniel William Coxe, his heirs and assigns, against all persons whomsoever claiming or to claim by, through, or under them, and their heirs The said tract of land was acquired by the said late Daniel Clark in his lifetime of Dominique Bouligny and Louis Bouligny, the said moiety is composed of the one (2) quarter part (undivided) of the whole tract, which still remained the property of the succession and heiress aforesaid, the other undivided quarter part, conveyed by this act, was acquired by the said Beverly Chew and Richard Relf as executors of the said late Daniel Clark, and as individuals, of Wade Hampton, by act passed before me, notary, on the 22d April, 1817, now extant in this my current register, and the same was acquired by the said Wade Hampton of the said late Daniel Clark, in his lifetime, by two several acts under private signature, which were deposited in and are now extant in this my current register, on the said 22d April, 1817 And it is expressly agreed and understood, by and between the parties hereto, he, the said D. W Coxe, is content with the title which the present seller have to the land hereby sold and conveyed, and with their rights to sell the same, and takes upon himself the strength and validity of said title, and hereby renounces all right to damages and indemnity in case of eviction or legal dispossession of the whole of said tract of land, or any part thereof. Thus done and passed at New Orleans, the second day of March, one thousand eight hundred and nineteen, in presence of George Pollock and John Dick, witnesses, who hereto sign their names with the parties, and me, notary.

> DANIEL W. COXE,
> JOHN DICK,
> GEORGE POLLOCK,
> RICHARD RELF,
> BEVERLY CHEW,
> CARLISLE POLLOCK,
> Not. Pub

I certify the foregoing to be a true copy of the original act, extant in my current notarial records

In faith whereof I grant these presents, under my hand and the [LS [impress of my seal of office, at New Orleans, on the twenty-ninth day of May, A D 1849.

> JOHN E HOLLAND, Notary Public

[8] Whereas, divers causes exist, (and especially the fire, by which the books of Mr D W C were burnt), to prevent an exact settlement of accounts between him and his partner, D C., and both being impressed with the fullest confidence in each

other, and desirous to avoid the trouble of a tedious investigation of accounts, they agree to the following articles, viz.

1. That after the payment of their joint debts, and a settlement
of accounts with the house of Chew & Relf, the remaining joint
stocks shall be equally divided between them, without reference
to the expenditures of either, or the state of their private accounts.

The joint landed property of D W C and D C., consisting
of the following tracts of land, shall be disposed of as soon as
possible, viz

52,000 arpents in the Ouachita, bought of Mons Boulignv
40,000   "   more or less, bought of Mr Filhiol & Co, with
           the house of Chew & Relf, one lot in the city of New
           Orleans, near the Rope Walk
120,000 arpents in West Florida, bought of Thomas Urquhart,
           George Pollock and Gilberto Andry
15,000 arpents more or less on the Bayou of the Rapides,
           bought of Miller and Fulton.
4,250 arpents in the Atakapas, being half of the Fusilier
           tract, bought of Gaspar Debuys
3,200 arpents in Opelousas, bought of widow Brunet
3,200   do   do   bought of Mons Gradenego
1,600   do   do.   bought of Mons Broutin.
200 arpents, more or less, on the right bank of the Missis-
           sippi, above the mouth of the Fourche, bought of
           Mons Ducourneau
240 arpents, more or less, on the Bayou of the Fourche,
           bought of Thos Dunford, agent of Mr Yarborough
1,163 arpents in the Mississippi Territory, bought of Fran-
           cisco Riaño.
1,000 acres in the Government of Baton Rouge on Bayou
           Sarah, granted to D C
1,000 arpents on Water's of Thompson's Creek, bought of
           J. Deville.
1,000 arpents on Water's of do, and the Amite, bought of
           Mons Mangey
2,500 arpents on the Missouri, granted to D C, being half
           of the original grant, the other half being, by agree-
           ment, given to John Watkins for locating and survey-
           ing
1,4000 arpents, more or less, in the neighborhood of St. Louis,
           bought of Mons Delassus.

Half of a tract of about 250 arpents on the Bayou Road,
bought in company with John Watkins, of Dñ Nicolas Maria
Vidal, and Mons. Blanc, with half of the slaves belonging to
said estate.

Half of a tract at the Terre aux Bœufs, in the Territory of Orleans bought in company with the Chevalier Delacroix

2 That after the pressure of their present debts is relieved, no shipments shall be made nor speculations entered into by either of the parties neither shall it be lawful for either from this date, to appropriate out of their joint stock, for his separate use, any greater sum than is necessary for his decent support, and maintenance of his family N B This is a rough copy of a fair draft hereof, in the writing of D W Coxe and which is in the hands of D Clark

Philadelphia April 18 1807

DANIEL W COXE
DANIEL CLARK

[9] NEW ORLEANS, 6th October, 1803

My dear Friend—I am happy to inform you that your ships, Thomas Wilson Mars and Matilda are in the river. the former even in town Mr Relf has been here two days You letters of the 20th and 29th August, and 8th ulto, by post, have just reached me, and I am overjoyed, that the land purchases I have made have met with your approbation They must infallibly very shortly make you an immense fortune and I will endeavor to add to it, without **putting** you under the necessity of making any large advances I shall now recapitulate the purchases made, and you may confidently rely on my adding to them some of the choicest sugar and cotton lands, in the whole province, which I am now in treaty for and for which I shall shortly have the titles (indisputable ones) in my possession 101,000 acres on both sides of the Ouachita, which falls into the Red River, in a new but thriving settlement, and which it will be impossible to set value enough upon the day our Government takes possession of this country, being on a navigable river, and consists of prairie and wood so that 100 plantations might be immediately settled on it and the plough set to work, without cutting down a tree. This is the country to which the whole of the emigration now tends from other parts of the province

50,000 acres in choice spots in the government of Baton Rouge, between the river Ibberville and the boundary line This country is too well known to you, and to every American, who ever visited this country, to need any thing to be said by me in praise of it

5 000 acres at the junction of the rivers Vermilion and Teche, and on the boundary between the Opelousas and Atacapas, without exception the first tract of land for intrinsic value in that rich country I should appear a madman, in your eyes, were I to **put** the value on it I know it to be worth, but when you recollect that it was disposed of here in a lump, at vendue, as the

property of an Englishman, who failed in London, and that till after the sale, none of those who knew the land had heard of its being about to be sold, you will not wonder at the immense sacrifice which has been made, and of the sum that you will probably gain by it

3 200 acres on both sides of the creek, called nez Coupeé, in the Opelousas, in a rich and thriving settlement, and one of the finest pieces of land in it

A plantation of 800 acres on the Mississippi, 7 leagues below Orleans, on this side the river, which, as you must know, it belonging formerly to Nicholas Duchesne, 2 leagues above Mons'r Gentilly s I shall say nothing further to you about

I have already promised you, and you may depend upon my honor, that you never shall have a dollar to pay for these acquisitions as I have of my own private funds wherewith to make good all the engagements hitherto entered into, and it will only be for those I may enter into, in future, that I shall call on you for assistance, and in no case whatever shall I make an engagement, without giving you timely advice, and in case the payments should be inconvenient, I will always have funds here in readiness to answer them, so that, in this respect, you may act with perfect freedom and convenience to yourself

I shall, in a short time, send you certified copies of the titles and plats of these lands, but at the same time, most earnestly advise you not to be tempted to make a sale of any of them, for the present, as they will shortly bring a much larger sum here than you can possibly ever procure from those who might be desirous of purchasing on speculation and with you there are few only who can possibly have a knowledge of the soil, situation and produce of these lands. Remember that my own plantation, which, in 1794, was called the desert, when my uncle first made a settlement on it, was then bought at $400 and is now worth $20,000, and be not surprised, if many of the present purchases should shortly be of equal value

I am now in treaty for a settled plantation, with 200 acres of land cleared, and under fence, on the Mississippi, with a front of 2 miles and a depth of half a league   I will honestly and ingenuously confess to you, that nothing, but the shame which I feel in not exceeding the terms of the unfortunate owner, has hitherto prevented this purchase being made.   You know the place, it is Bagnans s plantation, 12 leagues below Orleans, on the same side the river, and dire necessity compels him to offer it for $4,000   Before this reaches you, you may be assured it is yours

I set out in a few days, to look at some other lands, which I am in treaty for   It is unfortunate that I am so well known to be a purchaser, and that I cannot place implicit confidence in the judgment of others, as I might, in that case, only appear to be the purchaser, when the bargain was closed. If, however, any land should, in consequence be raised a trifle on me, I shall have the satisfaction to know that it is a choice tract, and that the money is not thrown away upon it.

I feel grateful to Mr Thomas Francis for his attentions to me, when in Philadelphia, and feel happy in having an opportunity of shewing him how much I wish to serve him. Do me the favor to assure him that I shall particularly attend to your requests to make a purchase for his son, Homer, and hope the boy will have as much reason to be pleased with the acquisition, as I was with him at first sight of him. I am sorry that a press of business prevents me from saying more to you at present. Remember me respectfully to Mr and Mrs Burd and family, and Mrs Coxe, whom I sincerely congratulate on her return, and on the re-establishment of her health.

Yours affectionately,   DANIEL CLARK

P S In order to shew you on what foundation I built my scheme of speculation in the Baton Rouge lands I forward you copies of two letters, which, having read, you will please to put carefully away, with other papers of a similar description of mine, and I am persuaded, you will think the information contained in them sufficient for purpose. Since I purchased, many other grants have been made, but as mine is the first, no surveys will be allowed of for others, before mine are completed and my agents will not choose the worst.   D. C

[10]   N. O, 13 July, 1803.

My DEAR FRIEND,—Forward these three letters herewith, by a safe conveyance, under cover, to your friends in France, and request that they be as careful to forward them by safe hands to Paris. Send them by different vessels. I leave one open for your perusal, which afterwards, seal and forward. They are all 3 copies of the same letter. Assist me, if possible to put this plan in execution. We have just heard, via Jamaica, that war is declared. Such is the report of the day but I have seen no papers.   Yours sincerely,

DANIEL CLARK

[11]   NEW ORLEANS, 18 Feb'y, 1804

My DEAR FRIEND,—Yours of the 21st ult came to hand yesterday. The express mail has stopped and the Post now takes its old course, so that I suppose our letters will in future be near a month getting to hand. I am glad you intended insuring the Mars and Fame, and hope you will not in future fail covering every thing. The Thomas must certainly be lost. We have begun to load the Sophia; she will have about 60 casks molasses, and 150 bales cotton, and you must insure accordingly. We have 200 more on hand, and according to what we may next hear from you, they shall be shipped by some other vessel, or kept for the Matilda. I approve much of your diminishing to a certain amount, your notes at home, before remitting to Barclay as all depends upon our credit there; and I will exert myself to the utmost to relieve you, but with all that can be done, remittances will fall far short of our expectations. I daily expect 200 bales more cotton in town and will use every exertion to assist you, and count on your doing the same; but I much wish to know what further sum will be essentially necessary to forward you after sending off the Sophia before I begin to remit to Barclay, and how long you can do without further remittances, that I may manage accordingly. If after the departure of the Sophia, you should want no further sums from me, I could positively assure you that two cargoes should be shipped to Barclay. Write me, therefore, particularly on this subject.

George is gone home to you, and you can settle with him yourself, therefore there is nothing lost, in not having brought him to a settlement here, which I could not do, if inclined, for want of a knowledge of the subject

general orders you saw published, fictious, they are perfectly

You know but little of Gen. W., when you suppose the in his style and I have seldom see anything from his pen less pompous than they are. People must be mad who talk of me as likely to obtain an office; I never could obtain an answer to a letter, even when employed; and altho' I flatter myself that I have rendered essential services am persuaded I am entirely forgotten. I am not sorry for it, as I would accept nothing but we really want somebody here in place of Claibourne, who is universally despised; he has literally done nothing but disgust the people by his want of energy and decision. We have not even been called on to take the oath of allegiance. All the forms and places, instituted by the Prefect, (à la Française) are preserved, and this will, in the end give the lower classes a hankering after the French Government. Thro' his fault, decided French and American parties are formed. All public business is (in statu quo) as when he came; the very public records shut by the prefect were only begun to be inventoried lately, and are not yet accessible; the poor creature is dirty slovenly a procrastinator, has no knowledge of the world, and out of the gates of New Orleans the American government is unknown by any act whatever; and, if we were not a very quiet people such supineness, irresolution, and want of action would have already produced bad consequences. The prefect, who is a turbulent man has more than once directly insulted the commissioners and Claiborne puts up with it. He has been writing to government that all is quiet, while two riots, which threatened the safety of the town, took place in the public ball room where he was present, and his conduct on the occasions has brought him into merited contempt even with his own friends. In short, if he is continued here the government itself will be despised. I wish you to keep these things to yourself, and not mention my name. It were to be wished that Dallas would come out governor. He is a gentleman, and a man of the world, and I make no doubt that the people would shortly by his endeavors, be attached to the U S, and I wish you to let him know my opinion. Dayton wrote to me lately, and seems hurt that I have not had an offer of something to my wish. The only thing I want is to be left quiet, as I am determined never to hold any office whatever. But, I confess to you, I am hurt at no notice being taken of the services I have rendered which deserved, at least a remembrance by a *complimentary epistle*, on the expiration of my Consulship. As no notice has been taken of me nor my representations, and as my functions have expired I shall not write a line to any member of the government. I am getting my correspondence with it copied and when finished will send it to you, that you may judge what I have done and attempted for it.

Our commissioners have hitherto done nothing, with respect to Florida; they, however, have orders to enter a protest, if it is not delivered up to them, as far East as the river Perdido, and when all the other business is done, I suppose they will comply with their orders and leave matters so. As soon as the estimate of the public buildings is finished, which now detains the French and Spanish commissioners, I suppose the latter will withdraw their troops, and the business of the American commissioners will then be over. They have yet to receive a part of the archives and some public buildings, which are still occupied by the troops and stores of the King of Spain. The Spaniards and Americans are on the best possible terms. It is not so with the Prefect and his party, with respect to us; they are conjuring up all possible hatred and opposition to us, with the Creoles, and thro' the incapacity of the Governor, are but too successful. I have hitherto done nothing for Francis, in the land way, but am going on a tour through the country, and before I get back will make a purchase for him, to the amount you mentioned. Let him know this, and that I am particularly desirous to serve him I send, by this post under cover, to Jon Dayton, in order to save postage, new titles and plots amounting, in the whole to 50,000 acres of land, being the first grant we obtained at Baton Rouge and if you can sell them, without guaranteeing title or for cash on obliging ourselves to refund the principal only, in case of being dispossessed by the U S I wish you would do it, but remember that these are all the best lands, and best situated in the country, and that the small tracts are particularly valuable. I

look on them, on an average, to be worth, at least, 2 dollars per
acre, and the choice spots, four   If you could get ground rents
or merchandize, that would suit us here, I would take them full
as soon as cash.   I have enclosed, with them, a certified copy of
the sale to me, and a certified copy of a special power of attorney
to you, to dispose of them

Ed Livingston has arrived here   I see that speculation is his
object   His manners are pleasing   I shall probably have an
opportunity of serving him, but shall have no connexion whatever, in any scheme or plan of business   Count on this, and be
at ease, with respect to money transactions

In my calculations, I count on your appropriating to your own
use, the cargoes, lately shipped to you, by the Matilda Thomas
Wilson, Mars, Fame, and now by the Sophia   If you could,
for some time, do without further remittances, I would, after this,
send a cargo or two, as soon as collected, to Barclay

By next post, C & R will, probably send you bills on London
for $4700   We shall want the amount of these bills here, as we
are pushed to extremities, for want of collections, and shall,
therefore, draw on you for their amount, as soon after remitting
them, as we can ourselves sell bills on you   You must, therefore, keep this sum sacred, for the purpose mentioned   I wish,
in order to help me out of my land payments, I could draw on you
for 4 or 5 thousand dollars   I am hard run, yet dare not attempt
relieving myself, by running the risk of embarrassing you   Write
me a word on the subject

I wish my mind could be relieved, by hearing the Thomas wa
insured, and for what sum   If this vessel does not come in, we
shall, I hope, hear of your sending back the Mars or Thomas
Wilson   If they are otherwise disposed of, I will not listen to
any new purchases.   I shall prefer shipping on freight

Let my parents know I am well, and endeavor to keep up their
spirits   Remember me respectfully to Mrs. Coxe, and believe
me, yours sincerely,   DANIEL CLARK

[13]   BALIZE, 26th March, 1806
My DEAR FRIEND.—I have this instant arrived here, safe, and
in good health   I am proceeding up to town, where my arrival
will rejoice Chew and Relf   I shall destine for Barclay the
remittances I bring with me, unless from your letters I see reason to dispose otherwise of them   The ship Patty arrived safe
at Vera Cruz, and there was every probability her cargo would
sell to advantage   Have insured on cargo by her, at least $55,-
000, at, and from Vera Cruz to Philadelphia, for joint accounts
of Benjamin Morgan and Chew & Relf   On this subject confer
with Price, who, no doubt, has been written to on the subject.

Let my family know that I am safe here, and that my intention is, to visit them shortly

Present me, respec'fully, to Mrs Coxe

Your affectionate friend   DANIEL CLARK.

Mr Daniel Wm Coxe, Philadelphia

[14]   New Orleans, 3 April, 1806

My Dear Friend—I arrived here on the 29th ultimo, much fatigued, and have since my arrival, only skimmed over your various letters to that of the 5th ultimo, per the Eliza, I shall not therefore, for the present, pretend to answer them, deferring it to another opportunity. I am glad to find that Chew & Relf have exceeded my most sanguine expectations, in remitting to you since my departure, having understood from them, that including a shipment of sugars, now making to you per the ship Mary, they have forwarded to you about $44,000. I flatter myself that this sum must have little or nothing to pay in Philadelphia, and that the previous remittances will have sufficed to pay off Chew's engagements in England and on the continent, so that now our whole exertions may be turned to two points, viz the establishment of a certain and lasting credit in England and on the continent, for shipments to us, and the payment of Barclay's debt, which must, by all means, be reduced to very near the sum which we may owe him, after deducting his overcharges, as by so doing, we shall convince every one that a sentiment of justice and not that of profiting by his capital, has induced us to refuse paying the balance demanded of us I have not before me, at present, any documents to refresh my memory, and do not therefore pretend to calculate with precision, but it appears to me, that since the first of August last, there has been an immense sum passed through your hands, viz $160 000, and I hope, on hearing from you, to learn that we owe nothing more, any where except in England, and that alone to Barclay. Calculating on this, and being desirous not to lose the fall sales, I have proposed to Mr Chew to go to England. to bring out another cargo, or rather to ship one, and then go to the continent, to ship another from thence, he has accepted my proposal, and will set off next week for Liverpool I shall put into his hands $22,000, which I brought in cash from Vera Cruz, and about $18,000 worth of cochineal, which was already here, so that he may have, on his arrival in England, with some other matters he will take with him, £10,000 sterling, and if, as I hope and rely, you want no part of this sum yourself, you can order here to pay as much as possible of it to Barclay, and keep the remainder to purchase such trifles as may be wanting to complete a winter assortment of goods for this country It will be in vain for you to cry out against this measure, it is the only one that suits our present circumstances, and our character, which must be supported and I firmly trust and rely, that nothing but necessity and the most absolute necessity, will induce you **to give** Mr Chew any directions whatever contrary to my intentions in this respect Should you however be so pressed as to make it indispensibly necessary and your effects such part of these resources, say, £1 000, or £2 000 I shall direct him to hold it at your disposal, but on this sacred condition, that you apply it to no new adventure as I will not consent or agree that any new one shall be attempted from your port, unless in cooperation with us here, until our debts are paid off when that is done, I care not what you do with the balance of our property Sell the shipping that remain, as I never will be brought to believe but they are a dead loss to us. as for instance, the New York will be here, perhaps, in June, there is then no freight to be had, and little or no produce but at an enormous price, no matter, she must be loaded to avoid the shame of sending away an empty ship and off she goes, to sell a cargo at a loss in a foreign country It is time to put an end to these things, sell her, and sell the Thomas Wilson and sell the Nancy & Katy I have sold the William Wright, and will sell the others as soon as possible By doing this, you will turn a bad property into an active one, and you will not be kept in eternal hot water, by contracting engagements to keep these vessels afloat Indeed, I now calculate, that in future you will undertake nothing, but in co-operation with us to aid our plans and not to keep us, as hitherto, the mere whippers in to such business as you would entrust to us I have enquired of C & R. what further sums they would probably have to remit to you and they assure me that between this and the first of July they cannot count on more than $20,000 I mention this that you may know what to look for There will, however be a shipment of about $55,000 worth of cochineal made, from Vera Cruz, in the ship Patty, by Robert Chew, and as we have advanced two-thirds of the first cost, you will receive two-thirds of the proceeds of it when it reaches you, and you ought, therefore, in concert with Price, to have this sum insured, at and from Vera Cruz to Philadelphia, per the Patty, Captain Lawson, and as she is a dull sailer you may expect her to be boarded, you ought, therefore, to take special care to have this property covered against every possible risk, although you should give a high premium, which the profit on the outward bound cargo will permit you to do, as it will be considerable. You know what risks are to be guarded against, as she went with one of Craig's Permissions, but she will, I am firmly persuaded, have no other property on board, at her return, but the proceeds of the shipment from hence, for accounts of Benjamin Morgan and

Chew & Relf, and some funds of Craig, for which she took bills on the Treasury, drawn in Pensacola, for the cargo of flour delivered there. I directed Robert Chew, before I left Vera Cruz, to ship no more than the amount of the first cost of his cargo, and leave the balance for another opportunity, being unwilling to expose all at one risk, and this risk should, by all possible means be guarded against. I urge this, for fear, in case of accident, the knowledge of the ship going to Vera Cruz in virtue of a special permission should be alleged by the underwriters as a reason for not paying the loss.

The amount of your shipment of sail cloth and copper shall be made to you in due time, as well as any thing else I may order on that way. For God's sake, do not neglect providing the ropewalk with yarns, I do not count on receiving any from Ormsby, as I formerly expected. Let my family know I am well, and present me respectfully to Mrs Coxe, to Mr and Mrs Bird and family.

Yours affectionately,   DANIEL CLARK

P S.—We daily look for the Caroline, whose cargo of logwood will be kept for the New York, which vessel we shall endeavor to fill up with an assorted cargo of sugar, tobacco, and cotton, and send to some port of the continent, to have the proceeds of the cargo held at Chew's disposal.

Memoranda of remittances made to D W C, since 1st August, 1805.

Shipment from Havana,	$17 500 lost,	$45,000
Appropriation from the Sally's cargo, returned,		15,000
Proceeds of insurance per the Eliza Claiborne,		15,000
Remittances in Post Notes,		2 000
do	in G T Philips' bills,	12,000
do	in 1100 bales sugar	22,000
do	in bill on Thibaut, (ab't)	,750
Remitted by C & R since my last trip to Vera Cruz, including therein a shipment of sugars now making,		44,000
		$155,750

Exclusive of Turner's remittances, and logwood from Campeachy, per Nancy & Katy and shipment of sugars to Bordeaux.

MR DANIEL WM COXE, Philadelphia

[15]   NEW ORLEANS, 17 April, 1806.

MY DEAR FRIEND.—I was somewhat unwell last postday, and therefore did not write to you. I have no letter from you by this post, and having been very busy since my arrival, in arranging one thing or another, have not set myself fairly down to write to you on the subject of our affairs generally. Next week, however, I shall do it   Chew will proceed to Europe we shall ship the cochineal to England, and lay out the funds as may be most advantageous, but on this subject I shall advise with you at length

I brought with me from Vera Cruz but about $22 000 on our own account, including in it $5,000 for the schooners, which I sold deliverable here   the balance of the funds was for the friends concerned in the former expeditions and I have still there $30,000 independent of the Patty's cargo They had however, here, about $20 000 worth of cochineal and they permitted me to make use of it, which I do, to forward our business and if I hear from you that insurance can be effected, and in case of loss by capture, that the amount will be recovered, I shall make another dash that way, to finish our *shopkeepers* a great many of which we have run off at good prices by the Patty

I have now to talk to you about an affair which concerns myself.

When I purchased about eighteen months since a tract of land on the Mississippi, it was my intention to bring all my negroes down immediately and set them there to work, to try to make sugar I cannot effect my purpose for two or three years, as the place must first be cleared, part of my people are there at work, for that purpose   A friend of mine, who had a large cleared plantation on the opposite side, sold it yesterday, with a number of slaves and the purchaser wishes me to take an interest in it, as I can afford to put a number of negroes on it, who will otherwise have but little to do, and by this means the interest of both will be advanced his, by getting an additional number of slaves to work the land , and mine, by getting land already cleared, for my hands to work on and this will suit me the better, as the instalments are at very distant periods and I shall be able to pay for the whole out of my own crops and the two places being directly opposite to each other, I shall be able to attend to both whenever I retire from business   To make this purchase, I wish for your consent as without it you might perhaps blame me or think I had invested any of our joint funds in a purchase on my private account, and the reason why I do not propose the thing on our joint account is, that the concern of each would be then trifling, and as the stock of slaves and cattle will be drawn from my other plantations, and the payments made out of my own crops, it would be next to impossible to keep a regular account of the plantation business between us Capt Turner, of Natchitoches, is the person who proposes the business to me, and if you consent to the purchase, you will, in your answer, mention a purchase to be made of, or on joint account with him

You have often in your letters, expressed a wish that we should jointly own a sugar estate, and I likewise wish it were the case, but we cannot pretend to do it, whilst more than our capital is already involved in other lands and shipping, and whilst we are engaged in trade. I will agree to make an immediate purchase of the best sugar estate to be sold here, on our joint account, provided you agree to leave off business at the expiration of our partnership, and that you permit me to apply to the payment of it, all such lands as we have at our disposal, after paying our present debts, till the plantation is paid for; but we cannot expect to get a good estate, with any number of slaves to make a revenue worth while, under $100,000, one-third of which we must consent to pay down and the balance in one, two, and three years after; the cash part it would be impossible for us to disburse, unless you could get a loan in your city for a few years, at a reasonable interest; this we could repay on a settlement of our business, and on a sale of our other property; and I beg you will write me without delay your intentions on the subject, as sugar lands are daily growing in value, and in a few months there will not be a single acre fit for sugar to be had, at any rate whatever.

The small plantation which about two years ago I recommended to Edward Burd, Jr., to purchase for $12,000, was sold in February of last year for $16,000 to James Brown, and he can now get $32,000 for it, when he pleases.

You will, perhaps, be surprised from this representation, that I sold the sugar estate we were concerned in with Bellechasse, but when you consider that to make it productive we should have had to erect sugar works which would cost $10,000, and buy twenty more slaves, which would have cost us a further $10,000, that we should have to make the whole disbursements while another derived half the benefits from it, and that at the time of the sale our credit would have been totally lost, without a stop to all further disbursements and without fascinating the eyes of the multitude by dazzling them with a great sale, you will allow that I did well to prefer present safety to future advantages.

The $100,000 laid out on a sugar estate with good management would annually give us a revenue of $25,000 while the principal would be increasing in value and we should pay, perhaps, near a half of the sum by the use of the place, before the credit was expired. But the thing is not to be done by halves, it must be followed up constantly, and if a few slaves are wanting they must be procured without delay. A beautiful place of this kind is now offered for sale, within four leagues of the city, on the upper side, it could probably be had for $85,000 payable $30,000 in cash and the remainder in three years, without interest; it has 54 slaves, and a beautiful set of works, but it will require thirty more negroes to get in the present crop, which would probably pay $15,000 of the purchase, after deducting all expenses

Could you borrow of Mr Burd, on our joint account and on our joint responsibility this sum, say $30,000 ? if you can. I will make the purchase, and we can give him a security on property to ten times the amount, but if the thing is done, it must be made known to me by return of post, or with as little delay as possible, and I must get authority to draw for the sum wanted We owe nothing here, and our whole landed property is free from any embarrassment whatever My landed property, and 140 slaves in the Mississippi Territory are likewise free of all incumbrances, except the annuity of $2,000 to my aunt, and that property alone, which is worth $250,000, I should engage to mortgage to Mr Burd, till the whole of the debt was cancelled I shall be impatient till I hear from you on these two subjects

Your sincere friend,　　　　DANIEL CLARK

Daniel Wm Coxe, Esq, Philadelphia

P S—People are running mad here, after Florida lands as soon as that business is settled by a cession to the U S, the whole of ours in that quarter will be worth from two to three dollars per acre The 50,000 acres, of which the patents are in your possession are the cream of the whole country, especially, the 12,000 acres on the east of the Amit If you make a sale of any of them, attend to this this last parcel is worth any sum you can in conscience ask for them

[12]　　　　　　　　Duplicate.

My Dear Friend,—I have this day put on board the Labooner a further quantity of *Bills at Sight*, amounting to $7,000, of which I advise you　　　　　Your's sincerely,
　　　　　　　　　　　　DANIEL CLARK

Vera Cruz, 15 March, 1806
Daniel W Coxe, Esq., Philadelhpia.

[16]　　　　　　　　New Orleans, 15 May, 1806

My Dear Friend —I have received your letter of the 4th ult . and feel what you must have suffered on the occasion mentioned in it Against these losses and sufferings we must bear up with fortitude, and must endeavor to repair them , but as it appears that in some matters ill luck has been against us, we must endeavor by all possible means to guard against its ill effects, and leave as little as we can exposed to chance I shall, by next week write you fully on our affairs here, and will forward you a statement, to show what we have to depend on here, in the mean time, guard against every sea risk, by insurance, that you can possibly cover, and do not expose us at this critical moment, to any new losses by even a moment's delay. Robert Chew was to sail on the 2d inst., in the Patty, for Philadelphia, and would take with him at least $50,000 worth of produce, of which two-thirds would be at your disposal, and I most earnestly and solemnly conjure you not to hesitate a moment in effecting insurance on it, as the loss of that sum might be more prejudicial to us at the present moment, than we can calculate. On this subject I have already written to you, and can say nothing new about it. Of these two-thirds of the produce, one-half is ours and the other half will remain with you to repay me the advance of the first cost, so that if you should be obliged to re-ship it and a loss should occur we can only lose what occurs on our one-third part. It will be proper you should, without delay, send me an affidavit made before the Spanish consul, respecting the loss of the titles for the 50,000 acres of land in Florida, granted to Thomas Urquhart in 1803 that I may obtain copies thereof, by a new application for them.

If it should be possible for you, I would thank you to send me a copy of your account with Turner, that I may have some idea of it.

The vessel which is to take the sail cloth, cordage, and copper, is arrived at Pensacola, and I daily look for her here, with the amount in cash which I shall forward you without delay.

Chew sails to-morrow, and will make use of the funds he takes with him to pay off our European engagements, that is to say, those contracted by himself; but with respect to Barclay, he will do nothing till he hears from you, and the fate of the Sally. Have insurance effected on this shipment of Chew's, without delay. The Caroline will go to Hamburg, with a similar cargo, on which subject we shall write you shortly. The cochineal shipped by the Alexander Hamilton, *is for account of our friends*, but the proceeds are to be disposed of for us, and we destine them to pay off Chew's shipment per the Brutus. We shall do all in our power to relieve you and I entreat you will get Mr. Burd to step forward to assist you, as we can most amply secure him. I feel thankful in the highest degree for that he has already done and request you will mention my gratitude for his kindness to us. I shall, without delay, proceed to sell off all the lands or lots we own jointly, in this country, except the Florida lands that we may be the better able to meet our engagements.

Your affectionate friend, DANIEL CLARK

Mr. Daniel Wm Coxe, Philadelphia.

Received about 15th July.

[17]   New Orleans, 11th June, 1806

My Dear Friend.—We have just heard of the arrival of the ship New York in the river, of that of the Sally at Antwerp, and of

Robert Chew being off the Havana, on the 24th ult, in the ship
Patty, bound for your port   The arrival of the latter with you,
would give me infinite pleasure, as the remittance he takes with
him would, I trust, *entirely relieve you from all embarrassments,*
and might probably put it in your power to appropriate a sum
equal to that lot in the Roebuck, to replace it ,—at any rate, I
shall be happy to learn that it will pay off the balance of your home
engagements, and permit us at last to breathe   For the ship
Mars, we have about 250 hogsheads prime tobacco, and about
100 tons logwood, we should have sold the whole of the latter
had it been possible, and would have remitted you the amount,
but we could not effect a sale, and we are, therefore, under the
necessity of shipping it for a market   I shall propose to Captain
George to take it on the ships account at the current price, as
there is but little freight, and indeed I do not know how we are
to complete the loading of this vessel   I most sincerely wish
that she were sold, that we might not be under the necessity of
running risks to give her freights   Chew & Relf have, doubtless,
informed you of Mr Chew's departure, and that the Caroline is
nearly ready to follow him   I request you will have insurance
effected on both these vessels, that we may not incur any further
losses   Barclays directions to the House at Antwerp, must
injure us, and I much fear the consequence of Willinks
attachment of that property will be a total loss of our credit
with him   Mr Chew's going there will be the only measure
that can possibly relieve us, and I long to learn that he has got
safe to Europe   I am uneasy at never having heard of the
arrival of the Hunter with you, nor that you had effected insurance on her   I hope, notwithstanding, she has got safely in,
and that her sugars, and those by the ship Mary, have sold to
advantage

   June 12th —Your letters of 26th of April 3, and 10th May,
have just reached me, and I am happy to hear of the arrival of
the Hunter, as her cargo of sugars, even sold at the price you
quote them, must pay a handsome freight   You mention, as if
with regret, that we did not ship dollars, but when you reflect
that we always mean for the best, you should not find amiss that
we prefer, when we have it in our power, to send anything to
you, to avail ourselves of the first opportunity, rather than wait
It may so happen we can send Bills by Post when there is no
vessel ready, and in the case of the Hunter, had we sent cash,
we could not have got her a freight   You will be induced rather
to approve of what we have done, than find fault with what you
think might be better effected

   I am happy to learn that you are likely to recover your insurance per the Mars

   If you should think proper to give Mr. Chew orders to defer

paying the £10,000 17s to Barclay which I wished paid him
out of the funds now going forwards, I must insist on their being
left in safe hands in Europe subject to that payment when
you and he shall come on terms, but I never will consent or
agree that the same be risked or made use of for any other purposes whatsoever

In addition to the other remittances made you, you must, I
hope, by this have received the Cochineal of the Patty, two-
thirds of which will be at your disposal, although one-third
will have to be sold for account of our friends in Vera Cruz,
as they were to make payment for their one-third of the first cost of
the cargo in Philadelphia,—the remaining one third is for account
of B Morgan

With respect to Craig, I do not know what he can claim of
us Benjamin Morgan and the Captain called on me, to inform
me that the ship Patty consigned to the former, was bound to
Vera Cruz, had a license to admit her to an entry, and if I would
give a freight I might make use of it I agreed to do so, and
besides pointed out to them the only way in which the vessel
would be admitted, by getting a certificate from the Spanish
agent here, that the ship went there in virtue of her license
this cost me $3000 to procure, and without it, the ship, with the
sixty pipes of wine which she carried on Craig's account, would
have been sent away empty On the vessel attempting to discharge,
some doubt arose in Vera Cruz whether the Marquis De Casa
Calvo was legally authorized to grant these certificates, and
bond has been entered into to prove that he was It is as much
Mr Craig's interest as ours to get a letter from the Marquis De
Casa Yrujo, stating that the Marquis De Casa Calvo was authorized as without it his own wine will 'be lost, and in future he
can do nothing there, and the Marquis de Casa Yrujo can
make no objection on Craig's application, as he sent such authority to the Marquis of Casa Calvo, and in his absence to Mr.
Castellan, who has now that right Although a large sum is
detained on that account in Vera Cruz, it is, for the present,
rather a nominal than a real injury to us, as I wished to leave
some funds there, in order to send another vessel, and I have,
besides, $20,000 belonging to my correspondents there in my
hands, which I shall not remit to them until this affair is concluded, as they being one-third interested must be at one-third
of the inconvenience It was always well understood by me
that the duties on the outward bound cargo from here must be
paid in Spain We did not pay any in Vera Cruz, and we shall
have the advantage of paying them in pesos sencillos, instead
of pesos en plata, which will make a difference of at least 25
per cent in their amount in our favor, you must, therefore, learn
from Robert Chew what these dutiesa mounted to, and take

measures for paying them—Chandler Price paying one-third of their amount, and you two-thirds, and if Craig has given any security for this in Spain, you must exonerate him   If he makes any rout he will injure himself, and you may make known that he undertook, when he entered into this trade, to cover all the property of the King of Spain, that might be put on board of his vessels even to one-third of their whole tonnage in bulk, he ought, therefore, to be careful

One thing you must always bear in mind, that I undertook this business with the object merely of getting rid of old shopkeepers, and I succeeded by selling $25,000 or $30 700 worth of goods, which, otherwise, would yet be on hand, and even under all circumstances I am persuaded the voyage will give 50 per cent clear profit   You must keep this in view when any of the disadvantages present themselves to your view.

By last post, we remitted you near $1000 on account of the young Duraldes; their father has, besides, paid me a further sum, so that the bill we have will not be presented   Please write to the old gentleman, who is a worthy, deserving man, respecting their progress, and forward me a general account of your advances and their expenses

Do me the favor to attend to the enclosed memorandum, addressed to me, and let me have your answer, it was delivered me by a man I respect, whose wife is in the unfortunate situation there mentioned.   Yours, sincerely,

                                        DANIEL CLARK

Mr. Daniel Wm. Coxe, Philadelphia.

                    Received about the 23rd July
[17.]   NEW ORLEANS, 18th June, 1806
MY DEAR SIR.—Your letter of the 17th ultimo has just reached me   I am sorry to learn the quality of the sugars by the Mary, and hope a small part only can be such as you describe them I never saw them, except a few hogsheads which were shipped on the bank of the river, as I passed upwards on my way from the Balize, when returning from Vera Cruz, but was always informed by Relf they were a choice parcel, it will, however, be a lesson to them which may be of service   Your last letter to C. & R., or to B. C., for I have it not before me, in which you state the funds he will find at his disposal, gives me pleasure, as I had not relied on such provision being made for the discharge of his engagements, and our late letters to you, will shew that we have entirely changed our plans, and that he and the property he takes with him will run no risk from Barclay   I hope by this time the Patty has got safe in, and that the funds by her, and the Cochineal by the Alexander Hamilton, if you are under the necessity of making use of them, will relieve you from all further embarrassments   It will be absolutely out of our power to make

you any further remittances before next Spring, without very great sacrifices, however, if they must be made, let us know in time, and to what amount.

The Caroline sailed on Monday last, for Hamburg The New York has not got up to town yet, but is, I understand, in the Turn The Maria we could not sell, but have, I believe, freighted her for the Windward Islands Do not fail to send me an authenticated affidavit of the loss of the Florida land titles, send me also, if you can Turner's accounts, with the statement of all the insurances on the Vera Cruz business Present me respectfully to Mrs Coxe, Mr and Mrs Burd and family

  Yours, affectionately,   DANIEL CLARK
Daniel W Coxe, Esq, Philadelphia

P S—Our loss by the fire, at the Rope Walk, was trifling, and will not exceed $2000 in the who'e, though for certain reasons, I have given out it was greater.

[18]   NEW ORLEANS, 26th June 1806
MY DEAR FRIEND —Yours of the 24th has just reached me, and I am pleased to learn that you have no objection to the acquisition made, in company with Capt Turner, for my account opposite to the Houmas Your letter of same date to C. & R, with its inclosures, I have seen and am glad you are likely to arrange with Barclay—be the terms what they will, as it will set my mind at ease in that particular I hope your insurance for the General Hamilton has been effected, as I am a decided enemy to delays in such cases and dear bought experience ought to convince you how necessary it is to attend instantly to them The arrival of the Patty, with you, which I flatter myself has happened, will enable you jointly with the proceeds of the cochineal per the Gen Hamilton, and sugars per the Mary, to get your paper very much reduced as we shall not require for the use of the house any part of these remittances, and we hope they will be exclusively applied to paying off your home engagements, indeed we flatter ourselves your home engagements will be then annihilated, as exclusive of the remittances to pay for the copper and sail cloth, we have forwarded you since the beginning of March, but including the shipments per the Patty and Gen Hamilton, very close on 100,000 dollars The shipments to

Europe per the Passenger and Caroline will be near	73,000
Per the New York ready to ship in tobacco and logwood,	21,000
Vanilla shipped to Bordeaux	5,000
	$99,000

And we propose investing the proceeds of the cargo per New York to this place, in such articles as will best suit, and which we suppose will produce from 5 to 6000 dollars more This last article will be on account of the ship, and we feel not a little embarrassed how to complete a freight for her We shall, however, act for the best, and will advise you in time to do the needful.

You will naturally advise with Chew how to dispose of the funds he has or will come into his hands, we counted that he would have wherewith to pay for the shipments made by himself per the Brutus, that he could pay £10 000 to Barclay, which I earnestly entreat may be done and that there would remain at his disposal 20 to 30 thousand dollars to employ as he might think proper, counting that the funds you had ordered to be left at his disposal, in Europe would pay off the balance of his first British engagements, and those on the Continent This is the state of our expectations, and it is to be hoped they will be realized

I already informed you that we should not have it in our power to remit you any thing further till the next spring, for altho we have a large amount of goods on hand and a considerable sum due, yet we have a great number of engagements which it will require all our resources to meet, until the ensuing spring sales and payments enable us to do any thing further You must besides, be sensible that the goods on hand are those which remain of various cargoes, and the least saleable, and can only be disposed of as people may call for them, and cannot be forced out of store at good prices I mention these things to you, that you may be prepared in time and not count on us for what we cannot do for you, or enter into any new projects in the hope that we can support you thro them

Were it possible to sell one half the New York I would do it without delay, and I beg you will sell the Thomas Wilson as soon as that vessel returns home

I have sold the lands we owned below this place, on the Mississippi, for $7000 being the sum I estimated them at in the little sketch of our affairs lately sent you The rope-walk is rebuilt, since the fire, and I have a hope of selling it, advantageously. The town wants to have the streets pushed through it, and I have demanded $20,000 as an indemnification for the loss of the business, and the breadth of the three streets, reserving to myself, however, all the lots of which the land is composed. The thing is at present in agitation, but let the purchase be made or not, I am very indifferent, as the walk now brings in very large profits, there being a greater sale of cordage, and better management than formerly

You talk of Mr Burd's name being on a great deal of our paper, can this possibly be the case, when the Patty's and Gen Hamilton's remittances are made use of to pay what it may now be on? and cannot it be possible to raise a sum with you on property here worth half a million of dollars, perfectly unincumbered with a clear title, and under our own Government? If it could be done, we should not lose the chance of purchasing a sugar estate, on joint account and stocking it with **negroes**, whilst the importation of them is allowed in this country I am already busied in making preparations for my intended trip, in October, to your country, that is to say, I am busied in **ransacking old papers**, to be ready to answer questions respecting **Louisiana**, and have wherewith to make claims for the landed property of the people with some hopes of success

It will be in vain to think of selling any lands in Florida, till the United States withdraw their claim when that is done, and we get possession, we may put our own price on the **greatest** part of them I remain yours, affectionately,

DANIEL CLARK

Daniel W Coxe, Esq Philadelphia

P S —I have need of the following articles immediately, for the use of my plantations which I beg you will forward without delay, as they cannot be procured here this season

75 pairs of 3 point blankets

120 Negro hats

60 pairs strong negro shoes large size, for men

60 pairs strong do, smaller size, for women

The shoes sent last year were good leather, but the **thread** was rotten and they were shortly of no service I intreat these things may be sent by first vessel

[19] New Orleans 7 August, 1806.

My Dear Sir —I have lately received two very long letters from you, dated 19 and 21 June, full of calculations and explanations These things are all perfectly needless to me, as my confidence in you is unlimited, and if I had it at my disposal, I would send you to the last farthing we own, to be made use of as you thought proper The only thing I find fault with you for is, for putting out of your hands the funds destined to pay off your home engagements which you know must be kept sacred, and for deviating unnecessarily from the plans once agreed on, by which means we are drawing against instead of helping each other out of our difficulties

I have already informed you of our inability to remit **you any** thing from here, for a long time to come, without injuring ourselves, and if you have suffered the cochineal, by the **Patty, to** escape you, you must look to Chew for relief In the **ensuing** spring, we shall be able to send you one hundred **thousand** dollars, as we count on selling, by that time, all the **goods on** hand, and receiving a considerable portion of the **outstanding** debts, while we hope to be able to defer the payment of **some** of our own engagements, for some months afterwards, until we can make further collections

In compliance with your wishes I have sold the remaining half of the rope-walk with the half of the six slaves belonging to it, for $15,000, and this sum, with the amount of cordage and materials sold, payable at the same time will bring us in 30,000 dollars   This has been a profitable concern and I regret from my soul to have parted with it but I saw the necessity of the thing, and preferred a loss of future profit to a loss of future reputation   The lot originally cost us $4000, and the six negroes about $2500   We sold the first half for $7500, the last for $15,000, so that we have gained on the purchase the sum of $16,500, independent of an equal sum, at least, by the profits of the establishment

I shall sell, as opportunities offer, our other lands, but it will not do to force a sale of them—they would in that case bring nothing compared to their real value

If you have made any contracts or engagements for yarns, in compliance with my directions, the purchasers of the walk are bound to take them and pay for them, with your commission, at such periods and in the place where you are to make your payments

Send me on without delay your account of the yarns shipped last year, with all the charges that I may settle that account

Mr Graham, the Secretary of this Territory, who is now in Washington, writes to Dr Watkins, our Mayor, on the 30th June, that he has had a conversation with the President who mentioned to him that our affairs with Spain were on the point of settlement, and he further mentions that the Florida land speculations would entirely fall to the ground   I know not whether he gives this as the President's opinion or his own, but I recommend to you to mention the matter to the *friend* who can inform you, and advise me of the result

No post has arrived to-day, so that I have no letters of yours to reply to since my last

I remain, my dear friend, yours, affectionately
                                        DANIEL CLARK.

Mr Daniel W Coxe

[20]   New Orleans, 4 Sept., 1806
My Dear Sir —I have just received yours, of the 25 July.   I now forward you a copy of Henry Turner's account, as stated by yourself, and add to it a memorandum received from him last year   Send, for God's sake, to Chew and Relf, as soon as you can make them out, statements of disbursements for the rope-walk last year, and the insurances on the Caroline and Wm Wright that we may settle these accounts   After receiving this letter it will be needless to write to me here.

How, in the name of God can I give you authority to draw on England who have neither money nor credit there. We have no produce at market, and our banks having left off discounting, we are reduced to the utmost distress. The only thing I can do is to send you a duplicate of what I wrote to Chew, by last post inform him what you indispensably want, and draw from him to the last farthing. Draw, by all means for the shipment for the Kentucky, as we can do nothing for you.

Damn the eclat which this shipment will give, when we are to pay for it with horror and vexation. I prefer Mr. Chew's returning without making a single shipment rather than you should be embarrassed. Draw on him, therefore, for every thing he can command.

You are much mistaken in your judgment of Relf, who is, in my opinion not only a good merchant, but possessed of great capacity and fully equal to any thing which can be entrusted to him.

It is laughable to hear you talk of our tobacco shipment per the New York. Do you think it was a matter of choice? was not that ship here at a moment when there was no other produce in market and with what could she have been otherwise loaded? One of two things she must either have taken, the tobacco, or remained here idle 4 or 5 months. I shall, however, act wiser another time, and will burn her and every other we own, as they return to port, rather than load them, in future, if freights can not be procured for them. Had you done this, instead of sending her to Cadiz it would have saved the loss on the tobacco at present.

It has always been impossible for us to lay up any produce, to wait for opportunities to ship it. You who know so well how we have lived by our invention, for years past, ought to be ashamed to write to me in this loose manner.

Yours, sincerely
DANIEL CLARK

P S —What is become of the Patty's business? have you totally lost sight of it? why do not you send me the certificates to cancel the bonds at Vera Cruz? I have a licence, and could easily bring home the balance of our money. I have not heard in answer to the line I wrote you for my negroes clothing.

Mr Daniel W Coxe

[21] NEW ORLEANS, 12th September, 1806.

Dear Sir—I have received yours of the 1st, and have seen that of the 8th, to Chew & Relf. You may perceive, by my letters, that I let no opportunity slip of selling our lands, that the Ropewalk and tract, bought of Francis, are already disposed of. The bank stock I hold, was necessary to ensure my re-election, without risk, as a Bank director, as the directors, by taking up a considerable number of shares, and voting one for the other, were then certain of their election, and the funds to pay for it being borrowed at a less interest than the dividend received, there was a clear gain of about 5 per cent on the amount. It shall, however, be sold, and our accommodations paid with it as soon as possible. They have been and are very considerable, as you may imagine from the remittances made you. I approve of your settlement with Barclay, and only regret that you did not leave Chew to pay him, it would have saved you from embarrassment and avoided the necessity of the purchase of the Kentucky, and cargo, the amount of which you must draw for as wanted, as I cannot possibly remit you a cent from hence, until after the new crop comes to market, and payments are made us

The reason why we invoice cargoes and get them ensured at the long price, is the fear, lest they should be stopped and carried into Halifax, in which case, we should have to return the drawbacks, as is the case with 2 or 3 of our merchants, who have met with this misfortune. Let this put an end to remarks on it, in future, you shall know the short and long ones, and can manage accordingly

I would rather, Mr. Chew should return without a cent, with our debts paid, than leave you embarrassed, and bring out large cargoes. Draw on him, therefore, to the last cent he may have, when you know what it is, and get yourself out of all trouble at once.

I know not on what you rely, to draw on Green & Wainewright for, and hope, if you do draw on them, you will have lodged funds in their hands to pay your drafts

Should the Hunter, contrary to all human probability arrive safe at Pensacola, and be permitted to sell, or rather not be seized, as I expect, the funds, when they get into our hands, shall be remitted you.

I thank you for shipping the articles ordered for my negroes, as they will be in the greatest need of them

It is said here, that the President is resolved on risking a war with Spain, for the Floridas, or the part we claim of them, if Spain refuses it. This news comes from Mr Graham, the Secretary of our Government, now at Washington.

When Craig obtains the papers, let them be forwarded without delay. I shall write fully to Aretlaga, on the subject.

My intention has been to pass through Charleston, on my way to Philadelphia, and I propose leaving this place the beginning of next month. You may, therefore, from the time this gets to hand, write to me at Charleston, directing your letters to the care of your friends there, and let there be one directed to be left at the post office, till called for, that I may know where to apply to for the others

You mention in your letters to C & R, that the tobacco, per the New York, is a bad purchase. But what could we do with that ship; it was the article that would fill her at least expense, and we were forced to the measure against our will

Yours sincerely,
DANIEL CLARK.

Mr Daniel W Coxe

[22]   WASHINGTON, 6th December, 1806

My dear Sir—I have hitherto no news of my trunks, and am not a little fearful that some accident has happened, which may deprive me of them, if not altogether, at least for a period very necessary to my objects in view. I have written to McDonald & Ridgeley but have received no answer. I forgot, in my last, to mention that all the members of Congress, of both parties, with whom I have conversed, have unequivocally informed me that the claim to West Florida, or a part of it, was supposed to be entirely given up, and in consequence, I feel very much at my ease, with respect to our lands in that quarter. On this subject I have written to Orleans, and hope by the time of my arrival, to find such confidence established in the titles as to enable me to make an immediate and advantageous sale, which will be the first object I shall attend to

I had mentioned to you, before I left Philadelphia, and you promised me to pay Capt Wilson's account. For God's sake, do it, therefore, without delay. A bill is now before the House, to suspend the non importation act, and altho' the Democrats, ashamed of their conduct, kick a little and flounce about repealing or suspending the act, yet it must go down. I am surprised you had no advices from Orleans, by the Comet, via Baltimore, which reports a number of vessels in the Mississippi, and hope the Baltic is among them. A knowledge of this circumstance would relieve me greatly, as I believe it would be a means of affording you some immediate relief, by procuring remittances, which might be afterwards replaced from another quarter. A number of the members of the Senate and House of Representatives have assured me of their support, in any thing reasonable for Louisiana. Remember me respectfully to Mrs Coxe, and believe me yours sincerely,

DANIEL CLARK.

Mr Daniel W Coxe

P S You are wonderfully precipitate, with respect to the St Domingo business. I have not hitherto seen Mons'r Turreau, I expect to have that *honor* to-morrow, and as soon as I can learn from him, whether he will oppose it or not, I shall advise you of the result, and act accordingly

It appears strange to me, that the proceeds of the brig Hunter's cargo, should not have purchased a great deal more than the small parcel of coffee she has on board. I understood from you that her outfit was near $9,000, and you now inform me that you expect a bill on you for $3,000, to pay the balance of the advance. If this is so, the adventure so far, will be a losing one, and I do not think the sales will pay the first cost freight and insurance.

The act for suspending the operation of the non importation law, to the 1st July next is just now carried. 101 to 5.

I shall write to-morrow, in answer to the questions from New York.

[23]   WASHINGTON, 25th December, 1806.

My dear Friend—I have received yours, of the 21st, and am glad you intend sending the maps, &c, but why, for the love of God, do you not send the tin case, by any of the stages to Baltimore, with directions to send it on from thence here, in the same way. If you send it otherwise, I shall never see it. If you can procure the Leges de Indias, send them, as I am much in want of them. I shall not approve of your sending any thing, but trifles, in the Thomas Wilson, unless you can get a long credit. I think 1st proof brandy will be too weak, and on that account, will not be in demand. There were a great many teas in Orleans, but good imperial or hyson teas, at the price you mention, must answer some time or other. Send. however, none but the best. Bulky articles, at low prices, must answer. I am afraid it will be too late for blankets, and that the Baltic has taken out a large supply, at a years credit, however, they will answer to sell in the beginning of the ensuing fall, counting on $5 per pair for the sale price. Table sets of china are not in demand. Crates of plates would probably command 3-1 dollar per dozen, and crates of pint bowls, and larger, as well as crates of chamber pots, and jugs, would sell, but no things, they must be *pots a bee* Malaga wine, I think, would sell, as well as good raisins, in small boxes, but they must be fresh. American porter, to sell, must be excellent, otherwise it will not go down. I do not precisely know the value of these things, but calculate they will always pay a freight. It is too late to ship flour, do not think of it.

It will be impossible for me to leave this, before the end of the session, my business is just commencing, and however ardently I desire to see you, I must give up the hope of it. The news from Ohio states that 13 or 15 of Burr's boats were seized at Marietta, while he, himself, was about the same time, acquitted on an indictment in Kentucky. Reconcile this, if possible. An anonymous letter from Pittsburg, to old Findlay, mentions me as the chief broker and paymaster to Burr   Have you heard of any of my drafts, for that purpose, or do you know of any funds, with which I am to answer the demands?   Present me most respectfully to the ladies of your family, and let them know I feel with deep regret my exile from Philadelphia

Yours affectionately,
DANIEL CLARK

Daniel W. Coxe, Esq

[24]   BALTIMORE 27 Dec'r, 1806.
MY DEAR FRIEND —After two or three letters from Mr Oliver of this city, and a visit from his brother at Washington, I determined on coming here to see whether anything could be done with respect to the licenses   We have this day come to the following agreement, which we are to ratify to-morrow, viz.

That D C cedes to R Oliver & Co, for their sole use and benefit, the three licenses he is in possession of, and undertakes to give the necessary directions for shipping their property in Vera Cruz though he does not bind himself to claim it•

R Oliver & Co, in return, bind and oblige themselves to receive D C's property in Vera Cruz, and to deliver to him an equal sum there at their risk and expense, provided, said sum does not exceed thirty thousand dollars, but, if it exceeds thirty, and does not pass fifty thousand dollars, then D C is to pay the export duty on the sum above thirty thousand dollars, and R. Oliver & Co are to deliver it at their risk and expense.

If I do not write you to the contrary to-morrow, you may conclude this affair is settled, and I shall give instant orders to pay whatever I may have there to their agent

Our house did not adjourn for the holidays   I set off for this place last night at 10 o'clock, and the roads were so horrible bad, that I did not get here till ten this morning, at the risk of being overset a thousand times.

I set off on Monday morning early for Washington   What think you of my negotiation? Remember me respectfully to Mrs. Coxe and the ladies of the family.

Yours respectfully,
DANIEL CLARK

Daniel W Coxe, Esq, Philadelphia.

[25]   WASHINGTON, 24 Feb., 1807
SIR —I have just received your letter of the 20th instant
Relf has been, I believe, been more frightened than he ought   I entertain, however, no other apprehensions respecting our property in Orleans, than the inconvenience resulting from a war in remittances, and I shall remedy that on arrival there   I am g   the shipments to Europe have such a promising appearance The William Harwood, whose name you mentioned, is totally un-

91

known to me, nor did I ever hear it mentioned in my life   I look on it as a trick of Burr or some of his adherents, to raise money, by persuading that they are authorized to draw on you or me   I shall certainly relieve you from all your embarrassments as soon as I can get home, and, on that account, mean that my stay in Philadelphia shall be as short as possible

I am sir, your humble servant,

DANIEL CLARK

Daniel W. Coxe, Esq   Philadelphia

[26]   BALTIMORE, 12 March. 1807

SIR :—I have directed Mr Stuart of Evan's tavern, to forward three trunks belonging and directed to me, to Philadelphia by the packet via New Castle   I take the liberty to request you will have them enquired for, and sent to your store until my arrival   In No 8, of which I enclose you the key, are two packets of letters, entrusted to me by Mr. Erskine, and directed to P Bond, Esq , I beg the favor of you to take them out and have them delivered.   I have reason to think that the last mail had several letters for me from Orleans   I hope you will receive and keep them for me

I have just received the enclosed   The land alluded to is about 546 acres   I shall make enquiry about it   It will serve to show that our Amite lands are known here

A prodigious emigration will shortly take place from this State and Virginia   A Mr Johnson will set off next month with 100 slaves, and many others are preparing to follow him

If I can sell my own estates advantageously to some of the emigrants, I shall sacrifice future views to present convenience, and return to Europe.   I shall be in Philadelphia in about 10 days   I remain, sir, your humble servant,

DANIEL CLARK

Daniel W. Coxe, Esq , Philadelphia.

[27]   NEW ORLEANS, 29 May, 1807

MY DEAR FRIEND .—I have little further to say since my last, except that we are straining every nerve to collect and remit you The New York has sailed   There are nearly 200 bales of cotton on the Four Friends, for Liverpool, and the Thomas Wilson will be shortly loaded.   With respect to the prices of cotton, I must refer you on that subject to Relf, as all the purchases were made before my arrival   I shall write you at length by next post, as I have been unable to occupy myself with anything since my arrival here but returning answers to the million of inquiries about myself, and what regarded the affairs of the country

I have written to Turner, on arrival, and directed him, if cheap purchases of cotton could be made, to count on any sum he might want instantly   Yours, sincerely,

DANIEL CLARK

[28]   HOLMAS PLNATATION, COUNTI OI }
                         ACADIA, 12th June, 1807.   }

MY DEAR FRIEND :—When I wrote you last, I mentioned that I was on the point of setting off for Natchez, and you must naturally conclude that I have had time enough to get there 'ere now   My departure from the city was caused by other reasons than business, and I shall now detail them.

Gov. Claiborne, stung to the quick by the few words I said in Congress respecting his conduct to the militia, and driven to despair by the flattering reception I met with on arrival, since when the most unbounded testimonies of affection have been heaped on me, thought fit after some preliminary correspondence, to challenge me.   To this step I believe him to have been spurred by one Gurley, att'y gen who has always hated me for my contemptuous treatment of him, and who preferred the Governor risking his person in a quarrel with me, rather than put his own in danger   We set off, therefore, for Manchac, in order to be out of the Governor's jurisdiction, and, immediately on crossing the Iberville we fought, and decided our quarrel, on Monday, the 8th at one in the afternoon   The aforesaid Gurley accompanied the Governor as his friend, Mr. Keene, a gentleman of the bar, and an intimate friend, was mine   We fired almost at the same instant, at 10 paces, and the Governor fell, shot thro' the thigh, and with a most severe contusion on the other.   I have received no injury   I look upon this business as settled, and will return to Orleans in three or four days   I keep away from it merely to avoid the congratulations and exultation of the public on the occasion   You will, doubtless, have some account of the affair from thence, and on my return, I will forward you the correspondence which took place previous to it   Wherever I have appeared since then, the inhabitants have mixed with the proofs of a most affectionate attachment, some bitter reproaches that I should have *dared* to risk a life, which, they think, ought to be reserved for them and the pain of his wound is not the only smart my unfortunate adversary will suffer under.   I have not written a line to Orleans since the affair, but my second will reach the city this morning, and should any misrepresentation of facts take place, he will correct it.

On my return to the city, I shall determine, without delay, on what I shall do during the summer, and will advise you   Let my parents know the fortunate result of this business, and that it will end here

I have found my plantations in better order than I expected, and with appearances of an excellent crop of sugar and cotton.

Present my respectful compliments to Mrs Coxe, to Mr and Mrs Burd, to Mr. Lea, and families, and believe me,

Yours, affectionately,

DANIEL CLARK

Daniel W. Coxe. Esq , Philadelphia

P S. I had forgot to mention, that the secret of the intended duel leaked out in Orleans from the Governor's friends who mentioned the thing publicly immediately after the Governor's departure on the third. This caused me to set off 36 hours before the appointed time, to avoid the sheriff, whose deputy pursued me 90 miles, without effect, and was within 6 miles of the place I was at on the night of the 7th, when he was informed that I had been seen crossing the Iberville but that very evening in consequence of which, he gave up the chase He was everywhere furnished with fresh horses by the planters in order to overtake and arrest me when the object of his journey was known Now that the affair has ended as it has done, they are in raptures that he did not succeed.

[29]   HOUMAS, 14 June, 1807.

MY DEAR FRIEND: I received. yesterday, your letter of the 24th April, and, at the same time the enclosed letters from New Orleans, which have been written without any communication between the parties. From their tenor you will judge of the public sentiment with respect to my affair with Claiborne and if I draw a true inference from that expressed by the hundreds who have waited on to reproach and congratulate me since my return here, on the issue of the business the portraits drawn by Relf and Davis are not too high colored.

You say with truth, that I should be ungrateful were I not to look on that country as my paradise whose inhabitants are so attached to me, and who take so lively an interest in my welfare

I am afraid you will lose much precious time in partly unloading the Caroline, and that the expenses caused by the delay and new insurance, will more than compensate for the profits The skins, especially, will run a great risk of suffering by it.

I return to Orleans to-morrow On arrival, I shall inform you what are our prospects, and will have more time to look into the details of matters Should it suit to make a shipment, I will either advise it to be done, or will set off to effect it.

I daily feel more and more what I owe to Mrs Coxe's kindness and wish that it depended in any manner on me to make a grateful return for it. Let her know I feel fully sensible of the obligations I am under, and that I long to tell her so myself.

Yours, affectionately,

DANIEL CLARK.

Daniel W. Coxe Esq. Philadelphia.

P S. You will, I believe find in the enclosed **verses**, the secret of my popularity here, the services I have rendered to so many of the inhabitants

[30]   New Orleans, 24th July, 1807

My Dear Friend —I received yesterday, your letter of the 5th June That of the 15th and 17th, by the Tombigbee mail, got to hand a week ago My former letters have advised you of the remittances made from hence, by which you will perceive that Relf has not been so inactive as you imagine, and if the shipments to Liverpool have been but small, it was because we had not funds enough to load our own vessels for foreign ports, and afterwards make shipments to England in other people's vessels On my arrival here, I found cotton rising, being at 23 1-2, and freights 4 1-2 per bbl. I did not think it safe to speculate at that price, and therefore declined receiving the $50,000 from Parish, as I am not fond of risk where there is nothing to gain I am now, notwithstanding your late directions, well pleased with having declined purchasing Our political horizon looks cloudy, and I wish we had still less property at sea than what we have afloat I have heard of the affair between the Chesapeake and the British 50 gun ship, and fear it will be but the commencement of difficulties between us   I have always blamed you, on the subject of insurances, for letting vessels sail before they were effected , and I see by your last letters, that, though you had heard near a month before of the New York's cargo being nearly shipped, and had received directions from C & R, to cause insurance to be made, yet, that it was not yet effected. You will one day be the cause of our ruin by this neglect, as vessels will sail be lost or taken, and the news arrive with you while you are thinking of these insurances.   You had, a year or two ago an instance of it with respect to Price's brig, which was wrecked on Cuba I feel much distressed on this account, and I now positively declare my firm determination to proceed to some violent extremity, if you do not, on first notice, cause insurance to be made on all shipments we are concerned in. I will likewise from hence refuse to be concerned in any underwriting, and entreat you to leave it off, and think of nothing but winding up our business

By my calculations, forwarded you at various times, there have been remitted you, since the first of January, from C. & R and Turner, including the 30,000 from Vera Cruz, $175,000.

Turner writes that he has drawn on you for about 20,000, leaving, therefore, $155,000, to be appropriated solely to the advantage of our engagements of one kind or another

I count, in addition to this, that the freight of the Creole, to be paid at Amsterdam, after deducting her expenses, there will be $7000

We shall load the Kentucky, for Rotterdam, with tobacco, as cotton is at $25 per C. and consequently too high to ship, which will leave a further sum at your disposal of $20,000

We have on hand, and daily expect, further small shipments of cotton from Turner, amounting to 10 000—$37,000

This will make in all the sum of $193,000, dollars, remitted you, and must, after paying off the balance due by Chew in Hamburgh, for the Caroline's outward cargo from thence, leave a large sum to be appropriated to the discharge of our debts to the manufacturers in England, independently of keeping $100,000 to pay off so much of your home engagements

I have made a further sale of 11,000 arpents of Florida land, at 1 1-2 dollars per acre, on condition that the person for whom it is bought, in England, shall approve it as the agent was only authorized to treat on these terms, the payments as before advised you This will make in all 24,000 arpents sold for $36,000, and seems to fix a price for the rest These ten sales have stamped a value on the lands which they did not before possess, and give much more confidence to others, as the conditional article of approbation remains unknown

I shall not, if I can possibly avoid it, return to Congress, my mind being made up on that subject I shall pass the time I would otherwise lose there, in collecting, and hope by that means to be free from debt, and ready to go in the spring to such part of the world as may best suit me. Do not, however, mention this to the family at Germantown

  Yours, sincerely,

        DANIEL CLARK

Daniel W Coxe, Esq., Philadelphia

[31.]   NEW ORLEANS, 6th August, 1807.

My dear Friend—I have just made an arrangement with two persons here, to the following effect, viz

To import for our account and risk, from your city, without delay, a quantity of Goods, as specified in the enclosed invoice, for which we are to be paid cost charges, and a neat profit of 12 1-2 per cent. I have received $30,000 in cash, and am to be paid the balance in 3 months after delivery. This is the state of the bargain with one of the houses.

With the other, it is as follows·

We receive here, to ship to your address, 1,000 quintals of Logwood, 220 boxes brown, 230 white Sugar, 70 bales Jalap, 70 do Sarsaparilla, the whole to be sold for account of the party interested, and the proceeds invested in German linens, and other articles, under my inspection in Philadelphia, and shipped here, to be delivered on arrival, by Chew & Relf. For all which we are to receive the usual commissions.

You may, therefore, count on the 30,000 being sent to you in bills, without delay, and the other articles shipped to you as opportunities offer, and I shall, myself, embark on the first vessel for Philadelphia, New York, or Baltimore, to superintend this business.

In consequence of this advice purchase as many German linens, without delay of the qualities mentioned in the enclosed note, as you can procure and at as long a credit as you can get, that we may have the longer use of the funds put into our hands.

The Mary Dexey is arrived at the Balize, and has, ere this, entered the river, she has on board 3700 quintals of wood.

The brig Maria has begun to load for Philadelphia, and will have 1800 quintals more wood for your account.

We will ship on the first vessel for Liverpool, 140 bales cotton, for your account, received of Turner.

The Kentucky will have 250 hhds tobacco for your account, and will go, without delay to Rotterdam, filled up with logwood, at $40 per ton.

You can easily calculate the amount of all these funds, to which we shall make all possible additions, and I hope they will relieve you from all embarrassments.

I have read your letters of 2d and 6th July, and have not now time to enter into an answer.

We can in addition to the amount of the German goods already contracted for sell immediately $100,000 worth, for cash, or a short credit.

Nothing but an immediate war, which I am not apprehensive of, can injure us as by this time our shipments must have all arrived in Europe and I do not see the necessity of making any more. In case of war, our ships will be lost, but that loss alone will not ruin us.

I look on the Caroline and New York, if not the Thos Wilson, out of danger, on their outward bound voyage.

Do not lose the opportunity of making purchases before my arrival.

When we meet we can explain everything viva voce.

Make my most respectful and affectionate remembrances to Mrs. Coxe, and assure her I feel particularly grateful for the interest she takes in my welfare. Remember me respectfully to Mr. and Mrs. Burd, to Mrs. Lee and families, and let my parents know they may shortly look for me. I have heard from General Wilkinson, that Mrs Anderson was at Washington. This augurs no good, and I tremble to learn the reason.

> Yours affectionately,
> DANIEL CLARK

Daniel Wm. Coxe, Esq.

The Kentucky is arrived. We have heard of the proceedings of Commodore Douglas, off Norfolk, to the 4th July. Should we hear of actual hostilities, we shall suspend all shipments, and at any rate, no vessel of ours shall sail till the next Fort Stoddart mail arrives, which will bring news from Washington, to the 20th July

POINTE A LA HACHE, 15 LEAGUES BELOW NEW ORLEANS,
[32]   7th September, 1807

My dear Friend—It blew a hard gale all day yesterday, increased almost to a hurricane last night and until now at 8 at night, has not abated. We have rode out the storm hitherto, without the least accident, and entertain no fears of any accident, until the return of good weather. I am very fearful this will not be the case with the shipping in Orleans, but as I repeatedly recommended to you to insure them, on account of the hurricane season, I feel at ease for the consequences.

I now enclose you a little sketch of our affairs here, as well those we are concerned in jointly, as my private ones, in order to satisfy any friend respecting our responsibility. The Florida lands I have only estimated at the same price I sold the others for before the news of the cession, and I am persuaded that if that event be realized I shall, at my return sell them for double the sum in the estimate. The cargo of tobacco and cotton per the Kentucky, valued at 26,000 and logwood, per the Mary are not included in it, and you may rest assured that the valuation put on all the lands is far below their present worth. I left town at 12 at night, on Thursday, the 3d inst, and the strong and contrary winds I have since met with, have prevented my further progress. I shall be much deceived in my conjectures, if my absence is not looked on, and felt as a real loss by the people of this country in general, who at present, seem to look on me, as their best friend. Remember me kindly to Mrs Coxe, and believe me ever yours,   DANIEL CLARK

Sept 10—It has continued to blow a gale until now. We have suffered nothing. I much wish I could hear from Orleans, before putting to sea.

DANIEL WM COXE, Esq

[33]   CHARLESTON, 29 Sept, 1807.

MY DEAR FRIEND —I sailed in the ship Comet from the Balize, on the 11th ult, and put in here, yesterday, to stop a leak, which is, I believe, in our upper works, and will require but little time or expense to stop. I propose, however, as I am ashore, to entrust this business to the captain, and intend to proceed, without delay, by the stage, to Philadelphia. If I can procure a draft, from the U S Branch Bank, for the money I have on board, for your account, and for Price, I shall deposit it here, and take a draft, indeed I should not have hesitated to deposit the cash, and take Branch Bank notes, but that it is absolutely impossible to procure them, there not being one in circulation

If I can get a draft, you will receive it by the post, but if it is not forwarded, you must count on the money being left on board the ship We were boarded, off the Tortugas, by the British sloop of war the Elk and overhauled rigorously for five hours On account of the drawback on the sugars, we cleared out for Amsterdam via Philadelphia The ship will make no delay here, but, after getting the upper works caulked, will proceed with the first fair wind I do not stay myself, as the fever rages here

We picked up, on the 21st, in the Gulf Stream, the mate and 5 of the crew of the ship Argo, of Philadelphia, in a small boat They had been wrecked on a reef to the east of the Little Isaac's Rocks, and on the 23d, we were fortunate enough to take off Mr Moore Wharton, with the captain and remainder of the crew, from the Great Isaacs, and have brought them all safe here The ship and cargo were totally lost, and we only succeeded in getting the people off the rock during an interval of calm of about two hours, in the most tempestuous weather I have known for a long time, and which continued till we got off the bar of this place further we could not get, on account of the violent north-east winds, and our leak had so increased as to keep one pump agoing. I believe the cargo has got no injury, Inform my parents that they may shortly look for me I hope the Kentucky and schooner Fidelity will shortly arrive with you. People here do not seem to fear an immediate war. Remember me respectfully to Mrs Coxe, and believe me yours, sincerely,

DANIEL CLARK

P S—It blew a hard gale in the Mississippi, from the 6th to the 9th inst, and I would not wonder that many vessels were blown ashore at New Orleans. you ought to attend to this.

[34] WASHINGTON, 15 Dec, 1807

MY DEAR SIR —I inclose you a letter, which I wish you to have thrown into your post office, as I have various reasons for wishing that the place or person from whence and whom it proceeds may remain unknown I have now a subject to mention, on which, if it is not already public, I wish you would not, for a day or two, at least, say any thing, altho', in the mean time, you may take your own measures, as far as our interest is concerned The circumstance is as follows Napoleon is determined to enforce his decree of 21 Nov., as far as respects all ships trading to and from England, or carrying British manufactures, and declares they shall, in those cases, be captured and condemned, when met with This information I have this moment received from the President, who, however, qualifies it by saying that he has not received it from the *highest source of authenticity*—these are his words, but that he has reason to believe that this was the answer given to an application made to the Emperor, on the subject of the application of his decree to us. Believe or disbelieve this, as you please, but the President thinks that it will be followed by a something similar by England. My reason for wishing you to keep this intelligence to yourself, for two or three days is that our mutual friend, Mr Goldsborough is much alarmed at the news, and by this post gives Mr Ashley directions to sell his insurance stock, and as this stock forms a very considerable part of his fortune. I hope you will not give currency to the news, for some days, and even then, I wish you to keep my name and the President's behind the curtain.

Times look alarming, and I much wish you would sell the shipment you are making to Nantz, instead of sending it on and, if possible, refrain from making others. I shall learn, in all probability, something new, to-morrow.

Remember me, respectfully, to Mrs Coxe.   Yours,

DANIEL CLARK.

DANIEL W COXE, Esq Philadelphia

[35]   WASHINGTON, 22d December, 1807

MY DEAR SIR —We were in conclave until 11 last night, and concluded our deliberations by passing a bill from the Senate, imposing an embargo on all shipping in port, whether cleared or not cleared, and all the ships hereafter arriving, whilst the embargo lasts. This embargo has no limitation.

This measure was recommended by the President in a confidential message, accompanied by a communication of Bonaparte's blockading decree, and an answer from Regnier, the Chief Justice, to some questions respecting the operation of it—but not a word of Armstrong's communications were laid before us, and the measure was hurried through the house with an indecent eagerness, whilst Munroe was hourly expected. The advocates of the measure mentioned that it was intended as a coercive measure against England, and it was warmly reprobated by Randolph, Dana, Livermore, Quincy, Rowan, Goldsborough, Kelly and others, who contended that it was a slavish submission to a mandate of the French Emperor. It has passed into a law, 82 to 44. Gallatin mentions that he looks on it as preparatory to war measures. You will now, I hope, acknowledge I have judged the administration right. I shall write you particularly to-morrow. The injunction of secrecy is taken off, but I wish my name to be kept behind the curtain. Shew this to Relf and let him make a paragraph from it in his own way, keeping my name concealed.   Yours,

DANIEL CLARK

D. W COXE, Esq Philadelphia

[36] Washington, 29th December, 1807

My Dear Friend —I rec'd, last night, on my return from the country your letters of the 21st 23d and 24th inst For one of them, which enclosed two letters from Orleans, with two newspapers I had $J 37 postage to pay When you send me new papers put them up two together, and no other paper with them, as I have to pay postage for all packets exceeding two ounces

I cannot think that G Britain will look on the embargo as cooly as you calculate on it I wish, however, that your inferences may prove more correct than mine

I shall advise you, as I can learn what is the temper of the times, and if anything can be done we must avail ourselves of it You would do well to reflect what price might be given in Orleans for Flour, to be shipped to England as soon as the embargo is taken off calculating only on a sale to the manufacturers for size, and as soon as there is a probability of things being settled, I shall advise Reil that he may have a chance of making purchases at a low rate The same hint may serve, likewise, for Cotton You say nothing in any of your letters of the Thomas Wilson? I am glad to hear the New York had sailed What is the fate of the Creole?

What I have now to mention you must only impart confidentially to Mrs Coxe

I met young Hamilton a few nights ago at a party, I wished to avoid him he however, introduced himself to me He inquired about Miss Lea, and as some of the party mentioned Lynch's name as that of one of her admirers, I laughingly congratulated his city on acquiring through Lynch so fine a girl He was thunderstruck assured the company it was not possible that, when in Philadelphia *he* had mentioned the subject to the young lady, that he was persuaded she cared nothing about him, and that she even *authorized him* to say so, or words to that effect The inference I drew was that Miss Lea had no objection to flirt a little with Hamilton in Lynch's absence, and his insufferable vanity had drawn therefrom conclusions highly favorable to himself When he was in Baltimore, a lady asked him how Miss Burd and Mrs Coxe were to which he replied that, although he had been to Mrs Coxe's house, he had seen, he had thought of Miss Lea only Such a fool and ungrateful coxcomb, ought not in the future be suffered to insult Mrs Coxe by his presence, wherever she might appear

There is nothing of importance now before either House When I give you my opinion that we shall have war, I do it on the knowledge that our Executive, through fear of France or weakness, is endeavoring to do such things as will bring it on, and with the unprincipled and base set of men who form a majority of the National Councils, I have little doubt of his influence

Remember me respectfully to Mrs Coxe

Yours, sincerely,　　　　　　DANIEL CLARK

Daniel W. Coxe, Esq

[37.]　　　　　　　　　　Washington, 1st January, 1808

My Dear Sir —I have now two of your letters before me, one of the 28th ult, the other received this evening, without a date　I have hitherto sold no lands to John Smith, as he is entirely occupied with other business, there being a report of a committee of the Senate of which John Adams was chairman, to expel him, and until that affair is got over, he can attend to no other　I cannot say when the first information of the embargo was sent to New Orleans, but suppose it was by the ensuing mail.　I have always given directions to Relf to follow your orders with respect to shipments, until the mail preceding the embargo, when I gave him directions to sell all he might have on hand, knowing that he might afterwards buy in at lower prices.　You reason much at your ease, on peace or war, I am still of opinion that it is the wish of our Administration to have it, and that Buonaparte has so commanded it; and even if we accommodate (contrary to my expectations) with England, France will go to war with us.　In that case, what will become of the cotton purchased?　How will it sell in England?　These are questions you must answer to yourself

I, from my soul, disapprove of the project of shipping flour in the Kentucky, as by the time she would get to Orleans, it will be there at two or three dollars per barrel, if the embargo lasts. it is now at $4 1-4, in Alexandria, and I am told, has been offered at $3 1-2

It is well understood that no foreign vessel, whether letter of marque, or otherwise, can take in a cargo, or depart with any thing else on board, than what she had when the embargo was notified to her.

I am of opinion that England will make a sweep at our shipping, as soon as she hears of the embargo. time will tell which of us is in the right.

There has been some talk among the members about returning to Philadelphia, but I believe it is all talk. and many of those who now confidently assure that they would vote for the measure, would certainly retract when the thing came to a vote Your city council would do well to make offers of accommodations; but I think they never will be tested　what would then become of the navy yard, and other presidential hobbies?

I flatter myself you have not already bought the flour, to ship in the Kentucky and consulted me afterwards

Before I left Philadelphia, I had very serious thoughts of exacting from you a solemn promise against underwriting, this was made to me last year but forgotten. I, however, wish you to know that I shall lose all confidence in you, if you continue it.

Mr Rose is somewhere below, in the bay, when he arrives here, I shall advise you of what is likely to be done with him.

Remember me respectfully to Mrs Coxe and believe me

Yours sincerely   DANIEL CLARK

P S —Send me, by return of post, $200 I believe it is the only sum I shall require of you until Congress breaks up

Daniel Wm Coxe, Esq Philadelphia

[38]   Private

My Dear Friend —I enclose you a publication respecting the circumstance that has occurred between Mr Randolph and Wilkinson.

I have refused to give any testimony in this business, until compelled by the House, in order to add more weight to what I shall declare.

Mr Rose had not landed when the last advices left Norfolk; some little difficulty had been made by the Collector, in consequence of an application to know whether the frigate would be treated as a ship of war of the most favored nations. Explanations, I understand, have been made, last night, by the Secretary of State, which will settle this business, satisfactorily.

I have just had it hinted to me that our Government has received dispatches of the most unpleasant kind, from France, which leave us no alternative between war or an alliance with them, and it is even said that war must ensue with them. Be on your guard. I hope there are no shipments on the way from Orleans to Nantz. I shall write you, to-morrow. Yours,

DANIEL CLARK.

Sunday, 3 Jan., 1808.

Mr Daniel Wm Coxe, Philadelphia

[39]   Washington, 4 Jan 1808.

My Dear Sir —It will be impossible for any one to say what will be the result of things, until Mr Rose arrives, who has been detained at Norfolk or Hampton by some little point of etiquette, or until certain assurances respecting the treatment to be offered to his frigate were given him. These, or what is considered here sufficient for the purpose, were sent from hence, two days ago, but a week or 10 days must elapse, before Rose gets here.

In the mean time, believe, firmly, that our Administration has taken a decided stand, and that Erskine is of opinion that the result is very doubtful. He is even, as he assured me, last night, very apprehensive, and believes that the first interview, or at most, 3 or 4 days, will settle the matter, in one way or the other I, who know the President, believe that he will think all his points gained, if Britain can be pushed on to commit hostilities, or declare war. The point of the blockade will be but a secondary consideration.

Nothing can be done, as you wish, on the Mobile, as the Collector of the Customs, at Fort Stoddart, will prevent any cotton being sent to Mobile, and none can be sent there from the Territory of Orleans

I mentioned to Gallatin, the day the embargo act passed, that the Spaniards would expect the crop of the Mississippi in their vessels, under British licenses. I did this to learn his opinion. He replied that it would be prevented. I remarked on the probability of retaliation, by the Spaniards, on our boats in the Mississippi, passing Baton Rouge, when he assured me that in this case our Government would dispossess them. From these circumstances, make your own deductions.

I am happy to learn that so much importance is attached to my visit to Anapolis, but it is perhaps unfortunate that the conjectures in my favor are so devoid of foundation

Remember me, respectfully, to Mrs Coxe, and believe me, very sincerely, yours,

DANIEL CLARK

Daniel Wm Coxe, Esq., Philadelphia

[40]   Washington, 18th Jan'y, 1808
My dear Friend—I have received yours of the 14th, and have now to mention to you that Mr Rose is supposed to have entered in business this morning with Mr Madison. It appears to me, that the administration is a little alarmed at the prospects of the embargo, and would take it off, if a decent pretence offered This is, however, mere suspicion. You would do well to have this in view, to calculate the chances of markets in Europe, and give C. & R. directions beforehand how to act, and be prepared, whenever the embargo is taken off, of the probability of which I shall inform them, as soon as I, myself know it. I shall write you again to morrow   Yours,

DANIEL CLARK.

Mr D W. Coxe

[41.]   (Private)
My dear Friend—I am very much inclined to believe, that since the news of the blockading decree has reached this city, affairs with England have assumed a very serious aspect. Rose will not treat until the President's proclamation, interdicting our ports and waters to the British ships, is done away. The President says, Great Britain must fall: and between the parties, I

believe little will be done You may rest assured, that the British ministers here have taken very high ground, and that they are not to be frightened by our non importation law or embargo I have been confidentially informed that it is even the opinion of the British envoys, that this state of things cannot last long, and that as G. B has now no interest in treating us well, it is more than probable she will adopt a different line of conduct You ought to make your calculations accordingly I forwarded the British blockading decrees and your letter to me, to Relf, and have directed him to follow your orders

The bills which you sent me to sign, and the letters of advice I have forwarded to you

Every thing which the administration can do, and all Wilkinson's friends, are conjuring up accusations against me, they are all become desperate and can only be saved by my ruin An attempt will be made to expel me, and one of the grounds, I understand to be, that a Mr Ogden, of New York, drew, in 1806, a draft on me, in favor of his brother, for $180, which was never presented to me I never corresponded with Ogden in my life, and the only intercourse I had with him was the visit he made me when I was in your house in Philadelphia, and the reception. I then gave him is known to you I have but little doubt that such is the temper of the House, that it will resort to some violent measures against me, and I wish you to be prepared for it Should they succeed, I shall just see you before I return to Louisiana, and then my future pursuits will be guided by circumstances, and I shall either stay there or go to Europe, as I may be able to sell my estate or not Keep what I now write to yourself alone, altho it cannot be long a secret

I remain, my dear friend, yours sincerely,
DANIEL CLARK.

Washington, 25th January, 1808
D$_{ANIEL}$ W$_M$ C$_{OXE}$ E$_{SQ}$

[42] W$_{ASHINGTON}$, 27th Jan'y, 1808
My dear Friend—I enclose you a letter, received last night, from Capt Truxton, with my answer, which please to seal and deliver to him You know his rage for publication, therefore, hint to him, that if any further explanation is necessary, I will give it to him, at my return to Philadelphia I cannot, for my soul, conceive who he got his information from I am fearful that Relf's publication will do me an injury, as it is come out before any formal attack is made on me by Wilkinson, and besides the half publication of my letter to him will have a bad appearance, of which he will avail himself The whole or no part of it ought to have been published

I am glad to learn that Chew was so near closing our affairs in Holland, and that the Comet and Concord had arrived. The Caroline will, I hope, soon follow them A few days will determine our situation with England, but I assure you I know not what to say on the subject of peace or war Reports and appearances are so contradictory from one hour to another that no dependence is to be placed on them

Remember me respectfully to Mrs Coxe, and believe me, yours affectionately, DANIEL CLARK

Daniel W. Coxe, Esq

[43] Washington, 31st Jan'y, 1808

My dear Friend—I received last night, too late to answer them by post, your letters, of 26th and 27th January I passed the evening yesterday at Erskine's, in company with Mr Rose, and from what I could learn, it strikes me that things are not settling with our Government You may rely on it that the affair of the proclamation is a great impediment, and that it is generally believed that affairs are no better than they ought to be.

Mr. Bayard and myself have it in contemplation to watch as far as lies in our power, the progress of the negotiation, and if we can learn beforehand, that affairs are likely to be amicably terminated, we propose advising you, that you may speculate in the different insurance stocks, which are now low In order that Mr B may determine, he wishes you to enquire which of the companies are best able to answer their engagements, and inform me, as it would be a folly to purchase at even the lowest rate, any stocks which would be affected by the pressure of its own demands Quote the prices and remark those which are affected by the rumor of war only from those which would probably be injured by the losses they have already sustained, and give your opinion as to the probable rise of each, and the amount you could purchase in case of any advices It will be prudent in your letters never to mention Mr B.'s name

I hope you will be able to obtain from Lewis, the paper you mention.

You talk much at your ease of the abuse poured out against me You ought to reflect that I am here among strangers, and consequently, that a great many, independent of the whole pack connected with the administration, may believe me to be as bad as I am represented to be.

Since writing the foregoing, I have seen Mr. Rose, who has informed me of the probability of a war between Russia and England, and that the respective ministers had withdrawn from Petersburg and London. This news he received since I left him last night. It will doubtless affect our politics, and make us take a more decided stand than before

Take care of the enclosed until Mr Keene calls for it.

I remain yours sincerely,

Daniel W. Coxe, Esq. DANIEL CLARK

[44] Washington 1 Feb'y 1808

My Dear Friend —The news of the rupture between Russia and England reached us very yesterday, and the inferences drawn from it by people of different parties, are strangely opposite to each other.

Those who favor the administration look to the downfall of England as the consequence, and a presumptuous adherence to, if not an addition to our former demands may be expected. I am much inclined to think that Mr Rose from something further to hope, will not protract his stay, and that after his departure, our difficulties will increase. He does not hesitate to say that the embargo is a measure he wishes to see us persist in, and I am told by one whom I believe, that Erskine says, as we have done all that was in our power to impair them we need not look for further forbearance. These are my impressions, and I communicate them to you in confidence. I am of the opinion that unless new orders or instructions are sent to Mr Rose from England, after the declaration on the part of Russia, that his mission will terminate without anything being done and the consequences you may afterwards calculate. In this state of things, as all depends upon the turn of a die you would do well to consider what directions you ought to give our agents in New Orleans respecting purchases and shipments, as I shall limit myself to directions to fulfil your views in every point. I shall keep you advised as circumstances occur and come to my knowledge but in the mean time, do not be too sanguine, and do not calculate too much on the pressure of affairs in England, she may become desperate.   Yours affectionately,
                                    DANIEL CLARK

Daniel W Coxe Esq. Philadelphia

[45] Washington, 4 February, 1808

My Dear Friend —I received, last night, your letter of the 31st ult and have to mention, that Ellicott had previously forwarded me a copy of his letter to which you allude. I much wish you would get some friend to enquire of the son of General Wayne what information he possesses, and if any, endeavor to procure it. Let me know, likewise, what the paper in Louis' possession states, and if it is of any importance. The president has this day communicated to the House some further information respecting the communications I made in 1803, which will, I think, fully corroborate all I said in the House respecting the views of Spain on Kentucky, my idea that my communications were not alluded to, and an offer to go to Washington to give elucidations that might be thought proper, all which were unattended to. These documents, when printed, I shall forward to you, and they will show how little any information was attend-

96

ed to.   It seems to be the president's view to lay the whole blame
on the old administration, by attempting to show that it was possessed of this same information, and made no use of it

We have been three days occupied with a resolution of Sloane
to remove the seat of government to Philadelphia, but it will not
be carried   Lewis, of Virginia, proposed that the resolution
should be deferred indefinitely and, after two days' discussion,
his just withdrawn his motion, in order that the subject may be
taken up immediately in Committee of the whole, hoping that it
would be then rejected   Sloan has moved that it should be committed for Monday two weeks, promising by that time to have
documents and arguments sufficient to point out the expediency
of this measure to the full conviction of the House   I think
Sloan will fail in his project, but the very idea of its being renewed and possibly carried at a future day, will put an end to
all further improvement here

What are the French doing with our shipping and commerce?
Have they become their prey?   We have no official communications on the subject

Present me respectfully to Mrs Coxe, and believe me
          Yours, affectionately
                              DANIEL CLARK
Daniel W Coxe, Esq. Philadelphia

[46]   WASHINGTON 6 Feb'y 1808
MY DEAR FRIEND —I have no news or letters from you since
the 31st ult , and am very solicitous to know whether my letter,
containing one for Mr Keene, has reached you in safety, as I am
fearful of unfair proceedings in the post office in your city.

Have you any news of what steps are likely to be taken by
France with respect to our commerce? and do you believe that
the shipments made just prior to the embargo will be permitted
by the British to proceed to their destination, and if they arrive,
whether they will be in safety in French ports, and not seized or
sequestrated?

I enclose you a printed copy of the president's last message,
which I beg you will deliver to Relf

I have no late news from New Orleans, nor anything respecting the state of our negotiations or foreign relations, on which
you can place any dependence.

Remember me respectfully to Mrs Coxe, and believe me
          Affectionately, yours,
                              DANIEL CLARK.
Daniel W Coxe, Esq , Philadelphia

[47]   WASHINGTON, 9 Feb'y 1808
MY DEAR FRIEND —I have just rec'd the enclosed, since
writing to you, and am much mortified at having to state the cir-

cumstances to you   Clay & Serrett we were in the habit of doing a great deal of business with and are well able to take up the bill   I beg you will make arrangements to have it sent back for that purpose to New Orleans, which, being my place of abode is the place where above can be responsible and where R.H can procure payment of the credit   At any rate, it would be needless to attempt to trouble you while here, as I could do nothing to collect payment until my return

Yours, sincerely,   DANIEL CLARK

Daniel W. Coxe, Esq., Philadelphia

[48]   SUNDAY, 14 Feb'y, 1808

My dear Friend,—I am just informed by the gentlemen of our house, on my return from Anapolis, that a communication will be made by the President on Monday to the House of Representatives, on the subject of our foreign relations, and that it is possible he will recommend an adjournment until June   It is the opinion of every one that the embargo will be continued until then   I shall, without a moment's delay, set off for New Orleans after seeing you, if the Session closes as soon as it is said

I am very fearful that England will take some desperate measure with respect to as as soon as she hears of the embargo and I would recommend to you to act in consequence

I believe that you had but 22,000 dollars insured on Bosch's shipment to Amsterdam   you would do well to endeavor to have the remainder effected at any rate as in case of loss we might find it difficult to recover of him   Write to him on the subject explaining why you have not been able to effect the whole insurance, and send the letter to Rell, that he may deliver it and require an answer   Yours affectionately,

DANIEL CLARK

Daniel W. Coxe, Esq., Philadelphia

[49]   •   WASHINGTON, 16 Feb'y, 1808

MY DEAR FRIEND —The negotiation with Rose is arrived at that point, that it must end one way or another, in two or three days   The greatest sacrifices are said to have been offered by Rose, but nothing that he can do is likely to produce any effect, and you may count that the Statira will not make a long stay   Mr Madison as been unwell for some days, otherwise the affair would have been terminated   All now depends perhaps on the turn of a straw, and though I fear the result and that from what I can learn Mr Erskine has little hopes, yet is in the verge of possibility that the parties may yet come to an understanding, and each yield a little I however, do not expect it   I now send you the paper respecting the explanatory decree, and believe you were right in your opinion of it

Mr Erskine preferred giving me the paper to copy, rather than an opinion in writing, which he never permits himself to give, but he believes that we may count on the literal execution of it

Yours, DANIEL CLARK.

Daniel W Coxe

[50] WASHINGTON, 18 Feb'y, 1808

MY DEAR FRIEND —I have now only to confirm, as far as my information goes, the opinion given you in my last, that the negotiation with Mr Rose would not be brought to an happy issue It is confidently stated and I believe with truth, that every thing is suspended, and that he will shortly return home I tremble at the consequences to the mercantile part of the community

The letter published in the Aurora was one written by me to Wilkinson, in answer to one from him, stating that attempts had been made to injure me with the Government. It is rather intemperate, but I see nothing else in it

I now inclose you a letter for Duralde and beg you will send him home without delay I had altogether overlooked the subject, but it is time to attend to it

You would do well to reflect seriously on the prices you may direct Relf to give for cotton, as I much fear that the embargo will continue so long as to reduce it almost to nothing.

Yours sincerely, DANIEL CLARK

Daniel W Coxe, Esq

[51] WASHINGTON, 21 Feb'y, 1808

MY DEAR FRIEND —I have received this morning your letter of the 17th, but my opinion is very different from yours, respecting the operation of the French decree dated at Milan The British blockading decrees, the embargo, and this French decree, must be productive of incalculable mischief and distress, and will, I fear, infallibly ruin all who have any thing exterior to count on I believe our affairs with England, that is to say the navigation is suspended, and that we are not likely to renew it. How will all this end for ourselves?

I am most ardently desirous of going to Philadelphia to see you, should it be but for a day or two, and will very shortly determine whether I shall go or not, of which I will advise you

Yours sincerely, DANIEL CLARK

Daniel W. Coxe, Esq. Philadelphia

[52] SUNDAY MORNING

MY DEAR FRIEND —Whether we shall have an immediate war with England, or not will be decided in an indirect way, to-morrow, in the House of Representatives according to the laudable custom of our administration which has endeavored to surprise Congress into a measure, (by a confidential message,) which would be it over soon be our ruin. We have been on Friday and Saturday in conclave and if Randolph does not succeed in having the doors thrown open to-morrow, I almost despair of salvation. Mr E... her this morning confidentially assured me that he has informed our Government, in words as strong as the English language would permit, that the British Government would look at the non-importation act as a war measure and act accordingly. You ought to be governed by these facts and no longer trust to reasonings on what good and wise men would do; these good and wise men are not those who are at the head of our affairs, and a little time will prove it. I think you would do wisely to give orders to Turner and Ref... to suspend such purchases.

I find there is an arrival from Nantz. has the New York sailed? have you any further news from the Thomas Wilson? I had no letter for you by the last mail

    Your,   DANIEL CLARK

Mr Daniel Wm Coxe, Philadelphia

[53]   Washington, 17 March, 1808

My Dear Friend —I have received yours enclosing that from Kennon. I wonder what he proposes to do, or can do, but I fear he means to take us in. It behoves us to be on our guard. I wish you would get the Felicity ready for sea, in ballast, as I may probably, after consulting you, step into her, and set off for Orleans; this is *entre nous* and not to be hinted to a soul. My reason for wishing her to be in ballast is, that I might call at Charleston and the Havanna on persons which I shall give you at our meeting. After the reception of this, direct no letters to me here, as I shall be with you on Tuesday. I wish you would mention my intentions to no one

    Yours sincerely,   DANIEL CLARK.

Daniel Wm Coxe, Esq, Philadelphia

[54]   Washington, 15 April, 1808

My Dear Friend —The enemies have at length broke out on me, in the Aurora, of your city, and the Whig, of Baltimore, and will continue, without doubt, until they sacrifice me. You may judge of my feelings which I cannot describe. I am now exposed to shame insult and disgrace.

I am of opinion that Congress will not break up as soon as was expected and that the embargo will continue until a change of measures takes place in Europe.

I have had no late news from Orleans, and am extremely solicitous to hear something from thence, and if possible, some good news from Europe respecting your shipments. Hoops is indefatigable in his exertions to serve me, and without him I know not how I should exist.

Yours, affectionately,   DANIEL CLARK.
Daniel Wm. Coxe, Esq, Philadelphia

[55]   Washington, 22d Feb'y, 1808
My Dear Friend,—The negotiation with Mr Rose was positively said to have been broken off on Thursday last, but it is now supposed to have been resumed   It is impossible to say what the result may be I can only give you the news of the day It is even stated that Mr Mansfied, Mr Rose's private secretary, was on the point of departure in the packet, but in consequence of the President's wish to resume the negotiation, his departure is put off.   Yours,

DANIEL CLARK

D. W Coxe, Philadelphia.

[56]   New Orleans 11th July, 1808
My Dear Friend·—I have just received yours of the 15th instant, and am happy to learn the important discoveries you made respecting Wilkinson, as stated in your evidence

I now inclose you an original letter from Col John Clay, of the 2d Regiment of Militia, of this city, in answer to one from me, by which you will find my statement of my visit to Wilkinson's Camp further corroborated   Col. Kingsbury has left Loftus' Heights, on furlough, as announced by Mr Gemmell in his letter   Col Clay is the brother-in-law of Governor Claiborne so that you may be sure he would not go a line beyond the truth in my favor

My last advised you of our purchases until then, since when there has come little or no cotton to town, and it has advanced a cent in price on account of our purchases   We shall follow your advice and shall purchase as opportunities offer.

We are only waiting for your Captains to load, and dispatch the Caroline and Kentucky, whose cargoes are in store   We shall load the New York as soon as she arrives

Present me, affectionately, to Mrs. Coxe, and believe me, ever yours,   DANIEL CLARK
Daniel W. Coxe. Esq, Philadelphia.

[57]   New Orleans, 23d July, 1808
My Dear Friend —I have just received yours of the 22d ultimo, by mail, inclosing Saludos' answer, which is a flattering compliment, and must have cruelly mortified Wilkinson's friends I have again to thank you for your services on the occasion, and beg you will forward me copies in Spanish of the Marquis' despatches, and hint how you came by them.   I have published your testimony, which operates most powerfully, and I much wish to see it published in Philadelphia

~ The Caroline, with 455 bales cotton, sails to-morrow. This vessel requires so heavy a cargo, or so much ballast, that we could get no more into her; it, however, makes up in weight, as the cargo amounts to upwards of 150,000 lbs French.

The Kentucky will sail in four or five days. I suppose she will carry from 500 to 550 bales

Mr Relf took the Comet for our account from the first start, as Bosch, who was to be half interested, could not pay his share; and, if you calculate her freight, to and from Philadelphia, the freight to Vera Cruz, you will find, on comparing her accounts, that she has cleared herself since bought.

I am in hopes the remittances made you in bills by the Felicity, with that from Vera Cruz by the Vanscap, and the shipments by the Felicity and Comet, have relieved you from your embarrassments We shall instantly load the New York on her return Remember me, respectfully, to Mrs Coxe

   Yours,   **DANIEL CLARK.**
Daniel W Coxe, Esq, Philadelphia

[58]   New Orleans, 16th August, 1808
My Dear Friend —I have just received yours of the 20th ultimo and am extremely sorry to learn your opinion of the fate of the Concoral and cargo; we must not, however, despair, but endeavor to support and repair the loss

Relf informs me that the cargo of the Felicity will sell well. I shall see that remittances are made you as fast as possible.

I much approve of your determination of not making any further shipments to Turner, until I can see him. I am happy to learn that Mrs Coxe and yourself are better I am present much engaged, and refer you to Relf.

   Yours,   **DANIEL CLARK.**
Daniel W Coxe, Esq, Philadelphia.

[59]   New Orleans, 22d Aug., 1808.
My dear Friend —I have just received yours of the 27th ult. I see now what I have always feared, that this embargo business would be a thorn in our sides which we could not easily get rid of and I much fear that our purchases will seriously injure us. I would advise you to sell as much of them as you can at home at as little loss as you can, for I much fear we can do nothing further here for the moment, remember that since I left you, there have been made shipments to you by the Comet and Felicity, to the amount of $15 000, that you have received $6,000 from Vera Cruz, and upwards of $3,000 in bills on your city, independent of the $25,000 in bills remitted the day after my arrival, all which amounts to near $50,000, and that situated as we are here, we cannot raise a dollar I do not, however, despair but I wish you to turn your attention to the means you

have in hand, and after reserving a sufficient quantity of produce to make Parish whole, sell the rest at any price to get out
of your difficulties.

We have no news of the New York or Felicity, although it
is said the Julia is in the river. Relf informs me that the shipments by the Felicity and Brutus will answer.

I propose setting off for Natchez in a few days, and will put
matters with Turner on a final footing. I am much pleased
with your determination of refusing all further credit. the state of
our affairs here has prevented me from leaving town sooner.

I inclose you a letter from Mr Daniel Holliday, of Baltimore,
who accompanied Mr Patterson to this country, and who was
to be interested in the purchase of my Sligo estate. I also inclose you my letter in reply; my only wish in selling *this Paradise,* is to relieve you, as I shall sacrifice more than the value of
it, before my slaves can bring me any income on another estate,
but this I do not care for—if you find you could make use of
the bonds you might receive in payment and get cash for them,
or otherwise make them useful in freeing you from difficulties
and diminishing your debts, you would in that case be authorised to sell the whole at a credit, in short, I trust implicitly to
you on the subject, only bearing in mind that I do not wish the
place sold on a credit, unless you can make use of the bonds, as
the interest on them is no object to me. Write to Holliday and
give him an invitation to see you. Something might be done. I
am offered in exchange for Sligo a most beautiful sugar estate in
perfect order, of twenty acres front, in the very heart of the
sugar country, with two hundred acres of cane planted, a good
work erected and handsome dwelling house, which I have refused. I will by next post send you the plat of Sligo, with the
date of the titles &c, &c., &c., so that you can make a conveyance, if necessary. Remember me affectionately to Mrs Coxe.
          Yours,   DANIEL CLARK
D. W Coxe, Esq, Philadelphia.

[60]   NEW ORLEANS, 12th Sept, 1808.
My dear Friend:—I have just received yours of the 17th ult,
and although you complain of the shortness of my letters, I
must for the present suffer under the charge, as I am to-day
somewhat indisposed, and consequently not inclined to write
much.

Relf has just come into my room in high spirits, with a letter
from you, which he says is the first you ever wrote in which you
tell him not to remit to you. I am made most happy by learning that you can, for the present do without assistance from us,
as it would be almost impossible to remit you anything on old
account.

[61.] New Orleans, 31 October, 1808.

My Dear Friend—Your letter of the 5th inst. has just reached me. I am as sorry as you express yourself in yours to C. & R. about the affair of the Comet, and hope, with the documents you must have received ere this reaches you, there can be nothing to apprehend respecting your securityship. We have just received copies of protest, survey, &c., which we do not send you, as Cap. Dixey informs us he will send you duplicates of them. The only thing I find fault with is, his not being particular enough in the protest, in stating the meeting of his crew, and place where the vessel was when he put ship about to proceed for Havana. I am glad to learn that the tide has turned against the Democrats, and hope they will be completely overwhelmed. It is, I hope, the first step to a good and more energetic form of Government, without the help of low intrigue and sacrifice of principle to popularity. I rejoice, from my soul, at every thing which militates against the French arms, and hope that Junot's capture will be followed by that of the destruction of every army which the Tyrant of Europe has now out, or may in future send out of France.

The letters you allude to from Chew have not come to hand. I am glad to hear of the arrival of the Concord, and that her freight is likely to turn out so well. The sale of the cotton in Liverpool is likewise flattering. It is impossible to say what cotton will be at here when the new crop comes in; it is now scarce 16 to 16 1-2 cents per lb. I have not yet gone to Natchez, as I must have gone there with my finger in my mouth, for want of the continuation of Turner's accounts from you, which never would have taken an hour to finish, and I suppose you never mean to send it. I shall, however, wait a fortnight before I determine on my future operations, in case you should have thought of it. Remember me, respectfully, to Mrs. Coxe, and believe me yours,

DANIEL CLARK.

Daniel W. Coxe, Esq., Philadelphia.

[62.] New Orleans, 8 November, 1808.

My Dear Friend:—I have just received yours of the 12th ult., inclosing Turner's accounts, and as the mail will close in an hour, I can only say that I am sorry they did not come to hand sooner. Chew & Relf have, as well as I recollect, furnished $50,000, or upwards, in addition to your account. I will, without delay, call on him, and if I can spare time, will personally wait on him, for his statement. Of the result you shall be advised.

I inclose you an original letter from Wilkinson, which, after reading, forward to Mr. Harper. It will fix the receipt of the money by Owens on him, and a further sum of $6,500, which I

97

knew nothing of. For reasons which I have mentioned in a letter to Harper, I wish you to keep the name of the person to whom it is addressed concealed for the present.

I have, this day, given Relf $3032, for a bill on you, at 60 days, in my favor. You may depend on having a bill remitted you, by next post, for a like sum, which will give you the use of the money for 60 days

I have an agent now gone to see Collins, and another to the Havana, and hope to obtain something material from thence.

We have no further news from the Comet, nor Cap. Dixey Relf has sent an agent to Havana, to see that remittances are made you, without delay   Yours, sincerely,

                                    DANIEL CLARK

P. S.—Since writing the foregoing, I have been advised not to trust the original letter by post. I send you, therefore, an extract   It is an answer to a friend of Wilkinson's, who had proposed a flour speculation   Wilkinson says, in his letter, that he rose from cool Madeira, to drop his friend a hasty line. There was truth in his wine

                                    DANIEL CLARK

Daniel Wm Coxe, Philadelphia

[63]   New Orleans, 24th October, 1808
My Dear Friend —Since my last, I have sold two tracts of land, of our joint stock, situated near Bayou Sarah, but both unimproved and of poor quality, for $4500, viz

1 tract of 1000 arpents, granted to me by the Spanish Government, sold to Patrick Walsh, payable in 1, 2, and 3 years, for $1500

1 tract of 1000 arpents, bought some years ago, of Col. Bellechasse, for $450, now sold to Bryan McDermott, payable 1000 dollars on the 1st January, and 2000 more with 6 per cent. per annum, from 1st January next, $3000

I am in treaty for various other tracts, and have hopes of selling   I shall let slip no opportunity

I hope you will do the same with our shipping and cotton in Philadelphia, should an opportunity offer   I am damnably afraid of the European market, on the taking off the embargo, and fear it may prove like another first year of a peace.

Yours of the 28th ult is just received. I am happy to hear that the Spaniards and Federalists continue to be successful. Present me, respectfully, to Mrs Coxe. Yours, affectionately,

                                    DANIEL CLARK

Daniel W Coxe, Esq, Philadelphia

[64]   New Orleans, 1 May, 1809
Sir:—I have received yours of the 29th March, and will do all in my power to bring Turner to a sense of honor and duty

Should he come this way, and there be no other means left, I shall endeavor to have him arrested, and held to bail; but this I shall keep sacredly to myself until I see what can be done with him. I now inclose you a letter, received yesterday, from him I should have set off long ago for Natchez, had not my presence been necessary here besides had I gone away I must have provided for some engagements which will fall due in my absence, and this I could not do without drawing on you. I probably shall be forced to do so, in the course of a fortnight; but if it should be so, I shall endeavor to replace the amount in your hands before the bills that may be drawn on you become due I did draw on you last week, for $1,225, in favor of Mr. Maury which I beg you will accept it was done on an emergency for the house, and was only resorted to as a matter of necessity We shall nothing by Clay and Street If I can make arrangements, without drawing on you before I leave town, I shall set off this week, for Natchez, and will not leave a soul who owes us in the country without a call before I return. The whole of my crop has been delivered to Relf I must request you to take up my note which is in Mr Oliver's hands, and I flatter myself it will be the last inconvenience you will be put to on my private account On writing to Mr Oliver, please to mention that, not hearing from him in answer to my letter inclosing a bill on you and finding, a few days afterward, that my note had come on here for payment, I resolved to wait until I should hear from him on the subject

I hope you will assist Mr Livingston in the publication he has undertaken for me, and that you will forward him any papers or documents, in your hand, relative to the subject. A Mr Samuel Hammond Jr of Georgia, may probably send you some, which, if he does, I beg you will also forward to Mr Livingston

Your late letters say nothing to us of your arrangements for getting home the sugars from Havana We suppose you have taken the necessary measures on that head, and, therefore, have done nothing more than recommend that your directions should be followed

Gov Folch is now here It is generally supposed that the object of our troops is to take possession of Florida, altho' the Governor's being here precludes the idea of its being intended to do any thing of the kind immediately I remain, sir, your humble servant,

DANIEL CLARK.

Daniel W Coxe, Esq., Philadelphia

[65] NEW ORLEANS, 8th May, 1809.
Dear Sir—I have received your letter of the 5th ulto, and am

as fearful as yourself, that we shall experience many difficulties in settling with Turner It will, however, be necessary to act with caution and prudence I shall shortly see him and will, if possible, come to some arrangement with him Should I find it out of my power to bring him to a sense of duty at home, I must patiently put up with some little delay, and have him arrested here whenever he may visit us This will require to be kept secret Relf received some time ago, 200 bales of cotton from him, which is all we have got this year He was excessively urgent to be permitted to draw on you, but I would never consent to it

I now enclose you an original letter from Wilkinson to Gen. Adair, which, after reading, forward to Mr E Livingston, at New York As I have put my whole crop of cotton into Relf's hands, I must count on your paying my note which is in Oliver's possession, and I hope it will be the last inconvenience of the kind I shall put you to As Oliver did not forward it here, I took no steps to remit him, and I entreat you will settle this business with him Write him, therefore, on the subject

I have lately sold 2 tracts of land in the Mississippi territory, which belonged to me, for $13,000, payable in 5 annual payments the obligations I have put into Relf's hands, and as they become due they will form a fund for the use of the house I have also been compelled to pay a balance of $5,500, due by mortgage on the Bayou plantation, which I have done without having recourse to Mr Relf for any assistance Without making this payment the place would have been sold In consequence of this, the half which belonged to Doctor Watkins has fallen to us, and if we can contrive to keep the wheel going, and sell it out in lots, it will shortly be a very productive property

Altho the sale of any lands, my private property, cannot relieve us for the moment yet it will eventually do so, and any that I can dispose of, I shall sell, and place the funds or obligations received for them in the hands of Chew & Relf It may be necessary to explain to you, how I found myself compelled to make the payment for the Bayou place It was purchased for security sake, in my name, altho' Doctor Watkins was half concerned, and a mortgage given for the sum of $5,500 which he owed on it As he could not pay for it, and the creditor was so urgent as to admit of no delay, I was under the necessity of completing the payment, or seeing the place sold for such sum as it would produce at public sale We now, therefore, own the whole of it, and it will shortly become a most valuable property, the more so, as Government proposes opening the canal of Carondelet. The payment I completed, by making a sacrifice of some property of my own, which I could do without affecting our credit. Whatever may be the hopes of future advantage, I shall, however, give them up, if cash can be realized for them and you may rely that I shall lose no opportunity of selling and that I shall make no acquisitions in future as every thing of my own has, and will be applied here to the liquidation of our joint affairs. I must entreat you to pay my respects to Mr. Oliver which I could have done myself had not the sum I mentioned above independent of my whole crop, been solely devoted to the payment of our joint engagements I must therefore rely on your writing immediately to Oliver on the subject

I am fearful that the latitude you allow to Blas Moran, in Havana, to sell your sugars and other produce for debt I wish from my soul those funds were in your hand We have given directions to Oriso, who had returned to Havana from Campeachy to remit you whatever funds he might receive for us there, which we estimated at about $5000 We are in daily expectation of hearing that he has done so Let us know what arrangements you have made about the produce you had on hand, and your shipping Would to God they were all sold

I remain your very humble servt

DANIEL CLARK

Daniel W. Coxe, Esq

[66] New Orleans, 11th May, 1809

Dear Sir—I have received yours of the 12th ulto and learned by it, with pleasure the prospect of an accommodation of our affairs with England Should it take place it will doubtless relieve us from the state of misery and distress which the whole country is involved in

I cannot for my soul, tell what can have induced you to think as you do, that I am surrounded by people, whom I suffer to prey on me without and without being able to discover the motives of their conduct I may, like others who have need of the world, be sometimes duped, but it would argue an incurable folly remain always so and you may depend upon it, that I have my eyes as open as you could wish them Those who have taken such pains to inform you, neither know my situation nor way of thinking and are endeavoring to deceive you as they have been deceived themselves Make yourself, therefore, easy on the subject of my pretended friends

I shall endeavor to make Turner think that I do not see in his conduct any thing amiss, until we come to a settlement, and I shall then be governed by circumstances I do not approve of making any use of Servoss, who has avoided me like death If Turner does not act the part of an honest man, I shall have him arrested, whenever he may set a foot in this territory.

I am sorry that circumstances should have induced you to purchase the other half the New York We would do better to burn our shipping than repair them   I shall only have this to say on the subject—sell them if you can   if not, give them away   As for George, himself, we shall serve him whenever opportunities offer

I must again most urgently intreat you will take up my note in the hands of Messrs Oliver, I have put into the power of the house here, all the funds I had   I am now about leaving town on a tour among our debtors, and I shall have no resource in my absence   For God's sake, therefore see Oliver, and make an arrangement with him respecting it   should it come on here, in my absence, it might ruin me.

I tremble, when I think of your cotton shipments   and would have preferred that it were sold at once at some loss   Your permission to sell your sugar in Havana, may, I fear be productive of further delay to you from that quarter

Remember me respectfully to Mrs Coxe

I remain yours sincerely
DANIEL CLARK

Daniel Wm Coxe Esq, Philadelphia

[67]   (Duplicate)   New Orleans, 25 May, 1808

My Dear Sir —I have been informed by persons of respectability, in whom I can place the greatest confidence, that it would be no difficult matter to make purchases of slaves to almost any number in Virginia, at a credit of one or two years, or perhaps longer, on giving a security by the signature of some well known merchant in the U S, for the punctual fulfilment of such engagements as might be entered into for the purpose   As the sale or employment of any number of negroes would give an immense profit, I have been induced to propose to you to enter into a plan for the purchase of as many as we could buy in Virginia, and after selling a sufficient number here to pay the cost of them, with all charges, I think a full third would remain to us, who might be most advantageously employed in cultivation, or sold in small numbers with a piece of land, either to the emigrants who daily flock here, or to people desirous of bettering their situation by becoming planters   On this subject we have often conferred, and believing the project to be an agreeable one to you I do not hesitate to propose to you to co-operate in it to the utmost of your ability   I therefore only wait for your consent in order to send a gentleman to make arrangements for carrying the plan into execution   He will first see you and after agreeing on the material points, will afterwards attend to all the rest of the business, viz. purchasing, shipping, and if it is necessary, accompanying the negroes to this place   The person I now allude to is well acquainted with Virginia, and with the manner in which this business ought to be carried on   I therefore entreat you will without delay, write to me in answer, and I shall not, after the receipt of your letter, lose a day in the business, which must be attempted on a large scale, or not entered into at all. I am sanguine in my expectations that at least a full third of all the number, and perhaps, the best of the slaves, would remain to us after paying off every expense and charge attending the speculation. I remain, dear sir,

Yours sincerely,

DANIEL CLARK

Daniel W. Coxe Esq.

[68]   NEW ORLEANS 16 December, 1809

My DEAR SIR.—We have received by post, this day, the news of the failure of the negotiation with Mr. Jackson and it has caused much alarm here. The effect of it may lower the price of cotton which since the receipt of your order has been scarce, and is now at 15 cents per lb. Should it fall to your limits, Chew & Relf will comply with your directions, and will make the shipment you have ordered.

I have received the letter you forwarded from Mr. Delacy, and I send it back to you with a request that you will forward it to your correspondent in Jamaica, to make inquiry on the subject. It strikes me that Mr. Corcoran must have either children or grand children in Sligo in which case if he has left anything, it goes to them of course. My mother however can give information to be depended on in this respect. I am not, however, inclined to believe that Mr. Corcoran could possess much property at the time of his death as I knew him to be embarrassed very frequently although he formerly possessed immense estates, and had I believe well grounded claims to others, of which he never got possession and the claiming of which kept him constantly involved in suits. It can however, cost nothing to make enquiry and for this purpose it would perhaps be well to send the letter from Delacy to your friends in Kingston and if Delacy is what he represent himself to be he can assist in the business. I would not, however, wish to expend any money in any doubtful claim or enter into any expensive investigation for the sake of a remote benefit to arise from it. I enclose you a letter for Delacy which I leave open that you may see it to request his services. When he was in this country, he was miserably poor and reduced to many shifts which brought him into disrepute, and I am somewhat doubtful of the truth of his representations respecting his own situation.

I wrote you, by last post about a set of copper boilers for my sugar works and forwarded you a copy of an invoice of a set similar to that I wished for. Let me entreat you to give immediate orders for the shipment of such a set to this place, if an opportunity offers the very instant they are ready, if not, to Philadelphia or New York   The fate of my next year's crop will depend on your assistance in this respect, and I must again entreat you to render me this service

I shall want, to set my mill agoing, five iron cylinders or mill cases, of the following dimensions

1 of 32 inches in diameter, and 32 inches in height, English measure

4 of 20 inches in diameter and 32 inches in height or length, English measure

These things must be turned as without it they will be of no use, and would neither serve me nor sell to anybody else

Write to me to let me know what steps you have taken in this business.

I also wrote to you for a double and single barrelled gun with their respective cases, and I beg you will forward them as early as possible

On the subject of our business I have written to you fully.   I have my statements nearly made out, and will forward them when finished   I request you will do the same, and give me your ideas respecting the closing of our concern with Chew & Relf, and what you mean to do with the shipping

Present me respectfully to Mrs Coxe, and believe me, dear sir
Yours, sincerely,

DANIEL CLARK

P S Do me the favor to forward a duplicate of my letter to Delacy which you can get one of your young men to copy If he should be still in Norfolk send it there   Should he however, go to Philadelphia, be on your guard against him he is a complete adventurer when here

Daniel W Coxe, Esq

[69]   NEW ORLEANS, 3 May, 1810.

MY DEAR SIR—I have just seen your letters of the 4th and 11th ult, to Chew & Relf, which arrived by this day's post The probability of the property under sequestration in Denmark being given up, fills my heart with gladness ; as when that is done, we shall at last know what we have to depend on, and act accordingly We shall here do all in our power to bring affairs within a small compass, so as to be prepared for a final settlement. I wish you had sold the Thomas Wilson for the $10,000, which you say were offered for her, and I hope you may not have reason to repent of refusing the offer made you That sum would have counted in the pressure of difficulties and would have so far diminished the burden which hangs heavy on you I recommend to you to get rid of her as soon as possible, and at such price as you may be able to get for her. I shall be glad to learn that you have abandoned the Kentucky, and settled with the underwriters for the amount insured on her

You are under a wonderful mistake, when you mention Barclay's affairs The arrangement you allude to was made, as well as I remember in June, 1806, and the payments I wished to call your attention to, were made between that period and November, 1807, in which month, as well as I recollect and just before Mr Thomas Barclay sailed from Philadelphia for New Orleans, I waited on him, by your directions and took his receipt for various sums you had paid him to that time amounting to upwards of £1 100 sterling and I delivered the receipt to you I am astonished beyond measure that you should have forgotten this circumstance, which Scofield himself admits but we cannot tell the exact sum I look, therefore, to the paper and if you have paid any thing since on account, advise me without delay With respect to the European payments, Chew is well acquainted and we can arrange them to satisfaction

You have expressed surprise at the small balance due by Turner The settlement was as favorable as I could make with such a man to whom I was obliged, in a country devoid of law and justice to yield some point, which I probably should not have done had I that gentleman or his property in Philadelphia, and had it been possible to have furnished him with account sales of all the cotton shipments That by the Jason particularly, is essential to us, and I have a thousand times demanded it Since our settlement he has remitted 200 bales of cotton 100 of which have been forwarded to you, the other 100 I have sold here in order to pay myself a balance of $3 600, due me on private account, and to pay a debt I had contracted, to put half a dozen slaves on a piece of land I owned at Coles Creek, in the Mississippi Territory, which land and slaves have been since sold for $13,500 dollars, payable in 4 annual payments, with interest, and the whole thrown into our joint stock, altho' the land had been my own private property. I shall in 2 or 3 weeks set off again for Natchez, and will do all in my power to procure further payments from him

Mr Relf sets off for Philadelphia to-morrow His object is not to come to a settlement with you there,—it is to procure business to support his house, which cannot subsist, if it remains idle You might probably find your advantage in proposing some plan to them at any rate, it is your interest and a duty incumbent on you, to serve and assist them in acquiring a share of the business doing to this port, by giving them the strongest recommendation to every merchant in the Union To him, I refer you for an ample detail of affairs here He takes on a statement of what respects themselves, which will show that the sums due them will about pay those they owe, and the statement I forwarded you myself some time since, will be about the true state of our joint affairs in this quarter

I have paid the sum of $212 for insurance effected on $6.000 dollars, by order and for account of Capt. Andrew Ehrenstrien, on the ship Franklin, at and from hence to Philadelphia, which please to charge him in account, and put to my credit.

You know the anxiety I feel to have our affairs settled, so that I may live out of misery. I will, therefore, thank you to forward me a statement as soon as you can effect it, of our situation. As to what may remain due to us, you may dispose of it as you please, and I shall do all in my power to put it in a safe state, and render it productive.

I remain, my dear Sir,

Yours sincerely,

DANIEL CLARK.

Daniel W. Coxe, Esq.,

[70]   NEW ORLEANS, 4th June, 1810

MY DEAR FRIEND —I have received yours of the 1st May, from Washington, and cannot express my thanks for the pains you have taken to serve me. I flatter myself that Wilkinson's reign is over, and that his power to injure me is ended. I shall endeavor to procure the affidavits you mention, which I shall forward to you, with the other papers, for safe keeping

We had no mail last week, and I impatiently wait to hear from you, to know the result of our business at Toningen, and the sale of the Franklin's cargo

I hear nothing of the copper kettles you ordered, their arrival would be of the utmost service to me. Forward, as soon as completed, the gudgeons, &c, that I may be prepared in time.

Young Bouligny is gone to Ouachita, to have the lands there surveyed, and to sell as opportunities offer. I am in hopes they will shortly sell to great advantage.

What is become of John Miller? I hear nothing of or from him

Should your advices encourage me, I am desirous of going to Philadelphia, but it will depend on what I may hear from you

On your business, I refer you to Mr. Chew, and remain,

Yours, sincerely,   DANIEL CLARK.

Daniel W. Coxe, Esq., Philadelphia

[71]   NEW ORLEANS, 15th February, 1811.

MY DEAR SIR —I expected to have written to you by this post from the Houmas, and have announced the fulfilment of the conditions on which I had made my bargain with General Hampton. I was prevented from setting out, as I had purposed the morning after writing, by his requiring some time to see the property again. I can only, therefore, say to you, with truth, tho if, as I believe, he will deal with me, no difference of price, however great, shall be an obstacle and no joy I ever felt will equal that I shall feel on remitting you the purchase money. My soul is narrowed up and my mind so tortured with fear and apprehension since the receipt of your letter of the 2d ultimo by Chew & Relf, that nature cannot long support what I now undergo. My body is so affected by what I suffer in mind, that unless Providence should relieve me, I must sink under it. I would, at this moment, give the best and whole of the property I own, for half the sum I should have taken the beginning of last week. I have, however, strong hopes that I shall still deal with Hampton.

Yours, affectionately, DANIEL CLARK
Daniel W. Coxe, Esq, Philadelphia

[72] NEW ORLEANS 1st March, 1811

My Dear Sir —I have received your letter of the 18th of January and feel so distracted since it came to hand, as to be almost incapable of answering it. I have sold my estates to General Hampton, and have his notes and bonds for $170 000, with 3 per cent interest, payable in four equal instalments, from the 25th ultimo. Had it been possible to sell them for a third less for cash I would have done it, and would have remitted you the amount. As the thing now stands, I will transfer them to you for the payment of your debts, if it will relieve you. With this security, payable at the State Bank, in Charleston, I hope your friends will have it in their power to serve you, and the more especially as Chew & Relf have given no bills on you. The bonds and notes are secured by mortgage on 200 slaves and the Houmas estate.

The effects of the failures, in New York especially, have been dreadfully felt here. Five or six houses who have drawn largely, have already failed, and twice the number of little ones have followed them. So great is the want of confidence, that scarce a man in the community can raise a dollar on property of any kind, and the reduction of the accommodations in the Branch Bank, and the absolute refusal of all new discounts, have put the whole town on the very verge of bankruptcy. Let me know what are the amount of your engagements.

Yours, sincerely, DANIEL CLARK
Daniel W. Coxe, Esq, Philadelphia

[73] NEW ORLEANS, 2d March 1811

My dear Sir —I wrote you yesterday by post, and have now only to repeat, in almost the same words, what I before stated. I have made a sale of my estates to Gen. Hampton, and have his notes and bonds secured by mortgage, payable at the State Bank of South Carolina, in four equal annual payments, for one hundred and seventy thousand dollars. If these objects will relieve

you and enable you, with the assistance of your friends, to pay
off your engagements, I will immediately forward them to you
It is in vain to hope for any relief from the sale of the property
we jointly own or from any outstanding debts, as the desperate
state of affairs here, where bankruptcy stares every one in the
community in the face, forbids me to flatter you with any prospects but from my own funds, late as this relief may get to you
or how little it may avail you, it is all I could do, and it would
have been worse to have waited any longer as things are getting
worse and property might not sell at all—at any rate let the worst
happen, there is the resource that you can injure no one and
must eventually satisfy all your engagements I have sold without regret what I looked on as invaluable and would sacrifice
my heart's blood, if by doing it I could relieve you sooner

Yours affectionately,

DANIEL CLARK

Daniel W Coxe Esq, Philadelphia

[74]　　　　　　　　NEW ORLEANS, 15th March, 1811

My dear Sir —I have received your letters of the 27th January and 6th February I feel to the bottom of my soul all that
you mention by the horror and distress here are so great and
confidence so completely lost that it is out of our power do anything either for your immediate relief or our own　On your
fate depends mine, and on mine that of Chew and Relf, as the
credit of the one is supported by the other Although I have
sold my private estate to Gov Hampton ever the payments being
not paid those goods can only eventually secure those we are indebted to and I every moment tremble lest some report of other may
deprive us of the confidence of the bank to which Chew &
Relf and myself are largely indebted Were I sure that the
bonds and notes secured by mortgage which I am received of
Hampton would really clear you of debt, I would instantly forward them　On this subject write to me and let me know what
your engagements amount to You must have received ere this,
the bills sent you to meet those I had drawn I can easily excuse your impatience and reproaches when I consider that you
thought yourself neglected in such a moment of distress

One consideration outweighs own my soul in agony and
despair my mother and her family in a foreign country without friends or protectors for God's sake, entreat your friends
to provide for them until I can take measures to do so, which
will be ere long I may, myself, become an outcast but, with
a little time and management there will be more than enough
to pay every one to whom we are jointly or separately indebted
It would, however, be ruinous to them, as well as to ourselves,
to have our landed property brought to the hammer and sold

for cash, as it would not then bring a tenth, perhaps, of its real value

I have been under the necessity of taking back the Florida and as the purchaser, McDonogh, could not pay for them, and I was fearful in case of any accident to him, that we might even lose the property itself If the sum of £120,000 of General Hammonds obligations will effectually relieve you, I shall send them and it will enable me to keep our property here from being sacrificed

    Yours, affectionately,   DANIEL CLARK

Daniel Wm Coxe Esq, Philadelphia

[75]   New Orleans, 22 March, 1811

My Dear Sir —I cannot describe to you my sensations, when I either receive a letter from or write one to you I tremble at the news I may receive and I regret, to my soul that I cannot relieve you The sums due to us are at distant periods, which we cannot make use of and however they exceed what we owe yet we are as hard run as any people whatever, and if the same total want of confidence which now prevails should continue and any more failures take place, in which we should be only involved for even a few thousand dollars, we could not raise them, such is our situation, and such the situation of almost every one in trade here Out of our landed property it would be impossible to raise a cent for the moment, and in case of any misfortune to you or myself it must be sacrificed Whilst we are in doubt and uncertainty respecting you, our efforts are paralyzed, as we are cut off from among the friends to whom we might apply to assistance in need, our only consolation is, that there is eventually enough to pay every one

I have only one favor to ask of you—to continue to assist my family until I can make arrangements to do it myself, as at present I could not remit them a dollar from hence

By next mail you will receive a statement from me of all our funds and resources here, with an account of my own, as well as Chew & Relf's engagements

    Yours affectionately,   DANIEL CLARK

Daniel Wm Coxe, Esq Philadelphia

[76]   New Orleans, 26 April, 1811.

My Dear Sir —It is my most earnest wish and desire to visit you in order to put you in possession of a statement of our affairs, and endeavor to take measures, in concert, to relieve ourselves effectually if it ever can be done To aid and assist in this business I have made some preparatory arrangements with the U S Bank here which was calling in its funds faster than either Chew & Relf, or myself, could collect from our outstanding debts, and a proposal I yesterday made to the board, to give

them in payment of our accounts, Wade Hampton or ?, at
eight and twelve months sight, drawn the ?5 ? ? was
accepted subject to the acceptance of the ? ? ? ?-
phia, and my proposal has been forward ? ? ? ?
You would serve Chew & Relf, and my? ? ? ?
acceptance of this proposition, as, if it is no ? ? ?,
utterly impossible for us to diminish ou? ? ? ? ?, ? ?
as I find it impossible either to sell any ? ? ? ? ? ?
or receive any thing from what is already ? ? Chew & R?
are making out a statement of their af? ? ? ? w? ?
ished, I will either transmit, or be the bearer of ? I c? ? ? ? ?-
age my affairs as to leave the place shortly I only wait for
this statement from C. & R to give you a full and entire detail
of every thing here, and refer you to their letters of this date,
respecting the business in their hands

Yours, affectionately,   DANIEL CLARK
Daniel Wm. Coxe, Esq, Philadelphia

[77]   Bayou St John, near New Orleans,)
                            6 September, 1811   (

My Dear Sir —I only arrived here yesterday, having had a
passage of forty-two days to the Balize, and a tedious time
coming up the river I found everything and everybody in confusion, owing to the fever. Mrs. Chew has been unwell, but is
recovering, Miss Chew is still unwell, but I believe in no danger My nephew has just recovered I have delivered your
letters to Chew & Relf, but they were together but for a moment, and I do not yet know what they think of the arrangement I have made for them By next post you shall hear from
me fully on the subject, as I shall lose no time in pressing them
to lend their aid, which I flatter myself they will do, to the utmost of their ability I have received your letter of the 24th
July, and regret the fate of the ship. I am well, though much
fatigued, and worn out with anxiety Remember me respectfully to Mrs Coxe

Yours,   DANIEL CLARK
Daniel Wm. Coxe, Esq, Philadelphia

[78]   New Orleans, 13 Sept, 1811
My Dear Sir —I have received yours of the 21st ultimo, and
must refer you, until next week, to what Chew & Relf write you
by this day's mail. You will learn from them, not only the embarrassments they have labored under, but also, that they were
obliged to appropriate to their use, before my arrival, the fund
on which I principally depended, and which I stated to you as
the sole resource I could rely on for the present The dreadful
state the city is in, on account of the sickness which prevails
there, and the stagnation of business, will not suffer me to in-

dulge a hope of doing any thing effectual to relieve you, until Chew & Relf can come to my assistance but whatever I may receive shall be solely destined for you Chew & Relf informed me on arrival that they had advised you of the failure of the house of Corral o Vera Cruz, which owed them $11,000, and on which they had counted to stop the breach, for which they had to apply to the Louisiana Bank, this with the loss sustained in the Wave sent to Havana, will diminish my resources considerably I shall set off, to make a tour through the country, to see all those who owe me, in the course of a fortnight, but before I go, I will lay before you a sketch of what I have to expect, and what you may count on.

Yours, sincerely,   DANIEL CLARK

D W Coxe, Esq, Philadelphia

[79]   BAYOU ROAD, 27th Sept, 1811

My dear Sir Altho' in the present distressing moment, I have nothing new to say, yet I dislike to let a post go out without writing, that you may not look on yourself as forgotten Sickness continues to make great ravages, and last week we had the misfortune to lose our friend, Don Josef Roxas Thomas Connellen and his wife died three or four days ago, and almost an entire stop is put to business. I shall endeavor, by next week, to send the copy of the conveyance you require for Mr Burd, and as soon as I can find it, the sale of the indigo, by Morgan. I stay out of town, not thinking it prudent to venture in, after an absence of 3 months, and were I to stay in the city, I could do nothing there at present I am sorry to learn, by your letter of 4th September, to Chew & Relf, that you have no news of the Thos Wilson Present me respectfully to Mrs. Coxe, and believe me yours, affectionately,

Daniel W. Coxe, Esq   DANIEL CLARK.

[80]   •   BAYOU ROAD, 18th October, 1811

My dear Sir Altho' I have nothing new to say, and that no post has arrived, yet I wish, in this time of calamity, that you should have a memorial of my being alive and well My friend, Capt Turner and wife, died this week and the situation of the country is really distressing. I have asked of Chew & Relf, the order you mention in your last, of Capt. Ehrenstrien on Capt. Turner, and they state that it never has been received When it gets to hand, I will attend to it I would give my heart's blood to relieve you, but I solemnly assure you that since my arrival I have not received a dollar. I have not been able to set out on my tour thro' the country, but expect to do it in the course of a week There is no business doing, nor will the country people trust themselves in town I remain sincerely yours,

Daniel W. Coxe, Esq   DANIEL CLARK.

DEFENDANTS

Signatures to Ecclesiastical Record of Prosecution of Desgrange, for Bigamy, &c., &c

Depositions of 1, Bishop Ant Blanc 2 Louis T Caire, 3, H B Eggleston, 4, J Bermudez, 5 A Cruzet

And afterwards, to wit on the sixth July, 1849, appeared the Right Reverend Archbishop Anthony Blanc, a witness on behalf of defendants, a person of sound mind and lawful age, who, being duly sworn, did depose and say

I am the Catholic Bishop of New Orleans embracing the State of Louisiana As such, I have charge of such of the records of the Bishopric as exist, but which are not entire some being lost I have searched among those records for a record of a prosecution against Jerome DeGrange for bigamy and have found it, and now produce it I have not been able to find the record of any other proceedings against Jerome DeGrange the one now produced is the only one I have been able to find Among the Catholic denominations of Christians marriage is a very solemn sacrament By the ecclesiastical laws of the diocese, there is an obligation imposed on Catholic priests to keep a record of the marriages they celebrate, and this ought always to be done by the Catholic priests when the priest is stationed in a regular parish There are circumstances where the priest, being called at a distance from the church, and not being provided with a regular record he may be called upon to celebrate a marriage which he is obliged to record on a separate sheet, which should generally be annexed to and made part of, the regular record

ANT BLANC, Bishop of New Orleans

Cross Examination

The record produced is a complete record of the whole proceedings in this case—the beginning, the proceedings, and the decree This is the proceedings in the Ecclesiastical Court Thomas Hasset was the Vicar General, representing the Bishop, that is, he was the first Canon of the diocese, the See being vacant, by the transfer of the Bishop to the Arch Episcal See of Gautimala, he became the administrator of the same

Question. Had the tribunal, from the record of which you take this record, the exclusive jurisdiction of proceedings of this nature, in the then Territory of Louisiana?

Answer As to exclusive jurisdiction, I could not affirm

Objection The complainant reserves all right of objection to the introduction of the record here referred to, except that a copy may be substituted for the original, which copy will be marked "Z" ANT BLANC, Bishop of New Orleans

J W. GURLEY, Commissioner,

And afterwards, to wit· on the 7th July, 1849, appeared Louis T. Caire, Esq., a witness heretofore examined on behalf of defendants, and now by them recalled, who deposes and says:

Question. Look at the signature of Marie Zulime Carrière DeGrange, in the record of proceedings had in the Ecclesiastical Court, in the prosecution of Jerome DeGrange, for Bigamy, in 1802, copy of which is marked Z, and state whether the signature of Marie Zulime Carrière DeGrange, in said proceedings, is, or not, in the same handwriting as her signature to three authentic acts in your office, dated 3d Nov., 1801, page 600, and 6th Nov., 1801, page 603, and 29th October, 1801, page 592

Answer To the best of my belief, those signatures are in the same handwriting, although the word Zulime has been omitted in the three authentic acts above referred to I have been a notary since 1826, and have been much in the habit of examining writings and signatures. There are in my office more of the ancient records and signatures than in any other office in town. I suppose I may safely say that I have examined more ancient records than any person in the city I do not doubt at all that the signatures here spoken of are all in the same handwriting.

LOUIS T. CAIRE.

J. W Gurley, Commissioner.

And afterwards, to wit on the 7th July, 1849, personally appeared H. B. Eggleston, attorney at law, in New Orleans, a witness on behalf of defendants, a person of lawful age and sound mind, who, being sworn, did depose and say

Answer. That on comparing the signature of Jerome De-Grange, in the record of proceedings from the Ecclesiastical Court, against Jerome DeGrange, for Bigamy, in September, 1802, copy of which is marked Z, with the signature of the said DeGrange to an authentic act in the office of Wm. Christy, notary public, New Orleans, dated 26 March, 1801, then kept by Narcisse Broutin, notary public, that he has no doubt that the two signatures are written by the same person. The material act referred to is a power of attorney, given by Jerome DeGrange to his wife Marie Zulime Carrière, written in the Spanish language

H. B. EGGLESTON.

J. W. Gurley, Commissioner,

And afterwards, to wit: on the seventh July, 1849, appeared Joachim Bermudez, a witness on behalf of defendants, a person of sound mind and lawful age, who, being duly sworn, did depose and say:

I was fifty-three years of age on the 29th day of May last. I was born in New Orleans, at the corner of Burgundy and Dumaine streets. I knew Mr. Francisco Bermudez; he was

99

my uncle   The signature to the Record from the Ecclesiastical Court, of the proceedings had against Gerome Desgrange for bigamy in 1802, the copy of which is marked Z, is his genuine signature.   Mr Francisco Bermudez was at that time a notary public.   He was a "Notario Real."

J BERMUDEZ

Cross examination waived by Mr Wright for complainants.

J. W. GURLEY, Commissioner

And afterwards, to wit on the 7th July, 1849, personally appeared Mr. Anthony Cruzat, a witness for defendants, a person of sound mind and lawful age, who, being duly sworn, did depose and say

I am seventy-four of age   I have lived the principal part of my life in New Orleans   I was born in St. Louis, and came here when I was twelve years of age.   I have examined the signature of Lavergne to the Record of the Ecclesiastical Court of the prosecution of Jerome DeGrange for bigamy in 1802, a copy of which is marked " Z," and the said signature is genuine.   I knew the late Daniel Clark.   I only knew one Daniel Clark

Question Was or was not the late Daniel Clark a married man

Objected to by complainants

Answer. I never heard that he was a married man   He was a man of high standing

Question.   Do you or not believe that Daniel Clark was capable of concealing his marriage from the public, had he been married ?

Answer. I do not believe it

Objected to by complainant, (the above).

Question Judging from the character of Daniel Clark, do you or not believe, he would have married a woman of doubtful reputation

Answer I do not believe he would

Objection. Objected to by complainant.

Question Was there or not a strong belief on the mind of the public, that Mr. Clark was impotent ?

Objected to by complainant

Answer. I do not know

A. CRUZAT.

Cross examination waived by P C Wright, Esq., for complainant.

J W GURLEY, Commissioner

Año de 1802 —T' M T No 141 —Criminales de oficio seguidos contra Geronimo DesGranges, sobre vigamia —Juez El señor Procurador Vico Gral y Gobor del Obispado —Notario Don Francisco Bermudez

Document Z referred to by bishop Blanc in his testimony given 6th July 1849, offered by defendants and filed this 16th of October, 1849 —M'GURLEY

"AUTO —En la ciudad de la Nueva Orleans, en quatro de
" Setiembre de mil ochocientos dos años, el señor Don Tho-
" mas Hasset, presvitero canonigo de esta santa iglecia cate-
" dral, provisor vicario general y gobernador del obispado de
" esta provincia, dijo Que se le ha partisipado correr de pu-
" blico en esta ciudad que Geronimo DesGrange, que casó el
" año de mil setecientos noventa y quatro, con Maria Julia
" Carrière, era entonces casado y aun lo es infacie Eclecie con
" Barbara Jeanbelle la misma que acava de llegar, è igual-
" mente que haviendo el dicho DesGranges, venido de Francia
" habra pocos meses, hizo tambien venir á otra muger, cuyo
" nombre so procurará saver, de manera que en toda la ciudad
" se dice con escarnio, de publico y notorio, que el expresado
" Geronimo DesGrange tiene tres mugeres, y no pudiendose
" disimular un hecho semejante y tan escandaloso, como opues-
" to á los preseptos de nuestra santa madre Iglecia Catolica,
" Apostolica Romana, mandó Su Sria que para proseder á la
" averiguazion y castigo correspondiente, se ponga testimonio
" de la informacion de solteria que produjo el expresado Des-
" Grange para verificar el matrimonio con la Carriere, que
" comparescan à declarar todas las personas qué puedan dar
" noticia del caso, è instructivamente el repetido DesGrange,
" nombrandose por interpretes á Don Celestino Lavergne y
" Don Antonio Formantin aseptando y jurando previamente
" cuya diligencia se comete   Yo por quanto tambien se tiene
" noticia de que el dicho Desgrange esta proximo á ausentarse
' con la ultima de las tres mugeres, se ponga en la carcel pu-
" blica á aquel, por via de deposito mientras se determina otra
" cosa previo el Auxo de uno de los SS Alcades ordinarios
" sirviendo este Auto de Recaudo politico en forma, que por
" este que Su Sria proveyó asi lo mandó y firmo de que yo el
" notario publico doy fe.
    (Signed)   "Thomas Hasset.—Ante my, Francisco
" Bermudez."
    "En la Nueva Orleans, en dicho dia pasa á la casa capitular
y sala de audiencia del señor Don Francisco Caisergues, Alcade ordinario de esta ciudad y su jurisdicion y partisipé á Su
Señoria el Auto antecedente del Sor Provor Vico Gral y gobernador del Obispado y de que quedó enterado doy fe
    (Signed)   Franco Bermudez "
        "Nueva Orleans, 1 de Setiembre de 1802

Cumplase lo que se suplica por el Sor. Gobernador del Obispado.

(Signed)   **Franco. Caisergues.**—Ante my Franco. Bermudez "

"En la Nueva Orleans en dicho dia, Yo el notario hise saver el nombramto. de interprete que por el Auto antecede se le hase á Don Celestino Labergne y dijo : que aseptava y asepto el encargo, y juro por Dios y la Cruz uzar lo bien y fielmente, y firmo de que doy fe.

(Signed)   Ctino. Lavergne.—Franco. Bermudez "

"En el mismo dia hise saver á Don Antonio Fromantin el nombramto de interprete que se le hace en el Auto antecedente y dijo . que aseptava y asepto, y juro por Dios y la Santa Cruz uzar bien y fielmente en encargo y firmo de que doy fe.

(Signed)   Antonio Fromentin —Franco Bermudez

"Visto.—Consedese licencia á Geronimo Desgrange, natural de Clermont, parroquia de Sn Gene en los Reynos de Francia, hijo de legitimo matrimonio de Juan Bautista DesGrange, y de Maria Francisca Roux, ambos difuntos y naturales del mismo lugar ; para que pueda contraer matrimonio con Maria Julia Carriere, natural de esta ciudad, hija de legitimo matrimonio de Juan Carrière y de Maria Chofert, el primero, natural de la ciudad de Libourne, y la segunda, de Bourdeux en dichos Reynos de Francia, ambos difuntos, para que pueda presentarse en el tribunal eclesiastico se le dará testimonio de este Auto, quedando las diligencias reservadas en el archivo Licenciado Manuel Serrado.—Proveyólo el señor licenciado Don Manuel Serrano, asesor de esta Intendencia, y Alcalde ordinario de primer voto de esta ciudad que lo firmó en la ciudad de la Nueva Orleans á trese de Nobiembre de mil setecientos noventa y quatro años Franco. Broutin, escrivano publico."

En dicho dia lo hise saver á Geronimo DesGranges doy fe Broutin, escrivano.

Concuerda con so original á que me remito, y queda en mi poder y archivo. Y en virtud de lo mandado por el decreto inserto doy este en la ciudad de la Nueva Orleans, trese de Nobiembre de mil setecientos noventa y quatro años Signado Franco. Broutin, escvo. publico "

"Pedimento —Geronimo DesGrange, natural de la Parroquia de San Gines, de la ciudad de Clermont, reyno de Francia, en la mejor forma que haya lugar en derecho, ante Usted paresco y digo · Que para mas bien servir á Dios Nuestro Señor, tengo tratado contraher matrimonio facie Eclecie con Maria Julia Carriere, natural de esta parroquia. En cuya virtud se servirá usted mandar se me reciba informacion, y que los testigos que presentare, declaren religiosamente como es cier-

lo me conocen, saven y les consta soy natural de dicha parro-
chia, hijo iegitimo de Juan Bautista DesGrange, y de Maria
Francisca Roux, catolico apostolico romano, que me han visto
hacer actos de cristiano, oyendo Missa y frequentar los santos
sacramentos, que no he prometido palabra de matrimonio á
otra persona mas que á la referida, con la que no tengo ningun parentesco, ni impedimento para contraher matrimonio.
cuya informacion dada por bastante, se servirá Usted mandar
que el cura de esta parroquia nos despose y vele en ella Por
tanto A Usted suplico se sirva proveer como pido, con justicia, &c, &c Otro si, presento devidamente la licencia del Sr.
Vice Parente para que obre los efectos que haya lugar que es
justicia ut supra.   Gerome DesGrange

"DECRETO—En lo principal recibase la informacion que
esta parte ofrece comparescan los testigos previa la explora-
cion del contenido Y en el otrosi hace por presentado el documento que refiere y dicho traigase   "Walsh" Proveyolo el
Señor Don Patrisio, Walsh, Clerigo, Presvitero, Vicario, Foraneo, Juez, Eclesiastico de esta Provincia y Comisario Sub-
delegado de Crusada que lo firmó en catorse de Nobiembre de
mil setecientos noventa y quatro   Estevan de Quiñones, notario publico"

" En la Nueva Orleans en dicho dia hise saver el decreto
que antecede à Geronimo DesGrange, doy fee. — Quiñones,
notario

"DECLARACION.—En la ciudad de la Nueva Orleans, en el
mismo dia mes y año, ante el señor Vicario, Foraneo, Juez
Eclesiastico, parecio Geronimo DesGrange, de quien, por
ante my el presente notario, recibió juramento que hiso por
Dios y la Cruz segun derecho, so cargo de el, prometió decir
verdad, y explorando su voluntad con la mayor proligidad, y
examinado al tenor del escrito que antecede, dijo· que es de
estado soltero que no ha prometido palabra de exponsales á
otra persona mas que á Maria Julia Carriere   Que no ha hecho voto de castidad ni de entrar en Religion, y que para esta
razon, no ha sido inducido, violentado ni atemorisado por persona alguna, y que la ha hecho de su libre y expontanea voluntad, por ser la verdad so cargo de su juramento; que es de edad
de treinta y quatro años, lo firmo, y dicho señor lo rubricó de
que doy fee, Rubrica, Gerome DesGrange, —Ante my, Este-
de Quiñones, notario publico.

"OTRA DECLARACION.—Yncontinente y para la informacion
que tiene ofresida dicho DesGranges, presentó por testigo ante
dicho Señor Vicario Foraneo, à Don Gabriel Mariano Dubuc,
de quien por ante my, dicho notario, recibió juramento que
hiso por Dios y la Cruz segun derecho, so cargo de él, prometió decir verdad, y examinado al tenor del escrito que antecede
dijo. Que conoce al que lo presenta, save, y le consta es natu-

ral de la Parroquia de San Gines de la ciudad de Cleremont Reyno de Francia, hijo legitimo de Juan Bautista DesGrange y de Maria Francisca Roux, catolico apostolico Romano, que lo ha visto hacer actos de cristiano, oyendo missa y frequentar los santos sacramentos, que no le consta haya prometido palabra de exponsales á otra persona mas que á la referida Maria Julia Carriere, con la que no tiene ningun parentesco, ni impedimiento para contraher matrimonio y responde que esta es la verdad so cargo de su juramento, que es de edad de quarenta y dos años, lo firmo y dicho señor lo rubricó, doy fee, Rubricado, Gabriel Dubuc.—Ante my, Estevan de Quiñones, notario publico '

" OTRA DECLARACION —Incontinente y presento por testigo ante dicho señor Vicario Foraneo Juez Eclesiastico de esta provincia á Don Antonio Benguerelle de quien por ante my dicho notario, recibio juramento que hizo por Dios y la cruz segun derecho so cargo de él prometio decir verdad y examinado al tenor de dicho escrito, dijo Que conose al que no presenta, save y le consta es natural de la Parroquia de San Gines de la ciudad de Cleremont reyno de Francia, hijo legitimo de Juan Bautista DesGrange, y de Maria Francisca Roux catolico, apostoltco, Romano, que lo há visto hacer actos de cristiano, oyendo misa y frequentar los santos sacramentos, y que no le consta haya prometido palabra de exponsales á otra persona mas que á la referida Maria Julia Carriere con la que no tiene ningun parentesco, ni impedimento para contraher matrimonio, y responde que esta es la verdad, so cargo de su juramento, que es de edad de quarenta y quatro años, lo firmó, y dicho señor lo rubrico, doy fee, rubricado, A Benguerelle—Ante my, Estevan de Quiñones, notario publico "

" DECRETO Nueva Orleans catorse de Nobiembre de mil setecientos noventa y quatro Vista la informacion antecedente producida por Geronimo DesGrange, para contraher matrimonio con Maria Julia Carrière, dijo su merced que devia aprovarla y la aprovó y dió por vastante, y para su mayor validacion, y firmeza interpuso en ella su autoridad y judicial Decreto quanto ha lugar en derecho y Mando, que el reverendo Padre Fray Juaquin de Portillo, cura de esta parroquia de San Luis, los despose, y vele en ella segun estilo, previas las proclamas ordinarias y todos los demas requisitos y formalidades que se requieren por parte de ella respecto á que el susodicho lo ha hecho constar en este Tribunal por la suya y no resultando ningun impedimento, a cuyo fin, se le libre la orden correspondiente, "Walsh"—Ante my, Estevan de Quiñones, notario publico."

" NOTIFICACION —En el mismo dia hise saver el Decreto que antecede á Geronimo DesGrange, doy fee, Quiñones notario "

" NOTA.—Libróse la orden que se manda al muy reverendo

Padre Fray Juaquin de Portillo, cura de esta parroquia de San Luis, doy fee, Quiñones notario —

Derechos del señor Vicario, treinta y dos reales, rubricado

" PEDIMENTO —Geronimo DesGrange en la informacion de mi libertad que he producido en la mejor forma que haya lugar en derecho ante usted expongo que previendo la proximidad del adbiento, que será el treinta del corriente á demas de serrarse las velaciones no se podrian verificar hasta que se abriesen con esta consideracion, y la de que mis asuntos en mi giro de comercio de licores nesesito una persona de confianza á quien fiarlos y no teniendo otra mas que mi futura esposa Suplico á usted se sirva dispensarme una proclama para que publicadas las dos Se verifique nuestro matrimonio Por tanto, á usted suplico se sirva proveer como pido con justicia y juro &a, &a, Geronimo DesGrange

" DECRETO —Nueva Orleans, catorse de Nobiembre de mil setecientos noventa y quatro Respecto á que las causas que esta parte expone para obtener dispenza de una proclama se graduan por suficientes Dijo su merced que uzando de venigindad se la dispensava y dispenso, y mando que publicadas las dos, se verifique su matrimonio como se ha mandado por anterior decreto, "Walsh —Ante my, Estevan de Quiñones, notario publico "

" En la Nueva Orleans en dicho dia hise saver el decreto que antecede á Don Geronimo DesGrange, doy fee, Quiñones notario "

' En dicho dia lo hise saver al reberendo Padre Fray Juaquin de Portillo, cura de este parroquia, doy fee, Quiñones, notario "

" Es conforme á un original que queda en el Archivo de mi cargo á que me remito y cumpliendo lo mandado en el Auto caveza de este espediente saque el presente en la Nueva Orleans, á quatro de Septiembre de mil ochocientos dos años "

(Signed)   (L S) Francisco Bermudez

" DILIGENCIA —En la Nueva Orleans, en el mismo dia, yo el Notario solicite en varias partes la recidencia de Doña Barbara Jeanbelle, y se me informó posava en la Havitazion de Don Bernardo Marigny, donde pase en seguida y cite para que el lunes seis del corriente se presentase á las siete de la mañana en el Tribunal por mandado de su señoria lo que pongo por diligencia de que doy fee "

(Signed)   Bermudez "

" En el propio dia hise saver al ministro de justicia Jose Campos el Auto antecedente en la parte que le comprehende, doy fee "

(Signed)   Bermudez.

" NOTA —Que el ministro anduvo toda la tarde con tres sol-

dados en solicitud de Geronimo DesGeange, y no le encontró
lo que se advierte para que conste."

(This note has been signed by the usual mark of said
Bermudez.)

" Declaracion de doña Barbara Zambelle.—En la ciudad
de la Nueva Orleans en seis de Setiembre de mil ochocientos
dos años compareció ante el señor Don Tomas Hasset, presvitero canonigo de esta santa yglesia catedral provisor vicario
general y gobernardor del opispado de esta provincia y Floridas
Doña Barbara Margarita Zambelle de Orsy, de quien se recibio juramento que hiso por Dios y la santa cruz segun derecho
so cuyo cargo ofrecio decir verdad en lo que supiere, y fuere
preguntada, y se le hisieron las preguntas siguientes

" Primeramente Si conose á Geronimo DesGrange, que
tiempo hace, y en que parage lo ha tratado, dijo. Que hace
trese años que lo conose, y que lo ha tratado en Nueva York
Estados Unidos de America y responde."

" Preguntada si es cierto ha sido casada con el ante dicho
DesGrange, en que parage, que yglesia, que tiempo, ha, quien
fue el parroco ó ministro, y quienes fueron testigos, Dijo que
no, aunque fué su intencion casarse con el ante dicho Des-
Grange, pero como este se ausentase para esta, la que responde
mudo de idea sin embargo de que hiso la diligencia de obtener
la venia de su Padre pasando á Filadelfia al intento, y que
estando aqui DesGrange la escrivio para que viniese á esta
ciudad á efectuar el matrimonio á que no consistio y que de
esto habra onse años y medio, y responde.

" Preguntada si há tratado á DesGrange en Francia despues
de la epoca que ha citada y si le ha buelto á tratar sobre el
mismo particular dijo Que el año pasado lo ha visto en Bor-
deux y que no le ha buelto á tratar sobre el matrimonio por
estar ambos casados y responde.

" Proguntada en el supuesto de que dice es casada diga con
quien, que tiempo hace, en que parage por que ministro y
quienes fueron testigos, dijo es casada con Don Juan Santiago
Sonmeylliatt, habra como dies años, en la ciudad de Filadelfia,
por un parroco catolico, y que fueron testigos el señor Bernardy
y su esposa, y responde

" Preguntada si tiene documento que lo acredite dijo que
no tiene documento que lo acredite, y responde

" Pregnntada si no ha oydo decir que DesGrange es casado
con tres mugeres, exprese á quienes, ó si es publico y notorio,
dijo Que nunca ha oydo nada de lo que se le pregunta, solo
desde anoche que le dijeron la reputavan como una de sus
mugeres, y responde que lo que ha declarado es la verdad en
cargo de su juramento, y haviendole sido leyda esta declaracion que ha dado por medio de los interpretes dijo ser conforme
en que se afirma y ratifica: que es de edad de treinta años,

firmô con los interpretes y su señoria, rubrico de que doy fee

(Signed)   B N Zambelle de Orsy, Hasset Celestino Lavergne Antonio Fromentin —Ante my, Fran'co Bermudez

" OTRA DI MARIA YEEAR, CITADA POR EL NOTARIO —En la ciudad de la Nueva Orleans en dicho dia mes y año comparecio ante su señoria, Maria Yeear de quien por medio de los interpretes se recibio juramento que hiso por Dios y la santa cruz so cuyo cargo prometio decir verdad en lo que supiere y fuere preguntada y siendolo por los que siguen dijo

" Preguntada que estado tiene, que tiempo há que llego á esta ciudad y con que objeto dijo Que es viuda de Juan Dupor (alias) Poulé que fallecio hase como dos años, con quien estubo casada como ocho años, que nunca ha tenido otro marido ni antes ni despues Que hase dose dias que llego á esta Y que el objeto ha sido para buscar su vida, instruhida de que era buen pais, por medio de su industria de costurera y responde

" Preguntada si conose á Geronimo DesGrange, desde cuando, y si ha sido llamada ó convidada por el á esta ciudad y con que motivo dijo Que conoció á Geronimo DesGrange en Francia habra ocho meses y que fue quien le dijo que viniese á esta ciudad donde podria buscar la vida mejor que en su patria, á quien fue recomendada, y responde

' Preguntada si ha dado palabra de matrimonio al referido Geronimo DesGrange, ó si ha mediado algun contrato particular referente á matrimonio ó otro trato con el ante dicho, dijo Que absolutamente no ha tenido con el repetido DesGrange ningun trato ni convenio semejante, pues no ignorava antes de embarcarse que el era casado en la Luisiana, y que su venida no ha sido con otro objecto que por lo que dijo dicho anteriormente, y responde

Preguntada si ha prometido al consabido DesGrange acompañarle en el viage que proyecto hacer ahora á Francia dijo Que muy lejos de acompañar á Desgrange en su viage pienza quedarse aqui en la casa de Cornelius Ploy (alias) Flamand donde la deja recomendada el mismo DesGrange con animo de buscar su vida con su costura, por ser el dicho Flamand de oficio sastre, y responde

" Preguntada si ha oydo decir de publico ó notorio que DesGrange ha sido casado con dos mugeres antes ó despues de su arribo á esta dijo que antes de su arribo no ha oydo nada sobre el particular, pero que en los dias que ha llegado á esta ciudad ha oydo decir de publico que DesGrange era casado tres veses graduandola á la que responde por la tercera, y responde que lo que ha dicho y declarado es la verdad en cargo de su juramento, que es de edad de veinte y cinco años, no

firmo por que dijo no saver, hizole su señoria, con los citados
interpretes de que doy fee

(Signed) Hasset, Antonio Fromentin, Celestino Lavergne —Ante my, Francisco Bermudez

" OTRA, MARIA JULIA CARRIERE, CITADA POR EL NOTARIO —
Incontinenty comparecio ante su señoria Maria Julia Carriere
de quien por medio de los interpretes se recibio juramento que
hiso por Dios y la santa cruz segun derecho so cuyo cargo
ofrecio decir verdad en lo que supiere o fuere preguntada y
siendolo por las que siguen, dijo

" Preguntada por su estado dijo que es casada con Geronimo
DesGrange, desde el quatro de Diciembre del año de mil setecientos noventa y quatro y responde

" Preguntada si ha oydo decir antes ó despues de su matrimonio que el dicho su marido ha sido casado con otra dijo. que
habra como un año que oyo decir en esta ciudad que su marido
era tambien (casado su marido) en el Norte, con cuyo motivo
quiso informarse por si misma de la validad y salio de este
puerto para los de Filadelfia, y Nueva York, donde pratico las
mas vivas diligencias para averiguarle y solo consiguio saver
que havia tenido amores con una muger cuyo Padre no haviendo querido consentir á ello no se verifico y que esta misma se
caso poco despues con otro y responde

" Preguntada si en estos dias ha oydo decir en este publico
que su dicho marido era casado con tres mugeres, si lo ha
creydo ó lo cree ó tiene alguna duda sobre el particular que la
inquiete ó perturbe su esposo, dijo Que aunque lo ha oydo
decir en el publico no solo no lo ha creydo sino que tampoco se
ha inquietado por estar satisfecha de lo contrario y responde que
lo que ha declarado es la verdad en cargo de su juramento, que
es de edad de veinte y dos años, firmo y su señoria rubrico de
que doy fee.

(Tigned) Marie Zulime Carrière DesGrange, Hasset,
(his mark,) Celestino Lavergne, Antonio Fromentin —Ante
my, Francisco Bermudez "

" OTRA DE GERONIMO DESGRANGE, CONDUCIDO POR EL NOTA-
RIO —En la ciudad de la Nueva Orleans en siete de Setiembre
de mil ochocientos dos años el señor Don Thomas Hasset,
presvitero canonigo de esta santa yglesia catedral, provisor vicario general y gobernador del opispado de esta provincia hiso
compareser ante si y por ante los interpretes á Geronimo Des-
Grange, se le recibio juramento que hiso por Dios y la cruz
segun derecho so cuyo cargo prometio decir verdad en lo que
supiere y fuere preguntado y siendolo por el tenor del auto de
quatro del corriente que hase cavesa de esta actuasion y demas
preguntas que se tubieron por convenientes dijo lo siguiente.

Preguntado si conose á Da Barbara Yanbel de Orsi, que
tiempo há y en que parage, dijo : Que la conocio en Nueva

York primero habra como onse años y despues en Filadelfia, y responde

Preguntado si es cierto fue casado con ella, diga en que parage, ante qué Ministro, que tiempo hace y quienes fueron testigos dijo. Que no ha sido casado con ella aunque lo pretendio solicitando la venia de su padre que le fue negada por careser el que responde de bienes de fortuna

Preguntado si despues de haverla dexado en Filadelfia la ha tratado en algun otro parage diga en donde y con que fin dijo. Que ha visto á la dicha Da Barbara en Bourdeux por la casualidad de que estando enfermo llamaron á Mr. Sonmeyllat su marido, y despues de su restablecimiento lo combidó á comer el dicho Sonmeyllat á su casa, donde la vio de que quedo admirado y siempre continuo vicitando la casa sin que llevase otro objecto que la amistad anterior y conocimiento del marido y responde.

Preguntado si conose á Da Maria Yllar, que tiempo hace en que parage y con que motivo, dijo. Que en Diciembre del año anterior al presente, conocio á la ante dicha estando en una posada empleada de criada en Bourdeux donde el que responde asistio y aloxava y responde

Preguntado si hiso algun trato con la ante dicha para que le acompañase en esta ciudad, diga qual fue, o con que motivo se halla en esta, dijo. Que no ha hecho ningun trato ni convenio con la referida, y que el motivo de hallerse en esta, ha sido por que preguntandola si le seria mas util este pais que el de Bourdeux para buscar su vida con, en el exersicio de la costura le aconsejo que viniese, que efectivamente le seria util y responde

" Preguntado si havia hecho intencion de llevarla consigo en el viage que esta proximo á haser, y si la ha solicitado al intento, dijo. Que no lo ha pensado pues que ha venido para el fin que lleva expuesto de ganar su vida y no para otro y responde

" Preguntado con que motivo paso al Norte Da. Maria Zuhine Carriere su consorte, el año proximo pasado, dijo. Que el principal motivo que le impulsó entre otros, fue que haviendose corrido en esta ciudad que el que responde era casado otra vez quiso indagar la verdad por si misma como lo hiso, y hago pasar á Francia á unirse con el, que no verifico por haver tenido noticia venia en derechura á esta y responde

" Preguntado que tiempo hace que corre en el publico la novedad de que havia sido casado con otra, dijo. Que habra como quatro años y responde.

" Preguntado si ha sido reconvenido ó requerido por algun Sor Juez eclesiastico sobre este asunto, dijo. Que no y responde

" Preguntado si es verdad que para satisfacer á su muger y

al publico ofrecio traher con sigo ó procurar documentos justi-
ficativos de su inosensia en el particular de que se trata, diga si
los tiene que los exhiva, dijo Que haciendose cargo que este
ruido caeria naturalmente, estando satisfecha su consorte de su
inocencia, ni haver juez que exhigiese tales documentos no ha
praticado diligencia alguna para conseguirlos, y responde que
lo que ha dicho y declarado es la verdad en cargo de su juramento en lo que se afirmo y ratifico leyda que le fue esta declaracion por los dichos interpretes exponiento ser todo conforme
á su intencion que es de edad de quarenta y un años, firmo con
los interpretes, y Su Sria rubrico de que doy fe entre Vs haver-
vale

[Signed]   J DesGrange —Husset, his mark —Ctino
Lavergne.—Antonio Fromentin   Ante my, Francisco Bermudez "

" Vistos.—No resultando comprovacion de la voz publica
de que se hace cargo el Auto caveza de este proseso, ni tanien-
dose mas noticias al presente, suspendanse por ahora para con-
tinuarlas en caso necesario, poniendose en libertad la persona
de Geronimo Desgrange, quien pagara las costas causadas "

[Signed]   Thomas Husset."

" Proveyolo el Sr Don Thomas Hasset, Presvitero Canonigo de esta Santa Iglecia Catedral, Provisor Vicario General y
Gobernador del Obispado de esta provincia de la Luisiana y
las Floridas que lo firmo en la Nueva Orleans en siete de Septiembre de mil ochocientos dos años

[Signed]   Franco. Bermudez "

" Notificacion —En la Nueva Orleans en dicho dia hise saver al Auto antecedente á Geronimo DesGrange á cuyo efecto
pase á la carcel publica, doy fe.

[Signed]   Bermudez."

" Otra.—En el mismo dia notifique dicho Auto á Joseph
Puche, en la parte que le comprehende como carcelero, doy fe

[Signed]   Bermudez."

"Tasacion de costas de las diligencias promovidas de oficio
contra Geronimo DesGrange sobre vigamia compuesto de f 15

Gratis.—Al Señor Don Thomas Hasset, Gobernador del
Obispado, por sus firmas   .   .   .   52 rs

Al Sr. Don Franco. Caisergues, Alcade
ordinario por las suyas   .   .   . .   .   2 "

[Signed]   Ctino Lavergne."

Al Sr Don Celestino Lavergne, inter-
prete, por sus derechos .   .   .   .   .   .   36 "

Amount brought for over   90

Recaby [Signed]
A Dn Antonio Fromantin por id   36 "
[Signed]
A Dn Franco Bermudez, notario por
los suyos y escrito   147
Pagado [Signed]
A Jose de Campos por sus derechos   5
Al tasador por id   3
[Signed]   Losada "

       286

       35 ps 6 rs

"Nueva Orleans 9 de Setiembre de 1802
[Signed]   Juan Losada

New Orleans 13th of October 1849

The undersigned Antoine Blanc Catholic Bishop of the Diocese of New Orleans residing at New Orleans and keeper of the Records of the Bishoprick of New Orleans hereby certifies that the foregoing twenty three pages are true and faithful copies of the original Records on deposit amongst the Archives of said Bishoprick, and to which he undersigned referred in his deposition taken before the Commissioner of the United States in the case of Mrs Myra Clark Gaines, against Chew and Relf and others, No 122 in the Circuit Court of the United States District of Louisiana, on the sixth day of July, 1849   ANT BLANC,

       Bp of N Orleans

Translation of document Z, referred to by Bishop Blanc, in his deposition of 6th July 1849, offered by defendants, and filed 16 Oct, 1849 "   J W GURLEY Commissioner

THE YEAR 1802

No 141

Criminal proceedings instituted against Geronimo Des Grange for bigamy

The Vicar General and Governor of the Bishoprick. Judge
     FRAN'CO BERMUDEZ, Notary

DECREE—In the city of New Orleans, the 4th day of September, 1802, Thomas Hasset Canonical Presbitary of this Holy Cathedral Church, Provisor Vicar General and Governor of the Bishoprick of this Provinc

Says, that it has been publicly stated in this city, that Geronimo

Des Grange, who was married in the year 1794, to Maria Julia Carrière was at that time married, and is so even now, before the Church, to Barbara Jeanbelle, who has just arrived, and also that the said Des Grange having arrived from France a few months since, he caused another woman to come here, whose name will be obtained. It is reported in all the city publicly and notoriously, that the said Geronimo Des Grange has three wives, and not being able to keep secret such an act as scandalous as it is opposed to the precept of our Holy Mother Church his Excellency has ordered that in order to proceed in the investigation and to the corresponding penalty testimony be produced to substantiate his being a single man, which the said Desgrange presented in order to consummate his marriage with said Carrière, that all persons should appear who can give any information in this matter, and also De Grange, with Celestin Lavergne and Antonio Fromantin interpreters they, the interpreters, first accepting the nomination, and swearing to act as such faithfully. And also, as it has been ascertained, that the said Des Grange, is about to leave with the last of these three wives, let him be placed in the public prison during these proceedings, with the aid of one of the Alcades this decree serving as an order which his Excellency has approved and as such it is signed by me, notary.

Signed—Thomas Hassett,—Signed before me, Franco Bermudez

New Orleans, in the same day it was passed to the Capitular House and Audience Hall of D. Franco Caisergues Alcade of this City, and in his Jurisdiction and I notified to his worship, the preceding decree and of which I have taken note.

(Signed)—Franco Bermudez

NEW ORLEANS, 4th September, 1802

Let the request of the Governor of the Bishoprick be complied with.

(Signed)—Fran'co Caisergue,—Before me signed, Fran'co Bermudez

In New Orleans, on the same day, I, the Notary notified Celestin Lavergne of his appointment as interpreter, and he said, that he accepted it, and swore by God and the Cross, that he would act well and faithfully in the premises, and he herewith signs his name

(Signed)—C'tino Lavergne—Fran'co Bermudez

On the same day I notified Antonio Fromantin of his appointment as interpreter, who accepted of it, and who swore by God and the Cross, that he would act well and faithfully in the premises, and he herewith signs his name

(Signed)—Antonio Fromantin—Fren'co Bermudez

APPROVAL —Let a licence be granted to Gerommo De Granges a native of Clermont, in the Parish of Gene in th Kindom of France legitimate son of John Baptist Des Grang and of Maria Francisca Roux who are bonafide inhabitants of the same place in order that he may solemnize his marriage with Maria Julia Carriere a native of this City legitimate daughter of John Carriere and of Maria Conteau in the faculty of the Curate of Livoudais in the second of the diocese in the Kingdom of France who in the best possible way may choose he is to present himself in the Ecclesiastical Tribunal at the foot of the number of this order the proceedings remaining in these the Archives

Lacrichende Navarro Serrano

It was approved by the Dr Maria Serrano Assessor of this Intendency with Maria Colonel of this City who signed in the City of New Orleans the 13th November, 17

(Signed)—Pedro Broutin, Not Pub

In the same by Inodore Geronimo De Grange
(Signed)—Broutin, Not Pub

A true copy of the Order to which I refer and which remains amongst the Archives of Order and events of the within deed I give the present in the City of New Orleans this 13th November 17

(Signed)—Pedro Broutin No Pub

PETITION —Geronimo Des Grange a native of the Parish of St Gines of the city of Clermont Kingdom of France, respectfully represent that in order the better to serve God, I am about to contract a matrimonial alliance with Maria Julia Carriere a native of this City, on account of which you will require that some of the witnesses allowed to testify and the same witnesses which you may order may declare religiously, that they actually know your petition that I am free of and that I am aware that I am in receive of that I am a legitimate son of John Baptist De Srang and of Maria Francisca Roux that I am a Roman Catholic and they may even to perform acts of a Christian bearing does are receiving the Holy Sacraments, that I have not promised marriage to any other person, but to the one to which I have referred with whom I have no relationship, nor impediment, which can prevent me from marrying her And being proof that and it being considered sufficient proof you may be pleased to order that the Curate of this not promised marriage to any other person than to Maria Julia Carriere, that he has taken oath of chastity, nor of orders in the Church and for this reason he has not been induced, either by force or fear, of any one, and that he has done it of his own.

Parish may marry us, and perform the subsequent religious ceremonies required by the Catholic Church

Wherefore, I pray that you may be pleased to grant what I ask, &c

SUPPLEMENT.—I duly present the license of the Vice Parente, in order that it may facilitate the object in view

Signed—Jerome Des Grange

DECREE.—Let the information, which the party interested offers be received and let the witnesses be present having first been made acquainted with the matter in the premises and as regards the supplemental petition, let the document be considered as presented, and let it be produced

Signed—Walsh

Approved by Don Patricio Walsh Presbiter, Vicar Ecclesiastical Judge of this Province and which, as Commissioner of the Cross, who signed it, this 11th November, 1794

Signed—Estevan de Quinones Notary Public

In New Orleans, on the same day, I informed Jeronimo Des Grange of the preceding decree

Signed—Quinones Notary

TESTIMONY.—In the city of New Orleans, on the same day of the month and in the same year, before the Ecclesiastical Judge appeared Jerome Des Grange who was sworn by me, Notary, and made oath by God and the cross, to tell the truth, and having examined him at length and having examined the tenor of the preceding petition, he said that he was a bachelor, that he had free will which is the truth. He also swore that he was thirty-four years old. I have signed, and the said gentleman has made his signature

Signed—Gerome Des Grange

Before me, Estevan de Quinones, Not Pul

Subsequently, and in accordance with the information which the said Des Grange had offered to give, I present, as a witness in presence of the said Vicar, Don Gabriel Mariano Dubac, who took oath, by God and the Cross, to tell the truth, and having examined the tenor of the preceding petition, said that he knows the person who has offered him, as witness he knows that he is a native of the parish of St Gines, of the city of Clermont, in the kingdom of France; legitimate son of Juan Bautista Des Grange and of Maria Francisca Roux, a Roman Catholic, that he has seen him perform christian acts, hearing Mass and attending the Holy Sacraments, that he does not know that he has ever promised marriage to any other person than to the said **Maria Julia Carrire**, with whom he has no relationship, nor impediment to contract marriage, and witness says that this is the truth; he also swears, that he, the witness, is forty-two years old I have signed, and the said witness has signed

(Signed)—Gabriel Dubac

Before me, Estevan de Quinones, Not Pub

Immediately after I present as a witness, before the said Vicar Ecclesiastical Judge of this province Don Antonio Benguerelle, who took oath before me, Notary, by God and the Cross, to tell the truth, and after having examined the tenor of the said petition, said that he knows the person who offers him, as a witness, and he knows that he is a native of the parish of St Gines of the city of Clermont, kingdom of France, legitimate son of Juan Bautista Des Grange and of Maria Francisca Roux, a Roman Catholic and that he has seen him perform christian acts, hearing Mass and attending the Holy Sacraments that he does not know that he has ever promised marriage to any other person than to the said Maria Julia Carrick, with whom he has no relationship nor is there any impediment to contract marriage, and he says that this is the truth he also swears that he, the witness, is forty-four years old I have signed, and the said witness has also signed with me

(Signed)—A. Benguerelle

Before me, Estevan de Quinones, Not Pub

NEW ORLEANS, 14th of November, 1794

Die ut.—Considering the preceding information, produced by Geronimo Des Grange, in order to contract marriage with Maria Julia Carrick his worship said that he should approve it, and it was approved and in order to give it full force and credit, he interposed thereon his authority and Judicial decree, and it is ordered that the Reverend Father Friar, Joaquin de Partillo, Curate of this parish of St Louis, shall marry them, with the requisite Religious Ceremonie as it is customary, having first made the necessary proclamations, and all other requisites and formalities as far as she is concerned the above mentioned having already performed all that is necessary on his side, and if there be no impediment found, let the necessary order be given

(Signed)—Walsh

Before me Estevan de Quinones, Not Pub

NOTICE.—On the same day I notified Geronimo Des Grange of the foregoing decree

(Signed)—Quinones, Notary Public

NOTE.—Let the order be served on the Very Reverend Father Friar Joaquin de Portillo, Curate of this Parish of St Louis

(Signed)—Quinones, Notary

Costs of the Vicar, thirty-two rials

PETITION—I, Geronimo Des Grange, most respectfully represent that being aware that the Advent which falls on the 30th day of the present month, and the time for receiving the nuptial benediction of the church will have passed, and that I cannot have that ceremony performed until the Church resumes its ceremonies, and that in order to carry on my business which is that of selling liquors I am in want of a confidential agent to whom to confide it, and having no other person but my future wife I pray that you may be pleased to dispense a proclamation which being duly published our marriage may be consummated

I, therefore pray that you will grant me this my request, &c

(Signed)—Gerome DeGrange

NEW ORLEANS, 14th November 1794

DECREE—In view of the causes that the petitioner has set forth in order to obtain a dispensation of a proclamation, and said causes being considered sufficient his Honor said that using of indulgence he will dispense and does dispense and does order that after due publication, the marriage be consummated as it has already been ordered in a previous decree

(Signed)—Walsh

Before me, Est van de Quinones Not Pub

NOTICE—In New Orleans on the same day I notified Geronimo Des Granges of the preceding decree

(Signed)—Quinones, Notary

On the same day notified the Rev Father de Portillo, Curate of this Parish

(Signed)—Quinones, Notary

A true copy of the original which is extant in my current register, to which I refer and in obedience to the preliminary decree at the caption of these proceedings I give the present copy in the city of New Orleans this 4th day of September 1802

(Signed)—Franco Permudez

CITATION—In New Orleans on the same day, I the undersigned Notary inquired at sundry places for the residence of Doña Barbara Jeanbelle, and I was informed she lived in Mr Bernard Marigny's house, where I then went, and there gave notice that, on Monday, the 6th instant, at seven o'clock in the morning, she must present herself before the tribunal as per order of his Excellency

(Signed)—Bermudez

On the same day I notified the Minister of Justice, Jose Campos, of the preceding decree

(Signed)—Bermudez

No 1.—The minister was out all the afternoon with three soldiers looking for Geronimo Des Grange, and could not find him, and notice is hereby given thereof.

This notice is signed Rev. John B— — — with the usual mark

Testimony.— Continuation of proceedings against Des Grange.—In the city of New Orleans on the 6th day of December 1802 appeared before Me. Thomas Hassett, Archdeacon Canon of the Holy Cathedral Church Provisor Vicar General and Governor of the Bishoprick of—— Louisiana, &c. the Señora Doña Barbara Maria——, native of the Observatory, who was sworn to tell the truth, and the following question were then propounded to her

First—Is she known Geronimo Des Grange, how long, and where did she know him

Answer—That she has known him for sixteen years, and that she was acquainted with him in New York

Second—Being asked whether it is true that she was married to the aforesaid Des Grange, in what place, in what church, how long ago, and what parson or what clergyman, and who were the witnesses

Answer—No, although it was her intention to marry the aforesaid Des Grange, but as the latter was going away she changed her mind, nevertheless she obtained the permission of her father to go? Placed——for that purpose, and that while there Des Grange, begged of her to come to this city to consummate the marriage, to which she did not consent, this took place about eleven years and half ago

Being asked whether she was acquainted with Des Grange in France, after the period above stated, and if she has ever spoken to him on this subject

Answer—That last year she saw him in Bordeaux, and that she did not ask to speak to him on the marriage because they were both of them married

Being asked that if she says she is married, with whom is she married, how long since, in what place, by what clergyman, and who were the witnesses

Answer—That she is married to Don Juan Santiago Soumevilliatt, about ten years ago in the city of Philadelphia, by a Catholic priest and that Mr Bernardy and his wife were witnesses

Being asked if she has any document to prove it

Answer—That she has no document to prove it

Being asked if she has not heard it said that Des Grange is married to three wives, say to whom and if it is not public and notorious

Answer—That she never heard any thing of what is asked her, until last night when she was told that it was said she was one of his wives and she says that what she has declared is the truth, and the testimony having been read to her which was interpreted by Dn Celestino Lavergne and Dn Antonio Fromantin, she declared it was what she had said and she now ratifies it, that she is thirty-four years old

(Signed)—B M Zambell De Orti——H———C——Celeo Lavergne— Antonio Fromantin.

Before me Franco Bermudes

Testimony of Maria Yllar.—In the city of New Orleans, on the same day, month and year appeared before his Excellency Maria Yllar, who being sworn to tell the truth the following questions were propounded to her

Being asked whether she is married or not how long it is since she arrived in this city, and with what object

Answers That she is the widow of Juan Dupre alias Poule who died two years ago to whom she was married two years, that she has never had any other husband, neither before nor since, that she arrived here two days ago and that her object was to gain a livelihood, having been informed it was a good country for seamstresses

Being asked if she knows Geronimo Des Grange, how long, and if she was invited or told by him to come to this city and with what object,

Answers That she knew Geronimo Des Grange in France about eight months ago, and it was he who told her to come to this city, where she could gain a better livelihood than in her own country

Being asked whether she has promised marriage to the said Geronimo Des Grange or if she has entered into any private contract with reference to matrimony or any other contract with him

Answers That she has not had any contract of the kind with the said Des Grange, because she knew before her departure from France, that he was married in Louisiana and that her coming here was only with the object that she has already stated

Being asked she had promised the said Des Grange to accompany him in the voyage he is going to make to France,

Answers That far from accompanying Des Grange during his voyage, she thinks of remaining in the house of Cornelius Ploy alias Flamand, to whom she has been recommended by the said Des Grange, for the purpose of gaining her livelihood, by sewing, as the said Flamand is a tailor by trade

Being asked if she has heard it publicly said that Des Grange has been married to two women before or since her arrival in this city,

Answers That before her arrival she heard nothing of the matter, but since she has been here she has heard it said publicly tha Des Granges born in the city... ... swears that what she has said is the truth and that she is twenty-five years old she does not sign not knowing how to write

(Signed)—Hasset—Antonio Fromentin—Ctino Lavergne
Before me, Franco Bermudez

TESTIMONY OF MARIA JULIA CARRIERE—Then appeared before his Excellency Marie Julia Carriere who through the interpreters, was duly sworn to tell the truth and the following questions were propounded to her

Being asked whether she was married or single

Answers That she is married to Geronimo De Grange, since the 4th of December, 1794

Being asked whether he heard before or since her marriage, that her said husband was married to another woman,

Answers That about a year since, she heard it stated, in this city, that her husband was married in the north and in consequence, she wished to ascertain whether it was true or not and she left this city for Philadelphia and New York, where she used every exertion to ascertain the truth of the report and she learned only that he had courted a woman, whose father not consenting to the match, it did not take place and she married another man, shortly afterwards

Being asked whether she had recently heard that her husband was married to three women if she believed it or does believe it, or has any doubt about the matter which renders (her) unquiet or unhappy

Answers That although she has heard so in public, she has not believed it, and the report has caused her no uneasiness, as she is satisfied it is not true she also swears that she is twenty-two years old

(Signed)—Marie Zulime Carriere Des Grange—Hasset, his mark—Ctino Lavergue—Antonio Fromentin

Before me, Franco Bermudez

TESTIMONY OF GERONIMO DES GRANGE.—In the city of New Orleans on the 7th day of September, 1802, Thomas Hasset, Presbytery Canon of this Holy Cathedral Church, Provisor Vicar General and Governor of this Bishoprick of this Province, caused to come before him, and in presence of the interpreters, Geronimo Des Granges, who was duly sworn to tell the truth, replied to the following interrogatories

Being asked whether he knows Barbara Tanbel de Orsi, how long, and in what place,

Answers That he first knew her in New York, about eleven years ago, and afterwards in Philadelphia

Being asked that if he was married to her, to state in what

2*

place before what clergyman, how long ago and who were the witnesses,

Answers That he was never married to her although he wished to do so, and had asked the consent of her father but he refused it as deponent was poor

Being asked whether ... in Bordeaux or has known her in any other place, and ... to deponent ...

Answers That he has seen her ... in Bordeaux, by mere accident, for deponent being sick Mr Sourneville her husband was sent for and ... he got well the said Sourneville invited him to dine with him, and ... where he saw her and was much astonished and there ... he continued visiting the house with no other ... token of friendship and with the knowledge of her husband

Being asked if he knows Maria Villa, to state how long he has known her, in what place and with what ...

Answers That in the month of December of last year he knew her when she was in a boarding house where she was employed as a servant in Bordeaux where the respondent lived

Being asked, if he made any arrangement with the aforesaid to accompany him to this city, to state what that arrangement was and what object she had in coming here,

Answer That he made no arrangement nor agreement with the aforesaid, and the reason she left there is that ... she asked him whether the country held out better advantages than Bordeaux, in order to gain a livelihood ... answered no and advised her to come as it would prove more advantageous to her

Being asked whether his intention is to take her with him on the voyage he intends making and ... her to do so

Answers That he has not thought of it, ... she came here to gain her livelihood, and for no other purpose

Being asked why Maria Julia Cannele his wife went to the north, last year

Answers That the principal reason was that a report had circulated in this city, that he was married to another woman she wished to ascertain whether it was true and she went

Being asked if he has ever been examined by any ecclesiastical Judge, in relation to this affair

Answers No

Being asked whether it is true that in order to satisfy his wife and the public he offered to ... him, with him or to procure documents to prove his innocence in this matter and that if he have them, to show them

Answer That taking it for granted that this charge would naturally fall, his wife being satisfied of his innocence, and no Judge having required the shewing of such documents he has used no exertions to obtain them, and that he is forty-two years old

(Signed)—.......... ....(his mark)—Antonio Pro-
........—.......... ....

Before ....—........ Bermudez

D........—No .... the public report which is
.... in a .... procedings, and hav-
..... no .... be pres ... . all procedings be suspended ... the ...... procee ..... em .... if necessary,
... ... p....... Geronimo Des ...ge be set at liberty ...
... ...

(Signed) Thomas Hassel

Don Thomas .... Presbitery Canon of the Holy Cathedral Ch.... .... and Gov.... of the Bishoprick of
this P........ or Lo .... of New Flori.. has approved
... signed the pro.... decree in New Orleans, this 7th September 1802 (Signed) Francisco Bermudez

In New Orleans on the same day, notified Geronimo Des
Grange of the ..... decree, and visited him in prison for
th.... p....

(Signed) Bermudez

G...... ...... notified and acc... to Joseph Puche the
P...... of ....

(Signed) Bermudez

Co..... the proceedings against Geronimo DesGrange
G........... To Don Thomas Hassel Governor
             of the Bishoprick for his signa-
             tures   52 rials
(Signed)   Don Franco Casegrues Judge,   2   "
Ch... ...... (Signed) Lavergne Interpreter, 36

                  Amount brought over   90   "
Amount brought forward - - - - - - 90 rials
Recd (Signed) Don Antonio Ravenin, interpreter, 36 "
(Signed) Don Franco Bermudez No 23, - 147 "
Paid (Signed) Don Jose Campo, justices, - 8 "
(Signed) Losada, taxation of cost - - - 5 "

                                            286 "
                  Dollars, - - 35 6 rials

New Orleans 9 of Sept. 1802
Signed—Juan Losada

I, the undersigned, do hereby certify that the foregoing twenty-
one pages are a true and faithful translation of the original pro

ceedings, instituted against Jeronimo des Grange, for bigamy in the year 1802, before Thomas Hassel, Presbytery Canon of the Cathedral Church of St Louis, of this city of New Orleans, and Governor of the Bishoprick of Louisiana, of which original proceedings thus translated, the R. R. Antoine Blanc, Bishop of this Diocese of New Orleans, has this day certified under his own hand, a true copy, as referred to in his testimony before the commissioner of the United States, in the case of Mrs Myra Clark Gaines against Chew & Relf and others, No 122, in the Circuit Court of the United States, district of Louisiana, on the sixth day of July, 1849

New Orleans, 12th of October, 1849

          I'DORE ANT QUEMPER

Filed, and opened, at request of Mr Duncan, under stipulation, this 3d October, 1849

          J W GURLEY, D'y Cl'k

Postage, 60 cents

Expenses of executing commission, forty dollars

          B D SILLIMAN, Commissioner.

CIRCUIT COURT OF THE UNITED STATES,
FOR THE 5TH JUDICIAL CIRCUIT, HOLDING SESSIONS IN AND FOR THE EASTERN DISTRICT OF LOUISIANA

To John Whitehead, or any other Louisiana commissioner, in the city of New York

Know ye, that reposing special trust and confidence in your integrity and ability, we hereby authorize and require you, that you call and cause to come before you, and   duly examine on oath touching and concerning certain matters and things in a case now depending in the said Court, wherein Myra Clark Gaines is plaintiff, and Relf, Chew et al, are defendants, and the same examinations, so taken and reduced to writing, you certify under your hand and seal, and send enclosed to this Court without delay, to be read in evidence on the trial of said cause, and send also this writ

Witness the honorable Roger B Taney, Chief Justice of the Supreme Court of the United States, at the city of New Orleans, this sixteenth day of July, Anno Domini 1849, and the 74th year of the Independence of the United States of America

[L.S]

          ED RANDOLPH, Clerk
          Per J W GURLEY, D'y Clerk.

The execution of this Commission appears by a certain schedule, hereto annexed, d'ted September 21st, 1 39

BENJ D SILLIMAN,
Commissioner in the State of New York,
For the State of Louisiana

In the Matter of E P Gaines and Myra Clark Gaines vs Chew & Relf, et al	IN CHANCERY In the Circuit Court of the United States, in and for the 5th Judicial Circuit, Holding Sessions in the Eastern District of Louisiana No 122

Interrogatories on the part of the defendants, propounded to Mrs Anne Frances Callendar, Mrs Caroline Matilda Stanard and Mrs Julia Ann Wood, now in the city of New York

1st. Will you and each of you be pleased to state your name, age, and usual place of residence, your maiden name, and whether or not your husband be now living, if not, when did did he depart this life, what was his business or calling, and where did he last reside?

2d Will you, and each of you, please state whether or not you are, or either of you is acquainted with the defendants, Beverly Chew and Richard Relf? If aye, how long have been so acquainted, and when, and where, and under what circumstances did you know them or either of them?

3d. Were you or was either of you or not ever in the city of New Orleans? If aye, state, with as much precision as your memory will permit, the time when you came to, and the period when you left, and where you resided when in New Orleans

4th Whether or not you were, or either of you was, acquainted with Daniel Clark, Esquire, formerly a merchant of New Orleans, and who departed this life in the month of August, 1813? If you answer affirmatively, state whether or not you were very intimately acquainted with him, where, and how frequently you saw him, at whose house and under what circumstances? Mention particularly and fully and state whether or not said Clark was a married man and what means you had of knowing, or your grounds of belief, as to this question whether or not he was married

5th. Whether or not Mr Clark was intimate with Mr Beverly Chew, or Mr Richard Relf or with either of them, and whether or not, that intimacy continued till the period of Mr. Clark's death? If you answer affirmatively state your means of knowledge.

6th Do you know or can you set forth any other matter or thing, which may be of benefit or advantage to the parties at issue in this cause, or to either of them, or that may be material

to the subject of this your examination, or the matters in question in this cause? If aye, set forth the same fully and at large in your examination.   J. G. DUNCAN.

Of Counsel for the defendants.

The complainant reserving all legal exceptions to the testimony sought to be elicited by the foregoing interrogatories, as evidence in this cause, propounds the following cross interrogatories to the said witnesses, produced and examined on the part of the defendants, to wit:

1st cross interrogatory. Were you or either of you on such terms of close intimacy with said Daniel Clark that he would have communicated to you any matter connected with his marriage? If aye, did he ever hold any conversation with you, or either of you, or in the presence of you or either of you upon that subject? If yea, when and where, and who did he say upon that subject? State fully and particular.

2d cross interrogatory. If Mr Clark had thought proper to marry privately, do you believe he would have been likely to have communicated the fact or his intention in that regard to you, or to either of you? If you answer, state why you think thus.   P. C. WRIGHT,

Counsel Solr.

The annexed depositions were taken by me, Benjamin D. Silliman, a Commissioner in the State of New York for the State of Louisiana, on the 7th, 11th, and 21st days of September 1849, under and by virtue of the annexed commission. The depositions of Mrs Julia A. C. Wood and of Mrs Caroline M. Stanard were so taken, at my office, No. 51 Wall street in the city, county, and State of New York; and the deposition of Mrs Anne M. Callender was taken at the residence of Mrs Callender, in Tenth street, in said city. I further certify that before taking and receiving the deposition of the said Mrs Julia A. C. Wood, on the 7th of September 1849, and before taking and receiving the deposition of the said Mrs Caroline M. Stanard on the 11th of September 1849, and before taking and receiving the deposition of the said Mrs Anne M. Callender, I did publicly administer to each of them separately, and apart, and out of the presence and hearing of each other, on the Holy Bible, an oath, or an affirmation, that the testimony to be given by them on the interrogatories and cross interrogatories proposed to them under said commission should be the truth, the whole truth, and nothing but the truth.

All which, with the depositions of said witnesses hereto annexed, I hereby certify to the Honorable the Circuit Court of the United States for the fifth judicial circuit holding sessions

in and for the Eastern District of Louisiana under my official
seal this 2st day of September 1849

[s]
BENJ D SILLIMAN

Commissioner of the State of New York for the State of Louisiana

Deposition ... produced sworn and executed by
virtue of ... commission on the seventh eleventh and
twenty ... September in the year of our Lord eighteen
hundred ... came 14th day in the county of New
York ... of New York before me Benjamin D Silliman ... in the State of New York for the State
of Lou ... in a cause now depending in the Circuit
Court of the United States for the 5th judicial circuit between
Maria Garcia &c plaintiff and Relf Chew &c defendants
... boundary Mrs Julia A C Wood of the
city of New York aforesaid being produced and sworn answers
as follows to the interrogatories propounded to her in this
cause

1 To the first interrogatory she saith My name is Julia A
C Wood my age is forty-nine years and my usual place of
residence is the city of New York My maiden name was
Julia A C ... and my husband is now living his name
is John Wood ... is a merchant in the city of New York,
where he ... resides

2 To the second interrogatory she saith I am acquainted
with Mr ... S Chew and Mr Richard Relf I have
been acquainted with Mr Chew since 1809 and with Mr Relf
since ... 1810 Mr Chew is my uncle and my acquaintance with I ... commenced on his return from Europe in 1809
... commenced in November 1809 from Fredricksburg
in Virginia ... New Orleans, where we went on our arrival,
on the house of Mr Relf and remained there as his guests for
some months and then and there I became acquainted with
him

3d To the third interrogatory she saith I arrived in New
Orleans in January 1810 I left there in the month of June 1813
I resided while there at Madame Florian's boarding school, part
of the time from the time of my arrival to about the month of
May at the house of Mr Relf and the rest of the time at my
uncle's whose house was always my home after the month of
May succeeding my arrival I think it was some time in the
month of June succeeding our arrival, that I was placed at
school

4th To the fourth interrogatory she saith I was acquainted
with Daniel Clark esq referred to in that interrogatory I was
intimately acquainted with him I went to New Orleans for
the purpose of being placed at school under the care of my un-

cle When we went to New Orleans Mr Clark lived in the family of Mr Relf. My uncle and his sister (then Miss Caroline Chew—now Mrs Col John Steward)a d myself were, on our arrival, invited to make our home, also at Mr Relf's, and did so. Mr Clark and Mr Relf received us on our landing in New Orleans. They came down to the boat and we went with them thence, to Mr Relf's house. We all, including Mr Clark, continued to reside in Mr Relf's house, and with him and his family, until he left it to visit the north which was not long before my uncle's marriage to which I have already alluded. My uncle, Mr Chew, then furnished the same house, and we all, including Mr Clark continued to reside with him there, until he, Mr. Clark had built and completed a house at the Bayou This, as nearly as I now recollect, was the summer before that in which we left New Orleans as above stated. My uncle's family then went and passed the summer with Mr Clark, at his new house, at the Bayou, and when the vacation in my school took place, I went there, and remained with them. At the close of the summer, my uncle and his family, including myself, returned to my uncle's house in the city. Mr Clark retained his residence at the Bayou, and whenever he was in the city, Mr. Chew's house was considered as his home and he dined there almost daily. Whenever I speak of my uncle in giving my testimony under this commission, I refer to Mr Beverly Chew. I am certain that Mr Clark was never married, my conviction on this subject results from my intimate knowledge of him, and I know that he was not married, as certainly as I know any other negative fact. I was indebted to him for great kindness. He took special interest in my education came for me frequently to the school, in his cabriolet, on Saturdays, to take me home, frequently heard me recite, selected books for me, took great interest in my studies, selected desirable books for me to read, from his own library, (which was an uncommonly large and good one) selected portions of poetry for me to commit to memory, and generally took great and constant interest in my education. In further reply to that portion of the interrogatory which requires the grounds of my belief, I may state, that he was, at the time, particularly attentive to my aunt, Miss Chew, and at the time of our parting, for Philadelphia, I think, indeed, I am almost sure of it that I heard him promise her, that he would be in Virginia, (whither she was then going,) in a short time. I know that after our arrival in Virginia we were looking forward with pleasure to the time of his expected visit It was reported in New Orleans, at the time, that he was paying his addresses to my aunt, Miss Chew. He died in the August following our departure from New Orleans. At the time Mr. Clark died, my uncle was with us in Virginia, with his family.

While I was in New Orleans I saw Mr Clark very frequently During the first three or four months I saw him almost daily I saw him almost daily during the summer we passed at the Bayou While at school I was at home during the vacations which were frequent and often at other times and on all these occasions saw him almost and as much as I saw other members of the family

5th To the fifth interrogatory she saith Mr Clark was on intimate and most friendly terms with both Mr Beverly Chew and Mr Richard Relf both of them being in New Orleans When I left New Orleans he came on board the vessel with us and took a kind and affectionate leave of my uncle and brought things of and ——

6 To —— Not ——special occasion to me which —— position —— of my answer already given except personal —— he —— would deem his position one and style of character we —— that he would have been one of the very last men on earth so far as I could judge likely or to marry any woman whose social position was not in all respects equal to his own, or whose personal character was not of the highest order

                    JULIA A. C. WOOD

Cross interrogatories

1 To the first cross interrogatory she saith My intimacy with Mr Clark was such that if he had been married I think it would have been made known to me I do not know that he would have made me specially a confidante, but it would never have been concealed from me He never held any conversation with me, or in my presence, on the subject of his being married

2 To the second cross interrogatory she saith If he had thought proper to marry privately and to keep it private, I do not suppose he would have informed me of it

                    JULIA A. C. WOOD

Examination taken reduced to writing and by the witness subscribed and sworn to before me this seventh day of September, 1849

                    BENJ D SILLIMAN
Commissioner in the State of New York for the State of Louisiana

Mrs Caroline Matilda Stanard, of Fredericksburg, Virginia, being duly and publicly affirmed pursuant to the commission hereto annexed, and examined on the part of the defendant doth depose and say as follows

1 To the first interrogatory she saith My name is Caroline Matilda Stanard I am fifty years of age, and upwards, my usual

3

place of residence is Fredericksburg in Virginia and I have at now in this city of New York on a visit. My maiden name was Caroline Matilda Chew, my husband, who was John Stothard Esq, is no living, he died about five years ago he was a colonel in the United States Army for some years and after that was Marshal of the Chancery Court in Virginia he last resided in Fredericksburg, he died in the city of Washington

2 To the second interrogatory she saith I am well acquainted both with Mr Beverly Chew, who is my brother and with Mr Richard Relf I have always been acquainted with Mr Chew I knew Mr Relf from January 1810 when I first met him in New Orleans, until the year 1813 when I left Mr Chew of course, I knew as my brother under the usual circumstances of family association and intimacy The circumstances of my acquaintance with Mr Relf were these I went to New Orleans under the care of my brother Mr Beverly Chew and in company with my niece, Mrs Silas Wood then Miss Julia Procie, in the month of January 1810 and with them went immediately to the house of Mr Relf, in New Orleans, where we all continued to reside as the guests of Mr Relf for several months, and until Mr Relf went to the north when my brother took the same house, and I continued to reside in his family until June 1813, when I left for the north

3 To the third interrogatory she saith I have already stated the time when I arrived at, and when I left, New Orleans While in New Orleans I resided as above stated, at the house of Mr Relf, from the time of my arrival until he left for the north, as aforesaid, which I think was about the month of May, 1810, but I am not positive as to the precise month, when he left I continued to reside in the same house and with my brother, who furnished it on Mr Relf's departure We continued there, as nearly as I can recollect about a year or two when we moved to another house in the same street, where we continued until our return to the north I resided in my brother's family all the time I was in New Orleans During this time I was in the convent for a few months, for the purpose of acquiring the French language

4 To the fourth interrogatory she saith I was well acquainted with Mr Clark, named in the interrogatory I was as well acquainted with him as with a brother He was a member of the family of Mr Relf from our arrival until Mr Relf departed for the north, and then continued to be a member of my brother's family until he built a house of his own at the Bayou, which, I think was the second summer after we arrived at New Orleans We passed a summer there with him, and from the time that he began to occupy his house at the Bayou, his home in town still continued at my brother's and he was there very frequently and

his room continued always in my brother's house, to be occupied by him and retained for his use. I was in the habit of seeing and meeting Mr. Clark as constantly and frequently as I met other members of the family at meal times and at other time... He was one of the family... intimate... any of...

He recovered... and made... he was... entirely took... part... I could say to a lady. I never heard... suggested the... married man whilst I was in New Orleans. I never heard such an idea expressed by any body... speak... heard of Mrs. Clark... He was the last person I took leave of on board the vessel in which we left New Orleans. He was standing by me on the deck until the vessel was actually cast off from the wharf, and his last words to me were, "God bless you." I hope to be with you in Virginia very soon.

5. To the fifth interrogatory she saith Mr. Clark was intimately and... connected with both Mr. Beverly Chew and with Mr. Richard Relf during all the period that I knew him. There never was the slightest interruption to their friendship that I ever knew. In reply to so much of the question as asks whether the intimacy continued until Mr. Clark's death I may answer affirmatively, inasmuch as my brother Mr. Beverly Chew left New Orleans with me in the same vessel and did not return to New Orleans until after Mr. Clark's death, which was in August, 1813. My uncle was with us, in Virginia, when the news of Mr. Clark's death arrived.

6. To the sixth interrogatory she saith. Nothing further occurs to me.

Cross Interrogatories.

1. To the first cross interrogatory she saith. I was on such terms of intimacy with Mr. Clark, that I can certainly say he would have communicated to me the fact of his marriage, had he been in fact married. The nature of my acquaintance with him and his communications to me necessarily precluded the possibility of his being married or of his ever having been married. He of course never intimated to me that he was or had been married.

2. To the second cross interrogatory she saith. I have no doubt that if he had thought proper to marry privately he would have communicated the fact to me and his intentions on the subject. The nature of my intimacy with him was such that I thus think.

Examination taken reduced to writing and by the witness subscribed and sworn to, before me this eleventh day of September 1849. CAROLINE M STANARD.

BENJ. D. SILLIMAN Commissioner the State of New York, for the State of Louisiana

Mrs Anna M Callender, of the city of New York, being duly and publicly sworn pursuant to the commission hereto annexed, and examined on the part of the defendants doth depose and say as follows

1 To the first interrogatory she saith My name is Anna Maria Callender. I am fifty years of age and upwards My usual place of residence is the city of New York My maiden name was Anne M Smith My husband, who was Thomas Callender, Esq is not living. He died in 1827. He was a merchant, and last resided in New York

2 To the second interrogatory she saith I know the defendants Messrs Chew and Relf I first knew them some forty years since, in New Orleans I then resided there Mr Chew and my brother married sisters, and I knew Mr Chew intimately.

3 To the third interrogatory she saith I went to New Orleans about forty years ago and left there about (35) thirty five years ago While there, I resided in Royal street part of the time but most of the time at Judge Prevost's on a plantation, four miles below town I cannot pretend to be precise about the dates

4 To the fourth interrogatory she saith I knew Mr Clark and saw him frequently at Judge Prevost's I knew him well but not intimately He dined often at Judge Prevost's, and I saw him then and on other occasions and at Mr Chew's I can't say how frequently I saw him He was not a married man, and I never heard such an idea suggested until I heard of Mrs Gaines suit I have no other grounds for my belief in this respect than his general repute in society as a single man

5 To the fifth interrogatory she saith I know Mr Clark was intimate with both Mr Chew and Mr Relf and I have every reason to believe his intimacy continued to the time of his death My means of knowledge on this point were my intimacy with Mr Chew, and my acquaintance with all the parties

6 To the sixth interrogatory she saith I can state nothing further unless, perhaps, that I heard and believe that he was engaged to be married to Miss Caton, within, I think, some three or four years before his death

Cross interrogatories

1 To the first cross interrogatory she saith. I was not on such terms of close intimacy with Mr Clark, that he would have been likely to have communicated to me any matter connected with his marriage, or to have made me his confidante in relation thereto

2 To the second cross interrogatory she saith Not to me, certainly

ANNE M CALLENDER

Examination taken, reduced to writing, and by the witness

subscribed and sworn to, this 21 September, A D 1849, before me   BENJ D SILLIMAN,

Commissioner in the State of New York,

for the State of Louisiana.

Filed 2d August 1849, and opened at request of Mr Duncan as per agreement on file   J W GURLEY

CIRCUIT COURT OF THE UNITED STATES, }
For the 5th Judicial Circuit, holding Sessions in }
and for the Eastern District of Louisiana }

To Charles C Whittlesey, Commissioner for the State of Louisiana St Louis

Know ye, that reposing special trust and confidence in your integrity and ability we hereby authorize and require you, that you call and cause to come before you Doctor John Barnes, and him duly examine on oath touching and concerning certain matters and things in a case now depending in the said Court, wherein Myra Clark Gaines is plaintiff and Relf Chew et al, are defendants and the same examinations, so taken and reduced to writing you certify under your hand and seal, and send enclosed to this Court without delay to be read in evidence on the trial of said cause and send also this writ.

Witness the honorable Roger B Taney, Chief Justice of the Supreme Court of the United States, at the city of New Orleans this twenty fifth day of June, Anno Domini 1849, and the 73d year of the Independence of the United States of America

[L S]

ED RANDOLPH, Clerk.
Per J W Gurley, D'y Clerk.

GAINES }
vs }   IN CHANCERY
CHEW & RELF, ET AL }   Circuit Court of the United States and District of Louisiana
No 122

Interrogatories propounded to Dr John Barnes residing in St Louis, Missouri, on behalf of the defendants

1st State whether or not you are acquainted with the parties to this suit, or any of them and which?

2d What is your age and residence?

3d Have you in your possession, or under your control, a letter purporting to have been written by Daniel Clark on or about the 14th day of October, 1805 in New Orleans, and addressed to his sister? If aye please annex the same to your answer to this interrogatory.

4th. If you have not the letter referred to in the last interrogatory, in your possession or under your control be pleased to state whether or not you ever had any such letter in your possession or under your control, and where the same was when you last saw it in whose possession or custody, where it is now, and do you believe it to be?

5th. If you have not the original, have you a copy? If so, annex it if you please

6th. The annexed paper is handed to you as a correct copy. Be pleased to examine it, and state whether or not it is an exact copy of the original.   G. B. DUNCAN,
                               Att'y for Chew, Relf and others.

Complainant waives all cross interrogatories, but reserves all legal exceptions to the evidence sought to be elicited by the said interrogatories, dated June 25th, 1849

                        P. C. WRIGHT, Sol for comp't.

                        NEW ORLEANS, 14th October, 1805.

My dear Sister—I have received your letter of the 3d May and thank you kindly for the pains you took in filling the toilette. I assure you that it would have given me infinite pleasure to have offered it, either to Mrs Clark or any person likely to become Mrs Clark, but this will not be the case for some time to come, for as long as I have the misfortune to be hampered with business, so long will I remain single for fear of misfortune or accident   Signed,   DANIEL CLARK.
   (A) C C W

The deposition of Dr John Barnes, of the city of St Louis, taken before the undersigned, Charles C Whittelsey, commissioner to take depositions for the State of Louisiana in the State of Missouri, in obedience to the annexed commission in a certain cause now pending in the Circuit Court of the United States for the fifth Judicial Circuit, holding sessions for the Eastern district of Louisiana, wherein Myra Clark Gaines is plaintiff, and Relf, Chew, and als are defendants

John Barnes being duly sworn, deposeth and saith, in answer to the interrogatories proposed

1st Int   State whether or not you are acquainted with the parties to this suit, or any them, and which?

Ans   I am acquainted with Myra Clark Gaines, and Chew and Relf.

2d Int   What is your age and residence?

Ans   I am fifty-eight years of age, and reside in the city of St Louis, and State of Missouri.

3d Int   Have you in your possession, or under your control a letter purporting to be written by Daniel Clark, on or about the 14th day of October, 1805, in New Orleans, and addressed to his sister? If yea please annex the same to your answer to this interrogatory

Ans I have no such letter in my custody or control

6th Int If you have not the letter, referred to in the last interrogatory in your possession or under your control, be pleased to state whether or not you ever had any such letter in your possession or under your control, and where the same was when you last saw it, in whose possession or custody, where it is now, where do you believe it to be?

Ans I have seen such letter which was in a large trunk in the office of the Clerk of Pro... among other papers of Daniel Clark's in the city of New Orleans where it is now I do not know

5th Int If you have not the original, have you a copy? If aye, annex it if you please

Ans I have no copy

6th Int The annexed paper is handed to you as a correct copy Be pleased to examine it and state whether or not it is an exact copy of the original

Ans According to my best recollection and belief, the paper here shown and marked (A) C C W, is a correct copy of the original letter that I have seen

JOHN BARNES

STATE OF MISSOURI |
County of St Louis | I, Chas C Whittelsey, commissioner in Missouri for Louisiana, do certify, that in pursuance of the annexed commission came before me, at my office, in the city and county of St Louis, Dr John Barnes and was by me duly examined on oath touching and concerning certain matters and things in a case now depending in the Circuit Court of the United States for the fifth Judicial District, wherein Myra Clark Gaines is plaintiff and Relf Chew and als, defendants, and the examination by me so taken was by me reduced to writing, and signed by him in my presence on the twentieth day of July eighteen hundred and forty-nine, and the examination so taken, with the papers thereto annexed, are herewith returned, according to the command of the commission hereto annexed

In testimony whereof, I have hereunto set my hand and [LS] affixed my seal at my office, in the city of St Louis, this 20th July, 1849

CHAS C WHITTELSEY,

Comm'r for Louisiana in the State of Missouri

Fees of commissioner, $5 Postage 30 cts Paid by L C & G B Duncan atts

Deposition of Sarah Hulings, for defendants

Received, filed, and opened at request of Mr Wright under stipulation, this, 14 October, 1849   [Postage, 40 cents]

J. W. GURLEY, D C

EDWARD RANDOLPH, Clerk

Circuit Court of the United States, for the 5th Judicial Circuit holding sessions in and for the Eastern District of Louisiana to Wm H. Rawle, Commissioner for State of Louisiana, residing in Philadelphia

Know ye that reposing special trust and confidence in your integrity and ability, we hereby authorize and require you, that you call, and cause to come before you, Mrs   Hulings and her duly examine on oath touching and concerning certain matters and things, in a case now depending in the said court, wherein Myra Clark Gaines is plaintiff, and Relf Chew et al, are defendants, and the same examinations so taken, and reduced to writing, you certify under your hand and seal, and send enclosed to this court, without delay, to be read in evidence, on the trial of said cause, and send also this writ

Witness, the Honorable Roger B Taney, Chief Justice of the Supreme Court of the United States, at the city of New Orleans, this, eighth day of August, anno domini 1849, and the 74th year of the independence of the United States of America

ED RANDOLPH Clerk

per J W GURLEY, D y Clerk

The execution of this commission appears in a certain schedule, hereto annexed   I certify that the examination was conducted as appears therein, all the interrogatories and cross interrogatories having been severally put to the witness, and severally answered, under solemn affirmation as therein set forth

WM HENRY RAWLE, Commissioner

The expense of executing this commission, is $5, five dollars

IN THE MATTER OF E. P. GAINES, AND MYRA CLARK GAINES, *vs* CHEW AND RELF, ET AL IN CHANCERY	No 122 IN THE CIRCUIT COURT OF THE UNITED STATES, IN AND FOR THE 5TH JUDICIAL CIRCUIT, HOLDING SESSIONS IN THE EASTERN DISTRICT OF LOUISIANA

Interrogatories on the part of the respondent, propounded to Mrs.   Hulings, widow of the late Dr Wm E Hulings, and now residing in Philadelphia

1st Be pleased to state your name, maiden name, your age, your present residence how long you have resided there, when you were married to Dr Hulings, and when, if be not living he departed this life

2d Whether or not you were in the city of New Orleans? If aye, at what time did you come, and how long did you remain and when depart?

3d Whether or not you are acquainted with the defendants, Beverly Chew and Richard Relf? If aye when and where did you know them?

4th Whether or not you knew Daniel Clark, Esq, merchant of New Orleans who departed this life in the month of August, 1813 if yea, state whether you knew him intimately, and can state whether or not he was a married man

State all means of knowledge on this subject and be as minute and particular in your answer as your memory will permit

And state whether or not your husband, Dr Hulings held an official station in New Orleans and what was his business if you answer that he held any official station state whether or not that station contributed to the closeness of intimacy, or frequent intercourse, between Dr Hulings and Mr Clark, at your house and in your presence

Do you know or can you state, any other matter or thing, which may be of benefit or advantage to the parties at issue in this cause, or either of them or that may be material to the subject of this your examination, or the matters in question in this cause? If yea, set forth the same fully and at large in your answer

L C DUNCAN,

of counsel for the Respondents

The complainant reserving all legal objection to the testimony sought to obtained by the foregoing interrogatories, as evidence in this cause propound the following cross interrogatories to wit

1st Cross Interrogatory Were you ever on such terms or close intimacy with the late Daniel Clark, as that he would have confided to you any matter or thing relating to his being married privately or otherwise? If aye state whether he at any time held a conversation with you upon that subject and if so when and where and what did he say to you? Did he at any time entrust you with any secrets, with regard to this matter of his marriage? If so, what was the secret confided to you?

2d Cross Interrogatory Was not Daniel Clark consul of the United States for New Orleans during the residence of yourself and your husband there? and did not your husband act as clerk of said consul and receive all or a greater portion of the emoluments of the said consulate, as a remuneration for his services? State fully and particularly

3d Cross Interrogatory If Mr Clark had chosen to marry clandestinctly, would he have entrusted you with the secret? If you answer affirmatively, say what reason you have for such belief?

P C **WRIGHT**, Comp Solicitor

Deposition of Sarah Hulings, a witness produced affirmed and examined by virtue of the annexed commission, on the fifteenth day of October, in the year of our Lord one thousand eight hundred and forty-nine, at the residence of said witness, at the south west corner of Schuylkill, Sixth and Vine streets, in the city of Philadelphia, before me, William Henry Rawle, the commissioner named in the annexed commission, and also the commissioner for the State of Louisiana to take testimony in the State of Pennsylvania, in a certain cause now depending in the Circuit Court of the United States for the fifth Judicial Circuit holding sessions in and for the Eastern district of Louisiana, wherein Myra Clark Gaines is plaintiff, and Relf, Chew, et al, are defendants

The said witness being duly affirmed (being conscientiously scrupulous of taking an oath), answers as follows to the interrogatories propounded to her in this cause

1 To the first interrogatory she answers and says

My name is Sarah Hulings my maiden name was Coren my age is seventy-nine my present residence is at the South West corner of Schuylkill, Sixth and Vine streets, in the city of Philadelphia, I was born and brought up in this city I have permanently resided here since 1804, I was married to the late Doctor Hulings, in this city, and he resided here at the time of his death

2 To the second interrogatory, she answers and says

I have been in New Orleans, I first left this city to go thither in July, 1791, and arrived there in September of that year, I remained there until May, 1804 when I left there to come to this city

3 To the third interrogatory, she answers and says

I am acquainted with both Beverly Chew and Richard Relf Mr Relf went with me to New Orleans in 1791 I had known him here for some years before I made the acquaintance of Mr Chew in New Orleans, some time after my arrival

4 To the fourth interrogatory, she answers and says

I was intimately acquainted with said Daniel Clark I do not know that Mr Clark was a married man I never had the least intimation that he was so. I made Mr Clark's acquaintance on the day I arrived in New Orleans, and he was every day at my house We lived, in the summer of the yellow fever, in the same house in the country My intimacy with Mr Clark continued while in New Orleans and subsequently, during his visits here From my long and continued intimacy with Mr Clark I have no hesitation in saying that he never was married, but was received in my house, and so far as I know, in the houses of others as an unmarried man. It was as perfectly understood that Mr Clark was an unmarried man as that Mr Relf and Mr Chew were married men, after they *were* married. From his language and conduct, he held himself out to society and the world as an unmarried man. My late husband Dr Hulings, was a merchant, and was vice consul of the United States. He acted as consul at the port of New Orleans then a foreign port. I do not think that the position of Dr Hulings, as vice consul, contributed to the intimacy between himself and Mr Clark, but they were both merchants together. I know that their personal and business relations were intimate, and Dr Hulings often lent money to Mr Clark, in whom he reposed great confidence. Dr Hulings acted as Mr Clark's agent in Philadelphia, in the payment of money to Mr Clark's mother, who resided in Germantown. He was subsequently named by said Mrs Clark one of her executors. I do not know that the official position of my late husband contributed to the closeness of the intimacy or frequent intercourse between Mr Clark and himself at my house and in my presence further than would have been the case from their personal acquaintance and confidence in each other.

5. To the fifth interrogatory, she answers and says

I do not know any other matter or thing, which may be of benefit or advantage to the parties at issue in this cause, or either of them, or that may be material to the subject of this my examination, or the matters or questions in this cause.

To the cross interrogatories, she answers and says

1. To the first cross interrogatory, she answers and says

The terms of close intimacy which I had with the late Mr Clark, were such that I certainly think he would have confided to me any matter or thing relating to his being married privately or otherwise. He never held a conversation with me on that subject. He never, at any time, entrusted me with any secret, with regard to this matter of his marriage.

2. To the second cross interrogatory, she answers as follows

Towards the close of our residence in New Orleans, Mr Clark held the commission of consul of the United States, for New Orleans and Dr Hulings acted as consul, discharging all the duties of his office, receiving all or a greater portion of the emoluments of the said consulate as a remuneration for his service.

3. To the third cross interrogatory, she answers and says

I can only answer this interrogatory by saying that from the closeness of our intimacy, I presume Mr Clark would not have married, without apprising me of it. If he had chosen to make his marriage strictly clandestine, of course he would have told no one   SARAH HULINGS.

Affirmed to and subscribed before me on the day and at the place first aforesaid

WILLIAM HENRY RAWLE, Commissioner

I, William Henry Rawle the commissioner named in the annexed commission, and also the commissioner for the State of Louisiana, to take testimony in the State of Pennsylvania, do hereby certify that the affirmant, Sarah Hulings, was by me duly affirmed (she being conscientiously scrupulous of taking an oath) to declare the truth on the questions put to her in this cause that the interrogatories and cross interrogatories were produced to her, and her answers thereto taken in writing by me and subscribed by her in my presence, on the day and at the place in that behalf first aforesaid

In testimony whereof, I have hereunto set my hand and [L S] affixed my seal of office, this fifteenth day of October Anno Domini one thousand eight hundred and forty-nine

WILLIAM HENRY RAWLE, Commissioner

Opened in court, by consent Nov 26, 1849 for J W Gurley, D C   ROB'T M LUSHER

CIRCUIT COURT OF THE UNITED STATES,
For the 5th Judicial Circuit, holding Session in and for the Eastern District of Louisiana

To Major John Mountfort, at Biloxi, Miss, or William H Cleveland of the same place

Know ye, that reposing special trust and confidence in your integrity and ability we hereby authorize and require you, that you call and cause to come before you Pierre Debuys, and him duly examine on oath touching and concerning certain matters and things in a case now depending in the said court, wherein Myra Clark Gaines is plaintiff, and Relf, Chew, et al are defendants, and the same examination, so taken and reduced to writing, you certify under your hand and seal, and send enclosed to this court without delay, to be read in evidence on the trial of said cause and send also this writ

Witness the honorable Roger B Taney, Chief Justice of the Supreme Court of the United States, at the city of New Orleans, this 29th day of June, Anno Domini 1849, [L S] and the 73d year of the Independence of the United States of America   ED RANDOLPH, Clerk,

Per J W Gurley, Dy Clerk.

MYRA GAINES
vs
CHEW, RELF, AND OTHERS
} CIRCUIT COURT OF THE UNITED STATES, FIFTH CIRCUIT.

Interrogatories to Pierre Dubuys, a witness for the defendants, to be qualified and examined under the annexed commission

Int 1st Do you, or not, know Madam Zulime DeGrange nee Carriere? and how long have you known her?

Int 2d What was her reputation for chastity, previously to the year 1808? was she, or not, a virtuous woman? State all your means of knowledge

Int 3d Did you know Madam Sophia Despau? and how long? what was her reputation for chastity? and what were your means of knowledge? what is her character for truth and veracity?

Int 4th Did you know the late Daniel Clark? did he, or not, live and die a bachelor? and if you answer in the affirmative, state all your means of knowledge

Do you know any other matter or thing that would be useful to defendants, who are sued for their property by Mrs Gaines, alleging herself to be the legitimate daughter of Daniel Clark, the issue of his lawful marriage with Zulime DeGrange née Carriere? If so, state every thing you know on these subjects, as fully as if particularly interrogated thereto

ISAAC T PRESTON,
Solicitor for defendants

The complainant, reserving to herself all right of exception to the foregoing interrogatories, declines to propound cross interrogatories at the present time New Orleans, July 3d, 1849

P C WRIGHT, Solicitor for complainant

MYRA GAINES
vs
CHEW, RELF, AND OTHERS
} CIRCUIT COURT OF THE UNITED STATES, FIFTH CIRCUIT

In pursuance of the annexed commission issuing out of said court, directed to Major John Mountford, at Biloxi, Miss, or me, William H Cleveland of the same place I, William H Cleveland aforesaid, did, on this 18th day of July, A D 1849, cause Pierre Dubuys, a witness therein named to come before me, and did him then duly examine on oath, by propounding to him the interrogatories annexed to said commission, and his answers did then reduce to writing, in his presence, and cause to be signed by him, which answers are the following

To the first interrogatory witness answers

I know Madam Zulime DeGrange nee Carriere I have known her from my youth

To the second interrogatory he answers

I do not know

To the third interrogatory

I did not know Madam Sophie Despau at all, consequently, I can state nothing further in answer to this interrogatory

To the fourth interrogatory

I knew the late Daniel Clark, from my childhood until his death. I have always been under the impression he was a bachelor. There was a report once, that he was to marry a lady at Natchez. I have no positive knowledge in regard to this matter. I cannot state the time when this report was current.

To the fifth interrogatory

No.

P DEBUYS

Signed and sworn to, this 18th day of July, A D 1849, at Biloxi, Mississippi, before me,

WM H. CLEVELAND, [Seal]
Commissioner

Filed 2d August, 1849, and opened at request of Mr Duncan, in accordance with agreement on file

J. W GURLEY, Deputy Clerk

CIRCUIT COURT OF THE UNITED STATES,
For the Fifth Judicial Circuit, holding Sessions
in and for the Eastern District of Louisiana

To Daniel D Avery

Know ye, that reposing special trust and confidence in your integrity and ability, we hereby authorize and require you that you call and cause to come before you Philip Hicky, and him duly examine on oath, touching and concerning certain matters and things in a case now depending in the said Court wherein E P Gaines and Wife are plaintiffs, and Relf, Chew, et al, are defendants, and the same examinations, so taken and reduced to writing, you certify under your hand and seal, and send enclosed to this Court without delay, to be read in evidence on the trial of said cause, and send also this writ

Witness the honorable Roger B Taney, Chief Justice of the Supreme Court of the United States, at the city of New Orleans, this twenty-ninth day of May, Anno Domini 1849, and the 73d year of the Independence of the United States of America.

[L S]

ED RANDOLPH, Clerk

J W GURLEY, D'y Clerk

IN CHANCERY

E. P. GAINES & WIFE ⟩ CIRCUIT COURT OF THE U. S. AND
vs EASTERN DISTRICT OF LOUISIANA
CHEW, RELF, ET AL ⟨ No. 122

Interrogatories propounded on behalf of the defendants Richard Relf, Beverly Chew and F. Dussuau Delacroix, to Col. Philip Hickey, residing in East Baton Rouge, Louisiana

1st What is your age, residence and occupation?

2d How long have you lived in Louisiana?

3d Were you acquainted with the late Daniel Clark of New Orleans?

4th Did you ever hear of Daniel Clark being a married man?

5th What was the general reputation of Daniel Clark in the community in which he resided, and in Louisiana generally, as to his being a married man or otherwise?

6th What was the general reputation of Daniel Clark, in New Orleans as to his relations or connection with Madame DeGrange?

7th Who was Jerome DeGrange, and what was his occupation or business and where did he carry on his business?

8th Do you know, either personally or by general report and reputation any thing about Daniel Clark having addressed a young lady with a view to marriage? If aye, state who the young lady was, and the time, as near as you can, when this transaction took place

9th Judging from your knowledge of Daniel Clark, and from his general reputation, do you, or do you not, believe that if he had been really a married man, and having a lawful living wife, that he would have been guilty of the outrage upon a lady's feelings of addressing her with a view to marriage? State fully

10th Is there any other matter or thing, within your knowledge, not yet related, and which would be of any benefit to either complainants or either of the defendants? If aye, please state the same as fully and particularly, as if you had been thereunto specially interrogated

G. B. DUNCAN

Counsellor and Solicitor for Chew, Relf, and Delacroix

The complainants in the foregoing entitled suit, by P. C. Wright, their solicitor, saving and reserving to themselves, now and at all times hereafter, all and all manner of exceptions, which may be had or taken to the form of the foregoing interrogatories, and to the admissibility of the testimony of said witness and all other legal ojection, propound the following cross interrogatories

1s cross interrogatory Have you at any time held or

claimed, or do you now hold or claim, any property, real or personal, of any name or kind, which belonged to Daniel Clark, deceased, during his lifetime, or which was found in his succession? State fully and particularly. Also, whether you have had, or now have any interest in such property?

2d cross interrogatory. Have you any interest in the result of this suit?

3d cross interrogatory. Were you on terms of close intimacy and friendship with said Daniel Clark? State particularly.

4th cross interrogatory. Did you ever visit the said Daniel Clark at his residence in New Orleans, or elsewhere? if yea, who have you met there? Who were Mr Clark's most intimate and confidential friends? Did you know either of those friends intimately, and which of them?

5th cross interrogatory. Did Daniel Clark ever speak with you respecting his domestic relations and affairs? if yea, what did he say? what time did this conversation take place? who else was present, if any one?

P. C. WRIGHT, Complainant's Solicitor

IN CHANCERY

E P GAINES AND WIFE
v
CHEW & RELF, ET AL

UNITED STATES CIRCUIT COURT, FIFTH JUDICIAL CIRCUIT HOLDING SESSIONS IN AND FOR THE EASTERN DISTRICT OF LOUISIANA

No 122

By virtue of the annexed commission to me directed, by the honorable the United States Circuit Court, in and for the Fifth Judicial Circuit, holding sessions in and for the Eastern District of Louisiana, as the Commissioner of said Court, to take the testimony of Philip Hicky, a witness in the above entitled suit. I caused the said witness to appear before me, at my office, in the town of Baton Rouge, on Monday the ninth day of July A D. eighteen hundred and forty nine, and having administered to him the oath required by law, I then propounded to him the interrogatories hereto annexed, propounded to him, by and in behalf of the defendants Richard Relf, Beverly Chew and F Dussuau Delacroix, as well as the cross interrogatories propounded by the plaintiffs, E P Gaines and wife to which said witness answers as follows:

To 1st interrogatory. I was on the 17th June last seventy-one years of age. I reside in the parish of East Baton Rouge, and am a planter

To 2d interrogatory. I have resided in Louisiana about sixty-two years

To 3d interrogatory. I was well acquainted with Daniel Clark

To 4th interrogatory I do not recollect ever to have heard that Daniel Clark was married

To 5th interrogatory As already stated, I have no recollection of his being spoken of as a married man

To 6th interrogatory Being but seldom in New Orleans and then but for a few days at a time since 1799 I knew nothing of Daniel Clark's connection with Mrs DeGrange

To 7th interrogatory I knew a DeGrange his first or given name I do not recollect he resided in one of the houses belonging then to Don Andres on the Place des Armes or Public Square He was at that time a confectioner

To 8th interrogatory I do not recollect any thing respecting Daniel Clarks having addressed a young lady with the intention of marrying her

To 9th interrogatory I do not believe that he would

To 10th interrogatory I know nothing further, that would be of interest or advantage to the defendants

Answers to cross interrogatories

To 1st cross interrogatory I never held or claimed, nor do I now hold or claim any property, real or personal, of any name or kind which belonged to Daniel Clark, or which was found in his succession, and consequently have no interest in any such property

To 2d cross interrogatory I know of no interest which I have in the result of this suit

To 3d cross interrogatory I was intimate with Daniel Clark he has often been at my father's house and frequently at my own

To 4th cross interrogatory I never visited Daniel Clark except at his store or counting room, in New Orleans and at this time I do not recollect who were his most intimate friends

To 5th cross interrogatory I do not recollect ever having had any conversation with Daniel Clark relating to his domestic affairs   PHILIP HICKY

And the said Philip Hicky, having carefully read the answers to the several interrogatories and cross interrogatories aforesaid as written by me and having signed the same as above I have closed these presents In attestation of all which I have hereunto subscribed my name and affixed my private seal, at Baton Rouge, the day and year above written

DANIEL AVERY   [seal]

DEFENDANTS EXHIBITS
D 3
Filed by Defendant 20 June 1849

J W GURLEY, Com'r

Be it known that this day before me Carlisle Pollock, a No

tary Public, in and for this city of New Orleans, duly commissioned and sworn, personally came and appeared, Richard Relf of this city, who produced and exhibited unto me, Notary three several documents, written in the English language purporting to be the last will of Mary Clark, the Governor's certificate thereunto annexed, and a power of attorney from Joseph Reed, the executor of the last will of the said Mary Clark, to Richard Relf and Beverly Chew, who having required of me Notary, to deposit said documents in my current register, I have, in compliance with his request, annexed the same to the margin of this act there to remain of record

Done and recorded at New Orleans, this 28th day of August eighteen hundred and twenty-four in presence of George Pollock and William Boswell witnesses, who have signed their names with the said appearer and me, Notary

[Signed]—Richard Relf—George Pollock—W Boswell—Carlisle Pollock, Notary Public

Copy of Document No 1, alluded to in the foregoing act of
deposit

In the fear of God' Amen I, Mary Clark, formerly of Ireland, now of the city of Philadelphia in the State of Pennsylvania, in the United States of America, being through the mercy of the Most High, of a sound disposing mind and in my usual state of health, do make and declare this my last will and testament

First, I order and direct, that all my just debts and personal expenses be fully paid and satisfied, as soon as conveniently may be, after my decease

Secondly, I give, devise and bequeath unto my executor herein after named, and to the survivor of them, and to the executors of said survivor, all my estate and property, real and personal, whatsoever and wheresoever, in trust, nevertheless, and to the intent and purpose that they shall and do immediately, or as soon as conveniently may be after my decease, collect all the monies and debts due to me, or received by any person for my account, acting under me, and also sell and dispose of all my lands and tenements, goods or chattels, rights and credits, for the best price that can be had or obtained for the same and on this further trust that they shall and do devise and distribute the monies arising from said sales, as the same may be received, into four equal parts and I do give, devise, and bequeath one share or fourth part thereof, to my daughter, Eleanor O'Bearn, of Sligo, in the kingdom of Ireland her heirs and assigns, forever, and in case the said Eleanor O'Bearn should be now dead, or should die before me I give and devise the share to the child or children of the said Eleanor their heirs and assigns, to be equally divided between them, share and share alike Further, I do give devise and bequeath one other share or fourth part of my said estate and property to my daughter Jane Green the wife of George Green of L__pool in the kingdom of Great Britain, her heirs _____ forever and in case the said Jane Green shall be _____ _____ _____ I give and desire the said share to _____ children of me said Jane Green ____ there ____ _____ ___ to be _____ belonging to them and shall _____ _____ _____ ___ proportion _____ one or both ____ ____ _____ the _____ proportion _____ grand-children to ____ _____ my Son ___ power to ____ ___ to hold the ____ ____ and to her heirs ____ _____ for ____ I _____ I do ____ ___ _____ adequate ____ ____ _____ _____ part of my said ____ and property _____ my grand-daughter, Caroline Clark _____ daughter of my ____ son Daniel Clark ____ _____ to her, _____ ___ of her age or ____ marriage ____ ____ whichever shall _____ _____ care and ___ age of eighteen years which ____ first ___ happen and ____ I die before either of the said events do take place then and in that case, the interest, profit or issue of the said share or fourth part of my said estate and property shall be paid and handed over to such person or persons, as she the said Caroline shall choose for her guardian or guardians to be appropriated by them for her support and maintenance until she shall by this my will, be entitled to receive the principal as aforementioned and in case the said Caroline Clark shall die unmarried or before she attains an age of eighteen years or if single, it is my will and desire that the said interest or principal sum to her devised, shall be paid and distributed in equal proportions to and among each of my heirs herein named, as shall be then living and to the legal representatives of such or others as shall be dead such representatives taking among themselves such share only, as their deceased parent, if living, would have taken. Further I do give, devise, and bequeath to my grand-daughter, Mira Clark, commonly called Mira Davis, a other natural daughter of my late son, Daniel Clark, the sum of two hundred dollars, to parents as a jewel as a remembrance of me I would have left her equal with my other heirs were she not already provided for. And I do further declare it to be my will, that no devise or legacy herein contained shall be deemed or held to be lapse, or become void by reason of the decease of the devisee or legatee in my life time but such devise or legacy shall be good and available in favor of the heirs or legal representatives of such legatee or devisee, under, and subject, nevertheless to the limitations herein before contained as if such devisee or legatee had survived me I do hereby nominate and appoint Joseph Reed, Esq attorney at Law, and Wm L. Hulings M D, both of the city of Philadelphia, to be the executors of this my last will and testament, hereby revoking all other

wills, testaments and powers, by me heretofore made and given,
and I do declare and acknowledge this to be my last will and
testament. witness whereof I have hereunto set my hand and
seal, this twenty-second day of November, in the year of our
Lord, one thousand eight hundred and seventeen.

(Signed)   MARY CLARK   [SEAL]

Signed, sealed, published, and released and declared by the
above named Mary Clark, as and for her last will and testament,
in the presence of us, who have, at her request and in her presence, and in the presence of each other subscribed our names as
witnesses thereto.—(Signed) John Connelly—Isaac Harvey Jr.
—L. Nicholson—John Bunting—Wm E Hulings

PHILADELPHIA June 3d, 1823

There personally appeared John Connelly Isaac Harvey Jr
and Lemdsay Nicholson three of the witnesses to the aforegoing
will, and on their solemn affirmation according to law, did declare and say that they did see and hear Mary Clark the testatrix
in the said will named sign, seal, publish and declare the same
as and for her last will and testament, and that at the doing
thereof she was of sound mind and memory and understanding, to the
best of their knowledge and belief.

CORAN EDMUND ROGERS, Deputy Register
CITY AND COUNTY OF PHILADELPHIA SS.

I certify that the foregoing writing is a true copy of the original last will and testament, and probate thereof of Mary Clark
deceased on file, and remaining on record in the Register's office
at Philadelphia.

Given under my hand and seal of office, the twenty-ninth day
of March, anno Domini 1824

(Signed)   JOS BARNES Register

The undersigned Notary does hereby certify the foregoing to
be a true copy of the original act of deposit made at the request
of Richard Relf of this city on the twenty-eighth day of August
1824, in the archives of my office, and also a true copy of the document No One annexed to said act of deposit, in said archives.

Witness, my signature, and seal of office at New Orleans, the
twenty-eighth of December, 1844

CARLISLE POLLOCK, Notary Public

[No 4]
Offered by Defendants   Filed 20th June 1849
J W GURLEY, Com'r.

Know all men, by these presents that I, Joseph Reed, of the
city of Philadelphia, in the county of Philadelphia, and State
of Pennsylvania executor of the last will and testament of Mary
Clark, late of Germantown of the county of Philadelphia

deceased have made, constituted and appointed and by these presents do make constitute and appoint and in my place and stead put and depute Richard Relf and Beverly Chew of the city of New Orleans in the State of Louisiana my true and lawful attorneys for me and in my name and for my use to ask demand sue for and recover and receive all such sum or sums of money, debts goods wares, and other demands whatsoever, which is or shall be due, owing, payable, and belonging to me as executor aforesaid by any manner or means whatsoever, and also to grant bargain and sell all the lands tenements and hereditaments whatsoever belonging to the said Mary Clark, or to which he is in any manner or way entitled to in, by, from, or under the will of the late Daniel Clark of the city of New Orleans, situate in the said State of Louisiana or the Territory of Florida, or elsewhere within the United States or the territories thereof and all the estate right, title and interest of the said Mary Clark therein, unto such person or persons, and for such price or prices as they, my attorneys may think proper, and also for me and in my name, place and stead, and as my proper act and deed to sign seal and deliver and acknowledge all such deed or deeds of conveyance as shall be necessary for the absolute granting and assuring the premises unto the purchaser in fee simple giving and granting unto my said attorney, by these presents my full and whole authority as executor aforesaid, in and about the premises, to have, use and take all lawful ways and means in my name for the purposes aforesaid and upon the receipt of any debts, dues, or sums of money, (as the case may be) acquittances or other sufficient discharges, for me and in my name to make, seal and deliver and generally all and every other act or acts, thing or things, device and devices in the law whatsoever needful and necessary, to be done in and about the premises for me and in my name to do so, execute, and perform, as fully largely and amply, to all intents and purposes, as I can so I might or could do, if personally present, and attorney one or more under them for the purposes aforesaid, to make and constitute and again, at pleasure, to revoke hereby ratifying and allowing and holding for firm and effectual all and whatsoever my said attorneys shall lawfully do in and about said premises, by virtue hereof

In witness whereof I have hereunto set my hand and seal, this second day of December in the year one thousand eight hundred and twenty-three

(Signed)   JOS REED

Sealed and delivered in the presence of us,

Jno Antrum—Roberton Wharton, Mayor

On this thirteenth of December Anno Domini 1823, personally appeared before me Robert Whart, mayor of the city of

Philadelphia, the above named Joseph Reed, and acknowledged the above written letter of attorney to be his act and deed and desired the same to be recorded as such, according to law

In witness whereof, I have hereunto set my hand and affixed the seal of the city, the day and year above written

(Signed)   ROBERT WHARTON Mayor

I, the undersigned Notary, do hereby certify the foregoing to be a true copy of an original instrument of procuration deposited in the archives of my office, and annexed to an act of deposit passed before me, on the thirtieth day of August eighteen hundred and twenty-four

In faith whereof, I have granted these presents under my signature and seal of office, at New Orleans, on the seventh day of December, eighteen hundred and forty-four

CARLISLE POLLOCK Not Pub

[No 5]

Offered by defendants.   Filed 20 June, 1849

J W GURLEY, Com

Sepan quantos esta carta vieren como yo Dn Geronimo Desgrange vecino de esta ciudad atorgo que doy todo me poder amplio bastante quanto por oro se requiera a Da Maria Zulima Carriere mi legitima esposa general para que en my nombre y representando mi propria persona dros y acciones haga demande perciva y scovre todas y quales quier cantidades de mis pesos de oro joyas esclavas mercaderias frutos de la tierra y otros efectos que al presente se me devan y en adelante me devieren por escrituras vales cuentas alcances conocimientos donaciones herencias clausula de testamento o por otro qualquier titulo a razon que sea aunque aqui no se especifiquen las cantidades ni las personas por quienes se me devan (y en adelante devieren por escrituras vales cuentas Alcances, conocimientos donaciones herencias) digo a las quales pida y tome cuentas haciendales cargos admitiendales justos des cargos nombrando terceros en discordia que ajusten liquiden resuelvan y determinen las dudas y dificultades que se ofrecieren confiriendo esperas si lo hallare por conveniente y de las cantidades que percivieren y demas que cobrare atorque recivos y cartas de pago finiquitos poderes y lastos con fee de la entrega o renunciacion de las leyes de este caso pueda administrar y administre todo y qualesquiera mis bienes asi raices como muebles arrendarlos venderlos hipotecarlos y comprar otros a los precios y plazos que ajustare y consentare otorgando sobre el particular las escrituras combenientes las que desde luego apruevo y ratifio como si presente fuere a su otorgamento y para todo mis pleitos causas y negocios civiles criminales, ordinarios y executivas movidos y par mover que de presente tengo y en adelante tuviere con qualquiere persona

demandando y defendiendo en todas y en cada uno de ellos
presentando escritos escrituras testigos probanzas y todo las
demas recaudos y papeles ql por bien tuviere sacandolos de
donde se halaren oiga ciertos y sentencios interlocutorias y defi-
atias lo favorable consienta y de lo perjudicial apele y suplique
... la apelacion y suplicacues y en todas instancias y
... y finalmente presente actue y obre quantas dilig-
... y esta juiciosse ofrescan sin exceptuar algunas
que el p ... que por todo lo incidente y dependiente necesité
... los y autigo sin limitacion con libre tranca y gral
administracion facultad de enjuiciar jurar substituir revocar
... y nombrar otros con relevacion en forma Al cumplimiento de todo ... obligo mis bienes havido y por haver
Doy p der a las justicias de **S M** para que me apremen a su
cumplimiento con todo rigor de dro como por sentencia consentida y pasada en autoridad de cosa jusgada sobre que renuncio
las leyes de ... con ra gral enforma que le prohive En
cuyo testimonio es fl lo carta en la ciudad de la Nueva Orleans
a veinte y seis de Marzo de mil ocho cientos y un años Yo
el Esno doy fee conozco al atorgante que lo firmo siendo
testigos Dn Santiago Felipe Guinault, Dn Simon Favre, y Dn.
Antonio Fromcain vecinos y presentes.

Original signed—J Des Grange—Ante mi Narco Broutin,
Esno Publico

I certify the foregoing to be a true copy of the original on file
and of record in this office

In truth whereof I grant these presents under my signature
and seal of office, at New Orleans, this 8th June A D 1849.

WM CHRISTY, Not Pub.

[No 6]

Offered by Defendants   Filed 20th June 1849

J W GURLEY, Com'r

Sepan cuantos esta carta vieren como nos Dona Felicite Carriere muger legitima de Dn Sintoriano Caillavet devidamente
autorisada par el dho mi marido para atargar la presente Dona
Maria Carriere muger legitima de Dn Bertran Lasabe ausente
y Dona Maria Sofia Carriere muger legitime de Don Guillermo Despaux teniendo en ausente y autorezadas par el Senor Dn
Nicholas Forstall Alcalde de primera eleccion para otargar la
presente Escritura Decimos que par la presente Damas todo
nuestros poder amplio bastante quanto por dro se requiera mas
pueda y deva valer a Dn Geronimo Desgrange vecino de esta
ciudad nuestro cuñado General para que en nuestro nombre y
representando nuestra propia persona dras y acciones perciva
y cobre todas las cantidades y efectos que nos corresponden
como lexitima conerederas a las bienes de nuestros Defuntos

Padre y madre Dn Juan Carriere natural de Libourne y Doña Maria Chauffert natural de Burdeos para lo qual siendo necesario haga y pratique quantas dilig's judiciales y extra Judiciales se ofrescan sin exceptuar alguna pueda reclamar y pedir cuentas a toda persona que tengan chos bienes, y de loque perciviere y cobrare otorgue recivos y cartas de pago finiquitos paderes y costas con fee de la entrega o renunciacion de las leyes de este caso oiga autos y sentencias interlocutorias y definitivas lo favorable consienta y de lo perjudicial apele y suplique siga las apelaciones y suplicaciones en todas instancias y tribunales que el pader que para todo lo incidente y dependiente necesite e se le damos y atargamos con libre franca y gral administracion facultad de enjuiciar jurar substituir revocar substitutos y nombrar otros con relevacion en forma   Al cumplimto de lo qual obligamos nuestros bienes havidos y por haver, damas poder a las Justicias de S M. para que nos apremen a su cumplimiento con todo rigor de dro como por sentencia consentida y pasada en autoridad de cosa gusgada sobre que renuncio las leyes de mi favor con la gral en forma que la prohine   En cuyo testimonio es fha la carta en la ciudad de la Nueva Orleans a veinte y seis de Marzo de mil ocho cientos y un anas   Lo el Escrivano doy fee conozco a las atorgantes que la firmaron siendo testigas Dn Antonio Boudousquie Dn Simon Favre y Don Antonio Fromentin vecinos y presentes

Original signed—Marie Carriere—Sophie Carrière—Felicit. Carrière—Simphe Caillavet—Ante mi Narco Broutin, E no Pub'co

I certify the above and before written, to be a true copy of the original on file, and of record in my office

In faith whereof, I grant these presents under my hand and seal of office, at New Orleans, this 5th June A D 1849

[L S]   W CHRISTY, Not Pub

[No 7]
Offered by defendants, filed 20th June, 1849
                    J. W. GURLEY, Commissioner

Aujourd'hui, seizieme jour du mois de Mai, de l'année mil huit cent onze et la trente cinquieme de l'Independance Americaine, pardevant nous, Pierre Pedesclaux Notaire Public des Etats Unis de l'Amerique, à la Nouvelle Orleans, est comparu Mr Daniel Clark, demeurant en cette ville, lequel a par ces presents, vendu, cede, quitte et transporte, sous la garantie de tous troubles dettes, hypotheques et autres empechements generalement quelconques, ce que certifie l'annotateur quant a l'ypotheque seulement

A Mons Joseph Deville Degoutin Bellechasse, demeurant en

cette dite ville, ici present et acceptant pour lui, ses hoirs ou ayant causes

Les terrains situés au faubourg St. Jean distant de cette ville d'une demie lieue, ou environ, dans l'Islet No onze, designés sous les Nos un, deux, trois quatre, cinq, sept, huit, neuf, dix, faisant face aux rues des Chênes Verts et Bellechasse, et à la septieme et sixieme rue

De plus tout, l'Ilet No vingt, borné par la sixième et cinquieme rue, et par les rues Bellechasse et des Chênes Verts

De plus, les terrains situés dans le dit faubourg, dans l'Islet vingt et un, désignés sous les Nos un deux, trois, quatre, cinq, sept, huit, neuf et dix, faisant face aux rues Bellechasse et des Chênes Verts, et à la cinquieme et quatrieme rue

De plus, tout l'Islet No vingt-neuf, borné par les rues Belle-chasse et des Chênes Verts, par les quatrieme et troisieme rues, et par le Sieur Le Blanc, finalement neuf terrains situés dans le dit faubourg dans l'Islet No quatorze, coté sous les Nos trois, quatre, cinq, six, sept, huit, nuef, dix et onze, faisant face aux rues Washington et Lepage et à la sixieme et septieme rue

Le tout conformement au plan figuratif fait par Mons. B y Lafon, et annexé à nos minutes, le neuf Juin, mil huit cent neuf, lesquels terrains, le sieur acquéreur a dit connaitre et en être content

La presente vente faite et acceptée entre les parties aux clauses et conditions ci-dessus, et en outre pour le prix et somme de six milles piastres, que le sieur vendeur declare avoir reçu comptant du sieur acquéreur, avant la passation des presentes, et dont il lui en donne quittance, au moyen de quoi, il s'est dé-sisté et separé de tous droits de propriété sur les dits terrains, ci-dessus vendus, en faveur du sieur acquéreur, qu'il en a saisi et revetu pour par lui en jouir, faire et disposer comme de chose à lui appartenant, dès maintenant et à toujours, et en prendre possession quand bon lui semblera, car ainsi, &c

Dont acte, fait et passé en notre etude, à la Nouvelle Orléans, le jour et an, que dessus, en presence des sieurs Joseph de Toca et Phi. Pedesclaux, temoins, qui ont signé avec les parties et nous, notaire

(Signé)—J D Degoutin Bellechasse—Daniel Clark—Phi. Pedesclaux—Joseph de Toca—Pierre Pedesclaux, Not Pub

Pour copie conforme à l'original, reste en mon étude pour recours, en foi de quoi j'ai signé les présentes, et y ai apposé le sceau de mon etude

LOUIS T CAIRE, Not. Pub

Nouvelle Orleans, le 21 Mai, 1849

[No 8]
Offered by defendants, filed 20th June, 1849
J W. GURLEY, Commissioner.

Pardevant Philp Pedesclaux, notaire public pour la ville et paroisse de la Nouvelle Orléans, et en présence des témoins ci-après nommés, fut present, M Fr. Dussuau Delacroix, demeurant en cette ville, lequel a, par ces présentes, vendu, céde et transporté, avec garantie de tous troubles, dettes, hypotheques, evictions et autres empéchements généralement quelconques,

A Demoiselle Myra Clark, mineure pubere, demeurant en cette ville, acquéreur pour elle, ses héritiers et ayant causes, ce qui à été accepté par le sieur Samuel B Davis, demeurant en cette ville, son curateur ad bona, à ce présent, un lot de terre situe au faubourg St Jean, à environ une demi lieue de cette ville, comprenant les deux Ilets, designes sous les Nos six et quinze, bornés aux nord par Messieurs Blanque et Fortier, à l'ouest par la sixième rue, au sud par la rue Lepage, et a l'est la dame veuve Kernion, le tout conformement au plan du dit faubourg déposé en notre etude; appartenant au vendeur pour l'avoir acheté de M Samuel B Davis, par acte devant feu Pierre Pedesclaux, lors notaire en cette ville, en date du premier du mois de Mai, de l'année mil huit cent douze

Cette vente est faite pour et moyennant la somme de deux milles piastres, que le vendeur declare avoir reçues de l'acquéreur, hors la vue du notaire, et des témoins soussignés, et dont il lui donne quittance et decharge, renonçant, à l'exception de la non numerata pecunia et autres lois á ces relatives, la dite somme ayant eté remise par le feu sieur Daniel Clark au sieur Davis, qui le reconnait, à l'effet de faire l'acquisition du dit lot de terre pour compte, et au nom de la dite Demoiselle Myra Clark.

Au moyen de ce payement, le vendeur met et subroge l'acquéreur dans tous les droits de propriete qu'il a, et peut avoir, sur le lot de terre presentement vendu, consentant que l'acquéreur en soit saisie et revêtue, pour par elle en jouir, faire et disposer comme de chose à lui appartenant en toute propriété, dès maintenant et à toujours.

D'après le certificat du conservateur, à la date de ce jour, il n'y a point d'hypothèques contre M François Dussuau Delacroix sur le lot de terre présentement vendu

Fait et passé en l'étude, à la Nouvelle Orleans, le seizième jour du mois de Mai, de l'annee mil huit cent vingt, en présence des sieurs Michel Fourcisy et J B'y Pedesclaux, témoins a ce réquis, et domiciliés en cette ville, qui ont signé avec les parties et le dit notaire.

(Signé)—Dussuau Delacroix—Sam B Davis—J. B'y Pedesclaux—Fourcisy—Phi Pedesclaux, Not Pub.

Pour copie conforme à l'original, resté en mon etude pour recours, en foi de quoi j'ai signé les présentes et y ai apposé le sceau de mon etude

LOUIS T CAIRE, Not. Pub.

Nouvelle Orléans, le 21 Mai, 1849.

[No 9]

Offered by defendants.   Filed 20th June, 1849

J W GURLEY, Com'r.

UNITED STATES OF AMERICA, }
STATE OF LOUISIANA, CITY OF NEW ORLEANS }

Be it known that on this day, the fourth of the month of June, one thousand eight hundred and thirty-three, and the fifty-seventh of the Independence of the United States of America,

Before me, Louis T Caire, notary public in and for the city and parish of New Orleans, duly commissioned and sworn, and in presence of the witnesses hereafter named and subscribed,

Personally came and appeared Mr William Wallace Whitney and Mrs Myra Clark, his wife, by him duly and specially authorized and assisted both lately of the State of New York, and now in this city of New Orleans, who delivered to the undersigned notary, and requested him to deposit in his current register, according to the laws and usage of this State, with full power to deliver copies of the same to whomsoever it shall or may belong, two documents in writing, purporting to be a power of attorney, under private signature, given by the said appearers to Mr Gaunaurd, and acknowledged before Charles Janin, then a notary public in this city, on the sixteenth day of March, one thousand eight hundred and thirty-three.   And a sale under private signature, made by Joseph Deville Degoutin Bellechasse, of Matanzas, to the said appearers, represented by the said Gaunaurd, of certain lots of ground, situated in the faubourg St John, near this city of New Orleans, bearing date the ninth day of April last past, containing the receipt of the sum of twenty thousand dollars, it being the consideration of said sale and acknowledged before Lewis Shoemaker, consul of the United States, of Matanzas, Cuba Island, on the same day

And in order to identify said documents with the present deed, they have both been signed *ne varietur* by the said appearers, in presence of the undersigned notary and witnesses, and at their request, are and remain hereto annexed, and the said Mr Whitney and Mrs. Whitney, authorized by her husband, as aforesaid, declared and said, that the following alterations and corrections have been made by them, in the power of attorney, hereto annexed and above mentioned, to wit one word scratched out in the fifth line and left blank; the word *Gaunaurd,* overwritten;

Consul of the United States of America, erased , three words in the sixth line, scratched and left blank , in the twenty-eighth line, *one mile and a half from the* overwritten, and that they acknowledge as null and no effect whatever the words so erased and left blank, and do hereby approve the words overwritten and here above mentioned

Thus done and passed in my office, at the city of New Orleans, the day, month and year aforementioned, in presence of Charles Darcantel and Philippe Lacoste, witnesses thereto required, and residing in this city, who have signed with the parties and me, notary, after the reading of the act

(Signed)—Wm Wallace Whitney—Myra Clark Whitney—Charles Darcantel—Phi Lacoste—Louis T Caire, not pub

A true copy of the original   One word erased null
New Orleans, May 21st, 1849

　　　　　　　LOUIS T. CAIRE, Not. Pub

　　　　　　[No 10]
Offered by defendants.   Filed 20th June, 1849
　　　　　　　J W GURLEY, Com'r.

Know all men by these presents, that I, Colonel Joseph Deville Degoutin Bellechasse, formerly of New Orleans, but now resident in the vicinity of Matanzas, in the Island of Cuba, have in the consideration of the sum twenty thousand dollars cash, the receipt whereof I hereby acknowledge, sold unto Myra Clark, the wife of William Wallace Whitney, Esquire, of Broome county, in the State of New York, by him duly authorized, the same being accepted by Joseph D Gaunaurd, citizen of Matanzas, as the attorney of the said Myra Clark, by virtue of a power to him for that purpose given, with the like authority of her said husband, bearing date the sixteenth day of March, eighteen hundred and thirty-three, and hereunto annexed, the following property, situate in the Faubourg Saint John and distant about one mile and a half from the city of New Orleans, to wit   1st Nine lots of ground, numbered one, two, three, four, five, seven, eight nine and ten, forming part of the square numbered eleven, and facing Live Oak, Bellechasse, Seventh and Sixth streets.   2d. The whole square numbered twenty, and bounded by Sixth and and Fifth, Bellechasse and Live Oak streets   3d Nine lots of ground, numbered one, two three, four five, seven, eight, nine and ten, forming part of the square numbered twenty-one, and facing Bellechasse Live Oak, Fifth and Fourth streets.   4th The whole of the square numbered twenty-nine bounded by Bellechasse and Live Oak streets, and by Fourth and Third streets, and by Mrs Le Blanc   5th Nine lots of ground, numbered three, four, five, six, seven, eight nine, ten and eleven, forming part of the square numbered fourteen, and facing Washington, Le Page, Sixth and Seventh streets, the whole comformable to a plan drawn by Mr B Lafon, in June, eighteen hundred and nine, and deposited in the office of Mr Pierre Pedesclaux, the notary in New Orleans, which said lots or parcels of ground are the property of the said Joseph Deville Degoutin Bellechasse, as purchaser of the same from Mr. Daniel Clark, of New Orleans, aforesaid, by virtue of an act passed before Mr Pierre Pedesclaux, the notary, in New Orleans, under date the sixteenth day of May, eighteen hundred and eleven And lastly, all other the property, situate in the said Faubourg Saint John, of what kind soever, which was purchased of the said Daniel Clark, by the said Joseph Deville Degoutin Bellechasse, together with all the buildings and improvements on the property hereinbefore described and referred to, erected and built

To have and to hold the said lots or parcels of ground and other the property, hereby sold unto said Myra Clark, the wife of the said William Wallace Whitney, as her paraphernal property, the sum of twenty thousand dollars, the consideration money aforesaid, having been part thereof, her heirs and assigns forever

In witness whereof, I have hereunto set my hand and seal in duplicate, this ninth day of April, eighteen hundred and thirty-three

(Signed)—Joseph D Degoutin Bellechasse—J D Gaunaurd, attorney for Myra Clara

Sealed and delivered in presence of us, Lewis Shoemaker—George Harris

Received the day of the date of the within deed poll of the within named Myra Clark Whitney, the sum of twenty thousand dollars, being the full consideration money therein mentioned

(Signed)— Joseph D Degoutin Bellechasse; and witnesses, Lewis Shoemaker—George Harris.

Ne varietur in conformity to a deed passed this day before me New Orleans June 1st, 1833 (Signed)—Wm. Wallace Whitney—Myra Clark Whitney—Charles Darcantel—Phi Lacoste   LOUIS T CAIRE, Not Pub.

Consulate of the United States of America, I, Lewis Shoemaker, consul of the United States at this port, do certify, that on this day personally, appeared the within named Joseph Deville Degoutin de Bellechasse, and in due form of law, executed the foregoing deed poll, and acknowledged the same to be his act and deed, and as such desired the same to be recorded. Also, appeared Joseph D Gaunaurd, attorney of Myra Clark, and in like manner executed the said deed poll, and acknowledged the same to be as well his own, as the act and deed of the said Myra Clark, and as such, desired the same to be recorded

Witness my hand and seal of office hereto affixed, this ninth day of April, in the year of our Lord, one thousand eight hundred and thirty-three.

(Signed)—Lewis Shoemaker, consul.

I hereby certify, that Mrs. Myra Clark, the wife of William Wallace Whitney, Esquire, of the State of New York, and the said William Wallace Whitney, personally appeared before me, and acknowledged the foregoing letter of attorney as their own act and deed, and in my presence signed the same, in testimony whereof, I have hereunto set my hand and seal, this sixteenth day of March, eighteen hundred and thirty-three, the said Myra Clark and William Wallace Whitney having signed with me.

(Signed)—Wm. Wallace Whitney—Myra Clark Whitney—Charles Janin, not. pub.

Ne varietur in conformity to a deed, passed this day before me. New Orleans, June 4th, 1833

(Signed)—Wm. Wallace Whitney—Myra Clark Whitney—Charles Darcantel—Phi. Lacoste.

LOUIS T. CAIRE, Not. Pub

Know all men, by these presents, that I, Myra Clark, with the authority of my husband, William Wallace Whitney, Esquire, of the State of New York, do hereby nominate and appoint Garnaud, Esquire, of Matanzas, my true and lawful attorney, in my name and on my behalf, to accept the sale of the property hereinafter described, and which I have purchased of Colonel Joseph Deville Degoutin Bellechasse, for the sum of twenty thousand dollars, paid out of my paraphernal property, to wit. Nine lots or parcels of ground, numbered one, two, three, four, five, seven, eight, nine and ten, forming part of the square numbered eleven, and facing Live Oak, Bellechasse, Seventh and Sixth streets. 2d. The whole square numbered twenty, bounded by Sixth, Fifth, Bellechasse and Live Oak streets. 3d Nine lots of ground, numbered one, two, three, four, five, seven, eight, nine and ten, forming part of the square numbered twenty-one, and facing Bellechasse, Live Oak, Fifth and Fourth streets 4th. The whole of the square numbered twenty-one, bounded by Bellechasse, Live Oak, Fourth and Third streets 5th. Nine lots, numbered three, four, five, six, seven, eight, nine, ten and eleven, forming part of the square numbered fourteen, and facing Washington, Le Page, Sixth and Eleventh streets, which said lots or parcels of ground are situate in the Faubourg Saint John, and distant about one mile and a half from the city of New Orleans. And lastly, all other the property of what kind soever, situate in the said Faubourg Saint John, which may have been purchased by the said Joseph Deville Degoutin de Bellechasse, of Mr. Daniel Clark, of the city of New Orleans, and for that purpose to sign the acts and deeds, and generally to do all things in the premises as fully as I myself could do, were I personally present, hereby confirming all that my said attorney may do, or cause to be done in the same.

(Signed)—Myra Clark Whitney, authorized by Wm. Wallace Whitney.

I certify, that the foregoing are the true copies of the documents annexed to an act of deposit by Wm. Wallace Whitney and Mrs Myra Clark, his wife, passed before me, the undersigned notary, on the fourth of June, eighteen hundred and thirty-three in faith whereof, I grant these presents, under my signature and seal of office.

New Orleans, 28th May, 1849.

    [L.S]   LOUIS T. CAIRE, Not. Pub.

[No. 11.]
Offered by defendants, and filed 20th June, 1849.
             J. W. GURLEY, Comm'r.

Inf on de Solt'a prod'da por Geronimo des Grange p'a contraer Matrim'o con Maria Julia Carrière.

DECRETO.—Vistos Concedese Licencia à Geronimo Des grange natural de Clermont Parroquia de San Gené en los Reinos de Francia hijo de legitimo Matrimonio de Juan Bautista Desgrange y de Maria Fran'ca Roux ambos difuntos y naturales del mismo lugar para que pueda contrajer Matrimonio con Maria Julia Carrière natural de esta Cindad hija de legitimo Matrimonio de Juan Carrière y de Maria Chofer el primero natural de la Ciudad de Libourne, y la segunda de Bordeos en Dhos. Reinos de Francia ambos difuntos, para que pueda presentarse en el tribunal Eclesiastico se le dara testimonio de este auto quedando las diligencias reservadas en el archivo—Lic'do Manuel Serrano —Proyeyolo el Señor Licenciado Dn. Manuel Serrano, Asesor de esta Intendencia y Alcalde Ordinario de primer voto de esta Ciudad que lo firmo en la Ciudad de la N. Orleans à trece de Noviembre de mil Settecientos noventa y quatro años—Francisco Broutin, Escrivano publico.

Nn.—En dho dia lo hoie saver a Geronimo Desgrange doy fee—Broutin, Escrivano.

Concuerda con su original à que me remito y queda en my poder y archivo y en virtud de lo mandudo por el Decreto Incerto. Doy esta en la Ciudad de la Nueva Orleans trece de Noviembre de mil settecientos nov'ta y quatro años.

          FRAN'CO † BROUTIN, S'no Pub'co.

Geronimo Des Granges, Nat'l de la Parroq'a de Sn Gines de la Ciudad de Clermot, Reyno de Francia, en le mejor forma q'e haya lugar en dro, ante V, paresco y Digo que p'd mas bien servir a Dios ñro S'or tengo tratado con raer matrim'o in facie eclesie, con Maria Julia Carriere, nat'l de esta Parroq'a en cuia virtud se serviren y mandar si me receba inf'on y q'e los tgos que presentare declaren Religios'un'te como es cierto me conocn saben y les consta soy natural de dha Parroq'a hijo lex'mo de Juan Bautista des Granges y de Maria Fran'ca Roux: cat'co app'o Romano que no han victo hacer actos de cristiano, oyendo misa y frequentar los S'tos Sacram'tos que no he prom'do palabra de Matrim'o à otra persona mas que à la referida con la q'e no tengo ning'n Parentesco, ni Impedim'to p'a contraer matrim'o cuia Inform'on dada for bastanle se servira y mandar q'l el Cura de esta Parroq'a nos despose, y vele en ella p'r tanto

A. V. Sup'co lesiroa proveir como pido con Sa g'les otron, presento debidam'te la licencia del S'or vice Parente p'a q'e obre los ef'tos q'e haya lug't q's x'a et supra

JEROME DES GRANGE

En lo pral recibase la inform'on q'e esta parte opece comparezcan los I'gos previa la exloracion del contenido, y eiselotrosi hase p'r pres'do el doeum'to q'e refiere y f'ho traigase

WALSH.

Proveyolo el S D. Patricio Walsh clerigo Presvitero vic'o Foranes, Jues Ecco de esta Prov'a y como subdeleg'do de exer'da que lo firmo en catorce de Nov're de mil setecientos noventa y quatro

ESTEVAN DE QUINONES, Not'o Pu'co

Notif'n. Y en la Nueva Orleans, en dho dia hice saber el D'to q'e antecede à Geronimo DesGranges, doy feè.

QUINONES, Not

Dec'on. En la ciudad de la Nueva Orleans en el mismo dia mes y año. ante el S. Vic'o Foranes, Jues Ecco parecio Geronimo Des Granges, de gn'pr antemi el pres'te Not'o recibio juram'to que hijo por Dios y la cruz seg'n dro socargo de el prom'o decir verd'd y explor'da su voluntd con la mayor prolijidad, y exam'do al thenda del escrito que antecede, dijo. que es de estado soltero, que no ha prom'do palabra de exponsales à otra persona mas que a Maria Julia Carrière· que no ha hecho voto de castid'd ni de entrar en Relig'n y q'e p'd esta res'on no havido Inducido, violent'do, ni atem'do p'r persona alguna, y q'e la ha hecho de su libre y expontanea vol'd p'r ser la verd'd socargo de su juram'to q'e es de ed'd de treinta y quatro a's lo firmo, y dho s'or lorubrico de q'e doy fee

JEROME DES GRANGE.

Ante my, Estevan de Quinones, Not'o Pub'co.

Otra y Incontinente p'r la Inf'on q'e tiene of'da dho Des
Granges pres'to p'r f'go ante dho s or vic'o Foranes a Don Gabriel Mariano Dubo.. de g'n pr ante me dho not'o recibio
juram'to que bro p'r Dio.. y la cruz seg'n dro, socargo de el
prom'o decr xc'd..v exam do d then'or del escrito q'e antecede,
dijo que conoce al q'e lo pre ta sbe.. y le cons't es nat'l de la
Porroq'a de ..n Gine de la ciud'd de C..mon.., Reyno de
Fr'ncia hijo legt'mo de Juan Bau.t..a des Granges y de Maria
G..ca Roux..q.. q.. p..Pon'mo q..lo..v..hacer actos
de cris'iano, oy'ndo mis..y re..ala..cos sa r..ch..os que no
le const.. n..a m..do p.. n.. de ex..cr..s..o o..persona
mas que a la re..cd.. Mar..a Jul..a C..re.., con l.. q.. no tiene
ning'n p..ent..sc.. p.. r.. ..o.. p.. c..t..ae' el matrim'o yo
esp de q'e esto es l.. ..d.. d..ra j..que su..r..m..t q'es de ed'd
de quaren..a a..s p.. ..a ..ma ..d..s..o lo..e..c doy fe

GABRIEL DUBAC

Ante m.., E.t..va.. de Q..n..es No o t..r..o

Otra.. y Ib..o.. l..nt..p..c..e p..r..m..ante di.. s or vic'o Fora-
ne.. Ju..l..o d..l..a Pr..t..l A..o..o Ben..g..rell.. de g'n
pr..m..ca..c.. ..ccer..a..nt..g..h..zo p'r Dio.. y la cruz
seg..n dr..s..c..rc..d..e pres.. s.. ..r'ca.a v ex..ndo al then'r
le dho es..r..t..y..p..conoce al c..lo pr..e..sb.. y le consta
es nat'l de l..P..rr..o..a..n..ines de la c..dd..de C..e..mont,
Reyno de Fr..nce.. hio legt'mo de J..n Bau.. De G..anges,
y d..Mar..e Fran..e..a R..u.. e..c.. t..pr..co Pon'mo que lo
ha visto hacer a..tos de cris..iano ay..do m..a.. ..c..p..los stos
sacram..os y con..le con..ta h..y d..n..ch..o..p..le.. de espon-
sales ..tra per..on..a..s q'e a la re..cd'a Mar..a Jul..a Curriere,
con l..g'e no ti..ne ningun parent..sco..n..i..pedim'nto para
com..er el mat..m..o..s..y re..p'de q'e est..e l..v..r'd socargo de
..u juram'to q'e es d..e..d de quarenta y quatro a..s lo firmo y
firmo y dho s or lo ..ub..co doy fe.

A BENGUEREL

Ante m..y, E..t..va.. de Q..i..one.. Nc..o P..b..o

N..c..e.., 14 N..vre de 1794

Vista la Inf..on anteced'te no l..t..m G..c..or..o d..s Grange,
pa contraer matrim.. o con Mar..a Ju..l..a C..rr..e.., dijo su Merced,
ge debia aprobarla y la apro..o y d..p..r..t..a..rte y p'a su mayor
val..on, y firme..a mt..t..preso en ell.. su a..t..or..d..s.. y j..d'l, Decreto
g t..ha lag r pr dho, y m..o..o..g'e..R..l Joachm de Portillo,
cura de e..ta Parroc..a de S..t..L..s..t..c..e v..lle en ella,
seg'n estilo, previas las Proclama..dra.. ..orio los ..n..s requisitos y form..s q'e se requien pr p..r..a..cha..r..p..c..o..q'e el
suso dho lo ha hecho constar en este m..l p'r la ..u..a y ..or..s..do

7*

ming'n impedimento; acuino fin se le libre la orn correspond'te

WALSH Ante my

Estevan de Quinones, Noto Pu'co

NOTIF'N.—Y en el mismo hce sabr el D'to qe antecede a Geronimo Des Granges, doy fee

QUINONES, Noto

Librose la orn qe se manda al M R P Fr Joachin de Portillo, cura de esta Parroqua de Sn Luis doy fee

QUINONES, Noto

Dros de Sr Vico treinta y dos r recebidos

Geronimo Desgranges en la informa'on de un libertad q'e he producido en la mejor forma qe hua lugar endro ante V M exponzo que previendo la proximidad del Adviento q'e sera el treinta del cori'te y ademas del errarse las velaciones no sepodrian verificar hasta q'e se abrieser conesta consideracion y la de q e mis assentos en mi gire de converso delicores necesiti una persona de confianza a quien pule y no teniendo otra mas qui mi futura espoa Sup'coa V M se sirva dispensarme unaproclama p'a q e publicadas las dos se verifique otro matrimonio por tanto

A. V M Sup'co se sirva proveer comopido con Just'a vuro, &c

JEROME DES GRANGE

Na Orleans, 14 de Nove de 1794

Respecto à que las causas que ester parte expone p a obtener dispensa de una proclama se graduan por suficientes dixo su mrd q'e usando de benignidad se la dispensaba y dispensaba y usando gue publicadas las dos se verifique su matrimo como se ha mandado por el anterior decreto.

WALSH. Ante my

ESTEVAN DE QUINONES Noto Puco,

N'N.—En la Na Orleans en dho-dia hice saber el decreto q'e antecede a Dn. Geronimo Desgranges doy f

QUINONES, Noto

N'N.—En dho dia lo hize saber al R P Fr Joachin de Portillo Cura de esta Parroq'a doy fe,

QUINONES, Noto

I certify the foregoing to be a true copy of the original, now in my possession In faith whereot, I grant these presents under my signature and seal of office, this tenth day of January, eighteen hundred and forty-five

WM. CHRISTY, Not Pub.

[No 12]

Offered by Defendants   Filed 20th June 1849

G W GURLEY, Com

MIRA CLARK AND HER CURATOR, STATE OF LOUISIANA,
ad litem, S B DAVIS,   FIFTH DISTRICT COURT
vs   OF
B CHEW AND R RELF, EXECUTORS   NEW ORLEANS
OF DANL CLARK, *dec'd*   No 1340

Petition filed 24th June 1817

To the Honorable Joshua Lewis, Judge of the District Court, for the First Judicial District

The petition of Myra Clark, an infant aged 13 years, and of Saml B Davis humbly showeth

That the said Myra Clark is about instituting a suit against the Executors of her deceased father, for the recovery of an alimony suited to the style and rank in life which her deceased father seemed anxious she should enjoy

Wherefore, your petitioners pray that Samuel B Davis may be appointed her Curator ad litem, to represent her in the said suit, and your petitioners, &c

(Signed)   DAVIS & PEIRCE,
                             Attorneys for Petitioners

ORDER —It is ordered that Samuel B Davis be appointed Curator ad litem to the petitioner, according to the prayer of the petition

(Signed)   JOSHUA LEWIS

Petition, filed 24th June, 1817

To the Honorable Joshua Lewis, Judge of the District Court, for the First Judicial District

The petition of Myra Clark, an infant aged thirteen years by Samuel B Davis her curator ad litem, specially appointed, humbly showeth—

That your petitioner is the natural daughter of Daniel Clark, late of the city of New Orleans deceased, acknowledged by him as such, that the said Daniel Clark died in the year 181— having made a will by which Richard Relf and Beverly Chew are the executors, but, making no provision by the said will, or for the continuance of her education, which had been begun during the lifetime of her said father, in a genteel and expensive style Her said father having frequently expressed his intention to his friends of educating and supporting her in his own rank of life, and providing amply for her, either in his lifetime or at his death And your petitioner shows that she has heard that some instrument was executed by the said father, making some provisions for her, and that the same has not been shown to her

Your petitioner, therefore prays that the said executors may produce all papers, if any there are which relate to her, and which may have been found among those of the said Daniel Clark, dec'd. That an adequate allowance for her education and support may be paid, and out of the estate of her said father, and that she may have such other and further relief as the nature of the case may require

And your petitioner, &c

(Signed)   DAVIS & PEIRCE,
                                  Attorneys for Petitioner

THE STATE OF LOUISIANA   ⎱ MESSRS BEVERLY CHEW
    FIRST JUDICIAL COURT   ⎰ AND RICHARD RELF

CITATION—You are hereby summoned to appear at the office of the Sheriff of the Parish of New Orleans and comply with the prayer of the annexed petition, or file your answer thereto in writing, in the Clerk's office of the First Judicial District Court at the city of New Orleans, ten days after the service hereof

Witness Joshua Lewis Judge of the said Court, the 24th day
  [L S] of June in the year of our Lord one thousand eight
        hundred and seventeen

(Signed)   STEPHEN PEDESCLAUX,
                                      Deputy Clerk

SHERIFF'S RETURN—Served copy of petition and citation on Richard Relf one of the defendants, June 25th, 1817   Returned June 27th, 1817

(Signed)   J H HOLLAND,
                                        Deputy Sheriff

Filed 3d July, 1817

ANSWER—The answer of Chew and Relf to the petition of **Myra Clark** exhibited by Samuel B Davis, her curator ad litem in the District Court for the First District

These defendants answering say it is true Daniel Clark, late of New Orleans deceased that in his last will and testament, and therein appointed these respondents executors, and they say it is also true that no provision is therein made for the support or maintenance of the plaintiff, nor is there any acknowledgment made by the testator in said will nor elsewhere, known to these respondents, of the said plaintiff being his child, nor do they know that he did ever, during his life, make any appropriation for her support or education

These defendants do, therefore, deny that the person represented **by said** Samuel B Davis is the natural child of said Daniel

Clark, deceased. They also deny that the said Daniel Clark had, at any time of his life ordered or given any instructions relative to the education of the said pretended Myra Clark; and they deny that her name was the same as Myra Clark by birth, baptism or reception of the said Daniel Clark, and that the same is as is therein alleged, and so far untrue.

These respondents say that Mrs —— Clark, the mother of the said Daniel Clark, is the sole and sole heiress to his estate, and is answerable to the plaintiff's demands, if any she lawfully hath, and not these defendants.

These defendants deny the right of the plaintiff to have a maintainance or an alimony decreed to her, out of the estate of the said Daniel Clark, deceased, and even if it should so appear that she hath such right, it can be for no more than a reasonable support, until majority or marriage. Wherefore, your respondents pray to be hence dismissed, with their costs, &c

(Signed) TURNER,
Attorney for Respondents

ORDER OF DISCONTINUANCE —19th February 1818

MYRA CLARK BY HER CURATOR
ad litem, SAML B DAVIS,
vs
B CHEW AND R RELF EXECUTORS OF D CLARK

No 1540

On motion of H Davis, Esq of counsel for the petitioner, it was thereupon ordered, by the Court, that he have leave to discontinue this case

STATE OF LOUISIANA,
FIFTH DISTRICT COURT OF NEW ORLEANS

I do hereby certify that the afore and foregoing three pages do contain a full and complete transcript of the record of the case wherein Myra Clark and her curator ad litem, Samuel B Davis, are plaintiffs and Beverly Chew and Richard Relf, executors of Daniel Clark, deceased are defendants instituted before the Late First Judicial District Court of the State of Louisiana, under the number 1540 the records of which Court have been, by law, transferred to the aforesaid Fifth District Court of New Orleans

In testimony whereof, I have hereunto set my hand and affixed the seal of the said Court at the city of New Orleans, this 15th day of June, in the year of our Lord one [L S] thousand eight hundred and forty-nine, and in the seventy-third year of the Independence of the United States of America.

Jno S. BARON, Deputy Clerk,

[No 13]

Offered by defendants   Filed 20 June, 1849

J W GURLEY, Com

STATE OF LOUISIANA,

THIRD DISTRICT COURT OF NEW ORLEANS

ZULIME C DESGRANGE)   No 178
              vs   > OF THE DOCKET OF THE LATE COUNTY
JEROME DESGRANGE)   COURT OF ORLEANS

Petition filed November 30th 1805

To the honorable James Workman, Judge of the County Court of Orleans

The petition of Zulime Carriere Desgrange, an inhabitant of the city of New Orleans humbly showeth—

That whereas it is provided by the first section of an act entitled an act concerning alimony and for other purposes, that the County Court shall have jurisdiction on application from wives against their husbands, for alimony, on the husband deserting his wife, for one year successively, and in cases of cruel, inhuman, and barbarous treatment, and whereas your petitioner may adduce proofs before this honorable court that she has been cruelly and barbarously treated by Jerome Desgrange, her husband, and likewise that she has been deserted by him, for three years past, to wit from the second day of September, one thousand eight hundred and two ever unto this day, although she has been told that the said Jerome Desgrange returned from France to New Orleans some time in the course of last month, and is now in the city of New Orleans

Wherefore, these are to pray that it may please your honor to order that the said Jerome Desgrange, your petitioner's husband, be condemned to pay to your petitioner a sum of five hundred dollars per annum, and that your petitioner be likewise entitled to all the other benefits and advantages belonging to her in virtue of the law of this Territory in that case made and provided, and your petitioner, as in duty bound, shall ever pray.

(Signed) ELIGIUR FROMENTIN, Att'y for plaintiff

A l'honorable James Workman, Juge de lacour du Comte d'Orleans.

La petition de Zulime Carriere Desgrange, de la ville de la Nouvelle Orleans

Represente humblement—

Que comme il est ordonne par la premiere section de l'acte intitulé act concernant les provisions alimentaires des maris envers leurs femmes que les cours du comte auront connaissances des demandes formus par les femmes contre leurs maris pour provision alimentaire dans le cas d'abandon de la femme par le mari pendant l'epoque d'une annee successivement, ou dans le cas de traitements cruels, inhumains, et barbares, et comme votre suppliante peut produire devant cette honorable cour des preuves qu'elle a été traitée d'une manière cruelle et barbare, savoir depuis le second jour du mois de Septembre de l'anne mil huit cent deux jusqu'à ce jour quoi qu'elle ait appris que le dit Jerome Desgrange est revenu de France à la Nouvelle Orleans En consequence votre suppliante vous prie d'ordonner que le dit Jerome Desgrange mari de votre suppliante, soit condamné a payer a votre suppliante une somme de cinq cents gourdes par an, et que votre suppliante soit aussi autorisée a se prévaloir de tous les autres avantages qui lui appartiennent en vertu de la loi de ce territoire faite à cet égard et votre suppliante comme de droit, etc

(Signé) ELIGIUR FROMENTIN,
Attorney for plaintiffs

CITATION

Mr Jerome Desgrange

You are hereby summoned to comply with the **prayer of the** annexed petition or to file your answer thereto in writing, with the clerk of the county of Orleans, at his office at New Orleans, in eight days after the service hereof and if you fail herein, judgment will be given against you by default

Zulime C Desgrange
     vs   No 178
Jerome Desgrange

Witness James Workman Judge of the said court, this **30th** day of November in the year of our Lord 1805

(Signed) THOS S KENNEDY, Clerk

Mr Jerome Desgrange

Vous etes sommé, par la presente de comparaitre aux fins de la petition ci annexée ou je remettre votre reponse par ecrit a la dite petition au greffier du comte d'Orleans, a son bureau a la Nouvelle Orleans en huit jours apres la notification de la cette petition et si vous y manquez jugement sera rendu contre vous par defaut

TEMOIN JACQUES WORKMAN, Judge

Tu dit comte, ce 30 jour de Novembre, de l'an de notre seigneur, 1805

(Signé) THOS S KENNEDY, Greffier.

Return on citation
6th December, 1805, served on the defendant

(Signé) JOHN T PROUILLARD, D S
FROMENTIN, Att'y.

ZULIME CARRIERE DSSGRANGE ⎫
　　　　　vs　　　　　　　　⎬　No 178
　　JEROME DESGRANGE.　　⎭

Petition filed 30th November, 1805, for alimony. Served December 6th, 1805　Judgment by default December 19th, 1805 The court doth award final judgment for the plaintiff December 24th, 1805　　　　　(Signed) JAMES WORKMAN

　　Attorney's fees, $19 62 1-2
　　Clerk's fees, $10 87 1-2
　　Execution issued December 24th, 1805

STATE OF LOUISIANA
THIRD DISTRICT COURT OF NEW ORLEANS

I, Ch's Weysham, Deputy Clerk of the Third District Court of New Orleans, do hereby certify that the above and foregoing four pages do contain a full and complete transcript of the record of the case, wherein Mrs Zulime Carriere Desgrange is plaintiff, and Jerome Desgrange is defendant, instituted in the late County Court of Orleans, under the No 178 and that by operation of law, the records of the said late County Court of Orleans, have been transferred to this court, and are now in the custody of the clerk thereof

　　In testimony whereof, I have hereunto set my hand and affixed the seal of the said court, at the city of New Orleans,
[L.S]　on this 12th day of June in the year of our Lord eighteen hundred and forty-nine, and in the 73d year of the Independence of the United States

　　　　　　　　　CH S WEYSHAM, D'y clerk

I, Thomas H Kennedy, sole Judge of the Third District Court of New Orleans, do hereby certify that Ch's Weysham, who signed the foregoing certificate, is, and was at the time of signing the same, deputy clerk of our said court, and that to all his acts as such full faith and credit are due and owing　And I do further certify that his said certificate is in due form of law.

　　Given under my hand, at the city of New Orleans, on this twelfth day of June, in the year of our Lord one thousand eight hundred and forty-nine.

　　　　　　　　　　　　T H KENNEDY

[No. 14]
By defendants filed 20th June, 1849.
　　　　　　　　J W GURLEY, Comm'r.

STATE OF LOUISIANA,
THIRD DISTRICT COURT OF NEW ORLEANS

ZULIME CARRIERE　⎫　　　No. 256,
　　　vs　　　　　⎬　OF THE DOCKET OF THE LATE COUNTY
JEROME DESGRANGES. ⎭　COURT OF NEW ORLEANS

CITATION—Mr Ellery (curator of Desgrange).

You are hereby summoned to comply with the prayer of the annexed petition or to file your answer thereto in writing, with the Clerk of the county of New Orleans, at his office, in New Orleans, in eight days after the service hereof; and if you fail herein judgment will be given against you by default.

Witness James Workman, Judge of the said Court, this 24th day of June, in the year of our Lord 1806.

Signed,   THOS S KENNEDY, Clerk

Mr Ellery, (curateur de Desgrange)

Vous êtes sommé par la présente, de comparaître aux fins de la pétition ci-annexée ou de remettre votre réponse par écrit à la dite pétition au greffier du comté d'Orléans, à son bureau, à la Nouvelle Orléans, huit jours après la notification de la dite pétition; et si vous y manquez, jugement sera rendu contre vous, par défaut.

Témoin Jacques Workman, Juge dudit comté, ce 24me jour de Juin de l'an de notre Seigneur, 1806.

Sign,   THOS S KENNEDY Greffier

Return on citation, served on Ellery 30th June 1806

Signed   GEO T ROSS, Sheriff

Plea filed July first 1806

ZULIME CARRIERE   } No 556

JEROME DESGRANGE   } COUNTY COURT OF NEW ORLEANS

The plea of Jerome Desgrange, defendant to the petition of Zulime Carriere plaintiff.

This defendant, by protestation, not confessing or acknowledging all or any part of the matters and things in the plaintiff's said petition contained to be true in such manner and form as the same are therein and thereby alleged, for plea unto the said petition said that this Court ought not to have cognizance of the same, because the laws by which this Court was created, and the jurisdiction thereof confided, do not extend the same to cases of divorce, or give to this Court any authority to pronounce therein; and because the damages in the said petition prayed for against this defendant cannot be enquired into or assessed, until after the judgment of the Court in touching the validity of the marriage between the prisoner and this defendant, shall be first declared.

Wherefore this defendant doth not suppose, that this Court ought in law to have or hold under cognizance of the petition aforesaid and therefore this defendant doth plead the premises in bar to the said petition, and humbly demands judgment of this honorable Court whether he shall be put to make further answer thereunto, and prays to be hence dismissed with his reasonable costs and charges in this behalf, wrongfully sustained

Signed,   A R ELLERY, for defendant

And the said plaintiff saith, that for any thing by the defendant above, in pleading, alleged she ought not be barred or precluded from having and maintaining her action aforesaid against the said defendant

Wherefore, for want of a sufficient answer in this behalf, the plaintiff prays judgment &c

Signed,   BROWN & FROMENTIN, for plaintiff

Answer filed July 24th, 1806

Zulime Carriere	No 356
vs	County Court of Orleans.
Jerome Desgranges	

Answer of Jerome Desgrange to the petition of Zulime Carrière

This defendant, saving and reserving to himself, all manner of benefit of exception to the many errors, untruths and imperfections in the said petition contained, for answer thereunto saith, that the facts in the said petition set forth are untrue, and prays that he may be hence dismissed, with his costs and charges in this behalf, most wrongfully sustained

Signed,   A R ELLERY, for defendant

Certificate of marriage, filed July 24th, 1806

Yo Fr Antonio de Sedella, Religioso Cap'no Cura de esta Yg'a Parroq'l de San Luis del Nueva Orleans certifico en la fra que puedo, y debo, como en uno de los libros de Matrimonios que es el septimo, al folio noventa y nueve hay una partida, que en numero, es la quatrocientas y treinta y quatro del tenor siguiente

Partida	Martes dia dosde Diciembre, de mil setecientos,
434	noventa y quatro, yo el infascripto missionero ap-

p'co cap no y cura de la Parroq'l de San Luis de esta ciudad de la Nueva Orleans, previas las diligencias necesarias y publicadas dos proclamas (dispensada la tercera por el Ser vicario) las quales se leyron a la Misa Parrogal de los domingos, dias, dies y seis, y viente y tres de Noviembre, de la q'e no resulto impedimento alguno, preparados con la confesion, y communion, y preguntados sobre el mutuo consentim to que prestaron con palabras expresas en mi presencia y la de los testigos, gunto legitimamte en matrimonio a Ceronimo Desgrange con Maria Julia Carrière el primero natural de la ciudad de Clermont en Francia, hijo legmo de Juan Bau'ta Desgrange, y de Maria Francisca Roux, naturales ambas de Clermont, y la segunda, natural de esta Parroq'l, hija legna de Juan Carriere natural de Ligourne en la Gascoña, y de Maria Choffir, natural de Bordeaux fueron testigos, Guillermo Maroe, Antonio Boudusquie, y Simphoriano Caillabet, no pudiendo ahora recivir las relaciones les previne se presentaran despues de la essfama para recivir la velacion y bendicion nuptial, y para que conste, lo firmo en el dia, mes y año arriba expresadas. Fr Joaquin Fornito.

Con aer tr an su partida on gi qu pueda en el estado libro de la referida y ga al que mi renuto, y e pedimento de parte, hay la presente, en la Nueva Orleans, a viente y quatro de Julio, de mil ochocientos, el sei años.

Signed,   FR ANTONIO DE SEDELLA

Brown & Thompson for Plff |
    Zulime Carriere |
            vs   }   No 356
        Desgranges |
    Tilery for Defendant |

Petition filed June 24th, 1806. Debt or damages, $100 nd 600. Plea filed July 1st 1806. Answer filed July 24th, 1806. Set for trial on Thursday, 24th July.

Summons issued for

M Coulram Chovot, Mary Marr Rose Carriere, Christopher Joseph Le Prevost, Jouque Le Breton d'Orgenoy and Joseph Villar, senior

Att'ys $10, | Mr Fourke, sworn
                | Mr d'Orgenoy
Clk's $7 57 1-2 | Madam Marr

Judgment for plaintiff. Damages, $100. July 24th, 1846

STATE OF LOUISIANA, }
Third District Court of New Orleans }

I, Charles Weysham, Deputy Clerk of the Third District Court of New Orleans, do hereby certify, that the above and foregoing five pages do contain a full and complete transcript of the record of the case, wherein Mrs Zulime Carriere is plaintiff and Jerome Desgrange is defendant, instituted in the late County Court of Orleans, under the No 356, excepting the petition that cannot be found. And that by operation of law the records of the said late County Court of Orleans have been transferred to this Court, and are now in the custody of the Clerk thereof.

In testimony whereof, I have hereunto set my hand, and affixed the seal of the said Court, at New Orleans, on this 14th fourteenth day of June, in the year of Lord, eighteen hundred and forty nine, and the seventy third year of the independence of the United States.

Signed, CHS WEY-HAM Dy Clerk

I, Thomas H Kennedy, Judge of the Third District Court of New Orleans, do hereby certify that Chs Weysham who signed the foregoing certificate, and who at the time of signing the same Deputy Clerk of our said court, and that so are his acts as such, full faith and credit are due and owing, and I do further certify that his said certificate is in due form of law.

Given under my hand at the city of New Orleans, on the fourteenth day of June in the year of our Lord one thousand eight hundred and forty nine and the seventy third year of the Independence of the United States

T H KENNEDY

[No 15]

Offered by Defendants Filed 20th June, 1849

J W GURLEY Comr

STATE OF LOUISIANA,
FIFTH DISTRICT COURT OF NEW ORLEANS

No 561	No 906	No 987
WILLIAM DESPAU,	SOPHIA C DESPAU,	WILLIAM DESPAU
vs	*vs*	*vs*
MARIE SOPHIA CAR-RIERE DESPAU	WILLIAM DESPAU	SOPHIA CARRIERE HIS WIFE

CUMULATED CASES

PETITION —Filed 10th June, 1805

To the Honorable, the Superior Court of the Territory of Orleans

The petition of William Despau residing in this city humbly showeth

That on account of in incompatibility of humor, and owing to several other reasons, the relation of which would be too afflicting, your petitioner has been laid under the necessity of wishing to be separated from Mary Sophia Carriere, his wife

That the aforesaid motives are fully explained in the suit of separation instituted before the Vicar General, Rev Patrick Walsh, on the application of the said Mary Sophia Carriere herself the whole of which may be laid before this Honorable Court

Therefore, may it please your Honorable Court, on the perusal of the formal consent of the said Mary Sophia Carriere to the aforesaid separation, in her said petition contained, to order and decree that your petitioner be separated of body and property from the said Mary Sophia Carriere, each party retaking his and her respective property, brought under the date of the 3d February, 1786, and that all community between them be dissolved from this day each party paying his costs, and your petitioner as in duty bound will ever pray

(Signed,)   P DERBIGNY, for petitioner

A l'Honorable Cour Supérieure dit Territorie d'Orleans

Guilaume Despau qui a cœur est le vœu a l'honneur de vous exposer que a cause de la considerable de l'honneur, et pour beaucoup de circonstances qu'il serait trop honoureux de retracer ici, votre petition s'est vu dans le nécessité de chercher a se séparer de Marie Sophie Carrière son épouse

Ces motifs sont amplement détaillés dans les pièces de la procédure qui s'est ouverte devant M. le Vicaire Général Patrice Walsh sur la propre demande de la dite dame Marie Sophie Carrière lesquelles seront mises sous les yeux de la Cour

Pourquoi votre petitionaire supplie l'Honorable Cour de la permission de citer par devant elle la dite dame Marie Sophie Carrière, pour y le consentement par elle donné a tout espèce de separation par s[...]ite ci-annexée, dire et juger que votre petition une soit separée de corps et de biens, de la dite dame Marie Sophie Carrière en consequence dire que toute communauté est dissoute entre les parties de ce jour et qu'elles rependront respectueusement tout ce qu'elles ont apporté en marriage a la date du 3 Février 1786, le depens compensés

(Signed,)   P DERBIGNY, pr le Pet're.

ANSWER—Filed 8th July, 1805

To the Superior Court in and over the Territory of Orleans

The answer of Mary Sophia Carriere Despau, wife of William Despau to the petition of her said husband

This defendant admitting the material facts in the said petition alleged, consents that the prayer of the same be granted, but saith that during the time of her marriage with the petitioner, they had two children, one now about the age of fifteen, the other about eight who are, as yet wholly unprovided for, this defendant therefore prays that previous to a decree of separation, as in the said petition is prayed, the petitioner be compelled to render to this Honorable Court a just and true account of all and singular, his estate, real and personal whether in possession, reversion, or otherwise, and of his rights and credits, that a division thereof be made, according to law, between the defendant and the said petitioner, and due provision thereout made for the said children, and that in case of the insufficiency of the said estates to satisfy the just expectations of this defendant in this behalf, that the said petitioner be also compelled to make further allowance to your petitioner and her children, according to his means.

(Signed,)   Ls KERR, Attorney,
                             and of counsel for Defendant

(TRADUCTION)

Dans la Cour Supérieure du Territoire d'Orleans.

La réponse de Marie Sophia Carrière Despaux, épouse de Guillaume Despaux, a la pétition de son mari

La defenderesse reconnait pour véritables les faits d'importance exposés par la dite pétition, et consent que la requête du demandeur soit accordée, mais dit que pendant son mariage ils avaient deux enfans, l'un age aujourd'hui d'environ quinze ans, et l'autre de huit et qu'in l'un ni l'autre n'ont pas jusqu'à ce jour reçu aucun etablissement. La defenderesse en conséquence prie avant que la dite séparation requête par la dite pétition soit décritée, que le dit Despaux soit obligé de rendre sous serment à cette honorable Cour, un rapport plein et véritable de tous ses biens, meubles et immeubles, ou actuellement entre ses mains, ou par des droits de reversion ou autrement, et de tous ses droits et ses credits de toutes espèces que ce soit, afin qu'en soit adjugé une partition conformément à la loi entre le dit Despaux, et la defenderesse, et que des arrangemens soient pourvus pour les enfans, et de plus si la dite propriété n'est pas suffisante pour contenter l'attente raisonnable de la defenderesse à cet égard, que le dit Despaux soit obligé en outre de faire des autres arrangemens pour cet objet proportion de ses moyens

(Signed,) L. KERR Procureur
and Avocat pour la defend'se

ORDER —(For separation of bed and board)

Superior Court, Saturday January 11th, 1806 }
Present the Honorable J B Prevost }

WM. DESPAUX, } On motion of Mr Derbigny by consent
vs } of parties Ordered that a separation of
MADAME DESPAUX } bed and board be made

ORDER —(Plaintiff to furnish account of his estate

26th March 1806

DESPAUX,
ADS
DESPAUX.
{ On motion of Mr Kerr, on the part of the defendant Ordered, that the plaintiff do on or before the first of April next, give, under oath, a full account of all his estate, real and personal, that partition thereof be made, according to law, unless cause be shown to the contrary.

CROSS PETITION.—Numbered 066 }
Filed September 1st, 1806 }

To the Honorable, the Judges of the Superior Court, in and over the Territory of Orleans

The petition of Sophia Carrière Despau, wife of William Despau, humbly showeth

That sometime since, her said husband commenced a suit in this honorable Court, to obtain a separation from your petitioner, and that in answer thereto your petitioner did make a like prayer, and that the estate of them might be divided between them, according to law, and that the said suit is now pending, and altogether undetermined.

That the said Despau hath not in possession to your petitioner's knowledge or belief any other property than two plantations or tracts of land at the Opelousas, and a grocery store in the city of New Orleans.

And that on the nineteenth of this present month of August, in the year 1806 in a public paper of the city of New Orleans, called the *Telegraphe*, the said Despau has advertised the said two tracts of land and his stock in trade in the said grocery store for sale, for ready money, and in the same advertisement declaring, that should not the said property be sold at private sale, before the twenty-fifth of the next month that then the same will be sold at public auction at the auction room of Messrs. Joseph Faurie & Co. as by the said advertisement herewith exhibited doth more fully appear; which sale, as your petitioner doth verily believe is about to be made by the said Despau, to the end that, by turning his property into money he may more easily conceal or remove the same, and intending thereby to defray your petitioner and defeat her just and lawful claims, as aforesaid.

Wherefore your petitioner prays that the said Despau may, by the order of your Honorable Court, be enjoined from making said sale, and declared incompetent to alienate in any manner, the property aforesaid until the suit above mentioned be terminated unless the said Despau shall give sufficient security that one half of the proceeds of said sale shall be forthcoming, to satisfy such eventual decree as your honorable Court may make in the premises. And your petitioner &c.

(Signed) L. KERR, for the petitioner.

Aux honorables Juges de la Cour Superieure du Tereritoire d'Orleans. La petition de Sophie Carriere Despau femme de Guillaume Despau humblement expose. Que quelque temps passe son epoux commencut un proces dans cette honorable Cour, pour obtenir un decret de separation de votre suppliante; et qu'en reponse votre suppliante faisait la meme requete, et que les biens dudit Despau et votre suppliante soient divises entre eux conformement a la loi, et que le dit proces est encore pendant.

Que le dit Despau autant que votre suppliante peut le savoir ou croire, n'a pas en possession aucune propriété, á la reserve de deux habitations ou portions de terre aux Oppelousas, et les fonds d'une boutique de graisseries dans la ville de la Nouvelle Orleans.

Et que le **19** du présent mois d Août 1806, dans une papier publique de la dite ville, nomme le Telegraphe le dit Despau annonçait la vente des dits habitations et des fonds de la dite boutique, au comptant, et dans le même avertissement déclarait que si les dits biens ne seront pas vendus à l'amiable avant le **25** du mois qui vient que ces biens seront vendus à l'encan chez Messrs Joseph Faurie & Co comme il paraît plus certain par le dit avis ci-annexé la quelle vente, votre suppliante croit sincèrement va d être faite par le dit Despau, afin que, en changeant sa propriété en l'argent, elle sera plus facilement cachée ou renvoyée, et qu il a l intention par ce moyen là a frauder votre suppliante et a frustrer ses droits justes et légales comme ci-dessus

Ce pourquoi que votre suppliante prie qu il soit défendu au dit Despau à vendre les biens ci-dessus, et qu il soit décreté qu il est incompétent pour les vendre jusqu a ce que le dit procès soit terminé, amoins qu'il donnera cautionnement suffisante que une moitié des produits de la dite vente sera mise en dépôt, ou gardé toujours pret à répondre a tel décret qui soit rendu finalement dans les premisses

Et votre suppliante, &c

(Signé)—Ls Kerr pour suppliante

(") Sophie Carriere Despaux

AFFIDAVIT —Compté D Orleans La suppliante ci-dessus après avoir été duement assermentée, dit que les allegations de la pétition ci-dessus, autant qu elle peut le savoir ou croire, sont **vrais** (Signed)—Sophie Carriere Despaux

Signé et juré à la Nelle Orleans le 23 Aout, A D 1806 avant moi (Signed)—B Cenas, Juge de Paix

ORDER.—By the Court ordered that an injunction issue in this case upon the plaintiff, according to the petition of the defendant, filed this day. September 1st 1806

ADVERTISEMENT ANNEXED —For sale a lot of land at the Appelousas, in the quarter of Bellevue said land contains 32 acres front and 40 in depth, about 2 leagues distant from the church, bounded on the north by the property of Mr Louis Lavergne, and on the south by that of Mr Joseph Chretien said property is of a fine soil, variegated and well known by its goodness and quality, fit for indigo, cotton, &c

For terms, apply to the editor of the Telegraphe, or to the owner, Mr Despau, No 48 Hospital street, who will give good conditions for ready money. If the said property is not sold by private contract, before the 25th of September next. it will on that day, be sold at public auction, by Joseph Faurie & Co to the highest bidder, agreeing to give up the titles and plans agreeable to the above description, together with the bill of sale for the same The said lot contains 1280 superficial acres

Also, for sale, another lot of land, consisting of **12 acres** front
and forty deep, being 480 superficial acres, situated at Point
Tauriac, at about 5 leagues distant from the church, is bounded
on the north by the land of Mr Michel Carriere, and on the south
by that of Mr Box, and lately surveyed and the boundaries marked out, by which it is found that the orchard and well lately occupied by Mr Box belongs to me. Said land is cultivated and of
a variety of situations rising and falling. Apply to the above
proprietor who has the plans and descriptions. It will be sold
on the same terms as the above lot. He wishes to dispose of his
stock in trade, consisting of provisions &c.

August 19 td

A VENDRE.—Une terre située aux Apelousses, quartier de
Bellevue, ayant 32 arpens de face sur 40 de profondeur, formant
1280 arpens de superficie distante de l'Eglise d'environ 2 heue,
bornée au nord par les propriétés de Mr Louis Lavergne, et au
sud par celles de Mr Joseph Carriera. Ladite terre est entiere-
ment labourable et en coteaux variés et bien connue par sa bonté
et sa qualité pour etre propre à la culture du coton, de l'indigo,
&c &c, pour plus amples informations et les conditions,
s'adresser au Redacteur du Telegraphe ou au Sieur Despau,
proprietaire, No 48 Rue de l'Hopital, qui en ferout bonne
composition pour du comptant.

N B.—Si la dite terre n'est pas vendue à l'amiable d'ici au
25 Septembre prochain elle se sera le dit jour à l'encan de MM.
Js Faurie & Co avec les titres plans &c, garantis.

Aussi.—Une autre terre de douze arpens de face **sur 40 de**
profondeur formant 480 arpens de superficie située **à la pointe**
Touriac distante de l'Eglise d'environ 5 heues bornée au nord
par Mr Michel Carriere et au sud par le sieur Box, venant **d'être**
recemment arpentée, d'après ce nouvel arpentage, **Mr Box se**
trouve avoir travaillé sur la dite terre, et le vergé qu'il y a établi
ainsi qu'un puits restent à la terre ci-dessus annoncée, qui est
intacte et sur un cote ce qui la met à l'abri des travaux propres
aux ecoulements des eaux. S'adresser comme ci-dessus, et tous
les titres et plans à ce necessaires qui sont garantis, seront donnés
à l'acquereur, avant, ou au moment de la vente, dont les conditions sont les mêmes que celles de **la terre précédente ci-dessus**
annoncée.

De plus.—Un fonds de boutique de graisseries, situé No. 48,
Rue de l'Hopital. S'addresser pour le dit objet à M. Despau
9*   2w td

ORDER ON MINUTES —1st September, 1806.

SOPHIE C DESPAU }
    ads
WM DESPAU   }

On motion of Mr Keir, ordered that an injunction issue in this case upon the plaintiff according to the prayer of the petition of the defendant, filed this day

PETITION —Numbered 987 —Filed 2d October, 1806

To the honorable —— Sprigg one of the Judges of the Superior Court of the Territory of Orleans

The petition of William Despau, of this city, humbly showeth—

That your petitioner has commenced a suit in your honorable court to obtain a separation from Sophia Carriere, his wife, and that in answer thereto, the said Sophia Carriere made a like prayer, and that the estate of your petitioner might be divided between them according to law, that your petitioner on that claim proved that the value of all his properties was far from being sufficient to satisfy his debt

That, moreover, your petitioner, urged by the creditors of the said debts, has been lately under the necessity of advertising the public sale of the said properties,

That, on this advertisement, Sophia Carriere prayed and obtained an order from your honor, directing that your petitioner shall be prohibited from making any sale of the said properties, unless he shall give sufficient security that the half part of the proceeds of the same shall be deposited or kept ready to satisfy such decree as your honorable court may issue in the said cause,

Therefore, your petitioner prays your honor to order that Joseph Faurie, of this city, merchant shall be approved as a good security, that the half of the proceeds of the aforesaid sale shall be kept in the hands of the said Faurie, or in such o her place of deposit that your honor will be pleased to appoint agreeably to your aforesaid order.

And your petitioner, as in duty bound will ever pray
          (Signed) G'ME DESPAU.

ORDER.—The petition is granted   October 2d, 1806
          (Signed) WM SPRIGG.

RECOGNISANCE OF DESPAU AND FAURIE —Filed 3d October, 1806.

Be it remembered, that on this 3d day of October in the year 1806, before me, J. W. Smith, Clerk of the Superior Court of the Territory of Orleans, personally appeared William Despau and Joseph Faurie, his security, and respectively acknowledged themselves indebted to the Government of the Territory of

Orleans in the sum of five thousand dollars, to be levied of their respective goods and chattels, lands and tenements, on the following condition.

Now the condition of this obligation is such that if the above bounden Joseph Faurie shall well and truly take charge and keep in his possession one half of the proceeds of the sale hereafter to be made of the lands and other property of the said Wm Despau, and now in question in virtue of a suit commenced by Sophie C Despau against the said Wm Despau, on the first day of September last, so that the said half of the aforesaid proceeds shall be forthcoming to answer such decree as may be rendered by said court in the case before mentioned then this obligation to be void, otherwise to be in full force and virtue.

(Signed) G'ME DESPAU   [L S]
J'H FAURIE   [L S]

Signed and sealed before me

(Signed) J W SMITH Clerk.

SUPPLEMENTARY PETITION—Filed 8th February, 1808

To the Honorable the Superior Court of the Territory of Orleans

The petition of William Despau, citizen of this city, humbly showeth—

That Sophia Carriere, his wife against whom he has since long while prosecuted on the purpose of getting a sentence to divorce him from her has (said Sophia Carriere) abused this honorable court's equity in such a manner, that in consequence of a petition by her presented under date of August eighteen hundred and six she has obtained the first of September following, an order forbidding your petitioner from selling any of his properties, unless he gave a sufficient security for the rights that may have the said Sophia Carriere his wife

That your petitioner respectfully obeying the order of your honorable court went to the clerk's office of said your honorable court, the third day of October following, and there gave, in the person of Joseph Faurie merchant, of this city, as security for said sum of five thousand dollars

That this measure, which was merely vexatory, from the part of said Sophia Carriere and for the only purpose of being hurtful to your petitioner has in fact thrown him under the impossibility of selling any part of his properties, though he very hardly want to do it in order to afford the feeding, the entertainment, and the education of his children, which are utterly forsaken by their mother.

That the depraved conduct said Sophia Carrière still continue to lead on by scandalously setting out from this Territory, where she left her children to the care of nobody, entitle your petitioner to pray your honorable court to render void the conservatory opposition formed by his wife, in consequence of in spite of all laws and regulations, her leading a wandering and rambling life, without any regard for the principles of honor and decency —living in open adultery

In these circumstances, and considering that your petitioner is ready and offers himself to take charge of the education and entertainment of the children legally born from his matrimony with said Sophia Carriere, his wife, and considering also that it is notoriously known that said Sophia Carriere has, several times, deserted the bed and board of your petitioner, and even that she is now out from the Territory without the consent of her husband, your petitioner humbly pray your honorable court to grant him replevy in full of the opposition formed to the sale of its property, by said Sophia Carriere, his wife which said Sophia Carriere shall be forfeited of all her rights, and also please your honorable court to discharge Joseph Faurie merchant, in this city, or his succession, of the security of five thousand dollars, which he has given in the clerk's office of your honorable court, for the account of your petitioner, by an act bearing date the third of October, eighteen hundred and six and in the mean time, to authorize your petitioner to sell and alienate, if he finds it proper, at whatever title it may be, all his property

And your petitioner as in duty bound, will ever pray

(Signed) GODOFREY, Att'y for Petit'r

Aux Honorables Juges de la Cour Supérieure du Territoire d'Orleans

Petition de Guillaume Despau, propriétaire deméurant en cette ville. Expose humblement—

Que Sophie Carriere Despau, son epouse, contre laquelle il poursuit depuis longtemps l'obtention d'une demande en divorce, a tellement surpris la religion de l'honorable cour que par suite d'une petition du mois d'aout mil huit cent six, elle a obtenu le premier September suivant un order portant defenses à votre pétitionaire de vendre aucune de ses propriétes, a moins qu'il ne donnât caution suffisante pour repondre des droits qui pourraient revenir à la dite Sophie Carriere son épouse

Que votre pétitionaire par respect a l'ordannance de l'honorable Cour, s'est transporté en son greffe le trois October de la même année, où il a fourni un cautionnement de cinq mille piastres, fortes en la personne du sieur Joseph Faurie, négociant en cette ville

Que cette mesure, qui était purement vexatoire de la part de Sophia Carrière, et dans l'intention de nuire à votre petitionnaire,

l'a effectivement mis dans l'impossibilite de vendre aucune partie
de ses proprietes, malgré le pressant besoin ou il etait et se trouve
encore davantage aujourd'hui, pour pouvoir, a son existence, à
l'entretien et a l'education de ses enfans qui sont totalement aban-
donnés de leur mere

Que la conduite depravée que continue de mener scandaleuse-
ment Sophia Carriere Despau, par son depart de ce territoire
ou elle laisse ses enfans a la merci d'un chacun, autorise votre
petitionnaire a reclamer la decheance pleine et entiere de la opposition conservatoire formée par son epouse, puisque au mepris
de toutes les lois elle mene une vie errante et vagabonde contre tous
les principes de l'honneur et de la bienseance, et dans le cas
d'adultere declaré. Dans ces circonstances et attendu que votre
petitionnaire est pret et offre de se charger de l'education et de
l'entretien des enfans issus legitimement de son union conjugale
avec Sophia Carriere son epouse, attendu aussi qu'il est no-
toirement connu que par recidive la dite Sophia Carriere a fui
et deserté la couche nuptiale, et qu'elle est même en ce moment
hors de ce territoire sans aucun consentement de son mari, votre petitionnaire supplie l'honorable Cour qu'il lui plaise, se con-
siderer lui accorder la main levée pleine et entiere de l'opposition
formée a la vente de ses biens par Sophia Carriere son epouse,
laquelle demeurera dechue de ses droits comme, aussi, dire et
ordonner que le sieur Joseph Faurie negociant en cette ville ou
sa succession sera bien et valablement dechargé du coutionne-
ment qu'il a fourni de la somme de cinq mille piastres pour le
compte de votre petitionnaire par acte en votre greffe du trois Octobre mil huit cent six, et autoriser en consequence votre petitionaire a vendre et aliener si bon lui semble et a quelque titre que
ce soit, les biens immeubles dont il est legitimement proprietaire ;
et lui ferez justice

(Signed) GODEFROY, Avt pr le petit'r

Affidavits Annexed

11 Novembre, 1807

Aujourd'hui onzieme jour de mois de Novembre de l'année
mil huit cent sep et, la trente deuxieme de l'independance Américaine

Par devant moi Cesar Alexis Bonamy, Juge de Paix de la
ville de la Nouvelle Orleans, est comparu le sieur Guillaume Despau domicilie en cette ville

Lequel a juré et affirmé sur le Saint Evangile que le six du
mois de juin dernier Maria Sophia Carriere, son épouse, est partie
clandestinement et pour la seconde fois de cette ville, quelle s'est
embarquée sans son consentement sur le navire *The Fair American*
pour le conunent d'Amerique—qu'il a donné avis de son depart
sur la gazette le **Thelegraphe No. 440**, et plusieurs autres sui-

vants, avec déclaration que son intention était de procéder en divorce contre la dite Marie Sophie Carriere son épouse, reclamant les lois pour se faire rendre compte des effets dont elle a disposé ou qu'elle a vendu sans son approbation, soutenant que, suivant toutes les lois, elle devait avoir perdu toutes reclamations de droit sur lui, comparant qu'elle a laissé et abandonné depuis sept ans. Et a signé.

(Signed,)   GME DESPAU

Juré et affirmé devant moi, Nouvelle Orleans, 11 Novembre, 1807   (Signed,)   A'IS BONAMY,
Juge de Paix.

Sont également comparus les sieurs François Poupard, citoyen domicilié en cette ville.

Lesquels après avoir aussi prêté serment sur le Saint Evangile de dire la verite, ont declaré qu'il est a leur connaissance que dame Marie Sophie Carriere épouse du sieur Guillaume Despau, a quitté ce territoire dans le mois de Juin dernier et qu'elle s'est embarqué pour le Nord d'Amerique, qu'ils sont intimement convaincus que le dame Despau est partie sans le consentement de son mari, puisque depuis longtemps elle ne vivait plus avec lui. Qu'il est également a leur connaissance que la dite dame Despau, ne tenant pas une conduite fort reguliere, et que son mari avait de justes raisons de s'en plaindre, et ont signé.

(Signed,)   F POUPARD.

Juré et affirmé devant moi Nouvelle Orleans, le 11 Novembre 1807   (Signed,)   A'IS BONAMY,
Juge de Paix.

Sont également comparus, Messrs Jean Jarreau, Jaques Mermet, citoyens de cette ville.

Lesquels après avoir prêté serment ont dit et declaré qu'il est à leur connaissance que dame Marie Sophie Carriere, épouse du sieur Guillaume Despau, a quitté ce territoire dans le courant de juin dernier, et qu'elle s'est embarquée pour le North Amerique, et qu'ils sont intimement convaincus qu'elle est partie sans le consentement de son mari.

Nouvelle Orleans, 11 Novembre, 1807

(Signed,)   JEAN JARREAU,
(Signed,)   J MERMET.

Juré et affirmé devant moi, Nouvelle Orleans, 11 Novembre, 1807.   (Signed,)   A'IS BONAMY,
Juge de Paix.

COPY OF RECOGNISANCE ANNEXED TO PETITION. See original pages, 8 and 9.

ENTRY ON MINUTES

Superior Court, Friday, February 12th, 1808

Present, the Honorable G. Mathews, the Honorable J. Lewis.

DESPAU, ⟩ Came on for trial
vs ⟩ Witnesses for Plaintiff —1 F. Pou-
MARIE SOPHIE CARRIERE, ⟩ pard —2 Bouhoud —3 Jarreau

Judgment rendered 21st May, 1808

Ordered by the Court, that the bond referred to in the petition on file in the office of the Clerk of this Court be cancelled, and the security discharged; and that as the defendant hath forfeited her right to the property acquired in the community, that the same vest in and belong to the petitioner.

May 24th, 1808   (Signed)   JOSHUA LEWIS
(Countersigned)—J. W. Smith, Clerk.

STATE OF LOUISIANA ⟩
FIFTH DISTRICT COURT OF NEW ORLEANS ⟩

I do hereby certify that the above, and foregoing thirteen pages, do contain a full and complete transcript (with the exception of the citations and writ of injunction, which are not among the papers,) of the record of the consolidated cases of William Despau vs Marie Sophia Carriere Despau No 561 Sophia C Despau vs William Despau, No 966, and William Despau vs Sophia Despau No 987, which suits were instituted before the late Superior court of the Territory of Orleans, under theer respective numbers of the docket of said Court.

In testimony whereof I have hereunto set my hand and affixed the seal of said Court at the city of New Orleans, this thirteenth day of June in the year of our Lord one thousand eight hundred and forty-nine, and in the seventy third year of the independence of the United States.

[L s]

JNO S BARON D'y Clerk.

[No 16]

Filed, by defendants, 20th June, 1849

J. W. GURLEY, Com'r

STATE OF LOUISIANA ⟩
CITY OF NEW ORLEANS ⟩

Be it known, that this day, before me, William Young Lewis, Notary Public in and for the city of New Orleans, duly commissioned and sworn, and in presence of the witnesses hereinafter named and undersigned,

Personally came and appeared, Edmund Pendleton Gaines, of lawful age, of the State of Tennessee, Major General in the service of the United States, now in this city, stipulating for himself.

And Madame Myra Clark, of lawful age, widow of the late William Wallace Whitney, of Broome county in the State of New York now in this city, daughter of the late Daniel Clark, stipulating for herself and with her own free will and accord, of the other part

Who severally declared that intending to join in the holy bonds of matrimony, the celebration whereof is to be forthwith, they do, by these presents, in contemplation thereof, mutually agree upon the following conditions and stipulations.

First   That there shall exist between them a community of acquets and gains, which said community of interest shall be regulated by the laws now in force in the State of Louisiana

Second   That the debt of each of said contracting parties prior to the celebration of their marriage, shall be paid out of their personal and individual funds nor shall either party in any wise be responsible for the debts of the other thus contracted

Third   That the party of the first part brings in marriage the following property, viz

Three thousand one hundred and forty acres of land, near Memphis, in the State of Tennessee, estimated, at forty-seven thousand dollars,	$47,000
Five thousand acres of East Florida land estimated at fifty thousand dollars,	50,000
Five lots of ground in the town of Memphis State of Tenessee, estimated at five thousand dollars,	5,000
Seven slaves, names not mentioned, estimated at five thousand dollars,	5,000
	$107,000

Making the sum of one hundred and seven thousand dollars; which said valuation the party of the second part acknowledges to be correct

Fourth   That the said party of the second part brings in marriage, sundry lots and squares of ground, situate in the Faubourg St John, near this city the exact description of which cannot be given at this time, but valued by her at one hundred thousand dollars, which said valuation the said party of the first part acknowledged to be correct, and that the said valuation is not intended to transfer said property to the said party of the first part

Fifth   That the said party of the second part also brings in marriage, her rights and claims as sole heir to the estate, effects, rights and credits of her deceased father, Daniel Clark, the amount whereof cannot be ascertained, it being now in litigation

Sixth.   That the said party of the second part, declares all property belonging to her, and brought in marriage. to be paraphernal, and retains the right of alienating or incumbering the same, whenever it is or shall be necessary

Seventh That the said party of the second part, further declares that she has three children by her marriage with the late William Wallace Whitney, viz William Whitney, Julia Whitney, and Rhoda Whitney

Eighth That the said party of the first part declares that he is a widower, and has two children, viz Henry Gaines and Edmund Gaines

Ninth That the said party of the second part, in consideration of the party of the first part being obliged to have considerable trouble and expense in attending to her law suits, for the recovery of the estate of her late father and the esteem and affection she entertains for him hereby makes a donation to him *inter vivos* out of her property, to be recovered from the said succession the sum of one hundred thousand dollars, provided, the same should produce an amount sufficient to render said donation legal and which the said party of the first part hereby accepts and the said party of the second part, further declares that she renounces all rights of dower upon the real and personal estates of the said party of the first part herein described also all rights of distribution of personal property of the party of the first part to which she might have under the statute of distribution in the State of Tennessee, or the Territory of Florida

Tenth That whenever the herein mentioned community of acquets and gains shall be dissolved by death of either of the aforesaid contracting parties or otherwise they hereby mutually agree, that it shall be lawful for the party of the second part, to retake all the property she brings in marriage, or that may devolve to her by succession donation or otherwise, and that she shall retake the same free of incumbrances

Eleventh That it is further agreed between the aforesaid contracting parties that in case the birth of children should revoke the herein mentioned donation, that the same shall be again renewed by the death of such children but that should the said party of the first part, depart this life before the said party of the second part, and without issue by her, that then the donation herein made to the said party of the first part, shall revert to the said party of the second part

Twelfth That whenever the said party of the first part shall receive property, money, and effects belonging to the said party of the second part, he shall acknowledge the same by act before a notary public

Done and passed at New Orleans, this sixteenth day of April, eighteen hundred and thirty-nine, in presence of William T.

10*

Lewis and Stuart H. Lewis, both of this city, witnesses, who have hereunto signed their names, with said contracting parties, and me the said notary

(Signed)—Edmund P Gaines—Myra Clark Whitney—William T Lewis—Stuart H Lewis—W Y Lewis, Not Pub.

I hereby certify that the foregoing is a true copy of the original, extant in my current register

In witness whereof, I grant these presents under my hand and [L S] seal of office, at New Orleans, this 7th day of May, 1840

W Y LEWIS. Not Pub

[No 18]
Offered by defendants   Filed 21st June, 1849.
J W GURLEY, Com'r.

COMPTROLLER'S OFFICE, January 29, 1841.

Sir I find, by looking on the balances on the books of the Register, a balance of $13 48-100 due you, as late collector of the Customs, per report No 70–540 dated Sept 5th, 1836, which has never yet been paid to you   You are hereby authorized to draw on the collector, at New Orleans, for the sum of thirteen dollars 48-100, and so close your accounts on the books of the Treasury

Very resp your ob't serv't,
J N BARKER Comp

Beverly Chew, Esq, late Col of Mississippi D,
At New Orleans, La

[No. 19.]
Offered by defendants   Filed 21st June, 1849
J W GURLEY, Com'r

TREASURY DEPARTMENT,
Comptroller's Office, 6th Sept, 1836

Sir Your accounts of the customs, for the district of Mississippi, have been adjusted at the Treasury, and a balance of $13 48, stated to be due to you from the U States

Very respectfully your ob't serv't,
GEO WOLF, Comptroller

Beverly Chew, Esq., late Col, Mississippi, Louisiana

[No 20]
Offered by defendants   Filed 21st June, 1849
J W. GURLEY, Com'r

NEW ORLEANS, 30th Nov'r, 1811

My dear Sir   I have this instant returned from a tour to the Mississippi territory, and on my arrival, your letters to the 6th inst., have been delivered to me   I cannot, therefore, reply to them, as the post closes in an hour, but by the next will state my means and resources and if I could, by the sacrifice of all I have, would relieve you. I feel as sensibly as yourself your wants, but I cannot in a moment of distress and total distrust, raise money here, and until the next election of directors, for the Louisiana bank takes place, I cannot dispose of the note you wish me to send you, as I informed you it was pledged for Chew & Relf's debt to that bank. I firmly believe that on Relf's re-election which I most confidently count on and which is to be the first Monday in January it will be possible to procure it, but an attempt to do so sooner would defeat the object, and would probably cause him to be rejected. The President's message has just got to hand and has caused a great sensation in this country, which in case of war, would be left without any possible resource. I most solemnly assure you that since my return I have not received a dollar from any debtor and my collections must be governed even in the spring by the price of cotton. I remain yours sincerely,

DANIEL CLARK

Daniel W. Coxe, Esq.

[No. 21]
Ordered by defendants. Filed 21st June, 1849

J. W. GURLEY, Com'r

CAPES OF DELAWARE, July 15th, 1811

Dear Sir. We are going to sea with pleasant weather, tho' the wind is light. I can only repeat that I shall remit you, conformably to our arrangements as soon as I return to New Orleans (say within four months from this time at furthest) a sum of at least twenty-five thousand dollars, and on this you may place the most implicit reliance in any arrangements you may have occasion to make. I beg you will keep me constantly advised of all political changes which can affect our market and the probable prices of our produce in Europe and in the U. S.

Yours sincerely,

DANIEL CLARK

Daniel W. Coxe, Esq,

[No. 22]
By defendants. Filed 21st June 1849

J. W. GURLEY, Com'r.

NEW ORLEANS, 13th Jan'y, 1812

My dear Sir. I set off to-morrow for the Houmas, to see what arrangements I can make with Genl Hampton, respecting the payment of his note, which the want of a sale for his crop of the two last years has prevented his affecting hitherto. I shall advise you from thence of what I do, and am in hopes I shall be able to do something to relieve you. It has not been in my power hitherto to get back the note from the bank but Relf informs me that he has hopes of obtaining it, in a few days

Yours affectionately,   DANIEL CLARK

Daniel W Coxe, Esq

[No 23]

By defendants   Filed June 21st 1849

J W GURLEY Com'r

NEW ORLEANS 15th June, 1812

My dear Sir I have before me your letters of 8th April and 24th May, and had begun a statement in answer to them which more than all I could say, would convince you that if I have not done for you all you could wish, it has not been my fault This statement I cannot finish in time, for the post, but you will receive it by the next Let it suffice for me to state to you for the present that since my return, instead of having, as I expected a large sum to receive of Chew & Relf to apply either to your use or my own, I have had to advance them since then $30 000 and I am utterly lost in conjecture as to the intention of the statement furnished me by Relf last year, copy of which I left with you and which served as the basis of the arrangement made with us I would now have written to you, as I could not, for the moment, forward you the complete statement which I wish were it not to put an end to your complaints about my silence, for I am heart broken, and have nothing new to say After you shall have received my next I will leave you to say yourself what I am to do, and believe me that if I could now sacrifice the little I have left, and after paying every thing, only reserve wherewith barely to keep me from starving in any other country I would do it in an instant, to escape from the hell I have lived in for the last 18 months I shall say nothing more until I can lay a complete state of affairs before you I remain yours sincerely,

DANIEL CLARK

Daniel W. Coxe, Esq

[No 24]

By defendants   Filed 21st June, 1849

J W GURLEY Com'r

NEW ORLEANS, 8th Sept, 1812

My dear Sir 'Altho' I understand, by a letter from Mr Relf to Mr Chew, which, during the sickness of this latter, has gone thro' my hands, that you are not desirous of hearing from me, except when I have remittances to make to you, yet I think it incumbent on me to trouble you, in order to clear up a point in which, perhaps, Mr Relf has deceived himself and you In the letter above alluded to, he states to Mr. Chew the communication I made to you of my having been under the necessity of ad vancing to their house the sum of $30,000, since my return from Philadelphia, last year, and he expresses surprise thereat, as if he doubted or disbelieved the assertion. As when I made this communication, it was done to show you how differently I found myself circumstanced from what I had expected, and that the funds which I had relied on to relieve you were made use of by them, I shall now briefly point out how and when these sums were paid to them

1st November, 1811, on receiving the news of the payment of one of Genl Hampton's bills which had been destined to pay off my account at the Louisiana bank the directors, at Mr Relf's request, agreed to let my account stand as it then was and he received from the amount of the bill,   - - - 10,000

Genl Hampton's crop of sugar delivered to them of which a part was sold here and the remainder shipped, supposed to amount to   - - - - - 13,000

Cash borrowed here for them since Relf's departure,   10,000

                                    $33,000

Should Relf be still in Philadelphia, I wish you to show him this letter, that if he still doubts, he may be convinced and from this you will be able to judge of the difficulties I have to struggle with and the agonies I suffer

When I left Philadelphia last year, I would not for fear of accident bring back with me the power of attorney, given me by Chew & Relf, to settle with you. It is, however, a very essential paper to me and I intreat you will forward it, as well as the letter you received from Chew & Relf, dated 13th September of last year approving of that settlement. On Mr Relf's return, it is my wish to come to a final understanding with them, and these two papers are indispensably necessary to me, if any thing should remain to ask from them

            I remain, dear sir, yours sincerely,

                    DANIEL CLARK

P S Mr Chew is not yet able to leave his room, altho' he is recovering

D W. Coxe, Esq

[No 25]

By defendants   Filed 21st June, 1849

                      J W GURLEY, Com'r

            NEW YORK, 13th August, 1802

Gentlemen I am so far on my way to England, and shall sail in the ship Oneida, on Tuesday, for London. I enclose you, by Mr Cox's order, the last letter he received from Green, it needs no comment. It is Mr. Coxe's orders, that all vessels whatever of his, bound to Europe, should call in the Delaware for orders, your directions to the captains, on this head, must be positive, tho' private and the captains, on arrival must protest, &c. Attend to what Green says, about a certificate. I request you will pay particular attention to the trunks containing the old papers of my uncle, as since I have been here I have heard that among the neglected papers, there are some which may be of advantage to me, especially a transfer of 1000 acres of land, by a person of the name of Callender, to my uncle, which paper I would wish you to look for, and put up carefully in my desk with the others; it is, I think, on a large sheet, and may probably be loose.

For God's sake, as you value our existence, push on remittances, and sell the shipping, when there are no more remittances to be made. I will return from England direct to Orleans if nothing new intervenes. Yours sincerely

DANIEL CLARK

P. S. Should the Thomas or Creole be still in Orleans, when this gets to hand, they must touch in the Delaware, and all others, in future.

Messrs. Chew & Relf

[No. 26.]

Copy of testimony taken on Shaumbourgh's application

By defendants filed 21st June 1849

J. W. GURLEY, Commissioner,

ESTATE OF DANIEL CLARK

COURT OF PROBATES, April 29th, 1834

Dussuau Delacroix, witness for the applicant Shaumbourg, sworn, says that he was very intimate with the late Daniel Clark for a great many years, and up to the time of his death, that some few months previous to the death of Daniel Clark, he visited deponent on his plantation, and expressed a wish that he, deponent, should become his executor, deponent at first refused, but after a little, from the persuasion of said Daniel Clark, he consented to become his executor, that in this conversation. Clark spoke of a young female, then in the family of Captain Davis, named Myra, that said Clark expressed a wish that deponent should become tutor to this female, and that she should be sent to France for her education, and that he, Clark, would leave her a sufficient fortune to do away with the stain of her birth. That a month or two after this conversation at the plantation of deponent, he, deponent, called to see Clark at his house, on the Bayou Road, he there found him in his *cabinet*, and had just sealed up a packet. The superscription on it was as follows *Pour être ouvert en cas de mort.* Clark threw it down in the presence of deponent, and told him that it contained his last will, and some other papers which would be of service. Deponent did not see the will, nor does he know anything about its contents, he only saw the packet with the superscription on it, as before related

In the conversation he had on his plantation as above related, Clark requested him deponent not to say anything about it to R Relf and B Chew, he observed to me that he had named R., Relf and B Chew as his creators in a former will, and on that account it was that he wished nothing said to said R Relf and B Chew. That after the death of Clark witness was not much surprised that the last will of Clark was not produced or found for it is to his knowledge that Clark had requested several other persons as he had done deponent to become his executor, he thinks he made the request to Mr Bellechasse and to Judge Pitot. That Clark never spoke to deponent about Myra, except on the occasion before related on deponents plantation, he then spoke of her as his daughter. Clark observed to deponent at the time he showed him the packet, which he said contained his will that in case of his death, it would be found in a small black trunk which he had there

Cross examined

That he does not know whether the will of which he speaks, was the same that was produced in Court, he knows nothing about the contents of the package shown him by Clark

APRIL 30TH

Dussuau Delacroix re-examined in chief says

That such a length of time having elapsed to wit, more than 20 years, it is impossible for him to say whether the conversation, wherein Clark enjoined secrecy about the will with regard to Chew and Relf was at the first interview deponent had with Clark on his, deponent's plantation, or whether it was at the second interview at the house of Clark on the Bayou Road He knows that the conversation took place as related by him, but precisely when and where, he cannot state.

Cross examined

That he has been acquainted with Mr Relf for about 30 years that his acquaintance with Relf proceeded from the intimacy deponent had with the late Daniel Clark, with whom Mr Relf was concerned, first as clerk, and afterwards, he believe, as a partner. During the whole of this time, he never heard anything against the character of Mr Relf, he always considered him to be a man of probity. That it is to his knowledge that Mr Relf has filled various public offices of trust, and among them the office of cashier of the Louisiane State Bank of which deponent himself was president for a number of years. That he is at the present day cashier of that Bank That deponent never heard anything against the integrity and correctness of Mr. Relf during the time he, deponent, was president. He supposes he must enjoy the confidence of the directors and stockholders to this day, from the circumstance of his continuing in his cashiership. That in the year 1820 when deponent went to France, he named Mr Deherriet and L G Hiligsberg, his attorneys in fact, and in case of their death, Mr Relf was named in their stead that if he had thought Mr Relf guilty of destroying the last will of Clark, he should not, most certainly, have named him to act for him. That very often when deponent would visit Mr Clark during his last illness, (which was short) he would meet Mr Relf there. He does not recollect if Mr Relf lived with Clark at the time. He thinks Mr Relf was there the day Clark died. That he never heard Clark say any thing, which would go to show that he had withdrawn his confidence from Mr Relf, except the circumstance of his enjoining the secresy of deponent towards him Relf & B Chew, when he spoke of making another will, and naming deponent as his executor.

Principal examination

Question. Have you any recollection of any case analogous to the present, in which Mr Relf was named executor in a will of prior date, when there was an alleged posterior will, that was said to have been destroyed made by the same testator in which Mr Relf was not named as an executor.

Answer No That when Clark showed deponent the sealed packet, as related before, telling him that it contained his will and other papers, deponent naturally supposed it to be the will, of which Clark spoke to him on his plantation, to wit, the one which contained the provision naming deponent executor and tutor to Myra

MAY 1 1834

Pierre Baron Boisfontaine, witness for applicant Shaumbourg, sworn, says that he was intimately acquainted with the late Daniel Clark, and was on very friendly terms with him, this intimacy was for many years prior to, and up to the time of his death Deponent was his agent on his estate. Deponent was with him during his last illness, and at the time he expired That he was acquainted with the wife of Mr Whitney formerly called Mirah Clark, that he knew her from the day of her birth, up to the time of Clark's death. She was born in deponent's house, in Barrack-street That Clark always acknowledged Myra to be his child, from her cradle up to the day of his, Clark's, death He was very much attached to her. He charged that she might be brought up by deponent's sister, the wife of Captain Davis That Clark in his last illness spoke to deponent about his last will and testament. He stated to deponent that he had made his last will, and that it was enclosed with some valuable papers, and deposited in a small trunk in a room below stairs. He told deponent that he had left the greater part of his property to his child Mirah, and that he had made a disposition in his last will to that effect. That deponent heard Clark tell Lubin, his confidential servant, that in case of his death, the small black trunk was to be delivered to Mr Dussuau Delacroix. That he heard Clark say when on his death bed that Bellechasse, Delacroix and Judge Pitot were the executors named in his last will. He also said that Mr Delacroix was named tutor to Mirah. Clark now the wife of Mr Whitney. That Mr Relf, at the time Clark expired, took the keys from the armon, as deponent initially supposed to lock up the effects of the deceased. Mr Relf went out of the room after he had taken the keys, and sent Lubin somewhere, he does not recollect where. Deponent never saw the last will of Clark; he only saw the package, when Clark handed it to Mr Delacroix. He was very much astonished after Clark's death, that the will did not appear, and his impression was at the time, that the will had been withheld or destroyed.

Cross examined

It was in the afternoon that Clark died. That Mirah in public passed by the name of Mirah Davis. This was through the park or Captain Davis, and deponent supposed his Davis', wife. The mother of Mirah Davis is J. Degrange. That he has known Mr Relf for upwards of forty years, and never heard his integrity called in question. He has always enjoyed the confidence of the public, and has filled many offices of trust, and fills one at the present day.

2D May, 1834

P. Baron Boisfontaine, re-examined on part of opponents

That he had charge of the plantation of Daniel Clark, called *Cann Bral*, and other plantations, for some years prior to, and up to the time of Mr Clark's death. That all this time, Mr Relf was charged with the business of said Clark in the city, and deponent always went to him about the plantation affairs of said Clark. That during the whole of this time, Mr Relf and Mr Clark were on the most intimate and friendly terms. Mr Relf lived in the same house with him. That witness does not believe from all he saw, that Mr Clark ever withdrew his confidence from Messrs Relf & Chew.

Examination in chief resumed

That he never heard Clark mention any other persons as his executors of his last will, of which he spoke to deponent, than Col. Bellechasse, Judge Pitot and Dussuau Delacroix

11*

Hubert Remy, witness for the opponents, sworn, says that he has been in the city of New Orleans for 42 years, and has known Mr. Richard Relf ever since he, Relf came to this place which was a few years after deponent—it is more than 30 years ago. Mr Relf was quite a boy at the time, he first went to live with Mr Huhngs—he Huhngs, was intimate with the late Daniel Clark and he, Clark, prevailed on him to let him have the services of Mr Relf, to assist him Clark, in his business, accordingly Mr Relf went to Mr Clark's, and continued many years with him in the capacity of clerk, and gained his esteem and confidence. That Mr Clark made a trip to Campeachy and other places, where he was gone several months, and Mr Relf was left charged with his whole business. That he never heard, during the long acquaintance he has had with Mr Relf, his integrity and honesty called in question. He has always sustained in this community the highest character for integrity and honesty. That he has filled many public offices of trust, and fills one at the present day. That it is to his knowledge, that Mr Relf resided with the late Daniel Clark, at his residence on the Bayou Road, both before and during the last illness. That deponent was himself intimately acquainted with the late Daniel Clark, and during his last illness, would frequently send his son and other persons to enquire after his health. Mr Relf would sometimes send word that Mr Clark was so ill, that no one could see him. From this circumstance deponent knows that Mr Relf was there. Deponent really believes that Clark reposed confidence in Mr Relf, to the last moment of his, Clark's life. Witness does not believe Relf capable of destroying a will.

Cross examined

Deponent never heard Clark mention any thing about testamentary dispositions

Jean Canon, being duly sworn for opponent, deposes that he is a native of the county, and knows Mr Relf from his childhood. Knew Clark very intimately. Clark rendered him many important services. Was a neighbor of Clark's, deponent living almost in front of Clark's house

Clark was as intimate with Relf as a father and son could be. Clark reposed entire confidence in Relf and Chew. Does not believe that Clark ever withdrew his confidence from Relf. The same day on which Clark died, Clark sent for deponent, to request deponent to attend to the delivery of certain negroes sold by Clark. Deponent not knowing the names of the negroes, called on Clark for them,—Clark called Relf, who gave their names to deponent, who then made the delivery. Towards sun down on the same day, deponent returned to Clark's house, and seeing all the doors open and Mr Relf walking to and fro on the gallery, suspected that Clark was dead, which was the case. Mr Relf then lived with Clark. Deponent does not believe Relf capable of destroying a will—he should have witness such a thing and even then he would not believe his eyes

Cross examined

Clark considered Mira to be his daughter. Clark told deponent that Mira was his daughter, and deponent recognizes Mrs Whitney to be the aforesaid Mira. Clark requested deponent to buy a small Choctaw horse and saddle for Mira, and deponent having complied with the request delivered the horse to Mira, who lived at Captain Davis' who resided at Terre aux Bœufs. Clark spoke to deponent very often about Mira, and manifested great affection for her. Deponent knows nothing of Clark's testamentary disposition. Clark always told deponent that Mira was his daughter, and that he loved her, and that he would leave her all that he could as a father

Gallien Preval, witness for opponents, sworn declares that he knew Relf for the last twenty years. Knew the late Daniel Clark. Thinks that the relations between those gentlemen were intimate. Deponent saw Relf at Clark's house when Clark died. He went there several times during Clark's sickness. Deponent was a magistrate and as such affixed the seals on the effects of the deceased. He recognizes the proces verbal as being made by him. Relf has filled several responsible offices in the community,—has and does enjoy the confidence. Deponent has no reason to suspect that Mr Relf would destroy a will

Cross examined

Judge Pitot told deponent that he Pitot, thought that Clark had made another will. From the manner in which the proces verbal is drawn up, deponent is inclined to think that Relf must have taken the will out of the trunk, in presence of him, Preval. It was not a custom with deponent to allow any person but himself to examine the contents of trunks of deceased persons. Witness does recollect that there was any seal upon the trunk, does not recollect that the trunk was locked, does not recollect whether the package, containing the will, was sealed or not, witness does not recollect any particulars, as, for the last 20 years, he has had a very great number of estates on which to affix seals, and too much official acts to recollect details

Louis Seré, witness sworn for opponent, deposes, he knows Relf since 1805, and Clark since 1805, witness came to New

Orleans in 1805, Clark was very intimate with Chew and Relf that intimacy lasted until Clark's death knows of no circumstance tending to show that Clark had withdrawn his confidence from Relf and Chew Relf lived with Clark until Clark's death that is, sometime before Clark's death Relf has always approved the reputation of an honest man never heard any thing derogatory of Relf—quite the contrary, in all the dealings deponent had with Relf, he found him correct for ten years consecutively, he dealt with Relf then transactions were very large Deponent considers Relf incapable of deceiving him

Cross examined

Knew nothing of Clark's testamentary dispositions from Clark himself, never heard any thing of a posterior will being made by Clark, the transactions of deponent with Clark were of a mercantile nature

A true copy of original

AND D DOURICOURT, Dy Reg'r

[No 27]

Filed 21 June, 1849   J W GURLEY, Com.

GERMANTOWN May 27th, 1803

I take up my pen at the desire of my dear brother at the same time, my performance will be so wretched that I need all your good nature and friendship to overlook the defects I debated whether I should, or not write but as I was to a brother, who, I hope, will kindly point out my errors and render me if not an elegant correspondent, at least a useful one   Some years back, had I the opportunity I now have, I flatter myself I might be worthy the correspondence of my dear brother as it is I venture to write, rather than not comply with your request How long does the time appear since you went away and how anxiously do I look forward when we may expect you' I often wish you had not been encumbered with such a family 'tis a serious subject, and where is the son or brother would do what you have done' May our conduct prove our gratitude 'tis there only we can make the return for such uncommon goodness My mother desires me to tell you all her wishes are gratified were you here Since you went, Mr Cox has given her whatever she called for I suppose, before this, you know Chew & Relf's bills were protested   be   my dear brother on that account, as we have every thing and situation

         to her more than I can express, her them improved at your return

         education improve equal to the

            since his removal, Sally

not yet sent to   are all so   to you, that I am determined shall not increase it for some time, indeed, she is at no great loss

—she writes and works at home every day, and returns you many thanks for your kind mention of her in your letters. This day, I heard from Mr Coxe and hear they are both well. In letter to me is express... ... ... He says in September we expect ... ... being him that time. Surely my dear ... ... who ... ... be with us before then. I should ... ... to be without you. Forgive me for pre... ... ... you we ... the case you the slavery of business were ... ... you might be at your ease now after all your ... ... my mother wishes

if she is to remain here for some time but I suppose ... aunt has informed all about it. We received the ... ... in excellent order. The time-piece is sent to be repaired ... we shall have it home in a few days. I sent some things to Mrs R. H. in the ship Dispatch but fear they are lost, their value was small, but as they were my own work, I am sorry to hear lost. I also wrote to you, by that conveyance. Will you my beloved brother add to the many obligations I already feel myself under to you by sending me word if they are really gone at present. I only suspect it. Remember me to Mr and Mrs Huling, Mr Chew, and all my friends. I remain with the sincerest affection,

Yours sincerely A ANDERSON

Dan'l Clark Esq. New Orleans

[No 28]

By Defendants. Filed 21st June 1849

J. W. GURLEY, Com

Liverpool May 3d, 1806

My Dear Brother —I scarcely know whether you will be obliged to me, or not for the share I had in setting up your truly elegant toilet, but the idea of its being intended for *Mrs D Clark* got strong possession of my mind, and so much do I wish to see one bear that name worthy of you that nothing in my opinion, could be too good to trust in it. I cannot think how the plan of such a thing could enter into your head for I assure you it has been exhibited in London as a master-piece of elegance and fashion. I sincerely hope it may reach you in safety and in as good order as we sent it off.

I had a letter from Ann, written after receiving your kind present to her, which she mentions in the most affectionate and grateful manner. She is my constant correspondent. Often do I breathe a prayer that, instead of writing, I had her to speak to, but that will never be until you bring her with you to England where you are hourly looked for by your nephews. The name of uncle seems to act like a charm, all the bits of paper they pick up are brought me for uncle's newspaper, on which, by the bye, you will see some of their handy-work. I had a mind to offended when you mentioned in your letter that they should be taught to know you Could you for a moment suppose that a child of mine would not be made familiar with the name of one to whom their mother owes all she possesses? When I forget that, I shall cease to live.

I hope Mr. Chew gave you an account of what a little prokle Clark is tell him he has not forgotten him, or likely to do so while the cordials last, for which I beg you will give him best thanks, we often drink his health in them

Mr. Green is working away in the counting-house, and not likely to leave it to-night. He is never so happy as when doing something for his family We are a very old-fashioned couple, for every day makes us more necessary to each other, there does not exist a kinder or more indulgent husband and father, all his pleasure is in his home At present, we are rather uneasy about Mr Green, I much fear my next will be an account of his death. He has been ill a long time, but now he declines rapidly, his complaint turns out to be water on the chest George is the doctor that does him most good, indeed, the greatest part of his time is spent at Crosby

The last accounts I had from Ireland, my aunt Crearn and Eleanor were both well, the latter truly sensible of your kindness in the very liberal allowance you made her

Do, pray, write soon to me, you cannot think how uneasy I made myself when I heard you went to Vera Cruz Why will you be forever toiling? Surely you should now sit down and enjoy life Let me know if my suspicions are right about the destination of the toilet, if they are, may you be as happy in your choice as is your truly affectionate sister.

JANE GREEN

P. S—Don't you think I have had a deal of forbearance to confine the mention of daughter to the end? She is a lovely little girl, and quite a beauty, like me.

Daniel Clark, Esq, New Orleans

[No 29]
Filed 20th June, 1849, by defendants.

J. W GURLEY, Com'r.

GERMANTOWN, March 30th, 1803

My Dear Child:—Your letter from Kingston we received last evening, and your enjoying good health has spread universal joy throughout the family, our fears have been very great for you, in the different voyages you have been compelled to make during the winter; but trust in the Almighty, they will soon have an end, that you may be restored to our wishes. Mr. Chew has sent the plate and the bills; the first I have received money for, the other you will know about before you receive this. Mr. Cox has conducted himself, in every respect, as you could wish, and complied, cheerfully, with every request made to him. What you mention about the happiness enjoyed by my dear Jane, fills my soul with gratitude to Heaven, and you, as being the means of placing her in a situation beyond what she could expect, but I hope not more than she is deserving of That she will ever continue the same line of conduct which has given so much pleasure to that worthy family, I have no doubt, for her slender opportunity, she made the most of it, and will, I hope, do credit to herself and friends

Ann received a letter from Mr Green, a day or two ago, in which he talks in raptures of the beauty of his son, and the likeness he bears to his mother, who he says, is handsomer than ever. The children are both well Richard we have removed to another school, and hope, when you return, to find him improved Ann wrote to you about a fortnight since, by a vessel going direct to New Orleans Your father continues much the same as when you left us, and longs impatiently to see you In your aunt's letter, you will have every particular you wish to be informed of concerning family affairs We want for nothing but the presence of him who has so largely contributed to our ease and comfort. Present my affectionate regards to Mrs Hulings and family, Madam Debuise and my little grandson, Mr Relf and family Your father sends his love and best wishes, your sisters and the children join in it May every happiness attend you, prays your affectionate mother,

MARY CLARK

Enclosed is the number of plate which came

Your father requests you to send him a couple of carrets of tobacco.

Dan'l Clark, Esq, New Orleans

[No 30]

Filed 21st June, 1849, by defendants

J W GURLEY, Comm'r

GERMANTOWN, July 9th, 1803

My Dear Child.—Your letter, which I yesterday received, has given me the most heart-felt pleasure I have for some time experienced The idea of your being indisposed had made me very uneasy—thank God, my fears are subsided on that score Your absence is a thing you can't avoid; therefore, I must be content until you can come with safety to yourself I am sorry the fate of the bill should cause you uneasiness, as I have not suffered any inconvenience by it, as yet, Mr Cox has complied with every demand I made on him with readiness and politeness, for which I feel greatly obliged, and I know you will be pleased at his attention. Your plantations I guessed would be in disorder from the time you left it, I suppose they have been little attended to; indeed, a person not living on them, in whom you could confide, must make it troublesome and expensive, besides the uneasiness it will give you to see them neglected, but I trust your presence will do a great deal in restoring them to what they ought to be. The children are well, and attend their school regularly. I hope Richard will, in a short time, be able to do something to forward himself in the world. he has lately been disappointed in his teacher, who left the place suddenly, and as yet there is none here so capable to supply his place. Your father enjoys perfect health, and sends his love and blessing. The things arrived in brig for me have not yet received, her quarantine not being expired. my dear child you are ever heaping benefits on us, the last sweetmeats are delightful, few, or none, indeed, would do what you are every day doing—adding comfort to the lives of their parents and family. I am happy to hear you sent Bil to Jane, he wished much for a removal, and I hope he will find the change to his advantage. By chance, I got a little black boy bound to me about 9 years old, which I intend sending her, he is a fine smart fellow, and will attend little Green. I know it will please them. I will send him by the first vessel of Mr Cox's that sails from here. 'Tis six weeks since we heard from Liverpool. perhaps you heard since, they were in perfect health, and blessed in the society of each other. they regret much your leaving them so soon. Jane says, I think, they would agree perfectly, Mr G. and Daniel are both slaves to business. what a blessing for Jane, to be so well provided for, 'tis through you, my dear boy, that all those comforts are derived.

Thomas is quite pleased at your attention to him, and ready to comply with all you desire. he is constant in his care of your father, in short I don't know what he would have done were it not for him. I suppose your aunt has informed you we remain in the same house still, and she with us. her nieces are returned to Virginia, and Mr A. Hoops is gone to the Genessee country, she talks of going in the fall to see her friends in V—; I hope, by that time, we will have you with us. Dejan is with us these two days. I was really glad to see him, I believe he goes to New York next week. Remember me to Mrs. Hulings, Madame Delus and family, Chew and Relf, Mrs Relf and family. The children join in love and best wishes to you; also your sisters. Ann writes, this post, to you. God bless and protect my child, prays your affectionate mother,

MARY CLARK

I am going to trouble you for a few handkerchiefs, I don't know what name to give them. they are cross-barred, and much worn by the ladies there, in New Orleans, on their heads, in winter. I admired them much, but did not think of getting them, when there, also, a few feather faro Your son, **William Dubui's**, you must kiss for me, and my god-son, Relf

[No 32]

Filed by Defendants, 23d June 1849.

J W GURLEY, Com'r

WILLIAM W WHITING &
MYRA C WHITING,
vs
ELEANOR O BEARNE AND
OTHERS

No 843.

IN THE PROBATE COURT, IN AND FOR THE PARISH AND CITY OF NEW ORLEANS

Interrogatories propounded by and on behalf of the above named defendants and by virtue of the annexed commission, to be answered under oath by William E Hulings Daniel W. Coxe, and others residing in the city of Philadelphia, State of Pennsylvania, and which together with the answers thereto to be made by said witnesses, the said defendants intend to offer and read in evidence on the trial of the above entitled cause

1st Will you, and each of you, be pleased to state your names, ages, and residence and whether not you are requested with the parties in the above entitled cause?

2d Will you and each of you be pleased to state whether or not you were acquainted with Daniel Clark, late of the city of New Orleans, who departed this life in the month of August, 1813? If *aye*, will you be pleased to state whether or not your acquaintance extended to friendly intimacy, and how long were you so acquainted with him previous to his death

3d Will you be pleased to state whether or not said Daniel Clark was ever married?

4th State, if you please whether or not you, or either of you, ever heard said Clark, during his lifetime say or acknowledge himself to be the father of any children? If *aye*, what were their respective names, sex, and probable age, and where are they at the time?

5th Did said Clark, during his lifetime, to the knowledge of either of you, make provision for the maintenance and education of any of his said supposed children? If *aye*, which ones? What where their names? and to what extent did he make such provisions to your knowledge, or from what you have heard said Clark say?

6th Do you, or either of you, know Mrs. Myra C Whitney? If *aye*, will you and each of you be pleased to state, if you know in whose family she resided from her childhood until her marriage with the said Whitney, and by what name she was known and generally received by the community at large, and from the

12*

general reputation which she bore in the community, whose child was she supposed to be

7th Do you, or either of you, know of any other fact or circumstance not mentioned by you in answer to some one of the foregoing interrogatories, which you suppose may be of any service to the defendants in this cause? If *aye*, be pleased to state the same as fully and particularly as if you had been thereunto specially interrogated   (Signed)   S DUNCAN,
     Attorney and curator ad hoc for defendants.

Cross interrogatories propounded by defendant to the above witnesses, reserving however, exceptions to the legality of the commission in this case, and all legal exceptions to the testimony taken under the same

1 Are you acquainted with the parties to this suit? If so, state how long you   known them

2 Are you interested in the event of this suit? If you answer in the affirmative, state in what manner

3 Have you not employed counsel to appear in the above suit?
(Signed,)   WM W WORTHINGTON, for Plaintiffs
Answers of William E Hulings to interrogatories propounded in the suit of William W Whitney and Mira C. Whitney, *vs.* Elenor O'Bearne and others in the Probate Court in and for the Parish and city of New Orleans

To Interrogatory 1st My name is William Empeson Hulings, aged sixty-nine years, residing in Philadelphia   I think I never saw Mr William W Whitney but once, when he at my house, and was introduced to myself and wife by the now Mrs Mira C Whitney, formerly called Mira Davis, with whom I had been slightly acquainted for some years, seeing her but very seldom. Mrs. O'Bearne I never saw, but have understood that she resided in Ireland, and was the sister of the late Daniel Clark, Esq, of New Orleans   The word "others" being indefinite, I have no answer to give as relates to it

To 2d interrogatory I say, my acquaintance with Daniel Clark, late of New Orleans, who died August 1813 began in the year 1789, in New Orleans, and continued in the closest personal intimacy until I left that city in May, 1804. Our friendship remained uninterrupted to the day of his death

To 3d interrogatory I answer, having been, as above stated, the intimate friend of the said Daniel Clark, had he been married, I cold not failed to know it I firmly believe he never was married.

To 4th interrogatory I say, that the said Daniel Clark never did acknowledge or intimate to me that he had a child or children, or that he ever had even had carnal connexion with any female; but I have frequently heard from Mrs Lyder, formerly Mrs. Alexander, late of our city, but now deceased, that a female child, named Caroline, placed (while she resided in Trenton) under her care by Daniel W Coxe, Esq, of this place was the daughter of the aforesaid Daniel Clark, and so frequently acknowledged by him to be That he, the said Daniel Clark, made many visits to see the said child and would fondly caress it, and make it handsome presents, and holding it before the looking-glass would trace his features in her face, and say that she should ride in her coach. Mrs Lynn continued to assert the same thing to the day of her death After the death of Mr Lynn the husband of said lady, Mrs. Mary Clark, mother of said Daniel, received the said Caroline into her family, at Germantown, as the undoubted child of her said son She remained there some time when as friends of the said Daniel Clark, Mr Daniel W Coxe and myself thought it time some attention should be paid to her education, in consequence, we, with the approbation and consent of the said Mary Clark, (who made an appropriation of money for the clothing, etc., of the said Caroline) placed her with Mr and Mrs Bazely, then keeping a boarding school for young ladies as an apprentice, her services to be as an equivalent for her board and education Said Caroline remained with Mrs Bazely I think, for the time stipulated, receiving from the said Mrs Mary Clark, as her grandmother, the sum appropriated to her use She afterwards was addressed by Dr Barnes of your city, a respectable man, and was married to him They moved to the Mississippi, and I believe now reside at or near Port Gibson The only knowledge I have of Mira Davis, now Mrs Mira C. Whitney being a child of the said Daniel Clark, was derived from Col Samuel B Davis who told me that Mr Clark *acknowledged* said Mira to be his child and had placed her under his care as such Caroline Clark, now Mrs. Barnes, I *believe* to be about thirty-three years of age, of Mira, now Mrs Whitney, I have no data on which to form an opinion. I have heard that she is in New Orleans

The 5th interrogatory I answered above, by my declaring that the said Daniel Clark never did acknowledge or intimate that he had a child, or children I have learned from Richard Relf, Esq, of New Orleans, that certain lots of ground out of New Orleans, on the Bayou road, were destined or appointed by said Daniel Clark, for the said Caroline and Mira Col Bellechasse, now or late of Matanzas, Cuba, informed me by letter, that he held a trust from the said Daniel Clark of some lots as aforesaid, for said Mira, but knew not of any provisions made for Caroline

To the 6th interrogatory I say, that I have precedingly acknowledged a slight acquaintance with Mira, now Mrs C Whitney, who, ever since I heard of her, has, I believe, resided in the family of Col Samuel B Davis, aforesaid, as his reputed daughter, being known in public, as far as I am aware, by the name of Mira Davis, and said Mira confess to my wife and self, that until some little time before she was married to said Mr

Whitney, she believed herself to be the daughter of the aforesaid Col. Samuel B Davis Further the deponent saith not. Philadelphia, 11th June, 1835

(Signed,)   WM E HULINGS

I answer to the cross examinations in the aforesaid suit, I say first· That I have slightly known Mrs Mira C Whitney, formerly Mira Davis, for some years, but cannot fix the period of our acquaintance   Of her husband I had no knowledge, until introduced to him by her, at my own house, sometime last summer, or early in the fall   I have never seen Mrs O Bearne, but have heard from Mrs Mary Clark, mother of aforesaid Daniel Clark, that said Mrs. O Bearne was her daughter   The "others" not being specified by name, I can say nothing as to them

To the 2d interrogatory I answer, that I am not either directly or indirectly interested in the suit of William W Whitney, Mira C. Whitney *vs* Elenor O Bearne and others.

Thirdly And to the last Interrogatory I say, that having no interest with the said suit, or any other relating to the persons within named, I have not employed any counsel in this suit, or any other cause   Further the deponent saith not   11th June 1835.

(Signed,)   WM E HULINGS

I hereby certify the foregoing to be true and correct copies of the originals on file, deposited in the office of the Sec-
[L. S] ond District Court of New Orleans

New Orleans, June 23d 1849

P M BERTON, D y Clerk.

[No 33]
Offered by defendants, and filed June 23d, 1849.

J W GURLEY, Com'r.

SUCCESSION OF DANIEL CLARK

Proces Verbal of opening and proof of the last will.
Recorded folio 298, vol 6

Know all men by these presents, that on the seventeenth day of August, in the year of our Lord, one thousand eight hundred and thirteen, and the thirty-eight of the Independence of the United States of America,

Personally appeared before me, James Pitot, Judge of the Court of Probates, in and for the city and parish of New Orleans, Paul Lanusse and Louis Seré, both residents in the city of New Orleans, who, being duly sworn, agreeably to law, declare and say, that a packet folded up, as a letter, sealed with a red wafer, which I presented to them, and bearing the following subscription. "This is my olographic will New Orleans, 20th May, 1811 Daniel Clark" That the same is the proper hand writing of him, the said Daniel Clark.

Signed—Paul Lanusse—Louis Seré.

Sworn to and subscribed before me, New Orleans, **August 17th, 1813** Signed—J Pitot Judge

Whereupon, I, the said Judge caused the said packet be broke open, in which was found one writing page, signed Daniel Clark and after, caused the same instrument to be read in presence of the above named witnesses, who did further recognize the same to be totally written by the late Daniel Clark

Signed—Louis Scre—Paul Lanusse

I do hereby declare that the said instrument is duly proved according to the laws of this State, as being the last will and testament, in scriptis, of the late Daniel Clark, and order the said last will to be deposited and recorded in the register office of this Court, that copies thereof may be delivered to all persons it may concern

Signed—J Pitot Judge

Deposition, filed July 6, 1835

W W WHITING AND WIFE VS ELEONOR O BIARN AND OTHERS

Deposition taken by virtue of a commission, issued by the honorable the Court of Probates in and for the parish and city of New Orleans

Mrs Callaret, being duly sworn, deposes and says, that she is the sister of Madame Gardet, formerly Madame Desgranges That some times after the marriage of her sister with Mr. Desgrange, her said sister discovered that Mr Desgrange had been previously married, that in order to ascertain this fact, she went to Philadelphia, in the absence of her husband, who was in France, that whilst at Philadelphia, Desgrange returned from France to New Orleans, and at the same time, or a very short time after, his first wife made her appearance in New Orleans Upon this, witness immediately apprized her sister of this fact, and she returned immediately to New Orleans On the arrival of the said first wife of Desgrange, she complained to the Governor, who caused Desgrange to be arrested, (it was under the Spanish government,) after some time, he obtained his release, and left the country Before his departure, he confessed, that he had previously married Witness understood afterwards from her sister, by letters which she received from her secretely, that she was married with Mr Daniel Clark the preliminaries of the contemplated marriage were settled by the husband of witness, at his house in the year 1802 or 1803, in the presence of witness, who went to France some time after the said arrangements, but previous to the said marriage alluded to.

Cross Examination

Mr Desgrange married the sister of witness, on or about the year 1796, her sister was then living at the house of witness, the marriage was celebrated at the church; there has been no children of that marriage. Mr. and Me Desgrange were recognized as husband and wife by every one, and no doubts have ever been entertained, with respect to their marriage. Witness has constantly resided in France, since she went there, and she returned here within the last days. When her sister wrote to her about her marriage with Daniel Clark, she informed her afterwards that she had had a a child (a daughter) by that marriage, who, she understood, was called Mira.

Signed,　　　　　　V. CAILLERET.

Sworn to and subscribed before me, New Orleans, May 22d, 1835.　　Signed,　　　GALLIEN PREVAL, Judge.

I do hereby certify, that the above deposition has been taken by me in the presence of C. Roselius, Esq., attorney for plaintiff, and L. C. Duncan, Esq., attorney for the defendant, at the house of Mr. Barnell, Chartres street, pursuant to the commission hereto annexed.

New Orleans, May 22d, 1835.

Signed,　　　　　GALLIEN PREVAL, Judge

I hereby certify the foregoing to be true and correct copies of the originals on file, deposited in the office of the second district court of New Orleans.

New Orleans, June 23d, 1849

[L S]　　　　　　BOISBLANC, D y Clerk

[No 35]

Offered by defendants, and filed 23d June 1849

J W GURLEY, Com'r

In pursuance of the annexed commission, directed to me, the subscriber, Mayor of the city of Cincinnati, appeared before me, William Miller, who being duly sworn to declare the truth on the questions put to him in this cause, answered to the interrogatories hereto annexed, in the manner following, to wit.

To the first and second interrogatories, this respondent says, that he was acquainted with Daniel Clark, and enjoyed, as he believed, his entire confidence.

In answer to the third, fourth, fifth, sixth, seventh and eighth interrogatories he says, that at the decease of Daniel Clark, he knows that he did leave a child; that during the pregnancy of the mother of said child, the said Daniel Clark told this deponent that the child of which she was then pregnant, was the child of him, the said Daniel Clark, that after its birth the said Daniel Clark acknowledged it to be his that the said child, for many years afterwards, lived in the family of Col Samuel B Davis, now of Philadelphia, and is now the wife of Mr Whiting, of New York; as this respondent believes the name of said child was Mira.

To the tenth interrogatory he answers, he does not.

To the 11th he answers, no

To the 12th, 13th and 14th, he says, that he, the said Daniel Clark, frequently expresssed much affection to the said child, Mira, and stated that he intended to make ample provision for her as one of his heirs.

To the 15th, this respondent answers, no

To the 16th, he answers, he knows nothing

To the 17th, he says, that he believes subsequently to the year 1811, he has frequently heard Daniel Clark speak of said child as her own, and that he would make provision for her as above stated. To the 18th, 19th and 20th, he answers as to the 17th.

To the 21st and 22d he says, that he saw Daniel Clark in 1812, he believes, but does not recollect any particular conversation at that time different from that before stated. To the 23d, 24th, 25th, 26th, 27th, 28th, 29th, 30th, 31st and 32d, he says, that he never heard Daniel Clark say, that he had made a will, and never saw him executed any will, although it was his impression and that of his friends, that he had made a will

In answer to the cross interrogatories, he says

To the 1st interrogatory he answers, his name is William Miller, that he resides in Cincinnati, that he is upwards of 60 years of age, and attends to the management of his own affairs

To the 2d and 3d, he answers in the negative.

To the 4th, that he was on his plantation in Louisiana, and Clark was in New Orleans

To the 5th he answers, that Daniel Clark was his merchant and commercial agent for many years, and his intimacy continued till his death, it commenced about 1796 or 1797

To the 6th, he says, that he was in the habit of conversing with this deponent confidentially, on general subjects, and with respect to his private affairs

To the 7th 8th or 9th, he answers he knows nothing further than already stated.

To the 10th, he says, that he does not believe Daniel Clark was ever married

To the 11th he says, he knows nothing more than has been stated in answer to the 3d 4th, 5th 6th, 7th & 8th interrogatories.

To the 12th, he says, that Daniel Clark acknowledged the child Mira to be his own, because he believed it to be so, and entertained no doubts with respect to it. The mother of said child was Madame DeGrange

To the 13th, he answers, no.

  Signed   W MILLER.

Which answers, being by me reduced to writing, were signed by the said witness in my presence. In testimony whereof, I have hereto affixed my hand and seal of said city, and also my private seal, this 21st day of July, 1834

Signed   G. W DAVIES, Mayor

I hereby certify the foregoing to be a true and correct copy of the original deposited in the office of the Second District court of New Orleans

New Orleans, 23d June 1849

[L S]   P M BERTON, Clerk

[No 36]

Offered by defendants, filed 25th June, 1849

J W GURLEY Commissioner

NEW ORLEANS, 29th June, 1812

MY DEAR SIR —I was unexpectedly called into the country last week, or I should have replied more in detail according to my promise in my last to your two letters of the 8th and 15th April and if what I shall now state is not satisfactory, it will, at least show that I have done everything which depends on me to serve and assist you

When I was about leaving Philadelphia, I stated to you what were my means and resources and what I wished, rather than believed, could be done I stated that I had a note of $50,000, of General Hampton, which would fall due in February, but that it was deposited in the Louisiana Bank, as a security for the sum of $25,000 due by Chew and Relf to that institution, and that I had until then destined the remainder to pay off an engagement on one of the estates sold to Gen Hampton, which would be due in three annual instalments I then mentioned my intention of endeavoring to meet these instalments in some other manner, and hinted the possibility only of deriving assistance from a friend of Chew & Relf who during last summer, had essentially served them, and even saved them and me at his own extreme peril Had this assistance been renewed I thought it were possible to remit you the whole of the note but nothing could be effected, and I now find it necessary to recall the whole of these circumstances to your memory, to prove that I never made you the promise of remitting these $50 000, which depended on contingencies and circumstances out of my power to control Had there been a possibility of doing it, I should have felt more pleasure in making, than you in receiving the remittance, and I can only refer you to Mr Relf to explain fully to you the state of painful anxiety in which, to his knowledge, I have passed the last eighteen months, occasioned solely by my inability to serve you To show you now that no part of these $50,000 has been applied to my use, I shall mention that, since my arrival here, such was the state in which I found Chew & Relf's affairs, that

I have been under the necessity of applying $30,000 to their relief, without which they and I must infallibly have sunk, ten thousand of which were appropriated in November last, and the remainder cut of the crops received from General Hampton, who still owes me, on account of this note from $8,000 to $10,000, which when received I shall forward to you but I cannot count on doing so before I learn from him that his crops in Carolina are sold and that I may draw for the amount It will strike you as it did me, with surprise, to learn that Chew & Relf's engagements have not been diminished at the Louisiana Bank, and that consequently the statement furnished me last year by Relf, on which I grounded the settlement with you, must have been erroneous, to the amount at least of the sum paid them since my return I can by no means account for this, and must wait Relf's return for an explanation of it If, however, to this sum you add the losses sustained by the failure of the house of Coval, of Vera Cruz who owed them near $15,000 and the number of small debts outstanding which it will be impossible ever to recover, with the sums necessary for their support you will find that from a source from which I expected much, I shall never have to receive a dollar

The annexed statement will show you the sums I have received since we parted last year from the persons who owed me, and also the sales of land which I have made, in conformity to the 4th article of our agreement

On seeing this you will naturally inquire how I have contrived to pay the debts which I owed, and to support myself in the meantime I can only answer it has been by getting, through Relf's influence a continuation of my credit in the Louisiana Bank, and by contracting new engagements to pay the old ones This will, however, show you that I do not sleep on a bed of roses, and if I can only convince you that I suffer equally with yourself every kind of privation, and feel my share of pain and anxiety, I shall at least be relieved from one load which weighs heavier on my mind than every other that of being thought forgetful of your situation to which I have and shall continue to sacrifice everything in my power

You may, perhaps have been deceived by the idea that I obtained by the inheritance which I have got from my deceased friend, Wilkins, the command of a large sum of money The thing is not so, for if I had, it should only have passed through my hands into yours This inheritance consisted of a beautiful and well cultivated estate of 2000 acres of land within five miles of Natchez, with 142 slaves, and everything necessary to carry it on without putting me to any expense and a crop of 410 bales cotton, which Heaven sent me at a most fortunate moment, to pay a debt of near 12,000 dollars which I contracted last year in the

13*

midst of our embarrassments, and the nature of which Relf will explain to you, as it is too tedious and disagreeable to state in writing The thing, however, was unavoidable in our then situation, to prevent an exposure which would have effectually ruined us

I have now to mention to you in confidence, that I should have had a large sum to receive from Wilkins' estate in cash and bonds, had it not been plundered by Minor, on the morning of Wilkins' death, and independent of the robbery he has now trumped up an account against the estate of 10 or 12 thousand dollars, after having stolen all the papers and documents which were in Wilkins house, at the time of his decease I have, however, strong proof against him and I shall endeavor to expose and bring him to justice At the worst however, I can lose nothing more than what I have lost already, the estate and slaves will remain clear, and according to what success I may meet with, I may or not force him to reimburse me $40 000 which is the least value of what he has villainously acquired He is now trembling, and I shall make him tremble more I shall shortly set off for Natchez, and if I cannot obtain legal redress, will challenge him and if he refuses to fight me, will publicly horsewhip him at the door of the bank of which he is president You may, therefore, expect something very serious to take place I have hitherto kept every thing quiet in order to give him time to reflect seriously, and not drive him to desperation by exposure but my mind is made up as to the course I mean to take, and I have informed him of it I shall leave every thing in which you have an interest, in the hands of Chew & Relf, that happen what will you may be no sufferer but the property which I have inherited, I shall make over in trust for the benefit of my mother and my family, as it would be equally unjust to them, to leave them exposed in a foreign land, when I had the means which I might honestly use to insure to them at least an independence Chew & Relf will, therefore, be the depositaries of the property mentioned in the schedule attached to our agreement, to the very last farthing out of which you will satisfy yourself, and if any thing remains it will go to my family I shall leave with them an ample explanation of every thing, so that they will be as well informed as myself on every particular, and in their hands your interest cannot suffer

What I have now communicated to you, I count on your religiously keeping secret from every one but Relf, as a knowledge of it would be injurious to my family, and productive of no good either to myself or those connected with me

You will from what I have written, perceive that the principal cause of my disappointments here has been that I have found the statement, furnished me by Relf last year, incorrect, and that his affairs were much more embarrassed than he thought. Mr Chew supposes he must have forgotten a sum of $18,000, which was borrowed of brokers at a high interest, which was indispensably necessary to pay to save their very existence, and in the present state of things, if Relf makes you any other payments than the $20,000 in bills on Charleston I will not answer for his finding his house in existence at his return home.

In your letters you make a merit of not reproaching me, but Great God! what can I do that I have not done. If there was any thing in my power, and that I refused or neglected to effect it, I should then think I merited reproach. But interrogate Relf, and learn from him the horrible situation, and distress of mind in which he has a thousand times seen me. I cannot work miracles, and if I had been mad enough to talk even of pushing Gen Hampton I could not in two years obtain from him what he has given already.

The sale of my property last year, ruined our credit here so much, that the friend who so essentially served us, on Mr Relf's departure, in a great measure withdrew that assistance which had so materially supported us, and we have had to make large sacrifices to make up the advances received from him.

You may perhaps think it strange that I do not attempt to recover by law the sums due me. I have had recourse to it in various instances, but what have I collected? The property for which these sums has been due is for lands sold, and by the law of the country these lands must bring 2-3ds of their valuation, or be sold on credit. In making the attempt, I have only changed the holders, as was the case with George Hart who owed $6,000 for a plantation, and Mons Perez, who owed $10,000 for another, and whom I sued to make pay a first or second instalment. I have, then, only succeeded in getting other debtors, and have had to pay the expenses of the suits which with the taxes on the large landed property I hold, has added to my difficulties by forcing me to borrow, to enable me to pay them.

You seemed impressed with the idea that I wish to make a fortune by the arrangement concluded with you last year, while I observed that nothing would remain to me after paying what was stipulated to be paid to you. To convince you of my firm belief of what I then asserted I will agree to receive of you $25,000 in full of every thing contained in the schedule, if you undertake to free me from all demands which might then be brought against me, and I will instantly transfer to you or your agents every thing therein mentioned.

The fall of cotton to 7 or 8 dollars has much contributed to the little success I have had this year in collecting, as that price would leave nothing to the planter to pay his debts, and would not generally suffice for the expenses of the year. Any change which will ameliorate our commerce, will be productive of benefit in this respect to us

I have now given you a full and plain statement of facts Show this letter to Relf, and let him judge between us You will observe that since November, I have been constantly on horseback, and that not a cent of debt has got to Chew & Relf's hands, which has not been procured thro my exertion, and with immense fatigue and exposure I have more than once since then rode 600 miles, and have not been able to collect as much as would defray the expenses, however trifling, of my journey I have given a letter of introduction to you to a Mr Lyman Harding, of Natchez, who will explain to you the state of things between Minor and myself, and I would thank you to attend to him He is a lawyer, and my friend in this business, on whose evidence and knowledge of Wilkins affairs, I must rely entirely to procure me justice.

I have now one word to say on a subject which I hope will be the last time that it will be necessary to touch upon it You tell me in a late letter, that I have lost one estate by sycophants, and express your hope that I will not endanger another by them. Nobody better than you ought to know how mortifying and injurious to my feelings such remarks must be, that they can be attended with no good, and may, perhaps, be thought to spring from an idea of great superiority of mind and intellect on the part of the adviser, to a kind of humble dependent, or debased slave, such as you may, perhaps in imagination, figure yourself, I may or ought to be to you I madden with indignation, when I ask myself what can authorize this liberty to be taken with me, and I only recover my reason on recollecting the habit you have acquired of saying mortifying things at the expense of others, perhaps, without sufficient reflection, and in the intimacy that subsisted between us, I have on more than one occasion suggested to you the necessity of paying more regard to other people's feelings If, therefore you set the smallest value on my friendship, I wish you to avoid this subject in future, and not lacerate my mind afresh, even by an explanation or allusion to it

If I have not written often to you of late, it was because, being myself oppressed with horror of mind, caused by my anxiety for you and the situation of things here, I knew my letters would partake of the gloom I felt, and could not be agreeable to you You must, therefore, attribute my silence to the true cause, and believe me when I tell you that I feel for you as much at least as I do for myself.

Present me respectfully to Mrs Coxe, to Mr. and Mrs Burd and family   Yours sincerely,

Daniel W. Coxe, Esq.   DANIEL CLARK.

[No. 37]
Offered by Defendants, and filed 25th June, 1849.

J W GURLEY, Com'r.

PLAQUEMINES, Sunday, 27th June, 1802

Messrs Chew & Relf

Gentlemen —We are still detained here, waiting for the register and sea letter, and have the mortification to see the sloop Sally pass, which will, in all probability arrive before us. What an unfortunate neglect this has been and how long shall we still suffer by it? I am almost afraid to think on the subject. I flatter myself my letter must have reached you yesterday morning, and that your answer ought to be here to-day, if I am disappointed, I shall be out of all patience

I recommended to you, before I left town, to try to settle Governor Sargent's business with Prosset, you have the accounts, but lest you should forget the principle, I shall now remind you the Governor's wish is that the balance as stated in the account which goes farthest back should be paid with interest at the rate of five per cent per annum, but not as stated in the accounts, in which compound interest is calculated From the amount, whatever it may be, you must deduct a sum due by me of the partners to David Williams, with the interest, calculating the pound of Carolina according to a rule laid down in the accounts, I think of four pounds, or thereabouts, to one dollar You will observe that the house changed its firm various times, and that the partners ought to pay the private debts of one of them, and there is as much probability that one was indebted on his private account to D W as D W to the whole, jointly, the same credit being due to each party You ought to settle the account with Prosset to the first of June of last year, and the interest from that time ought to be charged to ourselves, who had the sum of $1500 in our hands.

If Mr Relf has not sent Mr Britton's ring up to him, I request he will do it without delay Capt West spoke to me on the way down, respecting a letter said to be received from Mr Coxe by Mr Green, limiting his privilege I know nothing of it, and suppose the thing is misunderstood between them It was Mr. Coxe's intention to reduce the wages of his captains to the peace establishment, but in their privilege I know of no innovation intended

I forgot, I believe, to mention to you that Mr Joseph Higbie, of Philadelphia, wished me to advance to his brother, Wm Pitt Higbie, of the Atacapas $1000, provided it could be done in a way to assist him, and that it should be made known to William that the advance was a thing done by myself, without his family being concerned in it My idea was, to buy him a couple of negroes, to pay the $1000 on account, to give a mortgage on them for the balance, keep the title in my own name, and make him believe it was an advance I was willing to make him, for which he was to repay me in a certain number of years By this means, I thought he might have a way of doing something for himself and if he paid the instalments punctually a new advance of the same sum might be made him still under the persuasion that it was to be repaid until it could be clearly ascertained that he was entirely reformed as he is now a great drunkard I wrote to Higbie, to inform him that on his family's account I was willing to assist him and requested him to come to town I informed him that in my absence he might address himself to Mr Hulings, with whom he is well acquainted and I earnestly entreat you will on receipt of this call on Hulings shew him this part of my letter, and in concert with him devise such a plan for Higbie in future, as he may benefit by but by no means give him the cash to dispose of, as he will throw it away in liquor and extravagance I earnestly recommend this business to your and Mr Huling's attention you know it will be a meritorious action to relieve a man from distress and his family, which is a deserving one, will be ever grateful to you

I now enclose you Mons DesGranges note for the balance of his account to me, last year The negro Lubin, I took to prevent his being sold to any body else I wish you to offer him the preference of him at the same price if he does not choose to take him back, Chevalier Malarchai will buy him of you Independent of the note, I paid, after Mr DesGranges departure, $350 for him, by his direction, which last sum when received, is to be placed to my credit I have not charged myself with the money when I paid it I wish you not to push M D for payment, but wait, consistent with safety such time as he may find necessary Should he be inclined to go away before the sum is paid, you must insist on security

I request you will do all that you possibly can to be prepared for Power you know his situation and the obligations I am under to him and I entreat you will not limit your exertions to serve him to the mere reimbursement of the sum I owe him but assist him with any further one you can possibly spare

Examine well all the cotton before shipping particularly Dungier's, and try to keep a sum belonging to them in your hands, to answer any damages that may accrue from the bad quality of the cotton that may have been delivered by him

SUNDAY NIGHT 9 o clock

I have just received your letters, and hope to-morrow to get to sea we have lost four days of fair wind Remember me affectionately to all friends. Yours sincerely,

DANIEL CLARK

P S—Should you ship any sugars, for God's sake take care they are the best and brightest, and as dry as possible

[No 38]
Offered by defendants and filed 25th June, 1849.
J W GURLEY Commissioner

Duplicate (out and per mail)

Philadelphia July 23d, 1802

Messrs Chew & Relf

Dear Sirs —I only received a few days since your letters of
1, 4 5 & 19 June in New York and by the arrival of Mr Clark,
in the schooner Eliza at New Castle the 20th inst that of 21st
ult I shall this day go down to see him at Darby 7 miles from
here, where he now is when I hope to receive some consoling
information of the state of things at New Orleans In regard
to Bonnet's drafts I have only to repeat my former information
and instructions on that head Mr Wm Lynch denies all Bonnet's assertions and have nothing to say to him on the business
He knows no body in the agency of those bills but Mr Dickson,
of Norfolk from whom he received them, and continues to look
to me for payment of them I have already paid him $700 on
account to quiet him On seeing Mr Clark, I shall determine
whether the Eliza will return or not which I however, think probable All your drafts yet presented are accepted, and I am to
happy to find that no more are to appear If I can compass the
payment of those I have accepted it will be all I can do

Per sc Triton]   Philadelphia Aug 6th 1802

Dear Sirs —Mr Clark wrote you very fully, per mail some
days since since which he has come up to Germantown and
to-morrow sets out for New York there to embark for England
He has likewise written you a few lines, requesting your particular attention to the bills received per schooner Triton which
vessel goes to your address with a valuable cargo of $20,000
cost The schooner Eliza has been hove down and caulked at
Wilmington and will in a few days commence loading there
on freight and sail as soon as possible Mr Clark will write
Mons Delvids by her, informing of her purchase, deliverable
at Orleans for $3 500, according to Mr D s order

The Board of Health have advised a general removal of the
inhabitants, to prevent the effects of the fever, which has commenced 'tho' the deaths are yet very trifling in number 'Tis
generally expected that this precautionary measure will prevent
its spreading, should it be the yellow fever, which seems very
doubtful I send you a newspaper or two

I am dear sirs, yours very sincerely,

D W COXE

Let any of my small vessels coming here first stop at N
Castle, and send up to me for orders

[No. 39.]
Offered by defendants, and filed 25th June, 1849
J. W GURLEY, Commissioner

BORDEAUX, le 24 Juillet, 1801

MON CHER MONSIEUR ET AMI —Quoique tenu dans l'incertitude si vous êtes encore à la Nouvelle Orleans, je m'empresse à saisir une occasion qui part par le Natchez, pour vous donner de mes nouvelles   Je desire bien que ma lettre vous trouve en bonne santé   Quand on a un ami tel que vous, on ne saurait trop s'interesser a ce qui le regarde

J'ai reçu ici beaucoup d'honnêteté de Mr Jean Bernard, negociant, ami de M. Chew, qui fait de tres grandes affaires dans ce moment-ci   Il m'a beaucoup parle de Mr Chew, et de sa bonne conduite pendant son séjour a Bordeaux, qui lui avait éte recommende par Mr. Coxe

Je vous dirai qu'il est entré plusieurs batimens Americans dans ce port, depuis que je suis ici   Les denrées coloniales se sont tres bien vendues jusqu'à present   Je pense si votre ami de Philadelphie faisait une expedition pour ce port   que le retour pourrait lui donner de joli benefice

Faites-moi l'amitié, mon cher Monsieur, de me donner de vos nouvelles, ça sera pour moi un grand plaisir que vous me ferez   Quelques batimens Americains, pourront partir de chez vous pour venir ici en droiture   Je vous prie de faire bien mes compliments a Mr Chew, et le prier que si toutefois il ecrit a M. Bernard de lui parler de moi   Je prends la liberte de joindre sur votre couvert un paquet pour mon epouse que je vous prie de vouloir bien lui remettre   Permettez, mon cher ami, que je vous reiterer ma demande des offres honnetes que vous m'avez fait avant mon depart, que si mon epouse se trouve embarrassée pour quelque affaire, de vouloir bien l'aider de vos bons conseils   Je dois partir dans peu de jours pour me rendre dans ma famille   Je compte que je serai de retour à Bordeaux dans deux ou trois mois pour terminer les affaires que j'ai ici, et pour me preparer à venir vous rejoindre.   Je suis en procès depuis quelques jours, pour ce qui regard un bien de campagne appartenant à la famille de mon epouse   Je m'en vais charger M. Chicou St Brie de cette affaire pendant mon absence   Je crains bien de depenser beaucoup d'argent pour cette affaire   Je laisse M Bernard chargé de mes autres affaires   Je n'ai pas encore reçu aucunes nouvelles de mon epouse, ce qui me fait beaucoup de peine de partir pour la Provence, avant d'en recevoir   L'on parle toujours ici de paix pour la fin de l'année, mais je crains bien que nous ne jouirons pas ce bonheur-là. Et suis, en attendant le plaisir de recevoir de vos nouvelles, votre tres affectionné serviteur et ami,

DESGRANGE

Ecrivez-moi à l'addresse de M Jean Bernard, negociant, au Chartron, Bordeaux

[No 51]

Offered by defendants, and filed 25th June, 49

J W GURLEY, Commissioner

Marine Colonial Louisiane

NOUVELLE ORLEANS le 1er Fructidor, an 11

Le Préfet Colonial de la Louisiane. A MONSIEUR CLARK,

NOUVELLE ORLEANS

Je vous remercie Monsieur de la communication que vous avez bien voulu me donner, par votre lettre d'hier

Je felicite les Etats Unis de cette magnifique et importante acquisition

Je leur porte envie de l'avantage qu'ils auront de contribuer au bonheur et d'accelerer la prosperité de ce pays non moins interessant par la fécondité privilegiée de son sol que par l'excellente espece de ses habitans

En meme temps que, par un veritable interet pour lui j'en forme le vœu, je sens que tout de la part des Etats Unis lui en offre le presage

N'ayant, en ce qui me concerne aucun avis direct de mon gouvernement a cet egard, j'attends ses instructions et ses ordres pour m'y conformer

J'ai l'honneur de vous saluer, LAUSSAT

A Monsieur Clark, N O

N O, 18 Aug, 1803

CITIZEN COLONIAL PREFECT —Having received by his day's post from the Secretary of State of the U S, by order of the President, the news of the cession of Louisiana by France to the U S together with a copy of a few of the articles of said cession. I take the liberty of inclosing a copy for your information The President has been pleased to inform me that he has convened the Senate and Congress of the U S, to meet at Washington on the 17th October for the ratification of 'the treaty, and to make the appropriations for carrying it into execution I have the honor to remain with the greatest respect,

Sir, your most obedient and most humble servant, D C

[No 62]

Offered by defendants and filed 25th June 1849

J W GURLEY, Comr

DEPARTMENT OF STATE October 31st, 1803

Sir The present mail conveys to Gov Claiborne and Gen Wilkinson authority to receive or take possession of Louisiana, and to Gov Claiborne, authority to administer, for the present, the government of the ceded country The possibility suggested

14*

by recent circumstances particularly a protest from the Spanish
government against the cession from France to the U States
that Country may be restored at New Orleans on the part of
Spain required that provision should be made as well for adding
as receiving possession Should force be necessary Gov Claiborne and .... and in every probabi-
lity of a coup de main .... the civil courts,
which will require him to ...... put, and whild prepared to act
the other part In forming ... decision, they will need the best
and quickest information on the spot Gov Claiborne will
write to you on the subject in the re can be no doubt of the zeal
with which you will render them every aid of ... assort Should
a coup de main be resolved on there may be a call on you for
assistance of another sort A co-operating movement of the well
disposed part of the inhabitants ... be of critical advantage and
it is desirable that it should in concert with the military councils
be prepared and directed in a manner to give it its best effect
Your knowledge of local circumstances your acquaintance with
the disposition of the people and with the principal characters
and their views will enable you to render most acceptable services on such an occasion It is proposed that Mr Lausson may
also render his ... care over certain descriptions of the inhabitants, such to the object Mr Lausson has in the ...rongest terms,
press I than to do Such a ... well disposed a frank and
friendly communication and cooperation between yourself and
him is particularly to be wished and I doubt not, will be promoted on your part It will be ... to able to hear from you on
the receipt of this letter and in every good the interesting business which is the subject of it A courier will henceforward go
from this to Natchez in fourteen days and return in the same time
To double the chance of quick and certain conveyances, duplicates by water may also be expedient

I remain sir very respectfully your most obt serv't

                              JAMES MADISON

Daniel Clark Esq

Offered by defendant   Filed 25th June, 1849
                              J W GURLEY Com'r

                         Natchez, 16th Sept 1803

     Dear Sir I have received your favor of the 8th My own in-
discretion is but too apparent from the number of voluminous
documents you have taken the trouble to send me and several
of them copied perhaps, for no other purpose all I wished, was
general information, without particular or minute details, which
I knew could not be obtained without much trouble The particulars of the population being an interesting object I will be thank-

ful for I have already mentioned that the post, after receiving
the President's queries, I sent on such replies as were in my
power merely to gratify the first curiosity, referring to your information for correction. I made the white population to be a
little more than 50,000 without going further East than the river
Amit the black population near 36,000 and upwards of 10,000
white men able to bear arms. I am glad to observe that I paid
the same tribute of applause as you have done, to the virtuous
and worthy inmates of your convent perhaps our government
may see the propriety of preserving them in their present situation as an excellent female school for the rising generation. The
only object I wish to trouble you for now on the subject of our
western country is some geographical materials. I observe you
have said that from the mouth of Chatalaya to the R. Sabine is
3 deg. of longitude, how much then is it from Chatalaya to the
Balize or to the Regulets? I have been accustomed to believe
that the coast triple to be inundated by the Mississippi was not
less than 5 deg., and if the low grounds to the west of the mouth
of Chatalaya is only about 5 leagues the extent of Louisiana on
the sea coast in a line from E. and W. would be 300 geographical miles or about 247 English miles query whether it can be
so much? Would you suppose that the breadth of Louisiana,
opposite to the Natchez or the post of Adayes, come to more than
150 miles the general course of the coast from the bay of Mexico
is nearly south from Natchez to the Regulets? perhaps to
quite 2 1-2 deg. of longitude these parts would still fall
short of 300 English miles on a rough estimate the first calculation. Please to correct this as I have never had this map recol-
ected, but perhaps, the amount I at present estimate. I had
supposed that the extreme breadth could not exceed 250 miles
geographical. The rough sketch that Mr. Turner has made
would suit my purpose better than your own. Setting with delay I shall make correspondence and deliver your papers back by
next post. The trial by jury will be established as one basis on
so precious a nature all cases of ... and or ... ought to
be introduced immediately, but so far as respect to civil trials, I am
quite sick of the constitution ... others ... Every unprincipled student in the law grown by practice and education
with a few bad education ... a vast enormous reserve in mis-
leading our ignorant ... ... bringing about the greatest
injustice in general I would as soon ... throw on the dice as
submit to the decision of our inferior courts. I am not astonished at the late attempt of the Legislature of Pennsylvania the
cap of enormity is there no doubt been long since full on the
subject of which I complain the avarice and rapacity of the inferior members of the law with their industry in concocting a

contentious spirit among the people, with a view to fill their own pockets, is beyond all bearing. The people are blind, they see not thro' the designs of those blood suckers: their properties are squandered to satiate to inextinguishable apetites of their greatest enemies, and is an evil of still greater consequence to the State. Habits of idleness and licentiousness are introduced, the productive labor of the country is diminished, and the progressive riches of the State is arrested, which would not be affected merely by the transfer of property from one to another. Would it not be proper for the Louisianans to send an agent immediately to Congress, and present a memorial upon this subject? is it not possible to save this new province from so great a curse as will be entailed upon it by this villainous practice of extorting from the industrious and innocent part of the community, for pretended services, their hard acquired earnings, which ought to be applied to the improvement of their farms and the education of their families? What should prevent the institution of an honorable and virtuous court to try all civil causes upon the principles which guide the awards of arbitrators? Suppose a tribunal instituted by law, to consist of five (more or less) enlightened Judges, who shall associate with themselves, disinterested and enlightened inhabitants, forming in the whole the number 12, (if any virtue is supposed to reside in that number) Let those compose a court of arbitration for the trial of all civil causes, without the intervention of attorneys, let them proceed as arbitrators generally do, and let their awards be conclusive, or if you will, with such appeal as may be thought proper. The Judges and associated jurymen, to be paid out of the treasury, but I would not exempt the party cast from costs, which might be a per centage upon the amount of the object, to be paid into the treasury. Give me your ideas upon this subject, and if you think well of it why should not the Louisianans endeavor to secure their own peace and happiness by excluding an evil of such enormous magnitude, that they might hereafter be inclined to think that American liberty itself would scarcely compensate so great a breach upon their repose and prosperity.

I shall keep the translation of Don Andres' declaration until we can make out a list of interrogatories. We hear no more of the Moores revisiting Clarksville. I have got so much into the good opinion and confidence of the surveyors who are appointed by Court to verify the surveys, that I hope we shall evade partiality upon that point. Dear sir, your faithful   WM DUNBAR.

P. S. Moore and Don Zerbin have got into a newspaper war. they have honored each other with the appellation of accomplished villain. Pray what is meant by swindler and decree of the tribunal of New Orleans?

To Daniel Clark Esq, New Orleans

[No. 40]

Filed in open court, May 2d 1848   HOIT D C

THE STATE OF MISSISSIPPI

To all who shall see these presents—greeting

Whereas it appears, by the returns received at the office of the Secretary of State, that J A Talbot is duly and constitutionally elected to the office of Justice of the Peace, in the first police beat, in and for Harrison county in the State of Mississippi,

Now, know ye, that in consequence thereof and by virtue of the constitution and laws of this State, we do authorize and empower him, the said J A Talbot, to execute and fulfil the duties of that office according to law and to have and to hold said office, with all the powers, privileges, and emoluments, to the same of right appertaining, from the day of the date hereof, for the term prescribed by law

In testimony whereof, I, Albert G Brown Governor of the State

[LS]   aforesaid have caused these letters to be made patent, and the great seal of the State to be hereunto affixed

Given under my hand at the city of Jackson, the 28th day of July in the year of our Lord one thousand eight hundred and forty-five, and of the sovereignty of the State of Mississippi the twenty-eighth

By the Governor,   A G BROWN

WM HEMINGWAY, Secretary of State

EDMUND P GAINES AND HIS WIFE ⎫
MYRA CLARK GAINES,   ⎪
        vs   ⎬ UNITED
RICHARD RELF & BEVERLY CHEW, ⎪
SARAH CAMPBELL AND OTHERS ⎭

In pursuance of the annexed commission from the United States Circuit Court, I the undersigned Justice of the Peace in Harrison county, in the State of Mississippi have caused to come before me, in the village of Biloxi, this 16th day of October, 1845 Madame Sophia Despau, who, being duly sworn to declare the truth the whole truth, and nothing but the truth, touching each and every of the said interrogatories annexed to the said commission, she answers as follows

Answer to the first interrogatory I was well acquainted with the late Daniel Clark, of New Orleans

To the second (2d) Daniel Clark was married, in Philadelphia, 1803, by a Catholic priest I was present at this marriage. One child was born of that marriage, to wit Myra Clark, who married William Wallace Whitney, son of General T Whitney, of the State of New York, since then, to Gen E. P Gaines I was present at her birth, and knew that Mr Clark claimed and acknowledged her to be his child. She was born in 1806. I neither knew, nor any reason to believe any other child beside Myra was born of that marriage. The circumstances of her marriage with Daniel Clark were these. Several years after her marriage with Mr DeGrange, she heard that he had a living wife. Our family charged him with the crime of bigamy, in marrying the same Zulime. He at first denied, but afterwards admitted it, and fled from the country. These circumstances became public, and Mr Clark made proposals of marriage to my sister, with the knowledge of all our family. It was considered essential, first, to obtain record proof of DeGrange having a living wife at the time he married my sister; to obtain which, from the records of the Catholic church in New York (where Mr DeGrange's prior marriage was celebrated) we sailed for that city. On our arrival there we found that the registry of marriages had been destroyed. Mr Clark arrived after us. We heard that a Mr Gardette then living in Philadelphia was one of the witnesses of Mr DeGrange's prior marriage. We proceeded to that city, and found Mr Gardette. He answered that he was present at said prior marriage of DeGrange, and that he afterwards knew DeGrange and his wife of this marriage; that this wife had sailed for France. Mr Clark then said you have no reason longer to refuse being married to me; it will however be necessary to keep our marriage secret till I have obtained judicial proof of the nullity of your and DeGrange's marriage. They, the said Clark and the said Zulime, were then married. Soon afterwards our sister Mme Caillavet, wrote to us from New Orleans that DeGrange's wife whom he had married prior to marrying the said Zulime had arrived at New Orleans. We hastened our return to New Orleans. He was prosecuted for bigamy. Mr DeGrange was condemned for bigamy in marrying the said Zulime, and was cast into prison from which he secretly escaped by connivance, and was taken down the Mississippi river, by Mr Le Britten D'Orgenois, where he got to a vessel escaped from the country and according to the best of my knowledge and belief, never afterwards returned to Louisiana. This happened in 1803—not a great while before the close of the Spanish Government in Louisiana. Mr Clark told us that before he could promulgate his marriage with my sister it would be necessary that there should be brought by her an action against the name of DeGrange. The anticipated change of Government created delay, but at length, in 1806 Messrs James Brown and Eligeas Fromentin, as the counsel of my sister, brought suit against the name of Jerome DeGrange, in the City Court I think of New Orleans. The grounds of said suit were that DeGrange had imposed himself, in marriage, upon her at a time when he had a living and lawful wife. Judgment in said suit was rendered against said DeGrange. Mr Clark still continued to defer promulgating his marriage with her sister, which very much .... d an l ... t .... Mr Clark became a member of ... united ..t.. Congress in 1+.0. While he was in Congress his sister ...a.. that he was courting Miss Caton of B.lt.or. .... d ... ed .....t .. could not believe that .pos—k.ov .... he.se. to be his wife still his strange conta.t and t ..ing to promulgate his marriage with her had al.rm.d her. She ... ..l sailed for Philadelphia to get the proof of his marriage with her sister. We could find no record, and we ... told that the pr..st who married her and Mr Clark was gone to Ireland. My sister then sent for Mr Daniel W. Coxe, mentioned to him the rumor. He answered, that he knew it to be true that he (Clark) was engaged to her, my sister replied it could not be so. He then told her that she would not be able to establish her marriage with Mr Clark if he was disposed to co..t.t.. He advised her to take counsel and said he would ...l one. A Mr S...th, came and told my sister that she could no.. g h..es...blish her marriage with Mr Clark and pretended to ....d a letter in Eno.l.h (a language then unknown to my sister) from Mr Clark ...ing that he was about to marry Miss C.to.. In consequence of this information, my sister, Zulime, c.m. to the resolution of h...ing no further communication or intercourse with Mr Clark and soon afterwards married Mr .....t. of Philadelphia—Mr Coxe advising her to do so.

To the 3r.d (3d) I became acquainted with Mr Jerome DeGrange in 1793 when as I understood he first came to New Orleans. He was a no.l.man by birth, and passed for a single or unmarried man and courted and married Zulime nee de Corra.. at the age of thirteen the same who is the mother of Myra Clark Whitney. Zulime had two children by him—a boy and a girl. the boy died. the girl is still living, her name is Caroline, she is married to a physician, by the name of Barnes, I was present at the birth of these children.

To the 4th. Col Bellechasse who was well known throughout the island of Cuba as one of the most honorable of men, once the intimate friend of Mr Clark and as he informed me, one of the executors of Daniel Clark's last will of 1813. The plantation of my son-in-law, Chevalier de Moréjon was near that of Col Bellechasse. I made my home with my son-in-law. Col Bellechasse stated to Chevalier de Moréjon in 1827, that if Richard Relf had not destroyed Daniel Clark's last will, that his (Clark's) daughter would have been the richest lady in this country—these remarks were made in my presence—and that, in this will of 1813, Daniel Clark had acknowledged her to be his legitimate daughter, and that this will was written in Daniel Clark's handwriting. Bellechasse further stated, he had several times

written to the daughter of Daniel Clark, who was at that time
in Philadelphia but never received a reply, which he greatly
regretted

Answer to the 1st cross interrogatory I have already stated
that I was present at the marriage of Mr Clark with Zulime de
Carrière; they were married in the city Philadelphia, they were
married in a house which had been rented for us   I do not remember the name of the street   They were married by a Catholic
priest, whose name I cannot now remember   The parties did not,
to my knowledge, receive any certificate of their marriage   nor
was there any publication of their marriage made in the newspapers, to my knowledge   I have already stated that I was present
at her marriage (a private one)   Besides myself, Mr Dorsier,
wealthy planter of New Orleans, and an Irish gentleman friend of
Mr Clark's, from New York, were present at his marriage   The
first time I saw Mr Clark was in the latter part I think, of 1802
I was shortly after introduced to him by Col Bellechasse   My
acquaintance with Mr Clark ended in 1807   Mr Clark left Philadelphia, shortly after his marriage, on account of important business   Mrs Clark remained in Philadelphia until her departure for
New Orleans   Previous to my sister's marriage we remained
a short time with a lady in Philadelphia—a friend of Mr Clark
and Mr Coxe, I do not remember the name of the street   Mr
Clark called frequently to see us   The lady's name was Zulime
de Carrière   I have already stated the history of this lady in
answer to the first interrogatory   She had two children by her
marriage with Mr DeGrange   She was married to Mr Clark,
as Miss Zulime de Carrière   I do not remember the exact
month   Mr Clark left, as I have before stated, on important
business   I do not remember the exact time   His wife did not
accompany him.   I am not aware of his leaving Philadelphia
with any gentleman   We returned to New Orleans, in about
two months after Mr Clark left Philadelphia   I saw Mr Clark,
frequently, in New Orleans, after his marriage with my sister
He informed me that he had communicated his marriage with
my sister to Col S B Davis, Mr Daniel Coxe, and Mr Richard
Relf, and that the time was not distant when he would publicly
acknowledge it.   He kept a very handsome establishment for
her, in New Orleans, and was in a constant habit of visiting her
I do not remember the name of the street.   She resided with her
sisters, from the time she was separated from Mr de Grange,
until she left for the North.   I am her sister.   I was not in New
Orleans when Mr Clark died.   My sister was in Philadelphia
I have already stated that she was married at that time to Mr.
Gardette.   The history of that marriage has been given in my
answer to the second interrogatory   She had three children by
Mr. Gardette   Mr Gardette died in Bordeaux, (France,) in

1831 It was the misfortune of my sister, only a girl of thirteen, to be deceived in her first marriage with Mr DeGrange, who as I before stated was a married man at the time he married my sister Being satisfied that she had been imposed upon by Mr DeGrange and was no longer his wife, she married Mr Clark Had it not been for the interested wickedness of Mr. Coxe in assuring her, and employing counsel to aid him in misrepresenting to her that her marriage with Mr Clark was illegal she never would have married Mr Gardette

To 2d cross interrogatory I first became acquainted with Mr DeGrange 1793 He was a nobleman by birth he owned in New Orleans a large distillery I do not remember the street in which he resided He married my sister, in New Orleans, in a Catholic church I do not remember now, the name of the priest Her maiden name was Zuline de Carriere I have already stated that I know my sister is the mother of Myra Clark Gaines The last time I saw Mr DeGrange was in 1803 After he left New Orleans, he married as I was informed a widow lady residing in Vermont I have also been told that he died some years ago I do not remember the name of the place he died in I was not present at Mr DeGrange's first marriage He was married in New York I do not remember the name of the lady whom he married I never saw her

To the 3d cross interrogatory The mother of Mrs Gaines married Mr Gardette in Philadelphia, in 1808 I was not present at that marriage She lived with him twenty-three years She was always recognized by their friends and acquaintances as his lawful wife She had three children by this marriage, they were always regarded by their friends and acquaintances as legitimate It was the misfortune of my sister to have been deceived by those whose duty it was to protect her, and it is my firm belief that neither in the eye of God or highly honorable men or women will she be condemned but on the contrary be pitied for her unprecedented afflictions

To the 4th cross interrogatory I am the aunt of Mrs Gaines I have already stated that my sister is the mother of Myra Clark Gaines, and the only issue of her marriage with Daniel Clark, consequently I knew she was his heir and therefore, did not require any information upon a subject so well known to me I never received any letters on this subject from the parties in question I am at present residing at present, with my nephew and family at Biloxi Mississippi I have never received any promises or intimations of a pecuniary character from General or Mrs Gaines My only wish is, that justice which has been so long delayed, shall be finally done her

Signed SOPHIE DESPAU

Which answers, being reduced to writing, have been signed and sworn to, in my presence, this the sixteenth day of October, Anno Domini one thousand eight hundred and forty-five

In testimony whereof, I have hereunto set my hand and common seal, (having no seal of office,) the day and year first above written.   J A. TALBOTT,

J P. 1st Police District of Harrison co, State of Miss [L.S]

Interlineations and erasures in the above testimony
Page 1, line 21, "since then to Gen E. P Gaines"
   " 3, ' 11, "of"
   " 4, " 29, "in 1827 '
   " 5, " 14, "I think."
      5, ' 14, "after'
   " 5, " 30, "leaving"
   " 7, " 24 "on this subject ' were interlined
   " 2, part of line 28, the whole of line 29, and part of line
      30 erased
   " 6, part of 3d, the whole of the 4th, and part of 5th line
      from the bottom erased

                J A. TALBOTT, J P

              [No 87]
Offered by defendants, and filed 25th June 1849
             J W GURLEY, Com'r

(Duplicate)   VIRG'A, September 16, 1803

Sir —My present absence from the office of State, puts it out of my power to refer to all the letters from you not yet acknowledged The last received was of the 12th of August The preceding one, on the boundaries of Lousiana, &c , &c , has not yet reached me. All the information you may be able to give on that subject, and on every other made interesting by the late cession from France, will be highly acceptable You will have received an enumeration of various objects to which your attention will be particularly drawn To these, your own judgment, assisted by your local knowledge, will probably be able to make valuable additions

A letter from Governor Claiborne, received by the same mail with yours, conveys information concurring with the opinion that the Prefect meditates obstacles to the delivery of Louisiana into our hands It is presumable, however, that so much temerity, if not secretly favored by his government, must speedily yield to reflection , and it is not a natural supposition that the French Government should wish to embarrass or frustrate, in the midst of a war with Great Britian, a transaction, which the prospect of such a war contributed doubtless to enforce on its policy Still it will be proper, considering the peculiarities incident to personal character, and the vicissitudes incident to political affairs, that every circumstance should be marked and communicated, which may deserve attention in the arrangements to be made in so important a case

But whatever may be the real purposes of the French Prefect, there is ground to believe that Spain either alarmed by the cession of so much territory to the United States, or hoping to make her consent the price of concessions on their part, may be so unwise as to oppose the execution of the measure. With a view to such a posture of thing the President wishes you to watch every symptom which may show itself and to sound in every direction where discoveries may be most practicable proceeding at the same time with all the caution necessary to avoid suspicion You will please to let us know also, what force Spain has in the country, where is posted, what are its dispositions, how the inhabitants would act in case a force should be marched thither from the United States, and what numbers of them could be armed, and actually brought into opposition to it. You will be sensible that the value of information on these points may depend much on the despatch with which it is forwarded, and will therefore need no exhortation to that effect. With great respect and esteem, I am, sir,

Your obedient humble servant,

JAMES MADISON

DANIEL CLARK, ESQ, New Orleans

[No 98]

Private explanatory agreement between D Clark and D W Coxe, July, 1811

Offered by defendants and filed 26th June, 1849;

J W GURLEY, Commissioner.

Memorandum of private explanatory agreement, made at Philadelphia this 12th day of July 1811, between Daniel Clark, of New Orleans and Daniel Wm Coxe, of Philadelphia, viz

1st Daniel Clark agrees to settle with and pay Chew & Relf, of New Orleans (as one of the debts which he has contracted to pay under the first article of an agreement between the parties hereunto, of the same date), all and every claim or balance, which may be due or owing to them, on account of any connection or transactions, which either the said Coxe or Clark may heretofore have had with them, and as to mode of making which settlement, Daniel Clark is to be the sole judge D W Coxe agreeing to aid and assist therein, by all the means in his power

2d Daniel Wm Coxe also agrees, that if anything should ever

be recovered from John & Thomas Clifford, of this city, on account of an action now pending, wherein said Coxe is plaintiff, it shall be for the sole benefit and use of said Clark, deducting only therefrom the law charges

3d. Daniel Wm Coxe, further agrees that should Dan'l Clark (in case of any accident to said Coxe), ever be forced to pay any money on account of the blank endorsements of said Clark, lent him for the purpose of facilitating loans of money that then and in that case, the said sum or sums of money which said Clark might so be forced to pay for said Coxe, shall be deducted from the first payments which D Clark has agreed to pay said Coxe, by the other agreement of this date, herein before referred to

4th Daniel Wm Coxe hereby consents that Daniel Clark may sell and dispose of the lands in which they are jointly interested, (referred to in the other agreement of this date,) at such rates and prices, as he, the said Clark shall approve of, the restriction and limitation of value therein contained being intended to prevent the improper sacrifice or sale of such lands, by the heirs, executors or assignees of said Clark, should death or any other accident befal him

5th Daniel Clark agrees that certain premiums for insurances, which D W Coxe has effected on the schooners Sampson, Margaret and Young Hillman by order of Chew & Relf, of New Orleans, together with a balance due said Coxe by Joseph Vidal, of Orleans territory shall be remitted for account and benefit of said Coxe as also any small sums which he has just paid, or may yet be obliged to pay for either the said Daniel Clark or his friends and that all the balances, funds or remittances, which may remain in the hands of Green & Wainewright, of Liverpool, on account of any shipments or remittances heretofore made said Green & Wainewright, by order or for account of Chew & Relf, which after liquidating their, the said Green & Wainewright accounts, and paying the balances which might be due the British manufacturers, be and remain for the sole use and benefit of the said D W. Coxe, unconnected with any demands which Green & Wainewright may set up against said Clark for his guaranty of the debts of others, owing or indebted to Green & Wainewright And furthermore, should any of the property now in Europe, wherein D W Coxe is in any way interested, find its way to New Orleans, and go into the hands of Chew & Relf, or Daniel Clark, 'tis to be considered and remain for the sole use and benefit of said Coxe

Sealed and signed in duplicate, in presence of the subscribing

| | DANIEL CLARK. | (Seal) |
| | DAN. WM COXE | (Seal) |

Witnesses

JAMES MORPHY,

THOMAS SPARHAWK

[No 90]

Offered by defendants   Filed 25th June, 1849

J W GURLEY, Com'r

Extract of a letter written by the late Daniel Clark, Esq, Consul of the United States for the Port of New Orleans, to James Madison, Esq Secretary of State, dated New Orleans, 21st July, 1803

'The Marquis of Casa Calvo, who has no love for the French Government or French measures, had it in contemplation, in case of the surrender of the colony, to draw off from the island of New Orleans, and western bank of the Mississippi the whole of the inhabitants of three or four posts or settlements, *and place them on the lands reserved by the Spaniards between the Ibberville and our boundary line* I have strongly advocated the measure, as it will augment their mutual jealousy, and will weaken the French, it will be of service to ourselves by increasing the produce of a populous tract of country, already in a thriving situation, and whose commerce will be ours, as Spain, in order to strengthen their attachment, will make no attempt to raise a revenue there or prevent a trade with those who may be of most service to them"

See also his letter to same, of 26th of same month

(Private)   WASHINGTON, July 6th, 1803

DEAR SIR —Mr King has transmitted a letter to him from Messrs Livingston and Monroe, stating that on the 30th of April a treaty was signed by them and a French plenipotentiary, by which the *Island of New Orleans* and the whole of Louisiana, as held by Spain, is obtained for the United States   No particulars are mentioned, the treaty itself is every moment expected by a confidential bearer, for whom a passage was engaged at Havre on the 15th May, in a vessel which was to sail a few days after

I am, very respectfully, your most obedient servant,

(Signed,)   JAMES MADISON

DANIEL CLARK, Esq, Consul of the U S., New Orleans

[Mr. Clark's answer]

NEW ORLEANS, 12th August, 1816, (03)

SIR —I have been honored with your letter of the 6th ultimo, and feel the sincerest joy on the accomplishment of an object so dear to the heart of every American This important cession will insure the safety and prosperity of our western country, and I request you will accept my sincere congratulations on so great an event. I am now preparing, &c I sincerely wish that possession may soon be taken, and all our expectations realised.

I have the honor to be, etc.

(Signed,)   DANIEL CLARK.

The Hon JAMES MADISON.

[Copy of a letter from Mr Jefferson to Daniel Clark, Esq]

WASHINGTON, July 17, '03

DEAR SIR —You will be informed by a letter from the Secretary of State, of the terms and the extent of the cession of Louisiana by France to the United States—a cession which I hope will give as much satisfaction to the inhabitants of that province as it does to us, and the more, as the title, being lawfully acquired, and with the consent of the power conveying, can never be hereafter reclaimed under any pretence of force In order to procure a ratification in good time, I have found it necessary to convene Congress as early as the 17th of October It is essential that before that period we should obtain all the information respecting the province which may be necessary to enable Congress to make the best arrangements for its tranquillity, security and government It is only on the spot that this information can be obtained, and to obtain it there, I am obliged to ask your agency. For this purpose I have prepared a set of queries, now inclosed, answers to which, in the most exact terms practicable, I am to ask you to procure It is probable you may be able to answer some of them yourself, however, it will doubtless be necessary for you to distribute them among the different persons best qualified to answer them respectively As you will not have above six weeks from the receipt of them till they should be sent off, to be here by the meeting of Congress it will be the more necessary to employ different persons on different parts of them ; this is left to your own judgment, and your best exertions to obtain them in time are desired You will be so good as to engage the persons who undertake them to complete them in time, and to accept such recompense as you shall think reasonable, which shall be paid on your draft on the Secretary of State We rely that the friendly dispositions of the Spanish Government will give such access to the archives of the province as may facilitate information equally desirable by Spain on parting with her ancient subjects, as by us on receiving them, this favor will therefore, I doubt not, be granted, on your respectful application Accept my salutations, and assurances of esteem and respect

(Signed,)   THOMAS JEFFERSON

DANIEL CLARK, ESQ.

The queries enclosed consist of forty-three in number, a reference to a few only will be necessary

Q 1 What are the best maps, general or particular, of the whole, or parts of the province ? Copies of them, if to be had in print.

2 What are the boundaries of Louisiana, and on what authority does each portion of them rest ?

A number of questions follow, relative to W boundaries, Indian nations on the east side of the Mississippi, &c., &c., &c., till

9 What are the foundations of their land titles? their tenure?

10 Are there any feudal rights, &c., droits de moulin, &c., as in Canada?

11 What is the quantity of granted lands as near as can be estimated?

12 What is the quantity ungranted in *the Island of New Orleans, and in the settlements adjacent, on the west side?*

13 What are the lands appropriated to public use?

14 What public buildings, barracks, fortifications, and other fixed property belong to the public?

15 What the quantity and general limits of lands fit for the culture sugar?

16. What proportion granted? and what ungranted?

Various questions follow relative to code laws courts, number lawyers character people—are they litigious? effect of introduction of trial by jury in criminal and civil cases criminal jurisprudence colleges and schools church and clergy officers, civil and military—how many and how appointed? their emoluments, and how derived? taxes, duties, collectors, how paid? amount duties paid into treasury? any other taxes? expenses of the province paid from the treasury, under various heads? delapidations of the public treasury, &c? if annual expenditures exceed the annual revenues, and how deficiency made up? paper currency? funds for redemption, &c—do they bear interest, their amount, &c? are they due to the inhabitants or citizens of the U S, or to persons not inhabitants? exports and to where? imports, and from where? by land or sea? annual amount of indigo, cotton, sugar, molasses, &c, &c? what number vessels required for exports, and what for imports? coasting trade? ('The foregoing is merely the heads of the queries it being unnecessary to copy them verbatim.)

[Answer to the foregoing]

NEW ORLEANS, 18th August, 1816, ('03)

SIR—I had the honor of receiving this day your letter of the 17th July, to which I shall pay the strictest attention, and without waiting till the whole list of queries proposed can be answered, shall, by each successive post, forward such information as it is possible to procure, in obtaining which, I rely greatly on the friendly dispositions of the officers of the Spanish government I have, by this post, forwarded to the Secretary of State, as exact a manuscript map as could be procured of this country, on which the different parts or settlements are delineated and numbered, and hope to have a more perfect one completed in time to be of service I have joined to it some memorandums respecting the country, hastily put together, long before the news of the cession reached us, and am happy to have, so far, anticipated your wishes in this particular As I feel myself honored by your application to me, I request you will accept the assurance that I shall make every possible endeavor to show myself worthy of your confidence, and that if I do not succeed in acquitting myself to your satisfaction, it will not proceed from want of inclination or exertion Permit me to offer my sincere congratulations on an event which must forever insure the safety and prosperity of America I have the honor to remain, with sentiments *of the greatest respect,*

DANIEL CLARK

His Exc'y Thomas Jefferson, President of the U. S

Department of State, July 20th, 1803

Sir —I have the pleasure to inform you that the treaty and conventions entered into on the 30th of April, by our ministers extraordinary at Paris, with the French Government, were received here on Monday evening last For an outline of the agreement, I refer you to the inclosed newspaper, to which is added a copy of articles 2, 3, 4, 5, and 6, to these the President wishes you to give all the attention which may be due to the interests and the eventual rights of the United States

The property and papers specified in the second article will *particularly call for your attention* It is presumed that the authorities in possession will withhold no proper concurrence, and your prudence will, of course, cultivate their good dispositions

With respect to the 3d article, you may give the most ample assurances that all the rights of the inhabitants provided for, will be faithfully maintained, and in general, that their situation will experience every proper mark, not only of justice, but of affection and patronage The provision contained in this article was particularly enjoined in the instructions to our Minister and it is every reason to believe that it found a perfect coincidence in in the wishes and purposes of the French Government

Article 6th will suggest to you the proper inquiries into the relations subsisting between Spain and the Indian tribes and any ameliorations thereof, which the mutual consent of the United States and those tribes may introduce As far as there may be opportunities, t will be equally proper to prepare the Indians for the change which is to take place I have the honor to be, sir, respectfully, your most obedient servant,

JAMES MADISON

Daniel Clark, Esq., Consul U S, New Orleans.

[Answer to the foregoing]
New Orleans, 18th August 1803.

Sir —Your letter of the 20th ult came to hand this evening I shall, in every thing, as far as I am able, endeavor to fulfil your wishes, and regret that the immediate departure of the post pre-

...ents my reply to some of the subjects mentioned in it, I will take an immediate opportunity of doing. I flatter myself you will excuse me & &c

(Signed) DANIEL CLARK

Hon James Madison, Washington

New Orleans, 18th August, 1803

Citizen Colonial Prefect.—Having received by this day's mail the letter to the Secretary of State of the United States by order of the President, giving notice of the cession of Louisiana by France to the U. S. together with a copy of a few of the articles of cession, I take the liberty of inclosing a copy for your information. The President has been pleased to inform me that he has convened the Senate and Congress of the United States to meet at Washington on the 17th October for the ratification of the treaty, and to make the appropriations for carrying it into execution. I have the honor to remain, &c

DANIEL CLARK

[Answer]

Marine, Colonies, Louisiana

REPUBLIC FRANCAISE)

Nouvelle Orleans, le 1er Fructidor, An 11th (

Le Prefect Colonial de la Louisiane a Monsieur Clark, Nouvelle Orleans.

Je vous remercie, Monsieur, de la communication que vous avez bien voulu me donner par votre lettre d'hier. Je félicite les Etats-Unis de cette magnifique et importante acquisition. Je leur porte envie de l'avantage qu'ils auront de contribuer au bonheur, d'accélérer la prospérité de ce pays, non moins interessant par la fécondité privilégiée de son sol que par l'excellent espèce de ses habitants.

En même tems que par un véritable interet pour lui j'en forme le vœu je sens que tout de la part des Etats-Unis lui en offre le présage. N'ayant, en ce qui me concerne aucun avis direct de mon Gouvernement a cet egard, j'attends ses instructions et leurs ordres pour m'y conformer.

J'ai l'honneur de vous saluer LAUSSAT

Under due 20 November Mr Clark received information of the ratification of the treaty on the 21 October

On the 16th September Mr Madison acknowledged the receipt of Mr Clark's letter of 12th August

On the 26th August 1803, he forwarded answers to such of the queries as he could for the moment reply to, all which must be in the archives of the government

16*

[No. 88.]

Offered by defendants   Filed 25 June, 1849

J W GURLEY, Com

WASHINGTON, July 17   03.

DEAR SIR —You will be informed by a letter from the Secretary of State, of the terms and the extent of the cession of Louisiana by France to the United States; a cession which, I hope, will give as much satisfaction to the inhabitants of that province as it does to us, and the more, as the title being lawfully acquired, and with consent of the power conveying, can never be hereafter reclaimed under any pretence of force   In order to procure a ratification in good time I have found it necessary to convene Congress as early as the 17th of October   It is essential that before that period we should obtain all the information respecting the province, which may be necessary to enable Congress to make the best arrangements for its tranquility, security and government.   It is only on the spot that this information can be obtained, and to obtain it there I am obliged to ask your agency   For this purpose I have prepared a set of queries, now inclosed, answers to which in the most exact terms practicable, I am to ask you to procure   It is probable you may be able to answer some of them yourself, however, it will, doubtless, be necessary for you to distribute them among the different persons best qualified to answer them respectively   As you will not have above six weeks from the receipt of them till they should be sent off to be here by the meeting of Congress, it will be the more necessary to employ different persons on different parts of them   This is left to your own judgment, and your best exertions to obtain them in time are desired. You will be so good as to engage the persons who undertake them, to complete them in time, and to accept such recompense as you shall think reasonable which shall be paid on your draft on the Secretary of State   We rely that the friendly dispositions of the Spanish government will give such access to the archives of the province as may facilitate information equally desirable by Spain on parting with her antient subjects, as by us on receiving them. This favor, therefore, will, I doubt not, be granted on your respectful application.

Accept my salutations, and assurances of esteem and respect,

THOMAS JEFFERSON

DANIEL CLARK, Esq.

QUERIES.

1 What are the best maps, general, or particular, of the whole or parts of the province' copies of them, if to be had, in print

2 What are the boundaries of Louisiana, and on what authority does each portion of them rest?

3 What is the extent of the sea coast from the western mouth of the Mississippi called Peakemenes river?

4 What is the distance due west from the same mouth to the western boundary

5 Into what divisions is the province laid off?

6 What is the population of the province, distinguishing between white and black, but excluding Indians on the east side of the Mississippi? of the settlement on the west side next the mouth? of each distinct settlement in the other parts of the province? and what the geographical position and extent of each of those settlements?

7 Have they a militia? and what their numbers? what may be the number of free males from 18 to 45 years of age in the different settlements?

8 As good an estimate as can be had of the Indian nations, to wit their names, numbers, and geographical position

9 What are the foundations of their land titles? and what their tenure?

10 Are there any feudal rights such as ground rents, fines on alienation, droits de moulin, or any noblesse, as in Canada?

11. What is the quantity of granted lands, as near as can be estimated?

12 What is the quantity ungranted in the Island of New Orleans, and in the settlements adjacent on the west side?

13 What are the lands appropriated to public use?

14 What public buildings, fortifications barracks, or other fixed property belong to the public?

15 What is the quantity and general limits of lands fit for the culture of sugar? and what proportion is granted, and what ungranted?

16 Whence their code of laws derived? a copy of it if in print?

17 What are the courts in existence and their jurisdiction? are they corrupt? are they popular? are they tedious in their proceedings?

18 What is the number of lawyers, their fees, their standing in society

19 Are the people litigious? what is the nature of most law suits? are they for rights to land personal contracts, personal quarrels?

20 What would be the effect of the introduction of the trial by jury in civil and criminal cases

21 What is the nature of their criminal jurisprudence, number and nature of crimes and punishments?

22. What public colleges and schools have they? can the in-

habitants generally read and write? what degree of information do the people possess beyond that?

23 On what footing is the church and clergy? what lands or tythes have they? and what other means of support?

24 What officers, civil or military, are appointed to each division of the province and what to the general government, with a general definition of their powers?

25 By whom are they appointed? are any chosen by the inhabitants?

26 What emoluments have they? and from what source derived?

27 What are the local taxes paid in each division for the local expenses of such division such as roads poor, clergy, schools salary of local officers? and by whom are they imposed?

28 What are the duties on imports and exports respectively, the gross amount of each the place where levied? and the manner of paying them?

29 How are the officers paid who are employed in the collection? whether by fees, daily or annual salary or commission?

30 What is the nett amount of those duties paid in the treasury?

31 Are there any other taxes levied in the province? whether, 1, on land, income or capitation, 2 on transfer of real property, wills, and inheritances 3, on sales of merchandise 4, on stamps and records 5, on manufactures, by way of excise, 6, in any other way? the gross and nett amount of each? the time, place and manner of collecting them? and whether the collecting officers are paid by fee, commission or salary?

32 What are the expenses of the province paid from the treasury under the following heads 1 salaries of Governor, Intendant Judges and all other civil officers 2, military, including fortifications, barracks, &c 3 erection and repairs of public buildings 4 colleges and schools, 5 pensions and gratuities, 6, Indians 7, clergy 8, roads and all other expenses

33 What are the usual dilapidations of the public treasury, 1 before it is collected by smuggling and bribery 2, in its expenditure by the unfaithfulness of the agent and contractors through whom it passes?

34 If the annual expenditure exceeds the annual revenue in what manner is the deficiency made up?

35 What is the nature, amount, and depreciation of the paper currency?

36 On what funds does it rest? whether on provincial revenue, which will remain pledged for its redemption? or on the credit of the government?

37 Exclusively of paper currency, are there any other debts incurred by the Spanish government? their amount? do they

bear interest? are any evidences of the same in circulation? in what proportion are they due to inhabitants of the province or of the United States? and to persons not inhabitants of either?

38. What is the annual amount of exports of articles of the growth or produce of the province under following heads 1 cotton, 2 sugar and molasses 3 indigo 4, board, planks, and wood 5 rice 6 peltry 7 fur and deer skins, 8, horses, and 9 all other articles

39. What proportion of these articles were exported to the United States during the last year of the last war? and what to other countries? and what proportion of what was exported to other countries, was carried in American vessels?

40. What is the annual amount of imports under the following heads 1 articles of the growth of the United States coming down the Mississippi 2 articles of the growth of other countries, distinguished as follow th wines, quantity and quality, spirits and brandies do coffee teas, pepper, and spices, cocoa and chocolate refined sugar other West India articles, salt, segars, and Spanish tobacco also quantity and quality, all other articles of European and East India manufacture, being generally dry goods and hardware their value, and, as far as practicable, the quantities of each kind

41. What portion of these several importations is for the consumption of the province? what portion for reexportation, particularly the articles which are not the growth of the United States? where are these last reexported? by land or by sea? openly, or with a design to a contraband trade

42. What is the annual quantity of indigo, cotton sugar, and molasses, particularly the two last, made in the province? what are the domestic manufactures? are there any distilleries and sugar refineries?

43. What number of vessels and tonnage is required for the exportation of New Orleans? what for the importation? is there any coasting trade? what species of vessels and tonnage employed in ditto?

[No. 101]

Settlement between Daniel Clark, attorney for Chew & Relf, and D W Coxe, 11 July 1811

Offered by defendants, and filed 27th June, 1849, by defendants   J W GURLEY, Commissioner.

[Triplicate]

Articles of agreement made and concluded between Daniel Clark, of New Orleans, in virtue of a certain special power of attorney from Beverly Chew and Richard Relf, trading under the firm of Chew & Relf, at said place, bearing date, New Orleans, the twenty-fifth day of May last past, of the first part, and Daniel William Coxe, of Philadelphia, merchant of the second part, witness

That it being the wish of both parties to come to a final settlement of all their concerns and transactions of every kind whatever, it has been mutually agreed and stipulated as follows.

1st That all the debts owing by said Chew & Relf shall be first paid off, and discharged out of the assets of the house specified in a certain statement of their affairs, in the handwriting of Richard Relf, and signed at foot by the parties hereto, in order to identify the same, and also designated in a letter from said Chew & Relf to Daniel Wm Coxe dated New Orleans, thirty-first day of May last past, it being understood that the debts that were owing in Europe, to Green and Wainewright, the manufacturers, Hope & Co, and Etler & Co, have already been paid and liquidated

2d That after the payment of said debts of Chew & Relf, they shall retain each of them a sum of twenty-five thousand dollars out of the assets specified and designated in the aforesaid statement and letter of thirty-first of May last, in such items thereof, as may be agreed on between them and Daniel Clark, and which sum of twenty-five thousand dollars to each, shall be in full of all and every claim of every nature or kind, which they might or could have on the said Daniel William Coxe

3d. That after paying the aforesaid debts of Chew & Relf, and putting them respectively in possession of twenty-five thousand dollars in assets as aforesaid, then the residue and remainder of said assets and property in their possession shall be delivered up to the order of Daniel William Coxe, and each party to these presents will henceforth forever quit claim each on the other for all property which they may respectively possess of any nature or kind whatever, and thereby dissolve and terminate all concern and connexion in trade or otherwise, which may heretofore have existed And for the due and faithful performance of the conditions and stipulations of this agreement, the parties hereby bind themselves, their heirs, executors and assigns, each to the other, in the penal sum of sixty thousand dollars, to be paid by the non-complying to the complying party

In testimony whereof, we have hereunto affixed our seals and signed our names in presence of two witnesses, who have also subscribed their names, this agreement having been executed in duplicate, and one remaining in possession of each party

Philadelphia, eleventh of July, one thousand eight hundred and eleven   DANIEL CLARK, Att'y of Chew & Relf.
           DAN WM. COXE.

THOMAS SPARHAWK, } Witnesses
JAMES MORPHY

[No 103]

Offered by Defendants, and filed 27th June 1849

J W GURLEY, Com'r

Chew & Relf for them-
selves, and as Ex'ors for D
Clark Esq in their credits

Copies of sundry documents
March, 1814

STATE OF LOUISIANA,

FIRST JUDICIAL DISTRICT COURT.

Petition and schedule filed 3d

STATE OF LOUISIANA,
FIRST DISTRICT, ss

To the Honorable the Judge
of the said district

The petition of Beverly Chew and Richard Relf, acting for *themselves* and as *Executors of the last Will and Testament of Daniel Clark* Esq, deceased, of the city of New Orleans, respectfully showeth,

That owing to the peculiarity of the times, the scarcity of money, and the stagnation of commerce, arising from the oppressive political condition in which the United States have for some time been involved, as well as from the peculiar nature of their estate, they find it utterly impossible to produce either from sales or from collection a sufficiency of ready money, to meet their debts as they become due

They represent, that altho' they believe *the assets to be very abundant* to discharge every debt due and owing by them, and to leave a *large surplus to themselves* and to *the heirs of the late Daniel Clark*, yet they are apprehensive, that if sales are coerced at this time, for payments for ready money, or even at short credits, the whole landed and mortgaged property would be sacrificed at merely a nominal price, by which means speculators might enrich themselves on the ruin of your petitioners, and to the great loss of their creditors

Your petitioners further represent to your honor, that they deem it their bounden duty, as well to the heirs of the said estate, to claim of them a respite from the payment of their debts, and from all suits and prosecutions for the same until they can bring into action *the vast sums* that are in the hands of the debtors, residing in various parts of *this State* and the *Mississippi Territory*, and until they can call to their aid the proceeds of the large tracts of uncultivated lands which belong to them on sales to be made, on such credit, as will insure a fair price

To this end they pray your honor, the premises considered, to order a meeting of *their* creditors to take place, after the usual delay and notice, in John Lynd's notary's office in this city, to take into their consideration the affairs of the said estates, and the objects of this petition, when and where your petitioners will be ready to make *a full exposition of* the situation in which the affairs of *the estate* are involved   And inasmuch as your petitioners are threatened with law suits, which would be a useless expenditure of the moneys of *the estate*, they pray that all such proceedings against them may be stayed, &c

And they annex hereto a schedule, &c, but as the same *is not complete*, they reserve the privilege of rendering *a supplemental schedule*, in due time

      (Signed)   TURNER &c

PARISH OF ORLEANS, ss

Richard Relf maketh oath, that all the material facts and allegations contained and set forth in the foregoing petition are true, to the best of his knowledge and belief

New Orleans, March 28th, 1814

      (Signed)   RICHARD RELF

Sworn to before me

      (Signed)   JOHN P SANDERSON,

                    Justice of the Peace

THE SCHEDULE

Schedule of the debts due by Chew & Relf, and the deceased Daniel Clark, and of property belonging to, and debts due by

DEBTS DUE BY THEM

Chew & Relf's notes, favor J Pitot disc'd, in L B					45500
ditto	"	"	"	do in P B	4640
ditto	"	"	'	do in O B	1150
ditto	"	"	"	D Delacroix,	2000
ditto	'	"	"	J Tricou & Son,	1200
ditto	"	"	"	W. Brand, for work,	300

ditto " " " Rochelle & Shiff, in renewal of Wm Donaldson's notes, left with them as collateral securities,   3033

ditto to Villeneuve Le Blanc for account of Madame Barran,   710 93

ditto to Lewis Serre lent him   1000

ditto to Dan'l Wm Coxe, of Philadelphia discounted at bank of Pennsylvania   12000

To Marigny & Livaudais, for a bill on England,   900

To Phœnix Fire Insurance Company of London, balce of acc nt up to the 28th Feby inst   1050 50

To Syndics of C Bougand, for monies received   1500

To ditto of John Clay, for ditto   2000

To bills payable, our note to S Henderson.   1500

                              _____

              Dollars,   81,484 43

Daniel Clark's notes to Tricou & Son, due 4th

              April, 1814,   952 50

      Ditto   "   to do, due 4th, 1815,   952 50

Daniel Clark " to Louis Bouligny, 1st
    February, 1815   5000
    Ditto   notes to ditto due 1st Feb'y, 1816,   5000
Richard Relf, Executor's notes to Louisiana bank, 24800
    Ditto   to Harrod & Ogden's P B   440
    Ditto   " J Pitot & Delacroix   1300
    Ditto   "   and Chew & Relf,   2400
    Ditto   " E Sainet,   2700
    Ditto   ' Falzar,   1219
    Ditto   " M Abat,   141
    Ditto   " T A Claiborne,   150
    Ditto   " fav'd Betchtel   2621
    Ditto   " E Livingston,   1418
    Ditto   " ' Chew & Relf and S Elkins, 2000
    Ditto   "   do   do   3451 49
    Ditto   '   do and W Hampton, 2964 50
    Ditto   '   do   do   2964 25
    Ditto   do   do   5928 50
    Ditto acceptances on account of interest due
        Israel Trask, viz
        Bartlett & Cox,   416 21
        W & J Montgomery   93
        Philip Hickey   720   1229 21

    ditto note to C De Armas   70 50
Chew & Relf's note for act D Clark, to C Nagel, 188
    ditto   joint with E Clark, on account of
        wages of negroes on J Luke's place, 1000
Interest on note favor Dejean,   160
Amount of account for fees of office due T Beale 1066 87
Due to Stephen Henderson, for the 1st payment
    on plantation bot of him, to meet which
    he lent us his notes for   6000
And endorsed our notes for   7300   13300

Due the Estate of Wm Simpson, about   1500
   " the heirs of J McCarty,   2000
   "   W & J Montgomery,   981 89
   ' the heirs of E D Turner,   3000
   "   John Poulteney   1243
   "   Reynaud & Peytavin, 1, 2, and 3 years, 18581 95
Ditto to I E Trask, for balance of interest, 1170
   " Polydore, a free negro,   600
   " due Chev Delacroix   242 62 1-2
Due for sundry claims produced against the Estate,
    not liquidated, viz
17*

P St Amand,	$250	Aimé Pegneguy	191	
Vve Jourdain,	247	Mad e Bouregard,	200	
P K Wagner,	120	F Arrogo,	75	
Reynolds & Levy,	23 51	P Maspero,	22	
Duncan McCall,	168	Le Monier,	340	
Gray & Taylor,	18	Grandchamp,	269 25	
Berjac & David,	96	P Pedesclaux,	25	
D Rouguette,	92	P Marsia,	228	
Josh Nicholas,	3650	John Woodw'd,	96	
Porter & Depuyster,	1043 52		——	$3495 78

An annuity bond to Mrs Mary T Andry,   3000
A claim of Elijah Clark, for hire of negroes on
   John Luke s place

                                Dollars,   205722 78

DEBTS DUE THEM AND PROPERTY BELONGING TO THEM

By the following property mortgaged and debts transferred to
the Louisiana bank, in security of the sum owing it
Houses and lots, corner of Hospital and

Dauphine streets,	$12,000	
Houma's plantation, cost	30,000	
Robert Cochran's notes and mortgage,	3,560	
Navigation company stock	7,500	
Louisiana bank, do	3,000	
Wade Hampton's notes,	7,912	
	———	63,972
Insurance and navigation Co stock,		560
Fulwar & Skipwith s bond and mortgage,		1600
C B Dufau and M Pelletier, do		4200
Estate of Wm Donaldson, do		16200
Madame Barran, do		800
Horatio Sprigg, of Red River,		1200
Francis Wood,		300
J H Johnston, of Bayou Sarah,		2000
Simon LeBlanc, of German coast,		271
Elizabeth Bradford, of Bayou Sarah		341
Col Hamilton, of do		545
John Towles, of Attakapas,		218
Doct Davidson Fort Adams,		835
Edward Randolph, Pinckneville,		10,000
Michael Jones, St Helena,		600
Daniel Holliday, Fort Adams,		210 50

DOUBTFUL

Patrick Welsh, of Havana.	3000
B Bosque's Estate,	6000
Rich'd W Meade, of Cadez.	4500
R. & C Chew, of New York secured by	
a debt in Virginia	2600

Wm St Marc   1200
Gilbert Leonard judg's obtained,   500
Sundry book debts   4000
                                                   _____

And numerous other doubtful ones $21800
                                                   _____

5 acres front of land bot of Dejan cost   4500
40 000 ditto being an invaluable cypress swamp
    in Ouachita, bot of Filhiol cost,   8000
S B Davis note, with interest,   2300
                                                   _____

                    Dollars,   119155 50

By David Urquhart & Williams bond
    and mortgage, transferred to the
    Louisiana bank, $10,000
Henry Hunt's ditto   12,500
Wade Hampton ditto,   3 956   26456
                                                              _____

Seth Lewis and Wm Turner, by bond and mort
    gage on land and 55 slaves   17000
Robert Munson ditto,   3520
Levi Wells, ditto   3000
N W Kimball secured by bond and mortgage,   2514
W Witherspoon,   ditto,   3000
Josiah S Johnston,   ditto,   8000
Joseph LeBlanc   ditto,   3200
Col Hamilton,   ditto   7000
Zenon Cavelier and Louis Feriet, ditto   9000
J McDonough Sr,   1000
Thomas Power secured by Florida lands,   8000
Mons r Lafon's note   1229
Henry Turner, for Ouachita lands,   5000
Ditto, for unsettled outstanding debts of Natchez
    concern suppose,   10,000
Cavelier & Sons, for an assumption   2250
Major Hoops, of New York,   3500
P Guion, bond and mortgage,   8000
Michl Omer Fortier fils, for the balance due on the
    sale of the plantation, after paying to Hender-
    son the purchase money,   14733
Rent due the 1st May 1814, for lots sold at Su-
    burb St John,
A number (say 12 or 15) old and decrepid ne-
    groes, of little value
                Dollars   255557 50
                                                              _____
Landed Estate, at its appraised value, made
    by Mr Clark, *some time previous* to his death

Bayou estate, exclusive of the large house and
ground on which it stands, which are mortgaged to Wm Simpson, $100,000
Lands on Gentilly road, bo't of De-
    jean and others,   8,000
10 lots in the suburb St Mary,   4,000
Plantation on German coast bo't of
    Wm Simpson   10 000
Several tracts of land in Opelousas,   5,000
    do   do   in Attakapas,   3,000
    do   do   in Lafourche,   6 000
    do   do   in Bayou Bœuf   17 000
    do   do   in Ouachita,   26 000
120,000 acres in Florida,   120,000
                                   _____
                                    $342,000

There are, independent of the foregoing a number of doubtful
debts, but which it is impossible for the present, to state with any
precision, there may be likewise some claims against the estate
overlooked.

The following notes omitted
Abraham Aremeaux, $100
Manuel Perez,   100
Louis Boidore,   100
Eli R Trepagnier,   3000
John Lynd,   4461
Collson,   50
DeMagnan,   300 $8111
                                     _____

ORDER OF THE JUDGE ON THE PETITION AND SCHEDULE

Let a meeting of the creditors take place, after thirty days notice, according to law, at the office of Jno Lynd, notary public
in the city of New Orleans, and in the mean time ordered that
all proceedings against the petitioners be stayed And that Mr
A. Depeyster be appointed to represent the absent creditors
        (Signed)   JOSHUA LEWIS
2d March, 1814

AFFIDAVIT.

THE STATE OF LOUISIANA, }

PARISH OF ORLEANS, ss   }   The aforesaid Richard
Relf, one the plaintiffs, maketh oath, that the foregoing schedule
contains a representation of *their* creditors' debts, estate, and effects, as complete as he can exhibit at this moment But from
the peculiar situation of their affairs, it is probable *there are other
objects in existence* which it may be proper to exhibit in a supplemental schedule
        (Signed)   RICHARD RELF

Sworn to and subscribed before me, a Justice of Peace, for said parish, the 2d day of March, 1814

(Signed)   JOHN P ANDERSON

Justice of the Peace

Supplementary schedule of the debts due by Chew & Relf and the Estate of the late Daniel Clark, and property and debts due them

To amount of debts in first schedule presented				205722	78
" Chew & Relf's note, favor J Lynd lent him				1500	
" do do do do F Samou,				575	
" Dan'l Clark's do do L M Sigory,				730	90
" do do do do				2156	62
" Balance due estate Marty, by D Clark,				2275	18
" do do T Corn her				1885	
" D Clark's note, favor G Arhy,				2400	
" A claim of Madame J Andry for a negro,				400	
" D Clark's three notes favor L Leesnie,				2580	
" A claim of L Huding for law fees					
" M Thierry, account against estate D Clark,				285	

By amount of credits in first schedule presented				263,688	50
" amounts short entered in debts, due by the following persons					
	H Hunt,	2470	50		
	W Witherspoon,	360			
	J H Johnston,	59	18	2889	68

" Amount judgment against Lewis & Carpenter		600	
" do do against George Hart		700	
" do do against S Robinson,		1000	
" A P Walsh's note, favor Chew & Relf, balance,		525	
" R Duval's note, favor D Clark,		55	
" J Lynd's note for one lent him per contra,		1500	
" Jos A Parrott mortgage, favor D Clark,		100	
" Jno Dawson's do, favor P Chew, with interest,		1232	
" M Foye's do, favor D Clark,		2000	
" A claim against Kercheval & Co, due Wilkins,		2000	
" Three slaves, belonging to B Chew,		1300	
A tract of land, belonging to do, of $			
400 acres laying on Bayou Rapide, $2000			
" Amount advanced John Luque, sugar pl,		7788	
" Land bought of C Tessier, 500 acres,		1000	
" 24 sugar kettles, at $50, 25 cylinders, $50		2450	
" 3 barrels aniseed, 300 lbs 20,		60	
" A quantity of cotton gin machinery,			
" Judgment against C Keizer, for		2000	

" Sundry book debts, per list annexed, 6932 06
    Included in first part,   4000   2932 06

Sundry notes omitted in first part viz
R R Keene $2185, A Orso, $1200 L Lecesne,
$263 P Coulson, $43 C Ponnetor $50
G Pollock $90 Villanueva $120 Louis
Serré, $3000 Louis Dejsalles, $600 Min l
Salcedo, $600 E Marchand, $115 W Bel-
linger, $21,   8287
    (Signed)   CHEW & RELF

DISTRICT COURT—STATE OF LOUISIANA

I do hereby certify the foregoing to be copies of the original
petition, schedule, order, and affidavit, and supplementary schedule as filed in the office of the Clerk of this Court

Clerk's office, the 27th day of February 1836

  [LS]   JNO L LEWIS, Cl'k

[No 104]
Offered by defendants   Filed 27th June 1849
                        J W GURLEY, Com'r

Meeting of creditors of the estate of the late Daniel Clark and
Chew & Relf, praying for a respite, 6th April, 1814

Be it known, that on this sixth day of April, one thousand
eight hundred and fourteen, in virtue of an order issuing out of
the Honorable the District Court for the First District of this
State, directing that a meeting of the creditors of the succession
of the late Daniel Clark, *and of Chew & Relf*, should take place
at my office, in order that the affairs of said persons should be
taken into consideration, and such measures be pursued as may
seem best fitted to the interest of *all* concerned Before me, John
Lynd, notary public in and for this city of New Orleans, appeared
the persons hereinafter named, who proceeded in manner and
form following, that is to say

Beverly Chew and Richard Relf, acting for themselves, and
on behalf of *their mercantile firm* known by the name of Chew &
Relf, and for every member thereof, and as *executors testamentary
of the late Daniel Clark*, having exhibited a schedule of their
affairs, and called a meeting of their creditors thereupon, beg
leave to submit to them the following propositions for their consideration and concurrence, viz

That the embarrassment of *their* affairs is such as to render it
utterly impossible for them to make payment of all their debts at
the times of their respectively falling due, that such embarrassment has not proceeded from any mismanagement or fault on their
part, nor by any waste of the funds of the copartnership, but

solely by a concurrence of events beyond their control, that they have *abundant means* with good management and some indulgence to pay *every* creditor and *to leave for themselves a considerable surplus*, that the peculiar situation of their estate, and the complexity of their concerns are of such nature, as, if placed in the hands of a stranger would be managed with extreme difficulty, and, as they verily believe, would be attended with great loss

They, therefore, propose to their creditors that a *respite* may be granted to them from all demands and actions for and on account of the debts *due* and *to become due*, for the term of *one*, *two* and *three* years, without impairing or changing the nature of their securities, obligations, or privileges, and that they may be permitted to retain their estate in their own hands, and under their own management

And upon these propositions being agreed to by their creditors, they do hereby promise and agree to pay to each and *every creditor* such debt and debts as *are now due*, or *may become due*, within the space of three years from this date, by equal instalments of one third part of such debt and debts, at the periods of one, two, and three years

With permission, however to pay off, as soon as the funds will permit sundry small debts, which will not exceed in amount the sum of *four thousand dollars* or *thereabouts*, including *privileged claims, fees of Court, &c, &c*

Whereupon, appeared Pierre François Missonet, counsel for Madame Brosse Beauregard, who having been duly sworn, deposed that, according to the document placed in his hands, the heirs of the late Daniel Clark are justly indebted to his principal in the sum of two hundred twenty dollars, for negro hire and that he grants the respite demanded, reserving privilege. Signed—Missonet

Jean Baptiste Thierry also appeared, and, being sworn, deposed that the heirs of said Daniel Clark are justly indebted to him in the sum of two hundred eighty-five dollars, for funeral expenses, and advertising property for sale since decease, for which he grants the respite demanded, but reserves privilege. Signed—Thierry

G R Stringer, copartner of the firm of Montgomery & Stringer, having been duly sworn deposed that the heirs of said Daniel Clark are justly indebted to said firm in the sum of eighty-one dollars and ninety-four cents, for groceries furnished to his family; that he grants the respite demanded, reserving privilege Signed —G R Stringer

Dominique Rouquette, having been duly sworn, deposed that the heirs of the said Daniel Clark are justly indebted to him in the sum of ninety-two dollars for payment of which he grants the respite demanded   Signed—D que Roquette

Thomas Urquhart President of the Louisiana Bank, appeared, and having been duly sworn, deposed that the estate of the said late Daniel Clark and the said Chew & Relf   re justly in debted unto the said bank in the sum of seventy tho isand dollars and upwards, that for and in the name of said bank, he does hereby g ant the respite dem inded, reserving the privileges arising from the securities made over to said bank   Signed—Thos Urquhart, Pres't of La Bank

John Baptiste Dejan, the younger, appeared and, having been duly sworn, deposed that the heir of the said Daniel Clark are justly indebted to him in the sum of six hundred dollars and upwards remaining unpaid, for a purchase of land which is secured by mortgage that he grants the respite demanded, reserving privilege   Signed—Dejan

Thomas L Harman, being President of the Planters' Bank, appeared, and having been duly sworn deposed that the heirs of said Daniel Clark and the sa d Relf & Chew are justly indebted t the said bank in the sum of seven thousand dollars and upwards, that for and in the name of said bank, he gran's the respite demanded   Signed—Thos L Harm in, Pres t of the Planters' Bank

Pierre Joseph Tricou copartner of the firm of Joseph Tricou & Son, being sworn, deposed that the said heirs and Chew & Relf are justly indebted to the said firm in the sum of three thousand one hundred dollars and upwards, for the payment of which he grants the respite demanded   Signed—P J Tricou

Paul Lanusse, being sworn, deposed that the heirs of said Daniel Clark justly owe him a balance of account unsettled, amounting to about three thousand dollars and that for payment of same he grants the respite demanded   Signed—Paul Lanusse

Joseph Saul, Cashier of the Bank of Orleans, being sworn deposed that said Chew & Relf are justly indebted to said bank in the sum of eleven hundred and fifty dollars and that for the payment of the same, with bank interest thereon and without prejudice to their claims against endorsers he grants, for and in the name of said bank, he respite demanded   Signed—Jos Saul, Cashier of the Bank of Orleans

John Hughes, agent for Wade Hampton, being sworn, declared that the heirs of said Daniel Clark are justly indebted to his said principal in the sum of thirty thousand dollars and upwards, for his endorsements and accountability to Reynaud & Peytevin, that he grants the respite demanded, reserving to his said principal all right of resorting to the estate of said late Daniel Clark under the mortgage reserved in favor of said Reynaud & Peytevin for said sum of thirty thousand dollars with legal interest. Signed —John Hughes attorney for Wade Hampton.

William A. Montgomery copartner of the firm of W. & J. Montgomery being sworn deposed that the heirs of said Daniel Clark are justly indebted unto his said firm in the sum of about one thousand dollars, for payment of which he grants the respite demanded. Signed—W. W. Montgomery.

D. C. Williams copartner of the firm of Williams & Nathan, being sworn, deposed that the heirs of said Daniel Clark are justly indebted unto said firm in the sum of four thousand dollars by promissory note and endorsement, for payment of which with legal interest, he grants the respite demanded without prejudice to his claim against the other parties to said notes, and granting the same respite to Chew & Relf, who are parties to said notes. Signed—D. C. Williams.

Abner L. Duncan counsel for Mr. Mary Andry of this city, declared that the heirs of said late Daniel Clark are justly indebted to said Mr. Andry in the sum of ten thousand eight hundred dollars as appears by the schedule he has appeared having no other knowledge of the existence of such debt other than an obligation for eight thousand dollars and a note for two thousand four hundred dollars, and for payment of said sum he grants the respite demanded subject to legal interest on said debt. Signed —A. L. Duncan.

The same counsel for Philip Hickey, being sworn deposed that the heirs of said Daniel Clark are justly indebted unto said Philip Hickey in the sum of seven hundred and twenty dollars for the payment of which with bank interest, and reserving to said P. Hickey his resort against Israel L. Trask as well as his security under mortgage in favor of said Trask he grants the respite demanded. Signed—A. L. Duncan.

John Poultney junior being sworn deposed that the heirs of said Daniel Clark are justly indebted to him in the sum of twelve hundred forty-five dollars for payment of which he allows the respite demanded. Signed—John Poultney, Jr.

Matthew Bujac copartner of the firm of M. Bujac & J. S. David, having been sworn, deposed that the heirs of the said late Daniel Clark are justly indebted to his said firm in the sum of ninety-six dollars for payment of which he grants the said respite. Signed—Mew Bujac for self and J. S. David.

Reuben L. Rochelle, copartner of the firm of R. L. Rochelle & Shiff, being sworn, deposed that the heirs of said Daniel Clark, and Chew & Relf are justly indebted to his said firm in the sum of three thousand and thirty dollars for payment of which he grants the respite demanded in the name of his said firm. Signed —R. L. Rochelle for R. L. Rochelle & Shiff.

Ferdinand Alzar, being sworn, deposed that the heirs of said Daniel Clark, and Chew & Relf are justly indebted to him in the sum of twelve hundred nineteen dollars, or thereabouts, for payment of which he grants the respite demanded Signed—Fer'd Alzar

Louis Bouligny, comparait et ayant été dûment assermenté, deposait que la succession du feu Daniel Clark lui doit justement la somme de dix mille piastres, et que la dite somme etant assuree par hypotheque, il reserve son privilege et accorde le delai demande le comparant apres declarat de retracter toute cette declaration et s en allat sans faire une autre Signe—L Bouligny

William Brand, being sworn deposed that Chew & Relf are justly indebted to him in the sum of three hundred dollars and upwards, for payment of which he grants the respite demanded, reserving privilege Signed—Wm Brand.

Jozé Marias, being sworn, deposed that the heirs of the said Daniel Clark are justly indebted to him in the sum of two hundred twenty-three dollars, for hire as gardiner, and he grants the respite demanded, reserving privilege, and declaring he can not write, he hereto makes his usual mark Mark of Joze Marias—(†)

John W Smith, counsel for Thomas Augustine Claiborne, being sworn, deposed that, according to the documents in his possession and the schedule, the said succession of Daniel Clark is justly indebted to said T A Claiborne in the sum of one hundred and fifty dollars, for payment of which he grants the respite demanded Signed—J W Smith agent for T A Claiborne

James H Shepherd, attorney in fact for Rezin D Shepherd, one of the administrators of the estate of Edward D Turner, deceased being sworn, deposed that the heirs of the said Daniel Clark are justly indebted unto the said estate in the sum of three thousand dollars and for payment of same he allows the respite demanded Signed—J H Shepherd.

William A Depeyster, copartner of the firm of Porter & Depeyster, being sworn, deposed that the heirs of said Daniel Clark are justly indebted to said firm in the sum of one thousand dollars and upwards for payment of which said firm hereby grants the respite demanded, reserving privilege Signed —Wm A Depeyster, for Porter & Depeyster

William A Depeyster, Esquire counsellor at law appointed by the said court to represent the absent creditors, having been present from the beginning, declares by these presents that he sees nothing in the foregoing proceedings to object to Signed —Wm A Depeyster, for the absent creditors

L. M. Sagory, being sworn, deposed that the heirs of said Daniel Clark are justly indebted to him in the sum of five thousand eight hundred dollars and upwards, for payment of which he grants the respite demanded. Signed—L. M. Sagory.

Stephen Henderson having been sworn, deposed that the heirs of said late Daniel Clark are justly indebted to him in the sum of thirteen thousand and three hundred and thirty-three dollars and one-third of a dollar, which is secured by mortgage, and the further sum of fourteen hundred sixty six dollars and upwards is due to this appearer by *Chew & Relf*, for moneys advanced, and he hereby grants the respite demanded, so far as respects the Chew & Relf, but reserves to himself the right of immediate resort against the mortgaged property in the hands of the purchaser under the late Daniel Clark for the first mentioned sum. Signed—S. Henderson.

Louis Henri Lecesne being duly sworn, deposed that the heirs of the said Daniel Clark are justly indebted to him in the sum of three thousand seven hundred dollars and upward, for payment of which he grants the respite demanded. Signed—L. Lecesne.

Bernard Lafosse being sworn, deposed that the heirs of the said Daniel Clark and Chew & Relf are justly indebted unto this appearer, jointly and severally in the sum of one thousand and four dollars, for endorsements of two promissory notes made by Louis Lecesne, and he grants the respite demanded, right of recourse against the said maker reserved. Signed—B. Lafosse. Seghers of counsel for B. Lafosse.

John R. Grymes duly authorized by Samuel Elkins, appeared, and being sworn, deposed that, according to the account of the said Samuel Elkins the said Chew & Relf and the heirs of Daniel Clark are justly indebted to him in the sum of about eight thousand two hundred sixty dollars, for the payment of which he grants the respite demanded. Signed—Jno. R. Grymes, for Samuel Elkins.

Fielding L. Turner appeared and having been sworn, deposed that the heirs of the said Daniel Clark are indebted to him in the sum of one thousand dollars and upwards, for professional services, for the payment of which he grants the respite demanded. Signed—F. L. Turner.

François Dussuau Delacroix appeared, and, having been duly sworn deposed that the heirs of the said Daniel Clark, and the said Chew & Relf are justly indebted to him in the sum of about three thousand five hundred dollars for the payment of which he grants the respite demanded. Signed—Dussuau Delacroix.

Edward Livingston, having been sworn, deposed that the heirs of the said late Daniel Clark, and the said Chew & Relf are justly indebted to him in the sum of fourteen hundred and eighteen dollars for professional services rendered to said D Clark in his lifetime for which Richard Relf as executor granted a promissory note payable to the order of and endorsed by Chew & Relf, which note is now in the hands of another person in deposit and he grants the respite demanded subject to the decision of the Supreme Court with respect to the privilege of said debt and the priority of its payment Signed—Edw Livingston

Louis Sere, being sworn, deposed that the heirs of said late D Clark are justly indebted to him in the sum of five hundred dollars and upwards for payment of which he grants the respite demanded Signed—Louis Sere

John Soule being sworn, deposed that said Chew & Relf are justly indebted to him in the sum of one thousand dollars by their promissory note endorsed by Louis Sere and he grants them the respite demanded, reserving his right of recourse against the said endorser Signed—Jn Soule

Henry McCall copartner of the firm of Duncan & McCall being sworn deposed that the heirs of said Daniel Clark are justly indebted to said firm in the sum of one hundred sixty-eight dollars for which he grants the delay demanded Signed—Henry McCall

And no other persons concerned in this case having presented at the usual hour these proceedings were closed, the day and year first before written Signed—JOHN LYND Not Pub

I do hereby certify the foregoing to be a true and faithful copy of the original extant among the records of John Lynd formerly a notary public of this city, and deposited in my office for reference

In faith whereof I have hereunto set my hand and affixed the seal of my office at the city of New Orleans State of Louisiana on this twenty ninth day of October in the year of our Lord eighteen hundred and thirty-five and of the Independence of the United States of America the sixtieth

F GRIMA, Not Pub

[No 105]
Offered by defendants and filed 28th June 1849
J W GURLEY Commissioner

E P GAINES, ET UX COMPLAINANTS vs CHEW RELF, ET AL DEFENDANTS	CIRCUIT COURT OF THE UNITED STATES 9TH CIRCUIT IN AND FOR THE EASTERN DISTRICT OF LOUISIANA

IN CHANCERY

The answer of John Barnes, and his wife, Caroline Clark Barnes, two of the defendants to the original bill and to the amended bill of complaint of F. P. Gaines and his wife, Myra Gaines, complainants, against these defendants, and against Relf, Chew, et al, other defendants.

These defendants, now and at all times saving and reserving to themselves all advantages and benefit of exception to the errors and imperfections contained in the said original bill, and in its amendment of the said complainants, for answer thereto or to so much thereof as they are advised is material for them to make answer unto:—They answering, admit that the Daniel Clark mentioned in said bill did die seized and possessed of certain real and personal estate in Louisiana and elsewhere, as stated in complainant's bill; and they further answering, admit that the said Daniel Clark departed this life in the year 1813 testate, having devised all his real and personal estate to his mother Mary Clark by his will of 1811. But said defendants deny that he ever revoked said will of 1811 by a subsequent will of 1813 through which Myra Gaines, one of said complainants, by her bill claims to have been instituted testamentary heir. That the said Mary Clark died in the month of June 1823 and that prior thereto, to wit on the 22d day of November 1817, she made her last will and testament in which she bequeathed in trust, to the executor of said will, all her estate, both real and personal conditionally to wit with the further bequest, that the said executors, Joseph Reed, Esq., and Dr. Wm. E. Hulings, should dispose of her said estate and divide the proceeds into four equal parts: one-fourth part she bequeathed to her daughter Eleanor O Bearne, of Sligo, in the kingdom of Ireland, her heirs and assigns forever and in case the said Eleanor O Bearne should be then dead, or should die before her she gave and devised the share to the child or children of the said Eleanor, their heirs and assigns, to be equally divided between them, share and share alike. One-fourth part of her said estate and property she bequeathed to her daughter, Jane Green the wife of George Green, of Liverpool, in the kingdom of Great Britain, her heirs and assigns, forever and in case the said Jane Green should be dead, or die before her she gave and devised the said share to the child or children of the said Jane Green, their heirs and assigns forever, to be equally divided among them, share and share alike. One-fourth part of her estate and property she bequeathed to her grand-daughter late Sarah Anderson, then Sarah Campbell, and to her heirs and assigns forever. The other fourth part of her estate and property she bequeathed unto her grand-daughter Caroline Clark, a natural daughter of her late son, Daniel Clark, to be paid to her, (if received,) on the day of her marriage, or remaining unmarried, when she shall have obtained the age of eighteen years, whichever first should happen; and should the said Mary Clark die before either of the said events took place, in that case, the interest, profit or issue of said share or fourth part was to be handed over to such person or persons as the said Caroline might choose for her guardian or guardians to be appropriated for her support and maintenance, until by the will she would be entitled to receive the principal, as aforesaid And she further bequeathed to her "grand-daughter Myra Clark commonly called Myra Davis, another natural daughter of her late son, Daniel Clark the sum of two hundred dollars to purchase a jewel as a remembrance of her,' stating also 'that she would have left her equal with her other heirs had she not already been provided for "

And the said will of Mary Clark was duly admitted to probate, in the city of Philadelphia in the month of June 1823, and letters testamentary granted to Joseph Reed Esq, one of the executors named in said will, the other named executor Dr Wm E Hulings, declining to act an authenticated copy of which said will, with the probate thereof, was duly admitted to record in the Probate Court of New Orleans aforesaid, in the year 1838, for which, see the record and proceedings of said Court

But in this matter of allegation, these defendants would state, that according to their best information and belief, the said Daniel Clark had been induced to believe, that the said Myra was his illegitimate child, and as such, that he ought to provide for her. That he did provide to some extent for her support, in infancy, through the agency of the said Samuel B Davis, these defendants verily believe

Defendants are informed, and believe too, that some months before his death, he did meditate making a will, by which the said Myra should be thereby provided for after his death, and that he drew up memoranda for such will, expressive of this purpose, these defendants have been informed and believe That he may have shown such papers to his friends, and consulted with friends about becoming executors of such *proposed* will, defendants also believe probable. But that the contents of such *proposed* will were as stated in complainants bill, they do not believe , and so far as they know a negative, from knowing the character of Daniel Clark, and the circumstances surrounding him, the said contents *can not be true*

After having just made and executed a will in due form, by which he gave all his estate to *his mother*, it would impeach his sanity, if, without some rational explanation for his caprice, he had immediately made another will, by which he gave his mother and his openly acknowledged child, (this defendant Caroline,) so nearly *nothing* as by the complainants is represented. But, as respondents are informed and believe, the circumstances were as follows Daniel Clark's mother, the said Mary Clark, then resided in Germantown, near Philadelphia, where she died in 1823 This defendant, Caroline Clark passed her earliest infancy, partly in Philadelphia, and partly in Trenton New Jersey, in the vicinity of Philadelphia the acknowledged child of said Daniel Clark, was nursed, educated and boarded during his life-time, at his expense—bore his name, and was looked upon in her school days as his prospective heiress She was acknowledged *not only* by Daniel Clark's friends and acquaintances of the first respectability, in Philadelphia and New Jersey as his child, *but so known and kindly regarded* by said Daniel Clark's mother with **whom** she resided after the death of Daniel Clark, until she was placed at a boarding school in Philadelphia under the **charge of Mrs.** Bazeley, and at the expense of said grandmother Hence, Daniel Clark, in providing for his mother and this defendant, Caroline, did so, by the will of 1811, whereby he gave all his estate to his mother, with the purpose and assurance she would provide, as by *her will she did provide,* for this defendant Caroline, her acknowledged grand-child.

For the said Myra he also provided, as by her bill she hath shown, by conveying "property to Samuel B Davis, and others, to the amount of *several hundred thousand dollars'* to be held in trust by them for the said Myra This transaction, confessed in the complainant's bill to be true, is recited in Mary Clark's will of 1817, and is consistent with the well-known liberality, intelligence, and justice of Daniel Clark And the truth, thus consistent and sustained vindicates his memory from the gross folly and disparaging imputation charged in the bill that when he regarded himself as probably insolvent, by his partnership involvments in Philadelphia, that then he fraudulently conveyed "*several hundred thousand dollars'* worth of property, in secret and confidential trusts for an illegitimate child, and tantalised an aged mother with a residuary legacy of empty boxes Such version of Daniel Clark's character these defendants are well assured is fictitious and unjust

Having, as above stated arranged his testamentary matters in 1811, defendants admit that Daniel Clark did meditate some change therein *by will,* preferring no doubt, to provide **for Myra** by *will,* rather than by confidential discretionary trusts, which his trusted friends might find it convenient to forget to **execute.** With such view, he prepared his memoranda of a will, which defendants verily believe is the same paper referred to by complainants But instead of consulting with his servants, **and** overseers and the nurse of his reputed child, on the **subject of** making such will, your respondents are informed and **believe,** that he sent for, and consulted with, one of the most distinguished lawyers that then lived, or now lives, in the **State of**

Louisiana   That in conference with that eminent counsellor
Daniel Clark showed him this memoranda of his proposed will,
told him he regarded Myra as his illegitimate child, born of
the *wife* of Degrange and whom, if the law permitted he desired to provide for, by will, according to the memoranda exhibited. That learned counsellor assured him, that the said Myra being what the civil law denominated an adulterous bastard could
take nothing by *will*   Daniel Clark explained, that Degrange,
the husband of Myra's *mother*, was reputed a married man,
when she married him   His adviser replied, such a fact established would be sufficient to effect a divorce, but till the *divorce* was obtained, the prohibitions of the law were imperative
as to children so born before the divorce   And on all these
points, the learned counsellor produced the law books and instructed said Clark in chapter and verse   Daniel Clark satisfied
on these points, then further enquired by what means he could
lawfully provide for the said Myra, and was told by his counsellor,
the *laws* of *Louisiana* would sanction no provision by a father
for a child born under the circumstances then acknowledged by
Daniel Clark, and he could do no better than make absolute
conveyances in confidential trusts to his friends, and rely upon
their faith and honor to give them over to Myra   and the conference ended by Daniel Clark's acceeding to these views   This
conference was shortly before Daniel Clark's death, and his
counsellor and adviser left him with the full impression that
Daniel Clark's judgment was convinced, and his mind assenting
to conform himself accordingly   And the fact that Daniel
Clark left such *outstanding trust deed surviving him*, is almost
proof positive that he did so conform   And these defendants
have always been informed, and verily believe that Daniel Clark
died without leaving, or intending to leave, any other testament
than the will of 1811   And with respect to the further charge
of complainants, that the alleged will of 1813 in said bill set
up and relied on, was read by the said *Judge James Pitot* and
others, defendants answer, and upon their best knowledge and
belief, deny the allegation and say, that except to the extent
above admitted, it is without truth, and without any plausible
aspect of being true   Judge James Pitot was the Judge of
Probate before whom the will of 1811 was proven   The proceedings on that occasion show, that there were those with
whom Daniel Clark had probably spoken of his desires and
views of a contemplated will, subsequent to that of 1811, who
believed, perhaps, he had executed such a will   And before probate of the will of 1811 was permitted to be made, a full investigation on this subject was instituted, and thereupon due
search and judicial inquiry was made, and at a time too, when,
if the matters now charged in the bill were true, and had such

notoriety, as in said bill is pretended, they could, and most certainly would have been established, yet no such will was found and none such proved to have survived him. And it is incredible, that after a lapse of more than a quarter of a century, the delinquent friends of the orphan have had their memories so refreshed and their zeal to redress the injured so much stimulated, that their knowledge and memories can be now relied on to establish such will, and especially is it incredible, that the facts, as averred in the bill to be true, were *known to the same Judge Pitot* before whom the inquiry was pending, and who has left his judicial belief on record in the *judgment of probate executed under his oath of office*, that the will of 1811 was the last will of Daniel Clark.

Defendants not only rely upon Judge Pitot's *act* in this behalf, as proof that Judge Pitot *did not know*, or believe in this matter, as now averred in the bill but they rely upon it in bar as a judicial determination of the fact, that there was no such will executed as was then enquired after, and that the will probated was, in verity, the last will.

And as further answer to this pretension of complainants' bill respondents further say that said plaintiff Myra and her former husband Whitney, in the year 1834 or 5 or sometime about that period, and before filing this bill, instituted their proceedings to make probate of their alleged will of 1813 in the Probate Court of New Orleans, and after much and protracted effort to do so, the judgment of the Court was pronounced against them, and their proceeding dismissed. This direct judgment of the Court on this same allegation, having been submitted to without appeal, these defendants further interpose as if plead in bar to this pretension of the bill.

In respect to the averments of plaintiff Myra that her mother was the lawful wife of Daniel Clark, and that the plaintiff Myra is the only legitimate child of that marriage defendants answer and say, that a more exagerated fiction was never wrought up from a tissue of circumstances which comported so little with such conclusion and which these defendants are too painfully conscious, can admit of no apology, no explanation at which morality must not blush and these defendants especially deplore. They are informed and believe that about the year 1796, Zulime, née Carriere, of New Orleans, intermarried with one Jerome Degrange, and lived with him for several years, till about the year 1801, when, from some cause unknown to these defendants, they separated, having no children, as far as they are informed. After this time, an illicit intimacy intervened between the said Daniel Clark and the said Mrs. Degrange, of which this defendant, Caroline Clark Barnes, was the

19*

acknowledged issue, and the plaintiff Myra was the *reputed* issue, though this defendant Caroline, has been frequently assured by her mother, that she, Caroline, was the only child of Daniel Clark, and reports from others assuming to know have verified the same fact, that Daniel Clark was imposed upon and deceived into the belief that the said Myra was his child when she was, in truth, the child of another man This adulterous intercourse continued at intervals, as respondents are informed, till about the year 1804, when Daniel Clark withdrew from the said Mrs Degrange, and being absent from New Orleans about the year 1807, as a delegate in Congress, became. by report, an accepted lover of Miss Louisa Caton, of Baltimore, now, defendants believe, the present Duchess of Leeds

In the year 1808, the said Zulime being then in Philadelphia, and without having obtained any divorce from her husband Degrange, received the addresses of a Mr James B Gardette, and thereupon intermarried with him, which marriage, defendants believe, was publicly solemnized in the Roman Catholic Church of St Joseph, in said city of Philadelphia, and after residing with him in Philadelphia, until about the year 1822 or 23, went with said Gardette to France, and continued to live with him as his wife until his death, which took place a few years since in France   During which time she bore him a family of several children some of whom were christened in the said church of St Joseph, and some of whom, together with the said widow Gardette, now reside in the State of Louisiana All these facts the *complainants know, or have been informed of,* and these defendants would most gladly have suffered them to repose in oblivion, had not a perverted imagination attempted, from such humiliating circumstances, to work out a marriage of Mrs Degrange to Daniel Clark, and from thence the legitimacy of the complainant Myra, to the subversion of the established rights of this defendant Caroline, and with an accumulation of dishonor and reproach upon both her parents, greatly beyond that which a regard to truth, and the necessity of the occasion required, and which has extorted this answer, painful as it has been to the respondents to be constrained to make it

Defendents *expressly and positively deny* that they, or either of them, ever heard of the name of Caroline Degrange applied to the said Caroline Clark, until it was so applied by said complainants, in their said bill of complaint, but that, on the contrary, the said Caroline Clark Barnes, from her earliest infancy has always been regarded as the daughter of the said Daniel Clark, and never bore any other name then Caroline Clark, until she intermarried with her present husband, whose name she then assumed

These defendants in declaring their information and belief,

but give expression to the general knowledge and opinion of all Daniel Clark's friends and acquaintances, that he was *never married* to the said Mrs Degrange or any one else. And this defendant Caroline has heard from her mother, her repeated expression of sorrow and regret, that she had not succeeded in becoming the wife of said Daniel Clark. That she was not so in fact, and did not pretend to be, is further evidenced by the record of her suits for alimony and damages against the said Gerome Degrange in the City Court of New Orleans, in the years 1805 and 1806.

And that the said Myra was not a legitimate child, and that her guardian the said Samuel B Davis well knew she was not and, that he did *not conceal* the fact from Myra or the public, is evidenced by the record of a suit commenced in a court of New Orleans, sometime about the year 1817, in which the said Myra is represented to sue Chew & Relf as Clark's executors, alleging her cause of action to be, that as the illegitimate child of Daniel Clark she was entitled to a support out of his estate, and both of which last mentioned records will be relied on as proof in the cause.

And these defendants further represent, that in the year 1837, or sometime about that period, the present complainants, in conformity with their assumptions, now set up in their bill, of being entitled to the estate of Daniel Clark besides so giving out, in speeches, their pretensions aforesaid, did actually proceed to take possession of, or to assume ownership over certain lots of land in the city of New Orleans, belonging to Daniel Clark's estate; whereupon these defendants relying upon their title derived from Daniel Clark by his will of 1811, and by and through the will of Mary Clark of 1817, did institute suit against these complainants to contest their right of inheritance or devise on which trial the said complainants consulting their own policy and advice in their defence, did not, as they were bound to do if they could, establish their right as published by them to exist, and as relied on and set up in their bill, whereas these defendants did thereupon prove their right by bequest, and by the Supreme Court of the State of Louisiana, in contest with these opposing claimants, and have thus established themselves, and been, by the judgment of said Court, pronounced and decreed to be testamentarily entitled to the estate of the said Daniel Clark. And this judgment of the said Supreme Court these defendants here interpose, and will claim to rely upon on the final hearing of this cause as if formally plead in bar to the pretensions of the plaintiff's bill, in setting themselves up as heirs and devizees of the said Daniel Clark, deceased

In respect to the co-devizees and legatees with this defendant

Caroline, under the will of Mrs. Mary Clark, and in respect of the residence and interests of the parties, defendants say that the legacy to Mrs. O'Beirne never took effect in consequence of her death, in 1817 or 1818, and before the death of Mary Clark, but said legacy vested and took effect in her daughter and only child, Eleanor, now the wife of Peter Macniff, of St. Louis, in the State of Missouri.

And the interest which vested in Mrs. George Green of Liverpool, England, has, as these defendants are informed and believe, been duly released and set over to Mrs. Sarah Jane Campbell, of Germantown, Pennsylvania, another of the legatees under said will.

And these defendants except to the jurisdiction of this Court as incompetent and insufficient to decide this controversy, with only one of the four several legatees of Mrs. Clark's will before it, and the said Macniff and wife, and the said Sarah Jane Campbell being residents of other States of this Union, cannot be sued in this Court.

And answering to complainants amended bill, filed the 2d day of July, 1844, defendants say that, in respect to complainant, Myra's legitimacy and right of inheritance, and of Daniel Clark's supposed will of 1813, they answer as before they have answered.

And in respect to such supposed will, defendants further say that, the said Myra's illegitimacy being such as before set forth, such will would be null and void to give title to the said Myra to any property thereby bequeathed, even were such will proven to have been made, which defendants say never was made. And the property conveyed by the said Daniel Clark in his lifetime in secret trust, for the use of said Myra, as confessed in her bill, these defendants say was illegally conveyed as against the mother of said Daniel Clark, who was the lawful as well as testamentary heir of his estate, and these defendants claim the right to the property so conveyed to the extent of their share in said estate.

These defendants protest, also, to so much of said amended bill as pretends to introduce as a new claim of the complainant, Myra, the assignment of her mother, Zulime Gardette. First, because the said Zulime Gardette had no interest in Daniel Clark's estate to assign; and, secondly, that the said Zulime being then, and for a long time before, a citizen of Louisiana, she cannot by assignment to the complainant, Myra, suing as a citizen of New York or Tennessee, enable the said Myra to prosecute her controversy in this court, and to this end defendants except to the jurisdiction of this court, as if more formerly plead.

Said defendants further allege, and that such is true to the best of their information and belief that the defendant, Caroline Clark Barnes, is the daughter of the said Daniel Clark, by the said Zulime Nee Carriere, and that during the time the said Caroline was at the boarding-school of Mrs. Brazely in Philadelphia and also after her marriage the said Zulime Nee Carriere frequently visited her, and repeatedly assured her that she, Caroline, was the *only daughter* of the said Daniel Clark, and, therefore, the said defendants assert and maintain that if the said alleged marriage between said Daniel Clark and said Zulime did ever take place, as the complainants have averred, and it should be regarded of any validity by your honorable court, that then and in that case the said Caroline Clark Barnes would be, and must be regarded as the legitimate child of that marriage, for if even born before wedlock, she would be, by the laws of Louisiana, legitimated by the subsequent marriage of her parents, and the acknowledgment of the said Daniel Clark that she was his child and therefore would be entitled to all the rights and privileges of legitimate legal heirship and inheritance.

JOHN BARNES,

CAROLINE CLARK BARNES.

John Henderson solicitor for defendants.

STATE OF MISSOURI ss
County of St. Louis

Before me John M. Krum Judge of the Circuit Court, in and for the County of St. Louis, State of Missouri personally appeared the said John Barnes and Caroline Clark Barnes, and both being duly sworn, depose and say that the matters and things represented in the foregoing answer, as of their own knowledge, are true in all respects and those represented to be derived from the information of others, they believe to be true.

In witness whereof I have hereunto set my hand, this twenty-eight day of February, A. D., 1845

JOHN M KRUM.

STATE OF MISSOURI, sct
County of St. Louis

I, John Ruland, Clerk of the St. Louis Circuit Court, certify that the Hon John M. Krum, whose name is signed to the above and forgoing certificate, was at the time of signing the same, and now is the sole judge of the said Court, duly commissioned, qualified, and acting as such, and that full faith and credit are due to his official acts as such.

In testimony whereof, I have hereto set my hand and [Seal] affixed the seal of the said Court, at office, in the city of St. Louis, this first day of March, 1845

JN'O RULAND, Clerk

[No 109]
Offered by defendants, and filed 28th May, 1849

J W GURLEY, Com'r

CIRCUIT COURT OF THE UNITED STATES,
For the 9th Circuit, Eastern District of Louisiana

To any Judge or Justice of the Peace, in the county of Hancock, State of Mississippi

Know ye, that reposing special trust and confidence in your integrity and ability, we hereby authorize and require you, that you call and cause to come before you, certain witnesses, to wit Madame Caillavet and Madame Despau, and them duly examine on oath, touching and concerning certain matters and things in a cause now depending in the said Court, wherein Myra Clark Whitney is complainant in equity, and Richard Relf and Beverly Chew and others, are defendants and the same examinations, so taken and reduced to writing, you certify under your hand and seal, and send enclosed to this Court without delay, to be read in evidence on the trial of said cause, and send also this writ

Witness the honorable R B Taney, Chief Justice of the Supreme Court of the United States, at the city of New Orleans, this 22d day of March, Anno Domini 1838 and the 62d year of the Independence of the United States of America.

[L S]

T W COLLINS, D'y Clerk

IN THE DISTRICT COURT OF THE U STATES,
For the Eastern District of the State of Louisiana

WILLIAM W WHITNEY AND MYRA C WHITNEY, COMPLAINANTS,

AGAINST

RICHARD RELF, BEVERLY CHEW AND OTHERS, DEFENDANTS

IN CHANCERY

Interrogatories to be propounded on behalf of the complainants, to John Sibley, Madame Caillavet, Madame Despau and Mrs. Eliza Clark

1st Were you or not acquainted with the late Daniel Clark, of New Orleans?

2d. Was the said Daniel Clark ever married? if so, when and to whom, and was there any issue of said marriage? State all you may know or have heard of said Clark upon this subject

3d. Were you acquainted with a man in New Orleans, by the name of Desgranges? if so, when and where have you known him? was he or not married when he first came to New Orleans? and did he or not so continue until after he finally left it? State all you may know or have heard touching this subject

4th If you know any thing further material to the complainants, in the controversy, state it

(Signed)   GRYMES, CHINN &c for complainants

Filed 6th February, 1837

(Signed)   T W COLLINS D'y Cl'k.

CLERK'S OFFICE UNITED STATES COURT, }
New Orleans this 17th day of March, 1837. }

I do hereby certify the foregoing to be a true copy of the original on file in this office

[LS]   T W COLLINS, D'y Clerk

WM W WHITNEY AND }   IN EQUITY
MYRA C WHITNEY   }   IN THE DISTRICT COURT OF THE UNITED
        vs   }   STATES IN AND FOR THE EASTERN
RICHARD RELF, BEVERLY }   DISTRICT OF LOUISIANA
CHEW AND OTHERS   }   No 3823

Cross interrogatories to the interrogatories filed by the complainants on the sixth of February 1837, and by them propounded in their behalf to John Siblie, Madame Caillavet, Madame Dupau and Mrs. Eliza Clark

☞ The commissioner who may receive the answers to the interrogatories of the complainants, and to the following cross interrogatories is *notified,* that it will be required of him to certify that the said several interrogatories and cross interrogatories were answered by the deponents separately and apart from each other, and from other persons. and that neither the chief or cross questions were shown to or read by the deponents, or to or by either of them, and that *each question,* under each separate chief and cross interrogatory, was answered in the order in which the several questions are propounded, and that he did not permit any deponent to see or read any succeeding interrogatory, until his answer to the preceding had been fully taken down, and especially that no communications or suggestions were made in the presence of the commissioner, or to his knowledge or belief, by any attorney or agent of either of the parties to either of the deponents, and also to certify that he carefully cautioned each witness to distinguish accurately, in each answer, what he or she stated from his or her personal knowledge, and what from hearsay, and let it so be written down in the answers, what is of personal knowledge and what of hearsay

☞ *The complainants are notified,* that all legal exceptions are reserved to each one of their interrogatories, and especially do the respondents, in propounding these cross interrogatories, reserve to themselves the right to demur, plead, or answer hereafter as they shall be advised, and at all times to declare and show that this honorable Court hath not, either in equity or at law, any jurisdiction of the matter of the present bill of complaint, the same being only cognizable by the Probate Court of

the parish of Orleans, in the State of Louisiana, which Court is
already seized of the succession of Daniel Clark the pretended
ancestor of the complainant Myra, the same being a Court
where a plain, adequate, and complete remedy may be had at
law, by the complainants for any and all their supposed claims
against the succession of the said Daniel Clark, and full redress
for their many grievances set forth in their said bill of complaint
Protesting, therefore, against this proceeding, and not intending
to waive any right, or to admit any claim of the complainants in
the premises, but merely desiring and intending to provide
against the effect of error, accident, surprise or fraud, and wishing to advertise the complainants of the purposes of such respondents only as sign these cross interrogatories, said respondents
here acting in his, her and their own behalf only, and each one
acting for him or herself separately, propound the following

Cross interrogatories

1st Will you and each of you answering any interrogatory
of the complainants, state your age, employment and present
residence , and if a married woman, state your maiden name
and if married more than once, state the names of your husbands,
and by whom, and when and where you resided during each
year from 1810 and 1811 ?

2d If you answer the first interrogatory, in chief affirmatively, state how that acquaintance originated when and where did
you first see Mr Daniel Clark ? Was your acquaintance with
him intimate or not ? Was it ever interrupted and if so, for
what reason ?   Did it continue uninterrupted until the death of
Mr. Clark, and if so how long a period did it embrace ? Do
you say, that your intimacy with Mr Clark was of such a nature as to enable you to become acquainted with events in his
life, which were not disclosed to the entire circle of his acquaintance ? and if so, have you a distinct recollection of any such
event or events ? and state the circumstances which strengthen
your memory on this point

3d. Will you state where Mr Clark resided, when in New
Orleans ? Do you recollect the street and the house ? Did he
board or keep house ? If he boarded, did he also lodge at the
same house ? and if so, who was the keeper of this house, and
what was his or her general character ? If he kept house did he
have a house keeper ? and if so, what was his or her general
character ? Did he reside in New Orleans during the summer
months? and if not, where did he go ? At whose house did he
stop, or whom did he visit? and state what you know of the people whom he visited, and his own standing in society

4th If, in answering the second interrogatory, you say that
Mr. Daniel Clark was ever married, state *when, where,* and to
whom By what priest, clergyman, or magistrate ? and who

were the witnesses present? Were you among the witnesses What other witnesses were present with you? Did you ever see the lady whom you say Mr Clark married? and if so, what was her personal appearance, her age and name and family? Where did she reside before the time you say, she was married to Mr. Clark? How long did you know her before that time? Or were you unacquainted with her until then? Did not Mr Clark introduce her to you? State particularly every thing you know in regard to the connexion of Mr Clark with the lady whom you call his wife and state if she was ever married before or after the time you say she was married to Mr Clark, if so, when, where and to whom?

5th Did you ever know that there was any issue of said supposed marriage? if so who told you? State your means of knowing any thing about this circumstance What was the name, age, sex, and the time of the birth of the child, whose father you say was Mr Clark? Do you know who nursed and reared this child? and if so, who was the nurse? State if you please if you saw the mother shortly after this child was born? and if so, where was she? did she reside then at the house of Mr Clark? and if not, why not? and where did she reside? Did Mr Clark live with her at this time, and were they known generally to the neighbors as man and wife?

6th Was this supposed marriage of Mr Clarks (if you say he ever was married) public or private? If public, did Mr Clark introduce his wife to his friends and acquaintances in New Orleans? and if she was not so introduced state *why* she was not Or was his marriage private? if so, why was it private? and what circumstances could or did probably induce him to keep that marriage secret from his friends and the public?

7th Do you know Myra C Whitney one of the complainants in this controversy? if so, how long have you been acquainted with her? Did either of the complainents inform you by letter or otherwise that your testimony would be important to them in this suit? and if so, on what points did they wish you to be prepared?

8th If, in answering the third interrogatory, you say that you were acquainted with a man in New Orleans by the name of Desgranges, state if you please, where and when you first became acquainted with him in what year? Were you intimate with him? and if so, did this intimacy continue without interruption? was he born in the city of New Orleans? and if not, where was he born? and how long did he remain in said city? What was his employment? Was he married in New Orleans, or where was he married? Were you present at his marriage? and if so, state when and by whom he was married Have you ever seen his wife? and if so, what was her personal appearance

20*

and age, and what was her name prior to her marriage with Desgranges? Did you ever see Desgranges' wife and the lady whom you say Mr Clark married, in company together? if so, when and where, and how often? State particularly every thing you know, touching said Desgranges, his wife, and their connexion or relation with Mr Clark

9th Did you ever or not hear Mr Clarke acknowledge that he had any natural children in New Orleans and particularly, did you ever or not hear him acknowledge two female children, the one named Caroline and the other named Myra? and is or not that Myra, one of the complainants in this case? Did you ever hear him say that he intended to leave by will, money, or property enough to Myra to take the stain off her birth? If you heard him use such expressions or those of a similar character, state what you suppose he meant by taking off the stain from the birth of his own legitimate daughter?

10th Will you state who was the mother of the complainant Myra? and did the mother nurse Myra, if not why not? Who did nurse her? Did her mother die and leave her an infant, or was she too sick and too feeble to nurse that child? Did the mother of Myra, the complainant, nurse and raise her or not? If not, who did? Mention particularly any, and all the circumstances on which you found your opinion

11th. If you know when the complainant Myra was born, state the precise date, and place and state if you know by whom and where she was raised, and whose name she bore, and why she bore that name?

12th. State, if you please what are your feelings and affections towards the complainants? Whether you are related to, or connected with either of them? and if you are, how, and in what degree or way, and whether you have any interest in the event of this suit?

13th Will each one of you, answering any of these direct, or cross interrogatories state whether you have seen or examined, read or heard read, any one of them, or copies of them, at any time or place, before you were called upon by the commissioner to answer them? If aye, state when, where, and by whom they were thus so shown or read to, or by you, and for what purpose? State also, each one of you, whether you have had any conversation or correspondence within the last three or four years with the complainants or with either of them, respecting their supposed claims against the estate of Daniel Clarke? and if you answer affirmatively, state why when and where, such conversation or correspondence occurred, and the nature and amount of them, so far as your memory will serve you, and who was present at such conversations? If you have any letters from the complainants, or from either of them, or the matter referred to in the e direct and cross interrogatories, annex them to your answers if possible and if not possible, state why? If you have preserved and cannot annex them give true extracts from them, and if that be not possible, state your recollections

14th What is your maternal language? if not English, do you understand that language perfectly? and if you do not understand English how have you contrived to answer the foregoing chief and cross interrogatories? Who has translated them to you?

(Signed) L C Duncan, for R Relf and B Chew

(Signed) J J Mercier for the mayor, alderman, &c, of New Orleans Louis Dutossat and Louis Desdunes

(Signed) R M Shepherd, for P O Sorbe and Lemonier

(Signed) John Slidell for John Minturn, George Kenner, and Duncan Kenner

(Signed) Julien Seghers, for J H Petitpain, Claude Rivière, Samory and Louis Lalande Ferriere

(Signed) P A Rost for Marie Holiday and Dussuau Delacroix

(Signed) H Lockett for James Field

(Signed) J T Preston, for widow Jaubert and Luke Vignau, Charles Fonde Boletine Berdoule, Antoine Piernas, John Matthews Ramon Masana Manuel Marguez

CLERK'S OFFICE, New Orleans, 17th March, 1837

I hereby certify the foregoing to be a true copy of the original on file in this office

T W COLLINS, Dy Clerk

W W WHITNEY AND HIS WIFE MYRA CLARK WHITNEY, {
vs
RICHARD RELF, BEVERLY CHEW AND OTHERS }

In pursuance of the annexed commission issued from the United States Circuit Court for the Eastern District of Louisiana I, the undersigned Justice of the Peace, in Hancock County State of Mississippi have caused to come before me, Madame Sophie de Despau, who being duly sworn to declare the truth on the questions put to her in this cause, in answer to the interrogatories annexed to said commission, says

Answer to the first interrogatory

I was well acquainted with the late Daniel Clark, of New Orleans

Answer to second interrogatory

Daniel Clark was married in Philadelphia in 1803, by a Catholic priest I was present at this marriage One child was born of that marriage, to wit, Myra Clark, who married William

Wallace Whitney, son of General J Whitney, of the State
of New York I was present at her birth and know that
Mr Clark claimed and acknowledged her to be his child She
was born in 1806 I neither knew nor had any reason to believe that any other child besides Myra was born of that marriage The circumstances of her marriage with Daniel Clark
were these several years after her marriage with Mr Degrange,
she heard that he had a living wife, our family charged him with
the crime of bigamy in marrying the said Zulime, he at first
denied it, but afterwards admitted it and fled from the country
These circumstances became public, and Mr Clark made proposals of marriage to my sister, with the knowledge of all our
family It was considered essential first to obtain record proof of
Degrange having a living wife, at the time he married my sister,
to obtain which, from the records of the Catholic church in
New York (where Mr Degrange's prior marriage was celebrated), we sailed for that city On our arrival there, we found
that the registry of marriages had been destroyed Mr Clark
arrived after us We heard that a Mr Gardette then living in
Philadelphia, was one of the witnesses of Mr Degrange's prior
marriage We proceeded to that city, and found Mr Gardette
he answered that he was present at said prior marriage of Degrange, and that he afterwards knew Degrange and his wife by
this marriage —that this wife had sailed for France Mr Clark
then said, you have no reason longer to refuse being married to
me it will however be necessary to keep our marriage secret
till I have obtained judicial proof of the nullity of your and
Degrange's marriage They the said Clark and the said Zulime were then married Soon afterwards our sister, Madame
Caillavet, wrote to us from New Orleans, that Degrange's wife
whom he had married prior to marrying the said Zulime, had
arrived at New Orleans We hastened our return to New
Orleans He was prosecuted for bigamy Father Antoine, of
the Catholic church in New Orleans, taking part in the proceedings against Degrange Mr Degrange was condemned for
bigamy in marrying the said Zulime, and was cast into prison;
from which he secretly escaped by connivance, and was taken
down the Mississippi river by Mr Le Briton D Orgenois, where
he got to a vessel, escaped from the country, and according to
the best of my knowledge and belief never afterwards returned
to Louisiana This happened in 1803, not a great while before
the close of the Spanish government in Louisiana Mr Clark
told us, that before he could promulgate his marriage with my
sister, it would be necessary that there should be brought by her
an action against the name of Degrange The anticipated
change of government created delay, but at length in 1806,
Mr James Brown and Eligius Fromentin, as the counsel of

my sister, brought suit against the name of Gerome Degrange, in the City Court, I think of New Orleans. The grounds of said suit were that said Degrange had imposed himself in marriage upon her at a time when he had living a lawful wife. Judgment in said suit was rendered against said Degrange. Mr Clark still continued to defer promulgating his marriage with my sister which very much fretted and irritated her feelings. Mr Clark became a member of U S Congress in 1806. While he was in Congress my sister heard that he was courting Miss Caton, of Baltimore. She was distressed, though she could not believe the report, knowing herself to be his wife. Still his strange conduct in deferring to promulgate his marriage with her, had alarmed her. She and I sailed for Philadelphia, to get the proof of his marriage with my sister. We could find no record, and was told that the priest, who married her and Mr Clark, was gone to Ireland. My sister then sent for Mr Daniel W Coxe, mentioned to him the rumor,—he answered that he knew it to be true, that he, Clark, was engaged to her. My sister replied it could not be so. He then told her that she would not be able to establish her marriage with Mr Clark, if he were disposed to contest it. He advised her to take counsel, and said he would send one. A Mr Smyth came, and told my sister that she could not legally establish her marriage with Mr Clark and pretended to read to her a letter in English, (a language then unknown to my sister), from Mr Clark to Mr Coxe, stating that he was about to marry Miss Caton. In consequence of this information, my sister Zulime came to the resolution of having no further connexion or intercourse with Mr Clark, and soon afterwards married Mr Gardette, of Philadelphia.

Answer to the third interrogatory.

I became acquainted with Mr Gerome Degrange in 1793, when as I understood he first came to New Orleans. He was a nobleman by birth, and passed for a single or unmarried man, and courted, and married Zulime, nee Carriere, at the age of thirteen, the same who is the mother of Myra Clark Whitney. Zulime had two children by him a boy and a girl, the boy died, the girl is still living her name is Caroline. She is married to a physician by the name of Barnes. I was present at the birth of these children,

Answer to the fourth interrogatory.

I am not aware of knowing other important matter to the complainants in this cause.

Answer to the first cross interrogatory.

My name is Sophie, veuve Despau, nee De Carriere. My deceased husband was a planter. I was born in Louisiana. My

age is sixty-two   I now reside in Biloxi From 1800 to 1814,
I resided in Louisiana in Philadelphia, and in Cuba

Answer to the second cross interrogatory

I first knew Daniel Clark in New Orleans His being the
husband of my sister Zulime De Carrière placed me on a footing of intimacy with him during the time of their intercourse,
that intimacy was afterwards interrupted by their separation

Answer to the third cross interrogatory

I had reason to know that Mr Clark, at different times lived
in different houses in New Orleans I have before said that he
did not give publicity to his marriage with said Zulime   He
kept a very handsome establishment for her in New Orleans,
and was in the habit of visiting her

Answer to the fourth cross interrogatory

I have already stated that Mr Clark was married to my sister,
Zulime De Carrière, that I was present at the marriage, (a private one), in Philadelphia   Besides myself, Mr Dorsier, of
New Orleans, and an Irish gentleman a friend of Mr Clark's,
from New York, were present at his marriage A Catholic
priest performed the marriage ceremony   I have already before stated that Zulime was married to Mr Jerome Degrange,
before her marriage with Mr Clark, and that thereafter she was
married to Mr Gardette of Philadelphia

Answer to the fifth cross interrogatory

I have already stated that I knew Myra Clark to be the issue,
and the only issue of the marriage of Zulime De Carriere and
Daniel Clark   A few days after the birth of Myra Clark, she
was placed by her father under the care of Mrs Davis, the wife
of Col S B Davis, with whom she lived until her marriage with
Mr Whitney   I have heard that Col Davis, concealed from
the said Myra her true history, and that she bore his name after
her father's death   Zulime and Mr Clark occupied different
houses in New Orleans, but he always visited her, as heretofore mentioned, at her own house   Their marriage was known
only to a few friends Mr Clark told me he had informed
Col S B Davis, Mr Daniel W Coxe, Mr Richard Relf of his
marriage with my sister Zulime.

Answer to the sixth cross interrogatory

I always understood and believed, at least for the first years
of his marriage, that Mr Clark was prevented from making it
public, on account of her unfortunate marriage with Mr Degrange His pride was great, and his standing was of the
highest order in society, and that pride might have suggested
his opposition to the promulgation of his marriage He, however, always manifested by his coversations, which I frequently
heard, the greatest affection for his daughter Myra

Answer to the seventh cross interrogatory

I have already stated my knowledge of Myra Clark Whitney, from her birth. As I never made any secret of my knowledge of her being the daughter of Daniel Clark, nothing was more likely than she and her late husband should hear of my acquaintance with her parentage and true circumstances connected with it, as already related. And on this I was, I presume, that I have been called upon to give testimony in this chair. But neither of them, nor any body else, ever dared to ask of me any declarations in the least inconsistent with truth and justice.

Answer to the eighth cross interrogatory

I have already in my former answers stated, particularly the 3d and 4th my knowledge of Jerome DeGrange and of his first and second marriages. Before the detection of his bigamy, said Zulime had a son who died, and a daughter called Caroline, which bore his name. Since the death of Mr Daniel Clark, Mr. Daniel W. Coxe, and Mr Hulings of Philadelphia, gave her the name of Caroline Clark, and took her to Mr Clark's mother, and introduced her as the daughter of her son. She, of course, believed their story, which induced her, in her will, to leave a portion of her property to Caroline. Caroline was born in 1801, I was present at her birth, as well as that of her brother.

Answer to the ninth cross interrogatory

I never heard Mr Clark acknowledge his having any natural children, but have only heard him acknowledge one child, and that a lawful one, to wit, said Myra.

Answer to the tenth cross interrogatory

I have already given a full account of the mother of Myra, and of Myra herself, and her being with Mr Davis. I have stated all that I know of these matters, as called for by this interrogatory.

Answer to the eleventh interrogatory

The information called for by this interrogatory has already been given.

Answer to the twelfth interrogatory

I have already before stated myself to be the sister of Myra's mother. My feelings towards Myra are those of friendship and all becoming regard. I wish, however, that justice only be done towards her, but in or by the issue of the suit I have nothing to gain or lose.

Answer to the thirteenth cross interrogatory

I have never seen or heard read the interrogatories, or cross interrogatories, referred to, before called upon to answer them. Any conversation that I have had about this affair, I have already given an account of.

Answer to the fourteenth interrogatory

My natural language is French; but my nephew is well acquainted with the English language; and when in need of a translator, I apply to him

SOPHIE VE DESPAU NEE DE CARRIERE

Which answers, being reduced to writing, have been signed and sworn to, in my presence, this the twenty-eighth day of June, A. D eighteen hundred and thirty-nine. In testimony whereof, I have hereunto set my hand and seal, this the day and year afore written

HOLMES P WENTZELL, J P. of H C   [Seal]

One word erased on third page.
Also one word on fourth page
Two words interlined on fourth page.
Twenty-five words erased on fifth page
One word interlined on sixth page, before signing.

H P WENTZELL, J P of H C   [Seal]

W. W. WHITNEY AND MYRA C WHITNEY,
vs

RICHARD RELF, BEVERLY CHEW, AND OTHERS.

In pursuance of the annexed commission issued from the United States Circuit Court of the Eastern District of Louisiana, I, the undersigned Justice of the Peace, in Hancock county, State of Mississippi, have caused to come before me Madam Rose Ve Caillavet nee de Carriere, who, being duly sworn to declare the truth on the question put to her in this cause, in answer to the interrogatories annexed to said commission says

Answer to the 1st interrogatory

I was well acquainted with the late Daniel Clark, of New Orleans.

Answer to the 2d interrogatory

I was not present at the marriage of Zulime née De Carriére, who is my sister, with Daniel Clark, but I do know that said Clark made proposals of marriage for my sister, and subsequently, said Zulime wrote to me that she and said Clark were married. Mr Clark's proposals of marriage were made after it became known that her marriage with Mr. DeGrange was void, from the fact of his having then, and at the time of his marrying her, a living wife. These proposals were deferred being accepted till the record proof of DeGrange's said previous marriage could be obtained, and said Zulime, with her sister, Madame Despau, sailed for the north of the United States, to obtain the record proof

Answer to 3d interrogatory.

I was acquainted with Mr. DeGrange, in New Orleans. He was considered an unmarried man, on coming to New Orleans, and as such imposed upon my sister Zulime to marry him; but it was afterwards proved he had a lawful wife still living After this imposition of said DeGrange, his said lawful wife came to New Orleans, and detected and exposed his bigamy in marrying the said Zulime when he had a living and lawful wife at and before the time of his marriage with said Zulime He was prosecuted, condemned, and cast into prison, and escaped privately from prison He escaped from Louisiana, as it was reported, by the Spanish Governor's connivance Le Briton D'Orgenois was said to aid DeGrange in getting him off This happened some time before the Americans took possession of New Orleans Mr Clark's marriage with my sister Zulime was after the detection of DeGrange's bigamy The birth of their daughter Myra Clark was some years after the marriage

Answer to the 4th interrogatory

I am not aware of knowing any thing more of importance in this suit except the marriage of said Zulime with Mr Gardette, of Philadelphia, before the death of Mr Clark

Answer to the 1st cross interrogatory

My name is Rose veuve Caillavet née De Carrière. My age is sixty-eight years I was born in Louisiana and resided some time in France, after this marriage of Zulime and Mr Clark, and after that resided in the State of Mississippi.

Answer to the 2d cross interrogatory

I became acquainted with Mr Clark in New Orleans, in consequence of his attachment and marriage to my sister Zulime, an intimacy subsisted between him and myself Our friendly intercourse continued during my residence in New Orleans

Answer to the 3d cross interrogatory

When I resided in New Orleans, Mr Clark lived in his own houses with his own slaves to wait upon him He had the reputation of being a man of immense wealth He stood at the head of society, was considered a man of very great talents, and much beloved for his benevolence

Answer to the 4th cross interrogatory.

I have already stated all I knew about Mr Clark's marriage with Zulime, and of her marriage with Mr DeGrange By this marriage, she had two children—a boy, and a girl the boy is dead, the girl is still living her name is Caroline, and is married to Dr Barnes I have already stated that said Zulime also married Mr Gardette

Answer to the 5th cross interrogatory

It is to my knowledge that Myra Clark, who married Mr. Whitney is the child, and only child, of Mr. Clark by Zulime De Carrière It is to my knowledge that Mr. Clark put his daughter Myra under the charge of Mrs. Davis. Mr. Clark acknowledged to me that Myra was his lawful and only child

21*

Mrs. William Harper nursed her for some time, from kindness; Mr. Clark's gratitude towards this lady, for nursing his child, lasted with his life. Said Myra was brought up and educated in the family of Col Davis, and supposed herself their child, until within a few months of her marriage with Mr. Whitney

Answer to the 6th cross interrogatory

I always heard that Mr Clark's marriage with Zulime was private, and that he did not promulgate it, unless he did so in his last will, made a little before his death, and lost or purloined after his death   He never explained to me his reasons for not publishing his marriage in his lifetime

Answer to the 7th cross interrogatory

I have known Myra Clark Whitney for some years   Making no secret about my knowledge I possessed of the matters of which I have herein spoken, and it being known that I was an elder sister of Zulime De Carrière—therefor it was, I suppose, that I have been called on to testify in this case, but no one has ever taken the liberty to intimate a wish for me to declare anything but the truth

Answer to the 8th cross interrogatory

I have already said all I know about Mr. DeGrange

Answer to 9th cross interrogatory:

I never heard Mr. Clark make any acknowledgement of his having any natural children, and I never heard of his having another child than Myra Clark Whitney, and which, Mr Clark informed me, was his lawful child

Answer to the 10th cross interrogatory

I have already stated all I know as to the parentage and nursing and education of Myra Clark

Answer to the 11th cross interrogatory

I have already stated all I know about the parentage and name of Myra Clark, except that I have heard that after her father's death, she was called Myra Davis.

Answer to the 12th cross interrogatory

My feelings are friendly and kind towards Myra Clark Whitney, and I wish her such success only in her suit, as is compatible with justice.   I have no interest in the issue of it

Answer to the 13th cross interrogatory

I have never seen the interrogatories put to me, until called upon to answer them   I have already stated all I have to say about my conversations.   I am not aware of ever having any correspondence with either of them on this subject.

Answer to the 14th cross interrogatory

French is my mother tongue, but my son is well acquainted with the English language, and when in need of a translator, I apply to him.

VEUVE CAILLAVET NEE ROSE CARRIERE

Which answers, being reduced to writing, have been signed
and sworn to, in my presence, this the twenty-eighth day of
June, A D eighteen hundred and thirty-nine   In testimony
whereof, I have hereunto set my hand and seal, the day and year
above written

    HOLMES P WENTZELL J P H C [Seal]

One word interlined on the l page

    H P WENTZELL, J P H C Miss   [Seal]

[No 107]

Offered by defendants and filed 28th June, 1849

    J W GURLEY, Commissioner

STATE OF LOUISIANA, ⌉
  City of New Orleans   ⌋

Be it known, that this day before me, William Christy, a Notary Public in and for the said city and parish of New Orleans,
duly commissioned and sworn, personally came and appeared,
Madame Marie Zulime Carriere widow of the late Dan Clark,
late of the said city of New Orleans, deceased the said appearer
being at present a resident of the said city of New Orleans, who
declared, that whereas her said husband died in this city on or
about the 16th day of August 1813, leaving a large estate, real
and personal, and whereas her absence from the State at the time
of said death and ever since, until some eight or nine years past,
has prevented her from looking into the affairs of her said late
husband, and accepting or rejecting the community of acquests
and gains which existed between them, and whereas she has become satisfied that it will be proper for her to accept the said
community —

Now, therefore, she does hereby accept, purely and simply,
without benefit of inventory, the community of acquests and
gains which existed between her and her said late husband, with
all the advantages and responsibilities thereunto belonging, according to the laws in such case made and provided

Thus done and passed in my office, at the said city of New
Orleans, in the presence of W. G Latham, and Henry Rareshide witnesses, of lawful age, and domiciliated in this city, who
hereunto sign their names, with the said appearer, and me, said
Notary, on this tenth day of June, in the year of our Lord one
thousand eight hundred and forty-four

Original signed,—Marie Zulime Carriere, ve Clark—W. G
Latham—H Rareshide—Wm. Christy, Not. Pub.

I certify the foregoing to be a true copy of the original act
extant in my current register

In faith whereof, I grant these presents under my signature
    and seal of office, at New Orleans, this twentieth day
[L s] of June, eighteen hundred and forty-four

    WM CHRISTY, Not. Pub.

[No 108]

Offered by Defendants, and filed 28 June, '49

J W GURLEY Com'r.

EDMUND P GAINES AND WIFE,
MYRA CLARK GAINES,

vs

RICHARD RELF AND BEVERLY CHEW,
SARAH CAMPBELL AND OTHERS

In pursuance of the annexed commission from the United States Circuit Court aforesaid, I, the undersigned Justice of the Peace in Harrison county, in the State of Mississippi, have caused to come before me, in the village of Biloxi, this 16th day of October, 1845, Madame Rose Caillavet who, being duly sworn to declare the truth touching each and every of the said interrogatories annexed to the said commission, she answers as follows

Answer to 1st interrogatory —I was well acquainted with the late Daniel Clark of New Orleans

Answer to 2d interrogatory —I was not present at the marriage of Zulime nee de Carrière, who is my sister, with Daniel Clark, but I do know said Clark made proposals of marriage for my sister, and subsequently said Zulime wrote to me that she and said Clark were married Mr Clark's proposals of marriage were made after it became known that her marriage with Mr DeGrange was void, from the fact of his having then and at the time of his marrying her, a living wife; these proposals were deferred being accepted till the record from of DeGrange's said previous marriage could be obtained, and said Zulime with her sister, Madame Despau, sailed for the north of the United States, to obtain record proof

Answer to 3d interrogatory —I was acquainted with Mr De-Grange in New Orleans He was considered an unmarried man on coming to New Orleans, and as such imposed on my sister Zulime, to marry him, but it was afterwards proved he had a lawful wife still living After this imposition of said DeGrange, his said lawful wife came to New Orleans, and detected and exposed his bigamy in marrying the said Zulime, when he had a living and lawful wife at and before the time of his marrying with said Zulime He was prosecuted, condemned, and cast into prison, and escaped privately from prison He escaped from Louisiana, as it was reported, by the Spanish Governor's connivance Le Breton d Orgenois was said to aid DeGrange, in getting him off This happened sometime before the Americans took possession of New Orleans Mr Clark's marriage with my sister Zulime was after the detection of DeGrange's bigamy. The birth of their daughter, Myra Clark, was some years after the marriage

Answer to 4th interrogatory —1 am not aware of knowing anything more of importance, in this suit, except the marriage of said Zulime with Mr Gardette of Philadelphia, before the death of Mr Clark

Answer to 1st cross interrogatory —I have already stated that I was not present at marriage of my sister with Mr Clark I believe they were married, because my sister wrote me from Philadelphia that he was married to Mr Clark, Mr Clark also told me the same on his arrival at New Orleans They were married at Philadelphia Not being in that city at the time, I am unable to answer the numerous questions on that subject I first saw Mr Clark, I think, in the year 1802, I was introduced to him by Mr Dorsier, of Louisiana My acquaintance with him ended in 1806 My sister after her marriage with Mr Clark, arrived at New Orleans accompanied only by her sister Mme Despau. She was married to Mr Clark, as Miss Zulime de Carrière, in the year 1803, I do not remember the month I do not remember the season of the year that Mr Clark returned to New Orleans she did not accompany him I never left Louisiana until I went to France in 1806 I returned to New Orleans 1835 with my sister, Mrs Gardette I very frequently saw Daniel Clark after his marriage with my sister, as the marriage was a private one, it was not advisable that they should reside in the same house he however, provided her with all elegancies of life, and was devoted to his wife and child I was not in New Orleans at the time Mr Clark died, my sister was in Philadelphia, married to Mr Gardette, consequently, was unable to be with Mr Clark at the time of his death She had three children by Mr Gardette Mr Gardette died in France, 1831 My sister's peculiar situation, which has already been stated, was, of itself, sufficient to prevent her from asserting her rights, as she thought, at the time, to the estate of Daniel Clark She was, however, informed by Col Davis, that Chew & Relf had declared the estate of Daniel Clark insolvent.

To the 2d cross interrogatory. I first became acquainted with Mr DeGrange in 1793 He was the youngest son a wealthy nobleman of France, but in consequence of his wildness when a young man, had left home He had travelled a great deal throughout Europe, was in his manners an accomplished gentleman. He represented himself as unmarried and wealthy. I do not remember the name of the street he lived in. My sister was married to him and lived with him, until she was satisfied that she was not legally his wife; she was married in a Catholic church, I was present at that marriage; I do not remember the name of the priest. Her maiden name was Zulime de Carrière I am sure that the same lady that married Mr DeGrange is the mother of Myra Clark Gaines I last saw Mr. DeGrange, I think, in 1803;

I do not know when or where he died, although have been told that he died several years after he left New Orleans. I was not present at his marriage previous to his marriage with my sister, but do not entertain the least doubt of the fact. I do not know the name of the lady he first married

To the 3d cross interrogatory.—The mother of Mrs Gaines was married to Mr Gardette in Philadelphia, in 1805. I was not present at this marriage, I received a letter from my sister, during my residence in France, stating to me that she was married to Mr. Gardette. She lived with him twenty-three years, until his death, which took place in 1831. Some years after her marriage with Mr Gardette, she joined me in France, and visited in the first circles there, was always respected and beloved by all her friends and acquaintances, and to this hour corresponds with several noble, distinguished families of France—and was consequently recognised there by all her friends and acquaintances as the wife of Mr Gardette. She had three children by this marriage, and they likewise were always considered by the friends and acquaintances of the family as legitimate. After all that has been stated so repeatedly in former depositions, now upwards of ten years, with regard to the unexampled misfortunes of my sister, it is superfluous to add another remark on the subject

To the 4th cross interrogatory —I am her aunt. I first became acquainted from her birth that she was the legitimate daughter of Mr Clark; consequently, his heir. My sister, Mrs Clark, also Mrs. Despau, and Mr Clark, were my informants that she was his heir. I never received any letters from either General or Mrs. Gaines on this subject. I am at present residing at Biloxi, Miss., with my son. I do not expect any pecuniary benefit from the success of the said complainants, I am fortunately wealthy, and have all my wishes in a pecuniary point of view complied with. I have never received any promises or intimations from the parties in this suit. I will now close my answers by saying, that having great confidence in truth and justice, I hope and trust that the said Myra Clark Gaines will ultimately triumph over those who have so long withheld her property from her

(Signed,)   ROSE CALLAIVET NÉE CARRIERE

Which answers, being reduced to writing, have been signed and sworn to in my presence, this, the sixteenth day of October, anno Domini one thousand eight hundred and forty-five.

In testimony whereof, I have hereunto set my hand and common seal, (having no seal of office,) the day and year first above written.   J. A. TALBOTT, J P,
1st Police District of Harrison County,
State of Mississippi.

[L S]

Interlineations in the above testimony
Page 2, line 17, the words. "at New Orleans"
do 5 " 12, " "on"
do 5, " 18, ' "from"

J A TALBOTT, J. P

[No 114]
Offered by defendants, and filed 3d July, 1849
J W GURLEY, Com'r.

Sepase que yo Da Maria Carriere muger lexitima y apoderada Gral de Dn Geronimo Desgrange otorgo que vendo realm'to a Dn Gil Legoaster, de esta vecindad, una negra criolla nombrada Aleice, criolla de como treinta años de edad, que partenece a mi poderdante por haverla comprada a Dn Jose Zamora por escra en este archivo, fecha cinco de Agosto de mil setecientos noventa y tres, por cauptiva, sugeta a servir con todas tochas, vicios y enfermedades, a exception de las de ordinanza, de manera que al efecto todas las que se le descubran las doy aqui por inciertas y declaradas, por libre de grabamens, como le certifica el presente e Seno Anotador en precio de quatrocientos pesos que he recevido de contado a mi voluntad, renuncio la exception de la non numerata pecunia, y otorgo formal recivo mediante lo qual me aparto de la propriedad, posesion util, dominio, Señorio y demas acciones reales y personales que a dicha esclava havia y tenia que cedo y transfero en el comprador y en quien su dha y cahsa hubiere, para que como propia le posea o enagene a su voluntad, por esta escra que le otorgo en Señal de real entrega, con lo que es visto haver adquirido la posesion, sin otra prueva de que lo relevo, y obligo a mi poderdante à la eviccion y saneamento de esta ventren toda forma de dho: y estando presente yo, el nominado Dn Gil Legoaster, acepto esta escra y recivo comprada la Esclava en la contidad y conformidad que me va vendida en ella me doy por entregado y otorgo formal recivo y declaro que por tachas ni enfermedad no usace del derecho de redhibitoria, dolo ni quanto minory, pues lo renuncio En cuio testimonio, es fecha en esta ciudad de la Na Orleans, a tres de Noviembre de mil ochocientos y uno Yo el Escno. doy fe, conosco a las partes otorgantes que firmaron, Siendo testigos Dn Celestino Lavergue, Dn Fernando Percy y Dn Jacinto de Ayala, vecinos y presentes

(Fermado)—G Le Goaster—Marie Carrière Desgranges, ante mi Pedro Pedesclaux, Escno pub co.

Concuerda con el acto original que queda en el archivo de mi cargo a que me remito, en fe de lo que yo firmo el presente. A Nueva Orleans, a veinte y nueva de Junio de mil ochocientos buarenta y nueve.

[L.S]   LOUIS T. CAIRE, Not Pub

[No 45]
Offered by defendants, and filed 25th June 1849

J W GURLEY, Com'r

FORT ADAMS, December 7th, 1803

SIR —Your letters of the 29 and 30 ult have been duly received, and we feel happy on the interesting event which you communicate.

Every possible exertion has been made to hasten our departure from this post, and we trust that, on to-morrow, every thing will be in readiness for embarkation, and you may be assured that no time will be lost on the passage.

We shall descend with about 600 men, and until the period of our arrival, we flatter ourselves that the harmony of the city of New Orleans and its vicinity will be preserved

We are, sir, very respectfully,

Your most obed't serv'ts

WILLIAM C C CLAIBORNE,
JA. WILKINSON

DANIEL CLARK, Esq , Consul of the U S

[No 49]
Offered by defendants, and filed 25th June, 1849.

J W GURLEY, Com'r

U. S. DISTRICT COURT.

WM W. WHITNEY & WIFE, |
| *vs* |
| CHEW & RELF |

To MESSRS CHEW & RELF

GENTLEMEN —I hereby notify you that I shall proceed under the act of Congress of '89, to take the testimony of S. B Davis, at nine o'clock A M, on Monday next, the third day of March, at the court room of the District Court of the State of Louisiana, in this city, to be received in evidence, in the trial of the above cause.   C WATTS

New Orleans, 1st March, 1834

STATE OF LOUISIANA, |
| CITY OF NEW ORLEANS |

Nathan Jarvis being sworn, says that he served a copy of the above notice on Richard Relf yesterday, Sunday, 2d March, at half past three o'clock, and also to-day at eight o clock in the morning.   NATHAN JARVIS.

Subscribed and sworn, this 3d March 1834.

C. WATTS

STATE OF LOUISIANA |
| CITY OF NEW ORLEANS. |

Be it remembered, that on this third day of March, in the year

one thousand eight hundred and thirty-four, at nine o'clock in the
morning." Came before me, Charles Watts, Judge of
a first judicial district, in the court room of said court, Samuel
B. Davis, who being duly sworn to depose and answer to the
questions on the respective court of plaintiffs and defendant as
aforesaid. In behalf of said examination were present, A. M.
Wording on of plaintiffs; L. C. Duncan of counsel for R.
Relf, and also said R. Relf. Said L. C. Duncan objected to said
examination being taken on the ground that the notice was unreasonable.

Samuel Boyer Davis, being duly sworn as aforesaid, deposed
that in March, in the year one thousand eight hundred and twelve
he met Daniel Clark of New Orleans insisted on placing in the
hands of deponent of the sum of two thousand three hundred
and seventy-six dollars; which said Daniel Clark insisted deponent
should keep as a deposit for his daughter Myra Clark, who was
to receive the interest of deponent; and his house, as a member
of his family, and the money was to bear ten per cent interest, and
the interest to be applied to her education, and other sums were
to be furnished as it would become necessary. Deponent was
now trying to let it lie in more value; as deponent did not want
to use money at all, and to pay that rate of interest, but at the solicitation of Clark's witness took it and gave his note for it. The
agreement and terms upon which deponent received the money
was reduced to writing by Mr. Clark himself and appended to
the note, as deponent believes. A receipt for the note on the interest said of Chew & Relf, consigned to Samuel B. Davis, No. 372,
at the court of the parish, the register being produced, and
shown to witness in the office of the clerk of said court, where
this deposition is taken; and the petition in said suit being read,
deponent declares it is the note referred to in the preceding part
of his deposition, deponent never gave Daniel Clark any other
note at that time or at any other time, or for the sum deponent
left New Orleans in the month of May, or shortly after the transaction afterwards, viz: of the year one thousand eight hundred
and twelve. Previous to leaving New Orleans at that time, deponent had frequent conversations with Daniel Clark in relation
to this matter, and the said amount was placed in hands of deponent as a deposit for the benefit of his said daughter. Neither
D. Clark, nor Messrs. Chew & Relf nor any other person, ever
notified deponent that said note was endorsed, or made any demand of the money. If they had done so deponent would have
paid it: deponent was absent in the army at that time. Myra
Clark, the daughter of said Daniel Clark to whom deponent refers,
is now the wife of W. W. Whitney, the plaintiff in this case.
Deponent would have paid the note to the order of Daniel Clark,

22*

but to no one else, deponent had no knowledge of the suit above referred to, nor any opportunity of making a defence

Being cross examined deponent says he returned to New Orleans in the winter of 1815, after the battle of New Orleans Deponent was ordered here to join the 44th regiment, to which deponent had been transferred, deponent has been in New Orleans frequently since, deponent resided near New Orleans from 1816 to 1818, when he removed his family to the north deponent has been here frequently since deponent never said anything, that is, never took any judicial proceeding relative to this matter, because he had no interest in it Deponent was the protector of Myra Clark, who lived in deponent's family until she was married the girl considered herself the daughter of deponent, and went by his name deponent has possession of papers to show Daniel Clark's acknowledgment of her as his daughter deponent did not consider himself to be her legal guardian, and did not wish to wound her feelings by disclosing to her that she was not deponent's daughter, this was another reason why deponent never did any thing in relation to said matter About a year before her marriage said Myra Clark discovered that she was the daughter of Daniel Clark deponent entrusted the keys of his desk to her while he was absent and she there found and read her father's letters Previous to this occurrence, Daniel Clark deposited with deponent notes and titles to property to a large amount, for the benefit of Myra Clark they were put in bank in a trunk, as a special deposit to the order of deponent who gave a receipt for them when Clark returned, deponent gave them up to him again deponent took the money as a matter of friendship, and to oblige D Clark and his daughter Deponent was very intimate with Clark, and his daughter came into deponent's family when she was only eight days old

Clark had never offered witness any thing before but as she was now coming to an age when she must go to school Clark insisted on deponent's receiving the money deponent received it very unwillingly on these conditions it was absolutely forced on deponent Samuel Elkins was deponent's commercial agent in 1814 and 1815, deponent settled his account with him but did not receive the note when he settled his account with him Deponent was in partnership with Clark in a rope-walk, but had no moneyed transactions with him The first page and a half of a memorandum of notes receivable hereto annexed, is in hand writing of Daniel Clark

Direct examination resumed,

Myra Clark came of age about a year before she married, and she was married in September, 1832

SAMUEL B DAVIS.

Subscribed and sworn, this 3d March 1834

C. WATTS

The above deposition and examination was reduced to writing
by me   C. WATTS

I hereby certify that the foregoing deposition, reduced to writing by me were signed by the said S. B. Davis, in my presence and that the reason for taking the same was that the said Davis was about to go out of the District of Louisiana and to a greater distance than one hundred miles from the place of trial of the above action that the notice hereto affixed was issued by me and the defendant Relf, with L. C. Duncan, appeared to cross examine the witness

Witness my hand at the city of New Orleans this 22d day of March 1834   C. WATTS,

Judge of District Court in Louisiana

MEMORANDUM OF NOTES RECEIVABLE

Robert Munson's 4 notes dated 22d Nov 1809, with interest at 6 per cent $880 each		$3 520
Robert Semple — — , Note 3d February, Catherine Turnbull (due 1st Nov 1812		6 687 15
deld to Nott Gen Wade Hampton, 25th Feb		
Do 1811 payable in 1 year remained		50 000
Do Note of ditto same date D C		6 000
		56 000
Held D C W Hampton's 4 notes 19 May 1812, with interest at 6 per cent $3956 each		15 824
D C F Claiborne's note 18th Nov, 1811,		6 557 02
D C Ditto ditto		6 887 68
deld D C Wade Hampton's note 25th Feb 1811 for		5 000
Ditto ditto		1 500
Baron Boissontaine's ditto 7th March 1811, for		2 500
Levi Wells 4 notes of 1st Jan 1812 with interest 1000 each		4 000
S B Davis ditto 20th March 1812		2 361
Wm Witherspoon's 5 notes 1st Jan 1812 with interest for 600 each,		3 000
D C Edward Randolph's, 22d Nov 1811 for		12,321 42
one to D C Henry Hunt's 4 notes with interest, 15th March, 1810, of $3 125 each,		12,500
D C Henry Hunt's note		300
D C Patrick Walsh's 3 notes of 2d Aug 1808, for $500 each,		1,500

D C	John H Johnson's note 11th Nov 1811	3676 6.
	Jos Jenkins note 11th April at 6 months favor G Musson	600
	Mary Earle's note 31st March 1812, favor Mrs E Brooks at 12 months	500
	David Smith's note 7th April 1812 favor H Monroe & Co 12 months	150
Disco	P Derbigny's note 10th Jan 1809 D C, at 4 years,	965
Bank	Anto Orso's note, 27th Dec 1810, favor Madame Veuve Orso, at 2 years,	600
	Ditto, favor ditto 3 years	600
	Lockett & Carleton's note 13th May, 1812 payable 1st May, 1812	231
	Thos Villanueva's note 1st April, 1810 our favor, at one year	200
	Wm. S Marc's note, favor C B Defem of 6th July 1810	1000
	Francis Wood's note 3d March 1808, favor Sanderson & White	4576 69
Dr Towles	John Thompson (Jr) note, favor Geo Grery Jr 8th Feb 1810 (Delivered Doctor Towles for collection)	600

$18033 76

Mem referred to in deposition taken 31 March 1834 in W
W Whitney and wife vs Chew & Relf

                                    C WATTS

Offered by defendants and filed 3d July 1849

                J W GURLEY Commissioner

Sepase que yo Da Maria Carriere muger legitima y Apda
Generalde Du Geronimo DesGrange vecina de esta ciudad,
otorgo que vendo realmte Du Pasqual Pavillet de este comercio y vecindad un negro nombrado Pedro de como cincuenta y
ocho anos de edad que pertenece a mi merido por haberlo comprado a Du Louis Forneret, por escra en este Archivo digo
ante Dn Franco Broutin, fecha tres de agosto de mil setecientos
noventa y seis, par captivo, sugeto a servir, sano y sin tachas,
por libre de gravamen, comolo certifica el presente escno Anotador, en precio de trescientos pesos que he recivido de contada
à mi voluntad, renuncio la excepcion de la non numerata pecunia y otorgo formal recivo mediante lo qual me aparto de la
propriedad, posesion util, dominio, Senora, y demas acciones
leales y personales que a dho esclavo havia y tenir, que cedo y
transfiero en el comprador y en quien su dro y causa hubiere

para que como propri... lo p...sea o enagene ... su voluntad, por
esta escr... que le otorgo en s...al de real entreg... con lo que
es visto haver ...l...am... l... p... on sin o...ra prueb... de que lo
relevo y me oblig... a l... ... ...sa y ... m... anto de esta y... t... en
to la forma de drecho ... y e .... presente yo el nommad... D
Pasqual P...llet acepto est... e... ...y recivo comprador... esclavo,
en la cantidad y conf...rmi...d... que me va vendido, de el me doy
por entregado y otorgo for ma... recivo. En cuio testimo es fecha
en esta ciudad de la N... Orl...ns... a seis de Noviembre de mil
ochocientos y un años. Yo el escmo doy fe conosco a los otor-
g...ntes que firmaron ...endo testigos Dn. Celesino Lavergne,
Dn. Fernando Percy y don Facundo de Ayala vecinos y presentes

(Firmado)— Marie Carriere DesGrange — P Paillet
Ante mi Pedro P...di... ... y Esmo Pubco

Concuerda con el ... o o ...gin...l que queda en el archivo de mi
cargo a que me remito, en fe de lo que yo firmo el presente. A
Nueva Orleans a viente y nueve de Junio de mil ochocientos
quarenta y nueve

[L S]   LOUIS T CAIRE, Not Pub

[No 115]
Offered by defendants, and filed 3 July 1849
J W GURLEY, Comr

Sep...se que yo Da Maria Zulima Carriere, muger lexitima y
Apoderada Gral de Dn Geronimo DesGrange, como const... del
poder que le otorgo ante Dn Narciso Broutin, en viente y seis
de Marzo del corr...te año, otorgo que vende realmente a da Josefa
Moreno de esta m...zma vecindad una negra nombrada Maria
Marta de como treinta y tres años de edad que me p...rtenece por
haverla comprado m... p...derdante Dn Jose Navar...o por escr...
en este Archivo, en viente y nueve de Abril del ... o anterior,
por cauptiva sugeta a servir tal que se comporta, sin que pued...
repitir de redhis...tor... dolo ni quanto minor y en tiempo alguno,
libre de grabamen, como lo certifica el presente escmo. Anotador,
en precio de s...scientos pesos f...ertes del cuño Mexicano, de los
quales he recivido qu...trocientos de contado a mi voluntad, y de
cuio numeracion real y efectiva entrega yo el escmo doy fe, por
haverse hecho a mi presencia y la de los testigos instrumentales,
y los doscientos pesos dicho especie restantes que me devera satisfacer y pagar en el termino de tres meses de la fecha mediante
lo qual me aparto de la propriedad, posesion util dominio Seno-
rio, y demas acciones reales y personales que a dha esclava havia
y tenia que cedo y transfero en la compradora y en quien su drecho y causa hub ere para que como propria la posea o enagene à
su voluntad, par esto escr... que le otorgo en señal de real entrega,
con lo que es visto haver ...quirido la posesion, sin otra prueva

de que la relevo, y me obligo a la eviccion y saneamiento de esta
venta en toda forma de derecho. Y estando presente yo la nominada Dn Josefa Moreno acepto esta escra y recivo comprada
la esclava en la cantidad y conformidad que me va vendida de
ella me doy par entregado y otorgo formal recivo. Y me obligo
a satisfacer y pagar el plazo señalado lo doscientos pesos fuertes
del cuño Mexicano, que resulto deudora llanamente y sin pleito
alguno, y para mayor seguridad sin que la general obligacion
deroque la especial, ni por el contrario hypoteco especial y señaladamte la misma esclava que me va vendida que prometo no
vender ni en manera alguna enagenar hasta el real y efectivo
payo en cuio testimonio es fho en esta ciudad de la Na Orleans
a veinte y nueve de Octubre de mil ocochientos y un años. Yo
el esceno doy fe conosco a las otorgantes que firmo la vendedora
y por la compradora que dijo no saver a su ruego, una de los
testigos, que lo fueron Dn Celestino Lavergne Dn Fernando
Percy, y Dn Jacinto de Ayala, vecinos y presentes.

(Firmado,)—Marie Carriere DesGrange—Jacinto de Ayala

Antemi PEDRO PEDESCLAUX, Esceno Publico.

Concuerda con el auto que queda en el protoco de mi cargo,
a que me remito. En fe de lo que yo firmo el presente Nueva
Orleans a veinte y nueve de Junio de mil ochocientos cuaraenta.
y nueve

[L S]   LEWIS T CAIRE Not Pub

[No 116]

Offered by defendants, and filed 3d July, 1849

J W GURLEY Comr

En la ciudad de la Nueva Orleans a trece de Enero de mil
ochocientos y dos, ante mi el escribano y testigos, parecio Dn
Sinforiano Caillavet, apoderado substituido de Dn Guillermo
DesGrange a quien doy fe, conosco y dijo ha recivido de Da
Josefa Moreno doscientos pesos que debia a su poderdante por
escritura en este archivo, fha veinte nueve de Octubre del año
anterior, de que se da por entregado a su voluntad y de cuia numeracion real y efectivo entrega, yo el escrivano doy fe por haberse hecho en mi presencia y la de los testigos instrumentales
mediante lo qual da por rota y chancelada la obligacion e hipoteca y consiente se anote lo conducente, asi lo otorgo y firmo
Siendo testigos Dn Celestino Lavergue, Dn Fernando Percy y
Dn Jacinto de Ayala, vecinos y presentes.

(Firmado,)   SIMPHO CALLAVET

Antemi PEDRO PEDESCLAUX, Esceno Publico.

Concuerda con el auto original que queda en el archivo de mi
cargo, a que me remito, en fe deloque yo firmo el presente, a

Nueva Orleans a ciete y nueve de Junio de mil ochcientos cuarenta y nueve

[L S]   LEWIS T CAIRE, Not Pub

[No 108]

Offered by defendants and filed 21st August 1849
                         J W GURLEY Com'r

Original draft for decree

GAINES & DWITT vs PATTERSON

This cause having come on for final hearing by the consent of the complainants and the defendant Patterson, upon the bill, answer replication exhibits depositions and documents on file herein and the admission of the parties that the estate in controversy in this cause exceeds in value the sum of two thousand dollars and the said complainants and the defendant, Patterson expressly waiving and dispensing with the necessity of any other parties to the hearing or decision of this cause than themselves, and agreeing that the cause shall be determined alone upon its merits, and the court being now sufficiently advised of and concerning the premises doth finally decree and order, that the defendant Patterson do on or before the first day of the next term of this Court convey and surrender possession to the complainant Myra Clark Gaines all those lots or parcels of land lying and being in the city of New Orleans, and particularly described in his answer and exhibits and to which he claims title under the said will of 1811 Said conveyance shall contain stipulations of warranty against himself only and those claiming under him

It is further decreed and ordered that the defendant pay the complainant so much of their costs expended herein as has been induced by reason of his being made a defendant in the cause from which decree the defendant prayed an appeal to the Supreme Court of the United States, which is granted And by consent of the complainant bond and security is dispensed with By consent a copy of records of the Probate Court, with a full and complete transcript of the proceedings had in relation to the estate of the late Daniel Clark on file in said Court, (hereafter to be filed) is to constitute a part of the record herein

[No 169]

Offered in evidence by defendants and filed, this 30th Oct , 1849
                         J W GURLEY, Com'r

UNITED STATES OF AMERICA
DEPARTMENT OF STATE

To all to whom these presents shall come—Greeting

I certify, that the paper hereunto annexed, is a true copy, transcribed from and carefully collated with the original papers on file in this department , being a statement of letters written by

Daniel Clark, Esq, consul of the United States, for the port of New Orleans, showing to whom they are addressed from what place the month day of the month and year

In testimony whereof I John M Clayton Secretary of State of the United States have hereunto subscribed my name, and caused the seal of the department of State to be affixed

Done at the city of Washington this sixteenth day of October A D 1849 and of the Independence of the United States of America the 74th

[L S]   JOHN M CLAYTON

Statement of letters on the files of the Department of State written by Daniel Clark, Esq, consul of the U States for the port of New Orleans, showing to whom they are addressed from what place, the month, day of the month and year

To whom addressed	From what place	Month	Day of month	Year
James Madison,	New Orleans,	June	22d	1802
Elijah Cushing,	"	"	1st,	
James Madison	River Mersey	December	23	"
————————,	New Orleans,	March	8	1803
James Madison,	"	"	12	
"	Natchez,	"	24,	'
"	New Orleans,	April	27,	"
Gov'r Claiborne,	"	May	3,	"
James Madison,	"	"	"	'
"	"	"	13,	'
"	"	"	14,	"
'	'	'	17,	'
Brig'r Gen'l Wilkinson,	"	"	29,	"
James Madison,	"	June	1,	"
"	"	'	2,	"
Gov'r Claiborne,	"	"	3,	'
James Madison,	"	'	20,	'
"	"	July	1,	"
"	"	'	16,	'
Fulwar Skipwith,	"	"	20,	"
James Madison,	"	"	21,	"
"	"	"	26,	"
"	"	August	12.	"
"	"	"	17,	"
"	"	"	18,	'
"	"	"	20,	"
"	"	"	26,	"
Don Andrew Lopez de Armesto,	"	September	6,	"
Governor Claiborne,	"	"	7	"

James Madison,	"	'	8,	"	
"	"	"	"	'	
Governor Claiborne,	'	"	20,	'	
James Madison,	"	"	22,	"	
"		"	29,	"	
Albert Gallatin,	.	"	"	'	
James Madison,	'	"	'	'	
"	"	October	4	"	
"		"	6,		
"	"	"	13,	'	
'	"	"	20	"	
"	"	.	21,	.	
"	"	November	3,	"	
Don Monoel Salcedo, Gov'r of Louisiana, }	"	"	"	"	
Governor Claiborne,	"	"	7,	'	
—————————,	"	"	"	"	
James Madison,	"	"	8,	"	
Gov'r Claiborne,	"	"	9,	"	
"	"	"	"	"	
James Madison,	"	"	10,	"	
Governor Claiborne,	"	"	"	"	
"	"	"	"	"	
'	"	"	"	"	
"	"	"	11,	"	
"	"	"	14,	"	
"	"	"	15,	"	
James Madison,	"	"	16,	"	
Gov'r Claiborne,	"	'	17,	"	
"	"	"	21,	"	
.	"	"	22,	"	
"	"	"	23,	"	
"	"	"	24,	"	
"	"	"	25,	"	
James Madison,	"	"	28,	'	
Gov'r Claiborne, and Gen'l Wilkinson, }	"	"	29,	"	
James Madison,	"	"	"	"	
"	"	"	"	"	
"	"	December	3,	"	
Gov'r Claiborne, and Gen'l Wilkinson, }	"	"	6,	"	
"	"	"	12,	"	
James Madison,	"	"	13,	"	
"	"	"	31,	"	
"	"	January	24,	1804.	

[No 170]

Offered in evidence by defendants   Filed 30 Oct, 1849

J W GURLEY Com

(Copy)

RIVER MERSEY 23d December, 1802

SIR —At the very moment of departure I have received a letter from Paris, advising that General Victory, the Captain General of Louisiana, with his etat major, Mons J J Ayme, the Commissaire de Justice, with all the other officers of the new administration of that country had set off about the 11th instant, for Holland to embark for New Orleans without delay The Prefect had departed two or three days before for Rochefort to embark in a corvette, that he might arrive before, and prepare for the reception of the troops, &c I count on your indulgence to excuse the long letter I troubled you with, respecting this business, and as I shall be under the necessity of remaining some time among them to settle my private affairs I flatter myself my communications will not transpire I entreat you will favor me with your advice how to act on their arrival I am in the ship Thomas, bound direct to New Orleans, and hope to arrive a month before Victor and his army

With respect and esteem I remain, sir, your most obt servt

DANIEL CLARK

HON J'S MADISON.

It is stipulated that the foregoing is to be admitted as a true copy of the original on file in the office of Secretary of State, at Washington, and may be read in the hearing of the case of Gaines vs. Relf, Chew et al, subject to all objections to the same on the part of complainants as evidence

P C WRIGHT, Complainants' Solicitor

New Orleans, October 29, 1849

[No 1]

Filed by Defendants 20 June, 1849.

J W GURLEY, Com'r.

STATE OF LOUISIANA

PARISH OF ORLEANS, COURT OF PROBATES,
OFFICE OF THE REGISTER OF WILLS

Ne Varietur   (Signed) JS PITOT Judge

In the name of God, Amen

I, Daniel Clark, of New Orleans, do make this my last will and testament

Imprimis I order that all my just debts be paid

Second: I leave and bequeath unto my mother, Mary Clark. now of Germantown, in the State of Pennsylvania, all the estate. whether real or personal, which I may die possessed of

Third I hereby nominate and appoint my friends, Richard Relf and Beverly Chew my executors, with power to settle every thing relating to my estate

New Orleans, 20th May, 1811

(Signed) DANIEL CLARK.

Ne Varietur (Signed) JS PITOT, Judge

I do hereby certify the aforegoing to be a true and correct copy from the original last will and testament of the late Daniel Clark, deceased, and on file in the office of the Register of Wills.

In testimony whereof I have hereunto set my hand and affixed

[L S] the seal of our Court of Probates at this city of New Orleans, on this twenty-seventh day of November, in the year of Our Lord one thousand eight hundred and thirty-three and in the fifty-eighth year of the Independence of the United States of America

S BLOSSMAN,
Deputy Register of Wills

[No 2]

Offered by Defendants Filed 20 June, 1849

J W GURLEY, Comr

Be it known that this day before me John Lynd, Notary Public, in and for the city of New Orleans, personally appeared Beverly Chew and Richard Relf of this city, Esquires, who delivered to me notary an act of procuration made to them by Mary Clark of Germantown, State of Pennsylvania, and the said appearers required that the said instrument should be deposited in this my current register and remain of record to serve in case of need hereafter wherefore I now attach the said instrument to the margin of this act by my notarial seal. Thus done and passed at New Orleans, this twenty-second day of April one thousand eight hundred and seventeen, the appearers hereunto signing their names with me notary.

(Signed) RICHARD RELF,
BEV CHEW

N B—The signatures of the notary and of witnesses are wanting

ANNEX—Know all men by these presents, that I, Mary Clark of Germantown, in the county of Philadelphia, and State of Pennsylvania, widow, mother and sole heir, devisee and legatee of Daniel Clark, late of the city of New Orleans, and State of Louisiana, Esquire, deceased, have made ordained constituted and appointed, and by these presents do make ordain, constitute and appoint, and in my place and stead put and depute Beverly Chew and Richard Relf, of the city of New Orleans, merchants, and executors of the last will and testament of the said Daniel

Clark, deceased, jointly and severally to be my true and lawful attorney and attorneys, for me and in my name, to my use and in my behalf, to take possession of, and to hold all and every part and parcel of the real and personal estate of the said deceased; to manage, direct, bargain, agree for, and make sale of the same or any part thereof, to let, lease, rent or occupy the real estate, and to ask, demand, sue for and by all lawful ways and means recover and receive of and from all and every person or persons, bodies politic or corporate whatsoever, whom it shall, doth or may concern, all such sum and sums of money, debts and effects whatsoever, and of what kind soever as are or may be owing, payable or belonging to me, as sole legatee, devisee or heir at law of the said Daniel Clark, deceased, or under or by his last will and testament, whether by mortgage, bond, bill, book debt, account, contract, covenant, bargains, agreement or otherwise, by what other reason or means soever, none excepted or reserved, and to that end with whom it may concern to settle and adjust all accounts, and the balance thereof to receive, and on receipt in the premises to give one or more acquittances and discharges in due form of law, also, for me and in my name, and as my act and deed, to make, seal, execute, and deliver such act and acts, deed and deeds, as may be needful or necessary for the conveyance or assurance of any real estate, or for the letting or leasing of the same for a term of years or otherwise, or for the assignment or conveyance of any estate or effects, real or personal, and if need be to appear before any tribunals, judges and justices, in any court or courts, there to do, say, pursue, implead, arrest, attack and prosecute as occasion shall be and require, also, to compound, compromise, conclude and agree for the same, or in any way or manner respecting the premises by arbitration or otherwise, as my said attorneys, or either of them, shall think fit, and generally in the premises to do execute and perform all and whatsoever shall be requisite and necessary in as full and ample manner, to all intents and purposes, as I could do if personally present, with power of *substitution*, for all or any of the purposes herein before mentioned, and for revoking of the same hereby promising to ratify and hold for good and valid, all and whatsoever my said attorneys, or either of them, may lawfully do or cause to be done by virtue hereof.

In witness whereof, I have hereunto set my hand and seal, this first day of October, in the year of our Lord one thousand eight hundred and thirteen

(Signed)   MARY CLARK [L S.]

Sealed and delivered in the presence of us—

Mary Sweeny—Thomas Sparhawk—Dan Wm Coxe

CITY OF PHILADELPHIA, S C.

On this second day of October, in the year of our Lord one

thousand eight hundred and thirteen, before me, John Barker, Esq., Mayor of the city of Philadelphia, personally came Thomas Sparhawk who being duly sworn according to law, on his solemn oath deposes, and says that he was present and saw Mary Clark, of Germantown, in the county of Philadelphia, seal, and as her act and deed deliver the above and foregoing letter of attorney, and that he, together with Mary Sweeny and Daniel W Coxe, subscribed their names as witnesses thereto

(Signed)   THOMAS SPARHAWK

In testimony wereof I have hereunto set my hand, and caused
[L S]   the seal of the said city of Philadelphia to be hereunto affixed, the day and year above written

(Signed)   JOHN BARKER, Mayor

Recorded in my notarial register book N, folios 145 and 146,
[L S]   at Philadelphia, this fourth day of October, 1813.

(Signed)   CLEMENT BIDDLE, Not. Pub.

I, the undersigned Felix Grima, a notary public in and for the parish and city of New Orleans, duly commissioned and sworn, do hereby certify the foregoing to be a true and faithful copy of an act of deposit, and of the document annexed thereto, both extant among the records of John Lynd, late a notary public in this city, which records are now in the possession of me, the undersigned notary

In faith whereof I have hereunto set my hand and my seal of
[L S]   office, at New Orleans, on this twenty-first day of December, eighteen hundred and thirty-six

FX. GRIMA, Not Pub

[No 48]

Defendants   J W GURLEY, Com.

WASHINGTON CITY, Decem 5th, 1803

Dear Sir —I was not a little mortified at finding no letters from you, or any other of my friends in your quarter, in the mail which arrived, yesterday, from New Orleans and Natchez. Having regularly sent you our newspapers, which contain the details of our proceedings in Congress, especially such of them as relate to the newly acquired Territory of Louisiana; I have not, on that account, been so particular in my letters as otherwise I should have been. We wait for the intelligence of our being completely in possession, before we enter upon the provisions and regulations for the temporary government of the country. This will, doubtless, soon arrive, for I entertain no apprehension that there will be any serious opposition to it on the part of the Spaniards. They dare n provoke a war with us, especially under circumstances tha will leave them to contend without an ally. In the arrangements which have been made for occupying the city of New Orleans, I am apprehensive that some persons, not very agreeable to you, will present themselves among you, clothed with authority, and proud of their new duties, but you must consent to submit to and bear with it for a short time consoling yourself, as you certainly may, that it will not be of long duration If any thing should occur, unpleasant to your feelings, let me entreat you to repress them, and to act so circumspectly, as that your enemies, if you have any, can gain no advantage over you I do not mean to advise your submitting to insult or disgust for I know you have a spirit superior to such humiliation, but only that you should be more guarded in your language and deportment than it is in your temper to be   This hint is intended for your good, because your standing in the favor of our Government is now so good, that I look forward to your being offered one of the most respectable and honorable places under the new establishment, if no unfavorable representations should be made from thence to prevent it   The gentleman whom most you dislike will not be the Governor, but I flatter myself that one will be named, who will be acceptable, as unquestionably he will be respectable   It is not unlikely that the first stage of territorial Government will be established for you similar to that in the Indiana Territory, where the Governor and Judges have the most extensive powers, even to the enacting of laws, subject, however, to the revision of Congress   I hope that you will be called to the Judiciary, and if called, that you will accept it   No commissioner of limits will be immediately appointed   There must first be some convention or adjustment with the Spanish Government, relative to boundaries, and hitherto they have been in too bad temper about this cession, to admit even of our proposing it to them

I shall inform you, from time to time, of any transactions here, which may interest you, and must entreat you not to forget that you have a friend in me, to whom you ought to write more frequently   Have you made any operation, of the kind hinted at in your letter, in which you consider, or are disposed to consider, me concerned?   I left it to you, in my answer, to act as you pleased, upon the occasion   Are any of my acquaintance, especially the females, about to leave the city and country, in consequence of the change of Government?   Will Col Andre and Madame Sestine A remain?   The other Madame Andre must necessarily continue there, to look after her immense property   Let me know what movements are making, and what changes taking place with you   Are you and the prefect on better terms?   He has had, I am told, an open rupture with Gen Beurthe, whom he wished to send back to France

When do you mean to visit our country?

Do not neglect to present, in my name, to Mr. and Mrs. Hulings, the assurances of my most grateful remembrance and best wishes and believe me to be with sincere esteem, dear sir,

Your very humble servant,

JONA DAYTON

Dan'l Clark, Esq

[No 46]

Offered by defendants, and filed 25th June, 1849

J W GURLEY, Com'r

Natchez, 20th Dec'r, 1803.

Dear Sir I have received your favor of the 11th I am a good deal mortified that my cotton is not so good as I thought I had reason to expect and I would yet fain hope, that it may be a few bales of the last picking, which have first presented themselves to view, the latter cotton cannot be so fair as that of the middle season While my cotton was ginning it was much thought off by many who saw it Mr Wall (the friend of Mr Donaldson,) then here, was inclined to offer me 17 per (the curt price here, then was only 15 a 16), but I was then looking for better times if, nevertheless, it presents no better appearance, upon further examination, or that its reputation is already hurt so as to injure the sale, I would propose that we get clear of this parcel by remitting it to Philadelphia, where I have a payment to make, in hopes that the next parcel I send you will present a better aspect By the first opportunity, then, I will send you 50 more bales of cotton, those you have, please to ship by the first good vessel consigned to Messrs Matthew Pearce and James Crawford of Philadelphia, for my account and risk I must here stop short and make my apology for imposing this trouble upon you, my distance from N O has frequently obliged me to have recourse to one friend or another for similar services If you think it prudent to order insurance, please to write to those gentlemen to that effect, and send me one copy of the bill of lading, which I will forward by post I have a prospect of sending you this week a 2d remittance of 50 bales of cotton I have endeavored to be more than usually careful, this year, in picking my cotton, but it is nearly impossible to have the latter cotton quite pure There is an excellent improvement just made by a Mr Mills, which seems to take out nearly all the false green seeds, and shakes off the dirt and broken leaves The inventor has been here with me, and as he goes down, (he lives below the line,) I will get him to call and show Seeders how the improvement is to be made It is extremely simple, being nothing but a kind of grate or comb of wood, which joggles off (if I may use the expression) the impurities which lightly adhere to the cotton, just before it reaches the brush, its advantages are highly spoken of I am sensible we must be generally more careful, in order to recall the reputation of our cotton

With respect to the address in the Nat Intelligencer, we all wish it had been suppressed, now that we find no opposition was meditated, but what was to be expected from the ambassador's remonstrance, but that resistance and opposition, on the part of Spain were to be erected at New Orleans, against the demands of our commissioners'

From what you tell me, I suppose the calculation made by me, of the population of Louisiana, is too high   I was guided by Vidal, Minor and Walker, but I was careful in noting to the President, that it was to be considered only as conjectural, and to be corrected by your subsequent information   Your state- ment of the late census of the Atacapas, so far exceeding former accounts, has, I suppose, given some countenance to my list, and I am of opinion, it cannot do harm, but rather may be useful in pointing out the necessity of an augmented military establish- ment to assist the civil government of the province.

I have had Rees again with me, he has delivered me Bruin s and Truly's obligations, the former is accompanied by an am- ple mortgage.   I told Rees, that I must also have a mortgage with Truly's obligation, he replied, that the objects sold Truly, in order to raise this payment for you, are yet unconveyed to Truly, his bargain being that the sales will be made as soon as the money is paid; I then observed that nothing can prevent that same property being mortgaged to you, conditioned that the mortgage shall be released the moment Truly pays his obligation to you.   Rees observed, that all he has, nearly, is already mort- gaged to you, and was in doubt, whether the objects sold to Truly might not be included in your mortgage, which might have been his reason for selling conditionally, viz   that the money should be paid to you, before a conveyance, I desired he would exam- ine into that, for the condition of your indulgence was a security on the objects sold to Truly, in addition to the mortgage you held upon Rees' property, which was never to be released until the last farthing was paid   He went away, with a promise, that if the objects were not already included in his mortgage to you, he would immediately return and have it done   Rees' mortgage not being deposited with me, I could not have recourse to it my- self.   I often see Greenfield, and remind him of his payment to be made to you, he constantly promises me that as soon as his cotton is ready, he will send it to you, and seems more willing that you should forward it to Europe, on his own account, than take the country price, which, I suppose, will be equally agree- able to you   In all this transaction, I have been careful to pro- ceed only by your own instructions, and above all things, have been mindful of the good mercantile rule—to augment, but never to diminish a security.   We are now prepared to take notice of Harding's information to our good friend Mr. Turner.   I have been lately told from several quarters, that Harding takes every opportunity of saying unfavorable things of me. It is **very diffi-** cult for me to guess at the cause, because I have never ceased to treat him in a very friendly style, and he is the only attorney I ever employed for myself. I can only just surmise that he is offended at the *cold water* I threw upon Murray's proposition to aid your cause against the Moores, for a fee of 800 dollars, by which, no doubt, he conceives that he will himself, be disappoint- ed in receiving a like sum. I have also some idea, that he con- ceives me to be the cause of your new arrangement with Rees, by which (from his expressions, I judge) he may think himself delayed in seizing upon a commission.

Harding has been the grand promoter of petitions from the corporation, and from the citizens of the town of Natchez, to Con- gress, for what they call vacant lots and land within the limits of their city. they have also gotten a number of volunteer declara- tions, certifying that Gayoso had always insinuated that the green or commons, in front of the town should be kept for the use of the town, and should never be granted to individuals for the pur- pose of building houses. I need not tell you that this is the same which was granted to me. I have written on to our own dele- gate, (who I believe, is also against me, being a citizen of Nat- chez,) and to other members of Congress, pointing out the im- propriety of granting the prayer of the petition until the commis- sioners shall decide upon the legality of the titles of individuals, covering the lands within said city.

As to Ferral and Douglass, the only occasion upon which their names were ever mentioned was when Rees came forward with Brum & Truly's notes, and a promise of Greenfield's, to the full amount of the debt. he had also in his possession a note of 1500 dollars, from Ferral & Douglass in favor of B. Truly, and asked whether that note would be taken in lieu of so much to be paid by Truly. I told him, no, that I must have a security with Truly's note, and that I would have nothing to do with the other, unless he chose to deposit it as an additional security.

As to what Mr. Turner says of Pendergrast and the heirs of Carpenter, it is the first news I have had, nor do I clearly un- derstand how any such transaction can be carried on in silence; if any thing was delivered to Secders he would certainly adver- tise me. Dor. Pendergrast is gone down with the militia, and you can enquire into the truth of the report. if either of those had brought forward any demands well founded, I should have paid them or made arrangements for that purpose, otherwise, I should have written to you for authority to admit or reject, as I did in the case of Dor. Todd.

You have expressed a wish that I would not even hint to Turner, that I have seen his letter. I wish to be released from

24*

that injunction. We are on so good a footing, that there is no possibility of offence arising from such a circumstance Mr. Turner conducts himself always as your zealous friend I would, therefore, be much to blame, not to communicate every thing which I may conceive affecting your interest, if he is to blame in any thing, it is in not communicating his discoveries to me. From our mutual attachment to you, Mr T. and myself have always been extremely friendly, I am, therefore, desirous of communicating with him freely, and guarding him against Harding's insinuations

Your last letter came without a wafer or seal of any kind, but I do not believe there was time for any body to look into it, because I sent a messenger with letters for the northern mail immediately after the N O courier passed upwards

I have a letter from Philadelphia, which says, it is reported that Mr. Dawson is to be Governor of Louisiana, some of the newspapers say, it is a Mr Venable, of Virginia Gen'l Wilkinson wrote me in confidence, that he has it from the Secretary at War, confidentially, and, therefore, you have it from me as a profound secret, that W C. C C returns to his own government. and that Louisiana is to be divided into two territorial governments, upper and lower Louisiana The General must not know that I have betrayed him, but I cannot conceal it from you. He will certainly tell you himself   Your faithful

WILLIAM DUNBAR

You will remember that the commissioners of land claims are now sitting at the town of Washington, and that all our titles must be presented before the 1st of April next. The commissioners require that translations be made of any thing in a foreign languag , before the patents and chain of title be presented before their board   I am told they are not much flattered with the residence chosen for them at the town of Washington, by our Governor, and have written to the President to be allowed to adjourn their sittings to any place they please, which, it is supposed, will be Natchez

Do me the favor to place my name with the French and English editors, as a subscriber to their papers, in your city

To Daniel Clark, Esq , New Orleans.

[No 164.]
Offered by defendants, and filed
J. W GURLEY, Commissioner.

Testament de Simphorien Caillavet

Au nom de Dieu, amen Je, soussigné, Simphorien Caillavet, natif de la Paroisse de St. Profet, à Bordeaux, fils legitime de Joseph Caillavet, avocat en la Cour de Bordeaux, et de Dame Marie Fousal, ses pères et mères décédés. Etant sain d'esprit et de corps, en mon entier jugement et mémoire, craignant la mort, qui est naturelle à toute creature, je veux mettre ordre a mes affaires temporelles, et faire mon testament, et pour la plus grande validite et sureté j'invoque pour mon avocate la Soveraine Reine des Anges, Marie Notre Dame, pour qu'elle intercède pour moi auprès de son cher fils, notre Seigneur Jesus Christ, pour qu'il me pardonne la grandeur de mes péchés, et reçoive mon ame au rang de celle des bien heureux Elus avec cette priere et divine invocation, j'ordonne et octroge le présent, mon testament, et ordonnance de mes dernières volontés, de la maniere suivante

Je recommende mon âme au même Dieu qui me l'a donnée, crée, et rachettée, avec le prix et valeur infinie de son sang precieux, Passion et Mort, et je le supplie, que par la divine miséricorde, il daigne la pardonner

J'ordonne que mon corps soit mis en terre, de laquelle il a été forme, et quand je mourrai, je veux etre enseveli de la manière la plus simple, et qu'il me soit donné la sepulture dans le lieu et endroit, que mon executeur testamentaire, que je nomme ci-après, trouvera convenable

Item J'ordonne qu'il me soit dit les trois messes pour le repos de mon ame, et qu'il soit donne deux escalins à chacune des demandes forces pour etre ainsi ma volonte

Item Je declare être marie à Marie Rose Carrière, fille legitime de Monsieur Carriere, natif de Libourne, et de Marie Gooferte, née à Bordeaux, decedes, de laquelle femme j'ai eu plusieurs enfans, dont trois existent, savoir. Simphorien Guillaume Caillavet, agé de seize ans, Beltran Latour Caillavet, âgé de quatorze ans, Louis Arbaud Caillavet, age de douze ans, que je reconnais être mes enfans legitimes, nes de mon mariage avec la susdite, lesquels j'institue mes seuls et uniques héritiers par égale portions, pour qu'après ma mort ils héritent de mes biens avec la bénédiction de Dieu et la mienne, car c'est ainsi ma volonte Item Je nomme et institue mon executeur testamentaire la personne de sieur Jacques Moulon habitant de cette ville, a qui je donne le pouvoir aussi ample, que le requiert le droit, pour que par lui-meme, et sans qu'aucune justice intervienne, liquide ma succession, fasse l'inventaire, estimation, vente et partage de mes biens, nommant pour l'estimation deux personnes a sa satisfaction, et le tout conclu, qu'il le présent à un tribunal compétent pour être approuvé, le relevant de tout cautionnement Je revoque et annule, donne pour nul, d'aucune valeur, ni effet, tout autre testament, codicile, pouvoir ou dispositions tester qu'avant celui-ci, j'ai fait par écrit ou de parole, lesquels je veux ni fesant aucune foi en justice, ni hors, a l'exception de celui-ci, que j'ordonne, et pretends qu'ils valide comme mes dernieres volontés.

Item. Connaissant l'incapacité de ma femme dans les affaires,

je crains de compromettre l'intérêt de mes enfans en la char-
geant de leur tutelle, mais je declare lui connaitre dans tous
toutes les vertues qui doivent caractériser son sexe, c'est por-
quoi, je nomme pour tuteur de mes enfans Monsieur M. François Joseph Le Breton Dorgeais, habitant de cette ville, ancien
alcade ordinaire, le relevant de tout cautionnement

Item Mes biens consistent en Europe, en un bien de campagne, dans la Paroisse de Cardignard tout envigonnés
qu'autres terres cultivables, et landes detachées, par, une maison,
rue Bouquière et faire en la rue Veuve bornant dans le dernier
le cimitière de la Pooisse de Sent Colombe, une autre maison
hors la Porte S' Julien, rue Guérard a coté la rivière Ancien
Chanon

Item Je possède dans cette colonie une maison, rue Bourbon
une negresse domestique, nommée Julie, et mille piastres,
gourdes, en caisse dans ce moment

Item Si ma maison que j'ai intention de vendre, ne se vend
pas a mon décès, je veux et ordonne qu'il reste pour le loge-
ment de ma femme avec la negresse Julie, dont elle ne pourra
pas disposer sans vente ou autrement, ne lui laissant que l'usu-
fruit de la dite maison, qui est reversible à nos enfans après nos
décès

Item Elle pourra disposer de la negresse Julie, que j'estime
a la somme de huit cent gourdes, pour se remplir d'une somme
de six cents trente piastres de l'héritage de ses père et mères
ici, et de cent vingt-neuf piastres, qui m'ont été remis dernièrement par Monsieur Desgrange, provenant d'une partie de la succession de ses pères et mères en France

Item. Voulant que mes enfans soient envoyés en France,
adresser, par mon exécuteur testamentaire, a mes freres et a
ma sœur, denommés ci-dessus, et que leur passage soit payé
sur la somme en argent dans ma caisse

Item Je déclare ne devoir rien à qui que ce soit dans ce pays
ni ailleurs

Item Je nomme pour curateur ad litem, celui que jugera à
propos mon exécuteur testamentaire

Item Si après mon décès, mon epouse désirait passer en
France avec ses enfans, je donne ordre a mon exécuteur testamentaire de vendre la maison et la negresse Julie, ainsi que
tous les objets qui ne pourront point se transporter, mon epouse
ne se réservant que l'absolu necessaire pour son voyage, l'argent
du produit de la vente de toutes les choses mentionnées, sera
converti en denrees du pays, que seront adressés à mes freres, à
l'exception de ce qui faudra payer pour son passage, et d'une
somme de deux cents piastres, qui lui seront comptées pour avoir
les douceurs de son voyage

A la Nouvelle Orleans ce dix-neuf Juillet, mil huit cent deux
Signe,   SIMPHORIEN CAILLAVET

I certify the above to be a true copy from the records of the
late Probate Court   J BRIERRERE D'y Clerk

[No 47]
Offered by defendants and filed 25th June, 49
      J W GURLEY, Com'r

CITY OF WASHINGTON, October 22d, 1802

DEAR SIR —The treaty and conventions with the French Republic (as they still ludicrously style themselves,) were ratified, or rather approved by th Senate yesterday, and this morning received the ratification of the President I shall procure and enclose a copy of them that you may know what is to be your future destiny You will be surprised to hear that the Spanish government both in Europe and in this country have formally remonstrated against our purchase of the Province of Louisiana, and Island of New Orleans In the protest which they make to our Government against the ratification, they roundly and unequivocally charge the French Government with violation of faith and breach of promise, inasmuch as assurances had been given, as they aver that France would never part with it They also declare that the cession to us cannot be valid, because the conditions which were to entitle France to the possession of it were never fulfilled, and that consequently, having herself no title, she could convey none All this, and much more, is now unblushingly said notwithstanding the Royal order had been for some time previously given, and put into the hands of General Victor, and the Marquis of Casa Calvo had been sent out expressly character of Commissioner of Limits, to perform the ceremony handing over the possession, and altho' their own proclamation already avowed it There is not much danger that the Spanish officers will resist our troops coming to take possession, unless, indeed, they should be stimulated to send an additional force from the Havannah Even in this case they must be eventually unsuccessful because the whole force of the country   called forth, and directed to the effecting of that object, sooner   we would submit to its loss It will be in your power,   than in that of any other man to sound their intentions, to observe their movements, and to acq our Government and Gen Wilkinson of the result of your enquiry and observation It is unnecessary to say more, for it would be madness in them to attempt to resist us, possessing so good a title, and deter   to enforce it The question of limits, both on the ea   western boundary will become a serious one between   and us, as it would have been between them and France   not be allowed to possess the strip between **Manschac** or **Iberville** and our boundary West

Florida was understood by the French Government to be included in the cession, and we   entitled to as much. This will carry us to the Apalachicola The Rio Grande or Rio del Norte would have been insisted upon by France as the western boundary, and not a foot must be yielded to them there If we should ever consent to be bounded by the river Mexicano, the Adayes, and the Missour', it must be in consequence of an exchange of what we justly claim west of that line, for all that the Spaniards own or claim east of the Mississippi

Your name has been mentioned in such terms, and so ap   well received, that I flatter myself you will certainly be appointed as one of two or three commissioners for ascertaining the true limits of the ceded territory, if such a commission should be established, of which, however, I have very little doubt It is yet uncertain what system of government will be adopted for that country, but I am inclined to think that it will be temporary and provisional, intended to operate for one year only, in order to afford time for ac   more perfect knowledge of the temper, disposition, situation, numbers, &c, of the inhabitants, than can immediately be obtained. What form of government do you believe best adapted to that people? What plan of policy would be, in your opinion, the most advisable, in respect to them? Communicate to me freely your sentiments and your views, for you know my confidence in, and my friendship for you Write to me often, especially whilst Congress shall remain in session, which will be until sometime in March, perhaps until the month of April. Inform me of every occurrence that you may think sufficiently interesting, especially those which are connected with the cession to us, and our possession and government of the ceded territory.

I will not trouble you here with what relates to me personally, but must take leave to refer you to my letter addressed to Mr. Patton, which goes by this mail. You and my other friends will therein perceive a short, satisfactory explanation of the cause and probable result of the temporary embarrassment experienced by the house of trade in New York, in which I had an interest. My own separate and private fortune will not be affected ultimately or materially by it.

Is it true that the Prefect is to come here as   How do you agree, now. Is your rope-walk and other property placed by him under requisition, again restored? How is the Marquis of Casa Calvo? Is he pleased or displeased with the new arrangement?

Tell Madame S André that I shall never forget her polite attentions, and present me in respectful terms to her and to the Colonel, and believe me, your friend, &c.,

JONA. DAYTON.

DANL. CLARK, ESQ.

[No 49]
Offered by defendants, and filed 25th June, 1849

J W GURLEY, Com

City of Washington, October 31st, 1803.

Dear Sir —In my former letter, you were advised of the ratification of the treaty with France, for the purchase of Louisiana, and I have now to inform you, that this day has been passed the bill authorizing the President to take possession of the country, and estab'ish a temporary Government therein A copy shall be enclosed, if I can procure it before the departure of our expr s In the course of this session, it is intended, as you can perce 'e by this law, that Congress shall mature and pass other acts, or the more permanent Government of the newly acquired territories of which I will give you regular information

So numerous are we become, that it is impossible to ascertain, before hand, what those provisions will be, but I am much inclined to believe that, for the present, they will adopt and establish a form somewhat similar to that which has been heretofore established in the first stage of our territorial Governments.

I had a long conversation, last evening, with the President, confined, almost entirely, to the policy most proper to be observed towards Louisiana, and the means of taking and retaining possession of it No time will be lost in possessing ourselves of it, for if the Spaniards should venture to resist, we must only apportion our force to their means of resistance, and seize it even at the risk of a war with them We must have it immediately, and no time can be so fit as whilst the French are engaged in war, and will consequently be passive, even if we are compelled to resort to hostile measures against their allies of Spain

I have done all in my power (as indeed, my duty, as well as my friendship, induced me to do) to impress the President with the idea of your services, and the important benefits which may be derived from your knowledge and influence He speaks of Mr Du   and yourself as the two persons from whom he had received the most satisfactory information.

I enclose the newspaper of this city, and shall continue to send you such as shall be worthy of your perusal You will hear from me again by the mail of next week. In the mean time, believe me to be, with very sincere regard,

Your very humble servant,

JONA. DAYTON.

Daniel Clark, Esq.

[No 50]
Offered by defendants, and filed 25th June, 1849.

J. W. GURLEY, Com.

Germantown, 6th December, 1803

About two weeks since, I received my dear brother's very

affectionate letter, and thank you most sincerely for dedicating so much of your time to me. The hopes you give us of seeing you, in April, has given us all the highest delight and we look forward to that time, with pleasure. Long, very long, may it be before we are again deprived of your presence. Mr Coxe came to see us, a few days and showed me part of a letter of yours, desiring us not to mention any thing about house expenses to aunt Clark, we never have my mother. I believe, spoke something to Relf, concerning it, but forbore ever hinting the subject to aunt, till your return. She is gone to Virginia, since the 10th. November and we heard from Mrs Moylan, she has got safe to her journey's end

I hope your party has proved agreeable and that your health has not suffered from *excess* of any kind, indeed the idea of your *getting in that way highly diverted us, especially* our father, who enjoyed it very much. I had long letters from Jane and Mr. G, four days since they have been in London, in consequence of Mr Barclay's failure. She was sadly frightened, lest Mr G should suffer, but he tells me he will not be injured by it. Mr Wainwright has behaved very ungentlemanlike to Susan Green ever since he came to live with them his behavior was particular, and he seemed never well but when at Crosby—all at once, he quit visiting there, without giving any reason for such conduct and addressed some other lady that Mr G disapproved of very much. Jane was appointed to speak to him, he said 'twas only a little unmeaning gallantry, and as his visits were disagreeable. he would refrain from going any more. Mr G then said something against the lady, who was then the reigning favorite, the consequence was, Mr Wainwright sent him a challenge fortunately, Mr G was not at home, and Jane had a long tête-à-tête with the gentleman who brought it, when he found him not return, he left the challenge with Jane and departed she, true womanlike, opened it, but when she found what it was, you may guess her surprise—oh! she says, how did I long for my brother to advise with him how to act, however, when Mr. G. came home, she told him. Next morning, he went to the C House, and who should be there but the gentleman who left the challenge with Jane without any apology, Mr G showed him the shortest way down stairs, and wrote an account of the affair to Mr Barclay, expressing a wish to dissolve the partnership with Mr. Wainright, but Mr W will not till the expiration of the time at first proposed. At the time the letters were wrote, they had not met, and sincerely do I hope it may be prevented Poor Susan went to London, on a visit to some of her relations, and Jane says when she went there she hardly knew her; indeed, such conduct as Mr. W.'s, in my opinion, deserves punishment —only the innocent suffers with the guilty

Mr. Earle was so polite as to come to Germantown, to know if we had any commands I thought I would let you know the circumstance that perhaps you heard before myself Mary sends a small box directed to you, which she hopes you will take the trouble of opening, and give the contents according to the direction, with her love and compliments I spoke to Mr Coxe about the carriage, as you desired me, but our mother will not hear of such a thing, she says 'tis time enough when you come home, then, if you think it necessary, you may have one, she has no idea of running into so much expense, at present Your father and her send their love to you Mary also joins The children are both well, and send their duty to you May every good attend my dear brother is the sincere wish of his affectionate sister　　　　　　　　　　　　　　　A ANDERSON

Daniel Clark, Esq, New Orleans

[No 52]
Offered by Defendants, and filed 25 June, '49

J W GURLEY, Com'r

Natchez, 28th May, 1803

DEAR SIR —This will be handed to you by General Dayton, a member of the Senate of the United States, whose public character is so respectable, and I presume so well known to you, that it is unnecessary for me to say more, than that by extending to him your polite attention you will confer a singular favor on

Dear Sir, your friend and very humble servant,

JOHN STEELE

Mr DANIEL CLARK Consul at New Orleans

[No 53]
Offered by Defendants, and filed 25 June, '49

J W GURLEY, Com'r

WASHINGTON CITY, December 12th, 1803

DEAR SIR —Your favor of the 21st ult is this moment received, and affords the satisfactory information that no preparations have been made, nor disposition shown by the Spaniards to resist our taking possession of the Louisiana territory, and acknowledge myself disappointed upon learning that your name was not associated with Gen Wilkinson's, as commissioners for the purpose, but upon expressing my astonishment that it was not, was told that the bad understanding subsisting between Mr. Laussat and yourself, was the objection to such an arrangement No insinuation has been made that any censure should attach to you on account of the difference between the Prefect and yourself, but as he is the only intermediary for the transfer of the province from Spain to us, and his good will and good offices of course essential to us, it would be advisable to abstain from the appoint-

25

ment of any gentleman on an unfriendly footing with that officer.
I agree with you that the task imposed upon these commissioners
will be an Herculean one, and I am sure they will want that assistance and advice from you, which they cannot now hope to
receive, under all circumstances of the transaction. In leaving
town, and becoming a passive spectator, as you propose, of those
interesting scenes, you will not, I am sure, throw any obstacles
in the way, nor add any thing to those difficulties already sufficiently numerous and formidable   I trust that our affairs in relation to the newly acquired territory, will hereafter be better
managed than the first provision augurs, because, neither proud
Prefects, nor capricious, unaccommodating Intendants, will stand
in   way of our future regulations.

You promise me in a few days, more particular information,
which I shall be happy to receive, and in the mean time, subscribe
myself, with real esteem,

Dear Sir, your very humble servant,

JONA DAYTON.

Daniel Clark, Esq.

[No. 56]
Offered by Defendants, and filed 25 June, 1849.

J W. GURLEY, Com'r

Washinton Crty, Nov. 14th, 1803.

Dear Sir :—I have only time to send you   papers.
Nothing has been done in   to interest you, more than has
been   in former letters.

In haste, and with   yours,   JONA DAYTON
Daniel Clark, Esq., New Orleans

[No. 57]
Offered by Defendants.   Filed 25 June, 1849.

J. W. GURLEY, Com'r

Washington City, Nov 7th, 1803,

Dear Sir —In my two preceding letters you have been advised of the ratification of the treaty with the French Republic
by the President and Senate, and of the provisions made by
Congress for taking possession of the ceded territory, and for the
temporary government of the inhabitants, until more permanent
regulations   made for that purpose   It is difficult to
form any very satisfactory conjecture respecting the system
which a majority of the two Houses will think most advisable to
adopt in relation to this newly acquired country, but, it seems
to me most probable that, for the present, they will introduce the
territorial form of government, over the lower district at least,
appoint a Governor and three judges, officers of militia, &c., as in
the territories of Mississippi and Indiana.   The further settlement

of upper Louisiana, on the west side of the river, will not be encouraged, nor even permitted, from motives of policy, which I will detail to you hereafter. When we have so far matured our projects upon this subject as to enable me to judge more accurately what the result will be, you shall be informed thereof by the earliest conveyance, and of everything connected therewith which can be interesting to you. In the meantime you will oblige me by communicating regularly by letter your opinions, views and wishes to me without reserve, believing as you really may, that I possess the best disposition to promote and further them. I cannot believe that the Spaniards will oppose by force our possessing ourselves of the country, although they have protested formally against the ratification of the treaty. Our numbers (I mean of our troops,) will be sufficient to secure us against any violence or hostility their part, although I am prepared to hear that   possession of the territory reluctantly and with very bad grace.

The boundary on this side will certainly be claimed as far as the river Perdido, and possibly to the Apalachicola, as the French themselves would have claimed, but the   limits are more uncertain, and ought, it is said, extend to the Rio Bravo or Riviere du Nord. No commission   limits will be at present appointed, or you would   if you pleased, have been one, but it is possible that   to be passed hereafter will create such an office, although   more probable that we shall defer it, until it shall be found that the Spaniards contest our claim of limits, and then   remain to be adjusted by negotiations between the two governments.

In my opinion it would be best to settle every question of this sort as quickly as possible, whilst France is actually engaged in war, and Spain, her ally, in continual fear of being involved in it, but we do not always seize upon the happy moment for doing what ought to be done. You will be so good as to give my friends Mr. Hulings and Mr Patton, the perusal of such papers as I shall from time to time send to you. Give to them and to my other friends who enquire after me, the assurance of my best regards, and belive me,

Dear sir, with sincere esteem, your very humble serv't,

JONA. DAYTON

Daniel Clark, Consul, New Orleans.

[No 59

Offered by Defendants   Filed 25 June, 1849.

J W. GURLEY, Com'r.

GERMANTOWN, August 26th, 1803.

DEAR SIR :—Since writing to you on the 12th instant, in answer to yours by Mr Relf, nothing new has occurred and still in hopes of receiving the   of the bill I am progressing in my preparations for   to Virginia I had yesterday letters from my friends there   they are all well, and express great anxiety to see me among them again

We are to remove on the first of October to a house a little way above Doctor Blan s, on the opposite side of the street, the rent of it will be much lower than the one we at present occupy, and the house and its appurtenances are much more agreeable It is at £100 a year, and the one that we inhabit is at $400 a year

We are fully flattered by Mr Relf that we shall see you here by the time of our removal, and be assured we shall then have an apartment better prepared for your reception than when we last had that pleasure

I am, dear sir, with best wishes for   ever affectionate aunt

27th.—All things under the sun are changeable ! This morning we find that we cannot get possession of the house mentioned in the foregoing, which disappoints us very much   Mr Relf can give the   to our affairs

Daniel Clark, Esq , New Orleans

[No. 60]

Offered by defendants, and filed 25th May, 1849

J W GURLEY, Com

(Copy)   New Orleans, 26th Aug't. 1803

Sir I have the honor of enclosing to you, for the information of the President, answers to such of the queries forwarded me as I could, for the present, reply to   I have not observed the order in which they were put, as some will require further time to obtain information on, and others, tho not difficult to ascertain in the gross, cannot now be inserted on account of the details with which it will be necessary to accompany them, but I hope, in a short time, to finish the remainder, and will forward them without delay.   In favor of what I now send you, I have only to allege the diligence with which I have prosecuted the inquiries, and the fidelity with which I have endeavored to select the most correct information

My friend, Mr Dunbar, of the M T, having by yesterday's post, informed me that the President had likewise forwarded to him a copy of the same queries, I shall, in a few days, send him a copy of my answers, that he may add to them what is wanting, and expunge what is faulty, and thus render the whole more useful, being pursuaded that his judgment and information are infinitely superior to mine, and that our country may be better served by submitting my ideas and opinions to the correction of a person of his talents and judgment

I shall have the honor of addressing you again, in a few days, on this subject and remain very respectfully, sir,

Your most obedient and most humble serv't,

D. C.

The Hon James Madison

[No 61]

Offered by defendants, and filed 25th June, 1849.

J W..GURLEY, Com'r

(Private) WASHINGTON, July 6, 1803.

Dear Sir Mr King has transmitted a letter to him from Messrs Livingston & Monroe, stating that on the 30th of April, a treaty was signed by them, and a French plenipotentiary, by which the Island of N Orleans, and the whole of Louisiana, as held by Spain, is obtained for the L. States No particulars are mentioned The treaty itself is every moment expected by a confidential bearer, for whom a passage was engaged at Havre on the 15th of May, in a vessel, which was to sail a few days after

I am, very respectfully, your most obed't serv't,

JAMES MADISON

Daniel Clark, Esq, Consul U S, New Orleans

[No 63]

Offered by defendants, and filed 25th June, 1849

J W GURLEY, Com

NEAR NATCHEZ, May 15th, 1803

Sir Your letter of the 22d ultimo, was duly received The statement you made to the *intendant*, upon the subject of the Mobile and Tombigbee commerce, was highly proper, and well calculated to produce a revocation of *his* late decree It seems, however, that this man is firm to his purposes, and in the exercise of his discretionary powers, no concessions, with a view to conciliation or accommodation, are to be expected.

The Executive of the United States has been fully informed of the situation of our fellow citizens on the Tombigbee; their grievances will, no doubt, command immediate attention, and to me, it seems advisable, that no representation, upon the subject of the Mobile commerce, should be made, but by and under the immediate instructions of our government

The Prefect's motives, in advising the Spanish Governor, "to let things remain as they were, until advices could be received from Europe,' will, probably, be explained in a few weeks. It is not such councel, as a sincere friend to national faith and just rights would have given, and it seems to me, to have proceeded from some treacherous design.

I thank you for the information you give me, as to a certain Indian missionary; the movements of this person will be carefully watched, and any improper interference on his part, will soon be checked, and, probably, punished.

I have understood, that Mingo Pus Coos and other Choctaw chiefs, have lately, by invitation, visited Orleans, were received with every mark of attention, and that great presents were made them, accompanied with a long and friendly talk   Will you endeavor to ascertain the views of our destined neighbors, in relation to the Indians, and advise me thereof, in order that (if necessary) I may take immediate steps to counteract them.

I am well aware of your exposed situation, and shall confine to myself, any communications you may think proper to make ; I pray you, therefore, to write freely and without reserve, and if you are only careful as to the person to whose care you commit your letters for me, *all will be well.*

I presume my despatches of the 8th instant, have reached you, and that the deposit is restored.

From my late letters from the northward, it appears, that Mr. Munroe's success is confidently expected.

I am, sir, very respectfully your ob't serv't,

WILLIAM C C. CLAIBORNE

Daniel Clark, Esq.

[No. 64]
Offered by Defendants, and filed 25 June, 1849

J. W GURLEY, Com'r.

Near Natchez, 18th Nov., 1803

Sir :—Your letter of the 11th instant has reached me, and it affords me new proofs of your zeal in promoting the interest of the country.

As Louisiana has not yet been delivered to the French Commissioner, your application to the Spanish government for permission for one or more companies of cavalry to pass by land to New Orleans, as an escort to the commissioners to that place, was well timed, and I am solicitous to receive the response. My communications by Major Trask, I presume, have reached you, and your answer will greatly influence my future conduct.

A few of the militia of this territory will accompany the regular troops from Fort Adams to New Orleans. I have reason to believe that a printer, with all the necessary apparatus, will arrive at Orleans in the course of two weeks.

I take this occasion to renew to you assurances of my confidence and respect.

WILLIAM C. C. CLAIBORNE.

Daniel Clark, Esq., Consul U. S., New Orleans.

[No. 65]
Offered by Defendants, and filed 25 June, 1849.

J W GURLEY, Com'r.

NATCHEZ, Nov 22d, 1803.

SIR —Since my letter of yesterday, I have had a conversation with M——r, the particulars of which are not sufficiently interesting to relate. In the course of the conversation it was mentioned that I should descend the river from Fort Adams, in four or five weeks, and shortly after my arrival at Orleans, I doubted not but the province of Louisiana would be delivered up, since our government seemed to be convinced that every thing would be conducted with friendship and candor.

With respect and esteem, I am sir, your humble serv't,

WILLIAM C. C CLAIBORNE

Daniel Clark, Esq., New Orleans.

[No 66]
Offered by Defendants, and filed 25 June, 1849

J W GURLEY, Com'r.

ROCKY MILLS, near Richmond, December 13th, 1803.

DEAR SIR —Since writing to you from Philadelphia on the 9th ultimo, I arrived at this place on the 21st, and found all friends well. I saw Mr. Madison, on my way, at Washington. I took the liberty of speaking to him about the land warrants which you ceded to me, and he informed me, as before, that the law must be satisfied, that there is a residium estate before the executors can give or sell to each other, though they may to a third person, and that we cannot obtain patents separately, without an authenticated copy from the records of a final settlement, expressive of our right to a residium I know you must be greatly engaged in your official affairs, but must reiterate my entreaties that you will, if possible, attend to mine : a few moments dedicated to them would arrange the whole, and give me very great satifaction. Mr. Moylan was so obliging as to advance for me $500, for which I gave him an order on Mr Coxe, payable at the expiration of the current quarter, which will be the 10th of January ; and, also, left in his hands your notes, with orders to receive any cash or bills sent forward for me, until my return, which I expect will be in April ; and I hope then as you have as well as myself desired it, that all our accounts will be arranged and finally settled I have not heard from Germantown or Philadelphia since I left it. We are all in great suspense about Louisiana. I wish with all my heart that all was once amicably arranged, we are all fearful that the affairs of that country will oblige you to change all your plans, and induce a much longer separation than any of us had ever before contemplated.

God give you health and happiness, is the prayer of your
affectionate aunt,

                                        JANE CLARK

Daniel Clark, Esq , New Orleans

                    [No 68]

Offered by defdt

                    J W GURLEY, Commissioner
                                        April 20th, 1803

' Dear Sir :—Since writing to you on the 13th, Mr Coxe has
proposed that I shall send forward the legal power to Mr Dunbar, to sell whatever you choose   of that property which is under mortgage to me, in the manner you desire, and which I will do by the mail of Friday 22d He,
likewise, promises to give me proper security for my annuity as
soon as possible I have hiterto received it punctually, and
have had from him on your account
1,000 dollars there   without interest
        for one year and   months   were so good
as to allow me by agreement I am now about sending home
my two neices to Virginia , after that is done, I shall return to
Germantown, and look forward with the rest of the family for
your arrival amongst
with pleasure
        I am your affectionate aunt,   JANE CLARK
To Daniel Clark, Esq , New Orleans

                    [No 69.]
Offered by defendants, and filed 25th June, 1849
        J W. GURLEY, Commissioner

                    NEW ORLEANS, 8th June, 1803
Dear Sir :—I have not hitherto been able to procure the
antos, relative to your affairs with Mr Morgon, but am shortly
promised them, and shall then write you further Argote denies
having ever received anything on account of this business, and
is, I believe, now employed by Morgan, in assisting him in his
other affairs, and therefore will not be molested Morgan informs me that the mortgage given by Argote was declared null
and void by Miro, but he had no authority to do this extra-
judicially, and after seeing the papers, I shall be better able to
judge. It is a flat contradiction of what Argote asserts, that he
had no interest, that he should have given this mortgage, and
Morgan's attornies ought to have insisted on its validity Morgan further informs me, that when he was last here, and you
were called to acknowledge your signature to the bond, you
confessed you justly owed this money, but pleading inability to
pay, the matter was therefore deferred A Mr. John Clay, will

in all probability be sent some time next month to **Natchez**, on this and other business of Morgan's, and I presume will **have** orders to commence a suit against you   In a few days I shall write you more particularly

I remain, dear sir, yours sincerely,

DANIEL CLARK

Mr Thomas Wilkins, Natchez

[No 70]

Offered by Defendants, and filed 25 June '49

J W GURLEY, Com'r

NEW ORLEANS PRISON, August 8th, 1803

SIR —On Thursday last I arrived here in one of his Catholic Majesty's galleys, a prisoner as is said, from the Apalaches, where I was taken on the 25th of June last, at the town where I was transacting my private business, and interfering with no other business except that of my own private affairs, brought here and plunged into close confinement, without being acquainted with the nature of my capture or imprisonment   Now, the question stated is, if the citizens of the United States abroad cannot enjoy those privileges of trade which their own government admits of, and further, where they have appointed Consuls in the different ports for the purpose of   and assistance of all such citizens as may stand in need of relief—surprises me to find myself here, debarred of my liberty, and a confined prisoner, among many other of our citizens, whose sufferings have been much greater than that of mine, and am sorry to say that they have been destitute of the least assistance even from the Consul whose sole business is here for that purpose

Now, if the citizens of the United States who have served their country, are to be treated with thus much disrespect from their Consuls, I no longer remain a true Columbian which I have been from my youth   Any thing further I shall leave to your own discretion, and remain your humble servant,

WM BURNUM, Jun'r

DANIEL CLARK, ESQ, Consul for the United States, New Orleans

[No 71]

Offered by Defendants and filed 25 June, '49

J W GURLEY, Com'r

MILITARY AGENT'S OFFICE Philadelphia, 18 Oct, 1803

SIR —Agreeably to instructions from the Secretary of War, I have shipped to your address by the ship Benj Morgan, Captain Tedwell,   100 common tents, with poles complete
                22 horseman s "   "   "   "
                3 marquees,   "   "   "
                150 camp kettles
the property of the United States, the Invoice and Bill of Lading

26*

for which, you will find enclosed. On their safe arrival, be pleased to forward me an acknowledgment. These articles you will please to dispose of, agreeably to instructions you have, or will receive, from the Secretary of War

You will please to draw on me for any expense that may be incurred in the disposal of these stores The freight from Philadelphia to New Orleans will be paid by me, agreeably to the bill of lading I am, Sir, with sentiments of respect,
　Your humble servant,　　　　　WM LIMARD,
　　　　　　　　　　　　　　　　Military Agent.
DANIEL CLARK, Esq, Consul U S, New Orleans

[No 73]
Offered by defendants, and filed 25th June, '49
　　　　　　　J. W GURLEY, Commissioner
　　　　　　　　　　　NATCHEZ, 29th April, 1803

Dear Sir I have a dividend to pay to Mr Hulings of 190 4 1-2, and finding that I am in advance for you 220 collars, besides 100 dollars I have engaged to pay for a judgment against your uncle's estate, in favor of a fellow for a mule, I have taken the liberty of drawing upon you for this small sum, in favor of Mr Hulings By next post I will send you the particulars of our little account, being now a little pressed In the meantime any intelligence respecting your new masters, will be highly gratifying　　　　　Dea　　　　　　　your
　　　　　　　　　　　　　　　　　DUNBAR
Daniel Clark, Esq, U S Consul, New Orleans

[No 76.]
Offered by defendants, and filed 25th June, 1849.
　　　　　　　J. W GURLEY, Commissioner.
　　　　　　　　　　　NATCHEZ, Nov. 30th, 1803.

Sir I have only time to acknowledge the receipt of your letters of the 21st and 22d inst., and to add that the contents thereof afford me great pleasure.

I hope with you, that force will not ultimately be necessary , but if our claims should be resisted, you will find on the part of the commissioner as much *energy and promptitude* as you could wish

I shall　　a detachment of militia, from　　place, early on to-morrow morning, and on their arrival at the Heights, (if the General should have reached Fort Adams,) the army will immediately proceed to New Orleans.

With respect and esteem, I am, Sir, your humble serv't,
　　　　　　　　　　　　　　　DANIEL CLARK.
D Clark, Esq., New Orleans.
P. S. The rain has greatly retarded our movements · we have

not had a single clear day for near two weeks past; it is now raining, and no prospect of clearing up

[No. 89]
Offered by defendants, and filed 25th June, 1849
J. W. GURLEY, Com'r

NEW ORLEANS, 18th Aug't, 1803

Sir I had the honor of receiving, this day your letter of the 17th July, to which I shall pay the strickest attention, and without waiting till the whole list of queries proposed can be answered, shall, by each successive post, forward such information as it is possible to procure, in obtaining which I rely great'y on the friendly dispositions of the officers of the Spanish government I have, by this post, forwarded to the Secretary of State, as exact a manuscript map as could be procured of this country, on which the different posts or settlements are delineated and numbered, and hope to have a more perfect one completed in time to be of service I have joined to it some memorandums, respecting the country, hastily put together long before the news of the cession reached us, and am happy to have so far anticipated your wishes in this particular As I feel myself honored by your application to me, I request you will accept the assurance that I shall make every possible endeavor to show myself worthy of your confidence, and that if I do not succeed in acquitting myself to your satisfaction, it will not proceed from a want of inclination or exertion Permit me to offer my sincere congratulations on an event which must forever insure to the safety and prosperity of America

I have the honor to remain, with sentiments of the greatest respect,

Thos Jefferson, President of the U. S

[No 91]
Offered by defendants, and filed 25th June, 1849
J. W GURLEY, Com.

GERMAN TOWN, August 11th, 1803

Dear Sir. Mr. Digan, who will deliver you this, can inform you of our health and situation

I was happy to receive your letter, by Mr Relf. Flattering myself that you will expedite the payment of the bill and damages, so that I may receive it very soon, I am making preparations to visit my unfortunate friends in Virginia, to whom I have promised a visit a year ago but could not accomplish it for want of cash About the 15th of October, I hope to be able to set out I intend to remain there until the spring I regret leaving your family, but perhaps, you may be able to visit them before my return I hope the change of government at New Orleans, which now seems likely to take place, will be much to your advantage   I am, dear sir, wishing, as always, to you every happiness   Your affectionate aunt

JANE CLARK

I shall write you more fully by post to-morrow
Daniel Clark, Esq, New Orleans

[No 93]
Offered by Defendants.   Filed 25th June, 1849

J W GURLEY, Com'r

(Duplicate)   PARIS, 16th May, 1803

Dear Sir   The foregoing, my friend, is copy of my last respects to you, which was forwarded by Bordeaux, Liverpool, and the U. S.   If either of those letters, or this, should reach you before the great event of the cession of Louisiana to the U S by this government should be known in your country, I trust you will make the purchases I have desired, but should that event be divulged, you will please desist, for I am of opinion that so soon as the knowledge of the cession is known among you, individuals will hold their lands higher than they will a year or two afterwards   When being on the spot myself, I can act to my own satisfaction

Lord Whitworth, the B A, has just left Paris   War is not yet declared, but we momently expect to hear of its commencement at the mouth of British cannon   An American board of commissioners is forming here for a settlement of all American claims embraced by our convention of 1800   The moment this business is closed, which is not to exceed the term of 12 months, I shall shape my course for the banks of the Mississippi, of this, say nothing   I shall expect you to give me, in the meantime, every information possible of the climate, soil, and natural advantages of the various parts of L——.   It may happen that I turn the views of many wealthy people towards that country   Give me a statement also of such production of this country as will best suit your markets   It may suit me to invest my funds here in merchandize, and to accompany the same to N O, and as from my long residence in France, my property might be exposed to capture from the British, I wish you would furnish me with a regular order and invoice from your house, for a shipment to the amount of $50,000   Yours affect'y,

FULWAR SKIPWITH

Daniel Clark, New Orleans

[A]

Letter referred to in deposition of Mr Palfrey.

J. W GURLEY, U. S Com r.

LIVERPOOL, 7th October, 1802

MESSRS CHEW AND RELF—Gentlemen —I have been here

three days, and am on the instant of my departure for London Although prepared for the horrid tale I have heard, I could scarce stand it, as I never could bring myself to believe that your culpable neglect would have been so great as to suffer a fraud of such an enormous extent, and practiced with so little deception, to pass on you You may congratulate yourselves on having shaken Mr Cox's credit and fortune, as well as mine, and your own, and almost your future reputation to the very foundation, and had it not been for Mr Barclay's unexpected and unbounded confidence and support, shame would have long since overwhelmed me God grant he may not have withdrawn already, and may still continue his confidence, as on it at present under God is my only hope You were warned of the frauds by Green, Mr Cox, and myself, and yet so far from attempting to discover them and punish the authors, you make a shipment by the Mars, which you yourselves suspected, and advise that you entertained these suspicions Why not, therefore, verify them? Your madness, for such it must have been, has, I hope, passed off, and its effects will, I hope, alarm, warn and teach you to attend better in future to your business I shall send you, by the Creole, a large parcel of bales untouched, that you may perceive how grossly we have been deceived and injured by all the contractors, without exception, and I will probably return in her to assist in bringing them to punishment In future pay the most particular attention to all you ship, and endeavor, by a disclosure of the horrid and infamous practices, to make the planters careful to regain the lost credit of the cotton, without which ruin, unavoidable ruin awaits them Attend to Mr Green's directions about price, and do not, till you hear again from him or me, exceed 18 for the very best cotton, unless in cases where, by doing so, you secure a debt which would not otherwise immediately come in The cotton you ship must be of the very first quality, or ship none at all Endeavor by all possible means to procure certificates from Hulings of American growth, and try to get clearances from the custom-house at Loftus' Heights, when this can not be done let the vessels touch at a port in the United States, and let certificates such as you have already sent accompany their cargoes I find that large shipments have been made by the Matilda, Thomas, Mars and Washington, and the Thomas Wilson takes a small quantity of goods which remained of former orders As I neither know the particulars of these cargoes, nor how you may probably manage immediately on the port being shut, I will do nothing till I hear from you, but count on receiving ample information on all the particulars respecting trade for my government, when, if affairs there can be brought to bear, and they bear a good aspect with you, I will do all that can be done to serve you I fear in your orders you have not limited prices—

this I judge from the price of two bales of Cassimeres, which are now going to you, and which seem high, being charged at 7s., this proceeds from woollens having raised, and you should, in your orders, guard against these things   If you can not get good and excellent cotton at my limitations and as much of it as will load the shipping, sell as many of them as you can and remit the proceeds   On hearing from Mr Coxe and yourselves, and seeing Mr Barclay, I will write you fully, and will either stay here, travel to serve you, or return to Louisiana, as I may judge most for the general good

Do not neglect what I advised you about remitting to my parents   If you find a difficulty of selling my crop, and do not want it yourselves, ship it to Green & Wainwright separately, on account and risk of Richard Clark   If you sell it or take it to yourselves, the proceeds must be appropriated as before directed   I am and with reason almost mad with shame and vexation £30,000 to £40 000 sterling will be, at the lowest computation, the amount of our losses, and this, at a moment when I longed for retirement and ease after a life of toil and trouble, cannot be borne with patience   I wish you may have it in your power to punish the scoundrels who have been the cause of it   I am preparing a handsome present for the intendant, it will be elegant and valuable, of which advise him and shall consist at the same time of things rare and useful   I flatter myself he continues his protection to you, and I request you will cultivate his friendship, and advise me how you stand and how matters are likely to continue, that I may see how far I may venture to rely   Remember me to Gilbert and Barba, whom I shall not forget

Yours, sincerely,

DANIEL CLARK.

Messrs Chew & Relf, New Orleans

[B]

Referred to in deposition of Mr Palfrey

J. W GURLEY, U S Com'r

LONDON, 13 October, 1802.

MESSRS CHEW & RELF.

Gentlemen—I am under many obligations to Mr Robert Percy, the bearer of this, one of which, in particular, is known to your Richard Relf, and that alone entitles him to every assistance or service in my power to render him   Mr. Percy has been more than once at New Orleans, and will probably stand in need of no assistance, if any of his former acquaintances are still in business, as I know they will all feel happy in serving him   but so many changes have taken place lately, that fearful his old friends should have retired, I cannot avoid recommending him to you, and entreating you will serve him in all things, as if his affairs were mine. I have not had the pleasure of seeing Mr Percy since I arrived in London, and am ignorant of his views, but imagine he intends taking his family to Natchez, it is therefore presumable, that he may have employed his funds in goods to suit the upper country, which it might not be convenient for him to dispose of in New Orleans, if so, please to make him, on my account, any advance he may require, and do not let him or his family want any attention or civility in your power to bestow I remain, gentlemen, your sincere friend,

DANIEL CLARK.

[C]

Referred to in Mr Palfrey's deposition

J W GURLEY, U S. Com'r

LONDON, 13 October, 1802

MESSRS. CHEW & RELF

Gentlemen—You will learn with pleasure that on arriving here three or four days ago, I met with a very kind reception from Mr Salkeld, Mr Barclay's partner, the latter is at Margate, and I go there to-morrow, to see and thank him for past favors, and solicit a continuance of them I flatter myself all will yet go well I am requested by Mr Coxe to take out a large assortment, which I think I could procure, but I will enter into no speculations till I hear from you respecting the markets, the regulations, and facility or difficulty of importations, but if you delay in giving me advice I shall get impatient, and set off for New Orleans, to which I intend returning, after settling matters here Push all our debtors, and make as great remittances as possible; nothing else will keep the bark afloat Lauve. & Jarreau's cotton is as bad as that of Girod, Bringier, Peytavin and Remy, and 'tis hard to say which is worst I shall send you back a fine sample of bales, per the Creole or Thomas, and wish it may not, like Medusa's head, petrify you, on seeing it I am, and have been, ashamed and confounded, and cannot hold up my head when Green, or any body else talks of it. Mr Coxe has written to me that since the orders given to you while I was in the U. S., about ordering the ships to Philadelphia, that he has countermanded those orders yet, on account of the late act of Parliament of this country, it is indispensable that all vessels should touch in the United States for a new clearance you must therefore send the ships there, and give me as your authority for so doing Be careful about procuring certificates of American growth, to save the difference of duty I wish it were possible, in order to punish you for your negligence, that you should feel half the tortures of my proud heart, when forced to solicit favors. Heavens' how humiliating a situation, and how unused have I been to it' how painful is the reflection that this is my fate, when I thought myself in affluence   but for the present, no more of this   I expect cotton will be this season unusually good and well cleaned, if cheap, ship all you can, but not one bad bale, on your very existence   You must, from the shipments and resources in your power, have the most ample means, and you ought to avail yourselves of them   Cotton, I suppose, will be at 18 with you, you ought not to give more unless received in payment for dangerous or lingering debts   At that price ship all you can, and push your credit to the utmost to make large and early remittances   I wrote you by the Thomas Wilson, from Liverpool, to which refer you

    Yours sincerely,   DANIEL CLARK.

[D]

Letter referred to in Mr Palfrey's deposition

J W GURLEY, U. S Com'r.

LONDON, 13 October, 1802

MESSRS CHEW & RELF.—I have in this, to request you will not fail to attend to the directions I gave you from Cooper's ferry, about my family, and plantation affairs   If the crop will not sell for 20 cents, ship it to Mr George Green, or rather, to Green & Wainwright, for account of D C; only write to the overseer to pay the most particular attention to quality, otherwise, all will be ruined   I am doing all in my power to assist you, therefore do not forget my interest   Yours sincerely,

             DANIEL CLARK

[E]

Letter referred to in Mr Palfrey's deposition.

J W GURLEY, U. S Com'r.

MARGATE, 17th October, 1802.

Messrs Chew & Relf (New Orleans) Gentlemen —I have just received, at this place, (where I came on a visit to Mr Barclay,) a letter from Messrs Green & Wainwright, of Liverpool, advising that Capt. Jones, whom I was directed by Mr Coxe to displace, would not give up the command of the Thomas Wilson, nor deliver up her papers   You will be pleased on the arrival of the ship, to discharge him instantly, and appoint the mate in his place.   The papers must, if necessary, be taken from him by force, and in case of need apply to the authority of your Government   Mr. Coxe's powers are, by my substitution, invested in you, and neither he nor I will listen to any excuses whatever, for continuing Jones contrary to his positive orders   I will sail for Orleans in the first ship of Mr Coxe's that may arrive.   For God's sake, make every exertion to hasten collections and remittances.   Should it be possible to sell any of the ships, at a reasonable price do not fail to do it, as well as every other species of property whatever belonging to Mr Coxe, in Louisiana, in order that his credit may not suffer It is impossible to give you an idea of his immense losses by the villainous frauds practised on you and his friends here, who can not make sales, will not probably continue much longer to honor his drafts without new resources Should excellent cotton (but no other, on any account) be had at 1s you may purchase and ship till further orders and in this case while you have cargoes, you may send the vessels back here first touching at Philadelphia and New York rather than sell them In order to hasten remittances, I earnestly recommend to you to buy on credit as you must be sensible what risks Mr Coxe will run by delay Your own character as merchants, has suffered vastly in Liverpool and London by your shipments and to you alone shall we look, in time, for every thing respecting quality On your exertions our very existence depends do not, therefore, suffer us to perish

Yours sincerely

DANIEL CLARK

[Γ]

Letter referred to in Mr Palfrey's deposition
J W GURLEY, U S Com

London 19 October, 1802
(New Orleans)

Messrs Chew & Relf,

Gentlemen I have just seen Mr Morgan, who arrived yesterday from Madrid via Paris I asked him concerning the cession of your province, he replied that some difficulty had occurred on the part of Spain, to give an order to deliver up the colony, and he understood that this difficulty was occasioned by France not having yet performed what she was to do or had offered to do in exchange for the colony On his return thro' Paris, he was introduced to the officers appointed to govern Louisiana, among whom are Losat, Provincial Prefect Gen. Victor, Commander-in-Chief of the troops and Jean Job Ayme, Chief Judge This last is the person who was banished formerly to Cayenne who published a narrative of his sufferings, which I left with your Beverly Chew These people informed Mr Morgan, that the French Government had insisted on getting an order to take possession of Louisiana, offering to discuss the subject in dispute afterwards, and when Mr Morgan mentioned the difficulty on the part of Spain, they made light of it, and said that the Court of Madrid dare not refuse They talked of embarking at the end of this month, with 4000 men, and promised Mr Morgan their protection in Louisiana Inform Mr. Morales of these matters, confidentially, but make him promise to keep the business to himself, for fear of the consequences. If

27*

we have any property in deposit, ask him to let you have it, on paying the duties, and make what sales you can, that no accidents may happen   I will go out to you, in the first ship that arrives, to assist in settling matters   Keep this matter quiet after speaking of it to the intendant, and push remittances as fast as you can   I am in hopes the French will not embark as soon as they say   While Mr Morgan was in Paris, they had given Mr Livingston, our minister, notice of their intentions, and had visited him previous to going away   This is all I have heard, make the best use of it   Yours, sincerely,

DANIEL CLARK

P S—Mr. Percy is already at Gravesend, and I forward this letter, in hopes it will reach him

[G]

Letter referred to in Mr Palfrey's deposition

J W GURLEY, Com'r

LONDON, 22d October, 1802

Messrs Chew & Relf, Gentlemen —I have it from good authority that the French Government mean to take immediate possession of Louisiana   Mons Laussat is named Colonial Prefect, Gen Victor commands the troops, said to be 1000 men, who are to go out, and Mons Jean Job Ayme is commissaire de justice, or chief judge   I do not know how the province will be able to support so large a body of men   A friend from Paris has written to me that Pitot has been introduced to the prefect which gives me pleasure, as he is capable of giving him important information   These gentlemen expected orders to sail immediately, but I think circumstances have occurred which will delay their voyage

There is a great probability of a new war in Europe   The Emperor is dissatisfied with the plan of indemnities, and, from present appearances, seems to calculate on the assistance of Russia, where there has lately been a total change in the ministry, and, consequently, a total change of measures   Switzerland is convulsed, and has expelled its late governor, and overset the constitution made for it by Bonaparte, who threatens to send a French army into it without delay   England is displeased with his interference, will not give up Malta, has put a stop to disbanding the army, is fitting out her ships afresh   Couriers are daily passing to the continent, fast sailing vessels are daily sent off, at a moments warning, with dispatches—God knows where —and with sealed orders   The fleet in the Mediterranean (where France also is assembling her land and sea forces) is ordered to remain there, and all officers whose regiments are in Malta are ordered to join them   The heads of the ministry have been closeted with the commander-in-chief of the forces and head of the navy department. Holland expects a change in her Government and the Emperor is assembling and increasing his formidable armies. The moment is big with important events and the political horizon is more than usually gloomy, and portends a most dreadful storm. I set off for Paris on the 26th inst. to be introduced to the new constituted authorities there and will be the bearer of the strongest recommendations; after seeing them, I shall be able to judge what ought and must be done, and will, without delay, return to Louisiana for which purpose, shall keep one of the vessels now in Liverpool ready to sail at a moment's warning; the other will be sent back to you, in ballast. I shall be a fortnight on my journey from hence to Paris and back will stay a week in England at my return, and calculate with certainty on sailing for Orleans by the 20th of next month. My observations until then will be communicated to you verbally, at my return. Inform the Intendant and the Governor of what I have written to you and act with prudence, so as to be prepared for the event. It is said that Spain had hitherto refused to give an order to surrender Louisiana, as France had not complied with her stipulations; but the latter insists on it, and says she will afterwards settle the matter in dispute. I remain, gentlemen

Yours, sincerely

DANIEL CLARK

P. S.—Sell the rope-walk and negroes, if you can possibly do it with every thing else, and as many of the ships as you have not immediate use for, write to the Marquis of Casa Calvo to pay what he owes, and compel every one who is indebted, without any exception, to pay you without delay.

22d October, 1802. D. C.

[H.]

Letter referred to in Mr. Palfrey's deposition.

J. W. GURLEY, U. S. Com'r.

London, 22d October, 1802.

Messrs Chew & Relf. Gentlemen.—Since my last, the Creole and Thomas have arrived in Liverpool, the former, I am very sorry to learn, with another cargo of *damned bad cotton*. I know not yet at what reduced price you received it, but be it what it will it will be another loss in addition to the many already incurred by your shipments, and on my part, from the orders left with you, was totally unexpected. The least reflection ought to have taught you that to send another bad cargo to a market already overstocked with such trash, was to cause a reduction in price of the quantity on hand, and if you have sought to ruin Mr. Coxe, designedly, you could not take more effectual steps. You must have been, at the time this shipment was made, in-

formed that such cotton would not bring more than 5d per lb
and as the seller, by an offer of a reduction of price showed that
it was unmerchantable, it ought to have been thrown on his
hands. I shall leave you to settle this new business with Mr
Coxe, as well as you can. Hitherto I have succeeded in spite
of his immense losses, in excusing you but this last shipment,
with your eyes open, and a perfect conviction of the badness of
the cotton leaves me without a word to say and in my perturbed
state of mind, I almost wish for instant annihilation. This is
not all—one of the vessels brings a certificate of growth of
produce, the other has none, and if we succeed in getting the
cargoes landed, one will be subject to the additional duty, while
the other by having forwarded the usual document, will not
pay it. I am afraid all is not right with you. The ship's crew
not consisting of three-fourths Americans a difficulty has occurred
respecting an entry, which may or may not be got over. You
must, in future, attend to it most particularly, and see that each
seaman swears, before the Consul that he is an American and
has a certificate of it, in that case, by clearing the vessel out,
loaded with *American produce*, but not a single bale of any thing
unaccompanied with a certificate, and the vessel bringing a
clearance from the *port of deposit* for American produce, on the
Mississippi, things will go on as usual. I recommend to you
to push remittances as fast as possible, with the precautions
I have suggested, of clearing from the *port of deposit*, cargo of
American produce, for which the usual certificate will be sufficient
and the vessels legally navigated, they may come direct, as
heretofore. You should, on no account, pay more than 18c for
cotton, as there will otherwise be a loss on it, and you must ship
none but the very best.

The enclosed sketch will inform you what I am about and
what are the reports of the day attend, therefore, to them, let
certificates of property accompany your shipments, and should
war break out afresh, I will send or take you licenses

Yours, sincerely,
DANIEL CLARK

P S—It might be well to circulate the news of war it must
tend to raise your goods, and lower produce. Be cautious
about letters and passengers, and look to certificates.

[I]

Letter referred to in Mr Palfrey's deposition

J. W GURLEY, U S Com
Paris, 16th November, 1802.

Messrs Chew & Relf Gentlemen – I leave this city to-morrow,
for London, and hope, in a fortnight, to embark, at Liverpool,

for Orleans I have had the pleasure of being introduced to the persons appointed to govern your country in a civil and military capacity by whom I have been well received and have had from them assurances of countenance and protection The expedition will certainly take place in a very short time The Prefect and his family will go from l'Orient, in a few days the Capt. General with the troops from Helvoet-sluys, in Holland The Adjutant Gen. a Lt Colonel and an Ensign accompany me to England, and will go out with me I wish you to attend particularly to the directions forwarded you from England, respecting *early remittances* and to increase them, intreat you will not fail to sell the rope-walk, slaves, and any thing else which will command cash You may show this letter to Mr Morales, but must not hint its contents to any other soul whatever I shall shortly be with you, in the mean time, be active and diligent Yours, sincerely,

DANIEL CLARK

P S—A part of the Prefect's baggage is now embarking, at Havre

[K]

Referred to in Palfrey's deposition

J W GURLEY, U S Com

New Orleans, 20th Dec'r, 1811

My dear Sir We have had no mail to-day, and altho' anxious to know what effect has been produced by the communication of the Duke of Bassano's letter, yet we must remain in ignorance of it for another week

I shall particularly attend to and pay the taxes on the Marquis de Casa Yrujo's lands, in consequence of your directions, they were never taxed until this year, and even yet the amount is not, I believe, ascertained

I have every reason to believe that on the re-election of Mr Relf to a seat at the board of directors of the Louisiana bank, which takes place the beginning of next month, it will be in our power to remit you Gen'l Hampton's note, time enough to reach you before it is due which will be on the 25th February Chew & Relf, both promise me, to use every possible exertion to that effect, and I beg of you, for God's sake not to impute any want of disposition to us, as I would give my heart's blood to relieve you . Yours sincerely,

DANIEL CLARK

Daniel Wm Coxe, Esq, Philadelphia

[L]

Referred to in Palfrey's deposition.

J W GURLEY, U. S. Com.

New Orleans, 19th Jan'y, 1813.

My dear Sir I have received your letter, covering the original power of attorney from C & R and copy of their letter approving of the settlement with you which I shall hold to make use of, when necessary I am extremely concerned to learn that Gen'l Hampton's bills, on Schulz have not been paid I had every reason to believe from the General's assurances, that no difficulty would occur on that account and I now flatter myself that on his arrival, which must have been previous to this time, he will have taken measures to take them up if not and you should send them back here to C & R the recovery will neither be long nor difficult, and I am persuaded that there is scarce any sacrifice he will not make, rather than suffer the bills to return

The war and the total destruction of all crops by the hurricane in August last will prevent the recovery of any sums by the house here, and altho' my heart bleeds to learn the difficulties you are in, yet it would be unpardonable to give you hopes of relief from hence, which cannot be realized I do not foresee that it will be in my power to touch as much money as will pay our current expenses during the year Before Gen'l Hampton's departure from hence, I was under the necessity of settling with him, and taking his notes payable in 12 months from this time, for the balance due on his note, due 25th of February last There is no money here, credit is gone, and all our means are paralyzed by the war   I remain, my dear sir, yours sincerely,

DANIEL CLARK

Daniel Wm. Coxe, Esq, Philadelphia

[M]

Referred to by Mr Palfrey in his deposition

J W GURLEY, Commissioner

N'lie Orleans, 1 Mai, 1810.

Mon cher Lacroix On vient de m'offrir, pour six mois, une somme de six milles piastres, qui me mettra à meme de payer pleusieurs petits engagements qui me genent, je prends, en consequence, la liberte de vous prier d'endosser mon billet pour cette somme, que je vous envois inclus Aussitot le depart de Relf, je me propose le plaisir de passer une journee avec vous, et de vous engager à m'accompagner à la Terre aux Bœufs

Votre serviteur et ami,   DANIEL CLARK.

Lettre M, referred to in my testimony

H W PALFRY

[N]

Referred to by Mr. Palfrey in his deposition

J W GURLEY, U S Com'r.

Washington, 14 February, 1808

My Dear Friend.—Previous to setting off for Annapolis, I informed you of my intention I am sorry to have now to mention that it not only has not been effected but that the affair is for ever ended. The reasons I will give you when we meet, although they are too trifling in themselves to have caused the effect produced by them. I beg you to state to Mrs Coxe, and if you are spoken to on the subject, to state that you have had no knowledge whatever of it than

Yours, affectionately,

DANIEL CLARK

Addressed, on the back, to D. W. Coxe Esq, Philadelphia.

Originals of the three letters, annexed to a commission in the suit of Barnes et al *vs* Gaines et al.—No 19,150—in the First Judicial District Court of Louisiana

[O]

Letter referred to by Mr Palfrey in his deposition

J. W. GURLEY, U. S. Comr

WASHINGTON, 9th February, 1809

MY DEAR FRIEND—I have received your letters of the 4th and 5th inst., and in reply to that part of them which treats of the removal of the seat of Government have only to mention that I believe Sloan's motion will be negatived by a great majority, whenever the question is finally taken. The vote you allude to was on a resolution of commitment, and the majority of those who voted to commit the resolution, would have opposed the principles of it. It is supposed here that Mr Rose will have to wait fresh instructions from England

Mr Livingston, one of the judges, told Mr Harper, yesterday, that he believed we should have war with France in three months. I know not what he deduces his inferences from

I shall set off this evening for Annapolis, and shall pass two or three days there. If I find Miss Louisa Caton as favorably inclined towards me as you have hinted, I shall endeavor so to secure her affections, as to permit me to offer myself to her at my return to this country, in the course of the ensuing winter. I shall first go home to settle my affairs. On this subject I have never yet spoken to her, and I now communicate my intentions to you that you may inform Mrs Coxe, who will, I hope, as well as yourself, keep the affair quiet. At my return I shall inform you of the results

I know not what to say to you on the subject of affairs or purchases, and leave you entirely to your own discretion. I believe the embargo will last some months. We shall not, for the present, send any squadron against the Algerines

Present me, respectfully, to Mrs Coxe

Yours, affectionately,

DANIEL CLARK.

Daniel W. Coxe, Esq

[P.]

Referred to by Mr Palfrey in his deposition

J W GURLEY, U S Com

Washington 12th Janu y, 1808

My dear Sir It is now reported and I believe with truth, that Mr Rose is at last arrived in Alexandria It will take some days before we know what may be the probable result of his mission, but as I may learn any thing I shall inform you

I am sorry your last advices from Relf are so bad, but I flatter myself a great part of the difficulties he sees will be easily got over

With respect to underwriting, you must well know how much I have always been opposed to it If, however, you will continue to underwrite, it is a matter of indifference whether you mean to carry it on, on your private or our joint account, as I look upon our interests as indissoluble, and that what affects one must effect the other

My fears about cotton last year were you know very near being realized, it cost us more than we calculated on and but for an accident and state of things altogether unforeseen, the present benefits would not have been derived from the shipments

I have been so occupied lately, that I could not write to Duvalle, I will, however, endeavor to do it to morrow

Your accounts of my visits to Annapolis, have been, as usual, much ahead Whenever I am fortunate enough to induce any one to engage herself to me I shall let you and Mrs Coxe both know it , but until I see *jour a mes affaires*, I shall make no engagement

I am resolved on making my stay here as short as possible, and will hurry back to Orleans to assist relieving you by remittances from thence

What is the meaning of John Adam's motion? nobody I see can tell, and we are at a loss to know whether it is a ministerial measure, and he the cats paw, or an attempt of his own, to put an end to the embargo against the wish of the majority of Congress. Remember me respectfully to Mrs Coxe, and believe me, my dear friend, yours sincerely,   DANIEL CLARK

Daniel W Coxe, Esq

[Q]

Referred to in deposition of Palfrey

J W GURLEY, U. S. Com'r

UNITED STATES OF AMERICA,   }
State of Louisiana—City of New Orleans }

Be it remembered that, this day, the twelfth of the month of April, one thousand eight hundred and forty-one, and in the sixty fifth year of the Independence of the United States of America,

Before me, Louis T. Caire, a notary public in and for the city and parish of New Orleans, duly commissioned and sworn, and in presence of the witnesses hereafter named and subscribed,

Personally appeared Mr. Lucius Campbell Duncan, attorney at law, residing in this city, Royal street, who requested me, the undersigned notary, to file in my current Register, and to record a document under private signature, the purport and tenor whereof is in the following words and figures, viz:

Articles of agreement made and concluded between Daniel Clark, Esq., of the one part and Beverly Chew and Richard Relf of the second part, witnesses, that whereas in the year 1801, the aforesaid Beverly Chew and Richard Relf entered into partnership for the transaction of commercial concerns in this country with Daniel Wm. Coxe, Esq., of Philadelphia, who had previously thereto been carrying on business in this country in company with and under the name of Daniel Clark, Esq., aforesaid, to whose affairs the house of Beverly Chew and Richard Relf succeeded, and whereas on the 11th day of July, 1811, a supplementary agreement was entered into for the liquidation of said concern, fixing the profits that the aforesaid Beverly Chew and Richard Relf were to receive, and at the same time a distinct agreement was made between Daniel Wm. Coxe and Daniel Clark for their respective interests in the general concern, which several agreements it has, however, from the peculiar circumstances of the times and the nature of the affairs, been hitherto impossible to carry into effect, neither can the parties at this moment contemplate an early conclusion of them, but being mutually desirous of establishing the principles of a general settlement, when it may be found practicable, have agreed as follows:

1. That in lieu of the sum stipulated in the agreement, before referred to, dated the 11th July, 1811, fixing the profits of Beverly Chew and Richard Relf, they be from this day, concerned jointly and co-equally with Daniel Clark in all the property, debts, etc., held either in their own name or in that of Daniel Clark's, or Daniel William Coxe's, in this country, arising from the late concern of D. Clark or Chew & Relf, a schedule of which to be furnished by Daniel Clark and hereunto annexed, saving and excepting the house occupied by Daniel Clark on the Bayou road, as well as the estate inherited from T. Wilkins, which is hereby acknowledged to be said Daniel Clark's private property, and that after the payment of the debts of the concern, including those of Daniel Clark's, of which there is a schedule hereunto annexed, and a final settlement and payment of the balance that may be due D. W. Coxe, which payment is to be made out of the general funds, then the remaining property, either of lands.

28*

debts or other effects, to be equally divided between the parties, each one third.

2 That in order to promote the general good Daniel Clark engages to relinquish, in favor of the concern, the sum of *fourteen thousand dollars*, arising from the third installment of his contract with the navigation company, which Beverly Chew and Richard Relf are hereby authorized to receive and apply to the use of the house.

3 That for the better conducting the affairs in future, one of the parties shall, as early as practicable, remove to some city of the Atlantic States, and form an establishment of such a nature as may appear advantageous to the general concern

4 That neither of the parties during the term of this agreement, shall withdraw from the concern any funds for individual purposes other than for defraying'their personal expenses, which are hereby limited to   dollars per annum and that upon a final settlement the amount of the respective private accounts shall be brought into view in the division of property

In testimony whereof, we have hereunto affixed our seals and signed our names, in presence of witnesses, at New Orleans, this nineteenth day of June, one thousand eight hundred and thirteen

(Signed)   DANIEL CLARK.   [L S]
    "   BEV CHEW,   [L S]
    "   RICHARD RELF,   [L S]

Témoin
(Signed)   F. Dutillet,
              H W Palfrey

It is further understood that the plantation lately purchased by D. Clark, of S. Henderson, on account of which nothing has as yet been paid, is to remain on his private account

Which document, so recorded, has been signed *ne varietur* by the said appearer in presence of the undersigned notary and witnesses, to identify it herewith, and at his request, is and remains hereto annexed for reference

That he has for many years past been personally acquainted with Messrs Beverly Chew and Richard Relf, and has seen them write and sign their names, that the signatures of Beverly Chew and Richard Relf are the true and genuine signatures of Beverly Chew and Richard Relf, both now residing in this city, and the appearer signed

L C DUNCAN

And also personally appeared Messrs Francois Dutillet and Henry William Palfrey, residing both in this city, who, being duly sworn by me, the undersigned notary, declared and said that the signatures, Daniel Clark, Beverly Chew and Richard Relf have been written in their presence. that they have, themselves, signed as witnesses that they also acknowledge their own signatures and they have often seen them, the said Clark, Chew and Relf write and sign their names and the said H W Palfrey moreover declared that with the exception of few words, the main body of the document has been written by him, and the appearers signed

(Signed),—F Douillet—H Wm Palfrey

Done and passed in my office at the city of New Orleans, the day month and year aforementioned, in presence of Messrs Auguste Huard and Cyprien Courbe Ladreyere, witnesses thereto, required and residing in this city who have hereunto set their names with me, the notary

(Signed)—H Wm Palfrey—Cy Courbe Ladreyere—Aug Huard   LOUIS T CAIRE, Not Pub

A true copy of the original extant, in my current Register in faith whereof, I grant these presents under my signature and seal of office

New Orleans, the 2d of May, 1849

[L S]   LOUIS T CAIRE, Not Pub.

[A A]

Referred to in Mr Zacharie's deposition

J W GURLEY, Commissioner

Mon Ami—Je ne vous ai jamais méconnu, et votre dernière marque d'amitié ne prouve que la constance de la misère envers tout ce qui vous regarde, n'égale meme pas encore la votre

Ce que vous m'avez fait dire, mot à mot m'a été transcripté Je ne me rappele pas directement ce que j'ai pus ecrire Je n'ai jamais été l'ennemi des Américains,—je les aime, au contraire Mais, leur gouvernement, à la Louisiane au moins, m'a paru si vexatoire, que j'aurais tout sacrifié pour l'eloigner, ou pour m'en eloigner Je n'ai jamais accepté d'emploi, qu'à mon corps défendant, je n'en ai jamais accepté avec appointements, malgre, comme vous le savez, qu'ils m'en a été offerts, et des plus lucratifs Ceux que j'ai exercés, ont été avec honneur, je ne rien a me reprocher durant leurs exercises Si j'avais été rampant, capable de sacrifier l'amitié et la reconnaissance, a la basse intrigue, j'aurais pus etre un des bons dieux de la Louisiane, vous le savez, mais, comme ayant sacrifié l'intrigue à l'amitié je suis devenu une des betes-noires de son Excellence, surtout pour avoir decomposé et nui à ses projets relativement à l'insurrection de Mexico Mais ceci n'avait absolument rien contre le Governement, ou du moins, en apparence J'ai parlé avant mon depart sur le desir que j'aurais de revoir la Louisiane à l'Espagne, et j'ai écrit, je crois, sans pouvoir vous l'assurer combien j'étais flatté de voir que ce moment était près, et combien je serais flatté de co-opérer à l'accélérer, mais mes instants n'ont point été ici employés qu'à me procurer une terre pour m'y fixer, et y attirer tous ceux qui pensent comme moi,—c'est-à-dire, ceux qui préfèrent un gouvernement monarchique, a un gouvernement simplement libre que pour se dire des injures, et mettre en place l'intrigue et la fourberie.

Si j'étais seul et sans famille a la Louisiane il importerait peu d'avoir à m'y exprimer hautement et sans aucun ménagement. Je n'ai prêté au gouvernement aucun serment de fidélité, que dans les emplois que j'ai exercés, pour le temps de leur durée. Je n'ai pas demandé d'être Américain ni n'ai juré de l'être toute ma vie. Si j'avais fait l'un et l'autre je pourrais me réprocher un changement, mais je n'ai point changé. J'ai servi mon pays dans ce qu'il m'a forcé d'être et rien de plus, et puisqu'il ne peut redevenir Espagnole ou du moins qu'il ne le soit encore, il m'est bien libre de le laisser. C'est ce que je vais faire, et même pour ne le jamais revoir, s'il reste tel qu'il est. Néanmoins, comme il m'est indispensable d'aller y remplir des engagements sacrés que l'usure la fraude, et tout ce qui s'en suit m'a fait contracter j'attends de votre amitié, ce que vous pourriez attendre de la mienne, en me donnant avis par la même voie, de tout ce qui pourrait occasioner mon retard a la Louisiane, ce qui me causerait ici les plus grands préjudices, pour ce qui est de mon établissement.

Si par cas vous vous persuadez que je puisse être compromis ou par ce que j'ai dit ou par ce que j'ai écrit, voyez vous avec L......, et conjointement engagez ma famille a prévenir attendre à Pensa, sous prétexte que vous trouverez. Non seulement, mon ami, ni vous ni L... .... ne souffrît des avances que vous lui feriez à cet effet, mais encore je me trouverez en possibilité de vous être ici infiniment utile. c'est ce que je vous détaillerai dans un autre moment. En attendant, recevez mes remerciements, et croyez à la reconnaissance de votre dévoué et sincère ami,   BELLECHASSE

Havana, ce 9 gbre, 1814.

I hereby certify, that on this day, February 6th, 1835, I presented this letter to Mr Josef D Degouin Bellechasse, and upon enquiring whether it was signed and written by himself, received his reply that it was.

THE'RE. ZACHARIE

Matanzas Febr'y 6th, 1835.

[BB]
Referred to by Mr Zacharie in his deposition
J W GURLEY, Commissioner.

De meme date.

Vous devez mon cher ami, ne vous en prendre qu'à vous-meme, si je ne vous ai pas fait la retrocession des proprietées que notre ami Clark m'avait vendues Je vous en avais fait l'offre dans plusieurs occasions, et sous je ne sais quel prétexte, vous avez toujours remis a le faire, et m'avez laisse partir sans m'en parler, et si vous ne m'eussiez pas écrit a ce sujet, je vous jure que je n'y aurais jamais pense, ni comme une chose à restituer, ni comme une chose a laisser a mes infortunes enfants, si le ciel avait dispose de mes jours, bien qu'il m'eut pardonne un vol aussi innocent qu'involontaire, les miens n'en auraient pas moins ete les proprietaires puisqu aucun document ne pouvait prouver que cette vente n'etait que simulee.

Quoique peu a moi, ayant réfléchi d'apres la position ou l'infamie de M Livaudais m'a expose, que la chicane pouvait peut etre trouver matiere a vous nuire, en s emparent de ces proprietes, comme partie de ma propriete, j'ai crus en consequence devoir vous ecrire, comme je l'ai fait dans ma lettre, et vous envoie le document ci joint, afin de prouver que mon acte déclaratoire etait avant mon depart de la Louisiane, et depose entre les mains de Pedesclaux J'ai préféré celui-ci, persuade que vous lui ferais faire, a peu de frais, tout ce qui vous pourra convenir, et afin qu'il ne puisse pas, en cas de requisition, faire un faux, entendez-vous avec lui, remettez-lui le document, pour qu'il vous le remette sous votre reçu, et tout sera fini Cependant, si cela ne suffit pas, et que vous preferez que je vous fasse ici un acte notaire, faites-le moi savoir, et je ferai tout ce que vous me pourrais dicter, et en cas que Dieu dispose de mes jours, mon testament, qui etait entre les mains de MM Livaudais, père et fils, et qui doit avoir ete, ou qui peut etre retire par M Jumonville, Baron et Bore et en dernier, par Edouard Ducros, pourra attester, que je ne mentionne nullement ces propriets, ce qui servira de preuve qu'elles ne m'appartiennent pas.

J'ai dans plusieurs occasions, mon am, demandé à Baron et a ... deux charrues a boeuf ... deux petites à cheval, e ... S Pierre ... ns de me les envoyer, ... Vous pourrais les porter en compte à M Ynneravity, et les lui envoyer, pour qu'il me les fasse parvenir Je vous serais aussi oblige de m'envoyer par la même occasion, un petit barril de grains d'oranger mirtre, et une carabine que j'ai chez M Marigny Dautrive si elle n'est pas en etat, je vous serais oblige de la faire réparer, et de lui faire faire un moule.

Ma femme, à qui j'ai fait lecture de votre lettre a beaucoup pleuré, ma gré sa faiblesse, elle vous prie, ainsi que moi, de nous rappeller à votre chere epouse. Mille choses a tous nos amis, et croyez moi votre dévoué,

BELLECHASSE

Lorsque je serai plus à moi je vous recrirai, excusez moi pour cette fois. Cependant avant de finir je vous prierai d'aller voir ma sœur Foulon, et si, comme je n'en puis douter, elle à besoin de quelques secours, secourez-la, et vous ne perdera rien avec votre ami.

I hereby certify that on this day, February 6th, 1835, I presented this letter to Mr. Josef D. Degoutin Bellechasse and upon enquiring whether it was signed and written by himself, received his reply that it was

THE'RE ZACHARIE

Mantanzas, Febr'y 6th, 1835

[CC]

Referred to by Mr. Zacharie in his deposition

J. W. GURLEY, Comm'r.

A LA REUNION DESIREE, JURISDICTION DE MATANSAS,
ce 31 Janvier, 1816

C'est avec bien du plaisir, mon cher Relf que j'ai reçu votre lettre du 18 Decembre passé, mais je n'ai pas reçu celle que vous me dite m'avoir ecrit en réponse de celle que je vous écrivit de la Havane, en gbre ou zbre, je crois, de 1811. Par votre dernière, vous me souhaitez le bonheur, mais, mon cher ami, il est aussi loin de moi, que je suis éloigné d'avoir merité les calomnies que la malignité a exercée contre moi, et encore plus, les reflexcions défavorables que la conduite de M. Livaudais à mon égard, a pu faire naître parmi ses partisans, et ceux qui courrent à leur ruine en comptant sur son amitié et recevant ses services. Persuade de la justice que vous etes dans le cas de me rendre, connaissant par expérience, ma manière de traiter, ma loyauté dans les contrats, l'inviolabilité de ma parole, le deshonneur que j'ai toujours voué aux banqueroutes, de speculations, et mon dévouement à la reconnaissance et l'amitié, il m'est d'apres cela inutile, je pense, d'entrer avec vous dans des détailles justificatifs pour vous prouver que je n'ai pas emporté un sou avec moi de la Louisiane, reçus, à recevoir, ni avoir fait recevoir une obole, et que je n'ai pas dans ce moment un *maravesdis*, que je puisse dire m'appartenir. M. F. ron, jeune, pourra vous peindre ma position; il vous dira que j'ai l'espoir, si Dieu me donne des jours, d'avoir part aux bienfaits d'un ami genereux, et qu'en attendant que ma famille et moi n'existent que de ses secours.

Comptant sur l'amitié et la loyauté de Mr. Livaudais, j'ai parti de la Louisiane avec son agrément, et comptant y retourner de suite je n'ai pris aucune précaution ni ait eu aucune méfiance de sa perfidie, laissant l'arbitre de mon sort et de celui de ma famille, qu'il a ruiné, en abusant de ma confiance, et cherchant à flétrir ma réputation lorsque j'avais fait et que je faisais toute espèce de sacrifice pour le dégager, étant le seul qui, comme mon endosseur aura été victime d'une banqueroute, si j'avais eu l'âme assez basse d'en faire une surtout en y faisant participer ma femme contre son intérêt à lui. Cette conduite de ma part, ma résignation à tout sacrifier pour lui, était sans doute, dans le cas de l'obliger d'attendre mon retour, ou de m'écrire avant de m'exposer sur les papiers publics,—ce que j'ignorais, lorsque chaques personnes étonnés de ne pas me voir rougir, me regardaient comme un effronteur, de leur parler d'affaires, qui par eux m'était offert quelques temps avant, avec prières de les accepter! Non, mon ami, lorsque j'ai eu découvert la cause de ce changement, et que j'ai su que je le devais à M. Livaudais, toutes les foudres réunis ne m'eurent pas plus promptement écrasé je reste anéanti et ne pouvais en croire mes yeux, et si Mr Forbes n'eut eu de moi une connaissance aussi parfaite, ne serais-je pas aujourd'hui à mendier le pain que je pétris de mes sueurs pour mon infortunée famille? Mon ami, si vous m'êtes resté fidèle, comme je n'en puis douter, quoique mon pays me soit devenu odieux, je voudrais encore m'y voir rendre justice. A cet égard, j'avais pensé à vous pour vous charger de mes pouvoirs, mais voyant que je ne recevais aucune lettre de vous, j'ai dû croire que vous m'aviez aussi oublié, et en conséquence j'ai écrit à mon beau-frère, Edouard Ducros, en lui envoyant mon pouvoir pour protester contre ce que M. Livaudais a pu se permettre de faire à mon égard en abus de confiance, et comme il serait trop long d'entrer dans de nouveaux détailles, je vous envoie ci-joint la copie de la lettre que je lui ait écrit, ainsi que celle écrite à M. Livaudais, et comme cette dernière était dans celle d'Edouard s'il ne l'a pas reçue, remettez lui cette copie comme originale, ainsi qu'à M. Livaudais, celle qui lui est adressée, et priez Edouard de me servir en frère, comme je vous prie de me servir en ami.

Au sujet de ce que vous me dite dans votre lettre, touchant les propriétés de feu notre intéressant ami Clark, il est très vrai qu'il m'a vendu ses propriétés du Bayou, mais il est aussi très vrai que ces propriétés ne m'appartiennent pas, et que cette vente n'était que simulée, quoiqu'il n'existe aucun document qui puisse prouver le contraire qu'un document que j'ai remis à M. Pierre Pedesclaux, à votre adresse, pour vous être remis en cas de mort ou accident de ma part. Quoiqu'il m'ait donné un reçu

de ce document, il m'est impossible de vous l'envoyer, vu que
mes papiers sont encore a m'etre envoyes de la Nouvelle Orléans ; mais la présente sera pour lui un titre pour ne faire aucune
difficulté de vous le remettre, lui promettant sur ma parole de
vous l'envoyer aussitôt que mes effets seront arrivés, s'ils arrivent,
car je suis si malheureux que je ne puis plus compter sur rien.
Mais dans tous les cas, votre reçu lui servira, car étant mort pour
mon pays, grace à l'ingratitude, il aurait du même vous l'avoir
remit, comme sous ce rapport, je le prie de le vous remettre.

Je n'ai rien vu dans la nature de plus beau, de plus attrayant,
ni qui offre plus de ressources que le pays que j'habite. Je faisais
ma félicité d'y être apres mes revers de fortune. Mon infortunée
épouse y faisait aussi le sien , mais le sort, jaloux de notre paisi-
ble bonheur, envoya la mort nous visiter, qui dans sa retraite
nous enlevât notre fils, notre cher enfant mon cher Adolpe,
en frappant sa tendre mère de sa faux meurtrière ; oui, mon ami,
ma chere Adelaide est mourante depuis le 8 de ce mois, qu'elle
eut le malheur de perdre son fils' Pardonnez, je ne puis continuer ; adieu, plaignez votre ami,

BELLECHASSE

I hereby certify that on this day, February 6th, 1835, I presented this letter to Mr Josef D Degoutin Bellechasse, and upon
enquiring whether it was signed and written by himself, received
his reply that it was

THEO'RE ZACHARIE.

Matanzas, Feb'y 6th, 1836

[D?]

Referred to by Mr. Zacharie, in his deposition

J W GURLEY, Com'r.

REUNION DESIRFE JURISDICTION DF MATANZAS, }
                    23 gbre, 1822 }

MON CHER RELF —Il y en effet bien du temps que je me suis
crus oublié de vous, comme je l'ai été de tous ceux qui me donnait
le doux nom d'ami, lorsque j'étais dans la prosperite , mais vous
fait exception puisque vous me dites m'avoir en present à votre
ressouvenir C'est toujours plus que les autres n'ont fait, ainsi je
ne dois pas me plaindre

Voyant que je n'avais reçu de vous aucune reponse, au sujet
de l'acte déclaratoire que je vous ai fait parvenir, vous substi-tu-
ant à mon lieu et place pour remplir auprès M de Mira les intentions de feu notre ami Mr. Daniel Clark, j'ecrivis à divers,
entr'autre à Mr Baron, jeune, pour me donner avis si vous avez
reçu le dit acte ; et quoique j'ai reçu des lettres de lui, il ne m'a
nulement satisfait sur ma demande ; et sans votre dernière du 21
Août j'ignorais encore son sort

J'ai écris à cet egard a notre ami, Mr Huling, et a Mr Davis
Je les refer à vous et au susdit acte, qui est, je crois, aussi ex-
tensif que possible, et qui prouve assez surtout dans la position
malheureuse ou je me suis trouve, que si j'avais été capable de
dévier de mes principes, et ne pas remplir exactement les intentions de Clark, et mes instructions verbales, que j'aurais pu sans
que l'on eu rien a m'opposer, abuser de sa confiance, mais non,
il savait et connaissait le sein dans lequel il la deposait. Je ne
puis donc rien changer a ma declaration, sans me parjurer et
ouvrir la porte a un procès que Mad'lle Mira aurait droit de
me faire, de plus, que puis-je vous dire dans un nouveau pouvoir? surtout ne m'ayant par renvoyé le premier je ne puis
avoir exactement present les expressions de Clark, je pourrais
m'en écarter involontairement, ce que je n'ai pu faire a l'epoque
de mon acte declaratoire, ou elles se trouvaient encore gravée dans
ma memoire Neanmoins, et relativement a M'lle Caroline, je
puis dire, et même jurer, que Clark avait une trop belle ame et le
cœur trop bien place pour avoir été capable, ayant deux enfans
qu'il adorait, d'en avoir voulu favoriser une, en laissant l'autre
exposée a mendier son pain et livre aux vicissitudes qu'entraine
la misere Je ne doute pas que si le testament de Clark ne s'etait
pas perdu, que l'on aurait vu que la partie de ses biens confiés
au Chevalier de la Croix était designé a M'lle Caroline, comme peut l'affirmer Mr et Mde. Harper, qui assurent que Clark
leur en avair fait l'aveu

Mr Clark avait autant de confiance dans le Chevalier de la
Croix qu'en moi, et je crois qu'il la meritait également; c'est pourquoi, je regarde comme un effet du hazard qu'il m'ait designé
M'lle Mira au lieu de Caroline—si, donc, Caroline m'eut été designee Mira se trouverait dans l'hypothese ou Caroline se trouve
aujourd'hui, et comment prendrait-elle la chose? N'est-il pas du
devoir de celle que le hazard a favorise contre la volonté, sans
doute, d'un père tendre et vertueux, d'avoir en sa memoire un acte
de partage et de justice que le ciel benirait en la rendant prospere, et que je lui demande au nom de son digne pere, dont les
manes me sugere dans ce moment le conseil que je lui donne,
et qui lui meritera en le suivant le sufrage general si elle s'y
conforme et ce que je presume dans ce cas envoyez moi sa
declaration authentique et l'aveu du Colonel Davis, dans ce cas
et en me renvoyant mon acte declaratoire je vous enverrai telle
procuration que vous desirez, et conforme au modele que vous
pourrez me faire parvenir, et c'est tout ce que je puis vous dire
en reponse a votre lettre Votre d son et ami,

JOSEF D DEGOUTIN BELLECHASSE

P S—Si par cas ce que je vous propose ne peut avoir lieu
faites nommer une commission pour me prendre ma declaration
29*

et celle de Mr et Mde Harper. Elle ne peut se prendre devant l'agent Americain, parcequ'il n y en a pas ici, mais vous avez plusieurs Americains respectable a qui vous pourrez vous adaresser, tels que sont Messrs Jean Lattine George Miller, Philip Dickinson et autres, à qui vous pourrez vous adresser

I hereby certify that on this day, February 6th, 1835, I presented this letter to Mr Josef D. Degoutin Bellechasse, who acknowledged it to have been written by his dictation, and signed in his own handwriting; he says he does not exactly recollect who wrote it for him, but believes it to have been done by one of his daughters   THEO ZACHARIE.

Matanzas, 6th February 1835.

[No 112]

Offered and filed by defendants, 3d July, 1849

J W GURLEY, Com'r

Filed 18th June, 1834

To the honorable Charles Maurian, Judge of the Court of Probates, for the parish and city of New Orleans

The petition of Wm Wallace Whitney and Myra Clark Whitney his wife, residing in the State of New York, represents that, on the sixteenth day of August, in the year eighteen hundred and thirteen, one Daniel Clark, then residing in New Orleans, departed this life, having no descendant, except your petitioner, Myra Clark Whitney, who is the daughter of the said Clark your petitioners state that shortly after the death of the said Clark, a paper dated the twentieth day of May, eighteen hundred and eleven purporting to be the last will and testament of the said Clark, was produced, before the Court of Probates, as such last will That Richard Relf and Beverly Chew, both residing in New Orleans, are therein named as executors, and Mary Clark, the mother of the deceased, his heir or devisee, that the said will was admitted to Probate, and the administration of said estate assumed by the said Relf & Chew, who took possession thereof, and of all the papers and effects belonging thereto, in relation to all of which premises your petitioners refer to the said will recorded in this court, and the proceedings had thereon

Your petitioners further state that they are informed, and believe, that the aforesaid will is not the last will of the said Daniel Clark; that the said Clark, subsequent to the date of the aforesaid will, executed, in due form of law, an olographic will, by which he revoked the will aforesaid, and in which he instituted his aforesaid daughter, Myra Clark Whitney, his sole heir That the said will was left by the said Clark among his papers, at his decease, but that the same has not been produced, but is either lost or mislaid, or has been destroyed Your petitioners further state that the aforesaid Mary Clark, as they believe, during her life, accepted the succession of the said Daniel Clark, and, at her death left her last will and testament, by which she instituted as her heirs, Eleanor O Beirn, of Sligo in Ireland, Jane Green of Liverpool in England and Sarah Campbell and Caroline Clark your petitioners, therefore pray that the said Eleanor O Beirn, Jane Green, Sarah Campbell, and Caroline Clark, may be made parties to this suit and that as they are absent from the State of Louisiana, a curator ad hoc be appointed to represent them and all other persons who are absent and interested herein, and whose names are unknown to your petitioners, that the aforesaid Richard Relf and Beverly Chew be cited to appear and answer this petition, and that they be ordered to produce, at the trial of this cause, the aforesaid will of the said Daniel Clark, last above referred to, if in their possession

That they be further ordered to produce and deposit in this court all the documents and papers belonging to the said estate of the said Clark, and to render a full and true account of the administration of the said estate, and to surrender the property which remains in their possession unadministered

And your petitioners further pray that after due proceedings had, a judgment may be rendered in favor of your petitioners, that the said will, dated twentieth day of May, eighteen hundred and eleven, may be annulled and set aside and that your petitioner Myra Clark Whitney, may be declared to be the heir of the said Clark and entitled to all the rights of heir and that the said Relf and Chew may be ordered and adjudged to deliver to her the possession of all property belonging to said estate, and to pay over to her all sums of money which may have been by them received and to which they may not be entitled to a credit in the settlement of their accounts with the said estate of the said Daniel Clark

And that your petitioners may have all other and further just and equitable relief

WM M WORTHINGTON, for Pet'r.

ORDER —It is ordered, 1st that Lucius C Duncan, Esq, be appointed curator ad hoc of the absent defendants within mentioned 2d that said L C Duncan in his said capacity, and Richard Relf and Beverly Chew be cited to answer this petition

CHARLES MAURIAN, Judge.

New Orleans, 19th June, 1832

W W WHITNEY AND MYRA WHITNEY, ⎫
⎬ THE STATE OF LOUISIANA.
ELEANOR O BEIRN AND OTHERS. ⎭

Mr Beverly Chew, New Orleans. You are hereby summoned to comply with the prayer of the annexed petition, or to file your answer thereto, in writing, with the register of wills in and for the parish and city of New Orleans, at his office in New Orleans in ten days after the service hereof, and if you fail herein judgment will be rendered against you by default.

Witness the honorable Charles Maurian, Judge of the Court of Probates, the 23d day of June in the year of our Lord 1834

P L B DUPLESSIS, D'y Reg'r of Wills

Rec'd June 23d, 1834, and served on the 24th of said month Copy of petition and citation on B Chew, Esq, in person. Returned June 30th 1834.

J H HOLLAND, D'y Sheriff

WM. W. WHITNEY AND MYRA C. WHITNEY, } THE STATE OF
vs. } LOUISIANA
ELEANOR O'BEARN AND OTHERS. }

Mr L C Duncan, New Orleans, curator ad hoc of the absent defendants You are hereby summoned to comply with the prayer of the annexed petition, or to file your answer thereto, in writing, with the register of wills in and for the parish and city of New Orleans at his office in New Orleans in ten days after the service hereof, and if you fail herein, judgment will be rendered against you, by default

Witness the honorable Charles Maurian, Judge of the Court of Probates, this 23d day of June, in the year of our Lord 1834

P L B DUPLESSIS, D'y Reg'r of Wills

Ret'd June 23, 1834, and served on the 20th of said month Copy of petition and citation on L C Duncan, Esq in person Ret. June 30th, 1834

J H HOLLAND, D'y Sheriff

WM W WHITNEY AND MYRA C WHITNEY, } THE STATE OF
vs. } LOUISIANA.
ELEANOR O'BEARN AND OTHERS, }

Mr Richard Relf, New Orleans You are hereby summoned to comply with the prayer of the annexed petition, or to file your answer thereto, in writing with the register of wills in and for the parish and city of New Orleans, at his office in New Orleans, in ten days after the service hereof, and if you fail herein, judgment will be rendered against you, by default.

Witness the honorable Charles Maurian, Judge of the Court of Probates, this 23d day of June, in the year of our Lord 1834

P. L. B. DUPLESSIS, D'y Reg'r of Wills

Rec'd 23d June, 1834, and served on the 24th day of said month. Copy of petition and citation on Rich'd Relf, in person. Ret. June 30th, 1834.

J. H. HOLLAND, D'y Sheriff

In the Court of Probates in and for the city and parish of New Orleans, Thursday, 19th June, 1834

On motion of W. M. Worthington, and on his filing the

affidavit of William Wallace Whitney, it is ordered by the court that commissions issue to Cincinnati, State of Ohio, directed to the mayor thereof to Philadelphia, State of Pennsylvania to the mayor of said city and to Matanzas, in the Island of Cuba to Lewis Shoemaker, consul of the United States, to take the testimony of certain witnesses in behalf of plaintiffs.

WM WALLACE WHITNEY AND MYRA ⎫
   CLARK WHITNEY HIS WIFE,   ⎬   COURT OF PROBATES.
           vs   ⎪
ELEANOR O BEARN AND OTHERS   ⎭

Appeared Wm Wallace Whitney, one of the plaintiffs in the above cause who being duly sworn, deposeth and saith, that Wm Miller, of the city of Cincinnati, Samuel B. Davis, Mrs R Davis his wife, and Mrs E Clark, of Philadelphia and Joseph Deville Degoutin Belle chasse, and Harriet Harper, of Matanzas, in the Island of Cuba, are material witnesses for the plaintiffs in the above cause That the said parties a e all advanced in years, and he fears that unless their testimony is taken at once, he may be deprived of the advantage that he expects to derive from the same He prays that a commission may issue to Cincinnati, to the mayor thereof, to Philadelphia, to the mayor of said city, and to Matanzas, to Lewis Shoemaker, consul of the United States to take the testimony of the aforesaid witnesses That the same may be perpetuated to be used on the trial of the above cause.

             WM WALLACE WHITNEY

Sworn to and subscribed before me, New Orleans, 18th June, 1834

        W F C DUPLESSIS, Reg'r of Wills.

   Filed 19th June, 1834

        W F C DUPLESSIS, Reg r of Wills.

WM W WHITNEY AND WIFE, ⎫
        vs   ⎬
ELEANOR O BEARN AND OTHERS ⎭

Interrogatories propounded on the part of the plaintiffs ·

1st Were you acquainted with the late Daniel Clark, of New Orleans?

2d Were you at any time upon terms of intimacy with the said Daniel Clark? If you were so intimate with the said Daniel Clark as to enjoy his private confidence.

3d Do you know whether the said Daniel Clark, at his decease, left any child?

4th Have you heard the said Daniel Clark claim and acknowledge any child as his own?

5th. If the last question is answered in the affirmative, please state when and where you have heard the said Daniel Clark claim and acknowledge the said child as his own

6th. Please state where the said child then was protected by the said Daniel Clark; what became of it, and where it is at present.

7th. By what name was the said child called?

8th. Do you know Myra Clark Whitney? If you say whether she was the said child whom the said Daniel Clark claimed and acknowledged as his own.

9th. Are you acquainted with the circumstances of the said Daniel Clark, during his life, and at the time of his death?

10th Do you know whether the said Daniel Clark, at any time during his life, made any provision for the said child, in the event of his death? If yea, state particularly under what circumstances

11th Did the said Daniel Clark, at any time, place property in your hand, for the use and benefit of the said child? If yea, state under what circumstances, and how that property was disposed of.

12th. Did not the said Daniel Clark always manifest the fondest affection for the said child, and did he not express the intention to make her his heir?

13th Have you not often heard the said Daniel Clark say that he intended to leave to the said child his estate?

14th What intention of pecuniary advancement have you heard the said Daniel Clark express in regard to the said child?

15th. Are you acquainted with the circumstances under which the said Daniel Clark made a will, in the month of May in the year eighteen hundred and eleven? If yea, state the particulars of this subject, and whether, at that time, he had not otherwise provided for the said child.

16th Was the said will of May, eighteen hundred and eleven, made by the said Daniel Clark, a short time before his departure for the North? If yea, did the said Daniel Clark, after his return from the North, express to you his intention to make another will, and did the said Daniel Clark, after his return from the North, refer to the circumstances of the will of eighteen hundred and eleven?

17th Have you heard the said Daniel Clark subsequent to the date of the said will of May, of eighteen hundred and eleven, claim and acknowledge the said child as his daughter? If yea, at what times?

18th. Have you heard the said Daniel Clark, subsequent to the month of May, eighteen hundred and eleven, say that the said child was his heir, or that he would leave his estate to the said child? If yea, state particularly when, and the terms in which the said Daniel Clark spoke, in regard to the said child.

19th Had you, subsequent to the month of May, eighteen hundred and eleven, much intercourse with the said Daniel Clark?

20th Have you often, heard the said Daniel Clark speak of the said child subsequent to the month of May, eighteen hundred and eleven? If yea, state the particulars of his language, in regard to the said child

21st How long before the decease of the said Daniel Clark did you see him for the last time and, in your last interview with the said Daniel Clark did he speak of the said child? If yea, state the particulars of his conversation in relation to the said child

22d How long before his decease did the said Daniel Clark, for the last time speak to you in regard to the said child, and what did he say, at this time, in regard to the said child?

23d Have you heard the said Daniel Clark, subsequent to the month of May eighteen hundred and eleven, say that he was about to make or that he was engaged in making, or that he had made, his last will? If yea state the particulars of any conversation on this subject

24th Do you recollect at what time, or times, the said Daniel Clark spoke of being engaged in making his last will, or at what time he spoke of having made his last will?

25th Did you ever see the said will, or any writing, said by the said Daniel Clark to be his last will? If yea, when and where?

26th Was the said will in the handwriting of the said Daniel Clark, and was it signed by him, or was his name written in any part of it and was it dated?

27th Did you hear the said Daniel Clark say that, in his last will, he had left his estate to his daughter Myra? Recollect, as well as you can, his precise expressions.

28th When and where, for the last time, did you see the said will?

29th When and where, for the last time, have you heard the said Daniel Clark speak of the said will, and what did he say?

30th Did you hear the said Daniel Clark say who were named executors, in said will? If yea, state who

31st Did you hear the said Daniel Clark say who was named, in said will, tutor to his said daughter Myra? If yea, state all you know on this head

32d Did you, or not, ever read the said will? If so, state the contents as particularly as you recollect them, and whether the said will was not in the handwriting of the said Daniel Clark, and dated and signed by him

WM. M. WORTHINGTON, for Plaintiffs.

Cross Interrogatories.

1 Will you be pleased to state your name, age, residence, and employment?

2. Will you state whether you have any interest in the event this suit—the object of which to annul the will the late Daniel Clark, that is, a will made by him in the month of May 1811, and which at the period of his death, in August, 1813, was duly admitted to probate, in the courts of Louisiana?

3. Will you state whether, o not, you are related to or connected with the plaintiffs, or with either of them? If aye, state in what degree

4 Will you state where you were, in the spring and summer of the year 1813, and where Mr Daniel Clark was, at the same time?

5 If you state that you were intimate with the said Clark, mention the circumstances which led to that intimacy, how the same was formed, what was its particular character, and how long the same continued

6 Was the said Daniel Clark in the habit of consulting you about his affairs, whether personal, mercantile, or political? State fully and particularly

7. If you answer any one of the interrogatories in chief affirmatively, as to your knowledge of the will of Mr. Clark, state all the circumstances, the time when, and the place where, and what was the occasion of his mentioning the subject to you

8 If you say that you saw the will of Mr Clark, state where and when you saw it, and state who was present, and why he exhibited the same to you did you ask him whether he had made a will, and request him to show it to you? If not, state particularly and in detail the reasons why the same was shown to you.

9 If you answer that you saw the will about which plaintiffs interrogate you, will you state how you can, at this distant day, relate, with precision, the date of that instrument—so as to enable you to speak, with confidence of the year, the month, and the day? Did you take a copy of the will, or any memorandum to enable you to speak positively of the date? If you did annex that copy, or memorandum to answer, and when and why you made such copy or memorandum?

11 Was Mr Daniel Clark ever married, to your knowledge? If aye, when, where, and to whom?

12. If Mr. Clark was not married, state, if you please, all the circumstances attending the birth, the maintenance and education of the child Myra, whom you are asked whether he did not acknowledge. State when and where she was born; whether

to your knowledge whether she was not christened If so, by whom and where and who were her sponsors?

13 Will you state how, or why it was that Mr Clark come to acknowledge is the own ? … was she born in his house, or where? If … under his …, who was her mother and where did she reside?

14 Did you or not ever hear … Clark … own, any other child than this Myra? … that child and whether or not … did not appear to have as much affection for the one as for the other … who was the occasion of the difference of … the … reputed off-spring, and why did he acknowledge … the heir of his estate?

These cross interrogatories are proposed to be by the defendants, with a full reservation to … each and every of the interrogatories … exception thereto

TLCHUS C DUNCAN … and … attorney advocate … heirs … rights …

WM W WHITNEY AND MYRA C WHITNEY … PLAINT …

ELEANOR O BLAIN AND OTHERS … DEFENDANTS

To the Hon the mayor of the City of Philadelphia, State of Pennsylvania, greeting

Know ye that we reposing confidence in your prudence and fidelity do by these presents give … authority … to examine all witnesses whatsoever … will on the part of the plaintiffs as of the defendant in a certain suit now pending in your said court in which Wm W Whitney and Myra C Whitney are plaintiffs and Eleanor O Blain and others defendants—

Therefore, we desire you, that at certain times and places by you to be appointed for this purpose you cause the … witnesses to come before you that you then and there cause them apart, upon their respective corporal oaths … that you upon the Holy Evangelists that you examine … to writing and when you shall so have taken … that you send the same with this commission closed up under your seal, to us in our said court, at the city of New Orleans, without delay

Witness, the honorable Charles Maurian Judge of the said court, this twenty-fourth day of June, in the year of our Lord one thousand eight hundred and thirty four and in the fifty-eighth year of the Independence of the United States

Signed,   W F C DUPLESSIS, Regr of Wills
30*

Wm M. Whitney, Myra C Whitney, ⎱ Court of Probates,
                    vs   ⎰ State of Louisiana.
       Eleanor O'Beirn and al

A B C

Samuel B Davis, a witness for the plaintiff, being sworn, answers

Ne varietur, Aug 10, 1835

GALLIEN PREVAL, Judge

To the first interrogatory, on the part of the plaintiffs he answers as follows

1 I was

To the second interrogatory, on the part of the plaintiff, he answers as follows

2 I was

To the third interrogatory, on the part of the plaintiffs, he answers as follows

3 At the time of Mr Clark's death, he left a daughter named Myra, who was then living in my family

To the fourth interrogatory, on the part of the plaintiffs, he answers as follows

4 I have often heard Mr Clark acknowledge the said Myra as his child

To the fifth interrogatory, on the part of the plaintiff he answers as follows

5 Before her birth Mr Clark acknowledged her, to me, as his own child   Before her birth, Mr Clark came to me requesting me to make preparations for her birth   After her birth he placed her in charge of my family   He always claimed and acknowledged her, to me as his own child   He not only claimed and acknowledged her to be his child, but manifested the fondest paternal affection for her

To the sixth interrogatory, on the part of the plaintiffs, he answers as follows

6 This child, a few days after her birth, was placed in my care, and has been brought up in my family, where she remained till her marriage with Mr William Wallace Whitney   She and her husband are now on a visit in my family

To the seventh interrogatory, on the part of the plaintiffs, he answers as follows

7. She was named Myra   In Mr Clark's papers, respecting her, he called her Myra Clark

To the eight interrogatory, on the part of the plaintiffs, he answers as follows:

8 I know Myra Clark Whitney, wife of William Wallace Whitney.   She is the identical child, whom Mr. Clark claimed and acknowledged as his own.

To the ninth interrogatory, on the part of the plaintiffs, he answers as follows

9 In the month of May, eighteen hundred and eleven, Mr Clark requested me to go with him to his house. He appeared to be much agitated, and distressed in mind. He informed me that he was apprehensive on an account of the Daniel W Coxe, of the city of Philadelphia, with whom he had been a partner in business but become embarrassed by some bad speculations to the north of Europe and that he (Mr Clark) was in danger of suffering severely, as I were so far though he was not really a partner a short time ere the dissolution of the partnership had not been done in legal form. He showed me at the same time a schedule of the property, possessed by him and the debts for which he was accountable, to me to see by which it appeared there were of course a surplus of above five hundred thousand dollars, to the best of my recollection after all his debts were paid. The impression is the stronger on my mind as a coolness had subsisted between us for some time, and this was the first mark he gave me of his renewed confidence

To the tenth interrogatory on the part of the plaintiffs, he answers as follow

10 In our presence Mr Clark being about to leave Louisiana, placed to my order in the bank property to the amount of about twenty eight thousand dollars, which he said was contained in a trunk for which I gave him receipts, and received instructions from him that in case of accident to him, (the said Daniel Clark) to have the said property above mentioned secured for his daughters benefit. He returned in safety, and gave me up my receipts. Some short time before I left New Orleans, Mr Clark induced me to retain in my hands two thousand three hundred and sixty dollars, the interest of which was to go towards the education of his daughter, Myra, for which I gave him my note. This note was sued for, shortly after Mr Clark's death by Chew & Relf, and recovered, with interest while I was at the north, in the army, and the child lost the use of it. On the twenty seventh of May, eighteen hundred and eleven, Mr Clark wrote me from the Balize the following letter

Dear Sir We are preparing to put to sea, and I hope shall have a pleasant passage, my stay will be but short in Philadelphia unless a forced one in case of misfortune to me, be pleased to deliver the enclosed to Genl Hampton. I count on him, as a man of honor to pay the amount of notes mentioned in my letter to him, which, in that case, you will dispose of as I have directed. It will naturally strike you that the letter to the General is to be

delivered only in case of misfortune to me   Remember me kindly to Mrs Davis and all your family   Yours,
          Signed   DANIEL CLARK
    P S Of the enclosed letter you will say nothing, unless in case of accident when you may communicate it to Chew & Relf
    J B Davis Esq

His instructions to me were to place the money to the best advantage for his daughter Myra's interest   Mr Clark proceeded to Philadelphia and when he was about to sail for New Orleans, wrote to me the following letter, respecting his daughter Myra

                    PHILADELPHIA, 12th July, 1811
My dear Sir in case of any accident or misfortune to me, be pleased to open the letter addressed to me, which accompanies this, and act with respect to the enclosures as I directed you with respect to the other affairs committed to your charge, before leaving New Orleans

To account in a satisfactory manner to the person committed to your honor will I flatter myself, be done by you, when she is able to manage her own affairs, until when I commit her under God to your protection   I expect to sail to-morrow for New Orleans in the ship Orno and do not wish to risk these papers at sea   Yours,
          Signed   DANIEL CLARK
    S B Davis Esq

In this letter was the packet, referred to by Mr Clark, in his letter, which on his arrival in New Orleans, I gave to him unopened as also the letter addressed to Gen'l Hampton, in Mr Clark's letter from the Balize

    11 The tenth and eleventh interrogatories are intended to be answered by this

    To the tenth interrogatory on the part of the plaintiffs, he answers as follows

    12 Mr Clark always did manifest the warmest affection and deepest interest towards his daughter, Myra   He has repeatedly told me, that he intended to leave her his property, and I never doubted that he was entirely sincere

    To the thirteenth interrogatory, on the part of the plaintiffs, he answers as follows

    13 I have heard Mr Clark repeatedly say, that she was his heir

    To the fourteenth interrogatory, on the part of the plaintiffs, he answers as follows

    14 In answer to this, I can only repeat what I have already said in the preceding interrogatories that he intended to leave her his property

To the fifteenth interrogatory, on the part of the plaintiffs, he answers as follows

15 I have no knowledge of any written will At the time of Mr Clark's death I was absent in the army, at the north, and had been absent from Louisiana more than a year I have perfect knowledge that the property owned by him, commonly known as the Bayou property had been secured to her by a sale to Mr Delacroix and D D Bellechasse, in separate portions, wherein he confided in blind confidence to their honor This same property he had previously transferred to me in a bona fide sale in the same blind confidence, but in consequence of a coolness before mentioned in my reply to a former interrogatory, I gave it up

To the sixteenth interrogatory, on the part of the plaintiffs, he answered as follows

16 I never heard of any will until after his death

To the seventeenth interrogatory, on the part of the plaintiffs, he answered as follows

17 I have always, before and after her birth, up to the last hour I passed with him, heard him acknowledge her as his daughter, and received instructions from him relative to her education in the minute particulars about which he manifested the greatest anxiety

To the eighteenth interrogatory, on the part of the plaintiffs, he answers as follows

18 I have heard him on all occasions express himself in favor of her as his daughter and heir It was an every day conversation when we met

To the nineteenth interrogatory, on the part of the plaintiffs, he answers as follows

19 Mr Clark came, as he always had, to my house to see his child our intercourse was as usual I cannot pretend to say whether I possessed his confidence in the same degree that I thought I did before our estrangement

To the twentieth interrogatory, on the part of the plaintiffs, he answers as follows

20 I have very often heard him speak of her, she was always the subject of his conversation, when he visited my house, and he manifested, if possible more interest in his child, in proportion, as she grew older His language was always the same, but expressed with more enthusiasm, as she became more interesting

To the twenty first interrogatory, on the part of the plaintiffs, he answers as follows

21 I had not seen Mr Clark for upwards of a year, before his death, being absent in the army, as already related, at his last interview with his child, it was impossible for any father to have

manifested more solicitude and affection than he did   In my last interview with Mr Clark his conversation turned almost exclusively on the subject of his child   It was then I received instructions relative to her education, about which he seemed very solicitous, and alluded to the place that he wished her to take in society, when arrived at the years of maturity

To the twenty second interrogatory on the part of the laintiffs, he answers as follows

22. I have already related, I did not see Mr Clark for more than a year before his death   The conservations were always the same when on her subject, as I have so repeatedly said.

To the twenty third interrogatory, on the part of the plaintiffs, he answers as follows

23   I have no knowledge on the subject of any written will

To the twenty fourth interrogatory, on the part of the plaintiffs, he answers as follows

24   I have no knowledge on this subject

To the twenty fifth interrogatory, on the part of the plaintiffs, he answers as follows

25. I have no knowledge on this subject.

To the twenty sixth interrogatory, on the part of the plaintiffs, he answers as follows

26   I have no knowledge on this subject.

To the twenty seventh interrogatory, on the part of the plaintiffs, he answers as follows

27. I have no knowledge on this subject

To the twenty eighth interrogatory, on the part of the plaintiffs, he answers as follows.

28   I have no knowledge on this subject.

To the twenty ninth interrogatory on the part of the plaintiffs, he answers as follows

29. I have no knowledge on this subject

To the thirtieth interrogatory, on the part of the plaintiffs, he answers as follows

30. I have no knowledge on this subject

To the thirty first interrogatory, on the part of the plaintiffs, he answers as follows

31   I have no knowledge on this subject.

To the thirty second interrogatory, on the part of the plaintiffs, he answers as follows

32   I have no knowledge on this subject.

To the first cross interrogatory, on the part of the defendants, he answers as follows

1st. My name is Samuel B. Davis; gentleman; residence, Philadelphia, aged sixty-eight.

To the second cross interrogatory, on the part of the defendants, he answers as follows

2d I have no interest whatever in the event of this suit, that is in a pecuniary point of view.

To the third cross interrogatory on the part of the defendants, he answers as follows

3d I am in no degree whatever related to or connected with either of the plaintiffs

To the fourth cross interrogatory, on the part of the defendants, the answers as follows

4th I was in the spring and summer of eighteen hundred and thirteen, commanding officer at Lewistown, State of Delaware, first aid to the commander in chief of the State of Delaware. I believe Mr Clark was at that time in Louisiana

To the fifth cross interrogatory, on the part of the defendants, he answers as follows

5th I was very intimate with the said Daniel Clark, the circumstances that led to it were these I commanded the ship General Washington of sixteen guns and came to New Orleans, consigned to Mr Clark, in the year 1799, at this time our commerce had been much interrupted, and we were then in a state of open warfare with France in the service of which nation I had been several years, where I had acquired some reputation as an officer I had resigned my commission in this service as Lieutenant De Varsau and had lately returned to my country very poor and this was my first command Louisiana was then under the Spanish government The standing of Mr Clark in society, at that time inspired every stranger that came to the country, with the highest respect for his character and acquirements the kind reception which I met with from him, naturally gained my confidence was confirmed by the delicate attention which he shewed me on all occasions, and the interest which he took in every thing that related to me My intimacy continued with Mr Clark uninterrupted till 1809 or 1810, when, from some cause, of which I have been ignorant our mutual confidence was suspended

To the sixth cross interrogatory on the part of the defendants, he answers as follows

6th I was in partnership with Mr Clark for several years in the rope-walk establishment Mr Clark naturally conversed with me on the subject of our establishment

To the seventh cross interrogatory on the part of the defendants, he answers as follows

7th I know nothing on this subject

To the eight cross interrogatory on the part of the defendants, he answered as follows

8th. I never saw any will of Mr. Clark

To the ninth cross interrogatory on the part of the defendants he answered as follows:

9th. I have no knowledge on this subject

To the tenth cross interrogatory on the part of the defendants he answered as follows

10th. Answered in the preceding interrogatory

To the eleventh cross interrogatory on the part of the defendants, he answered as follows

11th. I do not know whether he was or not.

To the twelfth cross interrogatory on the part of the defendants, he answers as follows:

12th. I was not present at the birth of the child Myra, but at Mr. Clark's request, I had the necessary arrangements made for her birth. I have maintained and educated the child Myra at my expense. She was born in New Orleans, in June 1804 or 1805. I did not see her mother before her birth, nor had she any communication with me; the terms on which Mr. Clark and myself were at that time, precluded the possibility of his speaking to me of his child, in respect to the expense of her maintenance. I had been under so many obligations to him and I believe he knew my character too well to suppose that I would have tolerated such an allusion. Time rolled on and the child grew, and as she grew, she gained on our affection; and no conversations ever passed between me and Mr. Clark relative to the expense of her maintenance until we were about leaving that country for the north, in 1812, when her education became an object of deep interest to him; then he insisted in my retaining in my hands the two thousand three hundred and sixty dollars which I have already mentioned, the interest of which was to go towards her education; the requisite balance for her education was to have been remitted to me yearly. I never wrote to Mr. Clark on the subject of her expenses, nor ever should, his death put an end to our correspondence, had he lived, I am sure he would have attended to it. I cannot say whether the child was ever christened, or not; she was not christened at my house.

To the thirteenth cross interrogatory on the part of the defendants, he answered as follows

13th. It is impossible for me to answer this question in any other way, than that he, believing her to be his child, felt as a father towards her. She was not born at his residence, this question has been answered in my reply to a former interrogatory. Her mother's family name was Carriere, I do not know where her place of residence then was, but the child was born in New Orleans.

To the fourteenth cross interrogatory on the part of the defendants, he answered as follows

14th On one occasion Mr Clark spoke to me of a child called Caroline then living in New Jersey but we had no conversations on her subject if I remember rightly, but on one occasion, it was not for me to enquire what could produce a difference of feeling or attribute to him any cause of this difference of feeling

(Signed,)   SAMUEL B DAVIS.

[ABC]

WILLIAM M WHITNEY, AND
MYRA C WHITNEY,   COURT OF PROBATES, AND
       vs   STATE OF LOUISIANA
ELEANOR O'BEARNE & OTHERS

Marian Rose Davis, a witness for the plaintiffs, being sworn, answers—

To the first interrogatory on the part of the plaintiffs, she answers as follows

1st I was several years acquainted with Mr Clark

To the second interrogatory on the part of the plaintiffs, she answers as follows

2d I was upon terms of intimacy with Mr Clark, only so far as he was in the habit of coming very often to my house, to caress his daughter Myra, who was placed by him in the charge of my husband and myself

To the third interrogatory on the part of the plaintiffs, she answers as follows

31 When Mr Clark died, his daughter Myra was living in my family

To the fourth interrogatory on the part of the plaintiffs, she answers as follows

4th I have heard Mr Clark often claim and acknowledge as his own child the said Myra. He placed her in our family as his own child, he uniformly acknowledged her with pride and uncommon affection, as his own child

To the fifth interrogatory on the part of the plaintiffs, she answers as follows

5th Mr Clark himself placed his daughter Myra in charge of my husband and myself when she was about six or eight days old, and from that till our departure from Louisiana in 1812, he was accustomed to spend much of his time with his daughter Myra; he always claimed and acknowledged her as his own child

To the sixth interrogatory on the part of the plaintiffs, she answers as follows

6th This child was placed in my family by Mr Clark when she was six or eight days old, and she remained with her till her mar-

31*

riage with William Wallace Whitney   She is now with her husband on a visit in our family   She was protected by Mr Clark.

To the seventh interrogatory on the part of the plaintiffs, she answers as follows

7th She was named Myra

To the eighth interrogatory on the part of the plaintiffs, she answers as follows

8th I know Myra Clark Whitney   She is the very same person whom Mr Clark placed in care of our family as his own child, and whom he always claimed and acknowledged to us as his own child

To the ninth interrogatory on the part of the plaintiffs, she answers as follows

9th. I am not

To the tenth interrogatory on the part of the plaintiffs, she answers as follows.

10th. In May, 1811, at the time he heard that D W Coxe of Philadelphia had become very much embarrassed and went to that city on that account.   Mr Clark placed with my husband a large amount of property to be appropriated for the benefit of his daughter, Myra, if misfortune befell him, if not, they were to be returned to Mr Clark also, after his arrival in Philadelphia, as he was about to sail for New Orleans, Mr Clark wrote a letter to my husband, dated July 18th, enclosing, we supposed, written authority to invest his daughter with more property, in case of his death before his arrival in New Orleans

To the eleventh interrogatory on the part of the plaintiffs, she answers as follows.

11th Mr Clark never placed any property in my hands for his daughter

To the 12th interrogatory on the part of the plaintiffs she answers as follows

12th Mr Clark showed wonderful affection for his daughter Myra, and often spoke of her as the heir of his estate

To the thirteenth interrogatory on the part of the plaintiffs, she answers as follows

13th I have often heard him say that he would leave his estate to her.

To the fourteenth interrogatory on the part of the plaintiffs, she answers as follows.

14th. I have heard him speak of her as the heir of his estate

To the fifteenth interrogatory on the part of the plaintiffs, she answers as follows.

15th. I have no knowledge of any will of Mr. Clark.

To the sixteenth interrogatory on the part of the plaintiffs, she answers as follows.

16th. I have no knowledge of any will of Mr Clark.

To the seventeenth interrogatory on the part of the plaintiffs, she answers as follows

17th After Mr Clark's return from Philadelphia, in 1811, and until our departure from Louisiana in 1812, he came to our house very often to see his daughter Myra, and he always claimed and acknowledged her as his daughter

To the eighteenth interrogatory on the part of the plaintiffs, she answers as follows

18th When we were about to depart from Louisiana in 1812, Mr Clark said that she would be his heir, that he intended to leave his estate to her. He spoke in terms of great affection and pecuniary ambition about her

To the nineteenth interrogatory on the part of the plaintiffs, she answers as follows

19th After Mr Clark's return to New Orleans from Philadelphia in 1811, until our departure from New Orleans in 1812, he was in the habit of coming to our house very often to see his daughter Myra.

To the twentieth interrogatory on the part of the plaintiff, she answers as follows

20th After Mr Clark's return to New Orleans in 1811, as long as we remained in New Orleans, he came very often to see his daughter Myra. he spoke of her with great affection, said he should leave her all his estate, his ambition was stimulated to make her very rich

To the twenty-first interrogatory on the part of the plaintiffs, she answers as follows.

21st It was when we left New Orleans, in or near March, 1812, that I saw Mr Clark for the last time. I, with his daughter Myra, sailed about two months before my husband. On this occasion, Mr Clark said, as she was of an age to receive instruction, he wished that on our arrival at the north, teachers should be provided for her, he spoke of her as his heir and in speaking of her education, said that he wished her educated in a manner suitably, to take in society the standing of the heir of his estate.

To the twenty-second interrogatory on the part of the plaintiffs, she answers as follows.

22d I never saw Mr. Clark after I left Louisiana in the spring of 1812. On this occasion he spoke of his daughter Myra as the heir of his estate, manifested the immensest interest, affection and solicitude for her and pride and ambition for her.

To the twenty-third interrogatory on the part of the plaintiffs, she answers as follows:

23d. I never heard Mr Clark speak of any will.

To the twenty-fourth interrogatory on the part of the plaintiffs, she answers as follows

24 I never heard Mr Clark speak of any will

To the twenty-fifth interrogatory on the part of the plaintiffs, she answers as follows

25th I never saw any will of Mr Clark's, or any writing called by him his will

To the twenty-sixth interrogatory on the part of the plaintiffs, she answers as follows

26th. I have no knowledge on this head

To the twenty-seventh interrogatory on the part of the plaintiffs, she answers as follows

27th I never heard Mr Clark speak of any will of his own

To the twenty-eighth interrogatory on the part of the plaintiffs, she answers as follows

28th I never saw any will of Mr Clark

To the twenty-ninth interrogatory on the part of the plaintiffs, she answers as follows

29th I never heard Mr Clark speak of any will

To the thirtieth interrogatory on the part of the plaintiffs, she answers as follows

30th I never heard him speak of any will

To the thirty-first interrogatory on the part of the plaintiffs, she answers as follows

31st I never heard him speak of any will

To the thirty-second interrogatory on the part of the plaintiffs, she answers as follows

32d I never saw any will of Mr Clark's.

To the first cross interrogatory on the part of the defendants, she answers as follows

1st My name is Mary Ann Rose Davis, wife of Samuel B Davis. I reside in Philadelphia I have no employment

To the second cross interrogatory on the part of the defendants, she answers as follows

2d. I have no interest in the event of this suit.

To the third interrogatory on the part of the defendants, she answers as follows.

3d I am in no degree connected with either of the plaintiffs

To the fourth cross interrogatory on the part of the defendants, she answers as follows

4th I was at Lewistown in the spring and summer of 1813, I do not know where Mr Clark was

To the fifth cross interrogatory on the part of the defendants, she answers as follows

5th My intimacy with Mr Clark was only so far as was produced by having in my family his daughter, Myra; this continued till my departure from New Orleans, in 1812.

To the sixth cross interrogatory on the part of the defendants, she answers as follows

6th She was not

To the seventh cross interrogatory on the part of the defendants, she answers as follows

7th I have no knowledge of any will of Mr Clark's

To the eighth cross interrogatory on the part of the defendants, she answers as follows

8th I never saw any will of Mr Clark's.

To the ninth cross interrogatory on the part of the defendants, she answers as follows

9th I know nothing of any will of Mr Clark's.

To the tenth cross interrogatory on the part of the defendants, she answers as follows

10th I know nothing of any will of Mr Clark's

To the eleventh cross interrogatory on the part of the defendants she answers as follows

11th I do not know whether Mr Clark was married or not

To the twelfth cross interrogatory on the part of the defendants she answers as follows

12th Before the birth of this child Mr Clark came to my husband and requested him to have a house prepared for the reception of the child's mother She was born in New Orleans This child lived in our family till her marriage Before we left New Orleans, she had never had teachers, nor till Mr Clark's death, it was then alone at my husband's expense I do not know that she was ever christened Mr Clark purchased a servant for her, gave her costly dresses and play things

To the thirteenth cross interrogatory on the part of the defendants she answers as follows

13th I can only suppose it was from natural affection I believe that she was born in a house which my brothers then held, which, not the house of Mr Clark's residence Her mother's family name was Carrière I do not know where she then resided The child was born in New Orleans

To the fourteenth cross interrogatory on the part of the defendants, she answers as follows

14th His daughter, Myra, is the only child Mr. Clark ever acknowledged to me as his own

(Signed) MARIAN ROSE DAVIS, ⋈ her mark.
Indisposition prevents Mrs. Davis from signing her name.
(Signed) M. SWIFT.

WILLIAM M. WHITNEY AND }
MYRA C WHITNEY,   }   COURT OF PROBATES, AND
        vs.   }   STATE OF LOUISIANA
ELEANOR O BEARN.   }

A B C

Smith, a witness for the plaintiffs, being sworn to testify the truth, the whole truth, and nothing but the truth, answers as follows,

1st To the first interrogatory on the part of the plaintiffs, she answers as follows

I became acquainted with Mr Clark shortly after my arrival in New Orleans, which acquaintance continued until the period of his death, in August, eighteen hundred and thirteen

2d To the second interrogatory on the part of the plaintiffs, she answers as follows

When an infant, named Myra, claimed by Mr Clark as his daughter, was five or six weeks old, I suckled her, I did this because she had suffered from the imposition of hired nurses Mr Clark considered that this service constituted a powerful claim on his gratitude and friendship, and ever afterwards gave me his confidence respecting her

3d. To the third interrogatory on the part of the plaintiffs, she answers as follows

In his will of July eighteen hundred and thirteen, Mr Clark acknowledged Myra Clark as his legitimate daughter and designated her as then being in the family of Mr S J Davis

4th To the fourth interrogatory on the part of the plaintiffs, she answers as follows

I have frequently heard Mr Clark claim and acknowledge the said Myra as his own child

5th To the fifth interrogatory on the part of the plaintiffs, she answers as follows

Being at that period the wife of Mr Harper, a nephew of Mr S. B Davis, we became members of his family soon after our arrival in New Orleans While living in this family the infant Myra was introduced there, when this child was five or six weeks old, I suckled her, this led Mr Clark to caress her in my presence, to acknowledge her to me as his child, and to speak of her to me After I had left Mr Davis family to live at my own domicil, Mr Clark was accustomed to talk with me very often about her, always acknowledging her as his daughter.

6th To the 6th interrogatory on the part of the plaintiffs, she answers as follows

When this child was seven or eight days old she was placed in the care of Mr S B Davis' family, when that family left New Orleans in eighteen hundred and twelve, she departed with them, and I have since been told by Mr and Mrs Davis that she was brought up by them never having them till her marriage with Mr William Wallace Whitney She is now in Philadelphia with her husband, sojourning in the same family Mr Clark always protected her

7th To the seventh interrogatory on the part of the plaintiffs, she answers as follows.

She was named Myra Mr Clark, in his will of July, eighteen hundred and thirteen, called her Myra Clark

8th To the eighth interrogatory on the part of the plaintiffs, she answers as follows

I am acquainted with Myra Clark Whitney and recognize her as the same person whom Mr Clark claimed and acknowledged as his own child I recognize Myra Clark Whitney as the same person whom Mr Clark in his will of July, eighteen hundred and thirteen, acknowledged as his legitimate daughter

9th To the ninth interrogatory on the part of the plaintiffs, she answers as follows

I cannot give precise information in regard to Mr Clark's circumstances, I was under the impression that he was rich At the period of his making his will of eighteen hundred and thirteen he often spoke of the great wealth his daughter would possess as his heir From the inventory of property in this will of eighteen hundred and thirteen, I also judged that he was rich

10th To the tenth interrogatory on the part of the plaintiffs, she answers as follows

When Mr Clark was about to depart for Philadelphia, in May, eighteen hundred and eleven, he told me that he had placed in trust with friends, for his daughter Myra, a very large amount of property, consisting of notes and titles to real estate It was on the occasion of his hearing that D W Coxe, of Philadelphia, had been very unfortunate in his speculations

11th To the eleventh interrogatory on the part of the plaintiffs, she answers as follows

Mr Clark never placed property in my hands for the use of his daughter.

12th. To the 12th interrogatory on the part of the plaintiffs, she answers as follows

Mr. Clark always manifested great affection for her, it was shown in a greater degree after her departure from New Orleans, in March, eighteen hundred and twelve, after that period he spoke constantly of her as the impulse of all his ambition of accumulating property. When he told me that he intended to make his last will, he said it was the purpose of making her his heir; and while he spoke of being engaged in making it, he said that his object in making that will, was to institute her his heir to secure his estate to her.

13th. To the thirteenth interrogatory on the part of the plaintiffs, she answers as follows:

After her departure from New Orleans, in eighteen hundred and twelve, Mr. Clark often told me that he would leave her his estate; about four months before his death he told me that he intended to secure his estate to her by a last will.

To the fourteenth interrogatory on the part of the plaintiffs, she answers as follows:

14th. I have heard Mr. Clark frequently express the most extravagant pecuniary ambition for her; it was particularly after her departure from New Orleans, in eighteen hundred and twelve, that all his thoughts and feelings appeared concentrated on her. He would declare to me that all his desire and motive of accumulating property was for her sake; he would spend hours at my house in expatiating on his plans of aggrandisement for her. When he declared to me his intention of making his last will, he said it was for the purpose of securing his estate to her.

To the fifteenth interrogatory on the part of the plaintiffs, she answers as follows:

15th. Shortly before Mr. Clark's departure for Philadelphia, in May, eighteen hundred and eleven, he told me that he heard Mr. D. W. Coxe, of Philadelphia, had been very unfortunate in his speculations, that he (Mr. Clark,) must in consequence depart for Philadelphia as soon as possible. When he was about to start, he told me that the situation in which he was so suddenly placed, compelled him to make a will apparently in his mother's favor; that he had placed in trust a very large amount of property for his daughter, Myra.

To the sixteenth interrogatory on the part of the plaintiffs, she answers as follows:

16th. It was when Mr. Clark was on the point of departure, in May, eighteen hundred and eleven, from New Orleans, on the occasion just related by me, that he told me he had made and put into Chew & Relf's hands this will. After his return to New Orleans he told me ____ was a false report in respect to Mr. Coxe's affairs, several times referred to this will, always treating ____ in a light manner, said that he was in a false ____ when he made it, that it was designed to meet certain circumstances. About four months before his death, Mr. Clark told me that he intended to make his last will for the purpose of securing his estate to his daughter, Myra.

To the seventeenth interrogatory on the part of the plaintiffs, she answers as follows:

17th. After Mr. Clark's return from Philadelphia, in eighteen hundred and eleven, he was accustomed to talk to me a great deal about his daughter, Myra, but particularly after her departure from New Orleans in the spring of eighteen hundred and twelve, was he in the habit of coming to my house for the purpose it seemed of giving vent to his affection for her. Throughout he acknowledged her as his daughter. When he declared to me his intention of making his last will, in eighteen hundred and thirteen he told me that his object was to place her at the head of his estate, acknowledge her as his legitimate daughter and only heir. When he spoke of being engaged in making this will, he told me that she would be acknowledged in it as his legitimate daughter. When the will was done, Mr Clark expressed satisfaction that, by making his last will, he had established beyond chance the right that Myra had to his being acknowledged by him in it as his only and his legitimate daughter.

To the .... interrogatory on the part of the plaintiffs, she answers as follows:

18th. After the departure of his daughter from New Orleans, in eighteen hundred and twelve, Mr Clark often told me he intended to leave his estate to her, and about four months before his death he told me that he would secure his estate to her by a last will. During the period he spoke of being engaged in making his last will, he said he should acknowledge her in it as his legitimate daughter, and make her his only heir. After his will was done, he expressed satisfaction that, however soon he might die, his estate was secured to her beyond accident, that she would go forth to the world acknowledged by him as his legitimate daughter, and be educated according to his wishes.

To the .... interrogatory on the part of the plaintiffs, she answers as follows:

19th. After Mr Clark's return to New Orleans from Philadelphia, in eighteen hundred and eleven, he came frequently to my house, for the last year of his life I saw him almost every day when he was in town.

To the twentieth interrogatory, on the part of the plaintiffs, she answers as follows:

20th. After Mr Clark's return from Philadelphia, in eighteen hundred and eleven, he often talked to me about his daughter Myra. After his departure from New Orleans, in eighteen hundred and twelve, he came to my house nearly every day, if in town, to talk about her. He would say that all his ambition of accumulating property was for her sake, that he would cover her with fortunes, that he wished to live only for her sake. When he expressed his intention of making his last will, he said that he should acknowledge her in it as his legitimate daughter and only heir. At the times he told me he was en-

32*

gaged in making his last will, he always connected it with her saying, that the object of it was to place her at the head of his estate, in the quality of his legitimate daughter, and sole heir, and guarantee her the same course of education as he would direct if living At these times he talked a great deal on the subject of her education, and he spoke of the wealth she would possess as his heir, he dwelt upon the moral benefit to her, from being acknowledged by him, in his last will, as his legitimate daughter. When this will was done, he said to me, now Myra's rights are fixed beyond chance, now if I die to-morrow, she will possess the whole of my estate, she will go forth to society, and to my pious mother, acknowledged by me in my last will as my legitimate daughter, and will be educated according to my wishes

To the twenty first interrogatory, on the part of the plaintiffs, she answers as follows

21st The last time I saw Mr Clark was on the day he come out from his house for the last time, I cannot say how many days before his death, he come to my house about noon, on entering he complained of indisposition asked to have prepared for him a bowl of tea He made this visit of about two hours talking the whole time about his daughter Myra and his last will, he said that a burthen of solicitude was removed from his mind from the time he had secured to her his estate beyond accident, by finishing his last will He constantly carried with him the satisfaction of knowing that however soon he might die, she was his only heir, she would possess his estate, that she would go forth to society, to his relations, to his pious mother acknowledged by him in his last will as his legitimate daughter, and would be educated according to his wishes He said it would be the greatest boon from his God, to live to bring her up, but what was next to that, were his comprehensive instructions in his will, in regard to her education and her being committed in his will to the care of the Chevalier De Lacroix, who would have them rigidly complied with, and be as a parent to her He dwelt upon the pleasure it would give his aged and pious mother, if she survived him, that in his last will he had solemnly acknowledged her as his legitimate daughter. He dwelt upon the moral benefit to her in society, from being acknowledged by him in his last will as his legitimate daughter He talk about her education, about her great wealth as his only heir, as by the time she grew up. the value of his estate would be many fold increased He said that by acknowledging her as his legitimate daughter in his last will, and bequeathing to her all his estate in his last will, and by giving such particular instructions for her education, and then intrusting her to such a character as Chevalier Delacroix, as her tutor, in his last will and her interests to such characters as Chevalier Delacroix, Judge Pitot and Colonel Bellechasse, he had fulfilled the demands of affection, pride and honor. He said that as he might die while his daughter was a young minor, it was fortunate that such a character as Chevalier De la Croix was her tutor, in his will, and that such characters as Chevalier De la Croix, J. Pitot, and J. D. D. Bellechasse were executors in his will.

To the twenty-second interrogatory, on the part of the plaintiffs, she answers as follows:

22d. The last time Mr Clark spoke to me about his daughter, Myra, was on the day he came out from his house for the last time, which was the last time I saw him. He expressed satisfaction that he had effectually secured his estate to her, by finishing his last will, and he said that if he died to-morrow, she would go forth to the world with the moral as well as the pecuniary benefit of being acknowledged by him in his last will, as his legitimate daughter, and that she would be educated according to his wishes, under the superintendance of Chevalier Delacroix, in whom he had every confidence; and that such characters as Chevalier Delacroix, Judge Pitot and Colonel Bellechasse would have the care of her interests.

Mr Clark expressed a great deal of pride in regard to the position his daughter would be enabled to take in society. He spoke of the happiness he felt on his mother's account, if she survived him; that his daughter Myra was acknowledged by him in his last will as his legitimate daughter.

To the twenty-third interrogatory, on the part of the plaintiffs, she answers as follows:

23d. About four months before his death, Mr Clark told me that he felt that he ought no longer to defer securing his estate to his daughter Myra by a last will. Near this period he stopped one day at my house, saying to me, that he was on his way to Chevalier Delacroix's plantation, for the purpose of requesting him to be in his will one of his executors, and tutor to his daughter Myra. On his return he told me, with much apparent gratification, that Delacroix consented to conserve. He told me that Judge Pitot and Col Bellechasse had consented to be the other executors. About this time he told me that he had commenced his last will. Between this period and the time when he brought it to my house, Mr Clark spoke very often of being engaged in making his last will, he always spoke of it in connection with his daughter Myra, said he was making it for her sake, to make her his heir, to secure his estate to her, and and to ensure that she should be educated according to his wishes.

At the times Mr Clark spoke of being engaged in making his last will, he told me over and over again what would constitute its contents, that he should in it acknowledge the said Myra as his legitimate daughter, and bequeath all his estate to her, but direct that an annuity of two thousand dollars a year should be paid his mother during her life, and an annuity of five hundred dollars a year to a young female at the north of the United States, named Caroline De Grange, till her majority, then it was to cease, and five thousand dollars were to be paid her as a legacy, and that he would direct, that one year after the settlement of his estate, five thousand dollars should be paid to a son of Judge Pitot, of New Orleans, as a legacy, and at the same period five thousand dollars as a legacy to a son of Mr. Debuys, of New Orleans, that his slave Lubin was to be freed, and a maintenance provided for him   In his conversations respecting his being engaged in making his last will, he talked a great deal about the plan of education to be laid down in his will for his daughter Myra, he expressed frequently his satisfaction that the Chevalier Delacroix would be her tutor in his will   He often spoke with earnestness of the moral benefit to his daughter Myra, from being acknowledged by him in his last will, as his legitimate daughter, and he often spoke of the happiness it would give his mother   He expressed the most extravagant pride and ambition for her.   He would frequently use the emphatic language, that he was making her bill of rights. He mentioned at these times, that this will would contain a complete inventory of all his estate, and explanations of all his business, so as both to render the administration on his estate, plain and easy to his friends the Chevalier Delacroix. Judge Pitot and Col Bellechasse, and as a safeguard to his estate, in case he should not live long enough to dissolve and adjust all his pecuniary relations with others   About four weeks before his death, Mr. Clark brought this will to my house. As he came in, he said, now my estate is secured to Myra beyond human contingency, now if I die to to-morrow, she will go forth to society, to my relatives, to my mother, acknowledged by me in my last will, as my legitimate daughter, and will be educated according to my minutest wishes, under the superintendance of of the Chevalier Delacroix, and her interests will be under the care of Chevalier Delacroix, Judge Pitot and Col Bellechasse,— here is the charter of her rights, it now is completely finished, and I have brought it to you to read

When I saw Mr Clark for the last time, he said his mind had been greatly relieved from the time he had secured his estate to his daughter Myra by completing his last will, that it was a constant source of pleasing reflection, that however soon he might die, she would go forth to the world acknowledged by him, in his last will, as his legitimate daughter and only heir, that she would be educated almost as if under his own eye.

that she would be committed to the care of the Chevalier Delacroix, as her tutor and that her pecuniary interests would be under the care of such characters as the Chevalier Delacroix, Jugde Pitot and Col Bellechasse

To the twenty fourth interrogatory, on the part of the plaintiffs, she answers as follows

24th It was about four months before his death, that Mr. Clark said he intended to commence his last will, between this period and the time he brought it to my house, he many times spoke of being engaged in making it It was about four weeks before his death that he brought it to me to read, it was then finished

To the twenty-fifth interrogatory, on the part of the plaintiffs, she answers as follows

25th About four weeks before his death, Mr Clark brought to me at my house a writing which purported to be his last will finished, being then dated and signed with his name

To the twenty-sixth interrogatory, on the part of the plaintiffs, she answers as follows

26th The whole of this will was in Mr Clark's handwriting, it was dated and signed by Mr Clark at the time I read it

To the twenty-seventh interrogatary, on the part of plaintiffs, she answers as follows

At the time Mr Clark spoke of being engaged in making his last will, he told me that in it he should leave his estate to his daughter Myra, that he should acknowledge her in it as his legitimate daughter, and leave the whole of his estate to her. After it was done he referred to his having acknowledged her in his his last will, as his legitimate daughter, and having made her in his will his sole heir

To the twenty eight interrogatory, on the part of the plaintiffs, she answers as follows

28th It was at my own house, about four weeks before his death, that I saw for the first and last time this will.

To the twenty-ninth interrogatory, on the part of the plaintiffs, she answers as follows

29th The last time Mr Clark spoke to me about his last will, was on the day he came out from his house for the last time, he told me on this occasion that his mind was greatly relieved since he had secured his estate to his daughter Myra, by finishing his last will He expressed his satisfaction that such characters as Chevalier Delacroix, J Pitot and J D D Bellechasse, were executors in his last will and that Chevalier Delacroix was his daughter Myra's tutor in his last will He referred to the plan of education laid down in his will for her.

To the thirtieth interrogatory, on the part of the plaintiffs, she answers as follows

After this will was finished, Mr Clark referred to Chevalier Delacroix, Judge Pitot and Col Bellechasse being executors in his last will

To the thirty-first interrogatory, on the part of the plaintiffs, she answers as follows.

After this will was finished, Mr Clark in conversation with me, referred to Chevalier Delacroix being named in his last will as tutor to his daughter Myra   About the time he told me that he was about to commence this will, he told me that he was in his way to ask Chevalier Delacroix's permission to be named in his last will, tutor to his daughter Myra, on his return he told me that Delacroix consented to act

At the times he spoke of being engaged in making his last will, Mr Clark expressed his satisfaction that Chevalier Delacroix, would be tutor to his daughter in his last will   When Mr Clark brought his last will to me to read, he dwelt with much apparent pleasure, that by finishing his last will, he had ensured that however soon accident might befall him, his daughter Myra would be under the care of the Chevalier Delacroix, as her tutor, in his will   The last time I saw Mr Clark, he expressed his satisfaction with much earnestness, that Chevalier Delacroix was tutor to his daughter Myra, in his last will.

To the thirty-second interrogatory on the part of the plaintiffs, she answers as follows

I read this will about four weeks before Mr Clark's death. In this will Mr Clark acknowledged Myra Clark as his legitimate daughter, and only heir, designating her as then living in the family of Mr S. B Davis   Mr Clark, in this will, bequeathed all his estate to the said Myra, but directed that an annuity of two thousand dollars should be paid to his mother, during her (his mother's) life, and an annuity of five hundred dollars should be paid to Caroline DeGrange, till she arrived at majority, when the annuity was to cease—and five thousand dollars were to be paid her as a legacy   He directed that one year after his estate was settled, five thousand dollars should be paid as a legacy, to a son of Judge Pitot, of New Orleans, and that one year after his estate was settled five thousand dollars should be paid as a legacy to a son of Mr Debuys, of New Orleans   He provided for the freedom and maintenance of his slave Lubin.   He appointed Mr Dusuau De la Croix tutor to his daughter Myra   He gave very extensive instructions in regard to her education   This will contained an inventory of his estate, and explanations of his business relations   He appointed Mr Dusuau De la Croix, James Pitot, J D D Bellechasse, executors   The whole of this will was in Mr. Clark's hand writing, it was dated in July, eighteen hundred and thirteen, and was signed by him

To the first cross interrogatory on the part of the defendants she answers as follows

1st I am now the wife of George Smith M D Before my residence in New Orleans, and during my residence there, and for several years afterwards I was the wife of William Harper I am not now in any employment Since my marriage with Dr Smith I have had no settled residence I am now sojourning in Philadelphia my age is over forty-eight years

To the second cross interrogatory on the part of the defendants, she answers as follows

2d I have no interest in the event of this suit

To the third cross interrogatory on the part of the defendants, she answers as follows

3d I am not in any degree related to or connected with the plaintiffs, or with either of them

To the fourth cross interrogatory on the part of the defendants, she answers as follows

4th Mr Clark was in New Orleans in the spring of eighteen hundred and thirteen he was in New Orleans in the summer of 1813 I was in New Orleans in the spring and summer of that year

To the fifth cross interrogatory on the part of the defendants, she answers as follows

5th My suckling his daughter Myra led to it, and formed it, and the feeling of gratitude and friendship inspired in Mr Clark towards me, by this service—always kept it alive, this intimacy related to his daughter Myra, and continued as long as Mr Clark lived

To the sixth cross interrogatory on the part of the defendants, she answers as follows

6th Mr Clark was in the habit of communicating to me very freely in regard to his daughter, though it could not be called consulting me At the period he declared to me his intention of making his last will, he talked to me in regard to the plan of education to be presented in his will for his daughter Myra, though not in a manner of consulting me he talked freely to me of other points in that matter, though not in a manner of consulting me

To the seventh cross interrogatory on the part of the defendants, she answers as follows

7th It was about four months before his death, that Mr Clark told me that he intended to make his last will, it was in talking about his daughter Myra that Mr Clark introduced this subject he said he felt he ought no longer to defer securing his estate to her by a last will, that he wished to place her at the head of his estate, acknowledged by him in his last will as his legitimate daughter and heir; and he wished to render it certain that she would be educated according to his wishes, by prescribing particular instructions in a last will   Between this period and the time Mr Clark brought his will to my house, he many times spoke of being engaged in making his last will, he always connected it with his daughter Myra, as having in view to secure his estate to her, to ensure that she would be educated in the same manner as he would direct, if living   About four weeks before his death, Mr Clark brought his will to my house, when he came in, he said, now my will is finished, now, if I die tomorrow, my estate is secured to Myra, beyond chance Now she will go forth to the world, acknowledged by me in my last will as my legitimate daughter, be brought up precisely as I could wish, under the superintendance of Mr Delacroix, who will be a father to her Here is the charter of her rights all finished, I have brought it to you to read   The last time I saw Mr Clark, which was on the day he came out of his house for the last time, he spoke about his will— expressed the pleasure he had felt from the time he had secured his estate to his daughter beyond accident, by finishing his last will

To the eighth cross interrogatory on the part of the defendants, she answers as follows

8th It was at my own dwelling I saw Mr. Clark's will about four weeks before his death, he brought it to me to read, of his own volition, without my requesting to see it, I suppose his reason for wishing me to read it, was derived from the natural claim I had established on his feelings, in regard to his daughter, by having, in the first place, suckled her, then having heard for a long period, the expression of his feelings towards her, then during the period he spoke of being engaged in making his last will, his having again and again talked over to me this subject.

To the ninth cross interrogatory on the part of the defendants, she answers as follows ·

9th. I made no memorandum or copy of this will, but it may be that the circumstance of this will not appearing after Mr. Clark's death, contributed to fix in my mind the recollection of its contents, as it was then, has often been since, a matter of earnest and solemn reflection with me, especially, as I had not only read it so shortly before his death, but because the last time I saw Mr Clark, he had expressed in the most enthusiastic language, his happiness in knowing, that however soon he might die, his estate was secured to his daughter Myra by his last will, also, beause while he spoke of being engaged in making his last will, it seemed a matter to him of the most intense interest and solicitude. It may have contributed to fix my recollection of the date of this will, by my remembering that I playfully said to Mr. Clark, since the charter of Myra's rights, as you call your last will, is dated in July, what a pity that you had not finished it soon enough to bear the date of the fourth of July, the anniversary of the day the Americans promulgated their charter

To the tenth cross-interrogatory on the part of the defendants, she answers as follows

10th I made no memorandum or copy of this will

To the eleventh cross-interrogatory on the part of the defendants, she answers as follows

11th I do not know whether Mr Clark was ever married

To the twelfth cross-interrogatory on the part of the defendants, she answers as follows

12th This child was five or six weeks old when Mr Clark acknowledged her to me as his daughter After he acknowledged her to me, he told me that he had had all the arrangements prepared for her birth, and that he made arrangements with Mr S B Davis to receive her into his family Mr Clark purchased for his daughter a valuable servant he had made for her in Philadelphia a handsome coachee he furnished her with very costly dresses and playthings At the time she left New Orleans in eighteen hundred and twelve, she had never been at school In his will of July eighteen hundred and thirteen Mr Clark gave very particular instructions respecting her education Mr Clark told me that she was born in a house that was at that time in charge of the Messrs Baron in New Orleans I do not know that she has ever been christened She was born in or near the month of June 1804, or 1805

To the thirteenth cross-interrogatory, on the part of the defendants, she answers as follows

13th I can give no other reason than to judge that it was from parental affection, he told me that he had had the preparations made for her birth he told me that she was born in a house held by the Messrs Baron, which he obtained for that purpose, which was not the house of his own residence I believe that her mother's family name was Carriere I did not know her mother, and cannot say where her residence then was

To the fourteenth cross-interrogatory, on the part of the defendants, she answers as follows

14th Mr Clark never acknowledged to me any child as his own except his daughter Myra

HARRIET HARPER

Ne varietur
New Orleans, Jan'y 10th 1835

GALLIEN PREVAL, Judge

[A. B C]

BALIZE, 27th May, 1811

Dear Sir We are preparing to put to sea, and I hope shall
33*

have a pleasant passage My stay will be but short in Philadelphia, unless a forced one. In case of misfortune to me, be pleased to deliver the inclosed to Gen'l Hampton I

as a man of honor, to pay the amount of the notes mentioned in my letter to him, which, in that case, you will dispose of as I have directed. It will naturally strike you that the letter to the General is to be delivered only in case of misfortune to me. Remember me kindly to Mrs. Davis, and all your family

Yours,   DANIEL CLARK

P S Of the enclosed letter you will say nothing, unless in case of accident, when you may communicate it to Chew & Relf

S. B Davis, Esq.

Endorsed on the back, B 12 1-2 Samuel B. Davis, Esq, New Orleans.

Interrogatories propounded to witnesses, examined on behalf of the plaintiffs

Wm. W Whitney and wife   ⎫
          vs.   ⎬
Eleanor O. Bearn and al   ⎭

1st Were you acquainted with the late Daniel Clark, of New Orleans?

2d Were you at any times upon terms of intimacy with the said Daniel Clark ? If yea, were you so intimate with the said Daniel Clark, as to enjoy his private confidence ?

3 Do you know whether the said Daniel Clark, at his decease, left any child ?

4. Have you heard the said Daniel Clark claim and acknowledge any child as his own ?

5. If the last question is answered in the affirmative, please state when and where you have heard the said Daniel Clark claim and acknowledge the said child as his own ?

6 Please state where the said child then was, whether it was protected by the said Daniel Clark ? what became of it ? and where it is at present ?

7 By what name was the said child called ?

8 Do you know Myra Clark Whitney, one of the petitioners ? if you say whether she is the said child whom the said Daniel Clark claimed and acknowledged as his own ?

9. You acquainted with the circumstances of the said Daniel Clark, during his life, and at the time of his death ?

10 Do you know whether the said Daniel Clark, at any time, during his life, made any provision for the said child in the event of his death ? if yea, state particularly under what circumstances.

11. Did the said Daniel Clark, at any time, place property in your hands for the use and benefit of the said child ? if yea, state

under what circumstances, and how that property was disposed of?

12 Did not the said Daniel Clark always manifest the farthest affection for the said child, and did he not express the intention to make her his heir?

13 Have you not often heard the said Daniel Clark say, that he intended to leave his estate to the said child?

14. What intention of pecuniary advancement did the said Daniel Clark express, in regard to the said child?

15 Are you acquainted with the circumstances under which the said Daniel Clark made a will in the month of May, in the year eighteen hundred and eleven? if yea, state the particulars of this subject and whether, at that time, he had not otherwise provided for the said child?

16 Was the said will of May, eighteen hundred and eleven, made by the said Daniel Clark, a short time before his departure for the North? if yea, did the said Daniel Clark, after his return from the North, express to you his intention to make another will? and did the said Daniel Clark after his return from the North, refer to the circumstances of the said will of eighteen hundred and eleven?

17 Have you heard the said Daniel Clark, subsequent to the date of the said will of May eighteen hundred and eleven, claim and acknowledge the said child as his daughter? if yea, at what times?

18 Have you heard the said Daniel Clark, subsequent to the month of May, eighteen hundred and eleven, say that the said child was his heir? or that he intended to leave his estate to the said child? if yea, state particularly when, and the terms in which the said Daniel Clark spoke in regard to the said child

19 Had you, subsequent to the month of May, eighteen hundred and eleven, much intercourse with the said Daniel Clark?

20 Have you often heard the said Daniel Clark speak of the said child, subsequent to the month of May, eighteen hundred and eleven? if yea, state the particulars of his language, in regard to the said child.

21 How long before the decease of the said Daniel Clark, did you see him for the last time, and in your last interview with the said Daniel Clark, did he speak of the said child? if yea, state the particulars of his conversation in relation to the said child

22 How long before his decease did the said Daniel Clark, for the last time, speak to you in regard to the said child? and what did he say at this time in regard to the said child?

23 Have you heard the said Daniel Clark, subsequent to the month of May, eighteen hundred and eleven, say that he was about to make, or that he was engaged in making, or that he had made his last will? if yea state the particulars of any conversation on this subject

24 Do you recollect at what time or times the said Daniel Clark spoke to you of being engaged in making his last will, or at what time he spoke of having made his last will?

25 Did you ever see the said will or any writing said by the said Daniel Clark to be his will? if yea, when and where?

26 Was the said will in the hand writing of the said Daniel Clark, and was it signed by him, or was his name written in any part of it, and was it dated?

27 Did you hear the said Daniel Clark say, that in his said will he had left his estate to his daughter, Myra? recollect as well as you can his precise expressions

28 When and where, for the last time, did you see the said will?

29 When and where, for the last time, did you hear the said Daniel Clark speak of the said will, and what did he say?

30 Did you hear the said Daniel Clark say who were named in said will, executors? if yea state who

31 Did you hear the said Daniel Clark say who was named in said will, tutor to his said daughter Myra? if yea, state all you know on this head

32 Did you or not ever read the said will? if so, state as particularly as you recollect them, the contents and whether the said will was not in the hand writing of the said Daniel Clark, and dated and signed by him?

Signed,   WM M WORTHINGTON, for plaintiffs

Cross interrogatories

1 Will you be pleased to state your name, age, residence and employment?

2 Will you state whether you have any interest in the event of this suit, the object of which, is to annul the will of the late Daniel Clark, that is a will made by him on the month of May, 1811, and which, at the period of his death in August, 1813, was duly admitted to probate in this Court of Louisiana?

3 Will you state whether or not you are related to or connected with the plaintiffs, or with either of them? if aye, state in what degree

4. Will you state where you were in the spring and summer of the year 1813? and where Mr Daniel Clark was at the same time?

5 If you state that you were intimate with the said Clark, mentioned the circumstances which led to that intimacy? how the same was formed? what was its particular character? and how long the same continued?

6 Was the said Daniel Clark in the habit of consulting you about his affairs? whether personal, mercantile or political? State fully and particularly

7 If you answer any one of the interrogatories in chief affirmatively, as to your knowledge of the will of Mr Clark, state all the circumstances, the time when and the place where and what was the occasion of his mentioning the subject to you?

8 If you say that you saw the will of Mr Clark state where and when you saw it, and state who was present, and why he exhibited the same to you? Did you ask him whether he had made a will, and request him to show it to you? If not, state particularly, and in detail, the reasons why the same was shown to you?

9 If you answer that you saw the will about which plaintiffs interrogate you, will you state how you came at this distant day, relate with precision, the date of that instrument, so as to enable you to speak with confidence of the year, the month, and the day? Did you take a copy of the will or any memorandum, to enable you to speak positively of the date? If you did annex that copy or memorandum to your answer, and when and why you made such copy or memorandum?

10 Was Mr Daniel Clark ever married to your knowledge? if aye, when? where? and to whom?

11 If Mr Clark was not married, state, if you please, all the circumstances, attending the birth, the maintenance and education of the child Myra, whom you are asked whether he did not acknowledge? State, when and where she was born? whether to your knowledge she was not christened? if so, by whom? and where? and who were her sponsors?

12 Will you state how or why it was that Mr Clark came to acknowledge as his own, the child called Myra? was she born in his house? or where, if not under his roof? who was her mother? and where did she reside?

13 Did you or not ever heard said Clark acknowledge as his own any other child than this Myra? if aye, state the name of that child and whether or not he did not appear to have as much affection for the one as for the other? If not, what was the occasion of this difference of feeling towards his own reputed offspring? and why did he acknowledge the one to the exclusion of the other, as the heir of his estate?

These cross-interrogatories are propounded by the defendants, with a full reservation to them of all legal exceptions to each and every of the interrogatories in chief, and every the legal exception thereto

(Signed)   LUCIUS C. DUNCAN,
Attorney of Chew & Relf and Curator *ad hoc* to the other Defendants

Wm W Whitaly and Myra C Whitney,) Court of Probates,
                   vs   ) the State of
Eleanor O'Bearn and Others   ) Louisiana

To the Honorable the **Mayor** of Cincinnati, State of Ohio, greeting,

Know ye that we, reposing confidence in your prudence and fidelity, do by these presents, give unto you authority, diligently to examine all witnesses whatever, as well on the part of the plaintiffs as of the defendants, in a certain suit now pending in our said court, in which William W Whitney and Myra C Whitney are plaintiffs, and Eleanor O'Bearn and others are defendants

Therefore we desire you that at certain times and places, by you to be appointed for that purpose, you cause the said witnesses to to come before you, that you then and there examine them apart upon their respective corporal oaths, first taken before you upon the Holy Evangelists, that you reduce their examinations to writing, and when you shall so have taken them, that you send the same with this commission, closed up under your seal, to us in our said court, at the city of New Orleans, without delay

Witness the Honorable Charles Maurian, Judge of our said court, this twenty-fourth day of June, in the year of our Lord one thousand eight hundred and thirty-four, and in the fifty-eight year of the Independence of the United States

          (Signed)   W. F. C DUPLESSIS,
                                             Register of Wills.

In pursuance of the annexed commission, directed to me, the subscriber, Mayor of the city of Cincinnati, appeared before me. William Miller, who, being duly sworn to declare the truth on the questions put to him in this cause, answered to the interrogatories hereto annexed, in the manner following, to wit

To the first and second interrogatories this deponent say.

That he was acquainted with Daniel Clark, and enjoyed, as he believed, his entire confidence.

In answer to the third, fourth, fifth, sixth, seventh and eigl th interrogatories he says.

That at the decease of Daniel Clark, he says that he did have a child that during the pregnancy of the mother of said child, the said Daniel Clark told this deponent, that the child of which she was then pregnant, was the child of him, the said Daniel Clark, that, after its birth, the said Daniel Clark acknowledged it to be his that the said child, for many years afterwards, lived in the family of Col. Samuel B Davis, now of Philadelphia, and is now the wife of Mr Whitney, of New York, as this deponent believes ; the name of said child was Myra

To the tenth interrogatory, he answers

He does not.

To the eleventh, he answers, no

To the twelfth, thirteenth, and fourteenth, he says

That he, the said Daniel Clark, frequently expressed much affection for the said child, Myra, and stated that he intended to make ample provision for her as one of his heirs

To the fifteenth, this deponent answers

No

To the sixteenth, he answers

He knows nothing

To the seventeenth, he says

That he believes subsequently to the year 1811, he has frequently heard Daniel Clark speak of said child as his own, and that he would make provision for her, as above stated

To the eighteenth, nineteenth and twentieth, he answers as to the seventeenth

To the 21st and 22d, he says

That he saw Daniel Clark in 1812, he believes, but does not recollect any particular conversation at that time, different from that before stated

To the 23d, 24th, 25th, 26th, 27th, 28th, 29th, 30th, 31st and 32d, he says

That he never heard Daniel Clark say that he had made a will, and never saw him execute any will, although it was his impression and that of his friends that he had made a will

In answer to the cross interrogatories, he says

To the 1st interrogatory, he answers

His name is William Miller, that he resides in Cincinnati, that he is upwards of sixty years of age, and attends to the management of his own affairs

To the 2d and 3d, he answers in the negative

To the 4th,

That he was on his plantation, in Louisiana, and Clark was in New Orleans

To the 5th, he answers

That Daniel Clark was his merchant and commercial

for many years, and his intimacy continued till his death, it commenced about 1796 or 1797

To the 6th, he says

That he was in the habit of conversing with this deponent confidentially on general subjects, and with respect to his private affairs.

To the 7th, 8th and 9th, he answers

He knows nothing further than already stated

To the 10th, he says

That he does not believe Daniel Clark was ever married

To the 11th he says

He knows nothing more than has been stated in answer to the 3 4 5 6 7 and 8th interrogatories

To the 12th he says

That Daniel Clark acknowledged the child Myra to be his own because he believed it to be so and entertained no doubt with respect to it The mother of said child was Madame DeGrange

To the 13th he answers

No

   (Signed)   W MILLER

Which answers being by me reduced to writing were signed by the said witness in my presence

               In testimony whereof I have hereto affixed my hand

[L S]   and seal of said city and also my private seal this
          21st day of July 1834

   (Signed)   SAMUEL W DAVIS, Mayor

Filed 15th December 1834

               S BLOSSMAN Deputy R of Wills

Answers of Joseph Deville Degoutin Belchasse to the interrogatories propounded in the case of Wm W Whitney and wife vs Eleanor O Bearn and others under the commission hereto annexed

1st To the first interrogatory he answers

That he knew the late Daniel Clark deceased of New Orleans and enjoyed his confidence and intimate intercourse with him for many years before his death and until that event

2d To the second interrogatory he answers

That the said Clark at the time of his death in the month of August, 1813 left a daughter called Mira

3d To the third interrogatory he answers

That he knew that said Daniel Clark claimed and acknowledged said Mira for and as his daughter

4th To the fourth interrogatory he answers

That in various confidential conversations with said Clark both in his own house and that of Clarks and also in the house of Colonel S B Davis, whose wife had said Mira under her care, and treated her with maternal kindness he has heard said Clark acknowledge and claim said Mira to be his daughter At different times at said Daniel Clarks request, he has accompanied him in his visits to his said daughter in the house of said Davis and he always manifested for her the most ardent affection

5th To the fifth interrogatory he answers

That said Mira Clark, whilst in Louisiana lived in the house of said Davis under the care of his (Davis) wife, who was always accounted a woman of excellent character Said **Myra** is now the wife of said Wm W Whitney, he saw **them both** last year in this place when they were considered as husband and wife

6th To the 6th interrogatory he answers

That it is anticipated in the second answer

7th To the seventh interrogatory he answers.

That he knows Myra Clark Whitney and knows also that she is the same person that said Daniel Clark claimed and **acknowledged** to be his daughter in the manner above related

8th To the eight interrogatory he answers

He had a considerable knowledge of the circumstances of said Daniel Clark during his life, and at the time of his death

9th ninth To the ninth interrogatory he answers

That he knows that said Clark, some years before his **death**, and particularly in the year 1811 made provision for his said daughter Myra

10th To the tenth interrogatory he answers

That in proof of the provision at least in part, spoken **of in** the last answer said Daniel Clark transferred to him several lots of ground in the suburb or faubourg St John, near the bayou of that name, within the limits of the city of New Orleans, with **or** under the confidential understanding that they were to be and remain under his control or disposition for the use and benefit of said Myra and since the death of said Clark he has duly conveyed to her the said lots

11th To the eleventh interrogatory he answers

That said Daniel Clark always manifested the greatest affection for said Myra and never having given the deponent any charge or commission in favor of any other person, he necessarily considered her as the pre-eminent and predilect object of his **regard** and concern

12th To the twelfth interrogatory he answers

That said Daniel Clark always gave him to understand, **as** well by reason of his extraordinary affection for said **Myra, as** by his positive declarations to that effect that she, **said Myra,** would be the heir or heiress of his fortune

13th To the thirteenth interrogatory he answers

That the greatest object of the pecuniary cares of said **Daniel** Clark seemed always to be the said Myra

14th To the fourteenth interrogatory he answers

That in 1811, said Clark made known to him that on account of a special emergency that called him to the North he had **made** his will, (to the best of the deponent's recollection in the month of May, of that year) which he designed merely as a provisional will, in which, Richard Relf and Beverly Chew were named as

34*

his executors; and that, although he did not mention his said daughter in that will, yet, by confidential modes, he had made most ample provision for her   He, the said Daniel Clark, further told the deponent that he had deposited that will in the hands of said Relf, and after his return from the North in speaking of his testamentary dispositions, he told the deponent that he had it in contemplation to make his last will, and that he suffered the old will of 1811, already before spoken of, to remain in the hands of said Relf

15th To the fifteenth interrogatory he answers

That it is anticipated in the next preceding answer

16th. To the sixteenth interrogatory he answers

That down to his death the said Daniel Clark spoke of said Myra as his daughter, and left no doubt on the deponent's mind that she would be the heir of his fortune

17th To the seventeenth interrogatory he answers

That it is anticipated in answers 11th 12th 13th and 16th

18th To the eighteenth interrogatory he answers

That his communications with said Daniel Clark were constant, with the interval, for a long series of years until his death.

19th To the nineteenth interrogatory he answers

That he had often heard the said Daniel Clark subsequently to the month of May 1811 speak of his said daughter Myra, and always in the most affectionate terms and in such a manner as to show that she was destined by him to be his heir

20th To the twentieth interrogatory he answers

That a short time before the death-sickness of said Daniel Clark, and in the last interview, before that sickness, he conversed with the deponent, at the house of said Clark about his said daughter, in the same affectionate and paternal terms as theretofore He told the deponent that he had completed or finished his last will, that the deponent, Judge Pitot then present, and the Chevalier Delacroix were his executors named in it, (the deponent having given his consent before) and that apart from some legacies for his friends and a due pension for his mother, his said daughter Myra was the heiress of his fortune duly habituated for that purpose, and gave the said will open, to us to look at and examine The deponent saw that it was all in his own handwriting, and signed by him, the said Daniel Clark Some few days afterwards, the deponent called on him, and learned from said Relf that he, said Daniel Clark, was sick, in bed—too sick to be seen by the deponent However, the said deponent, indignant, at an attempt to prevent him from seeing his friend, passed forward into his room He took the deponent by the hand, and, with affectionate reprehension, said. ' How is it, Bellechasse, that you have not come to see me before, since my sickness? I told Relf to send for you" The deponent's answer was, that he had received no message or account, whatever, of his sickness from Relf Fearful of oppressing him, the deponent immediately retired, and told Relf that he would remain in the house, to attend occasionally to Clark He Relf, said there was no occasion for it that the doctor or doctors ordered that he, Clark, should be kept as quiet as possible, and not be allowed to talk and that if there should appear to be any danger, he, Relf, would send for him Without receiving a message, however, the deponent went, the next morning, and found that Clark was dead The funeral procession was arranged by said Relf, and in conformity with that arrangement much to the deponent's surprise and mortification, the said deponent was condemned to walk side by side, with Governor Claiborne, a well known enemy both of Clark and himself, to his Clark's, grave! On the return of the procession to Clark's mansion, on conferring with Judge Pitot, and other friend as to the mysterious disappearance of said Clark's said last will and the substitution in its place of said provision I will of anterior date, to wit of May, 1811, the deponent said, aloud Gentlemen, this mysterious occurrence surprises and afflicts me, I have heretofore received from our deceased friend Daniel Clark, a regular conveyance of several town lots which he after his return from his visit to the North, in 1811, refused to receive the reconveyance of from me I now pledge myself to convey them to his daughter Myra I have done so Judge Pitot as well as others, spoke with the utmost indignation of the suppression or destruction of said last will, of 1813 and the substitution of that of 1811, all of which we attributed to interested villainy

21st, 22d, 23d, 24th, 25th, 26th, 27th 28th and 29th, the witness answers

That it is anticipated in the twentieth answer

30th To the thirtieth interrogatory he answers

That he can not call to his mind any details of the matter referred to, in the interrogatory corresponding to this number

31st To the thirty-first interrogatory he answers

That it is anticipated in the twentieth answer

Answer to the cross interrogatories in said suit

1st To the first cross interrogatory he answers

That his name is Joseph Deville Degoutin Bellechasse, a retired lieutenant colonel of his Catholic Majesty's service, and a sugar planter of seventy years of age

2d To the second cross interrogatory he answers

He has no interest whatever in the event of this suit

3d To the third cross interrogatory he answers

He has no relationship with the plaintiffs in this suit

4th To the fourth cross interrogatory he answers

He was in New Orleans in the spring and summer of 1813 Said Daniel Clark died in said summer

5th To the fifth cross interrogatory he answers

That his intimacy with said Daniel Clark commenced in the latter part of the last century, and was continued until his death, with uninterrupted harmony and confidence

6th To the sixth cross interrogatory he answers

That said Daniel Clark was always in the habit of consulting him about his affairs generally

7th To the seventh cross interrogatory he answers

That said Daniel Clark spoke to him about his testamentary dispositions in the manner related in the deponent's answers in chief, and particulary in his answer 20th on account, as he supposed, of said Clark's confidence, of the deponent's great friendship and regard for him and of his belief of the deponent having been worthy of that confidence

8th. To the eighth cross interrogatory he answers

That the aforesaid last will, of 1813 of said Daniel Clark was shown by him, of his own accord, to the deponent and also to Judge Pitot, at the time mentioned by the deponent in his answer in chief No 20 at his, said Clark's house, and must have been so shown to us as a matter of course, considering his great confidence in, and intimacy with us both and considering also that we vere two of his executors named in that will

9th To the ninth cross interrogatory he answers

That altho' he took neither note nor copy of said will of 1813, yet from the *interesting nature* of those details that he has given of it, he had those details strongly impressed on his memory

10th To the tenth cross interrogatory he answers

That he has no satisfactory evidence of the marriage of said Clark, altho' he remembers to have heard no little talk about his marriage with Madame DeGrange the mother of said Myra

11th To the eleventh cross interrogatory he answers

That he has no recollection of the *minutiæ* expressed in the cross interrogatory, No 11, further than the maternal care and attentions of Madame Davis towards said Myra Clark

12th To the twelfth cross interrogatory he answers

That said Daniel Clark certainly acknowledged and claimed the said Myra to be his daughter because he believed her to be such The deponent always understood that said Myra was born in New Orleans, where her mother resided

- 13th To the thirteenth cross interrogatory he answers

That he had heard Daniel Clark speak of a daughter of Madame DeGrange, older than Myra, and called Caroline, whom he treated with great kindness But that the deponent never had any reason for satisfying himself that she was not the daughter of Monsieur DeGrange, begotten during his union with Madame DeGrange to be enthusiastically attached to her, the said Madame DeGrange, it seemed natural enough, particularly for a man of his warm and generous heart to treat his quasi step-daughter perhaps of *adoption*, with kindness and benignity, and even to acquiesce in her bearing his name   Signed

JOSEF DEVILLE DEGOUTIN BELLECHASSE

Sworn to and subscribed before me, this 22d day of August, 1834 Matanzas

Signed,   **LEWIS SHOEMAKER**
     Consulate of the United States of America,   Matanzas

I, Lewis Shoemaker, Consul of the United States of America, at this port and residing within the same, do certify that the execution of the accompanying commission to examine witness in the case of Wm W Whitney and wife, *is* Eleanor O'Bearn and others, issued out of the Court of Probate of the city and parish of New Orleans, will more fully appear by the schedule hereto annexed

Witness my hand and seal of office, this 22d day of August, 1834   Signed,   **LEWIS SHOEMAKER**, Consul.

Wм W. Whitney and Wife, }
           vs   }   COURT OF PROBATES
Eleanor O Biarn and Others }

Interrogatories propounded to witnesses on behalf of plaintiffs

1 Were you acquainted with the late Daniel Clark, of New Orleans?

1st Were you at any times, upon terms of intimacy with the said Daniel   ? If yea were you so intimate with the said Daniel Clark, as to enjoy his private confidence?

2d Do you know whether the said Daniel Clark, at his decease, left any child?

3d Have you heard the said Daniel Clark claim and acknowledge any child as his own?

4th If the last question is answered in the affirmative, please state when and where you have heard the said Daniel Clark claim and acknowledge the said child as his own

5th Please state where the said child then was, whether it was protected by the said Daniel Clark, what became of it, and where it is at present.

6th By what name was the said child called?

7th Do you know Myra Clark Whitney, one of the petitioners? If yea, say whether she is the said child whom the said Daniel Clark claimed and acknowledged as his own.

8th Are you acquainted with the circumstances of the said Daniel Clark, during his lifetime, and at the time of his death?

9th. Do you know whether the said Daniel Clark, at any time during his life, made any provision for the said child, in the event of his death? If yea, state particularly under what circumstances.

10th Did the said Daniel Clark at any time place property in your hands, for the use and benefit of the said child? If yea state under what circumstances, and how that property was disposed of.

11th Did not the said Daniel Clark always manifest the fondest affection for the said child? and did he not express the intention to make her his heir?

12th. Have you not often heard the said Daniel Clark say that he intended to leave his estate to the said child?

13th What intentions of pecuniary advancement have you heard the said Daniel Clark express in regard to the said child?

14th Are you acquainted with the circumstances under which the said Daniel Clark made a will in the month of May in the year eighteen hundred and eleven? If you, state the particulars of this subject, and whether, at that time, he had not otherwise provided for the said child

15th Was the said will, of May, eighteen hundred and eleven, made by the said Daniel Clark, a short time before his departure for the North? If yea, did the said Daniel Clark, after his return from the North, express to you his intention to make another will? and did the said Daniel Clark after his return from the North, refer to the circumstances of the said will, of eighteen hundred and eleven?

16th Have you heard the said Daniel Clark subsequent to the date of the said will, of May eighteen hundred and eleven, claim and acknowledge the said child as his daughter? If yea, at what times?

17th Have you heard the said Daniel Clark, subsequent to the month of May, eighteen hundred and eleven, say that the said child was his heir or that he would leave his estate to the said child?. If yea, state particularly when, and the terms in which the said Daniel Clark spoke in regard to the said child

18th Had you, subsequent to the month of May eighteen hundred and eleven, much intercourse with the said Daniel Clark?

19th Have you often heard the said Daniel Clark speak of the said child, subsequent to the month of May eighteen hundred and eleven? If yea, state the particulars of his language, in regard to the said child

20th. How long before the decease of the said Daniel Clark

did you see him, for the last time? and, in your last interview with the said Daniel Clark did he speak of the said child? If yea, state the particulars of his conversation in relation to the said child

21st How long before his decease did the said Daniel Clark, for the last time spoke to you in regard to the said child? and what did he say at that time in regard to the said child?

22d Have you heard the said Daniel Clark subsequent to the month of May eighteen hundred and eleven say that he was about to make any alteration in his making or that he had made his will? If yea, give the particulars of any conversation on the subject

23d Do you know at what time or times the said Daniel Clark spoke of his making or about his last will or at what time he spoke of his about his last will?

24th Did you ever see or was you witness to any writing, said by the said Daniel Clark to be his will? If yes, when and where?

25th Was the will or testamentary writing of the said Daniel Clark and was it signed by him or was his name written in any part of it and where was it?

26th Did you hear the said Daniel Clark say that in his said will he had left ... to his daughter Myra? Recollect, as well as you can ... his expressions

27th Where and when, for the last time, did you see the said will?

28th When and where for the last time, did you hear the said Daniel Clark speak of the said will, and what did he say?

29th Did you hear the said Daniel Clark say who were named in said will executors? If yes, state who?

30th Did you hear the said Daniel Clark say, who was named in said will tutor to his said daughter Myra? If yea, state all you know on this head

31st Did you or not ever read the said will? If so, state the contents as particular as you can recollect them, and whether the said will was not in the handwriting of said Daniel Clark, and dated and signed by him

(Signed) WM. M. WORTHINGTON, for Plaintiffs

Cross Interrogatories

1 Will you be pleased to state your name, age, residence, and employment?

2. Will you state whether you have any interest in the event of this suit, the object of which is to annul the will of the late Daniel Clark, that is, a will made by him in the month of May, 1811, and which, at the period of his death, in August, 1813, was duly admitted to probate in the Court of Louisiana.

3 Will you state whether or not you are related to, or connected with, the plaintiffs, or either of them? If aye, state in what
degree

4 Will you state where you were in the spring and summer
of the year 1813. and where Mr Daniel Clark was, at the same
time?

5. If you state that you were intimate with the said Clark,
mention the circumstances which led to that intimacy, how the
same was formed what was its particular character, and how
long the same continued

6. Was the said Daniel Clark in the habit of consulting you
about his affairs, whether personal, mercantile, or political? state
fully and particularly

If you answer any one of the interrogatories in chief affirmatively, as to your knowledge of the   of Mr Clark, state
all the circumstances, the time when, and the place where, and
what was the occasion of his mentioning the subject to you?

8 If you say that you saw the will of Mr Clark, state when
and where you saw it, and state who was present, and why he
exhibited the same to you? Did you ask him whether he had
made a will, and request him to show it to you? If not, state
particularly, and in detail, the reason why the same was showed
to you

9 If you answer that you saw the will about which plaintiffs
interrogate you, will you state how you can, at this distant day,
relate with precision the date of that instrument, so as to enable
you to speak with confidence of the year, the month, the day?
Did you take a copy of the will, or any memorandum, to enable
you to speak positively of the date? If you did, annex that copy
or memorandum to your answer, and when or why you made
such copy or memorandum.

10 Was Mr. Daniel Clark ever married, to your knowledge?
if aye, where, when, and to whom?

11. If Mr Clark was not married, state, if you please, all the
circumstances attending the birth, the maintenance and education
of the child Myra, whom you are asked whether he did not acknowledge? State when and where she was born, whether to
your knowledge she was ever christened, if so, by whom, and
where, and who were her sponsors

12. Will you state how or why it was that Mr Clark came to
acknowledge as his own, the child Myra? Was she born in his
house, or where, if not under his roof? Who was her mother,
and where did she reside?

13 Did you, or not, ever hear said Clark acknowledge as his
own, any other child than this Myra? If aye, state the name of
the child, and whether or not he did not appear to have as much

affection for the one as for the other, if not, what was the occasion of this difference of feeling towards his own reputed offspring, and why did he acknowledge the one to the exclusion of the other, as the heir of his estate?

These cross interrogatories are propounded by the defendants, with a full reservation to them of all legal exceptions to each and every of the interrogatories in chief and any other legal exceptions thereto.

(Signed)   LUCIUS C DUNCAN,

Attorney of Chew & Relf, and *curator ad hoc* to the other defendants

---

Wm W Whitney and Myra C Whitney,) Court of Probates,
                    vs   ) State of
     Eleanor O Beary and Others   ) Louisiana

To Lewis Shoemaker, Esq, Consul of the United States of America, Matanzas, in the Island of Cuba—Greeting

Know ye that we reposing confidence in your prudence and fidelity do by these presents give unto you authority diligently to examine all witnesses whatever, as well on the part of the plaintiffs as of the defendant, in a certain suit now pending in our said Court, in which Wm W Whitney and Myra C Whitney are plaintiffs and Eleanor O Beary and others are defendant. Therefore, we desire you that at certain times and places by you to be appointed for that purpose, you cause the said witnesses to come before you, that you then and there examine them apart upon their respective corporal oaths first taken before you upon the Holy Evangelists that you reduce their examinations to writing; and when you shall so have taken them, that you send the same, with this commission closed up under your seal, to us in our said Court, at the city of New Orleans without delay.

Witnessed, the Honorable Charles Maurian, Judge of our said Court, this twenty-fourth day of June in the year of our Lord one thousand eight hundred and thirty-four, and in the fifty-eighth year of the Indepence of the United States

(Signed,)   W F C DUPLESSIS, Register of Wills
Filed, December 15th, 1834   S BLOSSMAN,
                              Depy Register of Wills

Wm W Whitney & wife,)
            vs.   )
     O'Beary, & als   )

Personally appeared W. W. Whitney, one of the above plaintiffs, who being duly sworn, deposeth and saith, that Harriet Smith, now in New Orleans, is a material witness for the plaintiffs in the above cause, that she is about to depart from the

35*

State of Louisiana, and he fears the plaintiffs may be deprived of the benefit or advantage they expect to claim from her testimony He prays that a commission issue to take her testimony, &c

WM M WORTHINGTON, for Plaintiffs
WM WALLACE WHITNEY

Sworn to before me, this 3d January 1835

S BLOSSMAN D y R of Wills

Filed 3 January. 1835   S BLOSSMAN,
                               D y R of Wills

ESTATE OF DANIEL CLARK }
ELEANOR O BEARN, & ALS, }
        vs   }
WM W WHITNEY & WIFE }

On motion of Wm M Worthington Esq, of counsel for W W Whitney and wife, plaintiffs, and upon filing the affidavit of said W W Whitney it is ordered that a commission issue in this case to take the deposition of a witness or witnesses before Gallien Preval, Esq, associate Judge of the city Court of New Orleans, to be read in evidence on the trial

---

WM W WHITNEY,   }
        vs   }
ELEANOR O BEARN AND OTHERS }

Deposition taken by virtue of a commission issued by the Honorable, the Court of Probates, dated the   January, 1835

Mrs Harriet Smith being duly sworn deposes and says, that she recognises her signature affixed at the end of a deposition, made by her in Philadelphia, before John R Swift Mayor of said city, the said deposition now on file in the Court of Probates of this city, and hereto annexed, and signed by me, *ne varietur* , she also declares that the contents of said deposition are true, as therein stated

The signature of said deposition was by mistake signed of her former name, Harriet Harper, instead of Harriet Smith, the said deposition is marked at the beginning of it— A B C

HARRIET SMITH

Sworn to and subscribed before me
New Orleans, Jan y 10th, 1835
          Signed,   GALLIEN PREVAL, Judge

I do hereby certify that the following deposition has been taken before me on this day, the 10th of January instant, at Mrs. Woorster s boarding house, in Canal street, in the presence of Mr. Whorthington, attorney for plaintiffs, and Mr Duncan, attorney for Mr. Chew & Relf, and curator *ad hoc* of the absent heirs.

New Orleans, Jan y 10th, 1835

GALLIEN PREVAL, Judge

Costs of deposition $4 Notices issued and served twice, $4

W W Whitney and Wife   Court of Probates
      vs   The State of Louisiana
Eleanor O Beary and als   No 813

To the honorable G Preval, associate Judge of the City Court of New Orleans greeting

Know ye that we, reposing confidence in your prudence and fidelity, do by these presents give unto you authority diligently to examine all witnesses whatever as well on the part of the plaintiff, as of the defendant in a certain suit now pending in our said Court in which W W Whitney and wife are plaintiffs, and Eleanor O Beary and others are defendants

Therefore we desire you that at certain times and places by you to be appointed for that purpose, you cause the said witnesses to come before you, that you then and there examine them apart, upon their respective corporal oaths first taken before you upon the Holy Evangelists, that you reduce their examinations to writing, and when you shall so have taken them, that you send the same with the commission closed up under your seal, to us in our said Court, at the city of New Orleans, without delay

Witness the honorable Charles Maurian, Judge of our said Court, this fifth day of January, in the year of our Lord one thousand eight hundred and thirty-five and in the fifty ninth year of the Independence of the United States

      Signed, S BLOSSMAN, D'y R of Wills
Filed 10th Jan'y, 1835
      Signed, S BLOSSMAN, D y R of Wills.

W W Whitney and Wife
      vs
Eleanor O Beary and als

On motion of Lucius C Duncan, Esquire, and upon filing two separate answers of the defendants it is ordered that the judgment by default taken herein on the 10th instant, against said defendants be, and the same is hereby set aside, and considering the affidavits to said answers it is ordered that three commissions issue one directed to Thos P Barton secretary of American Legation, and Daniel Brent, consul of the U S at Paris in France, or either of them, and one addressed to John Swift, mayor, and John Binns, or S Rullgor, alderman, of the city of Philadelphia, Pennsylvania, or either of them, and the other to Lewis Shoemaker consul of the United States at Matanzas, Cuba

WILLIAM W. WHITNEY AND }   IN THE PROBATE COURT IN AND
   MYRA C. WHITNEY   } FOR THE CITY AND PARISH OF
          vs   }   NEW ORLEANS
ELEANOR O BEARN AND OTHERS } STATE OF LOUISIANA
                                No 843

For answer to the petition of the plaintiffs in the above entitled suit, or to so much thereof, as he believes it is necessary, and
material to answer, Lucius C Duncan, the curator ad hoc,
appointed to the absent defendants, named in said petition, comes
and says, that though soon after his said appointment he addressed letters to said absent defendants, advising them of the
institution of this suit, and of his appointment to represent them,
yet he hath received no answers to his said letters, and has seen
but one of said absent defendants, the said curator, therefore in
his said capacity, answering the aforesaid petition, denies the
right of the said plaintiffs to have or maintain this said action,
because there is no truth in any one of the allegations of the said
petition, tending to establish the pretended rights of the petitioner,
Myra, as the daughter or heir of Daniel Clark, deceased, and
named in said petition

It is further denied, that the said Daniel Clark was ever legally
married, or that he ever had any legitimate child, and especially
it is denied that the said Myra is his legitimate child or that she
is now, or ever had any rights as his heir.

It is further denied, that the said Daniel Clark ever made or
published according to any form of law, recognized in the late
territory of Orleans or in the present State of Louisiana, or elsewhere any other will or testament than that which the petitioners
allege, has been admitted to Probate in this honorable Court,
which said will he said curator in behalf of said absent heirs,
alleges and believes to be the only will said Clark ever made, and
to which he intended to give full legal effect

It is further denied that said Daniel Clark ever made any such
will, as the petitioners allege, constituting the said Myra, his sole
heir, and that if the form of such a will was ever contemplated
or made by him, it was by himself revoked and destroyed, and
would, moreover have been in derogation of the rights of his
mother, then living, and who survived him, and would further
have been in contraventions of positive law

It is alleged by said curator, that he is advised and believes
that the said Danl Clark left a natural child named Caroline
Clark, and who is entitled, by the will of his mother, who is his
universal heir, to inherit a considerable share of his estate, all
which this curator reserves in her behalf, (she being one of the
defendants represented by said curator) the right to prove on the
trial of this cause

And finally this curator denies all and singular the allegations of said petition so far as not hereinbefore admitted and which tend in any manner or form to establish any of the pretensions of the plaintiffs herein, and he prays for final judgment in behalf of the defendants, represented by him and for costs, and as in duty bound

Signed,   LUCIUS C. DUNCAN,

Curator ad hoc &c &c

L. C. Duncan the above named curator being duly sworn saveth that from information he has received, and from facts and circumstances known and communicated to him he verily believes that the testimony of Daniel W. Coxe and William E. Hulings, residing in Philadelphia Pennsylvania and Chevalier Dusuau Delacroix, a citizen of Louisiana presently absent and believed to be at Paris in France, and of J. D. D. Bellechasse, residing near Matanzas, in the Island of Cuba, is necessary and material to sustain the defence of the said absent defendants represented by him, this deponent that by said witnesses he will be able to disprove all the substantial allegations of said plaintiff's petition and to sustain the said defendants in the defence which he has deemed it his duty to present to the action of the plaintiffs herein that said testimony is competent and material and without it said curator believes he cannot safely go to trial, and that he knows of no other persons, than those above named, by whom he could prove and sustain the defence of the persons he is, herein, appointed to represent

Signed,   L. C. DUNCAN

Sworn to and subscribed before me, this 14th Jany, 1835

Signed   S. BLOSSMAN, Dy R. of Wills

Filed January 15th, 1835

       S. BLOSSMAN, Dy R. of Wills

WM W WHITNEY AND MYRA C WHITNEY vs ELEANOR O BEARN AND OTHERS	IN THE PROBATE COURT, IN AND FOR THE CITY AND PARISH OF NEW ORLEANS STATE OF LOUISIANA No 843

For answer to the petition in the above entitled suit, or so much thereof as they are advised and believe it is necessary and material for them to answer, Beverly Chew and Richard Relf, residing in New Orleans parties defendant, herein come and say, that so far as it concerns them personally to answer said petition, they deny all and singular the allegations therein, except so far as the said plaintiffs charge the execution and admission to probate of the will of Daniel Clark, now on file in this honorable Court, which will, these respondents alledge and believe to be the only last will and testament said Clark ever made, and which

he intended to have legal effect   These respondents further deny
that the plaintiff, Myra, has any such claim, in the premises, as
she pretends, they deny that the said Daniel Clark was ever legally married or that he ever had any legitimate offspring
especially do they deny, that the said Myra is his offspring   as
she pretends, or that she is entitled to any part or parcel of his
estate, whether in law or by testament   These respondents further say, in answer to the said petition, that if the said Myra is
the daughter of Daniel Clark, as in said petition, which these respondents deny, as alleged, that there is another person, named
Caroline Clark who is entitled equally with said Myra, to any
part or parcel of said Daniel Clark's estate she, the said Caroline, having been acknowledged as his natural daughter

And these respondents further deny all the other allegations in
said petition contained, so far as the same tend in any manner
or form to establish any right in the said Myra, either as daughter or heir of said Daniel Clark, and to whose estate she sets up
pretensions in the petition in this behalf

Wherefore these respondents pray for judgment in this behalf, in their favor so far as they are concerned herein, and for
costs, and as in duty bound, &c &c

Signed—Richard Relf—Bev Chew.

And by their attorney.

Signed,   L C DUNCAN

Richard Relf, one of the respondents in the foregoing answer,
being sworn, saith that the testimony of Dan'l W Coxe and
William E Hulings, residing in Philadelphia, Pennsylvania,
and of Chevalier Dusuau Delacroix, a citizen of Louisiana, presently absent, and believed to be at Paris, in France, and of J D
D Bellechasse, residing near Matanzas, in the Island of Cuba,
is necessary and material to the said respondents who expect to
be able to prove by said several witnesses, that all the allegations
or the chief part of the allegations of the petition, are untrue, except so far as they relate the execution and probate of the will
of Daniel Clark, on file in the Probate Court of the parish and
city of New Orleans, that the testimony of said witnesses is competent and material, and without it, they cannot safely go to the
trial of this cause, so far as the respondents, and deponent are
presently concerned therein.

Signed,   RICHARD RELF

Sworn to and subscribed before me, this 14th Jan'y, 1835.

Signed,   S. BLOSSMAN, D'y R of wills

Filed 15th January, 1835

S BLOSSMAN, D'y R. of wills

W. W. WHITNEY AND WIFE
vs
ELEANOR O'BEARN AND ALS

On motion of C. Roselius, Esquire, on behalf of plaintiff's counsel, it is ordered by the Court with consent of L. C. Duncan, Esquire that the rule taken on the 27th of March last, and returnable this day be enlarged until Friday morning next, the 3d instant, at 9 o'clock.

W. W. WHITNEY AND WIFE
vs } PROBATE COURT
ELEANOR O'BEARN AND AL

In answer to the rule served upon them, Bev. Chew and Rich'd Relf, come, and for cause to the same, show,

That the papers, books and documents pertaining to said succession are not all now in their possession some having been furnished to different tribunals, where they have instituted or defended suits for the heirs thereof, others have been furnished to the heirs, and some are now in the possession of Richard Relf, to be exhibited on the trial of this case, in compliance with the provisions of the law in said matters. The said Relf & Chew further answer, that the original will referred to in the said rule, is now, and ever has been on file in this Court, since the same was admitted to Probate, in the year 1813.

Signed,   L. C. DUNCAN,
           Att'y of Chew & Relf

Filed April 1, 1835

       S. BLOSSMAN, D'y R. of Wills

W. W. WHITNEY AND WIFE
vs
ELEANOR O'BEARN ET AL

On motion of W. M. Worthington, Esquire, on behalf of plaintiffs it is ordered by the Court, that a commission issue in this case directed to David B. Morgan, Esquire, at Madisonville Parish of St. Tammany, to take the testimony of Pierre B. Boisfontaine, to be used in evidence on the trial of this case.

W. W. WHITNEY AND WIFE
vs
ELEANOR O'BEARN, ET AL

On motion of W. M. Worthington, Esq., of counsel for the plaintiffs: it is ordered by the Court that, a commission issue in this case directed to Davis B. Morgan, Esq., Madisonville, Parish of St. Tammany, Louisiana, or to any justice of the peace in said parish, to take the testimony of Pierre Baron Boisfontaine, to be read in evidence on the trial.

W. W. WHITNEY AND WIFE ⎫
            vs   ⎬ PROBATE COURT
E. O'BEARN AND OTHERS ⎭

Personally appeared before me Clerk of the Probate Court
of the Parish of Orleans, W. W. Whitney, one of the plaintiffs
in this cause, who makes oath that Mad. Caillavet, a material
witness in this cause, is old and infirm, and about to depart out
of the jurisdiction of this Court, he, therefore, prays that a
commission be issued, directed to Gallien Preval, associate
Judge of the City Court, to take the testimony of said witness
            Signed,   WM WALLACE WHITNEY
Sworn to and subscribed before me New Orleans, 20th
May, 1835
      Signed,   W F C DUPLESSIS, Register of Wills

Filed 20th May, 1825.
      Signed,   W F C DUPLESSIS, Register of Wills.

W. W. WHITNEY AND WIFE ⎫
            vs   ⎬ PROBATE COURT.
ELEANOR O'BEARN, ET AL ⎭

Personally appeared W W Whitney, one of the plaintiffs
in the above case, who being duly sworn, deposeth and saith,
that Madame Sophie, veuve Despau nee Carriere, of Matanzas,
in the Island of Cuba, is a material witness for the plaintiffs,
prays that a commission be issued to Lewis Shoemaker, American Consul at Matanzas aforesaid, to take the testimony of
said witness   WM WALLACE WHITNEY

Sworn to and subscribed before me. New Orleans, 23d May,
1835   W F C DUPLESSIS, Register of Wills

Affidavit taken and filed, May 23d, 1835
      Signed,   S BLOSSMAN, D'y R of Wills

In pursuance of the annexed commission, directed to me, the
undersigned Justice of the Peace, personally appeared Pierre
Baron Boisfontaine, who being duly sworn to declare the truth
on the questions put to him in this cause, in answer to the following interrogatories, says
      In reply to the first interrogatory he answers
I was acquainted with the late Daniel Clark, of New Orleans,
and was many years intimate with him
      In reply to the second interrogatory he answers
Mr Clark left at his death a daughter named Myra, whom he
acknowledged as his own, before and after her birth, and as
long as he lived In my presence he spoke of the necessary
preparations for her birth, and asked my brother's wife to be

present at her birth, and in my presence he proposed to my sister and brother in law, Mr. ... B. Davis, that they should take th ... are of his ... br ... After ... birth, he acknowledged her to me ... his ... and ... tly ... at various places. He was very fond of ... her and ... ... ed the pleasure in talking to me about her. When he communicated to me he was making his last will, he told me he would acknowledge her in it as his legitimate child. ... two days before he died he spoke to me about her ... great affection and ... being acknowledged ... state in his last will. He conveyed to me the ... anxiety and the interest of a dying parent ... and as to ... that ... her ... will. She is still living, and is now the wife of Mr ... near Wemyss.

In reply to th ... interrogatory he answer.

About fifteen days ... Mr. Clark ... I was present at his house when he handed to Col. Delacroix a sealed packet and told him that his last will ... finished and was in that sealed packet. About ... days before his death had told me that it was done. Previous to this communication ... about four months before his death he had often told me he was making his last will, he said it in conversation to me on the plantation and at his house, and I have known him often on this subject at Judge Pitot's. I frequently heard at Judge Pitot's with Mr. Clark. On Sunday, the day before he died, he told me that his last will was below in his office-room in his little black case. The day he died he mentioned this last will to me.

In reply to the fourth interrogatory he answers.

I was present with Mr. Clark's house about fifteen days before his death when he took from a small black case a sealed packet, and told it to Col. Delacroix ... and said, my last will is finished, it is in this sealed packet with valuable papers, as you consented, I have made you in it tutor to my daughter, if any misfortune happens to me, will you do for her all you promised me, will you take her ... one ... Davis? I have given her all my estate in my will ... and ..., to my mother, and some legacies to friends. You, Pitot and Bellechasse, are the executors. About ten days before this, Mr. Clark talking of Myra, said, that his will was done; previous to this he often told me commencing about 6 months before his death, that he was making his last will. In these conversations he told me that he should acknowledge his daughter Myra as his legitimate daughter, and give her all his property. He told me that Chevalier Delacroix had consented to be her tutor in his will and had promised if he died before doing it, to go at once to the North, and take her from Mr. Davis. That she was to be educated in Europe. He told me that Chevalier Delacroix, Judge Pitot and Colonel Bellechasse were to be executors in this will. Two o ...

three days before his death, I came to see Mr Clark on plantation business he told me he felt quite ill I asked him if I should
remain with him, he answered that he wished me to I went
to the plantation to set things in order that I might stay with
Mr. Clark, and returned the same day to Mr Clark and staid
with him constantly till he died Tuesday before he died Mr
Clark speaking of his daughter Myra, told me that his last will
was in his office-room below, in the little black case That he
could die contented, as he had insured his estate to her in the
will. He mentioned his pleasure that he made his mother comfortable by an annuity in it, and remembered some friends by
legacies He told me how well satisfied he was that Chevalier
Delacroix, Judge Pitot, and Bellechasse were executors in it,
and Chevalier Delacroix Myra's tutor About two hours before
his death, Mr Clark showed strong feeling for and Myra, and
told me that he wished his will to be taken to Chevalier Delacroix, as he was her tutor as well as one of the executors in it,
and just afterwards Mr Clark told Lubin, his confidential servant, to be sure as soon as he died, to carry his little black case
to Chevalier Delacroix After this, and a very short time before Mr Clark died, I saw Mr Relf take a bundle of keys from
Mr Clark's armoire, one of which I believe, opened the little
black case. I had seen Mr Clark open it very often After
taking these keys from the armoire Mr Relf went below When
I went below I did not see Mr Relf and the office room door
was shut Lubin told me that when Mr Relf went down with
the keys from the armoire, he followed, saw him then, on getting
down go into the office room, and that Mr Relf on going into
the office room locked the office room door Almost Mr Clark's
last words were, that his last will must be taken care of on said
Myra's account

In reply to the fifth interrogatory he answers

I was with Mr Clark, when he died, I was by him, constantly
for the two last days of his life About two hours before he died,
he spoke of his last will and his daughter Myra in connection
and almost his last words were about her, and that his will must
be taken care of on her account

In reply to the sixth interrogatory he answers

When, after Mr Clark's death the disappearance of his last
will was the subject of conversation, I related what Mr Clark
told me about his last will in his last sickness, Judge Pitot and
John Lynd told me that they read it not many days before Mr
Clark's last sickness, that its contents corresponded with what
Mr Clark told me about it, that when they read it, it was finished,
was dated, and signed by Mr Clark, was an olographic will,
was in Mr Clark's handwriting, that in it he acknowledged the

said Myra as his legitimate daughter and bequeathed all his estate to her, gave an annuity to his mother, and legacies for some friends. The Chevalier Delacroix was tutor of his daughter, said Myra. Chevalier Delacroix, Colonel Bellechasse, Judge Pitot were executors. Judge Pitot and John Lynd are dead. The will and deposit of the same read in Colonel Bellechasse, and me, but Mr Clark showed it to him not many days before his last sickness, and I was then touched. Colonel Bellechasse and lately widow Mrs Maurine Harper are living.

In reply to first cross interrogatory he answers.

My name is Louis Baron Boisfontaine, my age about fifty-eight. I was born something in Madisonville. The place of my nativity, do do is near New Orleans, opposite side of the river. I was highly raised in Pointe Coupee. I was several years agent for Mr Clark's plantations, and I have been engaged in various ... The ... of the present suit, and I derive my interest born out of ... wealth ... I am in no manner connected with or interested in object of the particular suit. I have no interest in the suit.

In reply to second cross interrogatory he answers.

I knew Daniel Clark between nine and ten years. I knew him as the father of Myra Clark. She was born in my house, and was put by Mr Clark several days old with my sister and brother-in-law, Samuel Davis. I was Mr Clark's agent for his several plantations, first the Sligo and the Desert, then the Houmas the Houmas Point, and when he died of the one he purchased of Stephen Henderson. He respected our misfortunes, knowing that our family was rich and of high standing in St Domingo before the revolution. The mother of Myra Clark was solely on the Chevalier's family. Not being present at any marriage, I can only declare it my belief Mr Clark was her father. To answer this question in detail as is demanded, it is proper that I state what was communicated to me. It was represented to me by this Mr Clark and Mr DeGrange in good faith, but I learned a short time afterwards, that he already had a ... wife when the former Carrière separated from him. Mr Clark some time after this, married her, at the North West ... to escape the public, interested persons had probably ... these things between them, and this lady, being in ... that Mr Clark not here, was persuaded, by a lawyer ... that her marriage with Mr Clark was invalid, and she parted ... Monsieur Gardette, some time afterward, ... stated to me that this barrier to making his marriage public had been created. He spoke to me of his daughter, Myra Clark, from the first, as legitimate, and when he made known to me that he was making his last will he said to me, he should declare her in it as his legitimate daughter. From the above, I believe there was a marriage.

In reply to the third cross-interrogatory he answers.

Mr Clark made no question on this subject before and after her birth and as long as he lived he exercised the authority of a parent over her destiny. He was a very fond parent. He sustained the house of Mr Davis and Mr Harper, because my sister had her in care, and Mrs Harper suckled her. He sustained Harper as long as he lived and conferred great benefits on my brother-in-law. He spoke of her mother with great respect, and frequently told me of her marriage with Mr Gardette, and he would have made his marriage with her public, if that barrier had not been made. He frequently lamented to me that this barrier had been made but that she was blameless. He said he would never give Myra a step-mother. When in 1813 he communicated to me that he was making his last will for her, he showed great sensibility as to her being declared legitimate in it. While I was with him at his death-sickness, and even at the moment he expired, he was in perfect possession of his senses, and no parent could have manifested greater affection than he did for her in that period near his last words were about her, and that his will must be taken care of on her account. She, the said Myra is the only child Mr Clark ever acknowledged to me as his. She was born in July eighteen hundred and five.

In reply to the fourth cross-interrogatory he answers.

I was a friend of the confidential character from the time of said Myra's birth. Mr Clark treated me as a confidential friend, in matters relating to her and to his affairs generally. In reply to the fourth interrogatory I have stated what I know concerning Mr Clark's last will my recollection of these facts is distinct. The circumstances connected with them were of such a character that my recollection of them could not easily be impaired.

Signed   P. BARON BOISFONTAINE

Which answers, being reduced to writing were sworn to and signed by the said witness in my presence in testimony whereof, I have hereunto affixed my hand and private seal, at the parish of St. Tammany in the State of Louisiana, this twenty-ninth day of May eighteen hundred and thirty-five.

Signed,   DAVID B. MORGAN Justice of the Peace

WM. WALLACE WHITALY AND }
    MYRA HIS WIFE,   }   COURT OF PROBATES
      vs   }
ELEANOR O'BEARN & OTHERS }

Interrogatories to be propounded to witnesses, on behalf of the plaintiffs, in this cause.

1st Were you acquainted with the late Daniel Clark, deceased of New Orleans? If so were you at any time on terms of intimacy with him?

2 Did the said Daniel Clark leave, at his death, any child acknowledged by him as his own? If so state the name of such child and whether said child is still living, and, if living, what name it now bears, and also state when, and where, and in what terms such acknowledgement of said child was made

3 Have you any knowledge of a will said to have been executed by said Clark shortly before his decease? did you ever read or see the said will, or did Daniel Clark ever tell you that he was making said will, or had made said will? If so, at what time and place? and if more than one state how often, and when and where

4 If you answer the last question affirmatively, state whether the said Dan'l Clark ever declared to you or to any one in your presence the contents of said will and if so state the whole of said contents and the time place and name in which they were made before whom, and all the circumstances which occurred when such declarations were made

5 State how long before his death you saw the said Daniel Clark, for the last time how long before his death he spoke of his last will, and what he said in relation to his aforesaid child

6th State whether you ever heard any one say he had read the said will? If so, state whom what was said, and whether the said person is now living or not

Signed,   WM M WORTHINGTON, for Pl'ff-

Cross examined

1 Each witness examined, and answering any one of the foregoing interrogatories, is desired to state his name, age, residence, and employment, and whether he is in any manner connected with or related to any of the parties to this suit or has any interest in the event of the same

2 How long did you know Daniel Clark? and under what circumstances? And, if you presume to state that Daniel Clark had any child, at his death state who was the mother of said child and who was the husband of that mother State all the circumstances, fully and in detail and whether said Clark was ever married and if so to whom when, and where

If said Clark ever acknowledged to you that he supposed himself to be father of a child, state when and where he made such acknowledgement and all the circumstances of the recognition of such a child, or children, whether the act was public or private

4. Did said Clark consider you as an intimate friend, to whom

he might confide communications so confidential as these relating to his will? If aye, state what you know of your own personal knowledge, of the contents of said will, and be careful, if you please, to distinguish between what you know of your own knowledge and what from hearing.

The defendants propound the foregoing interrogatories with a full reservation of all legal exceptions to the interrogatories in chief, the same not being pertinent to the issue and the last of said interrogatories being calculated merely to draw from the witness hearing declarations.

Signed,   L. C. DUNCAN, for Defendants

WM. W. WHITEY AND
MYRA C. WHITNEY,
    vs
ELEANOR O'BEARN & AL. } COURT OF PROBATES
STATE OF LOUISIANA
No. 8

To David B. Morgan, Esquire, Madisonville parish of St. Tammany, Louisiana, or to any Justice of the Peace in said parish—greeting

Know ye, that we, reposing confidence in your prudence and fidelity, do by these presents give unto you authority diligently to examine all witnesses whatever, as well on the part of the plaintiffs as of the defendants, in a certain suit now pending in our said court, in which Wm. W. Whitney and Myra C. Whitney are plaintiffs, and Eleanor O'Bearn and als. are defendants

Therefore, we desire you, that at certain times to be properly you to be appointed for that purpose, you cause the said witnesses to come before you that you then and there examine, do properly, upon their respective corporal oaths, first taken before you upon the Holy Evangelists, that you reduce their examinations to writing, and when you shall so have taken the same you send the same with this commission, together with same closed to us in our said court, at the city of New Orleans as we command you

Witness the honorable Charles Maurian, judge of that said court, this fourth day of May, in the year of our Lord one thousand eight hundred and thirty five and in the fifty ninth year of the Independence of the United States

Signed   S. BLOSSMAN, D'y R. of wills

Filed July 6, 1835.

S. BLOSSMAN, D y R of wills

Wednesday, 22d July, 1835

WM. W. WHITNEY AND WIFE,
    vs.
ELEANOR O'BEARN AND OTHERS }

On motion of C. Roselius, Esquire, of counsel for the plaintiff

in this case, and upon filing two affidavits of **W. W. Whitney,**
one of said ____ ____ ____ by the court that four commis-
____ ____ ____ ____ ____ to the mayor of the city of
____ ____ ____ ____ ____ de____, one to the mayor
____ W____ ____ ____ ____ ____ ____, and the other to Louis
____ ____ ____ ____ ____ ____ peace, Hancock county,
____ ____ ____ ____ ____ ____ ____ of witnesses residing
in tho____ ____ ____ ____ ____ on the trial of this cause.

W____ W____ ____ ____ }
____ B____ ____ O____ }

De____ ____ ____ ____ of commission issued by the
h____ ____ ____ ____ ____ in and for the parish and city of
New O____

M____ C____ ____ being duly sworn, deposes and says that she
is the si____ of M____ ____ ____ formerly Madame Desgranges;
that some time a____ the marriage of her sister with Mr. Desgrange, her said sister discovered that Mr. Desgranges had
been previously married, that in order to ascertain this fact, she
went to Poland; ____ in the absence of her husband, who was in
France, the while in Philadelphia, Desgrange returned from
France to New Orleans, ____ of the same, or a very short time
after all his ____ made his appearance in New Orleans, upon
the ____ ____ ____ ____ of her sister of the fact and she
returned ____ ____ to New Orleans on the arrival of the
____ ____ ____ Desgrange; he complained to the Governor, who
ca____ Desgrange to be arrested (it was under the Spanish
Government) ____ ____ ____ ____ he obtained his release, and left
the country; ____ ____ ____ ____ ____ he confessed that he had previously married ____ ____ ____ ____ afterwards, from her sister,
by letters which she received from her, that she was married,
recently to M. David C____ the preliminaries of the contemplated marriage were settled by the husband of witness, at his
house, ____ ____ in 1802 or 1803, in the presence of witness, who
went to France, some time after the said arrangement, but previous to the said marriage alluded to

Cross examination

M____ Des____ange married the sister of witness, on or about the
year 1796, her sister was then living at the house of witness,
the marriage was celebrated at the church, there has been no
children of that marriage, ____ and Mde Desgrange were
recog____ ____ d as husband and wife by every one, and no doubts
have ____ ____ been entertained with respect to their marriage, witness
has constantly resided in France, since she went there, and she
re____ned here within the last fifteen days, when her sister wrote

to her about her marriage with Daniel Clark: she informed her, afterwards, that she had had a child (a daughter) by their marriage, who she understood was called Myra

Signed,   V CAILLAVET

Sworn to and subscribed, before me New Orleans May 22d, 1835.   Signed,   GALLIEN PREVAL, Judge

I do hereby certify that the above deposition has been taken by me, in the presence of C Roselius, Esq, attorney for plaintiff, and L C Duncan Esq, attorney for defendant, at the house of Wm Barruell, Chartres street, pursuant to the commission hereto annexed, New Orleans, May 22d, 1835

Signed,   GALLIEN PREVAL, Judge

Costs, $6, marshall's fees included

WM W WHITNEY AND WIFE,	COURT OF PROBATES,
vs	STATE OF LOUISIANA
ELEANOR O BEARN AND OTHERS	No 843

To the honorable Gallien Preval Associate Judge of the City Court of New Orleans—greeting

Know ye, that we, reposing confidence in your prudence and fidelity, do by these presents give unto you authority, diligently to examine all witnesses whatever, as well on the part of the plaintiff as of the defendant in a certain suit now pending in our said court in which W W Whitney and wife are plaintiffs, and Eleanor O'Bearn and als are defendants

Therefore, we desire you, that at certain times and places, by you to be appointed for that purpose, you cause the said witnesses to come before you, that you then and there examine them apart, upon their respective corporal oaths, first taken before you, upon the Holy Evangelists, that you reduce their examinations to writing, and when you shall so have taken them, that you send us, the same with this commission, closed up under your seal, to us in our our said court, at the city of New Orleans, without delay.

Witness the honorable Charles Maurian, Judge of our said court, this twenty-first day of May, in the year of our Lord one thousand eight hundred and thirty-five, and in the fifty-ninth year of the Independence of the United States

Signed,   S. BLOSSMAN, D'y R of wills.

Filed July 6, 1835.

Signed,   S BLOSSMAN, D y R of wills.

WM. W. WHITNEY & WIFE,	
vs.	IN THE COURT OF PROBATES.
E O'BEARN & AL.	

Wm W. Whitney being duly sworn, deposes and says, that

Edward Livingston, Esq, and Mrs Edward Livingston, are, as witnesses he avers material witnesses in the above cause, without the benefit of whose testimony the plaintiffs cannot safely go to trial, that said witnesses reside out of the State, in the city of Washington or the city of New York, and that it is necessary to issue commissions to said persons to take their testimony, and that this affidavit is not made for delay, but merely to have justice done

(Signed)   WM WALLACE WHITNEY

Sworn to and subscribed before me this 22d July, 1835

(Signed)   S BLOSSMAN, Dy R of Wills

WILLIAM W WHITNEY, AND WIFE, } In the Court of Probates
          vs
     E O'BEAR & AL

Wm W Whitney being duly sworn, deposes and says, that Samuel P Davis, residing in Philadelphia in the State of Pennsylvania, is a material witness for the plaintiffs, without the benefit of whose testimony they cannot safely go to trial, that said witness resides out of the State, as aforesaid, and that it is necessary to issue a commission to obtain his testimony, that this affidavit is not made for delay, but merely to have justice done

(Signed)   WM WALLACE WHITNEY

Sworn to and subscribed before me this 22d July, 1835

(Signed)   S BLOSSMAN, Dy R of Wills

Filed 22d July, 1835

(Signed,)   S BLOSSMAN, Dy R of Wills.

WM W WHITNEY, AND   }
MYRA WHITNEY, HIS WIFE, } COURT OF PROBATES
          vs
ELEANOR O BEAR, & ALS   }

The supplemental petition of Wm W Whitney, and Myra his wife, filed by leave of the Court first had and obtained, respectfully showeth, that your petitioners, on or about the   day of   in the year   , filed in this honorable Court their original petition against the above defendants, to which your petitioners refer, for the facts therein stated   your petitioners state that among other things it is there alleged, that on or about the   day of   , in the year 1813 the said Daniel Clark therein named, made an olographic will, which said will was the last will and testament of the said Daniel Clark, that the said will was left by the said Clark among his papers at his decease, and that the same has not been produced, but is either lost, or mislaid, or has been destroyed

37*

Your petitioners pray, that except so far as the said petition asks, that the devisees of Mary Clark therein named, may be made parties to this suit, and that a curator be appointed to represent them, and that Messrs Relf & Chew be cited to answer the petition, and to produce the aforesaid olographic will at the trial of this cause, the said petition may be amended by discontinuing the prayer therein contained, except so much of said prayer as asks for a revocation of the will of 1811, therein mentioned, and that the said olographic will of the said Daniel Clark before referred to, as the last will of the said Clark, may be admitted to probate upon the proofs exhibited in this cause and that your honor may do in the premises whatever is consistent with equity and justice, and your petitioners will ever pray

(Signed,)   WM M. WORTHINGTON, for Pl'ffs.
Filed 9 December, 1835.
          (Signed,)   S. BLOSSMAN, D'y R of Wills.

W. W WHITNEY & WIFE, ⎫
          vs.   ⎬
ELEANOR O'BEARN, & AL. ⎭

On motion of Wm. M Worthington, Esq, of counsel for the plaintiffs, it is ordered by the Court that this case be set for trial for Monday, the 11th of January next, 1836, at 9 A. M

WILLIAM W. WHITNEY ⎫
AND MYRA C WHITNEY, | No 843 IN THE PROBATE COURT, IN
          vs.   ⎬ AND FOR THE CITY AND PARISH OF NEW
ELEANOR O BEARN, | ORLEANS, STATE OF LOUISIANA.
     AND OTHERS   ⎭

Into the said Court by their *Curator ad hoc,* and attorney at law, come the defendants herein, and under leave of Court in this behalf first obtained, exhibit this their supplemental answer to the petition of the plaintiffs herein, and after reiterating all the matters of the defence heretofore set up by him in this case, say that the plaintiff, Myra C Whitney, hath no right to institute this suit, nor any such claim as she pretends therein, alleging that she is the legitimate daughter of Daniel Clark named in the petition herein; because, as these defendants say, if the said Myra be the daughter of said Clark, which the respondents expressly deny, she is an adulterous bastard child of said Clark, and hath no such claims as she pretends, nor any right to have or maintain this present suit: and the respondents further say that the said Myra has already received from the estate of said Clark more than in law she could legally receive from said estate

And for answer to the supplemental petition filed herein by the said plaintiffs, respondents deny the matters therein prayed for by said plaintiffs, and finally, the respondents pray to be hence dismissed with their costs and as in duty bound will ever pray

By their curator *ad hoc* and attorney at law,

L C DUNCAN.

Filed 2 January, 1836.

(Signed) CHARLES MAURIAN, Judge

WM W WHITNEY,
  vs   SATURDAY, 23d January, 1836
ELEANOR O'BEARN, & ALS

On motion of C Roselius, Esq, of Couns 1 for the plaintiffs, it is ordered by the Court that Richard Relf and Beverley Chew, Esqrs, late testamentary executors of a will of the late Daniel Clark, shew cause on Saturday next, the 30th inst, at 9 o'clock A M, why they should not bring into Court and deposite all the papers, books and documents which may have come into their hands as executors, aforesaid, in order to enable the plaintiffs to make search for the last will and testament of the late Daniel Clark, and for other papers and documents relative thereto

SATURDAY, 30th January, 1836

The rule taken herein on the 23d instant, by the counsel of plaintiffs, was called up for argument, and there being other business before the Court, the same could not be proceeded with, when, on motion of C Roselius, Esq., plaintiffs attorney, ordered that said rule of the 23d inst., be enlarged until Saturday next, the 6th of February, at 9 A M

TUESDAY, 9th of February, 1836.

On motion of C. Roselius, Esq., of counsel for the plaintiffs, it is ordered by the Court, that Richard Relf and Beverly Chew, Esqrs, late testamentary executors of a will of the late Daniel Clark, show cause on Monday next, the 15th inst, at 9 o'clock A. M, why they should not bring into Court and deposit all the papers, books and documents which, may have come into their hands as executors aforesaid, in order to enable the plaintiffs to make search for the last will and testament of the late Daniel Clark, and for other papers and documents relative thereto.

MONDAY, 15th February, 1836

W. W. WHITNEY AND WIFE,
         vs
ELEANOR O'BEARN, & AL

Came regularly on this day for argument, the rule taken herein on the 9th instant, by C. Roselius, Esq, on behalf of the plaintiffs.

C. ROSELIUS, for Plaintiffs.

L. C. DUNCAN for Defendants.

When after hearing argument, it is ordered by the Court that said rule be confirmed and made absolute, and that Beverly Chew and Richard Relf, Esqrs. bring into Court and deposit the papers, books and documents which may have come into their hands as executors of a will of the late Daniel Clark, in order to enable the plaintiffs to make search for the last will and testament of the said Daniel Clark, and for other papers and documents relative thereto

Monday, 7th March, 1836

WHITNEY AND WIFE,
    vs
ELEANOR O BEARN ET AL

On motion of C. Roselius, Esquire attorney for the plaintiffs, it is ordered that Mr. Richard Relf and Beverly Chew show cause, on Friday next, the 11th instant, at 9 o'clock, A. M., why they should not comply with the order of this Court, directing them to bring into court the books and papers in their hands as executors of a will of Daniel Clark, and in default of so doing, why a writ of distringas should not issue against them

WM WALLACE WHITNEY,
    vs   COURT OF PROBATES.
ELEANOR O BEARN AND OTHERS

Appeared W. Wallace Whitney, who, being sworn, deposeth and saith that P. Baron Boisfontaine is a material witness for him in the above cause, that said Baron is somewhat advanced in years, and he fears that unless his testimony is taken, he may be deprived of the advantage he expects to derive from the same. He prays a commission to issue to J. Bermudez, &c.

(Signed)   WM WALLACE WHITNEY

Sworn to and subscribed before me, this 31st day of June, 1834.

(Signed)   S. BLOSSMAN,
                    Deputy Register of Wills

Filed 1st July, 1834
(Signed)   W. F. C. DUPLESSIS,
                    Register of Wills

CONSULATE OF THE UNITED STATES OF AMERICA, PARIS

To the Honorable the Court of Probates, in and for the city and parish of New Orleans, in the State of Louisiana

The undersigned, Daniel Brent Consul of the United States, at Paris, in France, one of the persons named in, and to whom the annexed commission from your honorable court is addressed, hereby certifies, that on the 28th day of September, A. D. 1835, and of American Independence the 60th year, in the city of Paris, he caused to come before him François Dussuau de la Croix,

Esquire, now a resident of Paris, to answer the interrogatories propounded to him, in a suit pending in your honorable court, in which William W Whitney and Myra C Whitney are plaintiffs, and Eleanor O Bearn and others are defendants, and which interrogatories are attached to the aforesaid commission, and that after having first sworn the said François Dussuau de la Croix on the Holy Evangelists, to make answer truly, the whole truth and nothing but the truth, touching each and every of the said interrogatories, he answered as follows

To the first interrogatory

My name is François Dussuau de la Croix, I am fifty-eight years old, and reside ordinarily in New Orleans, but am now living at Paris rue de Bourbon, No 43 I have seen William W Whitney and Myra C Whitney at New Orleans, but I do not know Eleanor O Bearn and not knowing who are comprehended in the term ' others, I cannot say whether I am acquainted with them or not

To the second interrogatory

I was intimately acquainted with Mr Daniel Clark, late of the city of New Orleans, Louisiana, from the year one thousand seven hundred and ninety-five or thereabouts, until the time of his death

To the third interrogatory

I never knew that Mr Clark was married, nor I ever heard him or any one else say that he was married

To the 4th interrogatory

Mr Clark told me that he had one natural child which was a daughter named Myra. I cannot precisely say what her age was, but she was about four or five years old when I saw her, a long time before Mr Clark's death

To the 5th interrogatory

I remember that Mr Clark, some years before his death, transferred to me some property, with the verbal request that I should put his natural daughter, Myra in possession of it after his death, which I accordingly did, some years since, by a public act at New Orleans I am not aware of his having made any other provision for the maintenance and education of the said daughter

To the sixth interrogatory

Several months before his death Mr Clark came on my plantation, and told me that his intention was to make a will, and that he came to ask my consent to become his testamentary executor, I at first refused my consent, but Mr Clark having insisted on it, I did not feel authorized to persist in the refusal, on account of the intimate friendship which existed between us. Mr Clark asked my consent, also, to become the tutor of the said child Myra, and told me that his intention was to leave her a fortune, sufficient to efface, it possible, the dishonor of her birth. After the death of Mr Clark, the will which he had manifested to me the desire to make was not to be found and from what he told me before, I was certainly surprised at this.

To the seventh interrogatory.

I recollect perfectly well that, after his death, several persons told me that Mr Clark had asked them, also, to become his testamentary executors.

To the eigth interrogatory.

I know nothing else useful to the defendants, but, I may remark, that my private opinion is that Mr Clark was never *married, and I am the more confident in entertaining this opinion,* as Mr Clark, with whom I was very intimate would not have concealed from me this circumstance when he had the before mentioned conversation with me on my plantation, and he would not then have called his daughter a natural child. I ought to add that I have never had any knowledge of any circumstance which would induce Mr Clark to contract a secret marriage.

   (Signed)   DUSSAU DE LA CROIX.

Sworn to before me, this 28th day of September 1835.

   (Signed)   DANIEL BRENT.

               Commissioner U S Consul.

And, there being no cross interrogatories propounded by the plaintiffs, I certify that I caused the said François Dussau de la Croix to sign his answers to the eight interrogatories propounded by the defendants and I further certify that the same were received and reduced to writing by me, at my office in Paris, on the day and year first before written.

In testimony whereof I have hereunto set my hand, and seal of the United States Consulate and agency of claims, at Paris.

   (Signed)   DANIEL BRENT,

          Commissioner and U S Consul.

Wm. W Whitney, and Myra C Whitney,   Court of Probates,
          vs   The State of
  Eleanor O Bearn and others   Louisiana.

To Thomas P Barton, Esq, Secretary of American Legation, and Daniel Brent, Esq, Consul of the United States at Paris, in France or either of them Greeting.

Know ye that we, reposing confidence in your prudence and fidelity, do, by these presents, give unto you authority, diligently to examine all witnesses, as well on the part of the plaintiff as of the defendant, in a certain suit now pending in our said court, in which William W Whitney and Myra C Whitney are plaintiffs, and Eleanor O'Bearn and others are defendants.

Therefore, we desire you that, at certain times and places, by you to be appointed for that purpose you cause the said witnesses to come before you that you then and there examine them apart, upon their respective corporal oaths first taken before you upon the Holy Evangelists, and you reduce their examinations to writing and when you shall have taken them, that you send the same with his name and sealed up under your seal, to us in our said court at the city of New Orleans, without delay

Witness our Honorable Charles Maurian Judge of our said court, this twentieth day of December in the year of our Lord one thousand eight hundred and thirty-five, and in the fifty-ninth year of the Independence of the United States.

(Signed)   W. F. C. DUPLESSIS,
                       Register of Wills

The execution of the within commission will appear from the certificate hereunto annexed, for which I have received from the defendants the sum of (frs 25 00 X 10 66) thirty-five francs and sixty-six centimes

(Signed)   DANIEL BRENT

WILLIAM W. WHITNEY AND MYRA C. WHITNEY *vs* ELEANOR O'BEARN AND OTHERS	IN THE PROBATE COURT IN AND FOR THE PARISH AND CITY OF NEW ORLEANS No 843

Interrogatories propounded by and on behalf of the above named defendants, and by virtue of the annexed commission, to be answered under oath by Chevalier Dussuau Delacroix, of the city of New Orleans but now in the city of Paris, in the kingdom of France and which together with the answers thereto, to be made by said witness, the said defendants intend to offer and read in evidence on the trial of the above entitled cause

1st Will you be pleased to state your name, age, residence, and whether you are acquainted with the parties in the above entitled cause? if aye, how long have you been so acquainted with them and with each of them

2d Will you be pleased to state whether or not, you were acquainted with Daniel Clark late of the city of New Orleans, Louisiana, who departed this life in the month of August, 1813? If aye, state if you please whether or not, your acquaintance extended to terms of friendly intimacy and how long were you so acquainted with him previous to his death?

Will you be pleased to state whether or not, said Clark was ever married? and if you do not know this fact of your own knowledge, state if you have ever heard said Clark mention whether he had or not?

4th State if you please whether or not, you ever heard said

Clark during his life time, acknowledge himself to be the father of any children? if aye, what were their respective names, sex, and probable ages?

5th Will you be pleased to state if you know whether said Clark during his life time, made provision to the maintenance and education of any of said supposed children? if aye which ones? what where their names? and to what extent did he make such provision to your knowledge, or of what you have heard said Clark say?

6th Will you be pleased to state, whether or not you ever heard said Clark previous to his death speak of his intention of making a will for the disposition of his property? and whether he did or did not suggest to you his intention of mentioning you his testamentary executor? if aye state if you were, or not surprised, after the death of Clark, that said supposed will was not found? if nay, state why you were not surprised?

7th Will you have the goodness to state whether or not during said Clark's lifetime, and about the same time when he had mentioned his intention of appointing you his testamentary executor, you repeatedly heard from other persons that Clark had told them the same thing in reference to themselves?

8th Do you know of any other fact or circumstance which you have not already stated in answer to some one of the foregoing interrogatories and which you suppose may be of service to the above named defendants? if aye, will you be pleased to state the same as fully and particularly as if you had been thereunto specially interrogated?

Signed,   L. C. DUNCAN,
Att'y and Curator ad Hoc for defendants

As I protest against the commission in this case, I have no questions.

Signed,   WM M WORTHINGTON for Pl'ffs

Filed 28th Dec., 1835

Signed,   S BLOSSMAN, Dy R. of Wills

Saturday 23d January 1836

W. W. WHITNEY AND WIFE ⎞
           vs ⎬
ELEANOR O'BEARN et als ⎠

On motion of C Roselius Esquire of counsel for the plaintifs, it is ordered by the Court that Richard Relf and Beverly Chew, Esquires, late testamentary executors of a will of the late Daniel Clark, show cause on Saturday next, the 30th inst, at 9 o'clock A M why they should not bring into Court, and deposit all the papers, books and documents, which may have come into their hands as executors aforesaid, in order to enable the plaintiffs to make search for the last will and testament of the late Daniel Clark and for other papers and documents relative thereto

Saturday, January 30th, 1836

W. W. WHITNEY AND WIFE
vs
ELEANOR O'BEIRNE AND OTHERS

The rule taken herein, on the 23d instant, by the counsel of plaintiffs, was called up for argument, and there being other business before the Court, the same could not be proceeded with, when on motion of C. Roselius Esq. plaintiffs attorney, ordered that said rule of the 23d instant, be enlarged until Saturday next the 6th February at 9 A M

Tuesday 9th February 1836

On motion of C. Roselius Esquire, of counsel for the plaintiffs, it is ordered by the Court, that Richard Relf and Beverly Chew Esquires late testamentary executors of a will of the late Daniel Clark show cause on Monday next, the 15th instant, at 9 o'clock A M, why they should not bring into Court, and deposit all the papers books and documents which may have come into their hands as executors aforesaid, in order to enable the plaintiffs to make search for the last will and testament of the late Daniel Clark, and for other papers and documents relative thereto.

Monday 15th February, 1836

W. W. WHITNEY AND WIFE
vs
ELEANOR O'BEIRN & AL

Come regularly on this day for argument the rule taken herein on the 9th instant, by C. Roselius Esquire on behalf of the plaintiffs

C. ROSELIUS, for Pl'fs
L. C. DUNCAN for Def'ts

When after hearing argument it is ordered by the Court, that said rule be confirmed and made absolute and that Bev Chew and Richard Relf Esquires bring into Court and deposit all the papers, books and documents which may have come into their hands, as executors of a will of the late Daniel Clark, in order to enable the plaintiffs to make search for the last will and testament of the said Clark, and for other papers and documents relative thereto

Monday 7th March 1836

WHITNEY AND WIFE
vs
ELEANOR O'BEIRN

38*

On motion of C Reselius, Esquire, attorney for the plaintiffs, it is ordered that Messrs Richard Relf and Beverly Chew shew cause on Friday next, the 11th instant, at 9 o'clock, A M, why they should not comply with the order of this Court directing them to bring into Court the books and papers in their hands as executors of a will of Daniel Clark, and in default of so doing, why a writ of distringas should not issue against them

Wm W Whitney and Myra C Whitney, his wife, *vs* Elianor O Biann & Others	Court Probates for the Parish and city of New Orleans

Parish and city of New Orleans I William W Whitney one of the above plaintiffs, being duly sworn says, that Madame Louise Benquerelle Mr Louis Louaillier and Madame Carriere, residing in the parish of St Landry in the county of Opelousas and State of Louisiana Madame Caillavet residing at Biloxi, in Hancock County, in the State of Mississippi; Doctor John Sibley, residing at Nachitoches in the State of Louisiana and Madame Lassabe, and Colonel Joseph Deville Degoutin Bellechasse, residing at or near Matanzas in the island of Cuba are material and important witness and each of them is a material and important witness for the said plaintiffs in this cause, without the benefit of whose testimony the said plaintiffs cannot safely proceed to trial in said cause, and that it is necessary that commissions do issue from this honorable Court to fit and proper persons residing, or being, at the said places of residence of the said witnesses, respectively, to take the testimony of the said witnesses. And this deponent further says, that this application is not made for delay, or any other improper purpose, but solely that justice may be done. And this deponent also says, that he would have made application for the said commissions at an earlier day, if he had known that the testimony of the said witnesses would be necessary for the plaintiffs in this cause. That this deponent caused the petition of the said plaintiffs filed in this cause, to be amended in the month of December 1835, with a view to confine the inquiry before this Court to the single point of the making, and the existence at the death of Daniel Clark, of the will alleged by the said plaintiffs in their said petition, to have been made by Daniel Clark in 1813, that this deponent was informed and believed, that no answer had been made in this suit by the said defendants or by any one of them to the said amended petition, and that the said inquiry would be confined to the said point of the making, and the existence of the said will of 1813, at the death of the said Daniel Clark That this deponent was informed by his proctor, that no other testimony would be necessary for the plaintiffs on the trial of this cause upon the said amended petition than such as went to establish the said point of the marriage and the existence of the said will of 1813 at the death of the said Daniel Clark, and that this deponent did therefore believe as he reasonably ought, that no other testimony would be necessary, and the said plaintiffs omitted in consequence to procure the testimony which they now desire to obtain from the above named witnesses, that it was not until after the above cause was set down for trial, and on or about the ... year of April ... ..., that the ... deponent upon examining the papers on file in this cause ascertained for the first time that an answer to the said amended petition had been made and filed on the part of the said defendants, and that it was alleged in substance, in the said answer so filed to the said amended petition that if Myra C. Whitney one of the above plaintiffs was the child of Daniel Clark, she was an adulterous bastard child of said Daniel Clark and had no right to have or maintain this present suit. This deponent further says that the said allegation so made, as aforesaid in the answer of the said defendants, respecting the said Myra C. Whitney is a foul and malicious falsehood, and that the said plaintiffs will be able to prove it to be such by the testimony of the above named witnesses.

This deponent further says, that from the nature of the said answer and the allegation aforesaid contained therein, and from other sources of information, he has reason to believe and does verily believe, that the principal, if not the only point on which the said defendants intend to rely upon the trial of this cause will be an attempt upon their part, to show that Zulime Carriere mother of the said Myra C. Whitney, one of the above plaintiffs had another lawful husband to wit, one Jerome Degrange living at the time when she married the said Daniel Clark, and became the mother, by the said Daniel Clark of the said Myra. But this deponent says, that the said plaintiffs can abundantly prove by the said witnesses, that the said Degrange never was the lawful husband of the said Zulime Carriere, that if the said Degrange was at any time married to the said Zulime Carriere, previous to her marriage of the said Zulime Carriere with the said Daniel Clark, such marriage between the said Degrange and the said Zulime Carriere was wholly null and void ... because the said Degrange was a married man and had a wife still living previous, and at the time when he married (if at all) the said Zulime Carriere, which the said plaintiffs will be able, as aforesaid, to prove by the said witnesses. And further this deponent saith that, to the best of this deponent's information and belief the said plaintiffs cannot by any other evidence within their reach, sufficiently prove the facts, which they expect to establish by the testimony of the above witnesses, and that this deponent would have procured the testimony of the said witnesses before the cause had been set for trial, if he had had any cause to suppose that the fact of the legitimacy of the said Myra would be brought into question upon the trial of this cause but that he is now informed and believes that in the present state of the pleading the said plaintiffs cannot safely proceed to trial without the testimony of the said witnesses And this deponent also says, that on the morning of the 28th day of April last this deponent was in the said Court of Probates and intended to have the cause set down for trial for a day sufficiently distant to enable the said plaintiffs to procure the testimony which this deponent has so lately ascertained, might be indispensibly necessary for the said plaintiffs on the said trial but before this deponent had an opportunity to do so, Lucius C Duncan, Esq, attorney for the said defendants unexpectedly, and without the consent or approbation of this deponent, or, as this deponent believes, of any of the said plaintiff's counsel, set the cause down for the 5th day of May instant This deponent hoped, however, that under the circumstances, the said defendants would consent that the said commissions should issue and accordingly one of this deponent's counsel applied to the said Lucius C Duncan for such consent but he wholly refused to give it, and the said plaintiffs are therefore compelled to make the present application to the said Court for relief as otherwise said plaintiffs would be remediless in the premises, if forced to try their cause without the testimony of the said witnesses

Signed,   WM WALLACE WHITNEY

Sworn to and subscribed before me

New Orleans, 3d May 1836

W F C DUPLESSIS, Register of wills

Filed 3d May, 1836

In the Court of Probates in and for the parish and city of New Orleans, Wednesday, 4th May, 1836

Present the honorable J Bermudez, Judge.

W. W WHITNEY AND WIFE)
            vs   }
ELEANOR O BEARN AND ALS)

On motion of James M White, Esq, of counsel for the plaintiffs, and upon filing an affidavit of said plaintiff, W W Whitney, it is ordered by the Court that Richard Relf and Beverly Chew,

Esq, bring into Court, and deposit all the papers, books and documents, which may have come into their hands as executors of a will of the late Daniel Clark, in order to enable the plaintiff to make search for the last will and testament of the said Clark, and for other papers and documents relative thereto, ordered further that a copy of said affidavit be served upon said R Relf and B Chew, and that they produce the required papers and documents tomorrow the 5th instant, at 11 o'clock A M, the day and hour at which this cause is fixed for trial

Extract from the minutes   S BLOSSMAN,
Deputy Register of wills

In the Court of Probates in and for the parish and city of New Orleans, Wednesday, 4th May 1836

Present the honorable J Bermudez, Judge

W W Whitney and wife
vs
Eleanor O'Bearn et als

On motion of James W White Esquire of counsel, for the plaintiffs and upon filing an affidavit of W W Whitney, one of said plaintiffs, it is ordered by the Court that four commissions issue in this case, one directed to Michel Perrault, Robert Taylor and James Morgan, or any one of them, Justices of the Peace of the parish of St Landry county of Opelousas, Louisiana, one to Louis Arban Caillavet Justice of the Peace Biloxi, Hancock county Mississippi, one to Louis Shoemaker, U S Consul at Matanzas Cuba, or in his absence to the vice consul for the United States, at Matanzas, Cuba and the other directed to Silvester C Bossier, James W Sims, John Murrall Charles A Bullard and William Robertson, or to any one of them Justices of the Peace Natchitoches parish of Natchitoches, State of Louisiana, to take the depositions of witnesses residing in those places to be read in evidence on the trial of this suit

In the Court of Probates, in and for the parish and city of New Orleans, Monday 23d May 1836

Present, the honorable J Bermudez, Judge

Whitney and wife
vs
Eleanor O'Beara and als

On motion of James M White, attorney for plaintiffs, it is ordered, that Messrs Richard Relf and Beverly Chew show cause on Friday the 27th instant, at 10 o'clock in the morning, why they should not bring into and deposit in Court, all of the books, papers and documents, which may have come in their hands as executors of a will of the late Daniel Clark, in compliance with an order from this Court, heretofore obtained against them, by the said plaintiffs, and why they should not verify their compliance with said order by their affidavits, and in default of so doing, why a writ of distringas should not issue against them

In the Court of Probates, for the parish and city of New Orleans.

WILLIAM WALLACE AND MYRA C'
    WHITNEY, HIS WIFE
    vs
ELEANOR O'BEARN AND OTHERS

William Wallace Whitney, one of the above plaintiffs being duly sworn, says, that the above suit is brought to establish the last will of the late Daniel Clark of New Orleans, made in the year 1813, and in and by which the said Myra, one of the above plaintiffs, was made the sole heiress of the said Daniel Clark, that the said Myra is also the legitimate child of the said Daniel Clark, and was acknowledged and declared to be such by the said Daniel Clark, in his said last will of 1813 and this deponent further says, that he has received information and verily believes as well from said information, as from his examination of the records of this honorable court, and depositions already taken in this case; that immediately at or about the moment of the decease of the said Daniel Clark, the said will of 1813, was in existence unrevoked, amongst his, the said Daniel Clark's papers and effects, and that it was the dying intention and declared wish of the said Daniel Clark, that it should remain, after his decease, valid and effectual, as his last will, that from the same sources of information, and from said examination of the records of this court, and said depositions, this deponent has good reason to, and does verily believe that papers and documents, proving the legitimacy of the said Myra, were left by the said Daniel Clark, at his decease, amongst his said papers and effects, that upon the death of the said Daniel Clark, all the books papers and documents and effects of the said Clark, came into hands of Richard Relf, one of the defendants in this suit, and subsequently, as this deponent believes, into the hands also of Beverly Chew, another of said defendants, and that the said books, papers, and documents and effects have not been, at any time, since the decease of the said Clark, wholly surrendered or faithfully accounted for by the said Relf and Chew, or either of them, this deponent further says, that if all of the books, papers and documents of the said Daniel Clark, which came into the hands or control of the said Relf and Chew, or of the said Relf, were produced and deposited in court for the examination of the above plaintiffs, the said last will of 1813, and the papers and documents proving the legitimacy of the said Myra, would be discovered, and the said plaintiffs would thereby be able to make ample proof of the validity of the claims and rights of the said Myra to the estate of the said Daniel Clark; and further, this deponent says, that it would be necessary that the said books, papers and documents should be produced and deposited in court for the examination of said plaintiffs some days before the day set for the trial of this cause, in order to afford them and others a reasonable time to make search for the said will and other papers and documents, proving the right of the said Myra.

Signed, WM WALLACE WHITNEY

Sworn to and subscribed before me the 24th May, 1836

S BLOSSMAN

Deputy Register of wills.

In the Court of Probates, in and for the parish and city of New Orleans, Friday 27th May 1836

Present the honorable J Bermudez, Judge

W W Whitney and wife }
vs }
Eleanor O Beary and others }

Came on this day for argument, the rule taken herein, on the 23d instant

WHITE & GRYMES for plaintiffs

L C DUNCAN, for defendant

When, after hearing argument of counsel, ordered, that said rule of the 23d be discharged at plaintiffs costs.

In the court of Probate, in and for the parish and city of New Orleans, Saturday 28th May, 1836.

Present, the honorable J Bermudez, Judge

William W Whitney and Myra C }
Whitney his wife }
vs }
Eleanor O Beary and Others }

On motion of James W White, attorney for the above plaintiffs, it is ordered that Richard Relf and Beverly Chew, defendants in this suit show cause on Tuesday the 31st day of May, 1836 at ten o'clock A M why they should not produce and deposit in court under oath in compliance with a former order of this court made in this cause all books, documents, papers and other writings relating to the succession of the late Daniel Clark, of New Orleans which came to their hands as executors of a will of the said Daniel Clark, and also that which is hereunto annexed, and also why they should not produce and deposit in court certain private papers of the said Clark, amongst which the said Richard Relf has alleged that the will of the said Daniel Clark, of which he was appointed an executor, was found.

List of books, documents, papers, &c , relating to the succession of Daniel Clark, and which came to the hands of Richard Relf and Beverly Chew, as executors of a will of said Daniel Clark, and which are not yet deposited in court, and which are referred to in the foregoing order

1　A note made by John Lynd, in favor of said Daniel Clark, for $4461, dated April 10 1813 payable in 4 months, and inventoried under letter A, No 1 .... $4461 00

2　A note for $500 in favor of said Daniel Clark by Horice, empowered by his wife to act before Broutin, Not Pub, dated July 3d, 1813 and payable in December, 1813, and inventoried under letter C No 3 .... 500 00

3　A note for $100, in favor of said Daniel Clark, by L Boirdore, dated April 14th, 1812, payable at will, and inventoried under letter E No 5, ... $100 00

4　A note for $100, in favor of Daniel Clark, by Abraham Arunaux dated February 3d, 1813 payable at will, and inventoried under the letter H, No 8 .... $100 00

5.　A note for $6,557 92, in favor of William Brooks, by Ferdinand L Claiborne dated 18th November 1811 payable February 1st, 1813 endorsed by William Brooks H A Claiborne and Chew & Relf, and inventoried under the letter P, No 16, ... $6,557 90

6　Two notes, for the sum each, of $3,125, in favor of Daniel Clark by Hy Hunt, dated March 15, 1800, and payable at one and two years and inventoried under the letters XY, and Nos 24 and 25, ... $6,250 00

7　A note for $55, in favor of Daniel Clark, by Richard DeVals, dated Nov'r 23, 1811, payable in one year, and inventoried under the letter N, No 13, ... $55 00

8　A note for $300, in favor of Daniel Clark by Henry Hunt dated May 15, 1810, and bearing interest from its date and inventoried under the letter Z No 26. .... $300 00

9　A book with the Bank of Orleans, by which there appeared to be due the succession of Daniel Clark, at his decease, $3037 73, and inventoried under the double letter FF, No 32, ... $3,037 73

10.　Six of twenty-eight notes in favor of Daniel Clark, by persons supposed to be insolvent, contained in a bundle, inventoried under the double letter GG, No. 33

11 Nine of thirty-four documents, relative to Florida lands contained in a bundle inventoried under the double letter HH, No 34

12 Three of eighteen agreements contained in a
bundle inventoried under the double letter II,
No 35

13 Two of seven mortgages in favor of Daniel
Clark's succession contained in a bundle inventoried under the double letter JJ, No 36

14 A bundle containing 31 sale of slaves, and inventoried under the double letter KK, No 37

15 Five of fifty receipts, &c contained in a bundle inventoried under the double letter LL, No.
38

16 One of thirteen documents in relation to the
Canal Carondelet contained in a bundle inventoried under the double letter OO, No 41

17 Six of forty-four documents, in relation to the
settlement of accounts with Daniel W. Coxe, contained in a bundle inventoried under the double
letter OO No 43

18 Eighteen of sixty-six accounts contained in a
bundle inventoried under the double   RR,
No 44.

19 Two of forty-nine letters with several persons,
contained in a bundle inventoried under the
double letter SS, No 45.

20 Two acts of forty-eight acts of sales made by
Daniel Clark, of lands at the Bayou contained
in a bundle inventoried under the double letter
TT, No. 46

21. One of nine sales in favor of Wilkins, contained
in a bundle inventoried under the double letter
UU, No 47

22 Seven of forty documents contained in a bundle inventoried under the double letter VV, No.
48

23 Four of fourteen plans and titles to property,
contained in a bundle inventoried under the
double letter WW, No 49

24 Three of thirty-five documents relative to the
Bayou plantation, inventoried under the double
letter XX, No 50

25. A bundle containing twenty-nine titles or guarantees of lands at Ouachita, and inventoried
under the double letter YY, No 51

26 A bundle containing twelve documents relating to the plantations at Chapitoulas, inventoried under the double letter ZZ, No 52

27. One of two documents relative to lands in Attakapas, bought of Macarty's succession contained in a bundle inventoried under the treble letter EEE, No 57

28 A bundle containing two transfers of lands of the Bayou aux Bœufs, executed by Wm. Mover and Alexander Fulton, inventoried under the treble letter FFF, No. 58

29 A bundle containing five plans guarantees or transfers of 3200 arpents of land at Opelousas, bought of Mrs Broutin and inventoried under the treble letter GGG, No 59.

30 A bundle containing six plans, guarantees or transfers of 1600 arpents of land at Opelousas bought of Mr. Broutin and inventoried under the treble letter HHH, No 60

31 A bundle containing two documents in relation to the plantation Fusilier, at the Terre aux Bœufs, and inventoried under the treble letter KKK, No 63

32 A bundle containing four plans, transfers, or guarantees of 3200 arpents of land, situated at Opelousas, bought of Mr Gradnigo and inventoried under the treble letter LLL, No 64

33 One of four titles of lands of Mr Fusilier, contained in a bundle inventoried under the treble letter MMM No 65

34. One of twenty-two documentary papers of Jean Lingues, contained in a bundle inventoried under the treble letter OOO, No 67

35. Two of twenty-five documents to establish the accounts with L Claiborn contained in a bundle inventoried under the treble letter QQQ. No. 69.

36. Fifty-four of 4,105 letters contained in a packet or bundle, inventoried or numbered from one to sixty-three

Extract from the Minutes   S BLONSMAN,
                        Deputy Register of Wills

Received May the 30th, 1836, and on the same day served copy of the written order and list of documents on Richard Relf in person, and on Beverly Chew by leaving the same at his domicil, with his wife a free person above fourteen years of age, living in the house. Received May 31st, 1836.

FRED BUISSON, Sheriff.

In the Court of Probates in and for the parish and city of New Orleans.

MONDAY, 30th May, 1836.

Present, the Hon. J Bermudez, Judge.

W W WHITNEY & wife, }
                      } No. 43
ELEANOR O B   & c. }

On motion of James W White, Esq, of counsel for the plaintiffs, it is ordered by the Court that a subpœna duces tecum, issue in this case, directed to Henry P Leonard, English editor of the New Orleans Bee or for Jerome Bayon, that he bring with him into Court to be offered in evidence, in support of a motion to be made on the cause on Tuesday, the 31st day of May, A. D. 1836, the number that contains a copy of the newspaper called the New Orleans Bee, now in his possession and which was published on the 6th day of October, A. D. 1835, and in which is published a letter or communication relating in part to the succession of the late Daniel Clark of New Orleans, signed Richard Relf, and also, that he bring with him, at the same time and place, the original manuscript copy of the said letter or communication furnished to him by Richard Relf or by whomsoever the same was furnished to him for publication.

Extract from the Minutes.   P L B DUPLESSIS,
                             Deputy Register of Wills.

Received May 30th, 1836 and on the same day served copy of the written order on Jerome Bayon and H P Leonard, both in person.

Returned May 31st, 1836.

FRED BUISSON, Sheriff.

W W WHITNEY AND WIFE }   IN THE COURT OF PROBATES,
                  vs.   }   IN AND FOR THE PARISH AND
ELEANOR O BARNES & D & c. }   CITY OF NEW ORLEANS.

Tuesday, the 31st May, 1836.

Present, the Hon. J Bermudez, Judge.

On motion of James W White, attorney for plaintiffs, ordered that a subpœna duces tecum issue in this cause, directed to Mr. Jerome Bayon and Henry P Leonard, editors of the newspaper called the New Orleans Bee, that they personally appear before this Honorable Court, on the first day of June, A D 1836, at 10 o'clock A M of that day, and bring with them into said court at said time, to be offered in evidence in support of a motion, then and there to be made in this cause, the file number. or copy of the said ' The New Orleans Bee ' now in the possession of them, or either of them and which was published on the 6th day of October, A D 1835, and in which is published a letter or communication signed Richard Relf relating in part, to the succession of the late Daniel Clark of New Orleans and also that they bring with them at the same time and place the manuscript copy of the said letter or communication furnished to them, or either of them, by Richard Relf, or by whomsoever the same was furnished to them, or either of them for publication.

W W Whitnly and Wife ⎫
         vs   ⎬
Eleanor O'Beary and als ⎭

Came on this day, for argument, the rule taken herein on the 28th instant

GRYMES & WHITE, for Plaintiffs

SEGHERS & DUNCAN, for Defendant.

When, after hearing argument ordered that this case be continued over until to-morrow, the 1st of June, at 10 A M.

W W Whitnly and wife ⎫   In the Court of Probates,
        vs   ⎬   in and for the Parish and
Eleanor O'Beary and al ⎭   City of New Orleans

Wednesday, 1st June, 1836

Present, the Hon J Bermudez, Judge

Came on again, this day, pursuant to adjournment yesterday, the rule of the 28th day of May, last past.

GRYMES & WHITE, for Plaintiff.

DUNCAN & SEGHERS for Defendant.

When, after hearing further argument of counsel, ordered that the same be continued over until to-morrow morning, the 2d instant, at 10 o'clock

W W. Whitney and Wife ⎫   In the Court of Probates.
        vs   ⎬   in and for the Parish
Eleanor O'Beary et al ⎭   and City of New Orleans

Thursday 2d June, 1836

Came on again this day, pursuant to adjournment yesterday, the rule of the 28th day of May, last part

GRYMES & WHITE, for Plaintiffs

SEGHERS & DUNCAN, for Defendants

When, after hearing further testimony and argument of respective counsel, the same was submitted upon said rule, whereupon the Court delivered the following opinion, to wit

The private papers of the deceased, among which was found the will of the deceased, admitted to probate, cannot be viewed by the court as the papers contained in the black trunk mentioned in the inventory

The process verbal of the judge affixing the seals on the property of the deceased, the testimony of the said judge, the publication of one of the testamentary executors of the deceased in the columns of the Bee strongly impress upon the mind of the court that the private papers, amongst which was the will of the deceased, must have been contained in another trunk, elsewhere placed than in the room on the doors of which were placed the seals of the judge, as well the armoire, bureau and papers of the deceased, and afterwards inventoried by the Register of Wills The account which the executor gives of these private papers is, that they must either have been either lost or destroyed by moisture. Under this state of things, is the court to issue the order prayed for as a means necessary to the plaintiffs action? Can the court, by any order necessary for the exercise of its jurisdiction and for the protection of the rights of the plaintiffs, compel the production of what is lost or destroyed by moisture? It is thought not, and the only remedy of the party plaintiff seems indicated by the provisions of the code, which obliges him who causes damages to another to repair it when the same is the result of his negligence, imprudence or want of skill Should this remedy be inadequate to the purposes of the plaintiff, he may, from the insufficiency of the account of the private papers, the production of which he asks, draw such inferences as may be conducive to a fair and equitable decision of the present controversy It is, therefore, ordered that the rule be dismissed, and the cause having been set for trial upon the merits for this day, the defendants pleading ready, the plaintiffs moved for a continuance on the ground that they could not foresee the judgment of the court upon the rule taken by them and as they have not the documents, the production of which they asked it is necessary to obtain time to prepare themselves for trial The court declined using their discretion in granting the continuance as the judgment should have been foreseen by the plaintiffs and as the character and reputation of one of our respectable citizens has been for a long while involved in a controversy, and justice required that an end should be put to this controversy, the plaintiffs declining and refusing to proceed with their claim On motion of defendants, the plaintiff are non-suited they paying the costs of this suit.

New Orleans June 8 1836.

(Signed) J BERMUDEZ, Judge

W. W. WHITNEY AND WIFE
vs
ELEANOR O BEARN, ET AL.

On motion of L. C. Duncan, Esq, curator ad hoc for the defendants, under the appointment of the court, it is ordered by the court that the plaintiffs show cause, on Monday, morning next the 6th instant, at 10 o'clock why the sum of one thousand dollars should not be allowed said L. C. Duncan, as a fee for services rendered, and why the same should not be taxed by the Register of Wills, with the other costs incurred herein

SUCCESSION OF DANIEL CLARK	
WM. W. WHITNEY & WIFE,	COURT OF PROBATES,
vs	THE STATE OF LOUISIANA.
ELEANOR O'BEARN, & ALS	

To Michael Perrault, Robert Taylor and James Morgan, or any of them justices of the peace, parish of St Landry county of Opelousas, Louisiana, greeting

Know ye, that we, reposing confidence in your prudence and fidelity, do by these presents give unto you authority diligently to examine all witnesses whatever, as well on the part of the plaintiffs as of the defendants, in a certain suit now pending in our said Court, in which W. W. Whitney and wife are plaintiffs, and Eleanor O'Bearn and others, are defendants

Therefore, we desire you, that at certain times and places by you to be appointed for that purpose you cause the said witnesses to come before you that you then and there examine them apart, upon their respective corporal oaths, first taken before you upon the Holy Evangelists that you reduce their examinations to writing and when you shall so have taken them, that you send the same with this commission closed up under your seal, to us in our said Court at the city of New Orleans, without delay

Witness the honorable J. Bermudez, Judge of our said Court, this fourth day of May in the year of our Lord one thousand eight hundred and thirty-six, and in the sixtieth year of the Independence of the United States.

Signed,   S. BLOSSMAN D. R of Wills

W. W. WHITNEY, AND	
MYRA C. WHITNEY, HIS WIFE	IN THE COURT OF PROBATES,
vs	IN AND FOR THE PARISH
ELEANOR O'BEARN AND ALS.	AND CITY OF NEW ORLEANS

Interrogatories to be propounded to Madam Louise Benguerelle, Mr. Louis Louailier, Madam Carrière née Gradnigo, Madam Despau née Carrière and others residing in the parish of St Landry, in the county of Opelousas and State of Louisiana, witnesses on the part of the plaintiffs in this cause, and which are to be annexed to a commission, issued in said cause, from the said Court of Probates

First Will you please to state your name, age, occupation, and place of residence?

Second Are you acquainted with, or have you known or heard of, the above named William Wallace Whitney and Myra C Whitney his wife or either and which of them?

Third Are you or have you been acquainted with Zulime nee Carriere the mother of the said Myra? If aye, please to state when and where you were so acquainted with her, and whether the said Zulime was ever married to the late Daniel Clark, of New Orleans who died in the year 1813, and all you know on that subject, the time and place when such marriage took place if at all?

Fourth Did or did not, one DeGrange representing himself to be in true and pure estate himself as such in marriage upon the said Zulime and carried her at a time when in fact he had a lawful wife to whom he had been previously married, still living? If so please to state whether, after the said DeGrange had so imposed himself upon the said Zulime as above inquired of his said lawful wife did, or did not come to New Orleans and detect and expose the bigamy of which he had been guilty in marrying the said Zulime as has been inquired of in the first part of this interrogatory?

Fifth If you answer affirmatively in reply to the last preceding interrogatory please to state the time at which the said bigamy of the said DeGrange was detected and exposed. And was it, or was it not, many years before the birth of the said Myra?

Sixth Was it, or not proved and believed at that time and afterwards, amongst the friends and acquaintances of the said Zulime and the said DeGrange that he had a lawful wife living at and before the time of his marriage with the said Zulime?

Seventh If you have answered affirmatively in reply to the fourth of these interrogatories, please to state whether, when the said lawful wife of the said DeGrange came to New Orleans, as inquired of above he, besaid DeGrange, did, or did not, confess, or acknowledge that she was the   and that he had been guilty of bigamy in marrying the said Zulime

Eighth If you have answered affirmatively, in reply to the fourth of the above interrogatories please to state whether he, the said DeGrange did or did not escape or flee from Louisiana, when his said bigamy was detected and exposed, and many years before the birth of said Myra It aye, please to state whether the said DeGrange did, or did not, return again to Louisiana Describe the personal appearance of said De-Grange

Ninth Do you know of any other matter or thing of benefit or importance to the said plaintiff in this suit, which has been instituted for the purpose of establishing the claims of the said Myra C Whitney, one of the said plaintiffs to the succession o the said Daniel Clark? If aye, please to set forth the same, particularly

JAMES W. WHITE, att'y for pl'ffs.

The attorney who signs the foregoing interrogatories, a stranger to the laws of Louisiana and in disregard of the practice of the bar, having seen proper, (notwithstanding the admonition of the counsel of the defendants) to withhold the commission, the names, and the commissioner before whom he proposes to have said interrogatories answered exception is reserved to the entire proceeding and the counsel of the defendants desires the person who may be asked to receive the answers of any of the witnesses of the foregoing interrogatories to state whether he, the commissioner himself, is, or not, directly, or indirectly interested in the event of this suit whether he is not related to, or connected with the parties plaintiff therein, or with any of the witnesses, and if aye, with which of them

General cross interrogatories to be answered by every person answering any of the foregoing interrogatorie.

Having answered, categorically, the interrogatories of the plaintiffs, will you state whether you are related to, or connected with the plaintiffs, or with the mother of the plaintiff Myra? If aye, with which of them, and in what degree?

Also, how you derive your knowledge of the matters about which the plaintiffs interrogate you, whether it be personal or from hearsay, distinguish, in your statements, what you state on your personal knowledge from what you state of hearsay, and mention from whom, at what time, under what circumstances; where you were, when you obtained your information. And if you speak of any marriage of the late Daniel Clark, state, if you know, by whom, when, and where it was solemnized, whether you were present, and who was present with you and if D Clark ever publicly acknowledged his said wife If not, why? Whether she was divorced from him, and ever *married again.* If aye, and to whom.

L C DUNCAN, curator ad hoc to absent
defendants and of counsel.

Michael Perrault, Justice of the Peace in and for the parish of St. Landry. county of Opelousas, State of Louisiana, and one of the commissioners named in the annexed commission issued from the Court of Probates for the parish and city of New Orleans, in the suit of William Wallace Whitney and Myra C. Whitney, his wife, *vs* Eleanor O'Bearn and others, have caused to appear before me, Louise V've Benguerel, who, being duly sworn to declare the truth on the questions put to her in this cause, answers—

To the first interrogatory.

My name is Louise Vve Benguerel, age, about fifty-seven years, gentlewoman, place of residence, Opelousas

To the second interrogatory

I have heard of both.

To the third interrogatory

I am acquainted with Zulime née Carriere, the mother of said Myra, I knew her in New Orleans a long time ago I have no personal knowledge of such marriage

To the fourth interrogatory

Mr Jerome DeGrange married the said Zulime, which marriage proved, on his part, bigamy, for, after his marriage with the said Zulime, the lawful wife of said DeGrange, whom he had married previous to his marrying the said Zulime, came to New Orleans, and the said DeGrange was then prosecuted and condemned for bigamy in marrying the said Zulime, and he was thrown into prison from which he escaped, and fled from Louisiana this was in the year 1802 or 1803, since that period, I have never seen the said DeGrange, and do not believe that he ever returned to Louisiana.

To the fifth interrogatory

This interrogatory is answered under the preceding one

To the sixth interrogatory

It was The said lawful wife of the said DeGrange brought with her to New Orleans, proofs of her marriage with the said DeGrange The exposure at that time of the said DeGrange's bigamy, in marrying the said Zulime, was notoriously known in New Orleans

To the seventh interrogatory

My husband and myself were intimate with said DeGrange, and when we reproached him for his baseness, in imposing upon the said Zulime he endeavored to excuse himself by saying, that at the time of his marrying the said Zulime he had abandoned his said lawful wife, and never intended to see her again

To the eighth interrogatory

I have answered all this interrogatory in my answer to the fourth interrogatory except as to DeGrange's personal appearance, he was about six feet, English stout built, light complexion, blue eyes

To the ninth interrogatory

As well as I can judge I do not

To the general cross interrogatory

I am not related to or connected with plaintiffs, nor with either of them nor with the mother of said Myra nor am interested at all in this suit It was in New Orleans where I obtained my information It will be seen by my answers, how I knew the facts. I was well acquainted with the said DeGrange, and

40*

the said Zulime, and knew the said lawful wife of the said
DeGrange, whom he had married previous to his imposing
himself in marriage upon the said Zulime

Signed,   V'VE BENGUEREL.

Sworn to and subscribed, before me, this 27th day of May,
1836, at Opelousas, parish of St Landry   In testimony whereof,
I have hereunto set my hand and private seal, the day and year
above written.   I am not related to, nor connected with any of the
parties to this suit, nor with their relations nor with the witness.
I am not interested in this suit, nor of counsel.

[L S]   M PERRAULT, Justice of the Peace,
Parish of St Landry.

Filed 2 June, 1836.

Wm W Whitney and Myra C Whitney,   } Court of Probates,
vs.   } State of Louisiana.
Eleanor O'Bearn and Others.   }   No 813

To John Swift, Esq, Mayor, and John Binns, or S. Badger,
Aldermen of the city of Philadelphia, State of Pennsylvania—
greeting.

Know ye, that we, reposing confidence in your prudence and
fidelity, do by these presents give unto you authority diligently
to examine all witnesses whatever, as well on the part of the
plaintiff as of the defendant, in a certain suit now pending in our
said court, in which W W Whitney and Myra C Whitney
are plaintiffs, and Eleanor O'Bearn and others are defendants.

Therefore, we desire you, that at certain times and places, by
you to be appointed for that purpose, you cause the said witnesses
to come before you, that you then and there examine them apart,
upon their respective corporal oaths, first taken before you, upon
the Holy Evangelists, that you reduce their examinations to
writing, and when you shall so have taken them, that you send
the same with this commission, closed up under your seal, to
us in our our said court, at the city of New Orleans, without delay.

Witness the honorable Charles Maurian, Judge of our said
court, this twenty-first day of May, in the year of our Lord one
thousand eight hundred and thirty-five, and in the fifty-ninth
year of the Independence of the United States

Answer of Daniel W Coxe to interrogatories propounded in
the suit of William W Whitney and Myra C Whitney, *vs.*
Eleanor O'Bearn and others, in the Probate Court in and for the
parish and city of New Orleans

To the first interrogatory
My name is Daniel Wm Coxe, my residence in Philadelphia;
I am in my 66th year; am not acquainted with Mr. Wm. W.

Whitney, or Mrs Eleanor O'Bearn, but have seen the lady called Mrs Myra C Whitney, whom I suppose to be the same person who, under the name of Myra Davis, accompanied Col Sam'l B. Davis, as passenger, to New Orleans in the ship Ohio, Capt. Simeon Toby, about the year 1819 or '20, when I was also passenger on said ship but had never seen her before, nor have seen her since, that I recollect

To the second interrogatory

I was personally acquainted with the late Daniel Clark, Esq, of New Orleans, from the time of my first arrival in Louisiana, in 1791, till the period of his death, in 1813 Having been long associated with him in commerce, and in the purchase of real estate, in Louisiana, my knowledge of him was intimate, and our intercourse confidential The last time I saw him was in 1811, when he came to Philadelphia, to settle our co-partnership accounts, which was effected on that occasion.

To the third interrogatory

Mr Clark never was married, to the best of my knowledge and belief

To the fourth and fifth interrogatories.

Mr Clark communicated to me, in confidence, about the year 1802, that Madame Degranges, who came from New Orleans to Philadelphia, some time, I think, in that year, was pregnant by him and he requested me to assist him in placing her under the care of any reputable physician, and to furnish her with money during her confinement and stay in Philadelphia I accordingly employed the late Doctor William Shippen to attend her during her accouchement, who procured a nurse, and removed the child from her mother, immediately after its birth, and I paid the accounts The infant proved to be a girl, which was named Caroline Clark, (now Mrs Doctor Barnes) residing, as I am informed, in the State of Mississippi Mr. Clark never intimated to me that he had any other children, either by Mrs Degranges or any other woman, but after his death, I think for the first time, I was told by Doctor Hulings and Col Sam'l B Davis that he had another daughter born in New Orleans, subsequently to Caroline, by the aforesaid Mrs Degranges, called Myra; the same alluded to in my answer to the 1st interrogatory, who is now, I understand, in New Orleans, with Mr. Whitney, her husband. I am ignorant of her age, though I think Caroline, as far as I can ascertain, must be between 32 and 33 years of age Although so informed, yet I always doubted Myra being Mr Clark's child, because he confessed himself to be the father of Caroline, but never mentioned Myra to me, and because, in addition, Caroline was like him, and I saw no resemblance to him in Myra. After the early years of Caroline's childhood

had passed away with her nurse, Mr Clark, in his occasional
visits to Philadelphia, finding her health delicate, and the
place of her residence ineligible, required me to remove her
from it, and place her with some respectable person, who would
attend to her morals education and health, and I accordingly
placed her under the care of Mr and Mrs James Alexander, at
Trenton, New Jersey, with whom she continued to reside till
Mr Alexander died, I think in 1809 and subsequently with his
widow, till 1814 or 1815 Mr Clark always visiting her when
he came to Philadelphia, and treating her with the tenderness
of a parent, often making her presents, and remunerating Mr
and Mrs Alexander liberally for their care of the child After Mr
Clark's death, and the failure in trade of his executors and then
co-partners, Messrs Chew and Relf Dr Hulings and myself,
finding that remittances from those gentlemen to old Mrs Clark,
the mother and heir of Daniel, came on tardily, by reason
of their embarrassments, devised an economical plan for Caroline's benefit, by removing her from her grandmother, where she
was then staying, and placing her with Mrs. Bazeley, who
kept a boarding school in this city, under an agreement that
Caroline should assist in the school, while she was at the same
time acquiring education, and the knowledge necessary to fit her
for future usefulness

Previous to removing to Mrs Bazeley's, she spent a few days
in my house

Mrs Clark allowed twenty-five dollars per quarter for clothing, &c, during her residence with Mrs Bazeley with whom
she remained many years I annex hereto the original order on
Dr Hulings, drawn up by me, and signed by Mrs Clark, authorizing the payment of said allowance Caroline afterwards
married Dr Barnes, a respectable young man of this city It
is proper here to mention that Dr Hulings and myself, acting
as old confidential friends of Mr Clark, felt and took an interest in the welfare of his mother, then aged and infirm residing at Germantown, and as Myra was also said by Col Davis
to be his child, we thought it a duty to advise the old lady to
make a will, and provide for all who had natural claims upon
her, should any property remain after her son's executors and
partners had settled the estate

She accordingly made a will many years after her son's death,
and left Caroline (now Mrs Dr Barnes), a child's share, (I think
one quarter part), but for Myra she refused to make any provision, although Dr Hulings himself succeeded in persuading her to mention Myra also in her will and to leave her
something as a memento and recognition of her parentage This
we deemed proper to do, on the representation of Col. Davis,

with whom she lived and whose name she bore, that she was Mr Clark's child, notwithstanding our own doubts and uncertainty on the subject. It is necessary to add by way of explanation of a transaction which has been enveloped in partial mystery and concealment that after Mr Clark's death in 1813 I learned for the first time, he had made a certain provision for these girls in his lifetime, by creating two distinct trusts for their respective benefit the one to Col Bellechasse, and the other to Chevalier Delacroix, of New Orleans, to each of whom he conveyed certain lots of ground near the Bayou St Jean, and contiguous to New Orleans, a list of which Mr Relf furnished me, when I went to New Orleans in 1819, to recover an old partnership debt due me by Mr Clark which list I find corresponds with a similar one sent to Dr Hulings, many years ago by Mr Relf. Excepting Myra's portion of the aforesaid lots, and the memento in Mrs Clark's will, I know of no other provision made for her benefit nor do I know of any for Caroline's benefit, other than as already stated

To the sixth interrogatory I answer that old Mr Whitney, the father of Myra's husband called on me after his son's marriage, on a suggestion, as he said, that I knew something about Myra's property, and of her being the daughter of Daniel Clark, to whom I replied in substance ' Go to Col Davis, from whom this reference to me probably comes, and as he gave his own name, and not Mr Clark's to the girl, he can tell you all about her, as his house was her home" And I added, " I have no knowledge whatever, except what comes from Colonel Davis, and mere rumour, of her being Daniel Clark's child If she is, why was she kept in ignorance of her real name, and that of Davis given to her?

To the seventh interrogatory I answer that I do suppose it may be of service to the defendants in this cause to state that some time in the year 1808 after Madame DeGrange had re-returned to Philadelphia from New Orleans, and when lodging in Walnut-street, she sent for me, and during a private interview with her at Mrs Rowan's house, where she lodged, she stated that she had heard Mr. Clark was going to be married to Miss Caton, of Baltimore, which she complained was a violation of his promise to marry her, and added she now considered herself at liberty to connect herself in marriage with another person, alluding probably to Mr Gardette, who at the moment of this disclosure entered the room, when, after a few words of general conversation, I withdrew, and her marriage to Mr Gardette become public, a few days after; a certificate of which, authenticated by the Roman Catholic Bishops of the dioceses is hereto annexed, with an extract from the baptismal register, of the birth of two children by said marriage. Mrs. Rowan, with whom Madam Degrange lodged previous to her marriage with Mr Gardette, has told me that Mr Gardette engaged lodgings for her at her house next to Mr Gardette's own house, as a Miss Zulime Carriere, of New Orleans, by which name she was always known to her prior to her said marriage with Mr. Gardette

Cross interrogatories.

To the first cross interrogatory. I have already answered.

To the second   I am not aware of any interest whatever that I have in the result of this suit.

To the third.   I have employed no counsel in this suit, nor have I any concern or connexion with it, either directly or indirectly.

The words, "*to New Orleans*," interlined before signing in the first page.

The word "*Caroline*," stricken out in the third page

The syllable "*by*,' interlined in the 5th page, the word "*Caroline's*," interlined in the fourth page, in lieu of the word, "*her*," obliterated   The words, "*to her*," interlined in the 9th page. All done before signing

Philadelphia, June 15th, 1835

DANIEL W COXE

Answers of William E Hulings, to interrogatories propounded in the suit of William W. Whitney and Myra C Whitney vs Eleanor O'Bearne and others, in the probate court in and for the parish and city of New Orleans.

To interrogatory 1st   My name is William Empson Hulings, aged sixty-nine years, residing in Philadelphia   I think I never saw Mr. William W Whitney but once, when he called at my house, and was introduced to myself and wife by the now Mrs. Myra C. Whitney, formerly called Mira Davis, with whom I had been slightly acquainted for some years, seeing her but very seldom.   Mrs. O'Bearne I never saw, but have understood that she resided in Ireland, and was the sister of the late Daniel Clark, Esq, of New Orleans   The word, ' others," being indefinite, I have no answer to give to it

To the 2d interrogatory   I say my acquaintance with Daniel Clark, late of New Orleans, who died August 16th, 1813, began in the year 1789, in New Orleans, and continued in the closest personal intimacy until I left that city in 1804   Our friendship remained uninterrupted to the day of his death

To the 3d interrogatory   I answer, having been as above stated, the intimate friend of the said Daniel Clark, had he been married I could not have failed to know it.   I firmly believe he never was married.

To the 4th interrogatory I say that the said Daniel Clark never did acknowledge or intimate to me, that he had a child or children, or that he ever had carnal connexion with any female, but I have frequently heard from Mrs Lynn, formerly Mrs Alexder, late of our city, but now deceased that a female child named Caroline, placed (while she resided at Trenton) under her care by Daniel W Coxe Esq of this place was the daughter of the aforesaid Daniel Clark. and so frequently acknowledged by him to be, that he, the said Daniel, made many visits to see the said child, and would fondly caress it, and make it handsome presents, and holding it before the looking glass, would trace its features in his face, and say she should ride in her coach Mrs _____ continued to assert the same thing to the day of her death. After the death of Mr Lynn the husband of said lady, Mrs Mary Clark, the mother of said Daniel, received the said Caroline into her family at Germantown, as the undoubted child of her said son She remained there some time, when, as friends of the said Daniel Clark, Mr Daniel W Coxe and myself thought it time some attention should be paid to her education In consequence, we with the approbation and consent of the said Mary Clark, (who made an appropriation of money for the clothing, &c of the said Caroline) placed her with Mr and Mrs. Bazely, then keeping a boarding school for young ladies, as an apprentice, her services to be an equivalent for her board and education. Said Caroline remained with Mrs. Bazely, I think for the time stipulated receiving from the Mrs Mary Clark, as her grand mother, the sum appropriated to her use She, afterwards, was addressed by Doct Barnes, of our city, a respectable man, and was married to him They moved to the Mississippi, and I believe now reside at or near Fort Gibson The only knowledge I have of Mira Davis, now Mrs Mira C Whitney, being a child of the said Daniel Clark, was derived from Col Sam'l B. Davis, who told me that Mr Clark acknowledged said Myra to be his child, and had placed her under his care as such Caroline Clark, now Mrs Barnes, I believe to be about thirty-three years of age, of Mira, now Mrs Whitney, I have no data on which to form an opinion I have heard that she is in New Orleans.

The 5th interrogatory Is answered above, by my declaring that the said Daniel Clark never did acknowledge or intimate that he had a child or children I have heard from Richard Relf, Esq, of New Orleans that certain lots of ground, out of New Orleans, on the Bayou Road, were destined or appointed by said Daniel Clark, for the said Caroline and Mira. Col Bellechasse, now or late of Matanzas Cuba, informed me, by letter, that he held a trust from the said Daniel Clark, of some lots as aforesaid, for said Mira, but knew not of any provision made for Caroline.

To the 6th interrogatory. I say that I have precedingly acknowledged a slight acquaintance with Mira now Mrs. C Whitney, who, ever since I heard of her, has, I believe, resided in the family of Col S B Davis aforesaid, as his reputed daughter being known in public, as far as I am aware by the name of Mira Davis, and said Mira confessed to my wife and self, that until some little time before she was married to said Mr Whitney, she believed herself to be the daughter of the aforesaid Col Samuel B Davis Further, your deponent saith not

Philadelphia, 11th June, 1835

WM E HULINGS.

In answer to the cross examination in the aforesaid suit I say first, that I have slightly known Mrs Mira C Whitney, formerly Mira Davis, for some years but cannot fix the period of our acquaintance Of her husband I had no knowledge until introduced to him by her, at my own house, some time last summer, or early in the fa'l I have never seen Mrs O'Bearne, but have heard from Mrs Mary Clark, mother of aforesaid Daniel Clark, that said Mrs O'Bearne was her daughter The ' others" not being specified by name, I can say nothing as to them

To the 2d interrogatory I answer that I am not either directly or indirectly interested in the suit of W W Whitney, Mira C. Whitney vs Eleanor O Bearne and others

Thirdly To the last interrogatory, I say that having nothing to do with the said suit or any other relating to the parties therein named, I have not employed any counsel in it, or any other cause

Further the deponent saith not

Philadelphia, 11th June, 1835

WM E HULINGS.

WILLIAM W. WHITNEY AND MYRA C. WHITNEY *vs.* ELEANOR O'BEARN AND OTHERS	IN THE PROBATE COURT IN AND FOR THE PARISH AND CITY OF NEW ORLEANS No 843

Interrogatories propounded by and in behalf of the above named defendants, and by virtue of the annexed commission, to be answered under oath by William E Hulings, Daniel W Coxe and others, residing in the city of Philadelphia, State of Pennsylvania, and which, together with the answers thereto, to be made by said witnesses, the said defendants intend to offer and read in evidence on the trial of the above entitled cause

1st Will you and each of you be pleased to state your names, ages and residence, and whether or not you are acquainted with the parties in the above entitled cause ?

2d Will you and each of you be pleased to state whether or not you were acquainted with Daniel Clark, late of the city of

New Orleans, who departed this life in the month of August, 1813? If aye will you be pleased to state whether or not your acquaintance extended to friendly intimacy, and how long were you so acquainted with him, previous to his death?

3d Will you be pleased to state whether or not said Daniel Clark was ever married?

4th State if you please whether or not you, or either of you, ever heard said Clark during his lifetime say or acknowledge himself to be the father of any children? If aye, what were their respective names, sex and probable age, and where are they at this time?

5th Did said Clark, during his lifetime, to the knowledge of either of you, make provision for the maintenance and education of any of his supposed children? If aye, which ones? what were their names? and to what extent did he make such provision to your knowledge, or from what you have heard said Clark say?

6th Do you, or either of you know Mrs Myra C Whitney? If aye, will you and each of you be pleased to state if you know, in whose family she resided from her childhood until her marriage with said Whitney, and by what name she was known and generally received by the community at large? and from the general reputation which she bore in the community, whose child was she supposed to be?

7th Do you, or either of you know of any other fact or circumstance, not mentioned by you in answer to some one of the foregoing interrogatories, which you suppose may be of any service to the defendants in this cause? If aye, be please to state the same as fully and particularly as if you had been thereunto especially interrogated

Signed,   L C DUNCAN,

Att'y and curator ad hoc for defendants

Cross interrogatories propounded by defendant to the above witnesses reserving, however, exceptions to the legality of the commission in this case, and all legal exception to the testimony taken under the same

1st Are you acquainted with the parties to this suit? If so, state how long you have known them?

2d Are you interested in the event of this suit? If you answer in the affirmative, state in what manner?

3d Have you not employed counsel to appear in the above suit?

Signed,   WM W WORTHINGTON, for plaintiffs

STATE OF PENNSYLVANIA,
Mayor's Office— June 16th, 1835.

Pennsylvania City, ss.—Be it remembered, that on the six-

*41

teenth day of June, A D one thousand eight hundred and thirty
five, at the Mayor's office, in the city of Philadelphia, between
the hours of eleven A M and five P M by virtue of the annexed commission, issuing out of the Court of Probates, in the State
of Louisiana, bearing date the twentieth day of January 1835,
and in the fifty-ninth year of the independence of the United
States, personally appeared Daniel W Coxe and William E
Hulings who, being first sworn to testify the truth, the whole
truth, and nothing but the truth, did in my presence in their
own proper hand, reduce to writing and in my presence sign the
depositions hereunto annexed, and I further certify that no person appeared to cross examine the said deponents

In testimony whereof, I have hereunto set my hand and private seal, and caused the corporate seal of the city of Philadelphia to be affixed the   and year above written
                    JNO SWIFT, Mayor

W W WHITNEY AND WIFE)
            vs   }   COURT OF PROBATES,
ELEANOR O'BEARN AND AL'S)   June 2, 1836

G Preval Esq, witness for plaintiff sworn says that he was
the Justice of the Peace called upon to affix the seals upon the
effects of the late Daniel Clark being shown the original proces
verbal, made by him at the time, recognizes it to be the same
made by himself That he has no recollection of taking any papers out of trunks to deposit in the armoire and bureau upon
which he affixed the seals He thinks there were papers on the
tables, in the rooms of Mr Clark, which were gathered up and
put in the armoire and bureau It is now nearly twenty years
ago and he cannot possibly recollect where all the papers put
under seal by him were found that he has no recollection of
having seen Mr Relf take the will of Mr Clark out of a trunk
containing papers, that it is deponent's belief, that the seals had
already been affixed by him upon the chamber armoire and bureau,
when Mr Relf came and presented the will to him he says
that the seals had already been affixed, from the circumstance
of the keeper of the seals having signed the proces verbal before
mention is made therein of the said will He supposes that
it was about the time they were all going to sign, as the keeper
of the seals is generally the first person who signs the proces
verbal Deponent has no knowledge where Mr Relf got the
will from

Cross examination or examined

That deponent when called upon to affix the seals did not, in
any case, permit witnesses or others, to search over the papers
and effects under pretence of searching for a will or any other

paper, that he was not in the habit of permitting such searches to be made at the time the seals were affixed in this case, nor is he at the present time—the law now precludes such searches among the papers of accused persons, that deponent, at this time, cannot possibly recollect or state any particular places where the papers of said Clark were found. Deponent being asked by the court whether the procès verbal was signed in the room upon which the seals were affixed, answered that he thinks not, as the procès verbal mentions that the seals had been mixed, and he was asked to sign it in some other part of the house deponent was not told by Mr. Keil when he presented the will, said deponent, whether or not ....

In the Court of Probates, in and for the parish and city of New Orleans, Friday, 11th June, 1836

Present the honorable J. Bermudez, Judge

W. W. Whitney & Wife

vs.

Eleanor O'Beirne & al.

On motion of L. C. Duncan of counsel for defendants, ordered, that he have leave to withdraw the original documents attached to the commission, executed on behalf of defendants at Philadelphia

In the Court of Probates, in and for the parish and city of New Orleans, Tuesday, 14th June, 1836

Present the honorable J. Bermudez, Judge

Willim W. Whitney & wife

vs.

Eleanor O'Beirne & othrs

On motion of James W. White Esq, attorney for plaintiffs, it is ordered that L. C. Duncan Esq, produce and exhibit in open Court for the examination and inspection of the said plaintiffs, on Thursday the 16th day of June 1836 at 10 o'clock, A. M, upon the trial or argument of the rule taken by the said Lucius C. Duncan in this case, relative to the allowance and taxation of one thousand dollars in the taxed costs of a fee or compensation for the curator ad hoc for the absent defendants in said cause, of each and every power, letter or warrant of attorney, or other authority in writing executed by all or any of the said absent defendants, or by any one for both, or either of them appointing or constituting him, the said Lucius C. Duncan the attorney or agent of all or any of the said absent defendants, in order that the same may be offered in evidence upon the said argument or trial.

W W WHITNEY & WIFE,)
   vs.   }
ELEANOR O'BEARN)

Came on this day for argument, the rule taken in this case on the second instant

      L C DUNCAN, Plaintiff in rule

     GRYMES & WHITE for W W Whitney & wife

When, after hearing testimony and argument, the case was submitted, and the Court took time to advise.

In the Court of Probates in and for the parish and city of New Orleans

            FRIDAY, 8th July, 1836.

Present, the Hon J Bermudez, Judge

W. W. WHITNEY & WIFE,)
   vs   }
E. O BLARN, & als   )

On a rule to show cause why the plaintiff should not pay a fee of a thousand dollars to the curator ad hoc appointed by this Court to represent the absent debtors It has been ruled by the Supreme Court, in 2d L R. 166 and 7th L R p 71, that a curator *ad hoc* appointed at the institution of a suit, is not entitled to a fee or an allowance, which is to be taxed in the costs of suit, and paid by the party cast

 Hence it is, that a curator *ad hoc* is intended by law as a protector to the interests of the absentee, and should be considered as principally beneficial to the persons they represent, but should not the appointment of this officer be considered as also beneficial to the plaintiffs in this sense, that without him no proceedings can be had against the defendants ?

 Under the circumstances this case presents itself to the Court, I am of opinion that although the professional services rendered by the curator *ad hoc*, to represent absent defendants, are to be paid for by and out of the funds of the person whom he represents, yet that in case of a failure on the part of the plaintiff to prosecute with effect his action, he should be made to advance the remuneration for the services of the said curator

 The Court, therefore, considering that the services of L. C. Duncan, Esq, curator *ad hoc*, to represent the absent defendants, are proved to be worth the sum of one thousand dollars—It is ordered, adjudged, and decreed, that the register of wills do tax among the costs of suit the thousand dollars claimed by the said curator *ad hoc*, to be paid by the party cast in this suit, reserving to the plaintiffs their full and entire recourse for the recovery of this sum against the absent defendants represented by the said L. C. Duncan, Esq

In the Court of Probates in and for the parish and city of New Orleans

WEDNESDAY, 13th July, 1836

Present, the Hon J Bermudez, Judge

W W Whitney and wife, |

⎰

⎱ Estate of Daniel Clark.

Eleanor O Beary, et al |

On motion of L C Duncan, Esq, of counsel for Richard Relf, one of the defendants, ordered that the Register of Wills be authorized to return and deliver to said Relf all the papers, books and documents deposited with him in obedience to the former order of this Court

I, William F C Duplessis, Register of Wills in and for the parish and city of New Orleans, State of Louisiana, ex-officio clerk of the Court of Probates in and for the parish and city of New Orleans do hereby certify that the foregoing two hundred and forty-two pages contain a true copy of all the proceedings had in the suit No 843 entitled

WM W Whitney and

Myra C Whitney, |

⎰

⎱

vs

Eleanor O Beary, & others, | in the Court of Probates aforesaid

In faith whereof, I have hereunto set my hand, and affixed the seal of the Court of Probates aforesaid at the city of New Orleans, this twenty-ninth day of July, in the year of our Lord one thousand eight hundred and forty and the sixty-fifth of the Independence of the United States of America —Eighty-seven words erased and sixty-seven words interlined—all approved

[L S] W F C DUPLESSIS, Register of Wills

I, Joachim Bermudez, sole Judge of the Court of Probates in and for the parish and city of New Orleans, State of Louisiana, do hereby certify that Wm F C Duplessi, who signed the foregoing certificate, was at the time thereof, and still is, Register of Wills in and for the parish and city of New Orleans, ex-officio Clerk of the Court of Probates in and for the parish and city of New Orleans, as set forth in his certificate, which is in due form of law

Given under my hand, at the city of New Orleans, this 29th day of July, A. D 1840

J. BERMUDEZ, Judge.

[No 76]
Offered by Defendants and filed 25 June, 1849

J W GURLEY Com'r

NEW ORLEANS, 21 Nov 1803

SIR —I have just been honored with a letter from Gov Claiborne, of the M T, advising that the treaty between the U S and the French Republic has been ratified by the Senate and President, and that General Wilkinson and himself are appointed Commissioners on the part of the U S to receive the Province of Louisiana I take the liberty of making you an immediate communication of this intelligence, and have the honor to remain, with the greatest respect, sir,

Your most obedient servant,

Mon Laussatt, Colonial Prefect, &c.

[No 85]
Offered by defendants, and filed 25th June, '49

J W GURLEY Commissioner

CITY OF WASHINGTON, Oct 15th 1803

Dear Sir Your favor of the 2d Sept has been receiv but was unintentionally left at home in my hurry   prepare for my journey to this place You may be as   that the treaty with France for the   of Louisiana, and the island of New Orleans, will be ratif   by our Government The ratification of the first consul is already received, and before the last day of this month, every thing will have been done, which can be required on our part to give validity and sanction to that instrument, and to the conventions which accompany it As the Spanish Government have protested against the cession by France to us, and even against the right to sell it to the U States or any other power, you will render an essential service by having an eye upon the movements of the Spaniards, in order to ascertain whether there is any indication of a design to oppose or refuse   surrender of it to us If any symptoms of that sort appear, you ought to give immediate notice of it to our Govern   and to Gen Wilkinson or the commanding officer of the troops, in order that we may calculate our force accordingly. I have taken every opportunity of mentioning you in such terms, to influential men   , as will, I flatter myself, lead to your being actively as well as honorably employed, in completing the   necessarily growing out of the cession of   so valuable and so important

Consider me, if you please, associated with you in whatever adventure you may think advisable to make in consequence of this information, but advise me immediately whether you have done, or propose to do any thing

I shall write again by next mail, when I shall know more and have more leisure

I am dear Sir with sincere esteem

Your very humle serv t,   JONA DAYTON.

Daniel Clark Esq, American Consul, New Orleans

DOCUMENTS &c, FILED BY DEFENDANTS.

Be it remembered, that on this 20th day of June, 1849 the defendants by their counsel exhibited and filed with me Commissioner, to be by them offered in evidence on the trial of this case, the following documents, to wit

1st Authenticated copy of the Will of Daniel Clark, marked Exhibit No 1

2d Authenticated copy of the power of attorney from Mrs. Mary Clark to Beverly Chew and Richard Relf, dated October 1st, 1813

3d Authenticated copy of the will of Mrs Mary Clark, dated 22d November, 1817, together with authenticated copies of the probate thereof, in Philadelphia, in June, 1823

4th Authenticated copy of power of attorney from Joseph Reed, as executor of the will of Mrs Mary Clark, to Richard Relf and Beverly Chew dated 2d December, 1823

5th. Authenticated copy of power of attorney from Gerome de Grange to his wife Zulime Carriere, dated 26th March, 1801

The above objected to by complainants

6th Authenticated copy of power of attorney, from Felicite Carriere, et al, to Jerome Degrange, dated 26th March, 1801

Complainants object to introduction of the above.

7th Authenticated copy of act of sale from Daniel Clark to J. D. D Bellechasse, dated 16th May, 1811

8th. Authenticated copy of an act from Dussuau Delacroix to the complainant Myra, therein represented by Samuel B Davis, dated 16th May, 1820

Complainants object to introduction of the above

9th Authenticated copy of an act of deposit before Louis T Caire, on the fourth June, 1833, by William Wallace Whitney and Myra, his wife

Complainants object to introduction of above

10th Authenticated copy of act of deposit, together with authenticated copies of the documents therein referred to and annexed, made by William Wallace Whitney and Myra, his wife, before Louis T Caire, notary, on the 4th June, 1833

Complainant object to introduction of the above

11th. Authenticated copies of the marital proceedings of Jerome Degrange and Miss Carriere, before Broutin, notary public, and of Quinones, formerly notary public, in the year 1794 Defendants here re-offer the certificate of marriage between Jerome Degrange and Miss Carriere in 1794, already on file.

Complainants object to introduction of the above.

12th. Transcript of the record of the suit, entitled Myra Clark and her curator ad litem, S B Davis, vs B. Chew and R Relf, executors of Daniel Clark, deceased. No 1540 of the docket of late First Judicial District Court, now 5th District Court of New Orleans, La

Complainants object to the above

13th Transcript of a record, No 178, of the docket of the late County Court of Orleans, now Third District Court of New Orleans, entitled Zulime C Degrange vs Gerome Degrange

Complainants object to the above

14th Transcript of a record of a suit, No 356, of the docket of the late County Court of Orleans, now Third District Court of New Orleans, entitled Zulime Carriere vs Gerome Degrange, except the petition in said case, which the clerk certifies cannot be found

Complainants object to the above

15th. Transcript of a record of three suits, cumulated into one, the first No 561, entitled William Despau vs Marie Sophie Carrière Despau, the second No 966, entitled Sophie C. Despau vs William Despau and the third, No 987, entitled William Despau vs. Sophie Carriere, his wife, all from the docket of the former Superior Court of the Territory of Orleans, now Fifth District Court of New Orleans

Complainants object to admission of the above

16th Authenticated copy of a marriage contract between Gen E P Gaines and Myra C Whitney, dated 17th April, 1839

Complainants object to the above

17th Authenticated copy of the testimony of Daniel W Coxe, given in the suit entitled John Barnes and wife et als, vs. Edmund P. Gaines and wife, in the former First Judicial District Court, now Fifth District Court of New Orleans

Complainants object to the introduction of the above, as evidence, but waives all objections on the ground that it is a copy, and not the original of which it purports to be a copy, also on the ground that it was not taken in this suit

J W GURLEY, com

Be it remembered, that on this 21st day of June, 1849, the defendants, in the presence of the solicitor for the complainant, exhibited to and filed with me, commissioner, and to be used in evidence on the trial of this cause, the following letters and documents, to wit

18th Letter from J Barker, comptroller of the treasury department of the United States, dated 29th January, 1841, and addressed to Beverly Chew, the signature to which solicitor for complainant admits to be genuine

19th. Letter from George Wolf, comptroller of treasury de-

42*

partment of United States, dated 6th Sept, 1836, addressed to Beverly Chew; solicitor for complainant admits the signature to be genuine

20 Letter from Daniel Clark, dated 30th November, 1811, addressed to Daniel W Coxe, Esq, Philadelphia, the signature to which complainant admits to be genuine

21, 22, 23, 24 Four other letters from Daniel Clark to Mr Coxe No 21 dated 15th July, 1811. No 22 dated 13th January, 1812; No 23 dated 15th June, 1812, No 24 dated 8th Sept 1812 Solicitor for complainant here admits the genuineness of the foregoing letters

25 Letter from Daniel Clark to Messrs Chew & Relf, dated 13th August, 1802, admitted by complainant to be genuine

26 Certified copies of the testimony taken in the matter of the estate of Daniel Clark, in the Court of Probates for the parish and city of New Orleans, in the months of April and May, 1834, to wit. that of Dussuau Delacroix Pierre Baron Boisfontaine, Jean Canon, Louis Serc, Hubert Remy, and Gallien Préval.

27. Letter from Mrs. A Anderson to Daniel Clark, dated 27th May, 1803, complainant admits this to be genuine.

28 Letter from Jane Green to Daniel Clark, dated 3d May, 1806; admitted by complainant to be genuine

29. Letter from Mary Clark to Daniel Clark, dated, 30th March, 1803, admitted by complainant to be genuine.

30. Letter from Mary Clark to Daniel Clark, dated 9th July, 1803, admitted to be genuine by complainant

31. Document marked 31, and signed by me, to identify it herewith, containing 26 pages, and which said document is admitted by the solicitor for complainant to be a true copy from the original on file in the Court of Probates for the parish of Orleans, in the city of New Orleans, where it was filed, on the 27th August, 1838

J W GURLEY, com

And on this 23d June, 1849, the following documents were offered and filed by defendants

32. Certified copy of the testimony of William E Hulings, taken in the suit of William W Whitney and Myra C Whitney, *vs* Eleanor O'Bearn et al, No 843, of the docket of the Probate Court of the parish and city of New Orleans

33 Document, being certified copy of a proces verbal and proceedings of the proof, publication, and probate of the will of Daniel Clark, in the Court of Probates of the parish and city of New Orleans, and also a certified copy of the testimony of Madame widow Caillavet, taken in the suit of Wm. W Whitney and Myra C Whitney, *vs.* Eleanor O'Bearn et al,, No 843, of the docket of the Probate Court of the parish and city of New Orleans.

34 and 34 bis Certified copies of several papers, documents, and proceedings in the Court of Probates, parish of New Orleans, in the matter of the succession of Daniel Clark, all which will be seen by reference to the two documents of this number

35 Certified copy of the interrogatories propounded to William Miller, and his answers thereto, taken under commission in the suit of W W Whitney and Myra C Whitney, *vs* Eleanor O Bearn, No 843 of the docket of the Probate Court of the parish and city of New Orleans

36 Letter written and signed by Daniel Clark, addressed to Daniel W Coxe, dated New Orleans, 29th June, 1812, consisting of four sheets, which is admitted to be genuine

37 Letter from Daniel Clark to Messrs Chew & Relf, dated Plaquemine Sunday 27th June, 1802 being one of those brought into court by Mr Relf, under the orders of the court.

38 Two letters, from Daniel W Coxe on the same sheet, to Messrs Chew & Relf, first, dated Philadelphia 23d July, 1802; and the second, at Philadelphia 6th August 1802, and being of those brought into court by order of court

' 39. Letter from Desgrange to Daniel Clark, dated Bordeaux, 24th July, 1801

40 Letter (duplicate) dated Liverpool 29th November, 1803, addressed to Daniel Clark, signed P T O

41. Letter from Thos Connellin to D Clark, dated Germantown, 7th July

42 Letter from Wm Thayer to D Clark, dated Providence, 14th December, 1803

43 Letter from John Seeders to D Clark, Oct , 1803

44 Letter from same to same, 13th Sept , 1803, with note enclosed from William Mullon

45 Letter dated Fort Adams 7th Dec , 1803, to Clark, from W C C Claiborne and John C Kingsary

46 Letter from William Dunbar to D Clark dated Natchez, 20th Dec , 1803, on two sheets

47 Letter from Jona Dayton to Clark, dated Washington City, 22d Oct , 1803

48 Letter from Jno Dayton to Clark dated Washington City, 5th Dec , 1803

49 Letter from Jno Dayton to Clark, dated Washington City, 31st Oct , 1803

50 Letter from Anderson to Clark, from Germantown, 6th Dec , 1803

51. Two letters, 13th Dec , 1803 from Jane Clark to D Clark, on same sheet, dated Rocky Mills near Richmond

52 Letter dated Natchez, 25th May, 1803, from Jno. Steele to D. Clark

53. Bill of lading and invoice of public stores to be delivered to D Clark, at New Orleans, dated Philadelphia, 18th October, 1803.

54 Official note from D Clark to the Prefect Laussat, and his reply thereto, the latter dated New Orleans, 1 Fructidor, an 11, and the former New Orleans, 18th August, 1803

55. Letter dated Washington City, Dec 12th, 1803, frem Jona. Dayton to D. Clark

56. Letter dated Washington, 14th Nov, 1803, from Dayton to Clark.

57 Letter from same to same, dated Washington, 7th Nov, 1803

58 Letter dated City Washington, 21st Nov, 1803, from John Smith to D Clark

59 Letter dated Germantown, 26th August. 1803, from Clark's aunt to himself

60. Copy of letter dated New Orleans, 26th August, 1803, from Daniel Clark to Secretary of State of the United States

61 Letter dated Washington, 6th July, 1803, from James Madison to Daniel Clark

62 Letter dated Department of State, 31st Oct, 1803, from James Madison to D. Clark

63 Letter dated near Natchez, 15th May, 1803, from W. C C. Claiborne to D. Clark

64. Letter from same to same, dated same place, 18th Nov., 1803.

65 Letter from same to same, dated Natchez 22d November, 1803

66 Letter dated Rocky Mills, near Richmond, Dec. 13th, 1803, from Jane Clark to Daniel Clark

67. Letter dated Washington, 16th Sept, 1803, from James Madison to D Clark

68. Letter dated 20th April, 1803, from Jane Clark to Daniel Clark.

69. Letter dated New Orleans, 8th June, 1803, from Daniel Clark to Thos Wilkins

70 Letter dated New Orleans, 8th August, 1803, from Wm. Brunnan, Jr, to D Clark

71. Letter dated Philadelphia, 18th Oct, 1803, from Wm. Linnard to D Clark

72. Letter dated Havana, 18th July, 1803, from Maron Madan to D. Clark

73. Letter dated Natchez, 29th April, 1803, from Dunbar to D. Clark.

74. Letter dated Natchez, 27th Dec, 1803, from Wm. Dunbar to D. Clark.

75. Letter dated Havana, 23d May, 1803, from Mitchell, Grant & Kinnerston to D Clark

76 Letter dated New Orleans, 21st Nov., 1803, addressed to colonial Prefect Laussat, signed D C

77 Letter dated Natchez, 12th August, 1803, from William Dunbar to Daniel Clark

78 Letter dated Natchez, 22d Sept, 1803, from same to same

79 Letter dated Natchez, 23d May, 1803, from the same to same.

80 Letter dated Natchez, 9th September, 1803, from same to same.

81. Letter dated Natchez, 5th August, 1803, from same to same

82. Letter dated Natchez, 16th Sept, 1803, from same to same

83. Letter dated D   , 12th Dec, 1803, from John Seeders to Daniel Clark

84. Letter dated 8th October, 1803, from Archibald Palmery to D. Clark

85. Letter dated 11th June, 1803, from John to Daniel Clark

86 Letter dated Washington City, 15th Oct, 1803, from Jona Dayton to D Clark

87 Letter dated Virga, 16th Sept., 1803, from James Madison to D Clark

88 Letter dated Washington, 17th July, 1803, from Thos Jefferson to D Clark (on 2 sheets)

89 Draft of letter dated New Orleans, 18th August, 1803

90 Copies of letters, &c, on two sheets

91. Letter dated Germantown, 11th August, 1803

92 Letter dated 18th March, 1803, from G. E Pendergrast to Daniel Clark

93. Letter dated Paris, 16th May, 1803, from Fulwar Skipwith to Dan Clark.

94 Letter dated Desart Plantation, 28th April, 180 , from John Seeders to Clark

95 Letter dated Bayon Sara, Sept, 1803, from John S   th to Clark.

96. Letter dated Natchez, 30th Nov, 1803, from W C C Claiborne to Clark.

June 26th, 1849

97 Articles of agreement between Daniel Clark and Daniel W Coxe, dated Philadelphia, 12th July, 1811, together with a schedule thereto annexed as part thereof, and signed by the said parties; the signatures of which complainant admits

98. Document called memorandum of private explanatory

agreement made at Philadelphia, 12th July, 1811, between Daniel Clark and Daniel W. Coxe, the signatures to which are admitted (on two sheets).

99. The petition, answer, and other pleadings, together with a verdict and judgment, in the suit of W W Whitney and wife, *vs.* Chew & Relf, No 3393 in the District Court of the United States, for the Eastern District of Louisiana (copy to be furnished)

100. The petition, answer, and other pleadings, together with a verdict and judgment in the suit of W. W. Whitney and wife, *vs.* Chew & Relf, No. 3452, in the U S District Court of Louisiana (copy to be furnished).

101 Settlement between Daniel Clark, attorney for Chew & Relf, and D W Coxe, signed Philadelphia, 11 July, 1811.

102. Account current—D W Coxe with Chew & Relf, executors of D. Clark, New Orleans, 27th February, 1819

103. Petition of Chew & Relf in their own names and as executors of Daniel Clark, for a respite, filed in the first judicial District Court of Louisiana, now Fifth District Court of New Orleans, on the 3 March, 1814

104. Proces verbal of meeting of creditors of the estate of the late Daniel Clark and Chew & Relf, praying for a respite, before John Lynd, notary public, 6 April, 1814.

105 Answer of Barnes and wife, filed in this court 12th May, 1845, in the suit of Relf, Chew, Barnes and wife, et al.

106. Interrogatories propounded by complainants in the suit of E P. Gaines and wife, vs Richard Relf and B Chew, to Col Samuel B. Davis, and filed in said suit July 30th, 1839

107. Acceptance of community by Zulime Carriere, widow of Daniel Clark before William Christy, notary public of New Orleans, on 10th June, 1844

108. Depositions of Sophie Despau and Madame Callavet, taken in suit of Gaines and wife vs Relf, Chew, et al, in U S. Circuit Court, and filed in said cause 2 May, 1848

106. Depositions of the same parties, taken in suit of W W Whitney and Myra C Whitney his wife, vs Relf, Chew, et al, in U S. District Court, and filed in said suit 6th February, 1837.

110. Judgment in the case of W. W Whitney and wife, *vs* Eleanor O'Bearn, et al, in the Probate Court of New Orleans, dated 8th June, 1836; Bermudez, Judge.

3d July, 1849

111. Defendants offer in evidence, the "Memoirs of General James Wilkinson of his own times," published in Philadelphia, in 1816, in three volumes, also, the work of Daniel Clark, published in 1809, in Philadelphia, entitled, "Proofs of the corruption of Gen James Wilkinson, and his connection with Aaron Burr,

&c., &c.". Also, Martin's History of Louisiana, in two volumes. Complainant objects to the introduction of the above works as inadmissible in evidence for any purpose connected with this suit.

112. Record from the Probate Court of parish and city of New Orleans, petition filed there 18th June, 1834, in suit by W W. Whitney and wife *vs* Relf & Chew, &c

113 Act of sale of slave, by DeGrange Paillet 6 November, 1801

114 Act of sale of slave by DeGrange to Le Goaster, 3 November, 1801

115 Sale of slave by DeGrange to Moreno, 29 October, 1801

116. Mortgage by DeGrange in favor of Moreno, 13 January, 1802

117. Letter dated Wilmington, 30 May, 1808, from S White to D Coxe

118 Letter dated Baltimore, 27th September, 1808, from R. G. Harper to D Clark, (on two sheets)

119 Letter dated Baltimore, 12th September, 1808, from R. G Harper to Clark, (on two sheets)

120 Letter dated Washington, 3d May, 1809, from S White to Clark

121 Letter dated Washington, 20th November, 1808, from White to Clark.

122. Letter dated Washington, 2 December, 1807, from White to Clark

123 Letter dated Annapolis, 6 April, 1807, from Mrs Caton to D Clark

124 Letter dated 4 February, 1807, from Margaret Coxe to D Clark

125 Letter dated Philadelphia, 3 June, 1810, from Mary de la Roche to D Clark

126 Notarial act of sale of lot of ground, before Narcisse Broutin, Notary, from Gilberto Andry to D Clark

127 Statement of affairs of D W Coxe and D. Clark

128. Letter dated Natchez, 21 August, 1812, from Turner to Clark.

129 Receipt signed in duplicate, at New Orleans, 19 October, 1805

130 Letter dated New Orleans, 11 June, 1813, from Jas Innerarity to D Clark

131 Letter dated New Orleans, 5 February, 1813, from Z. Cavalier to Clark, (in French)

132. Letter dated Philadelphia, September, 1812, from Hulings to Clark

133 Letter dated Philadelphia, 23d December, 1812, from Coxe to Clark,

134. Account between D. Clark and D. W. Cxe, dated Phila-delphia, 19 May, 1813

135 Letter dated Norfolk, 2 May, 1813, from Wade Hampton to D W. Coxe

136 Letter dated Philadelphia, 30 October 1812, from Hulings to D. Clark.

137 Letter dated Philadelphia 30 August, 1802, from D W. Coxe to D Clark, (on three sheets)

138 Letter dated New Orleans, 31 May, 1811, from Chew & Relf to D Clark

139. Copy of letter dated 10 October, 1811, from D W Coxe to Jane Clark

140 Letter dated Philadelphia, 1 January, 1812, from Hulings to Clark.

141 Letter dated Houmas, 19 December, 1811, from W Hampton to D Clark

142 Letter dated Philadelphia, 4 May, 1813, from Hulings to Clark

143. Letter dated Philadelphia, 14 January, 1813, from Hulings to Clark

144. Letter dated 6 January, 1812, Philadelphia, from Hulings to Clark.

145. Letter dated 19 Nov, 1803, at New Orleans, from to Simon Poey & Co, Havanna.

146 Letter dated Liverpool, June, 1803, from Wm. Jones to Geo Green

147 Account with D Clark, of Green, dated Liverpool, 1802 and 1803

148. Letter dated Philadelphia, Nov 25, (1803?) from Coxe to Clark.

149 Letter dated 27 August, 1803, from Frederick Kimball to D. Clark.

150. Letter dated New Orleans, 18 August, 1803, enclosing two others, the one dated New Orleans, 21 July, 1803, and the other dated New Orleans, 25 July, 1803

151. Letter dated Philadelphia, August 26th, 1803, from Coxe to Clark, (on 5 sheets)

152 Letter dated Germantown, 25 August, 1803, to D Clark, from his sister. A Anderson

153. Memorandum or statement of debts, expenses, &c.

154 Letter dated 21 April, 1802, from Reed & Pera to D. Clark.

155. Spanish document, endorsed " Re-conveyance from Beverly Chew to D Clark, of half a plantation, &c &c.

156. French document with colored plan of tract of land on Mississippi, dated New Orleans 6 March, 1805.

157. Spanish document, endorsed "Transfer of lands on the Spanish side of the line, from Daniel Clark to Daniel Clark, Jr"

158 French document, from notarial office of Pedesclaux, dated 31 January, 1806

159 Deed from John Galloway to John Clark, of certain lands on Mississippi river, dated 23 Dec 1768

160 Notarial act, from the office of Narcisse Broutin, (in Spanish)

151 Written instrument, signed K. Claiborne, J P R., 5 Oct, 1812, from Parish Court of Rapides

162 Spanish document signed by Pedesclaux, endorsed, "Reconveyance from B Chew to D Clark, of lands formerly conveyed to said Chew

163 Record in suit of Richard Relf *vs* W W Whitney Transcript of record transferred from State Court to U S District Court, and filed 19 May, 1834—No 3452, of Docket of said U S District Court

164. Will of Simphorien Caillavet, dated 19th July, 1802

Complainant objects to admission of all the above documents from 111 to 164, both inclusive

J W. GURLEY, Com'r

165 Record in the case of W W Whitney and wife, *vs* Chew & Relf—No 3393, of the U S District Court of Louisiana. Petition filed 27 Feb'y, 1834

Complainant objects to admissability of above

August 2d, 1849 Offered by Defendants.

166 Deposition of Madame Despau, taken by the complainants in the Paterson case

167 Deposition of Madame Caillavet, also taken by the complainants in the Paterson case

August 21, 1849

168 Rough decree in the case of Gaines *vs* Patterson, filed 25 April, 1810 which complainants' solicitor admits to be in the handwriting of the late R H Chinn, Esq, who was, at the time of the filing of the same, the solicitor of the complainants.

Objection Complainant's solicitor objects to the introduction of the above as evidence.

Oct 30th, 1849.

169 Paper from Department of State, Washington, being statement of letters written by D Clark, Consul of the United States, for the port of New Orleans, showing to whom they were addressed, from what place, the month, the day of the month, and year

170 Copy of letter from D Clark to Jas. Madison, dated River Mersey, 23 Dec, 1802.

43*

NOTE.—New Orleans, 22d December, 1849—It was understood and agreed by and between the parties complainant and defendants, that, in order to avoid the trouble of making objection to each document and paper offered in evidence before the commissioner, that each should be at liberty to make, on the closing of the testimony, a general objection to all documents offered in evidence by either party

Such objection the complainant, by her solicitor, now makes to the documents and letters offered by the defendants

J W GURLEY, U S Com'r.

And the defendants do the like.

J W GURLEY, U. S Com'r.

COMPLAINANTS

[A]

Referred to by Mr. Patterson in his cross examination, 20th June, 1849

Introduced by Complainant

J W GURLEY, Com'r.

To the purchasers and present claimants of the estate of the late Daniel Clark, Esq

Notice is hereby given to the purchasers and present claimants of the estates devised by the late Daniel Clark, Esq, of the city of New Orleans, to his only daughter Myra Clark, (the wife of the undersigned,) or such parts of the said estate as were taken possession of and lawlessly sold by Richard Relf and Beverly Chew, the pretended executors of the said Daniel Clark, that having ascertained that the said Relf and Chew, with their co-partner or counsel, L. C Duncan and others, have been endeavoring to deceive and delude the said purchasers and claimants with the false impression that the claim of Myra Clark has been defeated in the courts of the State of Louisiana, and that the undersigned and his wife are unwilling to come to trial in the Circuit Court of the United States—In order therefore, to guard the said purchasers and claimants from further imposition, and to enable them to see through the veil behind which the swindlers are contriving their own escape from the infamy which they well know awaits them, the undersigned takes this method of assuring the said purchasers and claimants that no decision or trial upon his wife's claim has ever taken place in any of the State Courts—that she was twenty-four years of age before she was advised of her being the daughter and, heiress of her deceased father, Daniel Clark, who departed this life before she was seven years of age As soon as possible after being advised of the nature of her claim, proceedings were instituted in the Probate Court of New Orleans Previously to the day of trial, however, she had the good fortune to learn that a quorum of the Judges of the Supreme Court of the State had purchased valuable portions of the estate in question, and were consequently disqualified to sit in judgment in her cause. Inasmuch as the defendants would have appealed to the Supreme Court, when defeated in the Court of Probate, her only alternative was to bring the suit in Chancery now pending in the Circuit Court of the U S.

The undersigned, therefore, acting in accordance with the wishes of his wife, who has constantly desired only to have a speedy trial before an impartial tribunal, and to the worst of her adversaries she would most willingly *"return good for evil,"* even to those who have *publicly denounced her as an impostor*—and being anxious, as she has constanly been, to put it in the power of her calumniators to meet her before an impartial tribunal, (as she knows the Supreme Court of the United States to be,) by whose decision she will cheerfully abide —to prove the sincerity of these declarations, she is willing to make a liberal deduction in favor of all the purchasers who will, without further delay come to trial at the present term of the Circuit Court of the U S. Cordially concurring in these just and benevolent views and wishes, the undersigned and his wife make to the claimants aforesaid the propositions which follow.

1st To any one of the purchasers and present claimants aforesaid who will forthwith answer our Bill, and otherwise do whatever may be necessary and proper to meet us in fair trial in Chancery, without any further attempt to delay, we will make a deduction of 25 per centum in the amount of which we may ultimately be entitled from such person or persons, should the final decision be in our favor.

2d To any of the said purchasers and present claimants who may before the 22d instant desire a compromise, and take the necessary steps to render the compromise effectual, we will make a deduction of 50 per cent, in the amount of that part of the estate held by such claimant or claimants

The aforesaid purchasers and present claimants are respectfully advised to separate themselves from the lawless Executors and their co-partners in guilt, and take counsel of men who have no interest in shielding these high-handed robbers from condign punishment· as it must be obvious to all such purchasers and present claimants that they will be greatly benefitted, and in no possible event injured, by availing themselves of the above liberal propositions : to those who reject or disregard them, it is the painful duty of the undersigned to say, that no other effort on his part will be made to effect a compromise

EDMUND P GAINES,

for himself and his wife, Myra C. Gaines

New Orleans, April 14th, 1840.

[B.]

Referred to by Mr. Patterson, in his cross examination, 20th June, 1849.   J. W. GURLEY, Com.

Introduced by complainant.   GURLEY.

NEW ORLEANS, LA., May 11th, 1848.

CHARLES PATTERSON, ESQ—Sir: A final decree having been rendered by the Supreme Court, the highest judicial tribunal in the United States, settling forever in favor of the undersigned heir at law the painful controversy with you, and believing as we do, that you have acted in strict accordance with the sacred principles of EQUITY and JUSTICE—and that, in determining to meet us upon the MERITS OF THE CASE, you have incurred the displeasure of many of the lawless holders of the estate for so many years withheld from us, we take this occasion to assure you that we regard your long and strenuous opposition, and that of your counsel, though often of a character very harrassing to us, as under all the circumstances of the case, unavoidable, and perhaps, essential to facilitate the full and perfect establishment of our rights upon a firm basis without some years more of accrimonious controversy

Our rights being now established beyond the reach of mortal litigation, we freely and voluntarily assure you of our determination to guard you and your heirs from every expense or loss that may attend the result of our late controversy

With great respect your ob't serv'ts,
EDMUND P GAINES.
MYRA CLARK GAINES.

Filed and offered by complainant this 2d Jan'y, 1850.
J W. GURLEY, U. S. Cmm'r.

Hic IHS Jacet
DANIEL CLARK
Slegone in Hibernia natus.
a Puero Louisianæ in cola
in hac civitate,
dum sub Hispaniâ dictione esset,
Federatorum Statuum Consul
propter præclaras Virtutes
Renunciatus.
dein, Aurelianensis Agri
popularium unanimi voto
primus Gentis Americanæ
consilio, Delegatus assedit
amplas at sine maculâ
congestas Opes,
in egentium profudit necessitates
liberalitate tamen factus ditior
Obiit bonis omnibus flebilis
Augusti XVI, A. D. MDCCCXIII
Ætatis Suæ XLVII.

Amicus Amico
hoc Monumentum Erexit.

[Letter No 3]

Offered by Complainant　Filed 23 June, 1849

J. W. GURLEY, Com'r

(In hand writing of late Daniel Clark)

PHILADLIPHIA, 18　January, 1802

MESSRS CHEW & RELF

Gentlemen—Since the arrival of Mr Clark I have been constantly occupied, in conjunction with him, in devising the means of forwarding our mutual interests, and as the sudden peace must make a change in our views, will now communicate to you the result of our plans and ideas, confident that we shall find, on your part, the most extensive co-operation, and that you will use every exertion to carry into execution such part of our plans as you will find practicable

You must, however, always bear in mind, that some of our calculations, on account of the impossibility of knowing the extent and nature of your resources, and the length of time necessary to consult you on different subjects, must be founded on supposed *data*, and therefore great latitude will be always left you to exercise your own judgment, (when my ideas and wishes cannot be punctually complied with,) which I hope and trust will always be done with prudence and decision

That I may suffer as little as possible from want of information, I request you will be *more* than usually particular in writing to me, and never fail to answer with exactness any part of my letters which may require it, that this should never at any time be burdensome, by suffering matter to accumulate, accustom yourselves, on the receipt of my letters, to answer such part as you are then well informed on and as you may acquire further information, or procure other intelligence, commit it to paper while fresh in your memory, and by this means your letters will be finished, generally, before opportunities offer for forwarding them, without your being obliged to devote, at any period, a large portion of time to an object of such considerable importance; this mode I shall invariably follow myself, in future, and you may be fully persuaded that I shall pay the greatest attention to the most trifling matter contained in your letters, the receipt of which from the 28th October to the 15th December, including those of the 7th, 10th, 11th, and 25th November　　　to Mr Clark and myself I now acknowledge, and whose contents shall be attended to, though for the present I may but slightly, or for want of time may not at all touch on the subjects contained in them.

Previous to a knowledge of the Peace, wishing to make a great stroke, tempted by the flattering prospects of the price of cotton, and well knowing that ere long we should have many competitors, I wished to make the most of our time, and therefore forwarded you orders to make large purchases, which I knew from your usual exertions and activity I might depend on   To get the cotton to market at a proper season, before a fall in price was to be apprehended, I resolved, though at that time somewhat straitened for funds, to purchase the two ships, Thomas and New York, which I sent to your address their outfits and cargoes, as you may plainly percieve still further reduced my means, but as I hope they will afford you a supply of cash, and an early opportunity of getting cotton to market, I cheerfully put up with the inconvenience arising from it but have now serious thoughts of disposing of a part of the shipping as I shall afterwards more fully explain, and wish to have your ideas likewise, for my government

The inconveniences I feel have arisen from the cotton shipped to Europe since last spring remaining all on hand, and by late advices it had fallen again, after a considerable advance on the first news of peace. This will prevent Mr Barclay from selling, and I cannot consequently make free in drawing on him in advance, I shall, however, do all in my power to honor all the drafts you may give on me, but earnestly request and entreat they may be followed by shipments as soon as possible, and as my whole capital, time and attention is now, and will in future, as long as the trade is worth pursuing, be wholly turned to your country, without deviation, you may confidently rely on all the support in my power to give

As my shipping have been purchased with a view to your benefit as well as my own, you must be particularly careful of my interest, and diminish their expenses as much as possible, by reducing the wages of the masters and crews to the peace establishment, by keeping a strict eye on the disbursements, which in your port must positively be done with your consent and approbation, and by making no advances which are not indispensably necessary.   That you may not deprive yourselves of funds when so much wanted and in case of any difficulty or disagreement with any of the masters whose conduct may induce you to take such a step, I authorize and empower you to displace any of them you may think proper, and appoint others in their stead, always confiding you will use this power with great moderation, and only when the nature of the case indispensably requires it; should it ever be necessary to apply to the Spanish government for assistance to compel any captain to give up his command, you must then make use of the power of attorney given you by Mr Clark, as my attorney, which will at once remove all further difficulties To be, however, prepared on all occasions, make it an invariable rule on the arrival of my ships to get their papers into your hands, which must be done in order to procure an entry, and deliver them only on the day of departure . any change must be

certified by our Vice Consul, and any appointment you may make
must be an American citizen.

Although I have already mentioned in former letters the quantity of cotton which it will take to load the vessels already gone,
and on the way to you, yet I will place the calculation before your
eyes afresh, that you may see what I depend on, and that you may
perceive that my eyes are likewise open and attentive to the means
of procuring you funds to make good your engagements.

The following is therefore the calculation of the quantity of
cotton necessary for the shipping employed now to and from
New Orleans for one voyage

Brig Ohio,............... 400	bales	
" Creole,................. 300	"	
Ship Thomas,........................ 450	"	
" Washington,....................500	"	
" New York,.................... 800	"	
" Mars,............................ 600	"	
" Matilda,.................... 250	"	
" Thomas Wilson, ... 450	"	

                                    3,700 in all, at
the supposed average of 300 lbs each, making, at $25 per cwt,
a sum equal to $277 500, exclusive of shipping charges

To meet these engagements, Mr Clark informs me that the following calculations may be looked   as tolerably accurate, and
as offering what he thinks the whole of your resources, unless
some fortunate sales since his departure shall enable you to raise
more cash than he had before counted on—viz

$70,000   Paid in cash and goods, in advance for cotton,
            previous to Mr C s departure

30,000   Bills drawn for the purchase of the cargo for the
            statement, and all other bills from October to this
            date, supposed to be this sum.

20,000   Which, I calculate, will be the proceeds of the car-
            goes of the ship New York and brig Sophia the
            balance due on the Fame's sales, and the cargo
            of coffee per the Eliza, which I count on your
            selling

20,000   Which I am led to expect you will receive in cot-
            ton from Turner, and which will compose part
            Ohio, &c., which cargo is included in the former
            of the cargoes included in the estimate,

60,000   Collections during the Spring, from old debts, and
            sales made since the arrival of the Mars.

20,000   Which, I calculate, you will raise by the cargoes
            now sent you by the Mars, Washington and

Matilda, before your last payments will be made

——————

$220,000

In the whole, leaving a sum of $60,000, includingharges of shipment, which you must, doubtless, have recourse to me for, by drawing as opportunities offer.

In making these calculations, Mr Clark, to whom I am indebted for them, informs me that great allowances must sometimes be made for casualties, and that I must not, consequently, place too great reliance on them I therefore, by no means wish you to be impressed with the idea that you are to draw on me for no further sum than the balance or difference between the amount of the cotton to be shipped, and that of the calculation of funds which you may probably receive, as it may so happen that the cotton you have paid for in advance may not be delivered in time, and that you must supply its place with other parcels for which you will have payments to make, and that your collections, &c &c., may fall short or be delayed beyond the period when they are wanted For all this I am, and always will be prepared, knowing the nature of the business of your country, but, I again earnestly entreat you will avail yourselves of the first opportunity to make shipments and forward me the invoices and bills of lading, on which I must place my dependence for aiding and assisting you It will, I know, be unnecessary to put you in mind of availing yourselves of your credit in purchasing any parcels of cotton that you can get time for, by which means the payments may be made lighter to you, by enabling you to raise the amount from the sale of your goods, you must not, however, for this purpose give an extraordinary price, as the present sales will not admit of it

As peace has taken place, and a great competition in the market must be the result of it, I cannot too strongly impress you with the idea of selling every thing you can at such prices as will afford even a small profit, this will enable you to order out new cargoes, and the profits will be made up on the quantity of goods you sell I wish you would, therefore, in future look upon such as you order out, as the means only advanced you of making payments when cash cannot be forwarded, and by disposing of them at saving prices, make cash, if possible, from henceforward of all the shipments you may order. When your spring sales are concluded, and you see no further probability of effecting any move of importance for cash, would it not be worth your while to make a vendue at 6 months, of all such articles as you may think convenient, by way of making room for new orders, and having a fund ready before hand for any purpose that may be necessary in the beginning of the ensuing winter? This is a matter, however, which I merely suggest, leaving the adoption of it to your own judgment, if you think well of the measure.

As I intend to forward immediate orders to Mr Barclay to ship such of the goods as are mentioned in the intendant's list, which can be procured cheap in England, and complete the memorandum from hence. You would do well to order but such goods by the return of my vessels as you may be certain of making sale of, and forward your orders for return cargoes always before the departure of the ship which is to load them, that the goods may be got ready by her arrival, which will save a great deal of time, and consequently of expense, for want of attention to this point hitherto, the Mars and Washington have been delayed longer in England than I wished, and I know, by pointing out to you the propriety of taking this measure, you will without delay adopt it

Whenever you think any article that can be procured here, will afford a profit when sold with you, and will put you in cash, advise me, and I will forward it to you without delay, but be particular in describing the qualities, patterns and selling prices for my government. Many articles can often be sent from here nearly as cheap, and more expeditiously than from England, and liberal credits can be obtained, so that if it were only to procure you the means of making investments, after giving a very trifling profit, and free you from the necessity of drawing for large sums, it would be a great point gained. Forward me from time, sketches of sales, with the advance the goods have sold at, as near as you can judge, and try to get rid, as soon as possible, of the marble tiles, slate and coal, all which must be an incumbrance

With the cargoes you will now receive by the Mars and Washington, act as with those on hand—sell them cheap, and endeavor to attach those who pay well to you. Refuse no tolerable offer whatever to improve your finances, as you may always replace the goods in your store by a new order, in giving which attend to the prices, and always forward me a copy of it, with the calculation you make of its value, and let me know the ship you mean it to go by. You may readily perceive the anxiety I feel on the subject of your finances, by so often mentioning them

Always desirous of improving them I have determined on shipping, by the Thomas Wilson, a parcel of nails, and some other articles, which, I hope, will arrive as soon as any other things of the same kind, and that you will have an opportunity of selling them, if not to great advantage, at least for cash. I will, likewise, forward you such of the contract goods as can be got ready, for which I refer you to the invoice, and will forward you the remainder without delay. The pump tacks are as near the pattern as can be procured either here or in New York, and are put up in kegs, each keg resembling the pattern of a similar number, there is one keg assorted to make up the quantity of No 5, which could not be procured, and that no difficulty may take place, I send you back the patterns to compare with I have shipped, as nearly as possible, equal quantities of each, and hope the immediate attention I have paid to this business will give satisfaction, and procure you a preference of future contracts, which you may accept, calculating on the prices now quoted, and if any thing further can be done in that way which I very much wish for, on being advised, I will immediately execute the orders I flatter myself that the early supply of these goods will induce the intendant to wait patiently in case of any delay in the delivery of the cordage, as the unavoidable accident of Mr Clark s detention, by an embargo for 23 days in the Havana, delayed his arrival till the mountains are no longer passable, and may prove a difficulty in the way of getting of hemp, every attempt, however, will be made and I still hope with success, though I think you may, with perfect propriety for the reasons before alleged, crave considerable indulgence To show, however, my inclination to to do what I can I am about purchasing a large parcel of the very best Russia cordage here or in New York, which I propose shipping in the Fame and will calculate on having the hawsers and cables, which I cannot get here, made at Orleans, for which purpose I request you will destine particularly the yarn you will receive from Kentucky, and all the hemp you may have either shipped to you or can buy This last you must not miss if opportunities offer, as I am not sanguine in the hope of procuring a large supply, from the eagerness of the ropemakers above to speculate in cordage on their own account I will leave nothing, however, unattempted to procure as much as possible to be forwarded to you, and at the same time will recommend you to the merchants as a commission house, which I have already done in every other place where I had correspondents You would do well to write to your friend, Mons Bernard of Bordeaux, and request him to make your establishment known in the ports of France, from whence you may receive, in consequence of it, very valuable consignments

The scupper nails and spikes are making and will shortly be completed. I send you, for the present, a few of the latter to show that things are progressing By the next opportunity you will receive the remainder of them

In your attempts to procure further contracts of these or other articles, you will find the interest of Gilbert & Barba of the greatest service, and I recommend to you to cultivate their friendship. A great deal of trouble may be saved by them in the receipt of the contract goods, and you may assure them both, that I have already ordered from England the piano fortes for their daughters, which they requested Mr Clark to ship to them The piano forte, by the Thomas, was for Mad lle Durel, and was looked upon here, as the best that could be got in the city. With the piano fortes for Messrs Gilbert & Barba, will be shipped those for Mr. Deverges and Madame Roque, and you may, from me, request them not to get supplied elsewhere, as they may rely on receiving those I have ordered.

The order which our friend, Dn J M, furnished me with for goods, which would be wanted for the supply of the stores, I have forwarded to England, with directions to ship the articles mentioned in it, by the first of my vessels, after the goods are ready, a few of the articles can be had here on better terms than in England, and will be forwarded from hence In this shipment our friend will be interested 1-3, and I flatter myself, it will leave him a handsome profit on the sum he advanced, more especially as the share I now mention will considerably exceed his proportion of capital , you must give him to understand that I do not contemplate his running any risks, which will be guarded against by insurance and that in addition to the guarantee offered by Mr. Clark, I shall likewise offer mine for you Should you receive a parcel of nails and iron by the Mars, let him have an interest in the profits, and try to dispose of them to him, if no other purchaser offers

In speaking of yarn, I forgot to mention the quantity now at Frankfort. it is 18 hhds , being a part of last year's contract, with it you will receive 8 to 10 tons of baling rope, and I shall, in all probability, send you as much more of this latter article by the Fame, which I am about contracting for at 11 cents per lb , keep this in mind, in order to ensure supplies, in the course of a few weeks, to all those who may want it, with the baling rope, or before I may probably send you a quantity of sewing twine, which, if I can procure cheap, you will find mentioned in the invoice.

On the subject of my shipping, I have already written to you, but cannot refrain from mentioning again that I would wish you to dispose of the Fame, Sophia, Eliza and Matilda, immediately, if it can be done, at the prices quoted in the inclosed memorandum, and on their return from Europe, after completing this voyage, the ships Mars and Gen'l Washington, which you will order back from Liverpool, direct to you, for that purpose If a sale cannot be effected, you must try, in that case, to have cargoes of tobacco and some cotton ready for them, and before their return, I will forward orders where to send them to , keep me, therefore, advised of the price of tobacco, and should you be able to purchase a quantity, at any period between this and August, not exceeding 4 dollars per cwt, do it, if you can obtain a credit of a few weeks on the purchase I shall order a large quantity to be shipped to you from Kentucky, as a last resource for loading the shipping, if all others fail, but I request you will not hesitate to secure a quantity when it can be obtained If you can procure for the Thomas Wilson a freight of tobacco at a good price from the intendant, for Spain, you may accept it, and order her to Malaga, to load back with the proceeds, if she will not sell on being discharged, and before she incurs any expenses, for the sum of 8 to $9,000 Should no such freight offer, and one or the major part of one offer, at reasonable rates for France, you may accept it and fill up with cotton and tobacco on my account, on delivery of the cargo, if the vessel can be sold, let it be done; if not, let as good a freight for New Orleans, or this port, be procured, and in defect of both, let her return home in ballast, if I do not before order otherwise The small vessels, if you cannot sell them, you must endeavor to find employ for, either to some ports of the U S on freight, or elsewhere, as you may find most advantageous All the others, order directly back from Europe to Orleans, where I hope, by our mutual exertions, we shall have wherewith to load them I am of opinion that something may be done in the freighting way for the small vessels to Havana, if you can naturalize them and their Captains, now that the port is shut to our shipping, and you can always give directions to have any of them sold that will bring a good price, in this way, you may even employ the Matilda, if she does not sell in Orleans, and by the time they can return from Havana, I presume there will be flour freights in abundance for the U. S, tho' not at the great prices given last year In all cases I would prefer your abandoning rather than loading the small vessels on my account, and I wish them not to return home as long as they be employed abroad.

It is rumored here that the French chaige d'affaires, has orders to grant French papers to all vessels bought of our citizens; if so, I will not lose sight of this business, as by procuring these papers a great saving may be made, in case of loading any of them with tobacco for France

I shall immediately write to Havana to krow whether Spanish vessels, with flour from your country will be admitted there, and if it should, shall direct Mr Drake or Mr. Madan to advise you of it, with the formalities necessary to obtain an entrance The port, we hear, is now shut to the Americans, and I think flour will rise in consequence of it, so as to offer a good market for any quantity you could send there in my small vessels On this subject keep in mind what a mutual friend wrote to you from New York, and endeavor, as a last resource, to obtain a certificate for a quantity, as growth of the province, if the intendant can be brought to consent to it

I flatter myself you have, ere this, received a quantity of peltries from Chouteau, in conformity to his promise, if so, endeavor to dispose of them to some of the adventurers to France, rather than let them go forward on my account Should the peltries not have been shipped, you must write in the most urgent manner to Chouteau, whose conduct will be highly blameable, and likewise Clamorgan, who still owes a considerable sum, if not paid to Chouteau since his last visit to New Orleans I am informed by Mr Clark, that he left you statements of their accounts, so that you can be at no loss respecting their amount

As peace has taken place, your paper money will, no doubt, be shortly paid off, and the discount on it must fall, should you be in want of cash, you must sell the certificates received of Lassees, and I request you will write to him, urging the payment of the balance of his account

I have shipped by the Thomas Wilson, a few goods to complete an assortment for Mr. Turner, and enclose you the bill of lading, with a request that you will forward them to him by the first conveyance, with an attestation from the vice consul, that they are the same goods now embarked Be pleased to forward me, for my government, an account of the supplies and advances you have made to Mr Turner, and in addition to those already made, ship to him the following articles, which I expect you will be able to do on as advantageous terms as I could from hence, viz 2,000 lbs coffee, 20 boxes soap, a small assortment of paints, if not before supplied.

Keep me constantly advised of the remittances he may make to you in cotton, with your opinion of the state of affairs under his management, and the amount he may probably furnish in cotton between this and the first of May, if you can form any estimate of it.

Cotton is on the fall in Europe, and is expected by the best judges here to be down to 1-8d per lb Even at these prices, it will leave no loss, but I expect you have before now received, per the Washington, Mr Green's and Mr Barclay's opinions on the subject, by which you must be governed

You have not, I believe, mentioned in your letters what you ordered to be done with the Ohio, after her arrival in Liverpool. I request, in future, you will endeavor rather to let me know beforehand, than after the departure of my vessels, the destination you mean to give them, that I may be prepared to act accordingly

It would be imprudent to think, for the present, to contract for the next crop, and I would not advise your agreeing for any at a rate above $18, as the price will fall after the months of June and July, it is supposed, to 16 or 18d

Capt Tibbet, of the Sophia, has not pleased me by his conduct at Norfolk, and I fear he is not worthy of much confidence, you must therefore keep a strict eye to him, and put nothing in his power, make him no advances whatever, except what is indispensably necessary for his vessel, which I wish you would yourselves rather lay out than permit him to do, and if the brig should go on freight to any other port, give the strictest charge to your correspondents, respecting any advances being made him

January 19—I have this day received letters from Mr. Martin, from Havana, and suppose, from their tenor, he must be by this with you Please to employ him till I can devise some means of assisting him, on which subject I shall write you shortly

He might very probably assist you in disposing of bills in Havana, in case you are pushed for funds, and cannot sell bills at a good advance at home, they bore, when I was in Havana, a premium of 5 per cent, and I think will rise, now that the port is shut, when no remittances can be made to the U S in produce If the thing should become absolutely indispensable, Martin might sell your bills drawn in his favor at 60, 90, and 120 days, and remit you the amount in dollars, registering them on board any Spanish vessel, the expenses, including insurance, would not amount to more than four per cent, and if he obtained ten premium, there would still remain a handsome advance I think you might probably sell your bills on Martin at par, now that an intercourse has taken place, and by that means save the whole premium Your bills might be drawn for $500, $1000, and $2000 a set and forward him monthly a certain sum, according to your necessities and the probability of a sale of them; he should be furnished with a sufficient number of sets of each kind, and of different sights, that he might dispose of according as the call was greater or less and he ought by all means advise me as he sold a bill and made you a remittance, that I might be prepared for paying the one, or making insurance on the other This idea I only mention should all other sources fail, and wish you to think maturely on the subject before adopting it, perhaps when Martin is there he might assist you in other matters which you might put in his way so as to enable him to defray his expenses while employed by you His first care must be, on arrival in Havana, to mention that he is no longer employed by or for Mr Clark, and that he has no further connexion with him, nor funds of Mr Clark's in his hands.

Should you determine on sending the Thomas Wilson to France, Mr. Bonsel ought to go on her, to see that the cargo is disposed of advantageously, and that the funds are appropriated according to order, you must therefore advise me beforehand, if you mean to send the ship there, and what you think best to be done with her, in case he cannot sell her immediately after unloading, and before he goes to any expense for outfits

As the time limited by act of parliament for importing foreign commodities into England in American bottoms has expired, and that our vessels will now be exposed to seizure if not accompanied with certificates of *American growth* when they carry produce, you must by some means or another obtain them I flatter myself our friend H——, on account of the necessity of the thing, will not hesitate to let you have them, as you may assure him I would do so for him on a similar occasion, at any rate, they ought to be procured.

The cotton wick per the Sophia, and cotton per the Fame, belonging to Cavelier & Petit, are on hand, I will avail myself of the first opportunity of selling them, and will forward you the account sale when effected, as well as that of Mr Miller's peltries, which I daily expect to receive myself, from New York

I think it *necessary to mention, in order to avoid any misunderstanding* at a future period between us, that I am often under the necessity of having recourse to discounts to raise money to pay your drafts, and otherwise forward our joint views, and as my whole capital is now turned your way I mean to charge the concern with all the interest that may be paid from the 1st inst, as well as the loss on bills of exchange, and credit it with the premium when gained to this I shall expect your assent in writing, as it is not specified in the article of agreement between my attorney and you. I have chosen the first of January as the period at which interest was to commence, in order that any accruing on my former affairs might be settled and paid off, so that nothing but what was for account of the concern might be charged to it

Mons'r Theodore Bonnett goes out in the Thomas Wilson, he has business to settle with Messrs Roque & Lafon, and if he meets with any difficulty, will apply to you for assistance, which I request you will afford him, having assured him that he would find a friend in you, who would look upon his interests as your own As I flatter myself he will still settle amicably with them, keep *this advice to yourselves, that no remarks* may be made injurious to them

A very large proportion of the ship's cargo is consigned to Mr Poultney, a passenger on board her I have strongly advised him to apply to you, and if he does, it will be incumbent on you to assist him all in your power; he must, I am persuaded, employ somebody to do his business, and your conduct to him may be governed by his to you

Let me know without delay if you have written to Tunno &
Price, and to the house in Baltimore on the subject of Mr Harts
business if you have not I request you will do it immediately
It would be highly imprudent in you to make shipment, for account of any house in the U S in these unsettled times, and
draw upon it for the amount without first having an opportunity of consulting me respecting the responsibility of the persons
giving the order

I have informed Mr Chris Leet of this place that there is in
deposit in your hands the sum of $2400 or thereabout received
for his account from Mr Bubler's estate which he may dispose
of as he pleases you will shortly hear from him on the subject,
and I request you will as soon as possible forward him the
amount in the manner he may direct

Your letters of the 7th November per post with all their inclosures have got to hand this day The Lad drawn by Mr Dctor
be pleased to pay it being a just debt I will attend to your remark concerning Mr Porter and act in consequence Bran-
gier is right respecting any good from the store such being the
bargain made with him I am now preparing a *proyet* for a return cargo for Randle & Leech whose ship in all probability
will go again to your address from Bordeaux I have spoken to
many of the merchants who have made shipment lately to the
Havana, and offered to become guarantee for you in case they
consigned to you, if their vessels were refused admittance into
the ports of Cuba and I expect you will receive some consignments in consequence Should there be any houses to which
you wish to make yourselves known write to them under cover
to me, and I will add a guarantee for your transaction

The Russia goods necessary to complete your contract are
shipped in the Thomas Wilson, except 80 pieces of sheeting,
which could not be had, and which will be sent by the Fame,
these goods have been purchased low and will give a great
profit Thinking that a further quantity might be disposed of in
the same way I have shipped you 200 more pieces Russia duck,
and 240 pieces of Ravens duck, this last is not equal to the
parcel meant for the contract, but is laid in very low and I hope,
let matters be as they will they will bring you cash in a short
time, and afford you some profit With the same idea of putting
you in funds I have shipped you the large parcel of nails you
will see mentioned in the invoice and I advise you to sell these
things, and indeed every thing else, at a small profit rather than
keep them on hand as you may always order out supplies when
you want them, and as I have before mentioned, on being made
acquainted with what is wanted, that can be procured here, I
will immediately forward it The spikes are making and, in

order that you may have a sample, have now sent a cask of each
size, which be pleased to deliver, to show that I am mindful of
the business. The scupper nails are in hand and will be finished
shortly there are no Bramantes here but I will order them from
New York The Fame will take you out, in addition to a large
parcel of cordage, near 10 tons of baling rope, some cotton
bagging—if it can be procured a quantity of sewing twine,
some linseed oil and any thing else which your letters, between
this and the brig's departure may encourage me to buy. The
vessel is now heaving down and will sail in about 3 weeks
The 120 pieces of Russia sheeting, now shipped, are not as good
that is to say, as fine as I could wish, but I could get no others,
and you will, I hope find no difficulty in getting them received

Be pleased to forward me the account sales you have made
of marble tiles, codfish &c for account of Reed & Forde, and,
if you can by a reference to the books of Mr Clark, make out a
sale of a few medicine chests consigned to him in 1792, by
Jackson & Smith, to the brig Cayoso I would thank you to do
it, and advise me of it and see, at the same time, whether the
proceeds have not been credited to Reed & Forde, who have
called on Mr Clark for a settlement of it

The Russia duck sheetings Ravens duck, and 98 casks of
nails are entitled to draw back, you will, therefore, be particular
in forwarding the certificate of landing The spikes and scupper
nails, by being made here and the pump tacks, by forming parts
of various packages, are not entitled to any

As frugality is now indispensably necessary with the shipping,
you will, I trust, look to their disbursements, and suffer none to
be made but under your own eyes, and with your consent, make
no advances to the captains except what are indispensable, and
settle no accounts with them that you can avoid, give these
directions in every port you may send a vessel to

I conclude, by the time this reaches you, you will have secured
all the cotton you will have funds to pay for Be not alarmed at
the report of a fall, as even in that case, by being shipped direct,
there can be no loss, but let it stimulate you to ship, as soon as
possible, all you can get ready If a fall takes place with you to
20 or $22, continue to purchase and ship in any quantity you
can procure but take care to secure large quantities of tobacco—
that my vessels may not want freights when they return from
Europe, after making each a voyage this year On the second
voyage, I wish them sold if it can be done and if a good price
now offers for such of them as I have pointed out, do not miss
the opportunity

I strongly suspect that Capt Jones had a very considerable
sum in *bills* on board the Fame, of which he has given no

account, and has appropriated the freight to his own use. Among
others I believe Merdeaut shipped bills for $9000 Capt Lack
for $1500 Watson for 500 to Mr Brown and many others beside,
to the amount of near $50 000 in all. Jones denies this altho,
on the passage, he mentioned it to Mr Clark, mentioned. Be
pleased to make the most particular inquiry on this subject, and
advise me of the result, for my future government. I believe the
cash for Lack was received of Brooks and that Faurie shipped
$4000 for account of Capt Jones who commanded the Baltimore
pilot boat schooner that was sold to Benavest. From these advices you will be able to learn much and I trust that, in future, no
captain consigned to you will dare to sell bills on board without
advising you. It is likewise supposed that Capt Tibbets, of
the Sophia, had bills for 24 000 on board the freight of which he
likewise kept for his sole use, and which you must inquire into

I have authorized Capt Jones to take as many pieces of sail
duck and Ravensduck as he may want for making sails my
motive for not getting a small parcel separate for the ship was
to save the drawback the quantity, therefore, he may take, you
will be pleased to give the invoice short credit for

Should it be impossible to load any of my vessels in Orleans
without a long stay there, and you can procure them freights to
Havana, or elsewhere at a good rate, you may send them there,
and give directions to sell such as I have already mentioned,
you must, however, take care to keep a quantity of shipping
sufficient for your own purposes. You can always look upon
yourselves as authorised to dispose of any of my vessels much
lower than the general limitation, if they first earn a good freight,
as the gains on the freight will be looked on by me as so much
obtained in addition to the price

You must give general orders to all the shipping you send to
Liverpool to return back to you, direct, tho I should be in ballast
In this last case, give the most positive orders that there shall be
no delay made there it will not do to let vessels return from
Liverpool here as there will be no cargo here for them

Since writing the foregoing, I have shipped two barrels of
linseed oil for the use of the vessels, and that you may have a
little to get off your paints until I can send you a further supply,
and likewise three bales of twine for sewing cotton bales,
thinking it may be wanted you will find a separate invoice of
these articles inclosed

With sincere regard, I remain, dear sirs,
Your assured friend,
DAN WM COXE.

[Letter No 17]
Offered by complainant and filed 23d June 49
J W GURLEY, Commissioner

Bayou Sarah Nov 27th, 1802

MESSRS CHEW & RELF

Gentlemen —Yours of the 7th I duly received advising me that I might expect by Mr Forsythe the two tierces of bottled porter by him He has not yet arrived but I hope will in due time.

You also advise me of Mr Clark's departure for the U S, and that he has appointed you his attorneys in fact

This opens the way to lay a little business before you I hope no difficulty will occur —that none may, I send Mr Clark's account, his letters as well as Madam Clark's account and letter

Mr Clark's account, rendered 17th Apl last states a balance against me of $259 6 in which he has charged me $200 for my little daughter Jane advanced to Madam Clark This was not expended, as you will see by Madam Clark's account of expenditures This account is enclosed

Madam Clark expended $115 2

Mr Sterling the bearer of this, advanced $15 to my daughter, who handed it over to Madam Clark This is not stated in Mr Clark's account arising, I presume from her account being made out and sent forward before the money was paid by Mr Sterling

Mrs Clark paid for my daughter $100 2 deducting the $15 paid, as stated above

Mr Clark has stated in account $200 against me, but the case is as I have stated, and it arose from Mr Clark's goodness and friendly disposition, that there might be resources to meet any contingency of necessary expenses

I am only indebted to Mr Clark on his account of 17th April last, $159 1

July 18th, 1801, Mr Clark received on my account of Mr Hulings $809 7,—deduct $159 4,—there will be a balance of $650 3 coming to me

I presume Mr Clark's accounts or memoranda will show what I have stated

To make the matter more easy to you. I have sent Mr Clark's letter and account, also Mrs Clark's I would direct payment for what I owe you out of the monies coming from Mr Clark, but for two reasons 1st the monies coming are the monies of Mr Stokeley, 2d, I will send down my crop of cotton very shortly, when you shall be paid.

I send an order, by Mr Alex Sterling for the $650 3

       Your's respectfully,   DAVID BRADFORD

Messrs Chew & Relf merchants, New Orleans

[Letter No 5]

Offered by Complainant, and filed 23 June 1849

             J W GURLEY, Com

[Hand-writing of late Daniel Clark]

          Philadelphia 23 February, 1802

Messrs Chew & Relf —Gentlemen —Since my last I am
without any of your favors, but have received letters to the 17th
December from Messrs G Green & Son of Liverpool, advising
that the Mars and Washington were ready for sea and would sail
the first fair wind, the latter fully loaded the former nearly so, having in addition to the articles ordered by my agent, 10 tons of iron,
and as many of nails, which have been shipped on the recommendation of Capt George and would, doubtless have proved,
in any other circumstances than the present a very advantageous
shipment Let matters turn out as they will, I cannot but approve of Captain Georges intention in giving the order

As Mr Barclay forwards me no invoices be pleased to send
me copies of those you receive specifying generally the articles,
but without detailing all the different qualities and prices that I
may judge of the state of trade and form an exact opinion of the
articles suited for your country of changes in which I request
you will be particularly careful in giving me advice of Let me
know the value and extent of the trade to France, what new
manufactures are imported what old ones may be again generally used and, in fine give me an idea of everything that occurs,
how trifling soever it may appear to yourselves and whenever
you have a moment of time which you may not know how to
employ, devote it to writing to me Let not the political sentiments of the people of your country be forgot and if any changes
takes place in your officers of government let me know their
characters and the degree of esteem or fear they are held in
You may perceive how anxious I am to learn everything that
regards your country, and if you could prevail on your French
friends to write to Mr Clark, he would be thankful for it Should
you in future have any of my vessels nearly filled, you may, instead of keeping them waiting any time accept as much
freight as will complete their loading, always advising me in
time, that my orders for insurance which are given on the supposition of a full loading on my own account, may be regulated
accordingly Endeavor to procure freights for my small vessels,
or sell them if you can do it I would always prefer good
freights to foreign ports, and back again, but if they should not
offer and you can get freights here, or to New York or Baltimore,
take them I am endeavoring to make you known gener "

and wish you would, without delay send on printed circulars, which I shall address to all parts of the Union and to France, Holland and Hamburgh. At the time you send them give me a list of the houses to whom you have already forwarded them. Let me know what consignments you receive from other houses, that, if opportunities offer, I may give them information of the nature of the trade, and by that means direct their operation to the proper objects. I have before advised you that a parcel of rope yarn was sent to you from Kentucky: this you must manufacture into such work as will be immediately wanted by the Intendant. I shall send you at least 20 tons of cordage by the Fame, of the best quality and I hope this exertion will entitle you to a delay till the rest can be manufactured from the hemp that will either be shipped to you, or you buy as I am informed a great quantity will in all probability descend the river. Regulate your purchases of hemp and the price by the probable demand. I would have of my own accord ordered out from England to you a large assortment of goods, to reach you in August, but I fear there will be great quantities at market as every body who formerly was in the trade in France will be meddling in it again: and until things are settled and in their certain channel, it may be better to forego the prospect of gain, than run the risk of loss: besides, until I can get rid of some of my shipping, it may be necessary to be circumspect and keep within the compass of my capital. When matters are once arranged and trade in its channel, it will be proper to make regular importations, proportioned to the demand, and I will then put it in your power by establishing credits in all the manufacturing cities in Europe, to supply your customers cheaper and at a longer credit than other dealers.

Be pleased to send me an account of the money received of John Ellis, for account of Capt McFaden, and remit him the amount without delay.

With respect to freights it may be necessary to say something, in order that the rates may be ascertained, and thereby prevent future misunderstandings. I am far from desiring to engross any part of your profits by charging high freights: but as you know the circumstances under which I fitted out my ships in order to insure you an immediate conveyance of our purchases to market, the great length of time they have been delayed in Orleans, and the expense of sailing them under the disadvantages of high wages, which cannot be effectually reduced till their return home. You will not, I hope, find the following rates too high, especially when I assure you that I was offered them by Messrs Walker & Yard, of this city, if I had been willing to take freights on their account from New Orleans to Liverpool.

As Capt Davis may have met with some damage on his outward bound voyage from Liverpool to your place, when he lost his anchors and cables, which I hear are since recovered, I request you will in that case get a copy of his protest forwarded to me here, the ship being insured in this city

26th February — A Mr Wm Winn, of Liverpool, writes to me that he advanced the £10 8s 7d sterling, to the mate of the ship Mars, in 2 crates of ware. This man went, I understand, mate of the Matilda, and left the crates with you, on which you made an advance. When the sale is effected, remit the balance if it does not amount to more than the sum advanced in England, to Messrs G Green & Son, to be paid to Winn

The ship Diana has arrived at Baltimore but I have no advices from you. By newspaper accounts I learn that the ships Washington and Mars were spoken with early this month, the former near the Tortugas and the latter near the Hole in the Wall, and that the New York had arrived in the river. I am anxious to hear of the Matilda, Sophia and Eliza. I flatter myself you will be able to procure freights for my ships of sugar to Europe, as the price is low here if nothing better can be done with them

Should it be possible to forward good freights for one or two of the ships to the Havana, you may accept them and try to sell them there. if that cannot be effected while they are unloading they may return to you without delay to be in time for any freight or cargo that may afterwards offer. I wish my small vessels may be freighted, rather than loaded on my account, and if they come back here, I wish no produce sent in them for me, as it will deprive the large vessels of a part of their loading, and subject it to double charges. There will in all probability, be freight enough to be had and as long as this is the case keep them going till an opportunity offers of selling them. There must be plenty of passengers in the Spring and it is worth while to look after them

March 2 — Your letter of the 29th Jany, per the schooner Polly, has reached me as well as that by Stephen Minor. I am glad to hear of the safe arrival of the schooners Eliza and New York, and that the money by the last would arrive in time to be of service to you but I confess, I am very much surprised at the want of information in your letters. you do not mention the price of coffee, nor state of the market nor what you intend to do with the small vessels —leaving me in a state of uncertainty, which is painful. I suppose the Sophia is arrived, tho you do not say so, she is uninsured and a word respecting her would have been agreeable. I must request you will be more particular in future, and leave less to be guessed at. Let me know what quantity of cotton you have received from each of the people with whom contracts have been made, what you still expect to get from them and other quarters, and in what time, and every two months send me a sketch sale for my satisfaction, and advise me when you suppose each of the vessels, now with you, will sail   You well know what I must feel and therefore should be anxious to relieve me

4th March—Your letter of the 27th Jan'y, by the Lapwing, has just reached me, and tho' I have before touched on sugars, it may be necessary to remark again for your government that the very best bright grained sugars will not do to ship at a price exceeding 5 to 6 dollars, and inferior sugars will not do at any price   In shipping molasses you must pay the greatest attention that the quality be good, and that it be shipped in the best possible order

As the planters sell molasses by the gallon, or rather by the *Barrique of* 100 *Pots*, you should in future measure with the French vette, by which you will be gainer   there is an iron one at Jourdain, the coopers, which you should endeavor to bring into use

As peace is made, certificates of property are now useless, and you may in future avoid that expense

Mr Hollingsworth, a respectable merchant of this city, will forward you a power against Mr John O'Conner   I shall thank you to endeavor to secure this sum for him without distressing Mr. O'Conner by enforcing immediate payment

As long as you can sell the slate and tile you may receive by my ships, to advantage, do it   let those which do not go off be carefully stowed away   they will do to build with at the ropewalk   I have this so far at heart, that I wish you to see Dujarreau, and get from him the plan of the building with the elevation of it, and estimate of the expense, which send me, and if I approve it, I will write you instantly to contract with him, let him give you a list of the iron work, glass nails, locks, &c, that may be wanting, all which you can easily furnish

I hear that flour is at four dollars   if it is fresh, you ought not to have hesitated to load my small vessels with it at that rate, or even at 5 dollars, and let them touch at Havana, where, if they could not sell, they might proceed to other ports   In purchasing, you must in future weigh a good number of the barrels, as the cargo of the Fame wanted 20 lbs each barrel of the weight

It has lately become customary to forward letters to me under cover by post, I shall, therefore, in future request you to call on those who send them for the postage   Be pleased to ask *Le Brun* for 52c for the postage of a packet, and Jourdain 52c. for postage of his.

March 9—Your letters of 16th, 21st, 25th, 27th & 29th Jan and 1st & 8th Feb'y to the 9th February, have reached me, and all the bills, you mention in them, have been presented and duly honored Your bill on Rundle & Leech has come to hand, but as both partners of that house are absent from hence, it has not been accepted and such is the state of credit here, that I am not without apprehensions respecting it It is with regret I mention the stoppage of our mutual friends R S Hackley & Co If you should have orders from these ports to ship and draw I request you will not comply with them unless I have a knowledge of the parties and recommend them as trustworthy, and that you may take their bills let this be a general rule with you till times change and I advise you

I am sorry to observe your want of funds, and it is utterly out of my power to send you any at present If cotton keeps low, try to buy on credit even if you give a small advance for it the present appearances are that it will rise in England For the love of God, try to expedite the ships from your port, I am under heavy acceptances and have no other resource than drawing on the shipments My whole capital is now employed for our joint account and I must depend entirely on your exertions Your letter of the 8th Feb'y tho ten days latter than your preceeding one, mentions nothing about the schooner Eliza, nor what you propose doing with her, nor do you ever enter into any details of the markets, state of the trade, or regulations adopted or about to be adopted It is reported here, that the port was to be shut against importations in our shipping, unless for deposit Advise me in time of every thing likely to occur for my government You should, at any rate, endeavor to procure leave to sell all cargoes on the way there before the prohibition was known, and get leave for the ships to take cargoes away in return

The molasses by the Sophia will turn out a losing business, I fear it will not bring first cost, exclusive of charges Sugar is still worse, and if you should be under the necessity of taking any in payment, try to sell it again in New Orleans, rather than ship it I recommend the same thing to you with respect to peltries

Cotton pays now no duty on importation in England but for fear of accident, you had better get our friend to certify that it is of the growth of the Mississippi Territory, invoice it always as such, to avoid accident. I will write to Hulings on the subject

When you draw on me, I would prefer your drawing a single bill for a large sum, rather than give different bills to that amount,—the reason is this,—the banks seldom discount any

46*

bill or note above $2000, all bills, therefore, above that sum, must lie in the hands of the drawer, and I have by that means a chance of having less paper in the banks, and can get more of my own discounted for my own use I know well that it will not depend on yourselves to regulate this matter, and that you must draw as you can sell but I mention it for your government when an opportunity offers of attending to it

I have written to Mr J B Villanueva, of Charleston, and as well as your friend D C, have offered to guarantee your trans- actions, attend in these cases to orders, so as that no difficulties may occur, nor any room be left for claims in consequence

Inform me why Cayetano was put out of office, and what other changes are likely to take place, with the occasion of them

In the foregoing part of this letter I touched on the subject of freights, but did not continue to state what I had to say to you I shall, therefore, as briefly as possible state it the rate which I propose to charge you from Orleans to Liverpool, taking the vessels by the season will be 7 cents per lb, and half price for the frieght back calculating on the quantity of cotton she takes out with her   This has particularly reference to the Mars and Washington, whose voyages will commence at Liverpool, and will end there on their return I was offered 4d sterling per lb, on the departure of my ships Thomas and New York, freight, and could have engaged all the rest at the same rate, had I not thought it necessary to provide tonnage for ourselves, and not leave our business exposed to accident, if, owing to any particular reason, there should a momentary fall of freights you must recollect that my vessels by being sent out chiefly operate to cause it, and that without them, it would not in all probability occur, another thing to be con- sidered is that the very freights which my ships earn, are laid out for your benefit, which could not possibly be the case if paid to others

I believe I could prevail on Mr Clark to go to England and France, to make your house known and order you out cargoes from those countries, if you had kept me advised of the state of things, and the probability of my ships being admitted at their return, which since the peace, I have always been more or less fearful of Settle this point with the intendant, and for- ward me then your orders for future supplies, with patterns of any thing new that may be in demand Mr Clark will not only make you shipments and procure you consignments, but will from all places where he may visit, give you information respecting their manufactures and way of doing business, which must be highly necessary to you, and by giving orders in future to the manufacturers, an immense saving will be made I intend that your house shall always have a great and general assortment, so as to permit you to enter into competition with any, or all the other houses in your city

Forward me whether you want it or not, the most general list of goods you can procure, with the places they are to be had in, and prices, the colors, quantities and qualities for an assortment—for my future government inform me early what you want, that I may always supply you in time

March 11th

Your letter by the mail of 16th Jan'y is come to hand this moment, and Mr Derbigny's assurance will be attended to. A report has got here, previous to the receipt of the letter, that the Farmer grounded at the bar going out, and we do not know whether she got safe off or not. As the insurance could not be made while we are without a knowledge of the ship's safety, I shall defer doing any thing until we hear the ship gets off when the premium will be 4 per cent. If the ship should be lost at the Balize the property will doubtless be saved there, so that in either case Derbigny will not suffer. This letter of yours is the first which gives me a just idea of the quantity of cotton you bought, or what you intended doing with the small vessels, and I hope, in future, you will be as particular as possible

Mr Morales gave Mr Clark an order for sundry articles to furnish and ship for his account part of which I now send you, Mr Clark having requested me to comply with the order for him It seems to be Mr Clark's opinion that in general, the articles may be had cheaper in retail, in Orleans than here, and, as I forward you a copy of the order I request you will endeavor to supply some of the articles at home particularly the earthen ware, cambric, table linen, lawn handkerchiefs, cotton stockings, dimities, which I fear you have too many of on hand, and that you will put them to him at such a rate as to content him, such of the other things as you can conveniently get, you can include, (*haciendole alguna gracia en el precio*) as it is very difficult to procure them here. The *comestibles*, mentioned in the order, I have not meddled with, except the sherry, malaga, and spermaceti candles, knowing, since the peace, that all these things are far cheaper with you than with us, and I enclose you a memorandum of retail prices here, to show you that it is really impossible to do him justice. You must let him know the immense difference there is between the wholesale and retail prices, and make him comprehend the nature of drawbacks which are lost on the goods sold here in a small way, which adds considerably to the price I have ordered from England, to be shipped to you, a similar list of goods, and you may inform him that, besides taking the present parcel, or any part he pleases of it, he may have the whole or any part of the other parcel, at first cost, on its arrival

I have substituted a set of china instead of the set of blue ware, and have forwarded, besides, a small present, which you will be pleased to offer him in my name

I now enclose you invoice of sundries for joint accounts per the Fame, Capt Graisbury The cordage is for the contract, and is the best that could be made here I sent it that I might show my desire to fulfil all your engagements though we might have done it cheaper at home, and I hope it will impress the intendant advantageously The hemp and yarn you get from the Ohio, will do to manufacture into such cables and hawsers as I could not get here, and by this means the whole will, I hope, be delivered in time altho the delay by the embargo, which my vessel met with in Havana might be justly pleaded as an excuse for putting off the execution of the order for a length of time, by rendering the roads impassable through the mountain in winter In case of any unforeseen difficulty, you must represent this, and, as you have the advance made, will be better able to support your claim

After having had the scupper nails twice made, and returned to the workmen, I am under the necessity of sending off the brig with but a part of them; the remainder will go by next opportunity As these nails are of a very uncommon kind, I send, by Capt Graisbury, the sample and pattern I received from Mr Barba, that in case of any difficulty, you may have it compared with them. The sheeting and braimantes to complete the order, I now send you, and a ton of oakum, in hopes that it will sell; if it does not go off, immediately let be put up carefully, as you will yourselves always have need of it The remainder of the spikes, made after your model, are now shipped in the Fame, and in order to dunnage her well, I have put in her 750 staves, and 1954 feet of best pine boards for flooring, which I recommend to you to sell, on the levee as those things are put away, and forgot, amidst a hurry of more important concerns

I am much pressed by Mr Jordon to contract for a supply of yarn and baling rope, for next spring Let me have your opinion on this subject, and whether, in the present state of the rope-walk, we can expect to work them up, and afterwards sell cordage to advantage Until I hear from you, I shall give no answer on the subject

With respect to my small or large vessels, you have standing orders to sell as many as you please, reserving what you want for carrying our purchases to market When you cannot sell, try to freight, when you cannot do that, to advantage, especially with the little ones, and you load them for the Islands, unless on some extraordinary occasion, let them go to windward, and run down for market In all cases, a sale must be forced before ie vessel leaves the port, and I wish on all these occasions the funds should be returned to you, as no dependence whatever can be placed on remittances to me. In case of sale of vessel and cargo, let the captain be empowered to bring me the proceeds, in cash: in that case, his wages will run till his return home. I have already informed you that it is my opinion that the port of Havana is or will be shut to the Americans: could you not, therefore, put some of the little vessels under Spanish colors, and send them there loaded with flour (fresh and good), and have vessels and cargoes sold. If you could freight one or two of the large ones, if you have not wherewith to load them immediately for Europe, you may do it, but I request on no occasion, you will deprive yourselves of the means of transporting the produce bought or contracted for, to market, while such heavy payments hang over us. Write me the prospects of a freight or loading for them, after their return from Europe, that I may be prepared for all events. The Matilda is an unprofitable vessel, and ought to be got rid of: she would be the best to send to Havana, for sale. Flour on the Chesapeake is 5 to 5 1-2 dollars, and on the opening of the spring will not, in all probability exceed 6, on an average.

Cotton, by our advices to the 9th Jan'y had got up, in Liverpool, to 1-9, and was expected to be higher. There is now no duty on it there. By invoicing your cotton as American, you may continue to ship it: but it will be best to get our friend to give you certificates, which you must press him to do, for fear of accident—there is nothing to be gained or saved by doing so, except the risk of seizure, and I am almost certain that, seeing it in this point of view, he will not deny them.

Mr Pershouse, of the house of Clegg & Pershouse, of Manchester, have shipped you by the Fame, a bale of cassimeres, which were on hand here. I have informed him that a sale cannot be expected till the fall, and he is aware of it; let me entreat you to do your utmost to give them satisfaction, as it will procure you future consignments. I mean to get you, as before advised, into general credit with all the manufacturers, and by means of Mr Clark, who has an idea of going to Europe will forward particular information on every branch of them.

There is now some reason to believe that, altho' Louisiana was certainly by treaty ceded to France, yet posterior arrangements have been made, by which the province will remain in the possession of Spain, at least for some time to come. The reason supposed for this is, the uneasiness which the cession caused here and the certainty that it would sooner or later cause a breach with us, which it is the interest of France to avoid, as our weight would then be thrown into the scale of England, with which we should have to make a common cause. The United

States will never attempt to disturb Spain in her possession, but will see with a jealous eye any attempt of any other power whatever to get footing in that quarter. You may mention these circumstances to the intendant, and that I have them from good authority. I have sent to your care, by Capt Graisbury, the seal of the Mississippi Territory, which be pleased to receive of him, and forward to the Secretary, or, in case of the death of Col. Steel, to the Governor of that place.

Messrs Reed & Forde had a small parcel of cordage on hand, which they were desirous I should purchase, but would not, on account of its color altho' the quality is good. I have, however, agreed that you shall, if possible, pass it at the contract price, with our own, or if not practicable sell it for their account. I shall thank you to endeavor to make the most out of it, being desirous of serving them as much as in my power. When sold, remit them the amount in the way most advantageous to them. Their cordage can be distinguished from your own by having the mark on wooden tallies, and the captain can, beside, point it out to you.

I have already mentioned the difficulty occurring here with the scupper nails. One of the nail-makers, whose parcel I refused, has intreated permission to send out those nails to you, and I have consented. If they can be got off, with the others I will allow him the price at which they were to be furnished to me; if they do not go off to the King, try to sell them to the coopers, for sugar casks, at what they will bring, and advise me thereof, as soon as possible. The casks or kegs will be marked A. and, as they are the worst parcel, you must not have them first inspected, in order not to give a bad idea of our own which are marked D. W C / N , No. 1 a 3.

I remain, with esteem, gentlemen,

Your most obed't serv't,

DAN WM COXE

P. S—As long as you can command funds, and cotton is at 22, you may boldly purchase as a matter of speculation and profit. If it should be merely a matter of convenience to load my ships and prevent delay, you may go somewhat higher, there will be no loss at 25, as far as matters can be judged of at present.

[Letter No 6]

Offered by complainant, and filed 23d June, 1849

J W GURLEY, Com'r

PHILADELPHIA, 8th March, 1802.

Gentlemen—I have just received the enclosed letter from New York, advising that a bill I had on Mr. Lucet, of that place, will not be paid   I return it to you, requesting you will compel the drawer to reimburse me   Yours sincerely,

DANIEL CLARK

Messrs Chew & Relf, New Orleans

[Letter No 8]

Offered by complainant, and filed 23d June, 1849

J W GURLEY, Com

Philadelphia 14th March, 1802.
(Private and confidential)

Messrs Chew & Relf—

Gentlemen—I have received your letter of the 21st January, and your B C s letter of 20th December, from Natchez   I have been lately a good deal occupied, and shall, therefore, for want of time as the vessel is on the point of departure, touch but lightly on the subjects mentioned in them indeed, I think I have anticipated most of them in my former letters   I am sorry for the result of the suit brought by C Wilkins I did not expect it, the bill, however, you drew for its amount is accepted   Whatever things of the same nature occur in future, I wish you to settle at home   Should I be obliged to pay for Rapalge, have him arrested in the Spanish dominions if there, and compel him to settle with you without delay   With respect to the auditor you must be indulgent till we hear with certainty respecting Le Vergne, and whether there is any thing to be apprehended from that quarter   Give my respects to him and inform him that by next opportunity, I will forward the articles he gave me a memorandum of   I forgot them till now   You must, however keep this to yourselves, and make another excuse

I have sent a part of the articles, ordered by Morales, and have ordered out all the others from England except the comestibles   when these and the remainder arrive let him have what he pleases   I would have now sent the rest, but things are so extravagantly high in retail that I dare not buy them   I forward you the list of the things he ordered, and as you have, yourselves, a great many of them, and can possibly procure the others, (tho' you may lose somewhat in the price,) I recommend to you to procure what you can, you must, yourselves, have earthern ware, cambric, pocket handkerchiefs, cotton stockings, dimities, table linen, &c &c &c   I have not, in that account, made him out an invoice, that you may add to the list what you please, and have left my letter to him and the assessor, open, that you may see their contents, and be governed accordingly   The china you will offer, as a present from me, and not let him know the price that he may think it greater than it really is   I suppose you will not put his things in your custom house invoice, and by this

means he will not know what you have got till they are delivered   Should he not like any thing, or find it too high, let him
have it at his own price, you must keep in with him   The assessor must also be managed, have his cane or canes mounted.

Should Trouard not have it in his power to pay you this year,
you ought to make him give a security for payment the next, by
mortgage, this must not be neglected, your excuse must be, that
I am absent

I am sorry that Miller has acted as he has done towards you,
more for his sake than yours   When I refused to take his cotton, he knew well it was because I had not then money to pay
for it, if he can think he is under no obligation to yourselves or
me, I congratulate him on the goodness of his heart and memory
I had long contemplated an establishment on a larger scale, and
intended writing to him to come on here for the purpose   I suppose it will now be superfluous   mention in your next a word
on the subject, that I may know how matters go on

Mr Dunbar must, if he has paid none of the demands against
me, have a sum of mine in his hands   You know how the balance stood when I left home   he has since then recovered the
amount of the Vendue sale made for my aunt, and in all probability $1400 from Dougherty. See to this, and request him to
push Evans for what he owes

I shall write to Bellechasse particularly in a few days, inform
him of this

Dubigny wrote to me for some trifles   I could not in all
Philadelphia procure him more vignettes than two, which I send
him, with a few types   the whole got by your brother's means,
who has written directions which are in the bundle how to use
them   The cost of the things now sent is 8 dollars, which
charge   It will probably be your interest to foster him, by continuing to order out things in his line   Of this you must judge
by circumstances

Let Zerban know that I could not get his watch time enough
to send him now, I will forward it as soon as possible

I enclose you for your government, a letter from Mr Wagner,
chief Clerk of the Secretary of State's office, in answer to one
to him on the subject of Louisiana, which we have reason to
hope will not be given up at all to France, at any rate, it will
not be immediately   You will learn with pain the fate of St
Domingo, which might probably have been averted, by a little
policy on the part of my namesake, the General, but it suited the
interests of the expedition, that the whites should be murdered;
there would then be fewer claimants for estates, when the Island
was conquered, and more vacant lands to reward the officers
with   In this light things are looked on here and you may per-

ceive how cowardly the fleet acted from Lear's account of the business Keep Mr Wagner's letter a perfect secret, as it is a confidential one you may generally mention the subject, but particularise nothing respecting the advices from Chancellor Livingston, the ambassador

Forward to my plantation, without delay a hhd of claret, two of molasses, and a barrel of sugar if you have not before sent these things, and let me know how matters go on there

You have no idea how anxious we are here to know every detail about business with you Mr Coxe never thought my letters half long enough, and I now begin to think of them as he did

You will be pleased to keep Martin employed till I write you further respecting him, which will be in a few days, when I mean to take up every subject I have not hitherto touched on, and if any friend thinks himself neglected let him know he shall soon hear from me

Forward me the papers respecting the rope walk, including copies of grants survey and proceedings with your old Governor. Get Mr Argote to write a memorial to the Court on the subject which I shall sign, and forward from hence Send me at the same time some paper, such as is made use of for the purpose which Argote can get for you at some of the offices

I should like to know by what vessel you received my letters from Havana which I fear were delayed there They were to be forwarded by schooner John in case Walden sold his ship Did that schooner go consigned to you? and was young Van Zandt in her when wrecked in the late gales?

Let me know what quantity of bales you have received from each contractor, and how you go on with them It will behoove you, as cotton is falling, to act generously to have your name up for strict honor in future

Attend to my parents and let them come to this place in the month of April, by the return of any of Mr Coxe's little vessels, or any other if his are otherwise employed This is my determination respecting them and you must see to every thing else

You are doubtless to have an interest in all shipments made with funds which you have furnished

Request Mr Dunbar to pay Doctor Todd his account, that I may get rid of these demands

I will probably go to England and France, without delay, to push your business I would have already set off had you advised what would probably be the effect produced by the peace, whether the port will be shut or not, and, in general, what is or will be done Write particularly, and forward me general lists of goods, with particular ones of what you want immediately, and try to fix with the intendant, for the return of all Coxe's ships, even in case of a change of measures I will then send them all out loaded, that you may have a large stock on hand

I have hitherto said nothing to Mr C., on the subject of La Vergne, in order not to alarm him unnecessarily In writing, therefore, on this subject, enclose your letters to Earle, who will deliver them to me, and in the mean time, make the dispositions I already recommended, for fear of the worst

It is with extreme regret I have to mention the death of Capt Davis' mother, which happened about 8 days ago. Remember me kindly to him, and let him know I will see that his family does not suffer in his absence Remember me also to Capt George, and tell him that I fear he must have had a vast deal of trouble with my family He will find orders in Liverpool on his arrival there, to return home, unless you can find employment for him to your place another voyage, which I much fear

I have already mentioned to you that I will keep an eye here to every thing I will see that matters flow in one channel only I wish some of the vessels disposed of and only those kept that may be wanted Push on what you can, as for the reasons already given, funds are wanted here and neglect no means to make sales, there shall be no new enterprise whatever attempted Old Todd is here, and we have finally settled Brickwood s debt, tho' the old man and I have still some thing to finish I would not speak to Swan, whom he brought with him, and I believe the old man thinks me a very violent fellow

As the voyage to Amsterdam, by the Matilda has been a ruinous one, and it would be difficult to stipulate a freight out for her, as the small shipment will not afford a great one, and the ship cannot afford to take a small one, at the same rates she would a large one, I recommend to you to charge a commission on the sale, and if she loads for joint   from Orleans, let her freight then begin from that time

Let Debuys, Donaldson, Peytavin and Mr Hulings know that I will write them shortly

I have a thousand things to say, but my head is so confused that I cannot remember them.

I remain yours sincerely and affectionately,

DANIEL CLARK

P S—Seal my letters to Morales and the assessor, after reading them The things for Gilbert & Barba will go to you from England; let them know this I owe Riano 300 to $350 for balance of account; be pleased to pay it to him, he must want it.

[Letter No 14]

Offered by Complainant, and filed 23d June, 1849

J W GURLEY, Com'r.

(Duplicate)—Original, per Spanish lady

PHILADELPHIA July 3d, 1802

MESSRS CHEW & RELF

Dear Sirs—I yesterday heard by Mr ——, passenger in the brig Juliana, (who landed at Cape May and came up to town,) that the schooner Eliza had arrived in the Mississippi, with Mr. C—— He likewise mentioned that Mr C sent a letter on board the Juliana for me, which, if true, will reach me to-morrow or next day, on the Juliana's arrival. This information greatly relieves my anxiety for his early arrival with you. The above gentleman presented a draft dated 25th May, favor of Bustard & Eaton for $1000, at 75 days, which I accepted, and another has just been presented for the like sum at 90 days, dated 27th May, which I propose accepting at 120 days. Will your drafts then never cease pouring on me and increasing my difficulties? When or how I shall pay what I have accepted I know not, as it depends on Mr C and yourselves. By this vessel I send you a bundle of newspapers, a pamphlet entitled the "Suppression," and a book bound in boards, entitled, 'History of the late Administration.' I will continue to write you by post, and every opportunity, as any thing occurs and am, dear Sirs,

Yours sincerely, D W COXE

JULY 9th, 1802

DEAR SIRS —Since writing the foregoing, I have accepted the last mentioned draft in favor of Jno Crozier, at 90 days, pursuant to its tenor, the holder refusing to extend the time. I have also, *for the same reason* this day accepted your draft in favor of Josiah Pitts, at forty days, No 121 for $3200. Though I have accepted and must continue to accept such as the holders have not, or will not extend the time of I sacredly assure you that I shall be totally unable, from my present resources (or rather, want of resources,) ever to pay them. To afford, however, every chance to you and myself, I accept them, hoping a relief from you, if when only I can expect it. Every hour's reflection on the subject confirms my opinion that you committed an imprudence, (the consequences of which I will not yet decisively pronounce,) in continuing to draw on me, knowing in the first place how I was pressed, and secondly that cotton would not sell in England, and that *much* of your shipments to Barclay was of an inferior quality, and *hardly worth the charges.* I am placed between two evils, equally dangerous and alarming, to let your bills return on the one hand is ruin to you, and on the other, to draw on Barclay may be attended with the same consequences to me. You well knew that however you might be pressed for money in N w Orleans, that to protract, or even to have suspended your payme its would have been a trifling evil, *compared* with your bills or mine returning with 20 per cent damages, etc. The general want of money at New Orleans, and the deception which (before Mr Bensell's departure) heard had been practised by some of your contractors, would have afforded a justifiable pretext for delaying payments You have no banks with you to enforce the payment of notes to an hour, under the unavoidable penalty of a total stoppage and bankruptcy, and you therefore should have done what I cannot do.

Was it not unwise to refuse $25 000 for the Ohio and T Wilson, and to draw on me for the same amount? The goods you had on hand at Orleans were always a sure pledge to your creditors of your solidity Reflect for a moment on my situation, without a single dollar at any time, but what is derived from *confidence,* and then contrast your situation with mine If anything proves my destruction, it will be the badness of the cotton you have shipped, and but for which (Green states,) all the stocks would have been sold before the last depression To reason, in the situation to which I am reduced, is indeed but of little use at present it serves to show that the evil I complain of might have been prevented or mitigated by a more cautious mode of proceedings on your part On the arrival of our friend, Mr Clark, with you, I from time to time flatter myself with the hopes of receiving relief by some extraordinary exertions, which he was well informed were indispensably necessary at his departure, and which have since become *much more so* This letter, which is not copied, you had better destroy, after perusing it and showing it to Mr Clark

Affectionately yours,   D W. COXE

[Letter No 4]
Offered by complainants, and filed 23d June 1849
J. W GURLEY, Commissioner

Private]   PHILADELPHIA, 18th February, 1802
MESSRS. CHEW & RELF,

Gentlemen —I returned 3 or 4 days from Washington, where I had an opportunity of seeing the President, and the officers of Government, by whom I was very well received From all I could learn, there seems to be no doubt, but that France is to have Louisiana, and the news gives all parties here a great deal of concern The time when possession is to be given is not known, and you must endeavor to prepare for it It has been hinted that a great deal is expected from my services, and I very much fear I shall be requested to go back shortly, I will not do it, unless something serious is apprehended or news comes officially of a change taking place immediately. In either case you may then expect to see me. I shall shortly be more particular in writing to you on this subject. Let me know constantly what is going forward what is expected, and people's sentiments thereon that I may convey information to the fountain head and get some of my French friends to write me as often as possible, that I may learn their dispositions and sentiments. Keep me well advised of all occurrences in trade, and the changes and modifications that may take place. If our vessels must navigate under two sets of papers, it must be done, rather than have them thrown out of the trade for the present, till new arrangements can be made, and the Consul will give no difficulty in providing these vessels with the usual certificates, it being the wish of Government communicated to me, to favor the merchants in this particular. I will have an eye here to every thing that concerns the trade, and wish to be kept advised by you of all that occurs, that I may act in consequence.

Be pleased to let me know how my private account stands, after crediting me with the present crop, and charging the balance due by my late uncle, this is essential to me to know for various reasons. Settle as soon as you can with Pontalba's agents, and get the mortgage taken off. If you cannot pay him all, give him your own notes, or any other security for the balance, and dispose of the property as I before directed you. at any rate, you must deny having any property of mine in your hands, and if anything is attempted against me you must say that I have recalled my power of attorney, and refer them to me here.

When you write to me on private matters let your letters come directed to Mr Earle as things will often occur which I wish only to see. Should anything regarding ourselves occur which you intend for me only, take the same method, and you may rely on your communications being regarded as perfectly confidential.

Forward me the two thousand dollars which I wrote to you for, in one or two bills, in favor of some trusty friend at home, and by him endorsed in blank, that I may have some funds at my own disposal, without calling on Mr Coxe for trifles, as I may want money, this must be a business kept to ourselves, and charge me in account with the amount.

I am doing all in my power to assist you, and will not fail to recommend you, and procure you business by all means in my power.

The Fame will sail in about a fortnight, and will carry out

half the hawsers and all the small cordage , manufacture, therefore, only the cables, and a half of each quality of the hawsers, till you hear further from me   By the Fame you will probably receive a consignment of French goods from a house
here, whose interests you must in that case attend to   Try to
raise what funds you can at home, and sell as fast and as well
as you can , keep nothing on hand that you can dispose of for
cost and charges, or even on credit to sure hands   When you
cannot do better draw, but as sparingly as possible at first, as
all the cotton is still on hand in England   Keep the vessels
employed as long as you can

Yours sincerely and affectionately,

DANIEL CLARK

[No 21]

Offered by Complainant, and filed 27 June, 1849

J W GURLEY, Com'r

PHILADELPHIA, Dec 23 1802

MY DEAR FRIEND —I received per last mail yours of the 29th
ult , which was but 22 days coming   I am happy to find that
peaceable possession would so soon be taken of Orleans, not
that I expected the contrary, but doubts were entertained by many
here and the event once known it will render our affairs in
that quarter more secure, at least in public opinion   The
fears you suggested in your late letters, that our debt to
Barclay would become known, and affect my credit here, I am
sorry to say, proved in a degree well founded   A confidential
friend called on me, a few days past, to mention that it was
whispered abroad that I owed Barclay 20,000 guineas, that your
estate was mortgaged to Mr Burd, and that my Bloomsburg
estate had been left by my father's will in trust for my wife and
family, which *latter* circumstance (he added) had made the most
injurious impression of the three   I immediately convinced him
that the trust he alluded to was done away by my wife's consent,
after my father's death, and that the property was now on record
as mine, which fortunately is the fact, as the trust was dissolved
to enable me to mortgage my estate to the friends who loaned me
the $50,000, though that mortgage was *never recorded ,* though it
now exists to Mr Burd for all his endorsements, it is not known.

In regard to the mortgage on my estate, I told him that at a
period when Mr Burd endorsed my bills of each to £10 on
£15,000 sterling, at a time that you voluntarily *when here* offered
to secure him for such acts, though that no longer existed

With respect to Barclay's balance I told him I never made a
secret of any responsibility to him for a balance arising from his
large shipments for my concern in Orleans, and I fortunately

had by me a rough statement of Barclay's account, which showed a balance of about £15 000 sterling in his favor, though I informed him I could not aver that in settlement it would not prove with interest somewhat more. I next day made out a statement of my affairs generally and grounded on the documents brought on by Relf last summer showing a surplus of assets of above $200 000 independent of your and my real estates, and I gave him for perusal your letter respecting our land purchases, with all which impressions I sent him abroad to counteract any thing unfavorable he might hear and I therefore trust that though brokers and meddlers may talk, that I shall escape any serious inconvenience except what results from the indescribable press for money, arising from a rare combination of causes, and which is felt by every merchant in the city. My long experience in the fiscal line and my varied system of raising means, will, together with the lucky turn of our remittances from Orleans to this quarter, prevent anything more than the struggling against the difficulties to which I am already so much inured.

I feel that it will be indispensably necessary to wipe off as much as possible of my debts here, as in addition to the paper which I have myself issued to raise money a great deal that was given for the Matilda's cargo is now in the brokers hands. My plan is, on the arrival of the T Wilson to charter some vessel cheap and load her with N O Cotton, under the auspices of Willing & Frances, or A Baring, from whom I will get bills to relieve me. When you recollect that I cannot sell here to safe people, that the accounts from England are favorable, that exchange is 3 to 5 per cent above par that freights and insurance are both low, and that necessity besides, leaves no other safe alternative, you will agree that I ought not to hesitate.

Independently of the last consideration, I really believe a shipment to England the best that can be done with our cotton. Perhaps I may make the arrangement for a part to Antwerp, which I should prefer. Be easy, therefore, on my account, and let there be a clear understanding with Chew & Relf that they are to be concerned in these shipments, on account of the impossibility of selling here. The double freight will be but a trifle, if any more, than if the vessel went direct to Europe from Orleans. I hope soon to receive the titles and plots of the Baton Rouge lands, and also to learn whether the United States have given orders to our troops to occupy Florida or not. I sent you by Captain Donaldson, of the schooner Regulator, who sailed yesterday for Orleans, the handsomest guardette box, with a double set of best pearl counters, (say 160) that I could procure—price only $7. The chairs will go per Spanish Lady or ship John, in a few days. Being unable to engage a regular foreman for the rope walk, I fear I shall be obliged to send you too common, though good hands, the best of whom you must promote. 'Tis now said, (I know not on what authority,) that Venelle will not be your Governor, but that Gen Dearborn and Claiborne, Gov of the M T, are talked of Either of the latter would be infamous appointments, and yet I should not wonder at them

The tide of emigration to Louisiana is running strong, and you may expect to see in its train half the bankrupts, scoundrels and fortune seekers in the United States Beware, therefore, of the arts and knavery of many able men of talent who will visit that country Edward Livingston, of New York, late mayor of that city, and district attorney, a man of lost reputation and fortune, though of excellent abilities as a lawyer, sails for Orleans in a few days He is a very sanguine speculator, and more likely to endeavor to link himself with you than any one I know

You may make him useful, but never confide in him He possesses much plausibility, and will get into favor at Orleans, and may possibly hope for political preferment, though, having been lately dismissed from the office of District Attorney for misapplication, 'tis said, of public monies, he cannot be in favor with the cabinet

God bless you, my friend, and believe me, ever yours,

                                D W COXE

Your parents and sisters are all well Kingston's ward is also well He is poor devil, in the vocative, and has totally lost his spirits from perceiving, I believe, that he is really worse than nothing, which he could never persuade himself of till lately

Dan'l Clark, Esq

[Letter No 15]

Offered by Complainant, and filed 23d June, '49

                                J W GURLEY, Com'r.

COOPER'S FERRY, 20th July, 1802

MESSRS CHEW & RELF

Gentlemen—I arrived here last night, and have the pleasure of seeing, although I dare not enter, Philadelphia Our passage was short and pleasant from the Balize, being but 18 days to Newcastle, and the most perfect harmony reigned among the passengers during the whole of the voyage. To avoid a disagreeable quarantine at the Lazaretto, I had the schooner entered at Wilmington, where she will discharge, at the expiration of 15 days from the time of her arrival she will proceed to town, and will from thence return to Orleans, partly laded with freight for our Government, and filled up with such articles as you may find the means of landing with facility Give orders, therefore, how the Captain must proceed, which you may forward to the

Balize, so that he may, or may not, give a manifest of a part or the whole of his cargo, this you must particularly attend to.

Mr Coxe informs me that he has written you fully respecting the enormous and unfortunate frauds committed in the cotton business, which threaten us almost with total ruin The extent of these frauds is to me beyond comprehension, and their consequences personally, independent of the loss of fame and fortune, particularly dreadful I shall be under the necessity of embarking for Europe without seeing my parents, in order to face, and endeavor to avert our ruin, and you may possibly judge how I feel on the occasion Eternal damnation could only surpass the sufferings of mind and body which I must bear, when I thought it was almost out of the power of fortune to put me an inch out of my road I have made up my mind, and will sail this week, before my quarantine is over From my sacrifices you may see what exertions I must make to bring things to their old channel You are in a great measure to blame for too much confidence, and in future, more attention will be looked for from you I have carefully avoided, out of regard for you to hint that I think you blameable, and have inveighed against the scoundrels who imposed on you but you ought to have rendered it impossible for them to have done it to any extent I am fearful, from what I hear, that the whole of our shipments of this year will not bring above 1-2 My voyage is now undertaken to prevent any bills coming back which would bring on a stoppage here If I succeed, I will push matters and business as far as possible and will probably, before I return, travel through England, Holland, France and Spain, to procure you business and, if necessary to augment your credit, will avow the whole of the connexion between Mr Coxe, yourselves and me On your part there is no sacrifice you must not make to prevent any more bills being drawn, you must, on no account whatever, except in virtue of a decree of your tribunals, pay one dollar on account of any balances due to the cotton contractors, as I fear they are all culpable, and you should even try to get as many funds of them as possible into your hands I will re-ship to Orleans from England all the bad cotton—all that in which a fraud has been practised in packing, and will take such steps as will be necessary to procure you redress and damages for your losses, which I am led to fear will amount to a sum I can scarce dare to commit to paper I would gladly sacrifice one hundred thousand to be assured it will be no more What a situation, and how horrible are my feelings! For your own sakes, for my sake, for the sake of our own friends' reputation, and future success and ease in life, make uncommon exertions to push forward remittances, be strictly careful of the quality of the produce you may ship, put off your creditors at home, that **Mr. Coxe** may be kept full handed, and if the ship Thomas has, as I hope, arrived before the port was shut, and you have been able to effect a sale of her cargo to the Intendant, apply its proceeds exclusively to remit to Mr Coxe, if possible, in cash, and you will very, very shortly perceive the good effects of it. If you cannot do this, make no sacrifices on sales for the sake either of your own or our convenience, for small sums. It is impossible to describe what Mr C and myself suffer, and we will never forgive you, should you in a situation ten thousand times less difficult, do anything to liberate yourselves which at the same time would not assist us.

Again I repeat, and enjoin you as you prize my friendship and our responsibility in case of disobedience, to pay no further debts till you hear from me, Le Blanc and his partner excepted, whom I believe to be honest men and whom delay might ruin. You may plead Mr Coxe's orders, and the accounts from England, stand suit and ask for time to bring proof, which you will obtain without difficulty. Although I write you in a state of almost absolute despondency, and fearful of the worst that may happen, yet that Providence which has so often interposed in our favor, may yet secure us from this abyss be not therefore discouraged, but show by active exertions, by increased care and vigilance to put things in order comply with Mr Coxe's directions about returning any bad cotton on the hands of the contractors; examine it ingenuously send forward here all the remittances you can possibly make, in cash, and say nothing which may tend to injure your or our credit, though you may blazon the infamous conduct of those who have so shamefully deceived you. Write me instantly on the receipt of this, give me the fullest information respecting future prospects—how sales go on, whether they exceed or fall short of the estimation we put on the merchandize, whether the debts are now coming in which you must push for almost indiscriminately, and be particularly careful in advising me what steps I must take if I find it advisable to make you further shipments from England whether it can be done in American vessels, or if there will be a necessity of disguising them, as formerly, and if so, what are the regulations to which we will be subject respecting master and mariners if permissions are necessary, forward them, as well as all your letters, under cover, to Messrs Green Send me the *tariff* if the invoices are to be sent to the ambassador, and be careful to enquire if any royal order opposes *receiving* shipments from England, or British merchandize, with all other information that may be useful, and a list of any English goods that may be particularly wanted, or have grown into demand since I left you. Send me, likewise, your power of attorney, with orders to make you shipments, that eve.

rything may be fair and regular If you can do any thing with the Intendant, lose not the opportunity

On the return of the ships to you this winter if prospects are not flattering for further shipments to England, put them under Spanish colors if freights of boxes can be had for Havana there either sell or freight them for England—(say Europe) In the last case the ships must be well provided with sails, cables &c., and whatever is wanted in this way must be provided before they leave Orleans The captains who now command must be retained, and some Spaniard put in, for the form sake You, Richard Relf or B Chew, as you may agree between yourselves, ought to go to Havana, to see that no delay takes place If they can neither be sold nor freighted the first I should like best you must try to fall on some other plan—the molasses one perhaps, according to the price then coming on a sale of 32 cents here including 5 cents duty Perhaps freights might be had to and from Campeachy or Vera Cruz to Havana during the winter, until the new crops come in when vessels will be indispensably wanted in short do the best you can We have heard that vessels carrying horses are admitted in o Havana from the U S if this can be made certain, Mr Cox would put a few on board the New York when she returns here and send her there for sale, and order the proceeds forwarded to you make immediate inquiry, and advise him the result of it

A Mr William Bell is now loading a schooner called the Triton, Capt ———, to your address he puts in her part of a cargo which she brought from France, and will probably till up with such other articles as I may point out I have told him the risk there is of the port being shut but have assured him, that even in this case, you will find means of having the dry goods, if not even the wines and brandy, *landed at Natchez, as the nankeen and silks per the Eliza with very little costs* I wish you to serve him with all your heart and soul, as he is a worthy good man I have informed him that good sales are not to be made for cash but I wish you may have it in your power to procure a cargo for his vessel, such as he may offer, even if you do not sell immediately Should he wish his vessel sold, or put under Spanish colors, have it effected if possible, and if this business succeeds you will probably have many others in the same way The plaster of Paris that will go in the Eliza, is for Mons Dujameau he is to pay invoice cost, and ten dollars a ton freight, or half a sol per lb You may land it for ballast stores, as it will not be known for any thing else to the people of Orleans, and let Dujameau keep the matter to himself, till it is disposed of The state of things will not for the present admit of the building on the rope-walk therefore you can get an extraordinary price for the bricks there from the planters Sell them, and do not forget to make Faurie pay you for, or return, the 5000 to 6000 lent him I shall advise Mr Coxe to send you all Messrs Green's and Mr Barclay's late letters, as I believe they are more explicit respecting cotton than those to you The reputation of that of your country, and the mark D W C in particular is demanded, and I advise your immediately changing it, and substituting that of G B & Co, in its place, without the least delay, mortifying as this circumstance must be, you must adopt it and mention the reason of it in N Orleans. As sundry payments will be daily coming round here, for God's sake ship what money you can, independent of any remittances you make to England by the Creole and Thomas or to Mr Coxe, by the Fame and Sophia I count a great deal on the sale of the Thomas cargo, God grant I may not be disappointed do not appropriate any part of it or any other money you can procure, to any thing else than remitting here your own wants and embarrassments ought and must be second day considerations to you

I will write you again to go by the Eliza, which vessel, you may inform Mr Ferrielle, will be sent out to be delivered him agreeable to the terms he authorized me to propose for her, and I now mention it, that he may be prepared She will be hove down in Philadelphia at Mr Coxe's expense, and will be delivered him in better order than when she left New Orleans On this subject I will write him in a day or two, but in the meantime give him this information

I remain, very sincerely, yours,

[per mail]   Signed,   DANIEL CLARK

P. S I have written you on such paper as I could procure. Keep this from the eyes of your clerks.

Mention my intention of re-shipping sample bags of the bad cotton, with certificates of the quantity there may be of a similar kind Write a letter of directions to the captain of Mr Belt's schooner, respecting his manifest, how he is to make it out, &c, whether any ought or not to be made out if he reports for deposit. I will give directions either not to deposit the valuable trunks, or report them for deposit

[Letter No 9]

Offered by complainant, and filed 23d June, 1849

J W GURLEY, Commissioner

(Partly in handwriting of late D. Clark.)

PHILADELPHIA, 30th March, 1802.

Messrs. CHEW & RELF—

Gentlemen On looking over the accounts settled at the Havana by Mr Martin, I find I have credit for the sum of $594 21-2 received of John Mapothers of Merida This, I believe was in consequence of an order on him drawn by Charles McKiernan, of Natchez in favor of my agent Mr Daniel Clark, and I request you will take immediate measures to pay this sum to McKiernan, or his agents I shall by next post advise McKiernan that the sum has been received and direct him to apply to you for it By advices from London to 6th ult I find that the Ohio had arrived in Liverpool and discharged her cargo, and would return to your port I flatter myself she is by this time far advanced on her return and will meet with but little delay with you

Mr Barclay in his letters mentions that some of the bales, by the Mars and Washington were bad—full of seeds, &c I suspect them to have been Girods In future you would do well to mark in your cotton book the numbers as the bales are shipped, that you may have an opportunity of knowing who practices fraud, and expose him for it

April 1st—I have received letters from Mr Green to the 11th Feb y The Ohio had arrived, was discharged, and would sail on or about the 20th He complains bitterly of the frauds practised in the cotton which has almost ruined its reputation Pay particular attention to this in future and as I just before directed keep such a check on the marks and numbers you receive, compared with those shipped that, on information you may trace the roguery to its source On this subject, I will write to Green

Let me know if you have purchased any and what quantity of cotton below 25c since 1st November last what premium you have received, and how get on bills for my government you may either give me information in detail, by stating what your cotton cost by each parcel, or averaging the whole, and the same with respect to the premiums on bills by sending a list of those drawn, with the premium on each, or averaging the whole, till the time you write

By the annexed price current you will find that foreign cotton may be shipped in American bottoms to England avail yourselves of this knowledge, and purchase it if low, in preference

Continue to send me sketches of sales, and let me know what are the regulations likely to be adopted, that I may be among the first to make you shipments, and arrangements for a constant supply

Our friend Hackley, as I before wrote you, has resumed his business, with undiminished reputation, to the general satisfaction of his friends

The cotton, by the Sophia, turns out in the worst possible order—bags torn, a great part rotten, and the Captain, in excuse, alleges that it was a parcel which the captain of the New York refused, and beside that, it was sent down, on a rainy day   I must positively order that, in future, no bad bale be shipped, as the loss by such negligence is incalculable.

Your letter, by post of 13th Feb'y has got to hand, and its contents are noted   I wish it had been in your power to purchase largely, when cotton was low   I did all that it was in my power to do, by ordering the remittances from Jamaica and, until you forward invoices of the Mars and Washington when I can draw on their cargoes it will not be possible for me to forward any money to you, you must therefore do the best you can, and give bills on me, as opportunities offer of disposing of them

Should the port be shut you must use your influence with the intendant to give you leave to load the vessels you may have consigned to you so as to get all the produce you have on hand shipped   I have it now in contemplation to send you back the Sophia, with a large parcel of China and India goods, in hopes she will arrive a little before importations from hence are prevented, and as these things are cheap here, and can not be imported on such advantageous terms from other places I am in hopes that they may answer, and serve you as a fund, in the fall of this year   For fear the port should be shut when the brig arrives, I will have the major part of these articles put up in large, tight casks, that if you are forced to enter them for deposit, you may afterwards take out the contents and if necessary, supply the place of it with earthenware, which will always sell at Natchez   In this case, I recommend to you if there is any strictness observed, to take Christovals or Andres Fernandez' stores, which have back doors to them, the keys of which you must get into your possession, and of which you know by experience the use that a friend of ours was accustomed to make.

Molasses and sugar are a drug   I can get for that by the Sophia but 38 cents per gallon and shall lose freight duty, insurance, and shipping charges   I recommend to you to ship no more, unless you can get it on board at 25 cts per gallon, and sugar not to exceed 5 cts per lb

Mr Wm Conway had a tract of 20 or 24 acres of land, front, for sale, at the Houmas, which I think he offered to General Adair, for $2000   I wish you would purchase it for me, at the price he offered it at to Adair, or even something more, as I suppose lands have risen taking care to make some arrangement with him to keep up the levee, for two or three years, for a certain sum annually, and paying attention to have the whole depth, as far as the land extends, either to Galvez Town or the lakes.   He wanted this sum to pay a debt to Joyce, and I believe you will be able to manage the business with Norwood so as to get a credit, on paying him the interest for the stipulated sum Let me hear from you, immediately, on this subject, as I wish to advise the relative for whom I buy it, who is desirous of going to settle in that country

I remain dear friend yours,

DAN WM COXE

New York 17th August, 1802

Messrs CHEW & RELF—

Gentlemen I embark to-morrow in the ship Lydia, for Greenock, and according as I find matters in England will either stay there some time or return immediately to your country Great exertions will be necessary on your part to enable Mr Coxe to support his credit, and I earnestly entreat you will push remittances as fast as you can to enable him to make good his engagements You must depend for some time on your sales at home without drawing until the sale of our cotton in England is known The Genl Washington is arrived in Liverpool, and on the quality of her cargo and that of the Mars and New York, our fate depends I recommend to you to lose no opportunity, but on the contrary search for them to sell our real property and shipping, when you cannot keep them going If you could, at the return of the Mars and Washington, purchase cargoes for them at such prices as Mr Coxe will recommend, I would advise their being kept employed provided you can get credit, but it will not do to load them, and draw on Mr Coxe for the amount You must by all means, on this urgent occasion, push your credit to the utmost, and endeavor to get long credits yourselves so as to pay them, if possible, hereafter with the proceeds of the sale of your shipping or real property In short it behooves you to do all that mortals can to relieve yourselves and friends I am glad to hear the Thomas has arrived, and hope that you will send her and the Creole off with as little delay as possible You have done well to inspect the cotton rigorously had it been done before we should have had no embarrassments A thousand things occur which I have not time to mention Your letters by the Despatch I have received Push indiscriminately all who owe, buy as much as you can on long credits, and hasten on remittances you can have no idea of the necessity we are in for them Remember me kindly to all friends

Yours sincerely

DANIEL CLARK

P S—There are 3 French frigates now here, with about 900 negroes on board, which, under pretext of embarking at Guadeloupe, to take possession of one of the ceded Islands, they carried off, and wished to sell to the Spaniards at Carthagena They were ordered away from thence, and have come on here, with the gang, in great distress, it is said, for provisions. They have been refused permission to land any of the negroes here, and God only knows what they will do with them. Your Government had better be on its guard against them. We have nothing new on the subject of the cession to France; every report has its moment of belief. A vessel from Cadiz brings advice that the Emperor of Morocco has declared war against us, and that two of our merchantmen have been taken by the Tripolitans.

Remember me to Mons'r Castillan and Mons'r La Croix, and inform them that my sudden departure for Europe prevents my receiving answers to my letters on the business they recommended me to transact for them. Read this part of my letter to them, that they may know literally what I have said respecting their affair.

Take the first opportunity of remitting to Usher, of Baltimore, the balance of his account; he has twice written to me on the subject.

PHILADELPHIA, August 20.

The Eliza will sail in a week, when I will write you particularly. All your bills will be paid, but draw no more, unless to complete cargoes, and for very trifling sums. I am sacrificing my credit to save yours, and hope, at least, to keep you clear of difficulty.   D. W. C.

[Letter No. 18.]
Offered by complainants and filed 23d June, 1849
J. W. GURLEY, Commissioner

PHILADELPHIA, Nov. 18th, 1803.

My Dear Friend —I yesterday received your letters of 8th and 12th Oct., with a map of the Ouachita land. I am happy to find that you were lending your attention to the subject of good land, and note your different answers to my queries.

I fully agree with you in opinion, ' that no part of the gov't of Baton Rouge, *alias* W. *Florida*, has been ceded to France by Spain, and that if negociation takes place (which it actually has) between the U. S. and Spain for it, all the acts of the Governor must be valid."

I now briefly give you my view of the subject from my own investigation.

" Spain promises to cede to France, after the entire execution of the conditions relative to the Duke of Porsue, the province of Louisiana, with the same extent it *now has* in the hands of Spain, and that it had when France possessed it, and such as it should be after the treaties *subsequently* entered into between Spain and *other states.*" And 1st, its notorious that Louisiana, as *now possessed* by Spain, does not comprise West Florida 2d. **By** a clear inference from, and interpretation of the words ' *as when France possessed it*," they are merely part of an explanatory clause, which receives its final and complete elucidation from the *last* part of the sentence, viz *and such as it should be after the treaties subsequently entered into between Spain and other States*." Here let us enquire what are the *treaties*, and what the *States* here alluded to, which define what should constitute the remaining or future territory of Louisiana, seeing that some part of it had by these treaties been lopped off, and ceded to other powers. The answer is clear and unequivocal that these treaties are 1st., that very treaty of 1763, to which, France and Spain are both parties, and which cedes to Great Britain all the country east and south east of the Mississippi 2d. The treaty of 1783, by which England recedes to Spain or acknowledges her right by conquest of the *two Floridas* 3d. The treaty of San Lorenzo in 1795 by which the southern boundary of the United States is defined. Louisiana *is*, therefore, and *should be*, to use the words of the treaty, the country *west* of the Mississippi including the island of N Orleans. The Prince of Peace, when applied to by Mr Pinckney, at the request of Messrs. Monroe & Livingston, to know whether the Court of Spain did not acknowledge the claim of France to W. Florida, replied pettishly, "You may as well ask me if my shirt is yours," and treated the question with contempt and anger

I am, for my own part, quite easy as to the validity of our Baton Rouge grant, and am convinced that they will all be confirmed, even should the country become ours by negotiation, which I fully expect, but I have no fears of the West Bank being foolishly given up by the U S though I rather imagine that the part of Louisiana, *far west* of the river Mississippi, will be the boon we shall offer, and give in exchange for the Floridas. I should, therefore, advise your buying 50,000 acres more of the Baton Rouge good land, if well situated, as regards N O and navigation, even if you have to pay a small advance on the former price. As to the remonstrance by the Spanish Minister against the U S taking possession of Louisiana, and of which so much has been said in the public prints, I have no doubt that the leading point in that remonstrance is respecting the boundaries and the unfounded claim made by France and the U. S to W Florida. It may also be that the non-fulfillment of the engagement of France to Spain forms another ground of her opposition, and this, I rather believe, from the tricky character of the French, and the peculiar phraseology of the treaty, which is only a *promise* by Spain to cede, if certain conditions are performed

49*

If the U. S have an unsound title to Louisiana, 'tis the more favorable to our grant, as in that case we are safe on *two* grounds

I do not believe our Government will prohibit or discourage the importation of slaves into Louisiana at all events, they will be brought in as in South Carolina, where in spite of the prohibitory state-laws, they are landed off Charleston Bar by ship loads   I, therefore, strongly advise your immediately writing Green & W., to contract with some Guinea house, for the delivery of a cargo or two of the proper kind, at N O or in the river below, restricting them to such prices as can be afforded If you are averse to appearing in the business you   it under the cloak of C & Relf, writing Green confidentially to comply with C & R 's orders   I strongly advise this measure, as the one best calculated to ensure success to our plan of buying lands and cultivating a part, to increase the value of the remainder   It is a necessary branch of the speculation and the mode I suggest is the easiest safest, and will prevent (what you seem to fear) any odium attaching to it, as it will be the act of others and done in foreign vessels   The same ships which brought them could be loaded with cotton for Liverpool, and the proceeds applied by G & W, to pay for the slaves

You might safely venture to order 1000 to be sent, and that done, our fortunes would be made and we might quit trade forever   I will endeavor to send you the German or Swiss tradesmen you mention for your plantation   On the other points of your letter, I will write you more at large per next mail   Enclosed you have part of Randolph s

PHILADELPHIA, 29th March, 1802

MESSRS CHEW & RELF—

Gentlemen —I received yesterday afternoon the letters which you wrote to me, individually, respecting my family, and most sincerely thank you for your kindness and attention to them, which I have always anticipated and firmly relied on   I would have expressed my thanks to each of you separately, but am pressed for time, as the vessel by which this goes is on the point of departure, and have now only to mention that I confide in you to see the family accommodated with a passage to this place as soon after the 10th of April is past, as possibly you can procure one and to supply them with every thing necessary for their voyage   If you can procure a freight for the Fame home, it would be a good opportunity if not, avail yourselves of the best you can for this place or in defect of one for this city, to New York or Baltimore   My hopes and dependence are placed on you in this particular, and I will, therefore, say nothing more to you on the subject—you know how dear these objects must be to me. Inform Debuys that I have received his letter, and will answer immediately. Thank in the most expressive manner all such of my friends and acquaintances as show attention to my parents, and mention their names to me that I may acknowledge myself the obligation they lay me under. Your friend, Mr Coxe went out of town yesterday; he will be back in two or three days. In the meantime his head clerk writes to you, who is possessed of the same information with Mr C himself, on the subjects treated of.

I remain with esteem gentlemen your sincere friend,

DANIEL CLARK

Messrs Chew & Relf

Afidt of Gen Gaines filed March 18 1849

D N HENNEN, D'y Clerk

GAINES & WIFE
vs
CHEW & RELF

To the Honorable the Judges of the Circuit Court, Ninth Circuit, and Eastern District of Louisiana

Ed P Gaines one of the plaintiffs in the above mentioned cause, being duly sworn makes oath that the Reverend Dr Power, of the city of New York, is a material witness on the part of the plaintiffs in the above entitled cause; that the said Dr Power resides in the city of New York; that deponent fears that unless a commission should issue to take the deposition of the aforesaid witness, that the said plaintiff will be deprived of the advantage that they expect from the testimony of the aforesaid witness

EDMUND P GAINES,

Sworn to and subscribed before me this 18th March, 1840

F DE WINT, D'y Clerk

DEFENDANTS

Offered by defendants, and filed this 23d day of June, 1849.

J. W. GURLEY *Comm'r*

Record or Document D

Ne varietur (Signed)   W. F. DUPLESSIS

Register of Wills

To the honorable the Judge of the Court of Probates, in and for the City and Parish of New Orleans, State of Louisiana

The petition of Richard Relf and Beverly Chew, both residing in New Orleans, and here appearing in their capacity of testamentary executors of the estate of Daniel Clark, Esquire, whose succession is open in your honorable court, respectfully sheweth:

That your petitioners here tender to your honor their accounts of their administration of the said estate, and pray the usual order of publication, of the filing of the same, and after all due and legal proceedings thereon that the same be homologated, and they fully and finally discharged in the premises

The petitioners state, that the counsel heretofore appointed by this court to represent the absent heir of this estate hath departed this life, and that the said heir, the mother of said Daniel Clark, hath herself died, leaving heirs who succeed to her rights, two of whom, namely Caroline Barnes and Sarah T. Campbell, are now represented by C. Roselius Esq, one of the attorneys and counsellors of this court, and the other persons, Mrs Green, of Liverpool, England, and Mrs O'Bearn ——, Ireland, believed to be joint heirs of the said estate, have heretofore, through their agents conferred and have been represented by the present attorney of your petitioners, who therefore pray the court now to appoint another attorney to represent all the absent heirs of this estate

The petitioners deemed it an act of justice to themselves and respectful to this honorable court, to state in this petition, that the same may appear at all times of record the reasons which have hitherto and up to the present date influenced them in not complying with the requests of the law to exhibit their accounts as executors of said Daniel Clark and why a large amount of property in which said Clark was interested, was not included in the inventory of this estate, taken shortly after his decease

The petitioners annex to their petition a copy of their articles of co-partnership with said Clark, and acting under the advice of counsel at the time, and with the assent of the learned and respectable attorney appointed by this court, to represent the mother, the only heir of said Daniel Clark the partnership property of the firm of petitioners, and said Clark was excluded from the inventory of the private estate of said Daniel Clark and that alone inventoried, which appeared to belong to said, individually, of all which the petitioners now render a strict account and annex thereto a further account of the administration and disposition made of all the partnership property in which said Clark and petitioners were jointly interested say each for one part

2 The petitioners further represent as an additional reason for not presenting to this honorable court their accounts as executors of said Daniel Clark, that immediately after his death they received (the same being on file in this honorable court) a power of attorney from the mother and only heir of said Clark and that under the same, they continued to administer said estate to account to her up to the period of her death and subsequently thereto to account to and with her testamentary executor and heirs, from whom petitioners annex to this petition letters confirmatory of their accounts and proceedings up to the 31st December 1827, and from that date, the transactions have been inconsiderable as shown by the accounts hereto annexed

3 The petitioners further represent as another motive of delay in settling this estate, the pending of numerous suits against it, and the expectation which they indulged in common with many other citizens of the United States that a favorable action of Congress would ——— the titles to land in that part of Louisiana, called Florida, in which there are seventy thousand arpents, in one-third of which this estate is interested but no decision thereon hath yet been had notwithstanding repeated and unremitted applications to every department of the government of the United States

The petitioners have endeavored to preserve the rights of this estate to such interest in said lands as belong to the estate, by paying whenever presented all lawful demands for taxes and the same account the petitioners give of sundry parcels of lots of land in the State of Missouri in which the said Daniel Clarke was interested In these reasons the petitioners found their justification from all imputations of disregard either of their duty to the creditors and heirs of this estate or of proper respect for the authority of this court   Signed   RICHARD RELF,
BEVERLY CHEW

Petition filed 27th August 1838   *Executors, etc*
Order of Court thereon

Let public notice be given to the creditors of this estate, and to all others herein interested, to show cause within ten days from public notification, why the within account should not be approved and homologated, and the funds distributed accordingly   It is further ordered, that A. Hoa Esquire, be appointed to represent the absent heirs of the deceased

Signed   J BERMUDEZ, *Judge*
New Orleans, 27th August, 1838
[REC LXXV J T 1841]—53

*Accounts of the administration of the Estate of Daniel Clark, deceased,
by Richard Relf and Beverly Chew, testamentary executors*

A

*Daniel Clark's Private Estate distinct from his estate in co partnership with
Chew and Relf*

No	Funeral Charges,		
Paid 1	Church fees, per bill	- -	171 75
2	Ant Fernandez for funeral hangings	-	50 00
3	L Fourcand, for invitation cards and distributing	-	4 00
4	Sexton's bill	- - -	17 50
5	Caleb Stringer, for a coffin	-	100 00
6	Rob Mitchell hearse hire	- -	10 00
7	P Durell, for wax Candles	- -	93 75
8	V Durel, ame, bill for crape gloves, etc	-	505 00
9	Gurlut Guillot for erecting a tomb	-	100 00
10	Proper Fox, for a marble table engraved	-	200 00
11	T Turpin for refreshment furnished	-	116 50
12	Carriage hire	- - -	77 00
13	Clothes furnished his slaves in attendance	-	94 40
			1,581 00
Paid 14	Dr Lemonier, of his account as family physician for the years 1812 and 1813, including attendance on slaves employed at the canal	-	800 00
15	F Grandchamps apothecary bill	- -	269 25
16	Dr Dow, consultation fee	- -	18 00
17	Dr Montegut ditto	- -	25 00
18	Dr Harmann ditto	- -	36 00
19	Judge for affixing and raising seal	-	8 00
20	Fran Morales keeper of the seals	-	6 00
21	Moreau Laslet, counsel for absent heir	-	300 00
	Prosper Prieur and Blondeau, appraisers	-	82 00
22	Register of wills, commission on sale	-	1221 12
			2,76 1
	Personal Debts paid as follows		
24	To his gardener	- - -	97 00
25	ditto	- -	6 12
26	Nagel Tailor	- - -	344 00
27	ditto	- -	31 12
28	V LeBriton	- -	38 75
29	Pourre Goubur	- -	34 00
30	Joseph Martin	- -	26 75
31	Sugnauret -	- -	46 50
32	Chauvaux -	- -	39 12
33	Aime Pugnegery	- -	191 00
34	Bujac and David	- -	96 00
35	Reynald and Leuy	- -	23 81
36	Gube and Seaton	- -	19 18
37	D Rouguette	- -	92 37
38	Mrs. Zacharie	- -	17 00
39	Abram Mace	- -	35 50
40	Lewis Legerne	- -	1,339 00
41	Lewis Lere	- -	568 94
42	M Jutese -	- -	6 50
43	Breton Clark	- -	22 81
44	F Aime -	- -	27 00
45	Billegolly	- -	238 00
46	T Hagan	- - -	13 00
	Amount carried forward ———	3 29 4	4 346 3

A —Continued

No					
	Daniel Clark's private estate continued				4,346 37
	Personal debts continued and amount brt forward			3295 17	
Paid 47				11 00	
48				8 50	
49				9 25	
50				8 50	
51	Maspero	-		22 00	
52	John Moury	-		16 00	
53				36 87	
54	P K Wagner	-	-	93 50	
55	Lasseman	-		25 00	
56	Chantrelle	-		73 00	
57	Barbarin	-		8 00	
58	Sam Parton	-	-	5 25	
59	His barber	-		8 00	
A 59	Samuel Rey of Philadelphia			284 00	593 87
					3 889 34

Contract with New Orleans Navigation Company
Charges digging the canal from the time of Mr
Clark's death until the transfer of the contract to
Dussau De la Croix

Paid 60	Mr —— the superintendent for balance of accounts settled the 31st December 1813	-	1827 57	
61	Mon Auguste for fresh meat	-	-	321 94	
62	Mon Ferrand do	-	-	36 50	
63	F Avine 30 pair blankets	-		361 00	
64	H N Palfrey for 140 gallons whiskey	-	-	105 00	
65	James Bore, for 100 barrels corn	-		93 75	
66	Two pieces negro cloth	-		100 00	
67	Saulet for grinding corn			63 50	
68	for lumber	-		55 75	
69	for 3 ml bricks	-		36 00	
70	for mason work	-		22 25	
71	for lumber	-	-	20 25	
72	Marie Rose, for nursing sick negroes	-		24 00	
A 73	J B Jourdam, amount due him for negroes wages			247 00	
73	V Rabassa do do do			122 00	
74	Joseph Curtinco do do do	-		55 20	
75	Arm Dupresseur do co do			29 41	
76	Lafitte do do do			16 96	
77	Do do do do	-		14 40	
78	Mon Blache do do do			8 93	
79	Archer do do do	-		8 46	
80	Advertising	-		8 00	
82	Charles Murle & Co for supply	-		713 29	
	I L Turner for advice on contract	-		100 00	
	Dussau De la Croix, allowance made him for assuming the fulfillment of the contract			5038 00	
					9 511 16

Debts on the Inheritance of Thos Williams Estate

85	Y Lyman Harding, fees attending Mior's suit	-	500 00	
86	Edward Livingston		1418 00	
86	To F L Turner fees in suits with Mino	-	700 00	
87	Edward Turner ditto	-	-	209 62	
88	Costs in suit at Natchez	-	227 62	
89	Richard King, in satisfaction of a mortgage on Ridge's plantation		800 00	
90			398 00	
91	Recording paper on suit with Mino		8 12	
				4 256 36

No	Debts in relation to the Cannes Brule Estate		
92	To Steven Henderson, D Clark s notes given in payment of this estate	80000	00	
	Israel Trask, for amount of a mortgage held by him assumed by D Clark - -	10000	00	
	Interest due thereon - -	1000	00	
	Ditto, paid Stephen Henderson on different pay ments of sale to the Fortiers - -	5911	00	
93	Advertising sale	232	00	
94	S Henderson, for sugar furnished -	53	00	
95	Taxes	338	24	
96	Pasturage of cattle during inundation -	140	00	
97	Duncan & N Call, ditto - -	168	00	
98	St Armand, for plant cane	280	00	
99	Samuel Elkin, for corn - - -	822	00	
100	Bartlett Cox, for pork	36	00	
101	Doctor Glavered, for attendance -	100	00	
102	S Hughes, for apprehending a run away slave -	35	50	
103	S Danimor do do	69	00	
104	Baron Boisfontaine salary as overseer and expense -	1146	00	
105	Charles Marty & Co for supply -	685	05	
				131,015 79

Incidental charges		
Provision for slaves - - -	39	75	
Nurses drugs and interments - -	19	75	
Notarial fees and recorder of mortgages -	23	75	
Cartage and postage - -	19	37	
Tax on house in suburb St Mary - -	7	37	
F L Turner, professional services -	120	00	
Edward Turner do - -	413	32	
			643 31
			6060 63

To amount remitted to Mrs Mary Clark, his mother			
To allowance to partnership concerns, stipulated in the articles of agreement			14,000 00
To executor s commissions on $176,442 37 a ppll			4 411 05
By sales at auction by the Register of Wills			178,136 00
Household furniture - - -	793	00	
Library - - - -	1077	75	
Flowers - - - -	309	87	
Cattle received from the Cannes Brule estate -	1421	75	3,602 37
Sale by ditto to Mr C Fortier of the Cannes Brule estate and slaves			120,000 00
To Ed Macarty, 5 slaves, Peggy, Jenny, Reefe, Mary and William	1350	00	
M and C Fortier, 7 ditto Jack, Nan, Nerissa, Solomon, Sarah, William Jenny, Rose and son Bob, Fanny with her three children, Mayer, Nelson and Mary Winny with her three children, Ebe, Becky and Maria	5225	00	
F Labarre, 2 slaves Eliza, and child William -	690	00	
F Dupuis, 3 slaves, Hannah, Bird and Patty -	1260	00	
Mons Deynoul, 1 slave, Polly - -	460	00	
S Dufossat, 1 slave, Fanny - -	500	00	
C Avart, 4 slaves, Milly, Nancy, Keyley and Tom	1400	00	
C Bonnefoi, 1 slave, Nancy - -	415	00	
L M Sagory, 2 slaves, Waldrout and Charlotte -	800	00	
Mad Morant, 2 do Kitty and child Tom -	495	00	
Henry Elkins, 1 slave, old Richard -	260	00	
Mons Nachace, 2 slaves, Dinah and James -	500	00	

A —Continued

Desdunes fils, 1 slave, P che' - 41 00
I ——— 1 slave, Sack - 39 00
N z Tri au t slaves Ldie and two children Menny
Lucy Laurace Lill nd Nelly - 1705 00
N Forte 3 slaves, J us in fact two childr Henriette
and Rev - 850 00
Mons De i n, 1 slave Tilly - 39 00
Mon S i n 2 slaves Arthur and Rhob t - 839 00
Mon Fal r fils, 2 slaves Sally nd Betty - 83 00
Mons Verbes 3 slaves Ruby, B me n Anne - 145 00
Thomas Beale 1 slave Picture' - 32 00
Camille brule 1 slave P ggy - 36 00
Joseph 1 slave Dand - 315 00
La Barre, 1 slave, Pat os - 350 00
——— 21510 00

At Pr t S
Io Berru n fils 2 slaves ooa Sec - 200 00
N N 1 s c Bett - 150 00
M lobertson 1 slave' - 100 00
Jon McDonough 9 slaves Anthony Tiley Brown, James
Davis, Doctor D m Tu y t m cu crippled - 900 00
By set to Dusau D u Croix of 12 slaves Merot Phoebe ——— 1450 00
Hope Tom Turkey Joan Isadore Dan Levin John
Winny Esther Jos Mc C t Hamie Phil Betsy Mou-
ce Pine Mason Cambridge Tilly Jonn, Julien,
Fanny Esther P h Lucy R dolph Ned Fred
so Jack Jeremy bru H n Cox Sal Crin S in
Auguste Sp ncei Thomas Doriana Smith Little Nor
ny Judith, Dav In Turkey Victoire Joe Davis
Jonn, Hanson War o Andr in five orph n chadren,
Squire Tom Dav Arn and C rrel estimate in in
ventory - 21050 00
Abiten n mace thereon - 2922 00
——— 18128 00
By sale to B Livingston of a planta t on near Natchez, known
as the Ridge Plantation - 7500 00
By sale of a house and in Natchez to Joseph
received payment in cash - 1000 00
And o house in suburb S Mary afterward sold
to mary L Chauvin for rent - 2000 00
Received therefor - 333 00
Interest received of Mr I Chauvin - 60 67
——— 3393 67
By sale to Dassuau De l Croix of utensils in use at the can il 1000 00
By sale of a horse to Lew L ees n - 130 00
By sale of shrubbery - 39 00
By sale of a tract of land in the State of Mississippi to Mr
Hart with interest - 6721 01

Amount of assets 1833615
Do of debt 178137 01

Balance to the credit of Dan l Clark's private estate 8 239 01

B

Account of the liquidation of the Estate of Dani'l Clark, in partner-ship with Chew and Relf

	Bills payable to his accommodation notes at the Louisiana Bank						
1	A note of the 24th June 1813 to the order of W Donalson					2600 00	
2	Do	29th do	do	do	Chew & Relf	1200 00	
3	Do	2d July,	do	do	ditto	1400 00	
4	Do	20th do	do	do	W Donalson	1700 00	
5	Do	23d do	do	do	ditto	1500 00	
6	Do	6th Aug	do	do	ditto	700 00	
7	Do	10th do	do	do	James Pitot	1200 00	
8	Do	13th do	do	do	W Donalson	1500 00	$11 800 00
9	To his accommodation notes discounted at Planters Bank						
10	A note of the 21st June 1813 endorsed by J Pitot					500 00	
11	Do	3d July	do	do		2400 00	
12	Do	14th do	do	do	by J Pitot & Delacroix	1100 00	
13	Do	17th do	do	do		1500 00	
14	Do	24th do	do	do by W Donalson		440 00	
	Do	31st do	do	do	do	1100 00	7040 00
15	To his accommodation note discounted at Bank of Orleans						
16	A note of the 12th July, 1813 endorsed by J Pitot					800 00	
17	Do	5th do	do	do by W Donalson		250 00	
18	Do	19th do	do	do	do	1000 00	
19	Do	22d do	do	do	do	250 00	$2,300 00
20	His note of the 13th June, 1813 to Harrod & Ogden						875 31
21	Do	24th do	do	to Chew & Relf pd J Oliver			1000 00
22	Do	25th do	do	to Chew & Relf, pd E Sarrot			1000 00
23	Do	23rd July	do	to Chew & Relf pd ditto			1000 00
24	Do	6th Aug	do	to T Pitot paid do			1000 00
25	Do	5th July	do	to A R Hillery			470 00
26	Do	12th Aug 1812 to Dejan, cadet					560 00
27	Do	16th Jany, 1813 to	ditto				246 00
28	Do	12th Mar 1811, to Polidore a f m ot c					661 00
29	Do	6th Aug, 1813, endorsed by J Pitot & C & R paid L Lanoux					1000 00
30	Do	24th July	do	endorsed by C & R paid Labarre			1500 00
31	Do	27th do	do	to S Henderson paid V Vatte & Co			1000 00
31	Do	do	do	do			2000 00
32 33	Two notes of the 1st April, 1813 to E Tricou & Fils for $952 50 each						1905 00
34	His note 16th January, 1813 to	do					1200 00
35	Do	1st Febry	do	to L M Sagory			2346 52
36	Do	do	do	do			2456 51

B —Continued

37	To his note 11th March 1813 to J M Story	$730 00
38	} Three notes of the 11th Decr 1815 and by	
39	Chew and Relf paid Mr and	6000 00
40	} $2000 cts	
41	His note of the 9th June 1813 to L w s Tecesac	680 00
42	Do do do	600 00
43	Do 6th Dec 1813 to C Bere Andry	2100 00
44	Do 19th May 1813 to Rochele & Sheff	515 00
45	Harrod and Ogden note of 3rd March 1813, favor of H Munroe for his account	1000 00
46	Dussuau De La Croix note of the 6th July 1813, discounted at the Louisiana Bank for his use	2500 00
47	Do do of the 16th June 1813 co	300 00
		2800 00
48	His note to Dussuau De La Croix 11th Jan 1812	900 00
49	Samuel Elkins note of lent him	2500 00
50	} His three notes of the 15th January, 1812 to	
51	pay b on the 1st Feb 1813 1814	
52	} and 1815 of $5000	15000 00

Debts bearing mortgages.

	To Reynaud and Peytavin, balance due them on purchase of point Houm s estate recon veyed by Mr Clark to Wade Hampton with interest to 15th January 1817	37836 37
	William Simpson mortgage on bayou hous	14500 00
	Mad Boisfontaine secured by mortgage on slaves	13410 00
	Heirs of T B Macarty, mortgage on a tract of land in Attakapas	3500 00
	T B Dejan mortgage on Gentilly land	915 00
		71418 37

Debts to sundry individuals.

53	To W D Montgomery	941 87	
54	Samuel Elkins	3454 50	
55	To C de Armas	72 50	
56	J J Claiborne	150 00	
57	Fort Clement and Co	50 50	
58	act A L n an Harding	955 00	
86	John H Johnson	58 50	
87	Charles Olivier	651 75	
88	Patrick Murrel	33 00	
89	Dussuau De La Croix	784 62	
90	Heir Michell Cornelius	1529 17	
91	Thomas Cornelius	700 00	
92	M Popuius	23 62	
93	Porter and Depeyster	950 18	
94	Edward Turner	328 12	
95	Philip and Hermann	131 87	
96	S Woodward	97 65	
97	P Pecechus	15 00	
98	Jesse s n o to i	20 00	
104	act J Baron Boston	20 25	
99	Charles M	35 00	
100	Joseph Masse	150 00	
101	Harrod and Ogden	500 00	
102	J B Dejan	700 00	
	Moses Horn	6 00	
	J J Turner	809 81	13577 37

The estate of T B Curtinon on a judgment		1831 68
Amount paid on judgment in favor of Cath r e		
N vare in part of debt due James Fet		
cuer Esq		2000 00
Amount due D n d & Cox Price on o		
contract as agreed reimbursed D)		
Gar paid and put in price on obi ...		
and the ... limits	$15 000 0	
Bonds that were already due	$24 750 00	
Less payment made on account	19 797 54	4 952 46	154 952 16
Amount refunded Wade Hampton for recession of		
sale of Ouachit lands	-	21 790 37
		$443 259 49

By cash in bank at his death in the Louisiana bank		54 00
Planters		50 00
Bank of Orleans		60 00
In the hands of Chew and Relf arising from sums re		
ceived or and paid for them whilst sick		11 00	$500 00

Bills receivable collected

C Bonnefous note -	250 00
R Munsons	1 520 00
Wade Hampton	1 368 00
W Witherspoo	800 00
Lev Wells -	800 00
S B D vs	230 00
B Lyon	1037 57
M Amaux	100 00
Richard Duval	50 00
Lane le	1 00
R Dunlaps -	184 75
Desons	14 00
Sun Flower	5 75
Baron Boisfontaine	250 00
A Parro	250 00	30 956

Bonds and Mortgages

Louis Decrnet to Z Cavalier	11 000 00
Lewis and Tarner	12 215 88
Harry Hunt -	1 700 00
D v Urquhar and Williams	1000 00
Col Hampton	734 12
C M Xen -	450 00
Joseph Le Blanc	2931 31	62 670 3

Col treu of the Louisiana Bank special deposite	500 00
O Mons Le Burr balance of account	175 50
W Deacon	25 00
Jam s Gray - -	52 32
C Dean	50 00
George Hart - -	734 00
Rob Cochran -	1035 68
Henry Turner	255 66
Pierre Collson	28 00
John Watkins	2927 75

B —Continued

John L...d	-	421 00
W de Hampton	-	255 02
J B Nevill		557 7
Hugh Brown		2 03s
John Louque		801 37
		5443 11

B produce of sale of Real Estate

A tract of land in Ouachita known as the Cypress swamp to N Grod for the sum of	4000 00
An undivided right of the Masso Pengu...... in the Ouachita to H Turner	700 00
A tract of land ... Allemans to D W Cox	800 00
A tract of land in addition to W Kerner ... P Meier	500 00
A tract of Cypress swamps on canal Carondelet to L Partsi Blanc	400 00
A tract of land in Opelous... to C Layrn...	1500 00
A tract of land in Co..... to N b Le Breton	430 00
A tract of land do to V N....	470 00
Eleven arpents on the Island Conolly to Deg...h Lucand... he assuming the payment of 81.... thereon	750 00
Two arpents of land at Girods to Chas Moreau	901 00
Ten arpents of land Carondelet to P A Ducatorne	4400 00
A tract of land at Lafourche to P Guic...	400 00
A tract of land near Baton Rouge to S Piston	700 00
A lot Faubourg St Mary to Louis Bou...	10 00
A do do to A St Amand	810 00
A do do to Veu Ll...	852 00
Two do do to G Cortegues	610 00
Three do do to Thomas Bouse...on...	460 00
A do do to Phiacre and Cenr l	450 00
A do do to Vincent Rolich	590 00
A lot and house in suburb St John P Kern...	1050 00
A lot in do Joseph Conrade	160 00
A lot in do Das Abt	150 00
1000 arpents on the river Bouef to Hugh Brown	7 00 00
1050 do do to George M......	3150 00
	746 11 00

By transfer to Daniel W Cox of an interest in the Masson Rouge grant of Ouachita land in part payment of his claim under contract with Daniel Clark in dissolution of partnership	100 000 00
By transfer to Daniel W Cox of 5000 arpents of Texas land to balance of principal	50 000 00
	150000 00

Collected of Daniel Porter the principal in redemption of ground rents on lots sold him by D Clark in faubourg St John	1073 38
Ditto James Johnson on do	501 00
	1574 38

Remittances received from J Maulampi of St Louis for money received by him on sale of land do	700 00
From Edward Turner, for proceeds of a tract of land on the Homochitto Mississippi	525 00

By sale of slaves acquired of Clauborne Brooks and Samuel Elkins

To Mr C Portier, two slaves, Sam and Luke	1050 00
S Durossat J five slaves, Sam Harris Richard George Jem, Gurge and Champin	1260 00
John Blanque one slave Iago	400 00

Mons Massicot, four slaves, Darky, and her three children

    Dan Lewis, and Sally   790 00

Montigut fils, one slave, Mary -   -   -   310 00

Mons Guillet, one slave, David   410 00

C Avart, one slave, Losac -   -   520 00

J Trudeau, two slaves Tibby and Jeffry -   605 00

Mons Kerby, two slaves, Nelly and child Dace -   350 00

Ld Macarty, one slave, Phel -   -   -   450 00

Charles Adams, one slave, Washington -   250 00

J Ogdens, one slave, child Aime -   -   -   150 00

C Bonnefoi, one slave, Marie Marthe   50 00

Dussu au de la Croix, twenty two slaves, Rob, George, Gurge,

    Charles Cardinal Cloe, Davis, Jacques, Lucy, Mor

    row Mary, Solomon, Paid, Peter Wallace Rose and

    child Tom, Rachael, Jack, Strover, Austin

    Ben Gurge, estimated per inventory $9,500

Abatement made thereon -   1 178   8322 00

                                                        14917 00

Hire of slave Washington -   -   18 00

Sale of household furniture -   -   1306 00

Allowance to this concern, as stipulated in the article of

    partnership -   -   -   14000 00

                                                 $38620 81

C

Account of the liquidation of Chew & Relf's estate in partnership with Daniel Clark deceased

To bills payable owing on the 19th of June 1813 the date of
contract of partnership with Daniel Clark

Accommodation notes discounted at the Louisiana Bank	11 000 00	
Accommodation notes discounted at the Bank of Orleans	7 610 00	
Accommodation notes discounted at the Planters Bank	6 700 00	
Note to the order of D W Coxe discounted at the Bank of Pennsylvania, Philadelphia	15 000 00	
Note to Hugh Monroe & Co	1 517 32	
" William Brand	397 18	
" James Hopkins	125 00	
" R D Shepherd	750 00	
" Patton & Morgan	600 00	
" Mons Bellechasse	600 00	
Note negociated with Daniel Clark's endorsement	6 000 00	
		70 319 50

Balance due on open accounts

To the Phœnix Fire Company of London	1 353 44	
The estate of Meeker Williamson & Patton	853 12	
" C Bouzan	1 998 00	
" Clark Rodgers	153 37	
" John Clay	6 572 56	
" Jones & Lane	1,090 00	
" William Dunbar of Natchez	56 44	
" Elijah Smith of New York	776 94	
" Judah Touro	12 50	
" Widow Zachar e	1 000 00	
" John Frazer	15 37	
" Adams & Loughery of Philadelphia	290 56	
" Charles Marty & Co	31 31	
" J B Jourdan	71 75	
" Peter Segum	6 00	
" Bradford and Inskeep, of Philadelphia	573 31	
William Smith	115 94	
William Porter of Baltimore	44 00	
James Surret	4 00	
John Lynd	70 01	
W W Montgomery	116 94	
A Marshall	13 80	
John Morton, of Bordeaux	400 00	
		16,209 36

By cash on hand the 19th June, 1813		2,029 00

Bills receivable collected

W W Montgomery, note	995 50	
Louis Vealeo note	236 00	
F Aime, note	143 00	
A H Smith, note	165 07	
Caleb Stringer note	84 50	
Berry Tarrur, note	700 00	
William Kinner, note	385 25	
Daniel C Holiday, note	210 00	
Porter & Depeyster note	717 50	
Reynold & Levey, note	582 00	
Samuel Woodbridge, note	250 00	
Simon Le Blanc, note	600 00	
Peter Besse note	50 00	
George Pollock, note	150 00	

C —Continued

Cath Turnbull note	1654 68
Horatio Sprigg	1122 00
Per Colson	24 00
William Dewes	791 75
Nupard Davidson	835 00
Samuel Hamilton	545 00
A P Walsh	2025 69
S Voenel	90 00
William Miller	890 68
Robert Cochran	3560 68
John Powlls	218 31
William Kimball	2014 00
F Woods	209 68
S Robinson	1000 00
Locket & Carleto	234 00
Louis Le Carn	140 00
	20,613 53

By John Chew balance of accounts collected	239 81
John P Itrey do co	3899 12
Furwar Skipwith do do	1057 87
Joseph Walden & Co, do	1076 25
John Clay do do	2307 81
J H & J P Johnson co	1667 56
Edward Randolph co	6740 56
William Harper do do	159 24
P Pedesclaix do co	289 69
Louis Sere on acc	14 00
Robert and L Chew, on a c	2146 75
	19 648 98

Brig Aber balance of all collected	318 62
Daniel Patterson	100 00
Don Rougcutte	370 00
Edward Bradford	495 75
W A Dewes	89 75
Mad M xent	7 00
Joseph I y	60 00
J Murphy	78 81
C Bellengay	89 00
M Pacand	150 00
B Bernoudey	8 00
T Stone	32 12
Pable Grui pre	88 62
J W & P Kearney	212 00
Colddsugh & Thomas	17 68
Lewis C Carn	279 87
Dussuau de la Croix	606 31
Charles Paferke	47 68
Vabry Delassise	70 00
Mons Harang	25 50
Louis Deleru	39 00
Charles Marion	125 00
Isaac Johnson	238 75
M Populus	45 00
Ant Mendez	150 00
J Mercier	33 00
Charlotte Heyes	2 50
Gilbert Leonard	350 00
P T Phillip dividend	114 25
C Bougaud, dividend	285 25
M Sharpe dividend	269 60
	4,798 81

C —Continued

By proceeds of 31 shares Louisiana Bank stock		3100 00		
do	10 shares Planter Bank stock	1700 00		
do	10 shares Bank of Orleans	970 00		
do	4 shares Orleans Insurance stock	400 00		
do	96 shares Orleans Navigation stock	7995 00		
do	1 share Orleans Theatre stock	91 45		
			14256 45	
By sale of merchandise per account D annexed	-		3524 90	
By D n W Cox to his assumption of a debt due to Richard N Voy co			4036 95	
By sale of real estate —A tract of land and improvements situated in Acadia known as the Home as held in the name of B Chew sold to S Hendron and Destrehan			32000 00	
A house and lot situated on Hospital street, held in the name of Richard Relt to Pr Ice co		6600 00		
A house and lot contiguous to the above described held in the name of Richard Relt to J H co		6600 00		
A house and lot situated at the corner of Hospital and Burgundy streets held by Richard Relt to T Coulson		5620 00		
A house and lot Suburg L Course, acquired by Richard Relt from Bedchasse - 1000 00				
Less charges paid for repairs 70 00				
		930 00	14810 00	
A tract of land in the county of Acadia sold to William Kenner and Ph Minor -			6000 00	
			121718 63	

D

Chew and Relf, Estate in Partnership, Sales of Merchandise

1813				
July	21 To More Ony 2 barrel cam...	—		59 06
	31 Cash, ...			29 37
August	31 Cash, ...	—		11 6.
September	Mac Para...	—		30 7.
October	Charco... sugar ...	.	00
November,	Cash, a barrel linseed	—		2. 7.
1814				
February	At auction by P. ... & Mor... 3 hhds in ... asse...	—		113 56
March	Mon. Vanc 1 sugar reder			60 00
	Cash 1 barrel laniseed			19 18
April,	James Sers 1 sugar ... ter			70 18
May,	P H.. y 1 ...			7. 00
	N... ...	22 00		
June	M. Santo 1 ...	19 00		
	J & J thy ... sugar ... tes	—		550 00
	D ... & Lon ... 2 c ... ers			80 00
July,	Taour... & W... ms 3 sugar kettles			210 00
	Ma... S... cylinders			160 00
	I ... P... ared 1 cyl... ers			200 00
September	M... Rah... 1 cylinder	—		40 00
	B... & Cox 1 cylinder			40 00
	Bartell & Cox 1 sugar kettles	—		140 00
October	Jacob M... 2 cylinders			50 00
	C Deser, 7 sug... kettles			200 00
1...				
May,	1 Writ ... ...ed	—		75 00
July	Cash to run wines			50 00
August	P... ...on & Mor... 1 barrel damaged linseed	—		5 94
November	E Wr... t 9 ring wheels			131 81
December,	D B Mor...n, 30 rary wheels	75 00		
1...				
June,	A P... an 73 rary heel	—		109 50
N... v	A Bron... ...	—		40 00
October	H as ... 1 rary heels	—		90 00
	Cash 1 rary wines	—		75 00
18...				
January	John Cann, 2 rag wines	—		183 2.
September	Cash 16 rary ...	—		15 00
December	Cash, 51 rary w... and 75 r dragons			76 25
18.2				
January,	I Mill acon 1 cylinder	—		25 00
18...				
February,	Gerard Freres 2 cylinders			40 00
December	Jacob Hart, 6 cylinders			90 00
	Benj Morgan 1 p... ts debent	—		110 00
	I L Pu... 1 ...chest			100 00
	By Patton & Mor...s, at auction counting house tur			
	n...ture	—	—	66 2.
	Charges outstanding	—	5 4 00	3637 62
	Paid Lachapelle for rent of lot per kettle & cylinder	112 00		
	Cartage		6.	112 6.
				3524 92

F

Account of the charges incidental to the liquidation of the joint estates
of Daniel Clark and I Coxe and R Relf up the estate

Taxes on property in the parish of Orleans	1706 64
Taxes on property in the parish of Rapides	309 8?
Taxes on property in the parish of Concordia	20 50
Taxes on property in the parish of Iberville	396 42
Taxes on property in the parish of Pointe Coupee	38 63
Taxes on property in the parish of	3?
Taxes on property in the parish of Avoyelles	94 49
Taxes on property in the parish of Ascension	3 5?
Taxes on property in the parish of St Bernard	7 66
Taxes on property in the State of Mississippi	291 8?
Taxes on property in the State of Missouri	43 5?
United States direct tax	43 4?

Attorneys

Fee to J Mitchell our counsel in his several suits	250 00
I Moreau I Lislet on sundry cases	?? 00
Louisiana Bank Coxe L vs Coxe	?? 00
A Baxon's suit I Iberville suit and Pointe Coupee	1? 00
C A Wagner in suits with C L Petrie	5? 00
J Mazureau our Junior in cases	500 00
Alex Porter our assistant Pointe Coupee	200
Edward Livermore suits in various cases	1619 8?
Isaac Brown in various cases	375 00
F L Junes suits versus Bayou Sara	4776 36
James Turner our advice counsel	1559 18
J W Smith cases in various suits	945 00
Thomas C Scott cases versus Rapides	794 12
Nathaniel I Evans commissions on collections	80 00
Costs in various suits respecting lands in Orleans	1036 96
Costs in various suits respecting lands in Pointe Coupee	315 12
Costs in various suits respecting lands in Missouri	1161 83
Notarial records &c	633 87

Miscellaneous expenses

Repairs on levee respecting the land	56 18
Repairs of roads and bridges on Bayou Sara Concordia	190 00
Repairs on houses on Bayou and Concordia	44 23
Repairs on land of Concordia	56 25
Auctioneers commissions on sundry estates sold	650 50
Surveyor of lands in various parishes	50 00
Surveyor of lands in State Mississippi	20 00
Surveyor of lands	11 50
For various	100 00
Expenses incurred by I Coxe attorney and agent to recover property and effects of estate	14 00
Brokerage commissions on sundry monies	21 00
Counting house expenses Relf & Coxe suits	1603 18
Clerk hire in our counting house	248 18
Advertising	?0 ?0
Postage	04 ?0
Stationery	?? ??
Board lodging travelling expenses attending commissions &c	??? ??
Relf hire Pascott	118 00
Subpoena to witnesses	5 00
Subscriptions to three cases	1? ??
Board lodging expenses for Daniel Clark our friends in compensation to our friends through the years	1? 00

The accounts continued on page F

F

                                                                    INTEREST

Dʀ

To Thomas Beale - -	27	12
L Millaudon - -	136	00
Bartell and Coxe - - - -	21	68
J McDonough & Company - - -	45	00
Samuel Elkins -	211	81
Widow Zacharie -	13	00
John Soulee -	£140	25
Rochell & Schiff - - -	166	56
Tricou & Fils - - -	855	31
D Delacroix - - - -	667	68
Nathan & Williams	543	06
Heirs of J B Macarty	975	75
Heirs of Thomas Conelber -	1171	27
Gilbert Andry -	252	00
Renaud & Peytavin - - -	4858	92
Will Simpson, on D Clark s bond	7035	60
Mad Sertheme s annuity -	6333	33
Debit on LeBlanc s note	177	33
Do Butler & McCutcheon -	265	50
Do Mrs O Fortier - - -	392	18
Do Flower and Finleys - -	22	62
Do Henderson and Distrehan	7118	06
Do Longpress - -	12	00
Do Mrs A Fortier, note received in payment of Cannes Bru les - - -	6049	92
Do on notes received in payment of negroes -	2197	94
Do on notes received in payment of real estate -	5222	90
Do at banks and interest paid -	13653	67
Do at the Bank of Pennsylvania -	1027	43
Interest paid the Louisiana bank on settlement	15932	19
Do do Bank of Orleans	18	81
Do do Planters Bank - -	652	68
Do do on D Clark s bonds for Gentilly lands	1600	00
	78107	61

F —Continued

ACCOUNT

	Cr
By J Bedford	37 81
Potter & Dempster	6 37
Will Do	37 18
Horace Spring	111 44
J B Davis	452 00
Isaac Johnson	30 12
J C Stone	19 12
R Duval	. 31
J W and P Kearny	2 75
Locke and Carleton	37 00
A P Walsh	293 37
S Leblanc	26 31
A Mendez	6 75
W Witherspoon	525 37
Will Dewees	121 25
Lewis and Turner	775 87
D C Hobson	86 87
Colonel Hamilton	1851 81
Richard Davidson	172 37
Henry Hart	4945 39
Wade Hampton	5716 15
Rob Cochran	78 60
R Munson	1105 81
S Robinson	361 91
Kimerl and Wells	1205 51
John Palfrey	37 86
B Eason	128 87
J H and I Johnson	1868 73
J Woods	83 81
John Lynd	589 94
D W Coxe	219 22
L Le Corne	13 75
R Munson and other collectors for James Lyon	1591 35
Urquhart and Williams	5400 00
Dividends on stocks	5748 50
Rents of houses in Hospital street	3351 8
Ditto of Bayou and Gentilly property	9004 93
and rent of Brothers	2342 00
Balance	82 696 0
	78157 61

G

Consolidated State of the Partnership Account

To amount of Daniel Clark's partnership debts B	34,759.19
Do Chew & Relf's do to C	8,5.. 8.
Incidental charges D	..2..0
Daniel Clark's endorsements on W Ha per's protested notes	.. 00
Do do W Donelson's do	.750 0.
Chew & Relf's and D Clark's endorsements for James Pro.	16,731.55
Thomas Powers, for taxes on Florida lands held by Daniel Clark as security of a debt due by Powers	534.19
Taxes on Florida lands conveyed to the Marquis Trovo	337.03
Eugene de Flesneur, protested notes received in payment of Gentilly lands	.39..3.
	526,049.8.

The foregoing accounts made up to the 31st December 1827 embracing various statements transmitted to Mrs Mary Clark the sole legatee at different periods as the liquidation progressed during her life time and afterwards to Mr Joseph Reed, her executor were furnished to the date to Mr George Green Jun, the attorney of two of the heirs and were approved of by him to one exception as appears by his letter of the 12th April 18.. to Mr Joseph Reed, a copy of which is annexed hereto

G

Made up to the 31st December 18..

By amount of assets of D Clark's estate in partnership B	586,98.1..
Do do Chew & Relf's do C	121,718.6.
Balance unprovided for on the 31st December 1827	1,05..
	596,049.8.

H

Supplementary account of the liquidation of the joint estate of Daniel Clark's and Chew & Relf's made up to the 31st December, 1837

To balance of estate to the 31st December 1837 G		18,050

Incidental charges

Taxes on city property	-	01 25	
Taxes on Bayou Boeuf lands		77 31	
Taxes on Houma land		50 00	
Taxes on city and country lands $297, for Marquis Freigo		99 00	
Taxes on St Bernard or Terre aux Boeufs	-	24 97	
		651 53	

Less			
Received by W. W. Whitney his proportion of taxes on city lots	$150 00		
Received of D. D. Cross on Terre aux Boeufs	- 27 83	177 83	173 70

Law expenses

Fee to cashier Girod's D. W. Coxe	100 00	
Fee to Lucius C. Duncan, in suit of W. W. Whitney and R. R. Keene	2 650 00	
Fee to Maurian do do	1,200 00	
Fee to Soule do do	500 00	
Fee to F. Mazureau appeal of Florida land case	374 62	
Fee to Spalding for examining land title in Missouri	155 75	
Bowen and King fee in suit of Mr Lanusse	300 00	
Moreau J Isct fee of Breton's heirs	150 00	
J. W. Smith, fee in suit of L Breton's heirs	26 75	
Costs in suit of L Breton's heirs	74 18	
In Supreme Court in appeal Florida land case	66 00	
In suits with Keene and Whitney	$528 63	
Less recovered of Keene	125 83	402 81

Transcript of records in the District Court to be used in the defence of Mr Lanusse's suit	132 62	
Notarial acts for copies of documents in various suits	16 00	
Expenses of commissions sent to Matanzas and Philadelphia, in Whitney's and Keene's suit	110 00	
Expenses of a commission in Mr Lanusse's suit	20 00	
		6,608 73

Proportion of expenses surveying Terre aux Boeufs land	73 87	
Repairs of Bayou road and Bridges	88 75	
Publication of answer to Keene	20 00	
		182 62
Balance of interest paid		947 13
		26,262 56

To balance	-	9,166 68
July 1838, paid municipality taxes on Bayou property	17 50	

New Orleans 27th August, 1838

Signed RICHARD RELF,

BEV. CHEW

By amount received of Isaac Baldwin in compromise of sale of Bayou Boeuf, in dispute with Spencer's heirs		11,800 00
An undivided moiety of 14 arpents of lands held conjointly with D Delacroix, at Terre aux Boeufs, sold to Joseph Alphonse	$700 00	
Ditto of 6 arpents, sold to Felix Gonzales	300 00	
Ditto of 8 arpents, sold to J Alphonse	400 00	
Ditto of 1 arpent, sold to Corvin	50 00	
		1,450 00
A house and lots in suburb St Johns sold to widow St Cyr		900 00
Amount collected of Joseph Vidal through L C Duncan, Esq		120 00
Amount on a judgment obtained against R R Keene		592 57
Amount collected of Louis Sere		2,233 31
Balance		9,166 68
		26,362 56

Property remaining unsold

Bayou lots

Seventy thousand arpents Florida lands

An undivided portion of lands in the parish of St Bernard, held conjointly with Dassuau De La Croix

Several tracts of lands and town lots in the State of Missouri, title in dispute

I, William F. C. Duplessis, register of wills in and for the parish and city of New Orleans, State of Louisiana, ex-officio clerk of the Court of Probates in and for the parish and city of New Orleans do hereby certify that the foregoing twenty six pages contain a true copy of the petition filed by Richard Relf and Beverly Chew as surviving executors of Daniel Clark deceased, the ... of Construction of these courts by them filed, all in my office.

In faith whereof I have hereunto set my hand and affixed the seal of ... of said sessions at the city of New Orleans, this ... day of ... year of our Lord 1810, and the 66th of the Independence of the United States of America.

... in ... of ... pages ... and ... erased in eighth page ... the words ... erased in eighteenth page ... erased, in Louisiana Maryland, in twentieth page ... and six lines erased on twenty second page, seventeen lines erased, and ten figures interlined, on page twenty-five.

(Signed)   W. F. C. DUPLESSIS,
                                      Register of Wills

I Joachim Bermudez sole Judge of the Court of Probates in and for the parish and city of New Orleans, State of Louisiana do hereby certify that William F. C. Duplessis who signed the foregoing certificate was, at the and there ... as Register of Wills in and for the parish and city of New Orleans ex-officio Clerk of the Court of Probates in and for the city and parish of New Orleans ... a parish ... court ... which in due form of law.

Given under my hand at the city of New Orleans, this 29th day of July A. D. 1846

(Signed)   BERMUDEZ

[No 67,]
Offered by defendants, and filed 25th June 1849

J W CURLEY Com.

Virginia Sept 16, 1803

Sir—My present absence from the office of State put it out of my power to refer to all the letters from you not yet acknowledged   The last received was of the 14th of August   The preceding one on the boundaries of Louisiana &c has not yet reached me   All the information you may be able to give on that subject, and on every other made interesting by the procession from France, will be highly acceptable   You will have received an enumeration of various objects, to which your attention will be particularly drawn   To these your own judgment, assisted by your local knowledge, will probably be able to make valuable additions

A letter from Gov'r Claiborne, received by the same mail with yours, conveys information concurring with the opinion that the Prefect meditates obstacles to the delivery of Louisiana into our hands   It is presumable, however, that so much temerity if not secretly favored by his government must speedily yield to reflection, and it is not a natural supposition that the French government should wish to embarrass or frustrate in the midst of a war with Great Britain, a transaction which the prospect of such a war contributed doubtless to enforce on its policy   Still, it will be proper, considering the peculiarities incident to personal character, and the vicissitudes incident to political affairs, that every circumstance should be marked and communicated, which may deserve attention in the arrangements to be made in so important a case.

But whatever may be the real purposes of the French Prefect, there is ground to believe that Spain, either alarmed by the cession of so much territory to the U States, or hoping to make her consent the price of concessions on their part, may be so unwise as to oppose the execution of the measure   With a view to such a posture of things, the President wishes you to watch every symptom which may show itself, and to sound in every direction, where discoveries may be most practicable, proceeding at the same time with all the caution necessary to avoid suspicion   You will please to let us know, also, what force Spain has in the country where it is posted what are its dispositions, how the inhabitants would act, in case a force should be marched thither from the U States, and what numbers of them could be armed and actually brought into opposition to it   You will be sensible that the value of information on these points may depend much on the despatch with which it is forwarded, and will, therefore, need no exhortation to that effect

With great respect and esteem, I am, sir,

Your obedient humble servant,

JAMES MADISON

Daniel Clark, Esq. New Orleans

[No 117]

Offered by defendants, and filed 3d July 1849

J W GURLEY, Com

WILMINGTON, May 30th 1808

My dear Clark—I hope, ere this you have arrived safe and in health at N Orleans but my pleasure would be much heightened by having the fact from yourself. I should have solicited this information from you before but have been absent from Wilmington ever since you left here on a very unexpected tour through Maryland where I received a profusion of all the attention and hospitality of that most hospitable country During my absence Genl Wilkinson and Lt Pike spent some time in Wilmington and N Castle, with their friends, Rodney and Reed, the General dished in all his plumish glory, was marked in his attentions to every class of citizens and is certainly taking infinite pains to court popularity and support not a word, however, since you left us, has been said in the papers, even in the Aurora, relative to the affair between you and him or rather between the nation and him I received a letter from Van Rensselaer lately in which he mentions the names of eight Federalists elected from N York to the next Congress the embargo is operating gently but surely I hope, from what I see in the papers, that American property in France is like to share a better fate than you expected, and that yours will not be lost During my stay in Maryland, I had the pleasure of hearing from your capricious but sweet little La, she is well You must hasten back, my friend, and improve the fleeting hours of life for they are no where well spent but in the bosom of love and beauty. Betsey is yet in Philadelphia, and Miss Lee not married Bayard is well Let me hear from you I pray you on the receipt of this, and when we may anticipate the pleasure of seeing you again.

Accept my best wishes and believe me most sincerely yours,

S WHITE

Dan'l Clark, Esq

[No 118]

Offered and filed by defendants, 3d July, '49

J W GURLEY, Com'r

BALTIMORE, September 27th, 1808

MY DEAR CLARK —Your letter of August 22d reached me

on the 19th of this month, and yesterday I received one from Keene, dated at New Orleans on the 30th of August last. He speaks of seeing you every day, a... that you... he ad that you are much pleased with the po... ...t you got in Pa... ...ra... om Louisi... ...ich I... he is led... re communication ... ...this... ...den... to you... as to ... ...nication ...your p... b...

In request... ...bu...est... ...wh... ...e to av... visiting o...m becau... I canno... easily w...ewr...e ...sin... into so... c...pination which would be pain... h... hm... to... I was... hopes that my sile...ce would su...e p've... plain to him the disclosures which have ...een... e... d departure ... our Baltimore and would thus put... ... tercour... Being d...sa...pointed in this I r...s...ed... guy to write to him by this conveyance, and ... ... information relative to his son, which w... g...z...nd... true state of things here. We have of co...se...in no respect...e...ered our conduct towards the child whom o... the co...tra...y we regard with more interest since we have discovered that he has the additional misfortune of having so unworthy a father. B... Keene sent from the Havan...a box of ...eetm...es as a present to **Mrs. Harper** another to **M**... **C**...on some t...p strings to **Emily**, and a box of cigars each, to **Mr Caton, Charles Carroll,** and **Paterson**. As we could not think of accepting these presents, they were all placed in the hands of **Mr Pengu**, to be disposed of for the benefit of little Keene. Of this I have requested **Mr. Penguy** to inform **M**... **Keene**, in the hope that it may render any communication from me unnecessary.

Should you have any conversation with him on the subject, which probably may happen after he receives **Mr Perguy** letter, will you ask him, on my part, for a manuscript which I gave to him in Washington? It can now be of no use, and I wish to have it in my own possession.

We have lately heard that Mexico has declared for the council of Seville, but have not yet seen the particular account. This struggle in Spain must produce vast consequences in whatever way it may turn. Should it prove successful, it will certainly lead to the independence of all Spanish America, and open a vast and brilliant c...eer to those who may be in a situation to enter it. Should the Spaniards succeed in Europe, still their dominions in America, being accustomed, in a great degree, during the struggle to self government and free trade, will not return to their former state. While they will remain subject to the monarchy, their affairs will be conducted in a different manner, and on different principles from what has heretofore prevailed. In either case there will be far more security and greater advantages in the establishing of things among them than in Spain. The ... ... must be changed and am hope ... ... During the strug ... ... men of character ... our countries who with attacking any terms and from ... ... they go to join them. I am so strongly im ...

*   *   *   *   *   *   *

... heartily ... it speaks of me in the same manner. He ... ... to raise me on a ... ... Burr ... has great secret for blunting the ... ... him.

... from the Prince ... news that Keene has been taken by the English and carried into Port Royal, Jamaica, where he was left in detention, on the 13th of April. He is stated to have been taken on St Jago de Cuba, a circumstance for which I cannot account, except by supposing that he thought Jamaica a better market for his flour than the Havana and wished to be carried in. His taking a cargo from here contrary to his promise to me, has added very much to the disgust created by the other parts of his conduct. He probably by this time begins to think that he would have acted more wisely in following my advice, and fulfilling his engagements with me: in that case, he would have preserved his friends here his property, and his character, and might now have been quietly engaged in cultivating his coffee establishment in Cuba. The young man Mr Campbell, of this State, to whom he most unkindly refused a passage to the Havana, has been lost in an attempt to get there by another vessel.

We have your elegant present the medals handsomely framed, and hung up in our parlor where we constantly look at them with the interest inspired by every thing that is connected with you. Mrs H sends you her best wishes, she is in pretty good health at present and your little friends, Charles, Mary and Richard, are perfectly well. That you may long be so is the earnest wish of.   My dear Clark,

Your affectionate friend,

ROB G HARPER

P S—Betsey returned yesterday, from Philadelphia, she and the family are quite well.   R G H.

Hon DANIEL CLARK, Esq New Orleans

[No 119]

Offered by defendants, and filed 3d July, 1849

J. W GURLEY, Commissioner.

Baltimore Sept 12th 1808

My dear Clark—This morning your letter of August 16th reached me, and relieved me from great anxiety for it the first that I have received from you since you left New Castle I began to apprehend seriously that some accident had befallen you, and these apprehensions were much increased, when the Agenoria which carried out my letters, returned without an answer I am now not without some fears, on account of your letters, for I think it not at all improbable that we owe their failure to what Mr. Jefferson calls ' the curiosity of the post officers" To have the most delicate family affairs, our private concerns and our chit-chat with our friends, exposed to the view of such men as Gideon Granger and his master is not a very pleasant thing

I regret extremely my dear Clark, the unexpected embarrassment into which you were thrown by your own goodness, and the baseness of those whom you have served Could I have known them, nothing, not even my strong desire to save from ruin an old and most valued friend, would have induced me to add to them, although I knew that it would give you pleasure to do such an act, yet I felt the strongest reluctance to propose it to you, on account of the difficulties of the times, and the effect which I knew that they must produce, even on your resources As the step has been taken, the new proof which it has produced of your friendship to me, gives me the most heartfelt satisfaction

We heard of the revolution in Cuba sooner than you You will probably hear a similar one in Mexico sooner than us Probably you have already heard of it Will either of those revolutions open a field for enterprise and noble actions, that can be occupied by Americans?

I was preparing for a publication on Wilkinson s subject, when the Spanish news, and the political changes and arrangements in this country, combined to engross entirely the public attention I, therefore, thought it best to delay the publication till those novel and interesting events should in some degree pass over. But I have been constantly attentive to throw in all the new matter that came within my reach, and to make occasional and short explanations, as circumstances seemed to require The subject stands very well in the public mind All those whom party spirit has not blinded, or who have not, from party views resolved to appear blind, are convinced, and express their conviction The last documents which you laid before Congress, and Mr. Coxe's testimony, satisfied every candid and unprejudiced mind, both as to Wilkinson's corruption, and the purity of

your motives He came here after the trial and endeavored to
attract notice, but no respectable men, even of the Democratic
party, gave him any countenance He is now at Carlisle, where,
.... takes place Before he came
here he gave out .... to challenge me affecting, after my testimony, to consider me as his greatest enemy and p-
secutor but I made a answer......y for him, and he thought better of the matter He content himself with abusing me to
some of the leading democrats whom I gave to understand, as
soon as I heard of it that they were not to repeat any of his
slanders They took care to observe the caution, and there the
matter ended

Mrs Harper is now in the country, with the children, and is
very well Her health seems to be at length re-established That
of the children and of the whole family, except Mrs Patterson,
is excellent she sometimes complains Louisa is quite well,
and looks very well She very often gets her aunt to ask whether
I have heard from you, and when I expect to hear Mr Carroll,
Mr Caton, and Charles made a journey this season to Ballstown,
and have returned much benefited Mr Caton, in particular,
derived great advantage from the waters and the ride

I have not written to Keene nor shall I write Few occurrences of my life have given me more pain than his conduct It
is shocking to be found to think ill of a person, who has been
accustomed to possess your good opinion and your regard. The
impression made by the events which I developed to you, has
been very much strengthened, by matters which have come to
my knowledge since

God bless you, my dear Clark, sincerely and fervently prays
your affectionate friend, ROB G HARPER
I shall send a duplicate by post under cover to Chew & Relf

[No 120]

By defendants Filed 3 July, 1849

J W GURLEY, Com.

WASHINGTON, May 30, 1809

MY DEAR FRIEND —We have convened at this place once
more, but what will be the course of business is impossible to
say I have not written to you for some time past, expecting
every day to see or hear of you in our country, but in this I have
been disappointed Will you be so good as to let me hear from
you, as to what you are about and how you are? It will, I
assure you, give me great pleasure I have a nephew in New
Orleans in the compting house of W Morgan, a Mr Polk, should
he stand in need of your protection or friendship, you will
oblige me by extending it to him You shall hear from me
again very soon, but pray, my friend, let me likewise hear

from you. The Carrols and Catons are well, and L——a, it is said, has it in serious contemplation to take the veil

Yours, most sincerely,

S WHITE

Daniel Clark, Esq

[No 121]

By defendants Filed 3 July, 1849

J W GURLEY Com

WASHINGTON, Nov 29th 1808

MY DEAR FRIEND—Yours of the 25th ult I received last evening, but it was indeed a poor substitute for the pleasure I expected in seeing you, and I was the more disappointed as you say nothing of coming on My friend, you ought to be here considerations of high importance relating to yourself require that you should not fail to come I pray you let us see you We have done nothing, and the administration are, I believe, at a loss what to do They have blundered so deeply into difficulties, that they find it almost impossible to extricate themselves, and they have too much pride to retrace their steps, as that would be an acknowledgment of error They will for the present hold on upon the embargo, but I think will ultimately be driven out of that measure I have not received a line from you during the recess, though I have written to you several times and shall not frank this, lest it should be broken open I saw L——a the other day She is more blooming and charming than ever How can you stay away ? She wants to see you

God bless you! Come on immediately

Yours, most sincerely,

SAMUEL WHITE

Daniel Clark Esq

[No 122]

By defendants, 3d July 1849

J W GURLEY, Com'r.

WASHINGTON, Dec 2d 1807

My Dear Friend —We are out of all patience, in waiting for you. If you are not coming, in the course of 24 hours after the receipt of this, I pray you let us know the cause of your detention You cannot imagine how much we are at a loss for your agreeable society, or I if possible, the ladies infinitely more so Their inquiries on this interesting subject have wearied me out of my life, it is more mortifying than your pre-eminence when present You are not so much of an epicure as to be detained from your duties here, on account of the fine dinners given to their "*distinguished guest*," in Philadelphia, and, at all events, I think a hundred and twenty covers might have satisfied

you We have a small but agreeable mess consisting of Messrs.
Van Rensselaer Lewis, Kelly, Grimmer and Van Dyke at the
old place where rooms are reserved for you Goedsborough
will probably be with us Bayard has not yet come on You
have no doubt, seen detailed the proceedings instituted against
John Smith in the Senate the committee are likely to make a
very long business of it and I am told expect information from
you on the subject I suspect strongly that your love affair
keeps you in   how
unhappy such a suspicion even would render the fair Miss L of
Georgetown and Miss D of the 1st Avenue to both of whom,
it is reported here you are to be married—whether it once or
in succession public rumor has not decided The good old man
of one of the houses at every favorite spot whither Mr Clark
has come How can it be so cold! In th man of all that's
lovely has on the bosom and arms of beauty, swelling and
expanded to receive you

Got bless you! Come on or let us hear from you Adieu

                                                    S WHITE

Daniel Clark Esq

[No 123]

By defendants, 3d July, 1849

                                     J W GURLEY Com

                        ANNAPOLIS 16th April 1807

In consequence of Mr Clark's very kind promise Mrs Caton
takes the liberty of introducing Mr Naupa, the young French
gentleman whom she recommends to him He is a young man
of an excellent character and liberal education and Mrs Caton
trusts that any services which the benevolence of Mr Clark's
heart may induce him to render Mr Naupa, will not be ungrate-
fully required Mrs Caton and Miss Louisa unite with Mr
Caton in best wishes for Mr Clark's health and happiness.

Daniel Clark, Esq

                              Mr Naupa New Orleans

[No 124]

By defendants, 3d July 49

                                     J W GURLEY Com

                                   4th Feby, 1807

Dear   upon the
imp   making in yo
                until I see yo   for
the four p   here wish to see you a married
man from a conviction that you would be much happier in that
state than in any other and I feel quite delighted at the prospect

53

of my wishes being realized   I am not ac   Miss Lee,
but the preference you ha   sufficient to give her a high
place in   ations, and I feel great   patience to become
known to her.   Believe me, when I assure you that few things
would afford me more pleasure than to see you enjoy as much
happiness as is allowed to a mortal in this imperfect world
I was told, last night that you were to   perb ball,
on Friday next, in ho   it was supposed   It is said
that you   to be served up upon *gold* dishes, and that
all the other arrangements are to be made with corresponding
elegance.   If Cupid had not marvellously driven all your former
friends   it you would
                        of some
        d that   but at the most
                erica, might   But
I will   the little urchin shall
bear all the blame of your neglect of me and that none of it shall
be attached to you   I must now mention that I have not been
equally unmindful of you, and that   honed a party,
nearly a fortnight   have the pleasure of your
company   I have fixed upon Friday the 13th, to invite
my company and shall be greatly mortified if you do not make
your appearance here, before that time   There are some charming strangers with us, to whom I shall have great pl   in
introducing you   When the   situation wears off, I
hope you   forget to number amongst your

                Your very sincere one,
                        MARGARET COXE.

Honorable Daniel Clark, Washington City

                [O O O]
Referred to in Mr. Montgomery's deposition
                        J W GURLEY, Com'r

            New Orleans, 5th August, 1830
S**r** —In compliance with the pleasing duty assigned us by
our fellow citizens, we now present you with a service of plate,
as a testimonial of their esteem, and of their estimation of the
faithful performance of your duties as collector of the district of
Mississippi for upwards of thirteen years

We accompany it with a copy of the resolution of the public
meeting under which we have acted and will but add one circumstance, which we know will augment the pleasure and pride
you must feel in this expression of the good opinion of the community   After the publication of the above resolutions, more
than sixty masters of vessels came voluntarily forward, and sub-

scribed for the plate now presented you, offering larger sum
than the committee conceive necessary to accept. This approbation of those who had most frequent intercourse with you, as
Collector, is alike honorable to yourself and to them

We forbear suspending the further upon your time, and wishing
you a continuance of health so much to be enjoyed by one to
whom a long life of active virtue has secured peace of mind and
the general love,

We subscribe ourselves most respectfully &c

THOMAS URQUHART
WM NOTT
J HENDERSON,
J H SHEPHERD,
J LINSTONE,
L MILLAUDON

In behalf of the committee appointed at the meeting
To Beverly Chew, Esq

[P P P]
Referred to in Mr Montgomery's deposition

Office Bank United States,
New Orleans, Nov 25th, 1831

Bev Chew Esquire—

Dear Sir —I embrace most eagerly the opportunity which
the duty of transmitting to you an extract from the minutes of
our Board affords me of assuring you of my hearty concurrence
in the sentiments embodied in their resolutions

The uninterrupted harmony of the Board, and the pro perity
and popularity of our institution, during your administration,
must always be subjects of gratifying reflection In the performance of my own official duties I have uniformly enjoyed the
benefit of your friendly aid and advice, and my regret at being
now deprived of them is tempered only by the conviction that
your private interests required this step—that my loss is your
gain

With my best wishes that in your new situation the warmest
anticipations of yourself and your friends may be realized,

I am, dear sir, very sincerely yours,

S JAUDON, Cashier.

[Q Q Q]
Referred to in Mr. Montgomery's deposition
J W GURLEY, Com.

Office Bank United States,
New Orleans, 25th, Nov, 1831

At a meeting of the Board of Directors of this Office, held this

day, the following resolutions were, on motion, unanimously
adopted

"*Resolved*, That this Board view with deep regret the resigna-
tion of Beverly Chew, Esq our late worthy President who by
his amiable and conciliatory manners and his correct and gentle-
manly deportment endeared himself to us The able and impartial manner in which he presided at this Board secured him
the highest respect and esteem of all its members, and merits
their warmest gratitude and best wishes for his future happiness

'*Resolved*, That the foregoing resolutions be inserted on the
minutes, and a copy be transmitted to Mr Chew and to the
Parent Bank, by the Cashier"

S JAUDON, Cashier

Extract from the minutes

[No 125]

By defendants, 3d July, 1849

J W GURLEY Com'r

PHILADELPHIA, June 3d, 1810

MR DANIEL CLARK—

Sir I hope you will excuse a stranger for addressing you on
a subject in which you can be no otherwise interested than as
the cause of humanity I have been informed of the goodness
of your heart, and therefore have ventured to solicit you to use
your influence with William Harper in favor of his poor and
unfortunate sister and her orphan children From the time of
her husband's death until her arrival in Orleans he never sent
her one dollar, though he knew the situation she was left in
We did all we could for her, and as long as we could support
the expense She went to New Orleans, in hope that her
brother and uncle would do something for her and especially
as Davis' letters to her were very flattering, but she has been
disappointed

William promised her that, if she returned to Philadelphia, he
would allow her three hundred dollars per year and Davis was
to send her two hundred William desired her, immediately on
her arrival here, to go to boarding with her children, and rest assured he would, by the first post send on the money From that
time until this, she has not received one cent from him, except fifty
dollars he gave her at parting On her arrival she stayed with
me three or four weeks, waiting to hear from William but
nothing came I advised her to take rooms, and I lent her
furniture, she remained there until within four weeks of Toby's
arrival; we then paid the rent, and relieved the furniture She
has since been boarding here and her children, not doubting but
on the arrival of Capt Toby she would receive the promised

assistance or the contrary he has not wrote her a line, or sent her a dollar and what is become of her God only knows! If my husband had in his power to do for her, I would not apply to her untreating brother. He is willing, but the means are wanting. He like other people has felt the difficulty of the times and can just support his own family and meet his engagements. Though he has been obliged to do more for some time past he can do it no longer, and unless she receives speedy relief, she must part with her children to any person that will take them to be brought up in a line, perhaps very little differing from servants. Is it not a pity that such fine children should be so sacrificed when so near a relation has it in his power to prevent it? As to Davis, I place no dependence on his promise, if he has not injured her, nor does not, is all I ask; but if he should send her anything it will be very acceptable, and more than I expect. Thus, sir, I have given you a plain statement of facts. You will make your own comments, and let your heart plead for her poor children. I am sure from the character Sally has given me of you, that you will not think it too much trouble to inform me whether you succeed with William Harper or not.

I will thank you to let him suppose you have received your information through some other channel than from me, as it would make him very angry, and perhaps injure the cause I wish to gain. If he thinks Sally is not sufficient to manage for the children, let him place the money in my hands, or his sister Harriet's—either of us will see it properly applied—or any other person he may choose. She is to be sure as simple as a child, and any person may deceive her, in the way of business, ten times in a day. If time wont serve then turn, witness the terms on which she left New Orleans. I say this, because she had a right to expect some support from her brother, as 'tis certainly a duty incumbent on him to provide for her, when she has nobody else to do it, and especially as he can afford it, otherwise, circumstances would alter cases.

With the hope of soon having the pleasure of hearing from you, I remain, with respect and esteem,

Sir, your most ob't,

MARY G. DE LA ROCHE

N B.—Please to direct to me, No 123, South Second Street.
Daniel Clark, Esq, New Orleans

[No 132]

By defendants, 3d July, 1849

J W GURLEY, Commissioner.

(Duplicate)

PHILADELPHIA, Sept, 1812

DAN'L CLARK, ESQ —

Dear Sir   I wrote you, on the 15th July, in answer to your favor of the 1st June   The bill was regularly paid, and five hundred of the amount handed to your mother   the remaining thousand to your aunt, whose receipt you have enclosed

Your parent informed me that she was considerably in debt, and that little would be left of the $500, after she had discharged the claims on her, so that she will soon be in want of a further supply

She says that she does all that she can to economise, but that she is compelled to disburse, against her inclination   The deficiency is not of sudden accumulation but has been gradually increasing for a considerable time   I would recommend to you to send to me a sufficient sum to pay the claims,* and I will attend to it myself, and see them discharged

I have just put up (to send by Mr Relf) some melon seeds, you will have a part   As for other seeds I have not collected any, this year, having been occupied as an administrator, guardian, &c, &c   Should I obtain any thing of the kind, worth sending, I will endeavor to forward them to you

We had some hopes that you would have passed the winter with us, but from what Mr. Relf tells me, I have given over the expectation

War is the order of the day, and the opinions of its duration various as the hopes and interests of the individual   For my part, I see no prospect of a speedy adjustment   By Hull's disgraceful surrender, that desirable event must be considerably retarded   Had Canada been conquered, we should have had a quid pro quo to have offered to England

Mrs. Anderson has come, this morning, to town   Your family is well   I communicated your message to them

Sally joins me in friendship and good wishes for your health and happiness

            I am, with esteem and friendship,

                        Your most obed t, &c,

                              WM E HULINGS

                        PHILAD A, 20th Oct 1812

Mr. Relf, having been detained here, enables me to inform you

---

* The credits she will have recourse to, before she receives her next remittance

that, ten days ago your aunt Clark suffered an apoplectic stroke, in which she was speechless several hours. She revived, and on the third day was so much better as to sit up by the fire, and to give us hopes of her recovery. These were, however, delusory, and she now lies in a hopeless state. I shall leave my letter open until the latest hour that I may mark any change that takes place.

I hold a duplicate receipt from your aunt, so that if you have not received the original you may command it.

23d Oct. 2 o'clock, P. M.

Mrs. Clark is yet breathing but totally insensible, and I do not think will live many hours.

Your family are all well. We join in friendship and good wishes for your welfare.

I am, respectfully, your friend,
and most obed't, &c.
WM. E. HULINGS.

Daniel Clark, Esq., New Orleans.

[No. 133]

Defendants. 3d July, 1849.

J. W. GURLEY, Com.

(Private) Pittsburgh, 23d Dec'r, 1812.

My dear Sir—My mind is agonized by despair at the non-payment of Gen'l Hampton's debits for $20,000 which I had pledged to Mr. Burd for his additional endorsements, at 3 and 4 months, procured while Mr. Relf was here to relieve me from a debt that I had no other means of paying. My heart bleeds for him, whose kindness to you and myself has thus plunged into engagements, which instead of diminishing have been constantly augmenting, and whose situation has by this failure in Hampton to pay even this small amount of his debt held by Mr. Burd removed all confidence in the punctuality of the *others'* notes, which he held. This $20,000, which was extended to suit his convenience, had become a debt of peculiar obligation, gratitude and honor, and yet he has by deceiving us all, even deprived it of its original security. Great God, why am I thus doomed to suffer the misery and horrors due only to ingratitude and injustice. I have hitherto found a consolation in the reflection, that my friends were secure, and would soon be extricated from the embarrassments in which their disinterested kindness had plunged them; but alas, my friend, this hope is almost vanished. I am silent in my grief and sadness, which my wife (without yet knowing the cause) is in vain endeavoring to assuage. Tell me, my friend, what I am to do, and what I am to expect. Implore Hampton to save me by the payment, at least, of this

$20,000. You have claims on his feelings and justice. Exert all your powers and persuasion or indeed I cannot stand the shock. I had flattered myself that my late operations to Lisbon and Cadiz would have afforded me some relief but for the present they serve but to increase my embarrassments.

     Yours affectionately,   D. W. C.
Dan'l Clark, Esq

[No. 136.]
By defendants 3d July, 1849.

     J. W. GURLEY, Com.

    PHILADELPHIA, 30th Oct. 1812.

DAN'L CLARK, ESQ.—

 Dear Sir: I wrote you by Mr Rich'd Relf, who left this city on the 25th inst., in the ship Orleans, Capt Franklin. Your aunt, Mrs Jane Clark, then lay in a hopeless state. On the next day, at half past four o'clock P. M. she breathed her last, and on the 28th, I followed her remains to the Presbyterian Church in Market street.

 Mr William Todd, counsellor at law, is executor. Her property chiefly bequeathed to her brothers and two sisters, in Virginia.

 Your family are well. Your mother is in need of funds, on which subject I have before written you.

 Sally joins most cordially in wishing you health and happiness.   I am, with esteem,

     Your friend and most ob't

      WM. E. HULINGS

[No. 139.]
By defendant 3d July, 1849.

     J. W. GURLEY, Com.

  (Copy of Mr. Coxe's letter.)

    PHILADELPHIA 10th October 1811.

 Madam—I am favored with your note of this date. In adverting to my engagement to pay your annuity, it appears to be founded on your relinquishment to Mr Clark of a certain security held on property in the district of Natchez. On a settlement between him and myself last July, I made over to him my right and title to all my real and personal property in Louisiana, on a part of which he informed me you had consented to receive a fresh security in lieu of that formerly given up, and that he would himself, in future, remit you your annuity. He moreover stipulated to pay me a certain balance of account with interest thereon, half yearly, till paid. I, of course, concluded that your call on me would cease so soon as this new arrangement had taken effect, for which, however, there has yet scarcely been sufficient

...me A... Mr Cl... o... a... is thus about to be placed on ...s original footing and ...ea... ... a large creditor of his, its impossible fo... ... ...ithout... ... ...to... ... to pay you m... ...y ...her ...y ... ...Cl... ... ...m... ...ou ...o... ... ...o ... tha... Mr ... ...h... ...nd any ...o... ... ...o... y... du... ...a... I ...o... ... ...v... ...th C...k... ... 10 ...s...ith th... ...old w...t ...e... fom tu... of ... g... and a...other for $... p...ble out of 1... of ...ccou... ... 10... ...he prote... ...pa...t... du... th... 1... of J...ua...... ... 1... before ...u... ...p...e...t... Mr Clark will ha...e ma...e tho... ...arran...ments for ...h... ...a...ing th... in fu...e, ...n...te to your ...ati...on

Wi...h ...u...h ...r...spect, I am, madam your very obt serv...t,

DAN W COXE

Mrs Jane Clark.

[No 140]

By defendants 3d July 1849

J W GURLEY Com

PHILADELPHIA, 1st Jan...y, 181...

DANIEL CLARK Esq—

Dear Sir Your ...vor of 6th u...o enclosing W Phil...a ...aft on Messrs Clay & Dunning of New York for $500 was received last ...vening, and as I have no acquaintance whate...r in New York, to whom I could send it I ...id...order ...o...to...m... ...ow to have it collected through the b...n...of Penn...a...n... and ...hen received ...shall b... ...o...edi...e...y pai... to your a...ie...

You wi...h me to be...ome re...ch...nt for ...o... ...n a...ser...s o ...u...pure...a... I to ...oar ain... F... I ...o... ...are... i... ...o... ...o ...o on condit...n that you ke...n m...regul...ou...supp...d with ...e m...n...o... ...ing them sa... ...ou... as ...a...op...t...on...s would b ...unful ...f I had it...no... ...n ...y p...s...e...e g...a...t...a... I ...e...d not ...a...in...orm...n you that the ...o...e...o...my tra...e... b...n... suffi... ...ent of our own neces...... ... a by tho... ...he ...ro... co... com...s round th...pu...s is ... ...b...an...t...h ...d...o...s I were to sell sto...k or bo...s... ...t... ...m... ... ...h... a...u...e This necessity ...m...e...cily ...e...u... ... ...s you ...t... a...d th... funds suffi...ently ...ly ...o pa...t... ...c...t... ...u...d map... and no ca...e a... ...a...e...tion in ...h...ch ...a...ty ...ould b ...e...id... will be w...nting o... ...y p...t

Th... weather...tre...... ...o...nt ...m...p ...ne... ...o ...o ...r...e...s tion...g...... ...Go...m...... ... B... ...ou ...o ...er...p...t...b...c that you fr...dl... a... i...s ...t...i...u...d ...t...r... B...on...e... abou...1...me...a...o...el...5...) a...u...e...... ...e...r... ...t... ...o...y Anders...n and Mar... Cl...... ...h...... ...na...o...... ...s...y Th...la...r app...s to be ...e...l...... ...t ...i...k... ...s... ...a... advantage rathe... ...n...ot ...e...s ...o...o...r mother's househ...d

We had remarkable warm weather all the fall until the 16th ulto, when winter set in suddenly, since that time we have had some very cold days. We jog on in our old calm domestic manner, mixing but little with the bustling world, finding *satisfaction*, if not exalted happiness in pursuits where the more restless would in vain look for it

Sally joins me most sincerely in wishing you many happy returns of the season, and every blessing desired by you

　　　　I am, with esteem,

　　　　　　Respectfully your friend and most obed't,
　　　　　　　　WM E. HULINGS

[No 142]

By defendants　3d July, 1849.

　　　　　　J W. GURLEY, Com
　　　　　　Philadelphia, 4th May, 1813

Dan'l Clark, Esq —

Dear Sir I have been for some posts back expecting to hear from you in answer to my last, and also looking for funds for your parent, whom, I am mortified to say, has applied to me for what I have not to give to her You may remember that keeping me supplied for her use was a condition I made when I accepted the charge, and I did hope that it would have been as punctually kept as your pecuniary transactions, on my own account have invariably been It is impossible that the two sums last received, amounting together to $800, may, in your opinion, have been sufficient for the time, but, you must remember that a great part of that money had been anticipated, and if you have received *all* my letters, you will find that I pressed on you the propriety of sending on wherewith to pay off all her engagements, and to have a fund in my hands to meet her calls She is far advanced in life, is nervous, and ought, if possible, to be spared any cause of chagrin You will be sensible, my good friend, that in speaking so plain, I have no intention of hurting your feelings I am impelled to it by the situation in which you have placed me Were my means as ample as yours, your mother would not feel the delay, but you know that they are confined to periodical payments, not much more than sufficient to make both ends meet at the end of the year

We are in a gloom respecting our future political prospects Our port is completely blockaded, and even a part of our fire wood is intercepted Oak wood, which usually sells at this season for 4 1-2 to 5 dollars, brought yesterday from 6 to 7 nor was there a stick to be had at eleven, A M, from Chesnut street until you almost reached the lowest end of the town

Rich'd Smith paid us a visit on his arrival, and told us he was going to England. Since which Doct. Spencer has informed us that he met him at Washington, and that he understood him that he meant to return here in a few days, but we have reason to believe he has not come.

Sally joins me in friendship and good wishes for your health and happiness. I am respectfully yours, &c, &c

WM. L. HULINGS

[No 143]

By defendant, 3d July, '49

J. W. GURLEY, Com.

PHILADELPHIA 14th January 1813

DAN'L CLARK, Esq—

Dear Sir: Your favor of the 8th December, enclosing bills for the $300 came to hand three days ago, and have been forwarded for collection.

I informed you, in my last, that I had, by the assistance of a friend, advanced Mrs Clark $100 which would go but a *little* way towards paying her arrears of debt, and supplying her immediate wants. I learn, with pleasure, that they are likely both to be provided for by your arrangements. But my good friend, my duty to you obliges me, however unpleasant the task, to tell you that your presence with your family is much more wanted than even your money. There is a sad derangement in it, and I know of no remedy but your continual authority. I had determined never to say anything on this subject, and nothing but an increased conviction of the necessity there is that you should know it, would have altered my resolution. I am persuaded that, although the information be painful to you, you will justly appreciate my motives.

I have applied to your aunt's executor, Mr Wm Todd for your bonds, and expect to receive them in a few days. When I have them, I will erase your name, and hold them to your order.

I am requested to inform you, by Mr Todd, that there is sixteen days annuity due to the estate of your late aunt, amounting, I believe, to $89 66, which will close your account totally with her. If you should choose to remit it to me, I will take his final receipt for you.

We have nothing new to tell you. Sally joins me in cordial good wishes for your health and happiness.

I am, respectfully your friend,

and most obedient, &c, &c,

WM. E HULINGS

[No. 144.]

By defendants, 3d July, '49

J. W. GURLEY, Com.

Philadelphia, January, 1812

Dan'l Clark Esq.—

Dear Sir I received your favor of the 18th December, and was happy to hear that you were in actual and quiet possession. Mr. R. Nisbett, of the 7th ultimo, accounts the account of your affairs. I was much disappointed at not hearing from you or keeping good notices so as to regulate my use. There are debts to want and I have no means of means to advance them some......

I shall go to the ....

It is very .... to know .... and no to have it .... especially as I gave you timely .... now little care I have with .... has .... associated .... of .... the ..... of it .... immediate reach. I do trust that you will make such arrangements as will enable me cheerfully to discharge my agency.

I will apply to Mr. Todd your administrator for your bond.

Mrs. Hulings unites with me in friendship and in good wishes for your health and happiness.

Very respectfully, your most obed't &c,

WM. E. HULINGS

[No. 149.]

By defendants 3d July, '49

J. W. GURLEY, Com.

27th August, 1803

Dear Sir—I have waited with some degree of impatience, for the small sum which is due to me from the house of Chew & Relf. There has been many sole opportunities to have sent it by which many articles have been sent to other people. It is true, the sum is very trifling to them though would be of some consequence to me, could I get it, the principal reason is I owe it, and am regularly dunned for it and cash is so scarce, I could not borrow it if I was like to be sold for it.

I earnestly wish you to take the trouble to mention the circumstance to them. The fulfilment of the memorandum would be very acceptable, if they would send it.

I am, dear sir, your obed't serv't,

FREDERICK KIMBALL

Daniel Clark Esq., City of New Orleans

[No 150]

By defendants, filed 3d July, 1849

J W GURLEY, Commissioner

New Orleans 21st July 1803

Sir —I enclose you a copy of a letter I have just had an opportunity of forwarding to the Consul General in Paris and
I mentioned in it some matters chiefly respecting the population,
commerce, and resources of this country, thinking that they
might be of service in the present circumstances. It is generally supposed here that the war between England and France
now commenced will produce the latter getting possession of the
Colony, and the Prefect here and other French officers must and
should consider that their stay here will only be productive of
jealousy on the part of the Spaniards and perhaps mischief as
attempts are daily making on the one hand to usurp authority,
which are almost always as vigorously repressed on the other.
It is a fortunate circumstance for us that Mons. Laussat will not
be invested with authority, as all his actions and views are
directed to our prejudice. He violently opposed the restoration
of the deposit, even after the royal order had been read, and made
attempts to succeed in this matter with the Marquis de Casa
Calvo and Intendant separately, complained bitterly that the
order was so *tranchant*, and when I waited on him with a letter
from the French Minister advising of what was to take place he
lost his temper and betrayed the emotions and sentiments which
then prevailed within him. He had proposed a variety of vexa-
tious regulations respecting searches and visits of our shipping,
says we ought not to be regarded as a corps de nation, but as a
number of hordes spread over our country, and to his friends
his expressed his regret that he has not a small force to give
law to us. Whether these were his own or the views of his
Government we should not have the less to suffer from them.
To avoid fatiguing you with details I refrain from saying any more
on the subject.

The Marquis de Casa Calvo who has no love for the French
Government or French measures, has it in contemplation in case
of the surrender of the Colony, to draw off from the Island of
Orleans and western bank of the Mississippi the whole of the
inhabitants of 3 or 4 posts or settlements and place them on the
lands reserved by the Spaniards between the Iberville and new
boundary line. I have strongly advocated the measure, as it
will augment their mutual jealousy and hatred—will weaken
the French and will be of service to ourselves, by increasing
the produce of a populous trade country, already in a thriving
situation, whose commerce will be ours, as Spain, in order to

strengthen their attachment, will make no attempt to raise a revenue there, or prevent a trade with those who may be of most service to them

A second vessel, the Citoyen, loaded with slaves for account of the French Government, arrived, a short time since. She sailed from Rochport early in March

I have the honor to remain &c

James Madison, Esq

[No. 150]

By defendants, 3d July, '49.

J W GURLEY Com

New Orleans 26th June 1803

Sir I herewith take the liberty of enclosing to you a copy of some memorandums respecting the country, which I had an opportunity of forwarding to our Consul General in Paris, as advised in my last What respects the western boundaries of this country, and the respective ideas of the French and Spanish Governments, on that head may be new to you, and necessary to be informed of, in case of success in our pending negociations

The Spanish officers in this country as are of the immense importance of that part of Louisiana to the west of the Mississippi as well intrinsically as on account of the access it affords by rivers to the frontiers of New Mexico, have strongly urged to the Court of Madrid the necessity of proposing to the United States the cession of the 2 Floridas for the right bank of the Mississippi, in case we obtain it of France and they even flatter themselves with the hope of success. It must be needless to point out to you the immense difference there is in the value of the two countries, that the western part of Louisiana is valuable in every respect that it abounds with every advantage of soil, situation, navigable waters, has an immense Indian trade, and by possessing both banks, we   not   bad neighbors, while the other is almost barren and has only the port of Pensacola, which may be thought a valuable acquisition, and by its situation being surrounded almost by our possessions, must become ours whenever it may suit our purpose to demand it, or what is very probable, may, in a short time, on account of the expense and little benefit derived by Spain from retaining it, be offered us, without an equivalent You will, I hope, excuse me, and impute it only to the desire I entertain of being useful when I presume to advise that, in case the Government is successful in obtaining Louisiana, not a moment should be lost in taking possession of it, that no circumstance may occur which might either retard, or render that measure afterwards more expensive and difficult. The French and Spanish officers here are at open variance, on account of the presumption of the one, and the firmness of the other in resisting all attempts at encroachments on their authority and in this state of things, the interests of Spain and the United States being looked upon as the same, as it is supposed they must be equally governed by the views of France I enjoy with all the Spanish authorities, a degree of confidence almost unlimited and am consulted almost on all occasions that occur I have seen Gen Dayton, who remained here near 6 weeks gives a great many details which I was fearful to trouble you with and from whom you will be able to learn many things respecting the state of affairs and temper of many minds, which it would be too tedious to commit to paper I am instructed to inform you that the Governor and Intendant, though well disposed to grant the request made by Gen Wilkinson for permission to send two vessels in the spring and autumn, to our settlements on the Mobile river do not think themselves possessed of sufficient authority to comply with his wish, without consulting the court as they are fearful of committing themselves by granting anything unusual, at a moment when negotiations are supposed to be pending on the subject and their answer to the General's letter shows their readiness to permit anything for the use of the United States being transported from hence whenever permission shall be demanded I take the liberty of recommending that in future anything destined for the   should be deposited here where care will be taken of it until wanted, which will save the great expense hitherto incurred of transportation to Loftus Height and back to this place by which in addition to expense, a great risk is incurred and no good purpose answered

I have the honor to remain

Hon J. Madison

[No 130]

By defendants 3d July, 49

J W GURLEY, Com

New Orleans, 18th August, 1803

Sir —Your letter of the 20th inst came to hand, this evening. I shall in everything as far as I am able, endeavor to fulfil your wishes, and regret that the immediate return of the post prevents my replying to some of the subjects mentioned in it which I will take an immediate opportunity of doing I flatter myself you will excuse the hasty and incorrect manner in which the duplicate of the memorandums respecting this country now forwarded, are put together they were sent me out merely as hints for Mr Shipwith to make such use of as he might think proper, and time pressing, I had no leisure to attempt to correct the style of them, even had I been better calculated for such a busi-

ness The truth and exactness of these remarks must be my only
excuse, and I rely on your usual indulgence for me   The President having honored me with a letter, I enclose in answer open
to you   I am uncertain whether there is or is not impropriety
in replying directly to our first Magistrate   and if there be any
I intreat you will suppress the letter, and in lieu of it give to
him assurances of my disposition   to the utmost
on all occasions, in his and his country's service   If you see no
impropriety in its being delivered, permit me to request you to
seal and have it forwarded   The satisfaction generally expressed
throughout this country, on the event of the cession is great, and
no symptoms of discontent are manifested, except by a very
small portion of the merchants and merchants   but a number of
seamen and adventurers lately arrived from France   on whom
the Prefect has been practising his   since his
arrival   He is a violent and bad man, whose projects of plunder
and monopoly are ended   can brook no contradiction, manifests
a hatred and pretended contempt for our nation   has disgusted
all the Spanish authorities   and, by his conduct, has lost the
confidence of all the well disposed and thinking people   He
will not fail, should it be in his power to do us any possible
injury, and will stick at no measures to obtain his ends   I think
it necessary to inform you of this, that you may be prepared for
any event whatever

Hon J Madison

[No 151]

PHILADELPHIA August 26, 1803.

My dear Friend—Your several letters of 12 13 and 18th ult
covering those for Mr S, reached me on 22d inst, and afford me
a full view of what you had then accomplished and in *prospect*
I *greatly rejoice* at your prompt resolution of making a bold
stroke at lands, while the opportunity of procuring them on easy
and low terms was yet in your power   and I shall invoke all my
faculties of invention and contrivance to give you the fullest support in what I consider with you the fairest chance ever thrown
in our way of making a certain and immense fortune   The purchase of Boudigny is a propitious prelude to your entire success,
to which I look with the greatest confidence and certainty

  *   *   *   *   *   *   *

  *   *   *   *   *   *   *

I cannot sufficiently impress you with the necessity and great
importance of entering into an agreement about the division of
the property, whenever you buy in company with others   as the
death or a quarrel with your associate in the purchase might
hang up the property, and render it totally useless for a century
particularly if minor children should inherit your associate's part,

would indeed effectually prevent a division till they became of age   Undivided real estate is the source of tedious and expensive law suits, and ruinous of the value of property   Attend to this point.

*   *   *   *   *   *   *
*   *   *   *   *   *   *

I send enclosed to you three U States bank post notes, all dated this day, in my favor, and endorsed to your order for $2500, viz No 1304 and 1305, for $1000 each, and No 1801, for $500 , payable 10 days *after date*   And by next mail will send you, without fail a similar amount to be applied, together with the $20,000 (you are authorized to draw) to the purchase of lands for our joint accounts   I need not reiterate the very high opinion I entertain of judicious purchases in that line   Perhaps you might tempt Bouligny to let you have 50 000 more of his remaining 100,000 acres, by giving him half money   If you send me plats and an accurate description of any further purchases of large bodies of land, favorably situated for settlements I might sell to people here, or induce emigration thither on advantageous terms to ourselves   There is nothing like settlements for bringing lands into value

By Mr Relf I should have sent your friend the miniature picture of his little daughter Caroline, but she has been indisposed with a fever and ague, which has emaciated and reduced her so as to render it impossible to take a true likeness , when the weather becomes cooler and she recovers her looks, his request shall be attended to

God bless you, my friend, and prosper your speculations   From me, rely on the firmest support

Yours most affectionately,
DAN W COXE

Dan l Clark, Esq

[No 152]

By defendant   3d July, 1849

J W GURLEY, Com

GERMANTOWN, 25th August, 1803

Mr Relf leaves us to-morrow, and I again address my dear brother , by the time you receive this, you must certainly acknowledge yourself some letters in my debt, but if you write me just to say you don't think me too troublesome a correspondent, I shall freely forgive you   Could I like my much valued brother, say a great deal in a few lines, it would give me sincere pleasure , but as that is a perfection I can never arrive at, I will do all in my power to imitate his example   Aunt Clark is making preparations for her journey to Virginia , she has had her car-

riage handsomely repaired and spoke for horses, a son of Mr
John Barclay's accompanies her Some time ago, she asked me,
did I wish to see that country, and if I did, she would be happy
to have me with her I declined it, as I think we are not as yet
settled enough for me to undertake such a thing, particularly as
you are not here.

The fever rages with great violence in New York all communication is stopped between the cities 'Tis a fortnight since
Dejan left us and we have not heard whether he sailed or not
My father and mother are uneasy lest he should unfortunately
catch the distemper so far from home He remained with us a
month, and we were all pleased with his inoffensive manners;
indeed he seemed more like a child in the family than a visitor
A week since I had long letters from Jane and Mr G , tis easy
to perceive from them that they are happy she talks in raptures
of her son, and indeed of the whole family I don t know that
I ever met with an instance of a whole family being so much attached to a stranger as she certainly was at first to them, but to
you we are highly indebted for it all, and what we at present are
She is quite delighted with Bill and says little George is the
same Were I to tell you all she says of you, it would, perhaps,
seem like flattery but she declares there is not such a man on
earth , that we have reason to say so is beyond all doubt Richard is entirely recovered of the accident I mentioned in my letter
by Dejan and his old master is returned all the children seem
attached to him and Tom sure they can t get any person more
capable of instructing them

Did I not fear to offend you by all my nonsense, I would say
Sally wishes to add a few lines to you for your remembrance of
her in your letters I believe I shall let her exert her genius, and,
like her mother, trust to your goodness as an apology, for our
intrusion on your time and patience

Our father is tolerably well My mother writes by this opportunity, and I believe aunt Clark Mrs Coxe is returned, and
her health much mended Mary sends you her best wishes,
and a safe return here Richard also joins in it Last of all,
your father's and mother's blessing attend you Remember me
to Mrs Huling Mr Gayon and all my acquaintance

       I remain your truly affectionate sister,

            A ANDERSON

Will my dear uncle receive my thanks for all his kindness to
me and mama I am, as yet a bad writer but hope in a few years
to be all my friends wish me I go to school from eight to twelve
every day the remainder I spend at home

Cousin Richard is now quite well and able to attend school
I heard from aunt Jane a few days ago and she says I must

spend 2 years with her to finish my education It is hardly yet began, but you shall decide for me and I hope I shall not be undeserving your favor, at least I will strive to deserve it

My grandfather and grandmother are well so is aunt Clark and aunt Mary I am, my dear uncle's affectionate, but troublesome little niece, SARAH JANE ANDERSON

[No 51]

Off'd by Defendants and filed 2d ...

J W CURLEY Commissioner

Rocky Mills near Richmond December 13th 1849

Dear Sir—Since writing to you from Philadelphia on the 9th ultimo I arrived at this place on the 21st and found all friends well I saw Mr Madison, on my way, at Washington I took the liberty of speaking to him about the Land Warrants which you ceded to me and he informed me before that the law must be satisfied but there is a right ... before executors can give or sell to each other, ... land person, and that we cannot obtain ... without an authenticated copy from the records ... expressive of our right to a residuary

I know that you must be greatly engaged in your official affairs, but must re-iterate my intreaties that you will if possible, attend to mine A few moments dedicated to them would arrange the whole and give me very great satisfaction. Mr Moylan was so obliging as to advance for me $509 for which I gave him an order on Mr Coxe payable at the expiration of the current quarter, which will be on the 10th of January I also left in his hands your notes with orders to receive any cash or bills sent forward for me until my return which I expect will be in April and I hope then, as you have wished it to be as well as myself, that all our accounts may be finally settled I have not heard from Germantown or Philadelphia since I left it We are all in great suspense about Louisiana I wish with all my heart that all there was once amicably arranged—we are all fearful that the affairs of that country will oblige you to change all your plans and induce a much longer separation between us than we had ever before contemplated God give you health and happiness, is the prayer of your ever affectionate Aunt, JANE CLARK

SHELBURNE, near New Canton on ?
James River January 9th, 1804. }

Dear Sir—Since writing to you on the 13th of last month, nothing new has arisen It would give me much pleasure to hear from you before I left this State Any letter directed to me to the care of George Watt Esquire at Richmond, would find a safe conveyance—and could you send forward the necessary orders about the lands, herein mentioned, so that what relates to them might be adjusted as I passed through Washington on my return to Philadelphia, which I intend, please God to be about the first of April, it would spare me much pain and expense. Miss Syme and Miss Barclay desire me to make their best wishes and compliments to you as do my friends in general

I am your ever affectionate and obliged Aunt

JANE CLARK

P S Mr Madison promised to forward my letters to and from you the present I send to him

[No 86]

Offered by Defendants, and filed 25th June, '19

J W GURLEY, Com r

CITY OF WASHINGTON Oct r 15th, 1803

Dear Sir—Your favor of the 2d September has been received, but was unintentionally left at home in my hurry to prepare for my journey to this place. You may be sure that the treaty with France and the State of Louisiana and the Island of New Orleans will be ratified by our government. The ratification of the first consul is already received, and before the last day of this month, every thing will have been done, which can be required on our part to give validity and sanction to that instrument and to the conventions which accompany it. As the Spanish Government have protested against the cession by France to us and even against the right of France to sell it to the U. States or any other power, you will render an essential service by having an eye upon the movements of the Spaniards, in order to ascertain whether there is any indication of a design to oppose or refuse the surrender of it to us. If any symptoms of that sort appear, you ought to give immediate notice of it to our Government and to Gen'l Wilkinson, or the commanding officer of the troops, in order that we may calculate our force accordingly. I have taken every opportunity of mentioning you in such terms, to influential men amongst us as will, I flatter myself, lead to your being actively as well as honorably employed, in completing the arrangements, necessarily growing out of the cession of   so valuable and so important

Consider me, if you please, associated with you in whatever adventure you may think advisable to make in consequence of this information, but advise me immediately, whether you have done, or propose to do any thing

I shall write again by next mail, when I shall know more and have more leisure. I am Dear Sir, with sincere esteem.

Your very humble servant   JONA DAYTON

DAN'L CLARK ESQ

Extract from the Philadelphia Gazette and Daily Advertiser of September 17th 1832

MARRIED

On Thursday evening, the 13th inst , at Delamore Place, Del , by the Rev Mr Pardee, WILLIAM WALLACE WHITNEY, Esq , of New York, to Miss MYRA E daughter of Col. Samuel B Davis

---

COMPLAINANT

Offered by the complanant

En la Ciudad de la Nueva Orleans, á nueve de Noviembre de mil ochocientos y un años ante mi el escrivano y testigos pareció Da Maria Zelime Carriere, muger legitima de Dn Guillermo Desgrange a quien doy fe conosco y disco que confecha veinte y seis de Marzo ultimo pasado de este corriente año por escritura en este archivo el citado su marido le confirio su poder general el que confesa no estarle revocado, y usando de una de sus clausulas otorga por la presente que lo sustituye y substituve en Dn. Sinforiano Caillavet especiálmente para que pueda cobrar de Da Josefa Morena, la cantidad, de doscientos pesos que le esta deviendo por saldo de la negra Maria Marta, del nombrado Lacosta vecino de Pensacola ciento diez y siete ps quatro reales por su cuenta certificada, de Dn Leonardo Mazange diez pesos, y de Madama Lartigue ochenta y siete ps , otorgando recivos finiquitos poderes y lastos con fee de la entrega ó renunciacion de las leyes de este caso y practicando todas las deligencias judiciales y extrajudiciales se ofrezcan sin exceptuar alguna Al cumplim to de loqual obliga sus bienes havidos y por haver da poder á las justicias de S M para que la apremien a su cumplim'to con todo rigor de dro como por sentencia consentida y pasada en autoridad de cosa jusgada sobre que renuncia las leyes de su favor con la gral en forma que lo prohive En cuyo testimonio asi lo otorgo y firmo siendo tgós Dn Antonio Boudousquie, Dn Alexo Lesassier y Antonio Fromentin presentes

(Signed)   MARIE CARRIERE DESGRANGE

Ante mi Narco Broutin, Esno Peubo.

I certify the foregoing to be a true copy of the original act, now in my possession

In faith, whereof, I grant these presents under my signature, and the impress of my official seal, at the city of New Orleans, on this 18 January, 1850

WM CHRSTY, Not Pub

ERRATUM AND OMISSION.—*Complainant's Evidence.*

Page 1162, letter of David Bradford to Chew and Relf should be dated 1801 instead of 1802.

" 435—49 This endorsement omitted " Admitted by defendants as proved, reserving all legal objection to its admissibility as evidence

J W GURLEY, Comm'r."

[No. 34]

Orders appointing Chew and Relf Executors.—Oath.—Letters testamentary.—Petition to have seals removed.—Petition to have seals removed.—Filing account, order to publish.—Homologation of account.—Offered by the defendants and filed 23 June 1849. M. GURLEY, Comr

SUCCESSION OF DANIEL CLARK

Oath.—Recorded folio 300th, vol 6th.—Before me, John B M Brierre, Deputy Register of the Court of Probates for and in the Parish of Orleans, personally appeared Beverley Chew who solemnly swears that he will well and faithfully perform all and singular the Duties of testamentary Executor of the late Daniel Clark deceased

So help him God

Sworn and subscribed before me

Signed BLP CHEW

New Orleans this twenty first day of January 1814

Signed BRIERRE, Dy Rr

Oath.—Recorded folio 299th, vol 6th.—Before me, John B M Brierre, Deputy Register of the Court of Probates for and in the Parish of Orleans, personally appeared Richard Relf, Esquire, who solemnly swears that he will well and faithfully perform all and singular the Duties of a testamentary Executor of the late Daniel Clark deceased

So help him God

Signed RICHARD RELF

Sworn and subscribed before me

New Orleans this twenty seventh day of August 1813

Signed BRIERRE, Dy Rr

EXEMPLIFICATION.—Recorded folio 300th, vol 6th.—The Government of the State of Louisiana to all whom these presents shall come.—GREETING

Whereas Beverley Chew of the Parish of Orleans, named and appointed one of the Executors of the last will and testament of Daniel Clark, late of the Parish aforesaid deceased having duly proved the same, and applied to the Court of Probates in and for the Parish of Orleans by petition praying the said Court to grant Letters Testamentary thereon

Now know Ye, That the said Beverley Chew has been and he is hereby authorized and empowered to collect the goods and effects which were of the said estate of the late Daniel Clark deceased and to make a just inventory thereof, and all other lawfull acts to do and perform as Executor Testamentary of the said last will and testament

Witness, James Pitot Esquire judge of the Court of Probates for the Parish of Orleans this twenty first day of January in the year of our Lord one thousand eight hundred and four

18

teen, and the thirty eighth of the Independence of the United States

Signed   THOS BEALE, Register of Wills, for the Parish of Orleans

EXEMPLIFICATION.—Recorded folio 299th, vol 6th.—The Government of the State of Louisiana to all whom these presents shall come,—GREETING

Whereas, Richard Relf, of the Parish of Orleans, named and appointed one of the Executors of the last will and testament of Daniel Clark, late of the Parish aforesaid, deceased, having duly proved the same, and applied to the Court of Probates in and for the Parish of Orleans, by petition, praying the said Court to grant letters Testamentary thereon

Now know Ye, That the said Richard Relf has been and he is hereby authorized and empowered to collect the goods and effects which were of the said Estate of the late Daniel Clark, deceased, and to make a just inventory thereof and all other lawful acts to do and perform as Executor testamentary of the said last will and testament

Witness, James Pitot, Squire Judge of the Court of Probates for the Parish of Orleans this twenty seventh day of August in the year of our Lord one thousand eight hundred and thirteen and the thirty eight of the Independence of the United States

Signed   THOS BEALE, Register of Wills,
                        for the Parish of Orleans

PETITION of R. Relf, the Executor of D Clark, for the seals to be removed and inventory &c.—Recorded folio 298th vol 6th —State of Louisiana, Parish of Orleans.— To the honorable James Pitot, Judge of the said Parish

The petition of Richard Relf one of the testamentary Executors of the last will and testament of Daniel Clark, deceased. being desirous to cause the execution of said will as soon as possible completed, prays the seals affixed, may be removed and that an Inventory of the goods may be ordered to be made by your petitioner and that appraisers may be appointed to appraise the same, &c, and your petitioner will ever pray, &c

Signed   F L TURNER, Atty for the Petitioner
August 18th, 1813

ORDER.—Let the seals be removed to-morrow at ten o'clock, and let an Inventory and appraisement take place according to law M Moreau Lislet being appointed counsel for the absent heirs New Orleans this 18th of August, 1813

Signed   J PITOT, Judge

PETITION & AUTHORISATION FOR SALL.—Recorded folio 300th, vol 6th —To the Honorable James Pitot Judge of the Court of Probates in and for the District and City of New Orleans

The petition of Richard Relf testamentary Executor of the late Daniel Clark —Humbly sheweth

That your petitioner prays your honor to grant him the necessary authorisation that he might sell the moveable and unmoveable property of the estate of the deceased at public auction in the manner and form prescribed by law, that is after ten days advertisements for the moveable effects and after thirty days advertisements for the slaves and other unmoveable effects and your petitioner as in duty bound will ever pray

Signed   Signed   RICHARD RELF

MOREAU LISLET, of Counsel for the absent heirs

ORDER —Let the sale take place as prayed for and according to law   New Orleans, August 27th, 1813

Signed   J PITOT, Judge

In the Court of Probates and for the Parish and City of New Orleans

ORDER —Let public notices be given to the creditors of this estate and to all others herein interested to show cause within ten days from public notification, why the within account should not be approved and homologated and the funds distributed according thereto It is further ordered that A Hoa be appointed to represent the absent heirs of the deceased

New Orleans, 27 August 1838

Signed   J BERMUDEZ Jge   Saturday 17th, April, 1841

ORDER —Succession of Daniel Clark — On motion of L C Duncan of counsel for Beverley Chew and Richard Relf, testamentary Executors of Daniel Clark, and on shewing to the Court that due publications had been made of the account filed by said Executors in this Court on the 27th of August, 1838 it is ordered by the Court that said account be homologated and confirmed in all respects in which it is not opposed

New Orleans, 22d April, 1841

Signed   J BERMUDEZ, Judge

ORDER —In the Court of Probates in and for the Parish and City of New Orleans —Thursday, 1st February, 1844 —In the matter of the Estate of Daniel Clark, on the oppositions to the account filed by the Executors

On motion of L C Duncan, of counsel for Richard Relf and Beverley Chew, Executors of Daniel Clark, and on filing the consent of Caroline Barnes and Eleonore O'Brian, now Eleonore McNiff, it is ordered that the opposition filed in behalf of said Caroline Barnes and Eleonore McNiff on the 18th September, 1838, to the account of the Executors filed on the 27th August, 1838 be dismissed, and that said account be homologated so far as the same concerns the said Caroline Barnes and Eleonore McNiff

New Orleans, 8th February 1844 —J BERMUDEZ Jge

I thereby certify that the foregoing are a true and correct copies of the originals on file, deposited in the office of the Second District Court of New Orleans

In witness whereof I have hereunto signed my name and affixed the seal of said Court

New Orleans this 22d day of June 1849

THO C POOL Clerk

Aujourd'hui, le seizième jour du mois d'août de l'an mil huit cent treize de notre Seigneur et le trente huitième de l'Indépendance Américaine Nous Gallien Préval, l'un des juges de paix pour la ville et la Paroisse de la Nouvelle Orléans, nous étant trouvé présent au décès du sieur Daniel Clark, ce jour a dix heures du soir, avons été requis par Mr Richard Relf, d'apposer les scellés sur tous les papiers appartenants à la succession du dit sieur Daniel Clark ce à quoi nous avons procédé en présence de Mr James Pitot et F Dusuau Delacroix Ledit sieur Richard Relf ayant été requis par nous de représenter les papiers de ladite succession, nous a conduit dans la chambre dudit défunt, où en présence des témoins susdits, nous avons réunis tous les susdits papiers et les avons mis dans un bureau et une armoire que nous avons trouvés dans la chambre dudit défunt, après quoi nous avons apposé nos scellés sur les portes de ladite chambre, et en avons établi gardien le sieur Francisco Morales lequel a promis, sous la foi du serment de remplir bien et fidèlement les devoirs de sa charge, et a signé avec nous ainsi que les témoins susdits

Les mêmes jours mois et an que dessus, sa

Signed   FRANCISCO MORALES

                            ✝
                          Marque

Au moment de clore le présent procès verbal, le sieur Richard Relf ayant trouvé dans une malle du défunt son testament olographe nous l'avons pris en présence des susdits témoins pour en faire la remise à l'honorable juge de la Cour des Preuves

Signed   J PITOT

              GALLIEN PREVAL, Juge de Paix

DUSUAU DELACROIX

RICHARD RELF

To the honorable the judge of the Court of Probates of the Parish of New Orleans

The petition of Francis Dusuau Delacroix of this Parish, Planter   Respectfully sheweth

That your petitioner has strong reasons to believe and does verily believe that the late Daniel Clark has made a testament or codicil posterior to that which has been opened before your honorable Court, and in the dispositions whereof he thinks to be interested and whereas it is to be presumed that the double

of this last will whose existence was known by several persons
might have been deposited with any notary public of the city

Your petitioner wherefore prays that it may please your honor
to order as it is the usual practice in such cases that every
notary public of this city appear before your honorable Court
within the delay of twenty four hours, in order to certify on
oath if there does or does not exist in their office any testament
or codicil or any sealed packet deposited by the said late Daniel
Clark

And your petitioner as in duty bound will ever pray, etc

D SEGHERS of Counsel for petitioner

Francisco Dusuan Delacroix, the above petitioner maketh oath
that the material facts in the above peition set forth are true
to the best of his knowledge and belief

Signed   DUSUAL DELACROIX

Sworn to before me August 18th, 1843

THO BEALE, R Wills

It is ordered that the several notaries of this city do appear
before this Court at the office of the Register of Wills, to-morrow, the 19th instant, at 9 o'clock A M precisely in order to
comply with the prayer of this petition

New Orleans, August 18th 1843

Signed   J PITOT, judge

Recorded folio 298th, vol 6th.

State of Louisiana Parish of Orleans —To the honorable
James Pitot, judge of the said Parish

The petition of Richard Relf, one of the testamentary executors of the last will and testament of Daniel Clark deceased
being desirous to have the execution of said will as soon as
possible completed, prays the seals affixed, may be removed,
and that an inventory of the goods may be ordered to be made
by your petitioner and that appraisers may be appointed to
appraise the same, &c

And your petitioner will ever pray, &c

F L TURNER, atty for the plaintiff

August 18th 1843

Let the seals be removed to-morrow at ten o'clock and let
an inventory and appraisement take place according to law
Mr Morcan Liskt being appointed counsel for theabsent heirs

New Orleans, 18th of August, 1843

J PITOT, judge

Recorded folio 298th vol 6th

Parish of New Orleans Court of Probates —At a session of
the Court of Probates, in and for the Parish and city of New
Orleans holden at this city of New Orleans, at the office of the
Register of Wills on tuesday the 19th day of August in the

year of our Lord 1813 and the 28th year of the Independance of the U S of America

Personally appeared the undersigned, notary public of this city, who do depose and say that there is not, nor ever was any testament, nor codicil, nor any sealed packet deposited in their office by the late Daniel Clark, nor any other disposition *mortis causa* whatsoever passed before them, by the same or deposited in their office

In witness whereof, they have hereunto set their respective hands, the day and year first above written

Signed   PIERRE PIDETLAUX

CLAUDE DIJAU   STEPHON DE QUIÑONES

M LAFITTE   MICHEL DE ARMAS Not Pub

JOHN LYND   NARCISSUS BROUTIN,

Notary Public.

Ne varietur —JAMES PITOT, judge —DANIEL CLARK

In the name of God, I Daniel Clark of New Orleans do make this my last will and testament

In primis I order that all my just debts be paid

Second I leave and bequath unto my mother Mary Clark now of Jermantown, in the State of Pensylvania all the Estate whether real or personal which I may did possessed of

Third I hereby nominate my friend Richard Relf and Beverley Chew, my executors with power to settle every thing relating to my Estate

Ne varietur —J PITOT, judge —New Orleans, 20 May, 1811

Signed   DANIEL CLARK

Know all men by these presents, that on the seventeenth day of August in the year of our Lord one thousand eight hundred and thirteen, and the thirty eight of the Independence of the United States of America

Personally appeared before me, James Pitot, judge of the Court of Probates, in and for the City and Parish of New Orleans, Paul Lanusse et Louis Seré, both residents in the city of New Orleans, who being duly sworn agreably to law declare and say that a packet folded up, as a letter, sealed with a red wafer, which I presented to them, and bearing the following subscription, this is my olographic will.

New Orleans, 20 May, 1811.

Signed   DANIEL CLARK

That the same is the proper hand writing of him the said Daniel Clark

Sworn to and subscribed before me

New Orleans, August 17th, 1813

J PITOT, judge.   LOUIS SERE

Wherefore, I the said judge caused the said packet to be broken open, in which was found one writing page signed,

Daniel Clark, and after caused the same instrument to be read in presence of the above named witnesses, who did further recognise the same to be totally written by the late Daniel Clark   LOUIS SERE   PAUL LANUSSE

I do hereby declare that the said instrument is duly proved according to the law of this state as being the last will and testament, in scriptis of the late Daniel Clark, and order the said last will to be deposited and recorded in the register office of this Court, that copies thereof may be delivered to all person it may concern   J. PITOT, judge

Before me, John B M Brierre, deputy Register of the Court of Probates for and in the Parish of Orleans, personally appeared Richard Relf, Esquire, who solemnly swears that he will well and faithfully perform all and singular the duties of a testamentary executor, of the late Daniel Clark, deceased

So help me God
                    Signed   RICCHARD RELF
Sworn and subscribed before me
New Orleans this twenty seventh day of August 1813
                    BRIERRE, D y Ri of wills

Before me John B M Brierre, deputy Register of this Court of Probates for and in the Parish of Orleans, personally appeared Beverley Chew, who solemnly swears that he will well and faithfully perform all and singular the duties of a testamentary executor of the late Daniel Clark, deceased

So help me God   BEVERLY CHEW
Sworn and subscribed before me
New Orleans, this twenty first day of January 1814
          Signed.   BRIERRE, D y Rr

The Government of the State of Louisiana, to all to whom these presents shall come, greeting

Whereas Beverley Chew, of the Parish of Orleans, named and appointed one of the executors of the last will and testament of Daniel Clark, late of the Parish aforesaid, deceased, having duly proved the same and applied to the Court of Probates in and for the Parish of Orleans, by petition, praying the said Court to grant letters testamentary thereon

Now know you, that the said Beverley Chew has been and he is hereby authorized and empowered to collect the goods and effects which were of the said Estate of the late Daniel Clark, deceased and to make a just inventory thereof, and all other lawfull acts to do and perform, as executor testamentary of the said last will and testament

Witness, James Pitot, Esquire, judge of the Court of Probates for the Parish of Orleans, this twenty first day of January in the year of our Lord one thousand eight hundred and fourteen, and the thirty eighth of the Independence of the United State.

Signed   THOS. BEALE, Register of Wills, for the Parish of Orleans

The Government of the State of Louisiana, to all to whom these presents shall come, greeting

Whereas Richard Relf of the Parish of Orleans, named and appointed one of the executors of the last will and testament of Daniel Clark, late of the Parish aforesaid deceased, having duly proved the same and applied to the Court of Probates in and for the Parish of Orleans by petition, praying the said Court to grant letters testamentary thereon

Now know you that the said Richard Relf has been and he is hereby authorized and empowered to collect the goods and effects which were of the said Estate of the late Daniel Clark, deceased, and to make just inventory thereof, and all other lawful acts to do and perform as executor testamentary of the last will and testament

Witness, James Pitot Esquire, judge of the Court of Probates for the Parish of Orleans, this twenty seventh day of August, in the year of our Lord one thousand eight hundred and thirteen, and the thirty eighth of the Independence of the United States

Signed   THOS BEALE, Register of Wills for the Parish of Orleans

To the Honorable James Pitot, Judge of the Court of Probates in and for the Parish and City of New Orleans — The petition of Richard Relf testamentary Executor of the late Daniel Clark,—humble sheweth

That your petitioner has been duly empowered by the late Daniel Clark to settle all his affairs,—That by the situation in which your petitioner found the estate, it thought it impossible to discharge the debts of the said estate without the assistance of the Banks or of friends, who will be disposed to advance money for that purpose or without sacrificing the property of the deceased and the interests of the creditors as well as that of the heirs,

Wherefore your petitioner prays your honor to grant him the necessary authorisation with the consent of the counsel for the absent heirs to mortgage or give in pledge all such of the properties and effects of the estate he will think proper, to obtain money to discharge the debts of the said estate and even to bind himself as executor, to obtain the removal of such of the notes drawn or endorsed by the late Daniel Clark that he will find necessary or convenient to renew, in order to avoid the sacrifice of the estate by an immediate sale fore cost or at terms of credit so short that it would be impossible to obtain

price proportionate to the value of the property, and your petitioner as in duty bound will ever pray, &c
Signed   RICHARD RELF

I do consent that the prayers of the petitioner be granted as a proper mode the best calculated for the interests of the heirs of the deceased

New Orleans, August 27th, 1813

MOREAU LISLET, of counsel for the absent heirs

Let the prayer of this petition be granted with the consent of the counsel for the absent heirs

New Orleans, August 27th, 1813

J PITOT Judge

Recorded folio 299th, vol 6th.

To the honorable the Judge of the Court of Probates in and for the Parish of New Orleans —The petition of Richard Relf, of this City, merchant —Respectfully sheweth

That late Daniel Clark of this City deceased, by his olografic will, duly proved before your honorable Court on the seventeenth instant appointed your petitioner and Beverley Chew, of this city, merchants, his testamentary executors, with power to settle every thing relating to his estate

That in consequence of the absence of said Beverlley Chew of this State, your petitioner remains, for the present, sole testamentary Executor of said deceased

Wherefore he prays that it may please your honor to order that testamentary letters may be delivered to him according to law —And as in duty bound your petitioner will ever pray, &c
Signed   RICHARD RELF

Let testamentary letters be delivered to the petitioner according to law   New Orleans, 27th August, 1813
Signed   J PITOT, Judge   (Rec fol 299th vol 6th)

To the honorable James Pitot, Judge of the Court of Probates in and for the Parish and city of New Orleans —The petition of Richard Relf, testamentary Executor of the late Daniel Clark,—Humbly sheweth

That your petitioner prays your honor to grant him the necessary authorisation that he might sell the moveable and unmoveable property of the estate of the deceased at public auction in the manner and form described by law, that is after ten days advertisements for the moveable effects and thirty days advertisements for the slaves and other unmoveable effects and your petitioner as in duty bound will ever pray
Signed   RICHARD RELF
MOREAU LISLET,
of counsel for the absent heirs

Let the sale take place as prayed for according to law
New Orleans August 27th 1813   J PITOT Judge

2ᵗ

To the honorable James Pitot, Judge of the Court of Probates for the Parish of New Orleans.—The petition of Richard Relf one of the testamentary executors of the late Daniel Clark,—Humbly Sheweth

That by the appraisement made on the 5th of October last, of several slaves of the estate of Daniel Clark, they have been estimated so high that when they have been offered for sale on this day, at public auction, it was impossible to obtain the price of this apraisement,

And whereas there are now many respectable planters and others persons collected to become bidders to that sale who may be absent on another day, if the auction is postponed, whereby the estate may be greatly injured

Your petitioner prays your honor to order that a new appraisement be made immediately by three respectable planters or other persons having as far as possible a knowledge of the character and talents of the said slaves, and your petitioner as in duty bound will ever pray, &c &c

Signed   RICHARD RELF

I do consent to a new and immediate appraisement of the slaves, who have been offered for sale and whose price of appraisement has not been obtained

MOREAU LISLET, defendant of the absent heirs.

Recorded folio 304, vol 6

Aujourd'hui dix huitième jour du mois d'août de l'année de notre Seigneur mil huit cent treize et le trente huitieme de l'Independance des Etates-Unis d'Amérique quatre heures de relevée, à la requête du sieur Richard Relf, et en vertu de l'ordonnance de l'honorable juge de la Cour des Preuves, en date de ce jour, "portant qu'il sera procédé à l'inventaire du feu sieur Daniel Clark, conformément à la loi," nous Thomas Beale, Register des Testamens pour la ville et paroisse de la Nouvelle-Orléans, nous sommes transportés sur le chemin du Bayou en la maison où est décédé dit feu sieur Daniel Clark dans la soirée du seize du présent à l'effet d'y procéder à la levée et reconnaissance des scellés apposés par le sieur Gallien Préval, l'un des juges de paix de cette ville et paroisse, sur les propriétés du dit défunt, où étant, nous avons trouvé le dit sieur Richard Relf, executeur testamentaire du défunt, le sieur Moreau Lislet, avocat nommé par la cour pour représenter l'héritière absente et le sieur Gallien Préval, es-qualités qui précédent et avons en leur présence et en celle du sieur Pospère Prieur et Sébastien Blondeau témoins domiciliés, requis le sieur Francisco Morales, Gardien des dits scellés de nous les représenter ce qu'il à fait de la manière suivante

Premièrement sur une armoire en bois où étaient apposés les scellés, examen scrupuleux faits d'iceux par le sieur Gal hen Preval, ils ont été trouvés sains et entiers et nous les avons reconnu tels pour la décharge du dit Gardien

Ouverture et examen faits d'icelle, nous n'y avons trouvé que des papiers que nous avons soigneusement examiné, à l'effet d'en extraire les billets susceptibles de prompte échéance, pour ne pas perdre le recours contre les endosseurs, ainsi qu'il suit

Premièrement un billet à ordre de somme de quatre mille quatre cent soixante une piastres consenti en faveur du défunt par John Lynd en date du 10 Avril 1813 et payable à quatre mois de date, par nous coté et paraphé et inventorié sur la lettre A, numéro un to $4461

Item un autre billet à ordre de la somme de quatre cents piastres consenti en faveur du défunt par G Debuys, en date du 7 juillet 1813, et payable à soixante jours de date par nous coté, paraphé et inventorié sous la lettre B numéro 2 $400

                                                        $4861

Lesquels billets nous avons remis au dit sieur Richard Relf, exécuteur testamentaire qui s'en fait charge et tous les papiers de la dite armoire scrupuleusement examinés, ainsi que ceux d'un bureau en acajou, étant dans la même chambre, et n'y ayant trouvé ni testament ni autres billets prêts à échoir, nous avons réunis tous les papiers, que nous avons remis dans la dite armoire, sur laquelle nous avons re-apposé les scellés N° 1, et en avons de rechef confié la garde au sieur Francisco Morales, qui a promis sous serment de nous les représenter toutes fois et quantes il en sera légalement requis, et ont toutes les parties signé avec nous les mêmes jour mois et an que dessus et nous sommes retirés remettant la continuation du présent à demain six heures du matin ce dont toutes les parties et témoins se tiennent pour avertis

Signed	RICHARD RELF
THOS BEALE, Register of Will,	GALLIEN PREVAL juge de paix
BLONDEAU	L MOREAU LISLET
PROSPERE PRIEUR	Deffensor of the absent heirs

Et aujourd'hui dix-neuvième jour du mois d'août de l'an de notre Seigneur mil huit cent treize et le trente huitième de l'indépendence des Etats Unis d'Amérique, six heures du matin, heure indiquée au précédent procès verbal, nous Thomas Beale, Regester des Testamens pour la ville et paroisse de la Nouvelle Orléans, nous sommes transportés sur le chemin du Bayou, au domicile où est décédé feu sieur Daniel Clark, à l'effet d'y procéder à l'inventaire descriptif et estimatif de meubles, effets, bijoux, argenteries, terres, esclaves, titres et papiers provenant de la dite succession, ou étant, nous avons trouvé les sieurs Richard Relf, executeur testamentaire du défunt, Louis Moreau Lislet, avocat nommé par la cour pour représenter l'héritiere absente, et avons en leur présence pris le serment du sieur Prospère Prieur et Sébastien Blondeau de bien et fidèlement se conduire dans les devoirs d'appréciateurs de tout ce qui leur sera presenté comme provenant de la dite succession, après quoi nous avons procédé comme suit.

Premièrement dans une chambre en bas nous avons trouvé les objets suivants

Un lit à colonnes en bois de mérisier, garni de trois matelats en barbe espagnole, et de coutis, un traversin, deux oreillers, une mauvaise moustiquère en mousseline avec sa garniture, estimés par les sus dits appréciateurs, la somme de trente-cinq piastres $35

Item un petit bureau, en noyer, en forme de bibliotéque, estimé par les mêmes la somme de vingt piastres   20

Item une petite table en bois de mérisier, estimée par les mêmes la somme de trois piastres   3

Item une autre petite table ployante en mérisier estimée par les mêmes la somme de quatre piastres   4

Item une armoire en bois jaune, estimée par les mêmes la somme de trente piastres   30

Item douze chaises en bois, peintes en verd, estimées par les mêmes la somme de douze piastres.   12

Item une paire de pistolets d'arçon avec ses fontes, estimés par les mêmes la somme de douze piastres   12

Item un poignard garni en argent estimé par les mêmes la somme de trois piastres.   3

Item un sabre, garni en cuivre, estimé par les mêmes la somme de douze piastres   12

Item deux paires de razoirs avec un petit miroir de toilette estimés par les mêmes la somme de deux piastres.   2

Dans la salle du haut Un cabaret de porcelaine composé de douze tasses et onze sous-coupes une théière, un pot à crême, un sucrier, et trois assiettes, avec un plateau peint en rouge, le tout estimé par les mêmes la somme de trente piastres.   30

Item un autre cabaret de porcelaine composé de douze tasses, douze sous-coupes, une cafetière, un bocal et trois assiettes avec un plateau peint en ————

$ 163

Montant de l'autre part ⇒ 165

noir, le tout estimé par les mêmes la somme de vingt
piastres. 20

Item un pot à l'eau avec sa curette, estimé par
les mêmes la somme de dix piastres. 10

Item deux vieilles table à jouer, estimées par les
mêmes la somme de quatre piastres 4

Item une table pliante en merisier, estimée par
les mêmes la somme de huit piastres 8

Item un etui de mathematique et une petite poire
à poudre, estimés par les mêmes la somme de quatre piastres 4

Item une bibliothèque composée de sept cents
trois volumes de divers ouvrages, partie desquels
pourront être réclamés par divers estimés en bloc à
la somme de sept cent piastres 700

Dix huit cuillères et douze fourchettes une cuil-
lère à soupe seize cuillères à café, vingt-quatre
cuillères à crême et une pince à sucre le tout en
argent pesant cent vingt-huit onzes, six gros, estimés par les mêmes la somme de cent vingt-huit
piastres, soixant quinze cents 128 75

Item une montre anglaise à double boitier en or,
estimée par les mêmes la somme de trente six piast 36

Item dix pièces de grosse ratine bleu, estimées
par les mêmes à vingt-cinq piastres la pièce, ensemble la somme de deux cent cinquante piastres 250

Item un parti de fayence bleu dépareillé, estimée
par les mêmes la somme de cinquante piastres 50

Item six douzaines vin rouge, estimées par les
mêmes la somme de six piastres la donzaine, ensemble la somme de trente six piastres 36

Item dix douzaines de vin blanc, estimées par
les mêmes la somme de huit piastres la douzaine,
ensemble la somme de quatre vingt piastres 80

Qui est tout ce qui s'est trouvé de meubles et effets, provenant de la dite succession après quoi $1489–75
nous avons sans désemparer procédé à l'estimation
des esclaves de la succession

ESCLAVES —Un negre nommé *Will*, nègre de
champ, âgé d'environ trente ans, estimé par les mêmes la somme de cinq cents piastres $500

Item un nègre nommé Lubin, domestique, âgé
d'environ trente cinq ans, estimé par les mêmes la
somme de six cents piastres 600

Item Coks, mulatre commandeur âge d'environ

$ 1100

Montant de l'autre part $\times$ 1100

quarante cinq ans, estimé par les mêmes la somme
de cinq cents cinquante piastres   550

Item Salomon, nègre de champ âgé de quarante ans, estimé par les mêmes la somme de cinq
cents piastres   500

Item Jacob, nègre de champ, âgé de vingt cinq
ans, estimé par les mêmes la somme de six cents
piastres   600

Item John nègre de champ âgé de seize ans, estimé par les mêmes la somme de cinq cents cin-
quante piastres   550

Item Jacob, negre de champ, malade âgé d'environ dix-sept ans estimé par les mêmes la somme
de trois cent piastres vu son état de maladie   300

Item Jacques Lugen, nègre de champ, âgé d'environ dix-huit ans, estimé par les mêmes la somme
de cinq cents cinquante piastres   550

Item Antoine, nègre de champ âgé d'environ
quarante ans, estimé par les mêmes la somme de
cinq cents piastres   500

Item David, negre de champ, âgé d'environ cinquante ans, estimé par les mêmes la somme de qua-
tre cent cinquante piastres   450

Item Paul, griffe de champ âgé d'environ vingt
deux ans, estimé par les mêmes la somme de qua-
tre cent cinquante piastres   450

Item George, nègre de champ, âgé d'environ
cinquante ans estimé par les mêmes la somme de
deux cents piastres   200

Item Adam, nègre de champ âgé d'environ cinquante ans, estimé par les mêmes la somme de trois
cent piastres   300

Item doctor David, nègre médecin, âgé d'environ trente cinq ans, estimé par les mêmes la som-
me de cinq cent piastres   500

Item Randolphe, nègre de champ, âgé d'environ
trente cinq ans, estimé par les mêmes la somme de
quatre cent cinquante piastres   450

Item Etienne, nègre de champ âgé d'environ
cinquante cinq ans, estimé par les mêmes la somme
de quatre cent piastres   400

Item Lubin, nègre de champ âgé d'environ quarante ans estimé par les mêmes la somme de qua-
tre cent piastres   400

Item Relf, negre de champ âge d'anviron qua-

                                                                                ——————
                                                                               $\times$ 7800

Montant de l'autre part $ 7800

~~lante~~-cinq ans, estimé par les mêmes la somme de
quatre cent piastres   400

Item Providence, nègre de champ, âgé d'environ
quarante-cinq ans, estimé par les mêmes la somme
de quatre cent piastres   400

Item Figaro, nègre de champ, âgé d'environ trente ans, estimé par les mêmes la somme de cinq
cent piastres   500

Item Lindor, nègre de champ, âgé d'environ trente ans, estimé par les mêmes la somme de cinq cent
cinquante piastres   550

Item Nerihc, nègre de champ, âgé d'environ trente cinq ans, estimé par les mêmes la somme de
cinq cent piastres   500

Item Nese, nègre de champ, âgé d'environ trente
ans, estimé par les mêmes la somme de cinq cent
piastres   500

Item J. Sam, mulatre de champ âgé d'environ
dix-huit ans, estimé par les mêmes la somme de
cinq cent piastres   500

Item Jean nègre de champ âgé de vingt ans, estimé par les mêmes la somme de cinq cent piastres   500

Item Salomon, nègre de champ, âgé d'environ
quarante-cinq ans, estimé par les mêmes la somme de quatre cent cinquante piastres   450

Item Austin, negre de champ, âgé d'environ
vingt cinq ans, estimé par les mêmes la somme de
cinq cent piastres   500

Item James, negre de champ, âgé d'environ seize
ans, estimé par les mêmes la somme de cinq cent
piastres   500

Item Gibaud nègre de champ, âgé de quarante
cinq ans, estimé par les mêmes la somme de quatre
cent piastres   400

Item Wallis, negre de champ âgé d'environ trente ans, estimé par les mêmes la somme de cinq cent
piastres   500

Item Charles, mulatre de champ, âgé d'environ
quarante ans, estimé par les mêmes la somme de
cinq cent piastres   500

Item Jacques, mulatre de champ, âgé d'environ
trente cinq ans, estimé par les mêmes, la somme de   500
cinq cent piastres

$ 15000

Montant de l autre part $ 15000

Item Codio, nègre de champs, estimé par les mêmes la somme de cinq cent piastres — 500

Item Davis, nègre scieur de long, âgé d'environ soixante ans, estimé par les mêmes la somme de trois cent piastres — 300

Item Cardinal, nègre de pioche, âgé d'environ vingt-cinq ans, estimé par les mêmes la somme de quatre cent cinquante piastres — 450

Item Jérémie nègre de champ, âgé d'environ trente cinq ans, estimé par les mêmes la somme de cinq cent piastres — 500

Item L'Ebène, nègre de champ, âgé d'environ quarante ans, estimé par les mêmes la somme de quatre cent piastres — 400

Item John, nègre de champ, âgé d'environ quarante ans, estimé par les mêmes la somme de quatre cent piastres — 400

Item Mérode nègre de champ, âgé d'environ trente cinq ans estimé par les mêmes la somme de quatre cent cinquante piastres — 450

Item Willis, nègre de champ âgé d'environ dix-huit ans, estimé par les mêmes la somme de cinq cent cinquante piastres — 550

Item Moise, nègre de champ âgé d'environ seize ans, estimé par les mêmes la somme de cinq cent piastres — 500

Item Davis nègre de champ âgé de vingt ans, estimé par les mêmes la somme de quatre cent cinquante piastres — 450

Item André, nègre de champ, âgé d'environ vingt ans, estimé par les mêmes la somme de cinq cent piastres — 500

Item Dress, nègre de champ âgé d'environ quarante cinq ans, estimé par les mêmes la somme de quatre cent piastres — 400

Item André, nègre de champ, âgé d'environ cinquante cinq ans, estimé par les mêmes la somme de deux cent cinquante piastres — 250

Item Thom, nègre de champ, âgé d'environ quarante ans, estimé par les mêmes la somme de quatre cent cinquante piastres — 450

Item Bobe, nègre de champ, âgé d'environ vingt huit ans, estimé par les mêmes la somme de cinq cent cinquante piastres — 550

Item Alu, nègre de champ, âgé d'environ trente ——————

$ 21650

Montant de l'autre part $ 21650

cinq ans, estimé par les mêmes, la somme de qua
tre cent piastres   400

Item James, nègre de champ, âgé d'environ
soixante ans, estimé par les mêmes la somme de
cent cinquante piastres   150

Item Harry, mulatre domestique, âgé d'environ
quinze ans estimé par les mêmes, la somme de
cinq cent piastres   500

Item Stouder nègre vacher, âgé d'environ quarante cinq ans, estimé par les mêmes, la somme de
quatre cent piastres   400

Item Arthur négrillon âgé de douze ans, estimé
par les mêmes, la somme de trois cents piastres   300

Item Sam, nègre de picoche âgé d'environ quarante huit ans, estropié, estimé par les mêmes, la
somme de trois cent piastres   300

Item Ledger négrillon, âgé d'environ onze ans
estimé par les mêmes la somme de trois cent
piastres   300

Item Phébée, négresse de champ, d'environ
soixante ans, estimée par les mêmes la somme de
deux cent piastres   200

Item Fany négresse de champ, âgée d'environ
soixante ans, estimée par les mêmes la somme de
deux cent piastres   200

Item Ana négresse âgée d'environ vingt deux
ans, estimée par les mêmes la somme de trois cent
piastres   300

Item Geneviève negresse créole de Natchez,
âgée d'environ quarante cinq ans, estimée par les
mêmes la somme de quatre cent piastres   400

Item Betty negresse âgée d'environ cinquante
ans estimée par les mêmes la somme de quatre
cent piastres   400

Item Polly négresse âgée de vingt cinq ans,
avec ses deux enfans l'un nommé John, âgé de
cinq ans, et l'autre Julien, a la mamelle, estimés
par les mêmes la somme de six cent piastres   600

Item Liza, mulatresse âgée d'environ vingt ans,
avec son enfant nommé Williams, mulatre d'environ
quatorze mois, estimés par les mêmes la somme de
cinq cent piastres   500
                                                     _____
                                                     $ 26 600

qui font tous les esclaves qui nous ont été présentés pour être inventories comme provenant de la succession dudit défunt sieur Daniel Clark

Apres quoi, nous, Register sousdit et soussigne, avons sans desempasse procede a la description et estimation de la maison. sur laquelle nous operons, de la maniere suivante

MAISONS ET TERRAINS.—Une maison a etage, ayant soixante dix pieds de face a la place Bretonne et cinquante pieds de profondeur composee d'une grande salle, trois chambres, dont deux a feu, et une galerie au rez de chaussee, ayant au premier etage une grande salle, trois appartements dont deux a feu, et une galerie; la mansarde divisee en diverses petites chambres ladite maison batie en brique et couverte en bardeaux

Plus un batiment servant de cuisine et de cases a negres, ayant soixante dix pieds de long, bati en colombage et couvert en bardeaux estimee avec l'emplacement sur lequel elle est batie, conformement au plan de B J Lafon, et designe sous le No 5, et trop connu pour avoir besoin d'etre decrit plus amplement par les susdits appreciateurs, la somme de dix mille piastres $10,000

Monsieur Ridchard Relf. executeur testamentaire du defunt, nous a dit que, par egard pour sa memoire, il demandait qu'il ne fut pas procede a l'inventaire de sa garde-robe et de son linge de corps se reservant d'en faire approuver l'emploi par l'heritiere du defunt, et le sieur L. Moreau L'Islet, avocat nomme par la Cour pour la representer a accede à sa demande

Et attendu l'heure de trois de relevee survenue nous, Register susdit et soussigne, avons, du consentement des parties, arrête le present et avons remis la continuation pour l'eligement des papiers, lesquels nous avons soigneusement mis dans trois malles, sur lesquelles nous avons appose nos scelles. et que nous avons fait emporter en notre office, à demain quatre heures de relevée, ce dont toutes les parties se tiennent pour averties, et lecture faite de celui. nous avons trouve le montant du mobilier inventorie dans la presente vacation etre de la somme de quatorze cent quatre vingt neuf piastres soixante quinze cents, celui des esclaves aussi inventorie être de la somme de vingt six mille neuf cents piastres, et celui de la maison sur laquelle nous operons etre de la somme de dix-mille piastres, lesquels meubles et effets, esclaves et maisons nous avons laisses a la disposition dudit sieur Richard Relf, executeur testamentaire, qui s'en fait charge et a signe avec nous et les autres parties et temoins les mêmes jour, mois et an que dessus, et nous sommes retires

Signed   **BLONDEAU**   **MOREAU L'ISLET**
                                   deffenseur des heritiers absents
PROSPERE PRIEUR.   **RICHARD RELF**
RICHARD RUD   **THOS BEALE.** Register

Et aujourd'hui, vingtieme jour du mois d'Aout de l'an de notre

Seigneur mil huit cent treize, et le trente huitième de l'Indépendance des Etats-Unis d'Amerique, quatre heures de relevée nous, Thomas Beale, Register des Testaments pour la ville et paroisse de la Nouvelle Orleans avons procède en notre office en presence des parties et temoins reunis, à l'élégement et classifications des papiers contenus dans une petite malle sur laquelle était apposé le scelle No de la manière suivante

ACTIFS.—Premierement un billet à ordre de la somme de cinq cent piastres consenti en faveur du defunt par Morin, comme chargé des pouvoirs de son epouse, par acte par devant Broutin notaire, en date du trois Juillet 1813, et payable par tout Decembre prochain, ledit billet par nous cote, paraphe et inventorie sous la lettre C, No trois .... $ $ 500

Item un autre billet à ordre de la somme de deux cent quatre vingt quatre piastres cinquante cents consenti en faveur du defunt par P D Toley, en date du 6 Septembre 1810 et payable à demande par nous cote, paraphe et inventorie sous la lettre D. No 4, au dos duquel est un reçu de la main du defunt, de la somme de cent piastres, ce qui reduit ledit billet à celle de cent quatre vingt quatre piastres cinquante cents 184 50

Item un bon de la somme de cent piastres, consenti en faveur du defunt par L Boisdore, en date du 14 Avril 1810, payable à volonte par nous cote, paraphe et inventorie, sous la lettre E, No cinq..5 100

Item un billet de la somme de dix piastres, consenti en faveur du defunt par A J Lancell, en date du 29 Août 1812, payable à demande par nous cote, paraphe et inventorie, sous la lettre F et le numero six.... ....6 10

Item un billet de la somme de mille piastres, consenti en faveur du defunt par Gilberto Leonard en date du 13 Mars 1797, payable à volonte par nous cote, paraphe et inventorie, sous la lettre G, numero sept. 7 1000

Item un billet de la somme de cent piastres consenti en faveur du defunt par Abraham Arcenaus, en date du 23 Fevrier 1813, payable à volonte, par nous cote, paraphe et inventorie, sous la lettre H, numero huit........ ....8 100

Item un billet de la somme de cent piastres, consenti en faveur du defunt par Mr. Perez, en date du 4 Septembre 1811, par nous cote, paraphe et inventorie, sous la lettre I, numero neuf.... ....9 100
——————
$ 1991 50

Montant de l'autre part   1994 50

Item un bon de la somme de trois cent piastres, consenti a l'ordre du defunt par Magnau, en date du 23 Mars 1810, par nous cote, paraphe et inventorie, sous la lettre J, numero dix.... 10   300

Item un billet a ordre de la somme de trois mille piastres, consenti en faveur du defunt par Elizabeth Renaud Trepagnier en date du 20 Mai 1811, et payable au premier Mai 1812, par nous cote, paraphe et inventorié, sous la lettre K, No onze.....11   300

Item une reconaissance de la somme de cinquante quatre piastres et vingt-cinq sols consentis en faveur du defunt par Coisson, en date du 17 Octobre 1806, par nous cote, paraphe et inventorie, sous la lettre L, No douze..... 12   54 25

Item un billet a ordre de la somme de cinquante cinq piastres, consenti en faveur du defunt par Richard Devals, en date du 23 Novembre 1811 payable a un an de date, par nous cote, paraphe et inventorie, sous la lettre M, No treize 13   55

Item un billet a ordre de la somme de sept mille trois cent trente trois piastres quatre-vingt dix cents, consenti a John Clay par James Sterrot, en date du 3 Octobre 1808, et payable a six mois de date, lequel est endossé par John Clay et le defunt, au bas de la signature duquel est un reçu du montant dudit billet des mains de Mr. Daniel Clark, signe P Gryms, par nous cote, paraphe et inventorie, sous la lettre N, No quatorze. 14   7333 90

Item un mandat de ladite somme de cent soixante deux piastres, tire en faveur du defunt par le chevalier de Bellogent sur Mr Barriere, en date du 23 Juin 1812, par nous cote, paraphe et inventorie sous la lettre O, No quinze..............15   162

Item un billet a ordre de la somme de six mille cinq cent cinqante sept piastres quatre-vingt douze cents, consenti en faveur de William Brooks par Ferdinand L Claiborne, en date du 18 Novembre 1811, et payable au premier Fevrier dix-huit cent treize, ledit billet endosse par William Brooks, H A Claiborne, et Chew et Relf par nous cote, paraphe et inventorie sous la lettre P, No seize........16   6557 92

Item un billet de la somme de quarante deux piastres, consenti a l'ordre du défunt par Jean Raffray, en date du 15 Juillet 1799 par nous cote, paraphe et inventorie par la lettre Q, No. dix-sept...17   42   _____

$ 16799 57

Montant de l'autre part. $ 16799 57

Item une obligation de la somme de trente un mille
piastres, consentie en faveur du defunt par William
Harper en date du 8 Juin 1813, payable le 8 Juin,
par nous cotée paraphée et inventoriée sous la lettre
R No dix huit ... .13 31000

Item un billet de la somme de deux mille piastres,
consenti a l'ordre du defunt par William Harper en
date du premier mai 1813, et payable au premier
mai 1820, par nous cote, paraphe et inventorie sous
la lettre S numero 19 2000

Item un billet de la somme de deux mille piastres
consenti a l'ordre du defunt, par William Harper en
date du premier may 1813, payable le premier may
1816, par nous cote paraphe et inventorie sous la
lettre T N° 20 2000

Item trois billets de meme date pour la somme
de deux mille piastres chaque, ensemble la somme
de six mil piastres payable le 1er de mai 1817, 18
et 19, tiré par Wm Harper en faveur du defunt par
nous cotees, paraphees et inventoriees sous les lettres
U V, W et les numeros 21, 22 et 23 6000

Item deux billets de la somme de trois mille cent
vingt-cinq piastres chaque, ensemble la somme de
six mille deux cents cinquante piastres souscrits en
faveur du defunt, par Henry Hunt, en date du 15
mai 1810, payable a un et deux ans, par nous cotes,
paraphes et inventories sous les lettres XX et les numeros 24 et 25 6250

Item un billet de la somme de trois cent piastres,
souscrit en faveur du defunt, par Henry Hunt, en
date du 15 mai 1810, et portant interet depuis sa
date, par nous cote, paraphe et inventorie sous la
lettre Z, numero 26 300

Item une reconnaissance de la somme de neuf
cent trois piastres, souscrite en faveur du defunt par
John Watkins, en date du 24 aout 1807, par nous
cotée, paraphee et inventoriee sous la double lettre
AA N° 27 800

Item une reconnaissance de la somme de cinq
mille quatre cent quatre-vingt-quinze piastres et soixante-quinze cent, souscrite en faveur du defunt, par
Edward D Turner, en date du 19 Decembre 1808
par nous cotee, paraphee et inventoriee sous la double lettre BB N° 28 5195 75

Item une obligation hypothecaire de la somme de
———

$ 70145 32

                          Montant de l'autre part $ 70115 32

neuf mille six cent dix-neuf piastres, cinq escalins, souscrite en faveur du defunt, par John Walkins, en raport de Pierre Pederclaux, notaire public, en date du 29 Aout 1805 et portée ici uniquement pour memoire et par nous coté paraphée et inventoriée sous la double lettre CC numero vingt-neuf   29   9619 50

Item un livret de la Banque de la Louisiane, pour balance duquel il parait être du à la succession, la somme de quatre-vingt trois piastres quatre-vingt-dix-huit cents, article arrete au 13 Aout présente annee par nous coté et paraphe et inventorie sous la double lettre DD N$^\circ$ 30   83 98

Item un livret de la Banque des habitants, pour balance duquel il parait être du à la succession la somme de quatre mil cent huit piastres quarante trois cents, par nous cotes, paraphe et inventorie sous la double lettre E E N$^\circ$ 31   4108 43

Item, livret de la Banque d'Orleans, pour balance duquel il parait être du à la succession la somme de trois mille trente sept piastres, soixante treize cents, par nous cote, paraphe et inventorie sous la double lettre FF, N$^\circ$ 32.   3037 73

                                   $ 86994 96

Et attendu qu'il est sept heures de relevee, nous, Register susdit et soussigne, avons arrete le present, et du consentement des parties en avons remis la continuation a lundi vingt-trois du courant, ce dont toutes les parties et temoins se tiennent pour avertis, et lecture faite de celui, nous avons trouve le montant des actifs inventories dans la presente vacation, etre de la somme de quatre-vingt mille six cents soixante dix-huit piastres, quarante six cents, et ont toutes les parties et temoins signe avec nous les mêmes jour, mois et an que dessus, et nous sommes retires   Signed   **MOREAU L'ISLET,** defenseur des héritiers absents.

BLONDEAU,   **RICHARD RELF.**
PROSPERE PRIEUR   **THOS BEALE,** Register

Et aujourd'hui vingt troisième jour du mois d'Aout de l'an de notre Seigneur mil huit cent treize, et le trente huitieme de l'independence des Etats Unis d'Amérique, six heures du matin, nous, Thos Beale, Register des testaments susdits et soussigné, avons procede en notre office en présence de toutes les parties, et témoints reunis a l'eligement classification et inventaire des papiers de la succession de feu dit sieur Daniel Clark, de la manière et ainsi qu'il suit, apres avoir en presence des dites par nes et temoins levee les scelles de la petite malle renferment les papiers lequel a ete par eux reconnu sain et entier

Premierement une liasse, contenant vingt-huit billets souscrits en faveur du defunt par des personnes presumées insolvables s'elevant ensemble a la somme de huit mille quatre cents cinquante trois piastres quatre vingt neuf cents et demie, par nous cotes paraphes par premier et dernier et portes ici uniquement pour memoire la dite liasse par nous inventoriée sous la double lettre GG, N° 33

Item une liasse contenant trente-quatre pieces, relatives aux terres de la Florida, par nous cotes, paraphees par premier et dernier, et la dite liasse inventoriée sous la double lettre HH N° 34.

Item une liasse contenant dix huit accords ou conventions, par nous cotes paraphes par première et dernier, et la dite liasse inventoriée sous la double lettre I I N° 35

Item une autre liasse contenant sept actes hipothecaires en faveur de la succession, par nous cotes, et paraphees par premier et dernier, et la dite liasse inventoriee sous la double J J N° 36

Item une autre liasse contenant trente une ventes d'esclaves par nous cotes, paraphées et inventoriees sous la double lettre K K N° 37

Item une autre liasse contenant cinquante reçues ou quitances par nous cotes, paraphes par premier et dernier, la dite liasse par nous inventoriee sous la lettre L L N° 38

Item une liasse contenant trois lettres de change, supposées payées, par nous cotees, et paraphees par premier et dernier, la dite liasse par nous inventoriee sous la double lettre M. M numero trente-neuf.

Item une liasse contenant quatorze pieces d'estimation de terres par approximation et de notes d'argent dû au defunt par nous cotees, paraphees par première et derniere et inventoriees sous la double lettre N N et le n 40

Item une autre liasse contenant treize pieces d'estimation relatives au Canal Carondelet, par nous cotees, et paraphees par premiere et derniere la dite liasse par nous inventoriee sous la double lettre O O N° 41

Item une autre liasse contenant cinq procurations de divers, par nous cotees, et paraphees par premiere et deirnere, la dite liasse par nous inventoriee sous la double lettre P P N° 42

Item une autre liasse contenant quarante quatre pieces relatives au reglement de compte avec D W Coxe, par nous cotees, et paraphees par premiere et derniere. La dite liasse par nous inventoriee sous la double lettre Q Q N° 43

Item une autre liasse contenant soixante-dix comptes réglés ou a regler par nous cotes et paraphes par premiere et derniere la dite liasse par nous inventoriee sous la double lettre RR N ° 44

Item une autre liasse contenant quarante neuf lettres et correspondance avec divers, par nous cotes et paraphées par première et dernière, la dite liasse par nous inventoriee sous la double lettre SS N ° 45

Item une autre liasse contenant quarante huit actes de ventes, faites par feu D Clark a divers, de terres au Bayou, par nous cotes, et paraphes par premier et dernier, la dite liasse inventoriee sous la double lettre T T N ° 46

Item une autre liasse contenant neuf ventes en faveur de Watkins par nous cotees, et paraphees par première et dernière, la dite liasse par nous inventoriee sous la double lettre U U N ° 47

Item une autre liasse contenant quarante pieces pour renseignement, par nous cotes, et paraphees par première et dernière, la dite liasse par nous inventoriee sous la double lettre V V et le numero 48

Item une autre liasse contenant quatorze plans et titres de propriete, par nous cotes, et paraphes par premier et dernier, la dite liasse par nous inventoriee sous la double lettre W W N ° 49

Item une autre liasse contenant trente-cinq pieces relatives a l'habitation du Bayou par nous cotees, et paraphees par première et dernière la dite liasse par nous inventoriee sous la double lettre X X N ° 50

Item une autre liasse contenant vingt-neuf titres ou garanties des lettres de Ouachita, par nous cotes et paraphes par première et dernière, et la dite liasse par nous inventoriee sous la double lettre Y Y N ° 51

Item une autre liasse contenant douze pieces concernant l'habitation de Chapitoulas par nous cotes, et paraphees par première et dernière la dite liasse par nous inventoriee sous la double lettre Z Z. N.° 52

Item une autre liasse contenant treize pieces relatives a l'habitation achetee d'Arnaud Magnan, par nous cotees et paraphees par première et dernière, la dite liasse par nous inventoriee, sous la triple lettre AAA N ° 53

Item une autre liasse contenant sept pieces relatives au lot de terre, pres de la corderie, par nous cotees et paraphees par première et dernière, la dite liasse par nous inventoriee sous la triple lettre BBB N ° 54

Item une autre liasse contenant des transports de terres, achetées par D Carlos Duhault de Lassus pour Daniel Clark, a St Louis, en Septembre 1804, et retransportees par le dit Lassus a Daniel Clark a l'office de Broutin en 1805, par nous co-

ces paraphées par premiere et derniere et la dite hasse par
nous inventorie sous la triple lettre CCC. N.º 55

Item une autre hasse contenant deux pieces relatives a l'ha
bitation de limetairi par nous cotes paraphées, par premiere
et derniere et la dite hasse par nous inventorie sous la triple
lettre DDD N.º 56

Item une autre hasse contenant deux pieces relatives, aux
terres des Atakapas achetes de la succession Macarty, par
nous cotes et paraphees, et la dite hasse par nous inventorie
sous la triple lettre EEE N.º 57

Item une autre hasse contenant deux transports des terres
du Bayou aux Bœufs, faits par William Melies et Alexandre
Fulton par nous cotees paraphees et inventories sous la triple
lettre FFF N.º 58

Item une autre hasse contenant cinq plans, garanties ou
transports de trois mille deux cents arpents de terre, aux Ope
lousas achees de Madame Lamie Brunet par nous cotes pa
raphes par premier et dernier, et la dite hasse, par nous inven
torie sous la triple lettre GGG N.º 59

Item une autre hasse contenant six plans garanties ou trans
ports de seize cents arpents de terre, aux Opelousas, achetes de
monsieur Broutin, par nous cotes paraphés et inventories, sous
la triple lettre HHH N.º 60

Item une autre hasse contenant cinq plans titres ou transport
de terres situees à Baton Rouge au Sud de la ligne de de
marcation propriete exclusive de Daniel Clark, par nous cotes
paraphes, par premier et dernier la dite hasse par nous invento
riee sous la triple lettre III N.º 61

Item une autre hasse contenant deux titres ou plans de onze
arpens, quatre toises de face au Mississippi pres et audessus de
Lafourche, achetes de Simon Ducourneau, par nous cotes pa
raphes par premier et dernier, la dite hasse, inventoriee sous
la triple lettre JJJ N.º 62

Item une autre hasse contenart deux pieces de papiers relatives a l'habitation Ficher a la terre aux bœufs, par nous cotes
paraphees par premier et dernier, la dite hasse inventoriees
sous la triple lettre KKK N.º 63

Item une autre hasse contenant quatre plans, transports et
garanties de trois mille deux cents arpents de terre, situes aux
Opelousas, achetes de Mr Gradenigo par nous cotes paraphes
par premier et dernier la dite hasse par nous inventoriee sous
la triple lettre LLL N.º 64

Item une autre hasse contenant quatre titres de terre de Mr
Fletcher, par nous cotes paraphes par premier et dernier, ladite
hasse par nous inventorie sous la triple lettre MMM N.º 65

Item une autre hasse contenant trente-trois divers titres de
proprietes par nous cotes et paraphes par premier et dernier

ladite liasse par nous inventoriee sous la triple lettre NNN N ᵒ
66

Item une autre liasse contenant vingt deux pieces, papiers de
Jean Lucques, par nous cotés paraphes par premier et dernier
ladite liasse par nous inventoriee sous la triple lettre OOO N ᵒ
67

Item, une liasse contenant six comptes avec Mr P. Barrow,
par nous cotes, paraphes et ladite liasse par nous inventoriee
sous la triple lettre PPP, N ᵒ 68

Item, une autre liasse contenant vingt-cinq pieces pour etablir les comptes avec F L Claiborne, par nous cotes, paraphes
par premier et dernier ladite liasse par nous inventoriee sous
la triple lettre QQQ. N ᵒ 69

Item, un livre memorandum des terres tenues de societe entre
le defunt et le Dr William Coxe de Philadelphie, contenant
vingt sept folios ecrits par nous cote paraphe et inventorie sous
la triple lettre RRR, N ᵒ 70

Item, un autre livre memorandum des terres tenues de societe
entre le defunt et le Dr William Coxe de Philadelphie, contenant vingt folios ecrits, par nous paraphe et inventorie sous la
triple lettre SSS N ᵒ 71

Item, un autre petit livre de compte entre le defunt et feu le
Dr John Watkins contenant sept folios ecrits, par nous paraphe et inventorie sous la triple lettre TTT, N ᵒ 72

Qui est tout ce qui s'est trouve de papiers dans ladite petite
malle, et, attendu qu'il est six heures de relevee, nous Register
susdit et soussigne, avons du consentement des parties, arrete
le present et en avons remis la continuation a demain six heures
du matin ce dont elles se tiennent pour averties, et lecture faite
d'icelui, nous avons fait remise de ladite petite malle et de son
contenu au dit sieur Richard Relf, executeur testamentaire, qui
s'en fait charge et a signe avec nous et les autres parties et
temoins, les jour mois et an que dessus et nous sommes retires

(Signe) MOREAU L ISLET, Defensr des heritiers absens
BLONDEAU   RICHARD RELF
PROSPER PRIEUR,   THOMAS BEALE,
                                        Register

Et aujourd'hui, vingt-septieme jour du mois d'aout de l'an de
Notre-Seigneur mil huit cent treize et le trente huitieme de la
declaration de l'Independance des Etats-Unis d'Amerique,
quatre heures de relevee, nous Thomas Beale, Register des Testaments pour la ville et paroisse de la Nouvelle-Orleans, avons
procede en notre office en presence de toutes les parties et temoins reunis a l'elisement et classification des papiers de la succession renfermes dans une malle sur laquelle etait appose le
scelle N ᵒ deux, lequel a ete prealablement reconnu sain et en-

tier par les susdites parties et temoins, apres quoi nous avons procede comme suit

Premierement soixante-trois liasses contenant ensemble quatre mille cent cinq lettres de divers, par nous cotes et paraphees depuis le N.° 1 jusques et y compris le N.° 63

Item une autre liasse contenant cent trente-huit copies de lettres avec divers par nous paraphees et inventoriees dans le N.° 64

Item, une autre liasse contenant soixante-dix sept pieces relatives au tabac, avec James Wilkinson, par nous paraphe et inventoriees sous le N.° 65

Item, une autre liasse contenant dix pieces relatives a Walter Jones, par nous paraphees et inventoriees sous le N.° 66

Item, une autre liasse contenant huit pieces relatives au colonel Bill Chase, par nous paraphees et inventoriees sous le N.° 67,

Qui est tout ce qui s'est trouve dans la susdite malle, sur laquelle etait appose le scelle N.° 3, apres avoir prealablement examine scrupuleusement les scelles, lesquels ont ete trouves sains et entiers et reconnus tels

Premierement seize liasses, contenant ensemble quatre cent quarante-deux pieces relatives a diverses affaires tels que comptes, recus et quittances par nous cotes paraphes et inventories depuis le N.° 68 jusqu'au N.° 83 inclusivement

Et attendu qu'il ne s'est pas trouve d'autres papiers dans la susdite malle, nous, Register susdit et soussigne avons arrete le present et avons fait remise des susdites malles au dit sieur Richard Relf, executeur testamentaire, qui s'en fait charge et a signe avec nous et les autres parties et temoins les meme jour mois et an que cessus

(Signe) MOREAU L'ISLET, Defenseur des heritiers absents
BLONDEAU.   RICHARD RELF
PROSPER PRIEUR   THOMAS BEALE
                                                    Register

Et aujourd'hui vingt-huitieme jour du mois d'aout de l'an de Notre-Seigneur mil huit cent treize et la trente huitieme de l'independance des Etats Unis d'Amerique dix heures du matin nous, Thomas Beale, Register des Testaments pour la ville et paroisse de la Nouvelle Orleans, nous sommes transportes sur le chemin du Bayou, au domicile ou est decede le feu sieur Daniel Clark a l'effet d'y proceder a l'inventaire descriptif et estimatif des animaux provenant de ladite succession, ou etant nous avons trouve le sieur Richard Relf, executeur testamentaire du dit defunt, Louis Moreau Lislet, avocat nomme par la cour pour representer les heritiers absents, en presence desquels nous avons pris le serment des sieurs Prosper Prieur et Sebastien Blondeau de bien et fidelement se comporter dans les devoirs d'appréciateurs de tout ce qui leur sera présenté comme provenant de ladite succession, après quoi avons, en présence de tous, procédé comme suit

ANIMAUX

Premièrement, un cheval noir anglais, de cabriolet, estimé par les susdits appréciateurs la somme de cent piastres   100

Item, vingt trois vaches estimées les unes dans les autres a vingt-quatre piastres la piece, ensemble la somme de cinq cent cinquante deux piastres   552

Item, cinq taureaux estimés par les mêmes appréciateurs, l'un dans l'autre a huit piastres piece, ensemble la somme de quarante piastres   40

Item, trois paires de bœufs estimés par les mêmes, l'un dans l'autre a trente piastres la paire ensemble la somme de quatrevingt dix piastres   90

Item, douze mulets estimés par les memes, l un dans l'autre, a trente piastres le mulet, ensemble la somme de trois cent soixante piastres   360

Item un cheval rouge anglais estimé par les memes la somme de cinquante piastres   50

Item un cheval creole estimé par les memes la somme de vingt piastres   20

Qui sont tous les animaux qui nous ont été presentés pour être inventoriés comme provenant de la succession dudit feu sieur Daniel Clark, et lecture faite du present, nous avons trouve le montant de l'estimation faite être de la somme de douze cent quarante-deux piastres, lesquels animaux nous avons laisse a la charge du dit sieur Richard Relf executeur testamentaire qui le reconnait et a signe avec nous et les autres parties et temoins, les mêmes jour, mois et an que dessus, et nous sommes retirés

(Signe) MOREAU L'ISLET, Defens't des heritiers absents
BLONDEAU,   RICHARD RELF,
PROSPER PRIEUR,   THOMAS BEALE,
                                  Register.

VENTE DU MOBILIER —l't aujourd'hui dixieme jour du mois de septembre de l'an de Notre Seigneur mil huit cent treize et la trente-huitieme de l'Independance des Etats Unis d'Amerique, neuf heures du matin, nous, Thomas Beale, Register des Testaments pour la ville et paroisse de la Nouvelle Orleans, en vertu de l'ordonnance de l'honorable juge de la Cour des Preuves, de cette ville et paroisse, en date du vingt sept du mois d'aout dernier, et apres les publications prescrites par la loi, nous nous sommes transporte sur le chemin du Bayou, au domicil ou est decede feu sieur Daniel Clark, a l'effet d'y proceder a la vente les effets mobiliers et animaux provenant de ladite succession, ou etant, nous avons, en présence des sieurs Richard Rel, exécuteur testamentaire du defunt, Moreau Lislet, avocat nommé par la cour pour représenter les héritiers absents et celle des sieurs Prosper Prieur et Sebastien Blondeau, témoins domiciliés, proclamé la susdite vente à haute et intelligible voix aux termes et conditions suivantes, savoir

Au comptant pour les sommes qui ne depasseront pas celle de cent piastres, et pour celles au-dessus à soixante jours de credit payable en billets endosses à la satisfaction de l'executeur testamentaire

Premierement, un lit à colonnes en bois de merisier, garni de trois matelas en barbe espagnole et de coutil, un traversin, deux oreillers, une mauvaise moustiquaire en mousseline, ornée de garniture, adjugé à M. Hillebrough pour la somme de quarante neuf piastres cinquante cents   49 50

Item un petit bureau en noyer adjugé à M. Dusuau Delacroix pour la somme de vingt huit piastres   28

Item une petite table en bois de merisier, adjugée à M. Périllat aîné pour la somme de deux piastres et cinquante cents   2 50

Item, une autre petite table pliante, en merisier adjugée à M. Gougon pour la somme de six piastres soixante-quinze cents   6 75

Item, une armoire en bois jaune, adjugée à M. Millebrough pour la somme de cinquante piastres   50

Item douze chaises en bois vert, adjugées à M. Millebrough pour la somme de vingt-une piastres   21

Item neuf autres chaises en bois peintes en vert adjugées à M. Riano pour la somme de treize piastres   13

Item une paire de pistolets d'arçon avec ses fontes, adjugée à M. Samuel Elkins, pour la somme de dix-sept piastres   17

Item, un poignard garni en argent, adjugée à M. Castaing pour la somme de sept piastres   7

Item un sabre garni en argent, adjugé à M. Poultney, pour la somme de vingt piastres   20

Item, deux paires de rasoirs et un petit miroir, adjugés à M. Paul Darcantel pour la somme de trois piastres soixante-quinze cents   3 75

Item, un cabaret en porcelaine, composé de douze tasses et onze soucoupes, une théière, un pot à crême, un sucrier et trois assiettes et un plateau peint en rouge, adjugée à M. Dusuau Delacroix, pour la somme de trente-neuf piastres   39
                                                              ——————
                                                              257 50

Montant de l'autre part $ 257 50

Item un autre cabaret de porcelaine, composé de douze tasses douze soucoupes une cafetiere, un bow' et trois assiettes avec un plateau peint en oir adjugé à M Ogden, pour la somme de quarante piastres   40

Item, un pot à eau avec sa cuvette en porcelaine adjugé à M, Gros pour la somme de vingt-une piastres   21

Item, deux vieilles tables à jouer, en merisier adjugées à M Baran pour la somme de huit piastres   8

Item une table phante en merisier adjugée à M Fleytas pour la somme de dix piastres   10

Item, un étui de mathématiques adjugé à M Paul Darcantel pour la somme de neuf piastre cinquante cents.   9 50

Item dix-huit cuillers et douze fourchette une cuiller à soupe, seize cuillers à café vingt-quatre cuillers à crême et une pince à sucre le tout en argent, pesant cent vingt-huit onces six gros, adjugés à M Poultney Jr pour la somme de cent quarante-trois piastres   143

Item, une montre anglaise, à double boitier en or, adjugé à M Samuel Elkins, pour la somme de quatre-vingt-treize piastres   93

Item, une partie de faïence bleue dépareillée adjugée à M Ogden pour la somme de cent onze piastres   111

Item une piece de ratin bleu, 40 vardes, faisant 32 aunes à 109 l'aune, faisant la somme de trente-quatre piastres quatre-vingt-huit cents, ladite pièce adjugée à M P Guenon   34 88

Item, neuf autres pieces de ratine bleue, aunant ensemble 384 aunes, adjugées à M Herman, à raison de cent six cents l'aune, ensemble, la somme de quatre cent sept piastres et quatre cents   407 04

Une jarre de Provence, adjugée à M Fortier pour la somme de vingt-deux piastres et cinquante cents   22 50

Item, une autre jarre de Provence, adjugée à M Lecesne, pour la somme de vingt-deux piastres et cinquante cents   22 50

Une autre jarre de Provence adjugée à M Fortier pour la somme de vingt-trois piastres   23

—————

$ 1202 92

Montant de l'autre part $ 1202 92

Item une pierre à aiguiser et un poêle adjugés à Mr
Lefevre pour la somme de douze piastres   12

Item une selle adjugée à Mr Lynd pour la somme
de dix-neuf piastres cinquante cents   19 50

$ 1231 42

Qu'est-ce qu'il s'est trouvé d'effets mobiliers à vendre
comme provenant de la succession

Livres qui —Premièrement quatre volumes du
Trésor Espagnol, adjugés à Mr Edmond Forstall
pour la somme de sept piastres   7

Item huit volumes de l'Histoire Romaine (en
anglais) adjugés à Mr Smith pour la somme de
dix-huit piastres   18

Item dix volumes des Voyages du Nord-Amérique,
adjugés à Mr Dorteuille fils pour la somme de
douze piastres   12

Item huit volumes de divers ouvrages, adjugés à
Mr James Shephard pour la somme de dix piastres   10

Item six volumes de Milton, adjugés à Mr Wm
Ross, pour la somme de douze piastres cinquante
cents   12 50

Item vingt-quatre volumes des Œuvres de Swift
adjugé à Mr Samuel Elkins pour la somme de
quarante piastres   40

Item vingt-quatre volumes des Œuvres de Swift
adjugés à Mr Ellery pour la somme de cinquante
quatre piastres   54

Item vingt-cinq volumes de l'Histoire Universelle
adjugés à Mr Circulus pour la somme de quarante
cinq piastres   45

Item dix-sept volumes de Shakespeare adjugés
à Mr Samuel Elkins pour la somme de trente neuf
piastres   39

Item trois volumes de divers ouvrages, adjugés
à Mr Poultney pour la somme de treize piastres   13

Item vingt-quatre volumes de divers ouvrages,
adjugés à Mr Sevallos, pour la somme de quarante
quatre piastres   44

Item quatre volumes du Jeune Anacharsis, adjugés à Mr Dupuy pour la somme de onze piastres   11

Item six volumes de Mémoires du Temps de
Louis Seize, adjugés à Mr Albin Michel pour la
somme de douze piastres cinquante cents   12 50

$ 318 00

Montant de l'autre part	$ 318
Item vingt volumes du British Theatre, adjugés Mr Smith pour la somme de soixante une piastres	61
Item vingt cinq volumes de Chimie de Nicholson adjugés à Mr Wm Ross pour la somme de soixante et onze piastres	71
Item quatre volumes de l'Odissée (grec) adjugés à Mr Dupuy, pour la somme de sept piastres cinquante cents	7 50
Item quatorze volumes de divers ouvrages anglais, adjugés à Mr Guerlain, pour la somme de soixante quinze piastres	75
Item cinq volumes de Plutarque (grec) adjugés à Mr Millibrough pour la somme de six piastres cinquante cents	6 50
Item dix-huit volumes du Spectateur Anglais, adjugés à Mr Samuel Elkins, pour la somme de trente une piastres	31
Item sept volumes de divers ouvrages, adjugés à Mr Ellery pour la somme de neuf piastres et cinquante cents	9 50
Item huit volumes de divers ouvrages adjugés à Mr Poultney pour la somme de vingt piastres	20
Item trois volumes de tragédies de Sophocle (traduction latine), adjugés à Mr Allard pour la somme de quatre piastres	1
Item cinquante quatre trois volumes d'Encyclopédie Anglaise, adjugés à Mr Clague pour la somme de quatre-vingt-cinq piastres	85
Item trois volumes de la Maison Rustique, adjugés à Mr François Duplessis, pour la somme de vingt-une piastres	21
Item six volumes de divers ouvrages (en grec), adjugés à Mr Allard, pour la somme de quatre piastres	4
Item sept volumes des Œuvres de Bacon, adjugés à Mr Ellery pour la somme de trente une piastres	31
Item trois volumes de Don Quichotte en espagol, adjugés à Mr Simon Cucullu, pour la somme de dix-sept piastres	17
Item un volume Lexicon Manuale (anglais) adjugé à Mr Colombus Lawson, pour la somme de deux piastres	2
Item huit volumes latins, adjugés à Mr Edmond Forstall pour la somme de neuf piastres	9
	$ 772 50

Montant de l'autre part $ 772 50

Item sept volumes de divers ouvrages, adjugés à Mr Ma-péro, pour la somme de dix piastres ... 10

Item treize volumes de poetes anglais adjugés à Mr Fletcher pour la somme de trente-six piastres ... 36

Item quatre volumes de Virgile et Juvénal (latin) adjugés à Mr Morel, pour la somme de huit piastres ... 8

Item cinq volumes de divers ouvrages, adjugés à Mr Allard, pour la somme de sept piastres ... 7

Item neuf volumes de divers ouvrages, adjugés à Mr Riano pour la somme de sept piastres cinquante cents ... 7 50

Item trois volumes de divers ouvrages, adjugés à Mr Ellery pour la somme de sep piastres en cinquante cents ... 7 50

Item huit volumes de divers ouvrages, adjugés à Mr Ogden pour la somme de dix-neuf piastres ... 19

Item treize volumes de divers ouvrages, adjugés à Mr Morel, pour la somme de dix piastres ... 10

Item trois volumes de divers ouvrages, adjugés à Mr. Allard pour la somme de trois piastres ... 3

Item six volumes des Œuvres de Pope, adjugés à Mr Colombus Lawson, pour la somme de six piastres ... 6

Item douze volumes de divers ouvrages espagnols adjugés à Mr Hernan, pour la somme de sept piastres et cinquante cent ... 7 50

Item cinq volumes de Dictionaire de Géographie Commerçante adjugés à Mr Dupuy pour la somme de dix-sept piastres ... 17

Item sept volumes de divers ouvrages, adjugés à Mr Relf, pour la somme de onze piastres ... 11

Item cinq volumes de divers ouvrages, adjugés à Mr Samuel Elkins, pour la somme de six piastres ... 6

Item six volumes du Treatre d'Agriculture, adjugés à Mr Leroste, pour la somme de huit piastres cinquante cents. ... 8 50

Item cinq volumes d'Histoire Naturelle [Valmont de Beauman] adjugés à Mr Darcantel, pour la somme de dix piastres et cinquante cents ... 10 50

Item huit volumes de divers ouvrages, adjugés à Mr Elkins pour la somme de cinq piastres cinquante centimes ... 5 50

$ 952 50

50

Montant de l'autre part	$ 952	50
Item un atlas adjugé a Mr. Maspero, pour la somme de seize piastres	16	
Item onze volumes de divers ouvrages, adjuges a C Lawson pour la somme de onze piastres	11	
Item sept volumes de Voyage en Italie, par Lalande, adjuges à Mr. Garton, pour la somme de dix piastres.	10	
Item six volumes de divers ouvrages, adjuges a Mr. Taulent, pour la somme de cinq piastres	5	
Item trois volumes des divers ouvrages, adjugés a Mr. Ellery pour la somme de trois piastres cinquante cents	3	50
Item trois volumes espagnols, adjuges à Mr. Urcullu pour la somme de quatre piastres	4	
Item six volumes de divers ouvrages, adjuges a Mr. Périllat aine, pour la somme de dix piastres cinquante cents	10	50
Item sept volumes des Contes Moraux de Marmontel, adjuges a Mr Dupuy, pour la somme de sept piastres	7	
Item trente sept volumes de divei ouvrages, adjugés a Mr Sevallos pour la somme de vingt deux piastres	22	
Item trois volumes de divers ouvrages, adjuges a Mr Pierre Pédesclaux, pour la somme d'une piastre	1	
Item un volume, Dictionnaire Anglais et Espagnol, adjuge a Mr Castaing pour la somme de cinq piastres cinquante cents	5	50
Item deux volumes de Dictionnaire Italien et Anglais, adjuges a Mr Colombus Lawson pour la somme de quatre piastres cinquante centimes	4	50
Item six volumes de divers ouvrages, adjuges a Mr Morel pour la somme de trois piastres	3	
Item six volumes de divers ouvrages adjuges a Mr Clague pour la somme de quatre piastres	4	
Item sept volumes de divers ouvrages, adjuges a Mr Jacques Martin pour la somme de deux piastres vingt-cinq sols	2	25
Item huit volumes de divers ouvrages adjuges a Mr. Lawson pour la somme de cinq piastres	5	
Item dix-neuf volumes depareilles, adjuges à Mr Ellery pour la somme de cinq piastres	5	
Item deux volumes de divers ouvrages, adjugés a Mr. Poutney pour la somme de trois piastres cinquante centimes	3	50
	$ 1075	25

Montant de l'autre part $ 1075 25

Item deux volumes de divers ouvrages, adjugés a Mr Morel pour la somme de deux piastres cinquante centimes   2 50

Montant total de bibliotheque $ 1077 75

ARBRISSEAUX ET FLEURS.—Premierement six pots de fleurs, adjuges a Mr. Labosterie pour la somme de deux piastres   2

Item six autres pots de fleurs, adjuges a Mr Labosterie pour la somme d'une piastre quatre-vingt-sept cents et dem.   1 87½

Item six autres pots de fleurs, adjuges à Mr La bosterie pour la somme de trois piastres soixante-quinze cents   3 75

Item six autres pots de fleurs, adjuges a Mr. Joseph Abat pour la somme de douze piastres   12

Item six autres pots de fleurs adjuges a Mr. Labosterie pour la somme de six piastres douze cents et demi   6 12½

Item six autres pots de fleurs adjuges a Mr Honore Landreaux pour la somme de trois piastres trente-sept cents et demi   3 37½

Item sept autres pots de fleurs adjuges à Mr Labosterie pour la somme de cinq piastres vingt-cinq centimes.   5 25

Item neuf autres pots ou caisses des fleurs, adjugés a Mr Labosterie pour la somme de dix piastres vingt cinq cents   10 25

Item un pied d'agartrum ou rose myrte, adjuge a Mr Guerlain pour la somme de vingt-un piastres   21

Item un autre pied d'agartrum ou myrte rose, avec la caisse, adjuge a Mr Guerlain pour la somme de vingt cinq piastres.   25

Item un citronnier avec sa caisse adjugé a Mr. Henderson, pour la somme de neuf piastres   9

Item six pots de fleurs adjuges à Mr Lynd pour la somme de 5 piastres   5

Item six autres pots de fleurs, adjugés à Mr Lynd pour la somme de cinq piastres.   5

Item six autres pots de fleurs, adjugés a Mr. Ogden pour la somme de trois piastres   3

Item dix autres pots de fleurs, adjuges a Mr. Ogden pour la somme de cinq piastres vingt-cinq sols.   5 25

$ 117 87½

Montant de l'autre part $ 117 87½

Item un pied de reseda avec sa caisse, adjuge a Mr. Darcantel pour la somme de douze piastres cinquante cents.   12 50

Item six pots de fleurs, adjuges a Mr Roque pour la somme de trois piastres cinquante cents   3 50

Item cinq pots et un baril de fleurs, adjuges a Mr Henderson pour la somme de dix piastres   10

Item douze pots de fleurs, adjugés a Mr Lynd pour la somme de onze piastres et cinquante cents   11 50

Item un olivier adjuge a Mr Guerlain pour la somme de cinq piastres   5

Item vingt-quatre pots vides bons ou teles, adjugés a Mr Guerlain, pour la somme de sept piastres cinquante centimes   7 50

Item un pied de mengo avec sa caisse adjugé a Mr Guerlain pour la somme de quatre piastres vingt-cinq centimes   4 25

Item un citronnier avec sa caisse, adjugé a Mr Dupuy pour la somme de dix piastres   10

Item un floripondio avec sa caisse adjuge a Mr. Joseph Nicholas pour la somme de cinq piastres vingt-cinq centimes.   5 25

Item un bananier avec sa caisse, adjuge a Mr Lynd pour la somme de sept piastres cinquante cents   7 50

Item un pied de cachiman adjuge a Mr Darcantel avec sa caisse pour la somme de quatre piastres   4

Item un limonier avec sa caisse adjuge a Mr Roque, pour la somme de cinq piastres cinquante cents   5 50

Item deux pieds de pomellada, adjuges avec une caisse a Mr Guerlain pour la somme de quatre piastres   4

Item un citronnier avec une caisse, adjugé à Mr Guerlain, pour la somme de vingt piastres   20

Item un goyavier avec sa caisse, adjugé a Mr Dussuau Delacroix pour la somme de seize piastres.   16

Item un arbrisseau (nom inconnu) avec sa caisse, adjugé à Mr Roque pour la somme de huit piastres vingt-cinq centimes   8 25

Item un bananier avec sa caisse, adjugé a Mr. Roque pour la somme de six piastres.   6

Item un floripondio avec sa caisse, adjuge a Mr Roque pour la somme de neuf piastres vingt-cinq cents   9 25

$ 267 87½

Montant de l'autre part $ 267 87½

Item deux pieds de pomellada avec leurs caisses,
adjuges a Mr Darcantel pour la somme de huit piastres cinquante centimes   8 50

Item une petite caisse de fleurs, adjugée a Mr
Darcantel pour la somme de deux piastres   2

Item un citronnier avec sa caisse, adjuge à M.
Darcantel pour la somme de huit piastres cinquante
centimes   8 50

Item deux pieds de floripondio avec leurs caisses,
adjuges a Mr Dupuy pour la somme de huit piastres   8

Item une baignoire, adjugee a Mr Lynd pour
la somme de quinze piastres   15

Montant des arbrisseaux et fleurs . . . . $ 309 87½

Et attendu qu'il est six heures de relevée, nous, Register des
Testaments susdit et soussigné, avons arrête le present vente,
et en avons remis la continuation a demain six heures du matin ce dont nous avons prevenu le public a haute et intelligible
voix et lecture faite d'icelu, nous avons trouve le montant de
le vente du mobilier meublant etre de la somme de douze cent
trente quatre piastres quatre vingt douze cent, celui de la vente
de la Bibliotheque etre de la somme de mille soixante dix sept
piastres et soixante quinze centimes, et et enfin celui des arbrisseaux et fleurs, etre de la somme de trois cent neuf piastres
quatre-vingt sept cents et demi, lesquelles forment ensemble la
somme de deux mille six cent vingt deux piastres et cinquante
quatre cents et demi, laquelle somme nous avons laissée à la disposition du sieur Richard Relf, executeur testamentaire, qui le
reconnait et s'en fait charge, et ont toutes les parties et temoins
signe avec nous, les jour, mois et an que dessus et nous sommes
retirés

Signe   PROSPERE PRIEUR   BLONDEAU
     MOREAU L'ISLET,   defenseur des heritiers absents
     RICHARD RELF   THS BEALE Rr

VENTE DES ANIMAUX —Et aujourd'hui, onzieme jour du mois
de Septembre de l'an de notre Seigneur mil huit cent treize et
le trente huitieme de l'Indépendance des Etats Unis d'Amerique, dix heures du matin, nous, Thomas Beale Register des Tes
taments pour la ville et paroisse de la Nouvelle Orléans, nous
sommes transportes sur la route du Bayou, au domicile ou est
decéde feu sieur Daniel Clark, a l'effet d'y proceder a la continuation de la vente du mobilier provenant de ladite succession,
ou etant, nous avons en présence des sieurs Richard Relf, executeur testamentaire, Louis Moreau L'Islet, avocat nommé par
la Cour pour representer les heritiers absents et en celle des

sieurs Prospere Prieur et Sebastien Blondeau, temoins par nous réquis, proclamé la susdite vente aux termes et conditions suivantes. SAVOIR.

Au comptant pour les sommes qui ne depasseront, celle de cent piastres, et celles au dessous, a soixante jours de credit, payable en billets endosses a la satisfaction de l'executeur testamentaire

ANIMAUX.—Premièrement, un cheval noir anglais de cabriolet, adjugé à Mr. P F Dubourg pour la somme de cent trente piastres $ 130

Item une vache rouge et son veau, adjugés à Mr Millebrough pour la somme de vingt-cinq piastres et vingt-cinq sols   25 25

Item une autre vache rouge et son veau, adjugés à Mr Millebrough pour la somme de vingt-deux piastres   22

Item une autre vache rouge et son veau, adjugés à Mr Darcantel pour la somme de dix-huit piastres   18

Item une autre vache rouge et son veau, adjugés à Mr Darcantel pour la somme de seize piastres.   16

Item une autre vache blanche et noire avec son veau, adjugés à Mr. Lecesne pour la somme de dix-sept piastres   17

Item une autre vache blanche avec son veau, adjugés à Mr Baran pour la somme de vingt piastres   20

Item une autre vache brune avec son veau adjugés à Mr Jacques Guy Dreux pour la somme de cinquante-huit piastres   58

Item une autre vache cave avec son veau, adjugés à Mr Relf pour la somme de cinquante-quatre piastres   54

Item une autre vache brune prête à mettre bas, adjugée à Mr Cadet Déjean pour la somme de quarante-cinq piastres   45

Item une autre vache rouge sans veau, adjugée à Mr Coiron pour la somme de vingt-huit piastres   28

Item une autre vache noire sans veau, adjugée à Mr Cadet Déjean pour la somme de vingt-deux piastres.   22

Item une vache rouge bigarée sans veau, adjugée à Mr Coiron pour la somme de vingt-cinq piastres   25

Item une vache café au-lait sans veau, adjugée à Mr Cadet Déjean, pour la somme de vingt-cinq piastres   25
                                                                    ─────────
                                                                    $ 505 25

Montant de l'autre part $ 505 25

Item une vache rouge écornée sans veau, adjugée à Mr Louis Séré pour la somme de quarante-trois piastres   43

Item une vache rouge sans veau, adjugée à Mr Lecesne pour la somme de dix-neuf piastres   19

Item une vache barosse sans veau, adjugée à Mr Lecesne pour la somme de vingt-huit piastres   28

Item une vache noire sans veau, adjugée à Mr Bonnefoy pour la somme de dix-sept piastres   17

Item une vache rouge sans veau, adjugée à Mr Relf pour la somme de vingt-six piastres   26

Item une vache café au-lait sans veau, adjugée à Mr Cadet Déjean pour la somme trente-cinq piastres   35

Item une vache dos blanc sans veau, adjugée à Mr Darcantel pour la somme de treize piastres   13

Item une vache café au-lait sans veau, adjugée à Mr Cadet Déjean pour la somme de quinze piastres   15

Item une vache rouge sans veau, adjugée à Mr Coiron pour la somme de seize piastres   16

Item une vache soupe au lait, adjugée à Mr Hopkins pour la somme de dix-huit piastres   18

Item une jeune taure rouge adjugée à Mr Coiron pour la somme de treize piastres   13

Item une autre jeune taure rouge, adjugée à Mr Flevias pour la somme de neuf piastres.   9

Item une autre taure rouge, adjugée à Mr Pierre Guenon pour la somme de sept piastres et cinquante centimes   7 50

Item deux petits taureaux adjugés à Mr Blanc pour la somme de vingt piastres   20

Item une paire de bœufs adjugés à Mr Lecesne pour la somme de trente-six piastres   36

Item un autre paire de bœufs, adjugés à Mr Lecesne pour la somme de trente-sept piastres   37

Item une autre paire de bœufs blancs, adjugés à Mr Lecesne pour la somme de vingt-neuf piastres   29

Item deux mulets adjugés à Mr Cadet Déjean pour la somme de quatre-vingt piastres.   80

Item deux autres mulets, adjugés à Mr Coiron pour la somme de quatre-vingt quatorze piastres.   94

Item deux autres mulets, adjugés à Madame Faisandieu pour la somme de soixante piastres.   60

1120 75

Montant de l'autre part	1120 75
Item deux autres mulets, adjugés à Mr Coiron pour la somme de soixante une piastres	61
Item deux autres mulets, adjugés à Madame Faisandieu pour la somme de cinquante-trois piastres	53
Item deux autres mulets, adjugés à Mr. Coiron pour la somme de soixante-quinze piastres.	75
Item un cheval rouge anglais adjugé à Mr. Lecesne pour la somme de soixante piastres	60
Item un cheval créole, adjugé à Mr Lecesne, pour la somme de trente-deux piastres	32
Item un cheval souris, adjugé à Charles Decoudreau pour la somme de vingt piastres	20
Montant total des animaux	$ 1421 75

Et attendu qu'il ne nous a pas été présenté d'autres animaux à vendre comme provenant de la succession dudit feu sieur Daniel Clark, nous, Régister susdit et soussigné avons arrêté le present, et lecture faite d'icelui, nous avons trouvé le montant des animaux vendus être de la somme de quatorze cents vingt une piastres soixante quinze centimes, laquelle somme nous avons laissée à la disposition du sieur Richard Relf, qui la recconnaît, s'en fait charge et a signé avec nous et les autres parties et témoins, les mêmes jour, mois et an que dessus, et nous sommes retirés

Signé   BLONDEAU.   MOREAU L'ILET,
                                 deffenseur des héritiers absents
PROSPERE PRIEUR   RICHARD RELF.
THOS BEALE, Régister of Wills

INVENTAIRE DE L'HABITATION CHAPITOULAS

Et aujourd'hui, vingt huitieme jour du mois de Septembre de l'an de notre Seigneur mil huit cent treize et le trente huitieme de l'Indépendance des Etats Unis d'Amerique, quatre heures du matin, nous, Thomas Beale, Register des Testaments pour la ville et paroisse de la Nouvelle-Orleans, nous sommes transporté sur une habitation de la propriété du feu Daniel Clark sise à six heues de cette ville par en haut et du meme bord, a la côte des Chapitoulas, a l'effet d'y proceder a la continuation de l'inventaire descriptif et estimatif des proprietes delaissées par dit feu sieur Daniel Clark, où étant, nous avons trouvé le sieur Richard Relf, executeur testamentaire, L. Moreau L'Islet, avocat nommé par la Cour pour representer l'héritiere absente, et avons en leur présence pris le serment des sieurs P Baron, Boisfontaine et L'Ille Sarpy, appréciateurs choisis par l'exécuteur testamentaire de bien et fidellement se comporter dans leur fonction et d'estimer dans leur ame et conscience tout ce qui leur serait presente comme provenant de ladite succession , après quoi nous avons, en presence de tous, procedé comme suit .

MEUBLES ET FOURNITURES — Premièrement six chaises estimées par les dites appréciateurs la somme de six piastres $ 6

Item un matelat estimé par les mêmes la somme de cinq piastres 5

Item deux bois des lits estimés par les mêmes la somme de six piastres 6

Item deux tables, estimées par les mêmes la somme de trois piastres 3

Item deux coffre de medecines estimés par les mêmes la somme de vingt piastres 20

Item deux pares de chenais estimées par les mêmes la somme de dix piastres 10

Item une jarre a eau, estimée par les mêmes la somme de douze piastres 12

Item deux paires de draps estimées par les mêmes la somme de dix piastres 10

Item la batterie de cuisine tel quelle se pursuit et comporte estime par les mêmes la somme de vingt-cinq piastres 25

INSTRUMENS ARATOIRES — Quatorze charrues, évaluées par les susdits appreciateurs la somme de deux cent dix piastres le tout ensemble 210

Item deux socs de charrues estimés par les mêmes la somme de vingt piastres 20

Item deux grandes herses estimée par les mêmes la somme de dix piastres 10

Item quatre autres herses à roues estimés par les mêmes, ensemble la somme de douze piastres 12

Item huit charrettes estimée par les mêmes la somme de deux cents quatre-vingt piastres 280

Item deux brouettes, estimées par les mêmes la somme de cinq piastres 5

Item cinquante houes, estimées par les mêmes la somme de cinquante piastres 50

Item quinze beches estimée par les mêmes la somme de vingt-cinq piastres 25

Item un assortiment d'outils de forgeron, estimé par les mêmes la somme de deux cents piastres 200

Item trente haches, estimées par les mêmes la somme de quarante-cinq piastres **45**

$ 954

Montant de l'autre part $ 934

Item deux   estimées par les mêmes la **somme de deux piastres** 2

ANIMAUX.—Item douze paires de bœufs, estimés par les mêmes à quarante piastres la paire, ensemble la somme de quatre cent quatre-vingt piastres. 480

Item vingt-quatre mulets, estimés ensemble par les mêmes la somme de quatorze cents quarante piastres 1440

Item cinq chevaux, estimé par les mêmes à cinquante piastres pièce, ensemble la somme de deux cents cinquante piastres 250

Item quinze vaches, estimées par les memes la somme de vingt-cinq piastres chaque, ensemble la somme de trois cent soixante et quinze piastres 375

Item sept bouvillons estimés par les mêmes la somme de huit piastres pièce ensemble la somme de cinquante-six piastres 56

Item huit veaux estimés par les mêmes la somme de cinq piastres pièce ensemble la somme de quarante piastres 40

Item deux taureaux estimés par les mêmes la somme de dix piastres pièce ensemble la somme de vingt piastres 20

Item soixante-quatre moutons, estimés par les memes à quatre piastres pièce, ensemble la somme de deux cent cinquante-six piastres 256

$ 3873

qui sont tous les meubles, instrumens aratoires et animaux trouvés sur la dite habitation

ESCLAVES.—Premièrement Doctor nègre âgé de cinquante ans et estimé par le mêmes la somme de deux cent cinquante piastres 250

Item Hector negre âgé de vingt-sept ans, estimé par les mêmes la somme de cinq cents piastres 500

Item Janvier, nègre âgé de soixante ans, estimé par les mêmes la somme de soixante piastres 60

Item William, negre âgé de trente ans, estimé par les mêmes la somme de sept cents piastres. 700

Item Stuard, nègre âge de trent-cinq ans, estimé par les mêmes la somme de quatre cents piastres 400

Item Jem, nègre âgé de vingt-sept ans, estimé par les mêmes la somme de six cent cinquante piastres 650

$ 2560

Montant de l'autre part $ 2560

Item **Kersey**, negre aveugle âge de quarante ans, lequel vu son infirmité n'a pu être evalué par les susdits appréciateurs, et a été porté ici uniquement pour mémoire

Item Morice, negre d'environ trente ans, estimé par les mêmes la somme de trois cents piastres — 300

Item Kett negre âge de quarante-cinq ans, estimé par les memes la somme de deux cents cinquante piastres — 250

Item Brown negre âgé de soixante-six ans, estimé par les mêmes la somme de soixante piastres — 60

Item John negre âgé de trente trois ans, estimé par les mêmes la somme de sept cents piastres — 700

Item Wing negresse avec David son enfant, âgé d'un an estimé par les memes la somme de quatre cent cinquante piastres — 450

Item old Esther negresse âgée d'environ soixante ans, estimée par les memes la somme de deux cents piastres — 200

Item Betty negrillon âge de six ans, estimé la somme de cent piastres — 100

Item Ana negresse âgée de vingt ans estimée par les memes la somme de quatre cent cinquante piastres — 450

Item James McCah, negre âgé de vingt-trois ans estimé par les mêmes personnes à six cents piastres — 600

Item Pull, négrillon, âgé de douze ans estimé par les mêmes la somme de quatre cents piastres — 400

Item Betty, negresse, avec son enfant âgé de six mois, nommée Almee estimées par les memes la somme de quatre cent cinquante piastres — 450

Item Monthou, negre age de cinquante ans, estimé par les mêmes la somme de quatre cents piastres — 400

Item Esther âgé de trente-cinq ans estimée par les mêmes la somme de quatre cents piastres, — 400

Item, Morning négritte, âgé d'environ quatorze ans, estimée par les memes la somme de trois cents piastres — 300

Item Sam negre âgé de quarante-cinq ans estimé par les mêmes la somme de cinq cents piastres, — 500

Item, Old Cate négresse âgée de cinquante ans, estimée par les mêmes la somme de deux cents piastres — 200

$ 8370

Montant de l'autre part $ 8370

Item, Grace négritte, âgée de dix ans, estimée
par les mêmes la somme de trois cents piastres.   300

Item, Elijah, negrillon âgé de dix ans, estimé
par les mêmes la somme de quatre cents piastres,   400

Item, James nègre, âgé de trente ans, estimé par
les mêmes la somme de sept cents piastres,   700

Item, Rose, négresse âgée de trente ans, avec son
enfant nommé Den âgé d'un an estimés par les
mêmes la somme de quatre cent cinquante piastres,   450

Item Aaa négresse âgée de trente ans, estimée
par les mêmes la somme de trois cent cinquante
piastres   350

Item Bird negre âgé de quinze ans, estimé par
les mêmes la somme de quatre cents piastres,   400

Item Patty, négrillon âgé de treize ans, estimé
par les mêmes la somme de trois cents piastres,   300

Item, Lawrence nègre charpentier âgé de trente-
cinq ans estimé par les mêmes la somme de sept
cents piastres,   700

Item, Fanny, negre âgé de vingt ans estimé par
les mêmes la somme de quatre cents piastres   400

Item, John, négrillon âgé de dix ans, estimé par
les mêmes la somme de trois cents piastres   300

Item, Gaines, négrillon âgé de sept ans, estimé
par les mêmes la somme de deux cents piastres   200

Item McKinsy négrillon âgé de cinq ans estimé
par les mêmes la somme de cent piastres,   100

Item, Marguerite négritte âgée de trois ans, estimée par les même la somme de cent piastres.   100

Item, Fanny, négresse âgée de vingt-cinq ans
avec Marie son enfant, âgée d'un an estimées par
les mêmes la somme de quatre cents cinquante
piastres   450

Item, Nelson, âgé de neuf ans, estimé par les
mêmes la somme de deux cent cinquante piastres   250

Item, Major, négrillon âgé de sept ans, estimé
par les mêmes la somme de cent cinquante piastres   150

Item Wainy, négresse, de vingt-six ans et ses
trois enfans savoir Helech, âgé de cinq ans Bou-
ky, âgé de quatre ans, et Maria, de deux ans, estimés par les mêmes la somme de sept cents piastres   700

Item, Spencer, nègre âgé de quarante-sept ans,
estimé par les mêmes la somme de six cents piastres   600

Item, Themar, négresse âgée de vingt-cinq ans,   450
estimée par les mêmes la somme de quatre cent
cinquante piastres   ————
                                                      $ 15670

Montant de l'autre part $ 15670

Item Old Major, lequel vu son âge et ses infirmités, n'a été porté ici que pour mémoire.

Item, Darky, nègre âgé de trente ans, ayant un rhumatisme, estimé par les mêmes la somme de cent piastres — 100

Item, Doriana Smith âgé de seize ans, estimé par les mêmes la somme de deux cent cinquante piastres — 250

Item, Cambridge nègre âgé de quarante ans, estimé par les mêmes la somme de quatre cent cinquante piastres — 450

Item Rachel négresse âgée de vingt-six ans, et son enfant âgé de quatre mois nommé Gabriel, estimés par les mêmes la somme de quatre cent cinquante piastres — 450

Item St Wenny âgé de vingt ans, estimé par les mêmes la somme de quatre cent cinquante piastres — 450

Item Sarah négresse, âgée de vingt-six ans estimée par les mêmes la somme de cinq cents piastres — 500

Item Judith mulâtresse âgée de vingt-sept ans, estimée par les mêmes la somme de quatre cent cinquante piastres — 450

Item Polly négresse âgée de vingt-sept ans, estimée par les mêmes la somme de quatre cent cinquante piastres — 450

Item Fanny, négresse âgée de vingt-deux ans, estimée par les mêmes la somme de cinq cents piastres — 500

Item, Nace, nègre âgé de trente-six ans estimé par les mêmes la somme de six cents piastres — 600

Item, Molly, négresse âgée de quarante-six ans, estimée par les mêmes la somme de trois cents piastres — 300

Item, Nancy négresse de dix-huit ans, estimée par les mêmes la somme de quatre cent cinquante piastres — 450

Item, Kerry négritte âgée de douze ans estimée par les mêmes la somme de trois cent cinquante piastres — 350

Item, Tom, négrillon, âgé de huit ans, estimé par les mêmes la somme de trois cent cinquante piastres, — 350

Item, Nany, négresse âgée de dix-huit ans, estimée par les mêmes la somme de quatre cent cinquante piastres — 450

$ 21770

Montant de l'autre part. $ 21770

Item Washington, negre âgé de vingt-cinq ans
estropié d'une main, estimé par les mêmes la somme
de trois cents piastres, 300

Item, Ketty, négresse âgée de vingt ans, avec
son enfant Tom âgé de quatre mois, estimés par les
mêmes la somme de quatre cents piastres 400

Item, Betty, négresse âgée de vingt-six ans, estimée par les mêmes la somme de quatre cents piastres, 400

Item, George, nègre âgé de quarante ans, estimé
par les mêmes la somme de six cents piastres, 600

Item old Rachel, âgée d'environ cinquante ans,
estimée par les mêmes la somme de trois cents
piastres 300

Item Dina, négresse âgée de soixante ans, estimée par les mêmes la somme de cent cinquante
piastres 150

Item, un négrillon nommé Dave âge de cinq ans,
estimé par les mêmes la somme de cent cinquante
piastres, 150

Item Levy négrillon âgé de cinq ans estimé par
les mêmes la somme de cent piastres, 100

Item, Anthony, negre age de soixante-dix ans
estime par les memes la somme de cinquante piastres, 50

Item Rachel negresse agee de seize ans, estimee
par les memes la somme de quatre cents piastres, 100

Item, Charlotte, negresse âgee de seize ans, estimee par les memes la somme de trois cent cinquante
piastres, 350

Item, Waldran, negre age de quinze ans estime
par les memes la somme de quatre cents piastres, 400

Item, Patianne, négritte agée de treize ans estimee
par les memes la somme de trois cent cinquante
piastres, 350

Item, Sukey, négritte âgee de treize ans, estimee
par les memes la somme de trois cent cinquante
piastres, 350

Item, Lidly age de quarante ans, estime par les
memes la somme de quatre cents piastres, 400

Item, Mamny, négresse âgée de quinze ans, estimee par les memes la somme de quatre cents piastres, 400

Item, Sukey, negritte agee de treize ans, estimee
par les mêmes la somme de trois cent cinquante
piastres, 350

Item, Edmond, négrillon age de sept ans, estime —————

$ 27220

Montant ci-contre part $27220

par les mêmes la somme de deux cent cinquante
piastres,   250

Item, Nény, negritte agé de trois ans, estimée par
les mêmes la somme de cent cinquante piastres,   150

Item, Betsy, negritte agée de deux ans estimée par
les mêmes la somme de trois cents piastres   300

Item, Ben, négre agé de vingt sept ans, estimé par
les mêmes la somme de cinq cents piastres,   500

Item, Jenny, negresse age d' vingt six ans estimée par les mêmes la somme de quatre cent cinquan-
te piastres,   150

Item, Kitt, negritte agé de cinq ans estimée
par les mêmes la somme de cent cinquante piastres,   150

Item, Henriette, negritte agé de huit ans estimée
par les mêmes la somme de deux cent cinquante
piastres   250

Item, Bob quarteron agé de sept ans estimé par
les mêmes la somme de trois cents piastres   300

Item, Lacy, negre agé de trente neuf ans estimé
par les mêmes la somme de cent piastres *vu qu'il a
un ulcere*   100

Item, Kitty, negresse agée de trois plus estimée par les mêmes la somme de quatre cents pias-
tres   400

Item, Peggy, negresse agé de quarante ans, estimée par les mêmes la somme de quatre cents pias-
tres,   400

Item, Hottis, negrillon agé de douze ans estimé
par les mêmes la somme de quatre cent cinquante
piastres,   450

Item, Thomas negre agé de trente ans, estimé
la somme de deux cent cinquante piastres, *attendu
que leut negre a la gravelle*   250

Item, Sally, negresse de seize ans estimée par les
mêmes la somme de 500 piastres,   500

Item, Ritte mulatre agé de quinze ans estimé par
les mêmes la somme de quatre cents piastres   400

Item, Anny negre agé de trente-cinq ans, estimé
par les mêmes la somme de deux cents piastres,   200

Item, Williams, négrillon âgé de deux ans, estimé
par les mêmes la somme de cinquante piastres,   50

Item, Ben, forgeron, agé de cinquante ans, estimé
par les mêmes la somme de cinq cent cinquante piastres.   550

$ 32870

Montant de l'autre par　　$32870

Item Anny, negre, age de trente ans, estime par les memes la somme de quatre cents piastres　　400

Item Raily, négresse agée de vingt quatre ans, estimee par les memes la somme de cinq cents pias tres,　　500

Item, Jenny Tisserande, age d'environ trente-neuf ans estimee par les memes la somme de cinq cents piastres　　500

Item, James, negre age de quinze ans, estime par les memes la somme de quatre cents piastics,　　400

Item, Rachel, negresse agee de trente ans, estimee par les memes la somme de trois cent cinquante piastres　　350

Item, Jack, negre age de vingt six ans, estime par les memes la somme de six cents piastres　　600

Item Mary, negresse agee de trente ans, estimee par les memes la somme de cinq cents piastres,　　500

Item Joe, negre age de quinze ans, estime par les memes la somme de cinq cents piastres　　500

Item Sukey, negritte agee de douze ans, estimee par les memes la somme de trois cents cinquante piastres　　350

Item Victoire, négritte agee de dix ans estimee par les memes la somme de trois cent piastres　　300

Item Joe, mulatre age de seize ans, estime par les memes la somme de quatre cents piastres　　400

Item Rachael negresse agee de quinze ans, estimee par les memes la somme de cinq cent piastres

Item Piggy, negritte agée de dix ans, estimee par les memes la somme de trois cents piastres-　　300

Item James Harris, negre age de trente-sinx ans, estime par les memes la somme de cinq cent piastres　　500

Item Rachel, negresse agee de vingt cinq ans, estimee par les memes la somme d quatre cent piastres　　400

Item George, négrillon âge de huit ans, estime par les memes la somme de deux cent cinquante piastres　　250

Item James, négrillon âgé de dix ans, estimé par les memes la somme de cent piastres　　100

Jtem un negrillon nomme Campagne, estime par les mêmes la somme de cinquante piastres　　50

Item Rose, négresse âgée de vingt–cinq ans, estimée par les mêmes la somme de quatre cent piastres.　　400
──────
$ 39670

Montant de l'autre part   \$39670

Item Aimé, négrillon agé de cinq ans, estimé par les mêmes la somme de cent piastres   100

Item Thom, negrillon age d'un an, estime par les mêmes la somme de cinquante piastres   50

Item Zago, negre âge de quinze ans, estimé par les memes la somme de quatre cents piastres   400

Item Peter, negre âge de cinquante ans, estime par les mêmes la somme de quatre cent cinquante piastres   450

Item Mary, negresse âgee de trente-cinq ans, estimee par les mêmes la somme de deux cent cinquante piastres   250

Item Decke, negre âge de quarante ans, estimé par les memes la somme de trois cents piastres   300

Item Chloe, negresse agee de trente cinq ans, estimee par les mêmes la somme de trois cents piastres   300

Item James, negre âgé de cinquante ans, estimé par les memes la somme de trois cents piastres   300

Item Mary, negresse âgee de cinquante ans, estimee par les memes la somme de cent cinquante piastres   150

Item Nelly, negresse agée de trente ans, avec Daniel son enfant, âge de deux ans, estimée par les mêmes la somme de trois cent cinquante piastres.   350

Item Darky négresse âgee de vingt-cinq ans, estimée par les memes la somme de quatre cents piastres   400

Item Daniel, negrillon âge de six ans, estime par les mêmes la somme de cent cinquante piastres   150

Item Louis, negrillon âge de cinq ans, estimé par les mêmes la somme de cent piastres,   100

Item Sally, négritte âgee de trois mois, estimee par les mêmes la somme de cinquante piastres   50

Item Luke, negre âgé de trente ans, estimé par les mêmes la somme de cinq cents piastres   500

Item George, negrillon âge de dix ans, estimé par les mêmes la somme de trois cents piastres   300

Item Poggy, negre âge de vingt deux ans, estime par les mêmes la somme de cent cinquante piastres.   150

Item Yob, negrillon âgé de neuf ans, estimé par les mêmes la somme de trois cents piastres   300

Item Jack, nègre âgé de dix-huit ans, estimé par les mêmes la somme de six cents piastres.   600

Item Nathon, nègre âgé de vingt-huit ans, estime

\$ 34870

Montant de l'autre part.   34870

par les mêmes la somme de quatre cent cinquante
piastres   450

Item Yaby, nègre âgé de trente ans, estimé par
les mêmes la somme de trois cent piastres.   300

Item Geoffry, negrillon âgé de onze ans, estimé
par les mêmes la somme de trois cent cinquante
piastres.   350

Item Phil, nègre âge de quarante ans, cstimé par
les mêmes la somme de cinq cents piastres.   500

Item David, négrillon âge de douze ans, estime
par les mêmes la somme de trois cents piastres.   300

Item David, négrillon, estimé par les mêmes la
somme de trois cents piasttes   300

Item James Sheling, negre âgé de trente ans, im-
bécile, estime par les mêmes la somme de cinquan
te piastres.   50

Item Lucy Morrow, négresse âgée de quarante
ans, estimée par les mêmes la somme de quatre cents
piastres   400

Item George, négrillon âgé de dix ans, estimé par
les mêmes la somme de deux cents piastres.   200

Item Rose, negresse âgee de vingt-sept ans, avec
Rob son enfant, estimee par les mêmes la somme de
trois cents cinquante piastres   350

Item Rosette, negresse âgee de vingt quatre ans,
estimée par les mêmes la somme de quatre cent
cinquante piastres.   450

Item Hannah, negresse âgée de vingt six ans, estimee par les mêmes la somme de trois cents piastres.   300

Item Judich, négresse âgee de vingt-huit ans, estimee par les mêmes la somme de quatre cent pias
tres.   400

Item Ketty, négresse âgee de vingt-six ans, esti
mée par les mêmes la somme de trois cent cinquante piastres   350

Item Silva, négresse âgee de vingt-deux ans, estimée par les mêmes la somme de quatre cent cinquante piastres   450

Item Ketty, négresse âgee de vingt-cinq ans, estimee par les mêmes la somme de trois cent cinqante
piastres   350

Item Julia, negresse de vingt trois ans, avec ses
trois enfans, nommes John, âge de sept ans, Quako
âgé de cinq ans et Jenny âgée de trois ans, estimés
ensemble la somme de sept cent cinquante piastres.   750

$ 41120

Montant de l'autre part.#41,120

Item Louisa, négritte de treize ans, estimée par les mêmes la somme de quatre cent cinquante piastres.   450

Item Little Jem, négrillon âge de onze ans, estimé par les memes la somme de quatre cents piastres   400

Item Jerry, mulatre âge de seize ans, estime par les mêmes la somme de quatre cents piastres   400

42370

Qui sont tous les negres qui nous ont ete representes, comme provenant de la succession dudit sieur Daniel Clark, sur cette Habitation

HABITATION —Item l'habitation sur laquelle nous opérons, ayant vingt quatre acres et demie de terre face au fleuve sur la profondeur jusqu'au lac, borgne d'un cote par Mr Cadet Fortier et de l'autre par A William Kenner, sur laquelle il existe les batisses provisions et recoltes suivantes

BATISSES—Une purgerie, une petite maison de maitre, quatre-vingt cabanes a negre un pigeonier et une petite boutique de forgeron

PROVISIONS —Environ un millier de mais

RECOLTE —Et enfin, cinquante acres de terre plantees en cannes a sucre laquelle habitation telle qu'elle est decrite avec ses batisses, recolte et provisions a ete estimée par les mêmes appréciateurs la somme de cinquante mille piastres — 50 000

Et attendu, qu'il ne nous a plus rien ete presente comme appartenant a ladite succession, nous, Register susdit et soussigné, avons arrête le present a six heures de relevee, et lecture faite d'icelui, nous avons trouve le montant des meubles fournitures et animaux inventories dans les presentes vacations être de la somme de trois mille huit cent et treize piastres, celui des cent soixante cinq esclaves de tout sexe et de tout age, être de la somme de cinquante deux mille soixante-sept dix piastres, en enfin, celui de l'habitation telle qu'elle est decrite ci-dessus, être de la somme de cinquante mille piastres

Ce qui fait ensemble une somme de cent six mille, six cent quarante trois piastres, lesquels meubles, fournitures et animaux, esclaves et habitation nous avons laisses à la charge du dit sieur Richard Relf, executeur testamentaire, qui le reconait et a signé avec nous et les autres parties et temoins, les mêmes jour mois et an que dessus, et nous sommes retirés.

Signé MOREAU L'ISLET, deffenseur des heritiers absents
RICHARD RELF   L'ILLE SARPY.
THOS. BEALE, Register of Wills.

Et aujourd'hui, quatrieme jour du mois d'Octobre de l an de notre Seigneur mil huit cent treize, et le trente huitieme de l'In-

dependance des Etats-Unis d'Amérique, dix heures du matin.
nous, Thomas Beale, Register des Testaments pour la ville et Paroisse de la Nouvelle-Orleans, nous sommes transporté au Cafe
de la nouvelle Bourse à l'effet d'y procéder a la vente au plus
offrant et dernier encherisseur des esclaves provenant de la succession du feu sieur Daniel Clark ou étant, nous avons trouvé
les sieurs Richard Relf, Executeur testamentaire du defunt.
Louis Moreau L'Islet, avocat nommé par la cour pour represen
ter les heritier absents, et avons en leur presence et en celle des
sieurs Prospere Prieur et Sebastien Blondeau, proclame la sus
dite vente aux termes et conditions suivantes:

Les conditions de la vente sont a six mois de crédit payable
en billets endosses a la satisfaction de l'executeur testamentaire,
avec hypotheque speciale, jusqu'au parfait payment

Premierement, Sam Harris, negre âge de vingt-six ans, Rachel negresse, agée de vingt-cinq ans, George, âge de huit ans,
Jacques, age de six ans, et Champion âgé d'un ans, adjuges ensemble a Mr Soniac Dufossat, pour la somme de douze cent
soixante piastres $ 1260

Item Lago, negre age de quinze ans, adjugé à Mr
Blanque pour la somme de quatre cents piastres   400

Item Darky, negresse agee de vingt cinq ans, avec
ses trois enfants nommes Daniel, agé de six ans,
Lewis age de cinq ans, et Sally agée de trois mois,
ensemble, adjuges a Mr Augustin Massicot, pour la
somme de sept cent quatre-vingt-dix piastres   790

Item Mary, negresse agee de trente-cinq ans, adjugee a Mr Montegut fils, pour la somme de trois
cent dix piastres   310

Item David, negrillon âge de douze ans, adjuge a
Mr François Guillet, pour la somme de quatre cent
dix piastres   410

Item David, negrillon, âge de douze ans, adjuge
a Mr Beaulieu, pour la somme de trois cent quinze
piastres   315

Item Hannae, negresse agée de trente ans, avec
ses deux enfants, nommes Bud, negrillon, age de
quinze ans, et Patty, agee de treize ans, adjuges ensemble a Mr Dupuy, pour la somme de douze cent
soixante piastres   1260

Item Polly, négresse âgee de vingt sept ans, adjugee a Mr Denreu pour la somme de quatre cent
soixante piastres.   460

Item Fanny, negresse âgée de vingt deux ans, adjugee a Mr Soniac Dufossat, pour la somme de cinq
cents piastres.   500

Item Retty, negresse agee de vingt ans, avec son
       ————

       5,645

Montant de l'autre part. $ 5645

enfant, adjugés à Mr Morand, par la somme de quatre cent quatre vingt-quinze piastres   495

Item Old Rachael, negresse agée de cinquante
ans, adjugee a Mr Samuel Elkins, pour la somme de
deux cent soixante piastres.   260

Item Rachael, negresse agée de seize ans, adjugee
à Mr Dumas, fils, pour la somme de quatre cent
quinze piastres   415

Item Waldron negre âge de quinze ans, adjuge a
Mr Sagon, pour la somme de cinq cents piastres   500

Item Suckey negresse agee de treize ans, adjugée
a Mr Lachataignerais, pour la somme de trois cent
quatre vingt-quinze piastres   395

Item Jenny, négresse agee de vingt-six ans, avec
ses deux enfants nommés Harriette, de huit ans, et Rel
ly, âge de cinq ans, adjuges ensemble à Mr Norbert
Fortier, pour la somme de huit cent cinquante
piastres   850

Item Ben, âge de cinquante ans, et Amey, negresse agee de trente ans, adjuges ensemble a Mr
Verloins, pour la somme de neuf cent cinquante
piastres   950

Item Pegguy, negritte agee de dix ans, adjugée a
Mr Brusle, pour la somme de trois cent soixante
cinq piastres   365

Item Eliza et son enfant, adjugés a Mr François
Labaire, pour la somme de six cent quatre-vingt-
dix piastres   690

Item Isaac, mulatre âgé d'environ dix-huit ans,
adjugé a Mr Celestin Avan, pour la somme de
cinq cent vingt piastres   520

$ 11145

Et attendu que plusieurs autres esclaves ont eté exposes en
vente, et qu'ils n'ont pu s'élever au prix de l'estimation, qu'il est
deux heures de relevee et le peu d'enchérisseurs, nous, Register susdit et soussigné, avons du consentement des parties, renvo-
ye la vente a demain dix heures du matin, ce dont nous avons
prevenu le public a haute et intelligible voix, et lecture faite du
présent nous avons trouve le montant de la vente, être de la
somme de onze mille cent quarante-cinq piastres. laquelle nous
avons laissee en la disposition du sieur Richard Relf, Exécuteur
testamentaire du defunt, qui le reconnait, s'en fait charge, et a
signe avec nous et les autres parties et témoins les mêmes jour

mois et an que dessus, et nous sommes retirés

Signe   RICHARD RELF   MOREAU L'ISLET
   PROSPERE PRIEUR   defenseur des héritiers absens.
      BLONDEAU.   THOS. BEALE, Rr. of wills.

RE-ESTIMATION DES ESCLAVES — Et aujourd'hui cinquieme jour du mois d'Octobre de l'an de Notre Seigneur mil huit cent treize, et le trente huitieme de l'Independance des Etats-Unis d'Amerique, en vertu de l'ordonnance de l'honorable James Pitot, Juge de la Cour des preuves de la ville et Paroisse de la Nouvelle Orleans, nous, Thomas Beale, Register des Testaments de la susdite ville et Parroisse, avons procede à une nouvelle estimation des negres provenant de la succession de feu Daniel Clark, et ce en presence du sieur Richard Relf, Executeur testamentaire, Louis Moreau L'Islet, avocat nommé par la Cour pour representer les heritiers absens et par le ministere des sieurs Dussau de La Croix et Chevalier Macarty et P. Baron Boisfontaine, appreciateurs choisis par l'exécuteur testamentaire, lesquels ont prete en nos mains le serment de bien et fidèlement se comporter dans les devoirs de leur charge, et avons en presence de tous, procedé comme suti:

Premierement, Toby, negre agé de trente ans, avec Jeffry, agé de onze ans, estimés ensemble par les mêmes la somme de six cents piastres,   600

Item, Molly, negresse agee de quarante-six ans, avec ses trois enfans, Nancy, négresse agee de dix-huit ans, Kery, agée de douze ans, et Tom, agé de huit ans, estimes ensemble par les mêmes la somme de quatorze cents piastres,   1400

Item, Nancy, negresse agee de dix-huit ans, estimee par les mêmes la somme de quatre cents piastres,   400

Item, Dina, negresse agee de soixante ans, avec James, son enfant, age de quinze ans, estimes par les mêmes la somme de cinq cents piastres,   500

Item, Charlotte, négresse agée de seize ans, estimée par les mêmes la somme de trois cents piastres,   300

Item, Kitty, négresse agee de dix sept ans, estimee par les mêmes la somme de trois cent quatre-vingt piastres,   380

Item, Peggy, negresse agee de quarante ans, avec son enfant nomme Jerry age de dix ans, estimé par les memes la somme de sept cents piastres,   700

Item, Arthur, negre age de douze ans, estime par les mêmes la somme de quatre cents piastres,   400

Item, Sally, agee de seize ans, et Kitty, agée de quinze ans, estimees par les mêmes la somme de huit cents piastres,   800

Item, Rady, negresse agee de vingt-quatre ans.

estimée par les mêmes la somme de quatre cents
piastres,   400

Item, Rachel, negresse agée de quinze ans, estimée par les mêmes la somme de trois cents piastres,   400

Item, Rachel, negresse agee de trente ans, estimee
par les memes la somme de trois cents piastres,   300

Item, Luddy, negresse agee de quarante ans, avec
ses cinq enfants nommes Mimy, agée de quinze ans,
Sukey, agee de treize ans, Betsy, agée de dix ans,
Edmond age de sept ans, et Nelly, agee de trois ans,
estimes par les memes la somme de seize cents pias-
tres,   1600

Et attendu qu'il ne nous a point ete presente d'autres esclaves
pour être reevalues, nous Register susdit et soussigné avons
clos et arrête le présent, et lecture faite d'icelui, nous avons
trouve le montant des esclaves reevalues etre de la somme de
huit mille cent quatrevingt piastres et ont les parties, appreciateurs et temoins, signe avec nous les memes jour, mois et an
que dessus

(Signé) MOREAU L'ISLET, Defens'l des heritiers absents
BLONDEAU,   RICHARD RELF.
PROSPER PRIEUR,   THOMAS BEALE,
                                              Register

Et aujourd'hui, cinquieme jour du mois d'octobre de l'an de
Notre-Seigneur mil huit ceut treize et la trente huitieme de l'Indépendance des Etats Unis d'Amerique, dix heures du matin,
nous, Thomas Beale, Régister des Testaments pour la ville et
paroisse de la Nouvelle Orleans, nous sommes transportes au
Cafe de la nouvelle Bourse a l'effet d'y proceder a la continua
tion de la vente des esclaves provenant de la succession de dit
feu sieur Daniel Clark ou etant, nous avons, en presence des
sieurs Richard Relf, executeur testamentaire du dit defunt, Louis
Moreau Lislet, avocat nomme par la cour pour representer les
heritiers absents, et en celle des sieurs Prosper Prieur et Sebastien Blondeau, témoins par nous requis, proclame la susdite vente eux mêmes termes et conditions sus-enonces.

Premierement, Toby, age de trente ans et Jeffry,
agé d'onze ans, adjugés a M Jean Trudeau, pour la
somme de six cent cinq piastres,   605

Item, Molly, negresse agee de quarante six ans,
avec ses trois enfants, nommés Nanny, agé de dix-
huit ans Kery de douze ans et Tom de huit ans,
adjugés a M. Célestin Avare, pour la somme de
quatorze cents piastres,   1400

Item, Nancy, négresse agée de dix huit ans, adjugée à M. Bonnefoi pour la somme de quatre cent
quinze piastres,   415

Item, Dina, négresse agée de soixante ans, avec James, age de quinze ans, adjuges ensemble a M James Nado, pour la somme de cinq cents piastres,   500

Item, Charlotte, agee de seize ans, adjugee a M. Lecenne pour la somme de trois cents piastres   300

Item, Betty, negresse agee de dix-sept ans, adjugée a M Deyraud pour la somme de trois cent quatrevingt quinze piastres,   395

Item, Peggy, negresse agée de quarante ans avec son enfant nomme Jerry agé de dix ans, adjuges a M, Edmond Macarty pour la somme de sept cents piastres,   700

Item, Arthur, négrillon agé de douze ans, adjugé a M. Jaublanc pour la somme de quatre cents piastres,   400

Item, Sally agée de seize ans, et Ketty agee de quinze ans, adjugees à M Labarre pour la somme de huit cent trente cinq piastres,   835

Item, Ready, négresse agée de vingt quatre ans, adjugee a M Verbois pour la somme de quatre cent vingt-cinq piastres,   425

Item, Rachel negresse agee de trente ans, adjugée a M Thomas Beale pour la somme de trois cent vingt-cinq piastres,   325

Item Rachel, négresse agée de quinze ans, adjugée á M Jaublanc pour la somme de quatre cent trente piastres   430

Item, Lidley, negresse agee de quarante ans, avec ses cinq enfans, nommes Mimy, agée de quinze ans, Sukey, agée de treize ans, Betsy, agee de dix ans, Edmond, age de sept ans et Nelly agée de trois ans, adjugés ensemble a Madame veuve Louis Trudeau pour la somme de dix-sept cent cinq piastres   1705

Item, Patience, négresse agee de treize ans, adjugée a M. Pascalis pour la somme de trois cent cinquante piastres,   359

Item, Ruff, inny et William, adjugés à M. Macarty, pour la somme de six cent cinquante piastres,   650

Item, Nelly et son enfant adjugés a M. Kirby pour la somme de trois cent cinquante piastres,   350

Et attendu qu'il ne s'est point trouvé d'autres esclaves a vendre provenant de la succession de feu sieur Daniel Clark nous Register susdit et soussigné, avons clos et arrêté le present, et lecture faite d'icelui, nous avons trouvé le montant de la vente faite être de la somme de neuf mille sept cent quatrevingt cinq piastres, laquelle a étè laissée a la disposition de dit sieur Richard Relf, exécuteur testamentaire, qui le reconnait, s'en fait

charge et a signe avec nous et nos temoins les meme jour, e t
t an que dessus et nous sommes retires

BLONDEAU   RICHARD RELF
PROSPER PRIEUR   THOMAS BEALE
                                        Register

VENTE D'HABITATION ET D'ESCLAVES — And this day, the sixth
of November in the year of our Lord one thousand eight hundred and thirteen and the thirtieth of the Independence of the
United States of America,   o clock in the morning, I
Thomas Beale. Register of Wills in and for the parish of New
Orleans, went at the coast of Chapitoulas, on a sugar plantation
vulgarly called the *Cannes Brulées*, belonging to the estate of
the late Daniel Clark, for the purpose to see the said plantation
and some slaves belonging to said estate where being, I found
Mr Richard Relf, testamentary executor of said deceased Mr
Moreau Lislet, attorney appointed by the Court to represent the
absent heirs, and Mr Louis Lecesme and L A Pignegui, witnesses here present, and then and there I proclaimed the said
sale at the following terms and conditions, to wit

The plantation and forty slaves sold with it payable 40,000
dollars the 1st May 1822, with a yearly interest of six per cent
payable on the 1st May of every year, and the remaining in six
equal instalments, payable on the 1st of March of every year
beginning in 1815, with special mortgage until final payment

And the other slaves payable at six months credit, in notes
endorsed to the satisfaction of the testamentary executor in
special mortgage until final payment

A plantation situated six leagues above this city on the left
bank of the river, having twenty four and a half arpents more
or less in front and extending bank as far as the lake bounded
on one side by Mr Wm Kenner, and on the other side by
Mr. Jacques Fortier, and known by the name of *Cannes Brulées*,
with all the implements of husbandry, animals, cattle &c, and
forty slaves, viz Adam, Hector, Lubin, William, Ketty, Kate
Sylvia, James, Stephen, Doctor Davy Antoine, Figaro,
Stewart, Dave, Jem, Elysa, Maurice, Rose, Lindor, Providence, John, Julia, Anoreco, Mores, Hannah Ketty Rosette her
child, Bob, Mac Daniel, Lawrence, Franky and her four
children, John, Charles, Mc Kensey and Margaret, Judah and
her three children John Quakis and Jenny Toby, which
retired off and adjuged to Messrs Michael Fortier Jr and Omer
Fortier for the sum of one hundred and twenty thousand
dollars, & $ 120 000

A negro man named Luke, aged 30 years or
there about to the same for five hundred dollars   500

A ditto named James aged about   years to the
same for the sum of seven hundred dollars   700

Amount carried over, $ 121,200

A negro woman named Rose with her son Bob
to Mrs M. Fortier and Omer Fortier for four hundred and fifty dollars.   450

A ditto named Jacte to the same, aged about
, for   600

A ditto named Nau, aged about   , for   600

A ditto named Morese aged about   , to
the same for   500

A ditto named Solomon aged about   ,
to the same for   450

A woman named Sarah aged about   years, to
the same for   500

A man named Will aged about   years, to the
same for   550

A woman named Fanny with her children
Mayor, Nelson and Mary to the same for the sum of   850

A woman named Winy with her children Elick,
Buky and Maria to the same for the sum of   700

A woman named Jenny aged about   years, to
the same for the sum of   500

        $126,900

Which being all the property shewed to me by the testamentary executor, I have closed this proces verbal in the presence of the before mentioned witnesses and the parties with
the purchasers who hereby acknowledged the sale at the prices
and terms aforesaid

Signed   RICHARD RELF, Executor
A. PIGNIGUI   L LECESNE
    L MOREAU L'ISLET, défenseur des héritiers absents
    MICHEL FORTIER, J'r   OMER FORTIER
      THOS BEALE, Register of Wills.

Et aujourd'hui, vingt-septième jour du mois de Janvier de
de l'an de notre Seigneur mil huit cent quatorze et le trente
huitième de l'Independance des Etats Unis d'Amérique, heure
de midi, nous, Thomas Beale, Régister des Testaments pour
la ville et paroisse de la Nouvelle Orléans, nous sommes transportés au Café de la Nouvelle Bourse. à l'effet d'y procéder à la
vente de plusieurs nègres provenant de la succession du feu
sieur Daniel Clark, où étant, nous avons trouvé le sieur Ri
chard Relf, l'un des exécuteurs testamentaires du défunt Louis
Moreau L'Islet, avocat nommé par la Cour pour représenter les
héritiers absens, et avons en leur présence et en celle des sieurs
Prospère Prieur et Sébastien Blondeau, proclamé la sus-
vente à haute et intelligible voix aux termes et condi- tions sui
antes   SAVOIR

Payables à six mois de crédit en billets endossés à satisfaction de l'exécuteur testamentaire avec hypothèque spéciale jusqu'au parfait payament

Et après avoir successivement exposé en vente tous les divers nègres, provenant de la succession de feu dit sieur Daniel Clark, nous, Régister susdit et soussigné, les avons tous retirés du consentement des parties, attendu qu'ils n'ont pu s'élever au prix de l'estimation, et ont les parties et témoins signé avec nous, après lecture, les mêmes jour, mois et an que dessus, et nous sommes retirés

    Signed   RICHARD RELF
                    PROSPERE PRIEUR
                    BLONDEAU

I William F C Duplessis, Register of Wills in and for the Paris and City of New Orleans, State of Louisiana, do hereby certify, that the foregoing transcript contains a true copy of all the mortuary proceedings had in the matter of the succession of Daniel Clark, deceased, on file in Court of Probates aforesaid

In faith whereof I have hereunto set my hand and affixed the seal of said Court of Probates at the City of New Orleans, this twelfth day of August in the year of our Lord one thousand eight hundred and forty, and the sixty-fifth of the Independence of the United States of America—One hundred and thirty-three words erased, and forty-three words interlined, all approved   W. F. C. DUPLESSIS,
                    Register of Wills

I, Joachim Bermudez, sole Judge of the Court of Probates in and for the Parish and City of New Orleans, do hereby certify, that Wm F C Duplessis, who signed the foregoing certificate, was at the time thereof and still is Register of Wills, in and for the Parish and City of New Orleans, ex-officio Clerk of the Court of Probates in and for the Parish and City of New Orleans, as set forth in his certificate which is in due form.

Given under my hand, at New Orleans this 12th August
A D. 1840   J. J. BERMUDEZ, Judge

CPSIA information can be obtained
at www.ICGtesting.com
Printed in the USA
LVHW061639140822
725925LV00019B/124

9 781275 517080